Pr. 8-9 *a* Index: Year 1, 1.15; Year 2, 1.31; *b* Year 1, $761,250; Year 2, $652,000.
8-10 *a* Corrected pre-tax income: Year 2, $168,260; Year 3, $78,040; Year 4, $126,300.
8-11 *a* Inventories: (1) $52,000 and $82,750; (2) $63,250 and $79,500.
8-12 Cost of goods sold: *a* (1) $16,700; (2) $17,100; (3) $16,818; *b* (1) $16,700; (2) $17,700; (3) $17,179.
8-13 *a* Inventories (at cost), $80,635; *b* net income, $62,150; *c* total assets, $524,500; *d* retained earnings (ending), $278,650.

9-1 Contract revenue: Year 5, $300,000; Year 6, $375,000; Year 7, $525,000.
9-2 *a* Shrinkage, $46,500 (1.4%); *b* $265,584.
9-3 *a* (1) $300,000; (2) $310,000; *b* (1) $0; (2) $610,000.
9-4 *a* $33,872; *b* $185,000.
9-5 *a* $56,896; *b* $53,098.
9-6 *a* $20,575.
9-7 *a* $37,300; *b* net income for quarter ending: 3/31, $51,700; 6/30, $46,750; 9/30, $36,080.
9-8 *a* Understatement of physical inventories, $85,300.
9-9 *a* 12/31/7, billings in excess of cost, $370,000; 12/31/8, costs in excess of billings, $140,000; *b* contract revenue, $800,000.
9-10 Fire loss, $113,000.
9-11 Fire loss, $194,160; *b* $37,800; *c* gross profit: Year 10, $14,400; Year 11, $28,800; Year 12, $92,800.
9-12 *a* $88,440; *b* $81,240.
9-13 Fire loss, $52,450.
9-14 Loss before income taxes, $54,500.
9-15 *a* Total gross profit (net of $28,000 loss on Q), $113,375; *b* net costs and estimated earnings in excess of billings, $53,375.
9-16 *b* Gross profit: X, $15,200; Y, $2,400; Z, $30,300; *c* income taxes expense, $12,285.

10-1 Total current liabilities, $294,000.
10-2 *a* $66,000; *b* $60,000; *c* $34,408.
10-4 *a* Cost of machine, $51,520; *c* note payable (net), $42,592.
10-5 No journal entry required for (2), (4), and (5).
10-6 No journal entry required for (6), (7), and (8).
10-7 *b* Promotional Expense, $60,350.
10-8 *a* Additional rent, $870; income taxes expense, $7,252; sales tax payable, $27,000.
10-9 *a* Royalty paid in third quarter, $44,000.
10-11 Total current assets, $193,050; total assets, $396,150; retained earnings, $182,950.
10-12 *a* Estimated liability, $455,000.
10-13 *a* Credit liability for Coupons Outstanding, $79,350; *b* total current liabilities, $2,142,317.

11-1 *a* $735,000; *b* $3,453,500.
11-2 *a* Land, $1,501,000; buildings, $970,000; leasehold improvements, $640,000; machinery and equipment, $782,200.
11-3 *a* Loss, $5,400; *b* loss, $300; *c* land, $48,000; *d* $36,450.
11-4 *a* Policy A, $297,000; Policy B, $78,400; *d* $100,800; *e* gain, $5,000.
11-5 Loss on disposal of machinery, $3,520; cost of new machinery, $19,700.

Pr. 11-7 *a* Proceeds from sale of land, $87,378; *b* gain on disposal of building, $23,882; *c* cost of land, $93,450.
11-9 *a* Cost of land, $351,400; cost of building, $535,700.
11-11 *a* Gain, $82,805; *c* cost of building, $61,645.
11-12 *a* Fire loss, $66,000; *b* expected to be recovered, $111,500; *c* gain, $12,500.
11-13 *a* Fire loss, $57,600; *b* total claims, $55,800; *c* loss, $5,950.
11-14 Cost of land, $169,380.

12-1 *e* Year 3, $3,960; Years 4 and 5, $0.
12-3 *a* $66,000; *b* (2) Year 2, $19,000.
12-4 *a* Machinery, $46,000; accumulated depreciation of machinery, $17,190; *b* loss on disposal, $5,630; credit Retained Earnings, $5,010.
12-5 *a* Cost of land, $49,000; credit Depreciation Expense, $4,500; *b* (3) Year 3, $14,600.
12-7 *a* Machinery and equipment, $1,116,000; *b* loss on scrapping of machine Q, $7,550.
12-8 Total depletion and depreciation: Year 1, $145,500; Year 2, $261,525.
12-9 Balances, Dec. 31, Year 2: *a* $25,600; *b* $44,073; *b* $60,400.
12-10 *a* Machinery, $184,300; accumulated depreciation of machinery, $66,000.
12-11 *a* Net income, $1,091,000; *b* increase in pre-tax income if order is accepted, $175,000.
12-13 *a* $66,440; *i* $2,040; *l* $5,100; *m* $30,600.

13-1 *a* Research expense, $14,000; *b* patent amortization, $200.
13-2 Intangible assets, $1,650,000; related expenses for Year 8, $640,000.
13-3 *b* Goodwill: Logan, $132,000; Cabot, $469,200.
13-4 *a* $69,000.
13-5 *b* Amortization for first 40 weeks, $4,200 per telecast.
13-6 *b* Total intangible assets, $43,240.
13-7 *a* $13,000; *c* $71,475; *d* $32,359.
13-8 *a* Adjustment to retained earnings (debit), $164,410.
13-9 *a* (1) $94,700; (2) $56,800; (3) $40,500; (4) $81,800.

14-1 Pre-tax income: Year 9, $43,109; Year 10, $67,591.
14-3 *a* $9,000; *b* Year 3, $700,000; Year 4, $3,021,625.
14-4 Goodwill, $930,000; amortization for Year 8, $23,250.
14-5 *a* $3,018,000; *b* $277,000.
14-6 *a* Total gain, $37,210; *b* debit Investment account, $1,610.
14-7 *a* Investment in Womack Ltd., $2,099,250; Investment in Sandy Limited, $2,279,250.
14-9 *a* Imputed goodwill, $120,000.
14-10 *a* $450,909.
14-11 *a* Imputed goodwill, $950,000; *d* write-off, $182,875.
14-12 *a* Gain: (1) $565; (2) $528; (3) $525; *b* total, 4,740 shares at cost of $135,145.
14-14 *b* Total investments, $624,775.
14-15 *a* $1,096,505; *b* $538,800; *c* interest revenue, $156,705.

(Continued on back endpaper.)

intermediate
ACCOUNTING

fifth canadian edition

intermediate ACCOUNTING

fifth canadian edition

McGraw-Hill Ryerson Limited
Toronto Montreal New York
Auckland Bogotá Cairo Caracas
Hamburg Lisbon London
Madrid Mexico Milan
New Delhi Panama Paris
San Juan São Paulo Singapore
Sydney Tokyo

A. N. Mosich, Ph.D., C.P.A.
Ernst & Whinney Professor of Accounting
University of Southern California

E. John Larsen, D.B.A., C.P.A.
Associate Professor of Accounting
University of Southern California

Wai P. Lam, Ph.D., F.C.A.
Professor of Accounting
University of Windsor

D. Ross Johnston, M.B.A., F.C.A.
Associate Professor of Accounting
University of Windsor

INTERMEDIATE ACCOUNTING
Fifth Canadian Edition

ISBN: 0-07-549493-0

1 2 3 4 5 6 7 8 9 10 THB 7 6 5 4 3 2 1 0 9 8

Printed and bound in Canada

Care has been taken to trace the ownership of the copyright material contained in this text. However, the publishers welcome any information that will enable them to rectify any reference or credit in subsequent editions.

CANADIAN CATALOGUING IN PUBLICATION DATA

Main entry under title:

Intermediate accounting

5th Canadian ed.
Includes bibliographical references and index.
ISBN 0-07-549493-0

1. Accounting. I. Mosich, A. N.

HF5635.M526 1988 657'.044 C87-095186-6

c o n t e n t s

p r e f a c e

The fifth Canadian edition of ***Intermediate Accounting*** is designed for use in an intermediate-level financial accounting course following the introductory course in financial accounting. The book may be used in a two-semester or a three-semester course, or in a single course at the graduate level. The emphasis throughout is on underlying concepts and on analysis of the problems that arise in the application of the concepts to financial accounting. Appropriate attention is given to the use of accounting information as a basis for decisions by management, shareholders, creditors, and other users of financial statements.

This edition reflects the dramatic changes that have been occurring in the development and application of accounting principles, with special attention to the pronouncements of the Canadian Institute of Chartered Accountants (CICA) and those of the Financial Accounting Standards Board (FASB) and the Securities and Exchange Commission (SEC) in the United States that are relevant to the Canadian environment. In addition, it has incorporated the most current legal requirements.

New Features of This Edition

Every chapter has been updated to include relevant pronouncements by accounting rule-making bodies in Canada and in the United States; these pronouncements have been incorporated in a manner that we consider pedagogically sound. Also, many of the illustrations have been added or strengthened.

We have prepared a new chapter, ''Revenue and Expense Recognition; Income Measurement and Reporting,'' following the introductory chapters on accounting principles and information processing. We consider the concepts involved in the recognition of revenue and expenses (including gains and losses) as providing a useful foundation for much of the discussion in subsequent chapters dealing with the measurement of assets and liabilities. Because this new chapter appears early in the text, as Chapter 3, our illustrations of revenue recognition situations are designed to cover the important concepts without unnecessary complexities. In this chapter we cover revenue and expense recognition issues for service industries as well as for trading and manufacturing enterprises. The concepts of revenue recognition of section 3400 of the ***CICA Handbook***, ''Revenue,'' have been incorporated into the chapter. Because revenue and expenses are the primary determinants of net income, we conclude with a discussion of income measurement concepts and special problems accountants face in the reporting of income.

The new subject matter in Chapter 3 made it possible for us to present the discussion of financial statements in a single chapter, Chapter 4, thus maintaining this edition at 25 chapters. Chapter 4 also includes a new section, "Additional Disclosures," with special emphasis on annual reports issued to shareholders by publicly owned corporations.

Many additional and revised topics have been incorporated into this edition. These include unrealized intercompany profits in the application of the equity method of accounting for investments in equity securities; extinguishment of bonds through debt-equity swaps and in-substance defeasance; induced conversion of convertible debt; contingent stock warrants issued to customers and junior stock issued to employees; reporting a change in the reporting entity as a result of pooling-type business combinations; and complete revisions of the pensions chapter and the chapter covering the statement of changes in financial position on the cash concept that highlights operating, investing, and financing activities.

The financial section of the annual report of Provigo Inc. is included in an appendix at the end of Chapter 4, and reference is made to it in many of the subsequent chapters. The tables of present values and future amounts are included in an appendix at the end of Chapter 5.

The number of exercises and problems has been expanded significantly in many of the chapters. We have made a strong effort to cover all new topics added in the fifth Canadian edition in the questions, exercises, cases, and problems. The first exercise in each chapter consists of a series of multiple-choice questions, many adapted from recent Uniform CPA Examinations used in the United States.

Organization of Subject Matter

We have again organized the book in six parts to give focus to the subject matter and to provide a psychological benefit to students by making the contents more digestible. This arrangement should facilitate for instructors the planning and presentation of the subject matter and make it easier for students to learn and retain the concepts and procedures presented. A description of the contents of the six parts follows.

Part One: Basic Concepts and Financial Statements (Chapters 1–5). The first part includes an overview of accounting principles and professional practice, a concise summary of the accounting process, recognition of revenue and expenses, financial statements and additional disclosures, and the application of present- and future-value concepts to financial accounting measurements. Chapter 1 places in perspective the development and application of accounting principles. Increased emphasis is given to the objectives of financial statements and to the conceptual framework project of the FASB. The review of basic data-collecting processes in Chapter 2 reinforces the student's understanding of fundamental recording, classifying, and summarizing procedures. This chapter includes a new section on the type of analysis required for the preparation of correcting entries. The background developed in the first two chapters leads to a consideration in Chapter 3 of the revenue and expense recognition principles on which income measurement is based. Special problems in income reporting also are included in this chapter; financial statements and additional disclosures are covered in Chapter 4.

The discussion in these early chapters (and throughout the book) is not limited to a description of acceptable practices. We believe it is important at this stage in accounting education to encourage students to evaluate accounting principles critically and to make them aware of the conflicts and shortcomings that exist in the traditional structure of accounting theory. At the same time, it is important to provide students with an analytical foundation for making this evaluation and to stress that many controversial areas in financial accounting frequently revolve around the economic consequences of accounting principles. To this end, the critical evaluation of accounting concepts is correlated with the pronouncements of the accounting profession in Canada and in the United States.

The first four chapters of the book constitute an overview of the accounting process and financial statements and are designed to provide a gradual transition from the introductory course in financial accounting to the more rigorous level of analysis in subsequent chapters of this book.

The final chapter in Part One addresses the concepts of present and future values of cash flows. The early introduction of this material enables us to make appropriate use of present and future value concepts for receivables and liabilities, for the acquisition of plant assets, for investments in bonds and promissory notes, for amortization of bond discount and premium, and for pension plans and leases.

Part Two: Working Capital (Chapters 6–10). The second part of the book addresses the accounting for cash and short-term investments, receivables, inventories, current liabilities, and contingencies. The components of electronic banking are described with the purpose of introducing students to computer-induced changes in handling cash transactions.

The section on the use of receivables to accelerate cash inflows has been expanded and updated. The discussion and illustrations of accounting for notes receivable have been extensively revised.

The two chapters on inventories have been expanded and updated. For example, the section on accounting for construction-type contract has been rewritten, and a discussion of input and output measures of degree of performance on contracts and an evaluation of accounting practices for construction-type contracts are included. Accounting for contingencies, notes payable, and other current liabilities has been reorganized and improved.

Part Three: Long-Term Assets and Liabilities (Chapters 11–15). This part includes chapters on plant assets and depreciation, intangible assets, long-term investments, and long-term liabilities. Coverage of natural resources and depletion has been expanded to include a discussion of the successful efforts and full cost methods of accounting by oil and gas enterprises.

The chapter on long-term investments includes an expanded treatment of the equity method of accounting for equity securities. Among new topics are: unrealized intercompany profits, market value method of accounting for the conversion by investors of bonds to common stock, and long-term receivables.

We have attempted to sharpen the relationship of long-term investments to long-term debt. Accounting for debt-equity swaps, in-substance defeasance of debt, and restructured debt has either been added or significantly expanded.

The illustration of the type of analysis required for a refunding decision (a financial management topic) has been deleted from the current edition.

Part Four: Shareholders' Equity (Chapters 16–18). The coverage of accounting topics unique to corporations is again presented in three chapters. The first chapter includes the accounting for the traditional issues relating to contributed capital, retained earnings, and dividends. In the second chapter, we have significantly revised the discussion of stock warrants, convertible securities, and employee capital accumulation plans. New sections have been added on contingent stock warrants to customers, market value method of accounting by the issuer for the conversion of bonds to common stock, induced conversion of convertible bonds, accounting for terminated stock options, and accounting for junior stock. The coverage of stock option plans has been updated and made more cohesive.

Part Four concludes with consideration of accounting for treasury stock and earnings per share. These two subjects are combined in this chapter for two reasons—to achieve a better balance of learning modules in this part of the textbook and to emphasize the importance of treasury stock transactions and the "treasury stock method" for outstanding stock options and stock warrants in the computation of basic and fully diluted earnings per share.

Part Five: More Complex Accounting Topics (Chapters 19–22). The chapters in this part are grouped together because they address some of the more specialized and challenging financial accounting topics. Separate chapters are devoted to the accounting for employee pension plans, leases, and income taxes. The final chapter includes three topics—changes in accounting principles and estimates, correction of accounting errors, and the preparation of financial statements from fragmentary accounting records.

Among the improvements we have made in this part are the following: (1) Substantial rewrite and expansion of discussion of defined benefit pension plans; (2) presentation of differing views on the nature of pension liabilities; (3) an extensive example of the revised section 3460 in the ***CICA Handbook***, "Pension Costs and Obligations"; (4) discussion of the revised section 3460; (5) expanded coverage of accounting for deferred income taxes when reasonable assurance is and is not present; (6) coverage of accounting for investment tax credits; and (7) more complete discussion of income taxes for interim periods.

Part Six: Analytical Procedures and Statements (Chapters 23–25). The final part consists of three chapters on special financial statements (statements of changes in financial position, and constant-purchasing-power and current-cost financial statements), and the analysis and interpretation of financial statements. Special emphasis is given to the impact of inflation on financial statements and on business decisions. The chapter on the statement of changes in financial position has been thoroughly revised and illustrates both the cash and the working capital concept of financial resources. Emphasis is given to the flow of cash resources, and to a new statement format that highlights operating, investing, and financing activities of business enterprises.

Questions, Exercises, Cases, and Problems

The amount of learning and assignment material provided at the end of each chapter has been expanded. This material is divided into four groups: questions, exercises, cases, and problems.

The ***questions*** are intended for use by students as a self-testing and review device to measure their comprehension of key points in each chapter. Many of the questions are provocative, which makes them suitable for written assignments and class discussion.

Exercises generally cover a specific point or topic and do not require extensive computations. Instructors may use the exercises for homework assignments, for class discussion, and for examination purposes. We have class-tested all exercises included in this edition.

Cases generally require analytical reasoning but involve little or no quantitative data. In these cases, students are required to analyze business situations, to apply accounting principles, and to propose a course of action. However, they are not required to prepare lengthy working papers or otherwise to manipulate accounting data on an extensive scale. The cases also have been class-tested and are an effective means of encouraging students to take positions in the evaluation of controversial accounting issues. A number of the cases have been adapted from Uniform CPA Examinations used in the United States. The cases and questions are especially recommended as a means of sharpening students' skills in communicating accounting concepts and in weighing the merits of opposing arguments.

Many of the ***problems*** are new, and most of those carried over from the preceding edition have been updated and revised. Special care has been taken to include an adequate number of short problems in each chapter. The problems range in difficulty from easy to strong. Most of those problems in the Accounting Theory and Accounting Practice sections of recent Uniform CPA Examinations that are appropriate to intermediate accounting are included, through many have been considerably modified. In addition, several problems in each chapter are designed especially to demonstrate the concepts presented in the theoretical discussion included in the chapter.

Helping Students to Achieve Proficiency in Solving Professional-Level Problems

A feature of this edition is the inclusion of a large number of short problems closely correlated with the text material. The gradation in difficulty is carefully tailored to help the student progress smoothly from introductory accounting to a professional level of achievement.

A Checklist of Key Figures for Problems is provided on the inside covers of the book. Its purpose is to aid students in verifying problem solutions and discovering errors.

Contributions by Others

The many instructors and students who have used previous editions of this book have contributed to the improvements in this edition. Their suggestions for modification of certain problems and alterations of certain sections of the text material have been most valuable.

We are indebted to a number of other individuals who have contributed to the fifth Canadian edition. Our sincere appreciation goes to those who reviewed one or more chapters: T. Ross Archibald of the University of Western Ontario, John K. Courtis of the University of Waterloo, Esther Deutsch of Ryerson Polytechnical Institute, Mike Gibbins of the University of Alberta, Carol E. Dilworth of the University of Toronto, R. M. Callard, research manager at the CICA, Brian P. Duggan of the University of Manitoba, and G. R. Chesley of Dalhousie University.

We acknowledge the permission of the Canadian Institute of Chartered Accountants to quote from its pronouncements. We also acknowledge the permission of the American Institute of Certified Public Accountants to quote from many of their pronouncements and to adapt the Uniform CPA Examinations. All quotations and materials from the Canadian Institute of Chartered Accountants and from the Uniform CPA Examinations are copyrighted respectively by the Canadian Institute of Chartered Accountants and by the American Institute of Certified Public Accountants.

We are grateful to the Financial Accounting Standards Board, which granted us permission to quote from ***FASB Statements, Discussion Memoranda, Interpretations***, and ***Exposure Drafts***. All quotations used are copyrighted by the Financial Accounting Standards Board, High Ridge Park, Stamford, Connecticut 06905, and are reprinted with permission. Copies of the complete documents are available from the FASB.

We also are grateful to those companies who have given us permission to use all or part of their financial statements in this edition. We wish to especially thank Provigo Inc. for the use of their financial review and statements in the Chapter 4 appendix.

The assistance of David Scrimger and Rodney Rawlings, both of McGraw-Hill Ryerson, and of Sandy Berlasty of the University of Windsor, is much appreciated.

Finally, our families also deserve a great deal of appreciation for their assistance, patience, and understanding. In particular, thanks go to Jean, Angela, Lambert, and Gloria for their work in typing, proofreading, and editing Chapters 1 to 13; and to Norma for typing, proofreading, and editing and for assisting Sandi, Gord, and Sue in taking care of all the chores that were set aside so that Chapters 14 to 25 could be completed.

Wai P. Lam
D. Ross Johnston

intermediate ACCOUNTING

fifth canadian edition

p a r t o n e

BASIC CONCEPTS AND FINANCIAL STATEMENTS

Accounting principles evolve in a constantly changing business and economic environment. A conceptual framework of financial accounting and reporting is essential for the development of internally consistent accounting principles and reporting practices. Business transactions and events result in inflows and outflows of resources for a business enterprise. These resource flows are measured and summarized to facilitate the preparation of financial statements — that is, the income statement, the balance sheet, the statement of changes in financial position, and the statement of retained earnings.

The measurement of assets and liabilities is closely related to the measurement of revenue and expenses. Increases in assets result from revenue realization, and expense recognition is accompanied by a decrease in assets and an increase in liabilities. The measurement process in financial accounting frequently involves compound interest fundamentals discussed in Chapter 5.

Part One establishes the theme and general framework for subsequent sections of this book.

c h a p t e r 1

ACCOUNTING PRINCIPLES AND PROFESSIONAL PRACTICE

THE ENVIRONMENT OF ACCOUNTING

Fair presentation of financial affairs is the essence of accounting theory and practice. With the increasing size and complexity of business enterprises and the increasing economic role of government, the responsibility placed on accountants is greater today than ever before. If accountants are to meet this challenge, they must have a logical and consistent body of accounting theory to guide them. This theoretical structure must be realistic in terms of the economic environment and must be designed to meet the needs of users of accounting information.

Such information usually takes the form of a set of financial statements. Financial statements and reports prepared by accountants are vital to the successful working of society. Economists, investors, business executives, labour leaders, bankers, and government officials all rely on these financial statements and reports as fair and meaningful summaries of day-to-day business transactions. In addition, these groups are making increased use of accounting information as a basis for forecasting future economic trends. Accountants are being challenged to go beyond the timely reporting and interpretation of past events and to aid in the creation of useful forecasts of future operations. Consequently, accountants and the theoretical principles they use are at the centre of financial and economic activities.

Users of Accounting Information

The basic assumptions that underlie current accounting practice have evolved over many years in response to the needs of various users of accounting information. The users of accounting information may be divided into two broad groups: ***internal users*** and ***external users***.

Internal users include all the management personnel of a business enterprise who use accounting information either for planning and controlling current operations or for formulating long-range plans and making major business decisions. The term ***managerial accounting*** relates to internal measurements and reporting; it includes the development of detailed current information helpful to all levels of management in decision making designed to achieve the goals of the enterprise.

External users of accounting information include shareholders, bondholders, potential investors, bankers and other creditors, financial analysts, economists, labour unions, and numerous government agencies. The field of ***financial accounting*** is directly related to external reporting because it provides investors and other outsiders with the finanical information they need for decision making.

In this book we are primarily concerned with financial accounting; therefore, we emphasize the accounting principles and reporting standards that produce timely and informative financial statements. The increasing importance of financial accounting rests on the premise that the public has a right to know whether large business enterprises are functioning efficiently and in harmony with the broad goals of society.

Organizations and Laws Affecting Financial Accounting

Certain professional organizations, governmental agencies, and legislative acts have been extremely influential in shaping the development of the existing body of accounting theory and practices. In Canada, the Canadian Institute of Chartered Accountants (CICA) is the most prominent and influential in the development and improvement of accounting theory and practices. Other accounting organizations, such as the Society of Management Accountants of Canada, the Certified General Accountants Association of Canada, and the Canadian Academic Accounting Association, have also exerted an influence in this area, either through their participation, directly or indirectly, in the standard-setting process of the CICA, or through their research activities and publications. Legislative acts which have affected the development of accounting principles and practices include the federal and provincial business corporations acts, the Income Tax Act, and the provincial securities acts; their influence was particularly significant during the early periods of the formation of accounting principles and practices. Moreover, the geographic location and the economic and business relationships between the United States and Canada have produced another dimension in the development of accounting theory and practices in Canada—the influence of the accounting profession and the securities legislation in the United States. Most significant are the American Institute of Certified Public Accountants, the Financial Accounting Standards Board, the American Accounting Association, and the Securities and Exchange Commission.

Awareness of the roles of these organizational forces is helpful in gaining an understanding of current accounting principles and practices. Efforts to improve existing principles and practices will have a better chance of succeeding if they are made with full recognition of the needs of the various groups that use accounting information.

The Accounting Profession

There are a number of professional accounting organizations in Canada. Notably, these are the Canadian Institute of Chartered Accountants, the Society of Management Accountants of Canada, and the Certified General Accountants Association of Canada. Members of these organizations receive their respective professional designations as chartered accountants (CAs), certified management accountants (CMAs), and certified general accountants (CGAs). The education, training, and examination requirements vary considerably among the three professional organizations. Also, the Canadian Institute of Chartered Accountants places more emphasis on public accounting, the Society of Management Accountants of Canada is primarily interested in management accounting, and the Certified General Accountants Association of Canada is interested in both management accounting and public accounting.

The Canadian Institute of Chartered Accountants and the *CICA Handbook*

The history of the accounting profession in Canada stems from Scottish and English practices. In the early 1880s, two accounting organizations were formally established: the Association of Accountants in Montreal in 1880 and the Institute of Chartered Accountants of Ontario in 1883. As other provincial accounting organizations were formed, there was need to coordinate activities, strengthen relationships, and promote common standards of education, training, and admission qualifications. Consequently, a national organization, the Dominion Association of Chartered Accountants, was formed in 1902, and in 1949 its name was changed to the Canadian Institute of Chartered Accountants (CICA).

The CICA is governed by a 28-member board of governors, and its affairs are administered by the executive officers elected by the board. Its organization reflects the federalism of Canada. Thus, members of the various provincial institutes automatically become members of the national institute. While its primary objective is to promote and maintain high professional standards, the CICA not only serves the accounting profession at the national and international level, but also provides significant input to the public and private sectors throughout Canada regarding business practices, government legislation, and significant national policies and issues on which the public would expect leadership from the profession.

Through research studies, various publications such as the ***CICA Handbook*** and ***CA Magazine*** (a monthly journal), and its concern and involvement with national standards of education, recruitment, and business practices, the CICA performs a wide range of activities and carries out a variety of functions. All of these are designed to help its members serve their clients or employers better and to secure and maintain a uniformly high level of competence throughout the profession.

Although the profession of public accounting is not quite a century old in Canada, it is one of the fastest growing. Membership in the CICA has more than doubled in the past decade and is now in excess of 43,000.

Since its inception, the CICA has been concerned with the development of accounting and auditing practices for the enhancement of reliable and informative financial reporting. At present, three groups, the Accounting Standards Committee, the Auditing Standards Committee, and the Public Sector Accounting and Auditing Committee, are authorized by the institute's Board of Governors to issue recommendations in the ***CICA Handbook***. The Accounting Standards Committee is responsible for the development and promulgation of accounting principles, and its recommendations are contained in the volume ''Accounting Recommendations'' of the ***Handbook***. The Auditing Standards Committee is responsible for topics in the auditing areas, and its recommendations appear in the volume ''Auditing Recommendations.'' The Accounting and the Auditing Standards committees focus primarily on issues relating to the private sector; recommendations on accounting and auditing issues related to governmental and other entities in the public sector are issued by the Public Sector Committee.

The recommendations of all these committees become the generally accepted accounting principles and auditing standards of the profession. Both the Canada Business Corporations Act and the provincial securities commissions have recognized the ***CICA Handbook***'s accounting recommendations as generally accepted accounting principles. As well, the Canada Business Corporations Act essentially recognizes the auditing recommendations as generally accepted standards for auditing. Any departure from these recommendations by a member must be justified, and the responsibility for justification rests with the individual member. The ***Handbook*** states that ''where the accounting treatment or statement presentation does not follow the recommendations in this ***Handbook***, the practice used should be explained in notes to the financial statements with an indication of the reason why the recommendation concerned was not followed.''[1]

The issuance of a recommendation by one of these committees is generally preceded by thorough research on its conceptual validity and practicality. Next, an exposure draft on the recommendation is published to solicit comments and suggestions from Institute members and other interested parties. All comments and suggestions are given serious consideration. Only after due deliberation and with the approval of at least two-thirds of the committee members will a recommendation be incorporated into the ***Handbook***.

The Accounting Standards Committee normally comprises 22 persons, with terms of office ranging from one to three years. Although committee members include a cross-section of individuals with various backgrounds and occupations, some of whom may not be chartered accountants, at least two-thirds must be members of the institute. Thus, the committee's membership includes persons nominated by the Canadian Council of Financial Analysts, the Society of Management Accountants of Canada, and the Financial Executives Institute Canada, and, until late 1983, a person nominated by the Certified General Accountants Association of Canada. The Auditing Standards Committee is smaller, normally having only 18 members, all of whom are Institute members and at least 12 of whom are in public accounting. The terms of office also range from one to three years.

The Public Sector Accounting and Auditing Committee normally comprises 19 members and terms range from one to three years here as well. Also, at least 10 of

1 CICA, *CICA Handbook* (Toronto), p. 202.

the members must be from government; the balance of its membership may include legislators, economists, financial analysts, and academics.

Since the subject matter of the three committees is interrelated to a large extent, their activities are coordinated by the Joint Steering Committees.

Other Accounting Organizations

As mentioned earlier, three other accounting organizations also have an influence on the development of accounting theory and practices: the Society of Management Accountants of Canada, the Certified General Accountants Association of Canada, and the Canadian Academic Accounting Association. A brief description of each is presented below.

The Society of Management Accountants of Canada (SMAC) The SMAC is the national organization of professional management accountants. Its former name was the Society of Industrial Accountants of Canada and its members were designated as registered industrial accountants (RIAs). The majority of members are in industry, though many are with the government sector and some in public accounting. Since SMAC members are often responsible for the preparation of internal and external financial reports, they are intimately involved not only with management accounting and financial accounting but also with external reporting. Thus, the research interests of the SMAC, while primarily in the management accounting area, also extend to areas such as financial accounting and reporting and finance. Its research activities have resulted in the publication of a number of special studies and research monographs. In addition, the SMAC publishes the journal ***Cost and Management***. As mentioned previously, the SMAC is represented in the CICA's Accounting Standards Committee.

The Certified General Accountants Association of Canada (CGAAC) The CGAAC is the national organization for professional general accountants. Since the interests of CGAAC are in both management and financial accounting, its members are from both industry and government; also, in a number of provinces, they are from public accounting. The CGAAC has recently established a separate research foundation to sponsor research projects and to publish results in the form of monographs. The research areas include management and financial accounting, auditing, and taxation. In addition, the CGAAC publishes the journal ***CGA Magazine***.

The CGAAC was represented in the CICA's Accounting Standards Committee until late 1983.

The Canadian Academic Accounting Association (CAAA) The CAAA is a relatively new organization; it was established in the 1970s. Its membership includes people from academia, industry, and public accounting. The CAAA's main interests are to promote research in accounting and auditing education and in financial and management accounting, and to actively participate, through its committees, in the standard-setting process. It publishes the newsletter ***Canadian Accounting Education and Research News*** and the journal ***Contemporary Accounting Research***, and holds an annual conference for its members and other interested parties.

Legislation Concerning Business Corporations, Securities, and Income Tax
The federal and provincial government bodies involved in the enforcement of the legislation concerning business corporations, securities, and income tax have an inherent interest and influence in the development of accounting principles and practices because it is their responsibility to ensure that financial statements filed with them are fairly presented. At present, the federal and provincial legislature and regulatory authorities have generally delegated the accounting standard-setting to the CICA. For example, Regulation 44 of the Canada Business Corporations Act, and ***National Policy Statement No. 27***, issued in 1972 by the administrators of provincial securities commissions, have both stipulated that the accounting recommendations in the ***CICA Handbook*** constitute ''generally accepted accounting principles.'' Regulation 44 states:

> The financial statements referred to in paragraph 149(1) of the Act shall, except as otherwise provided by this Part, be prepared in accordance with the standards, as they exist from time to time, of the Canadian Institute of Chartered Accountants set out in the ***CICA Handbook***.

And National Policy Statement No. 27 states:

> Where the term ''generally accepted accounting principles'' is used, either in Securities Legislation, Regulations and Companies Legislation and Regulations, the Securities Administrators will regard pronouncements by the Accounting and Auditing Research Committee [names subsequently changed to Accounting Standards Committee and Auditing Standards Committee] of the Canadian Institute of Chartered Accountants to the extent set out in the research recommendations in the ***CICA Handbook*** as ''generally accepted accounting principles.''

It should be noted that under the Income Tax Act certain regulations for financial reporting are at variance with generally accepted accounting principles. These variances have often created reporting problems, as the amount of income taxes computed in accordance with generally accepted accounting principles is different from that based on income tax regulations. Such a difference does not necessarily indicate a superiority of one set of principles over the other, as the objectives for financial reporting are not the same as those for income taxation.

Accounting Organizations and Securities Legislation in the United States
As mentioned earlier, certain accounting organizations and certain securities legislation in the United States have an impact on the development of Canadian accounting principles and practices. The most important influences are the American Institute of Certified Public Accountants, the Financial Accounting Standards Board, the American Accounting Association, and the Securities and Exchange Commission.

American Institute of Certified Public Accountants (AICPA) The American Institute of Certified Public Accountants is the professional organization of practising certified public accountants in the United States. As a professional organization, the institute has been vitally concerned with developing standards of professional practice for its members. The AICPA publishes the monthly ***Journal of Accountancy*** as a forum for practitioners. Beginning in the early 1930s, the institute, in concert with the newly created Securities and Exchange Commission, began to develop standards of financial reporting. From 1939 to 1959, the AICPA published the ***Accounting Research Bulletin***, which dealt with a wide variety of accounting and reporting issues.

In 1959 the AICPA undertook a more comprehensive program of research into the problems of financial reporting. The Accounting Principles Board (APB) was established to formulate financial accounting and reporting principles based on this research. The board consisted of 21 (later 18) part-time members who served without pay.

The APB issued two separate series of publications. The more influential consisted of the 31 ***Opinions of the Accounting Principles Board***, issued between 1959 and 1973. Prior to 1964, pronouncements by the AICPA were not binding on practising CPAs. However, in 1964, the institute began requiring that departures from the ***Opinions*** be disclosed either in notes to financial statements or in the audit reports of AICPA members in their capacity as independent auditors. CPAs could not give their approval to financial statements that deviated from the ***Opinions*** unless they wanted to assume the considerable personal risk and burden of proof of defending the unauthorized practices. Few business enterprises or auditors were anxious to assume the burden of defending financial statements that so differed; thus, this requirement gave a new strength and authority to opinions of the APB.

After the creation of the Financial Accounting Standards Board, the AICPA established an Accounting Standards Division to influence the development of accounting standards. The Accounting Standards Executive Committee (AcSEC) of the Accounting Standards Division issues ***Statements of Position*** to propose revisions of AICPA-published ***Industry Audit Guides*** and ***Accounting Guides***. These ***Statements*** do not establish enforceable accounting standards; however, members of the AICPA must justify departures from practices recommended there. In addition, the Accounting Standards Division prepares ***Issues Papers*** to develop financial accounting and reporting issues that the division believes should be considered by the Financial Accounting Standards Board.

Financial Accounting Standards Board (FASB) The Financial Accounting Standards Board was established in 1972 to develop financial accounting standards for business enterprises and nonprofit organizations in the United States. This independent body consisted of seven full-time members and a large supporting staff.

Lending support and counsel to the FASB are the Financial Accounting Foundation, which appoints members of the FASB and raises funds for its operations, the Financial Accounting Standards Advisory Council, a Screening Committee on Emerging Problems, and numerous Task Forces consisting of financial executives, accounting educators, lawyers, and CPAs.

CPAs are not the only persons concerned with financial accounting and reporting. Consequently, the articles of incorporation creating the FASB require only four members to be CPAs from public accounting practice; the other three members need only be highly qualified in financial accounting and reporting. An individual appointed to the FASB must sever all connections with other organizations to avoid any suggestion of ***conflict of interest***. In a word, the public accounting profession is now engaged in a strenuous effort to improve the quality of financial accounting and reporting through an independent rule-making body that includes representatives from outside the field of public accounting.

The FASB is authorized to issue ***Statements of Financial Accounting Standards***, as well as ***Interpretations*** and ***Technical Bulletins***, to guide individuals and organizations in preparing and auditing financial statements. Before a formal ***Statement*** is drafted, the FASB frequently issues a ***Discussion Memorandum*** that identifies and analyzes the problems to be considered. Public hearings then are held on the problems. Next, an ***Exposure Draft*** of the proposed statement is circulated. These procedures are designed to encourage the widest participation possible by all interested parties before a new financial accounting standard is proclaimed.

American Accounting Association (AAA) The American Accounting Association, an organization of accounting educators and practitioners, has played an important role in the development of accounting principles. The activities of the AAA have emphasized the development of a theoretical foundation for accounting rather than the application of the theory to practical situations. The AAA encourages accounting research and continuous appraisal of accounting concepts through committee reports and the publication of a quarterly journal, ***The Accounting Review***.

Securities and Exchange Commission (SEC) The Securities and Exchange Commission was established in 1934 by the U.S. Congress to regulate interstate issuance of securities to the public and the trading of securities listed on stock exchanges and over the counter. The SEC has broad authority to prescribe accounting principles, forms to be filed, and information to be disclosed by business enterprises subject to its regulation. With regard to its authority to prescribe accounting principles, the SEC has generally relied on the private sector (FASB and AICPA) to perform this function. However, the commission has exerted strong influence on the development of accounting principles and reporting practices. SEC actions have included (1) continual review (and occasional rejection) of financial statements, (2) issuance of ***Regulation S-X***, which prescribes detailed accounting and financial reporting requirements, (3) publication of numerous ***Financial Reporting Releases*** and ***Staff Accounting Bulletins***, and (4) prodding the private sector to develop or revise certain financial accounting and reporting practices.

The primary concern of the SEC is ***disclosure*** of all relevant and material facts about the financial affairs of publicly owned business enterprises. In recent years, the SEC has become more active in its role as the watchdog for investors. The chief accountants of the SEC have pushed to expand the quality as well as the quantity of information disclosed to the public. The SEC has been primarily responsible for expansion of disclosure into such areas as inventory profits caused by inflation, replacement costs of inventories and plant assets, unusual risks and uncertainties, and replacements of independent auditors. Particular emphasis has been placed by the SEC on the concept of ***continuous disclosure*** of ***relevant*** information on a ***timely basis*** so that it is of maximum value to investors. Accordingly, it has required independent auditors to review quarterly financial reports and encouraged business enterprises to issue financial forecasts.

Attest Function of Public Accountants

A conflict of interest may exist between a business enterprise preparing financial statements and some of the users of those statements. For example, an enterprise applying for a bank loan may tend to be overly optimistic in portraying its financial position. Similarly, a corporation planning to raise cash by issuing common stock to the public has an incentive to overstate its reported net income. To protect the users of financial statements against a natural bias or outright misrepresentation, it is important to have ***auditors*** (independent public accountants) examine the statements (and supporting evidence) prepared by the accounting staff of an enterprise. The auditors then have a basis for expressing their professional opinion on the financial statements. This ***attest function*** is the primary role of public accountants. To attest to financial statements means to ***vouch for their validity***. Performance of the attest function requires the existence of an independent public accounting profession.

Because of the public interest in ***audited financial statements***, corporations are generally required by law to have their financial statements audited by independent public accountants. The attest function enhances the credibility and reliability of financial statements.

CONCEPTUAL FRAMEWORK FOR FINANCIAL ACCOUNTING AND REPORTING

The accounting profession in both Canada and the United States has been keenly aware of the need for a cohesive set of accounting concepts and principles as a framework for financial accounting and reporting. The CICA, the AICPA, and the FASB have published a number of studies in this regard.[2] However, the most comprehensive project has been the FASB's study on the entire conceptual framework of financial accounting and reporting, including objectives, qualitative characteristics, and the needs of users of accounting information. The purpose of the conceptual framework project was to provide a sound and consistent basis for the development of financial accounting standards. The figure on the next page depicts the elements of a conceptual framework for financial accounting and reporting.[3]

2 For example, the CICA's ***Corporate Reporting: Its Future Evolution*** (Toronto: 1980), the AICPA's ***Report of the Study Group on the Objectives of Financial Statements*** (New York: 1973), and the FASB's ***Statement of Financial Accounting Concepts No. 1:*** "Objectives of Financial Reporting by Business Enterprises" (Stamford: 1978).

3 FASB, ***FASB Discussion Memorandum***, "Conceptual Framework for Accounting and Reporting" (Stamford: 1974), p. 15.

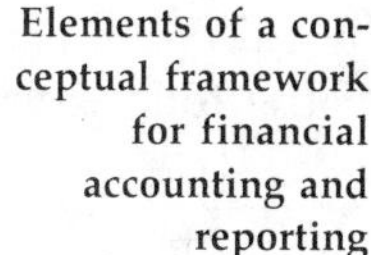
Elements of a conceptual framework for financial accounting and reporting

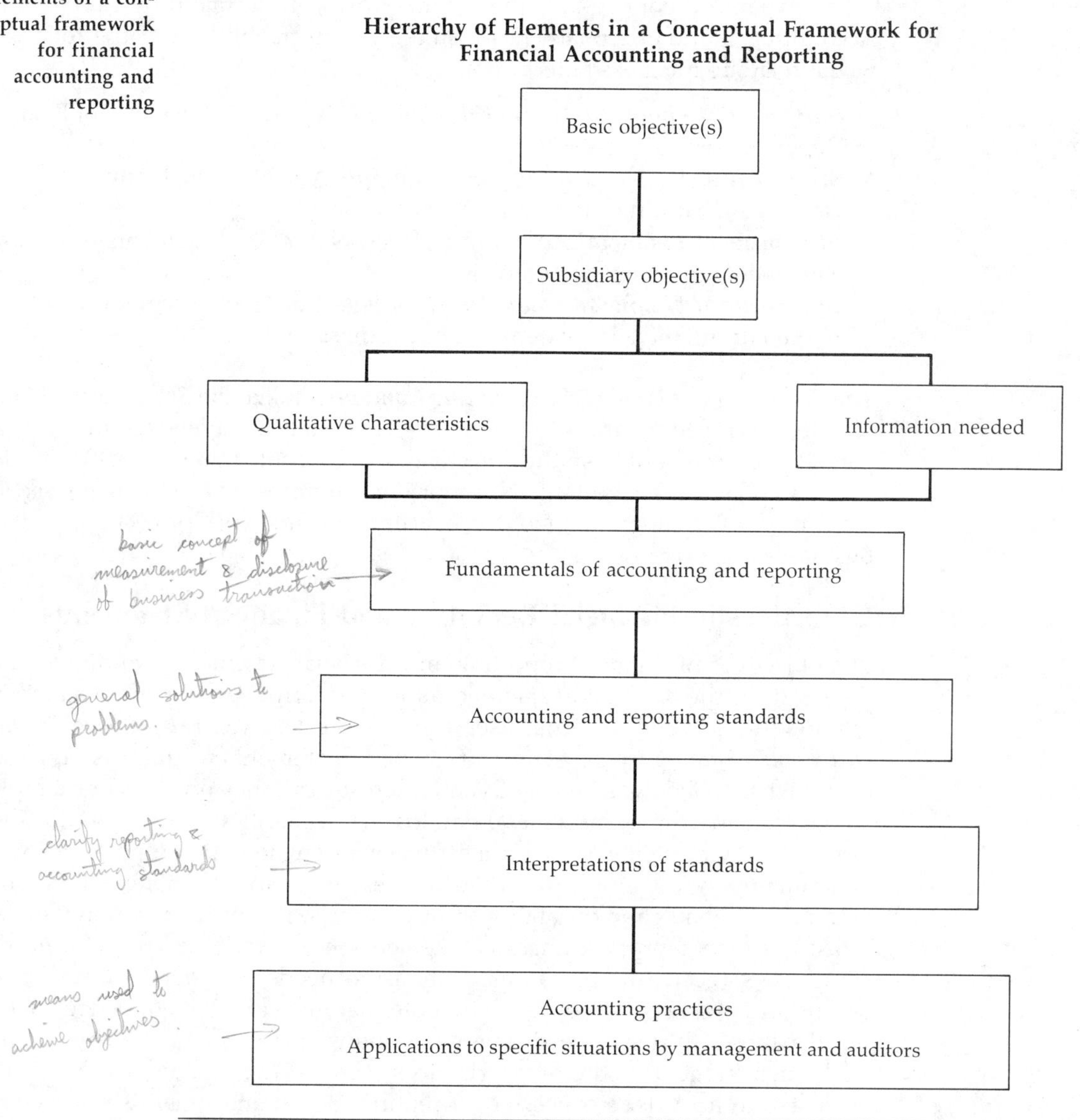

Hierarchy of Elements in a Conceptual Framework for Financial Accounting and Reporting

The ***fundamentals of accounting and reporting*** mentioned in the figure are the basic concepts underlying the measurement and disclosure of business transactions and events. Fundamentals might include the definitions of an accounting entity, assets, liabilities, net income, revenue, and expenses. ***Accounting and reporting standards*** represent general solutions to financial accounting problems, and ***interpretations of standards*** clarify the accounting and reporting standards as an aid to their application in accounting practices. ***Accounting practices*** are the means used by managements and independent auditors to achieve the objectives of financial statements and financial reporting.

The expanded conceptual framework project undertaken by the Financial Accounting Standards Board has resulted in the publication of the following, which relate to business enterprises:

- ***Statement of Financial Accounting Concepts No. 1:*** ''Objectives of Financial Reporting by Business Enterprises''
- ***Statement of Financial Accounting Concepts No. 2:*** ''Qualitative Characteristics of Accounting Information''
- ***Statement of Financial Accounting Concepts No. 3:*** ''Elements of Financial Statements of Business Enterprises''
- ***Statement of Financial Accounting Concepts No. 5:*** ''Recognition and Measurement in Financial Statements of Business Enterprises''

The ***Statements of Financial Accounting Concepts***, unlike the ***Statements of Financial Accounting Standards***, do not establish generally accepted accounting principles. Rather, they establish the objectives and concepts that the FASB will ***use*** to establish financial accounting and reporting standards. In the following sections we consider the components of the conceptual framework project applicable to business enterprises.

Objectives of Financial Reporting and Financial Statements

The objectives of financial reporting and financial statements are derived from the needs of the external users of accounting information. Financial statements intended to serve all external users often are called ***general-purpose financial statements***. Stating the objectives of financial statements would be simpler if all external users had the same needs and interests, but they do not. For example, a banker considering granting a 90-day loan is primarily interested in the short-term debt-paying ability of the business enterprise, whereas the long-term investor in common stock is more concerned with earning capacity, potential growth in earnings per share, and the ability of the enterprise to survive as a going concern.

Because general-purpose financial statements serve a variety of users, the needs of some users receive more emphasis than the needs of others. In present-day accounting practice the needs of the potential investor or creditor are subordinated to those who have already invested resources in the enterprise. This emphasis leads management of the enterprise to stress the uses made of the resources entrusted to it. A deep concern over reporting on management's role as custodian of resources may be one reason for the adherence to historical cost despite substantial changes in the general price level in recent years. This tradition may also explain, in part, the omission from the financial statements of what is known as ***social costs***, which may be increasingly important to a society becoming more aware of the need for preserving the quality of its environment.

In recent years the environment in which business enterprises operate has been changing at a rapid pace. Changes in the economic, political, and social structure of society cause changes in the informational needs of users of financial statements. Higher standards of measurement and reporting, along with a significant expansion of the amount of information disclosed, have been foremost among the new needs of users of financial statements.

The Financial Accounting Standards Board issued the above-mentioned "Objectives of Financial Reporting by Business Enterprises" to establish the objectives of general-purpose external financial reporting by business enterprises.[4] The objectives established by the FASB were as follows:[5]

1 Financial reporting should provide information that is useful to present and potential investors and creditors and other users in making rational investment, credit, and similar decisions. The information should be comprehensible to those who have a reasonable understanding of business and economic activities and are willing to study the information with reasonable diligence.

2 Financial reporting should provide information to help present and potential investors and creditors and other users in assessing the amounts, timing, and uncertainty of prospective cash receipts from dividends or interest and the proceeds from the sale, redemption, or maturity of securities or loans. The prospects for those cash receipts are affected by an enterprise's ability to generate enough cash to meet its obligations when due and its other cash operating needs, to reinvest in operations, and to pay cash dividends and may also be affected by perceptions of investors and creditors generally about that ability, which affect market prices of the enterprise's securities. . . .

3 Financial reporting should provide information about the economic resources of an enterprise, the claims to those resources, . . . and the effects of transactions, events, and circumstances that change resources and claims to those resources.

4 Financial reporting should provide information about an enterprise's economic resources, obligations, and owners' equity.

5 Financial reporting should provide information about an enterprise's financial performance during a period. Investors and creditors often use information about the past to help in assessing the prospects of an enterprise. . . .

6 The primary focus of financial reporting is information about an enterprise's performance provided by measures of earnings and its components.

7 Financial reporting should provide information about how an enterprise obtains and spends cash, about its borrowing and repayment of borrowing, about its capital transactions, including cash dividends and other distributions of enterprise resources to owners, and about other factors that may affect an enterprise's liquidity or solvency.

8 Financial reporting should provide information about how management of an enterprise has discharged its stewardship responsibility to owners for the use of enterprise resources entrusted to it.

9 Financial reporting should provide information that is useful to managers and directors in making decisions in the interests of owners.

Summarizing, the Financial Accounting Standards Board identified nine objectives of financial reporting, all of which focus on providing information

4 FASB, ***Statement No. 1*** (Stamford: 1978), p. 1.

5 FASB, ***Statement No. 1***, paras. 34, 37, 40–43, 49, 50, and 52. Also in ***Statement No. 2:*** "Qualitative Characteristics of Accounting Information" (Stamford: FASB, 1980), pp. 9–10.

needed by current and prospective investors and creditors of a business enterprise in their decision making. The primary emphasis was placed on information regarding the enterprise's earnings.

Qualitative Characteristics of Accounting Information

The Financial Accounting Standards Board issued ***Statement of Financial Accounting Concepts No. 2:*** "Qualitative Characteristics of Accounting Information" to examine the characteristics of accounting information that make it useful.[6] Thus, the FASB identified ***usefulness for decision making*** as the most important qualitative characteristic of accounting information.[7] To be useful, accounting information must be ***understandable*** to users (decision makers). The FASB summarized the qualitative characteristics in the diagram below.[8]

Qualitative characteristics of accounting information

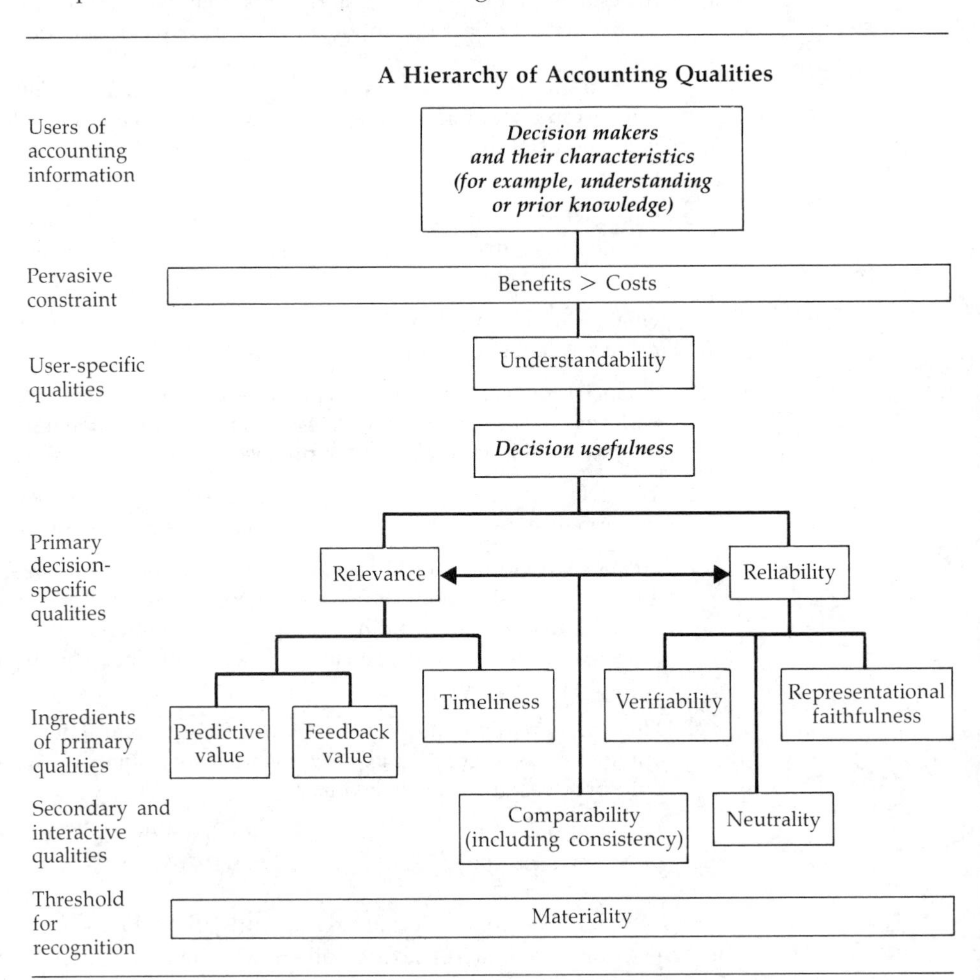

6 FASB, *Statement No. 2*, p. 1.

7 FASB, *Statement No. 2*, pp. 13–14.

8 FASB, *Statement No. 2*, p. 15.

The diagram identifies ***relevance*** and ***reliability*** as the two primary qualities of useful accounting information, with related ingredients of each primary quality also set forth. ***Comparability*** (including ***consistency***) and ***neutrality*** are identified as secondary qualities of useful accounting information, and the concepts of ***cost-benefit considerations*** and ***materiality*** are recognized as constraints. Let us now discuss the qualities set forth in this diagram.

Cost-Benefit Consideration

In recent years, the demands of many users of financial statements and other financial information have appeared insatiable to accountants. There has been an explosive growth in the amount of information disclosed in the annual reports of publicly owned corporations, and the cost of producing such information is substantial. The Financial Accounting Standards Board recognized the impact of cost-benefit considerations as follows:[9]

> Before a decision is made to develop a standard, the Board needs to satisfy itself that the matter to be ruled on represents a significant problem and that a standard that is promulgated will not impose costs on the many for the benefit of a few. If the proposal passes that first test, a second test may subsequently be useful. There are usually alternative ways of handling an issue. Is one of them less costly and only slightly less effective? Even if absolute magnitudes cannot be attached to costs and benefits, a comparison between alternatives may yet be possible and useful.

Relevance

Relevant accounting information may make a difference in a decision by helping investors, creditors, and other users to evaluate past, present, and future events (***predictive value***) or to confirm or correct expectations (***feedback value***).[10] For example, information concerning past dividends declared by a corporation enables investors to predict the prospects of dividends in future years; information on net income for the first three-quarters of a fiscal year enables investors to evaluate a prior estimate of net income for the entire fiscal year.

Accounting information is generally not relevant unless it is ***timely***, that is, unless it is accessible to decision makers before it becomes too dated to influence the decision.[11] The availability of computers has enabled accountants to make great strides in providing timely information.

Reliability

Accounting information is reliable if it is reasonably free from error and bias and faithfully represents what it purports to present.[12] To be reliable, information must be ***verifiable*** and must have ***representational faithfulness*** (validity).[13]

9 FASB, *Statement No. 2*, p. 58.

10 FASB, *Statement No. 2*, pp. xv, xvi.

11 FASB, *Statement No. 2*, p. 25.

12 FASB, *Statement No. 2*, p. xvi.

13 FASB, *Statement No. 2*, p. 26.

Supporting documents showing the details of complete "arm's-length" transactions provide clear evidence that may be verified. To ***verify*** means to prove something to be true by examination of the evidence of some underlying facts. If accounting information is free from bias, the same conclusions would be reached by different accountants working independently and following the same measurement techniques. In most cases, ***actual costs*** provide the most independently verifiable and reliable data.

However, financial statements are not completely factual; ***estimates*** on such matters as the economic life of plant assets, the net realizable value of inventories, and the collectibility of accounts receivable are inherent in the accounting process. The reliability quality calls for accountants to adhere as closely as possible to ***objectively verifiable evidence***. The alternative approach would be to establish accounting values through unrestricted use of appraisal reports, estimates of future events, and expressions of opinion. Such an approach to accounting, although often helpful in providing more relevant data, makes it more difficult for public accountants to perform independent verifications of financial statements. Today, accountants recognize that a tradeoff exists between ***relevance*** and ***reliability*** in financial statements. In recent years, the provincial securities commissions in Canada and the Securities and Exchange Commission in the United States have favoured relevance as the more useful criterion. For example, these commissions have encouraged the issuance of financial forecasts and the disclosure of replacement cost data (both based on estimates), on the grounds that such information is useful to investors in making decisions to acquire, sell, or retain corporate securities.

Conservatism

Although not a qualitative characteristic of accounting information, ***conservatism*** is a concept that may be discussed in connection with reliability. Many accounting measurements do not have a single "correct answer"; a choice must be made among alternative assumptions under conditions of uncertainty. The concept of conservatism holds that when reasonable support exists for alternative accounting methods and for different measurement techniques, accountants should select the method or technique with the least favourable effect on net income and financial position in the current accounting period.

Conservatism is generally regarded as a powerful influence stressing caution against the danger of overstating earnings or financial position. However, many business enterprises are not in favour of conservative accounting policies. Enterprises planning to issue securities to the public naturally try to project an image of superior management and increasing earnings. An enterprise that reports increased earnings year after year gains the reputation of being a "growth company"; financial analysts refer to its common stock as a "glamour issue"; and the market price of its common stock often rises to a high multiple of earnings per share. Once such a reputation is established, an enterprise finds it easier to raise needed capital through the issuance of additional securities or through bank loans. Attracting management talent is easier also. Executive compensation tends to increase both in salaries and through stock option and pension plans. All these pleasant ***economic consequences*** of a reputation for increasing earnings give enterprise management a powerful incentive to choose accounting policies that maximize current net income.

However, enterprises must be alert to the possible adverse economic consequences of following unconservative accounting policies. The issue we are raising relates to the ***quality of reported earnings***. The earnings of an enterprise using unconservative accounting policies are viewed as being of lower quality, and its common stock will tend to trade at a low price-earnings ratio. Small business enterprises that do not seek capital from the public and do not report their earnings to anyone other than income tax authorities have an incentive to choose acceptable accounting policies (and tax regulations) that hold income to the lowest level that can be justified.

Ideally, accountants should make estimates and select accounting policies that neither overstate nor understate the current net income and financial position of a business enterprise. The concept of conservatism should not be distorted to the point of deliberate understatement; however, the judicious use of conservatism in accounting may help to prevent the catastrophes that have befallen many investors and employees when enterprises with excessively optimistic accounting policies suddenly reached the limit of credibility and collapsed.

Comparability and Consistency

Comparability of the financial statements of a business enterprise from one accounting period to the next is essential if favourable and unfavourable trends in the enterprise are to be identified. If the financial statements for the current accounting period show larger earnings than for the preceding period, the user assumes that operations have been more profitable. However, if a material change in an accounting principle has occurred, the reported increase in earnings could have been caused solely by the accounting change, rather than by any improvement in the underlying business activity. Consistent application of accounting principles for a business enterprise from one accounting period to the next is needed in order that the financial statements of successive periods will be comparable.

The consistency principle does not mean that a particular method of accounting, once adopted, should not be changed. Accounting principles and methods change in response to changes in the environment of accounting. When an accounting change is desirable, it should be made, but with disclosure of the change and its effect in dollar amounts on the reported net income of the accounting period in which the change is made.

Comparability among financial statements ***within the same industry*** is also useful quality. However, differences in the operating policies among such enterprises result in the adoption of various accounting practices in such areas as valuation of inventories and depreciation of plant assets, so comparability within an industry is difficult to achieve.

Neutrality

The Financial Accounting Standards Board defined the quality of ***neutrality*** as the absence in reported information of bias intended to attain a predetermined result or to induce a particular mode of behaviour.[14] Because the users of general-purpose financial statements are many, freedom from bias is essential. For example, financial statements designed solely to influence the actions of investors could be damaging to the needs of creditors, who are another major user group for financial statements.

Materiality

Disclosure is necessary in financial statements or in notes to the financial statements only for ***material*** matters. The meaning of materiality in an accounting context is ***relative importance***. Items that are trifling in amount need not be treated in strict accordance with accounting theory but rather should be handled in the most economical manner. For example, most business enterprises establish a minimum dollar amount in considering whether an expenditure should be recorded as a depreciable plant asset. In theory, the cost of a new pencil sharpener should be capitalized and depreciated over its economic life. As a practical matter, the expense of making such allocations of cost would exceed the cost of the sharpener and represent an unjustifiably expensive accounting policy.

What is material for one business enterprise may not be so for another. To a small enterprise, an uninsured loss of, say, $50,000, might be considered material; for a large enterprise it would not be. In deciding on the materiality of an item in terms of financial statement disclosure, accountants should consider whether knowledge of the item would be likely to influence the decisions of the users of the statements.

In judging the materiality of an item, qualitative standards should be considered as well as the dollar amount. For example, a transaction between a business enterprise and its president is not at arm's length and suggests a possible conflict of interest. Disclosure of the transaction is appropriate, even though disclosure of such a transaction between independent parties would not be required.

In discussing quantitative measures of materiality, the Financial Accounting Standards Board has made the following statement:[15]

> The Board's present position is that no general standards of materiality could be formulated to take into account all the considerations that enter into an experienced human judgment. However, the position is not intended to imply either that the Board may not in the future review that conclusion or that quantitative guidance on materiality of specific items may not appropriately be written into the Board's standards from time to time. That has been done on occasion already (for example, in the Statement on financial reporting by segments of a business enterprise), and the Board recognizes that quantitative materiality guidance is sometimes needed. . . . However, whenever the Board or any other authoritative body imposes materiality rules, it is substituting generalized collective judgments for specific individual judgments, and there is no reason to suppose that the collective judgments are always superior.

14 FASB, *Statement No. 2*, p. xvi.

15 FASB, *Statement No. 2*, p. 53.

Elements of Financial Statements of Business Enterprises

In ***Statement of Financial Accounting Concepts No. 3:*** "Elements of Financial Statements of Business Enterprises," the Financial Accounting Standards Board identified 10 interrelated elements (building blocks) of financial statements: assets, liabilities, equity, investments by owners, distributions to owners, comprehensive income, revenues, expenses, gains, and losses. These elements were defined by the FASB as follows:[16]

- ***Assets*** are probable future economic benefits obtained or controlled by a particular entity as a result of past transactions or events.
- ***Liabilities*** are probable future sacrifices of economic benefits arising from present obligations of a particular entity to transfer assets or provide services to other entities in the future as a result of past transactions or events.
- ***Equity*** is the residual interest in the assets of an entity that remains after deducting its liabilities. In a business enterprise, the equity is the ownership interest.
- ***Investments by owners*** are increases in net assets of a particular enterprise resulting from transfers to it from other entities of something of value to obtain or increase ownership interests (or equity) in it. Assets are most commonly received as investments by owners, but that which is received may also include services or satisfaction or conversion of liabilities of the enterprise.
- ***Distributions to owners*** are decreases in net assets of a particular enterprise resulting from transferring assets, rendering services, or incurring liabilities by the enterprise to owners. Distributions to owners decrease ownership interests (or equity) in an enterprise.
- ***Comprehensive income*** is the change in equity (net assets) of an entity during a period from transactions and other events and circumstances from nonowner sources. It includes all changes in equity during a period except those resulting from investments by owners and distributions to owners.
- ***Revenues*** are inflows or other enhancements of assets of an entity or settlements of its liabilities (or a combination of both) during a period from delivering or producing goods, rendering services, or other activities that constitute the entity's ongoing major or central operations.
- ***Expenses*** are outflows or other using up of assets or incurrences of liabilities (or a combination of both) during a period from delivering or producing goods, rendering services, or carrying out other activities that constitute the entity's ongoing major or central operations.
- ***Gains*** are increases in equity (net assets) from peripheral or incidental transactions of an entity and from all other transactions and other events and circumstances affecting the entity during a period except those that result from revenues or investments by owners.
- ***Losses*** are decreases in equity (net assets) from peripheral or incidental transactions of an entity and from all other transactions and other events and circumstances affecting the entity during a period except those that result from expenses or distributions to owners.

16 FASB, ***Statement of Financial Accounting Concepts No. 3:*** "Elements of Financial Statements of Business Enterprises" (Stamford: 1980), pp. xi–xii.

Except for ***comprehensive income***, the foregoing elements are similar to the traditional concepts of components of financial statements. The FASB deliberately used the term ***comprehensive income*** rather than ***earnings*** to broaden the scope of measurements of the operating results of business enterprises.[17]

To allay fears that the foregoing definitions of elements of financial staements might suggest a radical change in financial reporting, the FASB stated:[18]

> The Board expects most assets and liabilities in present practice to continue to qualify as assets or liabilities under the definitions in this Statement. The Board emphasizes that the definitions neither require nor presage unheavals in present practice, although they may in due time lead to some evolutionary changes in practice or at least in the ways certain items are viewed. They should be especially helpful in understanding the content of financial statements and in analyzing and resolving new financial accounting issues as they arise.

Recognition and Measurement in Financial Statements of Business Enterprises

The Financial Accounting Standards Board essentially completed the conceptual framework project by issuing ***Statement of Financial Accounting Concepts No. 5:*** ''Recognition and Measurement in Financial Statements of Business Enterprises.'' In that ***Statement***, the FASB provided guidance on what information is to be included in financial statements and the timing of its inclusion (***recognition***) and on the quantification of the information (***measurement***). Among the provisions of the ***Statement*** are the following:[19]

1 A full set of financial statements for an accounting period should show financial position at the end of the period and earnings, comprehensive income, cash flows, and investments by and distributions to owners for the period. Disclosure is not a substitute for items that should be recognized in financial statements.

2 ***Comprehensive income*** is not the same as ***earnings*** because comprehensive income includes such items as changes in the market value of noncurrent marketable equity securities and gains or losses from holding nonmonetary assets during a period of changing current costs.

3 The use of different attributes, such as historical cost, current cost, current fair value, and net realizable value, which is a feature of current measurement techniques in financial accounting, is expected to continue. Information based on current prices should be recognized if it meets the qualitative characteristics of relevance and reliability and meets the cost-benefit test.

17 FASB, ***Statement No. 3***, p. 28.

18 FASB, ***Statement No. 3***, p. xiii.

19 FASB, ***Statement of Financial Accounting Concepts No. 5:*** ''Recognition and Measurement in Financial Statements of Business Enterprises'' (Stamford: 1984), pp. vii–ix.

Evaluation of Conceptual Framework Project

The Financial Accounting Standards Board worked more than 10 years on the conceptual framework project. The four numbers of ***Statement of Financial Accounting Concepts*** described in the preceding sections provide the FASB with a foundation for future issues of the ***Statement of Financial Accounting Standards***. For example, the definitions provided by the FASB in ***Statement of Financial Accounting Concepts No. 3*** have been used extensively in recent publications of the FASB dealing with proposed changes in accounting for pensions.

One wonders, however, whether the output of the conceptual framework project was cost-effective in terms of the substantial time, effort, and cost devoted to it. A close study of the four numbers of ***Statement of Financial Accounting Concepts*** outlined in the preceding sections discloses nothing revolutionary or even significantly different from present financial accounting concepts. The concept of ***comprehensive income***, for example, had roots in the "all-inclusive income statement" theory in effect many years ago. Perhaps the most significant impact of the conceptual framework has been an increased emphasis on ***cash flows*** as a measure of a business enterprise's performance during an accounting period. Only time will tell whether the benefits provided by the conceptual framework project, in terms of developing a cohesive body of financial accounting theory, were worth the energies devoted to it.

GENERALLY ACCEPTED ACCOUNTING PRINCIPLES (GAAP)

The term ***generally accepted accounting principles*** has long been used in financial accounting. This term also is used by public accountants in their audit reports to indicate whether the business enterprise being audited has prepared its financial statements in an acceptable manner, so that the statements may be compared with those of the prior year and to some extent with the statements of other enterprises. The principles of accounting are not rooted in the laws of nature as are the physical sciences. Therefore, ***accounting principles must be developed in relation to the stated objectives of financial reporting and financial statements***.

Although a body of generally accepted accounting principles has long been recognized, no complete official list of such principles exists. The most authoritative sources of generally accepted accounting principles in recent years have been the ***CICA Handbook recommendations*** in Canada, and in the United States the ***Statements*** issued by the ***FASB***, the ***Opinions*** issued by the ***APB***, the ***Accounting Research Bulletins*** issued by the ***AICPA*** Committee on Accounting Procedure, and the ***Financial Reporting Releases*** issued by the ***SEC***.

In the rest of this section we discuss a number of fundamental accounting principles and concepts. These are broad in nature and have been developed by accountants in an effort to meet the needs of the users of financial statements. The application of these principles and concepts to specific accounting and reporting issues is considered in later chapters.

Business Entity Principle

Because economic activity is carried on by various legal and economic entities, accounting results are summarized in terms of these entities. Accountants deal primarily with three general kinds of business entities: sole proprietorships, partnerships, and corporations. Regardless of the form of organization, the business affairs of the entity are distinguished from those of its owners. We see the effect of this principle when accounting income is measured as it accrues to the entity, not when it is distributed to owners. Similarly, an obligation of the entity to owners is treated as a liability, despite the fact that the owners owe a portion of the debt to themselves.

Accountants sometimes find it useful to prepare financial statements for economic entities that do not coincide with legal entities. For example, ***consolidated financial statements*** are often prepared for an economic entity that includes several corporate entities operating under common control exercised through common stock ownership. In contrast, separate financial statements may be prepared for divisions or segments of a large corporation.

Continuity or Going-Concern Principle

The ***continuity*** or ***going-concern principle*** means that accountants assume that a business entity will continue to exist indefinitely.[20] In deciding how to report various items in financial statements, accountants are often faced with this issue: ''Shall we assume that the business enterprise (entity) will continue to operate, or shall we assume that the enterprise will be terminated in the near future?'' The most probable situation for enterprises in general is that they will continue to operate for an indefinite period of time, and this is one of the most fundamental assumptions underlying financial acccounting.

To illustrate the significance of the continuity principle, consider the possibility that if an enterprise ceased operations, certain liabilities would mature immediately and require a payment in excess of their carrying amount. Productive assets such as machinery might have to be sold at a substantial loss. The assumption of continued existence provides the logical basis for recording probable future economic benefits as assets and probable future outlays as liabilities.

The continuity principle implies not permanence of existence but simply that a business enterprise will continue in existence long enough to carry out present plans and meet contractual commitments. This principle affects the classification of assets and liabilities in a balance sheet. Because it is assumed that assets will be used and obligations paid in the normal course of operation, no attempt is made to classify assets and liabilities in terms of their ultimate disposition or legal priority in case of liquidation.

There are times when the going-concern principle gives way to evidence that an enterprise has a limited life or intends to terminate operations. In such cases,

20 Sec. 5510.51 of the ***CICA Handbook*** defines ''going concern'' as the ability of the enterprise ''to realize assets and discharge liabilities in the normal course of business for the foreseeable future.''

accountants prepare financial statements under the assumption of a ***quitting concern*** rather than that of a going concern.

Revenue Realization (Recognition) Principle

Revenue may be defined as the value of goods and services that a business enterprise transfers to its customers. Thus, revenue is the principal factor responsible for increases in the net assets of a business enterprise apart from investments by owners. For a specific accounting period, revenue equals the inflow of cash and receivables from sales made during that period. For a single transaction, revenue equals the value of assets (cash and accounts receivable) received from the customer.

Any definition of revenue immediately raises questions as to timing — the essence of the ***revenue realization*** or ***recognition principle***. At what point or points during the creation of marketable products or services should revenue be recorded? What is the ***critical event*** that indicates revenue has been realized and justifies recording a change in net assets by replacing the carrying amount of assets such as inventories with a higher valuation representing their current fair value? Ideally, because each step in the process of producing and distributing goods is essential to earning revenue, the accounting ***recognition*** of revenue should be continuous rather than being linked to a single critical event. However, as a practical matter, reliable evidence is needed to support the recognition of revenue; and for most business enterprises, that evidence lies in an arm's-length transaction in which title to goods passes to the customer. Thus, the revenue realization or recognition principle dictates that assets such as inventories be carried ***at cost*** until appreciation in value is realized through sale. The reasoning underlying this practice is explained in Chapter 3.

Valuation Principle

Realization, which is a key principle in income measurement, also forms the basis for distinguishing methods of valuation used in the reporting of assets and liabilities in a balance sheet.

A general class of assets called ***monetary assets*** is usually carried in the balance sheet at amounts closely approximating current value. Examples are cash, term deposits or certicates of deposit, investments in bonds, and receivables; all these represent current purchasing power. Promissory notes receivable and notes payable that are non-interest-bearing, or that have an unrealistically low rate of interest, should be valued, not at face amount, but at their present value. ***Present value*** is determined by discounting all future payments on a promissory note at the current fair rate of interest. This discounting of receivables and payables to their present value applies principally to notes; it is not applicable to receivables and payables arising from transactions with customers or suppliers that are due within one year or less.

Another broad category of assets, termed ***nonmonetary assets*** or ***productive resources***, is reported in the balance sheet at ***cost***. Inventories and prepayments are examples of short-term productive resources that will be realized (used) at an early date. Buildings, equipment, patents, and investments in affiliated companies are examples of long-term productive resources that will be realized over a number of accounting periods. Until realization occurs, productive resources are measured and reported in the balance sheet at historical costs; after realization, valuations of the monetary assets received in exchange for productive assets generally approximate current fair value. These valuation principles govern the accounting for assets.

How should cost be measured when nonmonetary assets or services are acquired in noncash transactions — for example, when land is acquired in exchange for a corporation's own common stock? Cost is then defined as the cash equivalent (current fair value) of the land acquired or the cash equivalent of the common stock issued, ***whichever is more clearly evident***. If the common stock is listed on a stock exchange and is widely traded, the market price of the common stock may be stronger and more reliable evidence of the cost of the land than is an appraisal of the land.

Because a liability is an obligation to convey assets or perform services, the appropriate valuation of liabilities in a balance sheet is in terms of the cash (or cash equivalent) necessary to discharge the obligation on the balance sheet date. If payment is to be made later, liabilities are measured at the present discounted value (determined by use of the current fair rate of interest) of the future payments necessary to discharge the obligation. In the double-entry system of accounting, the present value of a long-term debt at the time it is incurred determines the cash proceeds of the borrowing or the cost of the asset received in exchange. As the maturity of a debt approaches, its carrying amount may change, and this change is a part of the computation of the interest expense on the debt. This topic is considered in Chapter 15.

Matching Principle

The ***matching principle*** means that after the revenue (accomplishment) for an accounting period has been determined, the costs (effort) associated with this revenue must be deducted from revenue to measure net income. The term ***matching*** refers to the close relationship that exists between certain costs and the revenue recognized as a result of incurring those costs.

Expenses may be defined as the cost of goods or services used to obtain revenue. The matching of a business enterprise's expenses (or expired costs) with its revenue for an accounting period is the primary activity in the measurement of the results of the enterprise's operations for that period. For example, expenditures for advertising attract customers and generate sales. The outlay for the advertising is one of the expenses to be deducted from the revenue of an accounting period. Similarly, the recognition of what is called ''doubtful accounts expense'' illustrates the importance of the matching of expenses and revenue in an accounting period. Doubtful accounts expense is caused by selling goods or services on credit to customers who fail to pay their bills. To match this expense with the related revenue, the expense must be recorded and deducted from revenue in the accounting period in which the sales are made and recorded, even though the receivables are not determined to be uncollectible until the following period. The use of estimates is necessary in this and in many other situations in order to implement the matching principle.

Monetary Principle

The ***monetary principle*** means that accountants assume money to be a useful ***standard measuring unit*** for reporting the effects of business transactions. Money is used as the common denominator throughout the accounting process. Of course, some of the information necessary to give a comprehensive picture of a business enterprise is difficult or impossible to quantify and express in money or other units of measurement. Examples are the competence, health, and morale of management and employees, and the effect of the operations of the enterprise on the natural environment. However, if information is to be included in financial statements, it must be expressed in monetary terms. If such measurement is not practicable, a possible alternative method of communication is to use notes to the financial statements.

In Canada the monetary unit is the dollar. To be a useful unit of measurement, the dollar, ideally, should be of unchanging value. For a long time the rate of price-level change in Canada was not considered to be significant enough to cast serious doubt on the usefulness of the dollar as a measuring unit. However, in many recent years, the continuing and relatively rapid inflation has reduced significantly the ''value of a dollar'' and has made the monetary principle one of the most controversial elements of generally accepted accounting principles. By the ''value of a dollar'' we usually mean the ***quantity of goods and services*** that the dollar will command in exchange. What kind of common denominator will enable us to measure the physical quantities of all the diverse goods and services that the dollar will buy?

The statistical solution to this question is a ***price index***, which is a device for measuring changes in the weighted-average price of a representative sample of goods and services between two points in time. Although they are somewhat imperfect, price indexes covering broad categories of goods and services are useful tools for measuring changes in the value of the dollar.

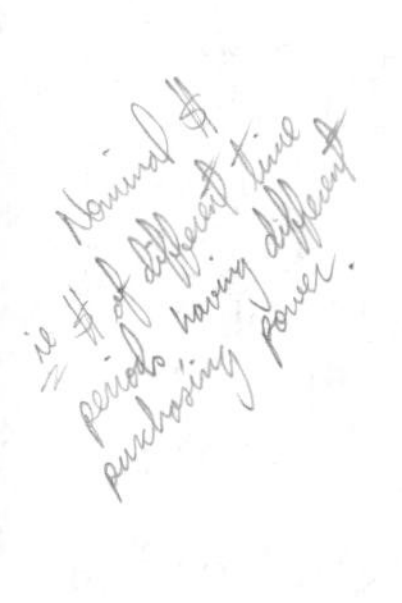

The monetary principle is reflected in a balance sheet by valuations of nonmonetary assets and shareholders' equity expressed in dollars of different time periods, that is, ***nominal dollars*** having different purchasing power (if the general price level rose or fell).

If the monetary assumption were changed, and balance sheets were expressed in ***constant purchasing power***, the two categories most affected would be nonmonetary (productive) assets (plant assets and inventories) and owners' equity. Monetary assets and most liabilities are stated at approximately their current fair values, and thus are expressed in constant purchasing power. However, the accounting valuation of nonmonetary assets is a mixture of historical costs. Similarly, capital stock and retained earnings in the shareholders' equity section of a balance sheet are expressed in nominal dollars that may have lost much of their significance because of changes in the general price level.

To illustrate this point, consider the case of Shan Corporation, which has been in business for 10 years, during which period the general price level has risen steadily. A balance sheet (in highly condensed and somewhat unorthodox form) for Shan is shown below, expressed in both ''nominal dollars'' and ''constant purchasing power.'' Compare the amounts under each approach.

SHAN CORPORATION
Balance Sheet
December 31, Year 10

Assets		*Nominal dollars (monetary assumption)*		*Constant purchasing power (revised assumption)*
Monetary assets (cash, investments in debt securities, and receivables — stated in fixed number of dollars)		$200,000		$200,000
Nonmonetary assets (inventories, plant assets, and intangible assets)		400,000		700,000
Total assets		$600,000		$900,000
Liabilities & Shareholders' Equity				
Liabilities (stated in fixed number of dollars)		$300,000		$300,000
Shareholders' equity:				
Common stock	$200,000		$400,000	
Retained earnings	100,000		60,000	
Unrealized purchasing power gain			140,000	
Total shareholders' equity		300,000		600,000
Total liabilities & shareholders' equity		$600,000		$900,000

Note the upward revision of nonmonetary assets and shareholders' equity when they are expressed in ''constant purchasing power.'' The decline in retained earnings expressed in constant purchasing power (from $100,000 to $60,000) occurs because the cost of goods sold, depreciation, and amortization of intangible assets are larger when they are expressed in constant purchasing power during a period of inflation. The ''unrealized purchasing power gain'' ($140,000) is more complex. It results from the fact that nonmonetary assets were financed in part by debt. Creditors are entitled to a repayment of only a fixed number of dollars. Thus, when nonmonetary assets are restated in terms of an increased amount of constant purchasing power, Shan gains at the expense of its creditors. Bear in mind that this illustration does not use current fair values for assets, but historical costs adjusted for the change in the general price level.

Financial reporting in terms of constant purchasing power has been tried in a few countries where price inflation has been extreme. In Canada and the United States, supplementary constant-purchasing-power data in annual reports to shareholders have attracted considerable attention. However, it appears unlikely that the monetary principle will be abandoned completely, barring a greater change in the value of the dollar than Canada has thus far experienced. The procedures for converting nominal-dollar financial statements to constant purchasing-power are discussed in Chapter 25.

Disclosure Principle

The ***disclosure principle*** requires that financial statements be complete in the sense of including all information necessary to users of the statements. If the omission of certain information would cause the financial statements to be misleading, disclosure of such information is essential. Thus, published financial statements include detailed notes that are considered to be an integral part of the statements. However, disclosures in the notes should supplement the information in the body of the financial statements and should not be used to correct improper presentation of information in the body of the statements.

Typical examples of information often disclosed in notes to financial statements are: a summary of significant accounting policies, related party transactions, descriptions of stock option and pension plans, status of litigation in which the business enterprise is a party, amount and nature of contingencies and commitments, and terms and status of proposed business combinations.

The concept of disclosure applies not only to transactions and events that have occurred during the accounting period covered by the financial statements, but also to material ***subsequent events*** that occur after the balance sheet date but before the financial statements are released. Such events are also disclosed in a note to the financial statements.

The disclosure principle does not require the listing of precise dollar amounts. In the published financial statements of most large companies, all amounts are rounded to the nearest thousand dollars. For example, if the general ledger has a balance for accounts receivable of $45,778,501.50 and a related allowance for doubtful accounts of $500,000.00, the balance sheet would show accounts receivable (net) at $45,279. In reading this amount, one must bear in mind that five digits have been omitted.

CASH FLOWS AND INCOME MEASUREMENT

Accountants assume that a business enterprise has continuous existence. Therefore, they record the prospect of future cash inflows as an increase in assets and as revenue whenever they have reliable evidence of the amount of the future cash receipt. Cash inflows often occur before an enterprise has performed its part of a contract. In this case, an increase in assets is recorded, but a liability is recognized instead of revenue. The liability indicates an obligation on the part of the enterprise to perform in accordance with the contract. When performance is completed, the revenue is recognized. Thus, cash inflows are closely related to revenue realization; however, the assumptions underlying the timing of revenue realization do not always permit cash inflows and revenue to be recorded in the same accounting period.

Similarly, cash outflows are closely related to expenses of a business enterprise; however, cash outflows and expenses may not be recorded in the same accounting period. For example, enterprises frequently acquire for cash in one period assets that will be productive over several future periods, and assets that are productive only during the current period are often acquired in exchange for a promise to pay cash in a future period.

Information concerning cash flows during an accounting period is valuable in judging the ability of the business enterprise to pay its debts, to pay regular dividends, to finance replacements of productive assets, and to expand its scope of operations. However, the increase or decrease in cash during a period is not useful in evaluating an enterprise's operating performance, because cash receipts and payments are not representative of the economic activities carried on in specific periods.

Accrual Basis of Accounting

The ***accrual basis of accounting*** is assumed throughout this book. Revenue is recorded when realized and expenses are recorded when incurred, without regard to the time of cash receipt or payment. The focus of the accrual basis of accounting is on the realization of revenue, the incurring of costs, and the matching of revenue realized with costs expired (expenses). Adopting the assumption that revenue is recorded when realization occurs and the related assumption that costs contributing to the realization of this revenue may be traced through the earning process requires the use of an ***accrual-deferral system*** of accounting.

The need for frequent measurement of the past performance of a business enterprise as the basis for decisions about the future has obliged accountants to adopt the accrual basis of accounting. Under the accrual basis, the accounting records are adjusted periodically to ensure that all assets and liabilities (and thus revenue and expenses) are correctly stated.

Cash Basis of Accounting

Under the ***cash basis of accounting***, revenue is recorded only when cash is received and expenses are recorded only when cash is paid. The determination of income thus rests on the ***collection*** of revenue and the ***payment*** of expenses, rather than on the ***realization*** of revenue and the ***incurring*** of expenses. Use of the cash basis of accounting is not compatible with the matching principle described earlier in this chapter. Consequently, financial statements prepared under the cash basis of accounting do not present the financial position or operating results of an enterprise in conformity with generally accepted accounting principles.

A strict cash basis of accounting is seldom found in practice, but a ***modified cash basis*** (a mixed cash-accrual basis) is more common. Under the modified cash basis of accounting, taxpayers who acquire property having an economic life of more than one year may not deduct the entire cost in the year of acquisition. They must treat the cost as an asset to be depreciated over its economic life. Expenses such as rent or advertising paid in advance are also regarded as assets and are deductible only in the year or years to which they apply. Expenses paid after the year in which they are incurred are deductible only in the year paid. Revenue is reported in the year received. However, in any business enterprise in which the purchase, production, or sale of merchandise is a significant factor, these transactions must be reported on an accrual basis. For example, when merchandise is sold on credit, the revenue must be recognized immediately. The cost of goods sold must reflect purchases on credit and inventories on hand, whether paid for or not. Thus, for a merchandising enterprise the revenue from sales, the cost of goods sold, and the gross profit on sales will be the same under the accrual basis of accounting as they are under the modified cash basis of accounting.

Illustration

The difference between the cash basis and the accrual basis of accounting is illustrated below for Tina Carson, a practising lawyer, who maintains accounting records on a cash basis. During Year 10, Carson collected $150,000 from her clients and paid $80,000 for operating expenses, resulting in a cash-basis net income of $70,000. Carson's fees receivable, accrued liabilities, and short-term prepayments on January 1 and on December 31, Year 10, were as follows:

Accrual-basis items of business enterprise that uses cash basis of accounting

	Jan. 1, Year 10	*Dec. 31, Year 10*
Fees receivable	$18,200	$37,000
Accrued liabilities	6,200	4,000
Short-term prepayments	3,500	2,500

A working paper showing the necessary adjustments to restate Carson's income statement from the cash basis to the accrual basis of accounting is illustrated below.

TINA CARSON, BARRISTER AND SOLICITOR
Working Paper to Restate Income Statement from Cash Basis to Accrual Basis of Accounting
For Year Ended December 31, Year 10

	Income statement under cash basis of accounting	*Adjustments to restate to accrual basis of accounting*		*Income statement under accrual basis of accounting*
		Add	*Deduct*	
Revenue from fees received in cash	$150,000			
Add: Fees receivable, Dec. 31, Year 10		$37,000		$168,800
Less: Fees receivable, Jan. 1, Year 10			$18,200	
Operating expenses paid in cash	80,000			
Add: Accrued liabilities, Dec. 31, Year 10		4,000		
Short-term prepayments, Jan. 1, Year 10		3,500		78,800
Less: Accrued liabilities, Jan. 1, Year 10			6,200	
Short-term prepayments, Dec. 31, Year 10			2,500	
Net income under cash basis of accounting	$ 70,000			
Net income under accrual basis of accounting				$ 90,000

Because the revenue from fees under the cash basis does not include the fees receivable on December 31, which were realized in Year 10, this amount is added to the cash collected in the restatement of revenue from fees to the accrual basis of accounting. Because fees receivable on January 1 were realized in Year 9 and collected in Year 10, this amount is subtracted from cash collections in the restatement of revenue from fees to the accrual basis of accounting.

The adjustments to restate operating expenses from the cash basis of accounting to the accrual basis of accounting are explained below:

1 The amount of accrued liabilities on December 31, Year 10, represents expenses incurred in Year 10 that will be paid in Year 11, and the amount of short-term prepayments on January 1, Year 10, represents services paid for in Year 9 that were consumed in Year 10. Therefore, both amounts are ***added*** to the amount of cash paid to restate the operating expenses for Year 10 to the accrual basis of accounting.

2 The amount of accrued liabilities on January 1, Year 10, represents expenses of Year 9 paid for in Year 10, and the amount of short-term repayments on December 31, Year 10, represents cash outlays in Year 10 for services that will be consumed in Year 11. Therefore, both amounts are ***deducted*** from the amount of cash paid to restate the operating expenses for Year 10 to the accrual basis of accounting.

REVIEW QUESTIONS

1 Identify the organizations or legislative acts that have been influential in the development of accounting principles and practices in Canada. What is the relationship between each of these organizations or acts and public accountants?

2 Do the accounting recommendations of the ***CICA Handbook*** constitute generally accepted accounting principles? Explain.

3 Describe the procedures followed by the CICA's Accounting Standards Committee in the development of a new accounting recommendation.

4 Briefly describe the Financial Accounting Standards Board's conceptual framework project for financial accounting and reporting.

5 What are four publications of the Financial Accounting Standards Board issued as parts of the conceptual framework project?

6 Briefly describe three objectives of financial reporting identified by the Financial Accounting Standards Board.

7 What is the most important qualitative characteristic of accounting information, according to the Financial Accounting Standards Board?

8 The two primary qualities of accounting information identified by the Financial Accounting Standards Board are ***relevance*** and ***reliability***. Are these qualities as likely to be present in a forecast of future earnings as in an income statement? Explain.

9 Is ***conservatism*** a qualitative characteristic of accounting information? Explain.

10 Briefly summarize the position of the Financial Accounting Standards Board on ***materiality*** as an influencing factor on the quality of accounting information.

11 What is ***comprehensive income*** as defined by the Financial Accounting Standards Board?

12 Are generally accepted accounting principles applicable to both financial accounting and managerial accounting? Explain.

13 What is meant by the ***continuity*** or ***going-concern principle*** of accounting? How does it affect the valuation of assets? When is this principle not applicable?

14 Define the ***revenue realization*** (***recognition***) ***principle***. How is this principle related to the ***valuation principle*** and the ***matching principle***?

15 Wembley Corporation acquired land in exchange for 50,000 shares of its common stock. How is the valuation principle of accounting applied in recording this transaction?

16 The ***monetary principle*** assumes that money is a useful standard measuring unit for reporting the effects of business transactions. State and explain two major criticisms or limitations of this accounting principle.

17 Hardy Corporation has total assets of $136,542,816.22. The balances of Hardy's Accounts Receivable and Allowance for Doubtful Accounts ledger accounts on December 31, Year 6, were $4,118,263.81 and $92,774.18 respectively.How may accounts receivable be presented in Hardy's December 31, Year 6, balance sheet under the ***disclosure principle***? Explain.

18 Distinguish between the ***cash basis of accounting*** and the ***accrual basis of accounting***. Do financial statements prepared under either method present the financial position and operating results of a business enterprise in conformity with generally accepted accounting principles?

EXERCISES

Ex. 1-1 Select the best answer for each of the following multiple-choice questions:

1 The valuation of a promise to receive cash in the future at present value in the financial statements of a business enterprise is valid because of the accounting principle or concept of:
a Entity *b* Materiality *c* Going concern *d* Neutrality

2 Which of the following is disclosed in the Summary of Significant Accounting Policies note to the financial statements?
a Amount of rent expense
b Maturity dates of long-term debt
c Methods of amortizing intangible assets
d Composition of plant assets

3 The imputation of interest for certain assets and liabilities is based primarily on the accounting principle or concept of:
a Valuation *b* Conservatism *c* Consistency
d Stable monetary unit

4 Which of the following is considered a pervasive constraint by ***Statement of***

Financial Accounting Concepts No. 2: "Qualitative Characteristics of Accounting Information"?
a Cost-benefit considerations *b* Conservatism *c* Timeliness
d Verifiability

5 According to ***Statement of Financial Accounting Concepts No. 2:*** "Qualitative Characteristics of Accounting Information," relevance and reliability are the two primary qualities that make accounting information useful for decision making. Is ***predictive value*** an ingredient of relevance? Of reliability? Choose ***a, b, c,*** or ***d*** in accordance with the table below.

	Relevance	*Reliability*
a	No	No
b	No	Yes
c	Yes	Yes
d	Yes	No

6 Under ***Statement of Financial Accounting Concepts No. 2:*** "Qualitative Characteristics of Accounting Information," which of the following is an ingredient of the primary quality of ***reliability***?
a Understandability *b* Verifiability *c* Predictive value
d Materiality

7 Under ***Statement of Financial Accounting Concepts No. 2:*** "Qualitative Characteristics of Accounting Information," ***timeliness*** is an ingredient of the primary quality of:
a Reliability *b* Relevance *c* Verifiability
d Representational faithfulness

8 Under ***Statement of Financial Accounting Concepts No. 3:*** "Elements of Financial Statements of Business Enterprises," does ***comprehensive income*** include changes in owners' equity resulting from investments by owners? Distributions to owners? Choose ***a, b, c,*** or ***d*** according to the table below.

	Investments by owners	*Distributions to owners*
a	No	No
b	No	Yes
c	Yes	No
d	Yes	Yes

Ex. 1-2 Norm Company debits all insurance premium payments to the Unexpired Insurance ledger account and prepares adjusting entries at the end of each month to recognize expired insurance premiums as an expense. Balances of the affected ledger accounts were as follows for Year 6:

Unexpired Insurance:	
Jan. 1, Year 6	$150,000
Dec. 31, Year 6	175,000
Insurance Expense, Dec. 31, Year 6	625,000

Compute the total insurance premiums paid by Norm Company during Year 6.

Ex. 1-3 Lemo Corporation owns a small building with offices that it rents under contracts calling for payments either monthly or yearly in advance. However, some tenants are delinquent in their rent payments. During Year 2, Lemo received $20,000 from tenants. Lemo's ledger account balances for Year 2 included the following:

	Jan. 1, Year 2	*Dec. 31, Year 2*
Rent Receivable	$2,400	$3,100
Unearned Rent	8,000	6,000

Compute Lemo Corporation's rent revenue for Year 2 under the accrual basis of accounting.

Ex. 1-4 Gilbert Company assigns some of its patents to other business enterprises under licensing contracts. Under some licences, advance royalties are received; under other licences, royalties are paid within 60 days after each licence year ends. During Year 5, Gilbert received royalty cheques of $200,000. Gilbert's ledger account balances for Year 5 included the following:

	Jan. 1, Year 5	*Dec. 31, Year 5*
Royalities Receivable	$90,000	$85,000
Unearned Royalties	60,000	40,000

Compute Gilbert Company's royalties revenue for Year 5 under the accrual basis of accounting.

Ex. 1-5 Cash paid by Langley Corporation for operating expenses during the month of October, Year 6, totalled $16,480. Short-term prepayments and accrued liabilities were as follows:

	Oct. 1, Year 6	*Oct. 31, Year 6*
Short-term prepayments	$1,240	$1,690
Accrued liabilities	2,570	1,820

Compute Langley Corporation's operating expenses for the month of October, Year 6, under the accrual basis of accounting.

Ex. 1-6 Identify each of the following phrases as being associated with either the cash basis of accounting or the accrual basis of accounting:

a Revenue recognized at time of collection
b Individual income tax returns
c Business enterprise with a material amount of inventories
d Minimum amount of record-keeping
e Generally accepted accounting principles

f Postponement of recognition of revenue
g Flexibility in recognition of expenses
h Emphasis on consistency and matching in the measurement of net income
i Sophisticated accounting system

Ex. 1-7 The general-purpose financial statements of Matt Corporation contain the following item and note to the financial statements:

Inventories	$1,760,000

NOTE 1—Summary of Significant Accounting Policies: Inventories are valued at the lower of cost and market; cost is determined on the first-in, first-out basis and market on the net realizable value basis.

Discuss the appropriateness of the foregoing in relation to the disclosure principle of accounting.

Ex. 1-8 Crocus Company uses the accrual basis of accounting. It reported advertising expense for Year 7 of $35,460. Prepaid advertising at the end of Year 7 amounted to $4,820, and cash paid for advertising during Year 7 amounted to $36,680. There was no advertising payable at either the beginning or the end of Year 7.

Compute the amount of Crocus Company's prepaid advertising at the beginning of Year 7.

Ex. 1-9 The financial statements of Weir Company include the items shown below, together with the related notes to the financial statements.

Cash (**NOTE 1**)	$ 96,500
Accounts receivable (**NOTE 2**)	210,300

NOTE 1: The amount reported as cash includes four chequing accounts, two petty cash funds, and one change fund.
NOTE 2: Accounts receivable include $48,400, representing the selling price of merchandise shipped on consignment and held for sale by consignees acting as agents. It is anticipated that this merchandise will be sold within six months and that none of it will have to be returned to the warehouse.

Discuss the appropriateness of Note 1 and Note 2 to Weir Company's financial statements as a means of carrying out the disclosure principle and the objectives of general-purpose financial statements.

CASES

Case 1-1 Generally accepted accounting principles require the use of accruals and deferrals in the determination of net income.

Instructions

a How does the accrual basis of accounting affect the measurement of net income? Include a discussion of what constitutes an accrual and what a deferral, and give examples of each.

b Contrast the accrual basis of accounting with the cash basis of accounting.

Case 1-2 During the first class meeting in an accounting course, Professor Logan asked three students to explain the nature of revenue and expenses as related to the preparation of financial statements for business enterprises. Carl Lucas stated that revenue and expenses reflect changes in the owners' equity of a business enterprise. Lois Chu stated that Carl was wrong and explained that revenue represents inflows of assets and expenses represent outflows of assets. Morris Dean responded as follows: ''Revenue and expenses are those items that determine net income.'' Professor Logan took the position that each student was on the right track, but that none had presented an entirely satisfactory explanation.

Instructions

Evaluate Professor Logan's response and describe the nature of revenue and expenses as these terms are used in financial accounting.

Case 1-3 The board of directors of DuPre Corporation is debating whether to adopt the straight-line method of depreciation or an accelerated depreciation method. Some directors are primarily interested in reporting steadily increasing earnings; others argue that the best way to achieve a favourable ''accounting image'' in the financial community is to adopt conservative accounting policies.

Instructions

Explain whether the conservative effect of accelerated depreciation on net income and financial position will be realized for only a few years or whether it will continue indefinitely to result in the reporting of lower earnings and a lower valuation of plant assets.

Case 1-4 A financial newspaper carried an advertisement of a small manufacturing enterprise being offered for sale by its owner. The advertisement emphasized the unusual profitability of the enterprise. Assume that you were interested in acquiring a business of this type and you therefore contacted the owner, Laura Griffin, who stated that Griffin Company in its first year of operations had realized net income of $95,000. You inquired whether the accrual basis of accounting had been used to determine the net income, and Griffin replied as follows:

> We use a mixed cash-accrual basis of accounting, just as many other small companies do. As you probably know, a strict cash basis is not satisfactory, but a modified or mixed cash-accrual basis meets our needs. For example, our purchases of merchandise are recorded only when cash payments are made. Our sales are recorded immediately, whether on a cash or a credit basis. We do not guess about doubtful accounts receivable in advance, but we do not hesitate to write off any receivable that proves to be uncollectible. We took a physical inventory at year-end and entered it in the accounting records. We did not record any depreciation on equipment because equipment was acquired by issuance of long-term promissory notes. No journal

entry will be made for these transactions until cash payments are made. We find this system gives us better results than a strict cash basis of accounting and requires less work than the accrual basis of accounting.

Instructions

Evaluate point by point the statement made by Laura Griffin. Do you regard Griffin Company's system as conforming with the usual standards of a "modified cash basis" of accounting? Is the net income of $95,000 during the first year of operations a valid measurement? Explain.

Case 1-5 In a discussion of the concept of conservatism as an influence on financial accounting and reporting, Alice Wu argued that conservatism is often used as a means of understating net income of the current accounting period and the financial position at the end of the period. George Case defended conservatism on the grounds that accountants frequently have to make choices among alternative assumptions under conditions of uncertainty and that making such choices on a conservative basis would help avoid dangerous overstatements of net income that could injure both investors and public accountants.

Wu and Case considered the five following situations but were unable to reach agreement on the proper accounting treatment for any of them.

1 A business enterprise has expended $125,000 (which is 5% of its annual sales) for research and development in an effort to develop new commercial products. No specific products have emerged from this research, but management believes that the research, if continued, eventually will lead to important new products. Furthermore, management believes that its existing products will lose their market appeal in a few years and that the enterprise must have new products to survive. Wu favours including the $125,000 in the balance sheet as an intangible asset, Deferred Research and Development Costs; Case favours treating the $125,000 as expense of the current year.

2 After occupying an old building on leased land for 17 years of a 20-year operating lease, the lessee enterprise constructed a new frame building, because the old building was unsatisfactory and the lessor refused to make repairs. Improvements on the land will revert to the lessor at the end of the lease term. There is a possibility, but no assurance, that the lessor will agree to renew the lease. Wu favours capitalizing the cost of the building; Case favours writing off the cost of the building as expense of the current year.

3 The products sold by a manufacturing enterprise are guaranteed for a period of one year. Wu favours the recognition of warranty expense only as claims are presented for repair or replacement of products; Case favours the recognition of warranty expense and crediting a liability for an estimated amount in the year of sale.

4 The inventory of a retailing enterprise contains a large quantity of item K for which demand has largely disappeared. Wu wants to include item K as an asset in the balance sheet on the grounds that the item is not subject to deterioration and customer demand for it may revive; Case favours writing off the cost of this item.

5 Credit terms of a retailing enterprise are 30 days. Case favours writing off a large receivable six months past due from a customer who went to Europe for an extended stay and cannot be located; Wu is opposed because the customer has been delinquent before and later paid in full.

Instructions
For each of the five situations, state your position on the proposed action and explain the reasoning underlying your position.

Case 1-6 Spivak Corporation owns several office buildings and rents space to tenants. One of these office buildings was acquired at a cost of $750,000 and has been depreciated for five years on a straight-line basis. Residual value is zero. The carrying amount, net of accumulated depreciation, will be $680,000 at the end of the current year.

At the time the building was acquired, Spivak Corporation had borrowed $750,000 from Curtis Evan, one of the founders of Spivak and presently a director and major shareholder. The promissory note payable issued for the loan made no mention of interest but called for repayment of $1,000,000 five years from the date of the note. In a directors' meeting near the end of the current year, Evan stated that, because of rising price levels, he considered the office building to be worth more than it had cost. Evan offered to accept the office building in full settlement of the $1,000,000 promissory note which was about to mature.

During a discussion of the offer by the board of directors, the following opinions were expressed:

Director Jacobs: ''If we give up the building in settlement of the $1,000,000 note payable, we shall increase our earnings this year by $250,000, and we shall have to correct our prior years' earnings by eliminating all depreciation on the building, because this transaction provides reliable evidence that the building has not depreciated. My understanding of generally accepted accounting principles is that our treatment of the transaction must use the reliable evidence provided by Evan's offer.''

Director Winton: ''In my opinion we could accept the offer and not have to recognize any gain. Spivak will not receive cash, receivables, or any other asset, so there is no gain involved. The revenue realization principle states that there must be an inflow of cash or receivables in order to have revenue.''

Director Toby: ''Spivak received only $750,000 when it issued the note payable, and it has not paid or recorded any interest. Now we shall give up an asset that cost $750,000 to discharge a recorded liability of the same amount, so this is a perfect example of the matching principle, and no gain or loss is involved.''

Instructions

a Evaluate the opinions expressed by each of the three directors, giving attention to the references made to accounting principles. Use a separate paragraph or paragraphs to evaluate each director's position and indicate what accounting principles are involved.

b Explain how the proposed transaction should be accounted for by Spivak

Corporation. Indicate the accounting principle or principles you consider to be applicable. Include in your answer whether interest and depreciation should be recognized and the amount of the gain or loss, if any, that would result from acceptance of Curtis Evan's offer.

c In the financial statements prepared immediately after completion of the exchange with Curtis Evan, is it necessary to make any disclosure of this transaction apart from the usual accounting for disposal of a building? Explain.

d Assuming that Spivak Corporation accepts Curtis Evan's offer, prepare a journal entry to record the transaction. Assume that depreciation expense has been recorded for the current year and that the accounting records have not been closed. No interest expense has been recorded on the promissory note payable. Assume also that the journal entry made at the time the note payable was issued consisted of a debit to Cash for $750,000, a debit to Discount on Notes Payable for $250,000, and a credit to Notes Payable for $1,000,000. ***Suggestion:*** The interest expense applicable to prior years may be debited to Retained Earnings (Prior Period Adjustment). Assume that the interest expense applicable to the current year is $55,000.

PROBLEMS

Pr. 1-1 Haig Corporation was organized by Howard Haig and Richard Haig for the purpose of operating a hardware store. Each invested $60,000 cash, and each received 3,000 shares of common stock. Howard Haig also lent $50,000 to Haig Corporation and received a two-year, 12% promissory note. Haig Corporation then issued 3,600 shares of its common stock in exchange for land and a building. The land had a current fair value of $30,000.

Merchandise costing $70,000 was purchased on credit, and a sales representative was employed to begin work the following week at a weekly salary of $500. Haig Corporation plans to use the periodic inventory system. Office supplies and office equipment were acquired for $15,000 cash. The office supplies were valued at $2,600 and the office equipment at $12,400.

Instructions

a What cost should be recorded for the land and the building acquired in exchange for Haig Corporation's common stock? Explain the reasoning underlying your answer.

b Prepare journal entries for the foregoing transactions of Haig Corporation.

c After one year of operations, Haig Corporation had a strong working capital position, but retained earnings amounted to only $20,000. Under these circumstances, would it be proper for Haig Corporation to pay the $50,000 note payable to Howard Haig? Explain.

Pr. 1-2 Carl Will and George Burr formed Will-Burr Corporation to operate a charter fishing boat. Each invested $54,000 cash, for which each received 6,000 shares of common stock. Will-Burr Corporation also issued 2,400 shares of common stock as part of the consideration to acquire a used boat. Wilma Todd, the former owner of the boat, had pledged it as collateral for a $50,000 bank loan, and this $50,000 liability was assumed by Will-Burr Corporation in the contract for acquisition of the boat.

Wilma Todd's accounting records showed that the original cost of the boat was $150,000 and that she had recorded depreciation expense of $90,000 by the straight-line method.

Will-Burr Corporation acquired for cash fishing equipment for $12,800 and supplies for $1,500. A crew member was hired to begin work the following week at a weekly salary of $550.

Instructions

a What effect, if any, does the amount of recorded depreciation and the depreciation method used by Wilma Todd have on the depreciation program to be used for the boat by Will-Burr Corporation? Explain the reasoning underlying your answer.

b What cost should be recorded for the boat acquired in exchange for 2,400 shares of Will-Burr Corporation common stock? Explain.

c Prepare journal entries to record the transactions completed by Will-Burr Corporation.

Pr. 1-3 Plumm Limited is a successful enterprise that is expanding rapidly. On May 1, Year 5, additional manaufacturing facilities were acquired from the Towne & Bates Partnership, which was terminating operations because of a dispute between the partners. The property had been advertised for sale at a price of $950,000. Bates asserted that the land alone was worth that much and that the building was insured for $500,000, its cost of construction.

Plumm acquired the property by issuing to the partnership 60,000 shares of its no-par common stock and agreed to assume a $250,000 mortgage note payable on the property.

Prior to the acquisition, Plumm hired a firm of industrial engineers to appraise the building. The report from this firm set forth a current fair value for the building of $480,000. The common stock of Plumm is listed on a stock exchange and was trading on May 1, Year 5, at a price of $12 a share.

Shortly after acquiring the property from the Towne & Bates Partnership, Plumm received a letter from a large corporation offering to acquire the property from Plumm for $1,000,000.

Instructions

a Prepare a journal entry to record the transaction of Plumm Limited.

b Explain the reasoning underlying your response to *a*.

Pr. 1-4 In borrowing from various sources, Gill Corporation issues promissory notes frequently. Some of the notes provide for payment of interest in advance; others do not. (For the purposes of this problem, you need not challenge the propriety of prepaid interest.) Gill uses the accrual basis of accounting. Interest expense under the accrual basis for Year 3 was $19,600. Information relating to prepaid interest and interest payable on two successive balance sheet dates appears below:

	Dec. 31, Year 2	*Dec. 31, Year 3*
Prepaid interest	$1,800	$ 400
Interest payable	1,700	2,200

Gill owns several buildings that it rents to tenants. Some tenants pay rent in advance; others do not. The amount of cash collected from the tenants during Year 3 was $56,400. The following information relates to rent receivable and unearned rent on two successive balance sheet dates:

	Dec. 31, Year 2	*Dec. 31, Year 3*
Rent receivable	$6,400	$5,000
Unearned rent	3,600	2,800

Instructions

a Compute the amount of cash paid by Gill Corporation for interest during Year 3.

b Compute the amount of Gill Corporation's rent revenue for Year 3, under the accrual basis of accounting.

Pr. 1-5 Lido Company uses the accrual basis of accounting. Lido owns buildings that it rents to tenants. Rent collected in cash during Year 5 amounted to $108,400. The amounts of rent receivable and unearned rent on two successive balance sheet dates were as follows:

	Dec. 31, Year 4	*Dec. 31, Year 5*
Rent receivable	$3,600	$4,900
Unearned rent	4,400	1,640

Lido advertises its merchandise through television, radio, and newspapers. Some of the advertising is paid in advance and some is paid on receipt of invoices. Advertising expense under the accrual basis of accounting for Year 5 was $64,200. The amounts of prepaid advertising and advertising payable at the beginning and at the end of Year 5 were as follows:

	Jan. 1, Year 5	*Dec. 31, Year 5*
Prepaid advertising	$5,360	$6,400
Advertising payable	7,840	2,930

Instructions

a Compute the amount of rent revenue that should appear in Lido Company's income statement for Year 5, under the accrual basis of accounting.

b Compute the amount of cash paid by Lido Company for advertising during Year 5.

Pr. 1-6 A summary of operating results for Perez Corporation for Year 2 is presented below:

Cash collected from customers	$466,000
Cash paid to merchandise suppliers	268,200
Cash paid for operating expenses	79,400

The following data were taken from comparative balance sheets prepared on the accrual basis of accounting:

	Dec. 31, Year 1	*Dec. 31, Year 2*
Accounts receivable	$52,400	$48,600
Inventories	75,000	72,100
Short-term prepayments	4,100	9,500
Accounts payable (merchandise suppliers)	32,000	37,400
Accrued liabilities	2,800	3,200
Accumulated depreciation (There were no disposals of plant assets during Year 2)	50,000	74,000

Instructions

Prepare income statements for Perez Corporation for Year 2, under ***a*** the accrual basis of accounting and ***b*** the modified cash basis of accounting whereby operating expenses (other than depreciation) are computed on the cash basis. Perez's income is taxed at 45%. Show supporting computations.

Pr. 1-7 The information listed below was obtained from the comparative balance sheets of Merk Limited for Year 4:

	Year 4	
	Jan. 1	*Dec. 31*
Accounts receivable	$ 77,500	$ 84,200
Inventories	110,000	125,000
Short-term prepayments	6,200	1,700
Accounts payable (merchandise suppliers)	49,500	38,000
Operating expenses payable	3,200	1,900
Accumulated depreciation (There were no disposals of plant assets during Year 4)	66,000	100,000

A summary of cash receipts and payments for Year 4 follows:

Cash collected from customers	$723,500
Cash paid to merchandise suppliers	440,000
Cash paid for operating expenses	122,800

Instructions

Prepare income statements for Merk Limited for Year 4, under ***a*** the accrual basis of accounting and ***b*** the modified cash basis of accounting whereby operating expenses (excluding depreciation) are computed on the cash basis. Merk's income is taxed at 45%. Show supporting computations.

chapter 2

INFORMATION PROCESSING AND THE ACCOUNTING CYCLE

Accounting has been called the ''language of business'' because it is a method of communicating business information. Like other languages, it is undergoing continuous change due to the attempt to develop better means of communicating.

The ***accounting process*** consists of three major parts: (1) the recording of transactions during an accounting period, (2) the summarizing of information at the end of the period, and (3) the preparation of financial statements.

During an accounting period business transactions and events are recorded as they occur, and at the end of each period the accounting records are summarized in order to prepare financial statements. After an unadjusted trial balance is prepared, adjusting entires are required to bring the accounting records up to date. Some adjustments must be made to the recorded data for changes that have occurred since the transactions were recorded; other adjustments are needed for events that have not been recorded but affect the financial position and operating results of the business enterprise. Examples of these unrecorded events are depreciation and other expirations of asset services, the accrual of expenses such as salaries and various taxes, and the accrual of revenue such as rent and interest.

When the accounting records have been made as complete, accurate, and up-to-date as possible, accountants prepare financial statements reflecting the financial position and the results of operations. An important measure of the success of the accounting process is the responsiveness of financial reporting to the needs of the users of business information.

RECORDING BUSINESS TRANSACTIONS AND EVENTS

If the accounting process is to provide the users of business information with reliable, timely reports, transactions and events during an accounting period must be interpreted in conformity with generally accepted accounting principles and recorded promptly and accurately. ***Business transactions*** and other ***events*** cause changes in the assets, liabilities, or owners' equity of a business enterprise. Transactions and events may be classified into two broad groups: (1) ***external transactions and events***, those between the business enterprise and another party, and (2) ***internal events***, such as the expiration or transfer of costs within the enterprise, the recording of depreciation of plant assets, the recognition of obsolescence in inventories, the transfer of production costs from the goods in process inventory to the finished goods inventory, and the recognition of estimated doubtful accounts expense.

Supporting Documents

A ***supporting document*** (sometimes called a ***business paper*** or a ***voucher***) is the first record prepared for a transaction. Such documents show the date, amount, and nature of the transaction, and the parties involved. Entries in the various journals are prepared from supporting documents. For example, sales invoices support entries in the sales journal: the original copy of a sales invoice is sent to the customer, who uses it as a basis for recording the purchase; a duplicate copy is retained by the seller as evidence of the sale. Some supporting documents may never leave the business enterprise, as, for example, cash register tapes, receiving reports, time reports, journal vouchers, and minutes of directors' meetings.

Any verification of financial statements or accounting records is likely to include tests in which summary amounts are traced to the supporting documents. The practice of identifying each type of document with serial numbers and accounting for all numbers in the series helps prevent the omission of transactions because of missing documents. Proper design and use of supporting documents is an important element in the system of internal controls, regardless of whether the enterprise uses a manual or a computerized accounting system.

Computerized Data Processing

The increasing use of computers by business enterprises, governmental units, and other organizations has changed significantly the methods of recording, summarizing, and classifying accounting information. The computer not only processes data with incredible speed and a high degree of accuracy, but also permits the classification and summarization of data in more forms and at lower cost than has been possible with manual systems.

In business enterprises that use computers, the recording, classifying, and summarizing steps used in creating accounting information may be combined into one process. With an ***on-line, real-time computer system*** (OLRT), the recording of a business transaction causes instantaneous updating of all relevant files. You have probably encountered OLRT systems at airline ticket offices and financial institutions. At banks and trust companies, a teller can update a depositor's account immediately by recording the deposit or withdrawal on a computer terminal. It is not difficult to envision a computer-based system that produces daily a set of financial statements or special reports updated to include all transactions to date and also provides the current amounts for such items as interest, depreciation, and labour costs.

Although the traditional forms of journals and ledgers are not essential to the processing of accounting information by computers, the concepts implicit in these records are also used in a computerized system. Furthermore, the output of the computers may be designed to provide information in a form similar to that of traditional journals and ledgers.

Because our primary focus in this book is on accounting principles and financial statements rather than on accounting systems, we will rely on manual recording methods as the simplest and clearest means of illustrating the application of accounting principles to business transactions and events.

Double-Entry System

The standard accounting model for accumulating data in a business enterprise consists of the ***double-entry system*** based on the basic accounting equation. As the name implies, the ***journal entry*** made for each transaction is composed of two parts: one or more debits and one or more credits. All journal entries are made within the framework of the basic ***accounting equation*** (assets = liabilities + owners' equity). Every transaction must be analyzed in terms of its effects on the elements of this equation. One of the advantages of the double-entry system is the fact that it includes built-in controls that automatically call attention to many types of errors, and offer assurance that once assets are recorded they will not be forgotten or overlooked. Management's responsibility for the custody of assets is thus strengthened by the inherent discipline of this system. The self-balancing nature of the double-entry system facilitates the preparation of a complete set of financial statements as frequently as desired.

The double-entry system, which is in practically universal use, takes its name from the fact that equal debit and credit entries are made for every transaction or event. The terms ***debit*** and ***credit*** may be related to the basic accounting equation ($A = L + OE$) in the following way:

Changes in balance sheet accounts

Asset accounts	=	*Liability accounts + Owners' Equity accounts*
Increases are recorded by debits Decreases are recorded by credits		Increases are recorded by credits Decreases are recorded by debits

Assets and liabilities are the two independent variables in the above equation; the dependent variable, owners' equity, is derived from the valuation assigned to assets and liabilities. One source of change in the owners' equity is the change in the ***net assets*** (assets minus liabilities) as a result of operations, measured by two classes of ledger accounts — revenue and expenses. ***Revenue*** accounts measure the inflow of assets resulting from the production and distribution of goods and services to customers. ***Expense*** accounts measure the outflow of assets necessary to produce and distribute these goods and services. The change in the net assets as a result of these two flows is reflected in the owners' equity. Revenue and expense accounts are subject to the same rules of debit and credit as applied to assets, liabilities, and owners' equity accounts:

Changes in income statement accounts

Expense accounts	*Revenue accounts*
Increases are recorded by debits Decreases are recorded by credits	Increases are recorded by credits Decreases are recorded by debits

In accounting, the terms ***debit*** and ***credit*** have no meaning except as a directive for recording data in ledger accounts: debit refers to the ***left side*** of a ledger account and credit refers to the ***right side***.

Accounting Period

The normal accounting period is one year, beginning on some specified day and ending 12 months later. A ***calendar-year*** accounting period ends on December 31; all other 12-month periods are known as ***fiscal years***. Business enterprises frequently adopt fiscal years that end when operations are at a low point in order to simplify year-end procedures and facilitate a better measurement of financial position and the results of operations. Such an accounting period is referred to as a ***natural business year*** because it conforms to the natural annual cycle of the enterprise.

Reports issued for shorter periods, such as one-quarter of the year or one month, are called ***interim reports***. Interim reports of the operating results of publicly owned corporations are needed to assist investors in reaching decisions to buy, hold, or sell securities. Traditionally, interim reports have not been audited by public accountants; but at present public accountants frequently do review their clients' interim reports to assure consistency with the annual financial statements.[1]

Accounting Cycle

The ***accounting cycle*** is a complete sequence of accounting procedures that are repeated in the same order during each accounting period. The cycle in a traditional manual system (and with modifications in a computerized system) includes the following steps:

1 Recording business transactions and events in the journals

2 Classifying data by posting from the journals to the ledger

3 Summarizing data from the ledger in an unadjusted trial balance (first pair of

1 For a discussion of the special reporting and measurement problems relating to interim financial reports, see CICA, ***CICA Handbook*** (Toronto), secs. 1750, 8100, and 8200; and AICPA, ***APB Opinion No. 28:*** "Interim Financial Reporting" (New York: 1973).

columns in the work sheet)

4 Adjusting, correcting, and updating recorded data; completion of the work sheet

5 Summarizing adjusted and corrected work sheet data in the form of financial statements

6 Closing the accounting records (nominal accounts) to summarize the operations of the accounting period

7 Preparation of a post-closing trial balance

8 Reversing certain adjusting entries to facilitate the recording process in the subsequent accounting period[2]

When these steps are completed, the cycle begins again for the next accounting period.

Let us now examine briefly the journals, the ledger, and the various steps of the accounting cycle.

Journals

The information shown in business papers is recorded in chronological order in the appropriate journals. Because a journal is organized chronologically by transaction and event, we might say the unit of organization for a journal is the individual transaction or event. Although a small business enterprise could conceivably record all transactions and events in a single journal (the general journal), this approach is seldom taken. When numerous transactions of the same nature occur (such as those involving the receipt of cash), ***special journals*** may be used as a more efficient means of recording and summarizing such recurring transactions. More specifically, the use of special journals helps to achieve division of labour, to minimize errors, to implement the system of internal control, and to reduce the clerical work of posting from the journals to the ledger.

The journalizing process requires the analysis of business transctions and events in terms of debits and credits to the ledger accounts they affect: (1) assets, (2) liabilities, (3) owners' equity, (4) revenue, and (5) expenses. To portray business transactions and events in a journal entry, we must identify and classify each important element of a transaction or event.

A growing business enterprise usually designs its accounting system to handle efficiently the increasing volume of transactions. One purpose of the accounting system is to facilitate the summarization of a large volume of transactions into meaningful totals for various uses. The basic accounting problems for large and small enterprises are quite similar; however, the procedures adopted for accumulating accounting data may differ.

Every business enterprise, regardless of its size, has certain established routines that are basic to the collection of accounting data. For example, documents are used to initiate transactions or to report their occurrence. As the

2 This is an optional step, as explained later in this chapter.

complexity of the enterprise increases, methods such as the preparation of several copies of these documents may be required, and various types of billing machines, mechanical registers, and preprinted forms may be used. In this way the time lag between the initiation of a transaction and its ultimate disposition may be shortened. Obviously, as the volume of similar transactions increases, the degree of automation possible in handling the data increases.

The great majority of business transactions are of four types, and for that reason most of the data may be recorded by the use of special multicolumn journals and a general journal. The four most commonly used special journals are: the ***sales journal***, the ***voucher register*** (or purchases journal), the ***cash receipts journal***, and the ***cash payments journal***. The primary types of transactions or events and the journals in which these are recorded are:

Types of transactions or events and the journals used for them

Type of transaction or event	*Journal*
Sales of merchandise on credit	Sales journal (S)
Purchases of merchandise, supplies, etc., on credit	Voucher register (VR) or purchases journal (PJ)
Receipts of cash	Cash receipts journal (CR)
Payments of cash	Cash payments journal (CP)
Other transactions or events........................	General journal (J)

A set of five journals similar to those listed above is adequate for the transactions of most small business enterprises. The general journal is necessary in addition to the special journals in order to (1) record unusual and nonrepetitive transactions and events and (2) record adjusting and closing entries at the end of the accounting period.

The following journals for Merchandise Mart, Inc., illustrate one possible form for each journal. The columnar headings are dictated by the needs of the enterprise. Merchandise Mart, Inc., uses special journals to facilitate the recording of transactions involving sales, purchases (where the periodic inventory system is used), cash receipts, and cash payments. Subsidiary ledgers are used for accounts receivable and vouchers (accounts) payable.

Sales Journal

The partial sales journal used by Merchandise Mart, Inc., is illustrated on the next page.

The procedure for recording sales requires that all credit sales be entered at the gross amount in the sales journal and all cash sales in the cash receipts journal. There is no need for a breakdown of sales by product or department, and the accounts receivable ledger is posted from the sales journal. When the individual accounts are posted, a check mark (✓) is placed beside the amount in the sales journal. The total of the one money column is posted monthly as a debit to the Accounts Receivable ledger account (ledger account no. 7) and a credit to the

Sales Journal **Page 50**

Date	*Customer*	*Inv. no.*	*Ref.*	*Amount*
Year 10				
Jan. 2	Emily Taylor	1001	✓	690
3	R. O. Black	1002	✓	850
3	Dan Crane	1003	✓	1,050
28	D. A. Adams	1025	✓	600
29	Jack Urbanks	1026	✓	1,215
				42,460
				(7) (115) Dr, A/R Cr, Sales

Sales ledger account (ledger account no. 115). All credit sales have terms of 2/10, n/30.

Cash Receipts Journal

All cash receipts are recorded by Merchandise Mart, Inc., in the cash receipts journal (see page 50) from a detailed list of cheques received by mail, a report of daily cash sales, store cash collections, and other cash sources. If a credit customer takes the cash discount offered, it is recorded at the time cash is received. The customers' accounts are posted daily from the cash receipts journal. The individual ledger accounts are posted weekly from the ''Other ledger accounts'' columns, and the column totals are posted monthly, except for the ''Other ledger accounts'' columns for which totals are not posted (***Not pos.***).

Voucher Register (Purchases Journal)

Merchandise Mart, Inc., has found that control over cash payments is improved by use of a voucher register. The voucher register serves both as a subsidiary ledger for vouchers payable and as a purchases journal. Purchases of merchandise are recorded net of cash discounts offered, and all cash discounts are taken.

A good system of internal controls requires that all cheques be supported by a voucher. At the time a voucher is paid, the cheque number is entered in the appropriate column of the voucher register. Any vouchers entered in the register without cheque numbers are hence unpaid and constitute the liability to vendors at that time. Note in the voucher register on page 50 that voucher no. 1500 has not been paid and that voucher no. 1501 was paid by cheque no. 1001. The totals of the special columns are posted monthly, and the individual ledger accounts in the ''Other ledger accounts'' columns are posted weekly or monthly. The total liability represented by unpaid vouchers may include vouchers from the preceding month.

Cash Receipts Journal — Page 42

		Debits					Credits					
				Other ledger accounts			Accounts receivable			Other ledger accounts		
Date	Explanation	Cash	Sales discounts	Account	Ref.	Amount	✓	Amount	Sales	Account	Ref.	Amount
Year 10												
Jan. 2	1st Union Bank	10,000								Notes Payable	71	10,000
5	D. A. Adams	833	17				✓	850				
6	Cash sales	452							452			
11	Dan Crane	1,029	21				✓	1,050				
31	Cash sales	800							800			
		46,807	256			1,240		31,780	3,423			13,100
		(1)	(117)			(Not pos.)		(7)	(115)			(Not pos.)

Voucher Register — Page 61

					Credit	Debits					
									Other ledger accounts		
Date	Payee	Explanation	Paid by chq. no.	Vou. no.	Vouchers payable	Purchases	Freight-in	Salaries expense	Account	Ref.	Amount
Year 10											
Jan. 2	Adams Supply Co.	Merchandise		1500	8,000	8,000					
2	Bross Trucking, Inc.	Freight-in	1001	1501	50		50				
5	1st Union Bank	Paid note and interest	1002	1502	4,040				Notes Payable	71	4,000
									Interest Expense	170	40
30	Media Services	Advertising		1597	2,000				Advertising Exp.	165	2,000
31	Ace Company	Merchandise		1598	900	900					
					48,720	25,680	980	8,220			13,840
					(70)	(104)	(105)	(72)			(Not pos.)

Cash Payments Journal

The requirement that all cheques be supported by a voucher means that only one column is needed in the cash payments journal of Merchandise Mart, Inc., illustrated below:

Cash Payments Journal **Page 60**

Date	*Payee*	*Voucher no.*	*Cheque no.*	*Amount*
Year 10				
Jan. 5	Bross Trucking, Inc.	1501	1001	50
5	1st Union Bank	1502	1002	4,040
31	Dart Brothers	1593	1090	570
				42,690
				(70) (1)
				Dr. V/P
				Cr, Cash

The total of the one column is posted to Vouchers Payable (ledger account no. 70) as a debit and to Cash (ledger account no. 1) as a credit. Recording the payment in the subsidiary ledger for vouchers payable (the voucher register) is done by entering the cheque number in the voucher register. The totals of the cash payments journal are posted monthly.

General Journal

The majority of transactions will normally be recorded in the special journals. However, to record all transactions and events that do not involve ledger accounts represented in the four special journals, and for adjusting, closing, reversing, and correcting entries, the general journal is used. A partial page of the general journal for Merchandise Mart, Inc., is illustrated below:

General Journal **Page 70**

Date	*Account titles and explanations*	*LP*	*Debit*	*Credit*
Year 10				
Jan. 24	Allowance for Doubtful Accounts	8	150	
	Accounts Receivable — Tyrone Kong	7/✓		150
	To write off uncollectible account receivable.			

The posting instructions for the illustrated entry in the general journal are: (1) Post the debits and credits to the accounts in the ledger indicated by the ledger account numbers in the *LP* (ledger page) column (the debit is posted to ledger account no. 8 and the credit is posted to ledger account no. 7); and (2) post the

$150 credit to the accounts receivable subsidiary ledger in the account of Tyrone Kong. The check mark indicates that the posting to the subsidiary ledger has been completed.

Ledger

We have indicated how the information contained in business papers is analyzed and expressed in terms of debits and credits by entries in the journals. Next is the step of transferring this information to ledger accounts. This transfer process is called ***posting***, which means that each debit and credit amount in the journals is entered in the appropriate ledger account.

A ***ledger*** consists of a number of accounts. Each ledger account represents stored information about a particular asset, liability, owners' equity, revenue, or expense. As previously indicated, the transaction is the unit of organization for the journal; similarly, the ledger account is the unit of organization for the ledger. When computers are used, accounting information may be stored on magnetic tapes or disks rather than on the pages of a traditional ledger. However, the printed form of ledger page is most convenient for our illustrations and analyses and is still used by many small- and medium-sized business enterprises.

Ledger accounts are often classified as ***nominal*** (temporary) and ***real*** (permanent) accounts. The nominal (revenue and expense) accounts are closed at the end of each accounting period by transferring their balances to other accounts. The real (balance sheet) accounts remain open and normally show a balance after the accounting records are closed. During an accounting period, a balance sheet account or an income statement account may contain both real and nominal portions. Such accounts are known as ***mixed accounts***. For example, the Unexpired Insurance ledger account may include both unexpired insurance premiums and expired premiums before the end-of-period adjusting entries are made. When the time arrives for preparation of financial statements, the nominal and real portions of a mixed account are separated by end-of-period adjusting entries. Thus, the nominal portion in the Unexpired Insurance account is transferred to Insurance Expense.

Two forms of the ledger account for Accounts Receivable are illustrated on the next page for Merchandise Mart, Inc. Note that the balance of $23,212 on January 31, Year 10, is the same as in the unadjusted trial balance on page 54. The three entries to the Accounts Receivable ledger account were posted from the journals illustrated earlier.

In many cases greater detail is desired for a particular ledger account, and a ***subsidiary ledger*** is set up to contain the details supporting the main or ***controlling account***. For example, the controlling account, Accounts Receivable, is adequate for general purposes; however, in order to facilitate the preparation of monthly statements to customers, it is desirable to have each customer's purchases and payments separately classified. In such situations a subsidiary ledger is established to provide the desired information. At all times, the total of the subsidiary ledger account balances should agree with the balance of the related controlling account in the ledger.

"T" form of ledger account

Accounts Receivable							Ledger Account No. 7
Date	*Explanation*	*Ref.*	*Amount*	*Date*	*Explanation*	*Ref.*	*Amount*
Year 10				Year 10			
Jan. 1	Balance		12,682	Jan. 24		J70	150
31		S50	42,460	31		CR42	31,780
				31	Balance		23,212
			55,142				55,142
Feb. 1	Balance		23,212				

Running balance form of ledger account

Accounts Receivable					Ledger Account No. 7
Date	*Explanation*	*Ref.*	*Debit*	*Credit*	*Balance*
Year 10					
Jan. 1	Balance				12,682 Dr
24		J70		150	12,532 Dr
31		S50	42,460		54,992 Dr
31		CR42		31,780	23,212 Dr

In addition to the use of a controlling account and subsidiary ledger for accounts receivable, other common examples of this concept include:

- A Vouchers Payable controlling account supported by a voucher register
- A Buildings controlling account supported by a subsidiary ledger that shows the individual buildings owned
- A Common Stock controlling account supported by a shareholders' ledger

Separate subsidiary ledgers not only provide the detailed information needed for certain purposes, but also strengthen internal controls by bringing to light most kinds of errors in the recording of business transactions and events. Moreover, the use of controlling accounts and subsidiary ledgers helps to achieve division of labour and to improve the system of internal control.

Trial Balance

At the end of each accounting period an ***unadjusted trial balance*** of the ledger is prepared (usually in the first pair of columns of the work sheet) to determine that the mechanics of the recording and posting operations have been carried out accurately. The unadjusted trial balance consists of a listing of all ledger accounts and their balances; it provides evidence that an equality of debits and credits exists in the general ledger. The following unadjusted trial balance summarizes the account balances in the ledger of Merchandise Mart, Inc., on January 31, Year 10.

Trial balance at end of first month of fiscal year

MERCHANDISE MART, INC.
Unadjusted Trial Balance
January 31, Year 10

	Debit	*Credit*
Cash	$ 15,454	
Accounts receivable	23,212	
Allowance for doubtful accounts		$ 850
Inventory (Jan. 1, Year 10)	47,860	
Unexpired insurance	200	
Land	45,000	
Building	80,000	
Accumulated depreciation of building		10,000
Equipment	16,000	
Accumulated depreciation of equipment		4,000
Notes payable—current		15,000
Vouchers payable		17,000
Common stock, no par		130,000
Retained earnings (Jan. 1, Year 10)		49,207
Sales		45,883
Sales discounts	256	
Purchases	25,680	
Freight-in	980	
Salaries expense	8,220	
Advertising expense	4,620	
Delivery expense	2,180	
Property taxes expense	1,220	
Interest expense	80	
Miscellaneous expenses	978	
Totals	$271,940	$271,940

Note that the dollar amounts of certain revenue and expense accounts in the trial balance for Merchandise Mart, Inc., may be traced to the five journals illustrated earlier. For example, the amount of sales consists of credit sales from the sales journal plus cash sales from the cash receipts journal ($42,460 + $3,423 = $45,883): the amount of sales discounts ($256) appears in the cash receipts journal; and the amounts for purchases, freight-in, and salaries expense appear in separate columns of the voucher register.

Trial balances of the subsidiary ledgers may also be prepared to prove that the totals of their balances agree with the balances in the related controlling accounts in the general ledger. These trial balances may also be used for other purposes; for example, a copy of the accounts receivable trial balance on the next page may be sent to the credit department for use in following up collections and as a basis for setting future credit policy.

Summary Comment

Although the number of accounts used, the type of financial statements prepared, and other aspects of the accounting system are determined by the needs of the particular business enterprise, the preceding examples illustrate the type of accounting system used by many small- and medium-sized enterprises.

List of accounts receivable from customers

MERCHANDISE MART, INC.
Accounts Receivable Trial Balance
January 31, Year 10

D. A. Adams	$ 1,500
R. O. Black	3,410
Other accounts (not listed here to avoid unnecessary detail)	18,302
Balance of Accounts Receivable controlling account (ledger account no. 7)	$23,212

ADJUSTING ENTRIES

Financial reporting on an annual, quarterly, or monthly basis requires accountants to summarize the operations of a business enterprise for a specific time period. The two types of end-of-period adjusting entries are (1) those to apportion ***prepayments*** of expenses and revenue and (2) those to record ***accrued*** expenses and revenue. Transactions that were recorded during an accounting period in balance sheet or income statement ledger accounts may affect two or more periods, and an end-of-period adjustment may be needed. Some financial events not recognized on a day-to-day or a continual basis must be recorded through ***adjusting entries*** at the end of the period ***to bring the accounting records up to date***. For example, if one should choose to record depreciation expense daily or to accrue interest expense daily, no adjustment for depreciation or interest expense would be needed at the end of the accounting period.

Note that every adjusting entry affects both a balance sheet account and an income statement account. This characteristic of adjusting entries reflects their dual purpose: (1) to measure all assets and liabilities accurately and (2) to measure net income correctly to matching expired costs (expenses) with realized revenue.

In illustrating the wide variety of adjusting entries, it is helpful to classify them into the following groups:

- Apportionment of recorded costs
- Apportionment of recorded revenue
- Accrual of unrecorded expenses
- Accrual of unrecorded revenue
- Valuation of certain assets and liabilities (for example, accounts receivable)

Apportionment of Recorded Costs

Costs that will benefit more than one accounting period are frequently incurred. These costs must be apportioned between periods in a manner that approximates the usefulness derived from the goods and services in the realization of revenue; this apportionment process is a necessary step under the matching principle to determine net income of each period. Recording periodic depreciation expense as shown on page 56 is an example of a cost-apportionment adjusting entry.

Journal entry for depreciation

	Debit	Credit
Depreciation Expense	12,000	
Accumulated Depreciation of Building		12,000
To record depreciation expense for one year.		

The periodic depreciation expense is considered a cost of production or a period expense to be deducted from revenue, depending on the nature of services derived from the asset. In the balance sheet, accumulated depreciation is deducted from the cost of plant assets.

Cost apportionment is also involved in accounting for all types of prepayments. However, the adjusting entry will vary according to the accounting procedure followed in recording the original transaction. To illustrate, assume that office supplies are acquired during the accounting period at a cost of $5,000. At the end of the period a physical inventory reveals that supplies on hand cost $550. At the time the supplies were acquired, the $5,000 may have been debited to either an asset account or an expense account. The required adjusting entry for each approach is illustrated below.

Prepayment Debited to Asset Account

The adjusting entry required is to transfer the ***expired*** portion of the cost to an ***expense*** account as illustrated below:

Adjusting entry reduces asset ledger account

	Inventory of Office Supplies (Dr.)	*Inventory of Office Supplies* (Cr.)	*Office Supplies Expense* (Dr.)	*Office Supplies Expense* (Cr.)
Balance, Dec. 31	5,000			
Adjusting entry		4,450	4,450	

Prepayment Debited to Expense Account

The adjusting entry required is to transfer the ***unexpired*** portion of the cost to an ***asset*** account as illustrated below:

Adjusting entry establishes asset ledger account

	Inventory of Office Supplies (Dr.)	*Inventory of Office Supplies* (Cr.)	*Office Supplies Expense* (Dr.)	*Office Supplies Expense* (Cr.)
Balance, Dec. 31			5,000	
Adjusting entry	550			550

Under either approach, the final result is the same: there is an asset of $550 and an expense of $4,450. In both cases the amount of the unexpired cost was determined, and an adjusting entry was necessary to make the ledger account balances agree with the information available.

Apportionment of Recorded Revenue

When a business enterprise receives payment for goods and services before the goods are delivered or the services are performed, a liability exists until performance takes place. If cash is received, the original transaction may be recorded by a credit to either a liability account or a revenue account. For example, assume that customers paid $500,000 for magazine subscriptions during the current accounting period; however, $75,000 represented payments for magazines to be delivered in subsequent periods. The adjusting entries for each of the two methods of recording cash receipts are as follows.

Liability Account Credited on Receipt of Cash

The required adjusting entry to record the ***earned*** revenue for the period appears below:

Adjusting entry reduces liability ledger account

	Unearned Subscriptions (Dr.)	*Unearned Subscriptions* (Cr.)	*Subscriptions Revenue* (Dr.)	*Subscriptions Revenue* (Cr.)
Balance, Dec. 31		500,000		
Adjusting entry	425,000			425,000

Revenue Account Credited on Receipt of Cash

The required adjusting entry to transfer the ***unearned*** revenue to a liability account is shown below:

Adjusting entry establishes liability ledger account

	Unearned Subscriptions (Dr.)	*Unearned Subscriptions* (Cr.)	*Subscriptions Revenue* (Dr.)	*Subscriptions Revenue* (Cr.)
Balance, Dec. 31				500,000
Adjusting entry		75,000	75,000	

Under either approach, the adjusted amount of the liability is $75,000, and the adjusted amount of the revenue is $425,000.

Accrual of Unrecorded Expenses

The incurring of certain expenses is related to the passage of time. These expenses are generally not recorded until payment is made, unless the end of an accounting period comes before the required date of payment. Interest and salaries are typical of the expenses that accrue with the passage of time and are recorded only when paid, except when the end of a period occurs between the time the expense was incurred and the time the payment is due. In order to measure expenses accurately for a period, an adjusting entry is necessary to record the accrued expense and the corresponding liability. For example, assume that interest of $18,000 on a $400,000 note payable is paid on March 1 and September 1 of each year. If expenses and liabilities are to be reported accurately on December 31, the following year-end adjusting entry is required:

Journal entry to record accrued expense

Interest Expense	12,000	
Interest Payable		12,000
To record the interest accrued on a 9%, $400,000 note for four months to Dec. 31.		

Accrual of Unrecorded Revenue

Revenue that has been realized but not recorded must be recognized at the end of an accounting period. For example, revenue that is realized on assets leased to others or on interest-bearing loans is seldom recognized until the cash is received, except at the end of a period. In order to measure accurately the results of operations under the matching principle, revenue is recognized in the period earned. For example, assume that rent totalling $625 that has been realized but not collected for the month of December has not been recorded. The following adjusting entry on December 31 is required to measure assets and revenue accurately:

Journal entry to record accrued revenue

Rent Receivable	625	
Rent Revenue..		625
To record rent revenue earned during December.		

Valuation of Accounts Receivable

A policy of making sales on credit almost inevitably results in some accounts receivable that are uncollectible. To achieve a satisfactory matching of revenue and expenses, the estimated expense arising from sales on credit should be recorded in the accounting period in which sales occur. This estimate of probable expense from the granting of credit requires an end-of-period adjusting entry to revise the valuation originally assigned to accounts receivable. For example, if doubtful accounts expense is estimated at $2,500, the following adjusting entry is made:

Journal entry to record doubtful accounts expense

Doubtful Accounts Expense	2,500	
Allowance for Doubtful Accounts		2,500
To record doubtful accounts expense.		

The Doubtful Accounts Expense (also called Uncollectible Accounts Expense or Bad Debts Expense) ledger account is generally reported as an operating expense in the income statement. Some accountants prefer to deduct it directly from sales to measure net sales, because no revenue is realized if accounts receivable are not collected. The credit balance of the allowance account is deducted from accounts receivable in the balance sheet to state accounts receivable at net realizable value.

The Work Sheet and Financial Statements

Adjusting entries are initially prepared in a work sheet, and adjusted account balances are then summarized in columns designed to facilitate the preparation of financial statements. A work sheet for a merchandising enterprise is illustrated on pages 66–67, and a work sheet for a manufacturing enterprise is illustrated on pages 72–73. Complete financial statements are illustrated in Chapter 4.

CLOSING PROCEDURES

Closing Revenue and Expense Accounts

Revenue and expense ledger accounts are closed at the end of each accounting period by transferring the balances of these ledger accounts to a summary ledger account called Income Summary. Revenue and expense accounts are extensions of owners' equity and are used to measure periodic net income. Once this information has been summarized, the revenue and expense accounts have served their purpose, and the net increase or decrease in owners' equity is transferred to an appropriate owners' equity ledger account. Thus, the closing of the revenue and expense accounts keeps the operating results of each period separate.

If we assume that a Subscriptions Revenue ledger account after adjustment has a credit balance of $425,000, the closing entry is:

Journal entry to close revenue ledger account

Subscriptions Revenue	425,000	
Income Summary		425,000
To close the Subscriptions Revenue ledger account.		

The balance of the Subscriptions Revenue ledger account is now zero. Temporarily, the Income Summary account has a credit balance of $425,000. All other revenue accounts are closed similarly.

To close an expense ledger account, one must transfer its debit balance to the left side of the Income Summary account. The following journal entry to close a Salaries Expense account with a debit balance of $61,625 is illustrative of this phase of the closing process:

Journal entry to close expense ledger account

Income Summary	61,625	
Salaries Expense		61,625
To close the Salaries Expense ledger account.		

The Salaries Expense account now has a zero balance, and the credit balance in the Income Summary account is reduced by the debit for salaries expense in the amount of $61,625. All other expense accounts are closed similarly. When there are numerous revenue and expense accounts, all may be closed in one journal entry as illustrated on pages 69 and 70 for Merchandising Limited.

Closing Inventories and Related Ledger Accounts

When the ***periodic inventory system*** is used, the journal entry to establish the cost of goods sold and the ending inventory balance for the accounting period may be viewed as an adjusting entry; however, because there may be little need for a ledger account for cost of goods sold, the adjusting and closing entries for inventories may be combined. This procedure is accomplished by closing the beginning inventory, ending inventory, purchases, and all related ledger accounts to the Income Summary account. At this point, the balance in the Income Summary account represents the cost of goods sold for the period. To illustrate, assume the following for Year 10: January 1 inventory, $80,000; purchases, $275,000; freight-in, $40,000; purchases returns and allowances, $2,500; December 31 inventory, including applicable freight-in, $60,000. The journal entry to close the accounts and to record the ending inventory is as follows:

Closing entry for inventories and purchases

Account	Debit	Credit
Inventory (Dec. 31, Year 10)	60,000	
Purchases Returns and Allowances	2,500	
Income Summary	332,500	
Inventory (Jan. 1, Year 10)		80,000
Purchases		275,000
Freight-in		40,000
To close beginning inventory and net purchases for the period, and to record ending inventory.		

Some merchandising enterprises prefer to use a separate ledger account, Cost of Goods Sold, to summarize the merchandising accounts when the periodic inventory system is used. The journal entry (which may be viewed as an adjusting entry) ***reflecting cost of goods sold in a separate ledger account*** is as follows:

Alternative: Record cost of goods sold in ledger account

Account	Debit	Credit
Inventory (Dec. 31, Year 10)	60,000	
Purchases Returns and Allowances	2,500	
Cost of Goods Sold	332,500	
Inventory (Jan. 1, Year 10)		80,000
Purchases		275,000
Freight-in		40,000
To record ending inventory and cost of goods sold for the period.		

When the perpetual inventory system is used, Cost of Goods Sold is debited and Inventory is credited during an accounting period as sales are made. An adjusting entry may be required if the carrying amount of inventory differs from the amount determined by physical count. At the end of the period, Cost of Goods Sold is closed to Income Summary, along with all other revenue and expense accounts.

Closing the Income Summary Account

After all revenue and expenses (including the cost of goods sold) have been closed, the balance of the Income Summary ledger account indicates the net income or net loss for the year. A credit balance in the Income Summary account indicates a profitable year and an increase in owners' equity; a debit balance indicates a net loss and a decrease in owners' equity. The Income Summary account is closed by transferring its balance to the Retained Earnings account or owners' capital accounts. Similarly, the dividends account is closed by transferring its debit balance to the Retained Earnings account.

REVERSING ENTRIES

After the accounting records have been adjusted and closed at the end of an accounting period, reversing entries ***may be made*** on the first day of the next period. The purpose of the reversing entries is to simplify the recording of routine transactions by disposing of the accrued items (assets and liabilities) that were entered in balance sheet accounts through adjusting entries. A reversing entry, as the name implies, ***is the exact reverse of an adjusting entry***. It consists of the same ledger accounts and dollar amounts as the adjusting entry, but the debits and credits are reversed, and the date is the beginning of the next period.

For example, assume that on July 31, Year 1, Clark Company borrowed $200,000 at 12% on a long-term note with interest of $6,000 payable every three months. The first payment of interest was made on October 31, Year 1; the next interest payment is due on January 31, Year 2. Clark is on a calendar-year basis. Before the accounting records are closed on December 31, Year 1, an adjusting entry must be made debiting Interest Expense and crediting Interest Payable for $4,000, the amount of interest for November and December. If no reversing entry is made on January 1, Year 2, the next quarterly interest payment of $6,000 on January 31, Year 2, will be recorded by a debit of $4,000 to Interest Payable, a debit of $2,000 to Interest Expense, and a credit of $6,000 to Cash. However, assume that on January 1, Year 2, the following reversing entry is made:

Reversing entry for accrued expense

Year 2			
Jan. 1	Interest Payable	4,000	
	Interest Expense..		4,000
	To reverse interest accrual made on Dec. 31, Year 1.		

This reversing entry has eliminated the liability account Interest Payable and has caused the Interest Expense account to have a $4,000 credit balance. Consequently, the cash payment of three months' interest on January 31 will not need to be apportioned. The January 31 entry will consist of a debit to Interest Expense for $6,000 and a credit to Cash for $6,000. In other words, the interest payment on January 31 (by reason of the reversing entry) may be recorded in the same manner as the three other quarterly interest payments during the year. After the January 31 interest payment has been recorded, the Interest Expense ledger account for Year 2 will contain a debit of $6,000 and a credit of $4,000, which produce a net debit balance of $2,000 representing interest expense for the month of January, Year 2.

An argument for reversing entries is apparent from this example. Employees with limited knowledge of accounting may be instructed to follow a standard procedure for recording all recurring transactions such as receipts and payments of cash. The reversing entries, as well as the year-end adjusting entries, are recorded in the general journal by an accountant who understands the concept involved.

General Guidelines for Reversing Entries

When a ***policy of using reversing entries is adopted***, the following general rules are followed:

1 When an adjusting entry affects an asset or a liability account that is not normally used during an accounting period, ***a reversing entry is required***. Thus, adjustments to accrue revenue and expenses are reversed because asset and liability accounts such as Rent Receivable and Interest Payable are not used in the normal course of accounting during a period. Similarly, if payments for insurance and supplies during a period are recorded in expense accounts, or if revenue received in advance during a period is recorded in revenue accounts, the adjusting entries would have to be reversed because asset and liability accounts not normally used during the period would be affected by the adjusting entries.

2 When an adjusting entry adjusts an asset or liability account that is normally used to record transactions during a period, ***no reversing entry is required***. Thus, if acquisitions of supplies and other short-term prepayments during a period are recorded in asset accounts, or if revenue received in advance is recorded in liability accounts, the adjusting entries would bring ***existing asset and liability balances up to date***, and no reversing entry would be required. For the same reason, adjusting entries for depreciation and doubtful accounts expense, for example, are not reversed.

Previously, we suggested that reversing certain adjusting entries is an ***optional*** procedure designed to simplify recording or recurring transactions. Another way of stating this is that reversing entries are never required as long as adjusting entries bring existing asset and liability accounts up to date.

To illustrate three alternative approaches for adjusting and reversing entries, let us return to the Clark Company example on page 61. Use of any of the three approaches illustrated on the next page results in a balance of $24,000 in Interest Expense and a balance of $4,000 in Interest Payable ***at the end of Year 2***.

Note that no adjusting entry was required under the third alternative because the amount of interest payable at the end of Year 2 was the same as it was at the end of Year 1. If the accrued interest at the end of Year 2 was other than $4,000, an adjusting entry would be required to alter the balance of the Interest Payable account, with a corresponding debit or credit to the Interest Expense account.

The three alternative approaches produce identical results

Alternative 1	*Alternative 2*	*Alternative 3*
No reversing entry; $4,000 of first interest payment in Year 2 is debited to the Interest Payable account.	***Reversing entry (R) is made;*** all interest payments in Year 2 are recorded in the Interest Expense account.	No reversing entry; all interest payments in Year 2 are recorded in the Interest Expense account.

Interest Expense

Alternative 1 Debit	Alternative 1 Credit	Alternative 2 Debit	Alternative 2 Credit	Alternative 3 Debit	Alternative 3 Credit
(a) 20,000		(a) 24,000	**(R)** 4,000	(a) 24,000	
(b) 4,000		(b) 4,000			
Bal. 24,000		Bal. 24,000			

Interest Payable

Alternative 1 Debit	Alternative 1 Credit	Alternative 2 Debit	Alternative 2 Credit	Alternative 3 Debit	Alternative 3 Credit
(a) 4,000	Bal. 4,000	**(R)** 4,000	Bal. 4,000		Bal. 4,000
	(b) 4,000		(b) 4,000		
	Bal. 4,000		Bal. 4,000		

LEGEND: (a) Payments of interest in Year 2; Cash account is credited for $24,000.
(b) Adjusting entry, Dec. 31, Year 2.
(R) Reversing entry, Jan. 1, Year 2.

CORRECTING ENTRIES

Correcting entries are not considered adjusting entries, because their function is to correct errors of omission or commission. For example, the failure to record a transaction would be rectified by a journal entry as it should have been made originally; the improper recording of a transaction requires a journal entry to ensure that ledger accounts are stated properly. When an error is made in one accounting period but discovered in a subsequent period, the effect of the error on the net income of the earlier periods is closed to the Retained Earnings ledger account. When an error is discovered in the period in which the error occurs, but before the accounting records are closed, revenue and expense accounts may require correction and the Retained Earnings account is generally not affected.

For example, assume that the following two errors were made in Year 1 and were discovered at the end of the accounting period when the work sheet for the year ended December 31, Year 1, was being prepared:

1 A purchase of merchandise for $500 cash was erroneously recorded by a debit of $50 to the Supplies Expense ledger account and a credit of $50 to Cash.

2 An acquisition of equipment for cash of $4,000 on April 1, Year 1, was recorded as a purchase of merchandise. The equipment had an economic life of 10 years with no residual value, and was depreciated by the straight-line method for nine months in Year 1.

The following table gives an analysis of the two errors, and the appropriate correcting entries:

Incorrect journal entry as recorded			*Journal entry that should have been made*			*Required correcting entry*		
1 Supplies Exp..	50		Purchases.........	500		Purchases.........	500	
Cash.........		50	Cash............		500	Supplies Exp..		50
						Cash............		450
2 Purchases	4,000		Equipment.......	4,000		Equipment.......	4,000	
Cash		4,000	Depr. Expense ..	300*		Dep. Expense....	300	
			Cash............		4,000	Purchases......		4,000
			Accum. Depr. of Equipment..........		300	Accum. Depr. of Equipment..........		300
			*$4,000 × 0.10 × ¾ = $300.					

A complete discussion of accounting errors and correcting entries appears in Chapter 22.

WORK SHEET

Accountants use many forms of work sheets and working papers. An ***end-of-period work sheet*** is a critical part of the accounting cycle. In this chapter we are concerned only with the end-of-period work sheet, and we shall refer to it simply as the ***work sheet***. The work sheet is a columnar working paper designed to facilitate the organization and arrangement of accounting data at the end of an accounting period. A major function of the work sheet is to uncover errors that otherwise might be entered in the accounting records. Accountants prepare a work sheet as an informal record strictly for their own purposes; a work sheet does not replace any financial statement and is never presented as the end result of the accountants' work. The work sheet is a tool that permits adjusting and closing entries and financial statements to be prepared informally before any part of this work is formalized.

The work sheet may be thought of as a ''testing ground'' on which the ledger accounts are adjusted, balanced, and arranged in the general form of financial statements. The satisfactory completion of the work sheet provides considerable assurance that all end-of-period accounting procedures have been brought together properly. The finished work sheet then serves as the source for the preparation of financial statements and for the recording and posting of the adjusting and closing entries.

Illustration of Work Sheet for a Merchandising Enterprise

A commonly used form of work sheet with appropriate headings is illustrated on pages 66–67 for Merchandising Limited for Year 4. The heading contains the name of the company, the title (''Work Sheet''), and the period of time covered.

The body contains six pairs of money columns, each consisting of one debit and one credit column. The procedures required in the preparation of the work sheet ***when the periodic inventory system is used*** are described below:

1 Enter the ledger account titles and balances on the work sheet, using the first two money columns, under the heading ''Unadjusted trial balance.'' Time and effort may be saved by arranging the ledger accounts (both in the ledger and in the trial balance) in the order in which they will appear in the financial statements. Frequently, several adjustments will affect a single ledger account; consequently, several lines should be left blank following such an account to facilitate listing the adjustments.

2 Enter the adjustments in the ''Adjustments'' columns. Adjusting entries should always be entered in the work sheet before they are journalized, for one of the functions of the work sheet is to establish the correctness of the adjusting entries. The information used as the basis for the adjustments illustrated in the work sheet for Merchandising Limited is stated below.

a The short-term investments consist of government bonds on which accrued interest amounts to $33 on December 31, Year 4.

b The accounts receivable arising from sales during Year 4 that are expected to be uncollectible are estimated to be ½% of gross sales.

c Accounts receivable totalling $520 are considered to be uncollectible, and the credit manager has authorized the write-off of these accounts.

d The balances in the Short-Term Prepayments ledger account are as follows:

	Jan. 1, Year 4	*Dec. 31, Year 4*
Unexpired insurance	$ 750	$ 450
Inventory of supplies	600	700
Prepaid rent	150	400
Totals	$1,500	$1,550

All cash payments for these items during Year 4 were recorded in expense accounts. Merchandising Limited ***does not reverse any adjusting entries***.

e The furniture and fixtures are estimated to have an economic life of 10 years, with no residual value at the end of that time.

f Accrued interest on the notes payable amounts to $40 on December 31, Year 4.

g Salaries accrued since the last payday total $818 on December 31, Year 4.

h Income taxes expense for the year ended December 31, Year 4, is estimated at $370.

i The inventory on December 31, Year 4, is $28,900.

After adjustments **a** through **i** are entered in the work sheet, the ''Adjustments'' columns must be ''footed'' (totalled) to prove the equality of the

MERCHANDISING LIMITED
Work Sheet
For Year Ended December 31, Year 4

	Unadjusted trial balance		*Adjustments*		*Adjusted trial balance*		*Income statement*		*Retained earnings statement*		*Balance sheet*	
	Debit	*Credit*	*Debit*	*Credit*	*Debit*	*Credit*	*Debit*	*Credit*	*Debit*	*Credit*	*Debit*	*Credit*
Cash	8,650				8,650						8,650	
Short-term investments	2,000				2,000						2,000	
Accounts receivable	15,700			(c) 520	15,180						15,180	
Allowance for doubtful accounts		800	(c) 520	(b) 875		1,155						1,155
Inventory (periodic system)	28,000				28,000		28,000	28,900			28,900	
Short-term prepayments	1,500		(d) 50		1,550						1,550	
Furniture and fixtures	6,000				6,000						6,000	
Accumulated depreciation		1,800		(e) 600		2,400						2,400
Notes payable — current		4,000				4,000						4,000
Accounts payable		10,000				10,000						10,000
Common stock, no par		40,000				40,000						40,000
Retained earnings (Jan. 1, Year 4)		3,170				3,170				3,170		
Dividends	1,500				1,500				1,500			
Sales		175,000				175,000		175,000				
Sales returns and allowances	2,500				2,500		2,500					

Sales discounts	3,150				3,150		3,150					
Purchases	128,000				128,000		128,000					
Purchases returns and allowances		3,000				3,000		3,000				
Salaries expense	22,500		(g) 818		23,318		23,318					
Rent expense	5,050			(d) 250	4,800		4,800					
Advertising expense	9,000				9,000		9,000					
Janitorial expense	1,500				1,500		1,500					
Miscellaneous expenses	2,000			(d) 100	1,900		1,900					
Interest expense	120		(f) 40		160		160					
Property taxes expense	600				600		600					
Interest receivable			(a) 33		33						33	
Interest revenue				(a) 33		33		33				
Doubtful accounts expense			(b) 875		875		875					
Insurance expense			(d) 300		300		300					
Depreciation expense			(e) 600		600		600					
Interest payable				(f) 40		40						40
Salaries payable				(g) 818		818						818
Income taxes expense			(h) 370		370		370					
Income taxes payable				(h) 370		370						370
Net income							1,860			1,860		
Retained earnings (Dec. 31, Year 4)									3,530			3,530
Totals	237,770	237,770	3,606	3,606	239,986	239,986	206,933	206,933	5,030	5,030	62,313	62,313

debits and credits. Without this proof of arithmetical accuracy, errors are likely to be carried forward in the remaining columns of the work sheet.

3 Determine the new account balances and enter these in the "Adjusted trial balance" columns. The purpose of this step is to prove the accuracy of the work of combining the adjustments and the original balances. However, the "Adjusted trial balance" columns are often absent from the work sheet, especially if adjustments are few.

4 Extend each balance from the "Adjusted trial balance" columns (or at least from the first four) to the "Income statement," the "Retained earnings statement," or the "Balance sheet" columns. ***Note that the beginning inventory of $28,000 is entered in the "Income statement" debit column.***

5 ***Enter the ending inventory in the "Income statement" credit column and the "Balance sheet" debit column.*** This procedure in effect deducts the ending inventory from the total cost of goods available for sale to leave the costs comprising the cost of goods sold for the year in the "Income statement" columns.

6 Foot (i.e., calculate the total of) the "Income statement" columns. The balancing amount is the net income or loss for the year. The difference of $1,860 between the credit and the debit columns in this illustration represents net income, and is entered in the debit column of the Income Statement and in the credit column of the Retained Earnings Statement.

7 Balance the "Retained earnings statement" columns and enter the difference in the debit column of the retained earnings statement and in the credit column of the balance sheet. This adjusts the retained earnings balance for changes during the year (net income and dividends).

8 Total the "Balance sheet" columns. Considerable assurance of the arithmetical accuracy of the year-end procedures is provided if these two columns balance.

Although the work sheet proves the mathematical accuracy of what has been done, it does not prove that some adjustments have not been omitted or that the amounts used in making the adjustments were correct.

Work Sheet and Year-End Procedures

The work sheet is the source of the formal adjusting entries. Once the adjusting entries are entered in the work sheet, the identical information is recorded in the general journal and the ledger. The adjusting journal entries for Merchandising Limited on December 31, Year 4, are given in the next illustration.

The data in the "Income statement" columns of the work sheet also may be used to prepare the closing entries. When a work sheet is prepared, the closing process is generally summarized in a series of closing entries as in the second Merchandising Limited illustration on page 69.

Adjusting entries at end of period

MERCHANDISING LIMITED
Adjusting Entries
December 31, Year 4

(a) Interest Receivable	33	
Interest Revenue		33
To accrue interest on short-term investments.		
(b) Doubtful Accounts Expense	875	
Allowance for Doubtful Accounts		875
To increase allowance for doubtful accounts by ½% of gross sales ($175,000 × 0.005 = $875).		
(c) Allowance for Doubtful Accounts	520	
Accounts Receivable		520
To write off uncollectible accounts.		
(d) Short-Term Prepayments	50	
Insurance Expense	300	
Rent Expense		250
Miscellaneous Expenses		100
To adjust Short-Term Prepayments ledger account to year-end balance.		
(e) Depreciation Expense	600	
Accumulated Depreciation		600
To record depreciation at 10% of cost of furniture and fixtures ($6,000 × 0.10 = $600).		
(f) Interest Expense	40	
Interest Payable		40
To accrue interest on notes payable.		
(g) Salaries Expense	818	
Salaries Payable		818
To accrue unpaid salaries.		
(h) Income Taxes Expense	370	
Income Taxes Payable		370
To record estimated income tax liability.		

Closing entries at end of period

MERCHANDISING LIMITED
Closing Entries
December 31, Year 4

Inventory (Dec. 31, Year 4)	28,900	
Purchases Returns and Allowances	3,000	
Income Summary	124,100	
Inventory (Jan. 1, Year 4)		28,000
Purchases		128,000
To close beginning inventory and net purchases for Year 4, and to record ending inventory.		
Sales	175,000	
Interest Revenue	33	
Sales Returns and Allowances		2,500
Sales Discounts		3,150

	Debit	Credit
Salaries Expense		23,318
Rent Expense		4,800
Advertising Expense		9,000
Janitorial Expense		1,500
Miscellaneous Expenses		1,900
Interest Expense		160
Property Taxes Expense		600
Doubtful Accounts Expense		875
Insurance Expense		300
Depreciation Expense		600
Income Taxes Expense		370
Income Summary		125,960
To close revenue and expense accounts.		
Income Summary	1,860	
Retained Earnings		1,860
To close Income Summary account.		
Retained Earnings	1,500	
Dividends		1,500
To close Dividends account.		

Post-Closing Trial Balance

After the closing entries have been posted and the nominal accounts closed, a post-closing trial balance is prepared to make certain that the debit and credit balances in the open ledger accounts are equal. The trial balance may be prepared on an adding machine tape or by computer, or it may be prepared more formally as illustrated below for Merchandising Limited:

MERCHANDISING LIMITED
Post-Closing Trial Balance
December 31, Year 4

	Debit	*Credit*
Cash	$ 8,650	
Short-term investments	2,000	
Interest receivable	33	
Accounts receivable	15,180	
Allowance for doubtful accounts		$ 1,155
Inventory	28,900	
Short-term prepayments	1,550	
Furniture and fixtures	6,000	
Accumulated depreciation		2,400
Notes payable—current		4,000
Interest payable		40
Accounts payable		10,000
Salaries payable		818
Income taxes payable		370
Common stock, no par		40,000
Retained earnings		3,530
Totals	$62,313	$62,313

Note that the balances in this post-closing trial balance are identical to those in the balance sheet columns of the work sheet on pages 66–67.

Illustration of Work Sheet for a Manufacturing Enterprise

The procedures for preparing a work sheet for a manufacturing enterprise are similar to those used for a merchandising enterprise. The addition of a pair of columns to summarize the manufacturing operation is the major difference. These columns allow for one more step in the classification of the data. The optional step of the adjusted trial balance is omitted from this illustration.

The following data are the basis for the adjusting entries included in the work sheet for Cole Manufacturing Limited for the year ended December 31, Year 4, on pages 72–73.

a Doubtful accounts expense for Year 4 is estimated to be $3,000.
b A three-year insurance policy was acquired on July 1, Year 3, at a cost of $1,800. The insurance expense is allocated to other factory costs and other general expenses in a 4:1 ratio.
c The wages accrued since the last pay period are direct labour, $1,800 and indirect labour, $950. The officers, office staff, and sales staff are paid on the last day of each month.
d Interest of $1,125 has accrued on notes payable.
e Depreciation expense for the plant assets is computed by the straight-line method on the basis of the following information:

Asset	*Estimated economic life, years*	*Estimated residual value*	*Cost allocation, %*	
			Factory	*General*
Building	40	$ -0-	80	20
Machinery and equipment	10	-0-	100	-0-
Furniture and fixtures	20	2,000	10	90

f The power bill for December has not been received as of December 31, Year 4. On the basis of past experience the cost applicable to December is estimated to be $1,450. All heat, light, and power costs relate to the factory.
g An inventory of factory supplies on December 31, Year 4, indicates that supplies costing $850 are on hand.
h The income taxes expense for Year 4 is estimated at $3,500.
i Inventories on December 31, Year 4, are as follows:

Finished goods	$41,500
Goods in process	26,350
Raw material	12,650

Work Sheet and Year-End Procedures

The journal entries for closing the manufacturing ledger accounts, for adjusting the inventory balances, for closing the revenue and expense accounts, and for

COLE MANUFACTURING LIMITED
Work Sheet
For Year Ended December 31, Year 4

	Unadjusted trial balance		*Adjustments*		*Manufacturing*		*Income statement*		*Retained earnings statement*		*Balance sheet*	
	Debit	*Credit*	*Debit*	*Credit*	*Debit*	*Credit*	*Debit*	*Credit*	*Debit*	*Credit*	*Debit*	*Credit*
Cash	32,000										32,000	
Accounts receivable	70,000										70,000	
Allowance for doubtful accounts		1,200		(a) 3,000								4,200
Inventories (Jan. 1, Year 4):												
Finished goods	48,000						48,000	41,500			41,500	
Goods in process	21,000				21,000	26,350					26,350	
Raw material	16,000				16,000	12,650					12,650	
Unexpired insurance	1,500			(b) 600							900	
Land	72,000										72,000	
Buildings	150,000										150,000	
Accum. depr. of buildings		45,000		(e) 3,750								48,750
Machinery and equipment	130,000										130,000	
Accum. depr. of mach. and equip.		52,000		(e)13,000								65,000
Furniture and fixtures	10,000										10,000	
Accum. depr. of furn. and fixtures		3,000		(e) 400								3,400
Notes payable — current		75,000										75,000
Accounts payable		41,300		(f) 1,450								42,750
Common stock, no par		200,000										200,000
Retained earnings (Jan. 1, Year 4)		88,875								88,875		
Dividends	6,000								6,000			
Sales		633,600						633,600				
Sales returns and allowances	3,600						3,600					
Raw material purchases	125,000				125,000							
Purchases returns and allowances		4,000				4,000						

Freight-in	3,500				3,500							
Direct labour costs	192,500		(c) 1,800		194,300							
Indirect labour costs	72,600		(c) 950		73,550							
Heat, light, and power	12,300		(f) 1,450		13,750							
Other factory costs	15,000		(b) 480	(g) 850	14,630							
Advertising expense	35,000						35,000					
Sales salaries expense	42,000						42,000					
Delivery expense	8,000						8,000					
Administrative salaries expense	50,000						50,000					
Office salaries expense	20,000						20,000					
Telephone and telegraph expense	1,800						1,800					
Other general expenses	2,800		(b) 120				2,920					
Interest expense	3,375		(d) 1,125				4,500					
Doubtful accounts expense			(a) 3,000				3,000					
Wages payable				(c) 2,750								2,750
Interest payable				(d) 1,125								1,125
Depreciation of bldg. (factory)			(e) 3,000		3,000							
Depreciation of bldg. (general)			(e) 750				750					
Depreciation of mach. and equip. (factory)			(e)13,000		13,000							
Depreciation of furn. and fix. (factory)			(e) 40		40							
Depreciation of furn. and fix. (general)			(e) 360				360					
Inventory of factory supplies			(g) 850								850	
Income taxes expense			(h) 3,500				3,500					
Income taxes payable				(h) 3,500								3,500
Cost of finished goods manufactured						434,770	434,770					
Net income							16,900			16,900		
Retained earnings (Dec. 31, Year 4)									99,775			99,775
Totals	1,143,975	1,143,975	30,425	30,425	477,770	477,770	675,100	675,100	105,775	105,775	546,250	546,250

closing the Dividends account are illustrated below, for Cole Manufacturing Limited.

Closing entries for manufacturing enterprise

COLE MANUFACTURING LIMITED
Closing Entries
December 31, Year 4

Account	Debit	Credit
Raw Material Inventory (Dec. 31, Year 4)	12,650	
Goods in Process Inventory (Dec. 31, Year 4)	26,350	
Purchases Returns and Allowances	4,000	
Cost of Finished Goods Manufactured	434,770	
Raw Material Inventory (Jan. 1, Year 4)		16,000
Goods in Process Inventory (Jan. 1, Year 4)		21,000
Raw Material Purchases		125,000
Freight-In		3,500
Direct Labour Costs		194,300
Indirect Labour Costs		73,550
Heat, Light, and Power		13,750
Other Factory Costs		14,630
Depreciation of Buildings		3,000
Depreciation of Machinery and Equipment		13,000
Depreciation of Furniture and Fixtures		40
To record cost of finished goods manufactured and ending inventories of raw material and goods in process.		
Finished Goods Inventory (Dec. 31, Year 4)	41,500	
Cost of Goods Sold	441,270	
Cost of Finished Goods Manufactured		434,770
Finished Goods Inventory (Jan. 1, Year 4)		48,000
To record ending finished goods inventory and cost of goods sold.		
Sales	633,600	
Cost of Goods Sold		441,270
Sales Returns and Allowances		3,600
Advertising Expense		35,000
Sales Salaries Expense		42,000
Delivery Expense		8,000
Administrative Salaries Expense		50,000
Office Salaries Expense		20,000
Telephone and Telegraph Expense		1,800
Other General Expenses		2,920
Interest Expense		4,500
Doubtful Accounts Expense		3,000
Depreciation of Buildings		750
Depreciation of Furniture and Fixtures		360
Income Taxes Expense		3,500
Income Summary		16,900
To close revenue and expense accounts.		
Income Summary	16,900	
Retained Earnings		16,900
To close Income Summary account.		
Retained Earnings	6,000	
Dividends		6,000
To close Dividends account.		

STATEMENT OF COST OF FINISHED GOODS MANUFACTURED

The cost of goods completed during an accounting period is summarized in a statement of cost of finished goods manufactured. The information for this statement, illustrated below for Cole Manufacturing Limited, is taken from the "Manufacturing" columns of the work sheet.

A statement of production costs for an accounting period

COLE MANUFACTURING LIMITED
Statement of Cost of Finished Goods Manufactured
For Year Ended December 31, Year 4

Goods in process inventory (Jan. 1, Year 4)		$ 21,000
Raw material used:		
Raw material inventory (Jan. 1, Year 4)	$ 16,000	
Raw material purchases (net)	124,500	
Cost of raw material available for use	$140,500	
Less: Raw material inventory (Dec. 31, Year 4)	12,650	
Cost of raw materials used	$127,850	
Direct labour costs	194,300	
Factory overhead costs (See work sheet for details)	117,970	
Total manufacturing costs		440,120
Total cost of goods in process during Year 4		$461,120
Less: Goods in process inventory (Dec. 31, Year 4)		26,350
Cost of finished goods manufactured		$434,770

Uses and Limitations of Accounting Information

The ultimate objective of accounting is the *use* of accounting information, through analysis and interpretation, as a basis for business decisions. Information derived from accounting records serves business executives in controlling current operations and in planning future business activities. Financial statements afford outsiders a means of analyzing the financial position and results of operations of business enterprises in which they have an interest. These financial statements essentially reflect past business transactions and events. The past is often the key to the future, however, and for this reason accounting information is highly valued by decision makers, both inside and outside the enterprise.

Among the main objectives of this book are: (1) to examine the basic accounting principles and their effectiveness as the underlying assumptions of accounting, (2) to explore the rules and conventions of accounting, and (3) to consider the possible uses of accounting information once it has been accumulated. However, we must be aware of the fact that accounting is justified only because the information accumulated is useful and that such information is often limited because many factors not measurable in terms of money have been omitted. Examples include the human resources of a business enterprise and the economic environment in which the enterprise operates. Furthermore, continuing inflation has made the dollar an imperfect tool for measurement of accounting information.

But even in the absence of inflation, it should be recognized that many business transactions and events are complex and inconclusive at the time they are recorded (pension costs and contingencies, for example). Thus, it may not be realistic to expect financial statements to achieve a higher level of certainty than the transactions and events they reflect.

REVIEW QUESTIONS

1 Describe the ***accounting cycle*** and list the sequence of procedures involved in the accounting cycle.

2 State in concise form the ***rules of debits and credits*** for the five basic types of ledger accounts.

3 Describe the function of ***journals***.

4 What is the function of a ***ledger***?

5 Explain the advantage of using ***controlling accounts*** and ***subsidiary ledgers***.

6 What is the purpose of an ***unadjusted trial balance***? Does it provide proof that there have been no errors in the recording, classifying, and summarizing of business transactions?

7 How are the ***temporary*** or ***nominal ledger accounts*** (revenue and expense accounts) related to the basic accounting equation, $A = L + OE$?

8 What is the objective of using ***special journals***?

9 With the advent of electronic computers, the cost of data-processing equipment and the complexity of operations increased significantly. What economies are available to the user to offset the added costs of converting to and using this type of equipment?

10 What are ***adjusting entries*** and why are they necessary?

11 Why is it necessary to prepare adjusting entries to change the carrying amount of accounts receivable when the journal entries for receivables are usually made only on objective evidence of credit sales and cash collections?

12 Prepare adjusting entries on June 30, Year 6, indicated by the following information:

a Accrued wages total $3,000.

b The estimate of doubtful accounts expense is $2,000, and the allowance for doubtful accounts has a zero balance.

13 What are ***closing entries***? Why are they made? What ledger accounts are closed?

14 You are given the following information about the merchandise ledger accounts of Foxx Company and are asked to prepare a single journal entry to adjust the Inventory account and close the relevant accounts to the Cost of Goods Sold account:

Inventory (Jan. 1, Year 10, ledger account balance)	$ 44,000
Purchases	276,400
Purchases returns and allowances	1,700
Purchases discounts	3,800
Freight-in	4,800
Handling and storage costs	26,800
Inventory (Dec. 31, Year 10, physical count; valued at net invoice cost plus freight-in, handling, and storage costs)	46,200

15 What are ***reversing entries***, and under what circumstances are they most commonly used?

16 Which of the following adjusting entries (explanations omitted) would be reversed when a business enterprise adopts a policy of preparing reversing entries? For each entry, indicate your reasons for reversing or not reversing.

a	Unearned Subscriptions Revenue	10,000	
	Subscriptions Revenue		10,000
b	Inventory of Office Supplies	5,000	
	Office Supplies Expense		5,000
c	Interest Expense	300	
	Interest Payable		300
d	Depreciation Expense	8,000	
	Accumulated Depreciation		8,000

17 What is the purpose of a ***work sheet***, and what benefits may be derived from using it?

18 List three limitations of accounting information.

EXERCISES

Ex. 2-1 Select the best answer for each of the following multiple-choice questions.

1 The accounting cycle for a business enterprise includes all the following procedures except:

a Closing the accounting records
b Classifying data by posting to ledger accounts
c Preparation of supporting documents for a business transaction
d Adjusting, correcting, and updating recorded data

2 The premium on a three-year insurance policy expiring on December 31, Year 3, was paid on January 2, Year 1. Assuming that the original payment was recorded in an asset ledger account, how would assets and expenses be affected in Year 3? Answer ***a***, ***b***, ***c***, or ***d*** according to the following table.

	Assets	*Expenses*
a	No change	Increase
b	No change	No change
c	Decrease	No change
d	Decrease	Increase

3 A business enterprise uses the periodic inventory system, and uses a closing entry to record the ending inventory (December 31). If the ending inventory is $56,200 and the beginning inventory (January 1) was $42,300, the correct closing entry (explanation omitted) is:

a	Income Summary	56,200	
	Inventory (Dec. 31)		56,200
b	Inventory (Jan. 1)	42,300	
	Inventory (Dec. 31)		42,300
c	Inventory (Dec. 31)	56,200	
	Income Summary		56,200
d	Inventory (Dec. 31)	13,900	
	Inventory (Jan. 1)		13,900

4 Chamber Company credits unearned fees received to an Unearned Fees Revenue liability account. On December 31, Year 2, before end-of-year adjusting entries, the credit balance in the Unearned Fees Revenue ledger account was $6,312. The credit balance in this account should be $4,286 on December 31, Year 2. The appropriate December 31, Year 2, adjusting entry (explanation omitted) is:

a	Unearned Fees Revenue	2,026	
	Fees Revenue		2,026
b	Cash	4,286	
	Unearned Fees Revenue		4,286
c	Fees Revenue	4,286	
	Unearned Fees Revenue		4,286
d	None of the foregoing		

Ex. 2-2 Total manufacturing costs for Latest Products, Inc., for Year 3 were $642,700. The cost of finished goods manufactured in Year 3 was $655,500.

Compute the amount of the goods in process inventory of Latest Products, Inc., on December 31, Year 3, assuming that the goods in process inventory on January 1, Year 3, was $62,000.

Ex. 2-3 The balance in the Accounts Receivable controlling account (ledger account no. 8) on January 1, Year 2, was $146,220. In January, sales on credit from the sales journal (page 22) were $109,800, and cash collections from the cash receipts journal (page 11) were $120,000 after sales discounts of $1,800. Accounts receivable of $2,200 were written off as uncollectible in the general journal (page 30) on January 22, and a provision of $1,460 for doubtful accounts was recorded on January 31.

Reproduce the ledger account (in three-column form) for the Accounts Receivable controlling account for the month of January, Year 2.

Ex. 2-4 For Year 5, the gross profit on sales of Oxnard Company was $102,000; the cost of finished goods manufactured was $340,000; the beginning inventories of goods in process and finished goods were $28,000 and $45,000 respectively; and the ending inventories of goods in process and finished goods were $38,000 and $63,500 respectively.

Compute the amount of Oxnard Company's sales for Year 5.

Ex. 2-5 During the month ended December 31, Year 3, Hope Company completed the following transactions:

Dec. 6 Acquired office supplies for cash of $12,000. The acquisition was recorded in the Office Supplies Expense ledger account. The December 1 balance of the Inventory of Office Supplies ledger account was $1,000; the inventory of office supplies on December 31, Year 3, was $2,500.

7 Borrowed $20,000 from National Bank on a 90-day, 12% promissory note. Hope Company computes interest on a 360-day year.

Prepare *a* journal entries to record the transactions described above, and *b* adjusting entries on December 31, Year 3, for each transaction. (Omit explanations.) Hope Company does not use reversing entries.

Ex. 2-6 Among the items requiring adjusting entries for Horizon Company on January 31, Year 2, were the following:

a Office supplies used, $64,290. Acquisitions of office supplies were recorded in the Inventory of Office Supplies ledger account.

b Rent revenue received in advance, $16,200. Advance rent received from lessees is credited to the Rent Revenue ledger account.

c Interest accrued on a 60-day, 18%, $60,000 note payable dated January 16, Year 2. Horizon uses a 360-day year to compute interest.

d Royalty revenue accrued from licensing a patent, $6,200.
e Doubtful accounts amounted to $82,800. The credit balance, before adjustment, in the allowance account was $64,600.

Prepare adjusting entries on January 31, Year 2, for each item described above. (Omit explanations.) Horizon Company uses reversing entries.

Ex. 2-7 The account balances below are taken from the ledger of Paradise Limited:

	May 1	*May 31*
Accounts receivable	$20,000	$28,500
Inventories	50,000	48,000
Accounts payable (suppliers of merchandise)	30,000	21,600
Retained earnings	28,000	40,400
Dividends declared and paid		12,900

Cash collections from customers in May were $106,000, and net purchases of merchandise were $65,000. No allowance for doubtful accounts is used, and no accounts receivable were written off. The only entries in the Retained Earnings ledger account were to close the Income Summary and Dividends ledger accounts.

Compute the following for Paradise for the month of May:

a Total net sales
b Cost of goods sold
c Amount of cash paid to suppliers of merchandise
d Net income
e Total expenses (other than cost of goods sold)

Ex. 2-8 The information below for Pinehurst Company provides a basis for making all necessary adjusting entries on December 31, Year 5, the end of Pinehurst's first fiscal year:

a On June 1, Year 5, borrowed $60,000 by issuing a 9% mortgage note payable that required interest to be paid quarterly, beginning September 1, Year 5.
b On October 1, Year 5, paid $2,700 for three years of insurance coverage commencing on that date. The Unexpired Insurance ledger account was debited.
c On November 1, Year 5, credited a nominal account when $4,800 in rent revenue was received from a tenant. This amount represented six months' rent paid in advance.
d On May 1, Year 5, acquired bonds with a face amount of $20,000 and an annual interest rate of 12% at face amount as an investment. Interest on the bonds is paid on April 1 and October 1.
e On December 31, Year 5, after an aging of accounts receivable, estimated that probable uncollectible accounts would total $4,000. The Allowance for Doubtful Accounts ledger account had an unadjusted credit balance of $900.

Prepare adjusting entries for Pinehurst Company on December 31, Year 5. Include in the explanation portion of each entry any computations required to prepare the adjusting entry.

Ex. 2-9 Selected ledger account balances of Lobo Corporation before and after the December 31 adjusting entries are listed below:

		Before adjustment	*After adjustment*
a	Allowance for doubtful accounts	$ 2,000 credit	$ 5,500 credit
b	Accumulated depreciation	14,000 credit	16,000 credit
c	Sales salaries expense	24,200 debit	24,650 debit
d	Income taxes payable	3,700 credit	6,250 credit
e	Interest revenue	6,500 credit	6,585 credit
f	Royalty revenue	5,000 credit	5,800 credit

Prepare the adjusting journal entries that were made by Lobo Corporation for each ledger account on December 31.

Ex. 2-10 Rainbow Company's accounting records provide the following information concerning certain ledger account balances and changes in the balances during Year 5:

a ***Accounts receivable:*** Jan. 1 balance, $15,000; Dec. 31 balance, $20,500; uncollectible accounts written off during the year, $4,100; accounts receivable collected during the year, $56,000. (Record sales on credit.)

b ***Allowance for doubtful accounts:*** Jan. 1 balance, $1,500; Dec. 31 balance, $2,200; adjusting entry increasing allowance on Dec. 31, $4,800. (Record write-off of uncollectible accounts receivable.)

c ***Inventory of office supplies:*** Jan. 1 balance, $1,600; Dec. 31 balance, $1,450; office supplies expense for the year, $9,500. (Record acquisition of office supplies.)

d ***Equipment:*** Jan. 1 balance, $20,500; Dec. 31 balance, $18,000; equipment costing $8,000 was sold during the year. (Record acquisition of equipment.)

e ***Accounts payable:*** Jan. 1 balance, $9,000; Dec. 31 balance, $11,500; purchases of merchandise on credit for the year, $48,000. (Record payments to suppliers.)

Transaction information is missing from each of the above. Prepare Rainbow Company's journal entry to record the missing information (indicated in the parenthetical instructions) for each ledger account.

Ex. 2-11 The accounting policies of Gina Publications, Inc., require that subscriptions received from customers be credited to Subscriptions Revenue when received. Acquisitions of supplies are regularly debited to Supplies Expense at time of acquisition. The post-closing trial balance on December 31, Year 5, includes the following ledger accounts:

	Debit	*Credit*
Accounts receivable	$ 24,000	
Allowance for doubtful accounts		$ 2,200
Inventory of supplies	1,710	
Equipment	135,500	
Accumulated depreciation of equipment		48,000
Notes payable		20,000
Interest payable		350 ✓
Wages payable		1,230 ✓
Unearned subscriptions revenue		2,940

Assuming that Gina Publications, Inc., follows a policy of reversing the adjusting entries that set up new balance sheet accounts, prepare the appropriate reversing entries on January 1, Year 6.

Ex. 2-12 The following transactions were completed in January (the first month of operations) by Lane's markets:

1 Sales on credit totalled $13,000. Terms 2/10, n/60.
2 Cash sales amounted to $24,000.
3 Purchases of merchandise totalled $50,000.
4 Payments of $28,600 were made to creditors in full settlement of purchase invoices totalling $29,000.
5 Accounts receivable in the amount of $10,000 were collected; one-half of these collections were made before the expiration of the 10-day discount period.
6 P. Lane, the owner, withdrew merchandise for personal use. This merchandise had a cost of $3,000 and had been marked to sell for $3,900. Lane also withdrew $500 cash during January.
7 Inventory of goods on hand at the end of January was $23,000.
8 Operating expenses for the month totalled $15,500.

Compute the net income or net loss of Lane's Markets for the month of January. Show supporting computations.

Ex. 2-13 During the review of the accounting records and the preparation of year-end adjusting entries for Sunburst Company, you discover the following errors:

a The perpetual inventory amount in the accounting records was overstated by $4,750 as a result of errors in pricing merchandise sold.
b Office equipment acquired for $10,500 was recorded in the Equipment Maintenance ledger account. The adjusting entry for depreciation expense has not been recorded.
c A payment to a supplier in the amount of $1,210 was debited to the Accounts Receivable ledger account.
d A sale on credit for $419 was recorded in the sales journal at $491. The correct amount of $419 was received from the customer and was recorded in the cash receipts journal.

e A fully depreciated piece of equipment costing $19,000 that was sold for $800 cash was recorded by a debit to Cash of $800 and a credit to Equipment of $800.

Prepare a correcting entry for each error described above. (Omit explanations.)

Ex. 2-14 All but one of the ledger accounts of Arnold's Store, a sole proprietorship owned by J. Arnold, appear in the following list on December 31, Year 1:

Accounts receivable (net)	$17,500
Accounts payable	21,000
Interest payable	1,300
Cash	8,500
Inventory	15,000
Notes payable	18,000
Plant assets (net)	41,000
Short-term prepayments	500

On January 1, Year 1, Arnold's equity in the proprietorship amounted to $27,000. In Year 1, Arnold withdrew $8,400 cash and made an additional investment of $5,000 of plant assets that had been part of another business enterprise owned by Arnold.

Compute the net income or net loss of Arnold's Store for Year 1, and show supporting computations. ***Hint:*** First prepare a trial balance to find the amount of the missing ledger account.

CASES

Case 2-1 Sharon Bebout, accountant for Arcadia Paint Store, Inc., has not recorded conventional closing entries for 10 years. Instead, she recorded the following journal entry annually and posted only the credit to the Retained Earnings account in the ledger:

Revenue and Expenses (not posted)	XXX	
Dividends (not posted)		XXX
Retained Earnings		XXX

In the ledger, Bebout skipped two lines to distinguish clearly the revenue and expenses for each year. For example, the Sales ledger account for the two most recent years appears as follows:

	Sales			Ledger Account No. 80	
Date	*Explanation*	*Ref.*	*Debit*	*Credit*	*Balance*
Year 9					
Dec. 31		S48		741,200	741,200 Cr
31		CR52		192,888	934,088 Cr
Year 10					
Dec. 31		S53		780,100	780,100 Cr
31		CR58		219,600	999,700 Cr

When a staff accountant working for Arcadia Paint Store's auditors objected to Bebout's closing procedure, she responded: "You should not object unless you can show me that the financial statements are in any way deficient. All assets, liabilities, shareholders' equity, revenue, and expense balances are 100% correct under my procedure. My only objective has been to be efficient and accurate; I wanted to dispense with the meaningless ritual of journalizing and posting closing entries to nominal accounts at the end of each year."

Instructions

Evaluate Sharon Bebout's response to the staff accountant.

Case 2-2 On January 2, Year 5, Paul Falk established a sole proprietorship, Falk's Nursery. He signed a three-year lease on a store building at a monthly rent of $300 and made the first monthly payment on January 2, Year 5. Also on that date, Falk acquired store equipment for $10,000 and purchased merchandise for $16,000. The store equipment had an estimated economic life of 10 years with no residual value. Falk made no other investment in the enterprise.

Both Falk and his wife worked in the enterprise; they had no employees. From time to time the Falks withdrew cash from the enterprise to meet their personal needs. Because the Falks had no prior business experience, they chose to minimize record-keeping. The only records maintained were a chequebook, which was reconciled monthly with the bank statement, a file folder of unpaid purchase invoices, and another file folder of uncollected sales invoices for a few customers.

On December 31, Year 6, Falk carried out the following procedures in an effort to see how the proprietorship stood after two years of operations:

1 Took a physical inventory of merchandise and priced the items, using invoice prices of recent purchases. This procedure indicated a total cost for the inventory of $45,000.

2 Reconciled the December 31 bank statement with the chequebook and found the correct cash balance to be $7,200.

3 Added the unpaid purchase invoices in the file, which showed a total liability to suppliers of $22,700.

4 Added the uncollected sales invoices and found that the total amount receivable from customers was $4,200.

5 Computed the withdrawals of cash for personal needs during the two-year period at $20,000.

Instructions

a Prepare a balance sheet for Falk's Nursery (a sole proprietorship) on December 31, Year 6. (Disregard income taxes, including the fact that apparently no personal income tax return was prepared to reflect Falk's tax liability for the first year of operations.)

b Explain to Falk the advantages of a double-entry accounting system over his present set of accounting records. Could the information obtainable from a double-entry system also be obtained from his present system?

c What conclusion can be reached about Falk's operations for the first two years?

Case 2-3 Carmen Garcia began her working career in the accounting department of Mod Company. Although Garcia had never taken a formal course of study in accounting, she gradually developed a thorough knowledge of Mod's accounting system, and eventually she was promoted to the position of chief accountant.

While attending a meeting of accountants, Garcia was puzzled by a statement made in a group discussion. The statement was: "Reversing entries are frequently helpful; however, they are not essential to the record-keeping function." Garcia was concerned because reversing entries had been used regularly by Mod Company, and she had always considered them an essential part of the accounting cycle.

Instructions

a Explain why reversing entries are not essential but why they may be helpful. Your answer should include an explanation as to when reversing entries are appropriate and when they should not be used.

b Using the data below, demonstrate with journal entries how reversing entries may be used or ignored. The accounting policy is to debit the Supplies Expense ledger account for all supplies acquired. The cost of supplies on hand on December 31, Year 4, was determined by count to be $1,150. The balance in the Inventory of Supplies ledger account was zero. The following adjusting entry was made:

Inventory of Supplies	1,150	
Supplies Expense		1,150
To record inventory of supplies on Dec. 31, Year 4.		

During Year 5, supplies were acquired at a cost of $17,500 and debited to Supplies Expense. The inventory of supplies on December 31, Year 5, was $850.

PROBLEMS

Pr. 2-1 The income statement columns in the work sheet for Billy Jack, Inc., for the year ended September 30, Year 2, are reproduced below:

	Debit	*Credit*
Inventory (periodic system)	$ 75,800	$ 94,200
Sales		875,000
Sales returns and allowances	10,800	
Sales discounts	12,500	
Purchases	588,000	
Purhases returns and allowances		15,000
Purchases discounts		10,200
Salaries expense	82,500	
Rent expense	24,000	
Advertising and promotion expense	52,100	
Other operating expenses	38,700	
Income taxes expense	26,750	
Net income	83,250	
Totals	$994,400	$994,400

Instructions

Prepare closing entries for Billy Jack, Inc., on September 30, Year 2, similar to those illustrated on pages 69–70.

Pr. 2-2 Verena Limited uses the periodic inventory system. Selected transactions and adjustments for Year 2 are listed below:

1 Sales on credit totalled $44,120.

2 A building and a tract of land were acquired at a cost of $300,000. The current fair value of the land was estimated at $90,000. One-fifth of the acquisition cost was paid in cash, and a 10% mortgage note payable was issued for the balance.

3 Merchandise costing $24,200 was purchased, subject to a cash discount of 2% if paid within 10 days. (Record invoice at net amount.)

4 Freight charges of $495 related to merchandise purchased were paid.

5 Uncollectible accounts receivable of $515 were written off. Verena uses an allowance for doubtful accounts and makes provisions for doubtful accounts at the end of each year.

6 The invoice for the purchase in item *3* was paid in full within the discount period.

7 Cash collections on customers' accounts totalled $27,400, after sales discounts of $350.

8 Equipment on which accumulated depreciation amounted to $3,000 was sold for $500 cash; the cost of the equipment was $5,000.

9 A cash dividend of $0.25 a share on 100,000 shares of outstanding common stock was declared and paid. (Prepare separate journal entries for the declaration and the payment.)

10 20,000 shares of no-par common stock were issued for $14 a share.
11 Defective merchandise purchased on credit for $650 (net amount) was returned for full credit.
12 An expense account was debited when supplies were acquired. The Inventory of Supplies ledger account had an unadjusted balance of $750, but the inventory of supplies at the end of Year 2 was $950.
13 The building acquired in item **2** was used in operations for nine months during Year 2. The building had an economic life of 25 years and no residual value. Depreciation was computed by the straight-line method.

Instructions

Prepare journal entries for Verena Limited to record the foregoing transactions and adjustments for Year 2.

Pr. 2-3 Marlboro Corporation uses the perpetual inventory system. A selected list of transactions and adjustments for Year 8 is presented below.

1 Sales on credit totalled $40,500; the cost of the goods was $27,500.
2 Marlboro acquired land and a building at a total cost of $310,000. One-tenth of the acquisition cost was paid in cash, and a mortgage note payable was issued for the balance. The building had an estimated current fair value of $192,000.
3 Merchandise costing $29,500 was purchased. The invoice amount was subject to a 2% cash discount if paid within 10 days. Marlboro records purchases invoices at the net amount.
4 Marlboro paid $850 for freight charges on merchandise purchased. Freight charges are recorded in a separate ledger account.
5 Accounts receivable of $350 were written off as uncollectible. Marlboro maintains an allowance for doubtful accounts and makes a provision for doubtful accounts expense at the end of each year.
6 The invoice for the purchase of merchandise in item *3* was paid within the discount period.
7 Cash collections on customers' accounts amounted to $39,880. No sales discounts were allowed.
8 Cash of $4,000 was received from disposal of equipment. The cost of the equipment was $20,000, and the accumulated depreciation was $17,500.
9 A cash dividend of $0.50 a share on 80,000 shares of common stock was declared and paid. (Prepare separate journal entries for the declaration and the payment.)
10 Defective merchandise was returned to a supplier for full credit. The merchandise had been purhcased on credit for $750 (net).
11 Marlboro issued 10,000 shares of its no-par common stock and received cash of $9 a share.
12 A customer's cheque for $180, received and deposited by Marlboro, was returned by the bank marked ''NSF'' (not sufficient funds).
13 The building acquired in item **2** was used in operations for 10 months during Year 8. The building had an economic life of 40 years and no residual value. Depreciation was computed by the straight-line method.

Instructions

Prepare journal entries for Marlboro Corporation to record the foregoing transactions and adjustments for Year 8.

Pr. 2-4 Tom Manufacturing Limited uses the periodic inventory system. Its adjusted trial balance on December 31, Year 2, follows:

TOM MANUFACTURING LIMITED
Adjusted Trial Balance
December 31, Year 2

	Debit	*Credit*
Cash	$ 35,100	
Accounts receivable (net)	62,000	
Inventories (Jan. 1, Year 2):		
Finished goods	40,000	
Goods in process	20,000	
Raw material	25,000	
Short-term prepayments	2,000	
Plant assets (net)	254,400	
Accounts payable		$ 48,500
Income taxes payable		40,000
Common stock, no par		250,000
Retained earnings (Jan. 1, Year 2)		82,000
Dividends	44,000	
Sales (net)		980,000
Raw material purchases (net)	210,000	
Direct labour costs	220,000	
Factory overhead costs	190,000	
Selling expenses	130,000	
General and administrative expenses	122,000	
Income taxes expense	46,000	
Totals	$1,400,500	$1,400,500

Inventories on December 31, Year 2, were as follows:

Finished goods	$45,000
Goods in process	25,000
Raw material	32,500

Instructions

a Prepare closing entries for Tom Manufacturing Limited on December 31, Year 2, similar to those illustrated on page 74.

b Prepare a statement of cost of finished goods manufactured for Tom Manufacturing Limited for the year ended December 31, Year 2.

Pr. 2-5 Dawn Merchandising Corporation has adopted a policy of not reversing any adjusting entries. All receipts and payments relating to revenue and expenses are recorded in nominal accounts, and the accruals and deferrals established at the end of the preceding year are adjusted to reflect current balances. The following unadjusted trial balance was prepared by Dawn Merchandising's accountant in the first pair of columns of the work sheet for the year ended October 31, Year 10:

DAWN MERCHANDISING CORPORATION
Unadjusted Trial Balance
October 31, Year 10

	Debit	*Credit*
Cash	$ 49,000	
Accounts receivable	32,000	
Allowance for doubtful accounts		$ 200
Inventory (Nov. 1, Year 9)	47,000	
Inventory of advertising supplies	3,000	
Land	264,000	
Building	210,000	
Accumulated depreciation of building		45,800
Equipment	252,000	
Accumulated depreciation of equipment		62,700
Notes payable		180,000
Accounts payable		45,000
Unearned rent revenue		3,200
Interest payable		4,000
Salaries payable		2,200
Bonds payable, 9%		100,000
Common stock		200,000
Retained earnings (Nov. 1, Year 9)		88,800
Dividends	8,000	
Sales		830,000
Rent revenue		18,600
Purchases	480,000	
Salaries expense	56,500	
Selling expenses	122,500	
General expenses	41,000	
Interest expense	15,500	
Totals	$1,580,500	$1,580,500

Additional Information

1 Aging of accounts receivable indicates that an allowance for doubtful accounts in the amount of $960 is required on October 31, Year 10.
2 Inventory of advertising supplies is $1,850 on October 31, Year 10.
3 The estimated economic life of the building is 30 years, and the residual value is zero. The estimated economic life of the equipment is 20 years, and the residual value is $12,000. (Use the straight-line method of depreciation.)
4 Unearned rent revenue is $2,700 on October 31, Year 10.
5 Interest payable is $6,400 on October 31, Year 10.
6 Salaries payable amount to $1,200 on October 31, Year 10.
7 The physical inventory on October 31, Year 10, is $35,000. (Prepare an adjusting entry to record cost of goods sold in a separate ledger account.)

8 Income taxes expense for the year ended October 31, Year 10, is estimated at $32,000.

Instructions

Prepare Dawn Merchandising Corporation's October 31, Year 10, adjusting entries for each item above. Record expenses in specific ledger accounts, such as Doubtful Accounts Expense, Advertising Supplies Expense, Depreciation Expense of Building, etc.

Pr. 2-6 Listed below are the adjusted ledger account balances of Rockingham Limited on January 31, Year 3, except for retained earnings, which is the January 1, Year 3, balance. There are no assets or liabilities other than those listed. The Dividends account represents the amount declared and paid during January, Year 3.

Accounts payable	$111,000
Accounts receivable	96,000
Accumulated depreciation	222,000
Cash	100,000
Common stock, no par	660,000
Dividends	24,000
Inventories	192,000
Plant assets	870,000
Retained earnings (Jan. 1, Year 3)	231,000

Instructions

a Compute the net income of Rockingham Limited for January, Year 3, by preparing a balance sheet on January 31, Year 3, that includes details showing the beginning balance, increases and decreases, and the ending balance of retained earnings.

b What was the amount of total sales for January, Year 3, assuming that the accounts receivable totalled $108,000 on January 1, Year 3, and that $480,000 was received on customers' accounts and from cash sales during January, Year 3?

c Determine the cost of goods sold for January, Year 3, assuming that inventories on January 1, Year 3, were $174,000 and that purchases of merchandise totalled $330,000 in January, Year 3.

d Compute the total of all other expenses for January, Year 3.

e Determine the total cash paid for merchandise purchases during January, Year 3, assuming that the January 31, Year 3, balance of accounts payable was $114,000 and that purchases (all on credit) amounted to $330,000 during January, Year 3.

Pr. 2-7 Subsidiary ledgers and related controlling accounts are maintained by Robin Company for accounts receivable and accounts payable. On December 31, Year 9, the two subsidiary ledgers were summarized as follows:

ROBIN COMPANY
Accounts Receivable Trial Balance
December 31, Year 9

Paul Davis	$ 2,000
Ed Fairly	6,000
Ken Iverson (credit balance)	(750)
Dolores Kiley	13,500
Balance of controlling account	$20,750

ROBIN COMPANY
Accounts Payable Trial Balance
December 31, Year 9

Joann Edwards	$ 588
John Gates (debit balance)	(570)
Julie Loomis	8,050
David Parks	2,330
Balance of controlling account	$10,398

Robin Company offers credit terms of 2/10, n/30 to all customers and records all sales at gross prices. Purchases of merchandise from suppliers are recorded net of purchases discounts because it is Robin's policy to take all purchases discounts available. When Robin fails to take the discount offered by suppliers, the Purchases Discounts Lost ledger account is debited.

Robin carried customers' credit balances as an offset against debit balances, and suppliers' debit balances as an offset against credit balances in the subsidiary ledgers. These balances are reclassified for reporting purposes to reflect customers' credit balances as liabilities and suppliers' debit balances as assets.

Transactions for January, Year 10, were as follows:

1 A cheque for $13,230 was received from Kiley in full settlement of her account within the discount period.
2 Purchases from Edwards totalled $11,000, terms 2/10, n/30. (Record net of purchases discounts.)
3 Payment to Loomis of $8,050 was made within the discount period.
4 Sales to Iverson were $23,000, terms 2/10, n/30.
5 Cash of $4,500 was received from Davis, including a $2,500 advance payment.
6 Payment of $11,380 was made to Edwards in settlement of the account payable balance. Because of an oversight, the payment was not made until after the discount period had lapsed on the December invoice for $600.
7 Purchases from Edwards totalled $13,200, terms 2/10, n/30.

8 Cash of $3,920 was received from Fairly in partial payment of his account balance. The discount was allowed on this portion of the account balance, because cash was received within the discount period.
9 Parks was paid $4,130, which represented payment of the balance due within the discount period and an $1,800 partial advance payment on a new order.
10 Purchases from Loomis totalled $5,000, terms 2/10, n/30.

Instructions

a Enter the December 31, Year 9, balances and the foregoing transactions of Robin Company directly in the appropriate accounts in both the general ledger and the subsidiary ledgers for accounts receivable and accounts payable. You need not maintain ledger accounts for Cash, Purchases, or Sales. (Because this problem does not include journals or monthly totals, each transaction should be entered individually in a general ledger controlling account as well as in a subsidiary ledger account. The three-column ledger account form is recommended.)
b Prove the accuracy of Robin Company's accounting records by preparing trial balances of the subsidiary ledgers on January 31, Year 10, and by determining that the totals agree with the balances of the respective controlling accounts on that date.
c Which accounts with customers and suppliers should be reclassified in Robin Company's balance sheet on January 31, Year 10? Explain how such accounts should be presented in the balance sheet.

Pr. 2-8 Suyanto Corporation adjusts and closes its accounting records at the end of each calendar year. The following information provides the basis for making the adjusting entries on December 31, Year 5:

1 On July 1, Year 5, Suyanto received $7,260 of rent revenue covering a one-year period beginning with the date of receipt. The Rent Revenue ledger account was credited.
2 Unexpired Insurance was debited on September 1, Year 5, when Suyanto paid a $2,700 premium for a three-year insurance policy effective on that date.
3 Suyanto borrowed $90,000 on March 1, Year 5, by issuing a three-year, 10% mortgage note payable, with interest payable quarterly. Interest payments were made on May 31, August 31, and November 30 of Year 5.
4 Bonds with a face amount of $20,000 and an interest rate of 12% were acquired at face amount as an investment on April 1. Interest payment dates are April 1 and October 1.
5 The building occupied by Suyanto has a cost of $96,000. Estimated economic life is 20 years, with no residual value. Straight-line method of depreciation is used.
6 An aging of the accounts receivable on December 31 indicated $4,100 to be a reasonable estimate of doubtful accounts. On that date the allowance for doubtful accounts had a ***debit*** balance of $260.
7 Office Supplies Expense was debited on July 2, Year 5, when $2,200 was paid

for office supplies. On December 31, Year 5, office supplies of $1,195 were on hand.

8 A contract was signed on December 20, Year 5, requiring Suyanto to deliver merchandise to Plainville Company on January 29, Year 6. The contract price was $14,500 and the estimated cost of the merchandise to be delivered was $9,000.

Instructions

a Prepare adjusting entries for Suyanto Corporation on December 31, Year 5. Include in the explanation portion of each journal entry any computations used to determine the amount of the adjustment.

b Prepare reversing entries for Suyanto Corporation on January 1, Year 6, assuming that Suyanto follows a policy of reversing the adjusting entries that include a balance sheet ledger account normally not used during the accounting period.

Pr. 2-9 Trijono Hardward Limited uses the periodic inventory system and maintains its accounting records on a calendar-year basis. The following unadjusted trial balance was prepared from the general ledger on December 31, Year 3, and no adjusting entries had been made.

TRIJONO HARDWARE LIMITED
Unadjusted Trial Balance
December 31, Year 3

	Debit	*Credit*
Cash	$ 8,000	
Accounts receivable	40,000	
Inventory (Dec. 31, Year 2)	23,000	
Land	80,000	
Building	200,000	
Accumulated depreciation of building		$ 42,000
Equipment	240,000	
Accumulated depreciation of equipment		59,500
Accounts payable		38,000
Interest payable		-0-
Salaries payable		-0-
Bonds payable, 12%		100,000
Common stock		200,000
Retained earnings (Dec. 31, Year 2)		75,200
Dividends	25,000	
Sales		806,000
Purchases	479,500	
Salaries expense	55,200	
Selling expenses	120,000	
General and administrative expenses	40,000	
Interest expense	10,000	
Totals	$1,320,700	$1,320,700

Reversing entries were made on January 1, Year 3, for interest payable and salaries payable that had been recorded by adjusting entries on December 31, Year 2.

Additional Information

1 Trijono has decided, after an aging and analysis of accounts receivable, to establish an allowance for doubtful accounts of $3,000.
2 The building and equipment are depreciated on the straight-line basis. The economic life of the building is 40 years and the residual value is zero; the economic life of the equipment is 15 years and the residual value is $15,000.
3 Interest on the bonds payable is paid on May 1 and November 1.
4 Salaries earned by employees but unpaid on December 31 amount to $6,000.
5 Income taxes are estimated to be $17,000.
6 The physical inventory on December 31, Year 3, was $28,000.

Instructions

a Prepare a 12-column work sheet for Trijono Hardware Limited on December 31, Year 3, to adjust the ledger accounts and classify the balances as to income statement, retained earnings statement, and balance sheet. (Include columns for an adjusted trial balance.)
b Use the work sheet as a source for preparation of closing entries for Trijono Hardware Limited on December 31, Year 3. (Adjusting entries are not required; do not record cost of goods sold in a separate ledger account.)
c Prepare reversing entries for Trijono Hardware Limited dated January 1, Year 4, with respect to salaries payable and to interest payable, for which adjustments were made on December 31, Year 3.

Pr. 2-10 The following unadjusted trial balance was prepared from the ledger of Rex Manufacturing Corporation on December 31, Year 10. Rex used reversing entries on January 1 of each year to reverse wages payable and interest payable.

REX MANUFACTURING CORPORATION
Unadjusted Trial Balance
December 31, Year 10

	Debit	*Credit*
Cash	$ 14,050	
Accounts receivable	80,000	
Allowance for doubtful accounts		$ 200
Inventories (Jan. 1, Year 10):		
Raw material	12,000	
Goods in process	56,000	
Finished goods	80,000	
Short-term prepayments	9,000	
Land	50,000	
Building	457,000	
Accumulated depreciation of building		54,800
Machinery and equipment	400,000	

Accumulated depreciation of machinery and equipment		120,000
Accounts payable		70,000
Wages payable		-0-
Interest payable		-0-
Bonds payable, 12%		200,000
Common stock		570,000
Retained earnings (Jan. 1, Year 10)		56,025
Dividends	15,000	
Sales (net)		992,000
Raw material purchases	310,000	
Direct labour costs	292,900	
Factory overhead costs	120,000	
Selling expenses	95,000	
General and administrative expenses	52,000	
Interest expense	20,075	
Totals	$2,063,025	$2,063,025

Additional Information

1 The allowance for doubtful accounts should be increased to a balance equal to 6% of accounts receivable.

2 Short-term prepayments at the beginning and end of Year 10 are as follows (insurance is an administrative expense):

	Jan. 1, Year 10	*Dec. 31, Year 10*
Unexpired insurance (two years remaining on Jan. 1)	$3,600	$1,800
Factory supplies	5,400	7,000
Totals	$9,000	$8,800

3 Invoices for raw material included in the ending inventory but not recorded in the accounting records total $12,000.

4 The straight-line method of depreciation is used to allocate the cost of plant assets. Other relevant data are presented below.

	Estimated economic life, years	*Estimated residual value*	*Percentage allocated to:*	
			Factory	*Administration*
Building	50	$7,000	70	30
Machinery and equipment	10	5%	80	20

5 Interest payments to bondholders are made semiannually on May 1 and November 1.

6 The factory power bill for December, Year 10, $3,200, has not been recorded.

7 Direct factory wages incurred but not paid on December 31, Year 10, total $1,800.
8 Income taxes are estimated at $4,700 for Year 10.
9 The ending inventories on December 31 are: raw materials, $18,000; goods in process, $53,000; and finished goods, $75,000.

Instructions

a Prepare a work sheet for Rex Manufacturing Corporation on December 31, Year 10, to adjust the accounts and classify the data as to manufacturing costs, income statement, retained earnings statement, and balance sheet. Do not include columns for an adjusted trial balance.
b Prepare Rex Manufacturing Corporation's closing entries on December 31, Year 10, to adjust the inventory accounts and to record the cost of finished goods manufactured and the cost of goods sold. You need not close any accounts to Income Summary.
c Prepare reversing entries for Rex Manufacturing Corporation as of January 1, Year 11, relating to wages payable and interest payable.

Pr. 2-11 The post-closing trial balance for Steve Shirt Corporation on June 30, Year 5, is shown below.

STEVE SHIRT CORPORATION
Post-Closing Trial Balance
June 30, Year 5

	Debit	*Credit*
Cash	$ 26,200	
Accounts receivable	32,600	
Allowance for doubtful accounts		$ 1,100
Inventory	54,950	
Unexpired insurance	600	
Store fixtures	38,400	
Accumulated depreciation of store fixtures		13,800
Vouchers payable		18,300
Income taxes payable		6,100
Wages payable		1,300
Common stock, no par value, 2,000 shares issued and outstanding		70,000
Retained earnings		42,150
Totals	$152,750	$152,750

Transactions recorded in the journals for the month of July, Year 5, are summarized on the next page. (To avoid unnecessary detail, all expenses are recorded in a single Operating Expenses ledger account.)

Additional Information

1 Aging of accounts receivable indicates that an allowance for doubtful accounts of $1,250 is required on July 31, Year 5.

Sales Journal (S)	
Debit to Accounts Receivable and credit to Sales	$82,100
Cash Receipts Journal (CR)	
Debits:	
Cash	$88,800
Sales Discounts	1,200
Credits:	
Accounts Receivable	$70,000
Common Stock (110 shares)	5,000
Sales	15,000
Voucher Register (V)	
Debits:	
Purchases	$45,200
Freight-In	900
Operating Expenses	13,800
Credits:	
Vouchers Payable	$59,200
Purchases Discounts	700
Cash Payments Journal (CP)	
Debit to Vouchers Payable and credit to Cash	$68,200
General Journal (J)	
Debits:	
Allowance for Doubtful Accounts	$ 200
Notes Receivable	5,000
Accumulated Depreciation of Store Fixtures	150
Credits:	
Accounts Receivable	$ 5,200
Store Fixtures	150

2 Depreciation expense for the month of July, Year 5, is $850.
3 Unexpired insurance amounts to $520 on July 31, Year 5.
4 Wages payable amount to $800 on July 31, Year 5.
5 Interest receivable is $40 on July 31, Year 5.
6 Income taxes expense for July, Year 5, is estimated at $10,000.
7 A physical inventory indicates that merchandise costing $51,000 is on hand on July 31, Year 5.

Instructions

a Post Steve Shirt Corporation's June 30, Year 5, balances and all transactions for July, Year 5, from the journals to ledger accounts.

b Prepare an unadjusted trial balance for Steve Shirt Corporation on July 31, Year 5, in the first pair of columns of a 12-column work sheet that includes an adjusted trial balance.

c Enter the adjustments in the work sheet and complete the work sheet.

d Record Steve Shirt Corporation's adjusting and closing entries on July 31, Year 5, in the general journal and post these entries to the ledger. (Reversing entries are not used.)

e Prepare Steve Shirt Corporation's income statement for the month of July, Year 5, and balance sheet on July 31, Year 5. (Disregard earnings per share.)

f Prepare a post-closing trial balance for Steve Shirt Corporation on July 31, Year 5.

c h a p t e r 3

REVENUE AND EXPENSE RECOGNITION; INCOME MEASUREMENT AND REPORTING

The measurement of periodic income of a business enterprise is perhaps the foremost objective of the accounting process. The concept of ***income*** (or ***net income***) is elusive, and the art of accounting will probably never progress to the point where "income" is defined to everyone's satisfaction. Accountants measure income for an accounting period by matching expired costs with realized revenue under a system of accrual accounting. This process requires workable standards for the recognition of revenue, expenses, gains, and losses applicable to each period. ***Terminology For Accountants*** defines ***accrual accounting*** as:[1]

> The method of recording transactions by which revenues and expenses are reflected in the determination of net income for the period in which they are considered to have been earned and incurred, respectively, whether or not such transactions have been settled finally by the receipt or payment of cash or its equivalent.

Similarly, the Financial Accounting Standards Board in the United States described ***accrual accounting*** as follows:[2]

> Accrual accounting uses accrual, deferral, and allocation procedures whose goal is to relate revenues, expenses, gains, and losses to periods to reflect an enterprise's performance during a period instead of merely listing its cash receipts and outlays.

1 Canadian Institute of Chartered Accountants, ***Terminology For Accountants***, 3rd ed. (Toronto: 1983), p. 5.

2 FASB, ***Statement of Financial Accounting Concepts No. 3***: "Elements of Financial Statements of Business Enterprises" (Stamford: 1980), pp. 41–42.

> Thus, recognition of revenues, expenses, gains, and losses and the related increments or decrements in assets and liabilities — including matching of costs and revenues, allocation, and amortization — is the essence of using accrual accounting to measure performance of business enterprises. The goal of accrual accounting for a business enterprise is to account in the periods in which they occur for the effects of transactions and other events and circumstances, to the extent that those financial effects are recognizable and measurable.

Our attention in this chapter focusses on the role of accrual accounting in the measurement and reporting of business income; the various forms of income statements are illustrated in Chapter 4.

RECOGNITION OF REVENUE

The concept of *revenue* originated in ancient times from the simple barter transactions involving goods and services between individuals. As societies matured and business organizations evolved, it was necessary to identify events and transactions that resulted in inflows of economic resources from customers (revenue) and to measure the value of such inflows in terms of a uniform standard of measurement such as money. In today's more complex and uncertain business environment, accountants are faced with the same two tasks relating to revenue — to determine ***when revenue is realized*** and the ***dollar amount at which it is recognized*** in the accounting records. Because of new and frequently complex ways of structuring business transactions, and because of the many new products and services developed in recent years, revenue recognition has become one of the most challenging problems in financial accounting.

The objective of any business enterprise is to generate income that will provide owners with a satisfactory return on their investment. The major source of income for most enterprises is from its operations — the process of generating revenue by providing goods and services to outsiders. Operations involve the incurring of costs and expenses; and unless a satisfactory level of revenue is generated, a loss or a low level of income will result, no matter how carefully costs and expenses are controlled. Consequently, the meaning of ***revenue*** and the criteria for its recognition are important not only to accountants but also to the enterprise and to the users of its financial statements.

Definition of Terms

Before undertaking the discussion of revenue recognition, a brief description of the following terms may be helpful:

- ***Revenue*** Section 3400.03 of the ***CICA Handbook*** defines ***revenue*** as the inflow of cash, receivables, or other consideration arising in the course of the ordinary activities of an enterprise, normally from the sale of goods, the rendering of services, and the use by others of enterprise resources yielding interest, royalties, and dividends. Similarly, the Financial Accounting Standards Board in the United States has defined ***revenue*** as the inflow or other enhancement of assets of a business enterprise or settlements of its liabilities (or a combination of both) during an accounting period resulting from delivering or producing goods, rendering services, or other activities that constitute the enterprise's ongoing major or central operations.[3]

- *Realization* (or ***recognition***) ***of revenue*** A common definition of ***realization*** or ***recognition*** is the process of converting noncash assets to cash or claims to cash.[4] In the measurement of revenue, ***realization*** or ***recognition*** generally means that a measurable transaction (such as a sale) or an event (such as the rendering of services) has been completed or is sufficiently finalized to warrant the recording of earned revenue in the accounting records. The selection of the ***critical event*** indicating that revenue has been realized (earned) is the foundation of the revenue realization or recognition principle.
- *Earning process* The profit-directed activities of a business enterprise through which revenue is earned is known as the ***earning process***; such activities may include purchasing, manufacturing, selling, rendering services, delivering and servicing products sold, allowing others to use enterprise resources, etc.

Conceptual Foundations of Revenue Recognition

Revenue is the measurable value of goods and services that a business enterprise transfers to its customers and clients, and realization refers to the ***timing of revenue recognition***. A practical working rule is needed to signal that revenue has been earned as a result of the enterprise's profit-directed activities. Each step in the earning process is essential to the earning of revenue. Ideally, the recognition of revenue should be ***continuous*** rather than being tied to a ***single critical event*** (such as the completion of a sale transaction) in the revenue-generating activities of the enterprise. In fact, increases in the value of the goods and services (output) produced by the enterprise take place continuously throughout the earning process. However, because continuous valuation of the output is not practical, alternative procedures must be found to measure these increases as objectively as possible in order to measure realized revenue.

Revenue Realization Conditions

When a business enterprise acquires asset services, accountants assume an ***even exchange*** of values—that is, that no gain or loss occurs at the time of acquisition. An arm's-length ***exchange price*** is viewed as the best evidence of value received at the time a cost is incurred. When accountants trace the flow of costs internally, the assumption of an even exchange continues to control accounting procedures. For example, the allocation of material, direct labour, and factory overhead costs to inventories is limited to the actual costs incurred, and the fact that there may be increases in the value of the output beyond the costs added is ignored. However, somewhere along the line reliable evidence will arise that the value of the output is greater (or possibly less) than the costs incurred in producing the output. When such evidence becomes conclusive, the value of the output is measured and

3 FASB, ***Statement No. 3***, pp. 31–32.

4 Revenue recognition is also defined as the process of recording revenue in the accounting records. However, the terms ***realization*** and ***recognition*** are used interchangeably in this text.

revenue emerges. Thus, revenue from the sale of goods is recognized in financial accounting at a specific stage of the earning process, generally when the following three ***revenue realization or recognition conditions*** are met:[5]

1 The ***significant risks and rewards of ownership*** have been ***transferred*** from the seller to the buyer.
2 ***Reasonable assurance*** exists regarding the ***measurement of the consideration*** from the sale, and the ***extent to which goods may be returned.***
3 ***Ultimate collection*** of the consideration from the sale is ***reasonably assured.*** [Emphasis added.]

Revenue from services and long-term contracts is recognized when the second and third conditions listed above are met. Thus either the percentage of completion method or the completed contract method may be used, depending on which method is more indicative of the fulfillment of these two conditions.[6] Similarly, these two conditions are used for the recognition of interest, royalties, and dividends revenue: interest, on a time-proportion basis; royalties, as they accrue, based on the terms of the agreement; and dividends, when the right to receive payment is established.[7]

Many of today's revenue-generating transactions are complex and involve considerable uncertainty. Consequently, sound professional judgement is essential in the proper application of the three revenue recognition conditions. However, further elaboration on each of these conditions will provide a better basis for making such a judgement. The significant risks and rewards of ownership are considered to have been transferred from the seller to the buyer when (1) all significant acts of performance relating to the sale have been completed and (2) the seller has no continuing managerial involvement in, or effective control over, the goods transferred to a degree that is usually associated with ownership.[8] In other words, the ***earning process*** is ***complete or virtually complete*** and all necessary costs have been incurred or may be estimated with reasonable accuracy. Reasonable assurance regarding the measurement of the consideration from the sale means that ***sufficient reliable evidence*** exists to ***measure*** the market value of the goods; such evidence is generally provided by an ***exchange transaction*** between independent parties. Reasonable assurance on the ultimate collection of the consideration from the sales exists when (1) the claims from buyers are legally enforceable and (2) the buyers are in a position to settle the claims fully and satisfactorily, or, in those cases where the claims may not be settled fully, the deficiency is reasonably determinable and provided for. In most cases, these three conditions are met and revenue is recognized when there is a passing of possession or legal title of the goods from the seller to buyer, such as in retail sales. On the other hand, there are situations in which one or more of the revenue recognition conditions are not met. For example, significant risks of ownership

5 CICA, ***CICA Handbook*** (Toronto), sec. 3400.06–.07.

6 CICA, ***CICA Handbook***, sec. 3400.08.

7 CICA, ***CICA Handbook***, sec. 3400.09.

8 CICA, ***CICA Handbook***, sec. 3400.07 and .12.

are considered ***not*** to have been transferred when (1) there is a liability for unsatisfactory performance not covered by normal warranty provisions, (2) the buyer has the right to rescind the sale, and (3) the goods are shipped on consignment.[9] Also, the measurement of the consideration from the sale is ***not*** considered to be reasonably assured when the sale is subject to ***significant and unpredictable*** amounts of goods being returned, as in the case where the market for returnable goods is untested.[10]

The Role of Evidence, Estimates, and Professional Judgement

In Chapter 2 we stated that changes in assets and liabilities, and related changes in revenue and expenses, result from either ***external transactions and events*** or ***internal events***. Acquisitions of asset services, hiring and paying employees, sales of goods and services, borrowing funds, and issuing shares of capital stock are examples of market transactions between a business enterprise and outsiders. Such transactions stem from express or implied contracts and generally represent exchanges between independent parties at arm's-length prices supported by ***external evidence***.

Internal events, such as accruals of revenue and cost allocations, leave a less distinct trail of ***internal evidence***. In such revenue and expense recognition situations accountants face some difficult problems. For example, the amounts spent for material, labour, and other services may be measured objectively; but the continuous transformation of these cost inputs into more valuable outputs is an internal process that requires estimates based on subjective judgement. In tracing the effect of this process and portraying it in terms of dollars, accountants do not have objective external evidence supporting market transactions as a basis for measurement and recording.

Whether revenue and expenses are recognized on the basis of external or internal evidence, accountants nevertheless rely on ***estimates*** and ***professional judgement*** in making many revenue and expense recognition decisions. However, generally accepted accounting principles provide few guidelines for making estimates and for exercising professional judgement in specific revenue and expense recognition situations. As you study the topics in this chapter, remember that ***accounting is an art, not a science***.

Pressures for Speeding Up Revenue Recognition

In an effort to enhance their ability to attract capital, some companies are tempted to recognize revenue at the earliest possible stage in the earning process. Instances of fictitious sales and sales to related parties lacking economic substance have been attributed to middle management personnel anxious to meet sales quotas and earnings performance goals set by top management. Although income may be overstated by deferral of costs as well as by premature recognition of revenue, the latter probably provides more opportunities for creative interpretation of accounting principles, also known as ''cooking the books.''

9 CICA, ***CICA Handbook***, sec. 3400.10.

10 CICA, ***CICA Handbook***, sec. 3400.18.

Because of the emergence of many innovative sales and sales financing arrangements in recent years, revenue recognition practices for the sale of products frequently occupy centre stage in some widely discussed cases of income manipulation. Today, accountants face a more difficult problem than ever before in determining when a ''sale'' has taken place or when a ''service'' has been substantially performed. In the next sections we discuss and illustrate the various stages of the earning process at which revenue may be recognized.

Revenue Recognized at Time of Sale and Delivery

In actual business situations, the most widely accepted evidence of revenue realization is the sale and delivery of a product or the performance of a service. There is little question about the reliability of evidence supporting the three revenue recognition conditions presented in the preceding section, because an arm's-length transaction has taken place that transfers title and possession of a product in return for cash or the expectation to receive cash. The transaction determines both the ***time*** at which to recognize revenue and the ***amount*** at which to record it.

One may question why accountants choose so late a stage in the earning process to recognize revenue and thus net income. The answer comes in two parts: (1) At any point prior to sale, the expected selling price of a product and the ability to sell it at a profit may be so uncertain that they do not constitute sufficient evidence to justify an upward valuation of the product, and (2) for most business enterprises the actual sale of a product is the most important step — the critical event—in the earning process. Until a sale is made and the product is delivered to and accepted by the customer, the significant risks and rewards of ownership have not been transferred and the future stream of revenue is uncertain in terms of both its measurement and its collectibility.

Shipments of goods on consignment do not constitute sales. In a ***consignment***, goods are transferred to another party (the ***consignee***) who acts as an agent for the owner of the goods (the ***consignor***). Title to the goods remains with the owner until the agent sells the goods to ultimate consumers, at which time a sales transaction takes place and revenue is recognized by the consignor.

Revenue Recognition When Right of Return Exists

Even when a sale occurs, the recognition of revenue may be delayed because of unusual terms surrounding the sales transaction. For example, in the recorded music and book publishing industries it is common practice to give retail stores ***the right to return products*** sold and delivered to them if they cannot resell them. When such a right exists, there are uncertainties regarding the measurement of revenue and the seller may continue to be exposed to significant risks of ownership. Thus, section 3400 of the *CICA Handbook* states that revenue would not be recognized when revenue ''is not determinable within reasonable limits''; such a situation occurs ''when payment relating to goods sold depends on the resale of the goods by the buyer.'' This section further states that revenue would not be recognized when sales are subject to ''significant and unpredictable amounts of goods being returned,'' as in the case where ''the market for a returnable good is untested.'' However, revenue may be recognized if the amounts of goods being returned are ***predictable*** and an adequate allowance is provided therefor.[11]

Similarly, the FASB has recommended that when a right of return exists, revenue is recognized on the date of sale only if ***all of the following*** conditions are met:[12]

1 The seller's price to the buyer is substantially fixed or determinable on the date of sale.
2 The buyer has paid the seller, or is obligated to pay the seller and the obligation is not contingent on resale of the product.
3 The buyer's obligation to the seller would not be changed in the event of theft or physical destruction or damage of the product.
4 The buyer acquiring the product for resale has economic substance apart from that provided by the seller.
5 The seller does not have significant obligations for future performance to bring about resale of the product by the buyer.
6 The amount of future returns can be reasonably estimated.

If these conditions are met and sales are recorded, provision for any costs or losses that may be expected in connection with any returns is made on the date of sale. The sales and cost of goods sold in the income statement exclude the portion for which returns are expected, and the allowance for estimated returns is deducted from trade accounts receivable in the balance sheet. Transactions for which revenue recognition is postponed are recorded as sales when the return privilege expires.

Sales on Instalment Plan

A sale of goods or services on the instalment plan generally provides for a cash down payment and a series of additional monthly payments. Because payments extend over a long period, the seller customarily charges interest and carrying charges on the unpaid balance of instalment receivables. Revenue from instalment sales is recorded in the same manner as from regular sales, unless the collection of the instalment receivables is not assured and there is no reasonable basis for estimating the probability of collection. If the accrual basis of accounting is not considered appropriate, an alternative method of revenue recognition such as the instalment method or the cost recovery method (discussed later in this chapter), must be used.

Thus, even though the completion of a sale has been widely accepted as a prerequisite to the recognition of revenue, the preceding discussion indicates that ''sale and delivery'' and ''revenue recognition'' are not necessarily synonymous. In some situations, accountants may record revenue at other stages of the earning process, such as ***before or after delivery*** of the product. These and other revenue recognition situations are discussed in the following sections.

11 CICA, ***CICA Handbook***, sec. 3400.18.

12 See FASB, ***FASB Statement No. 48***: ''Revenue Recognition When Right of Return Exists'' (Stamford: 1981), pp. 2–3. See also ***FASB Statement No. 49***: ''Accounting for Product Financing Arrangements'' (Stamford: 1981), pp. 1–5.

Revenue Recognition Before Delivery

We have seen that revenue must be realized before it is entered into the accounting records. Generally, realization does not occur unless a sale has taken place. However, in some cases revenue is considered realized before the product is delivered to customers, because a sale and a significant portion of the earning process, that is, performance by the seller, have taken place. Although performance by the seller is not completed, the amount of the partial performance may be both economically relevant and measurable. Under such circumstances, the postponement of revenue recognition until delivery of the product would be overly conservative and would assign the entire profit on the sale to the accounting period in which delivery is made. This may result in a shifting of income among periods and produce misleading financial statements.

Thus, accountants are faced with a perplexing question: When a sale occurs but is not considered to result in revenue realization, at what stage in the productive (earning) process might revenue be recognized? Possible answers to this question are: (1) prior to production, (2) during production, (3) on completion of production, and (4) at some other stage based, for example, on production, accretion, discovery, receipt of orders from customers, or billing of customers. These approaches to revenue recognition are discussed below.

Prior to Production

An agreement to enter into an exchange of property rights on some future date is a ***contract to sell***; a ***contract of sale*** is one in which property rights are exchanged between a seller and a purchaser. Neither a contract to sell nor a contract of sale without performance by the seller is a transaction that signals the realization of revenue.

Contracts to sell and contracts of sale in advance of production are common in many industries. For example, motion pictures, agricultural products, fashion goods, recorded music, and computer products may be "presold" for future delivery, perhaps months in advance of actual production. Such transactions should be entered in the accounting records merely in memorandum form, or not at all, unless a deposit is received by the seller. If a deposit is received, it is carried in a liability ledger account until the sale is completed and the goods are delivered to the purchaser, at which time a sale is recorded and revenue emerges.

Magazine subscriptions, insurance premiums, rents, and fees for most services may be received in advance of production or performance of the goods or services. Amounts received by the sellers of such goods or services represent deferred revenue (a liability) until delivery or performance takes place.

During Production

When revenue is generated from a large project — such as the construction of a dam or a bridge that requires two or more years to complete — production is the major element in the earning process. The contract for such a project generally specifies a fixed price, and completion of the "sale" is dependent only on the satisfactory performance by the contractor. If the revenue on such a contract were to be recognized only on completion of the project, a distorted pattern of net income may result for the years the project was in progress. A better matching of effort (costs incurred) and accomplishment (the portion of the contract price considered realized) is achieved by using the ***percentage-of-completion method*** for construction-type contracts.

Under this method, revenue is recognized on the basis of the amount of work (production) completed each year. Costs incurred each year are deducted from realized contract revenue to measure the gross profit earned in that year. The portion of the contract completed is generally measured by comparing the costs incurred to date with the total estimated costs of completing the contract. Thus, use of the percentage-of-completion method for revenue recognition is appropriate only when the actual costs incurred may be measured with reasonable precision and the estimate of the additional costs required to complete the contract is reasonably reliable.

As an illustration of the percentage-of-completion method, assume that in Year 1 Mori Company contracted to construct a dam for a fixed price of $10 million. In Year 1, Mori incurred costs of $2.2 million and expects to incur additional costs of $6.6 million to complete the contract. Mori's income statement for Year 1 includes the following contract revenue, costs, and gross profit relating to this contract:

Income statement amounts for first year of construction-type contract under percentage-of-completion method

Contract revenue ($10,000,000 × $2.2/$8.8)	$2,500,000
Less: Costs incurred	2,200,000
Gross profit	$ 300,000

At the end of Year 1, total costs to complete the contract are estimated at $8.8 million ($2.2 + $6.6 = $8.8). Thus, the percentage of completion to date is 25% ($2.2 ÷ $8.8 = 0.25), and 25% of the contract price of $10 million is recognized as contract revenue.

In Year 2, Mori incurred costs of $5 million on the contract, for a total to date of $7.2 million ($2.2 + $5.0 = $7.2), and it estimates that additional costs of $1.8 million will be incurred in Year 3 to complete the contract. Thus, at the end of Year 2 the total costs are estimated at $9 million ($7.2 + $1.8 = $9.0). On the basis of this information, Mori's income statement for Year 2 includes the following amounts:

Income statement amounts for second year of construction-type contract under percentage-of-completion method

Contract revenue [($10,000,000 × $7.2/$9.0) − $2,500,000 recognized in Year 1]	$5,500,000
Less: Costs incurred	$5,000,000
Gross profit	$ 500,000

At the end of Year 2, evidence indicates that total costs on the contract will be $9 million, a $0.2-million increase from the $8.8 million estimated at the end of

Year 1. Costs of $7.2 million have been incurred through the end of Year 2, indicating that the project is 80% ($7.2 ÷ $9.0 = 0.80) completed. Therefore, 80% or $8 million of the contract price of $10 million is considered realized in the first two years, and because $2.5 million of contract revenue had been previously recognized in Year 1, only $5.5 million ($8.0 − $2.5 = $5.5) of contract revenue is recognized in Year 2.

In Year 3, Mori completed the contract by incurring additional costs of $1.75 million (compare this with the earlier estimate of $1.8 million). Therefore, Mori's income statement for Year 3 includes the following amounts:

Income statement amounts for third year of construction-type contract under percentage-of-completion method

Contract revenue ($10,000,000 — $8,000,000 recognized in Years 1 and 2)	$2,000,000
Less: Costs incurred	$1,750,000
Gross profit	$ 250,000

Accounting for construction-type contracts is discussed in detail in Chapter 9; therefore, we purposely have limited our discussion to the use of the percentage-of-completion method for the recognition of contract revenue based on production. Discussion of the completed-contract method of accounting, progress billings to customers, treatment of projected losses, journal entries, and financial statement issues related to construction-type contracts is deferred to Chapter 9.

On Completion of Production

In some instances the recognition of revenue is delayed until production is completed, even though a contract of sale had occurred earlier. For construction-type contracts in which the use of the percentage-of-completion method is not appropriate, revenue is recognized when the project is completed or substantially completed, under the ***completed-contract method***. If the entire revenue is recognized on completion of production, any remaining "touch-up" costs should be accrued to achieve a proper matching of costs and revenue.

When special-order goods are produced to customers' rigid specifications, or when customers request that delivery of goods be delayed for their convenience, title generally passes to customers as soon as such goods are produced. In such circumstances, revenue is appropriately recognized on completion of production.

Other Methods

In unusual circumstances, it may be argued that revenue is realized before delivery of the product because the economic wealth of the seller has increased. Although this line of reasoning may have some conceptual merit, accountants have generally rejected the notion that revenue accrues before performance by the seller is essentially complete, or in the absence of an arm's-length sales transaction. Such an approach would violate the revenue realization conditions discussed earlier in this chapter. Some other methods that have been proposed, and generally rejected, for the realization of revenue prior to delivery of the product are:

1 *Production* This method is similar to the completed-contract method used for construction-type contracts, except that ***sales transaction is absent***. In the mining and refining of precious metals, or in the manufacture of other products that have a ready market at assured prices, the completion of production may be viewed as a source of realized revenue.

2 *Accretion* Revenue may be considered realized as certain products, such as agricultural commodities, increase in value through the various stages from planting to harvesting. This method has also been proposed for livestock, timber, and cultured products such as fish and mushrooms. Under accrual accounting, ''accretion'' in value does not fit the definition of revenue; ***it is a potential source of revenue***.

3 *Discovery* It is occasionally suggested that revenue results from the discovery of valuable deposits of ore or crude oil by business enterprises engaged in extractive industries. As in the case of accretion, ''discovery'' does not result in realized revenue because there is no sales transaction to provide reliable evidence for the measurement of revenue.

4 *Receipt of order* Some business enterprises in the book publishing, mail-order, and computer hardware industries, for example, record sales at the time orders from customers are received. This method of revenue recognition may be appropiate in rare cases when firm orders are accompanied by substantial and nonreturnable cash deposits or when legal title to the products ordered passes to purchasers as orders are received. For financial accounting, receipt of an order is seldom viewed as a ''critical event'' signalling the realization of revenue.

5 *Billing* A variation of the receipt-of-order method is to record sales when customers are billed, which may precede shipments to customers by several weeks. If the amount of such prematurely recorded sales is not material at the end of an accounting period, there is no serious distortion of revenue and net income; however, there is no theoretical support for use of the billing date to recognize revenue. Even though the billing is generally based on an existing sales contract, it is not a ''critical event,'' and the sales transaction is not considered completed.

The recognition of revenue prior to delivery is generally considered a departure from the revenue realization principle. Recognition of revenue on construction-type contracts under the percentage-of-completion method or on completion of ''special-order'' goods has considerable theoretical and practical support. In such cases a sale has occurred but delivery has not. Therefore, in the absence of a sales transaction, arguments supporting revenue recognition based on production, accretion, or discovery are generally rejected by accountants.

Revenue Recognition After Delivery

As stated in the preceding section, the most widely accepted evidence of revenue realization is the sale and delivery of products or performance of services. However, in the case of product sales, revenue recognition may be delayed until some stage in the earning process subsequent to sale and delivery because the sale and delivery may not provide sufficient evidence of revenue realization. In such instances revenue may be recorded under the instalment method, the cost recovery method, or some other method based on cash collections. These methods are discussed in the following sections.

Instalment Method

Business enterprises that sell goods on the instalment plan may use the ***instalment method*** of accounting only when accrual accounting is not considered appropriate. This method is not acceptable for financial accounting unless considerable doubt exists as to the collectibility of the receivables and a reasonable estimate of doubtful accounts expense cannot be made.[13]

Under the instalment method, the seller recognizes gross profit on sales in proportion to the cash collected. If the rate of gross profit on instalment sales is 40%, each dollar of cash collected on the instalment receivables represents 40 cents of gross profit and 60 cents of cost recovery. For example, assume that Galeria Sales Company sold merchandise on the instalment plan for $400,000 in Year 1, and that the cost of the merchandise sold was $240,000, or 60% of selling price. The terms of a typical sale required a down payment and a number of equal monthly payments. The cash collected, recovery of cost, and realized gross profit on these sales for Galeria Sales Company are summarized below:

Analysis of cash collected on instalment receivables

Year	*Cash collected (A)*	*Recovery of cost, 60% (B)*	*Realized gross profit, 40% (A – B)*
1	$180,000	$108,000	$ 72,000
2	150,000	90,000	60,000
3	70,000	42,000	28,000
Totals	$400,000	$240,000	$160,000

Galeria Sales Company uses the perpetual inventory system, and adopted the instalment method because it could not make a reasonable estimate of the collectibility of the instalment receivables. Deferred interest and carrying charges on the instalment receivables are disregarded for purposes of this illustration, and we have assumed that Galeria Sales eventually collected all receivables from these sales.

The journal entries during the three-year period for Galeria Sales Company under the instalment method are presented on the next page.

Instalment receivables from revenue transactions are included among current

13 AICPA, ***APB Opinion No. 10***: "Omnibus Opinion — 1966" (New York: 1966), p. 149.

GALERIA SALES COMPANY
Journal Entries — Instalment Method of Accounting
For Years 1, 2, and 3

Ledger accounts and explanation of transactions	*Year 1*		*Year 2*		*Year 3*	
	Debit	*Credit*	*Debit*	*Credit*	*Debit*	*Credit*
Instalment Receivables	400,000					
Cost of Instalment Sales	240,000					
Instalment Sales		400,000				
Inventories		240,000				
To record instalment sales and cost of instalment sales.						
Instalment Sales	400,000					
Cost of Instalment Sales		240,000				
Deferred Gross Profit (Year 1 Instalment Sales)		160,000				
To record deferred gross profit at end of Year 1.						
Cash	180,000		150,000		70,000	
Instalment Receivables		180,000		150,000		70,000
To record cash collections.						
Deferred Gross Profit (Year 1 Instalment Sales)	72,000		60,000		28,000	
Realized Gross Profit on Instalment Sales		72,000		60,000		28,000
To record realized gross profit on instalment sales at 40% of cash collections.						

assets in the balance sheet. The balance in the Deferred Gross Profit (Year 1 Instalment Sales) ledger account may be deducted from the receivables as a valuation account or included among current liabilities as a deferred revenue item. We prefer reporting the deferred gross profit as a valuation account because it is more in concert with the reason for use of the instalment method — absence of reasonable assurance that the full amount of the receivables will be collected.

Under the procedures illustrated above, the entire revenue and cost of goods sold are included in the income statement in the year instalment sales are made, and the unrealized gross profit of $88,000 ($220,000 × 0.40 = $88,000) applicable to instalment receivables outstanding at the end of Year 1 is deferred (deducted from total gross profit) and is recognized in Year 2 and Year 3 as the receivables are collected. In the income statements for Year 2 and Year 3, the gross profit realized from Year 1 instalment sales is added to each year's gross profit from regular sales.

An alternative procedure suggested by some accountants is to record revenue and cost of goods sold only as the instalment receivables are collected. This approach would produce the following results for Galeria Sales Company:

	Year 1	*Year 2*	*Year 3*
Instalment sales	$180,000	$150,000	$ 70,000
Cost of goods sold (60%)	108,000	90,000	42,000
Gross profit on sales (40%)	$ 72,000	$ 60,000	$ 28,000

If this approach is used, no ledger account for deferred gross profit is required, because the difference between the deferred portion of instalment sales and the deferred cost of goods sold represents the amount of gross profit deferred.

Application of the instalment method is complicated by variations in the gross profit rates from year to year, repossessions of goods sold on the instalment plan, uncollectible instalment receivables, interest and carrying charges on the receivables, and trade-in allowances. These issues are covered in advanced accounting texts; our purpose here is only to focus attention on the revenue recognition aspect of the instalment method of accounting.

Cost Recovery and Deposit Methods

The ***cost recovery*** and ***deposit*** methods may be used to account for revenue transactions when the terms of such transactions are ambiguous or the financial position of customers is so unstable as to make it virtually impossible to evaluate the collectibility of the related receivables. Under the ***cost recovery method***, no profit is recognized until the cost of the products sold is fully recovered. In the period of sale, the cost of the products is deducted from sales (net of the deferred gross profit) in the income statement. The deferred gross profit is also deducted from the related receivables in the balance sheet. Collections of principal reduce the receivables, and any collections of interest are credited to the deferred gross profit ledger account. Deferred gross profit subsequently recognized as earned is presented as a separate item of revenue in the income statement.

A situation in which the cost recovery method may be appropriate is the sale of recreational land. Such sales are often made to individuals who make only nominal down payments, have poor credit standing, and are able to cancel the sale at any time without penalty other than the loss of the payments already made. In many cases a seller has no legal right to take any action against customers other than to repossess the land. Because the seller has performed but the customer's ability to carry out the terms of the sale are very much in doubt in such cases, use of the cost recovery method of revenue recognition would be appropriate.

When a sales transaction is for any reason incomplete, performance by either the seller or the purchaser has not taken place. Even though the parties fully intend to consummate a sale, certain contingencies may have to be resolved before a sale is completed. Such contingencies may include the obtaining of permits or financing. Any cash received by the seller in such a ''potential sale'' is a deposit from customers rather than revenue. Thus, under the ***deposit method***, cash received from customers is a liability (advances from customers) until the sale is completed. On completion of the sale, the liability is transferred to a revenue account, consistent with an appropriate revenue recognition method such as the accrual method, the instalment method, or the cost recovery method.

Cash Collection Method

The recognition of revenue may be delayed beyond the point of sale until additional evidence confirms the sales transaction. For example, a significant degree of uncertainty may exist as to the collectibility of receivables resulting from revenue transactions, or a sales transaction may be lacking in economic substance and therefore may offer inadequate evidence of revenue realization. Under these circumstances revenue is recognized as cash is collected, and costs incurred are either recognized as expenses or deferred, as considered appropriate in a specific situation.

An extreme application of this test of revenue realization is the ***cash basis of accounting*** described in Chapter 1. In its most unrefined state, the cash basis of accounting calls for the recognition of revenue only when cash is received and for the recognition of expenses only when cash is paid. As previously pointed out, revenue recognition under the ***instalment*** and ***cost recovery*** methods of accounting is based to a considerable extent on the timing of cash receipts.

Other Revenue Recognition Situations

New industries and new ways of structuring business transactions have focussed public attention on numerous instances of ''managed'' and ''manipulated'' earnings, frequently as a result of creative approaches to the recognition of revenue. Financial statements issued by companies engaged in leasing, real estate development, banking, franchising, motion picture distribution, network television programming, and the assembly of computers and mobile homes have frequently been viewed as misleading because of the revenue recognition practices adopted by these companies. Because of the apparent obsession with growth in earnings on the part of corporate managements and investors, and because creativity is a pervasive human trait, it is likely that more examples of ''cute accounting'' in the area of revenue measurement and recognition will surface in the future.

The topics discussed in this section address a few additional revenue recognition situations encountered by accountants in today's business world.

Revenue from Service Transactions

Despite the large growth in service industries in the economy, the accounting for service transactions has received relatively little attention. Enterprises operating in service industries sell services, perform acts, agree to perform certain acts on a later date, or permit their resources to be used by others. Collectively these revenue-generating activities are called ***service transactions***. Examples of service enterprises include advertising and other types of agencies, computer services organizations, entertainment enterprises, banks, public accounting and law firms, hospitals, stock and real estate brokerage firms, and leasing and franchising enterprises. For the most part, service enterprises are small and privately owned; however, some are quite large and are publicly owned.

Generally, revenue is recognized from a service transaction when the provider has performed. *Performance* consists of the completion of a specified act or acts, or occurs with the passage of time. The following four methods of revenue recognition for service transactions have been suggested:[14]

1 *Specific-performance method* This method is similar to the sales method of revenue recognition for product sales and is appropriate when a service transaction consists of a single act; revenue is recognized at the time the act is performed. Examples of single acts include all types of entertainment performances, the sale of real property for a commission, and placement of a candidate on a job by an employment agency.

2 *Completed-performance method* This method is similar to the completed-contract method of revenue recognition for construction-type contracts. It is used when the amount of services to be performed in the ***last of a series of acts is so significant in relation to the entire service transaction*** that performance is not deemed to have occurred until this final act has been carried out. For example, an enterprise hired to move household furniture may pack, load, and store the furniture, but the final act of delivering it to its destination is so significant that the recognition of revenue is deferred until this has been performed.

3 *Proportional-performance method* This method is used when a service transaction consists of (a) a specified number of similar acts, (b) a specified number of dissimilar acts, or (c) an unspecified number of similar acts with a fixed period for performance. The implementation of this method requires considerable judgement to determine the appropriate pattern of revenue recognition. Examples in which this method may be used are:
   - A mortgage banker's processing monthly mortgage payments (specific number of similar acts)
   - A correspondence school's preparation and mailing of lessons, grading of completed lessons, administration of examinations, and grading of examinations (specified number of dissimilar acts)
   - A health club's sale of three-year memberships for unlimited use of its facilities (unspecified number of similar acts with a fixed period for performance)

   When the number of similar acts is specified, an equal amount of revenue is recognized for each act expected to be performed; when the number of acts is specified but the acts are dissimilar, revenue is recognized on the basis of the ratio of the direct costs incurred to the total estimated direct costs of the entire transaction; when the number of similar acts is unspecified and the period of

14 The discussion in this section is based on FASB, "Accounting for Certain Service Transactions," *Invitation to Comment* (Stamford: 1978).

performance is fixed, revenue is recognized ratably over the period of performance, unless evidence indicates that another method is more consistent with the observable pattern of performance.

4 *Cash-collection method* Revenue should be recognized only as cash is collected when considerable doubt exists that the revenue will be collected. This method is similar to the instalment and cost recovery methods of revenue recognition for sales of goods on the instalment plan.

Revenue from Franchise Sales

In the early years of the franchising industry it was common practice for a ***franchisor*** to recognize revenue at the time it sold a ***franchise*** (the exclusive right to engage in a business, such as a fast-foods outlet, in a specific geographic location) to a ***franchisee***. In some cases the contract of sale required the franchisor to help the franchisee locate a site, train the staff, commence operations, and provide consulting and other services for a specified number of years. In return, the franchisor generally received cash and promissory notes from the franchisee as an ***initial franchise fee***. The collectibility of the promissory notes in most cases was dependent on the business success of the franchisee.

Earnings of franchisors rose rapidly as they sold new franchises because the promissory notes and the franchise fee revenue were recorded at the face amount of the notes. This abuse of the revenue realization principle was curtailed when long-term notes receivable were required to be recorded at the discounted present value computed by use of an appropriate current rate of interest rather than at face amount.

Although the discounting of the promissory notes reduced the opportunities for the ***front-ending of income***, it did not answer the question of when the franchise fee revenue should be recognized. The main objectives in accounting for franchising contracts are: (1) to determine the point in the earning process when the franchise fee revenue is realized, (2) to measure the amount of franchise fee revenue to be recognized, and (3) to evaluate the collectibility of the promissory notes representing the unpaid portion of the franchise fee. Depending on the contractual provisions and circumstances surrounding the sale of a franchise, the initial franchise fee may be recognized as cash is received, ratably over the term of the franchise contract, or at the inception of the franchise contract. The principles for the recognition of franchise fee revenue are stated in ***FASB Statement No. 45***: ''Accounting for Franchise Fee Revenue,'' as follows:[15]

> Franchise fee revenue from an individual franchise sale ordinarily shall be recognized, with an appropriate provision for estimated uncollectible amounts, when all material services or conditions relating to the sale have been substantially peformed or satisfied by the franchisor. Substantial performance for the franchisor means that (a) the franchisor has no remaining obligation or intent—by agreement, trade practice, or law—to refund any cash received or forgive any unpaid notes or receivables;

15 FASB, ***FASB Statement No. 45***: ''Accounting for Franchise Fee Revenue'' (Stamford: 1981), pp. 2–3. The CICA has issued an accounting guideline, ''Franchise Fee Revenue,'' which contains similar requirements; however, it is also currently developing recommendations for the ***Handbook***.

(b) substantially all of the *initial services* of the franchisor required by the franchise agreement have been performed; and (c) no other material conditions or obligations related to the determination of substantial performance exist. . . . The commencement of operations by the franchisee shall be presumed to be the earliest point at which substantial performance has occurred, unless it can be demonstrated that substantial performance of all obligations, including services rendered voluntarily, has occurred before that time.

Installment or cost recovery accounting methods shall be used to account for franchise fee revenue only in those exceptional cases when revenue is collectible over an extended period and no reasonable basis exists for estimating collectibility.

To illustrate the accounting for one possible form of a franchise sale, assume the following:

1 On January 2, Year 1, Burito King, Inc., sold a franchise to El Paso Company for an initial fee of $100,000, payable $20,000 down and $40,000 on December 31, Year 1, and on December 31, Year 2. Two promissory notes with a face amount of $40,000 each were issued by El Paso to Burito King.

2 The current fair rate of interest on January 2, Year 1, was 12%, and the present value of the two notes discounted at 12% was $67,602 ($40,000 ÷ 1.12 = $35,714; $35,714 ÷ 1.12 = $31,888; $35,714 + $31,888 = $67,602). Burito King considers the notes to be fully collectible.

3 Burito King will provide substantial services to El Paso in opening the franchise and in operating it during the initial year. The cash down payment is not refundable; however, the additional payment of $40,000 on December 31, Year 1, will be paid by El Paso only if the franchise is opened or nearly ready to be opened on that date, and the final payment of $40,000 on December 31, Year 2, will be paid only if the franchise is operating profitably on that date. Burito King appropriately considers the value of the services and other consideration transferred to El Pasco on January 2, Year 1, to be worth at least $20,000. The value of services provided by Burito King in Year 1 and Year 2 is approximately equal each year.

4 The franchise was opened by El Paso in December of Year 1, and was operating profitably on December 31, Year 2; El Paso paid $40,000 to Burito King on each of these dates.

The journal entries for Burito King, Inc., to record the foregoing transactions are as shown on page 116.

Because cash of $20,000 was received and the current fair value of the promissory note is $67,602, the amount of franchise fee revenue to be recognized as services are provided by Burito King, Inc., over the two-year period is $87,602 ($20,000 + $67,602 = $87,602). Of this amount, $20,000 is considered realized on the date the franchise is sold, and the balance of $67,602 is considered realized equally in Year 1 and Year 2 because equal amounts of services are provided in each year. The discount on notes receivable is recognized as interest revenue, computed at 12% of the carrying amount (face amount less discount) of the notes at the beginning of each year. If the notes were initially recorded at face amount,

BURITO KING, INC.
Journal Entries for Year 1 and Year 2

Year 1			
Jan. 2	Cash	20,000	
	Notes Receivable	80,000	
	Franchise Fee Revenue		20,000
	Discount on Notes Receivable ($80,000 − $67,602)		12,398
	Deferred Franchise Fee Revenue		67,602
	To record sale of franchise to El Paso Company.		
Dec. 31	Cash	40,000	
	Discount on Notes Receivable [($80,000 − $12,398) × 0.12)]	8,112	
	Deferred Franchise Fee Revenue ($67,602 ÷ 2)	33,801	
	Notes Receivable		40,000
	Interest Revenue		8,112
	Franchise Fee Revenue		33,801
	To record collection of note receivable from El Paso Company, and to recognize realized interest and franchise fee revenue.		
Year 2			
Dec. 31	Cash	40,000	
	Discount on Notes Receivable ($12,398 − $8,112)	4,286	
	Deferred Franchise Fee Revenue	33,801	
	Notes Receivable		40,000
	Interest Revenue		4,286
	Franchise Fee Revenue		33,801
	To record collection of note receivable from El Paso Company, and to recognize realized interest and franchise fee revenue.		

interest revenue would be understated by $12,398 and franchise fee revenue would be overstated by the same amount over the two-year period; however, the amount of total revenue in each year would differ because franchise fee revenue and interest revenue are recognized in different patterns.

Revenue from Sales-Type Leases

When a lease contract meets the criteria of a ***sales-type lease***, the lease is recorded by the ***lessor*** as a sale, and the entire consideration received is recognized as revenue at the time the lease becomes effective. The consideration received generally consists of the present value of the monthly payments to be made by the ***lessee*** over the term of the lease.

As stated earlier, a lease contract is an example of a service transaction; yet in a sales-type lease the entire revenue and gross profit are recognized by the lessor despite the fact that the services from the leased asset are provided to the lessee over many years. Critics of accounting for sales-type leases argue that accountants give more weight to the ***form*** of the transaction than to its ***economic substance***. For example, a sales-type lease may be recorded as a sale based on provisions in the lease contract transferring ownership of the leased asset to the lessee at the end of the lease term or giving the lessee an option to acquire the asset at a bargain price. In addition, the collectibility of the lease receivables recorded by the lessor must be reasonably assured, and the lease term must cover at least 75% of the economic life of the leased asset. The criticism of accounting for sales-type leases revolves around the logic of recording a sale today for a transaction that transfers ownership of the asset (already consider ''sold'') to the lessee perhaps ten or more years from now, or gives the lessee an option to acquire the asset (already recorded as a ''sale'' by the lessor) at some future date. The ability of accountants (or anyone else) to estimate the collectibility of long-term receivables and the economic lives of assets, often subject to rapid technological obsolescence, also has been questioned.

In framing the accounting principles for sales-type leases, the accounting profession effectively eliminated some unacceptable accounting practices for leasing transactions. But as one writer has stated, ''No matter how many rules the accountants write, a smart fellow can find a way to bend them to his advantage.''[16] We have discussed sales-type leases at this point not only because of their relevance to revenue recognition but also because they involve some interesting theoretical issues. A complete discussion of accounting for leases is presented in Chapter 20.

Savings and Cost Offsets Are Not Revenue

Purchases discounts and other cost savings should not be confused with revenue. Discounts available on purchases of merchandise or supplies are reductions in the cost of the assets purchased, not revenue. ***Cost savings*** are potential outflows of cash that a business enterprise is able to avoid, not sources of revenue. For example, suppose that a machine may be acquired either for $1,000 cash or for $1,200 on the instalment plan. If the acquirer chooses the instalment plan, it has acquired two types of asset services — the machine for $1,000 and the option of deferring payment for $200; if the acquirer chooses to pay cash, the $200 of avoided interest is not revenue but a cost saving.

Revenue from the sale of a by-product (or scrap) is often recorded as a reduction of the cost of the main product. The main product and the by-product emerge from a single process; thus, a portion of total manufacturing costs applies to the by-product. However, because the sales value of the by-product is generally small, an allocation of the manufacturing costs would not be ''cost-efficient.'' Therefore, the revenue from the sale of the by-product is recorded as an ***offset*** to the cost of the main product. Similarly, when a plant asset is exchanged for another similar asset on terms that indicate a gain (a form of revenue) on the exchange, the gain is not considered realized but is deducted from the cost of the asset acquired.

Recognition of Gains

In financial accounting, ***gains*** may be defined as increases in a business enterprise's owners' equity from incidental transactions and from all other transactions and other events and circumstances except those that result from revenue or investments by owners. Gains from the disposal of assets or the extinguishment of debt

16 ''You Better Believe,'' *Forbes*, July 30, 1984, p. 112.

are generally recognized in the accounting period in which the related transaction is considered to have resulted in the completion of the earning process. The recognition of gains must pass a more severe test than the recognition of losses because of the influence of the concept of conservatism. The recognition and income statement presentation of extraordinary gains are covered in another section of this chapter. Other types of gains are discussed in subsequent chapters.

RECOGNITION OF EXPENSES

In the preceding pages our focus has been on the recognition of revenue, including gains. Similar issues arise in connection with the recognition of expenses and losses.

Expenses are outflows or some other using-up of assets or incurrences of liabilities during an accounting period from the sale of goods or the rendering of services. Initially, costs are incurred to acquire assets, and as assets are consumed or as the costs expire with the passage of time they become expenses.

Losses are decreases in a business enterprise's owners' equity from incidental transactions and other events and circumstances, except those that result from expenses or distributions to owners. Losses result when assets are consumed, costs expire, or liabilities are incurred without producing any discernible benefit for either the current or any future accounting period; thus, losses are never deferred because they have no future service potential.

Expenses and losses are generally recognized in the accounting records when a business enterprise's "economic benefits are consumed in revenue-earning activities or otherwise or . . . if it becomes evident that previously recognized future economic benefits of assets have been reduced or eliminated, or that liabilities have been incurred without associated economic benefits."[17]

In the measurement of net income the principles underlying the recognition of expenses and losses are as important as the principles for the recognition of revenue and gains. Before we outline the principles of expense recognition, a general discussion of the flow of costs in the operations of a business enterprise may facilitate our discussion.

The Flow of Costs

Ideally, all costs should be associated with some physical product or service. If all resources of a business enterprise are devoted to the production and sale of a single product, this approach may be reasonable, because all costs would be accumulated in inventory until the product is sold. However, even in a single-product case it is apparent that some costs are more directly related to the product than are others. The costs of direct material, direct labour, and some variable factory overhead, for example, may be traced to the product because the relationship between effort and accomplishment is relatively clear. At the other extreme,

17 FASB, ***Statement of Financial Accounting Concepts No. 5***: "Recognition and Measurement in Financial Statements of Business Enterprises" (Stamford: 1984), p. xi.

selling and administrative expenses are productive, but the relationship between effort and accomplishment is far more nebulous. In most cases it is virtually impossible to allocate these costs to specific products and accounting periods with any degree of precision. When we turn to the more realistic setting of an enterprise producing not one but many products and services, the difficulty of cost allocation increases. As a result, accountants must make reasonable assumptions for the allocation of costs to products and periods. It is not surprising that opinions as to what is "reasonable" in specific cases will differ.

Product and Period Costs

In the measurement of income for a manufacturing enterprise, certain ***product costs*** are traced to physical output and are accumulated in inventories until evidence of revenue realization is available. For example, the costs of direct material and labour used to manufacture a product ***attach*** to, and may be identified directly with, a unit of inventory. For a trading enterprise, product costs relate solely to the cost of goods acquired for resale; for an enterprise engaged in the sale of services, initial direct costs and direct costs (which will be described later) are analogous to product costs.

Other costs, called ***period costs***, are considered expenses of the accounting period in which they occur. Period costs, such as advertising and sales salaries, are generally not related to production and are ***expensed*** (deducted from revenue immediately), because the benefits are received in the same period the costs are incurred.

Making a theoretical distinction between product costs and period costs may be easier than the practical application of the concept. To illustrate this problem, consider the cost of goods purchased by a merchandising enterprise. There are certain costs directly related to the purchase, such as in the invoice cost of the product and freight-in. There are other indirect costs of purchasing, handling, storage, and display. The salary of a purchasing agent is an example, and decisions on the treatment of such costs are likely to differ among enterprises and are often resolved on the grounds of expediency. However, if the costs are material in amount, different practices may lead to significantly different net income amounts.

In addition to the distinction between product costs and periods costs, another issue arises when identical goods are acquired at different prices. As the goods are sold, decisions must be made as to which costs are to be assigned to the goods sold. The decision to assume a first-in, first-out, a last-in, first-out, or a weighted-average flow of costs is somewhat arbitrary, but important because different assumptions may produce materially different amounts of net income.

Expired Costs

Certain asset services, such as machinery and intangible assets, are acquired in advance of their use. For example, when a business enterprise acquires machinery, it acquires productive services. Some portion of the services will be used during the current accounting period; other portions will not be used for several periods. Accountants are faced with the problem of determining whether the cost of expired services is a product cost or a period cost. In addition, they are confronted with an even more perplexing question: How much of the asset services has been used during the current period, and what is the cost of the services used? In the case of material or merchandise, there is at least a physical flow of goods to indicate the changes that are taking place. In contrast, productive assets such as machinery exhibit little change in their physical condition as they provide services.

The expiration of the services of some productive assets is a function of time. If a three-year premium is paid for an insurance policy, the service acquired is three years of freedom from certain risks. It seems reasonable to assume that one-third of the cost of acquiring this service is used up in each of the three years. If the productive asset is an office building, the service acquired is floor space that may be rented to tenants. The value of the space in a new office building is greater than that of an older building, and thus the value of the services obtained from the building is greater in the early years. These facts should be considered in measuring the periodic cost (depreciation) of the building services used. Reliable evidence of the value of services used year by year is difficult to obtain. Furthermore, the economic life of the building is indefinite, and its residual value, if any, is not known. Therefore, any solution adopted for the measurement of periodic depreciation is highly subjective.

Principles of Expense Recognition

The expenses incurred by a business enterprise during an accounting period may be classified into the following three groups:[18]

1 Costs directly associated with revenue recognized in the period

2 Costs associated with the period on a basis other than a direct relationship with revenue

3 Costs that cannot reasonably be associated with any other period

The principles that provide accountants with guidelines for the recognition of expenses are: (1) ***associating cause and effect***, (2) ***systematic and rational allocation***, and (3) ***immediate recognition***.[19] These expense recognition principles are explained below.

Associating Cause and Effect

Costs may be recognized as expenses based on a presumed direct association with specific revenue. Costs that appear to be related to specific revenue are recognized as expenses concurrently with the recognition of the related revenue. Examples of costs related to specific revenue include the direct costs of goods sold or services provided, sales commissions, and direct costs incurred in relation to construction-type contracts. Accountants make assumptions regarding cost flows and the manner in which costs attach to products as they move through the productive process. For example, production costs may be considered to attach to

18 AICPA, *Statement of the Accounting Principles Board No. 4*: "Basic Concepts and Accounting Principles Underlying Financial Statements of Business Enterprises" (New York: 1970), p. 61.

19 AICPA, *Statement No. 4*, p. 61.

products on the basis of an association with a physical measure of activity such as labour hours or machine hours.

Systematic and Rational Allocation

If a direct means is not available to associate cause and effect, costs may be recognized as expenses on the basis of an orderly allocation to the accounting periods in which ***the costs appear to expire*** and presumably provide benefits. This approach involves assumptions as to the pattern of benefits and as to the relationship between costs and benefits received, because neither can be objectively measured. The allocation bases selected should be perceived as "reasonable" and should be applied systematically. Examples of costs that are recognized as expenses under this principle are depreciation of plant assets, amortization of intangible assets, and allocated amounts of property taxes and insurance.

Immediate Recognition

Expenses are recognized in the current accounting period when (1) costs incurred in the current period are not expected to provide any future benefit, (2) costs deferred as assets in earlier periods no longer provide benefits, and (3) allocation of costs to revenue or to accounting periods is impractical or is considered to serve no useful purpose. This principle requires such things as research costs, general and administrative costs, and amounts paid to settle litigation to be recognized as expenses in the period they are incurred. Costs deferred in earlier periods that have lost their service potential (such as obsolete plant assets or worthless intangible assets) are written off as soon as the loss becomes evident and measurable.

Application of these expense recognition principles requires costs to be associated, if possible, with revenue on the basis of cause and effect; if such an association is not practical, a systematic and rational allocation of the costs is attempted; if neither of these procedures is feasible, costs are expensed as incurred or as soon as expiration of the service potential of the costs becomes evident.

Expense Recognition for Service Transactions[20]

Generally, costs are recognized as expenses in the accounting period in which the associated revenue is recognized, and costs not expected to be recovered are not deferred. In the application of this principle to service transactions, costs may be classified into three categories as follows:

1 ***Initial direct costs***, which are directly associated with negotiating and closing service contracts. Such costs include commissions, legal fees, costs of credit investigations, document processing fees, and a portion of any salespersons' compensation applicable to a specific service transaction. Initial direct costs do not include any portion of indirect operating expenses such as rent or supervisory and administrative salaries.

20 This section is based on FASB, "Accounting for Certain Service Transactions."

2 ***Direct costs***, which are costs that have a clearly beneficial or causal relationship to the services performed for a specific customer or a group of customers. An example is labour and parts included in service contracts.

3 ***Indirect costs***, which comprise all other costs not included in the first two categories. Such costs include selling expenses, general and administrative expenses (including doubtful accounts expense), and any costs incurred in negotiating service contracts that are not consummated. Indirect costs are recorded immediately as expenses, regardless of the method used to recognize revenue.

When revenue from service transactions is recognized under the ***specific-performance method*** or the ***completed-performance method***, initial direct costs and direct costs are recognized as expenses in the accounting period in which the related revenue is recognized; such costs incurred before revenue is recognized are deferred and recognized as expenses at the time the related revenue is recognized in the accounting records.

When the ***proportional-performance method*** of revenue recognition is used, initial direct costs are recognized as expenses in the same manner revenue is recognized. However, direct costs are expensed as incurred, because a close correlation generally exists between the amount of performance and the amount of direct costs incurred.

Under the ***cash-collection method***, both initial direct costs and direct costs are recorded immediately as expenses because of the substantial uncertainty surrounding the collectibility of the claims from customers or clients.

Recognition of Losses

Under the accrual basis of accounting, losses are recognized in the accounting periods in which they occur as a result of transactions and other events and circumstances. Losses resulting from the disposal of assets or the retirement of debt are readily recognizable and measurable. Losses resulting from events and circumstances such as casualties, contingencies, declines in the market value of inventories and short-term investments in marketable securities, and impairments in the value of plant assets and long-term investments pose more difficult recognition problems. The current standards governing the recognition of losses resulting from events and circumstances are not highly developed and are not consistent with the standards for the recogniton of gains. For example, losses from holding short-term investments in marketable securities are recognized, but holding gains are not. Also, recoveries of such losses and similar recoveries of losses from write-downs of long-term investments are not recognized as gains.

As stated earlier, the standards for the recognition of losses are less severe than the standards for the recognition of gains. For example, a loss from an exchange of a plant asset for a similar asset is recognized; but a gain is not, because it is not considered realized. The recognition and income statement presentation of extraordinary losses are covered in another section of this chapter; discussion of the recognition of specific types of losses (such as those resulting from contingencies and impairments in the value of long-term investments) appear in other chapters of this book.

INCOME MEASUREMENT AND REPORTING

The concept of accounting income poses a double challenge for accountants — its ***measurement*** and the ***reporting of its components in the income statement***. Generally accepted accounting principles rest on a foundation of historical costs and measurable evidence provided by business transactions and events — that is, the accrual basis of accounting. Accountants have considered and rejected both the ***cash-basis concept*** and the ***economic concept*** of income measurement. Some critics of accrual-basis income still fret that such income portrays neither cash flows nor the change in a business enterprise's economic wealth. However, because both cash-basis income and economic income have serious shortcomings and are fundamentally incompatible, accountants have adopted the accrual basis of accounting as a reasonable approach to income measurement.

Probably no single concept of income would satisfactorily meet the widely divergent needs of various groups of users of financial statements. Perhaps some of these groups expect accountants to ***measure the unmeasurable***. Some groups admit that income must reflect ***past results*** and at the same time they insist that income must be ***predictive of future earnings performance***. In a rapidly changing and highly competitive business environment, income measurement is a complex process; the income for one accounting period probably predicts the income of the next period as accurately as today's score of a baseball game predicts the results of tomorrow's game between the same two teams. Furthermore, income tax laws, the effects of extraordinary items, changes in accounting principles, and the inclusion of earnings per share of common stock in the income statement further complicate the task of income measurement and reporting. These issues are discussed in the rest of this chapter.

Income and the Objectives of Financial Reporting

Among the objectives of financial reporting identified by the FASB that relate most directly to income measurement and reporting are the following:[21]

1 The primary focus of financial reporting is information about earnings and its components.

2 Information about enterprise earnings based on accrual accounting generally provides a better indication of an enterprise's present and continuing ability to generate favorable cash flows than information limited to the financial effects of cash receipts and payments.

3 Financial reporting is expected to provide information about an enterprise's financial performance during a period and about how management of an enterprise has discharged its stewardship responsibility to owners.

4 Investors, creditors, and others may use reported earnings . . . in various ways to assess the prospects for cash flows. They may wish, for example, to evaluate management's performance, estimate "earning power," predict future earnings, assess risk, or to confirm . . . or reject earlier predictions or assessments. . . .

21 FASB, ***Statement of Financial Accounting Concepts No. 1***: "Objectives of Financial Reporting by Business Enterprises" (Stamford: 1978), p. ix.

The highly condensed income statements issued by most publicly owned corporations are probably not achieving these objectives. In the opinion of the FASB, better information on earnings would help users of financial statements with their main need: the assessment of future earnings and cash flows.[22] Among the criticisms of the traditional income statement (illustrated in Chapter 4) are the following:

1 It does not provide enough information about past earnings to help users assess future earnings.

2 It does not require the separate disclosure of the effects of some unusual transactions and other events and circumstances.

3 It does not explain sufficiently the economic changes affecting the relationship between recurring revenue and expenses.

4 It places excessive emphasis on a single earnings amount, such as net income or earnings per share of common stock.

Improvements in the measurement and reporting of income are needed if income statements are to be of maximum value to users in predicting, comparing, and evaluating the earning power of business enterprises. For example, the earning of income consists of ***earnings cycles*** that may be ***completed, incomplete***, or ***prospective***; it may be useful to segregate "precisely measured results" from "estimated results." The basis of estimates might be explained so that users would be able to interpret the reported results in line with their own judgement and experience. Also, it may be useful to report the possible effects of changes in values of assets and liabilities on reported net income and to segregate expenses between fixed and variable components to help users predict cash flows and the possible effects of changes in volume of activity in future levels of net income.

The Complexity of Income Measurement

To illustrate the complexity of defining accounting income, let us assume that newly organized Pinecrest, Inc., acquired a tract of land to develop 500 lots for a residential community. The acquisition of the land required a small down payment that used up most of Pinecrest's available cash. Some of the land was level, some rolling, and some extremely steep. A golf course, riding stables, tennis courts, and a lake were to be constructed. Colourful sales brochures were prepared showing the attractiveness of the community after completion.

Residential lots were to be offered for sale by Pinecrest, Inc., with a down payment of only 3% of the selling price. Assume that 100 lots were sold with an average down payment of $400 received, along with long-term receivables calling for monthly payments of $175. How much income, if any, did Pinecrest earn when it sold the first 100 lots? The answer to this question depends on the answers to these related questions: How should revenue and expenses be measured? What is the value of the long-term receivables? How many of the 100

22 FASB, *FASB Discussion Memorandum*: "An Analysis of Issues Relating to Reporting Earnings" (Stamford: 1979), p. 1.

purchasers actually will make the monthly payments? What will it cost to develop roads, sewers, a lake, riding stables, and other recreational facilities? How many lots will be sold, and at what prices and on what terms? How should the total cost of the tract be allocated among the level lots, the hillside lots, and the lakefront lots?

Despite all the efforts to develop concise accounting principles, a wide range of answers may be given to the question of how much income, if any, was earned by Pinecrest, Inc. from the sale of the first 100 lots. We might even question whether "sales" really took place, or whether Pinecrest was a "going concern" capable of carrying out its commitments. Assuming that Pinecrest did carry the project to a successful completion, the income (or loss) from the project may then be measured as the amount of revenue received from customers less all costs and expenses of acquiring, developing, and selling the land. However, the objective of timeliness in financial reporting requires ***periodic measurement of net income*** long before the project is completed. This example illustrates some of the practical difficulties faced by accountants in the measurement of accounting income.

The Meaning of Income

In a very general sense, the objective of measuring income is to determine by how much a business enterprise has become "better off" during some period of time as a result of its operations. Economists define ***income*** as the maximum amount of assets that the enterprise could distribute to its owners during an accounting period and still be as well off at the end of that period as it was at the beginning. The key words in this definition are "as well off." Anyone who studies the concept of income will soon discover that controversies over the meaning and measurement of income centre on the problem of determining what the financial position of an enterprise is on a specific date, whether its position has improved or worsened during a specified period of time, and by how much.

Lifetime Income of a Business Enterprise

Let us begin with a relatively simple income measurement problem. If we were asked to measure the ***lifetime income*** of a business enterprise at the time it was being liquidated, we could probably agree on the following computation:

Lifetime income of a business enterprise

Total proceeds received on liquidation of enterprise	$800,000
Add: Amounts withdrawn by owners during life of enterprise	300,000
Less: Amount of cash invested by owners	(600,000)
Lifetime income of enterprise	$500,000

If we ignore the time value of money and effects of inflation, lifetime income of a business enterprise is easy to measure. The reason is that at the beginning and the end of the life of any enterprise, the value of its net assets may be measured with reasonable accuracy. The investments by owners and the proceeds received on liquidation are usually definite amounts of cash or other assets. However, at any stage prior to final liquidation, the ***net assets*** of an enterprise constitute a complex set of economic resources whose collective value depends largely on their future earning power. In theory, the only direct way to determine how "well off" an enterprise is on a given date is to compute the present value of its future net cash inflows. This is known as the process of ***direct valuation***.

Periodic Income of a Business Enterprise

Accountants readily concede their inability to determine at periodic time intervals the ***direct value*** of the net assets of a business enterprise. For this they should not be criticized for undue caution or modesty; they merely are being realistic about their limitations. Thus, in measuring how "well off" an enterprise is on a specific date in order to measure ***periodic net income***, accountants record only those changes in financial position that may be substantiated by reasonably reliable evidence.

As stated earlier, revenue increases assets or decreases liabilities as a result of an enterprise's providing goods and services to customers and clients; expenses decrease assets or increase liabilities in the enterprise's process of generating revenue. Thus, in the process of measuring assets and liabilities, accountants are at the same time measuring income. Income emerges if the ***effort*** (expenses) to generate revenue is less than the ***accomplishment*** (revenue) of that effort; a loss emerges if the effort exceeds the accomplishment.

The Impact of Changing Prices

We have seen how revenue and expense recognition procedures affect the measurement of income. Now let us look briefly at an accounting principle that is equally fundamental: the assumption that the dollar is a ***stable monetary unit*** for measuring the effects of business transactions and events.

Assume that in Year 1 a business enterprise invests $80 to manufacture a product that is expected to sell for $120. The cost of producing an identical product has risen to $130 in Year 2, and because demand is strong the enterprise is able to sell the product for $180 at the end of Year 2. During Year 2, the ***general price level*** throughout the economy rose by 10%. The gross profit on the sale of the product might be measured in three ways as illustrated below.

Three ways to compute gross profit on sale of a product

1	*Nominal-dollar gross profit*	
	Revenue realized	$180
	Less: Actual cost incurred in Year 1	80
	Nominal-dollar gross profit	$100
2	*Nominal-dollar gross profit, with price gain isolated*	
	Revenue realized	$180
	Less: Replacement cost on date of sale	130
	Operating margin	$ 50
	Add: Price gain or ***inventory profit*** (the difference between replacement cost of $130 on date of sale and actual cost of $80)	50
	Nominal-dollar gross profit (operating margin and price gain)	$100

3 *Constant-purchasing-power gross profit*

Revenue realized	$180
Less: Actual cost in constant (end-of-Year-2) purchasing power ($80 × 1.10)	88
Gross profit in constant (end-of-Year-2) purchasing power	$ 92

The ***nominal-dollar*** gross profit (method 1) reflects the entire difference between revenue realized and historical cost, without regard to differences in the purchasing power of the dollar. Under method 2, the effect of changes in ***specific prices*** is isolated (but without regard to the change in the purchasing power of the dollar), and the fact that one-half of nominal-dollar gross profit is attributed to rising replacement cost is disclosed. The difference between the actual cost of a product and its replacement cost at the time it is sold is known as ***inventory profit***. Under method 3, the measuring unit has been changed to ***constant purchasing power***; both costs and revenue are stated in end-of-Year-2 purchasing power; thus, the gross profit in constant (end-of-Year-2) purchasing power is only $92, because the enterprise must now recover $88 to be as well off in terms of purchasing power as it was when it invested $80 in the product in Year 1.

During a period of ***inflation*** (an increase in the general price level), a clear understanding of the limitations of the dollar as a unit of measurement is required to interpret accounting income and financial statements meaningfully. Supplementary measurement of net income in constant purchasing power is considered in Chapter 25.

Special Problems in the Measurement and Reporting of Income

The measurement and reporting of income has become complex as a result of requirements for the allocation of income taxes, extraordinary items, changes in accounting principles or policies, and the reporting of earnings-per-share data in the income statement. These topics are discussed briefly in the following sections.

Income Tax Allocation

Income taxes frequently constitute the largest single expense for many profitable corporations. ***Taxable income*** is a legal concept that is related to ***accounting income***, but there are significant differences that may cause a corporation's taxable income for a specific year to differ materially from the pre-tax accounting income reported in its income statement. In addition, the total amount of income taxes expense (or credit) included in the income statement must be assigned to any nonoperating sources of income or loss. Accountants have developed extensive ***income tax allocation procedures*** to deal with these issues. At this point only the general nature of income tax allocation in the income statement is considered, with attention focussed on the presentation of the income tax effects on extraordinary items and changes in accounting principles or policies.

Interperiod tax allocation is the process of apportioning income taxes among two or more accounting periods because of ***timing differences*** in the recognition of revenue and expenses. Timing differences result when revenue or expense items appear in the income statement either ***before*** or ***after*** they appear in the income tax return. By means of interperiod tax allocation, the income taxes expense in the income statement is related to the pre-tax income or loss reported in the income statement rather than to the amount of income or loss reported in the income tax return. Thus, income taxes are allocated among accounting periods as other expenses are.

In contrast, ***intraperiod tax allocation*** is the process of apportioning income taxes of a single accounting period among the different sources of income or loss that are presented separately in the income statement — such as income from operations, extraordinary items, and other sources of income and loss which require separate presentation in the income statement. Similarly, corrections of material errors made in prior periods are reported in the retained earnings statement net of any related income tax effect. Such allocation is a required practice in Canada.[23]

To illustrate the basic principles of interperiod and intraperiod allocation of income taxes, assume the following data for Irving Limited for the year ended December 31, Year 5 (a tax rate of 45% applies to all items):

Interperiod and intraperiod income tax effects

	Pre-tax amounts	*Income tax effects*
Income from operations	$200,000	$ 90,000
Extraordinary item (gain)	300,000	135,000
Additional depreciation (capital cost allowance) claimed in income tax return	(100,000)	(45,000)
Taxable income and income taxes payable for Year 5	$400,000	$180,000

Irving Limited elected to take the additional depreciation allowed by income tax regulations (depreciation is called ***capital cost allowance*** under the Income Tax Act) of $100,000 in its income tax return for Year 5 in order to postpone the payment of $45,000 of income taxes. This is an example of interperiod allocation of income taxes; the extraordinary item is an example of intraperiod allocation of income taxes. The various sources of income and loss are reported by Irving in the bottom portion of its income statement as follows:

Net-of-tax effects in income statement

Income from operations (after income taxes expense of $90,000); amount of income taxes payable currently is $180,000)....................	$110,000
Extraordinary item (gain), net of income tax effect of $135,000	165,000
Net income	$275,000

23 CICA, ***CICA Handbook***, secs. 3470, 3480, and 3600.

It is important to note that the income from operations and the extraordinary item of Irving are reported in its income statement net of the related income tax effect. Similarly, any other unusual components of net income should be reported in the income statement net of the related income tax effect, and any prior-period ajustment should be reported in the statement of retained earnings net of the related income tax effect. A complete discussion of accounting for income taxes appears in Chapter 21.

Extraordinary Items

A troublesome problem in reporting periodic income is the proper treatment of ***extraordinary gains and losses***. General agreement exists that unusual gains and losses, if material in amount, should be separately disclosed in the income statement. They should be distinguished from the ordinary operating revenue and expenses of the period. However, such gains and losses should be reported as extraordinary items in the income statement only when the events or transactions giving rise to the gains and losses are ***of an unusual nature*** and ***of infrequent occurrence***. This standard is summarized in section 3480.05 of the ***CICA Handbook*** as follows:

> Extraordinary items should include only gains, losses and provisions for losses which, by their nature, are not typical of the normal business activities of the enterprise, are not expected to occur regularly over a period of years and are not considered as recurring factors in any evaluation of the ordinary operations of the enterprise.

To be considered unusual in nature, the underlying event or transaction should be abnormal and clearly unrelated to the ordinary and typical activities of the entity. The scope of operations, the lines of business, the operating policies, and the environment in which an entity operates should be considered in applying this criterion. The environment of an entity includes such factors as the character-

Items which are and are not extraordinary items

Extraordinary	*Not extraordinary*
Loss due to major casualties (such as earthquakes or severe hailstorms in localities where such events are infrequent)	Write-down or write-off of receivables or inventories
Loss due to a prohibition under a newly enacted law or regulation	Gain or loss from exchange or translation of foreign currencies (including major devaluations and revaluations)
Loss from an expropriation of assets by a foreign country	Adjustments with respect to contract prices
Gain or loss from sale of investments not acquired for resale	
Gain or loss from sale or abandonment of a plant or a significant segment of the enterprise	

istics of the industry in which it operates, the geographic location of its activities, and the degree of government regulation.

If an event or a transaction is not reasonably expected to take place in the foreseeable future, it is considered to occur infrequently. Past experience of the entity is generally a helpful guide in determining the frequency of an event or transaction. Thus, only ***unusual*** and ***infrequent*** events and transactions produce "extraordinary gains and losses." However, these qualitative standards are difficult to apply in practice, and differences of opinion still exist in identifying extraordinary items. The table on page 129 shows how certain gains or losses should be classified in the income statement.

In a survey of 325 companies, more than one-third of them reported extraordinary items; of the 170 instances of extraordinary items reported, the most common were gains and losses from sales of assets and discontinued operations.[24] The presentations of extraordinary items, including the separate per-share effect in the income statement, are illustrated below.

Extraordinary item in income statement

Income before income taxes and extraordinary item	$500,000
Income taxes expense (actual income taxes payable are $80,000 as a result of the tax reduction from the extraordinary loss)	200,000
Income before extraordinary item	$300,000
Extraordinary loss from sale of a plant (net of income tax effect of $120,000)	180,000
Net income	$120,000
Earnings per share:	
Income before extraordinary item	$ 3.00
Extraordinary item	(1.80)
Net income	$ 1.20

The three examples listed in the "Not extraordinary" column are not considered extraordinary because they result from normal business activities. However, these items should be presented separately in, or by way of a note to, the income statement if they are caused by rare or unusual circumstances and are abnormal in amount.[25]

Accounting Changes

We have stated earlier that the use of the same accounting principles from one accounting period to another increases the usefulness of financial statements by facilitating comparison of the data. However, management may justify a change to an alternative acceptable accounting principle on the ground that it is more

24 CICA, *Financial Reporting in Canada*, 16th ed. (Toronto, 1985), p. 200.

25 CICA, *CICA Handbook*, sec. 3480.11–.12.

appropriate.[26] Basically, there are two types of accounting changes: (1) change in accounting policy, and (2) change in accounting estimate.[27]

Changes in accounting policy encompass changes in accounting principles as well as accounting methods used in the preparation of financial statements. For example, a change in determining inventory cost from a first-in–first-out to a weighted-average method, or a change in recognizing depreciation expense from a straight-line to a declining-balance method, constitutes a change in accounting policy. Since a change in accounting policy affects a number of accounting periods, the issue is how the effect of such a change should be treated in the financial statements. Section 1506 of the *CICA Handbook* recommends that the effect of an accounting policy change be reflected on a ***retroactive*** basis with a ***restatement*** of those prior period financial statements affected by the change. Thus, each of those prior period financial statements presented on a comparative basis is to be ***restated*** to reflect the new accounting policy. In addition, the cumulative effect of the change on the periods preceding the earliest period included in the comparative financial statements is treated as an adjustment to the beginning balance of retained earnings in the statement of retained earnings of that earliest period. It should be noted that the treatment for a change in accounting policy is the same as that for a prior period adjustment, even though the former does not meet the requirements of the latter.

Changes in accounting estimates include such items as a revision of the original estimate of the amount of allowance for doubtful accounts, or the revision of an original estimate of an eight-year economic life of a depreciable asset to a 12-year life. Since change in an estimate is a result of ***new*** information, section 1506 of the *CICA Handbook* recommends that the effect of such a change be accounted for in the period of change or in the period of change and the applicable future periods, depending on whether the change affects one or more periods. Accordingly, this differs from the treatment of a change in accounting policy in that a restatement of prior periods or a cumulative adjustment is ***not*** required.

Changes in accounting policy and accounting estimates are discussed and illustrated in more detail in Chapter 22.

Earnings Per Share

The amount of earnings per share of common stock for an accounting period is computed by dividing the net income available to common shareholders by the weighted-average number of shares of common stock (and in certain cases potentially dilutive common stock equivalents) outstanding during the period. The purpose is to show earning power on a per-share basis so that investors can relate the market price of a share to the income per share of common stock. However, when a corporation has outstanding stock options, convertible bonds or preferred stock, and other hybrid securities, we cannot compute a ***single*** meaningful

26 CICA, *CICA Handbook*, sec. 1506.02.

27 Sec. 1506 of the *CICA Handbook* also deals with the treatment of a correction of an error in prior period financial statements. This topic is covered in Chapter 22.

earnings per share amount. In such cases a ***dual presentation*** of ***basic*** and ***fully diluted*** earnings per share is required. When extraordinary items appear in the income statement, basic and fully diluted earnings per share are presented as illustrated below. This topic is covered in Chapter 18.

Dual presentation of earnings per share

	Year 2	*Year 1*
Earnings per share of common stock:		
Basic:		
Income before extraordinary item	$4.00	$3.35
Extraordinary item	(0.50)	1.65
Net income	$3.50	$5.00
Fully diluted:		
Income before extraordinary item	$3.55	$3.00
Extraordinary item	(0.42)	1.58
Net income	$3.13	$4.58

Significance of Income Measurement and Reporting

Income reporting is probably the most significant aspect of financial accounting because of the economic consequences it has for a business enterprise, its owners and creditors, and it potential owners and creditors. Net income is the lifeblood of any enterprise organized to earn a satisfactory return on the capital invested by its owners. The ability of an enterprise to compete effectively in its industry, and thus to prosper and survive, depends on its ability to generate income. Profitable operations represent the major source of cash and working capital, and it is unusual for a profitable enterprise to encounter difficulty making timely payments on its debt or to raise capital for expansion purposes.

Income measurement has to be based on sound principles of revenue and expense recognition to be of maximum value to management and other users of financial statements. The quality of a business enterprise's earnings depends to a large extent on the revenue and expense recognition practices it adopts. A reputation for reporting ***high quality earnings*** is a valuable asset to an enterprise. However, income measurement is only one side of the coin; the other is income reporting. The reporting of income must be timely and the sources of income must be presented in a meaningful and consistent manner. Nonrecurring sources of income or loss are ''nonrepeatable'' and are not considered as significant as the recurring sources.

A continuing challenge for accountants is to report the components of income in a manner that enhances the predictive value of the income statement. Users of financial statements face a different challenge: to interpret the significance of the reported income in the clear light of a highly complex and inflationary business environment.

REVIEW QUESTIONS

1 What is the objective of ***accrual accounting*** for a business enterprise as perceived by the accounting profession?

2 Describe two tasks accountants face relative to revenue. Why is the recognition of revenue so important in today's business environment?

3 Define each of the following terms:
   a ***Revenue***
   b ***Realization*** or ***recognition of revenue***
   c ***Earning process***

4 Would you support the argument that the recognition of revenue should be based on ***continuous activity*** rather than on a ***single critical event***?

5 Briefly decribe the three ***revenue realization (recognition) conditions*** for a business offering goods for sale.

6 Why does the implementation of the revenue realization principle pose significant challenges to financial accountants?

7 Briefly describe the importance of evidence, estimates, and professional judgement and experience in the process of recognizing revenue and expenses.

8 Business executives of publicly owned companies are at times under pressure to speed up revenue recognition. What is the possible explanation for this?

9 Assuming that revenue is usually recognized at the time of sale, what revenue-recognition problems are encountered in connection with each of the following:
   a ***Consignment*** of goods to retail merchants
   b Sale in which customer is given the ***right to return*** the goods purchased within 90 days of purchase
   c Sale of goods on the ***instalment plan***

10 When a sale of goods is not considered to result in revenue realization, at what other stages of the productive (earnings) process prior to delivery of goods to customers might revenue be recognized?

11 *a* Under what circumstances might revenue be recognized after the delivery of goods to customers?
   b Describe the ***instalment method***, the ***cost recovery method***, and the ***deposit method*** of revenue recognition for the sale of goods.

12 *a* Define ***service enterprises*** and ***service transactions***.
   b List and briefly describe four methods that may be used to recognize revenue for service transactions.

13 *a* What is meant by the expression ''front-ending of income'' in connection with the accounting of initial franchise fees received by a franchisor?
   b Evaluate the following note to financial statements that appeared in the annual report of Collins Foods International, Inc.:

> The Company recognizes initial franchise fees as income on the date the restaurant is opened, at which time the Company has substantially performed its obligations relating to such fees. Service fees (royalties) from franchise

agreements are taken into income on an accrual basis as the fees are earned and become due from the franchisee.

14 What possible objections might be made to the recognition of revenue on the date that the contract for a sales-type lease becomes effective?

15 Distinguish *a* between ***revenue*** and ***cost savings***, *b* between ***expenses*** and ***losses***, and *c* between ***product costs*** and ***period costs***.

16 *a* List the three groups into which the expenses of an accounting period may be classified.

b Describe the three principles of expense recognition.

17 *a* Define ***initial direct costs***, ***direct costs***, and ***indirect costs*** incurred by a service enterprise.

b How are the costs listed in part *a* recognized under the ***specific-performance***, the ***completed-performance***, the ***proportional-performance***, and the ***collection*** methods of revenue recognition for service transactions?

18 ''Big Mo'' Nikola owns and operates a commercial tuna boat, the ***Conte Blanco***. His fiscal year ends on January 31. On January 10, Year 3, Nikola presold 400 tonnes of yellowfin tuna at $800 a tonne to Pacific Packing Corporation. The tuna represented the expected catch of the initial Year 3 fishing trip to Central America by the ***Conte Blanco***. Because he felt that the success of the initial trip was ''reasonably assured,'' Nikola asked his accountant to record the presale in his accounting records on January 10, Year 3. Nikola also asked his accountant to record the estimated costs and expenses of the initial Year 3 fishing trip as deductions from the $320,000 (400 × $800 = $320,000) revenue recorded. The costs and expenses were estimated at $250,000, including ''shares'' to be distributed to the 12-member crew of the ***Conte Blanco***.

Do you agree with Nikola's proposed accounting for the presale of the 400 tonnes? Explain.

19 If earnings reports were to better meet the objectives of financial statements, what changes would you recommend in the content of income statements of publicly owned companies?

20 If 10 accountants were asked to measure the ***lifetime income*** of a business enterprise and to assume no change in the purchasing power of the dollar, they would probably agree within narrow limits on this long-run income measurement. The same 10 accountants might vary over a wide range in their measurement of the same enterprise's ***net income for an accounting period***. Why?

21 Define each of the following terms:

a ***Nominal dollars***

b ***Constant purchasing power***

c ***General price level***

d ***Specific price level***

e ***Inventory profit***

22 Explain the meaning of ***intraperiod tax allocation*** and ***interperiod tax allocation***, and explain how these procedures improve the usefulness of an income statement.

23 Describe the criteria for ***extraordinary items*** as set forth in section 3480 of the *CICA Handbook*.

24 List two examples of extraordinary items, and two of nonextraordinary items, caused by rare and unusual circumstances.

25 Describe two types of ***accounting changes*** and indicate how each type is reported in the income statement.

26 What is the purpose of reporting ***earnings per share*** of common stock in an income statement? Under what circumstances is a ***dual presentation*** of earnings per share of common stock required in the income statement?

27 How is each of the following material losses reported in the income statement of a business enterprise?

- *a* Loss due to shutdown of plant during a strike by employees
- *b* Loss due to abandonment of obsolete equipment
- *c* Loss due to tornado damage to the main warehouse (Assume that tornadoes are unusual and infrequent in the geographic area where the enterprise is located)
- *d* Loss incurred on the disposal of a professional football team (Assume that the business enterprise is a manufacturer of furniture)

28 An article in a business magazine once described examples of falsified accounting records designed to ''make the operating results of publicly owned companies look better.'' Some of the examples involved overstatements of inventories and premature recording of sales by executives in middle-management ranks whose salaries were based on earnings and who were under pressure from top management to report steady increases in net income.

What assurances do users of financial statements have that the statements of publicly owned companies are not based on falsified accounting records?

EXERCISES

Ex. 3-1 Select the best answer for each of the following multiple-choice questions.

1 Under generally accepted accounting principles, net income is measured:

- *a* By applying a value-added concept
- *b* By using a transactions approach and matching costs and revenue
- *c* As a change in the current fair value of owners' equity
- *d* As a change in the purchasing power of owners' equity

2 ***Realization*** or ***recognition of revenue*** refers to:

- *a* The timing of its recognition in the accounting records
- *b* The knowledge that it has been earned
- *c* Its receipt in the form of cash
- *d* Its recognition in an adjusting entry at the end of an accounting period

3 Which of the following is the most widely accepted evidence of revenue realization by a manufacturing enterprise?

a The process of production of products
b The completion of production of products
c The sale and delivery of products to customers
d The receipt of cash from the sale of finished products

4 "The determination of the periodic income of business enterprise depends on the measurement of its economic resources and obligations and changes in them as these changes occur." This pertains to:
a Disclosure *b* Accrual accounting *c* Materiality *d* The matching principle

5 Which of the following is not a basis for the immediate recognition of a cost as an expense of the current accounting period?
a The cost provides no discernible future benefit.
b The cost recorded in a prior accounting period no longer produces discernible benefits.
c The income tax savings under the immediate write-off method exceed the savings obtained by allocating the cost to several accounting periods.
d Allocation of the cost on the basis of association with revenue or among several accounting periods is considered to serve no useful purpose.

6 When costs may be reasonably associated with specific revenue but not with specific products, the costs should be:
a Charged to expense in the period incurred
b Allocated to specific products based on the best estimate of the production processing time.
c Expensed in the period in which the related revenue is recognized
d Capitalized and then amortized over a period not to exceed 60 months

7 An event or transaction is considered to occur infrequently, and thus possibly to qualify as an extraordinary item, if it:
a Is not reasonably expected to take place in the near future
b Is of an unusual nature
c Has not taken place for more than five years
d Is judged to be of infrequent occurrence by management of the reporting business enterprise.

8 Which of the following is an example of an extraordinary item in the income statement?
a A loss incurred because of a strike by employees
b The write-off of obsolete inventories believed to have no future benefit
c A gain resulting from the sale of an investment not acquired for resale
d A gain resulting from a settlement of a litigation

9 Marks Limited had the following ledger account balances for the year ended December 31, Year 5:

Interest expense	$123,000
Loss on disposal of long-term investments	80,000
Write-down of plant assets to estimated current fair value	60,000
Loss on disposal of a business segment	50,000

In its income statement for Year 5, how much should Marks Company report as total extraordinary items?
a \$50,000 *b* \$80,000 *c* \$110,000 *d* \$140,000 *e* \$130,000

10 Treiger Construction Company has consistently used the percentage-of-completion method of accounting for its construction-type contracts. During Year 4, Treiger started work on a \$3-million construction contract that was completed in Year 5. The accounting records include the following information:

	Year 4	*Year 5*
Progress billings to customers	\$ 950,000	\$2,050,000
Costs incurred	900,000	1,820,000
Collections from customers	800,000	2,110,000
Estimated cost to complete contract	1,800,000	

How much contract revenue should Treiger Construction Company have recognized in Year 4?
a \$800,000 *b* \$900,000 *c* \$950,000 *d* \$1,000,000 *e* Some other amount

Ex. 3-2 Network Company sells office-equipment service contracts, agreeing to service equipment for a two-year period. Cash receipts from contracts are credited to unearned service-contract revenue, and service-contract costs are debited to service-contract expense as incurred. Revenue from service contracts is recognized as earned over the term of the contracts. Here is additional information for the year ended December 31, Year 3:

Unearned service-contract revenue, Jan. 1, Year 3	\$600,000
Unearned service-contract revenue, Dec. 31, Year 3	720,000
Cash receipts from service contracts sold	980,000
Service-contract expense	520,000

Compute the service-contract revenue that Network Company should recognize for the year ended December 31, Year 3.

Ex. 3-3 Lovelace Company pays its outside salespersons base monthly salaries, plus a 3% commision on net sales. Sales commissions are computed and paid on a monthly basis (in the month following the month of sale), and the base salaries are treated as advances against commissions for this purpose. A commission is paid only when it exceeds the base monthly salary. However, if the base salaries for salespersons exceed their sales commissions earned for a month, such excess is not charged back to them. Here is information for the month of June for the three salespersons in the Eastern Region:

Salesperson	*Base salaries*	*Net sales*
A	$ 3,250	$ 90,000
B	3,500	260,000
C	4,200	350,000
	$10,950	$700,000

Compute the sales commissions expense for the Eastern Region of Lovelace Company for the month of June.

Ex. 3-4 For each of the following events and transactions, state whether Carr Company realized revenue or a gain. Give reasons for your conclusions.

a Gift certificates that may be exchanged by the holder for merchandise in a subsequent accounting period were sold for cash of $200.

b Land acquired for $45,000 two years ago has a current fair vlaue of $65,000.

c A new factory building was constructed by Carr's employees at a cost of $190,000. Bids of $205,000 and $210,000 from independent contractors were rejected.

d Securities with a current market value of $17,650 were received from a customer in settlement of a trade account receivable of $16,500 that was more than a year past due.

e Merchandise with a cost of $480 was sold under a 24-month instalment contract for a 10% down payment of $60. Title to the merchandise was to remain with Carr until all instalment payments had been collected.

f Land held for investment is planted in tomatoes. If the crop is harvested successfully and demand remains strong, cash receipts are expected to exceed expenses by $20,000. The crop growth is halfway to maturity at this time.

Ex. 3-5 Cowan Limited declared and paid cash dividends of $12,500 during Year 5. Cowan's accounting records show that changes in ledger account balances for the year ended December 31, Year 5, were as follows:

	Increase or (decrease)
Cash	$40,000
Trade accounts receivable (net)	(2,000)
Inventories	15,000
Buildings (net)	30,000
Equipment (net)	18,000
Notes payable	50,000
Trade accounts payable	(15,000)
Common stock	40,000
Retained earnings	?

The only journal entries to the Retained Earnings ledger account were for dividends and net income.

Compute Cowan's net income for the year ended December 31, Year 5.

Ex. 3-6 Ancaster Limited is subject to a 45% tax rate on all sources of income. Information for the current year follows:

Income before income taxes and extraordinary items	$600,000
Income taxes payable ($40,000 of current income taxes expense is deferred because depreciation is computed at an accelerated rate for income tax purposes)	297,500
Gain on sale of investments not acquired for resale (before income tax effect)	100,000
Loss from sale of discontinued business segment	150,000
Dividends declared on capital stock	165,000

Prepare a partial income statement for the current year with appropriate allocation of income taxes.

Ex. 3-7 On November 10, Year 2, Painting Contractors, Inc., commenced a $25,000 contract to sandblast and paint several buildings for a real estate investor. The direct costs of the contract (including subcontracting for the sandblasting, the paint, and the salaries of workers) were estimated at $20,000 on December 31, Year 2. The contract consisted of a large number of dissimilar acts. Through December 31, Year 2, the contract costs incurred amount to $14,000 and the acts performed to date amount to at least 80% of the total acts to be performed by Painting Contractors.

Compute three possible amounts of grosss profit that Painting Contractors, Inc., might recognize for the year ended December 31, Year 2, on the foregoing contract.

Ex. 3-8 The following information for Odds & Ends, Inc., relates to sales on the instalment plan:

	December 31:		
	Year 3	*Year 2*	*Year 1*
Instalment receivables, Year 1	$ 10,000	$20,000	$60,000
Instalment receivables, Year 2	40,000	80,000	
Instalment receivables, Year 3	280,000		
Instalment sales	400,000		
Gross profit on instalment sales	60%	55%	52%

Odds & Ends, Inc., uses the instalment method of accounting because it is unable to make a reasonable estimate of the collectibility of instalment receivables.

Compute the amount of realized gross profit that Odds & Ends, Inc.

recognizes for the year ended December 31, Year 3, under the instalment method.

Ex. 3-9 Slowe Construction Company uses the percentages-of-completion method of accounting for its construction-type contracts. The costs incurred and estimated additional costs to complete a $5-million fixed-price contract over a four-year period are summarized below:

Year ended Dec. 31:	*Cumulative costs incurred to date*	*Estimated costs to complete contract*	*Total cost of contract*
Year 1	$ 500,000	$3,500,000	$4,000,000
Year 2	2,100,000	2,100,000	4,200,000
Year 3	3,870,000	430,000	4,300,000
Year 4	4,250,000	-0-	4,250,000

Compute the contract revenue realized by Slowe Construction Company in each of the four years under the percentage-of-completion method.

Ex. 3-10 On January 5, Year 1, Fast-Fry Corporation sold a franchise to Horizon Enterprises for $20,000 cash. The initial franchise fee was nonreturnable; however, Fast-Fry agreed to help Horizon open the franchise and provide services for two years after the franchise opened. Horizon opened the franchise on October 1, Year 1. A reasonable estimate of the services Fast-Fry agreed to provide to Horizon follows:

In connection with opening of franchise	40%
For first 12 months of operations	36%
For next 12 months of operations	24%

Compute the amount of the initial franchise fee revenue that Fast-Fry Corporation should recognize for each of these years ended December 31: Year 1, Year 2, and Year 3.

Ex. 3-11 Orasco Limited was organized on March 1, Year 1 and was sold for cash by its three shareholders on August 20, Year 10. Orasco's activities during its lifetime are summarized below.

Proceeds from issuance of common stock in Year 1	$200,000
Proceeds from issuance of preferred stock in Year 4	50,000
Cost of treasury stock acquired in Year 8	19,800
Net income	845,200
Dividends declared and paid	590,000
Proceeds from sale of Orasco on Aug. 20, Year 10	900,000
Cash distributed on Dec. 31, Year 10, to shareholders after sale of Orasco	900,000

Compute the lifetime income of Orasco Limited.

Ex. 3-12 At the end of Year 5, Lash Corporation manufactured a machine at a cost of $10,000 with a selling price of $15,000. The cost of manufacturing an identical machine was estimated at $12,000 on December 31, Year 6, on which date the machine was sold for $18,750. The general price level rose by 15% in Year 6.

Compute the gross profit for Lash Corporation on the sale of the machine under each of the following procedures:

a Nominal-dollar gross profit
b Nominal-dollar gross profit, with price gain isolated
c Constant-purchasing-power (end of Year 6 purchasing power) gross profit

Ex. 3-13 Indicate which of the following gains and losses, which are material in amount, are reported as extraordinary items in the income statement:

1 Loss from earthquake in a city where earthquakes are extremely infrequent
2 Write-off of receivables, inventories, and intangible assets
3 Loss from prohibition under new law passed by the government
4 Gain or loss from the revaluation of foreign currencies
5 Loss from expropriation of assets by a foreign country
6 Gain or loss on disposal of a business segment
7 Gain or loss on disposal of investment in common stock that had been owned for 30 years
8 Gain or loss on disposal of a plant
9 Gain or loss on extinguishment of long-term debt
10 Loss from a prolonged labour strike

Ex. 3-14 The income statements of Duall Corporation for the latest two years include the following:

	Year 10	*Year 9*
Income before extraordinary item	$5,400,000	$4,200,000
Extraordinary item—gain (or loss), net of income tax effects	(720,000)	900,000
Net income	$4,680,000	$5,100,000

For both years, Duall had 500,000 shares of common stock outstanding for the computation of basic earnings per share and 600,000 for the computation of fully diluted earnings per share. Only common stock has been issued by Duall.

Show how basic and fully diluted earnings per share are presented in Duall Corporation's comparative income statements for Year 9 and Year 10.

CASES

Case 3-1 In a contract for the licensing of a new motion picture to network television, the producer of the motion picture generally recognizes revenue on commencement of the licence period and when all the following requirements have been met:

1 The sale price (licence fee) for the motion picture is known.
2 The cost of the motion picture is known or is reasonably determinable.
3 Collectibility of the licence fee is reasonably assured.
4 The motion picture has been accepted by the licensee in accordance with the conditions of the licensing contract.
5 The motion picture is available for delivery to the licensee on a date to be specified by the licensee.

Instructions
Evaluate the rationale of this revenue recognition standard for the licensing of a new motion picture for television viewing. Your discussion should be related to the three revenue realization or recognition conditions presented in this chapter.

Case 3-2 At the beginning of Year 10, Richard Nye, owner and operator of a large farm, had no inventories on hand. During Year 10, Nye produced 8,000 bushels of soybeans, 10,000 bushels of barley, and 16,000 bushels of rye, and sold one-half of each of his crops at the following prices: soybeans $8 a bushel, barley $4.25 a bushel, rye $3 a bushel. Nye followed the daily price quotations of these commodities closely, and at the end of Year 10, he noted that the market prices for the commodities were as follows: soybeans $8.50 a bushel, barley $4.50 a bushel, and rye $3.20 a bushel.

The expenses incurred in operating the farm during Year 10 totalled $75,200, including depreciation of buildings and equipment. Nye estimates that his cost of selling and delivering the crops is $1 a bushel. The selling and delivering costs applicable to the crops sold were included in operating expenses for Year 10.

Instructions
a Prepare an income statement for Richard Nye for the year ended December 31, Year 10. Explain the principle of revenue realization employed in your measurement of income and, in particular, the basis you used in assigning a valuation to the commodities on hand on December 31, Year 10.
b In measuring income before income taxes for Year 10, what consideration did you give to the possibility that the market price of the commodities might change between the end of Year 10 and the time Richard Nye finally sells them?
c What is the essential difference between the problem of measuring income for Richard Nye and measuring income for a manufacturer of farm machinery?

Case 3-3 Four different business enterprises recognized the following items in their accounting records during Year 2:

1 A pre-tax loss of $4 million resulted from the disposal of a chemical division (a business segment) operated by Grocery Chain Co. Ltd. The income tax rate is 45%, and the income (after income taxes) from operations is $8.2 million.

2 A loss of $6 million was recorded by XY, Inc., from write-offs of trade receivables and inventories caused by a severe business recession.

3 A loss of $8 million was recorded by Apparel Co. Ltd. from the sale of all assets used in the manufacture of sweaters.

4 Divisified Enterprises, Inc., sold a block of common stock from its portfolio of long-term investments. This was the first sale from its portfolio and resulted in a material gain of $4.5 million before income taxes. The income tax rate is 45%.

Instructions

Indicate how each of the items above should be reported in the business enterprise's income statements for Year 2. Give a brief explanation for each item.

Case 3-4 The financial statements of World Publishing Limited are presented to the board of directors for review after completion of the annual audit. Karen Young, a director, asks why the income statement is based on the assumption that an equal proportion of the revenue is earned with the publication of each issue of World Publishing's magazine. She feels that the ''critical event'' in the process of earning revenue in the magazine business is the cash sale of the subscription. She says that she does not understand why—other than for the smoothing of income — most of the revenue should not be recognized in the month of sale.

Instructions

a List three accepted methods for recognizing revenue and indicate the conditions under which each method would be appropriate. Do not limit your listing to the methods for the recognition of revenue by magazine publishing enterprises.

b Discuss the propriety of timing the recognition of revenue in World Publishing's accounting records with:

1 The cash sale of the magazine subscription
2 The publication of the magazine each month
3 Both events, by recognizing a portion of the revenue with the cash sale of the magazine subscription and a portion of the revenue with the publication of the magazine each month

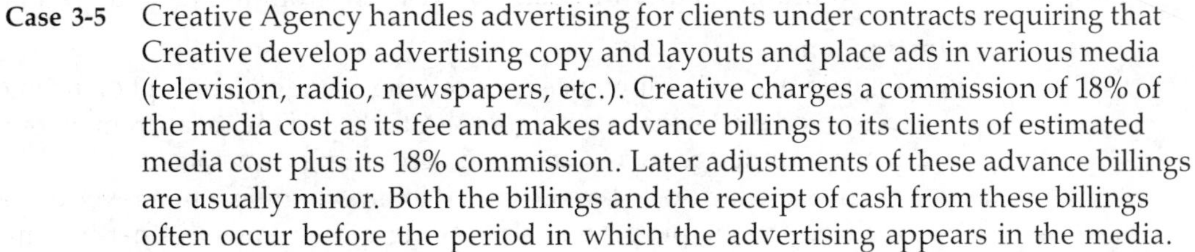

Case 3-5 Creative Agency handles advertising for clients under contracts requiring that Creative develop advertising copy and layouts and place ads in various media (television, radio, newspapers, etc.). Creative charges a commission of 18% of the media cost as its fee and makes advance billings to its clients of estimated media cost plus its 18% commission. Later adjustments of these advance billings are usually minor. Both the billings and the receipt of cash from these billings often occur before the period in which the advertising appears in the media.

In devising a system for measuring income, Creative Agency considered the following possible points at which revenue and expenses might be recognized and income measured: (1) at the time of the advance billing; (2) when payment is received from clients; (3) in the month in which the advertising appears in the media; (4) when the invoice for advertising is received from the media.

Creative Agency chose 1 above as the point at which it would recognize revenue and income, on the grounds that it has a contract with clients for specified advertising and thus revenue and income are earned when billed. At the time of billing, Creative records the accounts receivable from clients, the estimated liability to the media, and its 18% commission. Also at this time, Creative records an expense and a liability for the estimated expenses related to the client's billing. Adjusting entries are made to record actual cost and revenue amounts when billings are received from media, when actual expenses are determined, and when final billings invoices are sent to clients.

Instructions
Discuss each of the four points at which Creative Agency might recognize revenue and income, and state your opinion as to the proper basis for accounting for revenue and income in this case. If you disagree with the method followed by Creative, explain why, suggest an alternative point for revenue recognition, and justify your choice.

Case 3-6 On May 1, Year 1, Axel Corporation signed a contract with Westside Limited under which Westside agreed to (1) construct an office building on land owned by Axel, (2) accept responsibility for arranging financing for the project and finding tenants, and (3) manage the property for 10 years. The annual income from the project, after debt service, was to be divided equally between Axel and Westside. Westside was to accept its share of future income as full payment for its services in construction, obtaining financing, and managing the project.

By April 30, Year 2, the project was nearly completed, and tenants had signed leases to occupy 90% of the available space at annual rentals aggregating $3,300,000. It was estimated that, after operating expenses and debt service, the annual income would amount to $950,000. The owners of Westside believed that the economic benefit derived from the contract with Axel should be reflected in its financial statements for the fiscal year ended April 30, Year 2. Consequently, the owners of Westside requested their accountant to record revenue in an amount equal to the commercial value of the services Westside had rendered to Axel during the year, to record this amount in accounts receivable, and to deduct all expenditures incurred to date by Westside from the revenue recognized.

Instructions

a Explain the main difference between the economic concept of income as perceived by the management of Westside and the measurement of net income under generally accepted accounting principles.

b Discuss the factors to be considered in determining when revenue has been realized for the purpose of accounting measurement of net income.

c Is the belief of Westside's management in accord with generally accepted accounting principles for the recognition of revenue and expense for the year ended April 30, Year 2? Support your opinion by discussing the application to this case of the factors to be considered for asset measurement and revenue and expense recognition.

PROBLEMS

Pr. 3-1 Sonrisa Limited was organized in Year 1 to sell merchandise on the instalment plan and on regular 30-day open accounts. Sonrisa's activities for Year 5 are summarized below.

Regular sales on credit	$ 720,000
Instalment sales	1,200,000
Cost of regular sales	406,000
Cost of instalment sales	780,000
Operating expenses (all paid in Year 5)	354,000
Collections on regular sales	620,000
Collections on instalment sales	450,000

Sonrisa uses the perpetual inventory system. Income taxes and interest and carrying charges on the instalment accounts receivable are to be disregarded in this problem.

Instructions

a Prepare journal entries for Sonrisa to record all transactions and adjustments for Year 5, assuming that Sonrisa uses the accrual basis of accounting. Closing entries are not required.

b Prepare journal entries for Sonrisa to record all transactions for Year 5 (including the closing entry to establish the deferred gross profit and the adjusting entry to record the realized gross profit on instalment sales). Assume that Sonrisa uses the instalment method of accounting because the collectibility of instalment accounts receivable cannot be reasonably estimated. Other closing entries are not required.

Pr. 3-2 Sergio Corporation had 200,000 shares of common stock outstanding throughout Year 5. Sergio's results of operations for the year ended December 31, Year 5, are summarized as follows:

Sales (net of returns, allowances, and discounts)	$10,600,000
Costs and expenses	9,200,000
Gain on disposal of long-term investment in an affiliate	800,000
Loss from an expropriation of a subsidiary by a foreign government	960,000
Write-down of inventories due to unexpected obsolescence	200,000

The income tax rate for Sergio is 45%, and no potentially dilutive securities were outstanding.

Instructions

Prepare a partial income statement for Sergio Corporation for the year ended December 31, Year 5. Include earnings-per-share data and disregard notes to the financial statements.

Pr. 3-3 Gussman Limited is engaged in the manufacture of auto parts. Several years ago it acquired a small trust company, Halifax Trust, which has been operated at a loss since it was acquired. In Year 9, the board of directors of Gussman sold Halifax Trust for $5,100,000. Gussman's results of operations for the year ended December 31, Year 9, are summarized below.

	Auto parts	*Halifax Trust*
Revenue (net)	$26,000,000	$6,500,000
Costs and expenses	21,200,000	7,700,000
Loss on disposal of Halifax Trust, before income tax effect		400,000
Loss resulting from adjustments of contract prices	680,000	
Loss from an earthquake and hailstorms	300,000	

The income tax rate for Gussman is 45%. There were 400,000 shares of common stock (the only capital stock issued) outstanding during Year 9. No potentially dilutive securities were outstanding.

Instructions

Prepare a partial income statement for Gussman Limited for the year ended December 31, Year 9, including earnings-per-share data.

Pr. 3-4 Rosa Wong started a sole proprietorship on July 1, Year 3 by investing $60,000 cash and plant assets with a current fair value of $100,000. A few days later, Francis Wong was admitted as partner for an investment of $120,000 cash. The partners adopted the name ''Gentle Care'' for their business enterprise. Here is the balance sheet of Gentle Care on June 30, Year 11.

GENTLE CARE
Balance Sheet
June 30, Year 11

Assets		*Liabilities & Partners' Capital*	
Cash	$ 85,980	Trade accounts payable	$ 52,940
Trade accounts receivable (net)	57,820	Mortgage note payable	100,000
Inventories	64,200	Rosa Wong, capital	292,060
Plant assets (net)	392,000	Francis Wong, capital	155,000
Total assets	$600,000	Total liabilities & partners' capital	$600,000

The partners disagreed over business policies and decided to liquidate the partnership effective June 30, Year 11. Inventories were sold for $50,000 and plant assets for $560,000. Trade accounts receivable of $24,000 were collected, $32,000 were sold (without recourse) for $25,000, and $1,820 were written off as uncollectible. All liabilities were paid, including $400 of interest on the mortgage note payable not accrued at the time of the June 30, Year 11, balance sheet. During the life of Gentle Care, Rosa Wong and Francis Wong had withdrawn $300,000 and $196,000 respectively.

Instructions

a Compute the lifetime income of Gentle Care on the basis of the foregoing information. ***Reminder:*** A partnership is not a taxable entity.

b Explain whether there are any areas of uncertainty in your determination of the lifetime income of Gentle Care.

Pr. 3-5 Bolero Construction Corporation is engaged in the construction of small-boat harbours. During the first two years of its operations, Bolero completed three contracts and had two contracts in progress. Information relating to these contracts is summarized below:

Contract and fixed price	*Costs*	*Year 2*	*Year 1*
A, $100,000	Incurred:	—	$82,000
B, $150,000	Incurred:	$ 84,000*	40,000
	Estimated to complete:	—	80,000
C, $130,000	Incurred:	78,500*	20,000
	Estimated to complete:	—	80,000
D, $255,000	Incurred:	82,000	
	Estimated to complete:	123,000	
E, $500,000	Incurred:	210,000	
	Estimated to complete:	210,000	

*Completed during year.

Instructions

Compute the realized gross profit on Bolero's contract revenue for each year under the following methods of accounting for construction-type contracts:

a Percentage-of-completion

b Completed-contract

Pr. 3-6 On January 2, Year 1, Grove Corporation sold an idle machine to Anne Company for $350,000. On that date the machine had a cost of $600,000 and accumulated depreciation of $350,000 in Grove's accounting records. Under the contract, Anne paid $50,000 cash on January 2, Year 1, and signed a $300,000 promissory note bearing interest at the current fair rate of 10%. The promissory note was payable in instalments of $50,000, $100,000, and $150,000 on January 2 of Year 2, Year 3, and Year 4 respectively. The promissory note was not secured by any collateral. Grove appropriately accounted for the sale of the idle machine under the cost recovery method because there was no reasonable basis for estimating the collectibility of the promissory note. Anne made late payments on the note and interest as shown in the table at the top of page 148.

Instructions

a Prepare journal entries to record the foregoing transactions in the accounting records of Grove Corporation under the cost recovery method of accounting.

Date of payment	*Principal*	*Interest*
July 1, Year 2	$ 50,000	$ 45,000
December 31, Year 3	100,000	37,500
April 1, Year 5	150,000	18,750
Totals	$300,000	$101,250

Record the unrealized gain in a Deferred Gain on Disposal of Machinery account and any unrealized interest in a Deferred Interest Revenue ledger account. Assume that the gain on disposal of machinery is recovered before any interest revenue is recognized. Journal entries are required on the following dates:

1 January 2, Year 1
2 July 1, Year 2
3 December 31, Year 3
4 April 1, Year 5

b Show how the promissory note receivable, deferred gross profit on the disposal of machinery, and deferred interest revenue are presented in Grove Corporation's balance sheet on December 31, Year 3.

Pr. 3-7 In Year 1, Jeannie Bowman opened an ''exclusive'' exercise-diet studio in Windsor. After profitable operations for nearly three years, Bowman organized a separate company, EXDI, Inc., on January 2, Year 4, to sell and service franchises in several large cities. Each franchise was sold for $50,000, payable $14,000 down and $12,000 a year for three years starting one year after sale. No other payments were required from franchisees.

EXDI, Inc. was obligated to provide considerable services to franchisees in opening and operating their studios for the first three years, including the preparation of promotional brochures, the setting-up of accounting systems, and the training of employees. The down payment of $14,000 was designed to cover the initial direct costs of the franchise contract and for the right to use the name ''EXDI Studios.'' The three payments of $12,000 each were for annual services provided to the franchisee.

The fair rate of interest during Year 4 was 15% a year; thus, the present value of the three promissory notes of $12,000 each received from a franchisee was approximately $27,396 on the date a franchise was sold. However, the accountant for EXDI, Inc., recorded each franchise contract by debits to Cash and Notes Receivable for $14,000 and $36,000 respectively, and a credit to Franchise Revenue for $50,000. The notes were considered fully collectible.

Sales of franchises by EXDI, Inc., during Year 4 were as shown in the next table.

Operating expenses paid and accrued in selling the franchises and providing services to franchisees amounted to $271,800 for Year 4.

Date	*Number of franchises sold*
April 1	5
May 1	8
July 1	6
September 30	4
October 30	10
Total	33

Instructions

a Compute the income before income taxes for EXDI, Inc., for the year ended December 31, Year 4 under the accounting procedure adopted by its accountant.

b Evaluate the accounting procedure used by EXDI, Inc., for the sale of franchises and compute its income before income taxes in accordance with what you consider to be generally accepted accounting principles. Round all computations to the nearest dollar.

Pr. 3-8 The unadjusted trial balance of Selca Corporation included the following ledger account balances on March 31, Year 10:

Inventories (perpetual system)	$1,550,000
Deferred cost of unsuccessful contract proposals	19,500
Sales (regular and instalment)	6,500,000
Cost of goods sold (regular and instalment)	5,200,000
Contract revenue	500,000
Costs incurred on contracts	420,000
Purchases discounts revenue	40,000

Additional Information

1 Sales included $75,000, representing a shipment of goods on consignment to Milna Company. The cost of these goods was $51,000 and was included in cost of goods sold. Accounts receivable included $75,000 from Milna because none of the goods had been sold.

2 Sales also included $40,000, the estimated selling price of a special shipment of slow-moving goods to Diskonte, Inc. The $35,000 cost of these goods was included in cost of goods sold. Diskonte had the right to return 100% of these goods and to adjust the purchase price on the basis of its ability to sell the goods and to obtain reasonable prices on the sales. Diskonte had not sold any goods included in this shipment.

3 Instalment sales included $100,000, of which $40,000 had been collected through March 31, Year 10. Because the collectibility of the balance was not reasonably assured, the instalment method of accounting was used for this portion of instalment sales. The gross profit rate on this instalment sale was 32%. (Debit Deferred Gross Profit [to be offset from gross profit on sales in the income statement] and credit Deferred Gross Profit [to be offset from instalment receivables in the balance sheet].)

4 Sales included a deposit of $15,000 received from a customer who was considering a large order for the purchase of goods from Selca. No cost of goods sold was recorded.

5 Inventories and sales included $10,000, the value of old products discovered in the factory cellar, which had not been opened for at least 10 years.

6 Selca used the completed-performance method of revenue realization for its various service contracts, and it recognized contract revenue at the time the contracts were completed; however, all costs relating to contracts in progress had been recorded in the Costs Incurred on Contracts ledger account. It has been concluded that a contract for $30,000, on which 60% of the costs had been incurred, should be accounted for under the proportional-performance method of revenue recognition. An appropriate amount was debited to Accounts Receivable (not billed).

7 There were initial direct costs and direct costs in the amount of $15,880 related to contracts in progress for which revenue would be recognized under the completed-performance method. (Debit Costs of Contracts in Progress.)

8 Selca had deferred certain costs of unsuccessful contract proposals and planned to charge these costs against several outstanding proposals that were expected to result in significant service contracts.

9 Purchases discounts were recorded as revenue when invoices were paid within the discount period. Of the purchases discounts recorded, 15% relate to inventories on hand on March 31, Year 10, and 85% relate to Cost of Goods Sold (regular and instalment). The controller concluded that purchases discounts are cost offsets, not revenue.

Instructions

a For each ledger account listed in the partial trial balance for Selca Corporation, compute the correct amount on the basis of the information given in items 1 to 9.

b Prepare journal entries to correct or adjust the accounting records of Selca Corporation on March 31, Year 10, for each item from 1 to 9.

Pr. 3-9 Lobo, Inc., sells restaurant franchises to independent operators (franchisees) under a standard contract that includes the following terms:

1 The franchisee pays an initial fee of $40,000, of which 25% is payable at the time the contract is signed and $10,000 is payable at the end of each of the three subsequent years. The franchisee signs three non-interest-bearing promissory notes of $10,000 each for the balance payable to the franchisor. The initial $10,000 collected by the franchisor is to be refunded and the promissory notes cancelled if the franchisee fails to open the restaurant for any reason within one year.

2 For three years, starting on the date the restaurant franchise is sold, franchisor agrees to *a* assist the franchisee in selecting the location for the restaurant, *b* negotiate the lease for the land, *c* obtain financing and assist with building design, *d* supervise construction, *e* establish appropriate

accounting records, and *f* provide advice relating to employee training, quality control, and advertising.

3 In addition to the initial franchise fee, franchisee is required to pay a royalty of 2% of sales to Lobo for menu planning, recipe innovations, and the option to purchase food and supplies from Lobo at discount prices. This fee is payable on January 31 each year.

The management of Lobo estimates that the value of the services rendered to the franchisee at the time the restaurant is opened amounts to at least $10,000. The services relating to employee training, quality control, and advertising are considered significant and are expected to be provided by Lobo ratably over the three-year period. During the 30 months Lobo has been selling franchises, all franchisees have opened their restaurants on schedule and have made timely payments on the promissory notes and the 2% royalty.

The credit rating of the franchisees would enable them to borrow at the current annual interest rate of 15%. The present value of the three $10,000 promissory notes, discounted at 15%, is $22,832.

Instructions

a Given the nature of the standard contract with franchisees, how should revenue be recognized by Lobo? Discuss the question of revenue recognition for the initial franchise fee, the 2% royalty based on sales, and interest revenue.

b Assume that Lobo sold a franchise to Macon Company on December 31, Year 5, that Macon opened its restaurant on July 30, Year 6, and that sales for the restaurant were $480,000 for the year ended December 31, Year 6. Prepare journal entries for Lobo to record:

1 The sale of the franchise on December 31, Year 5

2 Recognition of franchise fee revenue on July 30, Year 6

3 Recognition of interest revenue on December 31, Year 6

4 Receipt of the second payment of $10,000 from Macon on December 31, Year 6, including recognition of franchise fee revenue on the straight-line basis

5 Accrual of the 2% royalty on December 31, Year 6

Pr. 3-10 Reseda Sales Outlet sells off-brand merchandise for cash and on the instalment plan. Information for the first three years of its operations is summarized below:

	Year 3	*Year 2*	*Year 1*
Cash sales	$500,000	$400,000	$300,000
Instalment sales	300,000	250,000	200,000
Collections on instalment receivables from sales made in:			
Year 1	50,000	85,000	60,000
Year 2	120,000	80,000	
Year 3	100,000		
Cost of goods sold:			
Cash sales	350,000	290,000	205,000
Instalment sales	186,000	150,000	130,000
Operating expenses	208,500	181,000	172,000
Gross profit percentages on instalment sales	38%	40%	35%

For purposes of this problem, interest and carrying charges on instalment receivables, doubtful accounts expense, and income taxes are disregarded.

Instructions

Compute the net income of Reseda Sales Outlet for each of the three years under each of the following methods of accounting for instalment sales (use one column for each year):

a Accrual basis of accounting

b Instalment method

Note: For *b* deduct unrealized gross profit on current year's instalment sales from the total gross profit on all sales for that year, and add realized gross profit on instalment sales of prior years to the total gross profit on all sales to compute realized gross profit for each year.

c h a p t e r 4

FINANCIAL STATEMENTS AND ADDITIONAL DISCLOSURES

In the previous two chapters we have stressed that the measurement of the resources and obligations of a business enterprise is fundamental to the accounting process. The ongoing recording of transactions and events and the preparation of end-of-period adjusting entries may be described as a process of measuring assets and liabilities. If assets and liabilities are measured correctly, it should be apparent that revenue, expenses, and total owners' equity also are measured correctly. However, the measurement of assets and liabilities is not an easy process, and the result of this process is summarized in ***general-purpose financial statements*** that provide decision makers with useful information. A set of general-purpose financial statements is the foundation of the financial reporting and disclosure system and includes an income statement, a balance sheet, a statement of changes in financial position, a statement of retained earnings, notes to the financial statements, and other, supplementary disclosures.

Both the form and the content of financial statements have received considerable attention from accountants for many years. It is widely agreed that the heading of each financial statement should include the name of the business, the title of the statement, and the date or dates of, or the period covered by, the statement (such as "For Year Ended March 31, 1987"). The title itself should include any qualifying or descriptive words such as "consolidated," "comparative," or "condensed." When financial statements are not audited by independent accountants, the word "Unaudited" ought to appear on the face of each. The manner of presenting information in the body of the financial statements will be discussed in this chapter.

The contents of a business enterprise's financial statements, including the supplementary disclosures, have ***significant economic consequences*** for the enterprise, its owners, its creditors, and all other parties who have an economic stake in its financial strength and profitability. Financial statements that are relevant, complete, objective, timely, and understandable are perceived by users to be credible. ***Credibility*** in financial reporting is an essential prerequisite to a healthy and efficient economic system.

INCOME STATEMENT

In Chapter 3 we emphasized that the task of measuring revenue, expenses, gains, and losses is formidable. Also, the presentation of these items in the income statement has been more than a routine process for accountants. A formal income statement consists of more than an itemized list of revenue, expenses, gains, and losses. Attention must be given to such issues as the system of classification, the amount of detail that is appropriate, the order of presentation, the relationship among the various components of net income, and the titles used to describe the ***line items*** in the income statement.

The information appearing in income statements issued to the public is usually highly condensed. But such an income statement may not be as useful to management as statements showing income by product, by department, or by division; managers are obviously interested in ***detailed*** accounting and statistical data, data that shed light on the contribution of the various segments of a business enterprise to its overall success; such information might also be useful to outsiders such as credit grantors and others having a special interest in the enterprise.

Even so, some income statements may still be quite complex. If an enterprise recognizes an extraordinary gain or loss, for example, the bottom portion of the income statement must be expanded. Also, ***earnings-per-share data*** are presented in the income statement of publicly owned companies, and this may be quite cumbersome when both ***basic*** and ***fully diluted*** earnings-per-share amounts are reported.

Alternative Forms of the Income Statement

Whether the ***multiple-step*** or the ***single-step*** form of income statement is generally better is an unsettled question. In the multiple-step form (illustrated on the next page for Model Corporation), various intermediate amounts, such as gross profit on sales, income from operations, and income before income taxes, are presented as separate ***line items***. The single-step form (illustrated on page 156) presents all revenue in one category, all costs and expenses in another, and derives net incomes as the final amount.

Those who favour the multiple-step form argue that there are several significant subtotals on the road to net income. The ***gross profit on sales*** indicates the markup on the merchandise sold that is available to cover operating expenses. The distinction between operating and nonoperating revenue and expenses permits the showing of ***income from operations*** as a measure of operating results. The ***income before income taxes*** reflects pre-tax earnings and emphasizes the special nature of income taxes expense.

Multiple-step form of income statement

MODEL CORPORATION
Income Statement
For Year Ended December 31, Year 5
(In thousands of dollars)

Sales (net of discounts, returns and allowances)			$18,108
Cost of goods sold:			
Inventories Jan. 1, Year 5		$ 1,000	
Purchases (net of discounts, returns, and allowances)	$10,302		
Freight-in	1,266	11,568	
Cost of goods available for sale		$12,568	
Less: Inventories Dec. 31, Year 5		580	
Cost of goods sold			11,988
Gross profit on sales			$ 6,120
Operating expenses:			
Selling expenses:			
Sales salaries	$ 1,260		
Advertising and promotion	880		
Building occupancy (including depreciation and property taxes on building)	420		
Other	80	$ 2,640	
General and administrative expenses:			
Salaries	$ 1,160		
Property taxes	308		
Depreciation of equipment	80		
Other	72	1,620	
Total operating expenses			4,260
Income from operations			$ 1,860
Other revenue (expenses):			
Investment income		$ 420	
Gain on disposal of equipment		50	
Interest expense		(230)	240
Income before income taxes			$ 2,100
Income taxes expenses (including $20 deferred)			1,043
Net income			$ 1,057
Earnings per share of common stock			$ 1.25

Proponents of the single-step form maintain that net income emerges as the overall amount by which a business enterprise is better off after taking into account all revenue and all costs and expenses incurred in producing that revenue. They object to the implication of the multiple-step form that there is a priority of cost recovery; that is, that cost of goods sold is recovered first, then operating expenses, then other expenses, and finally income taxes. The multiple-step form also implies relationships that do not exist. For example, showing investment income as "Other revenue" below "Income from operations" implies that such income is realized without cost, but in fact some general and administrative expenses are incurred to produce investment income.

The sequence of listing of expenses in income statements, and the amount of detail shown, vary considerably. The multiple-step form is more likely to be found in more-detailed income statements prepared for the use of management,

Single-step form of income statement

MODEL CORPORATION
Income Statement
For Year Ended December 31, Year 5
(In thousands of dollars)

Revenue:		
Net sales		$18,108
Investment income		420
Gain on disposal of equipment		50
Total revenue		$18,578
Costs and expenses:		
Cost of goods sold	$11,988	
Selling expenses	2,640	
General and administrative expenses	1,620	
Interest expense	230	
Income taxes expense (including $20 deferred)	1,043	
Total costs and expenses		17,521
Net income		$ 1,057
Earnings per share of common stock		$ 1.25

bankers, and other creditors. Many published income statements are closer to the single-step form and are almost always presented in ***comparative form*** like the one illustrated for Comcorp Inc., on pages 157 and 158. Financial statements prepared in comparative form highlight trends and changes, and emphasize the fact that financial statements for a single accounting period are only a small part of the continuous history of a business enterprise.

Classification of Revenue

As stated in Chapter 3, the major source of revenue for most business enterprises is the production and sale of goods and services. Examples of secondary sources are dividends, royalties, interest, rents, investment income from affiliated companies, and gains on the disposal of assets. An objective of reporting revenue in an income statement is to disclose the major sources of revenue and to separate primary from miscellaneous sources. For example, some enterprises report revenue from government contracts separately from revenue from nongovernment sources; this enables the user to form some opinion of future prospects in the light of projected governmental expenditures.

Revenue ***offsets*** should be distinguished from expenses; they are deducted from gross revenue in the income statement. Such items as sales discounts and sales returns and allowances are not expenses, but rather revenue that is never realized.

Classification of Costs and Expenses

Costs and expenses are classified in the income statement to help users understand the operating cost relationships of the business enterprise. Classification may be according to the nature of the expenses (***natural classification***), business functions (***functional classification***), areas of responsibility, or any other useful basis.

In many published income statements, costs and expenses are reported in single-step form, classified according to the ***nature*** of the expenses, that is, into categories that reflect the kind of resources used during the accounting period. Examples of such categories are merchandise and supplies, salaries and fringe benefits, purchased services, depreciation, property taxes, interest, and income taxes. This is called the ***natural classification***.

The multiple-step income statement for Model Corporation on page 155 illustrates a classification of expenses into five categories on a ***functional basis***: (1) cost of goods sold, (2) selling expenses, (3) general and administrative expenses, (4) other expenses, and (5) income taxes expense. In income statements prepared for different levels of management, the usefulness of the ***functional classification*** system may be improved by identifying additional functions. For example, material handling, production scheduling, assembly, inspection, and packing are examples of manufacturing subfunctions.

Illustration of Comprehensive Income Statement

The presentation of the results of extraordinary items and earnings-per-share data in the income statement is illustrated (with the related notes) below and on page 158 for Comcorp Inc. Observe that the unusual write-down of obsolete inventories is disclosed in a note to the income statement; as indicated in Chapter 3, such unusual items may alternatively be presented in the income statement as a separate item before income taxes expense and extraordinary items. The extraordinary gain and loss are presented as separate items (together with additional disclosure in a note) before the "bottom-line" net income figure of $9,750,000. Also note that the earnings-per-share data for extraordinary items are desirable but not mandatory disclosures.[1] Since Comcorp Inc. has no potentially dilutive securities, a ***dual presentation*** of earnings-per-share (***basic*** and ***fully diluted***) is not needed.

Comprehensive illustration of income statements in comparative form

COMCORP INC.
Income Statements
For Years Ended December 31, Year 3 and Year 2
(In thousands of dollars, except per-share data)

	Year 3	*Year 2*
Net sales and other revenue	$85,360	$75,750
Costs and expenses (**NOTE 1**)	65,880	60,390
Income from operations before income taxes and extraordinary items	$19,480	$15,360
Income taxes expense (including $1,200 deferred each year)	9,350	7,370
Income before extraordinary items	$10,130	$ 7,990

1 CICA, *CICA Handbook* (Toronto), sec. 3500.11.

Extraordinary items ((**NOTE 2**):		
Gain from sale of long-term investment, net of income tax effect of $820 in Year 3, $442 in Year 2	1,660	470
Loss on disposal of business segment, net of income tax effect of $1,880	(2,040)	
Net income	$ 9,750	$ 8,460
Earnings per share of common stock:		
Income before extraordinary items	$ 2.03	$ 1.60
Extraordinary items	(0.08)	0.10
Net income	$ 1.95	$ 1.70

NOTE 1: Costs and expenses for Year 3 include $675,000 write-down of obsolete inventories.
NOTE 2: In August, Year 3, the company sold its investments in an affiliate whose operations were deemed incompatible with the company's policies. This investment had been made 10 years ago. In October, Year 3, the company decided to dispose of its retailing segment that had consisted of 20 outlets in localities adjacent to its principal customers. Two of the outlets were closed in October, and the remaining 18 were sold prior to December 31, Year 3.

STATEMENT OF RETAINED EARNINGS

The statement of retained earnings is generally included with every set of financial statements. In fact, some legislation requires that such a statement be included in the annual financial statements for shareholders. Also, sections 1500 and 5400 of the ***CICA Handbook*** indicate that financial statements ***normally*** include a statement of retained earnings. The typical form of this statement includes the beginning balance, the net income for the accounting period as an addition, the dividends (both cash and stock) as deductions, and the ending balance. If operations for the latest period resulted in a loss, the beginning balance of retained earnings is reduced by the amount of the net loss. In addition, the beginning balance may be ***restated*** to reflect the effect of a ***prior period adjustment***.

Prior Period Adjustments

In contrast to extraordinary items described in Chapter 3, ***prior period adjustments*** are excluded from the determination of net income for the current accounting period and are applied retroactively to the income of the related prior periods. The financial statements affected by such an adjustment, when presented for comparative purposes, are to be restated accordingly, together with any related income tax effect. Also to be restated is the beginning balance of retained earnings for the periods subsequent to the period to which the adjustment relates. In the period wherein a prior period adjustment occurs, the information required to be disclosed includes: (1) a description of the adjustment, (2) its effect on the financial statements of the current and prior periods, and (3) the fact regarding the restatement of the financial statements of prior periods that are presented.[2] As noted in Chapter 3, prior period adjustments and changes in accounting policy, though very dissimilar in nature, are accorded the same retroactive treatment.

To qualify as prior period adjustments, adjustments must meet ***all four*** of the

2 CICA, *CICA Handbook*, sec. 3600.08.

characteristics stipulated in the *CICA Handbook*. Prior period adjustments:[3]

1 are specifically identified with and directly related to the business activities of particular prior periods;
2 are not attributable to economic events occurring subsequent to the date of the financial statements for such prior periods;
3 depend primarily on decisions or determinations by persons other than management or owners; and
4 could not be reasonably estimated prior to such decisions or determinations.

Because of the restrictiveness of these characteristics, prior period adjustments are rare. Section 3600 of the *CICA Handbook* provides only two examples:[4]

1 Nonrecurring adjustments or settlements of income taxes

2 Settlements of claims resulting from litigation

Alternative Forms of the Statement of Retained Earnings

The basic format of a statement of retained earnings which includes a prior period adjustment is illustrated below for Model Corporation. The related income statement (in multiple-step form) for Model Corporation was illustrated earlier; the related balance sheet and the statement of changes in financial position for Model Corporation will be presented later in this chapter.

Statement of retained earnings with a prior period adjustment

MODEL CORPORATION
Statement of Retained Earnings
For Year Ended December 31, Year 5
(In thousands of dollars)

Retained earnings, beginning of year, as originally reported		$2,800
Less: Prior period adjustment — settlement of lawsuit (net of applicable income tax effect of $240)		360
Retained earnings, beginning of year, as restated		$2,440
Add: Net income		1,057
Subtotal		$3,497
Less: Dividends on preferred stock	$ 57	
Dividends on common stock	400	457
Retained earnings, end of year		$3,040

As with other financial statements, the statement of retained earnings generally is presented in *comparative form*, that is, data are shown for two or more years. Some companies combine the income statement with the statement of retained earnings. Such a presentation has the advantage of displaying in one statement any prior period adjustments and extraordinary items, thus reducing the possibility that any of these items will be overlooked. One minor objection to this form is that the net income or net loss appears in the middle of the statement. An example of ***combined statements of income and retained earnings*** in comparative form for two years is given on the next page.

3 CICA, ***CICA Handbook***, sec. 3600.03.

4 CICA, ***CICA Handbook***, sec. 3600.02.

Combined statements of income and retained earnings in comparative form

RED LIMITED
Combined Statements of Income and Retained Earnings
For Year Ended December 31, Year 3 and Year 2

	Year 3	*Year 2*
Net sales	$1,295,100	$1,260,500
Less: Costs and expenses	1,014,000	1,021,600
Income before income taxes	$ 281,100	$ 238,900
Income taxes expense	142,100	126,900
Net income	$ 139,000	$ 112,000
Retained earnings, beginning of year	403,800	377,800
Subtotals	$ 542,800	$ 489,800
Less: Cash dividends	87,500	86,000
Retained earnings, end of year	$ 455,300	$ 403,800
Earnings per share of common stock	$ 2.78	$ 2.24

BALANCE SHEET

A ***balance sheet*** (or ***statement of financial position***) presents the financial position of a business enterprise on a specific date. A balance sheet provides a summary of assets, liabilities, and owners' equity, defined as follows:[5]

- ***Assets*** are probable future economic benefits obtained or controlled by a particular entity as a result of past transactions or events.
- ***Liabilities*** are probable future sacrifices of economic benefits arising from present obligations of a particular entity to transfer assets or provide services to other entities in the future as a result of past transactions or events.
- ***Equity*** is the residual interest in the assets of an entity that remains after deducting its liabilities. In a business enterprise, the equity is the ownership interest.

A balance sheet is basically a historical statement, because it shows the cumulative effect of past transactions and events. Generally, it is described as a detailed expression of the basic accounting equation:

Assets = Liabilities + Owners' Equity

The theoretical concept of an asset may be related to the discussion of revenue and expenses in Chapter 3. Assets are costs that have not been deducted from revenue; they represent ***expected future economic benefits***. However, the rights to assets have been acquired by a business enterprise as a result of past transactions.

5 FASB, ***Statement of Financial Accounting Concepts No. 3:*** "Elements of Financial Statements of Business Enterprises" (Stamford: 1980), p. xi. These definitions are more general and comprehensive than the ones in CICA's ***Terminology for Accountants***, 3rd ed. (Toronto: 1983).

If no future economic benefit is expected from a cost incurred by the enterprise, the cost in question is not an asset and should not be included in the balance sheet.

Liabilities also result from past transactions; they are ***obligations that require settlement in the future***, either by the transfer of assets or by the performance of services.

Implicit in these concepts of assets and liabilities is the meaning of owners' equity as the ***residual equity*** in the assets of a business enterprise.

Uses and Limitations of the Balance Sheet

At one time the balance sheet was considered the primary end product of accounting. However, experience pounded home the economic lesson that earning power is the prime determinant of the value of a business enterprise, and users of financial statements gradually placed more emphasis on the income statement. Today the balance sheet is recapturing much of the status it once had, because users of financial statements have come to realize that the income statement neither includes the economic resources and debts of an enterprise nor measures the enterprise's ability to raise sufficient capital for continued growth. Therefore, investors and creditors are placing more emphasis on an enterprise's current and acid-test ratios, debt-to-equity ratio, and rates of return on assets and shareholders' equity. After recent experiences with ''credit crunches,'' business recessions, high levels of interest rates, and inflation, enterprises are giving more attention to their balance sheets. In recent years, the accounting profession has taken significant actions to make the balance sheet more relevant and useful for decision makers. These actions have included a movement toward disclosure of the effects of inflation, immediate expensing of research costs and most development costs, mandatory amortization of goodwill, and the reporting of certain long-term leases as acquisitions of plant assets.

A balance sheet in ***comparative form*** provides valuable information to creditors, shareholders, mangement, prospective investors, and the public. Individuals with the ability to interpret comparative balance sheets may learn much as to the short-run solvency of a business enterprise, favourable or unfavourable trends in liquidity, commitments that must be met in the future, and the relative positions of creditors and shareholders.

In an ideal balance sheet, the list of assets and liabilities would be all-inclusive, and each would be reported at its current fair value. As a result, the residual equity (assets minus liabilities) would reflect meaningful ''net worth'' of a business enterprise. The major ***limitation*** of the traditional balance sheet lies in the inability of accountants to measure the ''current fair value'' of an enterprise's net assets. The inability of accountants (or anyone else) to foresee future economic events necessitates the preparation of balance sheets on a different basis. Indirect methods of valuation must be used to measure certain assets and liabilities in the balance sheet. Furthermore, accountants are unable to identify and provide a valuation for many factors that have a material effect on the financial position of an enterprise. The quality, morale, and character of management and other personnel, the market position of an enterprise and the reputation of its products, the growth potential implicit in the nature and diversity of its operations—all these are subjective and intangible factors of great importance in the evaluation of the financial position of an enterprise. None of these factors is reported directly in the dollars-and-cents framework of the accounting process that leads to a balance sheet.

Some critics, in discussing the merits of various accounting principles and procedures, take the position that because the balance sheet does not reflect "current fair value" it does not matter what amounts appear in it. There is a serious defect in such thinking. To imply that ***meaningful*** income statements may be prepared as an adjunct to ***meaningless*** balance sheets shows a failure to understand the relationship between these two financial statements. A consistently applied set of principles for the measurement of assets and liabilities is a prerequisite to a meaningful measurement of net income.

Balance Sheet Classification

On a balance sheet, the classifications, group headings, and number of items vary considerably according to the size of the enterprise, the nature of its operations, and whether the financial statements are intended for wide distribution or for the use of a few owners and creditors. As an example of the diversity encountered in published financial statements, public utility companies usually place plant assets at the top of the balance sheet, followed by current assets. Financial institutions generally do not use the current-noncurrent classification for assets and liabilities.

As a generalization, subject to many exceptions, the following classification of balance sheet items is suggested as representative:

Assets
Current assets
Investments (held for significant influence or control, or not readily marketable)
Plant assets
Intangible assets
Other noncurrent assets (including deferred charges)

Liabilities
Current liabilities
Long-term debt (including deferred income tax credits and deferred revenue)

Shareholders' equity
Capital stock (preferred and common stock)
Premium on capital stock
Retained earnings

This classification reflects the three elements of the basic accounting equation. In practice, it is not unusual to find a fourth category placed between liabilities and shareholders' equity (often with the heading "Deferred Credits"), to include items such as deferred income tax credits, unamortized investment tax credits, and minority interest in net assets of subsidiaries.

Working Capital

The ***working capital*** of a business enterprise is the excess of current assets over current liabilities. This amount has always been of considerable interest to credit grantors as a measure of short-run ***solvency***—the ability to finance current operations and to pay obligations as they mature. The amounts of current assets and current liabilities, and the relationship beteen them (the ***current ratio***), are widely quoted in financial circles and often incorporated in contracts between an enterprise and its creditors and preferred shareholders. Most such contracts do not define working capital but simply state that it ''shall be determined in accordance with generally accepted accounting principles.'' Thus, a generally accepted and consistent basis is needed for determining which items are included in, and which are excluded from, the current assets and current liabilities sections of the balance sheet.

Current Assets

As a practical matter, it is easy to grasp the conceptual difference between a current and a noncurrent asset. However, the boundary between these two categories is hazy, and defining an exact boundary is not an easy task.

Five general types of assets are usually included in the current assets classification:

1 ***Cash*** Money in any form — cash and cheques awaiting deposit, balances in chequing accounts, and expendable cash funds.

2 ***Secondary cash resources*** Various short-term investments that are readily marketable. Excluded are any such resources whose availability for current use is restricted by contract.

3 ***Short-term receivables*** Trade accounts receivable (including instalment receivables collected during the enterprise's operating cycle) and notes receivable with short-term maturities.

4 ***Inventories*** Material, supplies, goods in process, finished goods. This category includes items held for sale in the ordinary course of operations, items still in production, and items that will be consumed in the production of goods or services. Goods held on consignment from others are not included because title is not held to such goods.

5 ***Short-term prepayments*** The cost of various services, such as insurance, taxes, and rent, that have been paid for in advance of use. Short-term prepayments sometimes are referred to as ***prepaid expenses***.

There is little question about including cash, secondary cash resources, and short-term receivables in the current assets category. As might be expected, the troublesome area is the distinction between short-term and long-term investments in productive assets. The test usually applied in distinguishing current from noncurrent productive assets is whether or not the investment in these assets will be realized within the operating cycle or one year, whichever is the longer period.

The term *operating cycle* refers to the circulation of items within the current asset category. In a typical business enterprise, cash is invested in material, supplies, labour, and overhead costs, and these costs are traced through and assigned to inventories. Inventories are eventually realized by conversion to trade receivables, and trade receivables in turn are collected and once more become cash. The average period of time between the investment in goods and services and the conversion to cash is the length of the operating cycle of an enterprise. In most cases this is a matter of days or months, but in some industries the operating cycle may extend beyond one year. Thus, *the conventional time test for current assets is realization within one year or the operating cycle, whichever is longer*.

There are some theoretical flaws in the application of the time test. In a realistic sense, all asset services that will be used to produce revenue during the immediately succeeding operating cycle or accounting period will be realized and converted to liquid assets. A portion of the cost of plant assets will be realized in the same sense, as will be the investment in material. For example, it may be argued that standing timber that will be used to manufacture plywood in the next operating cycle has as good a claim to inclusion among current assets as the inventory of glue that will bind the layers of wood. Thus, the attempt to distinguish between assets that are consumed physically and assets that yield services gradually through use has some stumbling blocks in its way. These conceptual niceties are generally disregarded in the reporting of current assets in a balance sheet.

In any system of classification, there are troublesome items that do not fit neatly into designated niches. For example, if money is borrowed for the express purpose of constructing plant assets, it may be argued that its inclusion in working capital is misleading. If fire insurance covering a three-year period is acquired, a question may be raised about the logical consistency of including the full amount of unexpired insurance as a current asset.

In resolving these difficulties, accountants find themselves at odds with a neat, logical statement of the characteristics that distinguish current assets. They may explain their difficulties as an inevitable conflict between theory and practice, but the result is that the distinction between current and noncurrent assets is often based more on rules-of-thumb than on precise definitions.

Current Liabilities

The distinction between current and noncurrent is easier to make for liabilities than for assets. Generally, current liabilities are obligations whose liquidation is expected to require the use of current assets or the creation of other current liabilities. Three main classes of current liabilities fall within this definition:

1 *Obligations for the acquisition of goods and services that have entered the operating cycle* These include trade payables (including notes and accounts payable to suppliers) and accrued liabilities such as wages, commissions, income taxes, and property taxes.

2 *Other debts that may be expected to require payment within the operating cycle or one year* This includes short-term notes payable to banks and the currently maturing portions of long-term debt.

3 *Collections received in advance of the delivery of goods or the performance of*

services These advances are often described as ''deferred revenue,'' but it is the obligation to furnish the goods or services or to refund the payment that requires them to be classified in the current liabilities section of the balance sheet.

Some liabilities that will be paid shortly after the balance sheet date are excluded from current liabilities, because of the requirement that a current liability must involve the use of current assets or the issuance of new short-term debt for its extinction. Examples are (1) obligations due at an early date that will be retired by the issuance of new long-term debt, such as bonds that will be refunded or a loan secured by the cash surrender value of life insurance policies (the amount of cash that would be received if the policies were cancelled) that will be renewed, and (2) obligations that will be paid from a fund included among noncurrent assets, such as a life insurance policy loan that will be liquidated by offset against the cash surrender value of the policy, or by deduction from the proceeds of the life insurance policy at maturity.

Noncurrent Resources and Obligations

Noncurrent Assets

The definition of current assets determines by exclusion those assets reported as noncurrent. There are four categories of ***noncurrent assets***:

1 ***Long-term funds, investments, and receivables*** Many long-term commitments of funds do not qualify as secondary cash resources. Investments in the common stock of investees made for the purpose of significant influence or control are included in this category. Also included are noncurrent receivables (such as long-term advances to affiliated companies), the cash surrender value of life insurance policies, and funds established for such purposes as the payment of pensions, retirement of preferred stock, or repayment of long-term debt. Assets such as land held for speculative purposes and future plant sites are also included in this category.

2 ***Long-term tangible resources used in operations*** The distinguishing characteristics of assets in this category are that they are tangible (have physical substance) and are held for productive use in business operations. Land, natural resources subject to depletion, buildings, equipment, machines, tools, leased assets under capital leases, leasehold improvements, and plant assets under construction are included. Long-term prepayments for the use of physical assets, such as leaseholds, easements, or rights of way, also may be included in this category, though some accountants group these in the next category.

3 ***Long-term intangible resources*** Long-term property rights of an intangible nature may be of greater importance to a business enterprise than its tangible assets. Examples of such assets are patents, goodwill, trademarks, copyrights, organization costs, and franchises. However, under generally accepted accounting principles most of these items are recorded as assets only when an

expenditure has been made to acquire an intangible property right from outsiders. For example, internally developed goodwill is not recorded as an asset; instead, the costs incurred in building such goodwill are recognized currently as expenses. Similarly, all research and development costs, except those development costs that meet certain specified criteria as discussed in Chapter 13, are recognized as expenses.

4 ***Other noncurrent assets*** Most published balance sheets include a category titled "Other Assets," "Other Noncurrent Assets," or "Deferred Charges." Included in this category are items such as plant assets no longer used in operations and held for disposal, costs incurred in the issuance of long-term debt, and any other noncurrent asset that is not included in one of the first three categories.

Contingent Assets

A ***contingent asset*** is a property right whose existence is conditional on the happening of some future event (***gain contingency***). Generally, it is not appropriate to include contingent assets in the accounting records, because to do so would violate the principles of revenue realization. With a contingent asset there is little reliable evidence that an asset exists or that the earning process has been completed. However, disclosure of the existence of contingencies that are ***likely*** to result in material gains (and assets) is useful.[6] This topic is covered in more detail in Chapter 10.

Noncurrent Liabilities

A ***noncurrent liability*** is an obligation that will not require the use of current assets or the issuance of short-term debt within the next year or operating cycle (whichever is longer). There is some question whether there is any useful basis for subclassification within this category. In general practice, a distinction may be drawn between the following two classes:

1 ***Long-term debt based on security issues or related contractual arrangements*** Included in this category are notes and bonds, reported net of any unamortized discount and including any unamortized premium. The distinguishing characteristic is that there is a borrowing transaction supported by a contractual obligation to pay principal and interest.

2 ***Other noncurrent liabilities*** As the word "other" implies, this includes all long-term liabilities that do not belong in the first category. An amount received in advance on a long-term commitment to furnish goods or services is an example. Any portion of such advances that will be realized during the succeeding accounting period is reported as a current liability. Other examples are long-term advances from affiliated companies, noncurrent amounts payable under pension plans, deferred revenue, and deferred income tax credits.

6 CICA, ***CICA Handbook***, sec. 3290.21.

Contingent Liabilities

Liabilities that ***may or may not*** come into existence as a result of transactions or events that ***have not yet been finalized*** are usually not reported in dollar amounts in the balance sheet. Not only is the evidence with respect to such liabilities too vague to be called objective, but the events (***contingencies***) necessary to bring the liabilities into existence have not yet been completed. Such ***contingent liabilities*** are disclosed, usually by means of a note to the financial statements. Some examples of contingent liabilities are obligations to reimburse banks in case of default by the maker of discounted notes receivable and pending lawsuits that may result in the payment of damages.

Management would be imprudent to provide dollar estimates on anticipated unfavourable results from pending lawsuits, because such disclosure might be viewed as an admission of the merits of the opposing case. However, if the item is material, disclosure in general terms is essential.

A common error is the failure to distinguish between contingent liabilities and obligations that exist but are not definite as to amount, due date, or both. These obligations are called ***estimated liabilities***. There are varying degrees of uncertainty about liabilities; some may be estimated with a high degree of accuracy; others may rest on no more than an informed guess. The liability for income taxes or the amounts payable to employees under pension plans are examples of estimated liabilities that may be measured with reasonable precision on the basis of tentative income tax returns and other data. In contrast, it is difficult to estimate the cost of making good on potential product warranty claims. When such liabilities exist, they are estimated and included in the balance sheet.

Contra-Asset and Contra-Liability Ledger Accounts

Some assets and liabilities are reported in two amounts as a convenient means of disclosing more information about these items than would be afforded by a net valuation. For example, trade accounts receivable are reported as the difference between the gross amount due from customers and an allowance for doubtful accounts. Similarly, a bond discount is shown as a deduction from the face amount of bonds payable. The general criterion for determining whether to display a balance sheet item in one amount or two is the degree of usefulness of the added information. The amount of doubtful accounts receivable provides information about the expected collection experience on trade accounts receivable, and the amount of accumulated depreciation of plant assets provides information about depreciation policy and the age of plant assets. The disclosure may be made as a separate valuation ledger account or by a parenthetical note.

The use of valuation ledger accounts should be distinguished from an actual *offsetting* of assets and liabilities. When valuation accounts are used, the amount deducted from an asset is not a liability, and the amount deducted from a liability is not an asset. Offsetting assets and liabilities is improper, because it implies an association between the two that seldom exists. For example, if a business enterprise voluntarily accumulates a fund to pay a long-term debt when it matures, the intention may be revoked before the debt is paid. Thus, the fund is reported as an asset and the debt as a liability until payment is made.

Owners' Equity

The owners' equity in a business enterprise is the residual interest in assets, after liabilities have been deducted. The amount of owners' equity is thus directly dependent on the values assigned to assets and liabilities. When owners invest assets in an enterprise, the valuation placed on assets determines the amount added to owners' equity. When operating results are summarized, the increase in net assets determines the amount of net income added to the owners' equity. This point is worth noting, because accountants are sometimes tempted to reverse this process and assume that if an amount (for example, the value of common stock) is associated with an element of ownership, there must be an asset to match.

Because of the legal differences between incorporated and nonincorporated business enterprises, there are variations in the balance sheet presentation of owners' equity for such organizations.

Sole Proprietorships and Partnerships

The owners' equity in sole proprietorships and partnerships is usually reported in the balance sheet as a single amount for each owner. There is no reason why the amount of capital invested by each owner should not be shown separately from the reinvested earnings, but because there is no legal restriction on the amounts proprietors or partners may withdraw from the enterprise, such information is less significant than in the case of corporations. Contractual arrangements among partners governing investments, drawings, and the division of net income or loss require that each partner's equity be determined accurately and reported in the balance sheet. A sample statement of partners' capital is illustrated below.

ALLEN & BATES PARTNERSHIP
Statement of Partners' Capital
For year Ended June 30, Year 3

	Allen	*Bates*	*Combined*
Partners' capital, beginning of year	$25,000	$34,000	$59,000
Add: Net income	12,600	18,200	30,800
Subtotals	$37,600	$52,200	$89,800
Less: Drawings	15,000	10,000	25,000
Partners' capital, end of year	$22,600	$42,200	$64,800

The combined capital of $64,800 is reported as owners' equity in the balance sheet for Allen & Bates Partnership.

Corporations

The presentation of shareholders' equity in the balance sheet of a corporation is influenced strongly by legal considerations. Here is an outline of the main sections of owners' equity for corporations:

1 *Contributed or invested capital*

a ***Stated capital*** The amount assigned to shares of capital stock outstanding as par or stated value is known as ***legal capital*** or ***stated capital*** of a corporation. This amount usually appears under the heading "***Capital stock***." For each class of stock, the amount of par value per share if any, the number of shares issued, outstanding, and held in the treasury, and any dividend or liquidating preference should be disclosed. For capital stock ***without*** par value, the total amount of the consideration received is the legal capital.

b ***Additional contributed (paid-in) capital*** This category includes all amounts assigned to shares of capital stock in excess of par value. The terms ***premium on capital stock*** or ***premium on common stock***, etc., are commonly used.

In addition, it covers items such as the reissuance of treasury stock at more than cost, donations of assets to the corporation (donated capital), or transfers from retained earnings through stock dividends. Similarly, the cost of ***treasury stock*** (a debit balance) is a contra-shareholders'-equity item.

2 *Increase in shareholders' equity through the retention of earnings*

a ***Retained earnings*** Net income of past accounting periods that has not been distributed to shareholders as dividends falls in this category. The term ***retained earnings*** is used far more widely than any other to describe this part of shareholders' equity. Alternative terms are ***income retained for use in business*** and ***earnings reinvested in the business***. The term ***earned surplus***, though it is still used by a few companies, is obsolete.

b ***Appropriated retained earnings*** A corporate board of directors may sometimes wish to indicate that a portion of retained earnings has been appropriated. A formal segregation of retained earnings is a means of disclosing that future dividend payments are restricted to some degree, either because of legal or contractual agreements or by management intent. Section 3260 of the ***CICA Handbook*** recommends the term ***reserve*** to describe an appropriation of retained earnings. The use of appropriations of retained earnings as a means of disclosure has almost disappeared; other, more effective means of indicating the restriction of retained earnings are available, principally the use of notes to financial statements.

Use of the Term "Reserve"

In the past the term ***reserve*** was used by accountants in a number of different and somewhat misleading ways. Outside of accounting, a "reserve" is usually thought of as something held for a specific purpose, often for emergencies. This connotation leads to misinterpretation when the word is included in the title of an asset valuation or an estimated liability account. Currently, the trend is to avoid the use of the term, although some business enterprises continue to use it in the assets and the liabilities sections of the balance sheet.

When used to describe an appropriation of retained earnings, the term "reserve" is acceptable, although its use continues to decline.[7] ''Reserve for plant expansion'' is more likely to be misunderstood than ''Retained earnings appropriated for plant expansion.'' If it is used at all, the term ''reserve'' should appear only in the shareholders' equity section of the balance sheet. Because its purpose is to indicate a restriction of retained earnings, the nature of the restriction may be set forth more clearly in a note to the financial statements than by an appropriation of retained earnings.

Standards of Disclosure

Accountants use the disclosure principle as a basis for resolving a number of questions that arise in the preparation of balance sheets.

Account Titles

In providing titles for ledger accounts, considerable leeway is permissible, in deference to convenience and economy of space. The persons involved in the accounting function understand the nature of the item; thus, internally, short account titles are more convenient. However, in the preparation of financial statements, users of the information must be kept in mind, and a clearly worded description of each item is desirable. For example, what accountants call ''Accounts receivable'' may be stated in the balance sheet as ''Amounts due from customers.'' Clarity should prevail over brevity in the preparation of financial statements. Of course, several clearly-described ledger account balances may be combined under a single short heading such as ''Inventories.''

Basis of Valuation

Informed users of financial statements are presumed to be familiar with the general principles applicable to the valuation of assets and liabilities. However, variations in accounting procedures often produce balance sheet amounts whose significance is difficult to interpret unless the procedure used is disclosed. For example, the choice of first-in, first-out or last-in, first-out cost in inventory valuation results in materially different amounts for inventories during periods of inflation. The disclosure principle requires that the basis of valuation be indicated in the caption of all balance sheet items or in a note to the financial statements with some such title as ''Summary of Significant Accounting Policies,'' unless the basis is obvious (as in the case of cash, for example).

Notes to the Financial Statements

Explanatory comments and supplementary disclosure are made in ***notes*** to the financial statements. The notes include a complete description of significant accounting polices and may cover many pages of an annual report. For such matters as stock option plans, pension plans, leases, and business combinations, this is the only reasonable way to provide an adequate explanation. If the detail involved in a section of the balance sheet interferes with a concise presentation, it

7 CICA, *CICA Handbook*, sec. 3260.01.

may be desirable to summarize the item in the balance sheet and show the detail in a ***supporting exhibit*** — that is, in a note. For example, inventories may be reported in a single amount in the body of the balance sheet, and the detailed amounts of material, goods in process, goods on consignment, and finished goods presented in a separate exhibit. Business enterprises frequently show total long-term debt as a single amount and include a supporting exhibit in which the details are furnished. Thus, for users who want only "highlights," the balance sheet provides it; those who want more detailed information will find it in the notes.

Further discussion of notes to financial statements is presented later in this chapter.

Form of the Balance Sheet

Fairly standard ways of presenting balance sheet information have been developed, but there is no universal form. The objectives are ***clarity*** and ***adequate disclosure of all pertinent and material facts***; there are various ways of meeting these objectives, and experimentation should be encouraged. The arrangement of the major sections of the balance sheet also may vary. We shall describe the basic features of three forms of the balance sheet: the ***account form***, the ***report form***, and the ***financial position form***. Within the framework of these three forms a number of variations are possible. In a recent survey of 325 companies, 171 used the account form, 135 used the report form, and only 19 used the financial position form.[8]

Account Form

A balance sheet for Model Corporation in account form appears on pages 172 and 173. The distinguishing characteristics of this form is that all assets are listed on the left side and liabilities and shareholders' equity are "balanced" against them on the right side. The illustration includes typical accounts in each classification and follows current standards of disclosure and terminology. The appropriate degree of condensation in the balance sheet depends on the needs of users. Notes relating to the balance sheet are omitted from the illustration. An example of notes to the financial statements is included in the Appendix at the end of this chapter.

Report Form

The report form of balance sheet differs from the account form only in that the liabilities and shareholders' equity sections are listed below, rather than to the right of, the assets section.

Financial Position Form

Both the account form and the report form of the balance sheet express the basic accounting equation (Assets = Liabilities + Owner's Equity). However, a few

8 CICA, *Financial Reporting in Canada*, 16th ed. (Toronto, 1985), p. 96.

MODEL CORPORATION
Balance Sheet
December 31, Year 5
(In thousands of dollars)

Assets

Current assets:				
Cash				$ 485
Short-term investments (at cost, market value $220)				210
Notes and interest receivable				125
Trade accounts receivable			$1,162	
Less: Allowance for doubtful accounts			50	1,112
Inventories (at lower of average cost and net realizable value)				580
Short-term prepayments				60
Total current assets				$ 2,572
Investments:				
Common stock of affiliated companies (at equity)			$1,250	
Fund for retirement of preferred stock			60	
Land held for future expansion			100	
Cash surrender value of life insurance policies			50	1,460
Plant assets:				
	Cost	*Accumulated depreciation*	*Carrying amount*	
Land	$ 3,015		$3,015	
Buildings	10,950	$5,992	4,958	
Equipment	8,430	2,720	5,710	
Totals	$22,395	$8,712		13,683
Intangible assets (net of amortization):				
Goodwill			$1,105	
Patents			105	1,210
Other noncurrent assets: plant assets held for disposal				45
Total assets				$18,970

(For right-hand section see next page.)

enterprises prefer to use a format that emphasizes working capital; this usually carries the title "Statement of Financial Position" rather than "Balance Sheet." This is a ***vertical*** format in which current liabilities are deducted from current assets to derive working capital. Other assets are then added and other liabilities deducted, leaving a residual amount as shareholders' equity.

The balance sheet for Model Corporation is as of the date December 31, Year 5. However, in almost every published balance sheet comparative amounts for the previous year are presented. Such ***comparative balance sheets*** are illustrated in the Appendix at the end of this chapter.

STATEMENT OF CHANGES IN FINANCIAL POSITION

Along with an income statement and a balance sheet, a ***statement of changes in financial position*** is included in annual reports to shareholders of publicly owned companies and is covered by the auditors' opinion. The objectives of this state-

Liabilities & Shareholders' Equity		
Current liabilities:		
Trade notes and accounts payable		$ 460
Income taxes payable		200
Dividends payable		125
Advances from customers		50
Retirement benefits payable currently		40
Accrued liabilities		30
Total current liabilities		$ 905
Long-term debt:		
10% bonds payable, due Dec. 31, Year 15	$ 4,000	
Less: Discount on bonds payable	20	
Net bonds payable	$ 3,980	
Retirement benefits payable in future years	250	
Deferred income tax credits	300	
Total long-term debt		4,530
Total liabilities		$ 5,435
Shareholders' equity:		
6% cumulative, convertible preferred stock, $100 par, callable at $105 a share, authorized 10,000 shares, issued and outstanding 9,500 shares	$ 950	
Common stock, no par, authorized 1,000,000 shares, issued and outstanding 800,000 shares	9,500	
Premium on preferred stock	45	
Total contributed capital	$10,495	
Retained earnings	3,040	
Total shareholders' equity		13,535
Total liabilities & shareholders' equity		$18,970

ment are (1) to summarize the operating, financing, and investing activities of a business enterprise during an accounting period, including the amount of funds obtained from operations, and (2) to complete the disclosure of changes in financial position during an accounting period that are not readily apparent in comparative balance sheets. The term ***funds*** may mean either ***cash and its equivalents*** or ***working capital***. However, in Canada, the *CICA Handbook* now requires the statement of changes in financial position to be prepared on a cash basis (cash and cash equivalents).[9]

A complete discussion of the statement of changes in financial position is found in Chapter 23. In this chapter we merely illustrate the statement, without further explanation. The statement of changes in financial position on a cash basis for Model Corporation appears on page 174. The related financial statements for Model Corporation appear in this chapter. Note that the statement of changes in financial position is prepared in three sections disclosing the cash provided or used: (1) ***operating*** activities, (2) ***financing*** activities, and (3) ***investing*** activities. Statements of changes in financial position on a cash basis for a large public company appear in comparative form in the Appendix at the end of this chapter.

9 CICA, ***CICA Handbook***, sec. 1540.04.

MODEL CORPORATION
Statement of Changes in Financial Position
For Year Ended December 31, Year 5
(In thousands of dollars)

Operating activities		
Net income		$ 1,057
Add: Expenses not requring the use of cash:		
Depreciation	$ 186	
Amortization	64	
Decrease in inventories	420	670
Deduct:		
Increase in notes and interest receivable	$ 125	
Increase in trade accounts receivable	312	
Increase in short-term prepayments	40	
Decrease in trade notes and accounts payable	330	
Decrease in income taxes payable	150	
Decrease in advances from customers	88	
Decrease in accrued liabilities	50	(1,095)
Cash provided by operating activities		$ 632
Financing activities		
Issuance of preferred stock	$ 250	
Cash dividends	(402)	
Exchange of bonds payable for land	323	
Cash provided by financing activities		171
Investing activities		
Disposal of equipment	$ 100	
Acquisition of patents	(120)	
Acquisition of building	(280)	
Acquisition of land in exchange for bonds payable	(323)	
Cash used in investing activities		(623)
Increase in cash and cash equivalents		$ 180

ADDITIONAL DISCLOSURES

Publicly owned corporations play a dominant role in today's business environment. These corporations are managed by professional executives employed by the shareholders. Corporate managements are responsible for issuing periodic reports to shareholders to inform them of the corporation's operating and financial activities. Management's major means for communicating information to shareholders consist of the ***annual report***, the ***quarterly reports of earnings***, and the ***news releases*** of significant events and transactions.

The annual report of a corporation includes a complete set of financial statements prepared by management and examined by independent auditors. Management and the board of directors are responsible for the financial statements; shareholders are responsible for the selection of auditors who issue an opinion on the statements. The following excerpts from the annual report of Provigo Inc. describe the roles of management and independent auditors with respect to financial statements:

The consolidated financial statements of Provigo Inc. are the responsibility of management and have been approved by the Board of Directors. This responsibility includes the selection of appropriate accounting principles and the exercise of a careful judgement in establishing reasonable and accurate estimates in accordance with generally accepted accounting principles appropriate in the circumstances. Financial information shown elsewhere in this annual report is consistent with that contained in the consolidated financial statements.

Management of Provigo Inc. and its subsidiaries has developed and maintains accounting systems and internal controls designed to provide reasonable assurance that assets are safeguarded from loss or unauthorized use and that the financial records are reliable for preparing the financial statements.

The Board of Directors carries out its responsibility with regards to the consolidated financial statements principally through its Audit Committee, consisting solely of outside directors. The Audit Committee reviews the annual consolidated financial statements and recommends their approval to the Board of Directors. The Audit Committee periodically reviews the results of audit examinations performed by the internal auditors and independent external auditors with respect to the Company's accounting principles, practices and systems of internal control.

These financial statements have been examined by Clarkson Gordon and Raymond, Chabot, Martin, Paré, Chartered Accountants and their report stating the extent of their audit examination and their opinion on the consolidated financial statements is presented. . . .

Annual Reports to Shareholders

The annual report is the primary medium of publicly owned companies for communicating relevant information to its shareholders. Such information generally includes a summary of comparative financial highlights for the most recent years and a letter to the shareholders from the president (or from the chairman of the board and the president) in the report's first section. The next section generally includes a description of the company's products and any important corporate developments, followed by the financial statements, other financial data, and a list of the officers and directors of the company. At this point in our discussion, we are primarily concerned with the contents of the second section, specifically the financial statements and the other financial data. These generally consist of the following:

1 Two-year audited balance sheets, statements of income, retained earnings, and changes in financial position

2 Five-year selected financial data such as sales, income (or loss) from operations (including per-share amounts), total assets, amounts of long-term debt and redeemable preferred stock, cash dividends per share of common stock, and any additional items that enhance understanding and highlight trends in financial condition and results of operations

3 Management's discussion and analysis of the company's financial condition and results of operations, including liquidity, capital resources, favourable or unfavourable trends, significant events or uncertainties, causes of material changes in the financial statements, narrative discussion of the impact of inflation and changing prices, and (as an optional item) projections or other

forward-looking information

4 Highlights of selected two-year financial data such as sales, capital expenditures, earnings per share, working capital, and return on average capital ratio

5 Selected two-year data relating to industry segments, foreign and domestic operations, and export sales

Notes to the Financial Statements

As stated in Chapter 1, the disclosure principle requires that financial statements include all significant information needed by users of the statements. If the omission of certain information would cause the financial statements to be misleading, disclosure of such information is essential. The financial statements included in annual reports to shareholders are accompanied by detailed notes to the statements. However, disclosure in notes in used ***to supplement*** the information in the body of the financial statements, ***not to correct or justify improper presentations*** in the statements.

Some examples of information often disclosed in notes to the financial statements included in annual reports of publicly owned companies are:

1 A summary of significant accounting policies

2 A description of stock option, pension, and employee stock ownership plans

3 Disclosure of litigation in which the company is a party, loss and gain contingencies, and unusual commitments

4 The terms of proposed business combinations and a description of any unusual events or transactions, such as ***related party transactions*** (for example, transactions between the company and its affiliated companies, officers, or directors)

5 The depreciation methods used and the amounts of depreciation expense

6 An analysis of the composition of income taxes expense, including a reconciliation of the company's effective income tax rate with the statutory income tax rate

7 A detailed description or summary of receivables, inventories, investments, plant assets, intangible assets, borrowing arrangements with banks, long-term debt, and shareholders' equity

8 Segment reporting, disclosing financial information by industry and geographical area

This partial list suggests that such notes may be both numerous and complex. With the growing complexity of business and the pressure for ''full and complete disclosure,'' managements and independent accountants face a constant challenge to provide ***sufficient information in concise form*** in notes to the financial statements. Because of its relevance to topics covered throughout this book, the summary of significant accounting policies, usually presented as the first note to the financial statements, deserves special attention.

Summary of Significant Accounting Policies In 1982, the CICA's Accounting Standards Committee stated that:[10]

> The accounting policies adopted by an enterprise affect the financial position, results of operations and changes in financial position, as shown by its financial statements. Accordingly, the usefulness of financial statements is enhanced by disclosure of the accounting policies followed by an enterprise. The Committee has therefore concluded that information on significant accounting policies should be provided for the users of financial statements.

This requirement is also applicable to a ***complete set of interim financial statements***; but it does not apply to interim financial reports, unless the enterprise has changed its accounting policies since the end of the preceding fiscal year or the previous interim period. The disclosure includes a description of the accounting principles used, the methods of applying those principles, and judgements as to the appropriateness of principles relating to revenue recognition and cost allocations among accounting periods. It is particulary important to describe those principles and methods that (1) are peculiar to the industry in which the enterprise operates, (2) have been selected from among other acceptable alternatives, or (3) represent unusual or ''creative'' applications of generally accepted accounting principles.

Examples of disclosures by a business enterprise in a separate section (or a note) entitled ''Summary of Significant Accounting Policies'' include the following:

1. Basis for preparation of consolidated financial statements (principles of consolidation)
2. Method or methods used to compute depreciation, depletion, and amortization
3. Inventory valuation
4. Methods of revenue recognition (especially for revenue from construction-type contracts, instalment sales, franchising contracts, and leasing activities)
5. Any changes in accounting principles during the most recent accounting period

In the final analysis, the principles used in the preparation of financial statements largely determine the integrity and accuracy of financial statements and the ''quality of reported earnings.'' Consequently, the description of accounting policies in the annual report is viewed by many users of financial statements as the key element of the disclosure system of publicly owned companies. The summary of significant accounting policies of a large public company is given in the Appendix at the end of this chapter.

Segment Reporting Many large and highly ***diversified*** business enterprises sell products and services to distinct groups of customers in various geographical areas. Disclosure of information relating to product lines, major customers, export sales, and operations in foreign countries is required by section 1700 of the ***CICA***

10 CICA, ***CICA Handbook***, sec. 1505.03. The Accounting Principles Board in the United States reached the same conclusion; see AICPA, ***APB Opinion No. 22:*** ''Disclosures of Accounting Policies'' (New York: 1972).

Handbook and corporate legislation in order to enable investors to evaluate the activities, growth potential, profitability, and business risks of diversified enterprises. If a diversified enterprise were to report only aggregate results of operations, investors would not be able to assess meaningfully its future growth in revenue and earnings.

In reporting information relating to ***industry segments*** or ***lines of business***, a business enterprise (1) identifies the products and services from which it derives revenue, (2) combines the products and services into meaningful industry segments, and (3) identifies the ***reportable industry segments***, that is, those segments that are ***significant*** with respect to the enterprise as a whole. To be considered significant, and thus reportable, an industry segment must generally have 10% or more of the enterprise's total revenue, operating income, or identifiable assets. Examples of the information disclosed for each reportable industry segment include revenue, income or loss before income taxes, depreciation and amortization expense, identifiable assets, and capital expenditures. Also, similar disclosures for geographical segments and export sales are required.

Subsequent Events The objective of providing users of financial statements with "full and complete disclosure" cannot be achieved without considering material events and transactions that occur after the balance sheet date but before the financial statements are issued. Such ***subsequent events*** may require either an ***adjustment*** of amounts included in the financial statements or simply ***disclosure*** in a note to the financial statements

Adjustment of amounts included in the financial statements is required as a result of subsequent events that provide additional evidence with respect to ***conditions that existed on the balance sheet date*** and materially affect the financial statements. Information that becomes available prior to the issuance of the financial statements should be used by management and independent auditors to measure assets, liabilities, revenue, and expenses reported in the statements. For example, the filing for bankruptcy by a major customer shortly after the balance sheet date, resulting in a material uncollectible trade receivable, would be indicative of conditions existing on that date; thus, this evidence is used to measure the carrying amount of trade receivables and the amount of doubtful accounts expense included in the financial statements.

Disclosure in a note to the financial statements is appropriate when subsequent events provide evidence with respect to ***conditions that did not exist on the balance sheet date*** but have a significant effect on the enterprise's operations. For example, a material write-off of trade receivables as a result of a major catastrophe, such as an earthquake after the balance sheet date, is not indicative of a condition that existed on that date. Therefore, the financial statements would not be adjusted, but the amount of the write-off would be disclosed in a note to the statements. Other examples of subsequent events that ***do not require adjustment but require disclosure*** are listed below:

1 Issuance of material amounts of bonds or capital stock

2 Acquisition or disposal of significant amounts of assets, including those resulting from business combinations

3 Filing or settlement of important litigation

4 Material decline in the replacement cost of inventories not indicative of conditions existing on the balance sheet date.

5 Casualty losses and any other events that may have a material financial impact on the enterprise.

Supplementary Information in Annual Reports

Two special types of supplementary disclosures are discussed and illustrated in the final section of this chapter: (1) interim reports of earnings, and (2) prospective financial statements and forecasts. The first one is required by regulatory authorities and is considered desirable by the CICA's Accounting Standards Committee; and the second is optional. Information relating to inflation and changing prices is a recommended supplementary disclosure for certain large publicly owned companies.[11] This topic is described and illustrated in Chapter 25.

Interim Reports of Earnings

Interim financial information is generally issued quarterly by publicly owned companies and may include current data on financial position, results of operations, and changes in financial position. However, interim financial reports issued to shareholders seldom include a complete set of financial statements. Although practices differ somewhat, most publicly owned companies issue only highly condensed ***interim reports of earnings***, such as the one for Arlington Corporation illustrated below.

Interim report of earnings

ARLINGTON CORPORATION
Income Statements (Unaudited)
(In thousands, except per-share amounts)

	For three months ended		*For nine months ended*	
	Sept. 30, Year 2	*Sept. 30, Year 1*	*Sept. 30, Year 2*	*Sept. 30, Year 1*
Revenue	**$1,238,600**	$1,184,100	**$3,973,900**	$3,428,900
Costs and expenses	**1,221,300**	1,145,500	**3,876,200**	3,319,200
Income before income taxes	**$ 17,300**	$ 38,600	**$ 97,700**	$ 109,700
Income taxes expense	**4,100**	18,500	**39,100**	52,800
Net income	**$ 13,200**	$ 20,100	**$ 58,600**	$ 56,900
Earnings per common share:				
Basic	**$ 0.64**	$ 1.30	**$ 3.25**	$ 3.60
Fully diluted	**$ 0.62**	$ 1.23	**$ 3.20**	$ 3.40
Dividends per common share	**$ 0.40**	$ 0.30	**$ 1.20**	$ 0.90
Average number of common shares outstanding	**17,600**	15,800	**17,600**	15,700

NOTE: Shares outstanding and per-share data have been restated for the 3-for-1 split in Year 1.

11 CICA, *CICA Handbook*, sec. 4510.12.

Publicly owned companies are required by regulatory authorities to issue ***quarterly reports*** to their shareholders and to the regulatory authorities. Such reports are prepared in accordance with standards set forth in section 1750 of the ***CICA Handbook***, "Interim Financial Reporting to Shareholders." An audit of interim reports of earnings is not currently required. However, auditors generally perform a ***review*** of interim financial statements and convey their findings in a report addressed to the company, its board of directors, or its shareholders. The auditors' communication on interim financial statements includes an expression of negative assurance concerning the statements, and each page of the interim financial statements should be clearly marked as "unaudited."

Prospective Financial Statements and Forecasts

One of the objectives of financial statements is to provide information useful for the predictive process. The public accounting profession and the provincial securities commissions have sought to find a satisfactory basis for the preparation and issuance of ***prospective financial statements*** and ***forecasts***, including the expected results of future operations. Virtually every large business enterprise prepares forecasts of future operations as a means of defining goals and measuring performance. The problem is how to make such information available to the investing public yet avoid the danger of misleading the investors.

In 1976, the CICA published a research study on earnings forecasts.[12] Four years later, in response to the proposed regulations of the Ontario Securities Commission, the CICA published ***proposed*** accounting and auditing guidelines for forecast data intended to be included in ***prospectuses***.[13] In 1983, the CICA issued, for inclusion in the ***Handbook***, both the accounting and the auditing guidelines on ***financial forecasts*** which covered more than forecast data for prospectuses.

At one time the SEC in the United States proposed to require companies making earnings forecasts to meet detailed reporting standards, but it eventually withdrew its proposal. The commission currently does not require public companies to file financial forecasts with it; but to encourage such filing the SEC has developed the ***safe-harbour rule for projections***, which protects issuers of erroneous financial forecasts from liability if the forecasts were prepared in good faith and on a reasonable basis. In 1975, the Accounting Standards Division of the AICPA issued ***Statement of Position 75-4*** "as a guide for CPAs in the preparation of financial forecasts for clients."[14] Subsequently, the AICPA prepared a ***Guide for a Review of Financial Forecasts***, which neither requires nor recommends the preparation or review of financial forecasts.

At present, very few companies issue prospective financial statements and forecasts to the public.[15] However, many do issue such statements and forecasts to lenders, underwriters, and prospective investors in connection with raising capital.

12 R. H. Kidd, ***Earnings Forecasts*** (Toronto: CICA, 1976).

13 "Proposed Regulations and Guidelines on Earnings Forecasts," ***CA Magazine***, Aug. 1980, pp. 80–92.

14 AICPA, ***Statement of Position 75-4:*** "Presentation and Disclosure of Financial Forecasts" (New York: 1975).

15 CICA, ***Financial Reporting in Canada***, p. 95.

REVIEW QUESTIONS

1 What are the components of a set of ***general-purpose financial statements***?

2 What is usually included in the heading of a financial statement?

3 Explain the differences between the ***single-step*** form and the ***multiple-step*** form of the income statement. Are earnings-per-share amounts included in both forms?

4 Distinguish between ***functional*** and ***natural*** classifications of costs and expenses in the income statement. What are the advantages of the functional classification of expenses in an income statement prepared for use by management?

5 Define ***prior period adjustments*** and indicate how these are reported in financial statements.

6 What is the major advantage of a combined statement of income and retained earnings? What disadvantages are there in such a statement?

7 List three significant limitations of a balance sheet prepared at the end of a single accounting period as a source of information for use by investors.

8 Dennis Oba is a C.A. In auditing the financial statements of Newport Corporation, Oba found that Newport applied an accounting principle with which he agrees but which has not been accepted by the CICA's Accounting Standards Committee. Assuming that the difference in treatment has a material effect on the financial statements of Newport, what are the alternatives facing Oba in formulating an opinion on the financial statements of Newport?

9
- *a* How is the definition of a ***current liability*** related to the definition of ***current assets***?
- *b* Explain the term ***operating cycle*** and its significance to the classification of assets and liabilities as current or noncurrent.
- *c* Indicate circumstances under which liabilities payable within a few months after the balance sheet date might be excluded from current liabilities.

10 What is the distinction between an ***estimated liability*** and a ***contingent liability***? Give an example of each.

11 The term ***reserve*** has been used by business enterprises to describe, alternately, a contra-asset ledger account, an estimated liability, and an appropriation of retained earnings. Why are these uses objectionable? In which of the three uses is the term least misleading?

12 A balance sheet may be prepared in different forms. List these forms and indicate which is most widely used.

13
- *a* Briefly state the objectives of a ***statement of changes in financial position***.
- *b* What two approaches may be used to prepare the statement of changes in financial position? Which is recommended by the ***CICA Handbook***?

14 Is the independent accounting firm engaged to audit the financial statements primarily responsible for financial statements included in the annual report to shareholders? Explain.

15 What are the usual contents of the annual report to shareholders issued by a publicly owned company?

16 List some examples of information often disclosed in notes to the financial statements included in annual reports to shareholders of publicly owned companies.

17 Describe the type of disclosures made in a note to the financial statements entitled "Summary of Significant Accounting Policies."

18 Identify two types of ***subsequent events*** and indicate how each should be accounted for in the financial statements or disclosed in a note to the statements.

19 What is the usual form of ***interim reports of earnings***? Are such reports audited by independent accountants?

20 *a* What is the reason for disclosure of information relating to ***industry segments*** of a diversified business enterprise?

b What is a ***reportable industry segment*** and what information is disclosed for such a segment?

21 In what ways are ***financial forecasts*** useful to investors in making investment decisions?

EXERCISES

Ex. 4-1 Select the best answer for each of the following multiple-choice questions.

1 The preparation of notes to the financial statements complies with the:
- *a* Business entity principle
- *b* Continuity principle
- *c* Matching principle
- *d* Disclosure principle

2 When a business enterprise receives a deposit from a customer to protect itself against nonpayment for future services, the deposit is classified by the enterprise as:
- *a* Revenue
- *b* A liability
- *c* Part of the allowance for doubtful accounts
- *d* A deferred credit deducted from trade accounts receivable

3 The circulation of items within the current asset category of the balance sheet is termed the:
- *a* Accounting cycle
- *b* Current cycle
- *c* Operating cycle
- *d* Working capital cycle

4 Unamortized discount on bonds payable is presented in the balance sheet as:
- *a* Other noncurrent asset
- *b* A deduction from the face amount of bonds payable
- *c* Short-term prepayment (current asset)
- *d* Part of shareholders' equity

5 Which of the following is often excluded from current liabilities in the balance sheet?
   a Currently maturing portions of long-term debt
   b Income taxes payable
   c Life insurance policy loan payable, regularly renewed on maturity
   d None of the foregoing

6 Which of the following is disclosed in the balance sheet for each class of capital stock?
   a Par or no value of shares
   b Number of shares issued
   c Number of shares outstanding
   d Any dividends or liquidating preference
   e All of the foregoing

7 The following expenses and loss were among those incurred by Kerr Company during Year 2:

Accounting and legal fees	$160,000
Interest	60,000
Loss on disposal of office equipment	25,000
Rent for office space	200,000

One-quarter of the rented premises is occupied by the sales department. How much of the items listed above is included in Kerr's general and administrative expenses for Year 2?
a $310,000 *b* $335,000 *c* $360,000 *d* $370,000 *e* Some other amount

Ex. 4-2 The following are selected ledger account balances for Dinko Corporation for the year ended June 30, Year 10:

Inventories:		Selling expenses	$52,800
June 30, Year 9	$ 35,600	General and administrative	
June 30, Year 10	27,200	expenses	32,400
Sales	374,000	Interest revenue	1,800
Sales returns and allowances	6,480	Dividend revenue	4,000
Sales discounts	5,360	Interest expense	1,000
Purchases	218,200	Income taxes expense	22,000
Freight-in	25,320	Retained earnings:	
Purchases discounts	4,840	June 30, Year 9	80,000
Purchases returns	7,320	June 30, Year 10	88,000

From this information, compute the following for Dinko Corporation for the year ended June 30, Year 10:
a Total net revenue
b Total costs and expenses (including cost of goods sold)
c Net income
d Dividends declared

Ex. 4-3 For the year ended December 31, Year 2, Soledad Corporation had general and administrative expenses of 10% of sales (or 20% of cost of goods sold). Selling expenses equalled 20% of sales. Beginning inventories were $100,000, and purchases amounted to 55% of sales. Income before income taxes of 40% was $80,000.

Prepare Soledad's income statement for the year ended December 31, Year 2. (Show supporting computations.) ***Suggestions***: (1) Compute the cost of goods sold as a percentage of sales by using the information relating general and administrative expenses to cost of goods sold ***and*** to sales; (2) prepare an income statement in percentages, including all items from sales to income before income taxes, with sales representing 100%; and (3) prepare an income statement in dollars, using the dollar amounts given and deriving the other dollar amounts from the percentage relationships.

Ex. 4-4 Here is some information for Canyon Limited for the year ended December 31, Year 5:

Total assets	$2,255,000
Total liabilities	600,000
Preferred stock, no par, 10,000 shares	100,000
Common stock, no par, 300,000 shares	900,000
Prior period adjustment — loss on a lawsuit related to Year 4, net of income tax effect of $57,600	70,400
Net income	175,000
Dividends declared on common stock	60,000
Dividends declared on preferred stock	15,000

Prepare Canyon's statement of retained earnings for the year ended December 31, Year 5.

Ex. 4-5 Edmund Corporation had inventories at the beginning and end of Year 3 as follows:

	Jan. 1	*Dec. 31*
Raw material	$22,000	$30,000
Goods in process	40,000	48,000
Finished goods	25,000	18,000
Totals	$87,000	$96,000

During Year 3, the following costs and expenses were incurred by Edmund:

Raw material purchased	$300,000
Direct labour	120,000
Indirect factory labour	60,000
Property taxes and depreciation of factory building	20,000
Property taxes and depreciation of salesroom and office	15,000

Sales salaries	40,000
Office salaries	24,000
Utilities (60% applicable to factory, 20% to salesroom, and 20% to office)	60,000

Compute Edmund Corporation's cost of goods sold for the year ended December 31, Year 3.

Ex. 4-6 Prepare a skeleton balance sheet as of March 31, Year 5, for a hypothetical corporation, Bozajian Limited, in account form, showing only major classifications (approximately ten group headings).

Ex. 4-7 The balance sheet of Pocono Limited contains the following group headings, which we have coded with letters.

A Current assets
B Investments and restricted funds
C Plant assets
D Intangible assets
E Other noncurrent assets (including deferred charges)
F Current liabilities
G Long-term debt
H Deferred credits
I Invested capital
J Retained earnings

For each of the items listed below indicate the preferable balance sheet classification for Pocono by using the appropriate letter from the listing above. Place parentheses around the letter if the item is to be ***subtracted*** from other items in that classification.

1 Accrued interest on bonds payable
2 Convertible preferred stock
3 Mortgage note payable (outstanding for 12 years; due in two months)
4 Land held for price appreciation
5 Payroll account at Bank of Coe
6 Patents
7 Discount on bonds payable
8 Unexpired insurance
9 Costs for issuing bonds payable
10 Leasehold improvements
11 Allowance for doubtful accounts
12 Cash surrender value of life insurance policies
13 Premium on bonds payable
14 Accumulated depreciation
15 Donated capital
16 Short-term prepayments
17 Machinery retired from use and held for disposal
18 Salaries payable
19 Investment in common stock of Provigo Inc. (100 shares at cost)
20 Advance payments from customers

Ex. 4-8 You have been requested to assist the accountant of Polo Corporation to prepare a balance sheet. The outline presented below, which we have coded with letters, represents the various classifications suggested by the accountant; classification *L* has been added for items to be excluded from the balance sheet. (You are not asked to approve or disapprove the various classifications set forth below.)

A Current assets
B Investments and restricted funds
C Plant assets
D Intangible assets
E Other noncurrent assets (including deferred charges)
F Current liabilities
G Long-term debt (including deferred credits)
H Preferred stock
I Common stock
J Premium on preferred stock
K Retained earnings
L Items excluded from the balance sheet or reported in notes to the financial statements

Using the letters representing the various classifications, identify each of the following items according to the preferred balance sheet presentation for Polo Corporation. If an item is an offsetting or a valuation ledger account, place parentheses around the letter.

1 Dividend payable (on Polo Corporation's preferred stock)
2 Plant assets under construction
3 Goodwill
4 Bond issue costs
5 Land (held for possible future building site)
6 Merchandise (held by Polo Corporation on consignment)

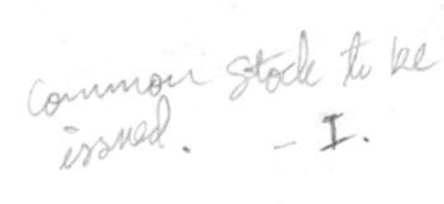

7 Stock dividend to be distributed (on Polo Corporation's common stock)
8 Inventory of office supplies
9 Sinking fund (First National Bank, Trustee)
10 Reserve for retirement of preferred stock
11 Instalment accounts receivable (average collection period 18 months)
12 Preferred stock was issued for more than its par value
13 Advances to officers (indefinite repayment date, non-interest-bearing)
14 Unredeemed merchandise coupons issued to customers
15 Shares of preferred stock held in treasury (at cost)

16 Small tools used in factory
17 Contingent liability from notes receivable discounted at Kong Bank

18 Allowance to reduce inventories to lower of cost or market
19 Common stock subscriptions receivable (considered currently collectible)
20 Common stock subscribed (Polo Corporation's common stock)

Ex. 4-9 From the following list of ledger account balances for Naughton Limited, compute ***a*** the amount of working capital, and ***b*** the equity (book value) per share of common stock:

Investment in affiliated companies (at equity)	$100,000
Cash surrender value of life insurance policies	10,000
Organization costs	5,000
Interest receivable	2,000
Reserve for contingencies (recorded by a debit to Retained Earnings)	50,000
Retained earnings — unappropriated	170,000
Common stock, 80,000 no-par shares	600,000
Deferred income tax credits	40,000

Cost of (construction) contracts in progress (for customers)	150,000
Bond sinking fund	80,000
Liability under product warranty	6,000
Creditors' accounts with debit balances	4,500
Plant assets (net)	426,500
Other current assets	198,000
Other current liabilities	108,000

Ex. 4-10 Listed below are selected ledger account balances of Glendale Company on December 31, Year 10:

Advances from customers	$ 15,000
Unused equipment held for sale	25,600
Bond sinking fund	260,000
Bonds payable (11% interest)	750,000
Discount on bonds payable	15,500
Instalment notes payable (13% interest, due $150,000 a year)	600,000
Salaries payable	72,000
Cash surrender value of life insurance policies	42,100
Unamortized bond issue costs	21,100
Advances to supplies (12% interest, no due date)	100,000

Prepare the Investments and Long-Term Debt sections of Glendale Company's balance sheet on December 31, Year 10.

Ex. 4-11 The December 31, Year 5, balance sheet and other data for Bren Corporation are presented below. These are the only items in Bren's balance sheet. Amounts indicated by ''?'' may be computed from the other data given.

BREN CORPORATION
Balance Sheet
December 31, Year 5

Assets	
Cash	$ 25,000
Trade accounts receivable (net)	?
Inventories	?
Plant assets (net)	294,000
Total assets	$432,000
Liabilities & Shareholders' Equity	
Trade accounts payable	$?
Income taxes payable (current)	25,000
Long-term debt	?
Common stock, no par	300,000
Retained earnings (deficit)	?
Total liabilities & shareholders' equity	$432,000

Additional Information

Current ratio, Dec. 31, Year 5	1.5 to 1
Total liabilities divided by total shareholders' equity, Dec. 31, Year 5	0.8 to 1
Turnover of ending inventories (based on sales) for Year 5	15 times
Turnover of ending inventories (based on cost of goods sold) for Year 5	10.5 times
Gross profit on sales for Year 5	$315,000

Compute the amount of each of the following for Bren Corporation on December 31, Year 5:

a Inventories
b Trade accounts receivable (net)
c Trade accounts payable
d Retained earnings (deficit)
e Long-term debt

CASES

Case 4-1 The combined statements of income and retained earnings shown below were prepared by Modern Fabrics Inc., a retail enterprise that makes most of its sales on credit. Accounts receivable are aged at the end of each accounting period, and the allowance for doubtful accounts is adjusted to an amount required to value receivables at estimated net collectible amount (net realizable value).

MODERN FABRICS INC.
Combined Statements of Income and Retained Earnings
For Years Ended December 31, Year 5, and Year 4

	Year 5	*Year 4*
Revenue:		
Sales, including sales taxes collected	$ 876,900	$ 782,500
Less: Returns, allowances, and sales discounts	18,800	16,200
Net sales	$ 858,100	$ 766,300
Dividends, interest, and purchases discounts	30,250	18,300
Recoveries of receivables written off in prior years	11,800	3,000
Total revenue	$ 900,150	$ 787,600
Costs and expenses:		
Cost of goods sold, including sales taxes paid	$ 415,900	$ 332,200
Salaries and related payroll expenses	60,500	62,100
Rent	19,100	19,100
Freight-in and freight-out	3,400	2,900
Doubtful accounts expense	24,000	26,000
Total costs and expenses	$ 522,900	$ 442,300
Income before extraordinary items	$ 377,250	$ 345,300

Extraordinary items, before income tax effects:		
Loss on discontinued styles (**NOTE 1**)	(24,000)	(4,800)
Loss on sale of short-term investments (**NOTE 2**)	(52,050)	
Loss on sale of investment in an affiliate (**NOTE 3**)	(117,950)	
Net income	$ 183,250	$ 340,500
Retained earnings, beginning of year	312,700	163,100
Subtotals	$ 495,950	$ 503,600
Less: Income taxes expense	(100,000)	(170,000)
Cash dividends	(41,900)	(20,900)
Retained earnings, end of year	$ 354,050	$ 312,700
Earnings per share of common stock	$ 1.83	$ 3.41

NOTE 1: Changes in customer preferences resulted in a loss on the disposal of discontinued styles.
NOTE 2: A short-term investment was sold at a loss.
NOTE 3: The shares of an affiliate were sold during the year at a loss.

Instructions

Identify and discuss any deficiencies in classification and disclosure in the combined statements of income and retained earnings of Modern Fabrics Inc. Explain why you consider these treatments to be deficiencies and what you consider to be the proper treatment of the items. Do not discuss form and terminology, and do not prepare revised combined statements of income and retained earnings.

Case 4-2 Here is the complete set of financial statements issued by Caldera Corporation for the year ended August 31, Year 5:

CALDERA CORPORATION
Combined Statement of Income and Retained Earnings
For Year Ended August 31, Year 5

Sales (net of $850,000 sales returns and allowances)		$10,700,000
Cost of goods sold		8,700,000
Gross profit on sales		$ 2,000,000
Operating expenses:		
Selling expenses	$1,500,000	
General and administrative expenses	940,000	2,440,000
Operating loss		$ (440,000)
Interest expense		(150,000)
Net loss		$ (590,000)
Retained earnings, beginning of year		1,700,000
Subtotal		$ 1,110,000
Dividends declared:		
Cash	$ 40,000	
Common stock	24,000	64,000
Retained earnings, end of year		$ 1,046,000
Average market price of common stock during the year		$ 15

- EPS - missing (not exempt)
- No income taxes expense
- loss carry fwd → notes to fin stat.

CALDERA CORPORATION
Balance Sheet
August 31, Year 5

Assets		
Cash		$ 104,000
Securities, at cost, which approximates market value		54,000
Trade accounts receivable (net of $65,000 allowance)		917,000
Inventories (at cost)		775,000
Plant assets	$3,200,000	
Less: Accumulated depreciation	1,475,000	1,725,000
Prepayments and other assets		125,000
Total assets		$3,700,000
Liabilities & Shareholders' Equity		
Trade accounts payable		$ 222,000
Miscellaneous liabilities		62,000
Bank loans and long-term debt		1,580,000
Total liabilities		$1,864,000
Common stock, no par (unlimited authorized shares, issued and outstanding 42,400 shares)	$ 790,000	
Retained earnings	1,046,000	1,836,000
Total liabilities & shareholders' equity		$3,700,000

Instructions

Identify and discuss any deficiencies and omissions in Caldera Corporation's financial statements for the year ended August 31, Year 5. Consider each deficiency or omission separately, and do not consider the cumulative effect of the deficiencies and omissions. There are no arithmetical errors in the financial statements. Assume that Caldera is not required to report constant purchasing-power or current-cost data.

Case 4-3 When Kelvin Chen, a consulting engineer, developed and patented a device for measuring temperatures encountered in space travel, he offered to sell the patent to Dymo Limited. A contract was signed under which Dymo acquired the patent and gave Chen in exchange $500,000 cash and a promissory note for $500,000. The note provided for payment only in shares of common stock of Dymo at the rate of 4,000 shares of common stock a year for each of the next five years.

The accountant for Dymo included $100,000 among the current liabilities, labelled ''Note Payable in Common Stock,'' and $400,000 among the long-term liabilities, similarly labelled. The accountant attached a note to the financial statements explaining the terms of the contract with Chen.

The president of Dymo, who was about to present Dymo's financial statements to a bank in support of a loan application, objected to this treatment of Dymo's liabilities, contending that they were overstated. The accountant replied that liabilities were obligations to convey something of value, and that

Dymo's common stock had a total value of $500,000, or $100,000 for each year of the five years.

Instructions

a Discuss the appropriate treatment of the note payable in common stock in Dymo's balance sheet, giving reasons for your conclusions.

b Suppose that under the terms of the note, Kelvin Chen had the option of accepting each year $100,000 cash or 4,000 shares of common stock. Would this change your answer? Why?

Case 4-4 Doris Tang owns a resort located on an excellent fishing lake. Her busy season begins May 15 and extends through to mid-fall. During the winter she engaged a contractor to build a boathouse for $50,000. The contract called for completion by May 15, because the resort was completely reserved for the week of May 15 to 22, the opening week of the fishing season. Because the completion date was so important to Tang, she specified in the contract that if the construction were not completed by May 15 the price would be adjusted downward by a penalty of $400 a day until completion.

In fact, the construction was not completed until June 9, at which time Tang paid the contractor $40,000, deducting $400 for each of the 25 days of delay. Tang is convinced that she lost goodwill because her facilities were inadequate and that several of her guests reduced their stay because the boathouse was still under construction.

In her balance sheet prepared on September 30, the end of her fiscal year, Tang included the boathouse at $50,000. Included in her revenue was an item ''Penalty payments received in lieu of lost revenue, $10,000.''

The auditor who examined Tang's balance sheet objected to this treatment of the penalty amount and insisted that the boathouse be recorded at its actual cost, $40,000. Tang could not understand the logic of this position. ''Accounting principles are so out of tune with reality!'' she complained. ''What if the contract had been 125 days late and the boathouse had cost me nothing; would you record in my balance sheet that I had no asset? I lost at least $400 a day in revenue because of the construction delay.''

Instructions

At what amount should the boathouse be reported in Doris Tang's balance sheet on September 30? (You may disregard any question of depreciation from June 9 to September 30.) Explain your position in terms of generally accepted accounting principles.

PROBLEMS

Pr. 4-1 The following information was compiled from the accounting records of Zee Corporation as a basis for preparation of an income statement for the year ended June 30, Year 3:

Inventories, July 1, Year 2	$ 496,300
Inventories, June 30, Year 3	542,700
Purchases returns and allowances	65,200
Common stock, no par, 20,000 shares (no change during year)	200,000
Sales	4,231,200
Sales returns and allowances	44,100
Depreciation expense (75% selling, 25% general and administrative)	220,000
Gain on disposal of equipment	13,500
Rent revenue	15,360
Purchases	3,100,850
Freight-in	123,400
Selling expenses:	
Salaries and wages	301,010
Purchased services	72,150
Supplies	66,050
General and administrative expenses:	
Salaries and wages	420,200
Purchased services	62,800
Supplies	101,100

Assume that Zee Corporation's income tax rate is 45% and that any loss for Year 3 may be carried back to obtain a refund of income taxes paid in the prior year.

Instructions

a Prepare a multiple-step income statement for Zee Corporation for the year ended June 30, Year 3. Include earnings or loss per share in the income statement.

b Prepare a single-step income statement for Zee Corporation for the year ended June 30, Year 3, under a functional classification of expenses. Include earnings or loss per share in the income statement.

Pr. 4-2 Eric's, Inc., is a merchandising enterprise with no par value common stock, of which 100,000 shares were outstanding throughout the year ended April 30, Year 10. In addition to its merchandising activities, Eric's obtains rent revenue of $28,324 a year for a part of its building leased to Western Wood Company.

The following information is available concerning the merchandising activities of Eric's for the year ended April 30, Year 10:

Inventories, April 30, Year 10 (a decrease of $54,264 during the year)	$ 100,944
Purchases of merchandise (of which $11,224 was returned)	737,696
Freight-in	63,504
Sales (of which $21,696 was returned by customers)	1,584,768
Selling expenses (salaries and wages, $122,340; purchased services, $31,248; supplies, $10,224)	163,812
General and administrative expenses (salaries and wages $100,688, purchased services $38,048, supplies $14,832)	153,568
Depreciation expense (75% selling, 25% general and administrative)	67,840

In addition to these operating revenue and expenses, Eric's Inc., incurred interest expense of $11,936 and declared dividends of $50,000. Income taxes expense was $154,000.

Instructions

a Prepare a multiple-step income statement for Eric's, Inc., for the year ended April 30, Year 10. Include earnings per share (rounded to the nearest cent) in the statement.

b Prepare a single-step income statement for Eric's, Inc., for the year ended April 30, year 10, classifying expenses on a natural basis (for example, merchandise and supplies, salaries and wages, purchased services, depreciation, interest, and income taxes) rather than a functional basis. Include earnings per share (rounded to the nearest cent) in the income statement.

Pr. 4-3 The following data were taken from the accounting records of Sunrise Limited for the year ended December 31, Year 5. Income taxes for Year 5 applicable to ordinary income were $72,600. Income taxes applicable to the extraordinary gain were $10,500. Income tax credit applicable to the extraordinary loss was $28,500. Sunrise had 10,000 shares of common stock outstanding throughout Year 5.

Cost of goods sold	$1,020,000
Depreciation expense	30,000
Cash dividends declared	45,000
Extraordinary gain, before income tax effect	35,000
Insurance expense	7,000
Sales	1,500,000
Extraordinary loss, before income tax credit	60,000
Salaries expense	195,000
Retained earnings, Jan. 1, Year 5	1,666,200
Other operating expenses	62,400

Instructions

Prepare a combined statement of income and retained earnings for Sunrise Limited for the year ended December 31, Year 5. Use the single-step form for the revenue and expenses part of the statement, and provide earnings per share (rounded to the nearest cent) in the income statement.

Pr. 4-4 The following ledger account balances (listed in random order) are available for Medov-Lance Corporation on December 31, Year 5, after the accounts were closed:

Income taxes payable (current)	$ 41,625
Cash surrender value of life insurance policies	10,800
Trade accounts receivable (net of $10,000 advances from customers)	92,000
Allowance for doubtful accounts	5,800
Cash on hand	800
Cash in First National Bank	44,025

Cash in Bank of Toronto	26,000
Short-term prepayments	3,500
Retained earnings	222,300
Current portion of 10% note payable	20,000
Long-term portion of 10% note payable (excluding current portion of $20,000)	230,000
Trade accounts payable	220,000
Inventories, at the lower of first-in, first-out and net realizable value	332,600
Short-term investments, at cost (market value, $58,500)	56,800
Buildings and equipment	300,000
Accumulated depreciation of buildings and equipment	109,600
Organization costs	16,000
Common stock, no par, unlimited authorized shares, issued and outstanding 110,000 shares	215,200
Long-term advance to affiliated companies	50,000
Patents (net of accumulated amortization of $18,950)	32,000
Land	100,000

Instructions

Prepare a classified balance sheet for Medov-Lance Corporation on December 31, Year 5, in report form. Use two money columns with rulings as necessary under subtotals. Notes to the financial statements are not required.

Pr. 4-5 The following memorandum contains information concerning the financial position of Valley Commuter Co. Ltd. on December 31, Year 10:

Our plant assets consist of aircraft and other flight equipment acquired at a cost of $10,880,000, on which we have recorded depreciation of $2,431,200 to date. In addition, we have one other aircraft that has been withdrawn from use and has been offered for sale. The carrying amount of this aircraft is $750,000, and we are currently negotiating for its sale at a price of $600,000. The negotiations for this sale soon will be completed; therefore, we have recognized a loss of $150,000.

When we acquired Commerce Parcel Service we paid $550,000 for goodwill, of which $348,000 has been amortized since acquisition.

We have cash in bank accounts amounting to $380,600, and a term deposit (short-term) of $801,600, including accrued interest at 15% a year. The controlling ledger account for trade accounts receivable shows a debit balance of $1,660,000, but this total includes a credit balance of $120,000 from a customer who made an advance payment. The allowance for doubtful accounts amounts to $44,400. Our inventories are carried at weighted-average cost, and amount to $91,200 (net realizable value, $93,000). Short-term prepayments amount to $42,000. The cash surrender value of life insurance policies naming the company as beneficiary amounts to $147,600.

Among our liabilities are $3,000,000 in 8% long-term notes payable, of which $300,000 is due in Year 11. Trade accounts payable total $780,000, accrued liabilities $100,000, and income taxes payable $385,200.

We have 5 million shares of no-par common stock authorized, of which 1,440,000 shares were issued at a price of $5 a share. Our reinvested earnings total $864,200.

Instructions

Use the above information to prepare a balance sheet for Valley Commuter Co. Ltd. on December 31, Year 10, in report form. Use two money columns, with rulings as necessary under subtotals. Notes to the financial statements are not required.

Pr. 4-6 Paradise Corporation had 200,000 shares of common stock outstanding throughout Year 4. Selected information on December 31, Year 4, is presented below:

Retained earnings, Jan. 1, Year 4	$2,444,100
Inventories, Jan. 1, Year 4	192,500
Gain on sale of a long-term investment, net of income tax effect of $32,000	96,000
Purchases	1,510,000
Sales	2,195,000
Royalties revenue	24,100
Inventories, Dec. 31, Year 4	208,000
Selling expenses	120,400
Sales returns, allowances, and discounts	25,100
Purchases returns, allowances, and discounts	23,450
Dividends declared	176,000
Gain on disposal of equipment	27,500
Income taxes applicable to results from operations	192,500
General and administrative expenses	197,550
Prior period adjustment: decrease in retained earnings on Jan. 1, Year 4, as a result of settlement of a litigation related to Year 3, net of income tax effect of $81,500	117,000
Loss from disposal during Year 4 of a business segment (net of income tax credit of $62,000)	84,000

Instructions

a Prepare an income statement for Paradise Corporation for the year ended December 31, Year 4, in single-step form. (A number of account balances may be combined to obtain summary amounts to appear in the single-step form for the income statement.) Include earnings per share (rounded to the nearest cent) in the income statement.

b Prepare a statement of retained earnings for Paradise Corporation for the year ended December 31, Year 4.

Pr. 4-7 The following information was available about Clark Corporation on December 31, Year 8:

Sales	$1,847,500
Extraordinary item (gain), net of income tax effect of $180,000	220,000
Prior period adjustment (debit balance, after applicable income tax credit of $90,000)	110,000
Dividends declared	240,000
Purchases	1,392,000
Purchases discounts	20,000
Inventories, Jan. 1, Year 8	146,000
Income taxes applicable to ordinary income	117,000
Selling expenses	100,000
General and administrative expenses	96,000
Inventories, Dec. 31, Year 8	152,000
Sales returns and allowances	25,500
Cumulative effect on prior years' net income of change in accounting principle (credit balance, net of income tax effect of $40,500)	49,500

The retained earnings on January 1, Year 8, were originally reported at $1,888,400. There were 100,000 shares of common stock outstanding throughout Year 8.

Instructions

a Prepare a multiple-step income statement for Clark Corporation, including earnings per share, for the year ended December 31, Year 8.

b Prepare a statement of retained earnings for Clark Corporation for the year ended December 31, Year 8.

Pr. 4-8 The condensed balance sheet of Tech Research, Inc., on June 30, Year 4, is presented below:

TECH RESEARCH, INC.
Condensed Balance Sheet
June 30, Year 4

Assets		*Liabilities & Shareholders' Equity*	
Current assets	$1,500,000	Current liabilities	$ 560,000
Noncurrent assets (net)	6,860,000	Long-term debt	2,500,000
		Contributed capital	3,800,000
		Retained earnings	1,500,000
Total assets	$8,360,000	Total liabilities & shareholders' equity	$8,360,000

Below are comments taken from an auditor's notes, describing certain components of the balance sheet. Some of them indicate that the accountant for Tech Research, Inc., has handled certain items improperly.

1 Included in long-term debt is a loan payable of $250,000 due on April 30, Year 5.

2 A $125,000 dividend to be distributed in the form of Tech Research's common stock is included in current liabilities.

3 Included in current liabilities is a contingent liability of $50,000 for possible lawsuits that may be filed. This amount was recorded by a debit to Retained Earnings.

4 Included in current assets is $90,000 in cash surrender value of life insurance policies on the lives of Tech Research's officers. Included in long-term debt is an $80,000 loan made against this cash surrender value. Tech Research intends to renew this borrowing annually on the maturity date of the loan.

5 Discount on long-term debt of $161,500 is included in noncurrent assets.

6 Included in long-term debt is a $500,000 appropriation of retained earnings for retirement of preferred stock.

7 Tech Research acquired 11,000 shares of its outstanding common stock for $400,000. This amount is included in noncurrent assets.

8 Rent received in advance, $74,800, is included in retained earnings.

9 A cash dividend of $80,000 declared on June 15, Year 4, and payable on July 22, Year 4, has not been recorded.

10 A fully depreciated plant asset was sold for $40,000, and the proceeds were credited to the Equipment ledger account.

11 Deposits of $25,000 made with suppliers for goods ordered have been netted against the balance in the accounts payable controlling ledger account.

12 An investment in the common stock of a supplier is included in current assets at a cost of $800,000.

Instructions

a List the dollar amounts of each of the six categories of the June 30, Year 4, balance sheet of Tech Research, Inc., on the first line of a six-column working paper. On separate lines below this show the effect of any necessary corrections to the accountant's amounts as a result of the information contained in the auditor's notes. Identify each correction with the related number above. Show as an end result the corrected balance sheet data on June 30, Year 4. If the information contained in any of the auditor's notes does not indicate any improper treatment, explain briefly why no adjustment is necessary in each case. Disregard income taxes.

b Would your appraisal of Tech Research's financial position on June 30, Year 4, be changed as a result of the revised data? Explain.

Pr. 4-9 The controller of Breeze Corporation must prepare a statement of working capital on June 30, Year 3. The purpose of this statement is to demonstrate that Breeze's working capital exceeds $750,000, the amount Breeze agreed to maintain under terms of a loan contract. The statement below was prepared by the assistant to the controller from information obtained from Breeze's accounting records:

BREEZE CORPORATION
Statement of Working Capital
June 30, Year 3

Current assets:		
Cash on hand and in banks		$ 157,500
Notes and securities		480,000
Receivables		542,500
Inventories and prepayments		562,300
Total current assets		$1,742,300
Current liabilities:		
Notes and accounts payable	$411,530	
Payroll taxes and pensions payable	495,000	
Reserve for contingencies	200,000	
Total current liabilities		1,106,530
Working capital		$ 635,770

The controller, after some investigation, made the following notes relative to the items included in the foregoing statement of working capital:

1 ***Notes and securities*** Includes $280,000 of notes receivable, of which $100,000 has been discounted at a bank. Also, $250,000 face amount of marketable securities (current market value $236,000) acquired for $216,000, on which $8,500 of interest has accrued since the last interest date. Breeze holds $84,000 in five-year notes receivable from a subsidiary company, on which $5,200 of interest is accrued on June 30 and is payable annually.

2 *Receivables* A single controlling account is used for receivables. The balance of the controlling account, $542,500, includes trade accounts receivable of $394,040, a current receivable from a subsidiary company of $40,000, current advances to employees of $28,460, and an instalment note receivable of $80,000 received in payment for the sale of a warehouse, due in four instalments of $20,000 a year; accrued interest on this note on June 30 was $4,800. Certain customers have credit balances in their accounts, totalling $35,000, because they have made advances prior to the shipment of merchandise ordered. Of the trade accounts receivable, $12,000 are worthless and should be written off; it is estimated that $20,000 of the remaining trade accounts receivable will prove uncollectible.

3 *Inventories and prepayments* The inventory of merchandise on June 30 on a last-in, first-out cost basis amounted to $320,750; its current replacement cost is estimated to be $471,000. Included in the $562,300 balance is $98,000 of equipment that is rented to customers and $19,750 of merchandise on order for delivery in six months, the full cost of which is included in trade accounts payable. Also included in the $562,300 balance are short-term prepayments of $94,800 and $29,000 representing a defalcation loss, of which $25,000 is expected to be recovered from an insurance company.

4 *Current liabilities* Current trade accounts payable amount to $261,530 and Breeze owes $150,000 on a 90-day note payable to the bank, on which unrecorded interest of $900 has accrued. Amounts withheld from employees for various payroll taxes amount to $70,000; Breeze's required contribution of $28,700 for such taxes has not been recorded. A provision for employee pensions amounts to $425,000, of which $51,500 will be paid in the coming fiscal year. The "reserve for contingencies" was set up to provide for ***possible*** losses that may result from the obsolescence of plant assets. The reserve was established by a debit to Retained Earnings.

Instructions

a On the basis of the foregoing information, prepare a corrected statement of working capital for Breeze Corporation on June 30, Year 3. List current assets in detail, followed by current liabilities. Provide supporting computations to show how specific items were determined.

b Is Breeze Corporation complying with the terms of the loan contract as to the maintenance of working capital?

c Compute Breeze Corporation's current ratio on June 30, Year 3.

Pr. 4-10 Here is the alphabetical list of account balances (before the Income Summary and Dividends ledger accounts were closed) taken from the ledger of Westmont Limited on December 31, Year 2:

Accounts payable	$ 743,400
Accounts receivable	1,016,000
Accumulated depreciation of buildings	1,104,000
Accumulated depreciation of leased equipment	220,000
Allowance for doubtful accounts	36,000
Buildings	3,951,800
Cash	164,100
Cash surrender value of life insurance policies	115,000
Common stock, no par, unlimited authorized shares, issued 50,000 shares	2,500,000
Dividends: common stock	125,000
Dividends: preferred stock	45,500
Goodwill (net)	62,400
Income summary (credit balance)	208,000
Income taxes payable	92,600
Insurance claim receivable (approved by insurance company)	250,000
Inventories, at lower of first-in, first-out and replacement cost	1,146,000
Issue costs on note payable	10,000
Land	800,000
Leased equipment under capital leases	1,400,000
Liability under capital leases (including current portion of $120,000)	1,050,000
Note payable, 9%, due Oct. 1, Year 10	1,000,000
Preferred stock, 7%, $100 par, authorized 10,000 shares	650,000
Premium on note payable	30,000
Premium on preferred stock	295,000
Retained earnings, Jan. 1, Year 2	1,344,800
Short-term investments (market value $205,000)	200,000
Unearned rent	12,000

Instructions

a Prepare a classified balance sheet for Westmont Limited on December 31, Year 2.

b Prepare a statement of retained earnings for Westmont Limited for the year ended December 31, Year 2.

Pr. 4-11 In the following trial balance for Chan Corporation, all amounts have been properly adjusted, except income taxes expense and related accounts:

CHAN CORPORATION
Trial Balance
December 31, Year 5

	Debit	*Credit*
Cash	$ 360,000	
Trade accounts receivable (net)	1,300,000	
Inventories	2,700,000	
Buildings and equipment	11,250,000	
Accumulated depreciation of buildings and equipment		$ 2,875,000
Land	1,750,000	
Notes payable (due in Year 6)		500,000
Trade accounts payable		1,200,000
Income taxes payable		125,000

Deferred income tax credits		410,000
Bonds payable (due in Year 14)		2,900,000
Common stock, no par (no change during year), issued and outstanding, 500,000 shares		5,200,000
Retained earnings, Jan. 1, Year 5		3,000,000
Dividends	550,000	
Net sales		12,840,000
Cost of goods sold	8,100,000	
Operating expenses	2,440,000	
Interest expense	210,000	
Gain on disposal of equipment		60,000
Gain on disposal of Disco Division		250,000
Loss from expropriation of assets by government	200,000	
Income taxes expense	500,000	
Totals	$29,360,000	$29,360,000

Additional Information

1 Income taxes expense in the adjusted trial balance consisted of the following:

Payments made in Year 5	$375,000
Add: Estimated amount accrued on Dec. 31, Year 5	125,000
Total debited to Income Taxes Expense ledger account	$500,000

The recorded income taxes expense does not properly reflect current or deferred income taxes expense or intraperiod income tax allocation.

2 The effective income tax rate for Chan is 40%, which is also applicable to extraordinary items. Its taxable income for Year 5 was $2,000,000 (an additional depreciation of $200,000 was claimed for income tax purposes).

3 On September 30, Year 5, Chan sold its Disco Division for $3,800,000. The carrying amount of the Disco Division was $3,550,000 on that date. For financial accounting, this was a disposal of a business segment.

4 On June 30, Year 5, Chan's subsidiary was expropriated by a foreign government, occasioning a loss of $200,000.

Instructions

a Prepare an income statement for Chan Corporation in multiple-step form for the year ended December 31, Year 5, including earnings per share rounded to the nearest cent. Allocate income taxes as required by generally accepted accounting principles and disregard notes to the financial statements.

b Prepare a statement of retained earnings for Chan Corporation for the year ended December 31, Year 5.

c Prepare a balance sheet in report form for Chan Corporation as of December 31, Year 5.

Pr. 4-12 In January, Year 11, Paramount Limited was seeking a short-term loan to finance a seasonal buildup of inventories and to pay a maturing instalment on its serial bonds payable. Anthony Manos, the loan officer of Coe National Bank, reviewed Paramount's loan application. Included there was the following balance sheet prepared by an inexperienced accountant employed by Paramount:

PARAMOUNT LIMITED
Balance Sheet
December 31, Year 10

Assets		*Equities*	
Cash	$ 78,700	Payable to suppliers	$ 186,000
Trade receivables	294,300	Miscellaneous accrued expenses	23,800
Inventories	376,200	Reserve for current income taxes	50,000
Land, buildings, and equipment	940,000	Serial bonds payable, 9%	450,000
Marketable securities	98,600	Reserve for depreciation	420,000
Prepaid expenses	18,400	Reserve for bad debts	11,800
Notes receivable	43,000	Reserve for product warranty	10,900
Patents (net)	75,000	Common stock	225,000
Discount on bonds payable	22,500	Preferred stock	206,000
Organization costs (net)	35,000	Earned surplus	398,200
Total assets	$1,981,700	Total equities	$1,981,700

After some study of this balance sheet, Manos decided to ask Paramount to have its financial statements audited by a firm of independent accountants. During the audit, the following additional information was accumulated:

1 Cash included demand deposits of $59,000, cash change funds of $800, and an IOU signed by Paramount's president for $18,900. (The IOU was collected on January 10, Year 11.)

2 The balance of trade receivables consisted of the following:

Trade accounts receivable	$331,500
Advances to employees for expenses, to be covered by expense reports submitted monthly	12,800
Claim for insurance recovery on damages to equipment	35,000
Less: Customers' deposits on goods ordered	(85,000)
Total trade receivables	$294,300

3 Approximately $14,700 of trade accounts receivable were uncollectible.

4 The cost of land owned by Paramount was $40,000, of buildings $750,800, and of equipment $299,200. The carrying amount of the buildings had been reduced by $150,000, representing an 11% mortgage note due on June 30, Year 15, on which interest of $8,250 was accrued but unrecorded on December 31, Year 10. The interest on the mortgage note was payable annually on June 30. Accumulated depreciation was as follows: buildings $240,000, equipment $180,000.

5 Marketable securities consisted of the following:

		Cost	Market value
Short-term investments		$20,000	$20,800
Second mortgage promissory note receivable from Rue Company, a supplier		66,390	?
Cash surrender value of life insurance policies		10,000	10,000
Accrued interest:			
Short-term investments	$ 250		
Second mortgage promissory note receivable from Rue Company	1,960	2,210	2,210
Total cost of marketable securities		$98,600	

6 The inventories listed below were valued at lower of weighted-average cost and net realizable value:

Raw material	$207,380
Goods in process	17,530
Finished goods	151,290
Total inventories	$376,200

7 Notes receivable were short-term and acquired in exchange for trade accounts receivable; unrecorded accrued interest on December 31, Year 10 was $900. It was estimated that $2,400 of the trade notes receivable would prove uncollectible.

8 In Year 9, Paramount issued $500,000 of 9% serial bonds maturing in annual instalments of $50,000. Of the total, $50,000, plus unrecorded accrued interest of $40,500, is due on January 1, Year 11. The bond discount had been correctly amortized in Year 10: the amount of discount applicable to the current portion of serial bonds payable was $500.

9 The reserve for product warranty represented the amount of the estimated obligation to service Paramount's products for a period of six months following sale.

10 Common stock consisted of 15,000 shares of no-par stock issued at $15 a share; preferred stock consisted of 2,000 shares of 10%, $100 par stock issued at $103 a share, callable at 105 a share. An unlimited number of shares of each class of stock was authorized to be issued.

11 Paramount was presently a defendant in a lawsuit with a potential loss that exceeded the insurance coverage. Paramount's lawyer was of the opinion that the outcome of the litigation would probably not have a material effect on Paramount's financial position and results of operations.

Instructions

Using the information accumulated during the audit, prepare a revised balance sheet on December 31, Year 10, with improved terminology for Paramount Limited. Prepare a separate supporting exhibit for the computation of the revised balance of retained earnings. Make adequate disclosure of the status of litigation against Paramount.

APPENDIX: FINANCIAL REVIEW AND FINANCIAL STATEMENTS FOR A LARGE PUBLIC COMPANY

FINANCIAL REVIEW

SEGMENTED ANALYSIS

Sector	System-wide sales	Growth	Net sales	Growth	Income	Growth	Return
Food	4,524	13%	3,692	13%	48.3	30%	21%
Provigo Corp.	446	1%	446	1%	6.2	(6%)	13%
Medis	824	35%	792	35%	8.0	3%	14%
C Corp.	474	–	319	–	8.7	19%	24%
Specialty Retailing	186	15%	152	9%	0.8	(77%)	2%
Total	6,454	13%	5,401	14%	72,0	16%	17%

Provigo once again experienced a year of rapid growth during which it met or surpassed all of its objectives.

System-wide sales, defined as the total retail sales of stores operating under its various banners, plus wholesale shipments to other clients, increased by 13% to $ 6.5 billion.

Net sales made up of wholesale shipments to affiliated and franchised stores and retail sales of corporate stores reached $ 5.4 billion, a 14% increase over the previous year. This growth in sales compares favorably with the 4% rise in the Consumer Price Index during the same period.

Earnings before income taxes increased by 30% to $ 115.0 million, due mainly to major improvements in the income of both Provigo Distribution and Loeb, which more than offset the decline in earnings at Sports Experts. Income before extraordinary items improved by 25%. Growth in income before extraordinary items was hampered by a $ 5.3 million increase in the Company's tax burden as a result of the elimination of the inventory tax allowance and the full-year effect of surtaxes on corporate income introduced last year.

Despite a 6% increase in the average number of outstanding shares following the issue of 2.5 million new shares in December 1985, earnings per share before extraordinary items amounted to $ 1.43, up 18% over last year. Return on average shareholders' equity once again surpassed 20%.

A $ 4.9 million net gain posted as an extraordinary item stemmed from an $ 8.6 million gain on the disposal of Montreal City and District Savings Bank shares; net of $ 3.7 million deducted to cover losses and provision for losses associated with the sale and closure of several supermarkets in the Montreal region and the termination of retail operations of the Company's American subsidiary.

Earnings per share after extraordinary items is $ 1.54, compared to $ 0.86 last year.

FOOD GROUP

The performance of all three companies comprising the Food Group improved in fiscal 1987.

Provigo Distribution Inc.

Wholesale and Retail Operations

The opening of new Maxi stores, Heritage stores and Provigo supermarkets, as well as the acquisition of the Octofruit chain and the launch of the new Proprio banner, generated a 18% increase in system-wide sales. The program to rationalize retail operations was completed and the number of corporate Provigo supermarkets was reduced from 77 to 44 during the year. Several other factors contributed to the increase in income. The most important of these were the growth in sales to affiliated stores and a reduction in the number of working days lost due to labor conflicts.

Food Service

Acquisition of Alphonse Allard Inc at the end of fiscal 1986, of Waldman Fisheries Company Limited and Le Groupe Landry Inc. during the last fiscal year had a positive impact on the growth of Provigo Distribution.

INCOME BEFORE INCOME TAXES

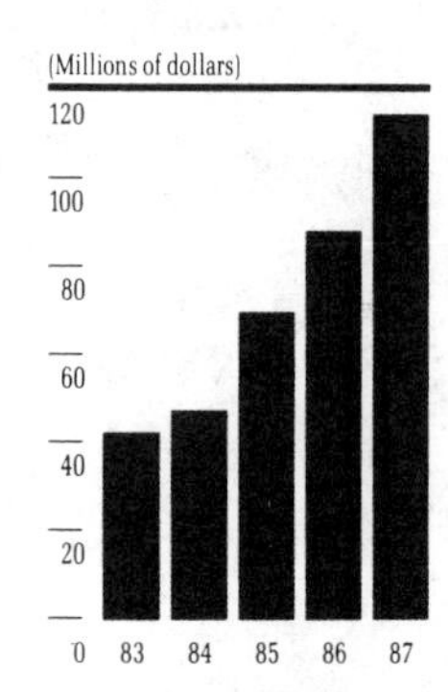

Loeb

An increase in productivity at Loeb IGA supermarkets, where sales per square foot increased by 12%, was the principal reason for both the 9% rise in system-wide sales and the growth in income.

Horne & Pitfield

In Alberta, Horne & Pitfield's income improved and system-wide sales grew 4% despite increased competition and an economic situation that remains difficult.

The Food Group's capital expenditures of $ 55.6 million, included primarily the construction of new Maxi stores, the renovation of several corporate supermarkets and the upgrading of distribution centers in Ontario.

The sale or closing of certain Provigo Supermarkets, however, led to a $ 30.0 million reduction in the amount of average net assets employed.

EARNINGS & DIVIDENDS PER SHARE

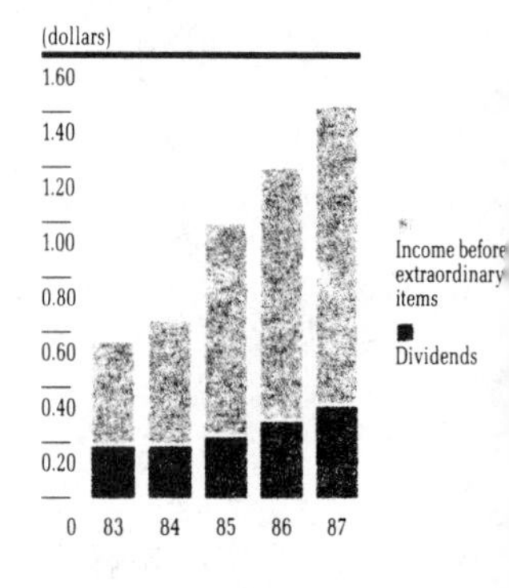

STOCK MARKET VALUE MONTREAL EXCHANGE

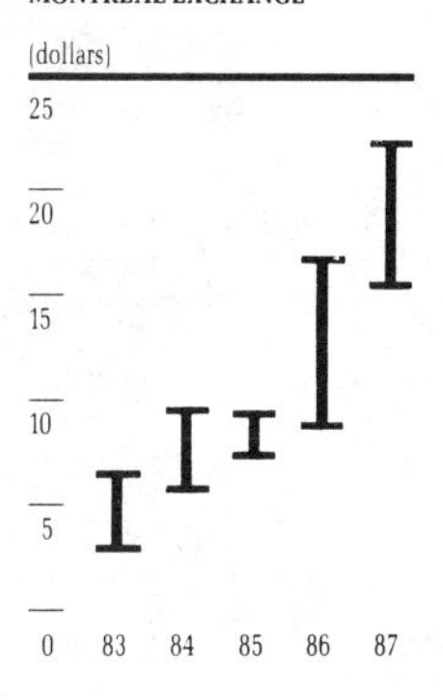

EQUITY & TOTAL DEBT

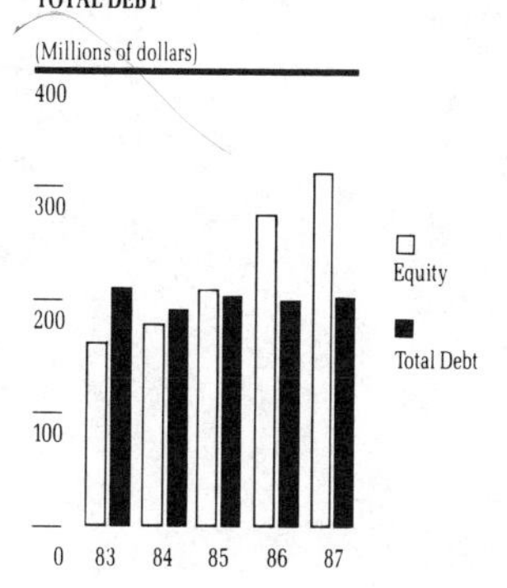

FUNDS FROM OPERATIONS

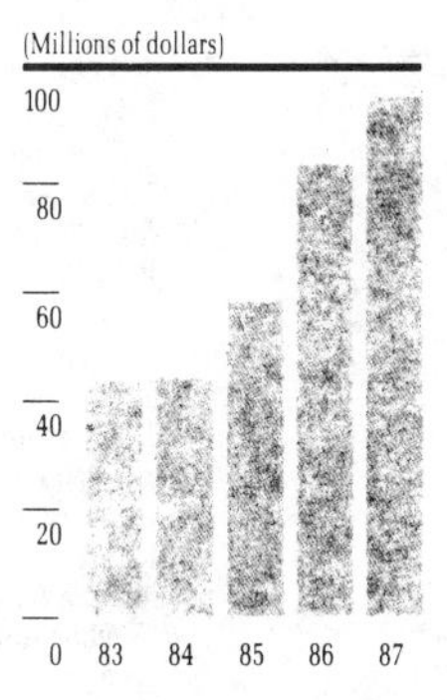

CAPITAL EXPENDITURES & DEPRECIATION

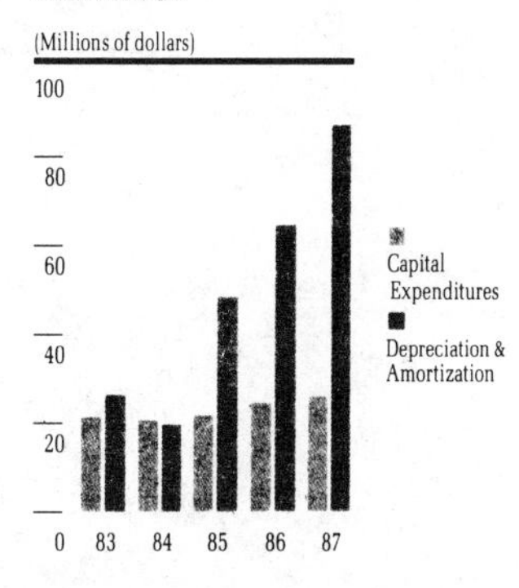

PROVIGO CORP.

The sales and profit margins of the USA Group were affected by the fierce competition in Northern California that comes essentially from the rapid development of super-warehouse stores. Despite this difficult situation, Provigo Corp. performed satisfactorily.

MEDIS

The supply contracts signed with Uniprix, Maxi-Santé and Lawton's, the acquisition of Southwestern Drug Warehouse Ltd in British Columbia and the strong growth in the demand for pharmaceutical products and health-care items contributed to the improvement in Medis sales.

Because of the start-up costs associated with the Uniprix and Boots supply contracts, income grew at a slower pace than sales.

To supply its fast-growing clientele, Medis built new distribution centers and increased its non-cash working capital. As a result, the value of average net assets employed increased by $ 20.3 million, $ 9.9 million of which was allocated to capital expenditures.

C CORP.

C Corp. was noteworthy for its improved income in Quebec as well as its program to rationalize stores in Ontario.

In Quebec, the 13% improvement in system-wide sales of convenience store products stemmed from a 6% average growth in sales per store, whose number grew by 9 outlets. The increase in the number of stores twinned with gas stations boosted the volume of petroleum product sales by 8%. These various factors account for the growth in C Corp.'s income in Quebec.

In Ontario, the rationalization program included the reorganizing of the Pinto stores and the opening of the first Winks convenience store.

C Corp.'s capital expenditures, which totalled $ 9.1 million, were applied to building Provi-Soir outlets in Quebec and a Winks store in Ontario. These expenditures account for the $ 2.0 million increase in average net assets employed.

SPECIALTY RETAILING GROUP

Sports Experts

Sales at Sports Experts climbed mainly due to an increase in the number of stores. The economic situation in Western Canada as well as poor weather conditions had a negative impact on the Company's income. In addition, the costs related to the consolidation of the administrative and distribution activities following the merger with Collegiate/Arlington and the closure of certain corporate stores whose profitability was considered inadequate, affected income growth. The reorganization and rationalization of activities in the Collegiate/Arlington post-merger period have now been completed.

Capital expenditures, which totalled $ 10.0 million, were primarily applied to expanding the Montreal distribution center and the construction of a store in Mont Ste-Anne. These investments, and the changes made to the method of paying for imported goods, led to a $ 9.0 million increase in average net assets employed.

Consumers Distributing

Provigo's share of Consumers Distributing's profits was $ 0.8 million higher than last year. Improved earnings from operations both in Canada and on the East Coast of the United States are the principal reasons for this improvement. However, these gains were partly offset by an increase in the tax burden in Canada, which led to an additional $ 4.2 million levy on Consumers Distributing income.

WORKING
CAPITAL RATIO

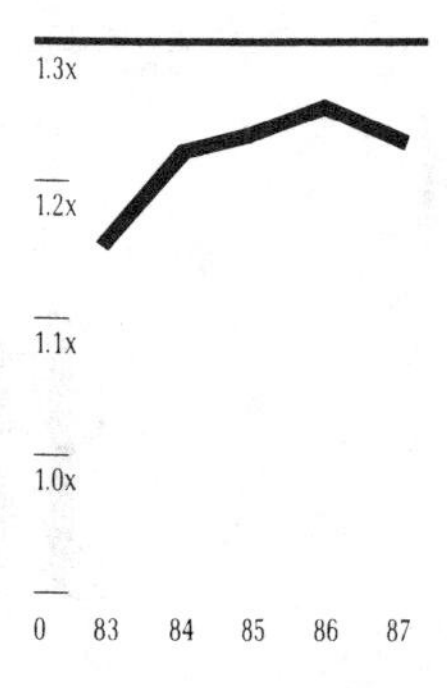

FIXED RATE DEBT

(in percentage of the total debt)

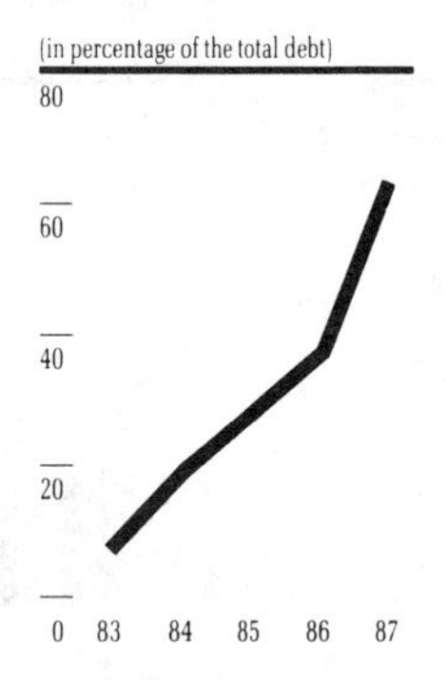

LIQUIDITY AND CAPITAL RESOURCES

The consolidated program of **capital expenditures** amounted to $ 86.2 million. Non-cash working capital was $ 48.0 million higher than last year. The acquisition of le Groupe Landry Inc., Octofruit, Pharmacom Systems Limited, Waldman Fisheries Company Limited and Southwestern Drug Warehouse Limited, cost $ 22.0 million. Dividends paid on common shares totalled $ 14.5 million, which represents 30% of the previous year's income before extraordinary items.

For fiscal 1987, **working capital** from operations, excluding extraordinary items, reached $ 95.4 million, up $ 12.5 million over last year. This growth stems mainly from the increase in income before extraordinary items. Sales of fixed assets amounted to $ 29.2 million, primarily the result of selling stores to new affiliates as part of the program to rationalize retail operations at Provigo Distribution and Sports Experts. Disposal of Montreal City and District Savings Bank shares generated $ 14.6 million net.

A $ 45.7 million net reduction in **liquidity** and $ 11.2 million increase in **long-term debt** were the other main sources of financing. The net reduction in liquidity meant a $ 30.5 million decrease in cash and a $ 15.2 million increase in bank loans and outstanding cheques. This change in liquidity is the major reason for the decline in the working capital ratio from 1.26 last year to 1.23.

Despite this $ 45.7 million reduction in liquidity and the $ 11.2 million increase in long-term debt, average total debt was lower than last year. This improvement reflects the impact of the 2.5 million share issue in December 1985 and the sale of Montreal City and District Savings Bank shares in the first half of the fiscal year. The reduction in interest expense is the result of this decline in average total debt.

The strengthening of the Company's financial position was confirmed by the Canadian Credit Rating Corporation and Dominion Bond Rating Services, which gave Provigo debentures an A rating. The Canadian Credit Rating Corporation also raised the rating of Provigo's promissory notes to A-1 while Dominion Bond Rating Service rated them R-1 (low). Following a $ 37.8 million increase in shareholders' equity and a slight rise in total borrowing of $ 4.2 million, Provigo's debt: equity ratio improved from 42:58 at the end of last year to 40:60 at the end of this year.

During the year, the Company reorganized its debt structure. $ 50 million of 9.80% unsecured debentures maturing in 1997 were issued with the proceeds applied to redeeming $ 20.0 million in Series D sinking fund debentures as well as to repaying various bank loans. Through the repayment of these floatin interest rate loans and an issue of fixed interest rate debentures, the percentage of fixed-rat borrowing this year climbed to 63% from 37% the year before. In addition, Provigo launched promissory note program.

As for its capital stock, the Company redeeme the 375,000 Series A preferred shares at par value for a total of $ 9.4 million.

SUBSEQUENT EVENTS

At the beginning of the fiscal year 1988, Provig continued its investments in the food service sector through the acquisition of Bronstein Bros (Que.) Limited and Pêcheries St-Laurent Inc. In addition, the Company sold its interest in Brico Centre (Canada) Inc.

CONCLUSION

With 18% growth in income per share, a 20.5% return on average equity, a 40% debt: equity ratio and dividends that represent 30% of its profits, Provigo attained or surpassed all of its financial objectives.

Henri A. Roy
Executive Vice President

PROVIGO INC.

MANAGEMENT'S RESPONSIBILITY FOR CONSOLIDATED FINANCIAL STATEMENTS

The consolidated financial statements of Provigo Inc. are the responsibility of management and have been approved by the Board of Directors. This responsibility includes the selection of appropriate accounting principles and the exercise of a careful judgement in establishing reasonable and accurate estimates in accordance with generally accepted accounting principles appropriate in the circumstances. Financial information shown elsewhere in this annual report is consistent with that contained in the consolidated financial statements.

Management of Provigo Inc. and its subsidiaries has developed and maintains accounting systems and internal controls designed to provide reasonable assurance that assets are safeguarded from loss or unauthorized use and that the financial records are reliable for preparing the financial statements.

The Board of Directors carries out its responsibility with regards to the consolidated financial statements principally through its Audit Committee, consisting solely of outside directors. The Audit Committee reviews the annual consolidated financial statements and recommends their approval to the Board of Directors. The Audit Committee periodically reviews the results of audit examinations performed by the internal auditors and independent external auditors with respect to the Company's accounting principles, practices and systems of internal control.

These financial statements have been examined by Clarkson Gordon and Raymond, Chabot, Martin, Paré, Chartered Accountants and their report stating the extent of their audit examination and their opinion on the consolidated financial statements is presented below.

Chairman, Chief Executive Officer
and President,

Pierre Lortie

Senior Vice-President,
Control and Corporate services,

David R. Friesen

AUDITORS' REPORT

To the Shareholders of Provigo Inc.

We have examined the consolidated balance sheet of Provigo Inc. as at January 31, 1987 and the consolidated statements of income, retained earnings and changes in financial position for the year then ended and have obtained all the information and explanations we have required. Our examination was made in accordance with generally accepted auditing standards, and accordingly included such tests and other procedures as we considered necessary in the circumstances.

In our opinion, and according to the best of our information and the explanations given to us, and as shown by the books of the Company, these consolidated financial statements are drawn up so as to exhibit a true and correct view of the state of the affairs of the Company as at January 31, 1987 and the results of its operations and the changes in its financial position for the year then ended in accordance with generally accepted accounting principles applied on a basis consistent with that of the preceding year.

Clarkson Gordon
Chartered Accountants

Raymond, Chabot, Martin, Paré
Chartered Accountants

Montreal, Canada
March 20, 1987

PROVIGO INC.

CONSOLIDATED STATEMENT OF INCOME

year ended January 31, 1987 (Millions of dollars)	1987 (53 weeks)	1986 (52 weeks)
Net sales	**5,401.6**	4,746.1
Cost of sales and operating expenses	**5,245.0**	4,614.2
Operating income	**156.6**	131.9
Depreciation and amortization	**25.7**	24.4
Interest – net	**16.6**	19.0
Share of net income of affiliated companies	**0.7**	(0.2)
Income before income taxes	**115.0**	88.3
Income taxes	**54.8**	39.4
Income before minority interest	**60.2**	48.9
Minority interest	**(0.1)**	0.6
Income before extraordinary items	**60.3**	48.3
Extraordinary items	**4.9**	(13.8)
Net income	**65.2**	34.5
Earnings per common share:		
Before extraordinary items		
basic	**$1.43**	$1.21
fully diluted	**$1.36**	$1.15
After extraordinary items		
basic	**$1.54**	$0.86
fully diluted	**$1.46**	$0.82

CONSOLIDATED STATEMENT OF RETAINED EARNINGS

year ended January 31, 1987 (Millions of dollars)	1987 (53 weeks)	1986 (52 weeks)
Retained earnings, beginning of year	**163.0**	141.6
Net income	**65.2**	34.5
Dividends paid	**(14.9)**	(12.0)
Share issue costs	–	(1.1)
Retained earnings, end of year	**213.3**	163.0

The summary of significant accounting policies and the accompanying notes are an integral part of the consolidated financial statements.

PROVIGO INC.

CONSOLIDATED BALANCE SHEET

	January 31, 1987 (Millions of dollars)	1987	1986
Current assets	Cash and deposit certificates	**5.6**	36.1
	Receivables	**263.6**	191.7
	Inventories	**345.2**	299.0
	Prepaid expenses	**11.0**	8.5
		625.4	535.3
Current liabilities	Bank loans and acceptances	**30.7**	35.0
	Cheques issued and outstanding	**53.3**	33.8
	Payables and accrued liabilities	**373.5**	322.1
	Income and other taxes	**47.5**	24.7
	Current portion of long-term debt and capital leases	**4.9**	9.1
		509.9	424.7
	Working capital	**115.5**	110.6
Other assets	Investments	**76.1**	63.9
	Fixed assets	**262.3**	230.8
	Deferred income taxes	**–**	3.7
	Sundry assets	**39.1**	30.2
		377.5	328.6
	Assets employed	**493.0**	439.2
Other liabilities	Long-term debt	**143.5**	127.8
	Obligations under capital leases	**27.6**	30.6
	Deferred income taxes	**3.4**	–
	Minority interest	**2.4**	2.5
		176.9	160.9
Shareholders' equity	Capital stock	**98.6**	105.7
	Retained earnings	**213.3**	163.0
	Foreign currency adjustments	**4.2**	9.6
		316.1	278.3
	Capital employed	**493.0**	439.2

The summary of significant accounting policies and the accompanying notes are an integral part of the consolidated financial statements.

Approved on behalf of the Board,

Marcel Bélanger

Director

Director

PROVIGO INC.

CONSOLIDATED STATEMENT OF CHANGES IN FINANCIAL POSITION

	year ended January 31, 1987 (Millions of dollars)	1987 (53 weeks)	1986 (52 weeks)
Operating activities	Income before extraordinary items	**60.3**	48.3
	Items not affecting working capital	**35.1**	34.6
	Working capital provided from operations	**95.4**	82.9
	Changes in non-cash working capital	**(48.0)**	(11.2)
	Foreign currency adjustments related to operations	**(0.7)**	1.5
	Total cash from operating activities	**46.7**	73.2
Investing activities	Investments	**(22.0)**	(51.7)
	Realization of investments	**3.7**	4.2
	Proceeds from sale of an investment	**14.6**	–
	Acquisition of fixed assets	**(86.2)**	(64.2)
	Sale of fixed assets	**29.2**	22.5
	Increase in goodwill	**(8.9)**	(2.6)
	Realization of goodwill	**–**	0.9
	Increase in deferred charges	**(4.3)**	(0.2)
	Costs related to extraordinary losses	**(5.0)**	(1.7)
	Total cash used for investing activities	**(78.9)**	(92.8)
Financing activities	Issue of common shares	**2.3**	43.9
	Share issue costs	**–**	(1.1)
	Increase in long-term debt	**81.0**	32.2
	Reimbursement of long-term debt	**(69.8)**	(20.1)
	Net increase (decrease) in obligations under capital leases	**(2.7)**	0.3
	Redemption of preferred shares	**(9.4)**	(3.1)
	Total cash from financing activities	**1.4**	52.1
Dividend payments	Preferred shares	**(0.4)**	(0.7)
	Common shares	**(14.5)**	(11.3)
	Total cash used for dividend payments	**(14.9)**	(12.0)
Cash and cash equivalents	Net increase (decrease) in cash for the year	**(45.7)**	20.5
	Beginning of year	**(32.7)**	(53.2)
	End of year	**(78.4)**	(32.7)

Cash and cash equivalents consist of cash and deposit certificates, less bank loans and acceptances and cheques issued and outstanding.

The summary of significant accounting policies and the accompanying notes are an integral part of the consolidated financial statements.

PROVIGO INC.

SUMMARY OF SIGNIFICANT ACCOUNTING POLICIES

year ended January 31, 1987

The consolidated financial statements have been prepared in accordance with generally accepted accounting principles in Canada, consistently applied, and conform in all material respects with International Accounting Standards with regard to the presentation of historical cost financial information. They include the following policies:

Basis of consolidation

The consolidated financial statements include the accounts of Provigo Inc. and all its subsidiaries.

Foreign currency

The accounts of the subsidiary in the United States have been translated into Canadian dollars as follows: assets and liabilities, at the year-end exchange rate; revenues and expenses, at the average exchange rate for the year. Foreign exchange gains or losses arising from translation are deferred and included in a separate component of shareholders' equity as foreign currency adjustments.

Inventories

Inventories are valued at the lower of cost, generally determined on a first-in, first-out basis, and net realizable value.

Pension plans

The Company and its subsidiaries participate in various defined benefit pension plans. The difference between the funding contributions and the amounts recorded as pension expenses or credits is reflected as deferred pension asset. Pension expense or credit includes the amortization, on a straight-line basis, of the difference between the pension fund's assets and the estimated actuarial present value of the accrued pension benefits attributed to services rendered, over the expected average remaining service life of the employee groups covered by the plans. Certain subsidiaries of the Company also participate in defined contribution pension plans. Substantially all the employees of the Company and its subsidiaries are eligible to participate in these plans.

Investments

Investments in affiliated companies consisting of a company subject to significant influence and a joint venture are accounted for using the equity method. The difference between the cost of the shares of affiliated companies and the underlying net book value of the assets acquired is amortized over the life of the assets to which the difference is allocated. Other investments are carried at cost.

Fixed assets

Fixed assets are stated at cost. Leases which transfer substantially all of the benefits and risks of ownership to the Company are accounted for as capital leases.

Depreciation is calculated according to the following methods and rates:

	Method	Annual rates
Buildings	Straight-line	2.5% @ 5%
Equipment	Straight-line	10%
Store equipment	Straight-line	12.5%
Automotive equipment	Diminishing balance	30%

Leasehold improvements are amortized over the terms of the related leases and the first renewal option period, if any. Fixed assets under capital leases are amortized over the terms of the related leases not exceeding 40 years.

Sundry assets

Goodwill is stated at cost less amortization accumulated on a straight-line basis over periods not exceeding 40 years.

Deferred charges are stated at cost less amortization accumulated on a straight-line basis over the life of the related items.

Store opening costs

Store opening and renovation costs are expensed as incurred.

Financial year

The Company's financial year ends on the last Saturday of January. Accordingly, the year ended January 31, 1987 comprises 53 weeks of operations while the preceding year ended January 25, 1986 comprised 52 weeks of operations.

PROVIGO INC.

NOTES TO CONSOLIDATED FINANCIAL STATEMENTS

year ended January 31, 1987
All tabular figures are in millions of dollars.

1. Acquisitions

During the year, subsidiaries of the Company acquired certain of the assets or the shares of three companies operating in the food sector and two companies operating in the health and pharmaceutical sector for a cash consideration of $16,000,000 and long-term debt of $6,000,000 assumed. The purchase price has been allocated as follows: $4,000,000 to working capital, $10,100,000 to fixed assets and $7,900,000 to goodwill. Operating results are accounted for from the dates of acquisition.

2. Depreciation and amortization

	1987	1986
Fixed assets	**24.6**	23.4
Goodwill	**1.1**	1.0
	25.7	24.4

3. Interest – net

	1987	1986
Long-term debt	**16.9**	18.6
Other	**5.3**	6.9
	22.2	25.5
Investment and interest income	**5.6**	6.5
	16.6	19.0

4. Income taxes

The Company's consolidated effective income tax rate is as follows:

	%	%
Statutory tax rate	**47.7**	47.8
Inventory allowance	**(0.2)**	(3.8)
Other	**0.2**	0.6
Effective income tax rate	**47.7**	44.6
The provision for income taxes consists of:		
Current taxes	**49.6**	39.6
Deferred taxes	**5.2**	(0.2)
	54.8	39.4

5. Investments

	1987	1986
Marketable securities	**0.4**	6.7
Long-term receivables, at rates approximating prime, maturing to 2000	**29.1**	10.5
Consumers Distributing Company Limited		
– shares	**45.2**	36.4
– debentures (converted during the year)	–	9.7
Brico Centre (Canada) Inc. – a 50% joint venture	**1.4**	0.6
	76.1	63.9

The company owns a 23.4% (1986 – 21.7%) interest in the shares of Consumers Distributing Company Limited representing 45.9% (1986 – 46.1%) of the voting rights. Summarized financial information is as follows:

Financial position	1987	1986
Current assets	**282.3**	296.9
Current liabilities	**164.1**	251.0
Working capital	**118.2**	45.9
Other assets	**90.6**	117.4
Assets employed	**208.8**	163.3
Other liabilities	**87.3**	61.5
Shareholders' equity	**121.5**	101.8
Capital employed	**208.8**	163.3

PROVIGO INC.

NOTES TO CONSOLIDATED FINANCIAL STATEMENTS

year ended January 31, 1987
All tabular figures are in millions of dollars.

	1987	1986
Operating results		
Sales	**933.4**	520.9
Net income	**5.6**	1.3
Share of net income, after amortization of the excess of the purchase price	**0.7**	(0.1)

Operating results for 1986 are reported from the date of acquisition in July 1985.

6. Fixed assets

	1987	1986	1987	1986
	Cost		Net Book Value	
Land	**29.8**	24.8	**29.8**	24.8
Buildings	**118.0**	98.5	**95.7**	80.5
Equipment	**182.6**	167.5	**78.5**	66.3
Leasehold improvements	**38.7**	30.7	**27.2**	20.7
Fixed assets under capital leases (consisting mainly of buildings)	**40.3**	48.3	**31.1**	38.5
	409.4	369.8	**262.3**	230.8

7. Sundry assets

	1987	1986
Goodwill, net of accumulated amortization	**32.4**	24.6
Deferred charges, net of accumulated amortization	**4.2**	0.6
Deferred pension assets	**2.5**	–
Future tax benefits	**–**	5.0
	39.1	30.2

8. Long-term debt

	1987	1986
Unsecured		
Series 1987 debentures, 9.8% maturing in 1997	**50.0**	–
Notes*	**22.2**	–
Other notes	**5.5**	3.4
Promissory notes, 6%, convertible to common shares, repayable starting in 1989, maturing in 1994	**20.0**	20.0
Bank loans and promissory notes**	**–**	31.0
Secured		
Series B sinking fund debentures, 9.5%**	**–**	1.2
Series C sinking fund debentures, 11.25%, maturing in 1995	**1.1**	1.2
Series D sinking fund debentures, at prime rate**	**–**	20.0
Series E debentures, 13.5%, maturing in 1993	**20.0**	20.0
Series F debentures, 11.875%, maturing in 1995	**20.0**	20.0
Mortgages	**7.4**	18.2
	146.2	135.0
Less instalments due within one year	**2.7**	7.2
	143.5	127.8

The secured debentures Series C, E and F are issued under a trust deed and are secured by a first floating charge on the assets of the Company. However, the Company has undertaken not to issue any additional debentures pursuant to the trust deed by virtue of which the floating charge was constituted.

*Notes consist of unsecured promissory notes issued at market rates, maturing within one year and supported by long-term credit facilities to November 1988. Accordingly, these borrowings have been classified as long-term debt.

**Reimbursed during the year.

Minimum annual instalments on long-term debt due in the next five years are as follows:

1988 – $2,651,000; 1989 – $2,959,000; 1990 – $2,653,000; 1991 – $2,474,000; 1992 – $365,000.

PROVIGO INC.

NOTES TO CONSOLIDATED FINANCIAL STATEMENTS

year ended January 31, 1987
All tabular figures are in millions of dollars.

Notes in the amount of $22,200,000 are excluded from the annual instalments due as a result of the Company's intention to renew annually the long-term credit facilities supporting these notes for periods of not less than twenty-four months.

9. Obligations and commitments under leases

Minimum lease payments under capital and operating leases are as follows:

	Capital leases	Operating leases Gross	Operating leases Net of sub-leases
1988	6.3	48.2	20.9
1989	5.7	45.0	18.7
1990	4.8	41.9	17.4
1991	4.0	38.5	15.6
1992	3.8	33.9	13.5
1993 and thereafter	96.1	248.0	110.7
Total minimum lease payments	120.7	455.5	196.8
Less:			
Imputed interest at the average rate of 13.3%	90.9		
Instalments due within one year	2.2		
Long-term obligations under capital leases	27.6		

The interest charged to income amounts to $3,976,000 (1986 – $4,916,000) and is included in interest on long-term debt. Operating lease expense charged to income during the year amounted to $21,320,000 (1986 – $19,977,000), net of sub-leases revenue.

10. Capital stock

	1987	1986
Authorized:		
1,000,000 preferred shares with a par value of $25 each.		
Unlimited number of common shares without par value.		
Issued and outstanding:		
Preferred shares (1986 – Series A: 375,000)	–	9.4
42,077,208 common shares (1986 – 41,907,030)	98.6	96.3
	98.6	105.7

During the year, 114,478 common shares were issued under employee stock purchase plans for a cash consideration of $1,894,000 and 55,700 common shares were issued under a stock option plan for the management of the Company and its subsidiaries, for a cash consideration of $475,000.

The Company has redeemed during the year the remaining 375,000 Series A preferred shares outstanding at their par value of $9,375,000.

As at January 31, 1987, common shares have been reserved for the following:

	Common shares reserved
Employee stock purchase plans	686,000
Stock option plans for the management of the Company and its subsidiaries	1,107,000
Conversion right attached to the convertible promissory notes	2,240,000

Of the 1,107,000 common shares reserved, 863,000 shares represent options that have been granted under stock option plans for the management of the Company and its subsidiaries which can be exercised at prices varying from $8.00 to $20.75 per share after certain vesting periods expiring up to 1992.

The conversion right attached to the convertible promissory notes is exercisable at a price of $8.95 per share until 1989 and $9.85 per share thereafter until 1994.

PROVIGO INC.

NOTES TO CONSOLIDATED FINANCIAL STATEMENTS

year ended January 31, 1987
All tabular figures are in millions of dollars.

Note		1987	1986
11. Foreign currency adjustments	Balance, beginning of year	**9.6**	5.2
	Effect of changes in exchange rates during the year	**(4.4)**	4.4
	Realized gain on repayment of long-term advances	**(1.0)**	–
	Balance, end of year	**4.2**	9.6
12. Extraordinary items	Gain on sale of an investment, net of related income taxes of $700,000	**8.6**	–
	Losses and provisions for losses on the abandonment of the retail operations in the United States, net of the related income tax recovery of $1,200,000	**(1.4)**	–
	Losses and provisions for losses on the sale and closing of supermarkets, mainly in the Montreal region, net of the related income tax recovery of $1,900,000 ($9,300,000 in 1986)	**(2.3)**	(12.2)
	Loss on the closure of the abattoir operation, net of the related income tax recovery of $280,000	**–**	(1.6)
		4.9	(13.8)
13. Items not affecting working capital	Depreciation and amortization	**25.7**	24.4
	Deferred income taxes	**10.2**	9.2
	Deferred pension assets	**(2.5)**	–
	Other	**1.7**	1.0
		35.1	34.6
14. Changes in non-cash working capital related to operating activities	Receivables	**(73.1)**	(24.2)
	Inventories	**(47.7)**	(37.7)
	Payables and accrued liabilities	**52.5**	39.4
	Other	**20.3**	11.3
		(48.0)	(11.2)

15. Pension plans

Effective at the beginning of the year and applied on a prospective basis, the Company has adopted the new recommendations of the Canadian Institute of Chartered Accountants. The effect of this change on net income for the year is not material.

The estimated value of the pension fund assets as of January 31, 1987 amounts to $80,499,000 (1986 – $63,988,000) and the estimated actuarial present value of accrued pension benefits attributed to services rendered amounts to $53,993,000 (1986 – $46,904,000).

16. Subsequent events

Subsequent to the year-end, a subsidiary of the Company acquired two companies operating in the food service sector for a total consideration of $12,500,000.

The Company disposed of its investment in the joint venture Brico Centre (Canada) Inc. for a consideration of $2,250,000.

NOTES TO CONSOLIDATED FINANCIAL STATEMENTS

PROVIGO INC.

year ended January 31, 1987
All tabular figures are in millions of dollars

17. Segmented Information

	Net sales		Segment operating profit		Performance income	
	1987	1986	**1987**	1986	**1987**	1986
Food Group – Canada The distribution and retail sale of food and related products.	**3,692.2**	3,258.3	**92.8**	67.3	**48.3**	37.1
Food Group – U.S.A.* The distribution in the United States of food and related products.	**446.3**	443.9	**12.3**	12.5	**6.2**	6.6
Total Food Group	**4,138.5**	3,702.2	**105.1**	79.8	**54.5**	43.7
Health and Pharmaceutical Group The distribution of pharmaceuticals and other drugstore products.	**791.6**	585.5	**16.2**	13.9	**8.0**	7.8
Convenience Group The sale of convenience products and related support to a network of franchise stores and the retail sale of petroleum products.	**319.4**	319.3	**15.9**	13.3	**8.7**	7.3
Specialty Retailing Group The distribution and retail sale of sporting goods and leisure wear.	**152.1**	139.1	**1.5**	5.2	**0.8**	3.5
Total	**5,401.6**	4,746.1	**138.7**	112.2	**72.0**	62.3
General Corporate Expenses			**7.8**	4.7	**3.7**	2.6
Interest – net			**16.6**	19.0	**8.8**	10.6
Share of net income of affiliated companies			**(0.7)**	0.2	**(0.7)**	0.2
Income taxes			**54.8**	39.4	–	–
Income before minority interest			**60.2**	48.9	**60.2**	48.9

	Identifiable assets		Net assets employed by segment		Capital expenditures		Depreciation and amortization	
	1987	1986	**1987**	1986	**1987**	1986	**1987**	1986
Food Group – Canada	**557.2**	482.1	**247.9**	245.6	**55.6**	35.8	**16.9**	17.0
Food Group – U.S.A.*	**76.7**	105.9	**40.6**	48.8	**1.5**	1.2	**1.9**	1.7
Total Food Group	**633.9**	588.0	**288.5**	294.4	**57.1**	37.0	**18.8**	18.7
Health and Pharmaceutical Group	**184.1**	111.3	**89.4**	46.1	**9.9**	3.1	**1.7**	1.0
Convenience Group	**64.1**	59.6	**40.2**	31.5	**9.1**	8.2	**3.6**	3.1
Specialty Retailing Group	**71.2**	49.8	**46.0**	25.2	**10.0**	14.7	**1.4**	1.2
Corporate	**49.6**	55.2	**58.9**	50.0	**0.1**	1.2	**0.2**	0.4
Total	**1,002.9**	863.9	**523.0**	447.2	**86.2**	64.2	**25.7**	24.4

Performance income corresponds to each segment's operating profit, net of related income taxes. General corporate expenses and interest-net shown in the same column are net of related income taxes.

Net assets employed correspond to each segment's identifiable assets, excluding cash and deposit certificates, net of all current liabilities except for bank loans and acceptances and the current portion of long-term debt and capital leases.

Corporate assets are principally marketable securities and investments in affiliated companies.

Inter-segment sales are not significant.

* The Company's only operation carried on outside Canada.

FIVE YEAR REVIEW

PROVIGO INC.

	1987	1986	1985	1984	1983
Operations (Millions of dollars)					
Net Sales	**5,401.6**	4,746.1	4,367.4	3,891.2	3,683.0
Operating income	**156.6**	131.9	110.4	88.4	91.6
Depreciation and amortization	**25.7**	24.4	21.8	20.6	21.3
Interest-net	**16.6**	19.0	18.6	19.6	30.3
Income taxes	**54.8**	39.4	29.6	21.5	16.5
Income before extraordinary items	**60.3**	48.3	40.3	26.5	24.1
Net income	**65.2**	34.5	40.3	26.5	22.5
Changes in financial position (Millions of dollars)					
Funds from operations	**95.4**	82.9	58.5	43.9	43.5
Capital expenditures	**86.2**	64.2	47.9	19.4	26.1
Dividends	**14.9**	12.0	10.2	9.0	9.7
Financial position (Millions of dollars)					
Current assets	**625.4**	535.3	453.0	404.4	358.2
Current liabilities	**509.9**	424.7	369.2	331.4	312.2
Working capital	**115.5**	110.6	83.8	73.4	46.0
Fixed assets	**262.3**	230.8	219.7	202.4	217.3
Total assets	**1,002.9**	863.9	728.9	660.8	624.2
Total debt	**206.7**	202.5	206.5	195.2	213.5
Shareholders' equity	**316.1**	278.3	211.7	180.9	163.7
Financial ratios					
Return on average equity	**20.5%**	22.0%	21.6%	16.4%	16.2%
Total debt: Equity	**40:60**	42:58	49:51	52:48	57:43
Current ratio	**1.23x**	1.26x	1.23x	1.22x	1.15x
Interest coverage ratio	**7.9x**	5.6x	4.7x	3.4x	2.4x
Per share					
Income before extraordinary items	**1.43**	1.21	1.01	0.655	0.58
1st quarter	**0.25**	0.26	0.25	0.075	0.09
2nd quarter	**0.41**	0.40	0.29	0.175	0.18
3rd quarter	**0.30**	0.29	0.21	0.21	0.15
4th quarter	**0.47**	0.26	0.26	0.195	0.16
Net income	**1.54**	0.86	1.01	0.655	0.535
Fully diluted:					
income before extraordinary items	**1.36**	1.15	0.98	0.655	0.58
net income	**1.46**	0.82	0.98	0.655	0.535
Dividends	**0.346**	0.288	0.238	0.20	0.20
Funds from operations	**2.27**	2.10	1.50	1.13	1.13
Capital expenditures	**2.05**	1.63	1.23	0.50	0.68
Shareholders' equity	**7.51**	6.42	5.10	4.25	3.73
Market value					
high	**22.25**	17.00	9.56	9.81	6.88
low	**15.25**	8.81	7.31	5.75	3.00
Common shares outstanding	**42,077,208**	41,907,030	39,031,612	38,936,474	38,839,392
Average number of shares traded weekly[1]	**243,967**	218,597	233,684	138,458	98,618
Shareholders of record	**7,346**	6,515	5,537	7,153	8,911
Effective income tax rate	**47.7%**	44.6%	42.3%	44.6%	40.7%

(1) Montreal and Toronto Stock Exchange

c h a p t e r 5

FUTURE AND PRESENT VALUES OF CASH FLOWS

THE TIME VALUE OF MONEY

Ignoring the effects of inflation, a dollar today is worth more than a dollar to be received a year from now. In other words, we would all prefer to receive a specific amount of money now rather than on some future date. This preference rests on the ***time value of money***. The term ***interest*** is used to describe the price charged for using money over time. When payments for the time value of money are made or accrued, ***interest expense*** is incurred; when payments for the time value of money are received or accrued, ***interest revenue*** is realized.

Business decisions often involve receiving cash or other assets ***now*** in exchange for a promise to make payments after one or more periods. A common example is a decision to borrow money. Another important group of business decisions involves investing cash now in order to receive cash, goods, or services in future periods.

Inflows of dollars on various future dates should not be added together as if they were of equal value. These future cash inflows must be restated at their ***present values*** before they are aggregated. The concept of the time value of money tells us that the more-distant cash inflows have a smaller present value than cash inflows to be received within a shorter time span.

Similar reasoning applies to cash outflows. Before we add together cash outflows on various future dates, we must restate these outflows at their present values. The more distant the date of a cash outflow, the smaller is its present value.

As a simple example of this concept of present value, assume that you are trying to sell your car and you receive offers from three prospective buyers. Buyer A offers you $8,000 to be paid immediately. Buyer B offers you $8,200 to be paid one year from now. Buyer C offers the highest price, $9,200, but this offer provides that payment will be made in five years. Assuming that the offers by B and C involve no credit risk and that money may be invested at 5% interest compounded annually, which offer would you accept?

You should accept the offer of $8,000 to be received immediately, because the *present value* of the other two offers is less than $8,000. If you were to invest $8,000 today, even at the modest rate of interest of 5%, your investment would be worth more than $8,200 in one year and considerably more than $9,200 in five years.

This example suggests that the timing of cash receipts and payments has an important effect on the economic worth and the accounting values of both assets and liabilities. Consequently, investment and borrowing decisions should be made only after a careful analysis of the relative present values of the prospective cash inflows and outflows.

USES OF PRESENT AND FUTURE VALUES IN FINANCIAL ACCOUNTING

Accountants find many situations in which a reliable measurement of a transaction depends on the present value of future cash inflows and outflows. For example, the amount received for a bond issue by the issuer reflects the present value of the issuer's promise to make a series of future interest payments and to repay the principal when the bonds reach maturity. Some other examples of the need for measuring present or future values of cash flows are listed below:

1 ***Promissory notes and mortgages*** Measurement of the present value of such assets or liabilities when the interest rate is not specified or differs from the current fair rate of interest (See Chapters 7 and 10)

2 ***Bonds payable*** Computation of interest expense and amortization of premium or discount by the effective interest method, and the determination of present value and interest revenue on investments in bonds (See Chapters 14 and 15)

3 ***Leases*** Measurement of amount to be recorded as an asset and liability under leases that are considered equivalent to acquisitions of assets, and the determination of periodic lease payments to obtain a desired rate of return on investment (See Chapter 20)

4 ***Pensions*** Measurement of pension costs (past and current) and funding programs for pension plans (See Chapter 19)

5 ***Plant assets*** Measurement of plant assets acquired by issuance of debt securities (including instalment contracts payable) when the interest rate is not specified or differs from the current fair rate of interest (See Chapter 11)

6 *Sinking funds* Determination of periodic payments required to provide a fund for the retirement of long-term debt or preferred stock (See Chapter 14)

7 *Depreciation* Computation of periodic depreciation under the sinking fund and annuity methods of depreciation (See the Appendix at the end of Chapter 12)

Measurement of the present and future values implicit in the foregoing examples involves the use of compound interest principles (defined below). In this chapter we illustrate the basic principles of compound interest in a format that will be useful throughout this book. We also stress the use of compound interest tables (presented in the Appendix at the end of this chapter) as a basis for solving a wide range of financial accounting problems.

SIMPLE INTEREST AND COMPOUND INTEREST

Interest is the growth in a ***principal amount*** representing the fee charged for the use of money for a specified time period. Because the concept of economic earnings is periodic, we typically think of return on investment in terms of ***a rate of return per year***.

Simple interest is the return on a principal amount for one time period. We may also think of simple interest as a return for more than one time period if we assume that the interest itself does not earn a return, but this kind of situation occurs rarely in the business world. Simple interest is usually applicable only to short-term investment and borrowing transactions involving a time span of less than one year.

Interest is most often expressed in terms of an annual rate. The formula for simple interest is $I = prt$ (interest = principal × annual rate of interest × number of years or fraction of a year that interest accrues). For example, interest on $10,000 at 8% for one year is expressed as follows:

Formula for simple interest

$$I = prt$$
$$I = \$10,000 \times 0.08 \times 1$$
$$I = \underline{\underline{\$800}}$$

Compound interest is the return on a principal amount for two or more time periods, assuming that the interest for each time period is added to the principal amount at the end of each period and earns interest in all subsequent periods. Because most investment and borrowing transactions involve more than one time period, business executives evaluate proposed transactions in terms of periodic returns each of which is assumed to be reinvested to yield additional returns.

For example, if interest at 8% is compounded quarterly for one year on a principal amount of $10,000, the total interest (compound interest) would be

$824.32, as is computed below:

Interest compounded quarterly

Period	*Principal* × *Rate* × *Time*	=	*Compound interest*	*Accumulated amount*
1st quarter	$10,000.00 × 0.08 × ¼	=	$200.00	$10,200.00
2nd quarter	10,200.00 × 0.08 × ¼	=	204.00	10,404.00
3rd quarter	10,404.00 × 0.08 × ¼	=	208.08	10,612.08
4th quarter	10,612.08 × 0.08 × ¼	=	212.24	10,824.32
Interest on $10,000 at 8% compounded quarterly for one year............................			$824.32	

Notice that in the computation of compound interest, the accumulated amount at the end of each period becomes the principal amount for purposes of computing interest for the following period.

FUTURE AND PRESENT VALUES OF A SINGLE AMOUNT

Amount of 1

The ***accumulated amount*** (small a) of a single amount invested at compound interest may be computed period by period by a series of multiplications, as illustrated in the foregoing table for $10,000 invested for one year at 8% compounded quarterly. If n is used to represent the number of periods that interest is to be compounded, i is used to represent the interest *per period*, and p is the principal amount invested, the ***series of multiplications*** to compute the accumulated amount a in the example above may be determined as follows:

Long-hand method for amount of 1

$$a = p(1 + i)^n$$
$$a = \$10{,}000\,(1 + 0.02)^4$$
$$a = \$10{,}000\,(1.02)(1.02)(1.02)(1.02)$$
$$a = \underline{\underline{\$10{,}824.32}}$$

It is important to observe that i is the ***rate of interest for each time period*** that interest is ***compounded***. For example, the formulas for the compound amount a of 1 at 12%, assuming different compounding patterns, are:

12% interest at different compounding patterns

Interest at 12% per year compounded *annually* = $(1 + 0.12)^1 = 1.12$
Interest at 12% per year compounded *semiannually* = $(1 + 0.06)^2 = 1.1236$
Interest at 12% per year compounded *quarterly* = $(1 + 0.03)^4 = 1.125509$
Interest at 12% per year compounded *monthly* = $(1 + 0.01)^{12} = 1.126825$

The symbol $a_{\overline{n}|i}$ is the amount to which 1 will accumulate at i rate of interest per period for n periods. This symbol is read as "small a angle n at i." If annual interest of 8% is compounded quarterly for one year, the rate of interest per time period (one-fourth of a year) would be 2%, and the number of interest periods n would be 4. Thus, the ***"amount of 1" formula*** at 8% compounded quarterly for one year is :

"Amount of 1" formula

$$a_{\overline{n}|i} = (1 + i)^n \quad \text{or} \quad a_{\overline{4}|2\%} = (1 + 0.02)^4$$

Tables are available that give the value of $a_{\overline{n}|i}$. Use of these tables involves reference to a line showing the number of periods and a column showing the rate of interest per period. For example, Table 1 in the Appendix (page 243) shows that $a_{\overline{4}|2\%}$ is equal to 1.082432, which means that $10,000 would accumulate to $10,824.32 in one year at 8% compounded quarterly. Compound interest tables generally are prepared for $1 and ***the dollar sign is omitted***. This provides a convenient means of finding the accumulated amount of any number of dollars by multiplying the amount of 1 at i interest for n periods by the number of dollars involved in a problem or a business transaction.

Summary and Examples

The amount of 1 formula, $a_{\overline{n}|i}$, is used to compute the future amount a of any given principal amount p that earns compound interest at a specified interest rate i per period for n periods. A diagram for the amount of 1 is shown below:

Diagram for amount of 1

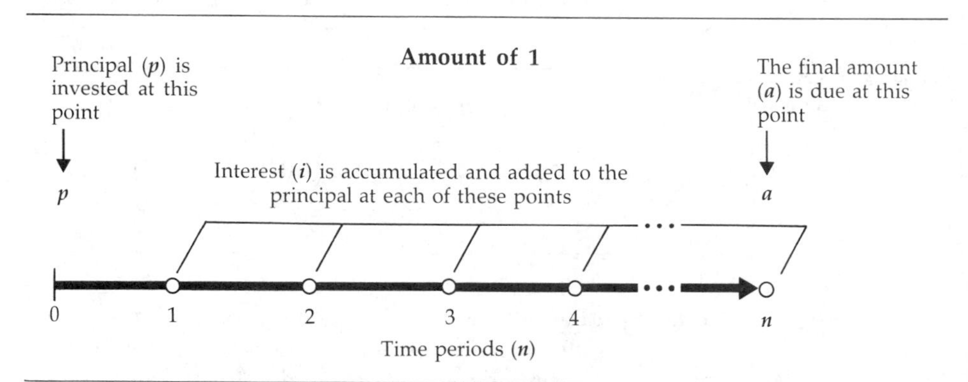

Example 1: Computation of the Amount of 1 for More Periods Than Are Available in Table 1 of the Appendix If on the day her daughter was born, Candace Carlo deposited $10,000 in a savings account that guarantees to accumulate interest ***quarterly*** at 10% a year, what will be the amount in the savings account on her daughter's 18th birthday?

Solution The amount in the savings account on the daughter's 18th birthday will be $10,000 (1 + 0.025)^{72}. Because Table 1 in the Appendix at the end of this chapter does not go beyond 50 periods, the amount in the savings account on the daughter's 18th birthday may be computed as follows:

$$\$10{,}000\,(1 + 0.025)^{50} \times (1 + 0.025)^{22}$$
$$\$10{,}000\,(3.437109) \times (1.721571) = \underline{\underline{\$59{,}172}}$$

Example 2: Determining the Interest Rate If $1,000 is deposited at compound interest on January 1, Year 1, and the amount on deposit on December 31, Year 10, is $1,806.11, what is the ***semiannual interest rate*** accruing on the deposit?

Solution The amount of 1 for 20 periods at the unstated rate of interest is 1.80611 ($1,806.11 ÷ $1,000 = 1.80611). Reference to Table 1 in the Appendix at the end of this chapter indicates that 1.806111 is the amount of 1 for 20 periods at 3%. Therefore, ***the semiannual interest rate is 3%***.

Example 3: Amount Accumulated When Interest Rate Changes Fanny deposited $10,000 in a fund that will earn 8% interest ***compounded quarterly for the first four years***, and 10% interest ***compounded semiannually for the next six years***. How much will Fanny have in the fund at the end of 10 years?

Solution Using Table 1 in the Appendix at the end of this chapter, we have the following amount at the end of four years at 8% interest compounded quarterly:

$$\$10{,}000 \times a_{\overline{16}|2\%} = \$10{,}000\,(1 + 0.02)^{16}$$
$$\$10{,}000 \times a_{\overline{16}|2\%} = \$10{,}000\,(1.372786) \quad \text{or} \quad \underline{\underline{\$13{,}728}}$$

And for the next six years at 10% compounded semiannually, we have:

$$\$13{,}728 \times a_{\overline{12}|5\%} = \$13{,}728\,(1 + 0.05)^{12}$$
$$\$13{,}728 \times a_{\overline{12}|5\%} = \$13{,}728\,(1.795856) \quad \text{or} \quad \underline{\underline{\$24{,}654}}$$

In this case the interest rate ***per period*** changed at the end of four years from 2% to 5%. Therefore, it was first necessary to compute the amount on deposit at the end of four years ($13,728) and then to accumulate compound interest on this amount for six additional years at 10% compounded semiannually.

Present Value of 1

Many measurement and valuation problems in financial accounting require the computation of the discounted present value of a principal amount to be paid or received on a fixed future date. As the next diagram illustrates, the ***present value of 1*** is closely related to the procedures used to compute the amount of 1:

Diagram for present value of 1

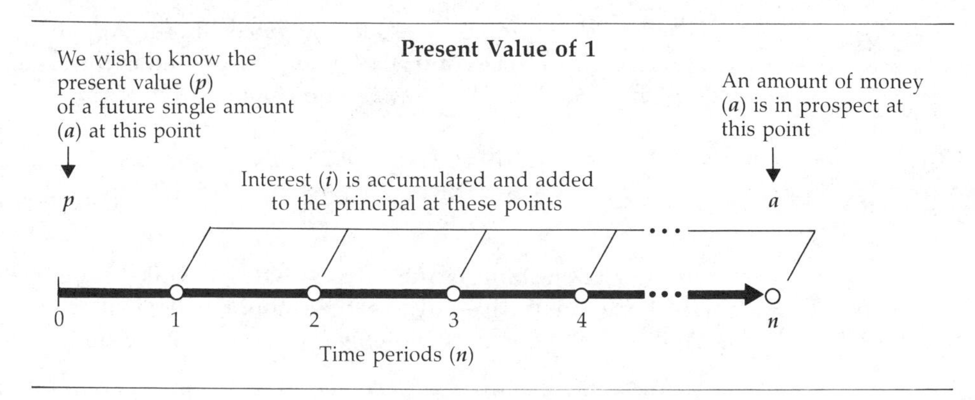

From this diagram we see that the computation of the present value of a single future amount is a ***reversal*** of the process of finding the amount to which a present amount will accumulate. For example, we have seen (page 222) that $(1 + 0.02)^4 = 1.082432$ and that the principal amount p of $10,000 will accumulate to $10,824.32 in one year if interest is compounded quarterly. To find the principal p that must be invested now at 8% compounded quarterly to give us $10,824.32 in one year, we may proceed as follows: We know that $a = p(1 + i)^n$, and when we solve for p by dividing both sides of the equation by $(1 + i)^n$, we have the following:

$$p = \frac{a}{(1 + i)^n}$$

Now we substitute $(1 + 0.02)^4$ for $(1 + i)^n$ and $10,824.32 for a, and we have:

$$p = \frac{\$10{,}824.32}{(1 + 0.02)^4} = \frac{\$10{,}824.32}{1.082432} = \underline{\underline{\$10{,}000}}$$

It should be clear that we may determine the present value p of any future amount a by dividing the future amount a by $(1 + i)^n$. Thus, the formula for the present value of 1 due in n periods at i rate of interest per period is:

"Present value of 1" formula

$$p_{\overline{n}|i} = \frac{1}{(1 + i)^n}$$

The symbol $p_{\overline{n}|i}$ is read "small p angle n at i." The ***"present value of 1" formula*** at 8% compounded quarterly for one year is:

$$p_{\overline{4}|2\%} = \frac{1}{(1 + 0.02)^4}$$

It is apparent that a table showing values for $1 \div (1 + i)^n$ at different interest rates i and different number of periods n would be useful. Table 2 in the Appendix at the end of this chapter provides such values. The value of $p_{\overline{4}|2\%}$ in that table is

0.923845; therefore the present value of \$10,824.32 discounted for one year at 8% compounded quarterly may be computed as follows:

$$\$10{,}824.32 \times 0.923845 = \underline{\underline{\$10{,}000}}$$

Summary and Examples

The present value of 1 formula, $p_{\overline{n}|i}$, is used to compute the discounted present value p of an amount a due or payable on some future date, discounted at a specified interest rate i per period for n periods.

Example 1: Proceeds from Issuance of ''Zero-Coupon Bonds'' Growth Corporation issues bonds that pay no interest when the market rate of interest on this type of bond is 14% compounded semiannually. How much will Growth Corporation receive from the issuance of 25-year ''zero-coupon bonds'' with a maturity value of \$100 million?

Solution The proceeds from the issuance of the bonds is equal to the present value of \$100 million discounted at 7% for 50 periods. Using Table 2 in the Appendix at the end of this chapter, the proceeds are computed as follows:

$$\$100{,}000{,}000 \times 0.033948 = \underline{\underline{\$3{,}394{,}800}}$$

Example 2: Present Value When Interest Rate Changes Paul Horsley wants to deposit cash into a savings account at the beginning of Year 1 so that he will have \$50,000 at the end of Year 6. How much must Horsley deposit at the beginning of Year 1 if the interest rate is 6% compounded semiannually for the first three years and 8% compounded quarterly for the next three years?

Solution Using Table 2 in the Appendix at the end of this chapter, we have the following present value at the beginning of Year 4 of the \$50,000 required at the end of Year 6:

$$\$50{,}000 \times p_{\overline{12}|2\%} = \$50{,}000 \times 0.788493 = \$39{,}425$$

And at the beginning of Year 1, we have:

$$\$39{,}425 \times p_{\overline{6}|3\%} = \$39{,}425 \times 0.837484 = \underline{\underline{\$33{,}018}}$$

Thus, Horsley must deposit \$33,018 at the beginning of Year 1 to have \$50,000 at the end of Year 6. Because the interest rate per period changed at the beginning of Year 4, it was necessary to prepare the solution in two steps.

Example 3: Determining the Approximate Interest Rate by Interpolation If the present value of \$100,000 discounted at an unstated rate of interest for 20 periods is \$64,162.10, what was the approximate interest rate per period used in computing this present value?

Solution From Table 2 in the Appendix at the end of this chapter, we obtain the following present values for different interest rates:

Estimating the rate of interest

$p_{\overline{20}|2\%} = 0.672971$ $\quad p_{\overline{20}|?\%} = 0.641621^*$ $\quad p_{\overline{20}|2\frac{1}{2}\%} = 0.610271$

difference (between 0.672971 and 0.641621) = 0.03135

difference (between 0.672971 and 0.610271) = 0.06270

*$64,162.10 ÷ $100,000 = 0.641621.

The unknown interest rate is exactly at the midpoint between 2% and 2½%. Therefore, the approximate interest rate per period is 2¼%, computed as follows:

$$0.02 + 0.005\left(\frac{0.03135}{0.06270}\right) \quad \text{or} \quad 0.02 + (0.005 \times \tfrac{1}{2}) = \underline{\underline{2\tfrac{1}{4}\%}}$$

Relationship of Amount of 1 and Present Value of 1 to *n* and *i*

In dealing with computations of accumulations and present values, it is useful to have some general idea of relationships as a basis for verifying the reasonableness of results. We may reason, for example, that $a_{\overline{n}|i}$ should grow *larger* for increasing rates of interest *i* and for an increasing number of periods *n*, because the longer a principal amount accumulates interest the larger it grows, and *the higher the rate of interest the larger the future amount*. The reverse is true of present values: the longer the time period *n* or the higher the rate of interest *i*, *the smaller the present value of any future amount*.

ANNUITIES

Many measurement situations in financial accounting involve periodic deposits, receipts, withdrawals, or payments (called *rents*), with interest at a stated rate compounded at the time that each rent is paid or received. These situations *are considered annuities if all the following conditions are present*:

1 The periodic rents are equal in amount

2 The time period between rents—e.g., a year, a quarter of a year, or a month—is constant

3 The interest rate per time period remains constant

4 The interest is compounded at the end of each time period

When rents are paid or received at the end of each period and the total amount on deposit is determined at the time the final rent is made, the annuity is an *ordinary annuity* (or *annuity in arrears*). Other types of annuities, that is, an *annuity due* (or *annuity in advance*) and a *deferred annuity*, are discussed in subsequent sections of this chapter.

Amount of Ordinary Annuity of 1

The amount of an *ordinary annuity* (or *annuity in arrears*) consists of the sum of the equal periodic rents and compound interest on the rents *immediately after*

the final rent. The amount A to which an ordinary annuity of n rents of R dollars each will accumulate in n periods at i rate of interest per period is illustrated below:

Diagram for amount of ordinary annuity

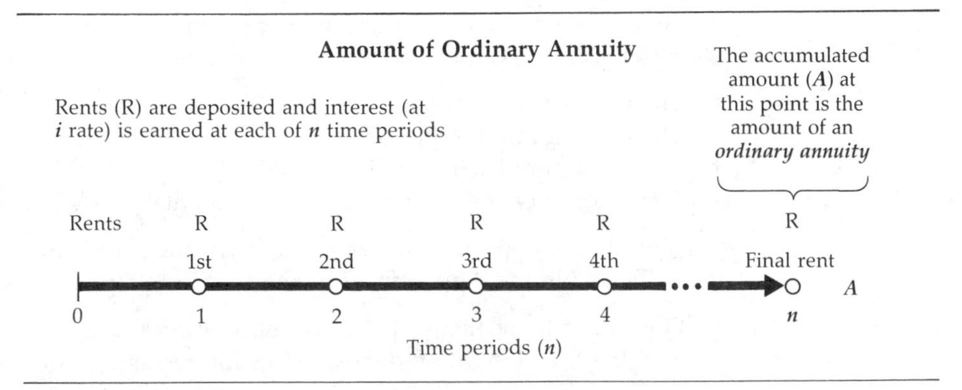

The amount A of an ordinary annuity of n rents of 1 at i interest rate per period is determined ***by dividing by* i *the compound interest*** that accumulates on a single deposit of 1 for n periods at i interest. This is expressed as follows:

Formula for amount of ordinary annuity of 1

$$A_{\overline{n}|i} = \frac{(1 + i)^n - 1}{i}$$

For example, the amount of an ordinary annuity of 16 rents of 1 at 2% is determined below:

Solving the formula

$$A_{\overline{16}|2\%} = \frac{(1 + 0.02)^{16} - 1}{0.02} = \frac{1.372786 - 1}{0.02} = \frac{0.372786}{0.02} = \underline{\underline{18.6393}}$$

The amount of 1 at 2% for 16 periods (1.372786) is taken from Table 1 in the Appendix at the end of this chapter. Dividing the compound interest of 0.372786 ($1.372786 - 1 = 0.372786$) by 0.02 gives the amount of an ordinary annuity of 16 rents of 1 at 2%. Tables such as Table 3 in the Appendix at the end of this chapter have been prepared to give the amount of ordinary annuities for different numbers of rents at varying interest rates. Note that in Table 3 the value for $A_{\overline{16}|2\%}$ is 18.64 (rounded to two decimal places). Table 3 in the Appendix is used to compute the amount of an ordinary annuity for rents of any dollar amount by a process of multiplication. For example, because the amount of an annuity of 16 rents of 1 at 2% is 18.64, the amount of an ordinary annuity of 16 rents of \$500 is \$9,320 (\$500 × 18.64 = \$9,320).

Other Applications of Formula for Amount of Ordinary Annuity of 1

In the example above the amount of an ordinary annuity of 16 rents of 1 at 2% (18.64) and the periodic rent ($500) were known. From the information available we were able to compute the amount of the ordinary annuity of 16 rents of $500 at 2% as $9,320. Thus, four variables were involved:

- The number of rents (16)
- The interest rate per period (2%)
- The amount of each periodic rent ($500)
- The amount of the ordinary annuity immediately after the last rent ($9,320)

If any three of these variables are known, the fourth may be determined by using Table 3 in the Appendix at the end of this chapter as illustrated below:

1 **Question** How many quarterly rents of $500 are required to accumulate $9,320 if the amount on deposit earns interest at 8% compounded quarterly?

   Answer $9,320 ÷ $500 = 18.64, the amount of an ordinary annuity of 1 at 2% for an unknown number of rents. The 2% column in Table 3 in the Appendix at the end of this chapter shows that ***the required number of rents is 16*** because the amount of an ordinary annuity of 16 rents at 2% is 18.64 (rounded to two decimal places).

2 **Question** If an amount of an ordinary annuity of 16 rents of $500 equals $9,320 immediately after the sixteenth rent, what is the interest rate?

   Answer $9,320 ÷ $500 = 18.64, the amount of an ordinary annuity of 16 rents of 1 at an ***unstated interest rate*** per period. The line for 16 rents in Table 3 in the Appendix at the end of this chapter shows that ***the interest rate per period is 2%.***

3 **Question** If the required amount of an ordinary annuity of 16 rents at 2% is $9,320, what periodic rents are required to accumulate this amount?

   Answer Table 3 in the Appendix shows that the amount of an ordinary annuity of 16 rents at 2% is 18.64 (rounded). ***The periodic rents are $500*** ($9,320 ÷ 18.64 = $500).

Summary and Example

The formula $A_{\overline{n}|i}$ for the amount of an ordinary annuity of *1* is used to compute the future amount A of n equal periodic rents of R dollars that earn compound interest rate i per period. The periodic rent is computed by dividing the dollar amount to be accumulated by the amount of an ordinary annuity of 1 at the specified interest rate for the number of periods equal to the number of rents (deposits).

Example: Accumulation of a Fund to Retire Debt Bloom Company wants to accumulate $600,000 on December 31, Year 5, to retire a long-term note payable. Bloom intends to make five equal annual deposits in a fund that will earn interest at 6% compounded annually. The first deposit is made on December 31, Year 1.

Compute the amount of the periodic deposits that Bloom must make and prepare a fund accumulation table to verify that $600,000 will be available on December 31, Year 5.

Solution The amount of the periodic deposits is $600,000 ÷ 5.637093 (the amount of an ordinary annuity of five rents of 1 at 6% from Table 3 in the Appendix at the end of this chapter), or $106,438 (rounded). The fund accumulation table appears below.

Example of fund buildup

BLOOM COMPANY
Fund Accumulation Table

Dec. 31, Year:	*Annual deposit*	*Interest earned at 6%*	*Increase in fund balance*	*Fund balance*
1	$106,438		$106,438	$106,438
2	106,438	$ 6,386	112,824	219,262
3	106,438	13,156	119,594	338,856
4	106,438	20,331	126,769	465,625
5	106,438	27,937*	134,375	600,000

*Adjusted for slight rounding error.

Amount of an Annuity Due

The amount of an ***annuity due*** (or ***annuity in advance***) is the total amount on deposit ***one period after the final rent***. This is illustrated below for an annuity due of 16 rents:

Diagram for amount of annuity due

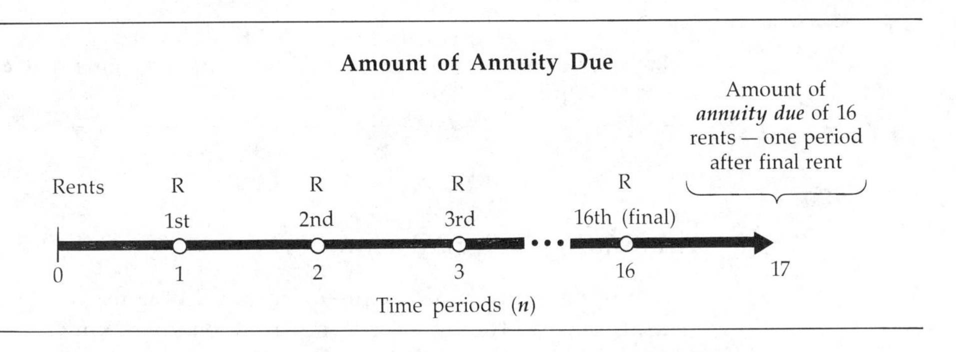

This diagram suggests that there are two ways of computing the amount of an annuity due of 16 rents of 1 at, say, 2% interest per period, as follows:

1 Take the amount of an ordinary annuity of 16 rents of 1 at 2% from Table 3 in the Appendix at the end of this chapter and accrue interest at 2% for one additional period.

$$18.639285 \times 1.02 = \underline{\underline{19.01207}} \qquad [A_{\overline{n}|i} \times (1 + i)]$$

2 Take the amount of an ordinary annuity of 17 rents of 1 at 2% from Table 3 in the Appendix at the end of this chapter and subtract 1, the rent not made at the end of time period 17:

$$20.01207 - 1 = \underline{\underline{19.01207}} \qquad (A_{\overline{n+1}|i} - 1)$$

The application of the amount of an annuity due is illustrated in the following example.

Application and Example

Example Greco Corporation needs $200,000 on March 31, Year 5. This amount is to be accumulated by making 16 equal deposits in a fund at the end of each quarter, starting March 31, Year 1, and ending on December 31, Year 4. The fund will earn interest at 8% compounded quarterly. Compute the periodic rents (deposits) that Greco must make.

Solution The balance in the fund on March 31, Year 5, represents the amount of an annuity due of 16 rents at 2% per period (19.01207 as determined above). Therefore, the periodic rents are: $200,000 ÷ 19.01207 = $10,519.63. This result may be verified as follows:

Ordinary annuity plus interest for 1 period = amount of annuity due

Amount of *ordinary annuity* of 16 rents of $10,519.63 at 2% on December 31, Year 4: $10,519.63 × 18.639285	$196,078
Add: Interest for first quarter of Year 5: $196,078 × 0.02	3,922
Balance in fund on March 31, Year 5 (amount of an *annuity due* of 16 rents of $10,519.63 at 2%)	$200,000

Amount of Deferred Annuity

When the amount of an ordinary annuity remains on deposit for a number of periods beyond the final rent, the arrangement is known as a ***deferred annuity***. The diagram on page 229 shows that the amount of an annuity due of 16 rents is also the amount of an ordinary annuity ***deferred for only one period***. Thus, when the amount of an ordinary annuity continues to earn interest for one additional period, we have an ***annuity due*** situation; when the amount of an ordinary annuity continues to earn interest for more than one additional period, we have a ***deferred annuity*** situation.

The amount of a deferred annuity may be computed by multiplying the amount of the ordinary annuity by the amount of 1 for the period of deferral to accrue compound interest. Alternatively, we may take the amount of an ordinary annuity for all periods (including the period of deferral) and subtract from this the amount of the ordinary annuity for the deferral period when rents ***were not made***, but interest continued to accumulate. The diagram below illustrates the relationship of an ***ordinary annuity*** of 16 rents, an ***annuity due*** of 16 rents, and an ***ordinary annuity of 16 rents deferred for five periods***:

Diagram for three types of annuity amounts

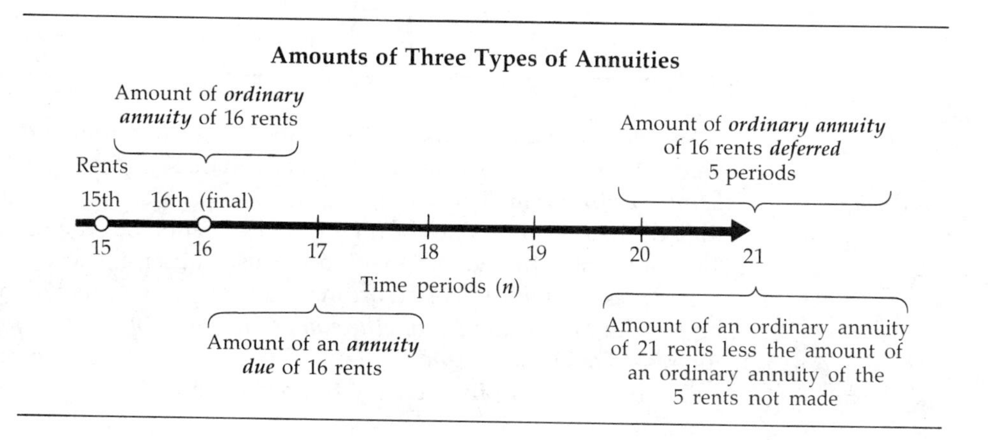

Using the Appendix at the end of this chapter, and assuming a 2% rate of interest per period, we have two ways of computing the amount of an ordinary annuity of 16 rents of 1 deferred for 5 periods (at time period 21):

Alternative computations for amount of deferred annuity

$$A_{\overline{16}|2\%} \times (1 + 0.02)^5 = 18.639285 \times 1.104081 = \underline{\underline{20.57928}}$$

or

$$A_{\overline{21}|2\%} - A_{\overline{5}|2\%} = 25.783317 - 5.204040 = \underline{\underline{20.57928}}$$

Present Value of Ordinary Annuity of 1

Present values of annuities are used more frequently in financial accounting than any of the compound interest concepts discussed so far. For example, the computations of (1) the proceeds of bond issues, (2) the value of plant assets acquired in purchase-type business combinations or through capital leases, (3) the amount of past service pension costs, (4) the amount of debt or receivables under instalment contracts, and (5) the amount of mortgage debt or investments in mortgage notes all require the application of the present-value-of-annuity concept.

The following diagram depicts the present value (P) of an ***ordinary annuity*** (***annuity in arrears***) of five rents (R):

Diagram of present value of ordinary annuity

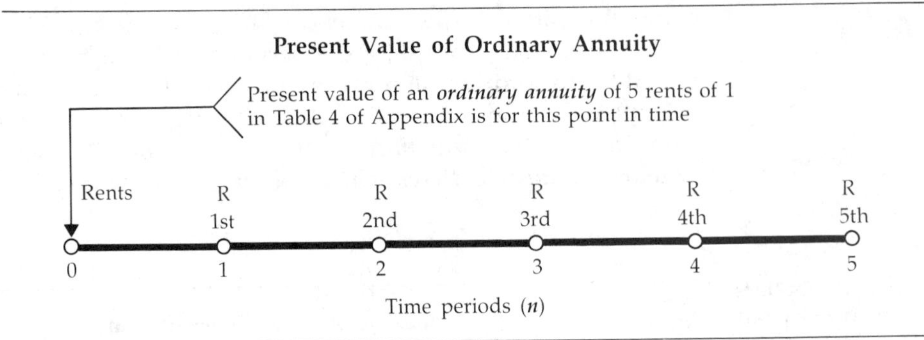

The present value of an ordinary annuity of five rents depicted above is the value of the rents, discounted at compound interest, at a point in time ***one period before the first rent***. The present value of an ordinary annuity is computed as the total of the present values of the individual rents, but the use of a table, such as Table 4 in the Appendix at the end of this chapter, is more efficient.

The ***present value*** (*P*) of an ordinary annuity of *n* rents at *i* rate of interest may be computed by ***dividing by* i *the compound discount*** on 1 for *n* periods at *i* rate of interest. This is illustrated below in the computation of the present value of an ordinary annuity of five rents at 8% per period:

Computation of present value of an ordinary annuity

$$P_{\overline{n}|i} = \frac{1 - \dfrac{1}{(1+i)^n}}{i} = \frac{1 - \dfrac{1}{(1+0.08)^5}}{0.08} = \frac{1 - 0.680583}{0.08}$$

$$= \frac{0.319417}{0.08} = \underline{\underline{3.99271}}$$

The present value of 1 at 8% for five periods (0.680583) is taken from Table 2 in the Appendix at the end of this chapter. Dividing the compound discount of 0.319417 (1 − 0.680583 = 0.319417) by 0.08 gives the present value of an ordinary annuity of five rents of 1 at 8%. In Table 4 in the Appendix, the present value of an ordinary annuity of five rents of 1 at 8% is given as 3.992710, thus confirming the computation above.

To illustrate the application of the present value of an ordinary annuity of 1, assume the following: Evans Company has outstanding a $500,000 non-interest-bearing debt, payable $100,000 a year for five years starting on December 31, Year 1. What is the present value of this debt on January 1, Year 1, for financial accounting, if 8% compounded annually is considered a fair rate of interest? The present value of the debt on January 1, Year 1, is equal to the present value of an ordinary annuity of five rents of $100,000 at 8% per period. Therefore, the debt should be reported at $399,271 ($100,000 × 3.99271) in the accounting records on January 1, Year 1. The ***repayment program (loan amortization table)*** for this debt is summarized in the following table:

Repayment program for debt

EVANS COMPANY
Repayment Program for Debt of $399,271 at 8% Interest

Date	*Interest expense at 8% a year*	*Repayment at end of year*	*Net reduction in debt*	*Debt balance*
Jan. 1, Year 1				$399,271
Dec. 31, Year 1	$31,942	$100,000	$68,058	331,213
Dec. 31, Year 2	26,497	100,000	73,503	257,710
Dec. 31, Year 3	20,617	100,000	79,383	178,327
Dec. 31, Year 4	14,266	100,000	85,734	92,593
Dec. 31, Year 5	7,407	100,000	92,593	-0-

As illustrated in our earlier discussion of the amount of an ordinary annuity, Table 4 in the Appendix at the end of this chapter may be used to compute other variables in the formula for the present value of an ordinary annuity. For example, if we know that $P_{\overline{5}|8\%} = 3.99271$ and the present value of an ordinary annuity of five rents at 8% per period is $399,271, we may compute the periodic rent of $100,000 by dividing $399,271 by 3.99271.

Summary and Examples

The formula for the present value of an ordinary annuity of 1, $P_{\overline{n}|i}$, is used to compute the amount P that would settle a debt one period before the first rent of n equal rents of R dollars discounted at compound interest rate i per period. In other words, $P_{\overline{n}|i}$ is used to compute the value one period before the first rent of a series of equal cash inflows or outflows, discounted at a constant interest rate per period.

Example 1: Proceeds from Bonds Issued at a Discount Murphy Limited issued $5 million face amount of 9%, five-year bonds on June 30, Year 5. The bonds pay interest on June 30 and December 31 and were issued to yield 10% compounded semiannually. Compute the proceeds of this bond issue.

Solution The proceeds of the bond issue may be computed as the total of (1) the present value of the $5 million to be paid at maturity, discounted at the 5% semiannual current rate of interest for 10 periods, plus (2) the present value of an ordinary annuity of 10 rents of $225,000 ($5,000,000 × 0.045 = $225,000) semiannual interest payments, also discounted at 5% per period. This approach can be illustrated as follows:

Computation of proceeds of bonds payable

Present value of $5 million discounted at 5% for 10 six-month periods: $5,000,000 × 0.613913	$3,069,565
Add: Present value of ordinary annuity of 10 rents of $225,000 discounted at 5%: $225,000 × 7.721735	1,737,390
Proceeds of bond issue	$4,806,955*

*$2 discrepancy between this amount and the amount computed below is caused by rounding in present value tables.

Alternative Solution Because the 9% interest rate on the bonds is less than the 10% current fair rate of interest, the bonds were sold at a discount equal in amount to the present value of the semiannual interest ***deficiency*** (interest that will not be paid to bondholders) of $25,000 [$5,000,000 × (0.050 − 0.045) = $25,000] for 10 semiannual periods discounted at the 5% ***current rate of interest per period***. Therefore, the proceeds from the bond issue may also be computed as follows:

Alternative computation of proceeds of bonds payable

Face amount of bonds	$5,000,000
Less: Present value of ordinary annuity of 10 rents of $25,000 interest deficiency discounted at 5% per period: $25,000 × 7.721735	193,043
Proceeds of bond issue	$4,806,957

Computation of the proceeds of "zero-coupon" bonds is illustrated earlier. In recent years some companies have issued bonds that bear a low nominal rate of interest. These have been issued at substantial discounts and are referred to as "deep-discount bonds." The proceeds of the issuance of bonds at a premium (when the interest rate paid on the bonds exceeds the current rate of interest) are computed similarly, as illustrated in Chapter 15.

Example 2: Note Receivable with Excessive Rate of Interest On March 1, Year 1, Crane Company sold land that cost $80,000 for a $100,000, two-year, 15% promissory note. Interest of $15,000 is due on March 1, Year 2, and $115,000 (interest and face amount of the note) is due on March 1, Year 3. The fair rate of interest on this promissory note on March 1, Year 1, was 10% a year. Crane recorded the transaction ***incorrectly*** on March 1, Year 1, as follows:

Note Receivable	100,000	
Land		80,000
Gain on Sale of Land		20,000
To record sale of land.		

Compute the current fair value of the note receivable and prepare a correcting entry required as of March 1, Year 1, as well as journal entries to record the cash receipts on March 1, Year 2 and Year 3. Disregard accruals of interest revenue.

Solution The current fair value of the note receivable is larger than its face amount because it bears an excessive rate of interest. The ***current fair value*** of the note receivable on March 1, Year 1, is computed as follows:

Computation of current fair value of note receivable on March 1, Year 1

Present value of face amount of note (discounted at 10% for two years): $100,000 × 0.826446*	$ 82,645
Add: Present value of interest on note for two years (ordinary annuity of two rents of $15,000 at 10%): $15,000 × 1.735537†	26,033
Current fair value of note receivable	$108,678

*Table 2 in Appendix at the end of this chapter.
†Table 4 in Appendix at the end of this chapter.

Shown below are the ***correcting entry*** as of March 1, Year 1, and the ***journal entries to record the cash receipts*** on March 1, Year 2 and Year 3:

Correcting entry and journal entries to record cash receipts

March 1, Year 1		
Premium on Note Receivable	8,678	
Gain on Sale of Land ($28,678 – $20,000)		8,678
To record premium on note receivable and increase the amount of the gain on the sale of the land from $20,000 to $28,678 ($108,678 – $80,000 = $28,678).		
March 1, Year 2		
Cash	15,000	
Interest Revenue ($108,678 × 0.10)		10,868
Premium on Note Receivable		4,132
To record receipt of interest and amortization of premium on note receivable.		
March 1, Year 3		
Cash	115,000	
Note Receivable		100,000
Interest Revenue [($108,678 – $4,132) × 0.10]...		10,454*
Premium on Note Receivable		4,546
To record receipt of principal and interest, and amortization of premium on note receivable.		

*Adjusted for $1 discrepancy because of rounding.

Present Value of Annuity Due

The present value of an ordinary annuity falls one period before the first rent. In contrast, the ***present value of an annuity due falls on the date the first rent is deposited or withdrawn***. For this reason, an annuity due is often referred to as an ***annuity in advance***. The difference between the present value of an ordinary annuity and the present value of an annuity due is illustrated below.

For example, we need the present value of an annuity due of ***n*** rents of 1 to compute the periodic rent payments on an instalment contract or a lease when the first payment is due at the beginning of each period. The diagram on the next page indicates that the present value at time period 1 of an annuity due of five rents may be computed (1) by adding interest for one period to the present value of an ordinary annuity of five rents or (2) by obtaining the present value of an ordinary annuity of four rents and then adding 1, representing the ''extra'' rent at time period 1. These two approaches are illustrated next, using Table 4 in the Appendix at the end of this chapter, to compute the present value of an annuity due of five rents of 1 at 8% per period.

Diagram of present values for ordinary annuity and annuity due

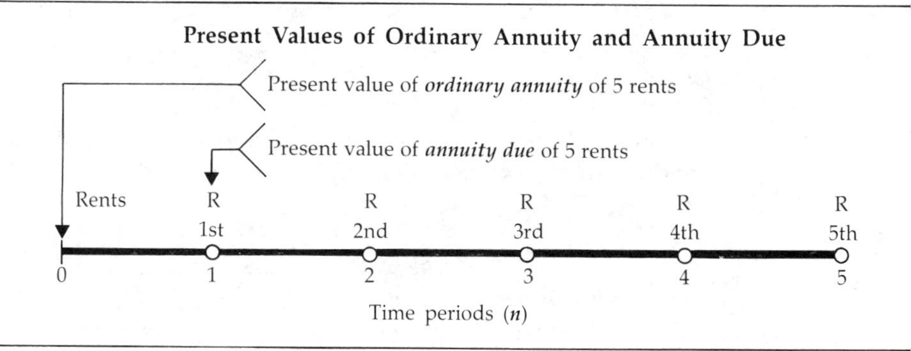

Two ways of computing present value of annuity due

Present value of ordinary annuity of five rents of 1 at 8%, plus interest at 8% on this present value for one period: 3.99271 × 1.08 = present value of annuity due $[P_{\overline{n}|i} \times (1 + i)]$	4.312127
or	
Present value of ordinary annuity of four rents of 1 at 8%, plus 1, the fifth rent at time period 1:3.312127 + 1 = present value of annuity due $(P_{\overline{n-1}|i} + 1)$	4.312127

To illustrate the application of the present value of an annuity due of 1, assume the following: On January 1, Year 1, Cinema Corporation acquired a plant asset for $64,682. Cinema agreed to make five equal annual payments starting on January 1, Year 1, and ending on January 1, Year 5, at 8% compounded annually. The annual payments on the debt are determined below:

$64,682 ÷ 4.312127 = $15,000

The repayment program for this debt is presented below:

Repayment program for debt

CINEMA CORPORATION
Repayment Program for Debt of $64,682 at 8% Interest

Jan. 1, Year:	*Debt at beginning of year*	*Payment at beginning of year*	*Balance accruing interest*	*Interest at 8%*	*Debt at end of year*
1	$64,682	$15,000	$49,682	$3,975	$53,657
2	53,657	15,000	38,657	3,093	41,750
3	41,750	15,000	26,750	2,140	28,890
4	28,890	15,000	13,890	1,110*	15,000
5	15,000	15,000	–0–	–0–	–0–

*Adjusted for $1 discrepancy due to rounding of computations.

Present Value of Deferred Annuity

When periodic rents are postponed for more than one period, the present value of such an annuity on some date prior to the first rent may be computed by using two different methods as follows: (1) Discount the present value of the ordinary annuity portion at compound interest for the periods the annuity is deferred, or (2) determine the present value of an ordinary annuity equal to the total number of periods involved and subtract from this the present value of the "missing" ordinary annuity for rents equal in number to the number of periods the annuity is deferred. To illustrate, assume that Jedi, Inc., wants to know the amount at time period 0 that would pay a debt of five payments of $100,000 each, payments starting at time period 4, and interest compounded at 8% per time period. A diagram of the periodic rents (payments) follows:

Diagram of present value of deferred annuity

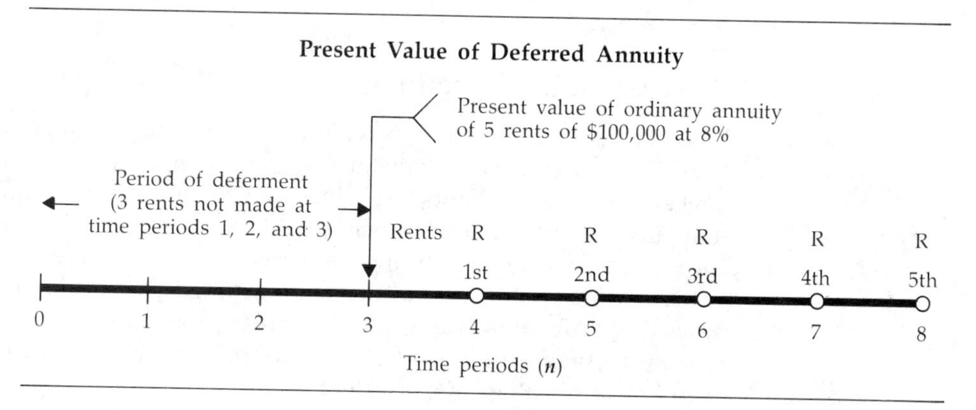

Using Tables 2 and 4 in the Appendix at the end of this chapter, we may compute the present value (at time period 0) of the ordinary annuity of five rents of 1 *deferred for three periods* as follows:

Two ways of computing present value of deferred annuity

Present value of ordinary annuity of five rents of 1 at 8% at time period 3, discounted at 8% for three periods: 3.992710 × 0.793832	3.169541
or	
Present value of ordinary annuity of eight rents of 1 at 8% at time period 0, less the present value of ordinary annuity of three rents of 1 (the rents not made) at 8% at time period 0: 5.746639 − 2.577097	3.169542*

*Slight discrepancy due to rounding of present values in the Appendix at the end of this chapter.

Thus, cash in the amount of $316,954 ($100,000 × 3.169542 = $316,954) is needed at time period 0 to repay the debt diagrammed above. The repayment of the debt is summarized as follows:

Proof that computation is correct

JEDI, INC.
Repayment Program for Debt of $316,954 at 8% Interest

Time period	*Interest expense at 8% per period*	*Repayments*	*Net reduction in debt*	*Debt balance*
0	Present value of debt			$316,954
1	$25,356			342,310
2	27,385			369,695
3	29,576			399,271
4	31,942	$100,000	$68,058	331,213
5	26,497	100,000	73,503	257,710
6	20,617	100,000	79,383	178,327
7	14,266	100,000	85,734	92,593
8	7,407	100,000	92,593	-0-

More Complex Situations

Many complex situations involving compound interest may be encountered in the business world. An understanding of the concepts discussed in the preceding pages enables accountants to analyze and solve problems requiring the application of compound interest principles. Because money may be invested readily to earn a return, there is a universal service charge (interest) for its use, and a specific amount of money available on a stated date has a different value at all other points in time. Compound interest procedures are a means of moving money inflows and outflows forward and backward in time on a basis that enables a comparison of values in equivalent terms.

For example, assume that you are given a choice of receiving $20,000 cash in two years or $30,000 in eight years. The choice is not obvious. Assuming a current fair interest rate of 10%, these amounts may be compared only by measuring their ***present value or accumulated amount on a particular date***. If we choose ***now*** (time point 0), the following ***present-value*** analysis shows that the $20,000 in two years is preferable to receiving $30,000 in eight years:

Comparing present values of future cash flows at 10% interest

$$\$20{,}000(p_{\overline{2}|10\%}) = \$20{,}000 \times 0.826446^{*} = \underline{\underline{\$16{,}529}}$$

$$\$30{,}000(p_{\overline{8}|10\%}) = \$30{,}000 \times 0.466507^{*} = \underline{\underline{\$13{,}995}}$$

*From Table 2 in the Appendix at the end of this chapter.

We may reach the same conclusion by comparing ***the accumulated amounts*** of the two dollar amounts eight years from now as follows:

Comparing amounts on a fixed future date at 10% interest

$$\$20{,}000(a_{\overline{6}|10\%}) = \$20{,}000 \times 1.771561^{*} = \underline{\underline{\$35{,}431}}$$

$30,000 at the end of eight years is equivalent to $\underline{\underline{\$30{,}000}}$

*From Table 1 in the Appendix at the end of this chapter.

Here, the receipt of $20,000 in two years is again shown to be preferable to the receipt of $30,000 in eight years, because if $20,000 is invested at 10% at the end of the second year, it would accumulate to $35,431 by the end of the eighth year. Any other point in time may be selected to make a similar comparison at 10% interest without changing the validity of the decision to receive $20,000 two years from today. However, if the interest rate were reduced materially, the option of receiving $30,000 in eight years would be more advantageous; for example, if we assume a 5% interest rate, the $20,000 received at the end of the second year would be worth only $26,802 ($20,000 × 1.340096 = $26,802) at the end of the eighth year. Thus, the option of receiving $30,000 in eight years would be preferable.

As another example, assume that, at the beginning of Year 1, Kay Park deposited $50,000 in a fund that pays 8% interest compounded annually, and that she planned to withdraw from the fund as follows:

1. Equal amounts for three years starting at the end of Year 1
2. Equal amounts starting at the end of Year 4 and ending at the end of Year 6 ***that are three times as large as the first three withdrawals***

The diagram below indicates that the deposit of $50,000 is equal to (1) the present value of an ordinary annuity of three rents (***R***) at 8% ***plus*** (2) the present value of an ordinary annuity of three rents three times as large as the first three rents (3***R***) deferred for three years.

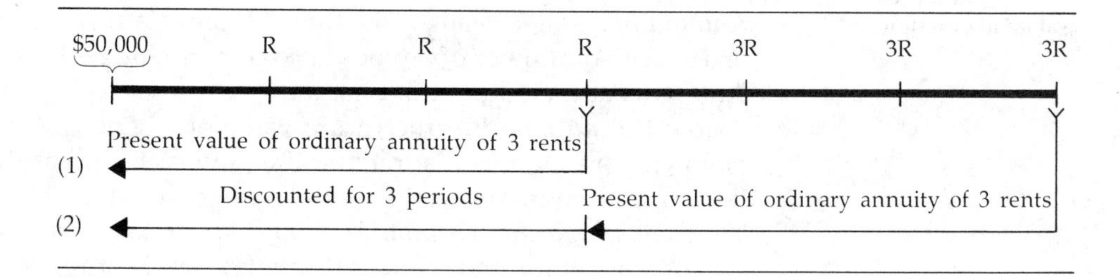

From the present-value tables in the Appendix at the end of this chapter, the amount of ***R*** may be computed as follows:

$$R\,(2.577097) + 3R\,(2.577097 \times 0.793832) = \$50{,}000$$

$$8.714443R = \$50{,}000$$

$$R = \underline{\underline{\$5{,}738}} \text{ (amount of each of the first three withdrawals)}$$

$$3R = \underline{\underline{\$17{,}214}} \text{ (amount of each of the last three withdrawals)}$$

The following table summarizes the compound-interest accumulations and withdrawals by Kay Park:

KAY PARK
Interest Accumulations and Withdrawals — Fund of $50,000

End of year:	*Interest revenue at 8% a year*	*Withdrawals*	*Net reduction in fund*	*Fund balance*
				$50,000
1	$4,000	$5,738	$1,738	48,262
2	3,861	5,738	1,877	46,385
3	3,711	5,738	2,027	44,358
4	3,549	17,214	13,665	30,693
5	2,455	17,214	14,759	15,934
6	1,280*	17,214	15,934	-0-

*Adjusted by $5 for rounding of amounts to nearest dollar.

Summary of Future Amounts and Present Values

The following list of future amounts and present values may be useful as a quick review of the essential concepts discussed in this chapter:

Essential concepts relating to future and present values of cash flows

1 **Future Amount:** the value on a future date of a ***single amount*** or a ***series of rents*** invested at compound interest.
  a *Amount of a single deposit:* the future value of a single deposit at the end of a specified number of periods at compound interest. (See Table 1 in the Appendix at the end of this chapter.)
  b *Amount of an annuity:* the future value of a series of equal receipts or payments (rents) made at regular time intervals and at the same rate of interest compounded each time the receipts or payments are made.
    1 *Amount of ordinary annuity* (*annuity in arrears*)*:* the amount accumulated at compound interest through a series of rents on the date the final rent is made. (See Table 3 in the Appendix at the end of this chapter.)
    2 *Amount of annuity due* (*annuity in advance*)*:* the amount accumulated at compound interest through a series of rents one period after the final rent is made. Thus, the amount of an annuity due of *R* rents is equal to the amount of an ordinary annuity of *R* rents plus interest for one additional period.
    3 *Amount of deferred annuity:* the amount of an ordinary annuity that continues to earn compound interest for more than one period after the final rent is made.

2 **Present Value:** the value now of a ***single amount*** or a ***series of rents*** to be received in the future and discounted at compound interest to an earlier date (usually the date of a transaction, as in the acquisition of equipment on the instalment plan).
  a *Present value of 1:* the value of a single amount due or payable on some

future date discounted at compound interest. (See Table 2 in the Appendix at the end of this chapter.)

b *Present value of an annuity:* the value of a series of equal future receipts or payments (rents) made at regular time intervals and discounted at the same compound-interest rate on each date rents are due.

1. *Present value of ordinary annuity* (annuity in arrears): the discounted value of a series of future rents on a date one period before the first rent. (See Table 4 in the Appendix at the end of this chapter.)
2. *Present value of annuity due* (annuity in advance): the discounted value of a series of future rents on the date the first rent is received or paid.
3. *Present value of deferred annuity*: the discounted value of a series of future rents on a date that is more than one period before the date the first rent is received or paid.

APPENDIX: COMPOUND INTEREST TABLES

Contents

Table 1 Future Amount of 1 at Compound Interest Due in n Periods: $a_{\overline{n}|i} = (1 + i)^n$

n \ i	½%	1%	1½%	2%	2½%	3%
1	1.005000	1.010000	1.015000	1.020000	1.025000	1.030000
2	1.010025	1.020100	1.030225	1.040400	1.050625	1.060900
3	1.015075	1.030301	1.045678	1.061208	1.076891	1.092727
4	1.020151	1.040604	1.061364	1.082432	1.103813	1.125509
5	1.025251	1.051010	1.077284	1.104081	1.131408	1.159274
6	1.030378	1.061520	1.093443	1.126162	1.159693	1.194052
7	1.035529	1.072135	1.109845	1.148686	1.188686	1.229874
8	1.040707	1.082857	1.126493	1.171659	1.218403	1.266770
9	1.045911	1.093685	1.143390	1.195093	1.248863	1.304773
10	1.051140	1.104622	1.160541	1.218994	1.280085	1.343916
11	1.056396	1.115668	1.177949	1.243374	1.312087	1.384234
12	1.061678	1.126825	1.195618	1.268242	1.344889	1.425761
13	1.066986	1.138093	1.213552	1.293607	1.378511	1.468534
14	1.072321	1.149474	1.231756	1.319479	1.412974	1.512590
15	1.077683	1.160969	1.250232	1.345868	1.448298	1.557967
16	1.083071	1.172579	1.268986	1.372786	1.484506	1.604706
17	1.088487	1.184304	1.288020	1.400241	1.521618	1.652848
18	1.093929	1.196147	1.307341	1.428246	1.559659	1.702433
19	1.099399	1.208109	1.326951	1.456811	1.598650	1.753506
20	1.104896	1.220190	1.346855	1.485947	1.638616	1.806111
21	1.110420	1.232392	1.367058	1.515666	1.679582	1.860295
22	1.115972	1.244716	1.387564	1.545980	1.721571	1.916103
23	1.121552	1.257163	1.408377	1.576899	1.764611	1.973587
24	1.127160	1.269735	1.429503	1.608437	1.808726	2.032794
25	1.132796	1.282432	1.450945	1.640606	1.853944	2.093778
26	1.138460	1.295256	1.472710	1.673418	1.900293	2.156591
27	1.144152	1.308209	1.494800	1.706886	1.947800	2.221289
28	1.149873	1.321291	1.517222	1.741024	1.996495	2.287928
29	1.155622	1.334504	1.539981	1.775845	2.046407	2.356566
30	1.161400	1.347849	1.563080	1.811362	2.097568	2.427262
31	1.167207	1.361327	1.586526	1.847589	2.150007	2.500080
32	1.173043	1.374941	1.610324	1.884541	2.203757	2.575083
33	1.178908	1.388690	1.634479	1.922231	2.258851	2.652335
34	1.184803	1.402577	1.658996	1.960676	2.315322	2.731905
35	1.190727	1.416603	1.683881	1.999890	2.373205	2.813862
36	1.196681	1.430769	1.709140	2.039887	2.432535	2.898278
37	1.202664	1.445076	1.734777	2.080685	2.493349	2.985227
38	1.208677	1.459527	1.760798	2.122299	2.555682	3.074783
39	1.214721	1.474123	1.787210	2.164745	2.619574	3.167027
40	1.220794	1.488864	1.814018	2.208040	2.685064	3.262038
41	1.226898	1.503752	1.841229	2.252200	2.752190	3.359899
42	1.233033	1.518790	1.868847	2.297244	2.820995	3.460696
43	1.239198	1.533978	1.896880	2.343189	2.891520	3.564517
44	1.245394	1.549318	1.925333	2.390053	2.963808	3.671452
45	1.251621	1.564811	1.954213	2.437854	3.037903	3.781596
46	1.257879	1.580459	1.983526	2.486611	3.113851	3.895044
47	1.264168	1.596263	2.013279	2.536344	3.191697	4.011895
48	1.270489	1.612226	2.043478	2.587070	3.271490	4.132252
49	1.276842	1.628348	2.074130	2.638812	3.353277	4.256219
50	1.283226	1.644632	2.105242	2.691588	3.437109	4.383906

Table 1 Future Amount of 1 (*continued*)

n \ i	$3\frac{1}{2}\%$	4%	$4\frac{1}{2}\%$	5%	$5\frac{1}{2}\%$	6%
1	1.035000	1.040000	1.045000	1.050000	1.055000	1.060000
2	1.071225	1.081600	1.092025	1.102500	1.113025	1.123600
3	1.108718	1.124864	1.141166	1.157625	1.174241	1.191016
4	1.147523	1.169859	1.192519	1.215506	1.238825	1.262477
5	1.187686	1.216653	1.246182	1.276282	1.306960	1.338226
6	1.229255	1.265319	1.302260	1.340096	1.378843	1.418519
7	1.272279	1.315932	1.360862	1.407100	1.454679	1.503630
8	1.316809	1.368569	1.422101	1.477455	1.534687	1.593848
9	1.362897	1.423312	1.486095	1.551328	1.619094	1.689479
10	1.410599	1.480244	1.552969	1.628895	1.708144	1.790848
11	1.459970	1.539454	1.622853	1.710339	1.802092	1.898299
12	1.511069	1.601032	1.695881	1.795856	1.901207	2.012196
13	1.563956	1.665074	1.772196	1.885649	2.005774	2.132928
14	1.618695	1.731676	1.851945	1.979932	2.116091	2.260904
15	1.675349	1.800944	1.935282	2.078928	2.232476	2.396558
16	1.733986	1.872981	2.022370	2.182875	2.355263	2.540352
17	1.794676	1.947901	2.113377	2.292018	2.484802	2.692773
18	1.857489	2.025817	2.208479	2.406619	2.621466	2.854339
19	1.922501	2.106849	2.307860	2.526950	2.765647	3.025600
20	1.989789	2.191123	2.411714	2.653298	2.917757	3.207135
21	2.059431	2.278768	2.520241	2.785963	3.078234	3.399564
22	2.131512	2.369919	2.633652	2.925261	3.247537	3.603537
23	2.206114	2.464716	2.752166	3.071524	3.426152	3.819750
24	2.283328	2.563304	2.876014	3.225100	3.614590	4.048935
25	2.363245	2.665836	3.005434	3.386355	3.813392	4.291871
26	2.445959	2.772470	3.140679	3.555673	4.023129	4.549383
27	2.531567	2.883369	3.282010	3.733456	4.244401	4.822346
28	2.620172	2.998703	3.429700	3.920129	4.477843	5.111687
29	2.711878	3.118651	3.584036	4.116136	4.724124	5.418388
30	2.806794	3.243398	3.745318	4.321942	4.983951	5.743491
31	2.905031	3.373133	3.913857	4.538039	5.258069	6.088101
32	3.006708	3.508059	4.089981	4.764941	5.547262	6.453387
33	3.111942	3.648381	4.274030	5.003189	5.852362	6.840590
34	3.220860	3.794316	4.466362	5.253348	6.174242	7.251025
35	3.333590	3.946089	4.667348	5.516015	6.513825	7.686087
36	3.450266	4.103933	4.877378	5.791816	6.872085	8.147252
37	3.571025	4.268090	5.096860	6.081407	7.250050	8.636087
38	3.696011	4.438813	5.326219	6.385477	7.648803	9.154252
39	3.825372	4.616366	5.565899	6.704751	8.069487	9.703507
40	3.959260	4.801021	5.816365	7.039989	8.513309	10.285718
41	4.097834	4.993061	6.078101	7.391988	8.981541	10.902861
42	4.241258	5.192784	6.351615	7.761588	9.475526	11.557033
43	4.389702	5.400495	6.637438	8.149667	9.996679	12.250455
44	4.543342	5.616515	6.936123	8.557150	10.546497	12.985482
45	4.702359	5.841176	7.248248	8.985008	11.126554	13.764611
46	4.866941	6.074823	7.574420	9.434258	11.738515	14.590487
47	5.037284	6.317816	7.915268	9.905971	12.384133	15.465917
48	5.213589	6.570528	8.271456	10.401270	13.065260	16.393872
49	5.396065	6.833349	8.643671	10.921333	13.783849	17.377504
50	5.584927	7.106683	9.032636	11.467400	14.541961	18.420154

Table 1 Future Amount of 1 (*continued*)

n \ i	7%	8%	9%	10%	12%	15%
1	1.070000	1.080000	1.090000	1.100000	1.120000	1.150000
2	1.144900	1.166400	1.188100	1.210000	1.254400	1.322500
3	1.225043	1.259712	1.295029	1.331000	1.404928	1.520875
4	1.310796	1.360489	1.411582	1.464100	1.573519	1.749006
5	1.402552	1.469328	1.538624	1.610510	1.762342	2.011357
6	1.500730	1.586874	1.677100	1.771561	1.973823	2.313061
7	1.605781	1.713824	1.828039	1.948717	2.210681	2.660020
8	1.718186	1.850930	1.992563	2.143589	2.475963	3.059023
9	1.838459	1.999005	2.171893	2.357948	2.773079	3.517876
10	1.967151	2.158925	2.367364	2.593742	3.105848	4.045558
11	2.104852	2.331639	2.580426	2.853117	3.478550	4.652391
12	2.252192	2.518170	2.812665	3.138428	3.895976	5.350250
13	2.409845	2.719624	3.065805	3.452271	4.363493	6.152788
14	2.578534	2.937194	3.341727	3.797498	4.887112	7.075706
15	2.759032	3.172169	3.642482	4.177248	5.473566	8.137062
16	2.952164	3.425943	3.970306	4.594973	6.130394	9.357621
17	3.158815	3.700018	4.327633	5.054470	6.866041	10.761264
18	3.379932	3.996019	4.717120	5.559917	7.689966	12.375454
19	3.616528	4.315701	5.141661	6.115909	8.612762	14.231772
20	3.869684	4.660957	5.604411	6.727500	9.646293	16.366537
21	4.140562	5.033834	6.108808	7.400250	10.803848	18.821518
22	4.430402	5.436540	6.658600	8.140275	12.100310	21.644746
23	4.740530	5.871464	7.257874	8.954302	13.552347	24.891458
24	5.072367	6.341181	7.911083	9.849733	15.178629	28.625176
25	5.427433	6.848475	8.623081	10.834706	17.000064	32.918953
26	5.807353	7.396353	9.399158	11.918177	19.040072	37.856796
27	6.213868	7.988061	10.245082	13.109994	21.324881	43.535315
28	6.648838	8.627106	11.167140	14.420994	23.883866	50.065612
29	7.114257	9.317275	12.172182	15.863093	26.749930	57.575454
30	7.612255	10.062657	13.267678	17.449402	29.959922	66.211772
31	8.145113	10.867669	14.461770	19.194342	33.555113	76.143538
32	8.715271	11.737083	15.763329	21.113777	37.581726	87.565068
33	9.325340	12.676050	17.182028	23.225154	42.091533	100.699829
34	9.978114	13.690134	18.728411	25.547670	47.142517	115.804803
35	10.676581	14.785344	20.413968	28.102437	52.799620	133.175523
36	11.423942	15.968172	22.251225	30.912681	59.135574	153.151852
37	12.223618	17.245626	24.253835	34.003949	66.231843	176.124630
38	13.079271	18.625276	26.436680	37.404343	74.179664	202.543324
39	13.994820	20.115298	28.815982	41.144778	83.081224	232.924823
40	14.974458	21.724521	31.409420	45.259256	93.050970	267.863546
41	16.022670	23.462483	34.236268	49.785181	104.217087	308.043078
42	17.144257	25.339482	37.317532	54.763699	116.723137	354.249540
43	18.344355	27.366640	40.676110	60.240069	130.729914	407.386971
44	19.628460	29.555972	44.336960	66.264076	146.417503	468.495017
45	21.002452	31.920449	48.327286	72.890484	163.987604	538.769269
46	22.472623	34.474085	52.676742	80.179532	183.666116	619.584659
47	24.045707	37.232012	57.417649	88.197485	205.706050	712.522358
48	25.728907	40.210573	62.585237	97.017234	230.390776	819.400712
49	27.529930	43.427419	68.217908	106.718957	258.037669	942.310819
50	29.457025	46.901613	74.357520	117.390853	289.002190	1083.657442

Table 2 Present Value of 1 at Compound Interest Due in *n* Periods: $p_{\overline{n}|i} = \frac{1}{(1 + i)^n}$

n \ i	½%	1%	1½%	2%	2½%	3%
1	0.995025	0.990099	0.985222	0.980392	0.975610	0.970874
2	0.990075	0.980296	0.970662	0.961169	0.951814	0.942596
3	0.985149	0.970590	0.956317	0.942322	0.928599	0.915142
4	0.980248	0.960980	0.942184	0.923845	0.905951	0.888487
5	0.975371	0.951466	0.928260	0.905731	0.883854	0.862609
6	0.970518	0.942045	0.914542	0.887971	0.862297	0.837484
7	0.965690	0.932718	0.901027	0.870560	0.841265	0.813092
8	0.960885	0.923483	0.887711	0.853490	0.820747	0.789409
9	0.956105	0.914340	0.874592	0.836755	0.800728	0.766417
10	0.951348	0.905287	0.861667	0.820348	0.781198	0.744094
11	0.946615	0.896324	0.848933	0.804263	0.762145	0.722421
12	0.941905	0.887449	0.836387	0.788493	0.743556	0.701380
13	0.937219	0.878663	0.824027	0.773033	0.725420	0.680951
14	0.932556	0.869963	0.811849	0.757875	0.707727	0.661118
15	0.927917	0.861349	0.799852	0.743015	0.690466	0.641862
16	0.923300	0.852821	0.788031	0.728446	0.673625	0.623167
17	0.918707	0.844377	0.776385	0.714163	0.657195	0.605016
18	0.914136	0.836017	0.764912	0.700159	0.641166	0.587395
19	0.909588	0.827740	0.753607	0.686431	0.625528	0.570286
20	0.905063	0.819544	0.742470	0.672971	0.610271	0.553676
21	0.900560	0.811430	0.731498	0.659776	0.595386	0.537549
22	0.896080	0.803396	0.720688	0.646839	0.580865	0.521893
23	0.891622	0.795442	0.710037	0.634156	0.566697	0.506692
24	0.887186	0.787566	0.699544	0.621721	0.552875	0.491934
25	0.882772	0.779768	0.689206	0.609531	0.539391	0.477606
26	0.878380	0.772048	0.679021	0.597579	0.526235	0.463695
27	0.874010	0.764404	0.668986	0.585862	0.513400	0.450189
28	0.869662	0.756836	0.659099	0.574375	0.500878	0.437077
29	0.865335	0.749342	0.649359	0.563112	0.488661	0.424346
30	0.861030	0.741923	0.639762	0.552071	0.476743	0.411987
31	0.856746	0.734577	0.630308	0.541246	0.465115	0.399987
32	0.852484	0.727304	0.620993	0.530633	0.453771	0.388337
33	0.848242	0.720103	0.611816	0.520229	0.442703	0.377026
34	0.844022	0.712973	0.602774	0.510028	0.431905	0.366045
35	0.839823	0.705914	0.593866	0.500028	0.421371	0.355383
36	0.835645	0.698925	0.585090	0.490223	0.411094	0.345032
37	0.831487	0.692005	0.576443	0.480611	0.401067	0.334983
38	0.827351	0.685153	0.567924	0.471187	0.391285	0.325226
39	0.823235	0.678370	0.559531	0.461948	0.381741	0.315754
40	0.819139	0.671653	0.551262	0.452890	0.372431	0.306557
41	0.815064	0.665003	0.543116	0.444010	0.363347	0.297628
42	0.811009	0.658419	0.535089	0.435304	0.354485	0.288959
43	0.806974	0.651900	0.527182	0.426769	0.345839	0.280543
44	0.802959	0.645445	0.519391	0.418401	0.337404	0.272372
45	0.798964	0.639055	0.511715	0.410197	0.329174	0.264439
46	0.794989	0.632728	0.504153	0.402154	0.321146	0.256737
47	0.791034	0.626463	0.496702	0.394268	0.313313	0.249259
48	0.787098	0.620260	0.489362	0.386538	0.305671	0.241999
49	0.783183	0.614119	0.482130	0.378958	0.298216	0.234950
50	0.779286	0.608039	0.475005	0.371528	0.290942	0.228107

Table 2 Present Value of 1 (*continued*)

n \ i	$3\frac{1}{2}\%$	4%	$4\frac{1}{2}\%$	5%	$5\frac{1}{2}\%$	6%
1	0.966184	0.961538	0.956938	0.952381	0.947867	0.943396
2	0.933511	0.924556	0.915730	0.907029	0.898452	0.889996
3	0.901943	0.888996	0.876297	0.863838	0.851614	0.839619
4	0.871442	0.854804	0.838561	0.822702	0.807217	0.792094
5	0.841973	0.821927	0.802451	0.783526	0.765134	0.747258
6	0.813501	0.790315	0.767896	0.746215	0.725246	0.704961
7	0.785991	0.759918	0.734828	0.710681	0.687437	0.665057
8	0.759412	0.730690	0.703185	0.676839	0.651599	0.627412
9	0.733731	0.702587	0.672904	0.644609	0.617629	0.591898
10	0.708919	0.675564	0.643928	0.613913	0.585431	0.558395
11	0.684946	0.649581	0.616199	0.584679	0.554911	0.526788
12	0.661783	0.624597	0.589664	0.556837	0.525982	0.496969
13	0.639404	0.600574	0.564272	0.530321	0.498561	0.468839
14	0.617782	0.577475	0.539973	0.505068	0.472569	0.442301
15	0.596891	0.555265	0.516720	0.481017	0.447933	0.417265
16	0.576706	0.533908	0.494469	0.458112	0.424581	0.393646
17	0.557204	0.513373	0.473176	0.436297	0.402447	0.371364
18	0.538361	0.493628	0.452800	0.415521	0.381466	0.350344
19	0.520156	0.474642	0.433302	0.395734	0.361579	0.330513
20	0.502566	0.456387	0.414643	0.376889	0.342729	0.311805
21	0.485571	0.438834	0.396787	0.358942	0.324862	0.294155
22	0.469151	0.421955	0.379701	0.341850	0.307926	0.277505
23	0.453286	0.405726	0.363350	0.325571	0.291873	0.261797
24	0.437957	0.390121	0.347703	0.310068	0.276657	0.246979
25	0.423147	0.375117	0.332731	0.295303	0.262234	0.232999
26	0.408838	0.360689	0.318402	0.281241	0.248563	0.219810
27	0.395012	0.346817	0.304691	0.267848	0.235605	0.207368
28	0.381654	0.333477	0.291571	0.255094	0.223322	0.195630
29	0.368748	0.320651	0.279015	0.242946	0.211679	0.184557
30	0.356278	0.308319	0.267000	0.231377	0.200644	0.174110
31	0.344230	0.296460	0.255502	0.220359	0.190184	0.164255
32	0.332590	0.285058	0.244500	0.209866	0.180269	0.154957
33	0.321343	0.274094	0.233971	0.199873	0.170871	0.146186
34	0.310476	0.263552	0.223896	0.190355	0.161963	0.137912
35	0.299977	0.253415	0.214254	0.181290	0.153520	0.130105
36	0.289833	0.243669	0.205028	0.172657	0.145516	0.122741
37	0.280032	0.234297	0.196199	0.164436	0.137930	0.115793
38	0.270562	0.225285	0.187750	0.156605	0.130739	0.109239
39	0.261413	0.216621	0.179665	0.149148	0.123924	0.103056
40	0.252572	0.208289	0.171929	0.142046	0.117463	0.097222
41	0.244031	0.200278	0.164525	0.135282	0.111339	0.091719
42	0.235779	0.192575	0.157440	0.128840	0.105535	0.086527
43	0.227806	0.185168	0.150661	0.122704	0.100033	0.081630
44	0.220102	0.178046	0.144173	0.116861	0.094818	0.077009
45	0.212659	0.171198	0.137964	0.111297	0.089875	0.072650
46	0.205468	0.164614	0.132023	0.105997	0.085190	0.068538
47	0.198520	0.158283	0.126338	0.100949	0.080748	0.064658
48	0.191806	0.152195	0.120898	0.096142	0.076539	0.060998
49	0.185320	0.146341	0.115692	0.091564	0.072549	0.057546
50	0.179053	0.140713	0.110710	0.087204	0.068767	0.054288

Table 2 Present Value of 1 *(continued)*

n \ i	7%	8%	9%	10%	12%	15%
1	0.934580	0.925926	0.917431	0.909091	0.892857	0.869565
2	0.873439	0.857339	0.841680	0.826446	0.797194	0.756144
3	0.816298	0.793832	0.772183	0.751315	0.711780	0.657516
4	0.762895	0.735030	0.708425	0.683013	0.635518	0.571753
5	0.712986	0.680583	0.649931	0.620921	0.567427	0.497177
6	0.666342	0.630170	0.596267	0.564474	0.506631	0.432328
7	0.622750	0.583490	0.547034	0.513158	0.452349	0.375937
8	0.582009	0.540269	0.501866	0.466507	0.403883	0.326902
9	0.543934	0.500249	0.460428	0.424098	0.360610	0.284262
10	0.508349	0.463193	0.422411	0.385543	0.321973	0.247185
11	0.475093	0.428883	0.387533	0.350494	0.287476	0.214943
12	0.444012	0.397114	0.355535	0.318631	0.256675	0.186907
13	0.414964	0.367698	0.326179	0.289664	0.229174	0.162528
14	0.387817	0.340461	0.299246	0.263331	0.204620	0.141329
15	0.362446	0.315242	0.274538	0.239392	0.182696	0.122894
16	0.338735	0.291890	0.251870	0.217629	0.163122	0.106865
17	0.316574	0.270269	0.231073	0.197845	0.145644	0.092926
18	0.295864	0.250249	0.211994	0.179859	0.130040	0.080805
19	0.276508	0.231712	0.194490	0.163508	0.116107	0.070265
20	0.258419	0.214548	0.178431	0.148644	0.103667	0.061100
21	0.241513	0.198656	0.163698	0.135131	0.092560	0.053131
22	0.225713	0.183941	0.150182	0.122846	0.082643	0.046201
23	0.210947	0.170315	0.137781	0.111678	0.073788	0.040174
24	0.197147	0.157699	0.126405	0.101526	0.065882	0.034934
25	0.184249	0.146018	0.115968	0.092296	0.058823	0.030378
26	0.172195	0.135202	0.106393	0.083905	0.052521	0.026415
27	0.160930	0.125187	0.097608	0.076278	0.046894	0.022970
28	0.150402	0.115914	0.089548	0.069343	0.041869	0.019974
29	0.140563	0.107328	0.082155	0.063039	0.037383	0.017369
30	0.131367	0.099377	0.075371	0.057309	0.033378	0.015103
31	0.122773	0.092016	0.069148	0.052099	0.029802	0.013133
32	0.114741	0.085200	0.063438	0.047362	0.026609	0.011420
33	0.107235	0.078889	0.058200	0.043057	0.023758	0.009931
34	0.100219	0.073045	0.053395	0.039143	0.021212	0.008635
35	0.093663	0.067635	0.048986	0.035584	0.018940	0.007509
36	0.087535	0.062625	0.044941	0.032349	0.016910	0.006529
37	0.081809	0.057986	0.041231	0.029408	0.015098	0.005678
38	0.076457	0.053690	0.037826	0.026735	0.013481	0.004937
39	0.071455	0.049713	0.034703	0.024304	0.012036	0.004293
40	0.066780	0.046031	0.031838	0.022095	0.010747	0.003733
41	0.062412	0.042621	0.029209	0.020086	0.009595	0.003246
42	0.058329	0.039464	0.026797	0.018260	0.008567	0.002823
43	0.054513	0.036541	0.024584	0.016600	0.007649	0.002455
44	0.050946	0.033834	0.022555	0.015091	0.006830	0.002134
45	0.047613	0.031328	0.020692	0.013719	0.006098	0.001856
46	0.044499	0.029007	0.018984	0.012472	0.005445	0.001614
47	0.041587	0.026859	0.017416	0.011338	0.004861	0.001403
48	0.038867	0.024869	0.015978	0.010307	0.004340	0.001220
49	0.036324	0.023027	0.014659	0.009370	0.003875	0.001061
50	0.033948	0.021321	0.013449	0.008519	0.003460	0.000923

Table 3 Future Amount of Ordinary Annuity of 1 per Period: $A_{\overline{n}|i} = \dfrac{(1+i)^n - 1}{i}$

n \ i	$\frac{1}{2}$%	1%	$1\frac{1}{2}$%	2%	$2\frac{1}{2}$%	3%
1	1.000000	1.000000	1.000000	1.000000	1.000000	1.000000
2	2.005000	2.010000	2.015000	2.020000	2.025000	2.030000
3	3.015025	3.030100	3.045225	3.060400	3.075625	3.090900
4	4.030100	4.060401	4.090903	4.121608	4.152516	4.183627
5	5.050251	5.101005	5.152267	5.204040	5.256329	5.309136
6	6.075502	6.152015	6.229551	6.308121	6.387737	6.468410
7	7.105879	7.213535	7.322994	7.434283	7.547430	7.662462
8	8.141409	8.285671	8.432839	8.582969	8.736116	8.892336
9	9.182116	9.368527	9.559332	9.754628	9.954519	10.159106
10	10.228026	10.462213	10.702722	10.949721	11.203382	11.463879
11	11.279167	11.566835	11.863262	12.168715	12.483466	12.807796
12	12.335562	12.682503	13.041211	13.412090	13.795553	14.192030
13	13.397240	13.809328	14.236830	14.680332	15.140442	15.617790
14	14.464226	14.947421	15.450382	15.973938	16.518953	17.086324
15	15.536548	16.096896	16.682138	17.293417	17.931927	18.598914
16	16.614230	17.257864	17.932370	18.639285	19.380225	20.156881
17	17.697301	18.430443	19.201355	20.012071	20.864730	21.761588
18	18.785788	19.614748	20.489376	21.412312	22.386349	23.414435
19	19.879717	20.810895	21.796716	22.840559	23.946007	25.116868
20	20.979115	22.019004	23.123667	24.297370	25.544658	26.870374
21	22.084011	23.239194	24.470522	25.783317	27.183274	28.676486
22	23.194431	24.471586	25.837580	27.298984	28.862856	30.536780
23	24.310403	25.716302	27.225144	28.844963	30.584427	32.452884
24	25.431955	26.973465	28.633521	30.421862	32.349038	34.426470
25	26.559115	28.243200	30.063024	32.030300	34.157764	36.459264
26	27.691911	29.525632	31.513969	33.670906	36.011708	38.553042
27	28.830370	30.820888	32.986679	35.344324	37.912001	40.709634
28	29.974522	32.129097	34.481479	37.051210	39.859801	42.930923
29	31.124395	33.450388	35.998701	38.792235	41.856296	45.218850
30	32.280017	34.784892	37.538681	40.568079	43.902703	47.575416
31	33.441417	36.132740	39.101762	42.379441	46.000271	50.002678
32	34.608624	37.494068	40.688288	44.227030	48.150278	52.502759
33	35.781667	38.869009	42.298612	46.111570	50.354034	55.077841
34	36.960575	40.257699	43.933092	48.033802	52.612885	57.730177
35	38.145378	41.660276	45.592088	49.994478	54.928207	60.462082
36	39.336105	43.076878	47.275969	51.994367	57.301413	63.275944
37	40.532785	44.507647	48.985109	54.034255	59.733948	66.174223
38	41.735449	45.952724	50.719885	56.114940	62.227297	69.159449
39	42.944127	47.412251	52.480684	58.237238	64.782979	72.234233
40	44.158847	48.886373	54.267894	60.401983	67.402554	75.401260
41	45.379642	50.375237	56.081912	62.610023	70.087617	78.663298
42	46.606540	51.878989	57.923141	64.862223	72.839808	82.023196
43	47.839572	53.397779	59.791988	67.159468	75.660803	85.483892
44	49.078770	54.931757	61.688868	69.502657	78.552323	89.048409
45	50.324164	56.481075	63.614201	71.892710	81.516131	92.719861
46	51.575785	58.045885	65.568414	74.330564	84.554034	96.501457
47	52.833664	59.626344	67.551940	76.817176	87.667885	100.396501
48	54.097832	61.222608	69.565219	79.353519	90.859582	104.408396
49	55.368321	62.834834	71.608698	81.940590	94.131072	108.540648
50	56.645163	64.463182	73.682828	84.579401	97.484349	112.796867

Table 3 Future Amount of Ordinary Annuity of 1 (*continued*)

n \ i	$3\frac{1}{2}$%	4%	$4\frac{1}{2}$%	5%	$5\frac{1}{2}$%	6%
1	1.000000	1.000000	1.000000	1.000000	1.000000	1.000000
2	2.035000	2.040000	2.045000	2.050000	2.055000	2.060000
3	3.106225	3.121600	3.137025	3.152500	3.168025	3.183600
4	4.214943	4.246464	4.278191	4.310125	4.342266	4.374616
5	5.362466	5.416323	5.470710	5.525631	5.581091	5.637093
6	6.550152	6.632975	6.716892	6.801913	6.888051	6.975319
7	7.779408	7.898294	8.019152	8.142008	8.266894	8.393838
8	9.051687	9.214226	9.380014	9.549109	9.721573	9.897468
9	10.368496	10.582795	10.802114	11.026564	11.256260	11.491316
10	11.731393	12.006107	12.288209	12.577893	12.875354	13.180795
11	13.141992	13.486351	13.841179	14.206787	14.583498	14.971643
12	14.601962	15.025805	15.464032	15.917127	16.385591	16.869941
13	16.113030	16.626838	17.159913	17.712983	18.286798	18.882138
14	17.676986	18.291911	18.932109	19.598632	20.292572	21.015066
15	19.295681	20.023588	20.784054	21.578564	22.408664	23.275970
16	20.971030	21.824531	22.719337	23.657492	24.641140	25.672528
17	22.705016	23.697512	24.741707	25.840366	26.996403	28.212880
18	24.499691	25.645413	26.855084	28.132385	29.481205	30.905653
19	26.357181	27.671229	29.063562	30.539004	32.102671	33.759992
20	28.279682	29.778079	31.371423	33.065954	34.868318	36.785591
21	30.269471	31.969202	33.783137	35.719252	37.786076	39.992727
22	32.328902	34.247970	36.303378	38.505214	40.864310	43.392290
23	34.460414	36.617889	38.937030	41.430475	44.111847	46.995828
24	36.666528	39.082604	41.689196	44.501999	47.537998	50.815577
25	38.949857	41.645908	44.565210	47.727099	51.152588	54.864512
26	41.313102	44.311745	47.570645	51.113454	54.965981	59.156383
27	43.759060	47.084214	50.711324	54.669126	58.989109	63.705766
28	46.290627	49.967583	53.993333	58.402583	63.233510	68.528112
29	48.910799	52.966286	57.423033	62.322712	67.711354	73.629798
30	51.622677	56.084938	61.007070	66.438848	72.435478	79.058186
31	54.429471	59.328335	64.752388	70.760790	77.419429	84.801677
32	57.334502	62.701469	68.666245	75.298829	82.677498	90.889778
33	60.341210	66.209527	72.756226	80.063771	88.224760	97.343165
34	63.453152	69.857909	77.030256	85.066959	94.077122	104.183755
35	66.674013	73.652225	81.496618	90.320307	100.251364	111.434780
36	70.007603	77.598314	86.163966	95.836323	106.765189	119.120867
37	73.457869	81.702246	91.041344	101.628139	113.637274	127.268119
38	77.028895	85.970336	96.138205	107.709546	120.887324	135.904206
39	80.724906	90.409150	101.464424	114.095023	128.536127	145.058458
40	84.550278	95.025516	107.030323	120.799774	136.605614	154.761966
41	88.509537	99.826536	112.846688	127.839763	145.118923	165.047684
42	92.607371	104.819598	118.924789	135.231751	154.100464	175.950545
43	96.848629	110.012382	125.276404	142.993339	163.575989	187.507577
44	101.238331	115.412877	131.913842	151.143006	173.572669	199.758032
45	105.781673	121.029392	138.849965	159.700156	184.119165	212.743514
46	110.484031	126.870568	146.098214	168.685164	195.245719	226.508125
47	115.350973	132.945390	153.672633	178.119422	206.984234	241.098612
48	120.388257	139.263206	161.587902	188.025393	219.368367	256.564529
49	125.601846	145.833734	169.859357	198.426663	232.433627	272.958401
50	130.997910	152.667084	178.503028	209.347996	246.217476	290.335905

Table 3 Future Amount of Ordinary Annuity of 1 (*continued*)

n \ i	7%	8%	9%	10%	12%	15%
1	1.000000	1.000000	1.000000	1.000000	1.000000	1.000000
2	2.070000	2.080000	2.090000	2.100000	2.120000	2.150000
3	3.214900	3.246400	3.278100	3.310000	3.374400	3.472500
4	4.439943	4.506112	4.573129	4.641000	4.779328	4.993375
5	5.750740	5.866601	5.984711	6.105100	6.352847	6.742381
6	7.153291	7.335929	7.523335	7.715610	8.115189	8.753738
7	8.654021	8.922803	9.200435	9.487171	10.089012	11.066799
8	10.259803	10.636628	11.028474	11.435888	12.299693	13.726819
9	11.977989	12.487558	13.021036	13.579477	14.775656	16.785842
10	13.816448	14.486562	15.192930	15.937425	17.548735	20.303718
11	15.783599	16.645487	17.560293	18.531167	20.654583	24.349276
12	17.888451	18.977126	20.140720	21.384284	24.133133	29.001667
13	20.140643	21.495297	22.953385	24.522712	28.029109	34.351917
14	22.550488	24.214920	26.019189	27.974983	32.392602	40.504705
15	25.129022	27.152114	29.360916	31.772482	37.279715	47.580411
16	27.888054	30.324283	33.003399	35.949730	42.753280	55.717472
17	30.840217	33.750226	36.973705	40.544703	48.883674	65.075093
18	33.999033	37.450244	41.301338	45.599173	55.749715	75.836357
19	37.378965	41.446263	46.018458	51.159090	63.439681	88.211811
20	40.995492	45.761964	51.160120	57.274999	72.052442	102.443583
21	44.865177	50.422921	56.764530	64.002499	81.698736	118.810120
22	49.005739	55.456755	62.873338	71.402749	92.502584	137.631638
23	53.436141	60.893296	69.531939	79.543024	104.602894	159.276384
24	58.176671	66.764759	76.789813	88.497327	118.155241	184.167841
25	63.249038	73.105940	84.700896	98.347059	133.333870	212.793017
26	68.676470	79.954415	93.323977	109.181765	150.333934	245.711970
27	74.483823	87.350768	102.723135	121.099942	169.374007	283.568766
28	80.697691	95.338830	112.968217	134.209936	190.698887	327.104080
29	87.346529	103.965936	124.135356	148.630930	214.582754	377.169693
30	94.460786	113.283211	136.307539	164.494023	241.332684	434.745146
31	102.073041	123.345868	149.575217	181.943425	271.292606	500.956918
32	110.218154	134.213537	164.036987	201.137767	304.847719	577.100456
33	118.933425	145.950620	179.800315	222.251544	342.429446	644.665525
34	128.258765	158.626670	196.982344	245.476699	384.520979	765.365353
35	138.236878	172.316804	215.710755	271.024368	431.663496	881.170156
36	148.913460	187.102148	236.124723	299.126805	484.463116	1014.345680
37	160.337402	203.070320	258.375948	330.039486	543.598690	1167.497532
38	172.561020	220.315945	282.629783	364.043434	609.830533	1343.622161
39	185.640292	238.941221	309.066463	401.447778	684.010197	1546.165485
40	199.635112	259.056519	337.882445	442.592556	767.091420	1779.090308
41	214.609570	280.781040	369.291865	487.851811	860.142391	2046.953854
42	230.632240	304.243523	403.528133	537.636992	964.359478	2354.996933
43	247.776497	329.583005	440.845665	592.400692	1081.082615	2709.246473
44	266.120851	356.949646	481.521775	652.640761	1211.812529	3116.633443
45	285.749311	386.505617	525.858734	718.904837	1358.230032	3585.128460
46	306.751763	418.426067	574.186021	791.795321	1522.217636	4123.897729
47	329.224386	452.900152	626.862762	871.974853	1705.883752	4743.482388
48	353.270093	490.132164	684.280411	960.172338	1911.589803	5466.004746
49	378.999000	530.342737	746.865648	1057.189572	2141.980579	6275.405458
50	406.528929	573.770156	815.083556	1163.908529	2400.018249	7217.716277

Table 4 Present Value of Ordinary Annuity of 1 per Period: $P_{\overline{n}|i} = \dfrac{1 - \dfrac{1}{(1+i)^n}}{i}$

n \ i	1/2%	1%	1 1/2%	2%	2 1/2%	3%
1	0.995025	0.990099	0.985222	0.980392	0.975610	0.970874
2	1.985099	1.970395	1.955883	1.941561	1.927424	1.913470
3	2.970248	2.940985	2.912200	2.883883	2.856024	2.828611
4	3.950496	3.901966	3.854385	3.807729	3.761974	3.717098
5	4.925866	4.853431	4.782645	4.713460	4.645829	4.579707
6	5.896384	5.795476	5.697187	5.601431	5.508125	5.417191
7	6.862074	6.728195	6.598214	6.471991	6.349391	6.230283
8	7.822959	7.651678	7.485925	7.325481	7.170137	7.019692
9	8.779064	8.566018	8.360517	8.162237	7.970866	7.786109
10	9.730412	9.471305	9.222185	8.982585	8.752064	8.530203
11	10.677027	10.367628	10.071118	9.786848	9.514209	9.252624
12	11.618932	11.255077	10.907505	10.575341	10.257765	9.954004
13	12.556151	12.133740	11.731532	11.348374	10.983185	10.634955
14	13.488708	13.003703	12.543382	12.106249	11.690912	11.296073
15	14.416625	13.865053	13.343233	12.849264	12.381378	11.937935
16	15.339925	14.717874	14.131264	13.577709	13.055003	12.561102
17	16.258632	15.562251	14.907649	14.291872	13.712198	13.166118
18	17.172768	16.398269	15.672561	14.992031	14.353364	13.753513
19	18.082356	17.226009	16.426168	15.678462	14.978891	14.323799
20	18.987419	18.045553	17.168639	16.351433	15.589162	14.877475
21	19.887979	18.856983	17.900137	17.011209	16.184549	15.415024
22	20.784059	19.660379	18.620824	17.658048	16.765413	15.936917
23	21.675681	20.455821	19.330861	18.292204	17.332110	16.443608
24	22.562866	21.243387	20.030405	18.913926	17.884986	16.935542
25	23.445638	22.023156	20.719611	19.523456	18.424376	17.413148
26	24.324018	22.795204	21.398632	20.121036	18.950611	17.876842
27	25.198028	23.559608	22.067617	20.706898	19.464011	18.327031
28	26.067689	24.316443	22.726717	21.281272	19.964889	18.764108
29	26.933024	25.065785	23.376076	21.844385	20.453550	19.188455
30	27.794054	25.807708	24.015838	22.396456	20.930293	19.600441
31	28.650800	26.542285	24.646146	22.937702	21.395407	20.000428
32	29.503284	27.269589	25.267139	23.468335	21.849178	20.388766
33	30.351526	27.989693	25.878954	23.988564	22.291881	20.765792
34	31.195548	28.702666	26.481728	24.498592	22.723786	21.131837
35	32.035371	29.408580	27.075595	24.998619	23.145157	21.487220
36	32.871016	30.107505	27.660684	25.488842	23.556251	21.832253
37	33.702504	30.799510	28.237127	25.969453	23.957318	22.167235
38	34.529854	31.484663	28.805052	26.440641	24.348603	22.492462
39	35.353089	32.163033	29.364583	26.902589	24.730344	22.808215
40	36.172228	32.834686	29.915845	27.355479	25.102775	23.114772
41	36.987291	33.499689	30.458961	27.799489	25.466122	23.412400
42	37.798300	34.158108	30.994050	28.234794	25.820607	23.701359
43	38.605274	34.810008	31.521232	28.661562	26.166446	23.981902
44	39.408232	35.455454	32.040622	29.079963	26.503849	24.254274
45	40.207196	36.094508	32.552337	29.490160	26.833024	24.518713
46	41.002185	36.727236	33.056490	29.892314	27.154170	24.775449
47	41.793219	37.353699	33.553192	30.286582	27.467483	25.024708
48	42.580318	37.973959	34.042554	30.673120	27.773154	25.266707
49	43.363500	38.588079	34.524683	31.052078	28.071369	25.501657
50	44.142786	39.196118	34.999688	31.423606	28.362312	25.729764

Table 4 Present Value of Ordinary Annuity of 1 (*continued*)

n \ i	3½%	4%	4½%	5%	5½%	6%
1	0.966184	0.961538	0.956938	0.952381	0.947867	0.943396
2	1.899694	1.886095	1.872668	1.859410	1.846320	1.833393
3	2.801637	2.775091	2.748964	2.723248	2.697933	2.673012
4	3.673079	3.629895	3.587526	3.545951	3.505150	3.465106
5	4.515052	4.451822	4.389977	4.329477	4.270284	4.212364
6	5.328553	5.242137	5.157872	5.075692	4.995530	4.917324
7	6.114544	6.002055	5.892701	5.786373	5.682967	5.582381
8	6.873956	6.732745	6.595886	6.463213	6.334566	6.209794
9	7.607687	7.435332	7.268791	7.107822	6.952195	6.801692
10	8.316605	8.110896	7.912718	7.721735	7.537626	7.360087
11	9.001551	8.760477	8.528917	8.306414	8.092536	7.886875
12	9.663334	9.385074	9.118581	8.863252	8.618518	8.383844
13	10.302738	9.985648	9.682852	9.393573	9.117079	8.852683
14	10.920520	10.563123	10.222825	9.898641	9.589648	9.294984
15	11.517411	11.118387	10.739546	10.379658	10.037581	9.712249
16	12.094117	11.652296	11.234015	10.837770	10.462162	10.105895
17	12.651321	12.165669	11.707191	11.274066	10.864609	10.477260
18	13.189682	12.659297	12.159992	11.689587	11.246074	10.827603
19	13.709837	13.133939	12.593294	12.085321	11.607654	11.158116
20	14.212403	13.590326	13.007936	12.462210	11.950382	11.469921
21	14.697974	14.029160	13.404724	12.821153	12.275244	11.764077
22	15.167125	14.451115	13.784425	13.163003	12.583170	12.041582
23	15.620410	14.856842	14.147775	13.488574	12.875042	12.303379
24	16.058368	15.246963	14.495478	13.798642	13.151699	12.550358
25	16.481515	15.622080	14.828209	14.093945	13.413933	12.783356
26	16.890352	15.982769	15.146611	14.375185	13.662495	13.003166
27	17.285365	16.329586	15.451303	14.643034	13.898100	13.210534
28	17.667019	16.663063	15.742874	14.898127	14.121422	13.406164
29	18.035767	16.983715	16.021889	15.141074	14.333101	13.590721
30	18.392045	17.292033	16.288889	15.372451	14.533745	13.764831
31	18.736276	17.588494	16.544391	15.592811	14.723929	13.929086
32	19.068865	17.873552	16.788891	15.802677	14.904198	14.084043
33	19.390208	18.147646	17.022862	16.002549	15.075069	14.230230
34	19.700684	18.411198	17.246758	16.192904	15.237033	14.368141
35	20.000661	18.664613	17.461012	16.374194	15.390552	14.498246
36	20.290494	18.908282	17.666041	16.546852	15.536068	14.620987
37	20.570525	19.142579	17.862240	16.711287	15.673999	14.736780
38	20.841087	19.367864	18.049990	16.867893	15.804738	14.846019
39	21.102500	19.584485	18.229656	17.017041	15.928662	14.949075
40	21.355072	19.792774	18.401584	17.159086	16.046125	15.046297
41	21.599104	19.993052	18.566109	17.294368	16.157464	15.138016
42	21.834883	20.185627	18.723550	17.423208	16.262999	15.224543
43	22.062689	20.370795	18.874210	17.545912	16.363032	15.306173
44	22.282791	20.548841	19.018383	17.662773	16.457851	15.383182
45	22.495450	20.720040	19.156347	17.774070	16.547726	15.455832
46	22.700918	20.884654	19.288371	17.880067	16.632915	15.524370
47	22.899438	21.042936	19.414709	17.981016	16.713664	15.589028
48	23.091244	21.195131	19.535607	18.077158	16.790203	15.650027
49	23.276565	21.341472	19.651298	18.168722	16.862751	15.707572
50	23.455618	21.482185	19.762008	18.255925	16.931518	15.761861

Table 4 Present Value of Ordinary Annuity of 1 (*continued*)

n \ i	7%	8%	9%	10%	12%	15%
1	0.934579	0.925926	0.917431	0.909091	0.892857	0.869565
2	1.808018	1.783265	1.759111	1.735537	1.690051	1.625709
3	2.624316	2.577097	2.531295	2.486852	2.401831	2.283225
4	3.387211	3.312127	3.239720	3.169865	3.037349	2.854978
5	4.100197	3.992710	3.889651	3.790787	3.604776	3.352155
6	4.766540	4.622880	4.485919	4.355261	4.111407	3.784483
7	5.389289	5.206370	5.032953	4.868419	4.563757	4.160420
8	5.971299	5.746639	5.534819	5.334926	4.967640	4.487322
9	6.515232	6.246888	5.995247	5.759024	5.328250	4.771584
10	7.023582	6.710081	6.417658	6.144567	5.650223	5.018769
11	7.498674	7.138964	6.805191	6.495061	5.937699	5.233712
12	7.942686	7.536078	7.160725	6.813692	6.194374	5.420619
13	8.357651	7.903776	7.486904	7.103356	6.423548	5.583147
14	8.745468	8.244237	7.786150	7.366687	6.628168	5.724476
15	9.107914	8.559479	8.060688	7.606080	6.810864	5.847370
16	9.446649	8.851369	8.312558	7.823709	6.973986	5.954235
17	9.763223	9.121638	8.543631	8.021553	7.119630	6.047161
18	10.059087	9.371887	8.755625	8.201412	7.249670	6.127966
19	10.335595	9.603599	8.950115	8.364920	7.365777	6.198231
20	10.594014	9.818147	9.128546	8.513564	7.469444	6.259331
21	10.835527	10.016803	9.292244	8.648694	7.562003	6.312462
22	11.061241	10.200744	9.442425	8.771540	7.644646	6.358663
23	11.272187	10.371059	9.580207	8.883218	7.718434	6.398837
24	11.469334	10.528758	9.706612	8.984744	7.784316	6.433771
25	11.653583	10.674776	9.822580	9.077040	7.843139	6.464149
26	11.825779	10.809978	9.928972	9.160945	7.895660	6.490564
27	11.986709	10.935165	10.026580	9.237223	7.942554	6.513534
28	12.137111	11.051078	10.116128	9.306567	7.984423	6.533508
29	12.277674	11.158406	10.198283	9.369606	8.021806	6.550877
30	12.409041	11.257783	10.273654	9.426914	8.055184	6.565980
31	12.531814	11.349799	10.342802	9.479013	8.084986	6.579113
32	12.646555	11.434999	10.406240	9.526376	8.111594	6.590533
33	12.753790	11.513888	10.464441	9.569432	8.135352	6.600463
34	12.854009	11.586934	10.517835	9.608575	8.156564	6.609099
35	12.947672	11.654568	10.566821	9.644159	8.175504	6.616607
36	13.035208	11.717193	10.611763	9.676508	8.192414	6.623137
37	13.117017	11.775179	10.652993	9.705917	8.207513	6.628815
38	13.193473	11.828869	10.690820	9.732651	8.220993	6.633752
39	13.264928	11.878582	10.725523	9.756956	8.233030	6.638045
40	13.331709	11.924613	10.757360	9.779051	8.243777	6.641778
41	13.394120	11.967235	10.786569	9.799137	8.253372	6.645025
42	13.452449	12.006699	10.813366	9.817397	8.261939	6.647848
43	13.506962	12.043240	10.837950	9.833998	8.269589	6.650302
44	13.557908	12.077074	10.860505	9.849089	8.276418	6.652437
45	13.605522	12.108402	10.881197	9.862808	8.282516	6.654293
46	13.650020	12.137409	10.900181	9.875280	8.287961	6.655907
47	13.691608	12.164267	10.917597	9.886618	8.292822	6.657310
48	13.730474	12.189136	10.933575	9.896926	8.297163	6.658531
49	13.766799	12.212163	10.948234	9.906296	8.301038	6.659592
50	13.800746	12.233485	10.961683	9.914814	8.304498	6.660515

REVIEW QUESTIONS

1 Briefly explain the difference between simple interest and compound interest.

2 *a* Explain the meaning of $(1 + i)^n$ and define the symbols i and n.
b Give the formula for each of the following:
1 Present value of 1
2 Amount of an ordinary annuity of 1
3 Present value of an ordinary annuity of 1

3 Define each of the following:
a ***Present value of an annuity due***
b ***Present value of a deferred annuity***
c ***Amount of an annuity due***
d ***Amount of a deferred annuity***

4 Write the formula, including the numerical value for i and n, for computing the compound amount of $500 invested for five years (do not compute the solution):
a At 10% compounded semiannually
b At 8% compounded quarterly
c At 12% compounded monthly
d At 6% compounded annually

5 The following values are taken from compound-interest tables for the same number of periods n and at the same rate of interest i:
a 13.180795
b 1.790848
c 0.558395
d 7.360087
What does each of the four values represent? Explain.

6 Indicate the compound-interest table that would be used in solving each of the following problems:
a Sheila Jones wants to know how much she would have in her savings account at the end of five years if she deposits a single amount and leaves it to accumulate interest.
b Eva Smith owes Olson $5,000 due in two years at no interest. Smith wants to know how much she should pay Olson now if they agree on a current fair rate of interest.
c Charles Harrison owes a debt to Andersen that is payable in semiannual instalments of $2,000 each. The first instalment is due today. Harrison wants to know the amount he should pay to Andersen today to eliminate his debt.
d Yo Takagaki wants to know what equal annual deposits he should make at the beginning of each of 10 years so that he will have $20,000 to acquire a cabin cruiser at the end of the tenth year. Interest at a fixed rate will be compounded annually on the cumulative amount in Takagaki's "cruiser fund."

7 Assume that you need the amount of 1 for 80 periods at 2% per period. You do not have access to a computer, and the compound-interest table that you have available includes amounts through only 50 periods. Explain how you would compute $(1 + 0.02)^{80}$.

8 What are the four prerequisites of an annuity situation?

EXERCISES

Ex. 5-1 Select the best answer for each of the following multiple-choice questions:

1 Which of the following is the present value of an ***ordinary annuity*** of 10 rents of 1 at an interst rate of 6% per period?
a 1.790848 *b* 0.558395 *c* 13.180795 *d* 7.360087 *e* Some other amount

2 Which of the following is used to compute the present value of an ***ordinary annuity*** of 20 rents of 1 at 16% compounded quarterly?
a $p_{\overline{5}|16\%}$ *b* $P_{\overline{5}|16\%}$ *c* $p_{\overline{20}|4\%}$ *d* $P_{\overline{20}|4\%}$ *e* Some other formula

3 Present values of an ***ordinary annuity*** of 1 at 15% a year compounded annually are as follows: $n = 5$, 3.352155; $n = 6$, 3.784483; $n = 7$, 4.160420. The present value of an ***annuity due*** of 6 rents of 1 at 15% a year compounded annually is:
a 3.784483 *b* 4.352155 *c* 3.160420 *d* Some other amount

4 The present value of an ***ordinary annuity*** is used in the accounting valuations of all the following, except:
a Proceeds of a bond issue
b Present value of a non-interest-bearing promissory note due in five years
c Cost of a plant asset acquired through a 10-year capital lease; lease payments are due monthly starting at the inception of the lease
d Cost of a plant asset acquired on the instalment plan with the first payment due one month after the date of acquisition

5 On January 10, Year 1, Irving Porton signed a contract to operate a fast-food restaurant for an initial franchise fee of $40,000. Of this amount, $15,000 was paid to Odom, Inc., when the contract was signed, and the balance is payable in five annual payments of $5,000 each beginning January 10, Year 2. The contract provides that the down payment is not refundable, and no future services are required of Odom, Inc. Porton's credit rating indicates that he is able to borrow money at 12% for a loan of this type. Information on present and future values (rounded) follows:

Present value of 1 at 12% for 5 periods	0.567
Future amount of 1 at 12% for 5 periods	1.762
Present value of an ordinary annuity of 5 rents of 1 at 12% a year	3.605

Porton should record the acquisition cost of the franchise on January 10, Year 1, at:
a $29,175 *b* $33,025 *c* $40,000 *d* $44,050 *e* Some other amount

6 For which of the following transactions would the use of the present value of an ***annuity due*** concept be appropriate in the computation of the present value of the asset obtained or liability incurred on the date of the transaction?

a A capital lease is entered into with the initial lease payment due one month subsequent to the signing of the lease contract.
b A capital lease is entered into with the initial lease payment due on the date the lease contract was signed.
c Ten-year, 8% bonds are issued on January 2 with interest payable semiannually on July 2 and January 2, yielding 7%.
d Ten-year, 8% bonds are issued on January 2 with interest payable semiannually on July 2 and January 2, yielding 9%.

Ex. 5-2 Below are the present values of 1 discounted at 8% for one through five periods. Each of the values is based on 8% interest compounded annually from day of deposit to day of withdrawal.

Periods	*Present value of 1 discounted at 8% per period*
1	0.926
2	0.857
3	0.794
4	0.735
5	0.681

Choose the best answer for each of the following four questions:

1 What amount should you deposit in a savings account today in order to have $5,000 three years from today?
a $5,000 ÷ 0.794
b $5,000 × 0.926 × 3
c ($5,000 × 0.926) + ($5,000 × 0.857) + ($5,000 × 0.794)
d $5,000 × 0.794

2 What amount should you have in your savings account today before withdrawal if you need $5,000 each year for four years, with the first withdrawal to be made today and each subsequent withdrawal at one-year intervals? (You will have a zero balance in your savings account after the fourth withdrawal.)
a $5,000 + ($5,000 × 0.926) + ($5,000 × 0.857) + ($5,000 × 0.794)
b ($5,000 ÷ 0.735) × 4
c ($5,000 × 0.926) + ($5,000 × 0.857) + ($5,000 × 0.794) + ($5,000 × 0.735)
d ($5,000 ÷ 0.926) × 4

3 If you deposit $8,000 in a savings account today, what amount will you have available two years from today?
a $8,000 × 0.857
b $8,000 × 0.857 × 2
c $8,000 ÷ 0.857
d ($8,000 ÷ 0.926) × 2

4 What is the present value today of $2,000 you will receive six years from today?
   a $2,000 × 0.926 × 6
   b $2,000 × 0.794 × 2
   c $2,000 × 0.681 × 0.926
   d Cannot be determined from information given

Ex. 5-3 Heidi Mealy plans to take a vacation starting July 4, Year 5, shortly after she graduates from college. Mealy estimates that the cost of her vacation will be $6,000 and wants to accumulate that amount in a fund that pays quarterly interest of 2% by making eight quarterly deposits starting on October 1, Year 3, and ending on July 1, Year 5. The last four deposits will be twice as large as the first four deposits.

Compute the amount of each of the first four deposits and the amount of each of the last four deposits, and prepare a fund accumulation table similar to the one illustrated on page 229. Use the Appendix at the end of this chapter and round computations to the nearest dollar.

Ex. 5-4 On June 30, Year 1, Levine Corporation purchased merchandise at an auction for $40,000. The current fair value of the merchandise, according to Levine's personnel, was at least $48,000. Levine paid $10,000 cash and signed a 16% one-year promissory note for $30,000. Interest of $1,200 is payable on the note quarterly, starting on September 30, Year 1. You conclude that the current fair rate of interest on the note is 12% payable quarterly.

Record the purchase of the merchandise in the accounting records of Levine Corporation, assuming that the periodic inventory system is used. Use the Appendix at the end of this chapter and round computations to the nearest dollar.

Ex. 5-5 From the compound-interest tables in the Appendix at the end of this chapter, compute the following values at 4%:
   a Amount of 1 for 10 periods
   b Present value of 1 for 20 periods
   c Amount of ordinary annuity of 15 rents of 1
   d Amount of annuity due of 15 rents of 1
   e Amount of ordinary annuity of 15 rents of 1, deferred for 10 periods
   f Present value of ordinary annuity of 25 rents of 1
   g Present value of annuity due of 25 rents of 1
   h Present value of ordinary annuity of 25 rents of 1, deferred for 5 periods

Ex. 5-6 Celestial Company acquired $10,000 face amount of noncallable 10% bonds that have a remaining term of 12 years. The bonds pay interest every six months. The present value of 1 at 4% for 24 periods is 0.390121, and the present value of 1 at 5% for 24 periods is 0.310068. The present value of an ordinary annuity of 1 at 4% for 24 periods is 15.246963, and the present value of an ordinary annuity of 1 at 5% for 24 periods is 13.798642.

Compute the amount paid for the bonds if the market rate of interest for bonds of comparable quality is 8% compounded semiannually. Round computations to the nearest dollar.

Ex. 5-7 On December 31, Year 1, Long Beach Development issued $10 millon of 8% bonds payable. Interest is payable on December 31 of each year. The bonds mature on December 31, Year 11. The bonds were issued to yield an annual rate of 10%. The present value of an ordinary annuity of 10 rents of 1 at 10% is 6.144567; the present value of 1 for 10 periods at 10% is 0.385543.

Compute the amount received from issuance of the bonds. Round computations to the nearest dollar.

Ex. 5-8 Fred Dryer sold a parcel of land for $44,000. He received $12,000 cash on the date of sale and 16 promissory notes of equal amount due serially, one each six months starting six months from the date of sale. It was agreed that the notes will include interest in their face amount at 12% compounded semiannually.

Using the Appendix at the end of this chapter, compute (to the nearest dollar) the face amount of each note.

Ex. 5-9 Sonar Products, Inc., wants to accumulate a fund of $80,000 at the end of Year 10 to retire a debt. The fund will be accumulated by making 20 equal semiannual deposits starting on June 30, Year 1.

If the fund will earn interest at 6% compounded semiannually, compute the amount of each deposit. Use the Appendix at the end of this chapter and round computations to the nearest dollar.

Ex. 5-10 Ken Krueger has a 6% loan with an unpaid balance of $17,169. The principal and interest are payable quarterly at the rate of $1,000. Krueger has 20 more payments to make, having just made the payment due December 31, Year 5. The lender approaches Krueger and offers to reduce the principal of the debt from $17,169 to $16,500 if Krueger would take out a new loan for $16,500 at 10% (the current market rate), payable quarterly for the next five years.

Should Krueger refinance the loan? Use the Appendix at the end of this chapter and present computations (to the nearest dollar) in support of your answer. Disregard income tax considerations.

Ex. 5-11 Denise Stevens deposited $1,000 each quarter starting on June 30, Year 1, into a savings account that earned interest at 8% compounded quarterly. She has already made seven deposits, the last one on December 31, Year 2.

Using the tables in the Appendix at the end of this chapter, compute the amount (to the nearest dollar) Stevens has on deposit on each of the following dates (assuming that she made no withdrawals from the savings account):

a December 31, Year 2, including the deposit made on that date

b March 31, Year 3, including the deposit made on that date

c June 30, Year 5, assuming that Stevens made the last deposit on March 31, Year 5

Ex. 5-12 On January 1, Year 1, Alameda Company leased equipment from Pico Corporation. This lease was noncancellable and was in substance an instalment purchase (a capital lease). The initial term of the lease was 12 years, with title passing to Alameda at the end of the twelfth year at no additional cost. Annual rent to be paid by Alameda was $10,000 at the beginning of each year. The first rent payment was made on January 1, Year 1. The equipment had an estimated economic life of 20 years, with no residual value. The interest rate generally paid by Alameda on similar financing arrangements was 8%. The present value of an ***annuity due*** of 12 rents of 1 at 8% is 8.138964.

a Compute the cost of the equipment to Alameda Company to the nearest dollar.

b Compute interest expense for Alameda Company for each of the first three years.

CASES

Case 5-1 The following letter was mailed by Hustler Finance Corporation to a resident of a large city:

> Dear Ms. Creditworthy:
>
> You are one of a select group of creditworthy individuals in your community who qualify for a unique opportunity. Without additional credit references or time-consuming technicalities, you are guaranteed a ''Prestiage Loan'' of $10,000 now.
>
> Because you are financially responsible, and you've always handled your financial obligations with efficiency, your loan ***has already been approved***. The enclosed certificate entitles you to a loan of $10,000 any time you'd like to have it. So please call or come to our office at your earliest convenience.
>
> Sincerely,
> Homer Hustler

The certificate referred to in the letter indicated that the repayment of the loan was to be made in 24 equal monthly payments of $534 each.

Instructions

a What is the total amount a borrower would have to pay to Hustler Finance Company over the two-year period of this installment loan?

b Compute the approximate ***annual rate*** of interest (as a percentage) compounded monthly, using Table 4 in the Appendix at the end of this chapter.

c Is the rate of interest computed in ***b*** attractive for ''creditworthy individuals'' if the current bank prime interest rate is 15%? Why?

Case 5-2 While on an audit with a CA firm at the end of Year 5, Michael Synn observed the following deferred compensation contract signed by his client:

> In lieu of any salary and bonus for Year 5, Mark Naughton will receive $25,000 at the end of Year 6 and each year thereafter through December 31, Year 11. Naughton will not be required to perform any services after December 31, Year 5. Six promissory notes in the amount of $25,000 each are hereby executed in evidence of this obligation.

The client of the CA firm recorded this contract as follows:

Salaries Expense ($25,000 × 6)	150,000	
Notes Payable		150,000
To record salary and bonuses payable to Mark Naughton.		

A staff assistant working under Synn's supervision stated: "This journal entry is proper; the expense is applicable to Year 5, and the notes meet all the traditional tests of a liability. The salary and bonus payments to Naughton had been over $130,000 a year for several years; therefore, the amount of $150,000 debited to Salaries Expense in Year 5 is reasonable."

Synn pointed out that there is no mention of interest in the contract with Naughton and that the client had to pay 8% interest on most of its bank loans in the last quarter of Year 5. He agreed that the notes were liabilities, but added that an auditor must ascertain not only that a liability exists but also that the amount of the liability on the balance sheet date is fairly stated.

Instructions

Use the appropriate table in the Appendix at the end of this chapter to reach your conclusions.

a Evaluate the positions taken by the staff assistant and by Michael Synn.

b What correcting entry, if any, would you recommend on December 31, Year 5, assuming that a Discount on Notes Payable ledger account is used?

c What journal entry should be made on December 31, Year 6, to record the first payment to Mark Naughton?

Case 5-3 Vincent Lee's godfather, Linton Chu, decided to make him a gift of $27,000. Chu gave Lee the option to receive the cash in any one of the following three patterns:

1 One thousand dollars at the end of each of the first three years, starting one year from now; $3,000 at the end of each of the next three years; and $5,000 at the end of each of the last three years. Chu suggests that this arrangement might be preferable because Lee is young and will need more money as he grows older, not only because he will learn to spend more but also because inflation will increase his cost of living.

2 Three thousand dollars at the end of each of the next nine years, starting one year from now. Chu pointed out that this option offers Lee the advantage of steady cash flow.

3 Five thousand dollars at the end of each of the first three years, starting one year from now; $3,000 at the end of each of the next three years; and $1,000 at the end of each of the last three years. Chu points out that he would not recommend this option to Lee because it would give him an excess of cash flow during the first three years that would be invested at a rate of interest lower than he (Chu) could earn. Lee had told Chu that he would invest all this money in Windsor at 6% compounded annually; Chu had responded that he invests his money at 10% compounded annually in a Hong Kong bank.

After discussing these alternatives with several philosophy students at Golden Shark University, Lee said to Chu: ''All three options are the same; obviously I shall receive an average of $3,000 at the end of each of the nine years, so it makes no difference. I'll take the first option.'' Chu responded, ''I am happy to know that you are in school; there is much to learn.''

Instructions

a Did Vincent Lee make the right decision? Why or why not?

b What is the present value of each option at 6% interest compounded annually, given the following present value of 1 at 6%?

Periods	*Present value of 1*	*Present value of ordinary annuity of 1*
3	0.8396	2.6730
6	0.7050	4.9173
9	0.5919	6.8017

c Briefly evaluate the observations made by Linton Chu relative to each of the three options he presented to Vincent Lee.

Case 5-4 Caledonia Corporation borrowed $500,000, payable in 12 equal annual instalments of $92,240. The effective interest rate is 15% a year and the total interest on the loan is $606,880 [($92,240 × 12) – $500,000 = $606,880]. The terms of the loan contract state that interest expense is to be computed in accordance with the ''Rule of 78.'' Under this rule, the interest expense for each year is determined by multiplying the total interest payable on the loan by a fraction the numerator of which is the number of periods remaining on the debt and the denominator of which is the sum of the periods' digits for the term of the loan. Thus, because the sum of the digits 1 through 12 is 78, Caledonia recorded interest expense of $93,366 ($606,880 × 12/78 = $93,366) in the first year of the loan.

Instructions

a Prepare a loan amortization table similar to the one on page 236 under the Rule-of-78 approach of recording interest expense. Round computations to the nearest dollar.

b Prepare a loan amortization table under the effective interest method; that is, interest expense is computed at 15% a year on the balance of the loan outstanding. Round computations to the nearest dollar.

c Evaluate the appropriateness of the results obtained under the two approaches.

PROBLEMS

Pr. 5-1 On July 1, Year 1, Sunset Company signed a three-year lease contract for a warehouse. The contract provided that Sunset has the option of either paying annual rent of $20,000 on July 1, beginning in Year 1, or paying total rent in advance at a 12% discount, compounded annually.

Instructions

(Use the Appendix at the end of this chapter and round computations to the nearest dollar.)

a What single amount would Sunset Company have to pay on July 1, Year 1, for the annual lease rent?

b Assume the same facts as above, except that the interest is compounded monthly. Compute the single amount Sunset Company would have to pay on July 1, Year 1.

c Explain the difference in the results obtained in ***a*** and ***b***.

Pr. 5-2 Fernando Slider has been a star baseball player for the Ancaster Boomers for many years. Before retiring to practice law, Slider decided to become a free agent and offered his services to the highest bidder for four more years. After many weeks of negotiations, Slider and his agent accepted the following offer from the Toronto White Shoes:

1 An annual salary of $600,000 for four years, payable in monthly instalments of $50,000, starting one month from today.

2 A deferred compensation of $480,000, payable in monthly instalments of $10,000 for four years, for services rendered during the four years of playing baseball for the Toronto White Shoes. These payments will commence one month after the last payment of $50,000 is made Slider.

3 A ''signing bonus'' of $120,000 cash, payable immediately.

Headlines in sport pages around the nation stated that Slider had signed a ''$3-million contract'' with the Toronto White Shoes.

Instructions

Assuming that interest at the rate of 1½% a month is charged on personal loans to professional athletes, compute the present value today of the ''$3-million contract'' signed by Fernando Slider with the Toronto White Shoes. Use the Appendix at the end of this chapter and round computations to the nearest dollar.

Pr. 5-3 The management of Sensormatic Company is evaluting a proposal to acquire a new drill press as a replacement for a less efficient old press that would be sold. The total cost of the new press is $180,000. If the new press is acquired, costs of $8,000 would be incurred in removing the old press. The old press has a carrying amount of $100,000 and a remaining economic life of ten years. Because of technical improvements that have made the old press uneconomical, it has a current resale value of only $50,000.

Additional Information

1 Management of Sensormatic provided you with the following comparison of annual production and operating costs:

	Old press	*New press*
Annual production (units)	400,000	500,000
Annual operating costs:		
Labour	$ 30,000	$ 25,000
Depreciation (10% of asset carrying amount)	10,000	18,000
Other costs	50,000	20,000
Total annual operating costs	$ 90,000	$ 63,000

2 Management believes that if the old drill press is not replaced now, it would have to wait seven years before replacement would be economically justifiable.

3 Both the old and the new drill press are expected to have a negligible residual value at the end of 10 years.

4 If the new drill press is acquired, the management of Sensormatic will require a 15% return on the investment before income taxes.

5 The present value of an ordinary annuity of 10 rents of 1 at 15% is 5.018769.

Instructions

a In order to assist the management of Sensormatic in reaching a decision on the proposal, prepare a working paper showing the computation of the following (disregard any effects of net incremental cash flow from increased sales of units produced by the new drill press):

1 Net initial cash investment, before income taxes.

2 Net present value of the net initial cash investment, before income taxes. Assume that the annual cash savings before income taxes are realized at the end of each year. Round computations to the nearest dollar.

b Would you recommend the acquisition of the new drill press? Explain.

Pr. 5-4 This problem consists of four independent parts, each related to the business activities of Eleanor Corporation. Compute the answer (to the nearest dollar) for each part by using the tables in the Appendix at the end of this chapter.

1 Eleanor plans to accumulate $500,000 on December 31, Year 10, to retire preferred stock. Eleanor deposited $125,000 in a fund on January 1, Year 1 that will earn interest at 10% compounded quarterly, and wants to know what additional amount it has to deposit in the fund at the end of each quarter for 10 years (starting on March 31, Year 1) to have $500,000 available at the end of Year 10. The periodic deposits also will earn interest at 10% compounded quarterly.

2 Eleanor plans to make five equal annual deposits in a fund beginning June 1, Year 4, in order to be able to withdraw $50,000 at six annual intervals beginning June 1, Year 9. The amount on deposit will earn interest at 12%

annually until the fund is exhausted. Compute the equal deposits that should be made to the fund.

3 On June 30, Year 1, Eleanor acquired a machine for $80,000. The down payment was $10,000, and the balance is to be paid in 48 equal monthly payments, including interest at 18% compounded monthly. What is the amount of the monthly payment if the first payment is due one month from the date of acquisition?

4 On April 1, Year 2, Eleanor made a deposit of $100,000 in a fund and left the fund undisturbed for four years to earn compound interest at a rate that did not change during the four-year period. At the end of four years, the fund had a balance of $132,088.60. If interest was compounded quarterly, what was the annual rate of interest earned on the deposit?

Pr. 5-5 This problem consists of four separate parts, each relating to the business activities of Situs Company. Compute the answer (to the nearest dollar) for each part by using the tables in the Appendix at the end of this chapter.

1 On July 1, Year 1, Situs issued $50 million of 20-year, 8% bonds, paying interest semiannually on January 1 and July 1. The bonds were issued to yield 9% compounded semiannually. What were the proceeds from this bond issue?

2 On April 1, Year 1, Situs acquired a plant asset by paying $8,000 down and $8,000 at the beginning of each of the next 19 calendar quarters. What was the cost of the plant asset for financial accounting purposes, assuming that the interest rate was 16% compounded quarterly?

3 Situs has a promissory note receivable in the amount of $300,000 issued by Kore Corporation. The note calls for payment of $100,000 of principal at the end of each year starting in three years, plus interest at the rate of 12% a year on the unpaid balance of the note. Only interest is due at the end of the first two years. Payments of $124,000 and $112,000 are due at the end of Year 4 and Year 5, respectively. Situs immediately discounted this note with a finance company at 10% interest compounded annually. How much did Situs receive from the finance company for the note?

4 Situs wishes to accumulate a $10-million fund with Ida Trust for the retirement of bonds in 10 years. Situs plans to make 20 equal deposits of $243,929.25 starting in six months, to accumulate the $10-million fund. What semiannual interest rate will be earned by Situs on the balance of the fund?

Pr. 5-6 As an accountant for Santa Rosa, Inc., you find the following memorandum on your desk from Howard Hinshaw, controller of Santa Rosa:

1 On December 31, Year 1, we shall sign a non-interest-bearing note for $400,000 due in five years. The lender wants to earn 10% compounded annually on the amount advanced to us. Please compute the proceeds on this borrowing transaction and prepare a table showing our interest expense and net liability for each of the five years of the loan.

2 Also on December 31, Year 1, the instalment sale of the land in Eureka will be completed. The purchaser will pay us $100,000 a year for ten years starting a year from now. Our contract includes interest at 10% a year in the face amount of the notes. The land is carried in our accounting records at $550,000. I want you to prepare a journal entry to record the sale of the land and to prepare a table that will show interest revenue for each year and the carrying amount of the notes receivable at the end of each year. We shall record the notes receivable at face amount.

Instructions

Prepare a memo to the controller of Santa Rosa, Inc., that includes the information he asked you to assemble. Use the Appendix at the end of this chapter and round all computations to the nearest dollar.

Pr. 5-7 Midland Oil Company has a debt for $300,000 maturing on June 30, Year 10. Midland Oil plans to deposit $25,000 in a debt retirement fund on June 30 each year for eight years, starting on June 30, Year 3. In addition, Midland Oil plans to deposit a single amount on June 30, Year 2, that, together with the eight annual deposits in the debt retirement fund, will be sufficient to repay the debt on June 30, Year 10. The amount in the debt retirement fund earns interest at 7% compounded annually.

Midland Oil also has made annual deposits of $40,000 in a ''contingency fund'' at the end of each of the last four years. The balance in the ''contingency fund'' after the fourth deposit on December 31, Year 4, was $180,244. Interest on the ''contingency fund'' is compounded annually.

Instructions

(Use the Appendix at the end of this chapter and round computations to the nearest dollar.)

a Compute the single amount that must be deposited on June 30, Year 2, if $300,000 is to be available on June 30, Year 10, in the debt retirement fund.

b What was the annual rate of interest earned on the ''contingency fund'' through December 31, Year 4?

c Compute the amount that may be withdrawn from the ''contingency fund'' at the end of each year for ten years, starting on December 31, Year 5, assuming that the amount on deposit in the ''contingency fund'' earns interest at 10% annually from January 1, Year 5, through December 31, Year 14.

Pr. 5-8 Lynne Kawagoe was recently hired as an accountant by Oahu Corporation, and the first assignment was given to her as follows:

To get your feet wet and to give you some practice with the calculator, I want you to prepare tables summarizing our interest expense or revenue and the liability or asset balance for these two transactions:

1 Today we acquired a machine for $54,173. We paid $10,000 down and agreed to make six equal semiannual payments, including interest at 12% compounded semiannually, starting six months from now.

2 We will need $200,000 five years from now to reline our furnaces. We want to deposit five equal amounts annually in a fund starting one year from now so that we will have the money we need in five years. We have arranged to invest the money with Punahoe Trust Corporation at 8% compounded annually.''

Instructions

a Compute (1) the amount of the semiannual payments on the contract for the acquisition of the machine and (2) the amount of the annual deposits in the furnace-relining fund. Use the Appendix at the end of this chapter and round computations to the nearest dollar.

b Prepare (1) a loan amortization table for the instalment debt incurred in the acquisition of the machine and (2) a fund accumulation table for the deposits to the furnace-relining fund.

Pr. 5-9 As a summer intern with Dugan and Ward, Chartered Accountants, you are presented with the following situations:

1 Client A inquired whether a proposed transaction made economic sense. The client sold a parcel of land for $51,000 and was given the choice of receiving $51,000 cash or $17,000 per year for four years starting one year from now. The client does not need cash but would like to earn 12% before income taxes annually on idle cash resources; consequently, the client wants to know what interest rate (to the nearest tenth) would be earned if the installment payment option is taken.

2 Client B wants to now how much to pay for $100,000 face amount of 8% bonds that mature in five years if interest is payable semiannually and if 10% compounded semiannually is a fair return on this type of investment.

3 Client C is negotiating to acquire a going concern and is uncertain whether the asking price for goodwill (present value of future superior earnings) is reasonable. The seller wants $60,000 for goodwill, but the client does not want to pay more than the present value of projected superior earnings for the next three years discounted at 15% annually. Superior earnings (to be realized at the end of each year) were estimated as follows:

At end of first year	$40,000
At end of second year	30,000
At end of third year	10,000

4 On June 1, Year 1, Client D plans to make the first of four equal annual deposits in a fund that will earn 9% and will amount to $180,000 immediately after the last deposit on June 1, Year 4. The client wants to know the amount of each deposit and wants proof that $180,000 would be available on June 1, Year 4.

Instructions

Prepare appropriate computations and a working paper that will give each of the four clients the information requested. Use the Appendix at the end of this chapter and round all computations to the nearest dollar.

Pr. 5-10 In the course of your December 31, Year 4, audit engagement for Dibble Limited, the following situations required you to apply compound-interest principles:

1 A non-interest-bearing note receivable in the face amount of $150,000 and maturing in three years was received on December 31, Year 4, in partial payment of an account receivable. The accountant for Dibble credited the customer's account for $150,000, despite a written agreement that the customer was to receive credit for the ''present value of the note discounted at 12% for three years, interest compounded semiannually.''

2 Dibble agreed to pay $20,000 a year for five years to a retiring executive, starting on December 31, Year 7. The liability ***was not recorded*** in the accounting records. The payments were in lieu of a year-end bonus that would have been taxed at an income tax rate of over 60%. Dibble regularly borrows money at a 9% annual rate of interest.

3 Dibble wants to accumulate a fund of $125,000 in six years (December 31, Year 10) to retire a long-term note. On December 31, Year 1, the board of directors had passed a resolution instructing the treasurer to make ten equal annual deposits in a fund earning interest at 8% compounded annually. Because no one knew how to compute the equal deposits, the treasurer decided to deposit $10,000 at the end of each year. The fourth deposit was made on December 31, Year 4. What equal annual deposits should be made during the next six years, starting a year from now, if exactly $125,000 is to be accumulated on December 31, Year 10? Prepare a fund accumulation table to confirm that $125,000 will be available on December 31, Year 10.

4 On December 31, Year 4, Dibble acquired a barge for $500,000. The contract calls for 20 payments of $32,629 every three months starting immediately. You have been asked by the president of Dibble to compute the approximate rate of interest charged on this contract every three months.

Instructions

Prepare journal entries for Dibble Company on December 31, Year 4, with supporting computations, to correct the accounting records for situations (1) and (2) above, and compute the answers for situations (3) and (4). Use the Appendix at the end of this chapter and round computations to the nearest dollar. Record notes receivable and notes payable at face amount.

Pr. 5-11 This problem consists of three independent parts relating to the business activities of West Company.

1 West invested $93,420 with Guardian Insurance Corporation on January 1, Year 1. The amount on deposit earned interest at 10% a year. West plans to withdraw the amount on deposit in three equal annual instalments starting December 31, Year 4.

2 West plans to accumulate a fund of $58,666 at Providence Bank at the end of five years by making five equal annual deposits starting one year from now. The fund will earn interest at 8% compounded annually.

3 On January 1, Year 1, West invested $270,358 at 12% compounded annually with Executive Annuity Corporation. The amount invested and accrued interest are to be withdrawn in five equal instalments starting on December 31, Year 1.

Instructions

(Use the Appendix at the end of this chapter and round computations to the nearest dollar.)

a Compute the three equal amounts that West Company will receive from Guardian Insurance, and prepare a table that shows that the entire amount on deposit will have been withdrawn by December 31, Year 6.

b Compute the annual deposits that West Company should make with Providence Bank and prepare a fund accumulation table for the five-year period.

c Compute the amounts West Company may withdraw each year from Executive Annuity Corporation, and prepare a table that shows that the amount invested will be exhausted by December 31, Year 5.

Pr. 5-12 Late in Year 1, Vronsky Corporation was negotiating to acquire machinery. An analysis of the proposed use of the machinery indicates that it will result in the following cost savings over its economic life of 10 years and residual value at the end of Year 11:

Estimated annual cost savings after income taxes	
(Assume that the savings will be realized at the end of each year)	
Year 2 through Year 6	$60,000
Year 7 through Year 10	50,000
Year 11	25,000
Estimated residual value of machinery	
End of Year 11	$10,000

Instructions

a Compute the amount that Vronsky Corporation should pay for the machinery, assuming that Vronsky requires a minimum of 12% annual rate of return on investments in plant assets. Use the Appendix at the end of this chapter and round computations to the nearest dollar.

b Assume that Vronsky Corporation acquired the machinery on December 31, Year 1, for the amount computed in *a*, and that it paid $100,000 cash as a down payment. The balance was payable in four equal annual instalments (including interest at 10% a year) starting on December 31, Year 2. Prepare a journal entry for Vronsky to record the acquisition of the machinery.

c Compute the amount of each of the four annual payments on the loan. Use the Appendix at the end of this chapter and round computations to the nearest dollar.

d Prepare a loan amortization table similar to the one illustrated on page 236, and a journal entry to record the first payment on the loan on December 31, Year 2.

p a r t t w o

WORKING CAPITAL

The motive power of a business enterprise is provided by its working capital components — cash, short-term investments, receivables, inventories, and current liabilities. Measurement of these components for balance sheet presentation also involves the recognition of revenue and expenses in the process of measuring periodic net income. Much of the criticism of financial statements in recent years has been directed at the accounting for doubtful accounts, inventories, profits and losses on construction-type contracts, and estimated liabilities such as product warranties.

Contingent losses are recognized to present the financial position and results of operations of business enterprises in accordance with generally accepted accounting principles; contingent gains are generally recorded in the accounting period in which realization takes place.

c h a p t e r 6

CASH AND SHORT-TERM INVESTMENTS

CASH

Cash is a medium of exchange that a bank will accept for deposit and immediate credit to the depositor's account. Cash includes currency and coin, personal cheques, bank drafts, money orders, credit card sales drafts, and cashiers' cheques, as well as money on deposit with banks. Items sometimes confused with cash include postage stamps, postdated cheques, and IOUs. Postage should be classified as a short-term prepayment; postdated cheques and IOUs should be classified as receivables.

Deposits with a trustee, for example, a bond sinking fund that is not under the control of management of a business enterprise, should not be included in cash. As another example, many airline companies have millions of dollars in cash deposits with manufacturers for the acquisition of flight equipment. Such deposits do not qualify as current assets because they are not available for payment of current liabilities.

Term deposits that are short-term are frequently classified as cash because they are available for immediate withdrawal.[1] Strictly speaking, savings deposits may not be withdrawn without prior notice to the bank; but banks seldom enforce this requirement, so savings deposits are usually viewed as cash. Petty cash funds and change funds are minor elements of cash under the control of management, even though these funds are mostly intended to be used for specific purposes. The limitations placed on the use of these funds do not remove them from the category of cash but simply aid in the control of cash on hand.

1 CICA, *Financial Reporting in Canada*, 16th ed. (Toronto, 1985), p. 97. These term deposits are generally identified as such even though they are combined with cash as one item in the balance sheet.

In summary, an item is ***cash*** if: (1) it is a medium of exchange; (2) it is available immediately for the payment of current debts; and (3) it is free from any contractual restriction that would prevent management of the business enterprise from using the item to pay its creditors.

Management of Cash

The management of cash is of major importance in any business enterprise because cash is a means of acquiring goods and services. In addition, careful scrutiny of cash transactions is required because cash can be readily misappropriated.

The management of cash is centred around forecasting and internal controls. The responsibilities of management with respect to cash are: (1) to assure that there is sufficient cash to carry on the operations, (2) to invest any idle cash, and (3) to prevent loss of cash due to theft or misappropriation. Cash forecasting is necessary for the proper planning of future operations and to assure that cash is available when needed but that cash on hand is not excessive. Internal controls are necessary to assure that the cash be used for proper business purposes and not wasted, misused, or stolen. Management is responsible for controlling and protecting all assets of a business enterprise. However, special problems exist in controlling cash because of its highly liquid nature.

Internal Controls

Internal controls may be defined as a system comprising "the plan of organization and all the coordinate systems established by the management of an enterprise to assist in achieving management's objective of ensuring, as far as practical, the orderly and efficient conduct of its business, including the safeguarding of assets, the reliability of accounting records and the timely preparation of reliable financial information."[2]

The purpose of a system of internal controls is to assure that assets which belong to the business enterprise are received when tendered, protected while in the custody of the enterprise, and used only for authorized business purposes. The system of internal controls consists of administrative controls and accounting controls, which are defined thus: "***Administrative controls*** include... the plan of organization and the procedures and records that are concerned with the decision processes leading to management's authorization of transactions... the starting point for establishing accounting controls for business transactions. ***Accounting controls*** comprise the plan or organization and the procedures and records that are concerned with the safeguarding of assets and the reliability of financial records...."[3]

A system of internal controls is not designed primarily to detect errors but rather to reduce the opportunity for errors or dishonesty to occur. In an effective system of internal controls, no one person carries out all phases of a business

2 CICA, ***CICA Handbook*** (Toronto), sec. 5200.05.

3 AICPA, ***Statement on Auditing Standards No. 1:*** "Codification of Auditing Standards and Procedures" (New York: 1973), p. 20.

transaction from beginning to end. For example, if a single person were permitted to order merchandise, receive it, write a cheque in payment, and record the transaction in the accounting records, there would be no protection against either fraud or errors. In large business enterprises, separate and independent departments are established for such functions as purchasing, receiving, selling, finance, and accounting, to assure that no one department handles all phases of a transaction.

The system of internal controls may frequently be improved by physical safeguards. Computers help to improve the efficiency and accuracy of the record-keeping function. Cash registers, safes, and prenumbered business forms are very helpful in safeguarding cash and establishing responsibility for it. Any system of internal controls must be supervised with care if it is to function effectively.

If an attempt is made to design a ''foolproof'' system of internal controls, it should be remembered that management's primary responsibility is profitable operation of the business enterprise. The cost of the system of internal controls must be balanced against the benefit to be derived in preventing errors and losses.

Controlling Cash Receipts and Payments

The objective sought in the control of cash receipts is to assure that all cash that is receivable by the business enterprise is collected and recorded without loss. The system of controlling cash payments should be designed to ensure that no unauthorized payments are made. Control is accomplished by division of responsibility to achieve independent verification of cash transactions without duplication of effort. Cash is safeguarded by keeping it in safes, depositing it in banks, and by using special, cash funds.

The Imprest Cash Fund or Petty Cash Fund

The term ***imprest cash fund*** or ***petty cash fund*** refers to a fund of fixed amount used for small expenditures that are most conveniently paid in cash. The imprest fund is restored to its original amount at frequent intervals by the issuance of a cheque on the general bank account payable to the custodian of the fund. The replenishment cheque is equal in amount to the expenditures made from the fund. Imprest cash funds placed in the custody of responsible employees thus serve to maintain control over cash without involved procedures for small payments.

The size of a petty cash fund should be sufficient to meet the normal need for small cash payments for a period of two or three weeks. As each cash payment is made, a ***voucher*** or ***receipt*** is placed in the fund. The vouchers or receipts are reviewed and cancelled when the petty cash fund is replenished. The petty cash fund is replenished when its cash is exhausted and at the end of the accounting period so that the expenses paid from the fund are recorded in the proper period and the year-end cash balance is stated correctly.

To illustrate the accounting for petty cash transactions, assume that on December 1, Year 6, Micro Systems Corporation established a petty cash fund of $250. On December 21, Year 6, the custodian requested replenishment for items paid to date. The following itemization of payments from petty cash was presented on December 21 for replenishment and on December 31 in connection with the Year 6 audit:

Summary of activity in petty cash fund for December, Year 6

MICRO SYSTEMS CORPORATION
Composition of Petty Cash Fund
December 21 and 31, Year 6

	Dec. 21	*Dec. 31*
Cash in fund	$ 9	$150
Office supplies expense	171	77
Miscellaneous selling expenses	65	25
Cash shortage (overage)	5	(2)
Totals	$250	$250

The journal entries required to record petty cash transactions for the month of December, Year 6, for Micro Systems Corporation are as follows:

Journal entries to record petty cash transactions

Year 6			
Dec. 1	Petty Cash Fund	250	
	Cash		250
	To record establishment of petty cash fund.		
21	Office Supplies Expense	171	
	Miscellaneous Selling Expenses	65	
	Cash Shortage (Overage)	5	
	Cash		241
	To record expenses incurred since Dec. 1, and to record replenishment of petty cash fund.		
31	Office Supplies Expense	77	
	Miscellaneous Selling Expenses	25	
	Cash Shortage (Overage)		2
	Cash		100
	To record expenses incurred since Dec. 21, and to record replenishment of petty cash fund.		

The Cash Shortage (Overage) ledger account in the foregoing journal entries is classified as revenue when it has a credit balance and as expense when it has a debit balance.

If for any reason the petty cash fund is not replenished at the end of an accounting period, it is still desirable that the expenses be recorded before the accounting records are closed. In this situation the journal entry for December 31, Year 6, illustrated above would be changed in only one respect: the credit of $100 would be to Petty Cash Fund rather than to Cash. The effect on the financial statements is the same as if the fund actually had been replenished.

Change Fund

A *change fund* is used to facilitate the collection of cash from customers. The amount of the change fund is deducted from the total cash (including cheques, money orders, etc.) on hand at the close of business each day to determine the daily cash collections. The cash should be counted and compared with the cash register tape daily. In general, change and petty cash funds are combined with cash on hand and in the bank and are presented as a single amount in the balance sheet.

Reconciliation of Bank Balances

The cash balance indicated in a bank statement seldom agrees with the cash balance indicated by the depositor's ledger account for cash. These two balances do not agree even though they purport to measure the same quantity, because there is a lag between the time transactions are recorded by the bank and the time they are recorded by the depositor. For example, the depositor credits the Cash ledger account when a cheque is prepared in payment of accounts payable. The bank does not reduce the depositor's account until the cheque is presented for payment by the payee. Another common difference between the two balances results when the deposit of cash receipts is made after the bank closes its records for the statement period. Both of these differences are self-correcting over time; the outstanding cheques are presented for payment and the deposit is recorded by the bank within a few days.

There are also time lags in transactions initiated by the bank. For example, a depositor is usually not notified of the bank's charges for servicing the account or for collecting a promissory note receivable for the depositor until the bank statement is received.

In addition to items that involve merely a lag in the recording process, various errors may be made by the depositor or by the bank. The process of reconciling the balances forces a careful review of all transactions involving cash and provides a means of proving the accuracy of the depositor's accounting records. The value of this review stems from the fact that two independent parties have recorded the same transactions and that their records are being compared. When differences arise, they must be explained. Differences that are self-correcting require no further action. However, corrections must be made for omissions or other errors in recording transactions in the depositor's accounting records. Errors made by the bank should be called to its attention for correction.

Two forms of bank reconciliation are in common usage: (1) both the bank balance and the balance in the depositor's records are reconciled to a correct balance, and (2) the bank balance is reconciled to the balance in the depositor's records. The first form is illustrated on page 277, and the second on page 279.

Bank Balance and Depositor's Balance Reconciled to Correct Balance

The Cash ledger account for Rossi Company shows a debit balance of $10,592.66 on December 31, Year 5. The bank statement indicates a balance on deposit of $12,269.02 on December 31. Receipts of December 31 in the amount of $1,144.60 were left in the bank's night depository on December 31 but were not included in the bank statement. The December bank statement included a debit memorandum for $13.50 for service charges for December. A credit memorandum included with the bank statement indicated that a note receivable in the amount of $2,000, left with the bank for collection, had been collected and credited to Rossi Company's account for $2,030, including interest revenue of $30. Comparison of the paid cheques with the cheque stubs indicated that cheque no. 821 for $463.90 on December 15, for the acquisition of office equipment, had been entered erroneously in the cash payments journal as $436.90. In addition, the following cheques issued in December, Year 5, had not been paid by the bank:

Cheques not paid by the bank in December

No. 811	$421.96
No. 814	93.00
No. 822	250.00
No. 823	116.50

Also included with the bank statement was a cheque for $50 drawn by Robert Reeves, a customer of Rossi Company. This cheque was marked ''NSF'' (''not sufficient funds''). Finally, an examination of the accounting records indicated that the bank had collected $10,000 for Rossi on December 31, Year 5, representing the maturity value of a Treasury bill, but that the bank did not credit Rossi's account until January 2, Year 6. The Treasury bill had been acquired by the bank for Rossi at a discount for $9,652 and had been recorded at cost in the Short-Term Investments ledger account by Rossi.

A reconciliation of both the balance in the depositor's records and the balance in the bank statement to the correct cash balance on December 31, Year 5, is presented below.

Reconciliation of bank balance and depositor's balance to correct cash balance

ROSSI COMPANY
Bank Reconciliation
December 31, Year 5

Balance in depositor's records		$10,592.66
Add: Note and interest of $30 collected by bank	$ 2,030.00	
Proceeds of Treasury bill that had been acquired for $9,652.00 (interest revenue = $348.00)	10,000.00	12,030.00
Subtotal		$22,622.66
Less: Bank service charges for December	$ 13.50	
NSF cheque drawn by Robert Reeves	50.00	
Error in recording cheque no. 821 ($463.90 − $436.90)	27.00	90.50
Correct cash balance		$22,532.16
Balance in bank statement		$12,269.02
Add: Deposit in transit	$1,144.60	
Proceeds of Treasury bill matured on December 31, Year 5	10,000.00	11,144.60
Subtotal		$23,413.62

Less: Outstanding cheques:		
No. 811	$ 421.96	
814	93.00	
822	250.00	
823	116.50	881.46
Correct cash balance		$22,532.16

This form of bank reconciliation serves three functions: (1) it determines the correct cash balance to be reported in the balance sheet, (2) it discloses errors made in recording cash transactions, either by the bank or by the depositor, and (3) it provides information necessary to bring the accounting records up to date. The journal entry required to adjust the accounting records for errors and omissions is taken from the adjustments to the depositor's records in the bank reconciliation. All items appearing in the reconciliation as additions to or deductions from the "balance in depositor's records" must be included in the journal entry. The journal entry on December 31, Year 5, to adjust the accounting records of Rossi Company is shown below.

Journal entry to adjust accounting records for items in bank reconciliation

Cash	11,939.50	
Office Equipment	27.00	
Accounts Receivable: Robert Reeves	50.00	
Miscellaneous Expenses	13.50	
Interest Revenue ($30.00 + $348.00)		378.00
Notes Receivable		2,000.00
Short-Term Investments		9,652.00
To adjust Cash ledger account per December 31, Year 5, bank reconciliation.		

The balance in the depositor's records, $10,592.66, plus the debit of $11,939.50 in the journal entry, equal the correct cash balance of $22,532.16.[4] If there had been arithmetic errors in balancing the Cash account, these would be corrected, and the balance in the depositor's records in the bank reconciliation would also be changed. Errors of this type are seldom found in bank reconciliation procedures if a trial balance of the general ledger is prepared prior to the preparation of the bank reconciliation.

The deposit in transit and the outstanding cheques will be processed by the bank in the regular course of business during January, Year 6.

Bank Balance Reconciled to Balance in Depositor's Records

The second form of bank reconciliation reconciles the bank balance to the unadjusted balance of the depositor's Cash account in the general ledger. Then, the

4 As a general rule, the journal entry resulting from a bank reconciliation is the only example of an adjusting or correcting entry that involves the Cash ledger account.

required adjustment to the Cash account is entered in the bank reconciliation, resulting in the correct cash balance. This type of bank reconciliation is illustrated below for Rossi Company.

Reconciliation of bank balance to unadjusted Cash ledger account balance

ROSSI COMPANY
Bank Reconciliation
December 31, Year 5

Balance in bank statement		$12,269.02
Add: Deposit in transit	$1,144.60	
Bank service charges for December	13.50	
NSF cheque drawn by Robert Reeves	50.00	
Error in recording cheque no. 821 ($463.90 − $436.90)	27.00	1,235.10
Subtotal		$13,504.12
Less: Outstanding cheques:		
No. 811	$ 421.96	
814	93.00	
822	250.00	
823	116.50	
Total outstanding cheques	$ 881.46	
Note and interest of $30 collected by bank	2,030.00	2,911.46
Balance in depositor's records, unadjusted		$10,592.66
Add: Adjustment to Cash ledger account (See page 278)		11,939.50
Correct cash balance		$22,532.16

Comparison of Two Forms of Bank Reconciliation

Each of the two forms of bank reconciliation has advantages and disadvantages. The form that reconciles both the bank balance and the depositor's balance to the correct cash balance has the advantages of being ''self-balancing'' and of clearly identifying items requiring adjustment in the depositor's accounting records. A disadvantage of this form is that is does not ***directly*** reconcile the bank balance to the unadjusted balance of the Cash ledger account.

The second form of bank reconciliation is preferred by many practising accountants because it verifies the balance in the Cash ledger account (unadjusted). Any required adjusting journal entries for posting to the Cash account are then prepared. A disadvantage of the second form of bank reconciliation is that it does not present in one place all items requiring adjustment of the Cash ledger account. However, this disadvantage is mitigated by the fact that, generally, all reconciling items in a bank reconciliation require adjustment of the Cash account, ***other than deposits in transit and outstanding cheques***.

A difference in the two forms of bank reconciliation is found in the handling of the $10,000 collected by the bank on behalf of Rossi Company on December 31, Year 5, for the matured Treasury bill. This item appeared as a reconciling item in both sections of the first form of reconciliation, because neither the bank statement nor the depositor's Cash ledger account (unadjusted) reflected the $10,000 item on December 31, Year 5.

Reconciliation of Cash Receipts and Cash Payments (Proof of Cash)

Cash balances in the bank statement and the depositor's ledger are reconciled to establish the accuracy of the cash records on a specific date. A full reconciliation of cash receipts and payments (known as a ***proof of cash***) may also be made to establish the accuracy of the cash balance and the effectiveness of internal controls over cash receipts and cash payments for a selected month or a longer period.

To illustrate a reconciliation of cash receipts and cash payments for Rossi Company, we need, in addition to the information already provided for the month of December, Year 5, the bank reconciliation for November and cash receipts and payments data for December from both the bank's and Rossi's records. This information is provided below.

1 The following bank reconciliation was prepared on November 30, Year 5:

Bank reconciliation on November 30, Year 5

ROSSI COMPANY
Bank Reconciliation
November 30, Year 5

Balance in bank statement		$6,947.26
Add: Deposit in transit	$1,055.52	
Bank service charges for November	3.25	
NSF cheque drawn by James Price	75.00	1,133.77
Subtotal		$8,081.03
Less: Outstanding cheques:		
No. 760	$ 244.18	
762	197.50	
763	88.49	
764	151.25	681.42
Balance in depositor's records, unadjusted		$7,399.61
Less: Adjustment to Cash ledger account (See journal entry below)		78.25
Correct cash balance		$7,321.36

2 The adjusting journal entry on November 30, Year 5, based on the bank reconciliation above, was as follows:

Journal entry to adjust accounting records for items in bank reconciliation

Miscellaneous Expenses	3.25	
Accounts Receivable: James Price	75.00	
Cash		78.25
To adjust Cash ledger account per November 30, Year 5, bank reconciliation.		

3 The cash receipts journal showed total cash received during December of $22,640.50, and the cash payments journal showed cash payments during December of $19,369.20. Thus, the unadjusted cash balance in Rossi's accounting records on December 31, Year 5, was $10,592.66, as follows:

Cash ledger account for December

Cash				
Date	*Explanation*	*Debit*	*Credit*	*Balance*
Year 5				
Nov. 30	Unadjusted balance.			7,399.61 Dr
30	Adjustment for items in bank reconciliation.		78.25	7,321.36 Dr
Dec. 31	Cash receipts for December.	22,640.50		29,961.86 Dr
31	Cash payments for December.		19,369.20	10,592.66 Dr

4 The bank statement for December indicated that the total deposits of cash during December were $24,581.42 and that the total cheques paid, including bank charges of $13.50, amounted to $19,259.66. This resulted in an unadjusted bank balance amount on December 31, Year 5, of $12,269.02 ($6,947.26 + $24,581.42 – $19,259.66 = $12,269.02).

The cash receipts, the cash payments, and the cash balances reflected in the bank statement and in the ledger of Rossi Company are reconciled to the correct balances for December, Year 5, as follows:

Proof of cash

ROSSI COMPANY
Proof of Cash
December 31, Year 5

	Balance, Nov. 30, Year 5	*Receipts*	*Payments*	*Balance, Dec. 31, Year 5*
Balances in bank statement	$6,947.26	$24,581.42	$19,259.66	$12,269.02
Deposits in transit:				
Nov. 30, Year 5	1,055.52	(1,055.52)		
Dec. 31, Year 5		1,144.60		1,144.60
Outstanding cheques:				
Nov. 30, Year 5	(681.42)		(681.42)	
Dec. 31, Year 5			881.46	(881.46)
Other reconciling items:				
Bank service charges for December			(13.50)	13.50
NSF cheque drawn by Robert Reeves			(50.00)	50.00
Error in recording cheque no. 821			(27.00)	27.00
Note and interest collected by bank		(2,030.00)		(2,030.00)
Balances in depositors' records	$7,321.36	$22,640.50	$19,369.20	$10,592.66
Add: Adjustment to Cash ledger account on Dec. 31, Year 5 (See page 278)				11,939.50
Correct cash balances				$22,532.16

The proof of cash for Rossi Company on December 31, Year 5, is explained below:

1 *Reconciliation of cash receipts in bank statement and in depositor's records* The $1,055.52 deposit in transit on November 30 is deducted from the deposits recorded by the bank in December because it was a receipt of cash in November. The $1,144.60 deposit in transit on December 31 is a receipt of cash in December and should be included in total cash receipts for December. The $2,030 proceeds of the note and interest collected by the bank must be deducted from the deposits recorded by the bank because the proceeds had not been entered in the accounting records (before adjustment) on December 31, Year 5.

2 *Reconciliation of cash payments in bank statement and in depositor's records* The outstanding cheques of $681.42 on November 30 are included in the bank debits for December. These do not represent cash payments during December but rather were shown properly as cash payments in November. The outstanding cheques of $881.46 on December 31 did not include any cheques that were outstanding on November 30; therefore, this total is properly classified as a cash payment by Rossi during December. The bank service charges of $13.50 and the NSF cheque of $50 were included in the bank's debits for December but not in the accounting records (unadjusted). The bank recorded cheque no. 821 at its correct amount of $463.90; that amount is $27 larger than the $436.90 amount recorded in the depositor's records.

3 *Reconciliation of bank and depositor cash balances* The last column of the reconciliation is identical to the reconciliation of the bank and depositor balances to the correct cash balance illustrated on page 279. The journal entry required to adjust the accounting records of Rossi Company on December 31, Year 5, is the same as that illustrated on page 278.

Cash Overdraft

The issuance of cheques in excess of the balance on deposit creates an ***overdraft*** in the bank account. Banks often (but not always) refuse to pay a cheque that exceeds the balance of the depositor's account. Such refusal prevents an overdraft from occurring. In the rare situation in which a business enterprise maintains only one bank account and that account is overdrawn on the balance sheet date, the overdraft amount is reported as a current liability. However, if an enterprise has other accounts in the same bank with larger positive balances, it is reasonable to present the net balance of cash as a current asset. This treatment is based on the reasoning that users of financial statements are interested in an enterprise's net cash position, rather than in the status of its individual bank accounts in a particular bank.

An overdraft in an account in one bank should not be offset against positive balances in other banks because no ***right of offset*** exists. The overdraft in the one bank account is a current liability, and the total of the positive balances is a current asset.

In rare instances, an accountant may discover a situation in which cheques are written (and recorded) in excess of the amount on deposit, but the cheques are not issued to creditors. In the preparation of financial statements, the credit balance in the Cash ledger account should be eliminated by a debit to the Cash account and a credit to the Accounts Payable account (or to other liability accounts) for the amount of the cheques written but not issued.

Disclosure of Compensating Cash Balances

A ***compensating balance*** can be defined as the portion of any demand deposit maintained by a depositor that constitutes support for existing borrowing arrangements with banks. Disclosure of compensating-balance arrangements is needed because such cash balances are not available for discretionary use by management on the balance sheet date. Because the maintenance of compensating cash balances affects liquidity and the effective cost of borrowing from banks, users of financial statements may find such information useful.

Credit Card Sales Drafts as Cash

Merchants making sales to customers who present bank credit cards prepare a ***sales draft*** to evidence the credit sale. One copy of the sales draft is given to the customer, another copy is retained by the merchant, and a third copy is deposited in the bank that issued the credit card. Thus, the copy of the sales draft deposited in the bank by the merchant is the equivalent of ***cash***. Accordingly, the journal entry to record a sale to a customer who presents a bank credit card is as follows:

Journal entry to record credit card sale

Cash	345	
Sales		345
To record sale (sales draft no. 4672).		

Any undeposited sales drafts at the end of an accounting period are reported as undeposited cash (an addition to the bank balance) in the bank reconciliation on that date.

The bank that issued the credit card charges a ***discount*** on credit card sales drafts deposited by the merchant. The discount, which varies on the basis of average amounts and monthly volume of sales drafts issued by the merchant, is either deducted from the gross amount of each sales draft deposited or subtracted monthly from the merchant's bank balance. In either case, the appropriate journal entry for the discount is a debit to an account such as Credit Card Discount Expense and a credit to Cash. The credit card discount expense is included with interest expense in the income statement for the merchant.

Electronic Banking

In recent years commercial banks have adopted various electronic systems for some of their services. ***Electronic banking***, or ***electronic funds transfer***, includes:[5]

- ***Automated banking services,*** such as automated teller machines
- ***Point-of-sale services,*** which include the verification or guarantee of cheques and direct charges to the bank account of a customer making a purchase from a retailer
- ***Home banking services*** such as pay-by-telephone arrangements between a bank and its depositors
- ***Automated clearinghouse services,*** which involve direct debits or credits to bank chequing accounts without the preparation of formal cheques or deposit slips

All these services have been designed to increase efficiency in the processing of banking transactions. However, because of limited documentary evidence provided by electronic banking, it is doubtful that cheques and deposit slips will disappear completely from banking in the foreseeable future.

SHORT-TERM INVESTMENTS[6]

Investment of Idle Cash

To achieve the efficient use of all resources, the management of a business enterprise frequently turns unproductive cash balances into productive resources through the acquisition of short-term investments. In some cases an enterprise may follow a policy of owning investments that may be converted to cash as needed.

The ***CICA Handbook*** states that short-term investments should be classified as current assets if they are "capable of reasonably prompt liquidation... [and] would include not only temporary holdings of marketable securities but also other investments, such as treasury bills, investment certificates, and call loans."[7] Thus, short-term investments held by a business enterprise for the purpose of earning a return on cash resources are characterized by their saleability at a readily determinable price. Stocks and bonds which are not widely held or frequently traded do not usually meet the marketability test; consequently, such securities are not considered in this discussion.

Investments in securities of other companies acquired by a business enterprise as a means of exercising influence or control over the operations of such companies are of a quite different character and should not be considered short-term

5 Howard G. Johnson, "Understanding Electronic Banking," ***Price Waterhouse Review***, 1983, no. 1, pp. 8–12.

6 According to the CICA's ***Financial Reporting in Canada***, 16th ed., p. 98, "short-term investments" is the term most widely used.

7 CICA, ***CICA Handbook***, sec. 3010.02.

investments. If the holding is for the purpose of exercising control, the effective operation of the enterprise may be hampered by the liquidation of the investment. Investments of this nature are discussed in Chapter 14.

In summary, short-term investments classified in the balance sheet as current assets must be readily saleable and should not be held for purposes of bolstering business relations with the issuing company. There is no requirement that short-term investments be owned for a limited time only or that management express its intent as to the duration of the investment. The objectives of acquiring short-term investments are two: (1) to maximize the return on assets, and (2) to minimize the risk of loss from price fluctuations.

When excess cash is available for short periods, the investment media typically used are term deposits, commercial paper, Treasury bills, and bonds (both government and corporate) with near-term maturities (in order to minimize price fluctuations). ***Term deposits*** are issued by banks for varying periods of time. ***Commercial paper*** is the term used for short-term unsecured promissory notes issued by corporations and sold at a discount to investors, generally other companies. ***Treasury bills*** are issued at a discount by the Government of Canada with varying periods of maturity, such as 30 or 90 days. Longer-term bonds and common stocks, although occasionally used as a medium for investing idle cash, do not necessarily meet the objective of limited price fluctuation. Long-term bond prices fluctuate with changes in the level of interest rates, as do prices of bonds with short-term maturities: the degree of fluctuation is greater for bonds with longer maturities. In contrast, common stocks are subject to wide price movements because of changes in investor sentiment, corporate earnings, and economic and political developments.

Recording Transactions in Short-Term Investments

At acquisition, short-term investments are recorded at cost, the price of the item in the market ***plus any costs incident to the acquisition***, such as brokerage commission. Bonds acquired between interest dates are traded on the basis of the market price plus the interest accrued since the most recent interest payment. The accrued interest is a separate asset acquired with the bonds. The cost of these two assets should be separated in the accounting records to achieve a clear picture of the results of the investment in bonds.

When short-term investments are sold, the difference between the carrying amount and the proceeds is recognized as a gain or a loss. A business enterprise that has numerous short-term investments may have a single Short-Term Investments (or Marketable Securities) controlling account in the general ledger and a subsidiary ledger account for each individual investment, showing cost, maturity date, interest or dividends earned, and gain or loss on disposal.

Illustration

On January 31, Year 5, Sawyer Corporation placed an order with a broker to acquire 100 Atlantic Railroad bonds in the amount of $1,000 at 9%. The bonds mature on November 30, Year 8, with interest dates May 31 and November 30. They were acquired on the same day ''at 103'' (103% of face amount), plus accrued interest of $1,500 for two months. The brokerage commission was $500. The total cost of the bonds and the total cash paid are computed below:

Computation of cost of short-term investment in bonds and total cash paid

Market price of bonds ($1,030 × 100)	$103,000
Add: Brokerage commission	500
Total cost of bonds	$103,500
Add: Accrued interest for two months on $100,000, at 9% a year	1,500
Total cash paid	$105,000

The journal entry required to record the acquisition of the bonds is shown below.

Journal entry for acquisition of short-term investment in bonds

Short-Term Investments	103,500	
Interest Receivable	1,500	
Cash		105,000
To record acquisition of 100 Atlantic Railroad bonds at 103 plus accrued interest of $1,500 and brokerage commission of $500.		

On April 30, Year 5, Sawyer Corporation sold the Atlantic bonds at 104¾ plus accrued interest for five months. The cash received from sale of the bonds, after brokerage commission of $500, is computed below.

Computation of cash received from sale of bonds

Market price of bonds ($1,047.50 × 100)	$104,750
Less: Brokerage commission	500
Net proceeds on sale of bonds	$104,250
Add: Accrued interest for five months on $100,000, at 9% a year	3,750
Total cash received	$108,000

The following journal entry is required for Sawyer Corporation on April 30, Year 5, to record the sale of the bonds:

Journal entry for sale of short-term investment in bonds

Cash	108,000	
Short-Term Investments		103,500
Interest Receivable		1,500
Interest Revenue		2,250
Gain on Sale of Short-Term Investments		750
To record sale of Atlantic Railroad bonds at 104¾, less brokerage commission of $500, plus accrued interest of $3,750.		

The gain of $750 realized on the sale of the Atlantic Railroad bonds is the result of a change in the market price of the bonds, which may have occurred for any number of reasons. The two most likely causes of such a gain are (1) a decline in the level of interest rates, or (2) a more favourable investor appraisal of this bond issue. If the level of interest rates had risen since January 31, Year 5, these bonds would probably have been sold at a loss.

The $1,500 of accrued interest on the bonds acquired on January 31, Year 5 might at that time have been recorded as a debit to the Interest Revenue ledger account. This procedure would require that the $3,750 of accrued interest received on April 30 be credited to the Interest Revenue ledger account. The net effect would be to show $2,250 ($3,750 − $1,500 = $2,250) as interest revenue for the three months the bonds were owned.

Discount or Premium on Short-Term Investments in Bonds

In accounting for short-term investments in bonds, it is usually unnecessary to amortize premiums or accumulate discounts. Such temporary investments generally have near-term maturities; consequently, any premium or discount is likely to be negligible. The holding period by the investor also is likely to be short, which means that any change in market price is usually attributable to changes in interest rates and risk factors rather than to the approach of the maturity date. In theory, the amortization of premium or the accumulation of discount on short-term investments in bonds is always proper, but as a practical matter such amortization or accumulation would add little to the accuracy of financial statements.

Cost Selection

The cost of short-term investments sold is not always as definite as in the preceding illustrations. If there are several acquisitions of the same bond or stock at different dates and prices, and a portion of the holdings is sold, some procedure of cost selection must be employed. Among the methods commonly used are specific identification, first-in, first-out, and average cost. For income tax purposes, only the average cost method is acceptable.

Stock and bond certificates generally have serial numbers that facilitate determination of the cost of specific investments. By using the specific identification method, management may influence the amount of realized gain or loss by deliberately selecting the certificates to be sold from a high-cost lot or a low-cost lot. As an example, assume that Kane Company acquired 100 bonds of Lowe Corporation for $96,000 and a few months later acquired another 100 bonds for $99,000. A month later Kane sold 100 Lowe Corporation bonds for $98,000. The sale will show a gain of $2,000 or a loss of $1,000, depending on which bonds are sold. Thus, the cost method used should be appropriate under the circumstances and should be used consistently so as to avoid deliberate manipulation.

Price Fluctuations and Valuation of Short-Term Investments

Normally, an asset is recorded at cost, and this cost is associated with the revenue generated from the use of the asset. If the asset loses its value without generating revenue, the cost is written off as a loss. As recommended by the ***CICA Handbook***, when the market value of short-term investments has declined below their carrying value, they should be shown at market value.[8] However, the ***revenue realization principle*** usually allows recognition of increases in the value of an asset only when it is sold. Whether realization should be limited to the point of sale for short-term investments is a question worth considering. By definition, short-term investments are readily saleable at a quoted market price. This same characteristic is usually not found in inventories or plant assets. This basic difference between these types of assets suggests that the traditional tests of revenue realization should not control the valuation of short-term investments.

The use of market prices to value short-term investments at the end of an accounting period has some advantages: (1) The income statement will show the results of decisions to hold or sell such investments period by period (for example, if the market price rises in one accounting period and falls in the next, the gain from holding short-term investments in the first period and the loss sustained by failure to sell at the higher price will be disclosed); (2) valuation at current market price eliminates the anomaly of carrying identical securities at different amounts because they were acquired at different prices; and (3) market value is more meaningful to creditors, who use the current section of a balance sheet to judge the debt-paying ability of the business enterprise.

The following example illustrates the issues that would arise if market value were used as the basis for valuation of short-term investments. On December 31, Year 1, Dixon Foundry has a portfolio of short-term investments that cost $148,000 and had a market value of $151,500. The question at issue is whether on December 31, Year 1, there has been a gain of $3,500 ($151,500 – $148,000) = $3,500). If we follow the traditional tests of revenue realization, ***no gain would be recognized until the investments are sold***. If valuation at market price is accepted, the following journal entry would be recorded:

Journal entry to record short-term investments at market value

Short-Term Investments	3,500	
Gain in Market Value of Short-Term Investments		3,500
To record increases in value of short-term investments.		

Thus, the gain would be recognized in the accounting period in which the price increased rather than in the period in which investments are sold.

On March 28, Year 2, the investments are sold for $149,800. Has there been a gain or a loss on the sale of investments? If the traditional revenue realization principle were followed, the increase in market price was not recognized earlier; because a sale has now taken place, a gain of $1,800 ($149,800 – $148,000 = $1,800) is recognized. If the investments were valued at market price on December 31, Year 1, the journal entry to record the sale on March 25, Year 2, would show a loss of $1,700 ($151,500 – $149,800 = $1,700) sustained since December 31, Year 1.

8 CICA, *CICA Handbook*, sec. 3010.06.

The question which must be answered is, "What event gives rise to the recognition of gains and losses from holding short-term investments?" The traditional answer has been "Sale of the investments," but the logic of this answer is questionable. In our opinion, the current market value of investments is the most relevant valuation because it is the one most likely to aid users in making decisions. It seems reasonable to anticipate that accountants will eventually find a satisfactory method of using current market prices to account for short-term investments.

Valuation at Cost or at Lower of Cost and Market

The forcefulness of the arguments in favour of reporting short-term investments at market value notwithstanding, most business enterprises continue to report marketable securities at cost when the market value is higher and at market value when it is lower than cost. This practice of valuation at the ***lower of cost and market*** for short-term investments is recommended by the ***CICA Handbook***, as mentioned earlier. Moreover, recoveries in the market value of short-term investments that have been written down are not recognized. The practice of not recognizing the recoveries in the decline of market value below cost lacks logical support. Consequently, the FASB in the United States has taken a positive step regarding this issue.

In the United States, the FASB issued in 1975 ***Statement No. 12*** to deal with the following questions regarding marketable ***equity*** securities:

- Under what circumstances should marketable equity securities be written down below cost?
- Should marketable equity securities that had been written down be written up at a later date?

FASB Statement No. 12 deals with ***marketable equity securities*** classified as current assets as well as marketable equity securities classified as noncurrent assets. In this section we are concerned primarily with the provisions of ***FASB Statement No. 12*** applicable to marketable equity securities carried as ***short-term investments***.

Definition of Terms

The FASB defined the following terms relating to marketable equity securities.[9]

1 ***Equity securities*** include instruments representing ownership shares or the right to acquire or dispose of ownership shares at fixed or determinable prices. Equity securities include common stocks, most preferred stocks (including convertible preferred stocks), stock warrants, and call or put options. The following ***are not*** equity securities: preferred stock that by its terms either must be redeemed by the issuing enterprise or is redeemable at the option of the investor; treasury stock; and convertible bonds.

9 FASB, ***Statement No. 12***: "Accounting for Certain Marketable Securities" (Stamford: 1975), pp. 3–5.

2 ***Marketable*** means that sales prices (or bid and ask prices) are currently available for an equity security on a securities exchange or in the publicly reported over-the-counter market.

3 ***Market price*** refers to the price of a single share or unit of a marketable equity security.

4 ***Market value*** refers to the aggregate of the market price times the number of shares or units of each marketable equity security in a portfolio.

5 ***Cost*** refers to the original cost of a marketable equity security, unless a new cost basis has been assigned on recognition of an impairment of value that was deemed other than temporary. In such cases, the new cost basis is the cost.

6 ***Valuation allowance*** for a marketable equity securities portfolio represents the net unrealized loss in that portfolio.

7 ***Carrying amount*** of a marketable equity securities portfolio is the amount at which that portfolio of marketable equity securities is reported in the balance sheet, that is, cost reduced by the valuation allowance.

8 ***Realized gain or loss*** represents the difference between the net proceeds from the sale of a marketable equity security and its cost. (Such gain or loss results only on sale of a security.)

9 ***Net unrealized gain or loss*** on a marketable equity securities portfolio represents on any date the difference between the aggregate market value and aggregate cost. (Such gain or loss is recognized for financial accounting only at the end of an accounting period.)

Accounting for Current Marketable Equity Securities

The FASB stated that the carrying amount of a marketable equity securities portfolio should be the lower of its aggregate cost and market value, as determined on each balance sheet date. The amount, if any, by which the aggregate cost of the portfolio exceeds market value is accounted for by use of a ***valuation allowance***. The treatment of changes in the valuation allowance depends on whether the securities are current or noncurrent assets. In the case of a classified balance sheet, marketable equity securities are grouped into separate ***current*** and ***noncurrent portfolios*** for the purpose of comparing aggregate cost and market value. In the case of an unclassified balance sheet, marketable equity securities are treated as noncurrent assets.

Realized gains and losses from sale of current marketable equity securities are included in the determination of net income of the accounting period in which they occur. Changes in the valuation allowance for a marketable equity securities portfolio ***included in current assets*** are also included in net income of the period in which they occur. Such changes in the valuation allowance result in ***unrealized gains and losses***. A recovery in the aggregate market value of securities that had been written down to a market value below cost requires the recognition of an

unrealized gain that is included in net income. However, increases in the aggregate market value of the current portfolio of marketable equity securities above aggregate cost are not recognized in the accounting records.

If there is a ***change in the classification*** of a marketable equity security between current and noncurrent, the security should be transferred between the corresponding portfolios at the lower of its cost and market value on the date of transfer. If market value is less than cost, ***the market value becomes the new cost basis***, and the difference is recorded as a ***realized loss***.

Illustration

To illustrate the application of ***FASB Statement No. 12*** to a current portfolio of marketable equity securities, assume that the changes in the portfolio of Weber Limited from December 31, Year 1, through December 31, Year 3, are as set forth below.

WEBER LIMITED
Changes in Current Portfolio of Marketable Equity Securities
For Years Ended December 31, Year 1 through Year 3

	Cost	*Market value*	*Unrealized gain (loss)*
Dec. 31, Year 1			
Security A	$100,000	$ 80,000	$(20,000)
Security B	200,000	160,000	(40,000)
Security C	50,000	75,000	25,000
Totals	$350,000	$315,000	$(35,000)
Dec. 31, Year 2			
Security A	$100,000	$ 75,000	$(25,000)
Security B	100,000*	70,000	(30,000)
Security C	50,000	60,000	10,000
Totals	$250,000	$205,000	$(45,000)
Dec. 31, Year 3			
Security A	$100,000	$ 80,000	$(20,000)
Security B	100,000	90,000	(10,000)
Security C	50,000	65,000	15,000
Totals	$250,000	$235,000	$(15,000)

*On March 1, Year 2, one-half of the holdings of Security B (cost, $100,000) was sold for $75,000. There were no other sales of securities in Year 2 or Year 3.

December 31, Year 1, the Date of Initial Application A valuation allowance of $35,000 is required for marketable equity securities included in the current portfolio to reflect the excess of total cost, $350,000, over total market value, $315,000. The unrealized loss of $35,000 is included in net income for Year 1. The journal entry to record the unrealized loss and the valuation allowance is:

Journal entry to establish valuation allowance for current portfolio of marketable equity securities

	Debit	Credit
Unrealized Loss in Value of Marketable Equity Securities	35,000	
Allowance to Reduce Marketable Equity Securities to Market Value		35,000
To establish valuation allowance for decline in total market value of current portfolio of marketable equity securities.		

March 1, Year 2, Sale of Security at a Loss The sale of one-half of the holdings of Security B for $75,000 resulted in a ***realized loss*** of $25,000. The loss is included in computing the net income for Year 2. The journal entry to record the sale is shown below:

Journal entry for sale of marketable equity security at a loss

	Debit	Credit
Cash	75,000	
Realized Loss on Sale of Marketable Equity Securities	25,000	
Short-Term Investments		100,000
To record sale of Security B at a realized loss.		

December 31, Year 2, Increase in Valuation Allowance A valuation allowance of $45,000 is required for marketable equity securities in the current portfolio to reflect the excess of total cost, $250,000, over total market value, $205,000. Because the balance in the valuation allowance account is $35,000, an increase of $10,000 is required. The journal entry to record the increase in the valuation allowance is:

Journal entry to increase valuation allowance

	Debit	Credit
Unrealized Loss in Value of Marketable Equity Securities	10,000	
Allowance to Reduce Marketable Equity Securities to Market Value		10,000
To record increase in valuation allowance as a result of further decline in total market value of current portfolio of marketable equity securities.		

December 31, Year 3, Recovery in Market Value of Portfolio There has been a market recovery during Year 3, as evidenced by the need to reduce the valuation allowance from $45,000 to $15,000. The difference of $30,000 is an ***unrealized gain*** and is included in net income for Year 3. The journal entry to record the reduction in the valuation allowance is:

Journal entry to reduce valuation allowance

	Debit	Credit
Allowance to Reduce Marketable Equity Securities to Market Value	30,000	
Unrealized Gain in Value of Marketable Equity Securities		30,000
To reduce valuation allowance as a result of recovery in total market value of current portfolio of marketable equity securities.		

After the foregoing journal entries have been posted, the Short-Term Investments and Allowance to Reduce Marketable Equity Securities to Market Value ledger accounts appear as follows:

Ledger accounts for marketable equity securities

Short-Term Investments

Date	*Explanation*	*Debit*	*Credit*	*Balance*
Dec. 31/1	Balance.			350,000 Dr
Mar. 1/2	Sale of one-half of Security B holdings.		100,000	250,000 Dr

Allowance to Reduce Marketable Equity Securities to Market Value

Date	*Explanation*	*Debit*	*Credit*	*Balance*
Dec. 31/1	($350,000 – $315,000.)		35,000	35,000 Cr
Dec. 31/2	[($250,000 – $205,000) – $35,000.]		10,000	45,000 Cr
Dec. 31/3	[($250,000 – $235,000) – $45,000.]	30,000		15,000 Cr

Note that on March 1, Year 2, the amount of the realized loss recognized was based on the actual cost of Security B ($100,000), not the market value at the end of the prior year ($80,000), and that ***the valuation allowance is adjusted only on December 31, Year 2, at the end of the accounting period***. It also should be observed that the valuation of the entire current portfolio at lower of cost and market results in the recognition of the unrealized gain on Security C in Year 1, which defers recognition of part of the unrealized loss of $60,000 on Securities A and B. Also, the current-verus-noncurrent approaches adopted by the FASB may result in possible manipulative practices to avoid recognition of unrealized losses in the current portfolio. This may be achieved by the transfer of a security with a market value above cost from the noncurrent to the current portfolio.

Disclosure Requirements for Current Portfolio of Marketable Equity Securities

The following information with respect to marketable equity securities included in the current portfolio is disclosed either in the financial statements or in a note to the financial statements:[10]

1 As of the date of each balance sheet presented, aggregate cost and aggregate market value, with identification as to which is the carrying amount

2 As of the date of the latest balance sheet presented, the gross unrealized gains representing the excess of market value over cost for all marketable equity securities in the portfolio, and the gross unrealized losses representing the excess of cost over market value for all marketable equity securities in the portfolio

3 For each accounting period for which an income statement is presented:
   a Net realized gain or loss included in the determination of net income

10 FASB, *FASB Statement No. 12*, pp. 7–8.

b The basis on which cost was determined in the computation of realized gain or loss (that is, average cost or other method used)

Financial statements are not adjusted for realized gains or losses or for changes in market prices when such events occur after the date of the financial statements but prior to their issuance. However, significant net realized and net unrealized gains and losses arising after the date of the financial statements but prior to their issuance, applicable to securities owned on the date of the most recent balance sheet, are disclosed.

Balance Sheet Presentation of Cash and Short-Term Investments

Cash is the most liquid asset a business enterprise owns, in the sense that it is most easily converted to other assets and services. This characteristic justifies its position as the first item in the current asset section of the balance sheet. There is seldom any reason to be concerned about the valuation of cash. There are few sources of possible loss except for theft, which cannot be anticipated. Loss due to bank failure has all but disappeared in recent years with the institution of the Canada Deposit Insurance Corporation. Therefore, cash is reported in the balance sheet at the amount that represents its current fair value. Terms of borrowing agreements, including requirements to maintain compensating balances, are disclosed in a note to the financial statements.

Short-term investments rank next to cash in liquidity and thus are listed below cash in the current assets section of the balance sheet. Whether short-term investments are reported at cost or at the lower of cost and market, disclosure of the current market value is required. The presentation of cash and short-term investments in a balance sheet, and the related notes to the financial statements on December 31, Year 4, are illustrated below.

Balance sheet presentation of cash and short-term investments

Current assets:	
Cash (**NOTE 1**)	$21,100,000
Short-term investments, at cost, which approximates market value .	9,000,000

NOTE 1: The company maintains lines of credit with a group of domestic banks for borrowing funds on a short-term and a long-term basis. The company has agreed to maintain an average compensating balance of 10% of the unused lines of credit and 15% of the amounts borrowed. On December 31, Year 4, the aggregate compensating-balance requirement was approximately $11,250,000.

REVIEW QUESTIONS

1 What are the usual components of *cash*?

2 How would you classify the following items in a balance sheet?
   a Travel advances to employees
   b Cash deposited with a trustee for the retirement of bonds payable
   c Undeposited cash representing receipts of the prior day
   d Customer's cheque returned by the bank marked "NSF" ("not sufficient funds")
   e A nonreturnable deposit with a real estate broker as an option on a tract of land

f Treasury bills temporarily held until cash is needed to make payments on building under construction
g A petty cash fund composed of the following:

Coin and currency	$110
Vouchers:	
Selling expenses	61
General and administrative expenses	29

3 What is ***management's responsibility*** with respect to cash? What techniques are used to aid in carrying out this responsibility?

4 *a* What is a system of ***internal controls***?
b What is the purpose of a system of internal controls?
c Differentiate between ***administrative control*** and ***accounting control***.
d Why is internal control over cash and short-term investments particularly important?

5 Parr Company has a change fund of $100 in its cash register. The cash sales tickets for May 25 total $2,049.60, and cash in the cash register, verified by count, totals $2,154.25. Prepare the journal entry necessary to record sales for May 25.

6 Why are adjusting entries usually not made to record outstanding cheques as liabilities or deposits in transit as cash on hand?

7 *a* What are three functions of a bank reconciliation?
b What function does the reconciliation of cash receipts and cash payments (proof of cash) serve?

8 *a* Describe two forms of bank reconciliation in common usage.
b Which form of bank reconciliation is preferred by many practising accountants? Explain.

9 How is a material ***cash overdraft*** reported in the balance sheet?

10 Define ***compensating cash balances*** and state the reasons for disclosure of such balances in a note to the financial statements.

11 Explain the appropriate accounting for the ***discount*** charged by a bank on credit card sales drafts.

12 What is ***electronic banking***?

13 Why is management concerned with investing cash that is temporarily in excess of current requirements in short-term investments? What may be done to eliminate or minimize the risk of loss from temporary fluctuations in the market price of securities held as short-term investments?

14 Do you support the use of current market value as the basis for valuing all short-term investments? Explain.

15 What two questions relative to marketable equity securities in a current portfolio did the Financial Accounting Standards Board in the United States attempt to answer in ***Statement No. 12***: "Accounting for Certain Marketable Securities"?

16 Define the following terms relating to the accounting for marketable equity securities according to ***FASB Statement No. 12***:

a *Equity securities*
b *Valuation alowance*
c *Carrying amount*
d *Realized gain or loss*
e *Net unrealized gain or loss*

17 Briefly describe the accounting treatment of the valuation allowance to reduce marketable equity securities to market value. Include in your answer the treatment of realized gains and losses and changes in market value in subsequent accounting periods.

18 Should term deposits be included in cash in the balance sheet for a business enterprise? Explain.

EXERCISES

Ex. 6-1 Select the best answer for each of the following multiple-choice questions:

1 When the aggregate market value of a business enterprise's current marketable equity securities portfolio is lower than its aggregate cost, the difference is:

a Accounted for as a current liability
b Disclosed in a note to the financial statements but not accounted for
c Accounted for as a valuation allowance deducted from the securities to which it relates
d Accounted for separately in the shareholders' equity section of the balance sheet

2 An analysis of Pickwick Corporation's short-term marketable equity securities portfolio acquired in Year 7 reveals the following totals on December 31, Year 7:

Aggregate cost of portfolio	$90,000
Aggregate market value of portfolio	80,000
Aggregate lower of cost and market value applied to each security in the portfolio	76,000

The amount of the valuation allowance that Pickwick should record on December 31, Year 7, is:

a $0 *b* $4,000 *c* $10,000 *d* $14,000 *e* Some other amount

3 Which of the following conditions generally exists before market value may be used as the basis for valuation of a business enterprise's current marketable equity securities?

a Management's intention must be to dispose of the securities within one year.
b Market value must be less than cost for each security held in the enterprise's current marketable equity securities portfolio.
c Market value must approximate historical cost.
d The aggregate market value of the enterprise's current marketable equity securities portfolio must be less than the aggregate cost of the portfolio.

4 Which of the following should not be included in cash in the balance sheet?
   a Petty cash funds
   b Postdated cheques from customers
   c Dividends bank account
   d Compensating balance for a 90-day note payable to bank
   e None of the foregoing

5 In preparing its bank reconciliaton for the month of March, Year 2, Derby Company has available the following information:

Balance in bank statement, Mar. 31, Year 2	$36,050
Deposit in transit, Mar. 31, Year 2	6,250
Outstanding cheques, Mar. 31, Year 2	5,750
Credit erroneously recorded by bank in Derby's account, Mar. 12, Year 2	250
Bank service charges for March, Year 2	50

The correct balance of Derby Company's cash on March 31, Year 2, is:
a $35,250 *b* $36,250 *c* $36,300 *d* $36,550 *e* Some other amount

6 In the form of bank reconciliation preferred by many practising accountants:
   a The unadjusted cash account balance in the depositor's records is reconciled to the bank statement balance.
   b The bank statement balance is reconciled to the unadjusted cash account balance in the depositor's records.
   c Both the bank statement balance and the cash account balance in the depositor's records are reconciled to a correct balance.
   d The correct cash balance is reconciled to the balance in the bank statement.

Ex. 6-2 The December 31, Year 5, balance of Wynn Company's Cash ledger account was $4,000. Wynn had the following items in its safe on December 31, Year 5:

1 Cheque of customer, Canna Company, payable to Wynn, dated and recorded on Jan. 2, Year 6	$1,000
2 Cheque of customer, Lowe Company, payable to Wynn, deposited by Wynn on Dec. 26, Year 5, but returned by bank on Dec. 30, Year 5, marked "NSF." No journal entry was made for the returned cheque. Wynn redeposited the cheque on Jan. 2, Year 6, and it cleared	200
3 Postage stamps received from mail-order customers	75
4 Cheque of Wynn Company payable to Keith Company, a supplier, dated and recorded on Dec. 31, Year 5. Wynn mailed the cheque on Jan. 2, Year 6	500

Compute the balance of cash to be included in Wynn Company's December 31, Year 5, balance sheet.

Ex. 6-3 The reconciling items in the February 28, Year 5, bank reconciliation of Dundee Company were as follows:

Balance in bank statement, Feb. 28, Year 5	$16,600
Balance in Cash ledger account, Feb. 28, Year 5	11,060
Bank service charges for February., Year 5	50
Deposit in transit, Feb. 28, Year 5	1,200
Error in Dundee's recording of cheque no. 654 to vendor, Ace Company ($400 cheque recorded by Dundee as $40)	360
Interest on note receivable collected by bank for Dundee on Feb. 28, Year 5	300
NSF cheque of customer, Bell Company, charged back by bank on Feb. 28, Year 5	250
Outstanding cheques (total) Feb. 28, Year 5	4,100
Principal of note receivable collected by bank for Dundee on Feb. 28, Year 5	3,000

Prepare a February 28, Year 5, bank reconciliation for Dundee Company in the form illustrated on page 279. Disregard the required adjustment to the Cash ledger account.

Ex. 6-4 The petty cash fund for Grant Company is $200. During March, Year 10, $30 was spent on entertainment expense, $36.20 was spent on office supplies expense, $53 was spent on postage expense, $40 was spent for merchandise, $32.90 was spent on miscellaneous items, and $7.90 remained on hand. Grant uses the periodic inventory system.

Prepare a journal entry to record the replenishment of the petty cash fund on March 31, Year 10.

Ex. 6-5 How are the following reconciling items included in a four-column reconciliation (proof of cash) for the month of November, Year 8? Explain.

a Outstanding cheques on November 30, Year 8
b Bank service charge for month of October, Year 8, recorded in general journal in November, Year 8
c Deposit in transit on October 31, Year 8
d NSF cheque returned to depositor by the bank on November 17, Year 8; redeposited on November 18, Year 8, with no journal entry in the accounting records

Ex. 6-6 In auditing the financial statements of Rohr Company for Year 10, you review the following ledger account:

Short-Term Investment — Weiss Limited Common Stock

Date	*Explanation*	*Debit*	*Credit*	*Balance*
Year 10				
Mar. 28	Acquired 200 shares at 26¼.	5,250		5,250 Dr
June 15	Dividend received.		80	5,170 Dr
Dec. 15	Dividend received.		80	5,090 Dr
23	Proceeds from sales of 100 shares.		2,940	2,150 Dr

You also find that a commission of $106 on the acquisition of the 200 shares of Weiss Limited common stock was debited to the Miscellaneous Expenses ledger account.

Prepare a journal entry on December 31, Year 10, to correct Rohr Company's accounting records.

Ex. 6-7 Presented below is a condensed version of the bank reconciliation prepared by Lowell Company on March 31, Year 1.

LOWELL COMPANY
Condensed Bank Reconciliation
March 31, Year 1

Balance in bank statement		$11,120
Add: Deposit in transit	$1,390	
Service charge for March	8	1,398
Subtotal		$12,518
Less: Outstanding cheques		2,008
Balance in Cash ledger account (before adjustment)		$10,510

Cash receipts and payments entered in the accounting records during the month of April, Year 1, are listed below:

Cash receipts	$29,400
Cash payments (including adjusting entry for March bank service charge)	26,950

On April 30, Year 1, cheques outstanding amounted to $2,950, and deposits in transit amounted to $1,911. There was no service charge for April, and no errors were made either by the bank or by Lowell.

Prepare a proof of cash for Lowell Company for the month of April, Year 1, similar to the illustration on page 281. Disregard the required adjustment to the Cash ledger account.

Ex. 6-8 Prepare journal entries to record the following transactions or events relating to short-term investments of Hadley Company during Year 4:

June 11	Acquired $50,000 face amount 15% bonds issued by Lamar Limited. Total acquisition price was $52,800, which included accrued interest of $1,250 from April 11.
Oct. 11	Received semiannual interest on Lamar Limited bonds, $3,750.
Dec. 11	Sold $20,000 face amount Lamar Limited bonds for total consideration of $23,500, which included accrued interest of $500 from Oct. 11.
31	Recorded accrued interest for 80 days on $30,000 face amount Lamar Limited bonds.

Ex. 6-9 From the following data of Skiff Company for December, Year 7:

a Compute the cash balance in the accounting records before adjustments are recorded.

b Prepare a journal entry to bring the accounting records up to date.

Balance in bank statement	$15,500
Cheques outstanding	6,400
Cash receipts recorded in the accounting records, not yet deposited	1,920
Bank service charges not recorded in the accounting records	22
Promissory note collected by bank, not recorded in the accounting records (includes interest of $40)	4,040

Ex. 6-10 The following bank reconciliation was prepared for Howe Corporation on June 30, Year 6:

HOWE CORPORATION
Bank Reconciliation
June 30, Year 6

Balance in bank statement, June 30, Year 6		$ 8,308
Add: Deposit in transit	$ 1,690	
Cheque incorrectly charged to Howe Corporation by bank	250	
Bank service charge for June	10	
NSF cheque from customer returned by bank	120	2,070
Subtotal		$10,378
Less: proceeds of bank loan arranged on June 30, Year 6	$10,000	
Outstanding cheques	2,940	
Error in recording cheques in payment of vendor's invoice	18	12,958
Balance in accounting records, June 30, Year 6		$(2,580)

a Compute Howe Corporation's correct cash balance on June 30, Year 6.

b Prepare a journal entry to adjust Howe Corporation's Cash ledger account to the correct balance. Interest on the bank loan is payable at maturity, and all payments on vendors' invoices are debited to the Accounts Payable ledger account.

Ex. 6-11 Pearl Company began investing idle cash in marketable equity securities in Year 3. The cost and market value of the securities held in its current portfolio at the end of its December 31 fiscal years were as follows:

End of Year	*Cost*	*Market value*
3	$200,000	$210,000
4	310,000	260,000
5	280,000	210,000
6	400,000	425,000

Prepare journal entries for Pearl Company at the end of each year to adjust the valuation allowance to reduce current marketable equity securities to market value.

Ex. 6-12 The items required for the September 30, Year 9, bank reconciliation of Leward Company's account follow:

Balance in bank statement, Sept. 30, Year 9		$12,367.43
Balance in depositor's records, Sept. 30, Year 9		4,977.47
Bank service charges for month of September, Year 9		6.50
Bank error in recording cheque no. 648:		
Drawn and recorded in depositor's records	$ 411.42	
Encoded incorrectly and paid by bank	41.42	
Net bank error		370.00
Outstanding cheques:		
No. 643	$ 10.00	
651	50.00	
654	750.00	
655	750.00	
671	55.00	
673	750.00	
674	2,000.00	
675	14.00	
676	250.00	
678	5.00	
679	2,390.96	
680	1.50	
Total outstanding cheques		7,026.46

Prepare a bank reconciliation for Leward Company on September 30, Year 9. Use the total for outstanding cheques on September 30, Year 9; do not list individual cheques. Reconcile both the bank balance and the depositor's balance to the correct cash balance.

CASES

Case 6-1 Management of Kingsley Corporation foresees a period of three to five years of reduced operations. During this period, management does not expect to replace any plant assets. Management presents the board of directors with a plan (1) to maintain the ratio of dividends to net income at 60% and (2) to invest all cash that accumulates in excess of normal operating needs in a diversified list of high-quality common stocks. Management also proposes that the common stocks be carried in the balance sheet at market value on the balance sheet date. Any change in market value from date of acquisition or the most recent valuation for financial statement purposes is to be included in the income statement.

Instructions

a What are the advantages of accounting for and reporting of investments in this manner?
b What objections might be made to this method of reporting the investments?
c Should the investments be reported as a current or a noncurrent asset? Why?

Case 6-2 Segura Company is projecting an increased level of operations for the coming year (Year 4), which will require an additional investment in inventories and accounts receivable. The minimum cash balance required is $50,000. After a detailed review of the prospects for Year 4, the controller prepared the following forecast of monthly cash balances (parentheses indicate a projected cash deficiency):

January	$110,000	July	$395,000
February	50,000	August	450,000
March	(100,000)	September	80,000
April	(230,000)	October	(250,000)
May	(150,000)	November	(290,000)
June	150,000	December	(50,000)

Short-term investment decisions are made and loans are negotiated on the fifteenth day of each month in an amount equal to the projected cash surplus or deficiency for the month. Changes in the short-term investment or loan positions are made in multiples of $5,000.

Assume that surplus cash is to be invested in short-term notes bearing 10% interest and that borrowed funds cost 15%. The cash balance on January 1, Year 4, was $50,000.

Instructions

a Prepare a working paper to compute the net cost (interest expense less interest revenue on short-term investments) of short-term borrowing to finance the operations of Segura Company for the year ended December 31, Year 4. Round computations to nearest dollar.
b If Segura Company is to avoid short-term borrowing, how much long-term debt or equity capital must be raised? Would you recommend that Segura attempt to raise the capital or follow a policy of short-term borrowing? Why

Case 6-3 Since the issuance of ***FASB Statement No. 12***: ''Accounting for Certain Marketable Securities,'' Coldwater Limited has intended to follow the practice of valuing its short-term investments in marketable equity securities at the lower of cost and market. On December 31, Year 10, the ledger account Marketable Equity Securities (Current Portfolio) had a balance of $260,000, and the ledger account Allowance to Reduce Marketable Equity Securities to Market Value had a balance of $40,000. The allowance account had been unchanged during Year 10; the balance of $40,000 was based on the following facts relating to the securities owned on December 31, Year 9:

Security	*Cost*	*Market value*	*Allowance required*
X Corporation common stock	$150,000	$120,000	$30,000
Y Corporation common stock	80,000	70,000	10,000
Z Corporation warrants to acquire common stock	30,000	75,000	
Totals	$260,000	$265,000	$40,000

During Year 10, the Y Corporation common stock was sold for $65,000, the difference between the $65,000 and the cost of $80,000 being debited to the Realized Loss on Sale of Marketable Equity Securities ledger account. The market values of the securities remaining on December 31, Year 10, were: X Corporation common stock, $90,000; Z Corporation warrants to acquire common stock, $40,000.

Instructions

a What argument supports the use of the lower-of-cost-and-market rule in the valuation of marketable equity securities?

b Did Coldwater Limited apply the lower-of-cost-and-market rule correctly at the end of Year 9? Explain.

c What correcting entries are required for Coldwater Limited on December 31, Year 10, assuming that any error made in Year 9 is corrected as an adjustment to the prior period? Disregard income taxes.

d Assume that the president of Coldwater Corporation does not wish to recognize any unrealized loss in the value of marketable equity securities at the end of Year 10. Instead, the president wants to transfer a block of K Corporation common stock from the noncurrent portfolio to the current portfolio. The common stock of K Corporation is listed on the Toronto Stock Exchange with a market value of $200,000. K is a major customer of Coldwater, and its common stock was acquired many years ago at a cost of $100,000 to maintain good business relations between Coldwater and K. Would you approve the president's proposal? Explain.

PROBLEMS

Pr. 6-1 The bank reconciliation for Linda Philip Limited at November 30, Year 3, included deposits in transit of $9,600 and outstanding cheques of $12,000. The following additional information is available at December 31, Year 3:

	Per depositor's accounting records	*Per bank statement*
Deposits during December	$ 98,400	$ 84,700
Payments during December	111,200	116,000
Collection of note by bank, including $100 interest revenue not recorded in the accounts		8,100

Bank service charges (including $160 consulting fee)		180
Cash balance at Dec. 31	40,800	32,620

Instructions

a From the foregoing information, prepare a bank reconciliation arriving at corrected balances at December 31, Year 3.

b Prepare a single journal entry to bring the accounting records up to date at December 31, Year 3.

Pr. 6-2 On January 2, Year 8, Mission Company, which adjusts its accounting records and prepares financial statements at the end of each month, acquired for cash 1,000 shares of common stock of three companies as short-term investments, as follows:

	*Cost**
1,000 shares of F Limited common stock	$12,000
1,000 shares of G Limited common stock	14,000
1,000 shares of H Limited common stock	16,000
Total	$42,000

*Includes brokerage commissions.

On February 14, Year 8, Mission sold 500 shares of G Limited common stock for $6,200, net of the brokerage commission. Market values per share of the three common stocks were as follows on January 31 and Feburary 28, Year 8:

	Jan. 31, Year 8	*Feb. 28, Year 8*
F Limited common stock	$13	$11
G Limited common stock	12	11
H Limited common stock	15	16

Instructions

a Prepare journal entries for Mission Company on January 2, January 31, February 14, and February 28 of Year 8, based on the requirements of *FASB Statement No. 12*.

b Would the amount for the short-term investments for statement presentation at January 31 and February 28 be different under the CICA recommendations? Explain.

Pr. 6-3 The bank statement for Dingle Corporation showed a balance of $70,688.88 on December 31, Year 9. The balance of the Cash ledger account was $65,194.43. In comparing the bank balance with the cash balance in the accounting records, Dingle's accountant discovered the following:

1 Cheques amounting to $18,830.00 had not cleared the bank.

2 A cheque in payment of an account payable was recorded in the accounting records for $857.20; the correct amount of the cheque was $875.20.

3 A customer's cheque for $739.90 was returned marked "NSF." No journal

entry had been made in the accounting records to record this cheque.
4 A deposit of $12,565.70 had not been recorded by the bank.
5 The bank's charge for printing cheques was $11.95.

Instructions

a Prepare a bank reconciliation for Dingle Corporation on December 31, Year 9, in the form illustrated on page 279.

b Prepare a journal entry for Dingle Corporation on December 31, Year 9, to bring the accounting records up to date. Record the journal entry's net effect on the Cash ledger account in the bank reconciliation prepared in *a*.

Pr. 6-4 The temporary investments owned by Lambert Corporation on September 30, Year 5 are shown below:

	Cost
9% government bonds, $400,000 face amount, due June 1, Year 8	$394,000
1,500 shares of $8 preferred stock of Tesla Power Limited	156,000
Total	$550,000

Accrued interest receivable on the government bonds on this date was $12,000. This amount has been recorded in the Interest Receivable account. Transactions relating to temporary investments for the three months ended December 31, Year 5, are summarized below:

Oct. 15	Purchased $40,000 face amount, 10% bonds of General Corporation at a price of 104, plus commission of $200 and accrued interest of $500 from September 1. Record interest acquired in the Interest Receivable account.
30	Received quarterly dividend on Tesla Power Limited $8 preferred stock.
Nov. 10	Sold entire holdings of Tesla Power Limited $8 preferred stock for $152,600, net of commission.
Dec. 1	Received semiannual interest on the 9% government bonds, $18,000.
31	Sold $200,000 face amount of 9% government bonds at 101, net of commission, plus accrued interest of $1,500.

Instructions

a Record the transactions in general journal form, including the adjusting entry to accrue interest on bonds owned at December 31, Year 5. Do not amortize premium or accumulate discount on bonds owned. Compute accrued interest (to the nearest dollar) on the basis of a 360-day year.

b Assuming that the market value of the bonds owned is $236,000, show three alternative ways that marketable securities might be presented in the balance sheet at December 31, Year 5.

Pr. 6-5 Seacoast Company was organized early in Year 1. During the next four years it completed the following transactions in the current portfolio of marketable equity securities:

Year 1	
Acquired the following marketable equity securities:	
Security A	$100,000
Security B	50,000
Security C	75,000
Year 2	
Sold Security A for $140,000, net of brokerage commission and other miscellaneous costs.	
Year 3	
Acquired Security D for $88,000.	
Year 4	
Sold Security B for $37,500, net of brokerage commission and other miscellaneous costs. Acquired Security E at a total cost of $180,000.	

The market values of the current portfolio of marketable equity securities on December 31 of each year were as follows:

	Year 1	*Year 2*	*Year 3*	*Year 4*
Security A	$125,000			
Security B	30,000	$ 45,000	$ 35,000	
Security C	50,000	90,000	70,000	$ 55,000
Security D			85,000	80,000
Security E				175,000
Totals	$205,000	$135,000	$190,000	$310,000

Instructions

a Prepare journal entries for Seacoast Company to record the transactions in marketable equity securities listed above for the four-year period ended December 31, Year 4, including appropriate adjustments to the valuation allowance account at the end of each year, as required by ***FASB Statement No. 12***. Disregard income taxes.

b Show how the current portfolio of marketable equity securities would be presented in Seacoast Company's balance sheet at the end of each of the four years ended December 31, Year 4. Supplementary disclosure pursuant to ***FASB Statement No. 12*** is not required.

c Would the amount for the market securities for the balance sheet at the end of Year 1 and Year 2 be different from that in ***b*** if the CICA's recommendations were followed? Explain. Which position appears to be more logical and why?

Pr. 6-6 On June 1, Year 2, Lew Corporation adopted a petty cash fund procedure for minor cash payments. Also on June 1, Year 2, Lew made an initial investment of idle cash in marketable securities. The fiscal year ends on June 30. The operations of the petty cash fund for the last month of the fiscal year ended June 30, Year 2, and the first month of the following fiscal year, and the acquisition of marketable securities, are summarized below:

June 1 The petty cash fund was established with a Lew cheque for $2,500 payable to the petty cash custodian.

1 Lew acquired 1,000 shares of Data Processing Associates, Inc., common stock at 40½, plus a commission of $825, as a short-term investment.

19 A request for replenishment of the petty cash fund was received by the accounts payable department, supported by appropriate signed vouchers summarized as follows:

Selling expenses	$ 468
Administrative expenses	678
Factory overhead costs	383
Special tools	192
Telephone, telegraph, and postage expenses	48
Miscellaneous expenses	308
Total	$2,077

20 A cheque for $2,077 was drawn payable to the petty cash custodian.

30 Lew's internal auditors counted the petty cash fund in connection with year-end audit work and found the following:

Cash in petty cash fund		$1,010
Employees' cheques with July dates (postdated cheques)		180
Expense vouchers properly approved as follows:		
Selling expenses	$249	
Administrative expenses	387	
Factory overhead costs	89	
Office supplies expense	96	
Telephone, telegraph, and postage expenses	56	
Miscellaneous expenses	428	1,305
Total		$2,495

The petty cash fund was not replenished on June 30, Year 2.

June 30 The internal auditors also noted that the closing market price of the Data Processing Associates, Inc., common stock on June 30 was $35 a share.

July 15 The employees' cheques that were in the petty cash fund on June 30 were cashed, and the proceeds were placed in the petty cash fund.

31 A request for replenishment of the petty cash fund was received by the accounts payable department, and a cheque was drawn to restore the fund to its original balance of $2,500. The supporting vouchers for July expenditures are summarized below:

Selling expenses	$ 160
Administrative expenses	164
Factory overhead costs	349
Telephone, telegraph, and postage expenses	35

Miscellaneous expenses	338
Total	$1,046

Instructions

a Prepare journal entries for the foregoing transactions of Lew Corporation, including any adjustment required on June 30, Year 2. Disregard income tax effects.

b Evaluate Lew Corporation's use of the petty cash fund.

c Show how the marketable securities should be presented in the balance sheet at June 30, Year 2, on the basis of the ***CICA Handbook*** recommendations.

Pr. 6-7 Gilson, Inc., received the following bank statement for the month of September, Year 6:

GILSON, INC.
In Account with Scotia Bank
London, Ontario

Cheques			*Deposits*	*Date*	*Balance*
				Sept. 1	3,658.74
310.00	35.48	130.00	820.00	Sept. 2	4,003.27
60.00	31.15	510.00	72.80	Sept. 5	3,474.92
70.00	515.00		361.00	Sept. 7	3,250.92
90.00			280.00	Sept. 8	3,440.92
13.30	62.50		510.00	Sept. 9	3,875.12
28.00			205.60	Sept. 12	4,052.72
650.00			180.14	Sept. 14	3,582.86
			345.00	Sept. 16	3,927.86
85.00			427.50	Sept. 19	4,270.36
24.10	125.06			Sept. 20	4,121.20
40.00	65.00		90.00	Sept. 21	4,106.20
162.40			360.00	Sept. 23	4,303.80
15.00			625.00	Sept. 26	4,913.80
355.00	270.00	225.00	130.25	Sept. 28	4,194.05
7.50s			280.50	Sept. 30	4,467.05

Legend:
s = Service charge.

The entries in Gilson's cash journals for the month of September are shown on the next page.

The Cash ledger account balance in Gilson's accounting records on August 31 agreed with the balance in the bank statement, although a deposit was in transit and two cheques were outstanding. The balance of the Cash ledger account on September 30 was $5,380.81.

Instructions

a Prepare a bank reconciliation for Gilson, Inc., on September 30, Year 6. Use the form illustrated on page 279.

Cash Receipts Journal

Date		*Explanation*	*Cash (debit)*
Sept.	1		72.80
	3		361.00
	6		280.00
	8		510.00
	10		205.60
	13		180.14
	15		345.00
	17		427.50
	20		90.00
	22		360.00
	24		625.00
	27		130.25
	28		280.50
	29		1,710.10
	30		315.25
			5,893.14

Cash Payments Journal

Date		*Explanation*	*Cheque no.*	*Cash (credit)*
Sept.	1		65	130.00
	1		66	90.00
	1		67	35.48
	2		68	31.15
	4–19		69–78	1,648.86
	20		79	24.10
	20		80	38.60
	20		81	65.00
	22		82	162.40
	23		83	150.00
	26		84	15.00
	28		85	270.00
	28		86	105.20
	28		87	225.00
	28		88	355.00
	30		89	25.00
	30		90	645.29
	30		91	155.00
				4,171.08

b Prepare the necessary journal entry to adjust Gilson, Inc.'s, Cash ledger account on September 30, Year 6. Record the journal entry's net effect on the Cash account in the bank reconciliation prepared in *a*.

Pr. 6-8 On February 1, Year 1, Ryder Company had cash in excess of its immediate needs. Management decided to invest this cash, and any other cash that appeared to be temporarily in excess of current needs, in short-term securities. The following transactions occurred during the fiscal year ended January 31, Year 2:

Year 1

Feb. 1 Acquired for $292,130, including accrued interest of $2,630, C.P. Ltd. 10% bonds, due in two years, $300,000 face amount, with interest payable June 30 and December 31. (Debit Interest Receivable for $2,630.)

May 31 Sold for $152,455, including accrued interest of $6,205, one-half of the C.P. Ltd. 10% bonds acquired February 1.

June 30 Received interest on C.P. Ltd. 10% bonds, $7,500.

Aug. 1 Acquired 40 Maritimes Ltd. 12%, $1,000 bonds, interest payable April 1 and October 1, at 102 plus accrued interest of $1,604 and a commission of $125. These bonds mature three years after the next interest date.

Oct. 1 Received interest on Maritimes Ltd. 12% bonds, $2,400.

Dec. 15 Sold for $148,054, including accrued interest of $6,904, the remainder of the C.P. Ltd. 10% bonds acquired February 1.

Year 2

Jan. 16 Acquired $100,000 face amount Sea Products 14% notes for a price of $102,250. Interest is paid on these notes on January 16 and July 16.

31 Adjusted the accounting records to reflect interest accrued to the end of the fiscal year. Management decided that the premium on bonds and notes acquired will not be amortized. Interest on bonds and notes is computed on the basis of the exact number of days elapsed, using a 365-day year. Compute interest on each security to the nearest dollar.

Instructions

a Prepare journal entries to record the foregoing transactions of Ryder Company.

b The closing market quotes for the Maritimes Ltd. bonds and the 14% Sea Products notes on January 31, Year 2, were 102 and 105 respectively. Prepare a partial balance sheet showing all data for short-term investments in accordance with the ***CICA Handbook*** recommendations.

Pr. 6-9 The following data pertaining to the cash transactions and bank account of Taurus Company for September, Year 4, are available to you:

1	Cash balance in accounting records, Sept. 30, Year 4	$28,104.50
2	Cash balance in bank statement, Sept. 30, Year 4	34,085.80
3	Bank service charge for September	14.00
4	Debit memo for printed cheques delivered by the bank; the charge has not been recorded in the accounting records	5.00
5	Deposit of Sept. 30 not recorded by bank until Oct. 1	3,870.00
6	Outstanding cheques, Sept. 30, Year 4	8,128.30
7	Proceeds of a bank loan on Sept. 30 not recorded in the accounting records (interest payable at maturity)	2,970.00
8	Principal and interest on customer's promissory note, face amount $800, collected by the bank, net of collection fee of $3 charged by the bank	810.00
9	Cheque no. 1086 to a supplier entered in the accounting records as $1,879.10; deducted in the bank statement in the correct amount of	1,789.10
10	Stolen cheque lacking an authorized signature deducted from Taurus Company's account by the bank in error	867.50
11	Customer's cheque returned by the bank marked "NSF," indicating that the customer's balance was not adequate to cover the cheque; no journal entry has been made to record the returned cheque	1,260.50

Instructions

a Prepare a reconciliation of the cash balances of Taurus Company and the bank to the correct balance on September 30, Year 4.

b Prepare a journal entry to adjust Taurus Company's accounting records on September 30, Year 4.

Pr. 6-10 You are the senior accountant in charge of the March 31, Year 2, audit of Lido Limited. Lido's inexperienced accountant has prepared the bank reconciliation shown below for your consideration. You have reviewed the dollar amounts in the reconciliation and have determined that they are accurate.

LIDO LIMITED
Bank Reconciliation
March 31, Year 2

Balance in general ledger, Mar. 31, Year 2		$69,316.66
Add: Deposit in transit, mailed Mar. 31, Year 2		8,197.66
$9,200 note receivable and $47 interest collected by bank Mar. 31, Year 2, less $1.07 service charge		9,245.93
Bank service charge for March, Year 2		10.88
Cheque in payment of account payable, drawn and paid by bank as $91.73, recorded in cash payments journal as $917.30		825.57
Subtotal		$87,596.70
Less: Outstanding cheques:		
No. 413	$ 185.22	
419	216.25	
420	96.44	
421	123.80	
422	314.55	
423	112.01	
Total outstanding cheques	$1,048.27	
Cheque of customer, J. K. Lane, deposited Mar. 26, Year 2, returned "NSF" by bank Mar. 31, Year 2	814.69	1,862.96
Computed balance in bank statement, Mar. 31, Year 2		$85,733.74
Unlocated difference		(14,320.54)
Balance in bank statement, Mar. 31, Year 2		$71,413.20

Instructions

a Prepare a corrected bank reconciliation for Lido Limited on March 31, Year 2, in the form illustrated on page 279.

b Prepare a correcting journal entry for Lido Company's Cash ledger account on March 31, Year 2. Record the net effect of the journal entry in the reconciliation prepared in *a*.

Pr. 6-11 You have completed your examination of the cash on hand and in banks in your audit of Harvey Corporation's financial statements for the year ended December 31, Year 7, and noted the following:

1. Harvey maintains a general bank account at National Bank and a payroll bank account at Provincial Bank. All cheques are signed by the company president, Douglas Harvey. Harvey uses a Vouchers Payable ledger account to accompany its voucher system for all cash payments.
2. Data and reconciliations prepared by Harvey's accountant on November 30, Year 7, indicated that the payroll account had a $1,000 general ledger and

bank balance with no in-transit or outstanding items, and the general bank account had a $12,405 general ledger balance with cheques outstanding aggregating $918 (no. 1202 for $575 and no. 1205 for $343) and one deposit of $492 in transit to National Bank.

3 Your surprise cash count on Tuesday, January 2, Year 8, revealed that customers' cheques totalling $540 and a National Bank deposit slip for that amount dated December 29, Year 7, were in Harvey's safe and that no cash was in transit to National Bank at that time. Your examination of the general account prenumbered cheques revealed cheque no. 1216 to be the first unused cheque; it was ultimately issued to a supplier.

4 Harvey's general ledger accounts are prepared on a posting machine, and all transactions are posted in chronological sequence. The ledger account for the general bank account for December, Year 7, is shown below.

General Ledger
General Bank Account
(National Bank)

Ref.	*Debits*	*Credits*	*Balance*
Bal.			$12,405
Dec. 1	$ 496		12,901
1206		$ 1,675	11,226
1207		645	10,581
Dec. 6	832		11,413
1208		1,706	9,707
Dec. 8	975		10,682
1209		2,062	8,620
1210		3,945	4,675
1211		6,237	1,562
Dec. 12	8,045		6,483
Dec. 15	9,549		16,032
1212		1,845	14,187
RT		241	13,946
1213		350	13,596
D		2,072	11,524
Dec. 22	1,513		13,037
1214		2,597	10,440
1215		1,739	8,701
Dec. 29	540		9,241
Dec. 31	942		10,183
1216		1,120	9,063
	$22,892	$26,234	

*Credit balance.

5 The December statements from both banks were delivered unopened to you. The Provincial Bank statement contained deposits for $1,675; $1,706;

$1,845; and $2,597 and 72 paid cheques totalling $7,823. The National Bank statement is shown below:

NATIONAL BANK
Account: Harvey Company (General Account)

Date	*Charges*		*Credits*	*Balance*
Year 7				
Nov. 30				$12,831
Dec. 1			$492	13,323
5	$1,675	$ 267 RT	496	11,877
8	575		832	12,134
11	1,706	654	975	10,749
14	1,987 D	2,062	8,045	14,745
18	6,237	1,845	9,949	16,612
21	241 RT	546 RT	546 CM	16,371
22	2,072 D		1,513	15,812
26	2,597			13,215
28	362	4 DM	1,010 CM	13,859
29	12 DM		362	14,209
	Total charges — $22,842		Total Credits — $24,220	

Legend:
CM: Credit memo D: Draft
RT: Returned cheque DM: Debit memo

6 You obtained cutoff bank statements from both banks on January 8, Year 8. The National Bank statement is presented below:

NATIONAL BANK
Account: Harvey Company (General Account)

Date	*Charges*		*Credits*	*Balance*
Dec. 29, Year 7				$14,209
Jan. 2, Year 8	$1,739	$3,945	$540	9,065
Jan. 5, Year 8	350		942	9,657

7 You determine that the bank statements are correct except that National Bank incorrectly charged a returned cheque on December 21; but it corrected the account with a credit the same day.

8 The $362 cheque charged by National Bank on December 28 was cheque no. 2000 drawn payable to Harvey Corporation and endorsed ''Harvey Corporation by Donald Hume.'' Your investigation showed that the amount credited by National Bank on December 29 was an unauthorized transfer from Provincial Bank Payroll Account to National Bank General Account that had been made by Harvey's accountant, who made no related entry in Harvey's accounting records. The cheque was charged to Harvey's payroll

bank account on January 2, Year 8, in the cutoff statement you received from Provincial Bank.

9 Drafts charged against the National Bank account were for trade acceptances signed by Douglas Harvey and issued to a supplier.

10 On December 28, a 60-day, 6%, $1,000 promissory note was collected by National Bank for Harvey for a $4 collection fee.

11 The $12 debit memo from National Bank was a charge for printed cheques.

12 Cheque no. 1213 was issued to replace cheque no. 1205 when the latter was reported not received by a vendor. Because of the delay in paying this account, Harvey was no longer entitled to the 2% cash discount it had taken in preparing the original cheque. Harvey completed a stop-payment order for cheque no. 1205.

Instructions

a Prepare a four-column reconciliation (proof of cash) for Harvey Corporation's general bank account for the month of December, Year 7. Use the form illustrated on page 281.

b Prepare an adjusting entry to correct the General Bank Account ledger account of Harvey Corporation on December 31, Year 7. Record the net effect on the account in the proof of cash prepared in ***a***. Use separate accounts receivable ledger accounts for customers' returned cheques and the unauthorized cash payment by Donald Hume.

Pr. 6-12 In connection with an audit of cash of Vail Company as of December 31, Year 15, you obtained the following information:

1 Balances in bank statements:

Nov. 30	$ 195,700
Dec. 31	313,674

2 Balances in accounting records:

Nov. 30	$ 164,826
Dec. 31	287,598

3 Cash receipts for month of December:

In bank statement	$1,670,450
In accounting records	2,751,445

4 Outstanding cheques:

Nov. 30	$ 63,524
Dec. 31	75,046

5 Dishonoured cheques are recorded as a reduction of cash receipts. Redeposited dishonoured cheques are recorded as a regular cash receipt. Dishonoured cheques returned by the bank and recorded by Vail amounted to $6,250 during the month of December; according to the accounting records, $5,000 of dishonoured cheques were redeposited. Dishonoured cheques recorded in the bank statement but not in the accounting records until the following months amounted to $250 on November 30 and $2,300 on December 31.

6 On December 31, a $2,323 cheque on which a stop-payment order was in force was charged by the bank to Vail's account in error.

7 Proceeds of a promissory note from Capp Company, collected by the bank on December 30, were not entered in the accounting records:

Principal amount of note	$2,000
Interest, $20, less collection charge of $5	15
Net proceeds	$2,015

8 Vail has pledged its accounts receivable with the bank under a contract whereby the bank lends Vail 80% on the pledged accounts receivable. Accounting for and collection of the accounts are performed by Vail, and adjustments of the loan are made from daily sales reports and daily cash deposits.

The bank credits Vail's account and increases the amount of the loan for 80% of the reported sales. The loan contract states that the sales report must be accepted by the bank before Vail is credited. Sales reports are forwarded by Vail to the bank on the first day following the date of sales. The bank allocates 80% of each deposit to the payment of the loan and 20% to Vail's account. Thus, only 80% of each day's sales and 20% of each collection deposit are entered in the bank statement.

The accountant for Vail records the pledge of new accounts receivable (80% of sales) as a debit to Cash and a credit to Loans Payable to Bank on the date of sales. Of the collections on accounts receivable, 100% is recorded as a cash receipt; 80% of the collections is recorded in the cash payments journal as a payment on the loan. In a review of the loan contract, you learned the following facts:

a Included in the deposits in transit is cash from the pledged accounts receivable. Sales were $40,500 on November 30 and $42,250 on December 31. The balance of the deposit in transit on December 31 was made up from collections of $32,110, which were entered in the accounting records in the manner indicated above.

b Collections on accounts receivable deposited in December, other than deposits in transit, totalled $1,320,000.

c Sales for December totalled $1,600,000.

9 Cash receipts from other sources that were deposited intact during December totalled $120,835.

10 Interest on the bank loan for the month of December, charged by the bank but not recorded in the accounting records, amounted to $6,140.

Instructions

a Prepare for Vail Company a four-column reconciliation (proof of cash) of beginning and ending cash balances, cash receipts, and cash payments for December, Year 15.

b Prepare the adjusting journal entry required to bring Vail Company's accounting records up to date on December 31, Year 15. Record the net effect on the Cash account in the proof of cash prepared in *a*.

c h a p t e r 7

RECEIVABLES

The balance sheet of every business enterprise includes a variety of claims from other parties that generally provide a future inflow of cash. These ***receivables*** arise from transactions and events such as sale of goods or services, loans made, subscriptions obtained from investors for capital stock or bonds, claims for income tax refunds, claims resulting from litigation, and amounts due from leasing of assets.

Receivables from customers frequently represent a substantial part of a business enterprise's current assets. Poor screening of applicants for credit or an inefficient collection policy may result in large losses. Consequently, strong accounting controls and effective management of receivables are typical characteristics of most profitable enterprises.

Valuation of Receivables

For most receivables the amount of money to be received and the due date can be reasonably determined. Accountants are thus faced with a relatively certain future inflow of cash, and the problem is to determine the net amount of this inflow.

A number of factors must be considered in the valuation of a prospective cash inflow. One factor is the probability that a receivable will actually be collected. For any specific receivable, the probability of collection might be difficult to establish; however, for a large group of receivables a reliable estimate of collectibility can generally be made.

Another factor to be considered in the valuation of receivables is the length of time until collection. As stated in Chapter 5, an amount of money due at some future time is not worth as much as the same amount due immediately. The longer the time to maturity, the larger the difference between the ***maturity value*** and the ***present value*** of a receivable. When the time to maturity is long, most contracts between debtors and creditors require the payment of a fair rate of interest, and the present value of such a contract is equal to its face amount. The present value of any non-interest-bearing receivable is less than the amount that will be received on the due date. If the time to maturity is short, this difference is usually ignored. For example, a 30-day unsecured trade account receivable is almost always recorded at its face amount. The difference between present value and face amount of longer-term receivables always should be considered, because this difference may be material.

Receivables From Sale of Goods and Services

The most common receivables result from revenue-producing activities, such as the sale of goods and services. The unsecured ***trade account*** is the most important of these. Contracts governing trade accounts receivable are typically informal and are supported by such documents as sales orders, invoices, and delivery contracts. Most trade accounts are non-interest-bearing. However, in the retail trade the addition of interest or a service charge to revolving charge accounts or installment receivables is a common practice. Manufacturers and wholesalers use disallowed cash discounts as a form of interest charge if payment is made after the discount period.

Some receivables from customers are represented by various commercial credit instruments such as promissory notes. Such instruments have a stronger legal status than ordinary trade accounts, and because the terms are specified in writing, the holder finds it easier to borrow against them.

A customer who requests an extension of time on a trade account often is asked to sign a promissory note so that the payee may discount the note and receive cash. Most notes and other commercial credit instruments bear interest, because they involve credit for long periods of time. Amounts due from employees and owners of a business enterprise may be included among trade receivables if they result from the sale of goods and services at the usual credit terms.

Receivables From Miscellaneous Sources

Some receivables result from transactions not directly related to the sale of goods and services. For example, short-term advances to affiliated companies, subcontractors, or customers are made in anticipation of future benefits. A claim against an insurance company and a claim based on a legal suit for damages are other examples of miscellaneous receivables. Prospective refunds of amounts previously paid, such as a claim for refund of prior years' income taxes, represent receivables whenever the collection of the claim is reasonably certain. Issuance of capital stock and bonds on a subscription basis and disposal of plant assets also represent sources of miscellaneous receivables. Any type of receivable that is material in amount should be listed separately in the balance sheet. Miscellaneous receivables expected to be collected in one year are classified as current assets; long-term receivables are classified under Investments.

Accruals of interest, dividends, rent, and royalties are current receivables that represent a prospective inflow of cash. Rent and interest receivable accrue as a function of time. Dividends usually are not recorded as receivables prior to the ex-dividend date. Royalties usually accrue as a result of the manufacture or sale of products or the extraction of natural resources.

Occasionally, a receivable arises out of a debit balance in trade accounts payable when, for one reason or another, overpayment has been made to a supplier. If the purchaser expects a cash refund, the amount involved is clearly a receivable. The rule against offsetting assets and liabilities requires that any sizeable debit balance in trade accounts payable be treated as a receivable rather than as an offset against other trade accounts payable. Similarly, a large credit balance in customers' accounts is reported as a current liability. An advance payment on a purchase contract is reported as a prepayment for goods rather than as a receivable. Receivables arising from leasing transactions are discussed in Chapter 20.

TRADE ACCOUNTS RECEIVABLE

A large portion of retail trade involves credit in some form; at the wholesale and manufacturing level almost all sales transactions are on a credit basis. Terms on ordinary trade accounts receivable range from the 10 days typically allowed for taking cash discounts to as long as six months or a year in some cases.

Accounting System and Internal Controls

Business enterprises with a large volume of credit sales usually computerize their accounting records. A computerized system enables the operator to record the credit sale, post to the controlling account, and post to subsidiary ledger accounts in a single operation. Such a system also facilitates the preparation of financial statements and an aging of trade accounts receivable (as illustrated on page 325) at appropriate intervals.

A procedure known as ***cycle billing*** may be used by department stores and public utilities with a large number of customers. Accounts receivable subsidiary ledgers are divided into a number of groups on the basis of geographical location, type of customer, or alphabetically, with each group having its own subcontrol account. The customers in each subcontrol group are billed at different times during a month. This procedure has the advantage of spreading the work of preparing customer statements more evenly during the month and assuring a more uniform cash flow from collection of trade accounts receivable.

It is possible to reduce record-keeping by the elimination of the formal subsidiary trade accounts receivable ledgers. Invoices for credit sales may be sorted by subcontrol groups, and the total amount is entered directly in the trade accounts receivable controlling account. The individual invoices are then filed according to customer. At the end of the month or cycle billing period, the amount receivable from each customer is summarized in a statement, the duplicate copy of which becomes the subsidiary ledger for that customer. Invoices are reproduced (to provide a file copy) and are mailed to each customer along with the statement of the customer's account.

Effective internal controls over the sale of goods and related cash collections are an integral part of the system for handling trade accounts receivable. The responsibility for recording sales and collections of trade accounts receivable should not be assigned to individuals who handle cash receipts or who prepare bank deposit slips and bank reconciliations. Without such segregation of duties, a dishonest employee could abstract cash collections from customers and conceal the theft by recording the collection as a debit to the Sales Returns and Allowances ledger account, or by writing off the receivable as uncollectible.

Recording Trade Accounts Receivable and Revenue

Two important questions faced by accountants in recording trade accounts receivable are:

1 At what point in the earning process should a trade account receivable be recorded?

2 How should the net amount of a trade account receivable be measured so that this asset and the related revenue and expenses will be recorded accurately?

Trade accounts receivable are generally recorded when sales are made and title to the goods passes. Receivables for services are recorded only as services are performed. Receivables are not recorded when a customer's order is received or when goods are produced; and shipments on ***consignment*** are not sales, because title to the goods does not pass until ***consignees*** sell the goods. However, receivables should be recorded for work completed on construction-type contracts.

When it is determined that revenue has been realized and recording of the claim against a customer is warranted, the question of measuring the amount of the receivable (and the revenue) still remains. For example, assume that a parcel of land is sold by a land developer for $5,000. The customer may pay either $5,000 cash or $1,000 down and $1,100 at the end of each year for five years. If the sale is made on the deferred payment plan, should the receivable be recorded by the land developer at $4,000 ($5,000 cash price less the $1,000 down payment) or at $5,500, the face amount of the five remaining payments of $1,100 each? Is the revenue realized by the land developer in the current year $5,000, $6,500, or some other amount? The amount of revenue is dependent on the valuation of the consideration received (including receivables) from revenue transactions. Thus, the land developer should record the receivable at $4,000 and recognize revenue of $5,000 at the time the land is sold. Accounting for trade accounts receivable centres on two issues: (1) the amount due, and (2) the estimate of the probability that the receivable will be collected. A number of problems relating to these issues are discussed in the following sections.

MEASURING TRADE ACCOUNTS RECEIVABLE

Trade Discounts

In some industries it is customary to bill customers a gross price subject to one or more trade discounts. The gross price is usually the suggested price for resale, and the trade discount represents the difference between gross (list) price and the price to the purchaser before cash discounts. The use of fixed list prices and varying trade discounts enables the seller to change prices, or to grant special discounts to certain customers, without reprinting catalogues or price lists. For financial accounting, these discounts should be recognized for what they are—a convenient means of pricing. The amount that a customer will pay is the net price after the trade discount, and this is the amount at which the receivable and the related revenue are recorded.

Cash (Sales) Discounts

Cash discounts are used to establish a ***cash price*** when payment is received shortly after delivery of goods, as distinct from a higher ***deferred payment price***. For example, if an invoice for $10,000 provides for terms of 2/10, n/30 the customer has two alternatives: (1) pay $9,800 in 10 days, or (2) wait the full 30 days and pay $10,000. The differential of $200 represents an effective interest rate of 36.7% for the use of the $9,800 for the extra 20-day period, and thus offers a strong incentive for payment before the 10-day discount period expires.[1]

A theoretical valuation of receivables subject to cash discounts should allow for the probability that discounts will be taken. In the case cited above, for example, if the probability is high that the customer will take the discount, the receivable is worth only $9,800. If the customer is expected to pay the face amount, the receivable is worth $10,000.

In dealing with a large number of receivables, accountants find that past experience is usually a good guide in estimating customer reaction to discounts that are available to be taken. In view of the generous saving inherent in the cash price, the assumption that most customers will take the discounts is probably justified.

Several approaches may be used to account for sales discounts. For example, entries to the Trade Accounts Receivable and Sales ledger accounts may be recorded at the face amount of the receivables, and discounts taken by customers are recorded by debits to the Sales Discounts ledger account. No journal entry is made at the end of the accounting period to anticipate discounts that may be taken by customers on outstanding trade accounts receivable.

Alternatively, the same procedure may be followed, except that an adjusting entry is made at the end of the accounting period to accrue discounts that may be taken by customers on outstanding receivables. The Sales Discounts ledger account is debited and the Allowance for Sales Discounts account is credited for the amount of potential discounts that may be taken on outstanding receivables. The balance in the Allowance for Sales Discounts ledger account is deducted from trade accounts receivable in the balance sheet. Actual discounts taken by customers at the beginning of the following accounting period may be debited to the Allowance for Sales Discounts ledger account. If a reversing entry is made to eliminate the allowance account, discounts taken may then be recorded in the usual manner by debits to the Sales Discounts ledger account.

Under the first approach, trade accounts receivable and pre-tax income are overstated by the amount of estimated sales discounts not accrued. These overstatements are eliminated under the alternative approach, which is consistent

1 There are eighteen 20-day periods in one year; therefore, the annualized rate earned may be computed as follows: (200 × 18) ÷ $9,800 = 0.367.

with the objective of reporting trade accounts receivable and revenue at ***net realizable values*** in the financial statements.

Estimated Collection Costs

Valuation of trade accounts receivable on the balance sheet date should take into account any direct costs (that are material in amount) of collecting outstanding receivables. For example, the estimated legal and other collection costs that may be incurred in the collection of outstanding receivables may be recognized as an expense of the current accounting period, and the related allowance account is deducted from trade accounts receivable in the balance sheet.

Sales Returns and Allowances

The value assigned to trade accounts receivable also should recognize the probability that some customers will return goods that are unsatisfactory or will make other claims requiring reduction in the net amount receivable. Potential sales returns and allowances reduce the amount that ultimately will be collected from customers and thus reduce the net realizable value of trade accounts receivable. If the amounts are material, as in the recorded music and catalogue sales industries, periodic income measurement is improved by an adjustment for estimated returns and allowances.

To illustrate, assume that experience shows that sales returns average 10% of accounts receivable, and that an average of 60% of the original selling price is ultimately realized from the returned goods. If trade accounts receivable at the end of the accounting period amount to $100,000 and the perpetual inventory system is in use, the appropriate end-of-period adjusting entry is illustrated below:

Accrual of sales returns

Inventory — Anticipated Sales Returns (at net realizable value) [($100,000 × 0.10) × 0.60]	6,000	
Sales Returns ($100,000 × 0.10)	10,000	
Cost of Goods Sold		6,000
Allowance for Sales Returns		10,000
To record anticipated sales returns.		

The effect of this journal entry is to reduce current assets and the gross profit on sales by $4,000 — the difference between the original selling price and the estimated net realizable value of the goods returned. This adjusting entry may be reversed on the first day of the next accounting period; then, as sales returns are made by customers, the Sales Returns ledger account is debited and Trade Accounts Receivable is credited.

Allowance for Freight-Out

Occasionally goods are sold with the understanding that a customer will pay the freight charges and then deduct that amount from the remittance. In such instances both trade accounts receivable and sales may be recorded net of the freight charges. Alternatively, both trade accounts receivable and sales may be recorded at the gross amount billed to the customer, along with a debit to Freight-Out and a credit to Allowance for Freight-Out. The balance in the allowance account is deducted from trade accounts receivable in the balance sheet.

Sales and Excise Taxes

Many government units impose sales and excise taxes on particular products or on sales transactions. Usually, the seller is responsible for the remittance of these taxes to the government. An excise tax imposed on the manufacture of a product is a part of the cost of production, but an excise tax on the sale of the product is imposed on the purchaser and is collected by the seller.

If sales and excise taxes are collected as separately disclosed additions to the selling price, they should not be confused with revenue but should be credited to a liability account. Whether this is done at the time of each sale or as an adjustment at the end of the accounting period is a matter of convenience. Generally, it is preferable to record the tax liability at the time of sale. For example, if a day's sales amount to $20,000 and are subject to a 6% sales tax, the sales tax payable is $1,200, and the journal entry to record sales is:

Recording one day's sales and sales tax payable

Trade Accounts Receivable (or Cash) ($20,000 × 1.06)	21,200	
Sales Tax Payable ($20,000 × 0.06)		1,200
Sales		20,000
To record sales and sales tax liability.		

Container Deposits

Customers may be charged for deposits on containers, with the understanding that the deposits will be refunded when the containers are returned. The containers, such as drums, are depreciable plant assets of the business enterprise that owns them. If container deposits are collected in cash, the only problem is the correct accounting for the refund obligation. When containers are returned, the liability is cancelled by the refund of the deposit; if containers are not returned, the liability no longer exists, and the difference between the amount of the deposit and the cost of the containers not returned represents a gain or loss which, as a matter of convenience, may be recorded in the ledger account for the depreciation of containers. At the end of an accounting period, an adjusting entry is required to record the estimate of the containers that will not be returned.

In some cases, container deposits billed to customers are debited to the Trade Accounts Receivable ledger account. This creates an uncertainty with respect to the amount that will be collected. Until the uncertainty is resolved, trade accounts receivable show a separate item for the amount billed to customers for containers.

Estimating Probability of Collection

Thus far we have considered the problem of determining the amount due from customers under the terms of credit sales. The other major valuation problem is to evaluate the probability that customers will pay their accounts. Because a business enterprise does not make a credit sale unless ultimate collection is reasonably assured, the probability of noncollection with respect to a specific sale is presumably low. However, the best efforts of a capable credit department cannot eliminate all uncollectible accounts. Furthermore, the managerial objective is not to minimize doubtful accounts expense but to maximize net income. Too stringent a credit policy may cause loss of sales volume, which more than offsets the reduction in the doubtful accounts expense.

Receivables that will never be collected have a zero value, and the related revenue will not be realized. The objective in the estimation of doubtful accounts expense (also called bad debts expense, uncollectible accounts expense) is to prevent an overstatement of assets and an understatement of expenses in the accounting period in which sales are made.

In the ledger, the estimate of doubtful accounts is carried as a credit balance in a valuation account titled Allowance for Doubtful Accounts or Allowance for Uncollectible Accounts. This is known as the ***allowance method*** of accounting for doubtful accounts expense. A separate valuation account is used, because it is not known which specific receivables will prove uncollectible and because the Trade Accounts Receivable controlling account must agree with the subsidiary ledger detail. In the balance sheet, the allowance account is deducted from trade accounts receivable to measure their net realizable value.

The doubtful accounts expense may be classified several ways in the income statement. Logically, doubtful accounts expense should be classified as an offset against gross sales, because it represents revenue that will not be collected. In practice, doubtful accounts expense usually appears among operating expenses, under the assumption that credit "losses" are a normal expense of operations. Finally, some consider doubtful accounts expense as a financial management item and report it as "other expense." Because each of these reporting practices produces the same net income, the issue is not a major one.

Two kinds of evidence are used in estimates of doubtful accounts expense: (1) the average relationship between sales and uncollectible accounts in past years and (2) an analysis of the quality and age of outstanding receivables at the end of an accounting period.

Estimate of Doubtful Accounts Expense Based on Sales

The average percentage of credit sales not collected in past accounting periods is a logical basis for estimating the portion of current credit sales that will prove uncollectible. This approach, often referred to as the ***income statement approach***, is simple to apply and makes possible an estimate of doubtful accounts expense as soon as credit sales are recorded. It results in a sound matching of costs and revenue, and is especially appropriate in the preparation of interim reports. For example, if credit sales for the first quarter of the current year are $250,000, and doubtful accounts expense is estimated at 2% of credit sales, the following adjusting entry is required:

Adjusting entry to record doubtful accounts expense

Doubtful Accounts Expense ($250,000 × 0.02)	5,000	
Allowance for Doubtful Accounts		5,000
To record estimated doubtful accounts expense at 2% of credit sales for first quarter of year.		

If the ratio of cash sales to credit sales is relatively constant, estimates of doubtful accounts expense as a percentage of ***total sales*** may produce reasonably accurate results. Strictly speaking, however, the estimate of doubtful accounts expense should be based on ***credit sales*** only. The estimate may be further refined by analyses of the experience for different classes of customers.

Application of the appropriate percentage to the credit sales for an accounting period provides an estimate of the sales of the period that will not be collected. The degree of error in the estimate cannot be determined until the record of collection experience is in. Because this approach initially ignores the balance in the Allowance for Doubtful Accounts ledger account, a periodic test should be made to make certain that the allowance account is neither overstated nor understated.

Estimate of Doubtful Accounts Expense Based on Receivables

An effective way to test the adequacy of the allowance for doubtful accounts and to estimate doubtful accounts expense is to make an analysis of accounts receivable by age group and probability of collection. This procedure is known as the ***balance sheet approach*** of estimating doubtful accounts expense. Generally, a significant correlation exists between the length of time an account receivable is past due and the collectibility of the receivable. A summary that classifies the balances of all accounts receivable according to whether the amounts are not yet due, or are past due by varying lengths of time, is known as an ***aging of accounts receivable***.

The number of different age classes to be used depends on actual experience and the terms of sale. An estimate of the average collection experience for each age class provides a basis for estimating the portion of outstanding trade accounts receivable that may prove to be uncollectible.

An aging summary of trade accounts receivable for Midwest Limited on December 31, Year 5, is illustrated below:

Analysis of trade accounts receivable by age

MIDWEST LIMITED
Aging of Trade Accounts Receivable
December 31, Year 5

Credit terms: Net 30 days

Classification by due dates	*Balances in each category (summarized from analysis of individual accounts)*	*Estimated uncollectibles, %*	*Estimated doubtful accounts*
Not yet due	$2,400,000 (75.0%)	1	$24,000
Under 30 days past due	416,000 (13.0%)	3	12,480
30–60 days past due	208,000 (6.5%)	5	10,400
61–120 days past due	96,000 (3.0%)	10	9,600
121–180 days past due	48,000 (1.5%)	30	14,400
Over 180 days past due	32,000 (1.0%)	Individual analysis	25,000
Totals	$3,200,000 (100.0%)		$95,880

The percentages shown next to the amount of each category are useful in detecting an imbalance between current and past-due accounts. When an aging of receivables is used as a basis for the estimate of doubtful accounts expense, the current provision is an amount sufficient to bring the balance in the Allowance for Doubtful Accounts ledger account ***to the amount indicated by the aging analysis***. For example, if the balance of the Allowance for Doubtful Accounts for Midwest Limited on December 31, Year 5, is $55,000 after interim provisions of $60,000 and write-offs of $70,000 during Year 5 (debit Allowance for Doubtful Accounts and credit Trade Accounts Receivable), the analysis above requires the following adjusting entry to bring the allowance account balance to the required $95,880:

Adjustment based on aging

Doubtful Accounts Expense ($95,880 – $55,000)	40,880	
Allowance for Doubtful Accounts		40,880
To adjust allowance to required balance of $95,880.		

A summary of the allowance account for the year ended December 31, Year 5, for Midwest Limited follows:

Allowance for Doubtful Accounts

Date	*Explanation*	*Debit*	*Credit*	*Balance*
Year 5				
Jan. 1	Balance.			65,000 Cr
Jan.–Dec.	Interim provisions during Year 5.		60,000	125,000 Cr
Jan.–Dec.	Write-offs during Year 5.	70,000		55,000 Cr
Dec. 31	Adjustment at year-end.		40,880	95,880 Cr

A simpler method sometimes followed is to increase the allowance ***to a specified percentage*** of receivables or to increase the allowance ***by a specified percentage*** of receivables. These procedures are not recommended because the results they produce are less accurate than those obtained through a comprehensive aging analysis.

In the process of aging trade accounts receivable, management should evaluate current financial statements of major customers to make a better assessment of the probability of collection. The credit department of a business enterprise is assigned responsibility for a continuing analysis of the financial statements of existing and prospective customers so that sales are not made to those who represent excessive risk of nonpayment.

Doubtful Accounts Expense and Income Measurement

It is unlikely that estimated uncollectible accounts receivable will agree with actual write-offs applicable to each year's revenue. As long as there is a reasonably close correlation between the annual estimate and actual experience, minor discrepancies from year to year may be ignored.

A major adjustment to reduce or increase the Allowance for Doubtful Accounts may involve receivables originating in prior accounting periods. Such adjustments are included in doubtful accounts expense and may be explained in a note, or listed as a separate item in the computation of income before extraordinary items. However, such adjustments should not be reported as extraordinary items or as prior period adjustments. Changes in Accounting estimates are discussed in Chapter 22.

In rare situations, an unusual and infrequent event may take place which results in a material or an abnormal write-off of accounts receivable. In such a situation, the effect of the write-off should be included in the income statement before extraordinary items and should be disclosed either as a separate item in, or by way of a note to, the income statement.[2]

Write-off and Subsequent Collection of Receivables

When the decision is made to write off receivables, the debit to the Allowance for Doubtful Accounts and the credit to the Trade Accounts Receivable ledger accounts have no effect on either the carrying amount of accounts receivable or the net income of the accounting period in which the write-off occurs. If a receivable that has been written off is collected later, Trade Accounts Receivable is debited and the Allowance for Doubtful Accounts is credited. This reverses the write-off, and the collection is then recorded in the usual manner. This method has the advantage of providing in the customer's subsidiary ledger account a complete record of credit experience with that customer.

Direct Write-Off Method for Doubtful Accounts Expense

Some business enterprises may elect to record doubtful accounts expense only as specific receivables are considered to be uncollectible. This ***direct write-off method*** of accounting for doubtful accounts expense overstates the carrying amount of receivables and does not match doubtful accounts expense with revenue, because receivables representing sales in Year 1, for example, may be recorded as an expense in Year 2, and receivables originating in Year 2, may be recorded as an expense in Year 3 or Year 4.

Under the direct write-off method, uncollectible receivables are written off by a debit to Doubtful Accounts Expense and a credit to Trade Accounts Receivable. Collection of receivables written off in a previous accounting period is recorded by a credit to Doubtful Accounts Recovered (a miscellaneous revenue item), and

2 CICA, ***CICA Handbook*** (Toronto), sec. 3480.12.

the recovery of receivables written off earlier in the current period is recorded by a credit to Doubtful Accounts Expense to eliminate an expense recorded prematurely.

Instalment Accounts Receivable

Many individuals and business enterprises find it convenient to buy certain items on the instalment plan. The instalment contract, in essence a promissory note providing for payment over an extended period of time, is widely used at the retail level. Most enterprises that sell goods on the instalment plan have adequate financial resources to carry their own instalment accounts receivable. Some enterprises, however, sell or assign their instalment accounts receivable to finance companies.

Instalment accounts receivable from the sale of goods or services in the ordinary course of business, including those due more than one year from the balance sheet date, are included in current assets (net of any unearned interest and finance charges). This classification is appropriate because instalment receivables arise in the operating cycle from revenue-generating activities. However, disclosure should be made for the instalment accounts receivable maturing beyond one year.[3] The unearned interest and finance charges are recognized as revenue only when realized and are disclosed separately in the income statement.

Analysis of Trade Accounts Receivable

Trade accounts receivable are an important factor in an analysis of financial liquidity and a projection of cash flows. Changes in the length of the average collection period or the number of days' sales in trade receivables, for example, should be analyzed carefully, and action should be initiated to correct unfavourable trends. A discussion of several analytical techniques for trade accounts receivable appears in Chapter 24.

USE OF RECEIVABLES AS A SOURCE OF CASH

Business enterprises generally raise the cash needed for current operations through the collection of trade accounts receivable. It is possible to accelerate this process by (1) ***pledging*** receivables as collateral for loans, (2) ***selling*** receivables, or (3) ***assigning*** receivables. In some industries, such procedures are quite common; in other industries, this may be done only in times of absolute necessity.

Enterprises engaged in the buying of receivables are known as ***factors***, and the process of selling receivables is called ***factoring***. Factors generally buy receivables outright, that is, ***without recourse***. Alternatively, factors or other lending institutions may buy receivables ***with recourse***, or may lend money to the owner of the receivables under a legal arrangement known as an ***assignment***. In such cases customers are usually instructed to make payments directly to the factors or other lenders. Factoring is an important source of ready cash in industries such as

3 CICA, *CICA Handbook*, sec. 3020.02.

textiles, apparel, furniture, and consumer electronics.

A pledge of accounts receivable as collateral for a loan involves no special accounting problems. Accounting for the sale and the assignment of accounts receivable is described in the following sections.

Sale of Receivables Without Recourse

The purpose of selling receivables ***without recourse*** is to shift to the purchaser of the receivables the risk of credit losses, the effort of collection, and the waiting period that result from the granting of credit. The ''without recourse'' applies only to the inability of customers to pay, not to disputes as to quality or price of the merchandise.

The acceptance of credit cards by retail merchants is a familiar form of sale (factoring) of receivables without recourse. For example, when merchants accept American Express, MasterCard, or Visa credit cards, they avoid accounting costs and doubtful accounts expense, and obtain cash almost immediately, in return for a 1.7-to-5% fee (discount). The amount of the fee depends largely on the volume of business a merchant generates for the credit card company. The fee or discount may be recorded by the merchant as a loss on sale of receivables, or as an interest and factoring expense because the sale of receivables is essentially a financing transaction.

Sale of Receivables With Recourse

When receivables are sold ***with recourse***, the seller (transferor) in effect guarantees the receivables, and the purchaser (transferee) is reimbursed for failure of debtors to pay the full amounts anticipated at the time of sale.

Generally, the sale of ordinary trade receivables with recourse results in receipt of proceeds that are less than the face amount of the receivables sold. Similarly, the sale of instalment accounts receivable that bear a lower interest rate than the discount rate used in the sale of the receivables results in proceeds that are less than the carrying amount of the receivables. For example, a sale for $18,500 of trade accounts receivables with a face amount of $20,000 and a carrying amount of $19,400 is recorded as follows:

Sale of accounts receivable

Cash	18,500	
Allowance for Doubtful Accounts	600	
Interest and Factoring Expense or Loss on Transfer (Sale) of Trade Accounts Receivable	900	
Trade Accounts Receivable		20,000
To record sale of trade accounts receivable on a recourse basis.		

However, the sale of instalment accounts receivable that bear a higher interest rate than the discount rate used to compute the proceeds on the sale would result in interest revenue or a gain. To illustrate, assume the following ledger account balances for instalment accounts receivable that are ***considered fully collectible***:

Carrying amount of instalment accounts receivable to be sold

Instalment accounts receivable, including interest at 1½% a month, payable at the rate of $723 a month for 36 months starting in one month	$26,028
Less: Deferred interest revenue	6,028
Carrying amount of instalment accounts receivable (equal to the present value of ordinary annuity of 36 payments of $723 a month at 1½% a month: $723 × 27.660684 [Table 4 in the Appendix at the end of Chapter 5] = $20,000)	$20,000

If these receivables are sold with recourse at a price to yield 1% a month to the transferee, the proceeds on the sale are computed below:

Proceeds on sale of instalment accounts receivable

Present value of ordinary annuity of 36 payments of $723 a month, with interest at 1% a month: $723 × 30.107505 (Table 4 in the Appendix at the end of Chapter 5)	$21,768

The *sale* of the receivables is recorded by the transferor as follows:

Transferor's journal entry to record sale of instalment accounts receivable on recourse basis

Cash	21,768	
Deferred Interest Revenue	6,028	
Instalment Accounts Receivable		26,028
Interest Revenue or Gain on Transfer (Sale) of Instalment Accounts Receivable		1,768
To record sale of instalment accounts receivable on a recourse basis. Receivables bear interest at 1½% a month but were sold to yield 1% a month to transferee.		

The *acquisition* of the receivables and the receipt of the first monthly instalment of $723 is recorded by the transferee as follows:

Transferee's journal entries to record acquisition of instalment accounts receivable and receipt of first monthly instalment

Instalment Accounts Receivable	26,028	
Deferred Interest Revenue		4,260
Cash		21,768
To record acquisition of instalment accounts receivable on a recourse basis at a price to yield 1% a month.		
Cash	723	
Deferred Interest Revenue	218	
Instalment Accounts Receivable		723
Interest Revenue ($21,768 × 0.01)		218
To record receipt of first monthly instalment.		

A sale of receivables with recourse frequently has the characteristics of a borrowing contract collateralized by the receivables. ***FASB Statement No. 77***: "Reporting by Transferors for Transfers of Receivables with Recourse" requires a transfer of receivables ***with recourse*** to be recognized as a ***sale*** if all the following conditions are met:[4]

1 The transferor surrenders control of the future economic benefits embodied in the receivables.

2 The transferor's obligation under the recourse provisions can be reasonably estimated.

3 The transferee cannot require the transferor to repurchase the receivables except pursuant to the recourse provisions.

If any of these conditions is not met, the amount of the proceeds from the transfer of receivables is reported as a liability resulting from a borrowing transaction.[5] When a transfer of receivables qualifies as a ***sale***, all ***probable adjustments***[6] in connection with the recourse obligations are accrued by the transferor in the measurement of the gain or loss on the transfer (sale) of the receivables. The proceeds received from the sale of receivables and the amount of transferred receivables that remain uncollected at the end of the accounting period are disclosed in a note to the transferor's financial statements.

Assignment of Receivables

Instead of selling receivables, a business enterprise may borrow money using the receivables as collateral. This may involve a pledge of the receivables under a contract providing that the proceeds from the collection of the receivables must be used to retire the loan. Alternatively, receivables may be ***assigned*** under a more formal arrangement whereby a borrower (***assignor***) pledges the receivables to a lender (***assignee***) and signs a promissory note payable. Assignment gives the assignee the same right to bring action to collect the receivables that the assignor possesses. The assignor retains the credit risks and continues collection efforts, and promises to make good any receivables that cannot be collected. In most cases, customers are not notified of the assignment and make payments directly to the assignor; however, they may be instructed to make payments to the assignee. The assignor generally has some equity in the assigned receivables because the financing company advances less than 100% of the face amount of the receivables assigned.

The primary accounting problem raised by assignment of receivables is to measure the assignor's equity in the assigned receivables and the liability to the assignee. Assigned receivables are transferred to a separate ledger account, Assigned Accounts Receivable, and a liability to the assignee is recorded. As collections are received by the assignor, assigned receivables are reduced, and the liability to the assignee is correspondingly reduced when cash is remitted by the

4 FASB, ***FASB Statement No. 77***: "Reporting by Transferors for Transfers of Receivables with Recourse" (Stamford, 1983), p. 2. There is no comparable recommendation in the ***CICA Handbook***.

5 FASB, ***FASB Statement No. 77***, p. 3.

6 Including, for example, adjustments for (1) failure to collect for any reason, (2) estimated effects of prepayments, and (3) defects in the legal title of the transferred receivables.

assignor to the assignee. Fees and interest charges are included in the remittance and are recorded as expenses.

To illustrate, assume that on January 2, Year 1, Adams Company assigned receivables of $50,000 to Finco Inc. and received $45,000, less a fee of 2% on the amount advanced. Interest at 1% of the unpaid balance of the loan was to be paid monthly. the journal entries for Adams to record the assignment and subsequent transactions are shown below.

Journal entries for assignment of accounts receivable

Transaction	*Journal entries in assignor's accounting records*		
Jan. 2: Assigned accounts receivable of $50,000. Finco, Inc., remitted 90% of receivables, less 2% fee ($45,000 × 0.02 = $900).	Assigned Accounts Receivable ..	50,000	
	Accounts Receivable		50,000
	Cash	44,100	
	Interest Expense	900	
	Notes Payable to Finco. Inc.		45,000
Jan. 31: Collected $30,150 and paid this amount to Finco, Inc., including interest at 1% a month on $45,000 unpaid balance of loan. Balances on Jan. 31 are as follows: Assigned accounts receivable ($50,000 − $30,150) .... $19,850; Note payable to Finco, Inc. ($45,000 − $29,700) 15,300	Cash	30,150	
	Assigned Accounts Receivable		30,150
	Notes Payable to Finco, Inc.	29,700	
	Interest Expense ($45,000 × 0.01)........	450	
	Cash		30,150
Feb. 28: Collected $17,000 and paid balance owed to Finco, Inc., plus interest at 1% a month on $15,300 unpaid balance of loan.	Cash	17,000	
	Assigned Accounts Receivable		17,000
	Notes Payable to Finco, Inc.	15,300	
	Interest Expense ($15,300 × 0.01)	153	
	Cash		15,453
Feb. 28: Transferred balance of assigned receivables to the Accounts Receivable ledger account.	Accounts Receivable	2,850	
	Assigned Accounts Receivable ($19,850 − $17,000).......		2,850

The assignor's equity in assigned receivables is generally reported in the assignor's balance sheet by deducting the balance of notes payable to the assignee from the amount of the assigned receivables. Offsetting the liability against the asset may be justified in this situation because collections of assigned receivables must be used to liquidate the loan. The presentation of assigned receivables by Adams Company on January 31, Year 1, is illustrated on the next page.

Disclosure of accounts receivable pledged, assigned, or sold, including any

Balance sheet presentation of assignor's equity in assigned receivables

Current assets:		
Accounts receivable		$200,000
Assigned accounts receivable	$19,850	
Less: Notes payable to Finco, Inc. (assignee)	15,300	
Equity in assigned accounts receivable		4,550
Total accounts receivable		$204,550

possible contingent liability, is made in the balance sheet or in a note to the financial statements.

NOTES RECEIVABLE

The term ***notes receivable*** (or ***promissory notes***) is used in accounting to designate several types of credit instruments. A promissory note is a written contract containing an unconditional promise by the ***maker*** to pay a certain sum of money to the ***payee*** under terms clearly specified in the contract. Most promissory notes used as a basis for business transactions are ***negotiable***, which means that a ***holder in due course*** may sell the notes, discount them, or borrow against them.

Notes receivable are often used when the goods sold have a high unit or aggregate value and the purchaser of the goods wants to extend payment beyond the normal 30-to-90-day period of trade credit. In the banking and commercial credit fields, notes are the typical form of credit instrument used to support lending transactions. Notes receivable may also result from sale of plant assets, or from a variety of other business transactions.

Valuation of Notes Receivable

As in the case of accounts receivable, the proper valuation of notes receivable and similar credit instruments is their current fair value (or present value) at the time of acquisition. Accountants can value notes receivable because their terms generally provide reliable evidence of the rights inherent in them. Except for questions of collectibility, there is little uncertainty with respect to the amounts that will be received and the dates on which the amounts will be received.

Notes receivable, like trade accounts receivable, may prove to be uncollectible. If a business enterprise uses notes as a regular credit medium and has a large volume outstanding, the amounts of probable uncollectible notes may be estimated, and an allowance for such notes established by procedures similar to those for accounts receivable.

Strictly speaking, there is no such thing as a non-interest-bearing note; there are only ***notes that contain a stated provision for interest and notes that do not***. The time value of money is present in any case, because the present value of a promise to pay a stated amount of cash on a fixed or determinable date is not as large as the amount to be paid at maturity. The so-called non-interest-bearing note has a lower present value than its face amount by an amount equivalent to an interest charge. In contrast, if a note bears a fair rate of interest, its ***face amount*** and ***present value*** are the same on the date of issuance.

This point may be illustrated by an example. Suppose that two promissory notes are received in connection with the sale of goods. In settlement of the first sale, Customer W gives a one-year 12% note, with a face amount of $25,000. In settlement of the second sale, Customer X gives a one-year note with a face amount of $28,000, but with no interest provision specified in the note. If accountants considered only the face amount of the notes, they might be tempted to record the two notes as follows:

Note from Customer X is not recorded correctly

Customer W			*Customer X*		
Notes Receivable	25,000		Notes Receivable	28,000	
Sales		25,000	Sales		28,000
To record sale in exchange for 12% promissory note.			To record sale in exchange for non-interest-bearing promissory note.		

A careful examination of the evidence indicates that the two promissory notes are identical, assuming that 12% is a reasonable annual rate of interest. Both customers have promised to pay $28,000 at the end of one year, and both notes have a present value of $25,000 ($28,000 ÷ 1.12 = $25,000). A logical method of accounting is to record both notes at $25,000, and to record interest of $3,000 as it is realized. Thus, the note receivable from Customer X may be recorded at $25,000 (the same as the note from Customer W), or preferably by use of a Discount on Notes Receivable ledger account (resulting in a ***carrying amount*** of $25,000) as illustrated below.

The correct way to record note from Customer X

Notes Receivable	28,000	
Discount on Notes Receivable		3,000
Sales		25,000
To record sale to Customer X in exchange for non-interest-bearing promissory note.		

The discount on notes receivable is amortized periodically as interest revenue, and any unamortized balance at the end of an accounting period is deducted from Notes Receivable in the balance sheet.

In practice, non-interest-bearing, short-term notes received from customers are often recorded at the outset at face amount (maturity value). The foregoing analysis shows that this procedure overstates assets and fails to recognize interest revenue. Although generally accepted accounting principles require that notes be recorded at present value, trade notes and accounts receivable with customary trade terms not exceeding one year may be recorded at face amount. When the amount of the unearned implicit interest is substantial, this procedure may result in a significant overstatement of assets, shareholders' equity, and net income in the accounting period that the notes and accounts receivable are recorded.

Discounting Notes Receivable

Negotiable notes receivable may be sold or discounted. The term ***sale*** is appropriate when a note is endorsed to a bank or finance company on a ***without-recourse*** basis; that is, in the event the maker of the note defaults, the bank or finance company has no recourse against the seller of the note. The term ***discounted*** applies when an enterprise borrows against notes receivable and endorses them on a ***with-recourse*** basis, which means that the borrower must pay the note if the maker does not.

The ***proceeds*** received when a note is discounted are computed by deducting from the ***maturity value*** of the note the amount of interest (discount) charged by the bank or finance company. Banks usually compute the discount on the maturity value of the note rather than on the proceeds (amount actually borrowed), which gives the bank a higher ***effective rate of interest*** than the rate of interest used to discount the note.

To illustrate these points and the accounting involved, assume that Scott Company discounts at a bank two notes receivable arising from the sale of merchandise. Both notes have a face amount of $100,000 and are due in one year. Note Y is non-interest-bearing; note Z bears interest at a 15% annual rate. The bank also charges a 15% discount rate. If we assume that the notes are discounted with recourse immediately upon receipt, the proceeds and the difference between the proceeds and the present value are determined as illustrated in the table given below.

Proceeds and present value of notes discounted

	Note Y (no interest)	*Note Z (15% interest)*
Face amount of notes	$100,000	$100,000
Add: Interest to maturity	-0-	15,000
Maturity value of notes	$100,000	$115,000
Less: Bank discount (15% of maturity value for one year)	15,000	17,250
Proceeds on notes	$ 85,000	$ 97,750
Present value at 15% (maturity value ÷ 1.15)	86,957	100,000
Difference between proceeds and present value	$ 1,957	$ 2,250

The difference between the proceeds and the present value of each note represents additional interest charged by the bank because the 15% discount is computed on maturity value rather than on the amount actually borrowed (proceeds). The additional interest is recognized as an expense over the remaining term of the note.

The journal entries to record the receipt and the discounting of the two notes are as shown on the next page.[7]

An alternative procedure for recording discounted notes is to credit Notes Receivable Discounted (a contra-asset account) rather than Notes Receivable. In the balance sheet, the balance in the Notes Receivable Discounted ledger account

7 An alternative approach is to view the proceeds received from the bank as the "true" present value of the notes. This interpretation calls for the recording of the two notes and related sales at $85,000 and $97,750 respectively; thus, the need to record deferred interest expense when the notes are discounted is eliminated.

Journal entries for discounted notes receivable

Note Y (no interest)			Note Z (15% interest)		
At time of sale:					
Notes Receivable	100,000		Notes Receivable	100,000	
Discount on Notes Receivable		13,043	Sales		100,000
Sales		86,957			
At time notes are discounted:					
Cash	85,000		Cash	97,750	
Discount on Notes Receivable	13,043		Deferred Interest Expense	2,250	
Deferred Interest Expense	1,957		Notes Receivable ...		100,000
Notes Receivable ...		100,000			

is deducted from Notes Receivable. When the note is paid at maturity, Notes Receivable Discounted is debited and Notes Receivable is credited. Because discounted notes are generally paid at maturity, this journal entry may be avoided by crediting Notes Receivable at the time notes are discounted.

If Scott Company had held the notes for some time before discounting them with recourse, interest revenue realized prior to the time the notes are discounted must be recognized. Assuming that Scott held the two notes for six months before discounting them at 12%, the following journal entries would be appropriate:

Note Y (no interest)			Note Z (15% interest)		
To accrue interest revenue for six months:					
Discount on Notes Receivable	6,522		Interest Receivable	7,500	
Interest Revenue		6,522	Interest Revenue		7,500
Interest revenue: $86,957 × 0.15 × 6/12 = $6,522.			Interest revenue: $100,000 × 0.15 × 6/12 = $7,500.		
To record discounting of notes at 12% for six months:					
Cash	94,000		Cash	108,100	
Discount on Notes Receivable ($13,043 − $6,522)	6,521		Interest Receivable		7,500
Notes Receivable		100,000	Notes Receivable		100,000
Deferred Interest Revenue		521	Deferred Interest Revenue		600
Proceeds: $100,000 − ($100,000 × 0.12 × 6/12) = $94,000.			Proceeds: $115,000 − ($115,000 × 6/12) = $108,100.		

The $521 excess of the proceeds of $94,000 over the carrying amount of $93,479 ($100,000 − $6,521 = $93,479) from the discounting of Note Y represents additional interest revenue to be recognized over the remaining six-month term of the note. Similarly, the $600 excess of the proceeds of $108,100 over the carrying amount of $107,500 ($100,000 + $7,500 = $107,500) from the discounting of Note Z is recorded as deferred interest revenue. In both cases, the additional interest revenue results from the fact that the notes were discounted by Scott Company at 12%, a rate ***less than the annual yield rate of 15%*** to Scott.

If a discounted note is ***dishonoured***, Scott Company would be required to pay the bank the maturity value of the note plus any protest fees charged by the bank. Notice of the dishonour of a discounted note must be given promptly; therefore, the endorser may assume that payment has been made if no notice is received within a few days after maturity date. When a note is dishonoured, the amount paid to the bank is debited to Accounts Receivable (or Dishonoured Notes Receivable). Subsequent collection from the maker of the note is recorded as a credit to this receivable; failure to collect requires that this receivable be written off against the allowance for doubtful accounts.

The party discounting notes receivable is contingently liable on the notes until the maker pays them in full at maturity. The ***contingent liability*** may be disclosed (1) in a note to the financial statements, (2) parenthetically in the balance sheet, or (3) by use of a Notes Receivable Discounted ledger account deducted from Notes Receivable. Disclosure by means of a note to the financial statements is by far the most common practice. A detailed discussion of contingencies is presented in Chapter 10.

Presentation of Receivables in the Balance Sheet

In the current asset section of the balance sheet, material amounts of the following classes of receivables should be reported separately: (1) notes and other receivables based on written negotiable contracts, (2) ordinary trade receivables, (3) instalment accounts receivable, (4) amounts owing by related parties, and (5) other current claims.[8] Negotiable notes and contracts have a special status because of the ease with which they can be converted to cash through discounting. Users of financial statements may be interested in the percentage relationship between trade receivables and credit sales as an indication of a business enterprise's collection experience.

Instalment accounts receivable maturing beyond one year are often included as current assets. The amounts and, where practicable, maturity dates of such receivables should be disclosed; in some cases, it may also be desirable to disclose the terms of such receivables.[9]

Receivables that have been pledged should be identified, and any receivables that will not be collected within a year or the operating cycle should be excluded from the current assets category. A credit balance in an individual account receivable, if material, should be reported as a current liability. Receivables from officers, employees, and shareholders are generally classified as noncurrent unless current collection is assured.

8 Sec. 3020.01 of the ***CICA Handbook*** provides only a very general recommendation on statement presentation: "Accounts and notes receivable should be segregated so as to show separately ordinary trade accounts, amounts owing by related parties, and other unusual items of substantial amount."

9 CICA, ***CICA Handbook***, sec. 3020.02.

The presentation of various types of receivables and related accounts in the balance sheet is illustrated below.

Presentation of receivables in the balance sheet

Receivables (current assets):	
Trade notes receivable (net of unearned discounts of $5,000)	$ 105,000
Trade accounts receivable (net of allowance for doubtful accounts of $47,000)	1,420,000
Instalment receivables (net of unearned interest and finance charges of $280,000 and allowance for doubtful accounts of $52,000)	600,000
Current amount receivable from affiliated company, interest at 11%	145,000
Miscellaneous (including $4,000 debit balance in accounts payable)	10,000
Total current receivables	$2,280,000

REVIEW QUESTIONS

1 Briefly discuss the significance of accounts receivable in an analysis of the financial position of a business enterprise.

2 What is meant by ***valuation of receivables***? If accountants generally require that assets be recorded at ***cost***, why are trade accounts receivable not recorded at the cost of the merchandise sold?

3 What is the distinction between ***trade receivables*** and ***miscellaneous receivables***? Give two examples of each type of receivable.

4 At what point are trade receivables recorded? Are shipments to consignees recorded as receivables?

5 Describe a ***cycle billing system*** and state its advantages.

6 Describe how the following items affect the valuation of trade accounts receivable: ***trade discounts***, ***sales discounts***, ***sales returns and allowances***, ***allowance for freight-out***, and ***sales and excise taxes***.

7 Describe two methods of accounting for cash (sales) discounts.

8 What is an ***aging of accounts receivable***? Describe how such an analysis may be used to estimate doubtful accounts expense and to analyze the quality of trade accounts receivable.

9 How should a major adjustment (increase or decrease) in the allowance for doubtful accounts be reported in the financial statements?

10 According to the ***CICA Handbook*** recommendations, how should an abnormal write-off of accounts receivable caused by an unusual or rare event be reported in the income statement?

11 Briefly discuss the logic of basing the estimate of doubtful accounts expense on ***a*** total sales, ***b*** credit sales, and ***c*** a fixed percentage of trade accounts receivable at the end of an accounting period.

12 Discuss the accounting procedures necessary to record recoveries of accounts receivable previously written off ***a*** if an allowance for doubtful accounts is used, or ***b*** if the direct write-off method is used.

13 Explain the distinction between ***factoring*** and ***assigning*** trade accounts receivable.

14 When receivables are transferred ***with recourse***, according to FASB requirements what three conditions must be met in order to record the transfer as a sale?

15 Equicorp sold merchandise with a selling price of $10,500 on an instalment contract covering 24 months. Payments of $500 were to be made by the customer each month. Interest charges of $1,500 were added to the sales price to compute gross instalment accounts receivable. Equicorp recorded the sale by a debit to Instalment Accounts Receivable and a credit to Sales for $12,000. Evaluate this procedure.

16 What errors would result if a non-interest-bearing note receivable due in one year were recorded at its face amount? Explain.

17 Describe various ways that a potential contingent liability relating to notes receivable discounted may be presented in financial statements or in a note to the financial statements.

EXERCISES

Ex. 7-1 Select the best answer for each of the following multiple-choice questions:

1 A method of estimating doubtful accounts expense that focusses on the income statement rather than the balance sheet is the allowance method based on:
a Direct write-off of uncollectible trade accounts receivable
b Aging of trade accounts receivable
✓*c* Credit sales
d The balance of trade accounts receivable

2 On March 28, Year 1, Swiss Company received a $120,000, 12%, 90-day note from a customer. Immediately, Swiss discounted the note at a bank; the discount rate was 16%. In its journal entry to record the discounting of the note, Swiss debits the Cash ledger account for:
a $118,800 *b* $115,200 *c* $118,656✓ *d* $120,000 *e* Some other amount

3 Balog Company received a $30,000, six-month, 10% promissory note from a customer. After holding the note for two months, Balog was in need of cash and discounted the note at Olympic Bank at a 12% discount rate. The amount of cash received by Balog from the bank was:
a $31,260 *b* $30,870 *c* $30,300 *d* $30,240✓ *e* Some other amount

✓*4* Hunt Company prepared an aging of its accounts receivable on December 31, Year 2, and determined that the net realizable value of the receivables on that date was $50,000. Here is some additional information:

Accounts receivable, Dec. 31, Year 1	$48,000
Accounts receivable, Dec. 31, Year 2	54,000
Allowance for doubtful accounts, Dec. 31, Year 1 (credit balance) .	6,000
Accounts receivable written off as uncollectible during Year 2	5,000

Hunt's doubtful accounts expense for the year ended December 31, Year 2, was:
a $3,000 *b* $4,000 *c* $5,000 *d* $7,000 *e* Some other amount

5 The following ledger account balances were taken from the December 31, Year 1, trial balance of Singer Limited:

Credit sales	$750,000
Sales discounts	15,000
Allowance for doubtful accounts (credit balance)	18,000

During Year 1, $30,000 of uncollectible accounts receivable were written off. Past experience indicates that 3% of gross credit sales proves to be uncollectible. What is the balance of the Allowance for Doubtful Accounts ledger account on December 31, Year 1, after provision for doubtful accounts expense is made for year 1?
a $10,050 *b* $10,500 *c* $22,050 *d* $34,500 *e* Some other amount

6 Kong Corporation provides an allowance for its doubtful accounts receivable. On December 31, Year 1, the allowance for doubtful accounts had a credit balance of $8,000. Each month Kong records doubtful accounts expense in an amount equal to 2% of credit sales. Total credit sales during Year 2 amounted to $2,000,000. During Year 2, uncollectible accounts receivable totalling $22,000 were written off against the allowance account. An aging of accounts receivable on December 31, Year 2, indicated that an allowance of $42,000 was required for doubtful accounts as of that date. Accordingly, doubtful accounts expense previously accrued during Year 2 should be increased by:
a $62,000 *b* $42,000 *c* $26,000 *d* $16,000 *e* Some other amount

Ex. 7-2 In auditing the financial statements of Status Corporation for the current fiscal year, you find that the following items are included in trade accounts receivable (both controlling account and subsidiary ledger):

Customer's accounts with credit balances	$ 2,950
Receivables from officers	12,500
Advances to employees	2,200
Customers' accounts known to be uncollectible	2,880

Prepare a correcting journal entry for Status Corporation to reclassify items that are not trade accounts receivable and to write off the uncollectible accounts receivable.

Ex. 7-3 On September 30, Year 1, the following notes receivable from customers are discounted at the bank. The bank charges a 10% discount rate on the maturity value of the notes. Compute the proceeds of each note, using 360 as the number of days in a year.

a 90-day, $24,000, 10% note dated September 30, Year 1
b 90-day, $18,000, non-interest-bearing note dated August 15, Year 1
c 60-day, $6,000, 8% note dated September 15, Year 1
d 6-month, $12,000, 15% note dated August 1, Year 1

Ex. 7-4 Wool Corporation began operations in Year 1 and had accounts receivable of $300,000 on December 31, Year 1. In determining the valuation of receivables on December 31, Year 1, management wished to recognize the following:

Estimated doubtful accounts	$6,240
Estimated collection costs	1,800
Estimated price adjustments and other allowances on outstanding receivables (no returns of merchandise are anticipated)	3,000
Estimated cash (sales) discounts	3,600

a Prepare an adjusting entry for Wool Corporation on December 31, Year 1, to recognize management's estimate of the net realizable value of accounts receivable. No accounts were written off in Year 1.
b Show how accounts receivable are reported in Wool Corporation's balance sheet on December 31, Year 1.

Ex. 7-5 Albert Company acquired merchandise at a cost of $4,000. The merchandise was offered for sale by Albert at a list price of $6,500, before a trade discount of 20% and a cash discount of 2% if the invoice was paid within 10 days. Albert bills customers net of the trade discount, records accounts receivable and sales at the invoice price, and uses the perpetual inventory system.

Prepare journal entries for Albert Company to record ***a*** the sale and the cost of the goods sold, and ***b*** the collection of the account receivable within 10 days.

Ex. 7-6 From the following information, compute the doubtful accounts expense for Year 1: Beginning balance in Trade Accounts Receivable was $80,000; beginning credit balance in Allowance for Doubtful Accounts was $6,000; ending balance in Trade Accounts Receivable was $110,000, of which 4% was estimated to be uncollectible. During Year 1, $7,490 of accounts receivable were written off as uncollectible.

Ex. 7-7 Certain information relative to the operations of Murphy Company for Year 10 follows:

Trade accounts receivable, Jan 1	$16,000
Trade accounts receivable collected during year	52,000
Cash sales	10,000
Inventories, Jan. 1	24,000
Inventories, Dec. 31	22,000
Purchases	40,000
Gross profit on sales	18,000

Compute the amount of Murphy Company's trade accounts receivable on December 31, Year 10.

Ex. 7-8 Your accounts receivable clerk, who earns a salary of $950 a month, has just acquired a new luxury car. You decide to test the accuracy of the accounts receivable balance of $30,400 as shown in the general ledger at the end of the year. All sales are on credit.

The following information is available for your first year of operation: Collections from customers, $125,000; payments for merchandise purchases, $130,000; ending inventories, $40,000; and ending accounts payable to merchandise suppliers, $30,000. All goods purchased were marked to sell at 40% above cost (selling price equals 140% of cost).

Compute the amount of any apparent shortage in trade accounts receivable at the end of the year.

Ex. 7-9 Watt Company prepared the following journal entry on April 30, Year 4:

Notes Receivable	20,000	
Discount on Notes Receivable		3,471
Sales		16,529
To record sale of merchandise and receipt of non-interest-bearing note due April 30, year 6. Present value of note at 10% annual rate of interest is $16,529.		

Prepare journal entries for Watt Company on April 30, Year 5, and April 30, Year 6, the end of the fiscal years.

Ex. 7-10 Cristy Company, which adjusts its accounting records and prepares financial statements at the end of each month, uses the income statement approach for estimating doubtful accounts expense. In past years, uncollectible accounts have averaged 3% of net credit sales. Relevant data for Cristy's doubtful accounts for the month of February, Year 3, follow:

Cash sales	$ 62,800
Credit sales	352,200
Cash discounts on credit sales	14,300
Sales returns and allowances on credit sales	3,900
Balance of Allowance for Doubtful Accounts, Jan. 31, Year 3 (credit)	69,900
Uncollectible trade accounts receivable written off, Feb. 28, Year 3	70,200

Prepare journal entries for Cristy Company on February 28, Year 3, to record the write-off of uncollectible trade accounts receivable and the provision for doubtful accounts for the month of February.

Ex. 7-11 The following accounts appear in the general ledger of Delphine Company on December 31, Year 7:

Sales	$1,200,000
Accounts receivable	500,000
Allowance for doubtful accounts (debit balance)	2,000

Prepare a journal entry for Delphine Company on December 31, Year 7, to record doubtful accounts expense for each independent assumption below:

√*a* The allowance for doubtful accounts is increased to a balance of $15,000.
√*b* Delphine recognizes 2% of sales as doubtful accounts expense.
c Through an aging of the accounts, $24,750 of accounts receivable is estimated to be uncollectible.

Ex. 7-12 On March 1, Beckman Company assigned accounts receivable of $60,000 to Rec-Fin, Inc., and received $54,000, less a 2% fee on $54,000. Interest is charged at the rate of 1% a month of the unpaid balance. Beckman made collections on the assigned accounts and remitted the proceeds at the end of each month to Rec-Fin, Inc. Collections in March were $30,000.

Prepare journal entries for Beckman Company to record the March transactions relating to the assignment of accounts receivable.

√ **Ex. 7-13** The information below is available for Terry Lanni Corporation:

	Amounts in thousands		
	Year 1	*Year 2*	*Year 3*
Credit sales	$ 900	$1,100	$1,000
Cash sales	600	800	700
Total sales	$1,500	$1,900	$1,700
Accounts receivable (end of year)	$ 170	$ 230	$ 220
Allowance for doubtful accounts (end-of-year credit balance)	47	30	46
Accounts receivable written off during the year	2	50	14

Assuming there was no change in the method used to estimate doubtful accounts during the three-year period, compute the balance of the Allowance for Doubtful Accounts ledger account of Terry Lanni Corporation at the beginning of Year 1.

Ex. 7-14 Olmstead Corporation operates in an industry that has a high rate of uncollectible accounts. On June 30, Year 6, before any year-end adjustments, the balance of the trade accounts receivable was $600,000, and the allowance for doubtful accounts had a credit balance of $48,000. The adjusted year-end balance for the allowance for doubtful accounts will be based on the aging analysis shown on the next page.

a Compute the required balance of Olmstead Corporation's allowance for doubtful accounts on June 30, Year 6.

Days outstanding	*Amount*	*Probability of collection*
Less than 15 days	$350,000	0.95
Between 16 and 30 days	110,000	0.90
Between 31 and 45 days	50,000	0.80
Between 46 and 60 days	40,000	0.70
Between 61 and 75 days	20,000	0.60
Between 76 and 90 days	10,000	0.40
Over 90 days	20,000	0.00
Total	$600,000	

b Prepare any journal entries required for Olmstead Corporation on June 30, Year 6.

CASES

Case 7-1 On July 1, Year 10, Rover Company, a calendar-year company, sold merchandise on credit and received in return an interest-bearing promissory note from the customer. Rover will receive interest at the prevailing rate for a note of this type. Both the principal and interest are due on June 30, Year 11.

On December 31, Year 10, Rover had significant amounts of trade accounts receivable as a result of credit sales to its customers. Rover uses the allowance method based on credit sales to estimate doubtful accounts expense. On the basis of past experience, 1% of credit sales will normally not be collected. This pattern is expected to continue.

Instructions

a When should Rover Company recognize interest revenue from the note receivable? Discuss the rationale for your answer.

b Assume that the note receivable was discounted without recourse at a bank on December 31, Year 10. How does Rover Company determine the amount of the discount and what is the appropriate accounting for the discounting transaction?

c Discuss the rationale for using the allowance method based on credit sales to estimate doubtful accounts expense. Contrast this method with the allowance method based on the balance of trade accounts receivable.

d How should Rover Company report the allowance for doubtful accounts in its balance sheet on December 31, Year 10? Also, describe the alternatives, if any, for presentation of doubtful accounts expense in Rover's income statement.

Case 7-2 Business transactions often involve the exchange of plant assets, merchandise, or services for promissory notes or similar instruments that may stipulate no interest rate or an interest rate that varies from prevailing rates.

Instructions

a When a promissory note is exchanged for plant assets, merchandise, or services, what value should be placed on the promissory note:

1 If it bears interest at a reasonable rate and is issued in a bargained transaction entered into at arm's length? Explain.

2 If it bears no interest or at an interest rate that varies materially from the prevailing rate? Explain.

b If the carrying amount of a promissory note differs from the face amount,

1 How is the difference accounted for? Explain.

2 How is the difference presented in the balance sheet? Explain.

Case 7-3 During the audit of accounts receivable of Daley Corporation, the president, Roberta Daley, asked why the current year's expense for doubtful accounts is debited because some accounts may become uncollectible next year. She then said she had read that financial statements should be based on reliable evidence, and that it seemed to her to be much more reliable and objective to wait until specific accounts receivable were actually determined to be uncollectible before an expense is recognized.

Instructions

a Discuss the theoretical justification of the allowance method as contrasted with the direct write-off method of accounting for doubtful accounts.

b Describe the following two methods of estimating doubtful accounts. Include a discussion of how well each accomplishes the objectives of the allowance method of accounting for doubtful accounts.

1 The percentage-of-sales method

2 The aging method

c What merit is there in the president's contention that the allowance method lacks the reliability of the direct write-off method? Discuss in terms of accounting's measurement function.

Case 7-4 The annual report for Year 10 of Allied Corporation, which operates a group of correspondence and resident schools, included the following relating to contracts receivable and sales:

Current assets:	
Contracts receivable, less allowance for doubtful contracts of $3,228,180 (**NOTE 2**)	$ 6,599,399
Current liabilities:	
Estimated costs to service contracts	$ 264,281
Unearned tuition revenue (**NOTE 2**)	1,074,226
Income statement:	
Sales, net of discounts and allowances of $2,076,911	$14,350,698
Doubtful contracts receivable expense	3,863,800

NOTE 2 — ***Contracts receivable:*** Students in home-study courses enter into contracts that contain various payment plans, generally for a term of one to three years. Similarly, home-study courses are generally completed over a term of one to three years. Revenue from home-study courses and estimated costs to service the contracts are recorded when the contract is received.

Many of the contracts receivable are due from resident students and represent advance registrations for classes that will begin subsequent to December 31, Year 10. Tuition revenue on these contracts and a portion of tuition applicable to the classes in progress on December 31, Year 10, net of an allowance for cancellations, have been deferred and will be credited to revenue as earned over the period of attendance.

It is estimated that gross contracts receivable of approximately $1,900,000 on December 31, Year 10, are not expected to be realized within one year. However, it is not practicable to state separately the long-term portion of contracts receivable in the balance sheet because of the difficulty of determining the allowance for doubtful contracts relating to the long-term contracts receivable.

Instructions

Briefly evaluate the accounting practices of Allied Corporation. Your answer should refer to such accounting concepts or principles as revenue realization, matching of costs and revenue, conservatism, reliability, and classification of contracts receivable as current assets based on the length of Allied's operating cycle.

PROBLEMS

Pr. 7-1 In the second half of Year 3, Jakarta Imports Limited required additional cash for its operations and used trade accounts receivable to raise cash as follows:

1 On July 2, Jakarta Imports assigned $300,000 of trade accounts receivable to Finance Corporation. Jakarta Imports received an advance from Finance of 85% of the assigned receivables, less a fee of 3% on the advance. Prior to December 31, Year 3, Jakarta Imports collected $190,000 on the assigned receivables, and remitted $185,000 to Finance, $13,500 of which represented interest on the advance (loan payable).
2 On November 10, Jakarta Imports sold $310,000 of trade accounts receivable for $280,000. The receivables had a carrying amount of $290,000 and were sold on a non-recourse basis.
3 On December 31, Jakarta Imports obtained a loan of $125,000 from Royal Bank by pledging $180,000 of trade accounts receivable.

Instructions

Prepare journal entries to record the foregoing transactions of Jakarta Imports Limited.

Pr. 7-2 The accountant for Kai Trading Company was hired at the beginning of Year 6. On December 31, Year 6, before making any adjusting entries, the accountant prepared a trial balance that included the following ledger account balances:

	Debit	*Credit*
Notes receivable (received in exchange for trade accounts receivable)	$ 50,000	
Trade accounts receivable	300,000	
Allowance for doubtful accounts	7,500	
Sales		$2,000,000
Sales returns and allowances	18,850	
Sales discounts	25,540	

Instructions

Prepare an adjusting entry for Kai Trading Company on December 31, Year 6, to provide for estimated doubtful accounts under each of the following independent assumptions. Explain the basis for each journal entry.

a Kai Trading's experience indicates that 70% of all sales are credit sales, and that on the average 3% of gross credit sales prove uncollectible.

b An analysis of the aging of trade accounts receivable indicates that potential uncollectible accounts and notes receivable on December 31, Year 6, amount to $30,000.

c Kai Trading's policy is to maintain an allowance for doubtful accounts equal to 5% of outstanding trade accounts receivable, including notes received from customers.

d The allowance for doubtful accounts is increased by 2% of gross sales, and an allowance for sales discounts of $9,000 on outstanding trade accounts receivable is established.

Pr. 7-3 On January 1, Year 1, Long Beach Corporation sold to Tab Tillman a parcel of land with a carrying amount of $450,000. Tillman gave Long Beach $80,000 cash and $600,000 non-interest-bearing promissory notes payable in six equal annual instalments of $100,000, with a first payment on the notes due on January 1, Year 2. Neither the land nor the notes had readily ascertainable current fair value. The market rate of interest for notes of this type is 15% a year. The fiscal year for Long Beach ends on December 31.

Instructions

a Prepare journal entries for Long Beach Corporation to record the sale of the land in Year 1, the collection on the notes receivable in Year 2, and adjusting entries on December 31, Year 1 and Year 2. Use the Discount on Instalment Notes Receivable ledger account. Include supporting computations as part of the explanation for each journal entry. Round all computations to the nearest dollar and use the Appendix at the end of Chapter 5.

b Show how the notes receivable are presented in the balance sheet of Long Beach Corporation on December 31, Year 2.

Pr. 7-4 The following information is taken from the trial balance Westwood Restaurant Supplies on September 30, Year 10, the end of its fiscal year:

	Debit	*Credit*
Notes receivable from customers (due within one year at 12% interest)	$100,000	
Trade accounts receivable	310,000	
Allowance for doubtful accounts and notes	7,300	
Allowance for sales discounts		$ 2,200
Allowance for sales returns		-0-
Sales — cash		250,000
Sales—credit		730,000
Sales returns	12,500	
Sales discounts	14,250	

Accounts receivable written off during the year were debited to the Allowance for Doubtful Accounts and Notes ledger account; merchandise returns by customers were recorded in the Sales Returns account; and sales discounts allowed to customers were recorded in the Sales Discounts account. Westwood Restaurant Supplies uses the perpetual inventory system.

Instructions

a Prepare journal entries for Westwood Restaurant Supplies on September 30, Year 10, to adjust the Allowance for Doubtful Accounts and Notes, the Allowance for Sales Discounts, and the Allowance for Sales Returns ledger accounts based on the following information:

1 Aging of trade accounts receivable and notes receivable indicates that the following balances are required on September 30, Year 10:

Allowance for doubtful accounts and notes	$20,800
Allowance for sales discounts	8,200

2 Based on many years of experience, management of Westwood Restaurant Supplies estimated that of the $310,000 of accounts receivable on September 30, Year 10, $20,000 selling price of merchandise will be returned. The net realizable value of the returned merchandise was estimated at $11,200. Westwood Restaurant Supplies follows the practice of establishing an inventory account for the merchandise expected to be returned by customers.

b Assuming that the allowance accounts are adjusted correctly on September 30, Year 10, show how sales, doubtful accounts expense, and receivables appear in the financial statements of Westwood Restaurant Supplies for the fiscal year ended September 30, Year 10. Doubtful accounts expense is reported as an operating expense in the income statement.

Pr. 7-5 In auditing the financial statements of Malta James Corporation for Year 5, you discover the following information:

1 On April 30, Year 5, Malta James received a non-interest-bearing promissory note for $30,000 maturing in one year, as payment for a consulting fee. The fee was originally established at $27,000, but, because the client was short of cash, Malta James agreed to accept the note. The note was recorded at $30,000 by a debit to Notes Receivable and a credit to Fees Revenue. A discount account representing unearned interest revenue is generally used by Malta James.

2 Malta James sold a parcel of land on June 30, Year 5 for $10,000 cash and a non-interest-bearing promissory note of $50,000 due in three years. The land had a cost of $39,600, and Gain on Disposal of Land was credited for $20,400. You ascertain that the present value of the note on June 30, Year 5, discounted at 12%, was $35,589.

3 A promissory note receivable of $9,000, on which interest receivable of $550 had been recorded in the Interest Receivable ledger account, was discounted at a bank at a rate of interest higher than the rate on the note. Proceeds of $9,440 were credited to Notes Receivable. Malta James does not use a Notes Receivable Discounted ledger account. The note matures early in Year 6.

4 Interest accrued on investment in bonds on December 31, Year 5, amounts to $7,115.

5 Malta James has recorded doubtful accounts expense only as specific accounts receivable were deemed to be worthless. You ascertain that an allowance for doubtful accounts of $11,200 is required on December 31, Year 5, after worthless accounts receivable of $4,100 are written off.

Instructions

Prepare an adjusting or correcting journal entry for Malta James Corporation on December 31, Year 5, for each item (1) through (5) above. The accounting records are still open for Year 5. Disregard income tax considerations and round all computations to the nearest dollar.

Pr. 7-6 From inception of its operations in Year 1, Ray-Randall Company had no allowance for doubtful accounts. Uncollectible accounts receivable were expensed as written off, and recoveries were credited to revenue as collected. On March 1, Year 5 (after the Year 4 financial statements were issued) management recognized that Ray-Randall's accounting policy with respect to doubtful accounts *was not correct*, and determined that an allowance for doubtful accounts was necessary. A policy was established to maintain an allowance for doubtful accounts based on Ray-Randall's historical uncollectible accounts percentage applied to year-end accounts receivable. The historical uncollectible accounts percentage is to be recomputed each year on the basis of all available past years up to a maximum of five years.

Information from Ray-Randall's accounting records is presented below.

Year	*Credit sales*	*Accounts receivable written off*	*Recoveries of written-off accounts receivable*
1	$1,500,000	$15,000	$ -0-
2	2,250,000	58,000	2,700
3	2,950,000	52,000	2,500
4	3,300,000	65,000	4,800
5	4,000,000	63,000	5,000

Accounts receivable balances were $1,450,000 and $1,660,000 on December 31, Year 4, and December 31, Year 5, respectively.

Instructions

a Prepare a journal entry for Ray-Randall Company to establish the allowance for doubtful accounts as of January 1, Year 5. Show supporting computations in the explanation for the journal entry.

b Prepare a working paper to analyze the changes in Ray-Randall Company's Allowance for Doubtful Accounts ledger account for the year ended December 31, Year 5. Show supporting computations.
c Evaluate Ray-Randall Company's policy.

Pr. 7-7 From inception of operations to December 31, Year 1, Ausman Corporation provided for uncollectible trade accounts receivable under the allowance method: provisions were made monthly at 2% of credit sales; accounts receivable written off were debited to the allowance account; recoveries of accounts receivable previously written off were credited to the allowance account; and no year-end adjustments to the allowance account were made. Ausman's usual credit terms are net 30 days.

The balance in the allowance for doubtful accounts was $130,000 on January 1, Year 2. During Year 2 credit sales totalled $9,000,000, interim provisions for doubtful accounts were made at 2% of credit sales, $90,000 of accounts were written off, and recoveries of accounts previously written off amounted to $15,000. Ausman installed a computer facility in November, Year 2, and an aging of trade accounts receivable was prepared for the first time on December 31, Year 2. A summary of the aging follows:

Classification by month of sale	*Balance in each category*	*Estimated percent uncollectible*
Nov.–Dec., Year 2	$1,140,000	2
July–Oct., Year 2	600,000	10
Jan.–June, Year 2	400,000	25
Prior to Jan. 1, Year 2	130,000	75
Total	$2,270,000	

On the basis of the review of collectibility of the trade accounts receivable in the "prior to Jan. 1, Year 2" category, additional receivables totalling $60,000 were written off on December 31, Year 2. Effective with the year ended December 31, Year 2, Ausman adopted a new accounting method for estimating the allowance for doubtful accounts at the amount indicated by the year-end aging analysis of trade accounts receivable.

Instructions

a Prepare a working paper for Ausman Corporation to analyze the changes in the allowance for doubtful accounts for the year ended December 31, Year 2. Show supporting computations.
b Prepare Ausman Corporation's journal entry for the year-end adjustment to the allowance for doubtful accounts balance on December 31, Year 2.

Pr. 7-8 The information given on page 351 appeared in the balance sheet for Wolfgang Company on December 31, Year 4.

The note receivable is a six-month, 10% promissory note for $24,000 from Ace Company dated July 31, Year 4. (A 60-day, 12% promissory note for $36,000 from

Burr Company dated November 15, Year 4 had been discounted at T-D Bank on November 30, Year 4.)

Note receivable			$ 24,000
Interest receivable			1,000
Trade accounts receivable		$280,000	
Less: Allowance for doubtful accounts	$11,200		
Allowance for sales returns	4,000	15,200	264,800
Total notes and trade accounts receivable			$289,800

A summary of transactions and other information relating to notes and trade accounts receivable for January, Year 5 follows:

Jan. 11 Received a 90-day, 12% promissory note from a customer, Karen Young, in exchange for a trade account receivable of $18,000. The fair rate of interest for the note is 12%.

13 Collected $732 from John Ruiz on a trade account receivable written off in Year 4.

15 Notice was received from T-D Bank that Burr Company paid the $36,000 note due January 14, together with the interest of $720. Wolfgang does not use a Notes Receivable Discounted ledger account.

20 Uncollectible accounts totalling $6,100 were written off.

30 Received payment on Ace Company note, including interest of $1,200.

31 Credit sales for the month totalled $712,400.

31 Collections on trade accounts receivable, not including the account of John Ruiz, were as follows:

1 From accounts outstanding on December 31, Year 4, after $5,000 in sales discounts, $244,000

2 From current month's sales, after $8,410 in sales discounts, $370,000

31 Recorded accrued interest for 20 days on note from Karen Young.

31 Aging of trade accounts receivable showed that $20,000 was required in the allowance for doubtful accounts, and $9,120 was required in the allowance for sales returns.

Instructions

a Prepare journal entries for Wolfgang Company for the transactions and other information given for the month of January. Wolfgang does not reverse any adjusting entries.

b Show how the information relating to notes and trade accounts receivable appears in Wolfgang Company's balance sheet on January 31, Year 5.

Pr. 7-9 The following is a summary of the Allowance for Doubtful Accounts ledger account of Arapaho Corporation for Year 5:

Allowance for Doubtful Accounts

Date	Explanation	Debit	Credit	Balance
Year 5				
Jan. 1	Balance.			29,800 Cr
Mar. 31	Provision.		10,530	40,330 Cr
31	Write-off, Year 3 accounts.	9,870		30,460 Cr
June 30	Provision.		9,720	40,180 Cr
30	Write-off, Year 4 accounts.	9,100		31,080 Cr
Sept. 30	Provision.		14,200	45,280 Cr
30	Write-off, Year 4 accounts.	6,840		38,440 Cr
Dec. 31	Provision.		12,550	50,990 Cr
31	Write-off, Year 5 accounts.	14,190		36,800 Cr

Arapaho sells on 30-day credit terms and has followed a practice of debiting Doubtful Accounts Expense in an amount equal to 4% of sales. Arapaho's accountant prepares quarterly income statements and makes adjusting entries at the end of each quarter in order to measure the interim net income. At the end of Year 5, the accountant suggested that an aging be made of trade accounts receivable to test the adequacy of the Allowance for Doubtful Accounts ledger account balance. The aging of accounts receivable on December 31, Year 5, follows:

Current accounts, outstanding 30 days or less	$290,000
31 to 60 days old	85,200
61 to 120 days old	50,000
121 days to 6 months old	31,000
Over 6 months old	26,800
Balance of controlling account, Dec. 31, Year 5	$483,000

After discussion with the credit manager of Arapaho, the accountant determined that the following percentages represented a reasonable estimate of the doubtful accounts in each category: current, 3%; 31 to 60 days old, 5%; 61 to 120 days old, 10%; 121 days to 6 months old, 20%; over 6 months old, 30%.

Instructions

a On the basis of the foregoing information, test the adequacy of the balance in Arapaho Corporation's Allowance for Doubtful Accounts ledger account on December 31, Year 5.

b Prepare an adjusting journal entry for Arapaho Corporation on December 31, Year 5 on the basis of your analysis. The accounting records have not been closed for Year 5.

Pr. 7-10 Paris Fashions Limited began operations on January 2, Year 3, and reported net income of $25,000 in Year 3, $33,000 in Year 4, and $50,000 in Year 5. The accounting records for the year ended December 31, Year 5, are closed.

Paris Fashions did not use the accrual basis of accounting for some items. It was agreed that adjustments should be made in the accounting records to report the assets, liabilities, and owners' equity on the accrual basis of accounting.

Trade accounts receivable at the end of each year consisted of the following:

	December 31:		
	Year 3	*Year 4*	*Year 5*
Relating to sales made in:			
Year 3	$20,000	$ 6,000	$ 3,000
Year 4		24,000	7,500
Year 5			35,000

Doubtful accounts expense was recorded when trade accounts receivable were deemed uncollectible. On the basis of an aging of the receivables, an allowance for doubtful accounts should be established as of December 31, Year 5, and should be estimated as follows: Current-year receivables, 5%; receivables relating to sales of Year 4, 20%; receivables relating to sales of Year 3, 60%. Doubtful accounts expense previously recorded and years of sale are summarized below:

Doubtful accounts expense recorded		*Doubtful accounts expense recorded for sales made in:*		
Year	*Amount*	*Year 3*	*Year 4*	*Year 5*
3	$1,500	$1,500		
4	2,000	1,400	$ 600	
5	5,500	500	2,000	$3,000
Totals	$9,000	$3,400	$2,600	$3,000

Salaries and insurance were recorded as expense when paid. The amounts of accrued salaries and unexpired insurance at the end of each year were as follows:

	December 31:		
	Year 3	*Year 4*	*Year 5*
Salaries payable	$ 800	$ 1,050	$ 1,420
Salaries paid	20,000	25,000	26,500
Unexpired insurance	600	800	150
Insurance premiums paid	2,500	2,000	2,200

Instructions

a Compute the required balance in the Allowance for Doubtful Accounts ledger account on December 31, Year 5, for Paris Fashions Limited.

b Compute net income for Paris Fashions for Year 5, under the accrual basis of accounting. First, prepare a working paper to compute each of the following expenses for Year 5, under the accrual basis of accounting. (Disregard income taxes.)
1 Doubtful accounts expense
2 Salaries expense
3 Insurance expense

c Prepare a correcting entry to restate the accounting records of Paris Fashions to the accrual basis of accounting on December 31, Year 5. Close the net adjustment to net income for the three-year period to the Retained Earnings ledger account. (Disregard income taxes.)

Pr. 7-11 Laser Research Company was organized in Year 1, and it adopted a policy of providing for doubtful accounts expense at the rate of 3% of credit sales. A record of Laser Research's experience for the past three years appears below:

	Year 3	*Year 2*	*Year 1*
Credit sales	$535,000	$380,000	$320,000
Cash collected on credit sales of:			
Year 1			$211,580
Year 2		$318,420	85,000
Year 3	$370,000	47,000	10,000
Accounts of respective years written off as uncollectible:			
Year 1			500
Year 2		8,180	8,800
Year 3	2,200	6,400	4,120
Balance of trade accounts receivable, Dec. 31, Year 3	162,800		
Totals	$535,000	$380,000	$320,000

Laser Research's accountant made no journal entries affecting trade accounts receivable other than entries to record sales, cash collections from customers, the annual provision for doubtful accounts, and the write-offs of uncollectible accounts against the allowance account.

Laser Research engaged you at the end of Year 3 to make an examination of its financial statements for the purpose of supporting a loan application. You have the foregoing data available as a basis for determining the adequacy of the allowance for doubtful accounts. You propose to adjust the allowance to conform to the actual experience relating to doubtful accounts expense during Years 1 and 2.

Instructions

a Set up ledger accounts in three-column form for Trade Accounts Receivable (controlling account), Allowance for Doubtful Accounts, and Doubtful Accounts Expense, and post all journal entries as Laser Research Company's accountant made them in Years 1 through 3. Also post closing entries for Year

1 and Year 2 to Doubtful Accounts Expense.

b Prepare and post to the accounts set up in part *a* any adjusting entries you deem necessary for Laser Research Company on December 31, Year 3, assuming that the accounting records have not been closed. Explain briefly the reasons for your adjustments and the basis for your determination of the proper allowance for doubtful accounts on December 31, Year 3. Laser Research Company records corrections of prior years' doubtful accounts expense in the current year's doubtful accounts expense.

Pr. 7-12 Kay Furniture Company operates a furniture manufacturing business in Vancouver. Although sales have been increasing rapidly, Kay Furniture has not been able to earn a consistently satisfactory net income because of price competition, losses as a result of excessive inventories, inability to collect on several large trade accounts receivable, and ineffective controls over manufacturing costs. Kay Furniture pays bills promptly, but its customers do not. As a result, Kay Furniture is short of cash and is unable to obtain material and equipment to start production of a new line of dining room furniture.

In an effort to obtain a loan, Mary Kay, the president of Kay Furniture, requested a working capital statement from her accountant with instructions to "make it look good." The accountant prepared the following statement of working capital:

KAY FURNITURE COMPANY
Statement of Working Capital
April 1, Year 5

Current assets:		
Cash		$ 8,925
Trade accounts receivable (net of $12,000 received from customers as deposits on special orders; allowances for doubtful accounts, sales discounts, and sales returns have not been used)		73,000
Inventories, at cost		49,150
Receivable for tax refund filed (net of income taxes payable of $4,000, which were due on Mar. 15, Year 5)		2,800
Receivable from subsidiary company (no due date)		34,000
Miscellaneous current assets		8,250
Total current assets		$176,125
Less: Current liabilities:		
Accounts payable	$50,450	
Wages payable	5,000	
Notes payable and miscellaneous current liabilities, including property taxes of $1,800 due on April 10, Year 5	15,000	70,450
Working capital (current ratio 2.5 to 1)		$105,675

Kay presented the foregoing statement to three bankers, hoping to obtain a loan of $50,000 for one year. Each turned her down, giving reasons as follows:

Banker A "We do not extend credit on the basis of partial balance sheets and without an income statement. We also like to see a cash forecast for the coming year. Incidentally, you should hire a chartered accountant who understands generally accepted accounting principles to audit your financial statements.''

Banker B ''You have a satisfactory working capital position and do not need a loan. Besides, we are fully loaned up at the present time.''

Banker C ''Because you do not need the money immediately, I would suggest that you take the following actions before we make a final decision on your loan request:

1 Make a stronger effort to collect trade accounts receivable, write off the worthless accounts receivable, and provide an allowance for additional uncollectible accounts

2 Curtail production until inventories are reduced, auction some slow-moving items to raise cash, and postpone payments on payables as long as possible

3 Obtain the services of an accountant who can help to implement a cost reduction program, improve inventory controls, and reduce credit losses.''

Instructions

a Evaluate the position taken by each of the three bankers.

b Assuming that $8,000 of the trade accounts receivable is uncollectible, that an allowance of 6% of the remaining accounts receivable is considered adequate, and that the market value (replacement cost) of inventories is approximately $41,200, prepare a revised statement of working capital for Kay Furniture Company as of April 1, Year 5.

c Prepare a reconciliation of the difference between the $105,675 working capital determined by Kay Furniture Company's accountant and your computation of working capital in part ***b*** above.

Pr. 7-13 Lydia Corporation finances some of its current operations by assigning accounts receivable to High Finance Limited. On May 1, Year 8, it assigned accounts receivable amounting to $300,000. High Finance advanced 80% of the accounts receivable assigned, less a fee of 2% of the total accounts receivable assigned. Customers were instructed to make payment directly to High Finance. Collections in excess of the loan and the fee were to be remitted to Lydia. At the time of remittance, the accountant for Lydia transferred any balance in Assigned Accounts Receivable to the Accounts Receivable ledger account.

The status of assigned accounts receivable at the end of May and June follows:

May 31 Lydia received a statement that showed that High Finance had collected $180,000 of the assigned accounts receivable and had made an additional charge for interest of 1½% of assigned accounts receivable outstanding on May 31. This charge was to be deducted from the first remittance of cash by High Finance to Lydia.

June 30 Lydia received a second statement from High Finance, together with a cheque for the amount due. The statement indicated that High Finance had collected an additional $66,000 and had made an additional charge for interest of 1½% of assigned accounts receivable outstanding on June 30, Year 8.

Instructions

a Prepare journal entries to record the foregoing transactions of Lydia Corporation. Debit all financing and interest charges to Interest Expense.

b Show how the information regarding assigned receivables is presented in the balance sheet of Lydia Corporation (1) on May 31, Year 8, and (2) on June 30, Year 8.

Pr. 7-14 Garment Factoring Limited was incorporated in December, Year 1 for the purpose of factoring (purchasing) accounts receivable. Garment Factoring was authorized to issue an unlimited number of no-par common stock; 100,000 shares were issued at $5 each.

Garment Factoring charges its clients a fee of 5% of all accounts receivable factored and assumes all credit risks. In addition to the 5% fee, 10% of gross accounts receivable is withheld on all purchases of accounts receivable and is credited to the Payable to Clients ledger account. This account is used for merchandise returns made by customers of the clients for which a credit memorandum would be due. Payments are made to its clients by Garment Factoring at the end of each month to adjust the Payable to Clients ledger account so that it equals 10% of the uncollected accounts receivable as of the end of the month.

Taking into consideration the collection experience of other factoring enterprises, the management of Garment Factoring decided to make monthly provisions to the Allowance for Doubtful Accounts ledger account on the basis of 1% of all accounts receivable purchased during the month.

Garment Factoring also decided to recognize fees revenue only on the factored accounts receivable that have been collected; however, for accounting simplicity all fees originally are credited to Fees Revenue, and an adjusting entry is made to Unearned Fees Revenue at the end of each quarter based on 5% of accounts receivable then outstanding.

Operations of Garment Factoring during the first quarter of Year 2 resulted in the following:

Accounts receivable factored:	
January	$400,000
February	500,000
March	800,000

Collections on accounts receivable for the first quarter of Year 2 totalled $950,000. Operating expenses paid during the first quarter of Year 2 were as follows:

Salaries expense	$19,500
Office rent expense	9,500
Advertising expense	800
Equipment rent expense	1,600
Miscellaneous expenses	1,450

On January 31, Year 2, a six-month, 12% bank loan was obtained for $200,000, with interest payable at maturity.

For the first three months of the year, Garment Factoring rented all its office furniture and equipment; however, on March 31, Year 2, it acquired office furniture and equipment for $20,200, payable within 10 days. This acquisition was not entered in the accounting records.

Instructions

a Prepare a six-column (two columns each for Transactions for Quarter, Income Statement, and Balance Sheet) working paper to summarize the activities of Garment Factoring Limited for the quarter ended March 31, Year 2. (Disregard all withholding taxes and the employer's liability for withholding taxes.)

b Prepare a balance sheet for Garment Factoring Limited on March 31, Year 2.

Pr. 7-15 Marten Company has not prepared financial statements for three years, since December 31, Year 1. Marten has used the accrual basis of accounting and had reported income on a calendar-year basis prior to Year 2. During the past three years (Years 2, 3, and 4), Marten has maintained cash records and has entered credit sales in an accounts receivable ledger; however, no general ledger postings have been made, and an allowance for doubtful accounts has not been used.

The balances at the beginning and the end of the three-year period accumulated as a result of your examination are presented below.

	December 31:	
	Year 4	*Year 1*
Aging of accounts receivable:		
Less than one year old	$14,562	$7,700
1 to 2 years old	1,900	600
2 to 3 years old	2,138	
Over 3 years old (known to be uncollectible)	1,100	
Totals	$19,700	$8,300
Inventories	$ 9,400	$5,800
Accounts payable (merchandise purchases)	6,500	4,305

Other information compiled from Marten Company's accounting records was as follows:

	Year 4	*Year 3*	*Year 2*	*Total*
Cash received on account, relating to:				
Current year's accounts receivable	$103,938	$80,900	$74,400	$259,238
Accounts receivable of the prior year	8,400	7,500	6,700	22,600
Accounts receivable of two years prior	262	200	300	762
Total cash received in Years 2 to 4	$112,600	$88,600	$81,400	$282,600

Accounts to be written off in addition to the $1,100 that are over 3 years old	$ 1,062	$ 820	$ 1,988	$ 3,870
Cash sales	15,600	13,200	13,500	42,300
Payments for merchandise purchases	86,900	70,600	62,500	220,000
Of receivables remaining Dec. 31, Year 4, estimated uncollectible percentage	10%	50%	80%	

No accounts receivable have been written off as uncollectible during the three-year period. The rate of gross profit for Marten Company has remained relatively constant for many years.

Instructions

a Prepare a working paper for Marten Company showing the gross profit on sales for Years 2, 3, and 4.

b Prepare adjusting entries for Marten Company on December 31, Year 4, to (1) establish an adequate allowance for doubtful accounts, and (2) write off accounts receivable that are uncollectible. Debit Retained Earnings for the amount required to establish the allowance for doubtful accounts. (Disregard income taxes.)

c Marten Company wishes to know what percentage of credit sales would be reasonable as an estimate of yearly doubtful accounts expense in the future, on the basis of Marten's experience of the past three years. Support your recommendation with appropriate computations.

Pr. 7-16 You are examining Marina Corporation's financial statement for the year ended December 31, Year 5. Your analysis of the journal entries for Year 5 in the Notes Receivable ledger account is summarized below:

MARINA CORPORATION
Analysis of Notes Receivable Ledger Account
For Year Ended December 31, Year 5

Date, Year 5	*Analysis of transactions*	*Notes Receivable, Debit (Credit)*
Jan. 1	Balance	$118,000
Feb. 28	Received 12%, $25,000 promissory note due Oct. 28, Year 5, from Daley Company, whose account receivable was past due. Memorandum entry only.	
28	Discounted Daley Company's note at 15% for 8 months	(24,300)
Aug. 31	Received principal of $10,000 and interest of $8,400 due from Allen Company and, in accordance with agreement, two principal payments of $10,000 each in advance	(38,400)
Sept. 4	Paid protest fee on promissory note dishonoured by Chark Company	25
Oct. 29	Paid protest fee of $30 and maturity value of Daley Company's promissory note to bank. Note discounted Feb. 28, Year 5 was dishonoured	27,030
30	Accepted fixtures with a current fair value of $26,500 in full settlement from Daley Company	(26,500)
Nov. 1	Received cheque in settlement of Bailey Company's promissory note	(8,960)

Dec. 31	Received non-interest-bearing demand promissory note from James Edge, Marina's treasurer	6,200
31	Received payment on Chark Company's promissory note, including interest for one year and late-payment penalty of $75	(43,700)
31	Accrued interest on Allen Company's note for 6 months at 12%	2,400
	Balance of Notes Receivable ledger account	$ 11,795

Additional Information

1 Notes receivable on January 1, Year 5, consisted of the following:

Note from Allen Company dated Aug. 31, Year 1, payable in annual instalments of $10,000 plus interest at 12% each Aug. 31 ..	$ 70,000
Note from Bailey Company dated Nov. 1, Year 4, due Nov. 1, Year 5, bearing interest at 12%	8,000
Note from Chark Company dated Dec. 31, Year 4, due Sept. 1, Year 5, bearing interest at 9%	40,000
Total notes receivable, Jan. 1, Year 5	$118,000

2 Balance in the Interest Receivable ledger account on January 1, Year 5, consisted of the following:

Allen Company's note ($70,000 × 0.12 × 4/12)	$2,800
Bailey Company's note ($8,000 × 0.12 × 2/12)	160
Total interest receivable	$2,960

3 No journal entries were made during Year 5 to the Interest Receivable ledger account, and only one credit entry for $2,400 on December 31 appeared in the Interest Revenue ledger account.

4 All promissory notes were from trade customers unless otherwise indicated, and were fully collectible (even if later dishonoured).

5 Debits and credits offsetting related credit and debit entries to the Notes Receivable ledger account were correctly recorded unless the facts indicate otherwise.

Instructions

a Prepare a working paper to adjust or correct each journal entry of Marina Corporation for Year 5 and to reclassify it, if necessary. Enter your adjustments in the proper columns to correspond with the date of each entry and use a Notes Receivable Discounted ledger account for notes that are discounted. Do not combine related entries for different dates. Your completed working paper will provide the basis for a single journal entry to correct all entries to the Notes Receivable ledger account and the related ledger accounts for Year 5. Use the following headings for the working paper:

			Adjustments or reclassifications required				
		Notes Receivable (as recorded)	*Notes Receivable*	*Accounts Receivable*	*Interest Revenue*	*Other ledger accounts*	
Date, Year 5	*Analysis of transactions*	*Debit (Credit)*	*Debit (Credit)*	*Debit (Credit)*	*Debit (Credit)*	*Account title*	*Debit (Credit)*
Jan. 1	Balance	118,000					

b From the ''Adjustments or reclassifications required'' section of the working paper in part ***a***, prepare a single journal entry to correct Marina Corporation's accounting records on December 31, Year 5.

c h a p t e r 8

INVENTORIES: COST AND COST FLOW ASSUMPTIONS

NATURE OF INVENTORIES

Inventories consist of goods held for sale to customers, partially completed goods, and material and supplies to be used in production. Inventory items are acquired and sold continuously by a merchandising enterprise; or acquired, placed in production, converted to a finished product, and sold by a manufacturing enterprise. The sale of merchandise or finished products is the primary source of revenue for most nonservice business enterprises.

In a retail or merchandising operation, inventories consist principally of products purchased for resale in their existing form. A retail enterprise may also have an inventory of supplies such as wrapping paper, cartons, and stationery. A manufacturing enterprise has several types of inventories: material and parts, factory supplies, goods in process, and finished goods.

Material and parts are basic commodities or other products obtained directly from natural resources or acquired from others, which will be incorporated physically into the finished product. ***Factory supplies*** are similar to material, but their relation to the end product is indirect. For example, in the manufacture of shirts, cloth is inventoried as material, whereas the cleaning supplies and the oil to lubricate the machinery are classified as factory supplies. ***Goods in process*** consist of partially completed products and include the cost of direct material, direct labour, and factory overhead. ***Finished goods*** are items that are complete and ready for sale and include the same cost elements as those in goods in process.

Inventory Procedures

Two methods may be employed to ascertain the inventory quantities on hand—the periodic system and the perpetual system. The two systems may be employed simultaneously for various inventories, such as material, finished goods, and goods in process.

The ***periodic inventory system*** relies on a physical count of the goods on hand as the basis for control, management decisions, and financial accounting. Although this procedure may give accurate results on a specific date, there is no continuing record of the inventory. The ***perpetual inventory system*** requires a continuous record of all receipts and withdrawals of each item of inventory. The perpetual record is sometimes kept in terms of quantities only. This procedure provides a better basis for control than is obtained under the periodic system. When the perpetual system is used, a physical count of the goods owned by the business enterprise ***must be made periodically*** to verify the accuracy of the inventories reported in the accounting records. Any discrepancies discovered must be corrected so that the perpetual inventory records are in agreement with the physical count.

COST AND QUANTITY ACCUMULATION

Timing Errors in the Recording of Purchases and Sales

When the cost of goods available for sale during a specific accounting period is being accumulated, decisions must frequently be made as to whether certain goods become the property of the purchaser in the current period or in the succeeding period. If acquisitions of goods are not recorded in the period in which they become the property of the purchaser, errors in the financial statements will result.

Three common types of timing errors in recording inventory purchases may occur. The errors and their effects on financial statements are:

1. A purchase is recorded properly, but goods are not included in the ending inventories. The result is to understate current assets and net income.
2. A purchase is not recorded, but goods are included in the ending inventories. The result is to state the assets properly but to understate current liabilities and overstate net income.
3. A purchase is not recorded, and goods are not included in the ending inventories. Net income in this case is unaffected because both purchases and ending inventories are understated by the same amount, but both current assets and current liabilities also are understated.

The first two errors are most likely to occur when the periodic inventory system is used; the third may occur under either the periodic or the perpetual system, but it is more likely when the perpetual system is used. In most cases, timing errors are counterbalanced in the following accounting period; however, the fact that the errors may be self-correcting does not remove the need for correct presentation of financial position and results of operations for each period.

The valuation of inventories has important effects on both the balance sheet and the income statement. The investment in inventories is frequently a major part of a business enterprise's total assets, and the valuation of inventories has a direct effect on the determination of the cost of goods sold. The effect of inventory valuation on the financial statements for a merchandising enterprise that has a single class of inventory is illustrated below.

Valuation of inventory determines the cost of goods sold

Beginning inventory (current asset in balance sheet on Dec. 31, Year 9)	$200,000
Add: Purchases during Year 10	700,000
Cost of goods available for sale during Year 10	$900,000
Less: Ending inventory (current asset in balance sheet on Dec. 31, Year 10)	150,000
Cost of goods sold during Year 10	$750,000

In this illustration the cost of goods available for sale is $900,000, composed of the beginning inventory and the cost of goods purchased during Year 10. The cost of goods available for sale is allocated between the inventory on hand on December 31, Year 10, $150,000, and the cost of goods that have been sold during Year 10, $750,000. The cost of goods sold for Year 10 is the difference between the cost of goods available for sale and the cost of the ending inventory. Any failure to determine accurately either the cost of goods available for sale or the ending inventory may have a material effect on financial statements.

Goods in Transit

Orders for goods that ***have not*** been filled by the seller present little difficulty for accountants. The orders that ***have*** been filled by the seller but not received by the purchaser are the crucial ones. The problem that must be resolved in these cases is to determine whether the goods in transit are the property of the purchaser or of the seller. The passage of title from the seller to the purchaser marks the time when the legal responsibility for the goods changes from one party to the other.

Contracts for purchases usually specify which party is responsible for the goods and the exact location where the responsibility changes. This point usually is indicated by the letters ''***FOB***,'' meaning ***free on board***, followed by the designation of a particular location, for example, ''FOB Halifax.'' This means that title is held by the seller until the goods are delivered to a common carrier in Halifax that will act as an agent for the purchaser.[1] The following example illustrates this concept.

KC Shirt Shop in Windsor orders 200 shirts from Atlantic Fashions in Halifax to be shipped ''FOB Halifax,'' the invoice to be paid within 10 days after shipment. When Atlantic Fashions delivers the goods to the common carrier that acts as an agent of KC Shirt Shop, title to the goods passes to KC Shirt Shop. At this time,

1 Other important FOB designations are ''FOB point of destination,'' which means that title passes at the purchaser's plant, and ''FOB point of shipment,'' meaning that title passes at the seller's plant.

KC Shirt Shop would record the purchase if it knew that the goods were shipped. The freight charges in this case must be paid by KC Shirt Shop; however, the liability for freight charges does not arise until the carrier delivers the goods to KC Shirt Shop.

If KC Shirt Shop also orders 1,000 shirts from Montreal Fabrics to be delivered "FOB Windsor," the shirts are the property of Montreal Fabrics until they are delivered, and KC Shirt Shop does not record an asset or a liability until the shirts are received.

Goods on Consignment and Instalment Sales

Goods may be transferred by one party to another without the typical sale and purchase contract. The party receiving the goods, the ***consignee***, agrees to accept the goods without any liability beyond that of providing reasonable protection from loss or damage, until the goods are sold by the consignee to a third party. At this time the consignee must remit to the shipper, the ***consignor***, the sales price less a commission and costs incurred in connection with the sale. The consignor retains title to the goods until the time of sale to the third party, and the consignee, acting only as an agent, never has title to the goods. Therefore, until the goods are sold by the consignee, they remain the property of the consignor and must be included in the consignor's inventories at cost, including the handling and shipping costs involved in the transfer to the consignee. The consignee does not own the consigned goods and, therefore, does not include them in its inventories.

When goods are sold on the instalment plan, the seller usually retains legal title to the goods until full payment has been received; however, such goods are excluded from the inventories of the seller. The expectation is that customers will make payment in the ordinary course of business; therefore, strict adherence to the "passing-of-title" rule is not considered a realistic approach to the recording of instalment sales transactions.

Inventoriable Costs

The two most important functions of accounting for inventories are to determine (1) the quantity of goods to be included in inventories, and (2) the cost of the inventories on hand. The first function involves the ***taking of inventory***, the second the ***valuation of inventory***.

Taking of Inventory

As we have already indicated, a complete physical inventory of goods owned by a business enterprise must be taken periodically under both the periodic inventory system and the perpetual inventory system. The physical inventory is usually taken on or near the end of the enterprise's fiscal year. The taking of a physical inventory is a complex and time-consuming activity that requires extensive planning and control to assure accuracy. Inventory teams consisting of the enterprise's employees or outside experts count, weigh, or measure the goods owned by the enterprise, using tags or sheets to record the counts. Care must be taken to assure that all goods owned by the enterprise, regardless of their location, are included in the physical inventory, and that customer-owned goods or consigned goods in possession of the enterprise are excluded.

Valuation of Inventory

After the quantity of goods owned has been determined, the starting point in the valuation process is to ascertain the inventoriable cost elements of goods purchased or products manufactured. For inventory items purchased from outsiders, the net invoice cost is generally considered to be the inventoriable cost. ***Net invoice cost*** is the invoice price of the item less any cash (purchases) discounts ***available*** to the purchaser. As stated in Chapter 3, cash discounts should not be included in inventory cost, regardless of whether the purchaser takes advantage of the discounts or fails to do so.

In theory, if a specific cost is expected to contribute to the production of revenue, that cost should be associated with the goods acquired. Thus, a theoretical justification exists for adding the indirect costs of ordering, freight-in, handling, and storing to the net invoice cost to determine the total cost of goods acquired. However, the work involved in the allocation of these costs to inventories often exceeds the benefits derived from the increased accuracy in the valuation of inventories. Furthermore, the allocation of some indirect costs to goods acquired may be highly subjective.

Although the assignment to inventories of all costs incurred in the preparation of goods for sale is desirable, unrealistic allocations of indirect costs should be avoided to prevent a false impression of precision in the measurement of inventory costs. When costs are incurred that are necessary for the acquisition or production of goods but are not expected to produce future benefits or are not material in amount, the costs are usually not included in inventories. Instead, such costs are considered ***period costs*** to be deducted from current revenue. The foregoing discussion is summarized in the diagram below:

Flow of inventory costs to the financial statements

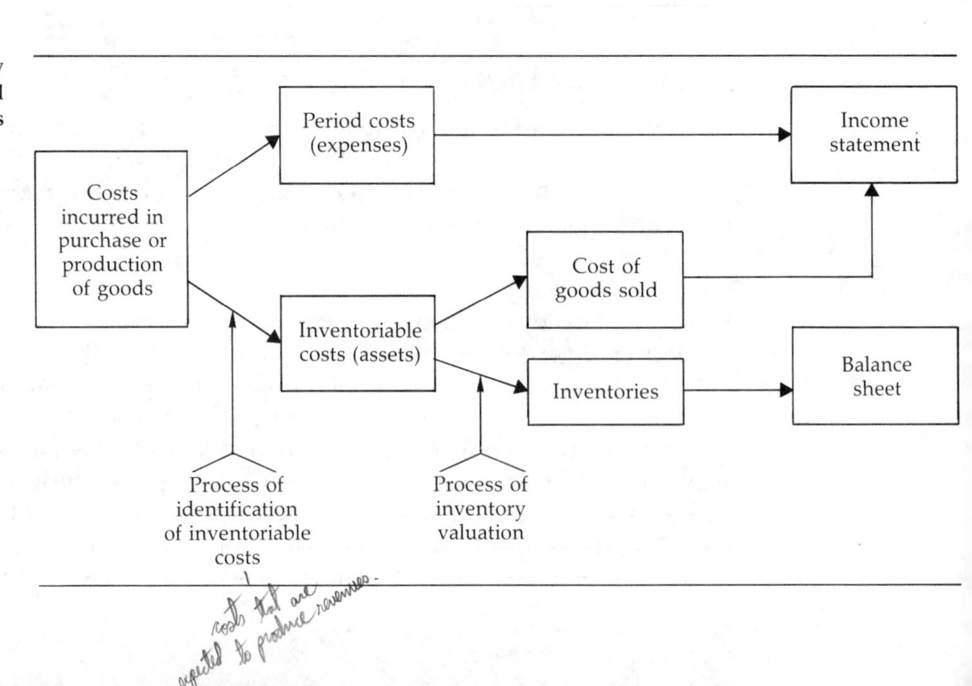

Purchased Inventories

All costs incurred in the ordering, securing, handling, and storing of goods are theoretically as much a part of the total cost of the goods as the net invoice cost itself. The following example involving the purchase of shirts by KC Shirt Shop described earlier illustrates the determination of the cost of goods acquired.

Assume that the invoice from Atlantic Fashions indicates the price of the 200 shirts to be $10 each, with terms 2/10, n/30. This means that KC Shirt Shop must pay Atlantic Fashions either $1,960 [(200 × $10) × 0.98 = $1,960] within 10 days of the date of the invoice or $2,000 (200 × $10 = $2,000) within 30 days after the date of the invoice. The net invoice cost is $1,960. If payment is not made within 10 days, the $40 ($2,000 − $1,960 = $40) cash discount lost is recorded in a Purchases Discounts Lost ledger account (a financing expense) and is not included in the cost of inventories.

The cost of deciding to order these particular shirts, the actual cost of ordering them, the transportation cost, and the handling and storage cost incurred after receipt of the shirts, are costs that logically might be added to the net invoice cost of $1,960. However, for the reasons discussed in the preceding section, these costs are typically expensed.

Manufactured Inventories

In many ways the problems of measuring inventory costs are the same for a manufacturing enterprise as they are for a retailing enterprise. This is particularly true of material and other purchased inventoriable items. The major difference is found in the measurement of the cost of finished goods and goods in process. Tracing the movement of goods and costs through the production process is often difficult, but if it is done with reasonable care, the resulting information is useful to management and outsiders.

As stated earlier, four classes of inventory are usually found in a manufacturing enterprise: (1) material and parts, (2) goods in process, (3) finished goods, and (4) factory supplies. The costs of these inventories emerge as a part of the general process of the measurement of the costs of the three elements (direct material, direct labour, and factory overhead) that flow through the manufacturing process, and of the tracing of these costs to specific quantities of partially finished and finished products as illustrated below:

Flow of production costs

Direct material
Direct labour
Factory overhead*

} → goods in process → finished goods

*Heat, light, and power; indirect material; indirect labour; rent; depreciation; insurance; supplies; maintenance; property taxes; etc.

For a manufacturing enterprise, a sound *cost accounting system* is an essential component of *financial accounting*. Two types of *cost systems* may be used to accumulate product costs for a manufacturing enterprise: the job order cost system and the process cost system.

The *job order cost system* is used when an enterprise manufactures several distinct products. For example, the job order system is used for a construction or specialty product enterprise. Each product or group of products is distinct in some way, and the production costs are identified with a specific job. ***Job order costs sheets*** are used to accumulate the cost of direct material, direct labour, and factory overhead incurred on each job. Costs entered in job order cost sheets make up the goods in process inventory until the jobs are completed. The cost of completed jobs is a part of the finished goods inventory until the goods are sold.

The ***process cost system*** is used when large numbers of similar units are produced on an assembly-line operation. The production process is typically divided into ***cost centres*** or departments, based on logical divisions for the assignment of responsibility. Direct material, direct labour, and factory overhead costs then are accumulated by cost centre, and the goods in process inventory is the sum of all costs incurred on the partially finished units in the various cost centres. The finished goods inventory is composed of all costs incurred to produce the completed goods on hand.

When the process cost system is used, the cost to produce a complete unit of product is usually determined from departmental ***cost of production reports***. Such reports show how the total costs incurred were assigned to any ***by-products*** (or scrap) and to the ***main products***. By-products are usually priced at net realizable value; if such value is immaterial, no cost is assigned to by-products.

Accountants frequently encounter situations in which production costs in a specific manufacturing process relate to two or more products. The allocation of these ***joint costs*** is necessary to determine the unit cost of each product and is frequently made on the basis of the ***relative sales value*** of the ***joint products***. Dividing the total costs by the total sales value of the joint product determines the ***cost percentage***, which then is applied to the unit selling price of each product to determine the estimated unit cost of each product.

Many enterprises engaged in manufacturing activities use standard costs as an integral part of their cost systems. ***Standard costs*** are estimates of what costs ***should be*** under relatively ideal conditions. The basic purpose of standard costs is to aid in measuring the efficiency of an operation, but standard costs may also be used for inventory valuation. The factors that make standard costs a useful control tool serve to reduce their usefulness for inventory valuation purposes. To be a good control tool a standard cost of a product should represent what cost ***ought to be***, not what it ***is*** or ***has been***. When standard costs are used for inventory valuation, accountants should ascertain that the standard costs are reasonable estimates of costs actually incurred.[2]

COST FLOW ASSUMPTIONS

The term ***cost flow*** refers to the inflow of costs when goods are purchased or manufactured and to the outflow of costs when goods are sold. The cost remaining in inventories is the difference between the inflow and outflow of costs.

2 CICA, ***CICA Handbook*** (Toronto), sec. 3030.04.

During a specific accounting period, such as a year or a month, identical goods may be purchased or manufactured at different costs. Accountants then face the problem of determining which costs apply to items in inventories and which apply to items that have been sold. The critical issue in accounting for inventories can be summarized as follows:[3]

> The selection of the most suitable method for determining the cost will depend upon the particular circumstances of each enterprise and the industry in which it is engaged. In some cases, the choice of method may have little effect on the financial statements. In other cases, where the choice of method of inventory valuation is an important factor in determining income, the most suitable method for determining cost is that which results in charging against operations costs which most fairly match the sales revenue for the period . . . regardless of whether or not the method corresponds to the physical flow of goods.

Thus the assignment of costs to inventories and to goods sold is based on the ***assumed flow of costs*** and need not conform to the physical flow of goods. In other words, ***cost flow assumptions relate to the flow of costs, rather than to the physical flow of goods***. The question of which physical units of identical goods were sold and which remain in inventories is not relevant to the accounting problem of income determination.

All methods of inventory valuation are based on the ***cost principle***; no matter which method is selected, the inventory is stated ***at cost***. In selecting an inventory valuation method (or cost flow assumption), we are matching costs with revenue, and the ideal choice is the method that most fairly matches the sales revenue for the period. The most widely used methods of inventory valuation are:

1. First-in, first-out method (fifo)
2. Last-in, first-out method (lifo)
3. Weighted-average method
4. Specific identification method

A recent survey of 325 corporate annual reports indicated that, of the 215 companies which disclosed the inventory costing methods, first-in, first-out was used by 134 companies; last-in, first-out was used by 11 companies; average cost was used by 86 companies; specific identification was used by 8 companies, and other companies applied a variety of other methods to the valuation of inventories. Obviously, many of the companies included in the survey used more than one method.[4]

3 CICA, ***CICA Handbook***, sec. 3030.08–.09.

4 CICA, ***Financial Reporting in Canada***, 16th ed. (Toronto, 1985), p. 104.

First-In, First-Out Method

The *first-in, first-out* or *fifo* method of cost flow is based on the assumption that the oldest goods on hand are sold first. This assumption about cost flow generally conforms to reality; management usually finds it desirable to keep the oldest goods moving out to customers in order to keep fresh or new goods on hand. The method is systematic and is easy to apply; it adheres to the cost principle; and the cost assigned to inventories is likely to be in close harmony with the current prices being paid for inventory replacements.

To understand the application of the fifo method, assume the following data for the month of January relating to item X in the inventories of West Company:

A total of 2,000 units was available for sale, and 1,300 units were sold

WEST COMPANY
Record of Purchases of Item X During January

Date	Description	Units	Cost
Jan. 1	Inventory on hand	200 units @ $7	$ 1,400
Jan. 8	Purchase	1,100 units @ $8	8,800
Jan. 25	Purchase	300 units @ $9	2,700
Jan. 30	Purchase	400 units @ $10	4,000
	Totals	2,000	$16,900

A physical inventory taken on January 31 shows 700 units on hand. The inventory could be composed of any combination of 700 units on hand at the beginning of January or purchased during January. If we follow the fifo procedure, however, we assume that the inventory on January 31 is composed of the items that were acquired *most recently*. The computation of the inventory cost of January 31, based on the fifo assumption, is illustrated below.

A fifo inventory of 700 units is on hand

WEST COMPANY
Inventory of Item X: First-In, First-Out Method

Jan. 30 (last purchase)	400 units @ $10	$ 4,000
Jan. 25 (next-to-last purchase)	300 units @ $9	2,700
Totals	700	$ 6,700

The cost of goods sold consists of the earliest costs incurred and amounts to $10,200 (total goods available, $16,900, less ending inventory, $6,700). *The fifo method gives the same result whether the periodic or perpetual inventory system is used* because each withdrawal of goods is from the oldest stock on hand.

Last-In, First-Out Method

The *last-in, first-out* or *lifo* method of cost flow is based on the assumption that the most recently purchased goods are sold first, because current costs are incurred to make current sales and to maintain adequate inventories on hand. Under this view, the latest costs are most closely associated with current revenue; thus, the matching principle of income measurement is carried out. In the balance sheet, inventories under the lifo method are valued at the ***earliest costs incurred***.

The following data for the month of January relating to item X in the inventory of West Company are the same as those used for the fifo illustration, except for the addition of the number of units sold and the dates when the sales were made:

Summary of purchases and sales

WEST COMPANY
Record of Purchases and Sales of Item X During January

Purchases					*Sales*	
Date	*Explanation*	*Units*	*Price*	*Total*	*Date*	*Units sold*
Jan. 1	Inventory on hand	200	$ 7	$ 1,400	Jan. 6	100
Jan. 8	Purchase	1,100	8	8,800	Jan. 9	200
Jan. 25	Purchase	300	9	2,700	Jan. 15	400
Jan. 30	Purchase	400	10	4,000	Jan. 27	600
	Totals	2,000		$16,900		1,300

The cost assigned to the ending inventory under lifo depends on whether the periodic or the perpetual inventory system is used.

Periodic Inventory System

Based on the information given above, the cost of the 700 units on hand on January 31 is computed under lifo periodic inventory procedures below.

A lifo inventory of 700 units is on hand

WEST COMPANY
Inventory of Item X: Last-In, First-Out Method
(Periodic Inventory System)

Jan. 1 (beginning inventory)	200 units @ $7	$1,400
Jan. 8 (first purchase)	500 units @ $8	4,000
Totals	700	$5,400

The lifo inventory on January 31 is composed of two layers: the 200 units on hand on January 1, plus the layer of 500 units added during January. Should sales exceed purchases in any subsequent period, the costs of units comprising the most recently added layer or layers would be removed from inventory and transferred to cost of goods sold. The cost of the original layer would not be reduced until all subsequently added layers had been assigned to cost of goods sold. The cost of goods sold for January is $11,500 ($16,900 cost of goods available for sale, less $5,400 cost of inventory on January 31, equals $11,500), and consists of the most recent purchases.

Perpetual Inventory System

Unlike the first-in, first-out method, the last-in, first-out method does not produce the same result when the perpetual inventory system is used. When the perpetual system is used, each withdrawal must come from the most recent purchase; however, this may mean that items may be withdrawn from the beginning inventory or the earliest purchase when purchases lag behind sales. If we assume the record of purchases and sales illustrated on page 371, the costs assigned to the goods sold under lifo perpetual inventory procedures is $10,600, as computed below:

Lifo method: cost of goods sold . . .

WEST COMPANY
Cost of Goods Sold (Item X): Last-In, First-Out Method
(Perpetual Inventory System)

Jan. 6	100 units @ $7	$ 700
Jan. 9	200 units @ $8	1,600
Jan. 15	400 units @ $8	3,200
Jan. 27	600 units { 300 @ $9	2,700
	300 @ $8	2,400
Totals	1,300	$10,600

The ending inventory under the lifo perpetual inventory system amounts to $6,300 ($16,900 − $10,600 = $6,300), and consists of the following:

. . . and ending inventory under perpetual inventory system

WEST COMPANY
Inventory of Item X: Last-In, First-Out Method
(Perpetual Inventory System)

Jan. 1 (Balance of beginning layer not sold)	100 units @ $7	$ 700
Jan. 8	200 units @ $8	1,600
Jan. 30	400 units @ $10	4,000
Totals	700	$6,300

Thus, it is apparent that the results of the lifo method of valuing the inventory under the perpetual inventory system may vary somewhat, depending on the timing of sales and purchases.

Unit-Lifo Method

The practical problems of determining the cost of inventory under the lifo procedure may be overwhelming, especially without the aid of a computer. When there are large numbers of similar items and numerous transactions, the weighted-average unit cost of the items purchased during an accounting period is considered the cost for purposes of pricing additions to inventory for the period. Such a procedure eliminates the need for identifying the cost of particular units. This adaptation is used in conjunction with the periodic inventory system and is called the *unit-lifo method.* Given the data presented on page 371 for West Company, the unit-lifo inventory on January 31 is computed below:

Illustration of unit-lifo method

WEST COMPANY
Inventory of Item X: Unit-Lifo Method

Beginning inventory	200 units @ $7.00	$1,400
Layer added in January	500 units @ $8.61*	4,305
Totals	700	$5,705

*Computation of weighted-average unit cost for units acquired in January:

Cost of purchases	$15,500
Total units purchased in January	1,800
Weighted-average unit cost of purchases ($15,500 ÷ 1,800)	$ 8.61

The unit-lifo method is applied only when there is an increase in the inventory during an accounting period. The layer added in January retains its identity in subsequent months as long as the inventory consists of 700 units or more. However, if the inventory decreased to 400 units in February, the inventory on February 28 would consist of 200 units at $7 and only 200 units at $8.61.

Dollar-Value Lifo Method

The determination of lifo cost for a single inventory item, as illustrated in the preceding sections, is not difficult. However, a business enterprise that has several product lines consisting of numerous items in its inventories would have difficulty in applying lifo cost to each of the individual items, especially if the earliest costs dated back many years. Such an enterprise might use the dollar-value lifo inventory method to simplify the application of lifo procedures. Under ***dollar-value lifo***, inventory items constituting a single product line or otherwise having similar characteristics are accumulated in ***pools***. Individual items in each pool are assigned lifo costs in accordance with the procedures described on page 371. The total lifo cost of each pool becomes base-year cost for that pool, with a ***cost index*** of 100. Total base-year costs for all pools constitutes the lifo inventories on the date of adoption of the dollar-value lifo method.

Subsequent ending inventories in each pool are valued first at ***current cost***; total current cost then is converted to equivalent base-year cost by use of the appropriate cost index. Any increase in the ending inventory for each pool, in terms of base-year costs, is valued at costs prevailing during the current year. In practice, the cost index as of the ***end of the current year*** is used to value the added layer; practical limitations of computing several indexes during a year have led to this procedure. A decrease in the ending inventory for each pool in terms of base-year cost is deducted from the most recent layer added to the inventory, at the costs prevailing in the year when the layer was added. Thus, dollar-value lifo measures changes in inventories in terms of ***dollar amounts*** rather than in terms of ***units***.

There are four techniques for applying the dollar-value lifo method: ***double-***

extension, index, link-chain, and ***retail***. These techniques differ primarily in the computation of the cost indexes. The dollar-value retail lifo method is illustrated in Chapter 9, together with other retail methods; the double-extension technique is described and illustrated in the following section.

Double-Extension Dollar-Value Lifo

Under the double-extension dollar-value lifo technique, the ending inventories subsequent to the base year for each pool are computed with two values—***current cost*** and ***base-year cost***. The ratio of total current cost to total base-year cost is the pool's ***cost index*** for the year, and is used to value any increase (***lifo layer***) in the pool for that year. The term "double-extension" refers to the two computations of quantities times unit costs.

To illustrate, assume that on December 31, Year 1, Lastin Limited adopted the dollar-value lifo method, with the double-extension technique, for costing its two inventory items, Alpha and Beta, which constitute a single pool. Details of quantities and unit costs for the two items on December 31, Years 1 through 4, follow:

Data for double-extension dollar-value lifo illustration

LASTIN LIMITED
Quantities and Unit Costs of Inventory Items
December 31, Year 1 Through Year 4

	Quantities on December 31:				*Unit costs on December 31:**			
Item	*Year 1*	*Year 2*	*Year 3*	*Year 4*	*Year 1*	*Year 2*	*Year 3*	*Year 4*
Alpha	4,000	5,000	6,000	5,600	$3.00	$3.60	$3.90	$4.20
Beta	6,000	8,000	9,000	8,400	4.00	4.80	5.20	5.60

*December 31, Year 1, unit cost is lifo cost; unit costs on December 31, Years 2 through 4, are current costs.

Lastin's December 31, Year 1, inventory at lifo cost is $36,000 [(4,000 × $3) + (6,000 × $4) = $36,000], which amount constitutes ***base-year inventory***. The cost indexes for Years 2, 3, and 4 are computed by the double-extension technique shown in the first table on the next page.

By use of total inventory for the base year, December 31, Year 1 ($36,000), and the cost indexes computed by the double-extension technique, Lastin computes its ending inventories by the dollar-value lifo method as shown in the next table (the inventories at base-year costs and the indexes are taken from the preceding table) on page 345.

The key feature of the dollar-value lifo method, regardless of the technique used to determine cost indexes, is the conversion of the beginning and ending inventories of each pool to base-year costs. The difference between the two converted inventory amounts indicates the increase or decrease in the inventory expressed in terms of base-year costs. The lifo layers then must be valued at costs prevailing when the layers were added to the inventory.

Computation of cost indexes for dollar-value lifo method by double-extension technique

LASTIN LIMITED
Computation of Cost Indexes for Dollar-Value Lifo: Double-Extension Technique
For Years Ended December 31, Year 2 Through Year 4

		Unit cost		*Total cost*	
Item	*Quantity*	*Current year*	*Base year*	*Current year*	*Base year*
Dec. 31, Year 2:					
Alpha	5,000	$3.60	$3.00	$18,000	$15,000
Beta	8,000	4.80	4.00	38,400	32,000
Totals.......	13,000			$56,400	$47,000
Cost index: $56,400 ÷ $47,000 = 1.20, or 120					
Dec. 31, Year 3:					
Alpha	6,000	$3.90	$3.00	$23,400	$18,000
Beta	9,000	5.20	4.00	46,800	36,000
Totals	15,000			$70,200	$54,000
Cost index: $70,200 ÷ $54,000 = 1.30, or 130					
Dec. 31, Year 4:					
Alpha	5,600	$4.20	$3.00	$23,520	$16,800
Beta	8,400	5.60	4.00	47,040	33,600
Totals	14,000			$70,560	$50,400
Cost index: $70,560 ÷ $50,400 = 1.40, or 140					

Dollar-value lifo method illustrated (double-extension technique)

LASTIN LIMITED
Computation of Dollar-Value Lifo Inventories: Double-Extension Technique
December 31, Year 1 Through Year 4

December 31:	*Inventories at base-year costs*	*Determination of inventory layers*	*Dollar-value lifo inventories at year-end*
Year 1	$36,000	$36,000 × 1.00	$36,000
Year 2	$47,000	$36,000 × 1.00	$36,000
		11,000 × 1.20	13,200
		$47,000	$49,200
Year 3	$54,000	$36,000 × 1.00	$36,000
		11,000 × 1.20	13,200
		7,000 × 1.30	9,100
		$54,000	$58,300
Year 4	$50,400	$36,000 × 1.00	$36,000
		11,000 × 1.20	13,200
		3,400 × 1.30	4,420
		$50,400	$53,620

Explanation of Computations

Year 2: The increase in the ending inventories, in terms of base-year costs, is $11,000 ($47,000 − $36,000 = $11,000). This increase is converted to year-end costs by multiplying it by 1.20, the end-of-Year-2 cost index. The $13,200 product is the Year 2 ***lifo layer***; this amount is added to the base-year ending inventories of $36,000 to obtain the $49,200 dollar-value lifo inventories on December 31, Year 2.

Year 3: The increase in the ending inventories, in terms of base-year costs, is $7,000 ($54,000 − $47,000 = $7,000). This increase is converted to year-end costs by multiplying it by 1.30, the end-of-Year-3 cost index. The $9,100 product is the Year 3 ***lifo layer***; this amount is added to the Year 2 ending inventories of $49,200 (at dollar-value lifo) to obtain the $58,300 dollar-value lifo inventories on December 31, Year 3.

Year 4: The decrease in the ending inventories, in terms of base-year costs, is $3,600 ($54,000 − $50,400 = $3,600). This decrease, termed a ***lifo liquidation***, is attributed to the Year 3 lifo layer, in accordance with the last-in, first-out cost flow assumption. Thus, the residual Year 3 lifo layer, in terms of base-year costs, is $3,400 ($7,000 − $3,600 = $3,400). The Year 4 cost index of 140 is not used in the computation of the dollar-value lifo inventories on December 31, Year 4, or at any subsequent year-end, because no lifo layer was added in Year 4. The $4,680 decrease ($58,300 − $53,620 = $4,680) in the December 31, Year 4, dollar-value lifo inventories may be verified by multiplying the $3,600 Year 4 lifo liquidation, at base-year costs, by 1.30, the cost index for Year 3 ($3,600 × 1.30 = $4,680).

Base Stock Method

The ***base stock method*** is similar to lifo. It has little theoretical support and is seldom used in practice. This method assumes a continuous existence of a minimum stock of goods, the cost of which is considered to be a permanent asset. Any excess over the base stock is considered a temporary increase and is priced at ***current replacement costs***; any decrease in the base stock is considered to be temporary and is assigned to cost of goods sold at current replacement costs.

The base stock method differs from lifo in that it uses current replacement costs as an element in the pricing of inventory; in contrast, lifo relies exclusively on actual costs.

Weighted-Average Method

The weighted-average method of inventory valuation is based on the assumptions that all goods are commingled and that no particular batch of goods is retained in the inventories. Thus, the inventories are valued on the basis of average prices paid for the goods, weighted according to the quantity purchased at each price. Given the information for West Company on page 370, the ending inventory and cost of goods sold are determined under the weighted-average method (periodic inventory system) as shown at the top of the next page.

This method produces a result, for both inventory valuation and income measurement, that lies between the results achieved under fifo and those achieved under lifo. The weighted-average method does not produce an inventory value consistent with the current cost of the items in inventory; by its nature it lags behind market prices. During a period of rising prices the inventory cost tends to be below replacement cost; during a period of falling prices it tends to be above replacement cost.

Weighted-average method under periodic inventory system

WEST COMPANY
Inventory and Cost of Goods Sold (Item X): Weighted-Average Method (Periodic Inventory System)

Cost of goods available for sale	$16,900
Total units available for sale	2,000
Unit cost = total cost ÷ number of units ($16,900 ÷ 2,000)	$ 8.45
Inventory valuation (700 × $8.45)	$ 5,915
Cost of goods sold ($16,900 − $5,915)	$10,985

When the perpetual inventory system is used, the weighted-average method gives the result of a *moving weighted average*. Under the perpetual system, a new weighted-average unit cost is computed after each purchase, and for this reason is known as the moving-weighted-average method. Units sold are priced at the latest weighted-average unit cost. Given the information for West Company on page 371, the moving-weighted-average method is illustrated below.

Weighted-average method under perpetual inventory system

WEST COMPANY
Inventory of Item X: Moving-Weighted-Average Method (Perpetual Inventory System)

	Units	*Amount*
Jan. 1 inventory	200 @ $ 7.00	$1,400
Less: Jan. 6 sale	(100) @ $ 7.00	(700)
Balance, Jan. 6	100 @ $ 7.00	$ 700
Add: Jan. 8 purchase	1,100 @ $ 8.00	8,800
Balance, Jan. 8 (new unit cost computed)	1,200 @ $ 7.92	$9,500*
Less: Jan. 9 sale	(200) @ $ 7.92	(1,584)
Balance, Jan. 9	1,000 @ $ 7.92	$7,916*
Less: Jan. 15 sale	(400) @ $ 7.92	(3,168)
Balance, Jan. 15	600 @ $ 7.92	$4,748*
Add: Jan. 25 purchase	300 @ $ 9.00	2,700
Balance, Jan. 25 (new unit cost computed)	900 @ $ 8.28	$7,448*
Less: Jan. 27 sale	(600) @ $ 8.28	(4,968)
Balance, Jan. 27	300 @ $ 8.28	$2,480*
Add: Jan. 30 purchase	400 @ $10.00	4,000
Balance, Jan. 31 (inventory at new unit cost)	700 @ $ 9.26	$6,480*

*Slight discrepancy due to rounding of average cost to nearest cent.

Specific Identification Method

At first thought one might argue that each item of inventory should be identified with its *actual* cost and that the total of these amounts should constitute the inventory value. Although such a technique might be possible for a business enterprise handling a small number of items, for example, an automobile dealer, it becomes completely inoperable in a complex manufacturing enterprise when the identity of the individual item is lost. Practical considerations thus make specific identification inappropriate in most cases.

Even when specific identification is a feasible means of valuation, it may be undesirable from a theoretical point of view. The method permits income manipulation when there are identical items acquired at varying prices. By choosing to sell the item that was acquired at a specific cost, management may cause material distortions in income. For example, assume that Grain Company acquires one million bushels of wheat in four equal lots of 250,000 bushels each, at costs of $3.50, $4, $4.50, and $5 a bushel. Grain Company receives an order to sell 250,000 bushels at $4.75 a bushel. If management is accounting for inventory in accordance with specific identification, it can determine the income reported for the period by selecting the batch of wheat that will produce the desired objective. The results of the transaction could range from a profit of $312,500 if the $3.50 wheat were sold, to a loss of $62,500 if the $5 wheat were sold. If an assumption regarding the flow of costs were adopted (fifo or lifo, for example), the effect of such arbitrary decisions on reported income would be removed.

Summary of Inventory Valuation Methods

The inventory valuation and cost of goods sold for West Company as determined in the preceding illustrations are summarized below. Results from use of the specific identification method are not shown, because we did not identify the composition of the units in inventory by date of purchase.

In the West Company example in which prices were rising, the costs assigned to inventory range from a high of $6,700 under the fifo method to a low of $5,400 when the lifo method is used in conjunction with the periodic inventory system. The disparity in inventory valuation under the various cost flow assumptions depends on the trend and volatility of prices paid for new purchases and, of course, on the length of time the lifo method has been in use.

Summary of cost flow assumptions

WEST COMPANY
Inventory and Cost of Goods Sold (Item X): Various Cost Flow Assumptions

Cost flow assumption	*Goods available for sale*	*Inventory*	*Cost of goods sold*
First-in, first-out method	$16,900	$6,700	$10,200
Last-in, first-out method:			
Periodic system	16,900	5,400	11,500
Perpetual system	16,900	6,300	10,600
Unit-lifo	16,900	5,705	11,195
Weighted-average method (periodic system)	16,900	5,915	10,985
Moving-weighted-average method (perpetual system)	16,900	6,480	10,420

INVENTORY VALUATION AND INFLATION

Although both lifo and fifo are accepted inventory valuation methods, they may lead to significant differences in the financial statements during a period of inflation. Neither method achieves an entirely satisfactory reporting of both inventories and cost of goods sold when prices are going up. Therefore, it is not surprising that a controversy has evolved around the relative importance of working capital and net income. In an inflationary period, the managerial implications of inventory valuation procedures should be considered.

Effect on Working Capital and Net Income

As illustrated earlier, the fifo method has the effect of assigning the most recently incurred costs to inventories, whereas the lifo assumption assigns the first costs incurred to inventories. During periods of rising price levels, inventories valued on the fifo basis approximate more closely the current cost of the inventories; the cost of items valued on the lifo basis are less than the current cost. The difference between the inventories valued at lifo and at current cost depends on the magnitude of the price level increases. The lifo method produces a seriously distorted inventory valuation when it is used over a long period during which the price level increases steadily or when the price level increases rapidly.

The understatement of inventories resulting from the use of the lifo method in a period of rising prices is objectionable because of the effect on working capital, current ratio, and inventories turnover rate. The problem is rather serious if no indication is included in the financial statements of the degree of understatement. The advocates of lifo minimize the importance of this understatement by arguing that the income statement is more important than the balance sheet. They argue that ***a more accurate measure of net income*** may justify a less meaningful balance sheet. Despite these views by proponents of lifo, it is essential that companies using lifo should disclose in a note to the financial statements the excess of replacement or current cost over the lifo value of inventories.[5]

Proponents of the lifo method argue that realized revenue should be matched with the cost of acquiring goods at or near the time the revenue is realized. They contend that during periods of rising prices, for example, two types of profits, inventory profits and operating profits, may be included in net income, unless diligence is exercised to avoid the inclusion of inventory profits. ***Inventory profits*** arise as a result of holding inventories during periods of rising inventory costs, and are measured by the ***difference between the original cost of the goods sold and their current cost at the time of sale. Operating profits*** result from sales of a product at a price above current cost. Because the lifo method matches the most recently incurred costs with realized revenue, it tends to exclude inventory profits from net income. Supporters of lifo favour the exclusion of inventory profits

5 *Regulation S-X* (Washington: Securities and Exchange Commission, 1984), Rule 5:02:6(c), requires those companies subject to its jurisdiction that use lifo to disclose the excess of replacement or current cost over the lifo inventory value.

from net income, on the premise that inventories that are sold must be replaced and that inventory profits are ***fictitious*** and ***illusory***.

Those supporting the fifo method of inventory valuation agree that there may be two types of profits, but they consider both to be an element of income realized at the time of sale. They argue that if the proponents of lifo are interested in measuring ***real*** rather than ***monetary*** income, they should extend their proposal to use current costs to value all assets. The cost of goods sold should not be the most recently incurred costs but rather the costs that ***will be incurred*** to replace the items that have been sold. This method has been referred to as the ***next-in, first-out (nifo)*** method of inventory valuation. At the present time, the nifo method is not acceptable, because it violates the cost principle.

The measurement of ***real income*** poses another problem during a period of inflation. To illustrate, assume that an inventory item was purchased for $100 when the general price-level index was 120, and was sold for $150 when the general price-level index was 132 and the current cost of the item was $124. The apparent gross profit of $50 ($150 − $100 = $50) on the sale of the item may be allocated between (1) the general price-level adjustment, (2) the holding gain, and (3) the operating profit as follows:

Analysis of gross profit

General price-level adjustment: ($100 × 132/120) − $100 (original cost) ..	$10
Holding gain: $124 (current cost) − $100 (original cost) − $10 (general price-level adjustment computed above)	14
Operating profit: $150 (selling price) − $124 (current cost)	26
Total difference between selling price and original cost ($150 − $100) ..	$50

The ***holding gain*** of $14 is the increase accruing as a result of owning the item while the specific price (current cost) of the item was rising. The holding gain does not include the $10 increase in price of the item caused by general inflation. The total of the price-level adjustment and the holding gain, $24, is the ***inventory profit*** (difference between the current cost of $124 and the original cost of $100). Finally the ***operating profit*** of $26 is the real economic reward to the enterprise for handling and selling the item.

Managerial Implications

The proponents of lifo argue that this method is an invaluable aid to management because it excludes inventory profits from net income. External factors that are beyond the control of management often create inventory profits. Moreover, inventory profits are reinvested in inventories, which means that disposable (spendable) income is measured more accurately by the use of lifo.

Fifo advocates agree that management may need information about the current cost of the inventory and its effect on net income; however, they maintain that this information may be compiled without distorting working capital and net income. Moreover, they argue that if the inventory profits are excluded from net income, similar profits derived from other investments also should be excluded. If management decisions regarding dividend declarations, wage negotiations, and prices are based on the concept of disposable income, a more extensive modification of the determination of net income is needed than that achieved by lifo. Adherents of fifo also criticize the distortions of net income caused by lifo liquidations. When these occur, cost of goods sold includes costs that may differ significantly from current costs. For example, in the Year 4 example for Lastin Limited (page 376), cost of goods sold includes $4,680 ($3,600 × 1.30 = $4,680) attributable to the lifo liquidation, compared with current cost of approximately $5,040 ($3,600 × 1.40 = $5,040). In recognition of this deficiency of the lifo method, the Securities and Exchange Commission in the United States requires companies that it supervises to disclose the effect of material lifo liquidations on their net income.[6]

Despite the theoretical arguments in support of lifo, the dominant reason for its popularity in practice is the income tax benefits that result from the use of this method. During periods of rising prices, taxable income and income taxes are reduced through the use of lifo. If prices later fall to the level at the time lifo was adopted, this reduction is simply a deferral of taxes. If prices continue to rise, the reduction will be permanent. In either case, the lifo user gains, because a postponement of taxes has economic value.

Since lifo is not allowed for income tax purposes in Canada, it is used by only a few companies. However, lifo is permitted under the income tax law of the United States, which stipulates that lifo must be used for financial accounting if it is used for income tax purposes. As a result, lifo is one of the most commonly used methods in that country. In addition, these companies in the United States also have influenced some of their subsidiary companies in Canada to use lifo so as to facilitate the preparation of consolidated financial statements. This helps to explain why certain companies in Canada use lifo even though it is not allowed for income tax purposes.

Disclosure of Inventory Profits

The accounting profession in Canada has long been concerned with the effect of changing prices on inventory, as well as on such long-term assets as property, plant, and equipment. After a number of exposure drafts and a discussion memorandum, the CICA issued, in December 1982, ***CICA Handbook*** section 4510 "Reporting the Effects of Changing Prices." This section of the ***CICA Handbook*** recommends the following disclosure in inventory as supplementary information to the basic historical financial statements of large publicly held enterprises:[7]

1 The current cost amounts of cost of goods sold and inventory

2 The amount of the changes in current cost of inventory during the accounting period

3 The portion of the changes in **2** above that is attributable to the effect of general inflation (general price-level changes)

6 Securities and Exchange Commission, ***Staff Accounting Bulletin 40*** (Washington: 1981), Topic 11F.

7 CICA, ***CICA Handbook***, sec. 4510.17–.18 and .24.

Thus, inventory profits are disclosed in such supplementary information.

The requirements of section 4510 of the ***Handbook*** are discussed fully in Chapter 25.

VALUATION OF INVENTORIES AT LOWER OF COST AND MARKET

We have indicated that valuation of inventories includes ascertaining the number of units, determining an appropriate unit cost, and computing the total cost. We now consider another possibility: that of a decrease in the economic value of inventories below their cost. If some items of inventories are used for display or demonstration, a part of the cost of these units should be expensed prior to their sale. Whenever an asset contributes to the realization of revenue and a part of the usefulness of the asset is consumed, a part of the cost of the asset should be deducted from such revenue.

Assume, for example, that the owner of Delphine's Dress Shop wants her store to have a reputation as ***the*** fashion shop in her area. To accomplish her objective she knows that she must stock the extreme styles in sufficient volume to satisfy a substantial part of her clientele. In many cases she will buy more dresses than she expects to sell in order to maintain her reputation. To obtain a proper measure of net income and to value her inventories properly, a part of the cost of the excess supply of dresses will have to be charged against revenue prior to the sale of these dresses. The problem is one of ascertaining the amount of the cost that should be charged off. The loss of economic value is believed to have contributed to the realization of revenue, and the selling price of dresses on hand will have to be reduced. The expired cost of dresses still on hand may be added to the cost of goods sold.

Obsolescence of Inventories

In other situations, part of the cost of inventories must be deducted from revenue even though no benefit has accrued to the business enterprise. Inventory items frequently become unsaleable at regular prices because of obsolescence, damage, or deterioration. If items that are to become a part of a manufactured article are damaged or spoiled during the production process, the loss need not be segregated, but may become a part of the cost of the completed product. This procedure is acceptable, provided the damage or loss is expected as a part of the normal operation of the plant. However, unusual loss or damage should not be included in the cost of manufactured goods.

Damaged or obsolete goods are frequently valued at ***net realizable value*** — estimated selling price less direct costs of completion and disposal. A more severe standard is to write the goods down to replacement cost—the price that would be paid for the goods in their present condition. In some cases an arbitrary percentage of the cost is written off; this is difficult to defend, but it may be necessary if a more objective basis is not available. Finally, when there is doubt about the existence of any net realizable value, the cost of the goods should be reduced to scrap value, or to zero in the absence of scrap value.

Price Fluctuations and Valuation of Inventories

Price changes that result in loss of economic usefulness of inventories should be deducted from revenue in the accounting period in which the loss takes place. Because the cost of the inventories is determined by negotiation between the purchaser and supplier on the basis of the purchaser's expectation of realizing a desired gross profit margin on resale, a significant decline in the selling price of inventories requires a reduction in the carrying amount of inventories. The inventory value that is most appropriate in such situations is ***replacement cost*** (or a "derived market" price), that is, a price that will allow recovery of the adjusted cost of the inventories and yield a desired gross profit margin.

At present, generally accepted accounting principles hold that gains attributable to price increases should not be recognized until inventories are sold. However, losses resulting from decreases in the replacement cost of inventories are recognized in the accounting period in which the losses occur. The basis for this ***lower-of-cost-and-market rule*** is found in the concept of conservatism.

Lower-of-Cost-and-Market Procedures

The lower-of-cost-and-market (LCM) rule requires that inventories be priced at the lower of these two values (cost price and market price). The benefits attributed to this method of inventory valuation are (1) that the loss, if any, is identified with the accounting period in which it occurred, and (2) that goods are valued at an amount that measures the expected contribution to revenue of future periods. The following principle established by the AICPA in the United States supports the lower-of-cost-and-market rule:[8]

> A departure from the cost basis of pricing the inventory is required when the utility of the goods is no longer as great as its cost. Where there is evidence that the utility of goods, in their disposal in the ordinary course of business, will be less than cost, whether due to physical deterioration, obsolescence, changes in price levels, or other causes, the difference should be recognized as a loss of the current period. This is generally accomplished by stating such goods at a lower level commonly designated as ***market***.

A precise measurement of ***utility*** is almost impossible, and the adoption of the LCM price is a practical means of approximating the decline in utility of goods in inventories.

What is meant by "market" in the expression "lower of cost and market"? Is it the price at which the item will be sold, or is it the price that would be paid to purchase the item? The ***CICA Handbook*** identifies several preferable possibilities:[9] replacement cost, net realizable value, and net realizable value less normal profit margin. Since the ***Handbook*** is silent on the choice among these three methods, it has implicitly sanctioned the use of any one of them, depending on

8 AICPA, *Accounting Research and Terminology Bulletins — Final Edition*, chap. 4, p. 30.

9 CICA, ***CICA Handbook***, sec. 3030.11.

the circumstances. In practice, net realizable value is the most widely used method, with replacement cost ranked as a distant second.[10]

In the United States, however, current practice requires the use of the current price, that is, ***replacement cost***, with certain limitations. Replacement cost is a broader term than purchase price because it includes incidental acquisition costs. Replacement cost may also be applied to manufactured inventories by reference to the prevailing prices for direct material, direct labour, and factory overhead. If replacement cost is not reasonably determinable or exceeds the amount expected to be realized by the sale of the items, ***net realizable value*** is used instead of replacement cost. The net realizable value is determined by subtracting from the expected selling price all prospective ***direct costs*** of completing and selling the item. The following limits (***ceiling*** and ***floor***) have been placed on ''market'' (''replacement cost'') by the AICPA.[11]

> As used in the phrase ***lower of cost and market*** the term ***market*** means current replacement cost (by purchase or by reproduction, as the case may be) except that:
>
> **1** Market should not exceed the net realizable value (i.e., estimated selling price in the ordinary course of business less reasonably predictable costs of completion and disposal); and
>
> **2** Market should not be less than net realizable value reduced by an allowance for an approximately normal profit margin.

In U.S.

Thus, the ***ceiling*** is equal to the selling price reduced by the estimated costs of completion and sale; and the ***floor*** is equal to the ceiling reduced by the normal gross profit. ***Replacement cost is used as ''market'' price if it falls between the ceiling and the floor; the ceiling amount is used as ''market'' price when replacement cost is above the ceiling; and the floor amount is used as ''market'' price when replacement cost is below the floor***. This general rule, established by the AICPA, is diagrammed on page 385 for a unit costing $40, with three different assumptions as to replacement cost ($38, $34, and $28), a ceiling limit on market price of $36, and a floor limit on market price of $30.

When the ceiling, replacement cost, and floor amounts are ranked from highest to lowest, the amount in the middle is used as the ''market'' price. Once the adjusted amount for market price is determined, ***the final step is to compare the cost of the inventory item with the adjusted market price*** to determine the LCM valuation. In each of the three assumptions in the diagram, the adjusted market price is less than cost, and is the value assigned to inventory under the LCM rule. This adjusted market price is used as the ''cost'' for future comparisons with market prices.

Although replacement cost is the basic concept of market, it should not be used blindly. When the replacement cost of an item is higher than its net realizable value, conservatism requires that the item be written down to its net realizable value. Otherwise, a loss that is already apparent would be deferred. For this

10 CICA, *Financial Reporting in Canada*, p. 105.

11 AICPA, *Accounting Research and Terminology Bulletins*, chap. 4, p. 31.

Applying the "ceiling" and "floor" tests of the AICPA's LCM rule

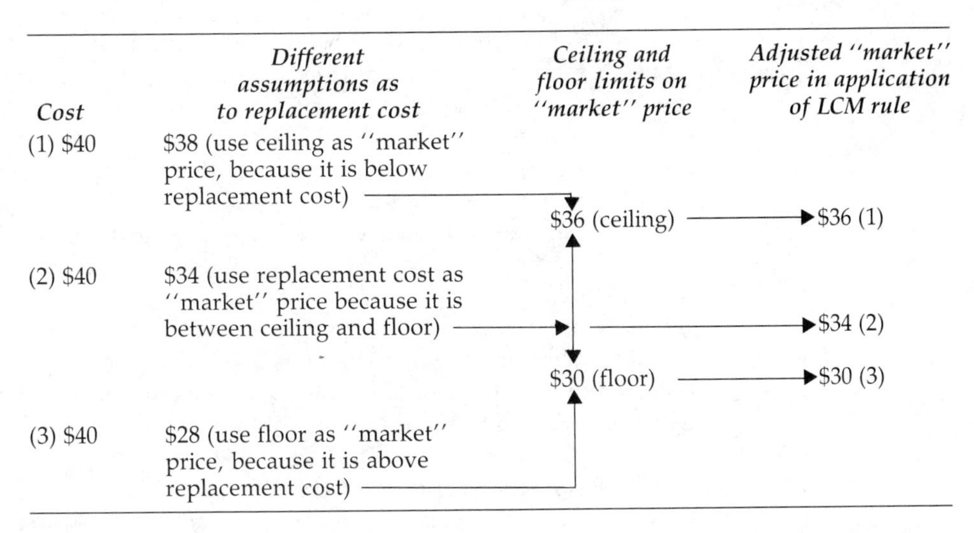

reason, net realizable value must be the ***ceiling***. In contrast, if a business enterprise is required to write down its inventories, it might be tempted to "take a big bath" and write off an excessive amount. In the following year, the gross profit on sales would be overstated; thus, investors would have an impression of a strong "turnaround." To prevent this type of manipulation, the write-down of inventories must not be below the ***floor***.

Illustrations of Selection of "Market" and "Lower of Cost and Market" Under the AICPA Rule

Because the AICPA requirements are far more involved than those of the CICA, the following additional examples illustrate the application of the AICPA's LCM rule. The inventory value for each item is in bold face type. Completion and selling costs are $6 for each item, and the normal gross profit margin is 25% of the selling price.

Application of the AICPA's LCM rule to five examples

	Inventory items				
	A	B	C	D	E
Selling price	$20	$20	$28	$36	$36
Cost (determined by specific identification, fifo, weighted-average, etc.)	16	15	20	25	***20***
Selling price less $6 completion and selling costs—net realizable value (*ceiling*)	***14***	***14***	22	30	30
Selling price less completion and selling costs and normal gross profit margin of 25% of selling price (*floor*)	9	9	15	***21***	21
Replacement cost on inventory date	15	16	***17***	20	19

Explanations

- ***Item A*** Replacement cost of $15 exceeds the ceiling of $14, which is the adjusted market price; because cost is $16, the inventory value is $14, the lower of cost and adjusted market price.

- *Item B* Replacement cost of $16 exceeds the ceiling of $14, which is the adjusted market price; inventory value is $14, although replacement cost of $16 exceeds cost of $15.
- *Item C* Replacement cost of $17 is between the ceiling-floor limit ($22 to $15); replacement cost is the adjusted market price; inventory value is $17, because it is less than cost of $20.
- *Item D* Replacement cost of $20 is below the floor of $21, which is the adjusted market price; the inventory value is $21, because it is less than cost of $25.
- *Item E* Replacement cost of $19 is below the floor of $21, which is the adjusted market price; the inventory value is $20, or cost, because cost is lower than adjusted market price of $21. In this case, the normal gross profit margin will be realized when the unit is sold; therefore, no loss in value is recognized.

Using Net Realizable Value as "Market"

Since the net realizable value method is selected by most Canadian companies in the application of the lower-of-cost-and-market rule, it is useful to compare this Canadian practice with the AICPA's rule used in the United States. The following illustration, based on the same information used in the five examples in the preceding paragraphs, shows the results of the application of the net realizable value as "market" and a comparison of these results with those produced by the AICPA rule. The inventory value to be reported for each item is in bold face type.

Application of net realizable value as market . . .

. . . and a comparison with the AICPA rule

	Inventory items				
	A	B	C	D	E
Cost	16	15	***20***	***25***	***20***
Market (net realizable value)	***14***	***14***	22	30	30
Inventory value based on:					
Net-realizable-value rule	14	14	20	25	20
AICPA rule	14	14	17	21	20

The inventory values to be reported for items A, B, and E are the same under both the net-realizable-value method and the AICPA rule. However, the values for items C and D are higher under the net-realizable-value method than the AICPA rule. This comparison indicates that the AICPA rule produced more conservative results for the current period than the Canadian practice of using the net-realizable-value method. On the other hand, the net-realizable-value method minimizes the extent of the shift of income from one period to the next and thus has an income-smoothing effect.

Application of LCM

The LCM rule can be applied to (1) each individual item in inventories, (2) major categories of inventories, or (3) inventories as a whole. Regardless of which of the three methods is adopted, each inventory item should be priced at cost and at market as a first step in the valuation process. The item-by-item method produces the lowest inventory value, and the application of the LCM rule to inventories as a whole produces the highest valuation. So far, the ***CICA Handbook*** has not taken a position on which is the preferable approach. However, we favour the application of the LCM rule to inventories as a whole because it is likely to produce a more logical and realistic matching of sales and cost of goods sold. The following illustration demonstrates the variations in LCM amounts that result from the application of these three methods.

Applying LCM to each item results in lowest inventory value

ANN COMPANY

Determination of Value of Inventories by Use of the LCM Rule—End of Year 1

Inventory categories	*Cost*	*Market*	*(1) Item by item*	*(2) Category of inventories*	*(3) Inventories as a whole*
No. 1: Item A	$ 6,000	$ 9,000	$ 6,000		
Item B	10,000	9,500	9,500		
Subtotals	$16,000	$18,500		$16,000	
No. 2: Item C	$15,000	$17,000	15,000		
Item D	20,000	14,000	14,000		
Subtotals	$35,000	$31,000		31,000	
Totals	$51,000	$49,500			$49,500
Valuation of inventories			$44,500	$47,000	$49,500

In the valuation of inventories for a manufacturing enterprise, goods in process and finished goods inventories must be adjusted for any decline in the price of material, direct labour, and factory overhead costs.

Subsequent Valuation Problems

Suppose that at the end of Year 2, item D in the illustration above is still on hand and that the market value has risen from $14,000 to $19,000. What valuation should be assigned to item D at the end of Year 2? Generally, accountants have held that, once an inventory item has been written down, this lower value ***is considered cost*** for future comparisons with "market." Therefore, in the application of the item-by-item method, the value of item D is $14,000 at the end of Year 2 because the item was written down to this amount at the end of Year 1.

For ***interim reporting purposes*** in the United States, this rule was modified by the Accounting Principles Board as follows:[12]

> Inventory losses from market declines should not be deferred beyond the interim period in which the decline occurs. Recoveries of such losses on the same inventory

12 AICPA, ***APB Opinion No. 28:*** "Interim Financial Reporting" (New York: 1973), pp. 524–525.

in later interim periods of the same fiscal year through market price recoveries should be recognized as gains in the later interim period. Such gains should not exceed previously recognized losses. Some market declines at interim dates, however, can reasonably be expected to be restored in the fiscal year. Such ***temporary*** market declines need not be recognized at the interim date since no loss is expected to be incurred in the fiscal year.

However, the CICA in Canada has no comparable recommendations.

Valuation Allowance for Write-Down of Inventories

When inventories are written down below cost, the reduction may be credited to an inventory valuation account rather than to the inventory account directly. This procedure accomplishes the objective of a write-down, and at the same time permits the cost of the inventory to be reported in the balance sheet. Use of a valuation account is especially appropriate with the perpetual inventory system, because it eliminates the necessity of adjusting the detailed inventory records (maintained at actual costs) to lower market prices.

Here is the journal entry to record the reduction of inventories at the end of Year 1 from a cost of $100,000 to a market valuation of $92,000 for Karen Company:

Recording inventory valuation account

Cost of Goods Sold (or Loss from Price Decline in Inventories) ($100,000 – $92,000)	8,000	
Allowance for Price Decline in Inventories		8,000
To record the reduction in value of inventories caused by declining prices.		

In the balance sheet at the end of Year 1, inventories may be listed at cost and may be reduced to a lower market by deduction of the allowance for price decline from cost. This procedure is illustrated for Karen Company below:

Balance sheet presentation of inventories after write-down

Current assets:		
Inventories (at first-in, first-out cost)	$100,000	
Less: Allowance for price decline in inventories	8,000	$92,000

Alternatively, inventories may be shown at the lower of cost and market of $92,000 only.

If the write-down of inventories is material, it may be shown separately from cost of goods sold in the income statement or disclosed in a note to the financial statements.

The inventory valuation allowance is not needed after the goods in question are sold. Therefore, at the time the cost of beginning inventories is transferred to Income Summary (or to the Cost of Goods Sold ledger account), the allowance account is also closed, to reduce the cost of beginning inventories to market value. For example, the following journal entry is made at the end of Year 2 by

Karen Company to close beginning inventories, assuming that the periodic inventory system is used:

Closing journal entry when inventory valuation account is used

Income Summary	92,000	
Allowance for Price Decline in Inventories	8,000	
Inventories (beginning)		100,000
To close beginning inventories to Income Summary.		

If the market value of inventories at the end of Year 2 is below cost, an allowance for price decline in inventories should again be established.

Valuation of Purchase Commitments at Lower of Cost and Market

If at the end of an accounting period a business enterprise has a contract to purchase goods at a fixed price that is higher than the current price of the goods, a loss should be recognized. In other words, the outstanding purchase commitment should be valued on a lower-of-cost-and-market basis by recognition of a current loss and the accrual of a current liability. These accounting procedures are described in Chapter 10.

Appraisal of the Lower-of-Cost-and-Market Rule

The lower-of-cost-and-market rule originated in an era of emphasis on balance sheet conservatism. It exemplifies an old accounting axiom: ''Anticipate no profit and provide for all possible losses.'' By reducing inventories to market, accountants also reduce net income for the current accounting period. However, if the price of the goods rises, generally accepted accounting principles do not permit the value of inventories to be increased. Such action would result in the recognition of income before revenue is realized.

The treatment of damaged and obsolete goods was discussed earlier, in accordance with the principle of valuing inventory at cost less an amount that measures any decline in utility. Also, the argument has been presented that a decline in prices casts a shadow over a part of the inventory cost because the revenue in future accounting periods may not be adequate to provide a normal margin of profit. Thus, accountants have been led to the conclusion that the goods have lost a part of their economic utility, and that the unrecoverable portion of inventory cost should be deducted from current revenue.

One should not dismiss such an argument lightly; unrecoverable costs are not assets. However, every price decline does not necessarily mean that the cost of goods in inventories will not be recovered. The price system is not so sensitive that it transmits related price movements quickly and uniformly throughout the economy. The indiscriminate application of the lower-of-cost-and-market rule should not be allowed to replace sound professional judgement in the valuation of inventories. There are instances when recognition of losses prior to sale is justified. However, a careful evaluation of the particular circumstances is necessary before the amount of the loss may be determined. This is perhaps why the

CICA has not taken a position on the three different methods of ''market.'' However, the AICPA's ceiling and floor limits on ''market'' do serve a useful function in making such an evaluation.

Anticipation of Price Declines

The lower-of-cost-and-market rule is applicable to price declines that actually have occurred, ***not to possible future price declines***. The AICPA has made the following distinction between inventory losses that may be measured objectively and those that are conjectural in nature.[13]

> It has been argued with respect to inventories that losses which will have to be taken in periods of receding price levels have their origins in periods of rising prices, and that therefore reserves to provide for future price declines should be created in periods of rising prices by charges against the operations of those periods. Reserves of this kind involve assumptions as to what future price levels will be, what inventory quantities will be on hand if and when a major price decline takes place, and finally whether loss to the business will be measured by the amount of the decline in prices. The bases for such assumptions are so uncertain that any conclusions drawn from them would generally seem to be speculative guesses rather than informed judgments.

Only ***actual*** losses on goods included in inventories that arise from price declines should be included in net income; ***possible*** future losses should not be entered in the accounting records.

Inventories and Financial Reporting Standards

The objectives of reporting inventories in the balance sheet are to reveal the type, the relative liquidity, and the basis of valuation of the inventories. In reporting the investment in inventories, as in reporting other assets, accountants are concerned with disclosing all significant information; they are particularly concerned that the investment in inventories has been determined on a basis consistent with that of preceding years. If a change is made in the method of determining inventory cost, the change should be explained fully as to its effect on the current and prior year's financial statements. The accounting problems of reporting changes in inventory valuation methods are discussed in Chapter 22.

When a valuation account is used as a means of valuing the inventory at the lower of cost and market, this account may be subtracted from inventory cost in the balance sheet as illustrated earlier, or the inventory may be reported net of the allowance account.

Financial accounting standards require that the various categories of inventories be indicated under the general caption ''Inventories,'' and that the basis of valuation and the method of determining costs be disclosed. The ***CICA Handbook*** requires disclosure of current cost of inventories by large publicly owned corporations in a supplementary section of the annual report.

13 *Accounting Research and Terminology Bulletins*, chap. 6, p. 42.

Inventories that have been pledged as collateral for loans are included in the Inventories section rather than being offset against the loans secured by the inventories. Such financing agreements are described in a note to the financial statements. Firm purchase commitments also are disclosed in a note to the financial statements. Most business enterprises report inventories in a single amount, accompanied by an explanatory note. Here is an example from an annual report of a publicly owned company:

Inventories in the balance sheet

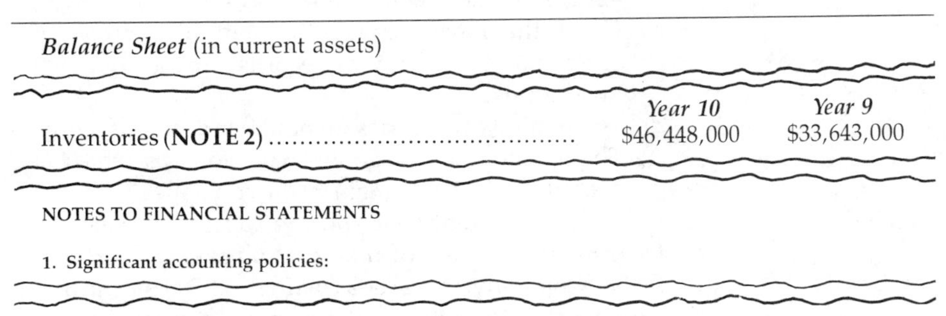

Balance Sheet (in current assets)

	Year 10	*Year 9*
Inventories (**NOTE 2**)	$46,448,000	$33,643,000

NOTES TO FINANCIAL STATEMENTS

1. Significant accounting policies:

(b) Inventories—
Inventories of raw materials and goods in process are valued at the lower of cost and replacement cost and inventories of finished goods at the lower of cost and net realizable value. Cost has been determined on the first-in first-out method for raw materials and on the moving average method for work in process and finished goods.

2. Inventories:

	Year 10	**Year 9**
Finished goods	$33,499,000	$19,854,000
Goods in process	4,513,000	4,250,000
Raw materials	8,436,000	9,539,000
	$46,448,000	$33,643,000

REVIEW QUESTIONS

1 What features distinguish inventory costs from other costs that are allocated between deferred and expired portions?

2 There are two systems of maintaining inventory records: ***a*** the ***periodic inventory system***, and ***b*** the ***perpetual inventory system***. What are the basic differences between the two systems, and under what circumstances should each be used?

3 Why is the valuation of inventories critical to financial reporting? What criteria should accountants use in deciding between alternative methods of valuation?

4 At the end of the accounting period, the following purchase invoices dated December 27 are on hand, but the goods have not been received. How would you treat each invoice in the determination of the ending inventories?

a Invoice amount $12,670; terms 2/10, n/30; FOB shipping point

b Invoice amount $14,860; terms 1/5, n/30; FOB destination

5 Indicate the effects on the financial statements for the current year and succeeding years of each of the following types of errors in accounting for

inventories. Indicate the direction of error—that is, overstatement, understatement, or no effect.

a An invoice for goods shipped FOB shipping point has been received, but no journal entry has been made to record the purchase. The goods have not been received and are not included in the ending inventories.

b An invoice for goods shipped, but not received, has been recorded correctly to indicate that the goods belong to the purchaser, but the items have not been included in the ending inventories.

c Goods that have been received, but the purchase of which has not been entered in the accounting records, are included in the ending inventories.

d The ending inventories do not include goods shipped on consignment. The transfer of these goods to the consignee has been recorded as a sale, even though they remain in the consignee's possession at the end of both the current year and the succeeding year.

6 Describe the process of ***taking of inventory***.

7 Lieber Company had goods costing $38,500 on consignment from Maxwell Company on June 30, Year 8, the end of Lieber's fiscal year. How should the consigned goods be treated in Lieber's June 30, Year 8, physical inventory under the periodic inventory system?

8 What costs should be included in the cost of inventories?

9 Midtown Corporation is licensed to manufacture and sell a certain product under a patent owned by Alan Bella. A royalty of 10 cents is payable to Bella for each unit sold. For financial accounting Midtown treats royalty payments as a selling expense and does not accrue a royalty liability on the unsold units in inventories. The property tax assessor claims that 10 cents should be treated as a production cost and included in the valuation of inventories. Do you agree with the tax assessor? Explain.

10 If two or more ***joint products*** are produced in a single department of a manufacturing enterprise, how are the total production costs incurred in the department allocated to the joint products?

11 The ***specific identification*** method of inventory valuation has been supported by some accountants as the ideal method of achieving a matching of costs and revenue. What objections may be raised to the use of this method for the valuation of inventories?

12 Differentiate between the ***weighted-average method*** and the ***moving-weighed-average method*** of determining cost of inventories.

13 In the application of the double-extension technique for the dollar-value lifo method of valuing inventories, it is necessary to value ending quantities of an inventory pool at both current costs and base-year costs. Why?

14 Under what conditions may a portion of the cost of inventories be written off prior to the sale of the items comprising the inventories?

15 Describe the term ***market*** as used in Canada in the inventory valuation procedure referred to as the lower-of-cost-and-market rule.

16 How does the AICPA define ***market*** in the inventory valuation procedure referred to as the lower-of-cost-and-market rule?

17 What are the general arguments against the use of the lower-of-cost-and-market rule in the valuation of inventories as it is practised in Canada and the United States?

18 Is there any difference, insofar as inventory valuation is concerned, between an item with a cost of $50 that regularly sells for $75 but has been so physically damaged that it may be sold for no more than $55, and a like item that has no physical damage, but whose replacement cost has declined to $30?

19 Under what conditions, if any, is it appropriate to enter anticipated inventory price declines in the accounting records?

20 Under what conditions, if any, should losses from price declines involving future purchase commitments be entered in the accounting records?

21 What objectives do accountants seek to achieve in reporting inventories in the balance sheets of business enterprises?

EXERCISES

Ex. 8-1 Select the best answer for each of the following multiple-choice questions:

1 Is the moving-weighted-average inventory cost flow method applicable to the following inventory systems? Answer *a*, *b*, *c*, or *d* according to the table.

	Periodic	*Perpetual*
a	Yes	Yes
b	Yes	No
c	No	No
d	No	Yes

2 The following pertains to an inventory item:

Cost	$60
Estimated selling price	68
Estimated cost of disposal	1
Normal gross profit margin	11
Replacement cost	51

Under the AICPA's lower-of-cost-and-market rule, this inventory item is valued at:

a $51 *b* $56 *c* $60 *d* $67 *e* Some other amount

3 During Year 4, Olsen Company discovered that the ending inventories reported in its financial statements were understated as follows:

Year	*Understatement*
1	$50,000
2	60,000
3	-0-

Olsen uses the periodic inventory system. Ending inventory quantities are converted to dollar amounts by the fifo cost flow method. Assuming no other accounting errors, Olsen's retained earnings balance on December 31, Year 3, is:

a Correct
b $ 60,000 understated
c $ 60,000 overstated
d $110,000 understated

4 Wye Company, which uses the periodic inventory system, failed to record a $6,000 purchase of merchandise that was received on March 31, Year 7, but included the cost of the merchandise in the March 31, Year 7, physical inventory (fifo basis). The effect of this error on Wye's financial statements for the fiscal year ended March 31, Year 7, was to:

a Overstate current assets and understate current liabilities
b Overstate net income and understate current liabilities
c Understate net income and understate current assets
d Understate current assets and understate current liabilities

5 Cash discounts on purchases should not be included in inventory cost:

a Only if the purchaser takes advantage of the discounts
b Only if the purchaser fails to take advantage of the discounts
c Regardless of whether the purchaser takes advantage of the discounts or pays the full invoice price
d If management of the purchasing enterprise decides to exclude the discount from inventory cost

6 Ending inventories differ depending on whether the perpetual inventory system or the periodic inventory system is used, under the following cost flow assumptions:

a First-in, first-out and last-in, first-out
b Specific identification and weighted-average
c Last-in, first-out and weighted-average
d First-in, first-out and weighted-average

Ex. 8-2 Janis Manufacturing Limited, which uses the perpetual inventory system, recorded the following data pertaining to material X:

	Units			
Date	*Received*	*Cost*	*Issued*	*On hand*
Jan. 1		$1.00		400
8	600	1.10		1,000
12			800	200
15	400	1.21		600

Compute the moving-weighted-average cost per unit of material X for Janis Manufacturing Limited on January 15.

Ex. 8-3 Stationers Company had 200 calculators on hand on January 1, Year 9 costing $18 each. Purchases and sales of calculators during the month of January, Year 9, were as follows:

Date	Purchases	Sales
Jan. 12		150 @ $28
14	100 @ $20	
29	100 @ $22	
30		100 @ $32

Stationers does not maintain perpetual inventory records. According to a physical count, 150 calculators were on hand on January 31, Year 9.

Compute the cost of Stationers Company's January 31, Year 9, inventory of calculators under ***a*** the fifo method and ***b*** the lifo method of inventory valuation.

Ex. 8-4 Dexter Corporation sells water beds. The perpetual inventory balance was $19,600 in the accounting records on December 31, Year 4. Some events that occurred near the end of Year 4 are listed below:

1 Beds shipped to a customer on January 2, Year 5, costing $2,000 were included in inventory on December 31, Year 4. The sale was recorded in Year 5.
2 Beds costing $9,000 received on December 30, Year 4, were recorded as having been received on January 2, Year 5.
3 Beds received costing $1,900 were entered twice in the perpetual inventory record.
4 Beds shipped FOB shipping point on December 28, Year 4, which cost $8,000, were not recorded as a sale by Dexter until January 3, Year 5. The beds were included in the ending inventory.
5 Beds on hand that cost $2,300 were not entered in the accounting records in Year 4.

Prepare a working paper showing the correct amount of Dexter Corporation's inventory on December 31, Year 4.

Ex. 8-5 Longo Company was established April 1, Year 1, and adopted the dollar-value lifo method, double-extension technique, for valuing inventories, which consisted of a single pool having two products, ergo and farad. Quantities and unit costs of the two products on March 31 of Year 2, Year 3, and Year 4, were as follows:

	Quantities, Mar. 31:			*Unit costs, Mar. 31:**		
Item	*Year 2*	*Year 3*	*Year 4*	*Year 2*	*Year 3*	*Year 4*
Ergo	10,000	12,000	16,000	$6.00	$6.20	$6.38¼
Farad	20,000	24,000	30,000	2.00	2.40	2.42

*March 31, Year 2, unit cost is lifo cost; unit costs on March 31, Year 3 and Year 4, are current costs.

Compute the cost indexes for Longo Company on March 31, Year 3 and Year 4, by the double-extension technique under the dollar-value lifo method. (The year ended March 31, Year 2, is the base year.)

Ex. 8-6 The following information relates to a commodity of Willis Company for the month of January:

Inventory, Jan. 1	100 units @ $5
Purchases	400 units @ $6; 100 units @ $7
Inventory, Jan. 31	200 units

a Compute the balance of Willis Company's January 31 inventory under the first-in, first-out cost flow assumption.

b Compute Willis Company's cost of goods sold for January under the last-in, first-out cost flow assumption.

Ex. 8-7 The following information was available from the inventory records of Rue Company for January:

	Units	*Unit cost*	*Total cost*
Balance, Jan. 1	2,000	$9.775	$19,550
Purchases:			
Jan. 6	1,500	10.300	15,450
Jan. 26	3,400	10.750	36,550
Sales:			
Jan. 7	(1,800)		
Jan. 31	(3,500)		
Balance, Jan. 31	1,600		

a Assuming that Rue Company maintains perpetual inventory records, compute the inventory on January 31 under the moving-weighted-average method, rounded to the nearest dollar.

b Assuming that Rue Company maintains periodic inventory records, compute the inventory on January 31 under the weighted-average method, rounded to the nearest dollar.

Ex. 8-8 Lansing Corporation uses the periodic inventory system and the first-in, first-out method to determine the cost of its inventories. The physical inventory on October 31, Year 6, is summarized in the next illustration.

Lansing regularly takes a 2% discount on all purchases (excluding freight-in) and allocates an appropriate portion of freight-in to the ending inventories. Additional information available on October 31, Year 6, is presented on the next page.

Item no.	*Unit cost**	*Inventory (units)*	*Freight-in applicable to inventory*
101	$ 3	6,000	$ 915
102	5	9,000	675
103	6	4,500	1,110
104	10	2,400	960

*Before cash (purchases) discounts.

Beginning inventories (Nov. 1, Year 5)	$100,500
Purchases (net of returns and discounts)	535,500
Freight-in	19,500
Sales (net of returns)	721,500
Sales discounts	9,300

a Compute the cost of Lansing Corporation's inventories on October 31, Year 6.
b Compute the amount of Lansing Corporation's gross profit on sales for the year ended October 31, Year 6.

Ex. 8-9 Presented below is the inventory activity for a product for the month of April:

Date	*Transaction*	*Units*	*Cost*	*Total*	*Units sold*
Apr. 1	Inventory	1,200	$8.00	$ 9,600	
4	Purchase	800	8.25	6,600	
7	Sale				600
10	Purchase	500	8.10	4,050	
13	Sale				1,000
16	Purchase	600	7.90	4,740	
19	Sale				900
22	Purchase	300	7.90	2,370	
25	Purchase	600	8.00	4,800	
28	Sale				500
	Totals	4,000		$32,160	3,000

Assuming that the periodic inventory system is used, compute the April 30 inventory cost under each of the following cost flow assumptions:

a First-in, first-out
b Last-in, first-out
c Weighted-average (round the average to the nearest cent)

Ex. 8-10 The following are three different sets of assumptions (cases) relating to an item in inventories:

	Case 1	*Case 2*	*Case 3*
Cost	$22,400	$20,000	$28,000
Selling price	$30,000	$30,000	$30,000
Cost to complete and ship to customers	$ 4,000	$ 4,000	$ 4,000
Normal gross profit on selling price	25%	25%	10%
Replacement cost	$20,000	$18,000	$26,500

Compute the inventory valuation at lower of cost and market for each case, basing it on:

a The AICPA rule

b the most common method of market used in Canada

Ex. 8-11 The controller of Grody Corporation, a retail enterprise that uses the periodic inventory system, made three different computations of gross profit for the first quarter ended March 31, Year 10. These computations appear below:

	Sales ($10 a unit)	*Cost of goods sold*	*Gross profit*
Computation 1	$280,000	$118,550	$161,450
Computation 2	280,000	116,900	163,100
Computation 3	280,000	115,750	164,250

The cost of goods sold in each computation is based on the following data:

	Units	*Unit cost*	*Total cost*
Beginning inventory, Jan. 1	10,000	$4.00	$ 40,000
Purchase, Jan. 20	8,000	4.20	33,600
Purchase, Feb. 12	5,000	4.13	20,650
Purchase, Mar. 14	7,000	4.30	30,100
Purchase, Mar. 27	12,000	4.25	51,000
Totals	42,000		$175,350

Nancy Rogers, the president of Grody, cannot understand how three different gross profit amounts were computed from the same data. As controller, you have explained to her that the three computations are based on three different assumptions concerning the flow of inventory costs; that is, first-in, first-out, last-in, first-out, and weighted average. ***Note:*** Computations 1, 2, and 3 were not necessarily prepared in this sequence of cost flow assumptions.

Prepare a working paper to compute the cost of goods sold and composition of the ending inventory of Grody Corporation under each of the three cost flow assumptions.

Ex. 8-12 You are given the following data about four items included in the inventories of Wold Corporation:

	Item			
	W	*X*	*Y*	*Z*
Cost	$50	$62	$29	$46
Replacement cost	52	48	25	44
Sales price less selling and completion costs	53	59	23	42
Sales price less selling and completion costs and less normal gross profit	47	51	20	38

Indicate which amount is to be used in valuing Wold Corporation's ending inventories in accordance with the lower-of-cost-and-market rule if one bases it on:

a the most common practice in Canada
b the AICPA rule

Ex. 8-13 The inventories for Calton Company consist of two major categories, listed below:

	Quantities	*Unit cost*	*Market*
Category A:			
Item XP	80	$ 7	$ 6
Item XQ	40	8	9
Item XR	30	10	8
Category B:			
Item YS	100	$ 4	$ 3
Item YT	150	9	8
Item YU	300	12	14

Prepare a summary similar to the one illustrated on page 387 to compute inventory values for Carlton Company under the lower-of-cost-and-market rule applied to (1) each item, (2) separate categories, and (3) inventories as a whole.

CASES

Case 8-1 Langley Company sells goods from its store and on consignment through Consignee Company.

Instructions

Answer the following questions:

a Should Langley Company include in its inventories goods purchased from its suppliers but not yet received if the shipping terms are FOB shipping point? Explain.

b Should Langley Company include freight-in costs as part of the cost of inventories? Explain.

c Langley Company purchased an item for inventories three times during the current year, each time at a higher cost than the previous purchase. What would have been the effects on ending inventories and cost of goods sold if Langley had used the weighted-average cost method instead of the first-in, first-out cost method in accounting for the purchases under the perpetual inventory system?

d What are ***goods on consignment*** and how should they be presented in the balance sheet of Langley Company? Explain.

Case 8-2 Paul Dunn, a partner in the law firm of Dunn, Ekker, and Finley, wants to withdraw from the partnership effective April 1, Year 1. Because the partnership maintains its accounting records on the cash basis of accounting, no recognition is given to accounts receivable and work (legal action suits) in process in the preparation of financial statements for the partnership. The partnership contract includes the following provision relative to the withdrawal of a partner:

> A partner who withdraws from the firm shall be entitled to an immediate cash payment equal to that partner's capital account balance, increased by (1) a share of uncollected accounts receivable, and (2) a share of work in process. No diminution in the withdrawing partner's capital will be made for outstanding liabilities.

The senior partner computed the carrying amount of work in process at March 31, Year 1, as follows:

Direct reimbursable costs (travel, outside experts, etc.) chargeable to clients	$ 4,000
Salaries paid to staff lawyers working on cases (excluding time of any of the partners)	29,500
Total carrying amount of work in process	$33,500

Dunn objected to this procedure on grounds that it does not include the value of partners' time spent on work in process, and the amount "represents a bare minimum value" of the work in process. He feels that the billable value of the work performed for clients to date amounts to at least $100,000, and that this amount represents the current fair value of the work in process.

An accountant who was asked to arbitrate the dispute suggested that the senior partner's amount of $33,500 should be increased by $10,000, representing "general office overhead" applicable to the work in process. The accountant feels that partners' time should not be treated as an inventoriable cost because partners' salaries are not expenses for the partnership.

Instructions

Briefly evaluate each of the three approaches to the valuation of work in process and recommend the procedure you consider equitable in this circumstance.

Case 8-3 Taylor Company purchases goods from various suppliers. Taylor's policy is to take all cash discounts offered by suppliers. Taylor uses the periodic inventory system and values its inventories at the lower of first-in, first-out cost and market.

Instructions

a Discuss the propriety of each of the following alternative methods for accounting for cash discounts on purchases:

1 Credit discounts taken to the Other Revenue ledger account when payments are made to suppliers.

2 Reduce cost of goods sold for the accounting period in which payments are made to suppliers.

3 Reduce cost of goods purchased from suppliers on the date of purchase.

b Identify the effects on both the balance sheet and the income statement of Taylor Company's use of the last-in, first-out method instead of the first-in, first-out method of inventory valuation for a substantial time period when purchase prices of goods are rising. State why these effects take place.

c Why is the lower-of-cost-and-market rule used in the valuation of inventories? Explain.

Case 8-4 In order to effect an approximate matching of current costs with related sales revenue, the last-in, first-out (lifo) method of pricing inventories may be used.

Instructions

a Describe the establishment of and subsequent pricing procedures for each of the following lifo inventory methods:

1 Lifo applied to units of product when the periodic inventory system is used.

2 Application of the dollar-value lifo method by the double-extension technique.

b Discuss the specific advantages and disadvantages of the dollar-value lifo method. Disregard income tax considerations.

c Discuss the general advantages and disadvantages claimed for lifo methods. Disregard income tax considerations.

Case 8-5 Lamb Corporation has valued its year-end inventories at the lower of first-in, first-out cost and market for many years. During this period purchases costs had tended to move in a rather general upward trend. For the past three years the general trend of purchases costs has been erratic, and management of Lamb has become concerned with the effect on net income of the lower-of-cost-and-market rule for inventory valuation. You have been requested to analyze the situation and make a recommendation to management supported by computations and accounting theory. The inventories on January 1, Year 1, were valued (both cost and market) at $60,000; additional data are given as follows:

	Year 3	*Year 2*	*Year 1*
Sales	$425,000	$325,000	$375,000
Net purchases	300,000	225,000	260,000
Year-end inventories:			
At fifo cost	75,000	70,000	60,000
At market	55,000	82,000	45,000

Instructions

a Prepare partial income statements for Lamb Corporation for each of the three years using (1) first-in, first-out cost and (2) lower of cost and market to determine cost of good sold.

b Draft a report to management of Lamb Corporation explaining the effect of their present procedure on net income. Assuming that this pattern of fluctuating net income is expected to continue, which method of valuation would you recommend. Why?

PROBLEMS

Pr. 8-1 Layne Corporation, a manufacturer of small tools that uses the periodic inventory system, provided the following information from its accounting records for the year ended December 31, Year 6:

Inventories, Dec. 31, Year 6 (based on physical count of goods in Layne's plant at cost on Dec. 31, Year 6)	$1,750,000
Accounts payable, Dec. 31, Year 6	1,200,000
Net sales (sales less sales returns) for Year 6	8,500,000

Additional Information

1 Included in the physical count of finished goods were tools billed to a customer FOB shipping point on December 31, Year 6. These tools had a cost of $28,000 and were billed at $35,000. The shipment was on Layne's loading dock, to be picked up by the common carrier.

2 Material was in transit from a vendor to Layne on December 31, Year 6. The invoice costs was $50,000, and the material was shipped FOB shipping point on December 29, Year 6.

3 Work-in-process inventory costing $20,000 was sent to an outside processor for plating on December 30, Year 6.

4 Tools returned by customers and held pending inspection in the returned goods area on December 31, Year 6, were not included in the physical count. On January 8, Year 7, the tools (cost $26,000) were inspected and returned to finished goods inventory. Credit memos totalling $40,000 were issued to the customers on the same date.

5 Tools shipped to a customer FOB destination on December 26, Year 6, were in transit on December 31, Year 6, and had a cost of $25,000. On notification of receipt by the customer on January 2, Year 7, Layne issued a sales invoice for $42,000.

6 Material with an invoice cost of $30,000, received from a vendor at 5:00 p.m. on December 31, Year 6, was recorded in a receiving report dated January 2, Year 7. The material was not included in the physical count, but the invoice was included in accounts payable on December 31, Year 6.

7 Material received from a vendor on December 26, Year 6, was included in the physical count. However, the related $60,000 invoice was not included in accounts payable on December 31, Year 6, because the accounts payable copy of the receiving report was lost.

8 On January 3, Year 7, a monthly freight bill in the amount of $4,000 was received. The bill specifically related to material purchased in December, Year 6, one-half of which was still in the material inventory on December 31, Year 6. The freight charges were not included in either inventories or accounts payable on December 31, Year 6.

Instructions

Using the working paper format shown below, prepare adjustments as of December 31, Year 6, to the amounts in Layne Corporation's accounting records. Show separately the effect, if any, of each of the eight transactions on the December 31, Year 6, amounts. If the transactions have no effect on the initial amount shown, leave the column blank.

	Inventories	*Accounts payable*	*Net sales*
Unadjusted amounts	$1,750,000	$1,200,000	$8,500,000
Adjustments — increase (decrease):			
(1)			
(2)			
(8)			
Adjusted amounts	$	$	$

Pr. 8-2 Roman Company began operations on January 2, Year 1, with 200 units of item X at a cost of $1,800. The data pertaining to purchases of item X taken from the accounting records at the end of Year 1 are shown on the next page.

A physical inventory on December 31, Year 1, revealed that 220 units of item X remained in stock. Roman Company uses the periodic inventory system.

Instructions

Based on the data provided, compute for Roman Company ***a*** the cost of inventory on December 31, Year 1, and ***b*** the cost of goods sold during Year 1, under each of the following cost flow assumptions:

1 Last-in, first-out

2 First-in, first-out
3 Weighted-average
For assumption *3* round unit cost to nearest cent and total cost to nearest dollar.

Purchase no.	*Number of units*	*Total cost*
1	24	$ 240
2	84	924
3	126	1,244
4	96	864
5	170	2,125
Totals	500	$5,397

Pr. 8-3 Lambert Corporation is a wholesale distributor of automotive replacement parts. Initial amounts taken from Lambert's accounting records are as follows:

Inventory, Dec. 31, Year 2 (based on physical count in Lambert's warehouse on Dec. 31, Year 2)		$ 920,000
Accounts payable, December 31, Year 2:		
Supplier	***Terms***	***Amount***
B Company	2/10, n/30	$ 265,000
C Company	n/30	210,000
D Company	n/30	50,000
E Company	n/30	225,000
F Company	n/30	-0-
G Company	n/30	-0-
Total		$ 750,000
Sales in Year 2		$8,200,000

Additional Information

1 Parts held on consignment from C Company, amounting to $155,000, were included in the physical count in Lambert's warehouse on December 31, Year 2, and in accounts payable on December 31, Year 2.

2 $22,000 of parts which were purchased from F Company and paid for in December, Year 2, were sold in the last week of Year 2, and appropriately recorded as sales of $28,000. The parts were included in the physical count in Lambert's warehouse on December 3, Year 2, because the parts were on the loading dock waiting to be picked up by the customers.

3 Parts in transit on December 31, Year 2, to customers, shipped FOB shipping point on December 28, Year 2, amounted to $34,000. The customers received the parts on January 6, Year 3. Sales of $40,000 to the customers for the parts were recorded by Lambert on January 2, Year 3.

4 Retailers were holding $210,000 at cost ($250,000 at retail), of goods on consignment from Lambert, the consignor, at their stores on December 31, Year 2.
5 Goods were in transit from G Company to Lambert on December 31, Year 2. The cost of the goods was $25,000, and the goods were shipped FOB shipping point on December 29, Year 2. The purchase was recorded on January 5, Year 3, when the goods were received.
6 A quarterly freight bill of $2,000 relating to merchandise purchased in December, Year 2, all of which was still in the inventory on December 31, Year 2, was received on January 3, Year 3. The freight bill was not included either in the inventory or in accounts payable on December 31, Year 2.
7 All purchases from B Company occurred during the last seven days of the year. These items have been recorded in accounts payable and were included in the physical inventory at cost before cash discounts. Lambert's policy is to pay invoices in time to take advantage of all cash discounts, to adjust inventory accordingly, and to record accounts payable net of cash discounts.

Instructions
Prepare a working paper for adjustments to the initial amounts on December 31, Year 2, using the format shown below. Show the effect, if any, of each of the transactions separately. Identify each adjustment with the number of the related paragraph above.

	Inventory	*Amounts payable (net)*	*Sales*
Initial amounts, Dec. 31, Year 2	$920,000	$750,000	$8,200,000
Adjustment — increase (decrease)			
(1)			
(2)			
(etc.)			
Adjusted amounts, Dec. 31, Year 2 ..	$	$	$

Pr. 8-4 The following information relating to product Q was taken from the accounting records of Dempsey Corporation for the three-month period ending March 31, Year 2:

	Units	*Unit Cost*
Jan. 1, Year 2 (beginning inventory)	800	$ 9.50
Purchases:		
Jan. 5	1,500	10.00
Jan. 25	1,200	10.50
Feb. 16	600	11.00
Mar. 26	900	11.50

The inventory on March 31, Year 2, consisted of 1,600 units. Dempsey uses the periodic inventory system.

Instructions

Compute the cost of Dempsey Corporation's inventory on March 31, Year 2, under each of the following inventory methods (show supporting computations):

a First-in, first-out
b Last-in, first-out
c Weighted-average

Pr. 8-5 Quebec Corporation manufactures and sells four products, the inventories of which are priced at the lower of fifo cost and market. Quebec considers a gross profit margin of 30% of selling price to be normal for all four products.

The following information was compiled on December 31, Year 4:

Product	*Units*	*Fifo unit cost*	*Cost to replace*	*Estimated cost to dispose*	*Expected selling price*
W	500	$35.00	$42.00	$15.00	$ 80.00
X	200	47.50	45.00	20.50	95.00
Y	480	17.50	18.00	5.00	21.00
Z	240	45.00	46.00	26.00	100.00

Instructions

a Why are expected selling prices important in the application of the lower-of-cost-and-market rule?
b On the basis of the most common method used by Canadian companies to apply the lower-of-cost-and-market rule, compute the total value for the inventory.
c Prepare a working paper containing unit values (including ''floor'' and ''ceiling'') for determining the lower of cost and market on an individual product basis. Underscore for each product the unit value for the purpose of inventory valuation resulting from the application of the AICPA's lower-of-cost-and-market rule. The last column of the working paper should contain the value assigned to each product and the total valuation of inventories.
d Comment on the results produced by the two different rules in ***b*** and ***c*** above.

Pr. 8-6 In the process of determining the inventory on June 30, Year 5, for Essex Corporation, you are presented with the summary on the next page relating to material J and finished part K.

Instructions

Prepare a summary similar to the one above, showing the cost of the various items comprising the inventory of material J and finished part K on June 30, Year 5. Place amounts (in dollars) in the two columns at the right. Give a brief reason for including or excluding each item.

	Material J (units)	*Finished part K (units)*
(1) Units on hand in warehouse per physical count. Cost is $4 a unit for material J and $20 a unit for finished park K	6,200	4,600
(2) Units in receiving department, to be refused because of poor quality. Invoice cost is $4.20 a unit	1,000	
(3) Units stored in parking lot considered worthless. Cost is $21 a unit		100
(4) Units in receiving department; no invoice has been received. Price on purchase order is $4.10 a unit	500	
(5) Units not received, for which invoice marked ''FOB shipping point'' has been received. Total cost of invoice, including freight, is $855	200	
(6) Units shipped on June 30, Year 5; invoice marked ''FOB shipping point'' has been mailed to customer. Total cost is $6,330		300
(7) Units completed in factory not transferred to warehouse. Cost is $21.50 a unit		150
(8) Units in shipping department; invoice marked ''FOB'' shipping point'' has been mailed to customer. Cost is $20 a unit		50
(9) Units in shipping department; invoice has not been mailed to customer. Cost is $20.30 a unit		80
(10) Units in possession of consignees with a total cost of $2,400		120

Pr. 8-7 Digby Company sells a single product that has been steadily increasing in selling price in recent months. The inventory on January 1, Year 9, and the purchases and sales for Year 9 are presented as follows:

	Number of units	*Unit cost*	*Average selling price*
Jan. 1, Inventory	8,000	$3.50	
Jan. 10, Purchase	3,000	4.00	
Jan. 21, Purchase	5,000	5.00	
Jan. 1–31, Sales for month	10,000		$ 9.00
Feb. 5, Purchase	4,000	6.00	
Feb. 18, Purchase	6,000	7.00	
Feb. 1–28, Sales for month	9,000		11.00
Mar. 5, Purchase	5,000	7.80	
Mar. 22, Purchase	10,000	8.25	
Mar. 1–31, Sales for month	13,000		13.00

Digby uses the periodic inventory system. Physical inventories are taken at the end of each month.

Instructions

a Compute the cost of Digby Company's inventories on hand at the end of each of the first three months of Year 9 under (1) the first-in, first-out cost flow assumption and (2) the last-in, first-out cost flow assumption.

b Prepare a comparative statement summarizing the gross profit on sales for each month, assuming that inventories are valued under (1) the first-in, first-out cost flow assumption and (2) the last-in, first-out cost flow assumption. Use the following form:

	(1) First-in, first-out			*(2) Last-in, first-out*		
	January	*February*	*March*	*January*	*February*	*March*
Sales						

Pr. 8-8 The following data were taken from the inventory records of Carney Tool Limited on December 31, Year 2:

Department	*Item number*	*Quanity (units)*	*Fifo unit cost*	*Market (per unit)*
Garden tools	10	140	$24.00	$25.00
	11	350	12.10	11.70
	12	10	8.00	9.60
Electric tools	20	60	4.00	3.00
	21	14	14.00	13.00
	22	8	36.00	37.00
Miscellaneous	30	70	2.40	2.00
	31	80	4.90	4.50
	32	100	1.20	1.30

Instructions

a Value Carney Tool Limited's inventories under the lower-of-cost-and-market rule applied to: (1) each individual item, (2) major categories, and (3) inventories as a whole.

b Which value in ***a*** would you recommend for inclusion in Carney Tool's financial statements for the year ended December 31, Year 2? Why is the value you recommend preferable to the other two?

Pr. 8-9 On January 1, Year 1, Lucas Inc. adopted the dollar-value lifo inventory method for external financial reporting. However, Lucas continued to use the fifo inventory method for internal accounting and management purposes. In applying the dollar-value lifo method Lucas used the double-extension technique and the multiple-pools approach under which substantially identical inventory items are grouped into inventory pools. The data shown on the next page were available for Inventory Pool No. 1, which is comprised of products A and B, for the two years following the adoption of dollar-value lifo.

Instructions

a Prepare a working paper for Lucas Inc. to compute the cost indexes for December 31, Year 1 and Year 2, under the double-extension technique. (January 1, Year 1, is the base year.) Round the indexes to two decimal places.

b Prepare a working paper to compute the dollar-value lifo inventory totals for Lucas Inc. on December 31, Year 1 and Year 2, under the double-extension technique. Round all amounts to the nearest dollar.

	Units	Unit cost	Total cost
Inventory, Jan. 1, Year 1:			
Product A	12,000	$30 (1)	$360,000
Product B	8,000	25 (1)	200,000
Totals	20,000		$560,000
Inventory, Dec. 31, Year 1:			
Product A	17,000	35 (2)	$595,000
Product B	9,000	28 (2)	252,000
Totals	26,000		$847,000
Inventory, Dec. 31, Year 2:			
Product A	13,000	40 (2)	$520,000
Product B	10,000	32 (2)	320,000
Totals	23,000		$840,000

(1) Lifo cost
(2) Current cost

Pr. 8-10 Malone Furniture Limited reported income before income taxes as follows:

Year 2	$132,600
Year 3	115,000
Year 4	125,000
Total	$372,600

Malone uses the periodic inventory system. An analysis of inventory on December 31, Year 4, indicates the following:

1 The inventory on December 31, Year 1, was correct.
2 Furniture costing $340 was received in Year 2 and included in the inventory on December 31, Year 2; however, the journal entry to record the purchase was made on January 6, Year 3, when the invoice was received.
3 The December 31, Year 2, inventory included 1,000 units of item Z, which cost $73 a unit, erroneously priced at $37 a unit.
4 Furniture that cost $500 and sold at $700 was shipped to a customer FOB shipping point on December 31, Year 3, and was not included in the December 31, Year 3, inventory; however, the sale was not recorded until January 5, Year 4.
5 Furniture costing $6,000 shipped FOB shipping point was recorded as a purchase in Year 3 when the invoice was received; however, it was not included in the December 31, Year 3, inventory because it was not received until January 6, Year 4.
6 Furniture costing $5,750 was sold on December 31, Year 3 for $8,000 and billed on that date. This sale was recorded on December 31, Year 3, but the furniture was included in the ending inventory because it had not been

separated from other stock and was not shipped until January 3, Year 4. (Assume that the sale should have been recorded in Year 4.)

7 The inventory on December 31, Year 4, was correct.

Instructions

a Compute Malone Furniture Limited's corrected income before income taxes for each of the three years and the total for the three years (Years 2 through 4).

b Prepare a journal entry to correct Malone Furniture's accounting records on December 31, Year 4, assuming that the accounting records have not been closed. Any corrections to income of Year 3 (or earlier) should be made to the Retained Earnings ledger account. Disregard income taxes.

Pr. 8-11 During the first two years of operations, Ritt Corporation, which uses the periodic inventory system, purchased units of a product as follows:

Year ended April 30, Year 3				*Year ended April 30, Year 4*			
Purch. no.	*Number of units*	*Unit cost*	*Total cost*	*Purch. no.*	*Number of units*	*Unit cost*	*Total cost*
1	13,000	$4.00	$ 52,000	6	12,000	$3.25	$ 39,000
2	4,000	3.75	15,000	7	6,000	3.50	21,000
3	12,000	3.50	42,000	8	4,000	3.50	14,000
4	5,000	3.50	17,500	9	5,000	3.75	18,750
5	8,000	3.00	24,000	10	16,000	4.00	64,000
	42,000		$150,500		43,000		$156,750

The replacement cost of the units on April 30, Year 3, was $4.00 a unit, and on April 30, Year 4, was $4.20 a unit. There were 16,000 units on hand on April 30, Year 3, and 21,000 on hand on April 30, Year 4.

Instructions

a Compute the inventory and the cost of goods sold of Ritt Corporation for each year under (1) the first-in, first-out method, and (2) the last-in, first-out method.

b If 800 units had been stolen during the year ended April 30, Year 4, and Ritt Corporation wanted to separate the theft loss from the cost of goods sold, how would Ritt determine the amount of the loss?

Pr. 8-12 The perpetual inventory records of Keylime Company indicate that the purchases, sales, and inventory quantities for product KB-80 for the month of March, Year 7, were as shown on the next page.

Instructions

a Compute the cost of the ending inventory and the cost of goods sold for Keylime Company for March, Year 7, assuming that the perpetual inventory system is used, under each of the following methods. The following

Date	Purchases		Sales (units)
	Units	Unit cost	
Mar. 1 inventory	800	$ 8	
6			500
10	700	9	
18			800
22	900	10	
30			600

columnar headings are suggested: Date, Transaction, Units, Unit Cost, Balance.

1 First-in, first-out
2 Last-in, first-out
3 Moving-weighted-average (Round unit cost to nearest tenth of a cent.)

b Assuming that the periodic inventory system is used, compute the cost of the ending inventory and the cost of goods sold for Keylime Company for March, Year 7, under each of the following methods:

1 First-in, first-out
2 Last-in, first-out
3 Weighted-average

For method *3* round unit cost to nearest tenth of a cent.

c Where differences occur between the results in ***a*** and ***b***, explain why they exist. Under what conditions would you recommend use of the perpetual inventory system? The periodic inventory system?

Pr. 8-13 The following trial balance for Marcia Limited has been adjusted for all items except ending inventories and income taxes.

MARCIA LIMITED
Trial Balance
December 31, Year 2

	Debit	Credit
Cash	$ 21,000	
Accounts receivable (net)	40,000	
Inventories, Dec. 31, Year 1 (at cost)	52,000	
Short-term prepayments	4,000	
Land	125,000	
Buildings	200,000	
Accumulated depreciation of buildings		$ 60,500
Equipment	225,000	
Accumulated depreciation of equipment		105,000
Accounts payable		55,000
Mortgage note payable ($12,000 due in Year 3)		50,000
Common stock, no par, 10,000 shares issued and outstanding		90,000
Retained earnings, Dec. 31, Year 1		266,500
Dividends	50,000	

Sales		505,000
Sales returns and allowances	10,000	
Sales discounts	5,000	
Purchases (including freight-in)	280,000	
Purchases discounts		3,500
Selling expenses	73,000	
General and administrative expenses	50,500	
Totals	$1,135,500	$1,135,500

Additional Information

1 Inventories on December 31, Year 2, consisted of the following:

	Cost	*Replacement cost (net of freight-in and purchases discounts)*
Inventories (cost includes freight-in but has not been reduced for 2% purchases discounts)	$87,000	$75,000

The controller of Marcia wants to recognize the decline in the market value of the December 31, Year 2, inventories by setting up an Allowance for Price Decline in Inventories; the write-down would be included in the cost of goods sold in the income statement. The cost of the December 31, Year 2, inventories should be reduced for purchases discounts that are normally taken. You also ascertain that the cost of ending inventories includes $4,700 of worthless goods and $2,300 of freight-in. Freight-in applicable to the worthless goods amounts to $65. Purchases discounts of 2% are offered on the invoice price of all purchases.

2 Assume that Marcia pays income taxes at the rate of 45%, and that it had 10,000 shares of common stock outstanding throughout Year 2.

Instructions

a Determine the adjusted cost of Marcia Limited's inventories on December 31, Year 2, and prepare a journal entry to record the estimated loss in value of the inventories caused by declining prices. Assume that the amount of the ending inventories had been entered in the accounting records by an appropriate closing entry.

b Prepare an income statement for Marcia Limited for the year ended December 31, Year 2. Include the write-down of inventories to market (replacement cost) in cost of goods sold.

c Prepare a balance sheet for Marcia Limited on December 31, Year 2.

d Prepare a statement of retained earnings for Marcia Limited for the year ended December 31, Year 2.

c h a p t e r 9

INVENTORIES: SPECIAL VALUATION METHODS

Inventory valuation methods based on cost flow assumptions and the application of the lower-of-cost-and-market rule are described in Chapter 8. Special inventory valuation methods, such as the ***retail*** and ***gross profit*** methods, are discussed in this chapter. In addition, the accounting for construction-type contracts (which involves the valuation of construction work in process inventories) is included in this chapter.

RETAIL METHOD

The retail method of estimating the cost of inventories is used primarily by retailing enterprises. Under the periodic inventory system, the cost of the ending inventories is subtracted from the total cost of goods available for sale to compute the cost of goods sold. Under the retail method, a record of goods available for sale at selling prices is kept separate from the accounting records, and sales for the accounting period are deducted from this total to determine the ending inventories at selling prices. The ending inventories valued at selling prices then are reduced to estimated cost by multiplying the inventories at selling prices by the cost percentage computed for the accounting period.

Some uses of the retail method of estimating the cost of inventories are:

1 To verify the reasonableness of the cost of inventories at the end of the accounting period. By using a different set of data from that used in pricing inventories, accountants may establish that the valuation of inventories is reasonable.

2 To estimate the cost of inventories for interim accounting periods.

3 To permit the valuation of inventories when selling prices are the only available data. The use of this method allows management to mark only the selling

prices on the merchandise and eliminates the need for reference to specific purchase invoices.

Illustration of Retail Method

The retail method of estimating inventories (at average cost) is illustrated by the following simplified example for Robb Company:

Key step in the retail method is the computation of a cost percentage

ROBB COMPANY
Estimate of Inventories by Retail Method
End of Current Year

		Cost	*Retail*
Beginning inventories		$ 40,000	$ 50,000
Net purchases		150,000	200,000
Goods available for sale		$190,000	$250,000
Cost percentage ($190,000 ÷ $250,000)	76%		
Less: Sales and normal shrinkage			220,000
Ending inventories, at retail			$ 30,000
Estimated ending inventories, at cost ($30,000 × 0.76)		$ 22,800	

Although the retail method enables estimation of the value of inventories without a physical count of the items on hand, the accountant should insist that a physical inventory be taken periodically. Otherwise, ***shrinkage*** due to shoplifting, breakage, and other causes might go undetected and might result in an increasingly overstated inventories valuation.

Normal shrinkage in the inventories may be estimated on the basis of the goods that were available for sale. The method frequently used is to develop a percentage from the experience of past years, such as 2% of the retail value of goods available for sale. This percentage is used to determine the estimated shrinkage, which is deducted, together with sales, from goods available for sale at retail prices to compute the estimated inventories at retail prices.[1] The cost of normal shrinkage is included in the cost of goods sold; the cost of abnormal shrinkage (theft, unusual spoilage, etc.) that is material in amount is reported separately in the income statement.

The estimated cost of the inventories is computed by use of a ***cost percentage***, that is, the relationship between the cost of goods available for sale during an accounting period and their retail value. The reliability of this procedure rests on the conditions that (1) a uniform relationship exists between selling price and cost for all goods available for sale during the period, or (2) if the markup on individual inventory items differs, the distribution of items in the ending inventories is roughly the same as the ''mix'' in the total goods available for sale during the

1 When sales are made to employees or selected customers at a special discount price, such discounts are added to sales to compute the estimated inventories at retail prices.

period. When one of these conditions is not present, the accuracy of the retail method is improved by applying it to the individual departments of the business enterprise, and adding the resulting departmental inventories to compute the estimated cost of the total inventories.

Retailing Terminology

The following terms are used in the application of the retail method of estimating the cost of inventories:

- *Original selling price* The price at which goods originally are offered for sale.
- *Markup* The initial margin between the selling price and cost. It also is referred to as ***gross margin*** or ***mark-on***.
- *Additional markup* An increase above the original selling price.
- *Markup cancellation* A reduction in the selling price after there has been an additional markup. The reduction does not reduce the selling price below the original selling price. Additional markups less markup cancellations are referred to as ***net markups***.
- *Markdown* A reduction in selling price below the original selling price.
- *Markdown cancellation* An increase in the selling price, following a markdown, that does not increase the new selling price above the original selling price. Markdowns less markdown cancellations are referred to as ***net markdowns***.

To illustrate these terms, assume that an item that cost $20 is priced to sell for $30 a unit. The ***markup*** is $10 (50% of cost or 33⅓% of selling price). In response to strong demand for the item an ***additional markup*** of $3 is added, so that the selling price is increased to $33. As the demand slackens, the price is reduced to $31 by a ***markup cancellation*** of $2. Subsequently, in order to dispose of the remaining units, the selling price is reduced to $25 by a markup cancellation of $1 and a ***markdown*** of $5. Finally, if management concludes that the remaining units will be sold at a price of $28, a ***markdown cancellation*** of $3 is required to increase the selling price from $25 to $28.

Retail Method — Valuation at Average Cost

An understanding of the meaning of each term defined above is important in the application of the retail method, because the treatment of net markups and net markdowns affects the estimate of the cost of ending inventories. The data below for Elmo Corporation are used to illustrate the treatment of net markups and net markdowns in the application of the retail method on December 31, Year 1.

Data for illustration of retail method

	Cost	*Retail**
Beginning inventories	$15,810	$ 27,000
Net purchases	75,190	110,000
Additional markups		5,000
Markup cancellations		(2,000)
Markdowns		(10,875)

Markdown cancellations	875
Net sales	(90,000)
Ending inventories, at retail	$ 40,000

*All amounts other than net sales are taken from separate records.

The inventories at ***average cost*** for Elmo Corporation on December 31, Year 1, are estimated by the retail method as follows:

Net markups and net markdowns are used to compute cost percentage for estimation of ending inventories at average cost

ELMO CORPORATION
Estimate of Inventories by Retail Method — Valuation at Average Cost
December 31, Year 1

		Cost	*Retail*
Beginning inventories		$15,810	$ 27,000
Net purchases		75,190	110,000
Net markups ($5,000 – $2,000)			3,000
Less: Net markdowns ($10,875 – $875)			(10,000)
Goods available for sale		$91,000	$130,000
Cost percentage ($91,000 ÷ $130,000)	70%		
Less: Net sales			(90,000)
Ending inventories, at retail			$ 40,000
Estimated ending inventories, at average cost ($40,000 × 0.70)		$28,000	

The cost percentage of 70% is determined after net markups are added to, and net markdowns are deducted from, the goods available for sale at retail prices. This procedure results in estimating the ending inventories at ***average cost***. The estimated cost of $28,000 for the ending inventories is accurate only if the goods on hand consist of a representative sample of all goods available for sale during Year 1. For example, if the ending inventories do not include any goods that were on hand on January 1, Year 1, the cost percentage should be computed without use of the beginning inventories amounts. Similarly, if all goods on which the net markups and net markdowns were made have been sold, both the net markups and the net markdowns should be excluded from the computation of the cost percentage. Under such circumstances, however, the net markups and net markdowns still are used to compute the ending inventories at retail prices.

Retail Method — Valuation at Lower of Average Cost and Market

The retail method may be adapted to produce inventory valuations approximating the lower of average cost and market when there have been changes in the costs and selling prices of goods during the accounting period. The crucial factor in the estimate of cost of the ending inventory by the retail method is the treatment of net markups and net markdowns in the computation of the cost percentage. The ***inclusion of net markups*** and the ***exclusion of net markdowns*** in the computation of the cost percentage produce an inventory valued at the ***lower of average cost and market***. This is sometimes called the ***conventional retail method*** and is illustrated for Elmo Corporation below.

Net markdowns are not used to compute cost percentage for estimation of ending inventories at lower of average cost and market

ELMO CORPORATION
Estimate of Inventories by Retail Method—Valuation at Lower of Average Cost and Market
December 31, Year 1

		Cost	*Retail*
Beginning inventories		$15,810	$ 27,000
Net purchases		75,190	110,000
Net markups ($5,000 − $2,000)			3,000
Goods available for sale		$91,000	$140,000
Cost percentage ($91,000 ÷ $140,000)	65%		
Less: Net sales			(90,000)
Net markdowns ($10,875 − $875)			(10,000)
Ending inventories, at retail			$ 40,000
Estimated ending inventories, at lower of average cost and market ($40,000 × 0.65)		$26,000	

Net markups and net markdowns change the relationship between the retail price and the cost for goods available for sale, and thus affect the estimate of the ending inventories and the cost of goods sold computed by the retail method.

In the illustration above, the cost percentage is 65%, and the estimate of the ending inventories at ***lower of average cost and market*** is $26,000. When both the net markups and the net markdowns were used in the computation of the cost percentage, the percentage was 70%, and the estimate of the ending inventories at ***average cost*** was $28,000. The inclusion of net markups in the computation of the cost percentage assumes that the net markups apply proportionately to items sold and to items on hand at the end of the accounting period; however, net markdowns are assumed to apply only to the goods sold. Because the retail price of goods to which the markdowns apply is less than the original retail price, the net markdowns as well as sales must be deducted from goods available for sale at retail price to determine the inventories at retail price. If these assumptions are correct, the exclusion of net markdowns in the computation of the cost percentage values the ending inventories at actual average cost. However, if the net markdowns apply both to goods sold and to goods on hand, the exclusion of net markdowns from the computation of the cost percentage results in an inventory valuation at the ***lower of average cost and market***.

As stated previously, the retail method is based on an assumption that the ending inventories are composed of the same mix of items as the total pool of goods from which sales were made. If there are markdowns for special sale promotions, this assumption implicit in the retail method may not be valid. Some markdowns may apply to goods available for sale and to goods in ending inventories in equal proportions, but others may apply only to goods that have been sold. In essence, we are saying that there are really two lines of merchandise, ''special sale'' items and regular items, on which the markups are different.

The two lines may not be held in equal proportions in the goods available and in the ending inventories. Attempts to handle the two lines in one computation are likely to prove inadequate as a means of estimating meaningful inventory cost amounts.

Retail Method — Valuation at Last-In, First-Out

The preceding discussion illustrated two variations of the retail method that produce inventory estimates at ***average cost*** and at the ***lower of average cost and market***. If the last-in, first-out method is used to estimate the cost of inventories, the conventional retail method must be modified.[2] The retail method may be adapted to approximate lifo cost of the ending inventories by the computation of a cost percentage for purchases of the current accounting period only. The objective is to estimate the cost of ***any increase*** (lifo layer) in inventories during the accounting period.

Because lifo is a cost (not lower-of-cost-and-market) method of inventory valuation, both net markups and net markdowns are included in the computation of the cost percentage for purchases of the current period, in accordance with the discussion of the average-cost procedure earlier.

The modification of the retail method necessary to value inventory at lifo cost is shown below for Elmo Corporation (using the same data as in previous illustrations). For purposes of this illustration, assume that selling prices have remained unchanged and that net markups and net markdowns ***apply only to the goods purchased during Year 1***.

Exclude beginning inventories from computation of the cost percentage when retail lifo method is used

ELMO CORPORATION
Estimate of Inventories by Retail Method — Valuation at Lifo Cost
December 31, Year 1

		Cost	*Retail*
Beginning inventories		$15,810	$ 27,000
Net purchases		75,190	110,000
Net markups ($5,000 − $2,000)			3,000
Less: Net markdowns ($10,875 − $875)			(10,000)
Goods available for sale, at retail			$130,000
Less: Net sales			90,000
Ending inventories, at retail			$ 40,000
Cost percentage for net purchases, including net markups and net markdowns ($75,190 ÷ $103,000*)	73%		
Ending inventories, at lifo cost:			
Beginning inventories layer		$15,810	$ 27,000
Add: Layer added in Year 1 ($13,000 × 0.73)		9,490	13,000
Ending inventories, at retail			$ 40,000
Estimated ending inventories, at lifo cost		$25,300	

*$110,000 + $3,000 − $10,000 = $103,000.

2 As pointed out in Chapter 8, the lifo method is not allowed for income tax purposes in Canada.

The inventories on December 31, Year 1, are composed of the cost of the beginning inventories plus the estimated cost of the layer added during Year 1. If in Year 2 the inventories decreased, the decrease would be taken from the layer added in Year 1, \$9,490, and then from the layer on hand at the beginning of Year 1, \$15,810. For example, if the ending inventories for Elmo Corporation totalled \$30,000 at retail prices (a decrease of \$10,000 during Year 2) on December 31, Year 2, the inventories at lifo cost would be computed as illustrated below:

Note the cost of layer added in previous year

	Cost	*Retail*
Inventories, Dec. 31, year 2, at lifo cost:		
Inventory layer, Jan. 1, Year 1	\$15,810	\$27,000
Layer added in Year 1 (\$3,000 × 0.73)	2,190	3,000
Ending inventories, at retail		\$30,000
Estimated ending inventories, Dec. 31, Year 2, at lifo cost	\$18,000	

Under retail lifo procedures, computation of a cost percentage for current year's purchases is required ***only when an increase in inventories (at retail) occurs during the current year***. The cost percentage is computed for the sole purpose of pricing the incremental layer in inventories. In contrast, if a decrease (lifo liquidation) in inventories takes place, the ending inventories consist of a fraction of the beginning inventories cost. For example, if the ending inventories at retail for Elmo Corporation on December 31, Year 2, amounted to only \$13,500, or one-half of the layer on January 1, Year 1, the estimated inventories at lifo cost would be determined on December 31, Year 2, as follows:

Inventories consist of one-half of prior year's beginning inventories

$$\$15{,}810 \times \frac{\$13{,}500}{\$27{,}000} = \underline{\underline{\$7{,}905}}$$

Retail Method — Valuation at First-In, First-Out

The cost of the inventories on a first-in, first-out basis may be estimated from the data used to determine the lifo cost. For example, the estimated cost of the inventories on December 31, Year 1, for Elmo Corporation on the first-in, first-out basis would be \$29,200 (\$40,000 × 0.73, the cost percentage applicable to Year 1 purchases). If the cost percentage for the following year (Year 2) was 68% and the inventories at retail amounted to \$30,000, the estimated inventories fifo cost would be \$20,400 (\$30,000 × 0.68 = \$20,400).

Changes in Price Levels and the Retail Lifo Method

Let us now remove the simplifying assumption of the stability of selling prices. In reality, retail prices do change from one accounting period to another, and this is particularly significant for pricing inventories at retail lifo. Because the procedure employed under these circumstances is similar to that used in conjunction with dollar-value lifo described in Chapter 8, it is known as the ***dollar-value retail lifo method***. The ending inventories at retail prices must be converted to beginning-of-year prices to ascertain the increase in the inventories at beginning-of-year prices. An appropriate cost index must be used to convert from end-of-year prices to beginning-of-year prices.

The procedure for estimating the cost of the ending inventories under the dollar-value retail lifo method and assuming increasing selling prices, is shown below for Todd Limited. The sales price index at the beginning of Year 5, ***when lifo was adopted***, is assumed to be 100, and the index at the end of Year 5 is assumed to be 110, an increase of 10%.[3] In order not to complicate the example, we assume that there were no net markups or net markdowns in Year 5.

Dollar-value retail lifo method when prices are rising

TODD LIMITED
Dollar-Value Retail Lifo Method
December 31, Year 5

	Cost	*Retail*
Inventories, Jan. 1, Year 5 (date lifo was adopted)	$18,000	$ 30,000
Purchases during Year 5 (cost percentage is 65%)	65,000	100,000
Goods available for sale during Year 5, at retail prices		$130,000
Less: Net sales during the period		75,000
Inventories, Dec. 31, Year 5, at retail prices		$ 55,000
Computation of increase in inventories, at end-of-year retail prices:		
Inventories, Dec. 31, Year 5, at beginning-of-year retail prices ($55,000 ÷ 1.10)		$ 50,000
Less: Inventories, Jan. 1, Year 5 at retail prices		30,000
Increase in inventories, at beginning-of-year retail prices		$ 20,000
Increase in inventories, at end-of-year retail prices ($20,000 × 1.10)		$ 22,000
Ending inventories, at dollar-value retail lifo cost:		
Beginning inventories layer	$18,000	
Add: Layer added in Year 5 ($22,000 × 0.65)	14,300	
Estimated ending inventories, at dollar-value retail lifo cost	$32,300[4]	

3 When the base period index is other than 100, the percentage increase is determined by dividing the index at the end of the current period by the base-period index and subtracting 100. For example, if the base-period index is 125 and the index at the end of the current period is 150, the increase would be 20% [(150 ÷ 125) − 1.00 = 0.20].

4 Failure to recognize the increase in the price level would result in an erroneous ending inventory cost of $34,250, as illustrated below:

	Lifo cost	*Selling price*
Beginning inventories layer	$18,000	$30,000
Incremental layer [lifo cost = ($55,000 − $30,000) × 0.65]	16,250	25,000
Estimated ending inventories	$34,250	$55,000

GROSS PROFIT METHOD

The gross profit method is useful for several purposes: (1) to control and verify the validity of inventory cost; (2) to estimate interim inventory valuations between physical counts; and (3) to estimate the inventory cost when necessary information normally used is lost or unavailable. The procedure involved is one of reducing sales to a cost basis; that is, cost of goods sold is estimated. The estimated cost of goods sold then is subtracted from the cost of goods available for sale to compute the estimated cost of the ending inventories.

In the event that both merchandise and inventory records are destroyed by fire, the inventory cost may be estimated by use of the gross profit method. The gross profit and cost of goods sold percentages are obtained from prior years' financial statements, which presumably are available. The beginning inventories amount for the current year is the ending inventories amount of the preceding year. Net purchases are estimated from copies of the paid cheques returned by the bank and through correspondence with suppliers. Sales are computed by reference to cash deposits and by an estimate of the outstanding accounts receivable through correspondence with customers.

Gross Profit Method Is Really a "Cost Percentage" Method

The key step in the application of the gross profit method is the development of an accurate ***cost percentage***, obtained by deduction of the gross profit rate from 100%. Frequently the best available measure is an average of the cost percentages for recent years, adjusted for any changes in costs and selling prices that have taken place in the current year.

To illustrate the computation of the cost of inventories by the gross profit method, assume the following data for Dubin Corporation for Year 4:

Cost percentage of 80% means that gross profit is 20%

Beginning inventories, at cost	$ 40,000
Net purchases	200,000
Net sales	225,000
Average cost percentage for past three years	80%

Assuming that the cost percentage for Year 4 remained at 80%, the cost of the inventories on December 31, Year 4, is estimated as follows:

The key step in the gross profit method is the estimate of cost of goods sold

DUBIN CORPORATION
Estimate of Cost of Inventories by Gross Profit Method
December 31, Year 4

Beginning inventories, at cost		$ 40,000
Add: Net purchases		200,000
Cost of goods available for sale		$240,000
Less: Estimated cost of goods sold:		
Net sales	$225,000	
Cost percentage	0.80	180,000
Estimated ending inventories, at cost		$ 60,000

The cost of the ending inventories estimated by the gross profit method is reasonably consistent with the usual method of valuing inventories. This follows from the fact that the gross profit percentage is based on historical records that reflect the particular method of valuing the inventories. If the inventories are valued at lifo, the estimated inventories will approximate lifo cost; therefore, if the gross profit method is used as a basis for recovering an insured fire loss, the inventories should be restated for insurance purposes to current fair value at the time of the fire.

Sometimes the gross profit percentage is stated as a percentage of cost. In such situations the gross profit percentage must be restated to a percentage of net sales to compute the cost percentage (based on net sales) for the period. For example, if the gross profit is stated as 25% of cost, the gross profit percentage may be restated to 20% of net sales as follows:

Restatement of gross profit percentage based on cost to percentage based on net sales

1 25% = ¼ gross profit based on cost
2 Add numerator of fraction to denominator to make ⅕
3 ⅕ = 20% gross profit based on net sales

When 20% is subtracted from 100%, we have the cost percentage of 80% of net sales. Alternatively, the cost percentage based on net sales may be determined directly as follows:

Direct computation of cost percentage

Let X = cost as percentage of net sales
$0.25X$ = gross profit percentage (based on cost)
Then $X + 0.25X$ = 100% of net sales
$1.25X = 100\%$

$$X = \frac{100\%}{1.25}$$

X = 80% (cost percentage based on net sales)

Applying the Gross Profit Method to Departments

If there are several classes of merchandise that have different markup percentages, the gross profit method yields accurate results only if the inventory for each class of merchandise is computed individually. The use of a combined cost percentage would require the unlikely assumption that the various classes of merchandise are sold in the same relative proportions each year. To illustrate this point, assume that the gross profit percentages for Dawson Company have averaged 50% for Department A and 30% for Department B in recent years. Thus, the cost percentage is 50% for Department A and 70% for Department B; the combined cost percentage has averaged 65% in recent years. The cost of the combined

Use of recent years' combined cost percentage does not work in this example

DAWSON COMPANY
Estimate of Cost of Departmental and Combined Inventories by Gross Profit Method
For Year 8

	Dept. A	*Dept. B*	*Combined*
Beginning inventories, at cost	$ 20,000	$ 40,000	$ 60,000
Net purchases	90,000	95,000	185,000
Cost of goods available for sale	$110,000	$135,000	$245,000
Less: Estimated cost of goods sold:			
Net sales	$150,000	$150,000	$300,000
Average cost percentage, ***prior years***	0.50	0.70	0.65
Estimated cost of goods sold	$ 75,000	$105,000	$195,000
Estimated ending inventories, at cost	$ 35,000	$ 30,000	$ 50,000

ending inventories for Year 8 may be estimated as shown above.

Use of the combined cost percentage (based on prior years' experience) produces an inventories estimate of $50,000, although the sum of the two departmental ending inventories is estimated at $65,000 ($35,000 + $30,000 = $65,000). The source of the error is clear when we note that the cost percentage for Year 8, determined by combining the departmental results, is not 65% but 60%, because a higher-than-usual proportion of total sales in Year 8 was made by Department A, which has a lower cost percentage. The ***actual*** combined cost percentage (60%) for Year 8 is determined below:

Actual combined cost percentage is 60%, not 65%

Total sales ($150,000 + $150,000)	$300,000
Total estimated cost of goods sold ($75,000 + $105,000)	$180,000
Combined cost percentage for Year 8 ($180,000 ÷ $300,000)	60%

If the combined Year 8 cost percentage of 60% is used, the aggregate ending inventories would be computed correctly at $65,000 ($245,000 – $180,000 = $65,000). Stated simply, separate departmental cost percentages should be used to estimate the cost of inventories by the gross profit method when the cost percentages differ materially among departments.

Gross Profit Method for Interim Reports

The gross profit method frequently is used in the preparation of interim reports. It should be clear that the use of the gross profit method results in an ***estimated cost*** of inventories. If the reporting enterprise normally values inventories at lower of cost and market for annual reporting purposes, it must follow the same procedure for interim reporting purposes. Thus, the estimated cost obtained by use of the gross profit method must be compared with market—which usually is either net realizable value or current replacement costs—to determine whether a write-down to a lower "market" is required.

The *CICA Handbook* suggests that it is preferable to use the same method to determine inventory for both the annual and interim financial reports and to disclose any changes from the inventory-valuation method used in previous annual or interim financial reports.[5]

> It is preferable that the determination of interim inventory be on the same basis as annual inventory. Procedures would have to be applied to give the best possible estimate of the figure which would be produced if all the normal inventory procedures had been carried out. In developing an inventory figure for interim financial reports, consideration should be given to declines which may have occurred in market or replacement value of stock on hand, obsolescence, shrinkages due to theft and unreported wastage, and the existence of quantities in excess of probable requirements. Temporary encroachments of base quantities of inventories maintained on a LIFO or base stock method should be taken into account. In industries where the retail inventory or ***gross profit*** methods are appropriate, these methods could be used.
>
> Interim financial reports ... are usually subordinate to annual financial statements, and the only necessary disclosure of accounting policies in interim financial reports would be any ***changes*** for those followed in either the previously issued annual statements or, if applicable, interim financial reports.

In the United States, the gross profit method may be used for interim financial reports even though annual inventories are determined by use of one of the cost flow assumptions described in Chapter 8. Enterprises that use the gross profit method for interim purposes "should disclose the method used ... and any significant adjustments that result from reconciliations with the annual physical inventory."[6]

OTHER VALUATION METHODS

Valuation of Inventories at Replacement Costs

The valuation of inventories at replacement costs has been advocated by accountants who believe that the current asset section of the balance sheet should reflect current fair values. The cost methods of inventory frequently understate the value of inventories, particularly during periods of rising prices. The significance of replacement costs as a measure of inventory value varies considerably depending on the type of inventories involved. In the retail market, the selling prices of staple commodities, such as sugar, copper, cotton, etc., tend to follow cost prices closely. In such situations, replacement costs of inventories are important to management and outsiders.

Replacement-cost valuation of inventories in the preparation of financial statements is not generally accepted. Perhaps the closest practical approach is the first-in, first-out method. Unless prices are rising rapidly, the fifo method of

5 CICA, ***CICA Handbook*** (Toronto), secs. 1750.23 and 1505.05 respectively, emphasis added.

6 AICPA, ***APB Opinion No. 28***: "Interim Financial Reporting" (New York: 1973), p. 524.

pricing presents inventories in the balance sheet at or near current replacement costs without a departure from the cost principle. The need for disclosure of replacement or current costs of inventories arises when the last-in, first-out method is used for pricing inventories.

The theoretical objection to the use of replacement costs as a method of inventory is implicit in the arguments previously presented. Some of the advantages of inventory valuation at replacement costs may be achieved by disclosure of current replacement costs of inventories in a note to the financial statements. Some accountants have argued for the adoption of replacement costs as a means of pricing inventories whether replacement costs are more than actual costs or less. They base their argument on the fact that the economic utility of inventories is indicated by the current costs of replacement. A valid point made by proponents of replacement costs is that if replacement costs are objective and more useful when they are lower than actual costs, they also possess those attributes when they are higher than actual costs.

The consistent use of replacement costs for the valuation of inventories would require some broadening of the revenue realization principle as presently applied. Under generally accepted accounting principles, revenue emerges at the time inventories are sold and converted to accounts receivable (or cash), as indicated in the following diagram:

Revenue is realized when inventories are sold

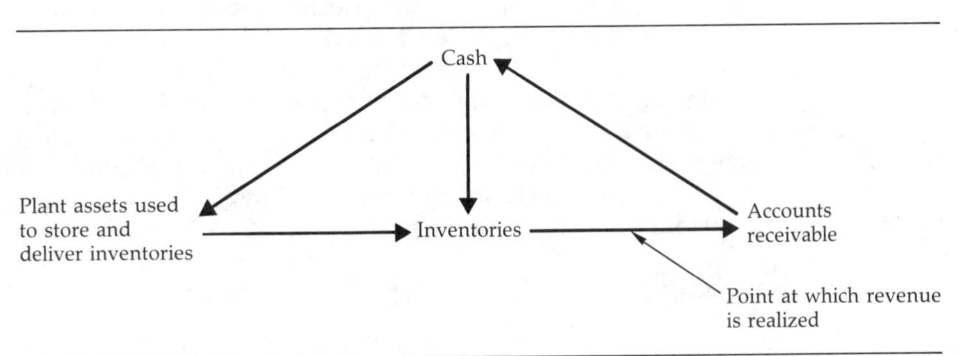

If replacement costs were adopted for inventory valuation, ***holding gains and losses*** represented by the difference between actual costs and replacement costs would be recognized and included in income prior to the sale of finished products. The information resulting from such a procedure would be useful in accounting periods when prices were changing significantly. The real issue is whether replacement costs can be determined with sufficient objectivity to provide a reliable basis for financial accounting. At present, valuation of inventories at replacement costs that are ***higher*** than actual costs is not acceptable.

In December, 1982, the Accounting Standards Committee issued ***CICA Handbook*** section 4510: "Reporting the Effects of Changing Prices." This section recommends that large publicly held enterprises should present their inventories at current cost (replacement or reproduction cost) as supplementary information to the annual financial statements. This subject is covered in Chapter 25.

Valuation of Inventories at Net Selling Prices

The valuation of inventories at ***net selling prices*** (sales prices less direct costs of completion and disposal) has some appeal, especially when one considers that economic value is added as the goods are brought to market. For example, in a retail store, goods are more valuable than they were at the wholesaler's warehouse; value is added by the process of bringing the goods nearer the ultimate market. In a manufacturing enterprise, costs are blended together, and a product emerges that is more valuable than the sum of the production costs. However, this method of inventory valuation has not been widely adopted for two reasons: (1) the lack of objectivity in determining the net selling price, and (2) the fact that the selling price has not been realized in cash or cash equivalents. Accountants generally consider revenue to be realized at the time of sale of goods, not at the time of production.

The valuation of inventories at net selling prices is appropriate for some types of business enterprises producing commodities that have readily determinable market prices. When the production of such commodities is complete, revenue may be considered realized. In some enterprises having selling prices established by contract, the sale is reasonably assured, and completed inventories may be valued at net selling prices.

The use of net selling prices to value inventories moves the point of revenue realization back one step in the earning process. As costs are incurred during the process of bringing an item to market, income is earned in the most fundamental sense. Each activity necessary to advance the goods closer to the customer and ultimately to close the sale transaction adds an element of income — the increase in selling price over the added cost. Therefore, if there are costs still to be incurred, there is still an element of income to be earned. The valuation of inventories at net selling prices means that a portion of income may be prematurely recognized before it is realized through sale.

Supplies and Short-Term Prepayments

In addition to inventories of merchandise, finished goods, material, parts, and goods in process, a business enterprise may have several types of supplies on hand. For example, inventories of supplies may include office supplies, promotional materials, shipping supplies, and factory supplies. The problems of determining cost and valuation of supplies are similar to those for inventories discussed in Chapter 8. Supplies are acquired for use in operations, and any quantities remaining on hand at the end of an accounting period are included in the current assets section of the balance sheet.

The term ***prepaid expenses*** is widely used to describe unexpired costs that are expected to be consumed within a relatively short period of time. However, this term is somewhat of a misnomer and should be replaced by a more descriptive title such as ***short-term prepayments***. Prepaid expenses are costs of goods and services that have not been consumed in the revenue-earning process. Strictly speaking, both depreciable plant assets and inventories fall within this definition. Plant assets are classified separately because they provide services over long time periods; inventories require separate disclosure because of their materiality and importance. There is a presumption that short-term prepayments will be consumed within one year or within the business enterprise's next operating cycle, and for this reason they are included in the current assets section of the balance sheet.

ACCOUNTING FOR CONSTRUCTION-TYPE CONTRACTS

Contracts for construction of buildings, roads, bridges, dams, and similar projects often require more than one year to complete. Such contracts present special problems of asset valuation and revenue recognition. There are four basic types of construction contracts:[7]

1 ***Fixed-price*** (or ***lump-sum***) ***contracts***, which provide for a single price for all work performed by the contractor

2 ***Unit-price contracts***, which include a fixed price for each unit of output under the contract

3 ***Cost-type contracts***, which provide for reimbursement of specified costs incurred by the contractor plus a fee for the contractor's services

4 ***Time-and-material contracts***, which provide for a fixed hourly rate for the contractor's direct labour hours, plus payment for cost of material and other specified items

Methods of Accounting for Construction-Type Contracts

As stated in Chapter 3, the two methods of accounting for construction-type contracts are the percentage-of-completion method and the completed-contract method. The two methods are not free-choice alternatives for the same circumstances.[8]

Most contractors employ the ***percentage-of-completion method*** of accounting for financial accounting.[9] This method requires the accrual of gross profit and revenue over the term of the contract to be based on the progress achieved each year. If the work performed in a year is estimated to represent 40% of the total work required on the contract, 40% of the total estimated gross profit and revenue is considered realized. Estimates of work performed on a contract during a year may be based on one of the following input or output measures:[10]

1 Input measures

a Costs incurred to date as a percentage of the total estimated cost (***cost-to-cost method***)

7 AICPA, ***Audit and Accounting Guide***: "Construction Contractors" (New York: 1981), p. 4.

8 FASB, ***FASB Statement No. 56***: "Designation of AICPA Guide . . . on Contractor Accounting . . . as Preferable . . ." (Stamford: 1982), p. 2. There is no comparable pronouncement in Canada.

9 According to the CICA's ***Financial Reporting in Canada***, 16th ed., p. 108, of the 30 companies reporting construction contracts, 22 used the percentage-of-completion method, 5 used the completed-contract method, and 3 used both methods.

10 AICPA, ***Audit and Accounting Guide***: "Construction Contractors," pp. 129–130.

b Labour hours, labour dollars, machine hours, or material quantities incurred to date as a percentage of the related estimated totals (***efforts-expended methods***)

2 Output measures

a Units produced, units delivered, or contract milestones (such as completion of the foundation of a building) completed to date as a percentage of the related estimated totals (***units-of-work-performed methods***)

b Value added to the project to date as a percentage of estimated total value of the completed project (***value-added method***)

Physical inspection of the project may be required to substantiate the percentage of completion estimated by one of the foregoing methods.

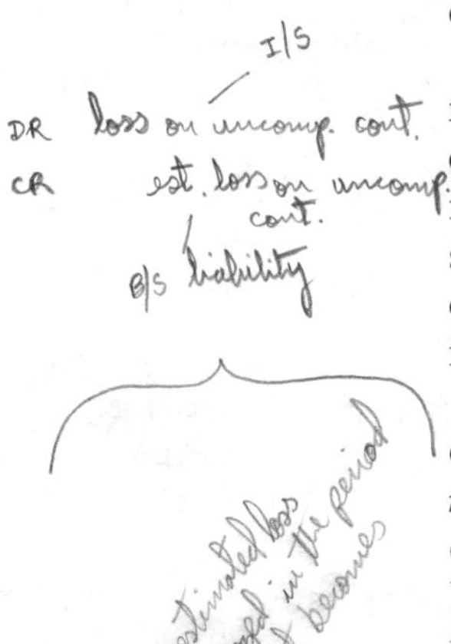

Under the ***completed-contract method*** of accounting, no gross profit is recognized for a construction project until it is ***substantially completed***; that is, when remaining costs and potential risks are insignificant in amount.[11] The completed-contract method is appropriate for financial accounting only if a contractor has primarily short-term contracts that are completed in a year or less or if estimates of input or output measures of completion are not reasonably dependable or are subject to inherent hazards such as those described on page 434.[12]

Under both the percentage-of-completion and the completed-contract methods of accounting, an estimated loss under a construction-type contract should be ***recognized in full in the accounting period in which it becomes apparent***, with a debit to Provision for Loss on Uncompleted Contracts and a credit to Estimated Loss on Uncompleted Contracts. The provision (debit-balance account) is included in the income statement as an element of cost of realized contract revenue, and the estimated loss (credit-balance account) is presented in the balance sheet as a liability or as a deduction from the cost of contracts in progress.

Accounting for a Construction-Type Contract: Profit Anticipated

To illustrate the accounting for a construction-type contract, assume that a small bridge is to be constructed by Cabot Construction Limited beginning in Year 1 at a fixed price of $900,000, with estimated construction costs totalling $750,000. The bridge is expected to be completed in Year 3. The construction costs incurred, cost estimates, and other data are presented below in summary form for each year of the three-year period:

Data for illustration

	Year 1	*Year 2*	*Year 3*
Construction costs incurred	$125,000	$495,000	$145,000
Estimated cost to complete the bridge	625,000	155,000	-0-
Progress billings to customer	110,000	565,000	225,000
Collections from customer on billings	90,000	520,000	265,000
Operating expenses incurred (selling, general, and administrative)	15,000	30,000	22,500

11 AICPA, ***Audit and Accounting Guide***: "Construction Contractors," p. 132.

12 AICPA, ***Audit and Accounting Guide***: "Construction Contractors," p. 21.

We illustrate the ***cost-to-cost method*** of estimating the percentage of completion of the bridge construction; other techniques for estimating work performed are similar in their application.

Percentage-of-Completion Method

If Cabot Construction Limited determines the estimated percentage of completion of the bridge by the cost-to-cost method, the percentages and the related contract revenue, cost of contract revenue, and gross profit are computed as follows:

Computations under percentage-of-completion method

CABOT CONSTRUCTION LIMITED
Computation of Contract Revenue, Cost of Contract Revenue, and Gross Profit:
Percentage-of-Completion Method
For Years 1, 2, and 3

	Year 1	*Year 2*	*Year 3*
Total estimated revenue (fixed price)	$900,000	$900,000	$900,000
Total construction costs incurred to date (*a*)	$125,000	$620,000	$765,000
Estimated cost to complete	625,000	155,000	0
Total estimated or actual cost (*b*)	$750,000	$775,000	$765,000
Total estimated or actual gross profit	$150,000	$125,000	$135,000
Percentage of completion (cost-to-cost method) [(*a*) ÷ (*b*)]	16⅔%	80%	100%
Contract revenue:			
Year 1 ($900,000 × 0.16⅔)	$150,000		
Year 2 [($900,000 × 0.80) – $150,000]		$570,000	
Year 3 [$900,000 – ($150,000 + $570,000)]			$180,000
Cost of contract revenue:			
Year 1 ($750,000 × 0.16⅔)	125,000		
Year 2 [($775,000 × 0.80) – $125,000]		495,000	
Year 3 [$765,000 – ($125,000 + $495,000)]			145,000
Gross profit for year	$ 25,000	$ 75,000	$ 35,000

Note that the computation of the cost of contract revenue for each year produces an amount equal to the actual construction costs incurred for that year (see data for illustration on page 428). This equality always results from the use of the cost-to-cost method of estimating the percentage of completion, but not from one of the other methods described on pages 427–428.

The journal entries for Cabot Construction for each year of the construction project under the ***percentage-of-completion method*** are shown on page 430.

Comments on these journal entries (identified by numbers) follow:

1 The Cost of Contracts in Progress ledger account is similar to the Goods in Process inventory account of a manufacturing enterprise. In the Cost of Contracts in Progress account are recorded the material, direct labour, and overhead costs incurred by the contractor, as well as costs associated with work performed by ***subcontractors.*** (like WIP account)

2 The Progress Billings ledger account ***is not a revenue account,*** despite its being associated with entries to the Contract Receivable or Accounts Receivable account.

Illustrative journal entries under percentage-of-completion method

CABOT CONSTRUCTION LIMITED
Journal Entries: Percentage-of-Completion Method

Accounts and explanations of transactions	*Year 1*		*Year 2*		*Year 3*	
	Debit	*Credit*	*Debit*	*Credit*	*Debit*	*Credit*
1 Operating Expenses	15,000		30,000		22,500	
Cost of Contracts in Progress	125,000		495,000		145,000	
Material Inventory, Cash, etc.		140,000		525,000		167,500
To record operating expenses and construction costs.						
2 Contract Receivable	110,000		565,000		225,000	
Progress Billings		110,000		565,000		225,000
To record billings on contract.						
3 Cash	90,000		520,000		265,000	
Contract Receivable		90,000		520,000		265,000
To record collections from customer.						
4 Cost of Contract Revenue	125,000		495,000		145,000	
Estimated Earnings on Contracts in Progress	25,000		75,000		35,000	
Contract Revenue		150,000		570,000		180,000
To record contract revenue estimated on the basis of cost incurred to total estimated cost. (See computations on p. 429.)						
5 Progress Billings					900,000	
Cost of Contracts in Progress						765,000
Estimated Earnings on Contracts in Progress						135,000
To record approval of project by customer.						

Progress billings to the customer are a means of financing (together with bank loans) for a contractor; the timing of progress billings is provided in the construction contract and may or may not bear a direct relationship to the percentage of completion of the project. Note, for example, that the $110,000 of Cabot Construction's progress billings in Year 1 represent approximately 12% of the total contract price ($110,000 ÷ $900,000 = 12.22%); compare this with the 16⅔% computation of the percentage of completion for Year 1 (see illustration on page 429).

Thus, the Progress Billings ledger account is a contra to the Cost of Contracts in Progress and the Estimated Earnings on Contracts in Progress ledger accounts. In essence, the balance of the Progress Billings ledger account on any date prior to completion of the construction project represents the ***customer's equity interest*** in the project.

3 The collections from customer, recorded by a credit to Contract Receivable, require no additional comments.

4 As indicated on page 429, when the cost-to-cost method is used to estimate the percentage of completion of a construction-type contract, the cost of contract revenue for an accounting period is identical to the total construction costs incurred in that period. Thus, the debits to the Cost of Contract Revenue account are the same as the debits to the Cost of Contracts in Progress account in journal entries in part 1 of the illustration. However, the Cost of Contract Revenue account, being similar to cost of goods sold of a manufacturing enterprise, appears in the income statement of the contractor and is closed at the end of each accounting period.

The Estimated Earnings on Contracts in Progress ledger account is a ***positive valuation account*** for the Cost of Contracts in Progress account. The use of a separate account for the accrual of earnings on a contract under the percentage-of-completion method preserves the record of actual costs incurred on the contract in the Costs of Contracts in Progress account and still achieves the goal of increasing the carrying amount of the contracts in progress asset.

The Contract Revenue ledger account is similar to the Sales account of a manufacturing enterprise. The total of the credits to this account during the term of the construction contract is equal to the total contract price.

5 When the construction project has been completed and approved by the customer, the asset and contra-asset amounts related to the project are removed from the related ledger accounts. No revenue or expenses are recognized by this journal entry because the total revenue and costs applicable to the contract were included in the journal entries in part 4 of the illustration.

The presentation of contract revenue and cost of contract revenue in the income statement is illustrated below for Cabot Construction Limited under the ***percentage-of-completion*** method:

Presentation in income statements: percentage-of-completion method

	Year 1	*Year 2*	*Year 3*
Contract revenue	$150,000	$570,000	$180,000
Less: Cost of contract revenue	125,000	495,000	145,000
Gross profit	$ 25,000	$ 75,000	$ 35,000

The balance sheets for Cabot Construction Limited include the amounts shown on the next page when the ***percentage-of-completion method*** is used.

If on the date of a balance sheet the balance of the Progress Billings contra-asset ledger account exceeds the total of the balances of the Cost of Contracts in Progress and Estimated Earnings on Contracts in Progress accounts, the excess is included

Presentation in balance sheets: percentage-of-completion method

	End of Year 1	*End of Year 2*	*End of Year 3*
Current assets:			
Contract receivables	$ 20,000	$ 65,000	$ 25,000
Costs and estimated earnings in excess of billings on uncompleted contract (NOTE)	40,000	45,000	

NOTE: Costs, estimated earnings, and billings on uncompleted contracts:

	End of Year 1	*End of Year 2*
Costs incurred on uncompleted contract	$125,000	$620,000
Estimated earnings	25,000	100,000
Subtotal	$150,000	$720,000
Less: Billings to date	110,000	675,000
Costs and estimated earnings in excess of billings on uncompleted contract	$ 40,000	$ 45,000

in current liabilities in the contractor's balance sheet. For example, suppose that the balance of Cabot Construction's Progress Billings ledger account had been $180,000 rather than $110,000, at the end of Year 1. The $30,000 excess ($180,000 – $150,000 = $30,000) of the contra-asset account over the total of the two asset accounts would be presented as follows in the current liabilities section of Cabot's end-of-Year-1 balance sheet:

Credit excess in balance sheet

Current liabilities:	
Billings in excess of costs and estimated earnings on uncompleted contract	$30,000

The billings in excess of costs and estimated earnings current liability of a contractor resembles the deferred revenue liability of a manufacturing enterprise that receives payments in advance for finished goods to be shipped subsequently to customers. Costs and estimated earnings in excess of billings and billings in excess of costs and estimated earnings are ***current*** assets and liabilities respectively, because the operating cycle of a contractor encompasses the total time required to complete construction contracts, even though that time exceeds one year.

Completed-Contract Method

Assuming that Cabot Construction Limited used the completed-contract method of accounting, rather than the percentage-of-completion method, for the small bridge construction project described on page 428, Cabot would record no gross profit on the project until Year 3, when the project was completed. The journal entries for Cabot to record the transactions related to the construction of the bridge under the ***completed-contract method*** are shown on page 433.

Assuming that the bridge construction contract was the only construction contract of Cabot Construction, its income statements for Year 1 and Year 2 would show pre-tax losses of $15,000 and $30,000 respectively, the amounts of operating expenses for those years. Cabot's income statement for Year 3 includes the following items under the ***completed-contract method***:

Presentation in the income statement for Year 3: completed-contract method

Contract revenue	$900,000
Less: Cost of contract completed	765,000
Gross profit	$135,000
Operating expenses	22,500
Income before income taxes	$112,500

The $135,000 gross profit recognized by Cabot in year 3 under the completed-contract method is equal to the total gross profit for Year 1, 2, and 3 under the percentage-of-completion income statements ($25,000 + $75,000 + $35,000 = $135,000).

Illustrative journal entries under completed-contract method

CABOT CONSTRUCTION LIMITED
Journal Entries: Completed-Contract Method

Accounts and explanations of transactions	*Year 1*		*Year 2*		*Year 3*	
	Debit	*Credit*	*Debit*	*Credit*	*Debit*	*Credit*
1 Operating Expenses	15,000		30,000		22,500	
Cost of Contracts in Progress	125,000		495,000		145,000	
Material Inventory, Cash, etc.		140,000		525,000		167,500
To record operating expenses and construction costs.						
2 Contract Receivable	110,000		565,000		225,000	
Progress Billings		110,000		565,000		225,000
To record billings on contract.						
3 Cash	90,000		520,000		265,000	
Contract Receivable		90,000		520,000		265,000
To record collections from customer.						
4 Progress Billings					900,000	
Cost of Contract Revenue					765,000	
Contract Revenue						900,000
Cost of Contracts in Progress						765,000
To record contract revenue and applicable construction costs on substantial completion of project.						

The balance sheets for Cabot Construction Limited include the amounts shown on the next page when the ***completed-contract*** method is used.

It is important to emphasize that, as pointed out on page 427, Cabot Construction does not have the ***option*** of using either the percentage-of-completion method or the completed-contract method of accounting for the bridge construction contract. Because the construction project extends over three years, Cabot may use the

Presentation in balance sheets: completed-contract method

	End of Year 1	End of Year 2	End of Year 3
Current assets:			
Contract receivables	$20,000	$65,000	$25,000
Costs in excess of billings on uncompleted contract (**NOTE**)	15,000		
Current liabilities:			
Billings in excess of costs on uncompleted contract (**NOTE**)		$55,000	

NOTE: Costs and billings on uncompleted contract:

	End of Year 1	End of Year 2
Costs incurred on uncompleted contract	$125,000	$620,000
Less: Billings to date	110,000	675,000
Costs in excess of billings (billings in excess of costs) on uncompleted contract	$ 15,000	$ (55,000)

completed-contract method only if estimates of measures of completion ***are not reasonably dependable or are subject to inherent hazards***. Estimates of costs are a critical part of the bidding and negotiating process for construction contracts; thus, situations in which estimates of completion under, for example, the cost-to-cost method would not be dependable are rare. With respect to inherent hazards, the AICPA in the United States has stated:[13]

> ... inherent hazards that make otherwise reasonably dependable contract estimates doubtful involve events and conditions that would not be considered in the ordinary preparation of contract estimates and that would not be expected to recur frequently, given the contractor's normal business environment.... Such hazards may relate, for example, to contracts whose validity is seriously in question (that is, which are less than fully enforceable), to contracts whose completion may be subject to the outcome of pending legislation or pending litigation, or to contracts exposed to the possibility of the condemnation or expropriation of the resulting properties.

Thus, the situations in which the completed-contract method of accounting is appropriate for construction-type contracts may be rare.

Accounting for a Construction-Type Contract: Loss Anticipated

We have indicated on page 428 that an anticipated loss on a construction-type contract should be recognized when it is identified, under both the percentage-of-completion and the completed-contract methods.

To illustrate, assume that City Contractors on January 2, Year 1, entered into a contract to construct a building on the customer's land at a fixed price of $1,000,000, with construction expected to be completed late in Year 2. In its bid on the project, City estimated total construction costs of $850,000, with an anticipated gross profit of $150,000. Construction costs incurred during Year 1 totalled $400,000;

13 AICPA, *Audit and Accounting Guide*: "Construction Contractors," p. 122.

estimated costs to complete on December 31, Year 1, totalled $640,000; and construction costs incurred during Year 2 totalled $650,000. Progress billings totalled $300,000 in Year 1 and $700,000 in Year 2. The building was completed on November 29, Year 2.

Under both the percentage-of-completion method and the completed-contract method of accounting, City Contractors would prepare the following journal entry on December 31, Year 1, to record the $40,000 estimated loss [($400,000 + $640,000) − $1,000,000 = $40,000] on the contract:

Journal entry to record estimated loss on contract

Provision for Loss on Uncompleted Contract	40,000	
Estimated Loss on Uncompleted Contracts		40,000
To provide for estimated loss on building contract.		

The income statement for Year 1 under the percentage-of-completion method would show contract revenue, $400,000 (the amount of the construction costs incurred in Year 1); cost of contract revenue, $440,000 ($400,000 construction costs incurred plus $40,000 provision for loss = $440,000); and a gross loss of $40,000 ($400,000 − $440,000 = $40,000). Only the $40,000 gross loss would appear in the income statement for Year 1 under the completed-contract method. An additional gross loss of $10,000 ($650,000 − $640,000 = $10,000) would appear in the income statement for Year 2 under both the percentage-of-completion method and the completed-contract method.

For the balance sheet for City Contractors on December 31, Year 1, the $400,000 balance of the Cost of Contracts in Progress ledger account would be reduced by the $40,000 balance of the Estimated Loss on Uncompleted Contracts account and the $300,000 balance of the Progress Billings account; the net amount of $60,000 ($400,000 − $40,000 − $300,000 = $60,000) would appear as ''costs in excess of billings on uncompleted contracts,'' under both the percentage-of-completion method and the completed-contract method of accounting.

Evaluation of Accounting for Construction-Type Contracts

Generally accepted accounting principles limit severely, and appropriately, the situations in which the completed-contract method of accounting may be used for construction-type contracts. The percentage-of-completion method is consistent with the accrual basis of accounting because it apportions total revenue under a construction-type contract to the accounting periods in which the construction activity took place. Although the percentage-of-completion method theoretically abandons the revenue realization principle, the abandonment is more conceptual than real. The customer under the construction contract realizes benefits throughout the course of construction; thus, for the contractor, the earning process may be considered to occur throughout the construction period, rather than solely when the project is substantially completed. In contrast, the purchaser of goods realizes no benefits from the goods before they are received; thus, recognition of revenue for sales of merchandise is appropriate when the goods are delivered. The only merit for the completed-contract method of accounting for a construction-type contract that extends over several accounting periods is the postponement of revenue recognition under conditions of substantial uncertainty, as described earlier.

Disclosures Regarding Construction-Type Contracts

Contractors should disclose the method of recognizing gross profit on construction-type contracts in the "Summary of Significant Accounting Policies" note to the financial statements.[14] In the United States, the Securities and Exchange Commission requires extensive disclosures regarding construction-type contracts extending over a period longer than twelve months. The SEC stated that such disclosure is necessary because long-term contracts involve inventories and receivables with ***unique risk and liquidity characteristics***. The disclosures required include the amount of inventoried costs, the nature of cost elements included in inventories, the amount of progress billings netted against inventories, and the principal assumptions used to determine total contract costs.[15]

REVIEW QUESTIONS

1 For what purposes may the ***retail method*** of inventory estimation be used?

2 **Differentiate between *a* *markup* and *additional markup* *b* *markup cancellation* and *markdown* *c* *markdown cancellation* and *additional markup*.**

3 Describe the computation of the cost percentage when inventories are valued at estimated average cost by the retail method.

4 Describe the computation of the cost percentage when inventories are valued at the estimated lower of average cost and market by the retail method.

5 What is the basic assumption as to the composition of the ending inventories when the retail method is applied on the basis of average cost or on the basis of the lower of average cost and market?

6 Describe the application of the retail method when cost is estimated on a last-in, first-out basis.

7 Describe the procedure required to estimate inventories on the ***retail lifo*** basis after retail prices have increased.

8 List three uses that may be made of the ***gross profit method*** of estimating inventories.

9 *a* Differentiate between gross profit as a percentage of net sales and as a percentage of cost.

b Convert the following gross profit percentages based on net sales to gross profit percentages based on cost: 16⅔%, 25%, 50%.

c Convert the following gross profit percentages based on cost to gross profit percentages based on net sales: 25%, 50%, and 150%.

10 Explain the possible limitations of the use of an average-cost percentage for prior years to estimate the cost of inventories by the gross profit method.

14 CICA, ***CICA Handbook***, sec. 1505.09–.10.

15 Securities and Exchange Commission, ***Regulation S-X*** (Washington: 1984), Rule 5-02-6 (d).

11 Under what conditions may inventories be valued at net selling prices? Explain.

12 Why are short-term prepayments included in the current assets section of the balance sheet?

13 Differentiate between ***fixed-price*** and ***unit-price*** construction-type contracts.

14 There are two methods of accounting for operations involving construction-type contracts. What are the two methods? What criteria are used in choosing between the methods? How do you justify a departure from the accepted practice of recognizing revenue only at the time of sale?

15 When a business enterprise adopts the percentage-of-completion method of accounting for construction-type contracts, there are several generally used methods of estimating the portion completed. What are three of these methods?

16 Under the percentage-of-completion method of accounting for construction-type contracts, anticipated profits are recorded only as the construction progresses, but anticipated losses are recorded in full as soon as they are ascertained. Why does this inconsistency exist?

EXERCISES

Ex. 9-1 Select the best answer for each of the following multiple-choice questions:

1 Under the retail method of estimating the cost of inventories, which of the following is included in the computation of goods available for sale at both cost and retail?

a Freight-in
b Purchases returns
c Net markups
d Net markdowns
e None of the foregoing

2 When a construction-type contract is expected to result in a loss, the loss is recorded as soon as it is determinable under:

a The completed-contract method only
b The percentage-of-completion method only
c Both the completed-contract method and the percentage-of-completion method
d Neither the completed-contract method nor the percentage-of-completion method

3 The completed-contract method of accounting for construction-type contracts is preferable when:

a A contractor is involved in numerous construction projects
b The contracts are of relatively long duration
c Estimates of costs to complete and extent of progress toward completion are reasonably dependable
d Lack of dependable estimates or inherent hazards cause forecasts to be doubtful

4 Included in the computation of the cost percentage for the lower-of-average-cost-and-market retail method of estimating cost of inventories are:
a Markups but not freight-in
b Net markdowns but not net markups
c Shrinkage but not purchases returns and allowances
d Net markups but not net markdowns

5 The gross profit method for estimating the cost of ending inventories is used for all the following except:
a Determination of end-of-year inventories under the periodic inventory system
b Control and verification of inventory cost
c Estimation of interim inventory valuations between physical counts
d Estimation of inventory valuation when necessary information normally used is lost or unavailable

6 The Progress Billings ledger account used in accounting for construction-type contracts is:
a An asset account
b A liability account
c A revenue account
d A contra-asset account
e A contra-liability account

7 The gross profit percentage for Rice Company has been 20% of cost for the past several years. Rice had net sales of $600,000 for the year ended February 28, Year 12. The estimated cost of goods sold of Rice for the year ended February 28, Year 12, is:
a $100,000 *b* $120,000 *c* $480,000 *d* $500,000 *e* Some other amount

8 Contractors, Inc., uses the percentage-of-completion, cost-to-cost method of accounting for its construction-type contracts. On January 2, Year 1, Contractors began work on a $6,000,000 contract, which was completed in Year 2. The accounting records included the following data for the contract:

	Year 1	*Year 2*
Construction costs incurred	$1,800,000	$3,600,000
Estimated cost to complete	3,600,000	
Progress and other billings to customer	2,200,000	3,800,000
Collections from customer on billings	1,400,000	4,600,000

The gross profit on the contract for Year 1 is:
a $200,000 *b* $220,000 *c* $300,000 *d* $400,000 *e* Some other amount

Ex. 9-2 Colby Company estimates its ending inventories by the lower-of-average-cost-and-market retail method. For the month ended August 31, Year 6, the following amounts were available:

Beginning inventories, at cost	$ 15,000
Beginning inventories, at retail	20,000

Net markdowns	3,000
Net markups	24,000
Net purchases, at cost	75,000
Net purchases, at retail	100,000
Net sales	85,000

Compute Colby Company's estimated inventories (under the lower-of-average-cost-and-market retail method) on August 31, Year 6.

Ex. 9-3 The following data were taken from the records of Dolby Department Store for the year ended January 31, Year 8:

	Cost	*Retail*
Inventories, Feb. 1, Year 7	$180,000	$260,000
Net markdowns		80,000
Net markups		20,000
Net purchases	660,000	920,000
Net sales		960,000

Dolby estimates normal shrinkage at 2% of the retail value of goods available for sale.

Compute the estimated inventories of Dolby Department Store on January 31, Year 8, under the lower-of-average-cost-and-market retail method.

Ex. 9-4 The following information was taken from the accounting and other records of Willoughby Company for the year ended May 31, Year 5:

	Cost	*Retail*
Beginning inventories	$ 25,000	$ 46,200
Purchases (net)	120,000	191,800
Net markups		12,000
Sales (net)		178,000
Net markdowns		3,800

You are to assume that all net markups and net markdowns apply to purchases of the year ended May 31, Year 5, and that it is appropriate to treat the entire inventories as a single department, with no markdowns having occurred during the year ended May 31, Year 4.

Compute the estimated ending inventories at last-in, first-out cost by the retail method.

Ex. 9-5 The following data are available for the month of May, Year 3, for Sharon's Store:

	Cost	*Retail*
Inventories, May 1, Year 3	$107,600	$160,000
Purchases	346,400	447,200
Purchases returns	6,000	7,200
Sales (net of returns)		489,000
Markdowns		42,000
Additional markups		58,000
Markdown cancellations		26,000
Markup cancellations		18,000

Compute the estimated inventories of Sharon's Store on May 31, Year 3, at the lower of average cost and market by the retail method.

Ex. 9-6 The following information is available for Chester Corporation for the three months ended March 31, Year 6:

Inventories, Jan. 1, Year 6	$ 900,000
Net purchases	3,000,000
Freight-in	200,000
Net sales	4,800,000

Chester's gross profit margin has averaged 33⅓% of cost of goods sold for the past several years.

Compute Chester Corporation's estimated inventories on March 31, Year 6, under the gross profit method.

Ex. 9-7 Higbie Company's gross profit margin on sales has averaged 30% for many years. Higbie suspects that employees may have been stealing goods from its inventories during Year 4. Physical inventories under the periodic inventory system were $550,000 on January 1, Year 4, and $600,000 on December 31, Year 4. Net sales and net purchases for Year 4 were $3,000,000 and $2,250,000, respectively.

Compute the estimated cost of goods stolen by Higbie Company's employees during Year 4.

Ex. 9-8 Seeley Company uses the gross profit method to estimate monthly inventories. In recent months gross profit has averaged 35% of net sales. The following data are available for the month of January, Year 9:

Inventories, Jan. 1, Year 9	$ 26,580
Purchases	120,000
Purchases returns	5,000
Freight-in	6,000
Gross sales	169,000
Sales returns and allowances	10,000

Compute the estimated cost of Seeley Company's inventories on January 31, Year 9, by the gross profit method.

Ex. 9-9 You took a physical inventory for your sole proprietorship at the close of business on July 20, Year 2. The inventory totalled $20,500. Your fiscal year ends on June 30; therefore, you must estimate an inventory amount on June 30, Year 2. You find that during the period July 1 through July 20 sales were $70,500; sales returns, $1,800; gross purchases, $65,000; purchases returns, $1,200; freight-in, $600.

Compute the estimated cost of the inventory on June 30, Year 2, assuming that goods are sold at prices 20% above cost.

Ex. 9-10 On July 10, Year 10, a fire destroyed the goods in process inventory of Tallman Company. Inventories of material and finished goods were not damaged. Physical inventories taken after the fire were as follows:

Material	$ 65,000
Finished goods	120,000
Total	$185,000

Inventories on January 1, Year 10, were as shown below:

Material	$ 45,000
Goods in process	80,000
Finished goods	150,000
Total	$275,000

The accounting records disclosed the following for January 1 through July 10, Year 10:

Sales (net)	$380,000
Purchases of material (net)	117,500
Direct labour costs	92,000
Factory overhead costs	58,200

The gross profit in recent years has averaged 25% of cost of finished goods sold.

Compute the estimated cost of the goods in process inventory of Tallman Company destroyed by the fire.

Ex. 9-11 Haywood Construction Limited records gross profit under the percentage-of-completion method for its construction-type contracts. During Year 8, Haywood entered into a fixed-price contract to construct a bridge for $15,000,000. Construction costs incurred and estimated cost to complete the bridge were as follows:

	Cumulative construction costs incurred to date	*Estimated cost to complete*
Dec. 31, Year 8	$ 1,000,000	$8,000,000
Dec. 31, Year 9	5,500,000	5,500,000
Dec. 31, Year 10	10,000,000	2,000,000

Compute the amount of gross profit that Haywood Construction Limited should recognize on the bridge contract under the percentage-of-completion, cost-to-cost method of accounting for the year ended December 31, Year 10.

Ex. 9-12 On April 1, Year 10, Lary Construction Corporation entered into a fixed-price contract to construct an apartment building for $6,000,000. Lary accounted for this contract under the percentage-of-completion, cost-to-cost method. Information relating to the contract is as follows:

	Dec. 31, Year 10	*Dec. 31, Year 11*
Percentage of completion	20%	60%
Estimated total cost when completed	$4,500,000	$4,800,000
Cumulative gross profit recognized	$ 300,000	$ 720,000

Compute the amount of construction costs incurred by Lary Construction Corporation during the year ended December 31, Year 11.

Ex. 9-13 In Year 1, Dodd Construction Limited contracted to construct a building for $800,000. The building was completed in Year 2. Dodd uses the percentage-of-completion, cost-to-cost method of accounting for construction-type contracts. Data relating to this contract are summarized below:

	Year 1	*Year 2*
Construction costs incurred	$180,000	$442,800
Estimated cost to complete the building	420,000	-0-
Progress and other billings to customer	200,000	600,000
Collections from customer on billings	160,000	590,000

Prepare journal entries for Dodd Construction Limited for Year 1 and Year 2 relating to this contract. Journal entries to close nominal accounts are not required.

Ex. 9-14 In Year 1, Garcia Corporation began work under a construction-type contract. The fixed price was $800,000, and the construction was expected to be completed in three years. Garcia uses the percentage-of-completion, cost-to-cost method of accounting. The revenue to be recognized each year is based on the proportion of construction costs incurred to total estimated costs to complete the contract.

The information relating to this contract in the financial statements for the year ended December 31, Year 1, follows:

Balance sheet:		
Contract receivables		$20,000
Costs incurred and estimated earnings on uncompleted contract	$200,000	
Less: Billings to date	188,000	
Costs and estimated earnings in excess of billings on uncompleted contract		12,000
Income statement:		
Gross profit		$20,000

a Compute the amount of cash collected by Garcia Corporation on this contract in Year 1.

b Compute the total estimated gross profit of Garcia Corporation on this contract.

Ex. 9-15 Rey Construction Company began operations in Year 3. By December 31, Year 3, the first construction project was finished and a second project was partially completed. Information as of December 31, Year 3, follows:

	Project no. 1	*Project no. 2*
Construction costs incurred	$ 80,000	$105,000
Percentage of completion	100%	70%
Fixed price	$100,000	$200,000
Progress and other billings to customers	$100,000	$115,000
Collections from customers on billings	$ 92,000	$ 75,000

a Prepare journal entries for Rey Construction Company for Year 3 (excluding closing entries) to record the transactions relating to the two projects, assuming that the percentage-of-completion, cost-to-cost method of accounting for construction-type contracts is used.

b Prepare a partial balance sheet for Rey Construction Company on December 31, Year 3, under the percentage-of-completion method of accounting.

Ex. 9-16 Carson Contractors, Inc., entered into a $600,000 fixed-price construction-type contract on January 2, Year 6. Because Carson's estimates of measures of completion were subject to inherent hazards, Carson adopted the completed-contract method of accounting. Data regarding the contract for Year 6 are shown below:

Construction costs incurred	$280,000
Estimated cost to complete construction	410,000
Progress billings to customer	250,000
Collections from customer on billings	220,000

Prepare journal entries for Carson Contractors, Inc., for Year 6 for the contract. Journal entries to close nominal ledger accounts are not required.

Ex. 9-17 Krone Construction Company adopted the percentage-of-completion, cost-to-cost method of accounting for its $2,800,000 fixed-price construction-type contract with Biggers, Inc., dated April 1, Year 3. The following data relate to the contract for the year ended December 31, Year 3:

Construction costs incurred	$1,152,000
Estimated cost to complete construction	1,728,000
Progress billings to customer	1,080,000
Collections from customer on billings	900,000

Prepare all journal entries for Krone Construction Company, except entries to close nominal ledger accounts, for the contract for Year 3.

CASES

Case 9-1 Dru Department Store uses the conventional retail method as a means of controlling the investment in inventories at its branch stores. Dru's main accounting office summarizes the recorded activity at each branch and estimates the ending inventories monthly. The estimate is then compared with a normal inventory investment based on expected volume. Normal shrinkage is estimated at 1% of the retail value of goods available for sale. Store managers are required to explain deviations of 5% or more from the expected normal inventory. The following data have been accumulated for the South Branch on April 30, Year 5:

	Cost	*Retail*
Net sales		$630,000
Beginning inventories	$150,000	222,000
Net purchases	560,000	823,000
Net markups		20,000
Net markdowns		9,000

Instructions

a The normal inventories of the South Branch total $220,000 at lower of cost and market. Compute the estimated amount of the ending inventories at retail and at lower of average cost and market and indicate the nature of the explanation to be made by the South Branch store manager.

b What effect, if any, would the following factors have on the effectiveness of the retail method as a control device?

1 A widely fluctuating shrinkage factor

2 A shift in the volume of goods handled at various markups

3 Additional markups related to goods sold by the end of the accounting period
4 Markdowns incorrectly treated as markup cancellations
5 Additional markups included with markdown cancellations

Case 9-2 Broadmoore Company has used the gross profit method for estimating the investment in inventories and as a test of the physical inventory at the end of each year. Broadmoor has two lines of merchandise that have produced gross profit margins of 25% and 35% respectively on selling price over the past several years. The gross profit margin for Broadmoor's total sales has averaged 30% of sales.

The operation data for the year ended January 31, Year 7, were as follows:

	Economy line	*Quality line*	*Total*
Sales	$100,000	$200,000	$300,000
Beginning inventories	10,000	25,000	35,000
Purchases	90,000	130,000	220,000
Gross profit margins on selling price	25%	35%	30%

A physical inventory of the merchandise on January 31, Year 7, totalled $50,000, but the manager's estimate by the gross profit method indicated ending inventories should be $45,000. The manager of Broadmoor is of the opinion that the discrepancy is too large to accept without explanation. A test sample selected revealed that the gross profit margins on the two lines were unchanged at 25% and 35%.

Instructions

a Show how the manager of Broadmoor Company computed the January 31, Year 7, inventories by the gross profit method.

b Compute the January 31, Year 7, inventories of Broadmoor Company by the gross profit method in the manner in which it should be used in this situation.

c Explain to the manager of Broadmoor Company why the difference exists between the physical inventory and the estimate of the value of inventories on January 31, Year 7, under the gross profit method.

Case 9-3 Lalo Construction Limited had three construction-type contracts in progress on December 31, Year 1, the data for which are presented in the next table.

Instructions

a Prepare partial income statements and balance sheets for Lalo Construction Limited for Year 1 reporting the details of the foregoing contracts under (1) the completed-contract method, and (2) the percentage-of-completion, cost-to-cost method. Use adjacent columns for both methods. Show total revenue and applicable costs in the partial income statements, and show supporting computations.

Contract	*Fixed price*	*Estimated total costs*	*Construction costs incurred to date (all in Year 1)*	*Progress billings to date*	*Collections from customers to date*
X	$ 750,000	$ 600,000	$400,000	$450,000	$415,000
Y	1,000,000	1,050,000	525,000	400,000	380,000
Z	900,000	675,000	202,500	225,000	202,500

b What are the differences between the two sets of financial statements?

c Which set of financial statements do you think presents the more meaningful data about the construction-type contracts of Lalo Construction Limited? Explain.

Case 9-4 The two methods of accounting for construction-type contracts are the percentage-of-completion method and the completed-contract method.

Instructions

a Discuss how realized contract revenue and gross profits on construction-type contracts are computed and recorded under these two methods.

b Under what circumstances is it preferable to use one method instead of the other?

c Why is realized contract revenue as measured by progress billings not generally accepted for construction-type contracts?

d How are construction costs and progress billings reported in the balance sheet under the percentage-of-completion method and under the completed-contract method?

PROBLEMS

Pr. 9-1 Con-Tract Limited has a construction-type contract with Customer Company with a fixed price of $1,200,000, which it entered into on April 1, Year 4, the beginning of a fiscal year. Data with respect to the contract for the three years ended March 31, Year 7, were as follows:

	Year ended March 31:		
	Year 5	*Year 6*	*Year 7*
Construction costs incurred	$200,000	$250,000	$400,000
Estimated cost to complete construction at end of year	600,000	350,000	-0-
Progress and other billings to Customer Company	300,000	400,000	500,000
Collections from Customer Company on billings	270,000	360,000	450,000
Operating expenses incurred	50,000	60,000	70,000

Instructions

Prepare journal entries for Con-Tract Limited's operations during the three years ended March 31, Year 7, under the percentage-of-completion, cost-to-cost method of accounting for the construction-type contract. Round all amounts to the nearest dollar. Use the following format for your working paper:

	Year ended March 31:					
	Year 5		*Year 6*		*Year 7*	
Accounts and explanation	*Debit*	*Credit*	*Debit*	*Credit*	*Debit*	*Credit*

Pr. 9-2 The controller of Retail Sellers, Inc., estimated that normal inventory shrinkage of Retail ranged between 1% and 1.5% of the retail value of goods available for sale. To test that estimate, the controller authorized the taking of a physical inventory on July 31, Year 7, midway through the fiscal year ending January 31, Year 8. The July 31, Year 7, physical inventory totalled $301,800 at retail prices. Data for the conventional retail inventory method for the six months ended July 31, Year 7, follow:

	Cost	*Retail*
Beginning inventories	$ 247,400	$ 288,400
Net markdowns		40,600
Net markups		120,400
Net purchases	2,674,200	2,911,200
Net sales		2,931,100

Instructions

a Compute the estimated inventories of Retail Sellers, Inc., on July 31, Year 7, and compare it with the physical inventory at retail on that date to determine whether normal inventory shrinkage falls within the range estimated by the controller.

b Compute the estimated lower of average cost and market of the physical inventory of Retail Sellers, Inc., on July 31, Year 7.

Pr. 9-3 Ward Construction Corporation began operations on March 1, Year 2. During Year 2, Ward entered into a contract with Stevens Corporation to construct a building. At that time, Ward estimated that it would take four years to complete the building at a total cost of $4,800,000. The fixed price for the construction of the building was $6,200,000. During Year 2, Ward incurred $1,250,000 of construction costs related to this project, and Stevens was billed and paid 30% of the contract price. The remaining costs to complete the contract were estimated at $3,750,000 on December 31, Year 2.

Instructions

Prepare working papers for Ward Construction Corporation to compute (1) the amount of gross profit realized on the construction-type contract for the year ended December 31, Year 2, and (2) the amount to be shown as "costs and estimated earnings in excess of billings on uncompleted contract" or "billings in excess of costs and estimated earnings on uncompleted contract" on December 31, Year 2, under each of the following accounting methods:

a Percentage-of-completion, cost-to-cost method
b Completed-contract method

Pr. 9-4 This problem consists of two unrelated parts.

a Logan Company uses the retail method to estimate its inventories. Information relating to the computation of inventories on December 31, Year 1, is as follows:

	Cost	*Retail*
Inventories, Jan. 1, Year 1	$ 55,000	$ 90,000
Net sales		620,000
Net purchases	355,000	580,000
Freight-in	7,600	
Additional markups		60,000
Markup cancellations		10,000
Markdowns		25,000
Markdown cancellations		5,000

Estimated normal shrinkage is 3% of the retail value of goods available for sale.

Instructions

Compute the estimated cost of Logan Company's inventories on December 31, Year 1, at the lower of average cost and market. Use the retail method and show supporting computations.

b On June 28, Year 1, a fire at Watt Company's warehouse caused severe damage to its inventories. Watt estimated that the cost of the undamaged inventories after the fire was $30,000, and that its gross profit rate was 30% of net sales. The following information was available from the accounting records:

Inventories, June 1, Year 1	$250,000
Net purchases from June 1 to June 28, Year 1	350,000
Net sales from June 1 to June 28, Year 1	550,000

Instructions

Compute the estimated cost of Watt Company's inventories lost in the fire. Use the gross profit method and show supporting computations.

Pr. 9-5 Information relating to the operations of the sportswear department of Amy's Fashion Shop for the year ended December 31, Year 10, is presented below:

	Cost	*Retail*
Beginning inventories	$ 49,600	$ 83,600
Purchases	257,800	406,900
Freight-in	10,400	
Purchases returns	4,200	7,000
Additional markups		15,000
Markup cancellations		8,500
Markdowns		8,000
Markdown cancellations		1,600
Sales		396,500
Sales returns		6,700

Normal shrinkage is estimated at 1% of the retail value of goods available for sale.

Instructions

a Compute the December 31, Year 10, inventories of Amy's Fashion Shop at the lower of average cost and market by the retail method.

b Compute the December 31, Year 10, inventories of Amy's Fashion Shop by the retail lifo method.

Pr. 9-6 San Remo Company uses the retail method to estimate ending inventories for its monthly financial statements. The following data pertain to a single department for the month of May, Year 8:

Inventories, May 1:	
At cost	$ 19,000
At retail	30,000
Purchases (exclusive of freight-in and returns):	
At cost	83,558
At retail	146,495
Freight-in	5,100
Purchases returns:	
At cost	2,100
At retail	2,800
Additional markups	2,500
Markup cancellations	265
Net markdowns	800
Sales (net of sales returns)	138,200

Normal shrinkage is 1½% of the retail value of goods available for sale.

Instructions

a Using the conventional retail method, prepare a working paper to compute San Remo Company's estimated inventories at lower of average cost and market on May 31, Year 8. Round all amounts to nearest dollar.

b Assume that San Remo Company used the conventional retail inventory method to estimate the cost of its May 31, Year 8, inventories at $30,600, and that a physical inventory revealed only $26,000 of inventories at lower of cost and market. Identify factors that may have caused the difference between the computed inventories and the physical inventory.

Pr. 9-7 This problem consists of two unrelated parts, one for Archer Company and one for Bowman Limited.

Archer Company uses the retail lifo method. Information relating to the computation of Archer's inventories on December 31, Year 5, follows:

	Cost	*Retail*
Inventories, Jan. 1, Year 5	$ 30,200	$ 45,000
Purchases	120,000	171,000
Freight-in	22,000	
Net sales		190,000
Net markups		40,000
Net markdowns		11,000

Bowman Limited prepares quarterly financial statements and estimates inventories at the end of each quarter by the gross profit method, because the relationship of selling prices and costs remains relatively stable during each year. The inventories on December 31 are determined by a physical count. The data below for the first three-quarters of the year ending December 31, Year 5, were taken from Bowman's accounting records:

	Mar. 31	*June 30*	*Sept.30*
Sales	$993,600	$963,000	$808,500
Sales returns	13,000	20,000	8,000
Sales discounts	600	3,000	500
Purchases	745,000	735,000	665,000
Freight-in	9,500	9,100	8,210
Purchases returns and allowances	500	2,400	4,630
Operating expenses	102,000	103,000	94,400

The physical inventories for Bowman Limited on December 31, Year 4, totalled $105,000.

Instructions

a Assuming that there was no change in the price index during the year, compute the estimated cost of the inventories on December 31, Year 5, for Archer Company by the retail lifo method.

b Assuming that the gross profit rate for the prior fiscal year was 20% of net sales and that this rate is expected to prevail throughout Year 5, prepare quarterly income statements for Bowman Limited for the first three-quarters of Year 5. Income taxes expense is estimated at 45% of pre-tax income.

Pr. 9-8 This problem consists of two parts.

a The June 30, Year 3, physical inventories of Dalbert Company, which uses the periodic inventory system, totalled $623,300 at first-in, first-out cost, which was lower than market. The controller of Dalbert, believing that the physical inventories might be understated, decided to use the gross profit method, because Dalbert's gross profit percentage had been constant at 33⅓% of cost of goods sold for several years. Data for the gross profit method for June 30, Year 3, follow:

Beginning inventories, at fifo cost	$ 482,400
Net purchases	6,822,000
Net sales	8,794,400

Instructions
Using the gross profit method, estimate the June 30, Year 3, inventories of Dalbert Company at fifo cost, and compute the difference between the estimate and the physical inventories amount of $623,300.

b In reviewing the records of purchases, sales, and consignments for the year ended June 30, Year 3, Dalbert Company's controller found the following items:

1 Goods costing $23,800, shipped FOB shipping point by the supplier on June 28, Year 3, had been recorded in the Purchases ledger account on June 30, Year 3, but had not been included in the physical inventories on that date because the goods were not received until July 2, Year 3.

2 Goods billed to a customer at $20,000 on June 30, Year 3, and physically segregated in the shipping department for the customer's later pickup had been included erroneously in the June 30, Year 3, physical inventories at cost.

3 Goods with a selling price of $102,000, on consignment from Dalbert to Consignee Company, had not been included in Dalbert's June 30, Year 3, physical inventories.

Instructions
Correct Dalbert Company's June 30, Year 3, physical inventories total of $623,300 for any effects of the foregoing items, and compute any remaining difference between Dalbert's corrected June 30, Year 3, physical inventories and the estimated inventories computed in ***a***.

Pr. 9-9 This problem consists of two unrelated parts.

a On July 2, Year 7, Crewe Construction Limited entered into a $4,000,000 fixed-price contract with Farley Company, which was expected to be profitable, to construct an office building over a two-to-three-year period. Because of inherent hazards in estimates of input or output measures, Crewe adopted the completed-contract method of accounting for the project. Information with respect to the contract for Years 7 through 9, follows:

	Year ended Dec. 31:		
	Year 7	*Year 8*	*Year 9*
Construction costs incurred	$ 350,000	$2,150,000	$1,750,000
Estimated costs to complete	3,150,000	1,700,000	
Progress and other billings to customer ..	720,000	1,440,000	1,840,000

Instructions

Compute the amounts to be shown in Crewe Construction Limited's balance sheets on December 31, Years 7 through 9, as ''costs in excess of billings on uncompleted contract'' or ''billings in excess of costs on uncompleted contract.'' Show supporting computations of gross profit or loss to be recognized on the contract by Crewe Construction for the years ended December 31, Years 7 through 9.

b On April 1, Year 9, Builder Corporation entered into a $2,400,000 fixed-fee contract to construct a building for Dalton Company. Builder estimated a two-year construction period at an estimated total cost of $2,000,000. For the year ended December 31, Year 9, Builder incurred construction costs of $700,000 under the contract, and billed Dalton a total of $500,000. Estimated costs on December 31, Year 9, to complete the building totalled $1,400,000. Builder adopted the percentage-of-completion, cost-to-cost method of accounting for the contract.

Instructions

Prepare a journal entry on December 31, Year 9, for Builder Corporation to recognize contract revenue and cost of contract revenue for the construction-type contract.

Pr. 9-10 Adam Corporation is a small manufacturing company. On March 31, Year 6, a fire completely destroyed the inventory of goods in process. The material and finished goods inventories were not damaged. After the fire a physical inventory was taken. The material was valued at $37,500 and the finished goods at $62,000, at first-in, first-out cost.

The inventories on January 1, Year 6, consisted of:

Material	$ 15,500
Goods in process	60,500
Finished goods	85,000
Total	$161,000

A review of the accounting records disclosed that the sales and gross profit on sales for the last three years were:

	Sales	*Gross profit on sales*
Year 3	$400,000	$120,000
Year 4	380,000	110,500
Year 5	250,000	88,800

The sales for the first three months of Year 6 were $150,000. Material purchases were $62,500, freight-in on purchases was $5,000, and direct labour cost for the three months was $50,000. For the past two years factory overhead cost has been applied at 75% of direct labour cost.

Instructions
Compute the estimated cost of Adam Corporation's inventory of goods in process destroyed by the fire on March 31, Year 6, using the weighted-average gross profit for the last three years.

Pr. 9-11 This problem consists of three unrelated parts.

a Arn Company lost all its inventories by fire on January 1, Year 10. A physical inventory had not been taken on December 31, Year 9. The following data are available for the three preceding years:

	Year 7	*Year 8*	*Year 9*
Inventories, Jan. 1	$161,600	$168,000	$170,160
Sales	724,000	788,000	812,000
Sales returns	12,000	8,000	12,000
Purchases	644,000	656,000	720,000
Purchases returns	36,000	32,000	40,000
Operating expenses	198,000	221,000	240,000
Accounts receivable, Dec. 31	55,000	50,000	60,000
Accounts payable, Dec. 31	28,000	35,000	40,000

Instructions
Assuming that the gross profit percentage for Year 9 was estimated to be the same as the weighted-average gross profit percentage for the two previous years, compute the estimated cost of Arn Company's inventories destroyed by fire on January 1, Year 10.

b Burr Company uses the retail method to estimate its inventories. The following information was available for Burr Company for Year 10:

	Cost	*Retail*
Beginning inventories	$ 40,500	$ 65,000

Purchases (net of returns)	290,000	405,000
Freight-in	2,000	
Net markups		5,000
Net markdowns		9,000
Employee discounts		2,000
Net sales		410,000

Instructions

Compute Burr Company's estimated inventories by the retail method on December 31, Year 10, on the basis of lower of average cost and market.

c Corb Company entered into a construction-type contract early in Year 10. The fixed price was $800,000, and Corb expected to earn a gross profit of $180,000 on the contract. The following information was available through the end of Year 12:

Year ended Dec. 31:	*Cumulative construction costs incurred to date*	*Estimated costs to complete construction*
Year 10	$ 49,600	$570,400
Year 11	172,800	467,200
Year 12	504,000	126,000

Instructions

Compute the gross profit to be recognized by Corb Company in each year (Years 10 through 12) under the percentage-of-completion, cost-to-cost method for the construction-type contract.

Pr. 9-12 On January 1, Year 2, Moy Company adopted the retail method of accounting for its inventories. When you undertook the preparation of Moy's interim report of earnings for the six months ended June 30, Year 2, the data below were available:

	Cost	*Retail*
Inventories, Jan. 1, Year 2	$ 76,200	$120,000
Markdowns		31,500
Additional markups		58,500
Markdown cancellations		19,500
Markup cancellations		13,500
Purchases	265,860	335,400
Sales		366,000
Purchases returns and allowances	4,500	5,400
Sales returns		20,000

Instructions

a Prepare a working paper to compute Moy Company's estimated June 30,

Year 2, inventories under the retail method of accounting. The inventories are to be valued at last-in, first-out cost. Assume that net markups and markdowns apply only to purchases.

b Without prejudice to your solution to part ***a***, assume that you computed the June 30, Year 2, inventories to be $132,300 at retail and the cost percentage to be 80%. The general price level had increased from 100 on January 1 to 105 on June 30, Year 2. Prepare a working paper to compute Moy Company's estimated June 30, Year 2, inventories at the June 30 price level, using the dollar-value retail lifo method. Round amounts to nearest dollar and percentage.

Pr. 9-13 On April 15, Year 5, a fire damaged the office and warehouse of Weeden Company. The only accounting record saved was the general ledger, from which the following trial balance was prepared:

WEEDEN COMPANY
Trial Balance
March 31, Year 5

	Debit	*Credit*
Cash	$ 23,800	
Accounts receivable	27,000	
Inventories, Dec. 31, Year 4	36,000	
Land	24,000	
Building and equipment	120,000	
Accumulated depreciation of building and equipment		$ 46,000
Other assets	3,600	
Accounts payable		23,700
Accrued liabilities		7,200
Common stock		100,000
Retained earnings		47,700
Sales		135,400
Purchases	103,000	
Operating expenses	22,600	
Totals	$360,000	$360,000

Additional Information

1 Weeden's fiscal year ends on December 31.

2 An examination of the April, Year 5, bank statement and paid cheques disclosed that cheques written during the period April 1 to 15 totalled $11,600: $5,700 paid on accounts payable as of March 31, $2,000 for April purchases, and $3,900 for operating expenses. Deposits during the same period amounted to $10,650, all of which consisted of receipts on account from customers, with the exception of a $450 refund from a vendor for goods returned in April.

3 Correspondence with suppliers disclosed unrecorded purchases on April 15, Year 5, of $3,500, including $1,300 for shipments in transit on April 15.

4 Customers acknowledged indebtedness of $26,400 as of April 15, Year 5. It

also was estimated that customers owed another $5,000 that will never be acknowledged or recovered. Of the acknowledged indebtedness, $700 probably will be uncollectible. All sales were on credit.

5 Assume that the weighted-average gross profit percentage for the past two years was in effect during Year 5. Weeden's financial statements included the following:

	Year ended Dec. 31:	
	Year 3	*Year 4*
Net sales	$300,000	$400,000
Net purchases	174,000	226,000
Beginning inventories	35,000	45,000
Ending inventories	45,000	36,000

6 Goods with an estimated cost of $8,250 were salvaged and sold for $4,800. The remainder of the inventories was lost in the fire.

Instructions

Prepare a working paper to compute the amount of Weeden Company's inventory fire loss on April 15, Year 5, including a supporting computation of the cost of goods sold percentage.

Pr. 9-14 Provo Construction Limited constructs water treatment plants for small communities. All its construction-type contracts are accounted for by the percentage-of-completion method, except for two contracts that are accounted for by the completed-contract method because of inherent hazards in estimates of input or output measures.

The following information on construction-type contracts is available for the year ended December 31, Year 5:

Information on Construction-Type Contracts

Percentage-of-Completion Method Fixed prices of construction-type contracts accounted for by the percentage-of-completion method totalled $6,050,000. Costs incurred on these contracts were $1,500,000 in Year 4 and $3,000,000 in Year 5. On December 31, Year 5, it was estimated that additional costs of $1,000,000 were required to complete these contracts. Revenue of $1,750,000 was recognized in Year 4, and progress billings totalled $4,900,000, of which $4,600,000 had been collected. No construction-type contracts accounted for by the percentage-of-completion method were completed in Year 5.

Completed-Contract Method The two construction-type contracts accounted for by the completed-contract method were started in Year 4. One had a fixed price of $5,000,000. Costs incurred were $1,400,000 in Year 4 and $1,600,000 in Year 5. Progress billings totalled $3,100,000, of which $2,900,000 had been collected. Although it was difficult to estimate the additional costs required to complete this contract, Provo expected the contract to be profitable.

The second contract had a fixed price of $4,000,000. Costs incurred were $1,200,000 in Year 4 and $2,600,000 in Year 5. Progress billings totalled $3,200,000, of which $2,900,000 had been collected. Although it was difficult to estimate the additional costs required to complete this contract, Provo expected a loss of approximately $100,000.

Additional Information

1 Operating expenses totalled $200,000 for Year 5.
2 Other revenue amounted to $45,500 for Year 5.

Instructions

Prepare an income statement for Provo Construction Limited for the year ended December 31, Year 5, stopping at income (or loss) before income taxes. Show supporting computations. Disregard income tax and deferred tax considerations. Notes to the income statement are not required.

Pr. 9-15 Dykes Construction began operations on January 5, Year 10. Construction activities for Year 10 are summarized below:

Contract	*Fixed price*	*Construction costs incurred*	*Estimated cost to complete*	*Progress and other billings to customers*	*Collections from customers on billings*
P	$ 310,000	$187,500	$ 12,500	$160,000	$155,000
Q	415,000	195,000	248,000	249,000	210,000
R	350,000	320,000	-0-	350,000	300,000
S	300,000	16,500	183,500	20,000	
Totals	$1,375,000	$719,000	$444,000	$779,000	$665,000

The controller of Dykes Construction has asked you to compute the amounts of contract revenue for the year ended December 31, Year 10, to be recognized under the percentage-of-completion method of accounting for construction-type contracts.

Additional Information

1 All contracts are with different customers.
2 Any work remaining to be done on the contracts is expected to be completed in Year 11.
3 Dykes Construction's accounting records have been maintained by the percentage-of-completion, cost-to-cost method.

Instructions

a Prepare a working paper for Dykes Construction to compute the amount of contract revenue, cost of contract revenue, and gross profit or loss realized on each contract for the year ended December 31, Year 10, under the percentage-of-completion, cost-to-cost method. Show supporting computations.

b Prepare a working paper under the percentage-of-completion method to compute the amounts that would appear in Dykes Construction's balance sheet on December 31, Year 10, for:
   1 Costs and estimated earnings in excess of billings on uncompleted contracts
   2 Billings in excess of costs and estimated earnings on uncompleted contracts

Pr. 9-16 Pacific Corporation began operations on October 15, Year 1, with contract X as its only construction-type contract during Year 1. A trial balance on December 31, Year 2, follows:

PACIFIC CORPORATION
Trial Balance
December 31, Year 2

	Debit	*Credit*
Cash	$ 23,300	
Contract receivable	136,480	
Cost of contracts in progress	461,120	
Estimated earnings on contracts in progress	8,000	
Progress billings		$459,400
Plant assets	135,500	
Accumulated depreciation of plant assets		13,880
Accounts payable		70,820
Common stock		235,000
Retained earnings		5,900
Operating expenses	20,600	
Totals	$785,000	$785,000

Additional Information

1 Pacific determines gross profit on construction-type contracts under the percentage-of-completion, cost-to-cost method for both financial accounting and income taxes.

2 During Year 2, there were three contracts in progress, the fixed prices of which had been estimated as follows:

	Contract X	*Contract Y*	*Contract Z*
Material and labour costs	$169,000	$34,500	$265,700
Indirect costs	30,000	5,500	48,000
Total costs	$199,000	$40,000	$313,700
Add: Gross profit	40,000	3,000	30,300
Total fixed price	$239,000	$43,000	$344,000

3 Progress billings to customers are credited to the Progress Billings ledger account. Contract revenue is recognized at year-end by offsetting debits to the Cost of Contract Revenue and Estimated Earnings on Contracts in Progress ledger accounts.

4 All contract costs are debited to the Cost of Contracts in Progress ledger account. Original cost estimates compiled by engineers are considered reliable. Data on costs to December 31, Year 2, are shown below:

Contract	Original cost estimates	Costs incurred to date		
		Total	Material and labour costs	Indirect costs
X	$199,000	$115,420	$ 92,620	$22,800
Y	40,000	32,000	26,950	5,050
Z	313,700	313,700	265,700	48,000
Totals	$552,700	$461,120	$385,270	$75,850

5 On December 31, Year 1, accumulated costs on contract X were $39,800, or 20% of the total; no costs had been accumulated on contracts Y and Z. All work on contract Z was completed prior to December 31, Year 2, and the full contract price had been billed to the customer.

6 Pacific is subject to an income tax rate of 45%.

Instructions

a Prepare a working paper for Pacific Corporation to compute the percentage of completion of contracts on December 31, Year 2.

b Prepare a working paper for Pacific Corporation to compute contract revenue, cost of contract revenue, and gross profit to be recognized in Year 2.

c Prepare a working paper for Pacific Corporation to compute estimated income taxes expense for the year ended December 31, Year 2.

d Prepare journal entries for Pacific Corporation on December 31, Year 2, to record (1) contract revenue, cost of contract revenue, and gross profit for Year 2; (2) income taxes for Year 2; and (3) approval of completed contract Z by the customer.

c h a p t e r 1 0

CURRENT LIABILITIES AND CONTINGENCIES

In Chapter 1, ***liabilities*** are defined as ''probable future sacrifices of economic benefits arising from present obligations of a particular entity to transfer assets or provide services to other entities in the future as a result of past transactions or events.'' Liabilities are recorded when obligations are incurred, and are measured at the amounts to be paid or at the present value of these amounts. The distinction between current liabilities and long-term liabilities is important in an evaluation of the financial position of a business enterprise and its ability to meet maturing obligations. Some liabilities are definitely determinable, both as to existence and as to amount; other liabilities exist, but their amount is estimated; and certain contingencies require the accrual of liabilities. Current liabilities and contingencies are discussed in this chapter.

Distinction Between Current Liabilities and Long-Term Liabilities

Traditionally, one year marked the accounting boundary between current and long-term liabilities. When strictly applied, this one-year rule may result in a misleading financial picture, particularly when the ***operating cycle*** of a business enterprise exceeds one year.

The modern viewpoint is that current liabilities are obligations for which payment will require the use of current assets or the creation of other current liabilities in one year or during the next operating cycle, if longer. Section 1510.03 of the ***CICA Handbook*** states that current liabilities ''should include amounts payable within one year from the date of the balance sheet or within the normal operating cycle, where this is longer than a year (the normal operating cycle should correspond with that used for current assets).'' The definition of current liabilities is closely related to the definition of current assets. Thus, current liabilities include obligations for items that have entered into the operating cycle, such as payables to suppliers and employees, cash advances from customers and accruals for rents, taxes, product warranties, etc. Obligations incurred outside of the operating cycle and not payable in one year are not current liabilities; obligations that will be liquidated by the issuance of shares of capital stock are included in shareholders' equity in the balance sheet.

Current liabilities also include obligations that are or will be payable on demand within one year (or the enterprise's operating cycle, if longer) from the balance sheet date, even though liquidation may not be expected within that period. Similarly, long-term obligations that are or will be callable by creditors because of the debtor's violations of provisions of the debt agreement also are included among current liabilities. However, the reclassification of such obligations from long-term to current is not appropriate if creditors have waived or lost their right to demand payment, or if it is probable that the violations will be cured within a specified grace period.[1]

The amount of current liabilities reported in the balance sheet is of great interest to users of financial statements. Short-term credit is an important source of financing for most business enterprises. Certain current obligations such as trade accounts payable and accrued liabilities regularly arise from business operations; however, other obligations result from decisions by management to obtain cash during periods of expanding or peak business activity. Financial analysts keep a close watch on the amount of current liabilities, the relationship of current assets to current liabilities, and the relationship between cash balances and current liabilities. These relationships are important indicators of financial stability and ***solvency***—the ability to pay debts as they mature.

Recognition and Valuation of Current Liabilities

Every business enterprise faces the prospect of a wide variety of future cash outlays in order to continue in operation. For example, an enterprise must purchase material, pay wages, pay for services, replace plant assets, and pay taxes. We might take an extreme view and consider the ***present value*** of all these future cash outflows as the total debt of the enterprise at a specific time. This would correspond to the concept of assets as the present value of all future cash inflows. However, these theoretical extremes are beyond the accountants' power of measurement. As a practical matter, we need a basis for establishing some limits on the liability concept.

A logical starting point is to say that the amounts of all legally enforceable debts should appear as liabilities in the balance sheet. But what about legal obligations that are highly uncertain in amount? Because liabilities must be quantified, the ability to measure them with reasonable accuracy is essential. Then we must consider whether a strict legal test excludes any obligations to convey assets that are significant in an economic sense. The process of measuring net income may

1 FASB, ***FASB Statement No. 78:*** "Classification of Obligations That Are Callable by the Creditor" (Stamford: 1983), pp. 2–3.

require that a valuation be placed on highly uncertain future cash outflows that result from past transactions and events, because the costs incurred must be matched with current revenue.

These two elements, ***measurability*** and ***relation to past transactions and events***, lead us to conclude that liabilities should be defined to include all future cash outflows that result from past transactions and events and that may be measured with reasonable accuracy. Because we are dealing with ***future payments***, the element of uncertainty plays an important role in accounting for current liabilities.

In theory, the measure of any liability at the time it is incurred is the present value of the required future cash outflow.[2] In practice, however, most current liabilities are recorded at face amount. The difference between the present value of a current liability and the amount that will be paid at maturity usually is not material because of the short time period involved.

To emphasize the importance of the degree of uncertainty, the measurement of current liabilities is discussed under the following headings: (1) definitely measurable liabilities, (2) liabilities dependent on operating results, (3) estimated liabilities, (4) contingencies, and (5) future liabilities and commitments.

DEFINITELY MEASURABLE LIABILITIES

Liabilities in this category are the result of contracts or the operation of federal and provincial statutes such that the amount of an obligation and its due date are known with reasonable certainty. The accounting problems are to ascertain that an obligation exists, to measure it as accurately as possible, and to enter it in the accounting records.

Trade Accounts Payable

The accounting procedures for recording and controlling the payments for the purchase of goods and services generally are designed so that the existence, amount, and due date of such liabilities are readily determinable. Accountants give particular attention to transactions occurring near the end of one accounting period and at the beginning of the next period to see that the recording of purchases of goods and services is consistent with that of the related liability. For example, if goods are purchased and received near the end of a period but an invoice has not arrived, the goods may have been included in inventories, but the recording of the liability may have been overlooked.

Trade accounts payable may be recorded at ***face amount*** or ***net of purchases discounts offered*** by suppliers. When trade accounts payable are recorded at face amount, the Purchases Discounts ledger account is credited for discounts taken, and a material amount of discounts available to be taken at the end of an account-

2 The present value of a liability is the sum of expected future payments discounted to the present date at an appropriate rate of interest. ***APB Opinion No. 21:*** ''Interest on Receivables and Payables'' states that presentation of liabilities at their discounted present value is not required for ''payables arising from transactions with customers or suppliers in the normal course of business which are due in customary trade terms not exceeding approximately one year.'' ***APB Opinion No. 21*** also does not apply to estimates of warranty obligations assumed in connection with sales of property, goods, or services. The CICA has not taken a position in this area.

ing period should be accrued by a debit to Allowance for Purchases Discounts (a contra-liability ledger account). The balance of the Purchases Discounts account is deducted from the amount of purchases in the income statement. When trade accounts payable are recorded net of purchases discounts, the Purchases Discounts Lost account is debited for discounts ***not taken*** and for any estimated discounts that ***will not be taken***. In the income statement, the amount of purchases discounts lost is reported under Other Expenses.

To illustrate, assume the following activity relating to trade accounts payable for Year 10:

1 Purchased $900,000 of merchandise on terms of 2/10, n/30.

2 Paid invoices for purchases of $600,000 within the discount period and for purchases of $100,000 after the discount period lapsed.

3 Estimated at the end of Year 10 that 25% of the $200,000 outstanding trade accounts payable would not be paid within the discount period.

The journal entries (explanations omitted) for Year 10 and the presentation of trade accounts payable in the balance sheet at the end of Year 10 under the two alternative approaches are presented below:

Trade accounts payable recorded at face amount or net of purchases discounts

	Trade accounts payable recorded at face amount			***Trade accounts payable recorded net of purchases discounts***		
1	Purchases	900,000		Purchases ($900,000 × 0.98)	882,000	
	Trade Accounts Payable		900,000	Trade Accounts Payable		882,000
2	Trade Accounts Payable	700,000		Trade Accounts Payable ($700,000 × 0.98)	686,000	
	Cash		688,000	Purchases Discounts Lost ($100,000 × 0.02)	2,000	
	Purchases Discounts ($600,000 × 0.02)		12,000	Cash		688,000
3	Allowance for Purchases Discounts	3,000		Purchases Discounts Lost [($200,000 × 0.25) × 0.02]	1,000	
	Purchases Discounts [($200,000 × 0.75) × 0.02]		3,000	Trade Accounts Payable		1,000
	Presentation in balance sheet at end of Year 10:					
	Trade accounts payable		$200,000	Trade accounts payable		$197,000
	Less: Allowance for purchases discounts		3,000			
	Carrying amount of trade accounts payable		$197,000			

Most business enterprises plan to take advantage of all cash discounts available and thus prefer to record trade accounts payable at the net amount. The added cost of departures from this policy is indicated in the Purchases Discounts Lost ledger account.

Loan Obligations and Refinancing of Short-Term Debt

In this category are included short-term promissory notes issued as evidence of borrowing, and any portion of long-term debt due within one year. If long-term debt currently maturing is expected to be retired from sinking funds, from the proceeds of new long-term debt or equity securities, or through conversion to common stock, current funds will not be required. Therefore, such debt is reported as long-term, and the reason for this classification is described in a note to the financial statements. Similarly, short-term debt that is expected to be refinanced on a long-term basis may be excluded from current liabilities.[3]

Promissory Notes

The accounting for promissory notes payable is similar to the accounting for promissory notes receivable described in Chapter 7. When a promissory note bears a current fair rate of interest, its face amount is equal to its present value at the time of issuance; however, when a promissory note bears no interest or an unreasonably low rate of interest, the present value of the note payable is less than its face amount. The discount on such a note represents an adjustment (increase) to interest expense over the term of the note.

To illustrate the accounting for a promissory note issued at a discount, assume that on July 1, Year 1, Karlinsky Company issues a one-year non-interest-bearing note as consideration for the acquisition of office equipment. The face amount of the note is $150,000 and the current fair rate of interest on the note is 12% compounded quarterly. From Table 2 in the Appendix at the end of Chapter 5, we find that the present value of this note is $133,273 ($150,000 × 0.888487 = $133,273). The journal entries for the last six months of Year 1 and the presentation of the note in Karlinsky's balance sheet on December 31, Year 1, are on page 465.

On March 31, Year 2, interest expense of $4,242 ($141,389 × 0.12 × $\frac{3}{12}$ = $4,242) would be recorded, and on June 30, Year 2, interest expense of $4,369 [($141,389 + $4,242) × 0.12 × $\frac{3}{12}$ = $4,369] would be recorded. These journal entries increase the carrying amount of the note to its maturity value of $150,000.

Promissory notes payable that bear an unreasonably high rate of interest require the recording of a premium. The accounting for such notes is illustrated on pages 234–235 of Chapter 5.

Refinancing of Short-Term Debt

Refinancing means replacing short-term debt with either long-term debt or equity securities, or renewing, extending, or replacing the short-term debt with other short-term debt for more than one year (or beyond the operating cycle of the business enterprise, if applicable) from the date of the balance sheet. ***Ability to refinance*** on a long-term basis must be demonstrated either by (1) actually having

3 CICA, *CICA Handbook* (Toronto), sec. 1510.06.

Accounting for promissory note payable issued at a discount

Journal entries

Year 1			
July 1	Office Equipment	133,273	
	Discount on Note Payable	16,727	
	Note Payable		150,000
	To record issuance of a one-year non-interest-bearing promissory note. The current fair rate of interest on the note is 12% compounded quarterly.		
Sept. 30	Interest Expense	3,998	
	Discount on Note Payable		3,998
	To record interest expense for three months ($133,273 × 0.12 × 3/12 = $3,998).		
Dec. 31	Interest Expense	4,118	
	Discount on Note Payable		4,118
	To record interest expense for three months [($133,273 + $3,998) × 0.12 × 3/12 = $4,118].		

Presentation in balance sheet on December 31, Year 1:

Note payable	$150,000
Less: Discount on note payable ($16,727 − $3,998 − $4,118)	8,611
Carrying amount of note payable................................	$141,389

issued long-term debt or equity securities to replace short-term debt after the date of the balance sheet but before the balance sheet is issued, or by (2) having entered into a firm financing contract that will enable the debtor enterprise to refinance short-term debt at maturity.

When a short-term debt is classified as other than a current liability, the reasons for such classification are disclosed in a note to the financial statements. Specific disclosures required include a general description of the refinancing contract, the terms of any new debt incurred or to be incurred, and the terms of any equity securities issued or to be issued pursuant to the refinancing. An example of such disclosure from a balance sheet dated December 31, Year 10, follows:

Disclosure of refinancing contract in balance sheet

Current liabilities:	
Trade accounts payable	$1,800,000
Income taxes payable	1,150,000
Other current liabilities	370,000
Total current liabilities	$3,320,000
Long-term debt:	
12% notes payable (**NOTE 1**)	3,200,000
Total liabilities	$6,520,000

NOTE 1: The company has entered into a refinancing contract with Scotia Bank to borrow up to $5,000,000 at any time through Year 12. Amounts borrowed under the contract mature three years from the date of the loan and bear interest at 2% above Scotia Bank's prime interest rate. The contract requires the company to maintain working capital of at least $6,000,000 and prohibits the payment of cash dividends and acquisition of treasury stock without prior approval by Scotia Bank. Because the company intends to borrow at least $3,200,000 under the refinancing contract to retire the 12% notes payable that mature on March 31, Year 11, the notes have been classified as long-term debt.

A related issue is whether a short-term debt should be excluded from current liabilities if it is repaid after the balance sheet date and then is replaced by a long-term debt before the balance sheet is issued. Because repayment of the short-term debt before funds are obtained through a long-term refinancing requires the use of current assets, the Financial Accounting Standards Board in the United States concluded that the short-term obligation ***shall not be excluded from current liabilities*** on the balance sheet date.[4]

Liabilities Relating to Payrolls

Employers act as tax collectors for the federal and provincial governments with respect to taxes withheld from employees. Employers also may withhold from salaries and wages amounts for such items as union dues, group life insurance, and contributory pension plans. Accountants must be familiar with the general provisions of payroll tax legislation.

Canada Pension Plan

The Canada Pension Plan Act requires, with a few exceptions, both employers and employees, including those who are self-employed, to make contributions to the Canada Pension Plan. Its purpose is to provide retirement, disability, and similar benefits. The employers are responsible for withholding an appropriate amount of contribution from the pensionable earnings of each of their employees and are required to contribute an amount equal to that of the employees. The amount withheld together with the amount contributed by the employers is remitted monthly to Revenue Canada, Taxation. The Canada Pension Plan applies to all provinces except the Province of Quebec, which has its own, similar pension plan. The two plans are closely coordinated so that contributing employees are protected wherever they may work in Canada.

Unemployment Insurance

The federal Unemployment Insurance Act requires, with a few exceptions, both employers and employees to contribute to unemployment insurance. The employers are responsible for withholding an appropriate amount of unemployment insurance premium from their employees. The employers' premium contribution is more than the employees'. The amount of premium withheld from the employees together with that of the employers' premium is remitted monthly to Revenue Canada, Taxation.

Income Tax Withholding

Our pay-as-you-go system of income tax requires employers to withhold a portion of the earnings of their employees. The amount withheld depends upon the amount of the earnings and upon the amount of income tax exemptions to which the employee is entitled. On the basis of the earnings and the amount of exemp-

4 FASB, ***FASB Interpretation No. 8:*** "Classification of a Short-Term Obligation Repaid Prior to Being Replaced by a Long-Term Security (An Interpretation of ***FASB Statement No. 6***)" (Stamford: 1976), p. 2. There is no comparable CICA recommendation in this area.

tions, the employer can determine the income tax to be withheld from the employee by referring to the income tax deduction tables provided by Revenue Canada, Taxation. The amount withheld from the employees is remitted monthly to Revenue Canada, Taxation. This amount includes both the federal and the provincial income taxes for all provinces except the Province of Quebec, which collects its own income taxes. Thus, employers in Quebec must withhold separate deductions for federal and Quebec income taxes.

Compensated Absences and Special Termination Benefits

Vacation, holiday, and illness pay (collectively referred to as ***compensated absences***) are a standard element of most employment contracts. The right to such pay usually depends on the length of employment, and may increase after an employee completes a specified term of service.

When does a liability for compensated absences come into existence for financial accounting? Does it arise only when an employee has met all the conditions, or does it accrue through the employment period? For example, it seems clear that an employee who earns $500 a week and is entitled to a two-week vacation is paid $26,000 for 50 weeks of work, or $520 a week ($26,000 ÷ 50 = $520). This reasoning suggests that the vacation pay accrues at the rate of $20 a week during the 50 weeks prior to the vacation. Whether a legal liability exists for the vacation pay depends on the terms of the employment contract and the relevant labour law. If the paid vacation is contingent on the employee's remaining in service until the vacation period, the legal obligation does not arise until this condition has been met. However, an obligation exists that meets the tests of a liability, because the employer estimates the liability for vacation pay on the basis of employee turnover experience. Generally, the probability is high that a future cash outflow for vacation pay will take place, and the recording of a liability is appropriate.

Liabilities for employees' compensation for future absences are accrued if ***all*** of the following conditions are met:[5]

1 The employer's obligation to compensate employees for future absences is attributable to services already rendered by employees.

2 The obligation relates to rights that ***vest*** (are not contingent on an employee's future service) or ***accumulate*** (may be carried forward to one or more accounting periods subsequent to that in which it is earned).

3 Payment of the compensation is probable.

4 The amount can be reasonably estimated.

Inability to estimate a liability for compensated absences that meet the first three tests above is disclosed in a note to the financial statements.

Special termination benefits may be offered by employers to their employees as consideration for early retirement. Such termination benefits may consist of a

5 FASB, ***FASB Statement No. 43:*** "Accounting for Compensated Absences" (Stamford: 1980), pp. 2–3.

lump-sum payment, periodic future payments, or a combination of these. The Financial Accounting Standards Board in the United States requires that employers record an expense and a liability when their employees accept the offer and the amount may be reasonably estimated. The amount thus recorded consists of the lump-sum payment to employees plus the present value of any expected future payments.[6]

Recording Payroll Liabilities

The liability aspect of the problem of accounting for payroll centres on the amounts due employees, the liabilities associated with withholdings from employees' earnings, and the employer's share of payroll taxes and fringe benefits. There is also a cost side to the problem. The total costs incurred for employee services, including gross earnings, payroll taxes, and other fringe benefits, must be allocated to cost centres or profit centres to provide useful cost information for management.

To illustrate the recording of a payroll in the accounting records, we assume the following payroll data for Corbin Company for the month of May. Because May is the fifth month of the year, some employees have received salaries in excess of the limits subject to payroll taxes, so that the amount subject to payroll taxes is less than the total amount earned. The employer's assumed total payroll costs, including fringe benefits, are summarized below:

Employers' total payroll costs

Payroll costs	*Total*	*Sales Salaries*	*Administrative salaries*
Total salaries earned	$100,000	$60,000	$40,000
Unemployment insurance	2,100	1,300	800
Canada Pension Plan	2,300	1,400	900
Group insurance	1,600	1,000	600
Vacation pay ($100,000 × 4%)	4,000	2,400	1,600
Total payroll costs	$110,000	$66,100	$43,900

The assumed amounts withheld from employees' salaries and the computation of employees' net take-home pay are summarized below:

Amounts withheld and employees' take-home pay

Total salaries earned		$100,000
Withholdings:		
Unemployment insurance	$ 1,500	
Canada Pension Plan	2,300	
Income tax withheld	12,800	16,600
Employees' net take-home pay		$ 83,400

6 FASB, ***FASB Statement No. 74:*** "Accounting for Special Termination Benefits Paid to Employees" (Stamford: 1983), p. 1.

Assuming that payroll taxes are combined with gross salaries for accounting purposes, the following summary journal entry would be prepared to record the payroll for the month of May.

Journal entry to record payroll

Selling Expense—Salaries	66,100	
Administrative Expense—Salaries	43,900	
Liability for Unemployment Insurance		3,600
Liability for Canada Pension Plan		4,600
Liability for Group Insurance		1,600
Liability for Income Tax		12,800
Vacation Pay Payable		4,000
Salaries Payable		83,400
To record payroll for the month of May.		

Payroll taxes on employers become a legal liability when salaries and wages actually are paid, rather than at a time services are rendered by employees. For example, if salaries and wages accrued at year-end amount to $4,500, payroll taxes would not be levied on these earnings until the following year. However, the matching principle requires that payroll taxes be accrued for financial accounting when payroll taxes are material in amount.

Other Current Liabilities

Cash Dividends

When a cash dividend is declared by a corporation's board of directors, the corporation incurs a legal obligation to pay the dividend on a specified date. Because the time between declaration and payment is short, a dividend payable in cash is a current liability. ***Dividends in arrears*** on cumulative preferred stock are disclosed in a note to the financial statements because no liability exists until such dividends are declared by the board of directors. Undistributed ***stock dividends*** are not included among current liabilities, because no cash outlay will be required; the balance in the Stock Dividends to Be Distributed ledger account is included in the shareholders' equity section of the balance sheet. Dividends are discussed in more detail in Chapter 16.

Advances from Customers

When a business enterprise receives payments in advance from its customers, a liability is created. This liability is sometimes referred to as a ***deferred revenue*** or ***deferred credit***. The enterprise is obligated to perform by delivery of goods or services, or to refund the advance if it fails to perform. Generally, the cost of performance will not be as large as the advance, because there is an element of unrealized profit in the price charged. The profit element emerges as goods are delivered or services are performed; prior to this time the enterprise essentially is a trustee of the funds received from its customers. As performance takes place, the amount of the liability diminishes and is transferred to revenue. The costs of performance are recognized as expenses, and income (or loss) emerges.

Advances from customers that are expected to be realized as revenue within a year or during the next operating cycle (if longer than a year) are classified as current liabilities. Examples include deposits on sales orders received, magazine subscriptions received in advance, and billings in excess of estimated earnings and costs incurred on construction-type contracts. Advances from customers that are not expected to be realized as revenue within one year or the next operating cycle are classified as noncurrent liabilities. It may be argued that certain short-term deferred revenue, such as rents and interest received in advance, should be classified as noncurrent liabilities because the realization of such revenue is not expected to require current expenditures. Although this position has some merit, it has not been widely accepted, because the amounts involved generally are immaterial and because it may be difficult to estimate the expenditures to be incurred in the process of realizing such deferred revenue items.

Amounts received from customers as ***container deposits*** generally are refunded when the containers are returned (usually within a short period); therefore, such deposits are classified among current liabilities in the balance sheet.

Accrued Liabilities

The term ***accrued liabilities*** (or ***accrued expenses***) is used to designate obligations that come into existence as the result of past contractual commitments or laws that levy taxes on income, real and personal properties, payrolls, and sales. Because of their materiality, income tax liabilities are listed separately among the current liabilities. Most other accrued liabilities may be combined under one heading, or, as is the case of accrued interest on short-term loans, combined with the liability to which they relate. The problems involved in accounting for property taxes and accrued losses on firm purchase commitments require special attention.

Property taxes are based on the assessed value of real and personal property and usually represent the primary source of revenue for local governmental units. Legally, property taxes arise as of a particular date on which the taxes are levied and become a lien against the property.

The two accounting issues relating to property taxes are: (1) When should the liability for property taxes be recorded? (2) To which accounting period does the tax expense relate? Because the legal liability for property taxes arises on the date on which the taxes are levied and become a lien against the property (the levy or lien date), the liability may be recorded on that date. However, the AICPA in the United States took the position that accrual of property taxes during the fiscal year of the taxing units generally is the most acceptable method.[7] Because property taxes are expenses associated with the use of property during the fiscal year of the taxing units, it seems reasonable to expense the property taxes during that period.

To illustrate, assume that Morris Company's plant assets are subject to property taxes by local taxing units. The fiscal years of the local taxing units cover the period from July 1 to June 30. Property taxes of $36,000 are assessed on March 15, Year 1, covering the fiscal year starting on July 1, Year 1. The levy or lien date is July 1, Year 1, and taxes are payable in two instalments of $18,000 each on December 10, Year 1, and on April 10, Year 2.

7 AICPA, ***Accounting Research and Terminology Bulletins — Final Edition*** (New York: 1961), pp. 83–84.

Property taxes accrued over fiscal year of taxing units

Explanation	*Journal entries*		
July 1, Year 1. Liability of $36,000 comes into existence on July 1, Year 1, the levy or lien date.	(No journal entry required.)		
At the end of July, August, September, October, and November, Year 1, to record ***monthly*** property taxes expense.	Property Taxes Expense ($36,000 ÷ 12)	3,000	
	Property Taxes Payable		3,000
Dec. 10, Year 1. To record payment of first instalment of property tax bill.	Property Taxes Payable ($3,000 × 5)	15,000	
	Prepaid Property Taxes	3,000	
	Cash		18,000
Dec. 31, Year 1. To record ***monthly*** property taxes expense.	Property Taxes Expense	3,000	
	Prepaid Property Taxes		3,000
At the end of January, February, and March, Year 2, to record ***monthly*** property taxes expense.	Property Taxes Expense	3,000	
	Property Taxes Payable		3,000
Apr. 10, Year 2. To record payment of second instalment of property tax bill.	Property Taxes Payable ($3,000 × 3)	9,000	
	Prepaid Property Taxes	9,000	
	Cash		18,000
At end of April, May, and June, Year 2, to record ***monthly*** property taxes expense.	Property Taxes Expense	3,000	
	Prepaid Property Taxes		3,000

The accounting for property taxes for the period from July 1, Year 1, to June 30, Year 2, assuming that Morris accrues property taxes monthly, is illustrated below.

Under this method of accounting for property taxes, neither prepaid property taxes nor property taxes payable would appear in the December 31, Year 1, balance sheet of Morris Company.

An ***accrued loss on a firm purchase commitment*** at the end of an accounting period requires the recording of a current liability. To assure a steady supply of merchandise or material, a business enterprise may enter into a contract for the future delivery of such goods at a fixed price. It is assumed in this discussion that the contract is ***not subject to cancellation***, regardless of changes in market price. As stated in Chapter 8, if the price of the goods at the end of an accounting period is less than the contract price, the lower-of-cost-and-market rule is applied to the purchase contract and the loss is recognized in the accounting records. However, if a loss will not ***in fact*** be incurred because of the price decline, no loss or liability is recorded. According to the AICPA in the United States, "The utility of such commitments is not impaired, and hence there is no loss, when the amounts to be realized from the disposition of the future inventory items are adequately protected by firm sales contracts or when there are other circumstances which reasonably assure continuing sales without price decline.''[8]

A sustained loss is recognized in the accounting period in which the price decline occurs, and the value of the goods under contract is reduced as though these goods were on hand. The journal entries to record an assumed loss of $15,000 and the subsequent purchase of the goods at a fixed price of $100,000 are illustrated below:

Journal entries for loss on firm purchase commitment

Year of price decline:		
Loss on Firm Purchase Commitment	15,000	
Liability Arising from Firm Purchase Commitment		15,000
To record loss due to decline in price of goods ordered.		
Year of purchase:		
Inventories (or Purchases)	85,000	
Liability Arising from Firm Purchase Commitment	15,000	
Trade Accounts Payable		100,000
To record purchase of goods under contract on which a loss due to price decline was recorded in the previous year.		

The loss on firm purchase commitment is listed separately in the income statement if it is material in amount. The liability recorded in the year of price decline is the estimated amount the purchaser would be required to pay if the contract were cancelled. When the goods are purchased, this estimated liability is transferred to Trade Accounts Payable. If the expectation is that the purchase will be made during the operating cycle of the business enterprise, the liability arising from the firm purchase commitment is presented as a current liability in the balance sheet.

If contracts to purchase goods at fixed prices may be cancelled by the prospective purchaser without penalty, no liability is recognized for declines in market prices because such unfavourable contracts generally would be cancelled.

LIABILITIES DEPENDENT ON OPERATING RESULTS

The amount of certain obligations cannot be measured until operating results are known. These include income taxes, bonuses, profit-sharing distributions, and royalties. There is no particular accounting problem in determining such liabilities at the end of a fiscal year, when the operating results are known. However, difficulties may arise in estimating such obligations for ***interim reports***.

Income Taxes

The most familiar example of a liability whose amount is dependent on operating results is income taxes. Individual proprietors and members of a partnership are subject to personal income taxes on their share of the net income of the business

8 AICPA, *Accounting Research and Terminology Bulletins*, p. 35.

enterprise. Thus, sole proprietorships and partnerships are not taxable entities and therefore do not report income tax liabilities in their balance sheets.

Corporations, estates, and trusts are taxable entities and are subject to income taxes. Income tax liabilities, therefore, appear in the balance sheets of such entities. In most cases a corporation is required to make payments of its estimated income tax liability in advance. The remaining tax not covered by the estimated payments is payable by the due date of the income tax return. The estimated tax payments may be debited to the Prepaid Income Taxes ledger account, to the Income Taxes Expense account, or to the Income Taxes Payable account if the accrued tax liability previously was recorded. A credit balance in the Income Taxes Payable ledger account is reported as a current liability at the end of the accounting period.

As stated in Chapter 3, a problem arises in accounting for income tax obligations because of timing differences between ***taxable income*** and ***pre-tax accounting income***. As a result of these differences, interperiod allocation of income taxes is required, and the amount of current income taxes payable at the end of a fiscal year may differ materially from the amount of income taxes expense reported in the income statement. Consequently, Prepaid Income Taxes and Deferred Income Tax Credits ledger account balances appear in the balance sheet. These balances may be current or noncurrent, depending on the reasons for the differences between taxable income and pre-tax accounting income. A complete coverage of this topic appears in Chapter 21.

Bonus and Profit-Sharing Plans

Contracts covering rents, royalties, or employee compensation sometimes call for conditional payments in an amount dependent on revenue or income for an accounting period. We use the term ***bonus*** to describe conditional payments of this type.

Expenses based on revenue cause little difficulty. For example, if an operating lease specifies rent of $500 a month plus 1% of all sales in excess of $100,000 a year, rent expense accrues at the rate of $500 a month, and when sales reach $100,000 each additional dollar of sales creates an additional rent obligation.

Some bonus plans provide for a bonus based on income. The plans generally are drawn so that the income amount used to compute the bonus is clearly defined. For example, the bonus may be based on (1) income before income taxes and bonus, (2) income after bonus but before income taxes, or (3) net income.

To illustrate the computations involved, assume that Larson Limited has a bonus plan under which a branch manager receives 20% of the income over $20,000 earned by the branch. Income for the branch amounted to $80,000 before the bonus and income taxes. Assume for purposes of illustration that income taxes are 40% of pre-tax income. The bonus under each of the three plans listed above is computed as follows:

Plan 1

The bonus is based on income in excess of $20,000 before deduction of income taxes and the bonus:

$$\text{Bonus} = 0.2(\$80{,}000 - \$20{,}000) = \underline{\underline{\$12{,}000}}$$

Plan 2

The bonus is based on income in excess of $20,000 after deduction of the bonus but before deduction of taxes:

$$
\begin{aligned}
B &= \text{Bonus} \\
B &= 0.2(\$80{,}000 - \$20{,}000 - B) \\
B &= \$16{,}000 - \$4{,}000 - 0.2B \\
1.2B &= \$12{,}000 \\
B &= \underline{\underline{\$10{,}000}}
\end{aligned}
$$

The computation of the bonus may be proved by taking 20% of the amount by which the income after the bonus exceeds $20,000. Thus, 20% of $50,000 ($80,000 – $10,000 – $20,000 = $50,000) equals the bonus of $10,000.

Plan 3

The bonus is based on net income in excess of $20,000 after deduction of both the bonus and income taxes:

$$
\begin{aligned}
B &= \text{Bonus} \\
T &= \text{Income taxes} \\
B &= 0.2(\$80{,}000 - \$20{,}000 - T - B) \\
T &= 0.4(\$80{,}000 - B)
\end{aligned}
$$

Substituting for T in the first equation, the bonus is computed as follows:

$$
\begin{aligned}
B &= 0.2[\$60{,}000 - 0.4(\$80{,}000 - B) - B] \\
B &= \$12{,}000 - \$6{,}400 + 0.08B - 0.2B \\
1.12B &= \$5{,}600 \\
B &= \underline{\underline{\$5{,}000}}
\end{aligned}
$$

The computation of the bonus may be proved by taking 20% of the amount by which the net income after the bonus of $5,000 and income taxes of $30,000 ($75,000 × 0.40 = $30,000) exceeds $20,000. Therefore, 20% of $25,000 ($80,000 – $5,000 – $30,000 – $20,000 = $25,000) equals the bonus of $5,000.

The journal entry to record the bonus under Plan 3 follows:

Journal entry to record bonus

Bonus Expense	5,000	
Bonus Payable		5,000
To record liability for bonus to branch manager.		

Bonus Expense is presented as an operating expense in the income statement and Bonus Payable as a current liability in the balance sheet.

Some current liabilities may be based on operating results other than income. These include, for example, royalties for use of patents, royalties based on extraction of natural resources, and rentals for the use of films or other artistic works.

ESTIMATED LIABILITIES

The term ***estimated liability*** is used to describe an obligation that definitely exists but is uncertain as to amount and due date. The primary accounting problem relating to an estimated liability is to obtain a reasonable estimate of the amount of the liability. An estimated liability may be current or long-term. The accounting for some estimated current liabilities is described in the following sections.

Product Warranties

Estimating the liability that arises in connection with various kinds of product warranties often poses a difficult problem. Warranties to replace or repair a product if it proves unsatisfactory during some specified time period are made by most business enterprises. Such liabilities arise at the time of sale and may be recorded at the time of sale or at the end of the accounting period. The following journal entries are made if the liability is recorded at the time of sale:

Journal entries for product warranty liability recorded at the time of sale

Product Warranty Expense	XXX	
Liability Under Product Warranty		XXX
To record estimated liability under product warranty.		
Liability Under Product Warranty	XXX	
Cash (or Accounts Payable, Inventories of Parts, etc.)...		XXX
To record costs of servicing customer claims.		

The balance in the liability ledger account at the end of an accounting period should be reviewed and adjusted if necessary to make certain that it is a reasonable measure of potential customer claims on outstanding product warranties.

An acceptable alternative is to make no journal entry in the liability account at the time of sale; Product Warranty Expense is debited as actual costs are incurred in servicing customer claims and outstanding potential claims are recorded at the end of the accounting period.

Gift Certificates

Some business enterprises issue tickets, tokens, or gift certificates that are promises to perform services or to furnish merchandise on some later date. The amount of the liability is equal to the amount advanced by customers. As redemptions are made, the liability ledger account is debited and a revenue account is credited. Examples of this type of transaction are coupons issued by garages and gasoline stations, tickets and tokens issued by transportation enterprises, and gift certificates sold by retail stores. Because such advances are in small individual amounts and numerous, it is almost certain that some never will be presented for redemption. Estimating the amount of forfeited claims is simplified when there is an agreement that the obligation expires after a stated time. When the offer is of indefinite duration, it is necessary to estimate the amounts of potential claims that will not be redeemed and to transfer this amount from the liability ledger account to a revenue account.

Service Contracts

Business enterprises selling or servicing household appliances often sell service contracts to customers under which the enterprises agree to service the appliance for a specified period of time. The amounts received for such service contracts constitute unearned revenue that will be earned (realized) by performance over the term of the contract. To illustrate, assume that an enterprise sells television service contracts for $150 each, agreeing to service customers' sets for one year. If 1,000 such service contracts are sold, the journal entry is:

Journal entry for sale of service contracts

Cash (or Trade Accounts Receivable)	150,000	
Unearned Service Contract Revenue		150,000
To record sale of 1,000 service contracts at $150 each.		

During the ensuing 12-month period, the unearned service contract revenue will be realized, and actual costs of servicing the television sets will be recognized as expenses. On the basis of experience, it often is possible to establish a pattern of probable service calls as a guide for recognizing revenue. For example, if the bulk of the service calls tend to be made in the first part of the year covered by the service contract, a policy of recognizing revenue for, say, 30% of the contract price in the first month, 20% in the second month, and 5% in each of the 10 subsequent months might be reasonable. The journal entries below are illustrative of this procedure for the first month of the service contract period, if we assume that costs of $30,735 were incurred in servicing the contracts during the first month:

Journal entries for revenue realized and costs incurred under service contracts

Unearned Service Contract Revenue	45,000	
Service Contract Revenue		45,000
To recognize 30% of unearned service contract revenue as realized revenue for the first month of the contract period ($150,000 × 0.30 = $45,000).		

Service Contract Expense	30,735	
Inventory of Parts		14,250
Cash, Accrued Payroll, etc.		16,485
To recognize expense incurred under service contracts.		

At the end of the first month, the balance of $105,000 ($150,000 – $45,000 = $105,000) in the Unearned Service Contract Revenue ledger account is reported among current liabilities in the balance sheet.

Coupons and Trading Stamps

In an effort to promote the sale of certain products, a business enterprise may issue coupons exchangeable for prizes such as cash or merchandise. In such cases, the enterprise incurs a liability equal to the cost of the prizes that are expected to be claimed by customers.

The liability for prizes to be distributed is based on the enterprise's past and anticipated experience with redemptions of coupons. For example, assume that in Year 1 Lena Company issued coupons that may be redeemed for prizes costing $2,500 if all the coupons are presented for redemption. If past experience indicates that only 80% of the coupons issued will be presented for redemption, the liability is $2,000 ($2,500 × 0.8 = $2,000), the maximum cost of prizes that are expected to be claimed by Lena's customers.

The purchase of prize merchandise to be given to customers is recorded in an inventory ledger account. For example, the journal entry to record the purchase of $2,800 of prize merchandise by Lena Company in Year 1 is illustrated below:

Journal entry for purchase of prizes

Inventory of Prize Merchandise	2,800	
Cash (or Accounts Payable)		2,800
To record purchase of merchandise to be offered as prizes.		

Generally, the cost of the coupons is immaterial in amount and is not accounted for separately; if the cost of coupons is material, the cost also may be recorded in an inventory ledger account. Assuming that Lena Company's customers present coupons during Year 1 in exchange for prize merchandise costing $1,500, the following journal entry would be required:

Journal entry for redemption of coupons for prizes

Promotional Expense	1,500	
Inventory of Prize Merchandise		1,500
To record redemption of coupons by customers in exchange for prize merchandise costing $1,500.		

An adjusting journal entry is required at the end of each accounting period to recognize the estimated expense and liability relating to the coupons outstanding. In our example, the total cost of prizes expected to be claimed by Lena

Company's customers was estimated at $2,000, of which $1,500 was redeemed during Year 1. Thus, an additional expense and a liability of $500 ($2,000 – $1,500 = $500) are recorded at the end of Year 1 as follows:

Adjusting entry to record liability for unredeemed coupons

Promotional Expense	500	
Liability for Coupons Outstanding		500
To record estimated liability for coupons outstanding at the end of Year 1.		

At the end of Year 1, the inventory of prize merchandise is $1,300 ($2,800 – $1,500 = $1,300). This inventory is listed among the current assets in Lena Company's balance sheet; the liability for coupons outstanding, $500, is included among current liabilities; and the promotional expense for the year, $2,000 ($1,500 + $500 = $2,000), is classified as a selling expense in the income statement.

A slightly different situation exists when a retailer gives its customers ***trading stamps*** to be redeemed by another enterprise engaged in the sale and redemption of trading stamps. The retailer pays a fixed price for the trading stamps, which are recorded in an Inventory of Trading Stamps ledger account. When stamps are issued to customers, an operating expense ledger account is debited, and the Inventory of Trading Stamps ledger account is credited. The obligation to redeem the stamps is assumed by the enterprise that sells and redeems trading stamps. The trading stamp enterprise usually records the proceeds from the sale of stamps in a revenue ledger account and also records a liability for the cost of merchandise and related service costs to be incurred when stamps are redeemed. When merchandise is issued for redeemed stamps, the liability is debited and the inventory of merchandise is credited.

CONTINGENCIES

Contingencies were briefly introduced in Chapter 4 as potential gains or losses, the existence of which is conditional upon the happening of some future event. Until the issuance of ***CICA Handbook*** section 3290: "Contingencies," the distinction between potential liabilities from contingencies and estimated liabilities was not clear to many accountants. Similarly, some confusion existed as to which contingencies require the accrual of a loss, which contingencies simply call for disclosure in the notes to the financial statements, and which general-risk contingencies inherent in a business enterprise may be disclosed in the financial statements. The purpose of section 3290 of the ***Handbook*** was to establish more definitive standards of accounting for contingencies.

A ***contingency*** is "an existing condition or situation involving uncertainty as to possible gain or loss to an enterprise that will ultimately be resolved when one or more future events occur or fail to occur."[9] Resolution of the uncertainty surrounding a contingent gain generally results in an acquisition of an asset or a reduction of liability; resolution of the uncertainty surrounding a contingent loss

9 CICA, ***CICA Handbook***, sec. 3290.02.

generally results in a reduction of an asset or an incurrence of a liability. The probabilities that the future event or events will confirm the contingency may be ***likely*** (chance of occurrence or nonoccurrence is high), or ***unlikely*** (chance of occurrence or nonoccurrence is slight), or ***not determinable*** (chance of occurrence or nonoccurrence cannot be determined).[10]

The preparation of financial statements requires estimates for many business activities, and the use of estimates does not necessarily mean that a contingency exists. Thus, ''the mere fact that an estimate is involved does not of itself constitute the type of uncertainty which characterizes a contingency.''[11] For example, the measurement of depreciation and of income taxes expense involves estimates, but neither is a contingency. There is no uncertainty regarding the expiration of the cost of depreciable assets nor the incurrence of the obligation to pay income taxes; the uncertainty relates solely to the use of estimates of the periodic amounts to be recognized in the accounting records.

Examples of Contingencies

The following items are contingencies:[12]

1 Pending or threatened litigation

2 Threat of expropriation of assets

3 Guarantees of the indebtedness of others

4 Possible liabilities arising from discounted bills of exchange or promissory notes

However, there are other items which may possess many of the characteristics of contingencies but which are not considered contingencies. The items that are explicitly excluded as contingencies include allowances for doubtful accounts and provisions for product warranties.[13] In the United States, the FASB, in its ***Statement No. 5***: ''Accounting for Contingencies,'' took a different view and treated allowances for doubtful accounts and provisions for product warranties, and other, similar items, as contingencies.

Accrual of Contingent Losses

According to the ***CICA Handbook***, an estimated amount of a contingent loss should be accrued by a charge to income if ***both*** of the following conditions are met:[14]

1 It is ***likely*** that a future event will confirm that an asset had been impaired or a liability incurred at the date of the financial statements.

10 CICA, ***CICA Handbook***, sec. 3290.06.

11 CICA, ***CICA Handbook***, sec. 3290.04.

12 CICA, ***CICA Handbook***, sec. 3290.03.

13 CICA, ***CICA Handbook***, sec. 3290.05.

14 CICA, ***CICA Handbook***, sec. 3290.12.

2 The amount of the loss can be ***reasonably estimated***.

When the range of loss can be reasonably estimated and a single amount within the range appears to be a better estimate than any other, ***this single amount would be accrued***.[15] On the other hand, if no single amount within the range of estimated loss appears to be a better estimate than any other amount within the range, ***the minimum amount in the range would be accrued***.[16] For example, assume that at the balance sheet date a business enterprise had learned that a foreign government had expropriated the assets of a major subsidiary of the enterprise and that there would be a compensation by that government for the expropriation. Assume also that a reasonable estimate of the loss to the enterprise would be for not less than $16 million or more than $30 million. No amount between $16 million and $30 million appears to be a better estimate than any other amount. Thus, $16 million is accrued as a loss, and the possibility of an additional loss is disclosed in a note to the financial statements.[17] If the contingent loss meets the criteria for classification as an extraordinary item, such as the expropriation loss cited in the example, it should be presented as an extraordinary item in the income statement.

Disclosure of Contingent Losses Not Accrued

It was discussed earlier that note disclosure was required when there was an exposure to loss in excess of the amount accrued. In addition, note disclosure is required if one of the following conditions exists.[18]

1 The occurrence of the confirming future event is likely but the amount of the loss ***cannot be reasonably estimated***.

2 The occurrence of the confirming future event is ***not determinable***.

In essence, a contingent loss should be disclosed in a note to the financial statements when it does not meet the two conditions (''likely'' and ''reasonably estimated'') for accrual as described earlier.

Moreover, it is desirable to disclose in a note to financial statements those ***unlikely*** contingent losses if their occurrence would result in a material adverse financial effect on the business enterprise. Such contingent losses include lawsuits and guarantees on behalf of others.[19]

While the absence of insurance or the lack of adequate insurance covering property damages or injury claims expose a business enterprise to possible losses, this does not indicate that an asset has been impaired or that a liability has been incurred. Thus, mere exposure to risk does not require the accrual of losses.

15 CICA, *CICA Handbook*, sec. 3290.13.

16 CICA, *CICA Handbook*, sec. 3290.13.

17 CICA, *CICA Handbook*, sec. 3290.15.

18 CICA, *CICA Handbook*, sec. 3290.15.

19 CICA, *CICA Handbook*, sec. 3290.17.

However, it may be desirable to disclose the lack of adequate insurance against a material risk that is normally insured.[20]

Contingent Gains

Contingencies that might result in gains should not be recognized in the accounting records until the gains are realized or realizable. This is consistent with the general principle of revenue recognition. Accordingly, if a contingent gain is likely, that is, the chance of the occurrence of a future event or events is high, it should be disclosed in a note to the financial statements only.[21]

Note Disclosure of Contingent Gains and Losses

There should be adequate disclosure regarding contingencies. Even though a contingent loss is accrued in the financial statements, it still may be desirable to disclose the nature and the amount of the accrual. For those contingencies that are not accrued in the financial statements, the following disclosure should be made:[22]

1 The nature of the contingency

2 An estimate of the amount of the contingent gain or loss or a statement that such an estimate cannot be made

3 Whether any settlement resulting from the resolution of the contingency is expected to be accounted for as a prior period adjustment or as a charge to income of the period in which the settlement occurs

The following are examples of note disclosure of contingencies from published annual reports:[23]

> 1 The Company has received claims of approximately $2,300,000 arising from guarantees that the Company allegedly made on behalf of clients of a brokerage firm; however, the Company has denied any liability with respect thereto. One of these claims formed the basis of an action against the Company in the Supreme Court of Nova Scotia, Trial Division, which was dismissed by the Court on February 29, 1984, but has subsequently been appealed.
>
> The Company does not anticipate that a loss will result; accordingly, no provision has been made in the accounts for such an occurrence. If any loss is eventually incurred, it will be treated as a prior period adjustment.
>
> 2 An action was commenced against the Company in 1972 by . . . claiming damages for alleged breach of contract. A court decision has held that there was an enforceable agreement. The issue of the amount of damages is being considered. While a provision for loss is not presently determinable, in its latest damage claim the

20 CICA, ***CICA Handbook***, sec. 3290.16.

21 CICA, ***CICA Handbook***, sec. 3290.21.

22 CICA, ***CICA Handbook***, sec. 3290.22.

23 CICA, ***Financial Reporting in Canada***, 16th ed. (Toronto, 1985), pp. 36–38, adapted.

plaintiff seeks $3,910,000. A loss, if any, would be treated as a prior period adjustment.

3 ... The Company has the following contingent liabilities:

a The Company is contingently liable for $225.0 million advanced to Dome Canada by the Arctic Petroleum Corporation of Japan.

b In 1983, Revenue Canada — Taxation issued reassessments to the Company disallowing the frontier exploration allowance claimed in 1980. Management believes that these amounts were validly claimed and intends to contest the issue. If the Company is not successful, a prior period adjustment will be made relating to 1980 which will increase the deficit and deferred income taxes by $44.3 million.

There are no pending legal proceedings to which the Company or any of its subsidiaries is a party or of which any of their properties is the subject, that in management's view would have a material effect on the Company's consolidated financial position or results of operations.

4 The Corporation has filed a claim in the amount of $1,564,000 with two insurance companies covering repair costs and business interruption losses related to a two-week shutdown of a paper machine in January 1984. The insurance companies have denied coverage and the Corporation has instructed its attorneys to institute legal proceedings to recover the said amount less any applicable deductibles. In the opinion of management and legal counsel, the Corporation has a valid claim and is entitled to its payment. Because legal proceedings are involved, settlement of the claim could be delayed for a prolonged period and it has therefore not been reflected in the financial statements. Any recovery will be treated as a prior period adjustment when received.

FUTURE LIABILITIES AND COMMITMENTS

Most business enterprises are continuously planning future operations. In many instances, commitments may be made that will result in substantial liabilities in the near future. On any balance sheet date, an enterprise ordinarily will have made certain commitments that are of a recurring nature and normal in amount; these do not require special disclosure. However, when unusual and material commitments have been made, their nature and amount should be disclosed.[24] Examples are commitments for an unusually large purchase of material, a major acquisition of plan assets and natural resources, payments to be made contingent on earnings of acquired enterprises, or unusually large commitments for advertising and product development costs. An example of disclosure of commitments appears below:

The company has commitments under contracts for the purchase of land and for the construction of buildings. Portions of such contracts not completed at year-end are

24 CICA, *CICA Handbook*, sec. 3280.01.

not reflected in the financial statements. Such unrecorded commitments amounted to approximately $58,575,000 at the end of 1989 as compared to $83,757,000 for 1988.

Presentation of Current Liabilities in the Balance Sheet

The two issues that arise in connection with the presentation of current liabilities in the balance sheet are (1) the order of presentation and (2) the extent of disclosure necessary for different types of current liabilities. Current liabilities can be reported in the ***order of maturity*** or according to ***amount*** (largest to smallest). It is difficult to satisfy both objectives, and the usual compromise is to rank current liabilities in order of size unless differences in maturity dates are significant. However, cash overdrafts and promissory notes maturing shortly after the balance sheet date usually are listed first.

The main classes of current liabilities should be shown separately; such classes include bank loans, notes payable, accounts payable, taxes payable, dividends payable, deferred revenues, and current payments on long-term debt.[25]

The matter of detail will depend to some extent on the purpose for which the balance sheet is prepared. In a balance sheet prepared in support of a loan application or for use in forecasting short-term financial requirements, a listing of current liabilities in greater detail is desirable. For financial statements presented in annual reports, the classification illustrated below is recommended:

Balance sheet presentation of current liabilities

Current liabilities:	
Notes payable to banks	$ 600,000
Notes payable to trade creditors	445,000
Accounts payable	325,200
Current maturities of long-term debt (including bonds payable, mortgage notes payable, and equipment contracts payable)	150,500
Income taxes payable	112,500
Other accrued liabilities (payroll, interest, royalties, guarantees, etc.)	29,000
Dividends payable	25,000
Miscellaneous current liabilities (advances from customers, credit balances in customers' accounts, etc.)	21,800
Total current liabilities	$1,709,000

If the due date of any liability can be extended, the details should be disclosed parenthetically or in notes accompanying the financial statements. Short-term obligations for which ''contractual arrangements have been made for settlement from other than current assets'' should be excluded from current liabilities.[26] For example, a short-term obligation which is expected to be liquidated by the issuance of additional shares of capital stock is reported in the shareholders' equity section of the balance sheet. When current liabilities are secured, they should be so described and shown separately.[27]

25 CICA, ***CICA Handbook***, sec. 1510.07.

26 CICA, ***CICA Handbook***, sec. 1510.06.

27 CICA, ***CICA Handbook***, sec. 1510.08.

REVIEW QUESTIONS

1 Liabilities sometimes are described as "equities of outsiders in the assets of a business enterprise." Do you agree with this description of liabilities? Explain.

2 Distinguish between a ***liability*** and a ***commitment***. Should the currently maturing instalment of a deferred compensation contract that is to be liquidated by the issuance of common stock be reported as a liability in the balance sheet? Explain.

3 What is the basis for distinguishing between a ***current liability*** and a ***long-term liability***?

4 Distinguish among the following: ***definitely measurable liability, liability dependent on operating results, estimated liability, contingent loss***. Give one or more examples of each.

5 Under what circumstances is it proper to report a currently maturing debt as a noncurrent liability in the balance sheet?

6 *a* What are the liabilities that generally arise in connection with a payroll?
b When are ***special termination benefits*** recorded by an employer?

7 When should deferred revenue (or unearned revenue) be reported as a current liability? When should deferred revenue be reported as a noncurrent liability?

8 When is the liability for property taxes entered in the accounting records? Over what period are property taxes recognized as expenses? Explain.

9 Describe the generally accepted accounting principles for an accrued loss on a ***firm purchase commitment***.

10 Where should the liability for current year's income taxes appear in the balance sheet of a partnership? Explain.

11 Motowne, Inc., acquired certain patent rights in return for royalties equal to "10% of income." What difficulties may arise in the interpretation of this contract?

12 *a* Define a ***contingency*** and differentiate between a ***contingent gain*** and a ***contingent loss***.
b Give some examples of contingent gains and contingent losses.
c What two conditions must be met before a contingent loss is accrued?

13 On December 31, Year 6, Granite Limited had an investment of $2 million in the bonds of Coe Corporation, which was likely to go bankrupt. A reasonable estimate of the probable loss ranges from $600,000 to $900,000. No amount of the estimated loss in this range appears to be a better estimate than any other. How should Granite account for this contingent loss in its financial statements for the year ended December 31, Year 6?

14 Briefly describe the accounting for promotional plans involving coupons and prizes, product guarantees, and the sale of service contracts.

15 Describe three situations under which a contingent loss should be disclosed in a note to financial statements.

16 Indicate how each of the following items is reported in the balance sheet:
a Bank overdraft
b Customers' accounts with credit balances

c Service guarantee on products sold
d Bonds maturing in three months, to be paid from a sinking fund
e Stock dividend to be distributed in the form of common stock of the issuing corporation
f Dividends in arrears on cumulative preferred stock
g Interest (discount) on a note payable, deducted from the face amount of the note to determine the net proceeds received
h Estimated payments to be made to employees under a three-year union contract

17 Under what circumstances are commitments for future expenditures disclosed in financial statements? How should this disclosure be made?

18 List some general guidelines for reporting current liabilities in the balance sheet of a business enterprise.

EXERCISES

Ex. 10-1 Select the best answer for each of the following multiple-choice questions:

1 According to section 3290 of the ***CICA Handbook***, an estimated loss from a contingency is accrued if the amount of the loss can be reasonably estimated and information available prior to issuance of the financial statements indicates that, on the date of the financial statements, the impairment of an asset or the incurrence of a liability is:
a Likely *b* Reasonably possible *c* Certain *d* Remote

2 In July, Year 7, Nyquist, Inc., filed suit in a court against Dean corporation seeking to recover $750,000 for patent infringement. A court verdict was rendered in August, Year 9, awarding Nyquist $500,000 in damages. Dean has appealed the verdict, but a final decision is not expected before Year 12. Nyquist's counsel believes it is probable that Nyquist will be successful against Dean for an estimated amount of $400,000. What amount does Nyquist recognize as a gain in the year ended December 31, Year 11?
a $0 *b* $400,000 *c* $500,000 *d* $750,000 *e* Some other amount

3 Cone Corporation, a manufacturer of paint, is preparing annual financial statements on December 31, Year 3. Because of a recently proven health hazard in one of its paints, the federal government has indicated clearly its intention of having Cone recall all cans of this paint sold in the last six months. The management of Cone estimates that this recall would cost $800,000. What accounting recognition, if any, should be accorded this situation?
a No recognition
b Disclosure in a note to the financial statements
c Operating expense of $800,000
d Appropriation of retained earnings as a reserve for the $800,000

4 Lucero, Inc., provides an incentive compensation plan under which its president is to receive a bonus equal to 10% of Lucero's income in excess of $100,000 before deduction of income taxes but after deduction of the bonus.

If income before income taxes and the bonus is $320,000, the amount of the bonus is:

a $20,000 *b* $22,000 *c* $32,000 *d* $44,000 *e* Some other amount

5 Swanny's is a retail store operating in a province with a 5% retail sales tax. The law provides that the retail sales tax collected during the month must be remitted to the province during the following month. If the amount collected is remitted on or before the twentieth day of the following month, the retailer may keep 2% of the sales tax collected. On April 10, Swanny's remitted $16,905 sales tax for March retail sales. What was the amount of the March retail sales subject to sales tax?

a $331,340 *b* $331,480 *c* $338,100 *d* $345,000 *e* Some other amount

6 Monica Limited was sued for negligence in permitting local residents to be exposed to toxic chemicals from its plant. Monica lost the suit, and its lawyers have concluded that it is likely that Monica will be liable for a judgement costing anywhere from $250,000 to $1,250,000. However, the lawyers state that the most likely cost is $500,000. As a result of the above facts, Monica should accrue:

a A contingent loss of $250,000, and disclose an additional contingency of up to $1,000,000
b A contingent loss of $500,000, and disclose an additional contingency of up to $750,000
c A contingent loss of $500,000, but not disclose any additional contingency
d No contingent loss, but disclose a contingency of $250,000 to $1,250,000

7 On January 2, Year 5, Lee Company borrowed $200,000 from its major customer, Sun Corporation, evidenced by a promissory note payable in three years. The note did not bear interest. Lee agreed to supply Sun's merchandise needs for the loan period at favourable prices. The market rate of interest for this type of loan is 14%. Assume that the present value (at the market rate of interest) of the $200,000 note is $135,000 on January 2, Year 5. What amount of interest expense is included in Lee's Year 5 income statement?

a $0 *b* $18,900 *c* $21,667 *d* 28,000 *e* Some other amount

8 Ability to refinance a short-term debt on a long-term basis is evidenced by:

a Actually having issued other short-term debt to replace the short-term debt after the date of the balance sheet but before it is issued
b Planning to issue equity securities to replace the short-term debt after the date of the balance sheet
c Having entered into a firm financing contract that will enable the debtor to refinance the short-term debt when it becomes due
d None of the foregoing

9 Reyes Company estimates its annual warranty expense at 2% of annual net sales. The following data are available:

Net sales for Year 5	$4,000,000

Warranty liability ledger account:	
December 31, Year 4 balance	$60,000 credit
Warranty payments during Year 5	50,000 debit

After estimated warranty expense for Year 5 is recorded, the warranty liability ledger account will show a December 31, Year 5, balance of:
a $10,000 *b* $70,000 *c* $80,000 *d* $90,000 *e* Some other amount

10 During Year 1, Charles Company introduced a new line of machines that carry a three-year warranty against manufacturer's defects. Based on industry experience, warranty expense is estimated at 2% of net sales in the year of sale, 4% in the year after sale, and 6% in the second year after sale. Net sales and actual warranty payments for the first three years were as follows:

	Net sales	*Actual warranty payments*
Year 1	$ 200,000	$ 3,000
Year 2	500,000	15,000
Year 3	700,000	45,000
Totals	$1,400,000	$63,000

What amount does Charles report as a liability under product warranty on December 31, Year 3?
a $0 *b* $5,000 *c* $68,000 *d* $105,000 *e* Some other amount

11 Laura Company sells its products in reusable, expensive containers. The customer is charged a deposit for each container delivered and receives a refund for each container returned within two years after the year of delivery. Laura accounts for the containers not returned within the time limit as being sold for the amount of the deposit. Information for Year 3 is as follows:

Containers held by customers on December 31, Year 2, from deliveries in:		
Year 1	$ 50,000	
Year 2	145,000	$195,000
Containers delivered in Year 3		260,000
Containers returned in Year 3 from deliveries in:		
Year 1	$ 30,000	
Year 2	85,000	
Year 3	95,000	210,000

What amount does Laura report as a liability for returnable containers on December 31, Year 3?
a $165,000 *b* $215,000 *c* $225,000 *d* $245,000 *e* Some other amount

12 The balance in Ashe Company's Trade Accounts Payable ledger account on December 31, Year 2, was $700,000 before any necessary year-end adjustments relating to the following:

1 Goods were in transit from a vendor to Ashe on December 31, Year 2. The invoice cost was $50,000, and the goods were shipped FOB shipping point on December 29, Year 2. The goods were received on January 4, Year 3.
2 Goods shipped FOB shipping point on December 20, Year 2, from a vendor to Ashe were lost in transit. The invoice cost was $25,000. On January 5, Year 3, Ashe filed a $25,000 claim against the common carrier.
3 Goods shipped FOB destination on December 21, Year 2, from a vendor to Ashe were received on January 6, Year 3. The invoice cost was $15,000.

What amount does Ashe report as trade accounts payable on its December 31, Year 2, balance sheet?
a $725,000 *b* $740,000 *c* $750,000 *d* $775,000 *e* Some other amount

Ex. 10-2 On December 31, Year 3, Muriel Company issued a two-year non-interest-bearing promissory note with a face amount of $58,320 for the purchase of scrap metal. The transaction was recorded as follows:

Purchases	58,320	
Note Payable		58,320

a Prepare a correcting journal entry for Muriel Company on December 31, Year 3, assuming that a fair rate of interest is 8% a year and that the accounting records are still open for Year 3. Use the Appendix at the end of Chapter 5 to determine the present value of the note.
b Prepare an adjusting entry for Muriel Company on December 31, Year 4, to record interest expense on the note.
c Show how the note is presented in Muriel Company's balance sheet on December 31, Year 4.

Ex. 10-3 Rio Corporation had $6 million of short-term promissory notes outstanding on June 30, Year 6, the end of its fiscal year. On that date, Rio had a firm contract to refinance these notes by issuance of long-term debt. However, because Rio had excess cash in July, it retired $2 million of these notes. On August 10, Year 6, Rio issued $12 million long-term bonds, and on August 15, it issued financial statements for the year ended June 30. The proceeds of the $12-million long-term bond issue were to be used as follows:
1 To increase working capital, $2 million
2 To pay balance of promissory notes, $4 million
3 To finance construction of new warehouse, $6 million

Indicate how the foregoing information is to be presented in Rio Corporation's balance sheet on June 30, Year 6.

Ex. 10-4 On October 29, Year 5, Ernst Company contracted to purchase 7,500 tonnes of material in Year 6 at a fixed price of $100 a tonne. The contract was not subject to cancellation. On December 31, Year 5, the replacement cost of the material was

$88 a tonne.

Prepare a journal entry for Ernst Company on December 31, Year 5, to recognize the loss on the firm purchase commitment.

Ex. 10-5 Raymond ZeBrack has an employment contract under which he is to receive a bonus of 20% of Kyle Company's net income in excess of $100,000. Kyle's income before the bonus and income taxes for the year is $385,000. Income taxes are 45% of taxable income.

Compute the amount of Raymond ZeBrack's bonus, rounded to the nearest dollar, assuming that it is based on Kyle Company's net income in excess of $100,000 after deduction of both the bonus and income taxes.

Ex. 10-6 At the end of a fiscal year, the auditors for Moran Company found the following contingencies that had not been entered in the accounting records:

a Stella Davis, a former officer of Moran, has threatened to sue Moran for $1 million "to recover the contributions she made to the success of the company's marketing program for which she was not compensated adequately." In the opinion of Moran's management and outside legal counsel, the suit has absolutely no merit and probably will never be filed by Davis.

b Moran has guaranteed a debt of $500,000 issued by certain affiliated companies. The affiliated companies are in a strong financial position, and Moran's management does not consider that any of the companies will default on their debt.

c Moran's management is of the opinion that $100,000 should be set aside for general business risks that cannot be identified at the present time.

d Moran has been sued for industrial espionage, and the damages sought by the plaintiff amount to $200,000. Moran's outside legal counsel and management are of the opinion that the suit has merit and that the amount of the damages may range from a minimum of $25,000 to a maximum of $75,000. No amount in this range is a better estimate than any other amount.

For each situation described above, prepare a journal entry for Moran Company to record the contingency or briefly explain why a journal entry is not required.

Ex. 10-7 Adams Company sold a machine (which it had manufactured) on credit early in Year 5 for $1,200, along with a one-year warranty. Maintenance on each machine during the warranty period averages $100.

Prepare journal entries for Adams Company to record the sale of the machine and the cash expenditure of $85 to service the machine during Year 5, assuming that the Product Warranty Expense ledger account is debited at the time of sale and that Adams uses the periodic inventory system.

Ex. 10-8 In Year 1, Palmer Corporation began selling a new line of products that carry a two-year warranty against defects. Based on past experience with other products, the estimated warranty costs related to dollar sales are as follows:

First year of warranty	2%
Second year of warranty	5%

Sales and actual warranty payments for Year 1 and Year 2 are presented below:

	Year 1	*Year 2*
Sales	$500,000	$700,000
Actual warranty payments	10,000	30,000

Compute Palmer Corporation's estimated warranty liability at the end of Year 2.

Ex. 10-9 In an effort to increase sales, Remo Company launched a sales promotional campaign on June 30, Year 5, whereby Remo placed a coupon in each package of product sold, the coupons being redeemable for a premium. Each premium costs Remo $2, and five coupons must be presented by a customer to receive a premium. Remo estimated that only 60% of the coupons issued will be redeemed. For the six months ended December 31, Year 5, the following information is available:

Packages of product sold	*Premiums purchased*	*Coupons redeemed*
800,000	60,000	200,000

Compute Remo Company's estimated liability for premium claims outstanding on December 31, Year 5.

Ex. 10-10 Cord Company distributes to consumers coupons that may be presented (on or before a stated expiration date) to grocers for discounts on certain products of Cord. The grocers are reimbursed when they send the coupons to Cord. In Cord's experience, 40% of the coupons are redeemed, and generally one month elapses between the date a grocer receives a coupon from a consumer and the date Cord receives it. During Year 8, Cord issued two separate series of coupons as follows:

Date issued	*Total value*	*Consumer expiration date*	*Amount disbursed as of Dec. 31, Year 8*
Jan. 1, Year 8	$100,000	June 30, Year 8	$34,000
July 1, Year 8	120,000	Dec. 31, Year 8	42,000

Compute Cord Company's liability for unredeemed coupons on December 31, Year 8.

Ex. 10-11 Sinbad Company offers a coupon with each unit of product sold. A customer who submits 100 coupons is given a choice of prizes consisting of a football, a basketball, or a baseball glove. These prizes cost $5 each. The Promotional Expense ledger account is debited as redemptions are made during the year and also at the end of the year when an estimate is made of outstanding coupons that will be redeemed. The following summary transactions occurred in Year 1:

a Acquired for cash 800 coupon books, each containing 1,000 coupons, for a total cost of $800. (Debit Inventory of Coupons.)
b Issued 500,000 coupons to customers.
c Acquired for cash 2,200 items of prize merchandise (footballs, basketballs, and baseball gloves).
d Issued 1,500 prizes to customers.
e Of the coupons issued, it is estimated that an additional 120,000 will be redeemed.

Prepare journal entries to record each of the transactions of Sinbad Company.

Ex. 10-12 On January 6, Year 1, Plaga, Inc., acquired prize merchandise costing $5,000 for distribution in a promotional campaign, and related coupons costing $100 (an immaterial amount). During Year 1, prize merchandise costing $3,100 was distributed to customers in exchange for coupons. Coupons redeemable for $8,000 of prize merchandise were issued to customers. The controller of Plaga estimated that 90% of the coupons would be presented by customers who obtained the coupons from cartons of Plaga's product. No expiration date appeared on the coupons.

Prepare journal entries for Plaga, Inc., in connection with the promotional campaign.

CASES

Case 10-1 Salcedo Limited has been sued for $2,000,000 for an injury caused to a child as a result of alleged negligence while the child was visiting Salcedo's plant on March 10, Year 5. The lawsuit was filed on July 6, Year 5. Salcedo's lawyer states that it is likely that Salcedo will lose the lawsuit and be found liable for anywhere from $200,000 to $900,000. However, the lawyer states that the most probable estimated loss is $400,000.

Instructions

How should Salcedo Limited report the probable effect of the lawsuit in its Year 5 financial statements? Discuss the rationale for your answer. Include in your answer disclosures, if any, that should be made in Salcedo's financial statements or in a note to the financial statements.

Case 10-2 On June 30, Year 3, Horsley Limited has a bank loan due on September 30, Year 3. The loan has been in existence for five years, but both Horsley and the bank intend to renew it indefinitely. The loan is collateralized by the cash surrender value of life insurance policies.

For several years, Horsley has been offering to officers and employees the right to acquire its 15% bonds that are redeemable at face amount at the holder's request at any time after two years from the date of issuance. In the past, executive incentive bonuses have been paid by the issuance of these bonds. During the past 10 years, bonds redeemed were less than 10% of bonds outstanding, and evidence indicates that no bondholders intended to redeem their bonds in the year ending June 30, Year 4.

Instructions
State how you would classify the cash surrender value of the life insurance policies, the bank loan, and the 15% bonds payable in the balance sheet of Horsley Limited on June 30, Year 3. Give reasons for your answer.

Case 10-3 The balance sheet of Denny Limited on December 31, Year 5, ***did not*** include among the current liabilities the following items (all of which are material in amount):

1 Promissory notes payable to a group of 12 shareholders, the notes to become due and payable on demand of at least 8 of the shareholders
2 A promissory note payable due March 31, Year 6, in settlement of which the holder accepted 1,000 shares of preferred stock on January 15, Year 6
3 Rent collected one year in advance
4 Bonds payable maturing on March 31, Year 6

Instructions
Assuming that in each case the exclusion from current liabilities was based on sound reasoning, give the arguments in support of the financial statement presentation used by Denny. If your answer involves assumptions as to facts not given in the case, state your assumptions.

Case 10-4 Promotek Company was organized on January 2, Year 1, to sell trading stamps to retailers who distribute the stamps gratuitously to their customers. Books for accumulating the stamps and catalogues illustrating the merchandise for which the stamps may be exchanged are given free to retailers for distribution to stamp recipients. Centres with inventories of merchandise have been established for redemption of the stamps. Retailers may not return unused stamps.

The analysis at the top of the next page shows Promotek's expectations as to percentages of a normal month's activity that will be attained. For this purpose, a "normal month's activity" is defined as the level of operations expected when expansion of activities ceases or tapers off to a stable rate. Promotek expects that this level will be attained in the third year and that sales of stamps will average $2,000,000 a month throughout the third year.

Promotek adopted a fiscal year ending on December 31, Year 1.

Instructions
a Discuss the accounting alternatives that should be considered by Promotek Company for the recognition of revenue and related expenses.
b For each accounting alternative discussed in ***a*** above, identify the ledger

Month	Actual stamp sales, %	Merchandise purchases, %	Stamp redemptions, %
6th	30	40	10
12th	60	60	45
18th	80	80	70
24th	90	90	80
30th	100	100	95

accounts that are used and indicate how each is classified in Promotek Company's balance sheet.

Case 10-5 A condensed balance sheet of Candide Corporation on December 31, Year 5, is presented below:

CANDIDE CORPORATION
Condensed Balance Sheet
December 31, Year 5

Assets	
Current assets	$15,000,000
Other assets	25,000,000
Total assets	$40,000,000

Liabilities & Shareholders' Equity	
15% Note payable to bank, due Feb. 1, Year 6	$ 2,500,000
18% Note payable to insurance company, due July 10, Year 6	1,500,000
Accounts payable and accrued liabilities	5,000,000
16% Bonds payable, due Dec. 31, Year 25	12,500,000
Shareholders' equity	18,500,000
Total liabilities & shareholders' equity	$40,000,000

Before Candide issued a classified balance sheet on March 1, Year 6, as of December 31, Year 5, you ascertained that Candide intended to refinance the two notes payable on a long-term basis. During December, Year 5, Candide negotiated a financing contract with Equitable Bank for a maximum amount of $4 million at any time through December 31, Year 6. The terms of the contract are as follows:

1 Funds will be made available at the request of Candide, and any amount borrowed will mature three years from the date of borrowing. Interest at the prevailing bank prime interest rate will be due quarterly.

2 An annual commitment fee of 1% will be charged by the bank on the difference between the amount borrowed by Candide and $4 million.

3 The contract is cancellable by the bank only if:

i Candide's working capital, excluding borrowings under the contract, falls below $6 million.

ii Candide becomes obligated under a lease contract to pay annual rent in excess of $1 million.

iii Candide acquires treasury stock without prior approval of the bank.
iv Candide guarantees indebtedness of other business enterprises in excess of $200,000.

Instructions

a Is Candide Corporation's intention to refinance sufficiently finalized to permit the classification of the two notes payable as noncurrent liabilities in a classified balance sheet dated December 31, Year 5?

b Assuming that the two notes payable are properly excluded from Candide Corporation's current liabilities in the balance sheet dated December 31, Year 5, prepare a note to the financial statements to describe the refinancing contract.

PROBLEMS

Pr. 10-1 Account balances and other data relating to liabilities, contingencies, and commitments of Computer Memories, Inc., on December 31, Year 5, are as follows:

Notes payable, due Feb. 1, Year 6	$ 80,000
Notes payable, due Oct. 31, Year 8	100,000
Discount on notes payable, due Oct. 31, Year 8	4,100
Notes payable to officers (renewed annually)	60,000
Trade accounts receivable (excluding $40,000 sold to a factor on a recourse basis)	171,200
Trade accounts payable	101,750
Bonds payable ($100,000 due on June 30 of each year)	800,000
Payroll payable	4,280
Liability for income taxes and payroll taxes	1,770
Miscellaneous accrued liabilities	2,600
Stock dividend to be distributed	20,000
Income taxes payable	32,100
Deferred income tax credits	145,000
Liability for coupons outstanding	7,500
Unearned service contract revenue (Contracts are for one year)	6,000

On October 10, Year 5, Computer Memories signed a noncancellable contract to purchase merchandise in Year 6 at a fixed price of $60,000; this merchandise had a market value of $52,000 on December 31, Year 5. On January 3, Year 6, $50,000 of the $80,000 principal amount of notes payable due February 1, Year 6, was refinanced on a long-term basis due February 1, Year 9.

Instructions

Prepare the current liabilities section of the Computer Memories balance sheet on December 31, Year 5, and list any contingencies and commitments that should be disclosed in a note to the financial statements.

Pr. 10-2 The general manager of Incentive Systems, Inc., wants a bonus based on income of the current accounting period, which the general manager estimates will be approximately $660,000 before the bonus and income taxes.

Instructions

If the bonus rate is established at 10% and income taxes amount to 45% of taxable income, compute the estimated amount of the bonus to the general manager under each of the following assumptions. (Round all amounts to nearest dollar.)

a Bonus is based on income before income taxes and bonus.
b Bonus is based on income after bonus but before income taxes.
c Bonus is based on net income (after income taxes and bonus).

Pr. 10-3 Listed below are selected transactions and events for Innovative Design Limited relating to current liabilities during the year ended December 31, Year 8:

Jan. 10 Purchased merchandise for $30,000. A 2% discount is offered by suppliers. Innovative Design records purchases and accounts payable net of discounts and uses the periodic inventory system.

19 Paid $21,560 on invoice of January 10. The invoice amount was for $22,000 and was paid within the discount period.

31 Paid balance of January 10 invoice, $8,000, after the discount period.

Apr. 1 Issued one-year promissory note to a supplier in settlement of an invoice for $12,500 dated March 31. The invoice had been recorded net of 2% purchases discount; that is, $12,250. The face amount of the note was $14,210, including interest at 16% on $12,250 for one year. The note was recorded at face amount.

30 Wages for April were $16,000 before the following withholdings:

Income taxes	$2,380
Unemployment insurance	106
Canada Pension Plan	260

The company records payroll taxes at the end of each month in Payroll Taxes Expense account. The company's contributions were: Unemployment insurance $148, Canada Pension Plan $260.

May 20 Declared dividends on common stock as follows:

Cash	$18,000
Stock	3%

The dividends were to be paid or distributed to shareholders on June 25. There are 300,000 shares of $1,500,000 common stock outstanding; the current market price of the common stock is $30 a share. (Debit Retained Earnings for total amount of dividends.)

June 25 Paid the cash dividend and distributed the stock dividend declared on May 20.

Dec. 31 Innovative Design sells service contracts on its products and credits Deferred Service Contract Revenue when payments are received from customers. For Year 8, $7,400 of the service-contract revenue was considered realized.

31 Recorded interest expense for Year 8 on the promissory note issued to the supplier on April 1.

Instructions

Prepare journal entries to record the foregoing transactions and events of Innovative Design Limited.

Pr. 10-4 Southern Milling Company acquired a machine on July 1, Year 1, for $10,000 and an 18-month, $45,000 face amount promissory note on which interest was payable at the annual rate of 10% on December 31 and June 30. The current fair rate of interest on a note of comparable quality was 16% compounded semiannually.

Instructions

(Round all computations to the nearest dollar.)

a Compute the cost of Southern Milling Company's machine and record the acquisition of the machine on July 1, Year 1. Use the Appendix at the end of Chapter 5 to determine the present value of the note payable.

b Prepare journal entries for Southern Milling Company to record the following:

1 Payment of interest on the note and adjustment of the Discount on Note Payable ledger account on December 31, Year 1.

2 Payment of interest on the note and adjustment of the Discount on Note Payable ledger account on June 30, Year 2.

3 Payment of the note (principal and interest) and adjustment of the Discount on Note Payable ledger account on December 31, Year 2.

c Show how the note payable is presented in Southern Milling Company's balance sheet on December 31, Year 1.

Pr. 10-5 Greenly Corporation, a publisher of trade magazines, is preparing its December 31, Year 5, financial statements and must determine the proper accounting treatment for each of the following situations:

1 Greenly sells subscriptions to several magazines for a one-year, two-year, or three-year period. Cash receipts from subscribers are credited to Unearned Magazine Subscriptions Revenue, and this account had a balance of $2,400,000 on December 31, Year 5. Outstanding subscriptions on December 31, Year 5, expire as follows:

During Year 6	$650,000
During Year 7	900,000
During Year 8	400,000

2 On January 2, Year 5, Greenly discontinued collision, fire, and theft coverage on its delivery vehicles and became "self-insured" for these risks. Actual losses of $45,000 during Year 5 were debited to Delivery Expense. The Year 4 premium for the discontinued coverage amounted to $100,000, and the controller wants to set up a reserve for self-insurance by a debit to Delivery Expense of $55,000 and a credit to Reserve for Self-Insurance of $55,000.

3 A suit for breach of contract seeking damages of $1,000,000 was filed by an author against Greenly on July 1, Year 5. Greenly's legal counsel believes that an unfavourable outcome is likely. A reasonable estimate of the court's award to the author is in the range between $200,000 and $550,000. No amount in this range is a better estimate of potential damages than any other amount.

4 During December, Year 5, a competitor filed suit against Greenly for industrial espionage claiming $2,000,000 in damages. In the opinion of management and Greenly's legal counsel, it is likely that damages will be awarded to the plaintiff. However, the amount of potential damages awarded to the plaintiff cannot be reasonably estimated.

5 An investment of Greenly's in a foreign country has been expropriated. The carrying amount of the investment is $800,000, but Greenly is likely to recover at least $1,000,000 on insurance policies covering this investment.

Instructions

For each situation above, prepare a journal entry for Greenly Company on December 31, Year 5, or explain why an entry is not required. Show any supporting computations.

Pr. 10-6 While auditing the financial statements of Tao Limited for the year ended December 31, Year 3, you found that the following contingencies had not been entered in the accounting records:

1 In prior years, Tao had not accrued estimated claims for injuries to customers as a result of their using Tao's products because such claims were covered by insurance. In Year 3, Tao discontinued the insurance. A reasonable estimate of outstanding claims (which are likely to be successful) on December 31, Year 3, was $31,000.

2 A former employee has sued Tao for $500,000, alleging age discrimination. Tao's lawyer does not think the suit has any merit but has suggested that Tao pay the former employee an out-of-court settlement of $8,000, because the cost of defending the suit was estimated at $50,000. Tao agreed, and the former employee signed appropriate settlement papers.

3 Tao has lost a breach of contract suit, but the amount of damages has not been determined. The plaintiff is seeking damages of $100,000. Management and legal counsel are of the opinion that the damages the court would find for the plaintiff would be a minimum of $12,500 and a maximum of $50,000. No amount within this range is a better estimate of potential damages than any other.

4 Tao is an endorser on notes receivable discounted at a bank in the amount of $150,000, including interest. All but one of the makers of the notes are financially sound companies. The one maker had issued a one-year 10% unsecured promissory note of $20,000 to Tao. The note matures on January

30, Year 4, but the maker's bankruptcy trustee has estimated that only 50% of the maturity value of unsecured notes will be paid.

5 A lower court has awarded $200,000 in damages to Tao in litigation in which Tao was the plaintiff. The defendants have appealed the decision to a higher court, which is not expected to issue a decision for a year or more.

6 During Year 3, Tao discontinued collision coverage on its motor vehicles and assumed the risk for this contingency. Actual losses of $15,000 during Year 3 were debited to Delivery Expense. Because the premiums for collision insurance in past years averaged $45,000, the controller wants to record a "reserve for self-insurance" by increasing the balance of the Delivery Expense ledger account by $30,000.

7 Management has requested your consent to record a provision for unspecified general business risks for $120,000 by a debit to an expense ledger account.

Instructions

For each contingency described above, prepare a journal entry for Tao Limited to record the contingency, or briefly explain why an entry would not be in accordance with generally accepted accounting principles.

Pr. 10-7 Sandra Corporation sells tomato juice in six-packs, cases, and through vending machines. In order to promote the drink, Sandra launched in Year 10 a promotional plan called "Toma." For every 10 bottle caps and 10 cents turned in, customers receive a pen and become eligible for a grand prize of $100 cash, one of which is awarded for every 12,500 bottle caps turned in. Sandra estimates that only 30% of the bottle caps will be presented for redemption. A summary of transactions for Year 10 follows:

1 Sold 4,000,000 bottles of juice for $2,261,600 cash.

2 Acquired 80,000 pens for $32,000 cash. (Debit Inventory of Prize Merchandise.)

3 Expenses paid in cash and attributable to the promotional plan were $8,750.

4 A total of 60,000 pens were distributed as prizes to customers, and an appropriate number of grand prizes were awarded on December 31, Year 10.

At the end of each year, Sandra recognizes a liability equal to the estimated cost of potential prizes outstanding. The 10 cents received for each pen is considered sufficient to cover the direct expenses of handling each request; therefore, neither the estimated direct expenses nor the potential remittances from customers are accrued at the end of the year.

Instructions

a Prepare journal entries for Sandra Corporation to record the transactions relating to the promotional plan for the year ended December 31, Year 10. Expenses of the promotional plan are recorded in a Promotional Expense ledger account.

b Compute the balances of all ledger accounts relating to the promotional plan of Sandra Corporation and explain how each account would appear in the financial statements for the year ended December 31, Year 10.

Pr. 10-8 Described below are selected transactions and events of Plainview Limited for the year ended December 31, Year 6:

1 Plainview is obligated under an operating lease for the payment of minimum monthly rent of $1,000 in advance, plus additional rent (payable by the tenth day of the following month) equal to 8% of the net income earned by its branch store, after both total rent and a 40% provision for income taxes have been deducted. Operating income of the branch store during January, Year 6 (before rent and income taxes), was $20,000. Income taxes expense is recorded monthly. (Compute rent expense to the nearest dollar and debit Rent Expense for both the rent advance on January 2 and the accrual of rent on January 31.)

2 Plainview issues gift certificates in denominations of $5, $10, and $25. The certificates are redeemable in merchandise having an average gross profit of 25% of selling price. During March, Plainview sold $31,000 of gift certificates and redeemed certificates having a sales value of $27,400. It is estimated that 8% of the certificates issued will not be redeemed. Plainview uses the periodic inventory system, and thus does not compute the cost of goods sold until the end of the year. The sales of gift certificates are recorded in a Liability for Gift Certificates Outstanding ledger account.

3 Sales during June totalled $777,000, of which $487,500 were on credit. Plainview operates in a province that has a 6% sales tax. Included in the sales amount are sales taxes to be collected from customers on all items except food, which is exempt from sales tax. Food sales amounted to 40% of total sales before the sales tax was added.

Instructions

a Prepare journal entries for Plainview Limited to record the transactions and events described above. An entry to record the accrual of income taxes for January should be made in part *1* above.

b Prepare a list of all current liability ledger accounts of Plainview Limited involved in the journal entries in ***a***. (Do not include account balances.)

Pr. 10-9 Monte Rico Corporation started mining in Year 5 on certain land leased from Highlands Company. Monte Rico previously had paid minimum royalties of $56,000 to Highlands, none of which was earned, during a 3½-year period prior to Year 5. The royalty provisions in the lease contract are as follows:

1 Minimum annual royalty is $16,000, with a minimum of $4,000 payable quarterly. Unearned minimum royalties may be recovered in any subsequent quarter from earned royalties in excess of minimum royalties.

2 Earned royalty shall be 10 cents per tonne shipped from the mine plus a per-tonne amount equal to 3% of the amount that the market value of the ore at the mine exceeds $4 a tonne.

Operations of Monte Rico for Year 5 are summarized as follows:

Quarter	Tonnes shipped	*Market value at destination, per tonne*	*Freight from mine to destination, per tonne*
1st	None		
2nd	150,000	$11.50	$3.50
3rd	300,000	12.50	3.50
4th	None		

Instructions

a Compute the amount of royalty to be paid to Highlands Company by Monte Rico Corporation for Year 5, and the amount of unearned minimum royalty on December 31, Year 5.

b How is the unearned minimum royalty paid reported in the balance sheet of Monte Rico Corporation on December 31, Year 5? Explain.

Pr. 10-10 Four transactions completed by Bavaria Company during the year ended December 31, Year 7, are described below:

1 On February 20, Year 7, Bavaria was offered a stock of merchandise being closed out by a manufacturer. Bavaria purchased the merchandise on February 26 for $72,000, and paid for it on March 1 by issuing a non-interest-bearing promissory note for $81,000, due on March 1, Year 8. Bavaria uses the periodic inventory system and records notes payable at face amount. The discount of $9,000 on the note payable is amortized by the straight-line method and represents a fair rate of interest.

2 On July 2, property taxes on Bavaria's retail stores for the ensuing 12-month period were levied and became a lien against the property. Bavaria's controller estimated that property taxes for the year in the amount of $13,200 would be paid on November 1. Taxes in the amount of $13,300 were paid on November 1.

Bavaria does not record the liability for property taxes on the levy or lien date; however, it records the current year's portion of taxes as an expense at the time of payment.

3 On November 2, Bavaria purchased $30,000 of merchandise from Y Company, terms 2/10, n/30; and $10,000 of merchandise from Z Company, terms 2/10, n/e.o.m. Bavaria records accounts payable net of cash discounts offered. The invoice from Y Company was paid on November 10, but the invoice from Z Company was not paid until November 25, and the cash discount was lost.

4 On December 1, Bavaria launched a special one-month promotion of one of its products. Included in each product package sold during December was a coupon that, if returned to Bavaria with $1 enclosed, entitled the customer to receive a toy. Bavaria's sales manager estimated that 50% of the customers would accept the offer, which would cost Bavaria $1.20 for each toy claimed plus 30 cents in packaging and shipping costs. Bavaria acquired 50,000 toys for cash. During December, Year 7, 100,000 of the products were sold for $4 cash each, and 30,000 coupons were presented for redemption. (Credit the Packaging and Shipping Expense ledger account for 30 cents for each coupon redeemed because actual costs incurred in packaging and shipping were recorded in that account.) On December 31, Year 7, on the basis of experience to date, it was estimated that only 12,000 additional coupons will be presented by customers before the offer expires. Toys that will not be distributed as prizes may be sold for 40 cents each. The inventory of prize merchandise expected to be sold should be written down to net realizable value by a debit to the Promotional Expense ledger account.

Instructions

a Prepare journal entries for Bavaria Company to record the transactions described above.

b Assume that no journal entries have been made other than the entries to record the foregoing transactions as they occurred. Prepare adjusting entries for Bavaria Company on December 31, Year 7, relating to each of the four transactions.

c Prepare a list of ledger accounts used in ***a*** and ***b*** and indicate the financial statement classification—that is, current asset, current liability, cost of goods sold, operating expense, etc.—for each account. (Do not include ledger account balances.)

Pr. 10-11 A summary of the financial position of Sorrento Limited on December 31, Year 8, is presented as follows.

Cash — includes an overdraft of $1,250 with Suburban Bank, receivables from employees of $300, and cheques from customers of $3,500 dated January 10, Year 9, that have been recorded as cash receipts		$ 44,300
Customers—includes promissory notes of $20,000 (accrued interest of $800 has not been recorded), trade accounts of $77,500 (including an uncollectible account of $1,200 that should be written off), and an allowance for doubtful accounts of $1,300. Aging of accounts indicates that an allowance of $4,200 is required on December 31, Year 8. Customer's promissory note of $12,000 maturing on March 31, Year 9, has been discounted at a bank		96,200
Inventories—include $2,000 of prize merchandise, $6,800 of worthless goods, and $5,000 of goods on consignment from Capri Company		60,000
Prepayments — include tools of $2,000, cash surrender value of life insurance policies of $3,100, long-term utility deposits of $1,000		12,500
Fixtures — net of $34,500 accumulated depreciation		197,000
Total assets		$410,000
Current liabilities, recorded in a single ledger account that includes the following:		
Promissory note payable due in three annual instalments; interest at 15% since Sept 1, Year 8, has not been accrued	$45,000	
Trade accounts payable	46,000	
Payable to Capri Company for consigned goods	5,000	
Liability for coupons outstanding	1,500	$ 97,500
(Sorrento has been sued for damages of $25,000 but does not anticipate that any liability will result.)		
Shareholders' equity—100,000 shares of no-par value common stock issued for $120,000 (less 1,000 shares of treasury stock reacquired for $2,800) and retained earnings of $195,300		312,500
Total liabilities & shareholders' equity		$410,000

Instructions

Prepare a revised balance sheet for Sorrento Limited, including appropriate notes to the financial statements. Disregard the income tax effect of any corrections to previously reported net income. A working paper to determine correct ledger account balances is recommended in the following form:

Ledger accounts	*Unadjusted ledger account balances*		*Adjustments and corrections*		*Corrected ledger account balances*	
	Debit	*Credit*	*Debit*	*Credit*	*Debit*	*Credit*

Pr. 10-12 Systems Dynamics Corporation requests that you make an estimate of its product warranty liability on June 30, Year 9.

Systems Dynamics manufactures television parts and sells them under a six-month warranty to replace defective parts without charge. On December 31, Year 8, Systems Dynamics reported a Liability for Product Warranty of $374,800. By June 30, Year 9, this account had been reduced to $55,920 by debits for the net cost of defective parts returned that had been sold in Year 8. The net cost of replacing defective parts sold in Year 9 (January to May) was recorded in the Product Warranty Expense ledger account.

Systems Dynamics began Year 9 expecting part returns to equal 8% of the dollar volume of sales for the year. However, as a result of the introduction of new models during Year 9, this estimated percentage of returns was increased to 10% on May 1. It is assumed that no parts sold during a specific month are returned in that month. Each part is stamped with a date at the time of sale so that the warranty may be administered properly. The following table indicates the likely pattern of sales returns during the six-month period of the warranty, starting with the month following the sale of the parts:

Month following sale:	*Percentage of total returns expected*
First	20
Second	30
Third	20
Fourth, fifth, and sixth (10% each month)	30

Gross sales of parts for the first six months of Year 9 were:

January	$3,600,000	April	$2,850,000
February	3,300,000	May	2,000,000
March	4,100,000	June	1,960,000

The warranty offered by Systems Dynamics also covers payment of the shipping cost on defective parts returned and on new parts shipped as replacements. This shipping cost averages approximately 10% of the selling price of the parts returned. The manufacturing cost of the parts is roughly 80% of the selling price, and the residual value of returned parts averages 20% of their selling price. Returned parts on hand on December 31, Year 8, were carried in inventories at 20% of their original selling price.

Instructions

a Prepare a working paper to estimate Systems Dynamics Corporation's liability under its product warranty on June 30, Year 9.

b Prepare an adjusting journal entry for Systems Dynamics Corporation on June 30, Year 9. (Ignore income tax considerations.)

Pr. 10-13 The following list of Synchronicity Corporation's liabilities on December 31, Year 1, was prepared by an inexperienced accounting intern:

Trade notes payable (rates of interest, 12 to 15%)	$ 480,000
13% equipment contract payable (due $25,000 plus interest at the end of each month)	500,000
14% note payable (due June 1, Year 2)	350,000
12% note payable (due in annual instalments of $100,000 on Jan. 31 of each year)	600,000
Trade accounts payable	1,050,000
Income taxes payable (net of $200,000 previously paid on the estimated amount due for Year 1, and including $135,000 of deferred income tax credits as a result of use of accelerated depreciation for income tax purposes)	174,000
Allowance for sales returns	25,000
Deposits on returnable containers	14,500
Interest payable	74,167
Miscellaneous current liabilities	32,100
Total liabilities	$3,299,767

Additional Information

1 The financial statements for the year ended December 31, Year 1, were to be issued on February 1, Year 2. On January 23, Year 2, the principal amount of the 12% note payable was refinanced on a long-term basis by the issuance of an $800,000, 13½% mortgage note to Knapp Mortgage Corporation. The mortgage note matures on January 23, Year 7.

2 On January 25, Year 2, a noncancellable agreement was reached with Troy Bank to refinance the principal amount of the 14% note payable on a long-term basis. The terms of the agreement are readily determinable but will not be finalized until February 4, Year 2. Both Synchronicity and Troy Bank are financially capable of honouring the agreement, and there have been no violations of any provisions of the agreement as of January 31, Year 2.

3 Trade accounts payable were recorded at gross invoice amounts. A 2% cash discount is offered by suppliers on 80% of the trade accounts payable outstanding on December 31, Year 1. Synchronicity wishes to establish an allowance for purchases discounts on December 31, Year 1.

4 On November 28, Year 1, Synchronicity signed a noncancellable contract to purchase merchandise at a fixed price of $2,000,000 during the second

quarter of Year 2. The market value of the merchandise under contract was $1,910,000 on December 31, Year 1. Neither the contract nor the price decline of the merchandise has been entered in the accounting records.

5 During Year 1, Synchronicity issued coupons with a face amount of $280,000 to its customers. The expiration date of the coupons was December 31, Year 1, but redemptions are honoured up to three months after the expiration date. Approximately 80% of the coupons issued are expected to be redeemed, and handling costs of 15% of the face amount of redeemed coupons generally are incurred by Synchronicity. Through December 31, Year 1, the face amount of the coupons redeemed amounted to $155,000, and handling costs of $23,100 were incurred and recorded in the Promotional Expense ledger account. The estimated amount of outstanding coupons on December 31, Year 1, and the related handling costs have not been recorded.

6 The allowance for sales returns, the deposits on returnable containers, the interest payable, and the miscellaneous current liabilities were measured and recorded in conformity with generally accepted accounting principles.

Instructions

a Assuming that the accounting records have not been closed for Year 1, prepare a single journal entry as of December 31, Year 1, to correct Synchronicity Corporation's accounting records. Disregard income tax considerations.

b Prepare the liabilities section of Synchronicity Corporation's December 31, Year 1, balance sheet, including notes to the financial statements required by generally accepted accounting principles. ***Reminder:*** The financial statements for the year ended December 31, Year 1, are to be issued on February 1, Year 2.

p a r t   t h r e e

LONG-TERM ASSETS AND LIABILITIES

Accounting for long-term assets and liabilities provides accountants with some of their most challenging problems. The cost of plant assets, intangible assets, and long-term investments are measured and recorded; the cost of plant assets (other than land) and intangible assets is allocated to revenue over their economic lives; disposals of long-term assets require the recognition of gains and losses; exchanges of plant assets may result in deferral of an indicated gain if no monetary assets are received; accounting for long-term investments in equity securities may require the application of the equity method of accounting or the lower-of-cost-and-market rule, depending on the amount and nature of such investments; and the issuance and retirement of long-term liabilities involve some unusual accounting issues.

The use of long-term assets and proceeds from long-term borrowing requires periodic depreciation, depletion, and amortization. The differentiation between capital expenditures and revenue expenditures, selection of appropriate methods of depreciation, depletion and amortization for long-term assets, and the method of amortization for discount and premium on long-term debt have a significant impact on the measurement of income.

Other accounting problems arise in connection with long-term assets and liabilities, such as the capitalization of interest during construction, research and development costs, the estimate of goodwill for a business enterprise, and the restructuring of debt. These and additional topics are discussed and illustrated in this Part.

c h a p t e r 1 1

PLANT ASSETS: ACQUISITION AND DISPOSAL

Nature of Plant Assets

The terms ***plant assets***; ***plant and equipment***; ***property, plant, and equipment***; and ***fixed assets*** often are used to describe the tangible assets used by a business enterprise in its operations. ***Use in operations*** distinguishes these assets from other tangible assets that are reported in the balance sheet as investments. Land held as a prospective building site, for example, is an investment. When a building is constructed on the land and is placed in service, the land is reported in the balance sheet under plant assets. A characteristic common to all plant assets is that they yield services over many years. Plant assets other than land have a limited economic life; consequently, the cost of such assets must be allocated as depreciation expense to the accounting periods receiving benefit from their use.

Classification of Assets Used in Operations

Assets used in Operations may be divided into ***tangible*** and ***intangible*** categories as follows:

Tangible Assets

Tangibility is the characteristic of bodily substance, as exemplified in a tract of timber, a bridge, or a machine.

1 ***Plant assets*** Included in this category are properties acquired for use in operations. Examples are land, buildings and structures of all types, machinery, equipment, furniture, tools, orchards, returnable containers, and leasehold improvements. Plant assets generally are acquired for use rather than for sale. In yielding services over many accounting periods, a plant asset does not

change in physical characteristic; that is, it does not become physically incorporated in the finished goods of a business enterprise. For example, a building or machine wears out and eventually loses its ability to perform efficiently, but its physical components remain relatively unchanged. In contrast, material is incorporated in finished goods.

a ***Land*** Unlike the other kinds of tangible property, land has an indefinite economic life. In general, land does not deteriorate with the passage of time and is not physically exhausted through use. There may be exceptional cases. Agricultural land may suffer a loss of usefulness through erosion or failure to maintain fertility. Building sites may be damaged or destroyed by slides, floods, or earthquakes. Generally, however, land is accounted for as a nondepreciable asset.

b ***Property having a limited economic life*** With the exception of land, all other plant assets have limited economic lives. The cost of such assets is allocated through the process of ***depreciation*** to the cost of the goods and services produced. Depreciation is discussed in Chapter 12.

2 ***Natural resources*** This term includes ***wasting assets*** that are subject to exhaustion through extraction. The principal types of wasting assets are mineral deposits, oil and gas deposits, and standing timber. In essence, natural resources are long-term inventories acquired for sale or use in production over a number of years. The cost of acquiring and developing wasting assets is allocated to expense in the form of ***depletion*** charges. Depletion also is discussed in Chapter 12.

Intangible Assets

Intangibility denotes a lack of physical substance. Examples of intangible assets (as this term is used in financial accounting) include patents, copyrights, trademarks, franchises, organization costs, and goodwill. The cost of intangible assets is ***amortized*** over their estimated economic lives, but generally not in excess of 40 years.[1]

Accounting for Plant Assets

A plant asset is a ***bundle of future services***. The cost of acquiring such an asset is a measure of the amount invested in future services that will be provided by the asset. At the time of acquisition, cost is also an objective measure of the exchange value of an asset. The market price represents the simultaneous resolution of two independent opinions (the acquirer's and the seller's) as to the current fair value of the asset changing ownership. There are cases where the acquirer pays too high a price because of errors in judgement or excessive construction costs, and it is sometimes possible to acquire plant assets at bargain prices. These, however, are exceptional cases; accountants seldom have objective evidence to support either "unfortunate" or "bargain" acquisitions. Accountants use cost as the

1 For a more complete discussion of intangible assets see Chapter 13.

basis of recording and reporting plant assets because it is reliable and because it is a measure of the investment in future services.

The problem of determining ***carrying amount*** (often referred to as ***carrying value*** or ***book value***) subsequent to acquisition is also important. As a plant asset is used in operations, a portion of the original bundle of services (cost) is used up. This is illustrated in the diagram below. The carrying amount of a plant asset thus is reduced by depreciation, because a smaller bundle of potential services remains at the end of each accounting period.

Bundle of asset services is used up and is called depreciation

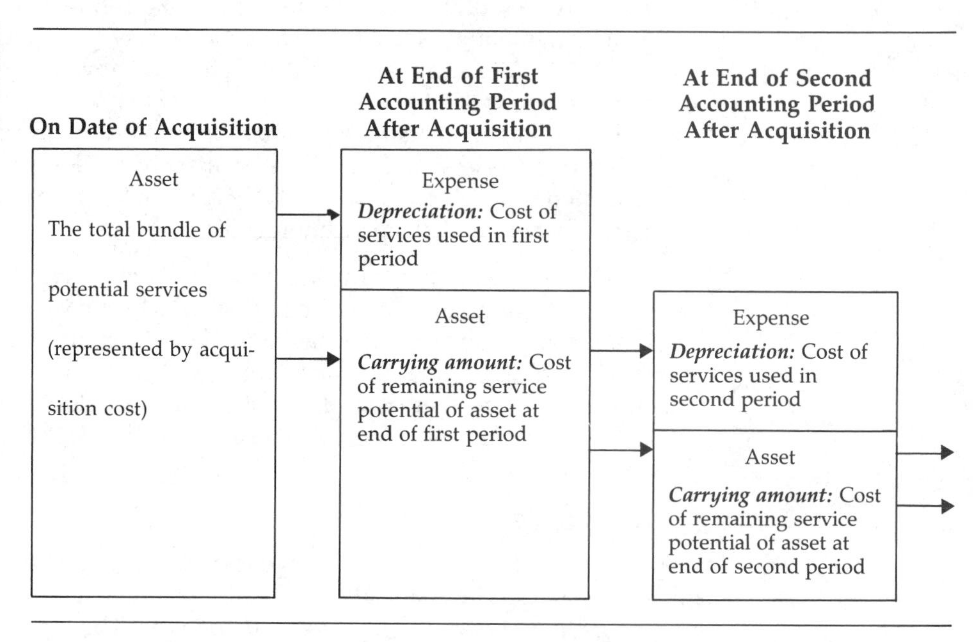

Because plant assets generally have long economic lives, it is possible that their current fair value may rise above or fall below carrying amount between the time of acquisition and the time the services are used. When such price movements are material, a question arises about the continuing significance of historical cost. This issue is discussed in Chapter 25.

COST OF PLANT ASSETS

The total cost of a plant asset is the cash outlay, or its equivalent, made to acquire the asset and place it in operating condition. This is a clear and simple statement of the principle involved; however, problems arise in the application of this principle to practical situations. In essence, these problems raise three questions: (1) What is included in the cost of plant assets? (2) How is the cost of plant assets measured? and (3) How are costs incurred subsequent to the acquisition date recorded? Each of these questions is examined in the following sections.

What Is Included in the Cost of Plant Assets?

Until a plant asset is ready to perform the services for which it was acquired, it is not complete. Some plant assets, such as a truck or a computer, are complete and ready to function at acquisition. The cost of such assets may be measured by the total of the invoice price (including sales tax) and transportation costs. Other assets, for example an automobile assembly line or the machinery for a paper mill, must be assembled, installed, and tested. ***All expenditures*** connected with the assembling, installing, and testing logically are viewed as a part of cost of the asset.

Capital Expenditures and Revenue Expenditures

Initial and other expenditures that are included in the cost of assets are called ***capital expenditures***, and such expenditures are said to be ***capitalized***; expenditures treated as current expenses are called ***revenue expenditures***. The distinction between capital expenditures and revenue expenditures is important in the periodic measurement of net income. If the cost of acquiring plant assets is recorded as a current expense, income of the current accounting period is understated, and income of future periods, when the asset services are used, will be overstated.

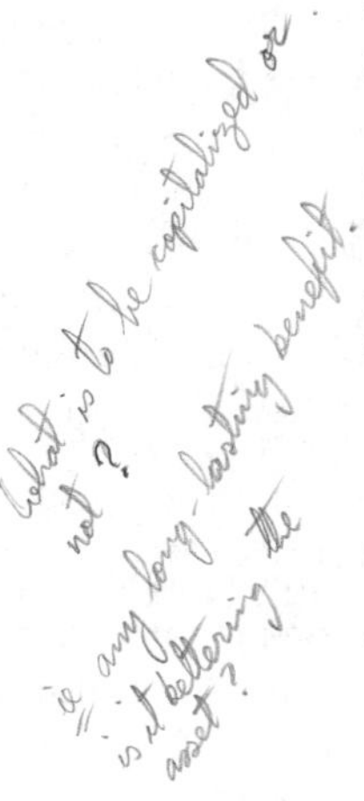

The theoretical test to distinguish a capital expenditure from a revenue expenditure is simple: Have the services acquired been consumed entirely within the current accounting period, or will there be a carryover of services to future periods? As we shall see, this test is not always easy to apply. Many business enterprises follow the arbitrary procedure of debiting all asset expenditures of relatively small amounts (for example, those under $250) to expense accounts, to minimize accounting effort. Unless these small expenditures are significantly large in the aggregate, such practices, if consistently followed, are reasonable and efficient. They are condoned as a matter of expedience, because they do not materially distort periodic measurement of net income.

Specific types of capital expenditures and revenue expenditures after acquisition, such as additions, betterments, replacements, and repairs, are covered in a subsequent section of this chapter.

Land

Special problems arise in the determination of the initial cost of land. Generally, the acquisition cost of land includes: (1) the acquisition price; (2) all costs of closing the transaction and obtaining title, such as real estate commission and legal fees; (3) all costs of surveying, clearing, draining, or filling to make the land suitable for the desired use, including the cost of demolishing existing unneeded structures; and (4) costs of land improvements.

It sometimes is necessary to examine the terms of the aquisition contract to determine the price paid for land. Suppose, for example, that an acquirer agrees to pay $80,000 for a parcel of land in addition to delinquent property taxes of $5,000 and past-due mortgage note payments of $1,500. The acquisition cost of the land in this case includes all the additional consideration and is $86,500 ($80,000 + $5,000 + $1,500 = $86,500), not $80,000.

When newly acquired land is not in the condition necessary for the intended use, the acquirer will incur certain costs that should be recorded as part of the cost of the land. For example, costs of clearing trees, or of levelling hills or filling low spots, are included in the cost of the land. Any salvage material recovered in the process of clearing land represents a ***cost offset***.

Land held as a potential building site or for investment purposes is not currently used in operations and should be reported under Investments in the balance sheet rather than as a part of the plant assets category. The ***carrying costs***, such as property taxes and weed control incurred prior to the time that the land is placed in use, are capitalized (added to the cost of the land). When the site is placed in use, the land is reclassified from the investment category to the plant assets category, and future carrying costs are recognized as expenses.

Land Improvements

Land improvement costs are capital expenditures and are either recorded as a part of land cost or recorded in a separate Land Improvements ledger account. Improvements such as landscaping and drainage, which have indefinite economic lives, are added to land cost. The cost of land improvements such as sidewalks, streets, and sewers may or may not have indefinite economic lives. In many localities, the cost of streets, sewers, and similar improvements are paid by the owners of the benefitted property, but the local government unit agrees to maintain and replace them if they are built to standard specifications. In such cases the special assessment expenditure is a part of land cost, because it is permanent in nature. If the property owner is responsible for eventual replacement of land improvements, however, they have limited economic lives and are recorded in a separate Land Improvements ledger account to facilitate depreciation accounting.

Buildings

The distinction between land and building costs may be of considerable importance because of the potential effect on net income. For example, suppose that a parcel of land is acquired as the site for a new building. On the land is an old building that must be razed before the new building can be constructed. Is the cost of tearing down the old building (net of any salvage recovery) a current expense, a part of the cost of the new building, or a part of land cost? If it is a current expense, it is deducted from revenue immediately; if it is a part of the cost of the new building, it will be depreciated over the economic life of the building; if it is a part of land cost, it will not be depreciated. What are the standards to be used in the application of these guidelines?

The primary issue is the nature of the relationship between the expenditure and a particular plant asset. Accountants must ask: What is the asset that has been acquired, and is the cost at issue reasonably related to the acquisition of this particular asset? If land is acquired for a building site, the entire cost of bringing the land into suitable condition as a building site, including cost of razing existing structures, is allocated to the land; in contrast, excavation costs incurred to construct the foundation for a new building are a part of the cost of the building.

The line of reasoning outlined above may be used to determine the appropriate accounting for various costs incurred during the construction of a new building. The following examples are illustrative:

	Cost incurred	Accounting treatment
1	Cost of temporary structures used for offices or for storing tools and material during construction of a new building.	***Record as cost of new building.*** This is a necessary cost of constructing the new building.
2	Cost of tearing down an old building previously used in operations in order to construct a new building.	***Record as a loss on retirement of old building.*** This cost is related to the services of the old building.
3	Cost of liability insurance coverage during construction of a new building.	***Record as cost of new building.*** This is an ordinary and necessary cost of constructing the new building.

When a building is constructed, all costs necessary to complete the construction should be included in the cost of the building. These may include architects' fees, building permit, and a variety of overhead costs. When a completed building is acquired, all costs relating to the acquisition (termite inspection fee, for example) that are applicable to future revenue should be capitalized. Separate ledger accounts may be used for the building shell (foundation, walls, and floors), partitions, air conditioning units, roof, wiring, and siding.

Cost that will not benefit future accounting periods should not be capitalized. For example, suppose that immediately after the acquisition of a building it is found that extensive repairs are necessary. The proper treatment of such costs must rest on evidence as to the circumstances of the acquisition. If the acquirer recognized the need for these repairs at the time of acquisition, the repair costs are a part of the cost of placing the building in serviceable condition and should be capitalized. The reasoning is that paying $100,000 for a run-down building and $50,000 for renovation is equivalent to paying $150,000 for a renovated building. However, if a building is acquired for $150,000 under the assumption that it is in condition for occupancy and it is later discovered that there are serious defects requiring an expenditure of $50,000 to correct, any portion of the $50,000 expenditure that does not result in an improved structure or add to the originally anticipated economic life of the building should be deducted from revenue as incurred.

A similar line of reasoning may be used to reject proposals to treat the carrying amounts of obsolete plant assets replaced as part of the cost of the new plant assets acquired. The cost, and thus the service potential, of the new assets is not increased by the obsolescence of assets no longer in service. Future periods will benefit from the ownership and use of new assets, not from the retirement of the obsolete plant assets or from the failure to depreciate such assets fast enough.

Leaseholds and Leasehold Improvements

A ***leasehold*** is a personal property right granting to the ***lessee*** the use of real property for a specified length of time. The contract under which this right is granted is called a ***lease***, and the owner of the property is known as the ***lessor***. A lease contract generally requires monthly rent payments. On rare occasions, leases provide for a lump-sum payment of the entire rent in advance. A lease contract gives the lessee the right to use the property in exchange for a contractual obligation to make future rent payments. Thus, it may be appropriate to record both the leased asset and the corresponding obligation to pay rent in the accounting records of the lessee. This topic is discussed in Chapter 20.

Leasehold improvements in the form of buildings or structural alterations sometimes are made on leased property. Accounting for leasehold improvements by the lessee is comparable with accounting for similar owned property, except that economic life should be related to the term of the lease. If the economic life of the leasehold improvements is less than the lease term, the cost of the improvements is amortized over their economic life. However, a building expected to last 20 years that is built on land leased for 15 years with no renewal option has a 15-year economic life to the lessee, and a residual value equal to any amount that the lessor agrees to pay to the lessee at the end of the lease term. When the lease contract contains a provision to renew at the option of the lessee, the length of economic life becomes uncertain, except in terms of the present intentions of the lessee. In the foregoing example, if the lease contract contained a renewal option for an additional five-year period, the economic life for the building would be either 15 or 20 years, depending on the intent of the lessee with respect to renewal.

The lessor generally does not record leasehold improvements made by the lessee. However, if the lessor pays for any of the improvements, the cost should be recorded in a plant asset ledger account by the lessor and depreciated over the estimated economic life of the improvements.

Machinery and Equipment

This category may encompass a wide variety of items, including all types of machinery, furniture, fixtures, ships, vehicles of all types, tools, containers, patterns and dies, computers, and other office equipment. Cost of machinery and equipment items is determined and allocated to revenue through the process of depreciation. Several topics relating to the acquisition of machinery, equipment, and buildings are discussed in the following pages.

Self-Constructed Plant Assets

Occasionally, a building, a machine, or equipment may be constructed by a business enterprise for its own use, either because this is an economical method of acquisition or because the quality and specifications of the asset may be controlled better if the asset is self-constructed. Determining the cost of the completed asset in this situation raises a number of issues.

Accountants generally agree that all direct costs incurred in construction activities should be capitalized. ***Direct costs*** are defined as costs that are identified specifically with the construction project in the sense that they would not have been incurred otherwise. Direct costs include the cost of material, labour, design, engineering, etc. Whether any overhead should be included in the cost of the self-constructed asset is a controversial issue.

The basic issue is whether overhead costs that will not change as the result of a self-construction project should be included in the cost of the new asset. Some enterprises have engineering and construction departments that regularly engage in new construction. The overhead costs incurred in these departments benefit current revenue-producing activities as well as the new construction. But what of the overhead costs of a regular producing department that undertakes the construction of a plant asset? It is difficult to imagine a situation in which any significant self-construction project could be undertaken without some increase in overhead. However, there are several fixed overhead costs that will not increase as a result of construction activities. If these fixed costs are allocated between regular production and self-construction projects, the result may be that the average manufacturing cost for units produced will be reduced during accounting periods in which self-construction activities are undertaken. Pre-tax income during the construction period thus would be increased by the amount of the fixed overhead costs allocated to the self-constructed asset. The three possible approaches to this issue are the following:

1 ***Allocate no overhead costs to the self-constructed asset.*** This approach has little to recommend it. At least some overhead costs are the direct result of new construction, and charging such incremental overhead costs to current operations is a clear case of distortion of income by the failure to recognize a capital expenditure.

2 ***Allocate only incremental overhead costs to the self-constructed asset.*** This approach may be defended on the grounds that incremental overhead costs represent the relevant cost that management considered in making the decision to construct the asset. Fixed overhead costs, it is argued, are period costs. Because they would have been incurred in any case, there is no relationship between the fixed overhead costs and the self-constructed project. This approach has been widely used in practice because it does not distort the cost of normal operations.

3 ***Allocate a portion of all overhead costs to the self-constructed asset.*** The argument for this approach is that the proper function of cost allocation is to relate all costs incurred in an accounting period to the output of that period. If an enterprise is able to construct an asset and still carry on its regular activities, it has benefitted by putting to use some of its ***idle capacity***, and this fact should be reflected in larger income. To charge the entire overhead to only a portion of the productive activity is to disregard facts and to understate the cost of the self-constructed asset. This line of reasoning has considerable merit.

If a plant asset is constructed for less than the lowest bid received from an outside contractor, the asset is recorded at actual cost; no "profit" is recognized. Profits are generated from asset ***use and disposal***, not from asset ***acquisition***; the ***cost saving*** will be realized through lower depreciation expense over the economic life of the asset.

Interest During Construction Period

During the time it takes to complete a self-construction project, cash is tied up in material, labour, and other construction costs. Is the interest cost incurred in borrowing funds for this purpose a part of the cost of the constructed asset? This has been a controversial question in financial accounting.

Generally, accountants regard interest as a cost of financing, not as a cost of obtaining asset services. If X pays cash for an asset and Y borrows cash to acquire an identical asset, there is no logical basis for claiming that Y has an asset with a higher cost because it has paid interest on borrowed funds. This reasoning, applied to self-constructed assets, suggests that interest on funds borrowed and used in construction should not be capitalized.

The opposing view is that interest during construction is a cost of acquiring future asset services. Funds are immobilized during the construction period. In deciding to construct an asset, management of the business enterprise must have determined that the value created would be sufficient to cover all costs, including interest. Furthermore, interest on investment is included in the price of the asset if it is acquired in finished form. Therefore, it may be argued, the interest on funds employed in construction of an asset should be added to the cost of the asset rather than expensed.

In 1979, the FASB in the United States issued ***Statement No. 34***: ''Capitalization of Interest Cost,'' which established the current standards of accounting and reporting for capitalized interest cost.[2] The FASB pointed out that the cost of any asset includes all costs ''incurred to bring it to the condition and location necessary for its intended uses.'' When a period of time is needed to bring the asset to that condition and location, the interest cost incurred in these efforts should be included in the cost of the asset. Such a period of time is called the ***acquisition period***. The objectives of this accounting treatment of interest cost are (1) to measure more accurately the total investment in the asset, and (2) to charge this investment, including interest cost, to future revenue that will benefit from the use of the asset.

Capitalization of interest cost ***is required*** for assets that are constructed for a business enterprise's own use, and for assets intended for sale or lease that are constructed as clearly identifiable projects, such as ships and parcels of real estate; interest cost ***is not capitalized*** for inventories that are routinely produced in large quantities on a repetitive basis, assets that are either in use or ready for use, and assets that are not intended for use in the activities of the enterprise. For example, the interest cost relating to idle land is not capitalized; however, if the land is being developed for a particular purpose, the interest paid on any debt incurred in the acquisition and development of the land is capitalized. Thus, if land is to be used as a parking lot or sold as developed land, interest is included in the cost of the land. However, if land is to be used to construct buildings for the enterprise's own use or for resale, interest is added to the cost of the buildings.

The amount of interest properly capitalized is that portion of interest cost during the acquisition period that ***could have been avoided if the asset had not been acquired***. Needless to say, the application of this concept is not easy. ***If a project is financed by a specific loan, the interest actually paid on the loan is capitalized***. However, if a project is financed from internally generated funds or from general borrowings, the average effective interest rate on all outstanding debt is used to compute the amount of interest capitalized. The total amount of interest capitalized in an accounting period must not exceed the total amount of

2 FASB, ***FASB Statement No. 34:*** ''Capitalization of Interest Cost'' (Stamford: 1979). The remaining discussion in this section is based on pages 2–8 of this ***Statement***. There is no comparable pronouncement in Canada.

interest cost actually incurred by the business enterprise in that period. The acquisition period begins when the following three conditions are present:

1 Expenditures for a specific asset have been incurred.

2 Activities to prepare the asset for use are in progress.

3 Interest cost is being incurred.

Interest capitalization continues as long as all three of these conditions are present and ends when the asset is completed and is ready for use. The total interest cost incurred and the total interest cost capitalized in an accounting period must be disclosed in a note to the financial statements.

To illustrate the computation of interest cost capitalized as part of the cost of an asset, assume that Clark Steel Limited constructed a blast furnace in the current year. The construction activity started on March 1, and the furnace was ready for use on December 1. Thus, the acquisition period was nine months. On March 1, Clark borrowed $400,000 at 15% for five years to pay for the parts and material acquired on that date, and financed additional costs of $360,000 from its general borrowing of approximately $4,000,000, which carried an average interest rate of 12%. The additional costs of $360,000 were incurred at a rate of $40,000 a month from March 1 through December 1. Thus, the average amount of the accumulated additional costs was $180,000 ($360,000 ÷ 2 = $180,000) during the acquisition period. The total interest cost included in the cost of the blast furnace is computed below:

Computation of interest capitalized as part of cost of plant asset

	Interest capitalized
Specific borrowing on Mar. 1 ($400,000 × 0.15 × $\frac{9}{12}$)	$45,000
Average accumulated additional costs from Mar. 1 to Dec. 1 ($180,000 × 0.12 × $\frac{9}{12}$)	16,200
Total interest cost included in cost of blast furnace	$61,200

Assuming that Clark Steel debits interest cost to the Interest Expense ledger account when it is incurred, the journal entry to capitalize the interest cost included in the cost of the blast furnace is as follows:

Journal entry to record capitalized interest cost

Machinery and Equipment	61,200	
Interest Expense		61,200
To capitalize interest cost included in cost of blast furnace.		

The total cost of the blast furnace for financial accounting is $821,200 ($400,000 + $360,000 + $61,200 = $821,200). Note that no interest cost is capitalized after the furnace is placed in use on December 1, even though interest continues to accrue on the $400,000 loan for the acquisition of parts and material needed for the construction of the blast furnace.

Ledger Account for Self-Constructed Plant Assets

A Construction in Progress ledger account generally is used to record the costs incurred in the self-construction of plant assets. This account is debited with the material, labour, overhead costs, and interest cost incurred in the construction of the assets. During the period of construction, depreciation is not recorded for the self-constructed assets because they are not producing revenue. If several plant assets are being constructed in an accounting period, a subsidiary ledger may be established for the ***work orders*** used to record costs accumulated for each asset, similar to job order cost accounting for manufactured goods. When construction is completed, the appropriate plant asset ledger account is debited and the Construction in Progress ledger account is credited for the total cost incurred in the construction of the asset.

How Is Cost of Plant Assets Measured?

We have reviewed some of the problems that arise in the determination of what is included in the cost of plant assets. Now, let us examine the problems that arise in the measurement of the cost of plant assets when the method of acquisition obscures the acquisition price. The objective of cost measurement is to determine the cash outlay or its equivalent necessary to obtain the asset.

Cash Discounts

When assets are acquired under terms that allow the deduction of a discount for the payment of cash in a specified period of time, the term ''cash equivalent'' may be interpreted to mean the invoice price, net of the discount. For example, if M Company acquires a plant asset for $10,000, terms 2/10, n/30, it has the choice of either paying cash (in a 10-day period) of $9,800, or deferring payment for an additional 20 days, at an added cost of $200. If payment is made in the 10-day period, the cost of the asset is only $9,800; if payment is deferred for 20 days, the additional $200 paid is a penalty for late payment and is not included in the cost of the asset.

Deferred Payment Contracts

In many cases, payment for a plant asset is delayed for long time periods. For example, suppose that equipment is acquired under a contract calling for payments of $1,490 at the end of each year for 10 years. To assume that the present value of the liability, and thus the cost of the equipment, is $14,900 ($1,490 × 10), is to ignore the fact that there is an interest charge included in the contract. To arrive at a basis for recording this acquisition, accountants must look for evidence of the cash-equivalent price of the equipment. If the equipment may be acquired for $10,000 cash, this amount becomes the measure of cost. If no conclusive evidence of a cash price is available, the rate of interest implicit in the contract price should be determined. The present value of an ordinary annuity of 10 rents or payments of 1 at an unstated interest rate is 6.71 ($10,000 ÷ $1,490 = 6.71), and Table 4 of the Appendix at the end of Chapter 5 shows that 6.71 is the present value of 10 equal payments of 1 ***at 8% interest***. Thus, the present value of 10 equal payments of $1,490 at 8% interest is approximately $10,000.[3] Assuming that an 8% rate of interest is reasonable, the acquisition of the equipment and the first two payments are recorded under the interest method as illustrated below.

Journal entries for acquisition of plant asset on instalment plan

On acquisition date:		
Equipment	10,000	
Discount on Equipment Contract Payable	4,900	
Equipment Contract Payable		14,900
To record acquisition of equipment under contract requiring payment of $1,490 at the end of each of 10 years. Present value of equipment contract payable at 8% is $10,000.		
Payment on contract at end of first year:		
Interest Expense	800	
Equipment Contract Payable	1,490	
Cash		1,490
Discount on Equipment Contract Payable		800
To record interest expense on equipment contract for first year [($14,900 – $4,900) × 0.08 = $800] and payment of first instalment.		
Payment on contract at end of second year:		
Interest Expense	745	
Equipment Contract Payable	1,490	
Cash		1,490
Discount on Equipment Contract Payable		745
To record interest expense on equipment contract for second year [($13,410 – $4,100) × 0.08 = $745] and payment of second instalment.		

When payment is deferred for relatively short time periods, the amount of interest implicit in the acquisition price may not be material in amount and may be ignored. However, if the length of time and the amount of interest involved are material, a reasonable estimate of the cash-equivalent acquisition price is required.[4]

Property often is acquired by assuming a purchase-money obligation. A ***purchase-money mortgage***, for example, is a loan created at the time property is acquired, collateralized by the property, and having priority over any subsequently created lien on the property.

Lump-Sum Acquisitions

A single negotiated price may be paid for two or more assets. If the assets have different economic lives, it is necessary to allocate the total lump-sum cost among them to provide a proper basis for the computation of depreciation. The most common example of this situation is the acquisition of real property — land and building — for a single price. Because the economic life of land is indefinite and the economic life of a building is limited, an allocation of the total cost is necessary. Assume, for example, that a building and the land on which it is located are acquired for $250,000 (see entry on page 518). How is an accountant to determine how much of the $250,000 applies to the land and how much to the building? An

3 $1,490 × 6.71 = approximately $10,000.

4 See AICPA, *APB Opinion No. 21:* "Interest on Receivables and Payables" (New York: 1971).

examination of the negotiations that preceded the transaction may show that the price was settled on under the assumption that $200,000 applied to the building and $50,000 to the land. If such evidence is not available or is considered to be unrealistic, the accountant must look elsewhere for more objective evidence of ***relative values*** as a basis for cost allocation. If, for example, the assessed valuation for property tax purposes is $161,000 for the building and $69,000 for land, the allocation of the total cost of $250,000 is made as follows:

Allocation of joint costs by relative value method

	Assessed valuation	*Relative value*	×	*Total cost*	=	*Allocation of cost*
Building	$161,000	70%		$250,000		$175,000
Land	69,000	30%				75,000
Totals	$230,000	100%				$250,000

Parties to a real estate transaction generally engage a lawyer to handle the details of the transaction. When the transaction is closed, each party receives a statement (often referred to as a ***statement of trust account*** or ***statement of adjustment***) which shows the complete details of the transaction. It shows (as charges and credits) items such as: selling price of the property, mortgage note assumed by the acquirer, transfer taxes, commission charged to the seller, cash received from the acquirer, any amount paid to either party to complete the transaction, etc. The allocation of property taxes, interest on the mortgage note, insurance, rents, and other items also is summarized in the statement. Such a condensed statement for the acquirer of the property discussed in the preceding section is shown below:

Statement for building and land

Items	*Charges*	*Credits*
Acquisition price of property	$246,700	
Balance of mortgage note assumed		$104,000
Interest at 12% from Oct. 16, Year 1, to Nov. 1, Year 1		520
Property taxes prorated, $6,600 a year from July 1, Year 1, to Nov. 1, Year 1		2,200
Fire insurance prorated, $480 a year from Nov. 1, Year 1, to May 1, Year 2	240	
Deposited in trust by acquirer		143,570
Legal fees	3,000	
Deed registration and transfer tax	300	
Cheque to balance (made payable to acquirer)	50	
Totals	$250,290	$250,290

The statement for the acquirer shows that the acquisition price of the property was $246,700. The acquirer was charged $240 for unexpired insurance, and additional costs of $3,300 ($3,000 + $300 = $3,300) allocable to the property. Thus, the total cost of the property is $250,000 ($246,700 + $3,300 = $250,000). The acquirer was credited for $104,000, representing the unpaid balance of the mortgage note assumed, $520 of accrued interest on the mortgage note and $2,200 of accrued property taxes that the acquirer must pay on a later date, and $143,570 of deposit to apply on the acquisition price. (The cash deposit had been recorded in the Deposit in Trust ledger account.) The "cheque to balance" of $50 is the amount of cash returned to the acquirer to close the transaction on November 1, Year 1.

The statement for the acquirer provides the information needed to record the acquisition of the property as illustrated below.

Journal entry to record acquisition of property

Cash	50	
Building	175,000	
Land	75,000	
Unexpired Insurance	240	
Interest Payable		520
Property Taxes Payable		2,200
Mortgage Note Payable		104,000
Deposit in Trust		143,570
To record acquisition of building and land. The total cost of $250,000 is allocated on the basis of property tax valuation of building and land. (See allocation on page 518.)		

A similar statement prepared for the seller provides the required information to record the sale of the property by the seller.

Securities Issued in Exchange for Plant Assets

When a corporation issues shares of its common stock for a plant asset, the appropriate basis for recording such a transaction is not always clear. The current fair value of the plant asset acquired is the cash equivalent received by the corporation for its shares of common stock. Conversely, the current fair (or market) value of the common stock given in exchange is a measure of the consideration for the asset. Thus, accountants are faced with the problem of obtaining independent evidence of (1) the current fair value of the plant asset, and (2) the current fair value of the common stock given in exchange. We should expect these two values to be roughly equivalent; if they are not, a choice between them must be made based on the factors considered by management in completing the transaction and on the validity of each valuation.

Shares of common stock represent an interest in the net assets of a corporation, including the plant asset being acquired. The market price of the common stock issued thus is not an entirely independent variable, because it depends to some extent on the value of the asset received in exchange. This reasoning indicates that our first choice should be independent evidence of the current fair value of the asset acquired, determined by appraisal, from previous bid prices, or from other objective sources. For example, if a machine that was appraised at $180,000 is acquired in exchange for 2,000 shares of no-par common stock, the exchange is recorded as follows:

Issuance of common stock for a plant asset

Account	Debit	Credit
Machinery	180,000	
Common Stock		180,000
To record exchange of 2,000 shares of common stock for machine appraised at $180,000.		

In some cases, evidence of the market value of shares of common stock is easier to obtain and more reliable than evidence as to the current fair value of an asset. This is particularly true if the common stock is listed on a stock exchange and daily quotations of market price are available.

Assets Acquired by Gift and with Government Assistance

In enhancing the long-run well-being of the community and the business enterprises, shareholders of a corporation may contribute assets as a gift to the corporation, and government may provide the corporation with financial assistance for the acquisition of assets. For example, assume that the City of Stillwater is trying to attract industry to its area. In order to induce Tanner Limited to locate a manufacturing plant in its city, the City Council agrees to provide $800,000 for the construction of a building for the company, in return for which the company promises to have its shareholders donate a building site and operate a plant in the city for a number of years. The land to be donated by the shareholders is purchased by the shareholders for $400,000; the construction cost for the building is $2,000,000, for which $800,000 is paid by the city.

How should accountants record this transaction? If we adopt the view that the sole responsibility of accountants is to keep track of costs incurred, we might argue that no cost is involved in the receipt of the land and part of the building in this instance, and therefore no journal entry is required to record these two items. This, however, is too narrow a view of the scope of accounting. A primary justification for recording asset acquisitions at cost is that cost at that time represents more satisfactory evidence of current fair value than any other basis. When cash outlay no longer is a reasonable basis for asset accountability or income measurement, accountants should be prepared to deal with the problem on its merits rather than adhering solely to the cost principle. If a business enterprise receives an asset at no cost, the asset should be recorded at its current fair value, determined on the basis of the best evidence available. Referring to the Tanner Limited example, the donation of the land and part of the building results in an increase in the net assets of the company, and is recorded as follows:[5]

Recording a donated asset and government assistance ...

Account	Debit	Credit
Land	400,000	
Building	2,000,000	
Donated Capital		400,000
Cash		1,200,000
Unearned Government Assistance		800,000
To record the land donated by shareholders and $800,000 government assistance from the City of Stillwater for part of the cost of the building.		

5 CICA, *CICA Handbook* (Toronto), sec. 3800.26.

If the economic life of the building is 10 years without any residual value and depreciation is based on a straight-line method, the Tanner company will charge depreciation expense of $200,000 a year. The unearned government assistance of $800,000 from the City of Stillwater will be amortized on the same basis as the building, by amortizing to income $80,000 a year.[6] Accordingly, the entries for depreciation and amortization will be as follows:

... and recording of related depreciation and amortization

Depreciation Expense	200,000	
Accumulated Depreciation		200,000
To record depreciation on the building (1/10 of $2,000,000).		
Unearned Government Assistance	80,000	
Income from Government Assistance		80,000
To record amortization of unearned government assistance on the same basis as the depreciation of the building (1/10 of $800,000).		

The effect of the depreciation expense and the amortization of the unearned government assistance to income is to charge to operation of Tanner Company a net expense of $120,000 ($200,000 − $80,000). The rationale for such an accounting treatment is to recognize that the government assistance affects the profitability of the company by conferring the financial benefit in exchange for the company's commitment to operate a plant in the community.[7]

The ***CICA Handbook*** states that, as an alternative, the building can be recorded on a net basis at $1,200,000 — that is, the $800,000 government assistance is deducted from the $2,000,000 cost of the building.[8] Consequently, there will be no amortization, as the government assistance is already deducted from the cost of the building. Also, the annual depreciation expense will be $120,000 (1/10 of $1,200,000). Thus, this alternative produces the same effect on income as the one discussed in the preceding paragraph.

How Are Costs Subsequent to Acquisition Recorded?

Expenditures relating to plant assets normally are made throughout the economic life of the assets. Whether these expenditures should be charged against current revenue (***revenue expenditures***) or whether they should be capitalized (***capital expenditures***) often is a difficult question. The general approach for dealing with these expenditures may be stated as follows: Expenditures that result in additional asset services, more valuable asset services, or extension of economic life are capitalized and allocated to future revenue; expenditures to maintain plant assets in good operating condition are recognized as expenses. This approach is consistent with the principle of matching expired costs and revenue and should be applied to any expenditure of significant amount. ***Future benefit is a characteristic of all capitalized costs relating to plant assets; costs that are applicable to***

6 CICA, ***CICA Handbook***, sec. 3800.26.

7 CICA, ***CICA Handbook***, sec. 3800.09.

8 CICA, ***CICA Handbook***, sec. 3800.26.

current or past revenue are recognized as expenses or losses.

Although the general approach outlined in the preceding paragraph enables accountants to distinguish between capital expenditures and revenue expenditures incurred subsequent to acquisition of plant assets, a brief discussion relating to different types of such expenditures is appropriate.

Additions

An ***addition*** is a capital expenditure for a new and separate plant asset or an extension of an existing asset. The construction of a new wing on an existing building is an example of an addition to buildings. The installation of two-way communication radios in a fleet of delivery trucks is an example of an addition to equipment. The addition of entirely new units is identical in nature to the acquisition of new plant assets and raises no accounting problems not discussed previously. When the addition involves an enlargement or extension of an existing plant asset, the only problem is to determine whether any portion of the service potential of the existing asset has been removed or lost in the process. For example, if in connection with the construction of a building addition, it is necessary to remove the old heating unit and install one with a larger capacity, the old heating unit should be retired. The journal entry to record the addition is accompanied by another entry to remove the cost of the old heating unit and its related accumulated depreciation from the accounting records and to recognize any resulting loss.

Improvements, Renewals, and Replacements

Improvements (or betterments), renewals, and replacements are nonrecurring capital expenditures that add to the service potential of plant assets. The additional value may be the result of extending the economic life, increasing the rate of output, or lowering the cost of operation per unit of output. Therefore, such capital expenditures are related to future services and should be matched with revenue in the accounting periods in which the services are used. Improvements and renewals may be accomplished through the substitution of better component parts and thus may be labelled "replacements." The distinction between these different expenditures is obscure and is not relevant to the basic accounting issues involved. Costs of this type often are referred to as ***plant renovation*** (or ***plant modernization) costs.***

To the extent that renovation involves the substitution of a new part for an old one, the proper accounting is to remove the cost of the old part from the asset ledger account (and the appropriate amount from the related accumulated depreciation account) and to substitute the cost of the new part. If the renovation does not involve a substitution but results only in some modification of the plant asset, the costs incurred are added to the carrying amount of the asset by a debit to either the asset ledger account or the accumulated depreciation account. These three procedures are explained below:

1 A considerable improvement in accounting for plant assets is possible if property units are defined in terms of major components and separate economic lives are used to depreciate these components. To illustrate, suppose that a glass-

lined food storage tank is constructed at a cost of $200,000, of which $40,000 is estimated to be the cost of the glass lining. The estimated economic life of the tank is 20 years; the lining must be replaced approximately every five years. If a single ledger account, Storage Tanks, is used, there will be a problem of dealing with the periodic replacement of the lining. A better procedure is to use two ledger accounts, Storage Tanks and Tank Lining, and to depreciate the former over 20 years and the latter over five years. Now, assume that at the beginning of the fifth year the glass lining had to be replaced at a cost of $54,000, but a new material was used that is expected to last ten years, with no net residual value. The journal entries to record the lining replacement are shown below:

Journal entries for replacement of a component of a plant asset

Accumulated Depreciation of Tank Lining ($40,000 × ⅘) ..	32,000	
Loss on Retirement of Tank Lining	8,000	
Tank Lining		40,000
To record removal of old tank lining. Carrying amount of old tank lining is recognized as a loss.		
Tank Lining	54,000	
Cash		54,000
To record replacement of old lining with new material.		

Depreciation of the new lining is recorded at $5,400 ($54,000 ÷ 10 = $5,400) in each of the next ten years, and the Storage Tanks ledger account is undisturbed by these events.

2 A capital expenditure that does not replace an existing part may enlarge the capacity or improve the efficiency of a plant asset without prolonging its economic life. Such an expenditure is recorded in the asset ledger account and depreciated over the remaining economic life of the asset. This procedure is similar to the one previously suggested for additions.

3 The cost of plant asset renovation often is debited directly to Accumulated Depreciation. The rationale for this procedure is that such an expenditure extends the economic life of the asset and thus restores some of the service potential (cost) previously written off. This procedure is sound in theory, but it should not be followed indiscriminately, particularly when capital expenditures for additions and replacements are involved.

Rearrangements and Moving Costs

Costs of rearranging machinery and equipment to provide a more efficient plant layout may be recorded in a separate ledger account and amortized over the period of time expected to benefit from the rearrangement (usually a short period because of the possibility of further rearrangements). Costs of moving the entire plant or office may be recorded similarly, unless the moving results from some unusual or infrequent event, in which case the costs of moving may be included as part of the related extraordinary loss. In practice, most business enterprises record moving costs as expenses.

Ordinary Repairs and Maintenance

Minor repair and maintenance revenue expenditures usually are required throughout the economic life of a plant asset to keep it in efficient operating condition. The distinguishing characteristic of such expenditures is that they neither add to the value of the asset nor materially prolong its economic life. The preferable procedure is to recognize these costs as expenses, because maintenance activities are recurring and the costs are related to current revenue. However, any unusual or extraordinary repairs arising from fire or other casualties are recognized as losses if not covered by insurance.

A questionable approach to the problem of dealing with repair costs that vary widely from one accounting period to another and are significant in amount is to ***anticipate*** such costs and allocate them to expense over the economic life of the appropriate plant asset. Under this procedure, the total expected repair costs are estimated at the time each asset is acquired, and Repairs Expense is debited each accounting period for a portion of the estimated lifetime repair costs. The offsetting credit is to an account titled Allowance for Estimated Repairs. Actual repair expenditures are debited to the allowance account. For income tax purposes, only the actual expenditures are deductible in the year incurred.

To illustrate, assume that repair costs for an item of equipment are expected to average $250 a year, that no repair costs are incurred in Year 1, and that repair costs of $400 are incurred in Year 2. The journal entries required during the first two years are shown below:

Journal entries for accrual of repair costs

End of Year 1:		
Repairs Expense	250	
Allowance for Estimated Repairs		250
To record estimated repairs expense.		
During Year 2:		
Allowance for Estimated Repairs	400	
Cash, Parts, Accrued Payroll, etc.		400
To record actual costs of repairs.		
End of Year 2:		
Repairs Expense	250	
Allowance for Estimated Repairs		250
To record estimated repairs expense.		

At the end of the second year, the allowance ledger account has a credit balance of $100 ($500 − $400 = $100). Conceivably, a debit balance might appear in the allowance account if major repairs occurred early or if the estimate of repair costs were too low.

A number of criticisms of this method may be raised. Some accountants have argued that it is an ***operating reserve*** (income-smoothing device) and that it tends to obscure the fact that repair costs may increase as an asset becomes older. Others question whether reliable estimates of repair costs can be made. Finally, the classification of the Allowance for Estimated Repairs ledger account poses difficulties. A credit balance in the allowance account is not considered a part of shareholders' equity because it is illogical to debit an expense and increase shareholders' equity. Classification as a liability may be questioned, because no legal obligation for an expenditure exists. Treating the allowance as an asset valuation ledger account (to be deducted from or added to the cost of the related plant asset in the balance sheet) assumes that the "accrued repairs" represent additional depreciation and thus reduce the carrying amount of the asset. This is probably the least objectionable alternative, because it is consistent with the reporting of a debit balance in the allowance account as an asset—in the nature of a prepayment of repair costs.

Anticipation of repair costs does not fit neatly in the conceptual model of financial accounting. Year-to-year accrual of estimated repair costs lacks sufficient objectivity and might encourage managements of business enterprises to adopt other income-smoothing practices.

RETIREMENTS, DISPOSALS, AND EXCHANGES

When a plant asset is retired, sold, or exchanged, the accumulated depreciation on the asset first is brought up to date. The second requirement is to remove from the accounting records all ledger account balances relating to the asset and to recognize any gain or loss from the disposal of the asset. Some of the more common situations involving the retirement, disposal, or exchange of plant assets include the following:

1. A fully depreciated plant asset with no residual value is ***retired*** without receipt of any proceeds; no gain or loss is recognized on such retirement.
2. A partially depreciated plant asset is ***retired*** without receipt of any proceeds; a loss is recognized on such retirement.
3. A fully or partially depreciated plant asset is ***retired*** or ***sold*** with some recovery of net residual value; a gain or loss is recognized on such retirement or sale.
4. A fully or partially depreciated asset is ***exchanged*** for other assets without any cash being received or paid; the guidelines for the recognition of a gain or loss on such a ***nonmonetary exchange transaction*** are:
   a. If a loss is indicated by the terms of the transaction, the ***loss always is recognized.***
   b. If a gain is indicated in an ***exchange of dissimilar assets that results in the completion of the earning process*** (such as the exchange of an inventory item that cost $1,000 for a plant asset with a current fair value of $1,500), the ***gain is recognized***.
   c. If a gain is indicated in an ***exchange of similar assets that does not complete the earning process*** (such as an exchange of an inventory item for another inventory item or an exchange of a plant asset with a similar plant asset), the ***gain is not recognized.***
5. A fully or partially depreciated plant asset may be exchanged for a ***similar asset***, with cash being paid or received by the parties to the transaction. In such exchanges, ***an indicated loss is recognized in full, but only a portion of any indicated gain is recognized by the party receiving cash.***

The accounting procedures for the foregoing situations are described in the following sections.

Retirements and Disposals of Plant Assets

When a fully depreciated plant asset with no net residual value is retired, and no proceeds are received, the retirement is recorded by a debit to the accumulated depreciation ledger account and a credit to the plant asset account; when a partially depreciated plant asset is retired and no proceeds are received, a loss is recognized equal to the difference between cost and accumulated depreciation; when a fully or partially depreciated plant asset is retired or sold with some recovery of net residual value, a gain or loss is recognized equal to the difference between the carrying amount of the asset and the proceeds received. For example, assume that equipment with a cost of $6,000 with no net residual value has been depreciated at an annual rate of 10% for eight years. In the middle of the ninth year the equipment is sold for $1,750 cash (net of any direct costs incurred on the sale). The journal entries to record this sale are shown below:

Depreciation first is brought up to date when a plant asset is sold

Depreciation Expense ($6,000 × 0.10 × ½)	300	
Accumulated Depreciation of Equipment		300
To record depreciation at 10% for six months on equipment costing $6,000 with no net residual value.		
Cash	1,750	
Accumulated Depreciation of Equipment ($6,000 × 0.10 × 8½)	5,100	
Gain on Disposal of Equipment		850
Equipment		6,000
To record sale of equipment.		

The proper interpretation of any gain or loss that may result from the retirement or sale of a plant asset often is uncertain. To the extent that it stems from errors in estimates of economic life or net residual value, the "gain" or "loss" is an adjustment of previously reported net income. To the extent that it is caused by changes in the current fair value of the asset, the gain or loss is also an element of net income for the current year. In most cases a combination of these factors is present. Material gains and losses (or provisions for losses) from the sale or abandonment of individual plant assets are included in the determination of income before extraordinary items.

Standby Plant Assets

Plant assets sometimes are retired from active service and are neither sold nor abandoned but are kept on a ***standby status*** for use in emergency or to meet peak-load requirements. When this occurs, the plant assets are written down to their standby or residual values. Depreciation of such assets is discontinued while they remain idle. When the amount of standby plant assets is significant, it should be reported under the "Other noncurrent assets" caption in the balance sheet.

Exchanges of Plant Assets

Prior to the issuance in the United States of ***APB Opinion No. 29:*** ''Accounting for Nonmonetary Transactions,'' exchanges of plant assets for similar plant assets were recorded in a variety of ways for financial accounting. Such a transaction frequently was recorded at the carrying amount of the plant asset given in exchange plus any cash paid or less any cash received, and no gain or loss was recognized. Alternatively, a gain or loss was recognized when the current fair value of the plant asset given in exchange was used to record the transaction, and the plant asset acquired generally was recorded at the current fair value of the asset exchanged, plus any cash paid or less any cash received. Since the ***CICA Handbook*** is silent in this area, key provisions of this ***Opinion*** are discussed in the following paragraphs.

APB Opinion No. 29 differentiated ***monetary exchanges*** involving cash and receivables or payables from ***nonmonetary exchanges*** involving, for example, inventories, investments in common stocks, and plant assets. An ***exchange*** was defined as a transfer between business enterprises that results in one enterprise receiving assets or services or satisfying obligations by surrendering other assets or services or incurring other obligations.[9] The portion of the ***basic principle*** in ***APB Opinion No. 29*** that relates to exchanges of plant assets appears below:[10]

> The Board concludes that in general accounting for nonmonetary transactions should be based on the fair values of the assets (or services) involved which is the same basis as that used in monetary transactions. Thus, the cost of a nonmonetary asset acquired in exchange for another nonmonetary asset is the fair value of the asset surrendered to obtain it, and a gain or loss should be recognized on the exchange. The fair value of the asset received should be used to measure the cost if it is more clearly evident than the fair value of the asset surrendered.

The Accounting Principles Board modified this basic principle in several important respects. First, the accounting for exchanges is based on the current fair values of assets unless such values are not reasonably determinable. If current fair values are not reasonably determinable, the asset acquired is recorded at the carrying amount of the asset given in exchange plus any cash paid, and no gain or loss is recognized. Second, if an exchange transaction does not result in the completion of the earning process (realization), the asset acquired also is recorded at the carrying amount of the asset surrendered. An example of such a transaction is an exchange of a plant asset for a similar plant asset. However, if the terms of the transaction indicate that the asset surrendered has a current fair value that is less than its carrying amount, a loss is recognized. Finally, if cash (or other monetary consideration) is received in an exchange of assets, the recipient of the cash is deemed to have realized a gain on the exchange equal in amount to the excess of the cash received over the proportionate share of the carrying amount of the asset given in exchange. A transaction in which a plant asset and cash are received in

9 AICPA, ***APB Opinion No. 29:*** ''Accounting for Nonmonetary Transactions'' (New York: 1973), p. 541.

10 AICPA, ***APB Opinion No. 29***, p. 547.

exchange for another plant asset ***is viewed as a sale to the extent of cash received, and as an exchange to the extent of the current fair value of the plant asset received***.

The procedures to be followed in recording exchanges of plant assets pursuant to ***Opinion No. 29*** are summarized below:

1 Compute the indicated gain or loss on the exchange. The gain or loss is equal to the difference between the current fair value of the asset surrendered and its carrying amount.

2 If the computation in **1** results in a loss, the entire indicated loss is recognized for financial accounting, and the asset acquired is recorded at the current fair value of the asset surrendered plus any cash paid (or less any cash received). ***An indicated loss is always recognized.***

3 If the computation in **1** results in a gain, and the earning process is completed, the full indicated gain is recognized; if the earning process is not completed and cash is paid (or no cash is involved in the exchange), no gain is recognized; if cash is received in the exchange, only a portion of the gain is recognized, as follows:

Gain is recognized on the cash part of the "sale" when the earning process is not completed

$$\text{Gain} \times \frac{\text{cash received}}{\text{cash received} + \text{current fair value of asset received}} = \text{gain recognized}$$

The procedures for recording exchanges of similar plant assets are illustrated in the examples on page 529. The plant asset exchanged has a carrying amount of $6,000 (cost of $20,000 less accumulated depreciation of $14,000). Each example involves similar plant assets with comparable current fair values, adjusted for any cash paid or received. For each example, the indicated gain or loss is the difference between the current fair value of the old asset and its carrying amount.

The indicated losses in each of the first three examples are recognized for financial accounting. In the next two examples, no gain is recognized because no cash was received in example **4** and because cash was paid in example **5**. However, in example **6**, 10% of the indicated gain of $4,000 is recognized because 10% of the total consideration received consisted of cash, and to that extent ***the earning process was completed***.

If the exchanges in the last three examples involved ***dissimilar*** assets, the entire indicated gain would be recognized for financial accounting ***because the earning process would be considered completed***. Exchanges of plant assets that are material in amount, either individually or in the aggregate, are disclosed in the financial statements. Such disclosure includes the nature of the exchanges, the basis of accounting for the assets transferred, and the amount of gain or loss recognized.

Involuntary Conversions

The services of plant assets occasionally are lost through condemnation, fire, or other involuntary means. In the accounting for such events, the amount of any

Examples of exchange transactions involving similar plant assets (earning process not completed)

	Exchange transaction	*Journal entry (Explanation omitted)*		
1	***Loss of $2,000 is indicated; no cash is involved.*** Current fair value of old asset is $4,000. (Cost of new asset is $4,000 current fair value of old asset.)	Plant Asset (new) .... Accumulated Depreciation ...... Loss on Exchange of Plant Asset .... Plant Asset (old)	4,000 14,000 2,000 	 20,000
2	***Loss of $2,500 is indicated; cash of $1,000 is paid.*** Current fair value of old asset is $3,500. (Cost of new asset is $3,500 current fair value of old asset plus $1,000 cash paid, or $4,500.)	Plant Asset (new) .... Accumulated Depreciation ...... Loss on Exchange of Plant Asset .... Cash .... Plant Asset (old)	4,500 14,000 2,500 	 1,000 20,000
3	***Loss of $1,000 is indicated; cash of $200 is received.*** Current fair value of old asset is $5,000. (Cost of new asset is $5,000 current fair value of old asset less $200 cash received, or $4,800.)	Cash .... Plant Asset (new) .... Accumulated Depreciation ...... Loss on Exchange of Plant Asset .... Plant Asset (old)	200 4,800 14,000 1,000 	 20,000
4	***Gain of $6,500 is indicated; no cash is involved.*** Current fair value of old asset is $12,500. (Cost of new asset is $6,000 carrying amount of old asset.)	Plant Asset (new) .... Accumulated Depreciation ...... Plant Asset (old)	6,000 14,000 	 20,000
5	***Gain of $6,500 is indicated; cash of $1,000 is paid.*** Current fair value of old asset is $12,500. (Cost of new asset is $6,000 carrying amount of old asset plus $1,000 cash paid, or $7,000.)	Plant Asset (new) .... Accumulated Depreciation ...... Cash .... Plant Asset (old)	7,000 14,000 	 1,000 20,000
6	***Gain of $4,000 is indicated; cash of $1,000 is received.*** Current fair value of old asset is $10,000, indicating a current fair value of new asset of $9,000. The portion of indicated gain recognized is: $\$4{,}000 \times \left(\frac{\$1{,}000}{\$1{,}000 + \$9{,}000}\right) = \$400$ (Cost of new asset is $6,000 carrying amount of old asset, less $1,000 cash received, plus $400 gain recognized, or $5,400; alternatively, the cost of new asset may be computed by deducting the gain not recognized from the current fair value of the new asset: $9,000 − $3,600 = $5,400.)	Cash .... Plant Asset (new) .... Accumulated Depreciation ...... Plant Asset (old) .... Gain on Exchange of Plant Asset	1,000 5,400 14,000 	 20,000 400

loss or gain is recognized, and all amounts relating to such assets are removed from the accounting records. For example, assume that certain land and buildings owned by a business enterprise are expropriated for the construction of a highway, and that the government sets a price of $140,000. Accumulated depreciation of the building is $120,000, and its cost was $160,000; the cost of the land was $40,000. The journal entry to record this involuntary conversion follows:

Recording involuntary conversion

Cash	140,000	
Accumulated Depreciation of Building	120,000	
Building		160,000
Land		40,000
Gain on Expropriation of Property		60,000
To record property expropriated by government.		

Since the ***CICA Handbook*** has yet to deal with involuntary conversions, the position of the Financial Accounting Standards Board in the United States on this topic is highlighted below.[11]

> Involuntary conversions of nonmonetary assets to monetary assets are monetary transactions for which gain or loss shall be recognized even though an enterprise reinvests or is obligated to reinvest the monetary assets in replacement of non-monetary assets.

The FASB addressed this topic because many business enterprises applied the income tax rule for an involuntary conversion of plant assets. In most cases no gain is recognized for income tax purposes at the time of an involuntary conversion if the owner of the property uses the funds received to replace the involuntarily converted asset within a certain time period.

When depreciable plant assets or merchandise are destroyed by fire or other casualties, accountants often assist in measuring and recording the losses sustained. For example, inventories on hand at the time of fire may have to be estimated by the gross profit method described in Chapter 9.

Insurance on Plant Assets

Most business enterprises insure assets for possible losses resulting from fire, theft, explosion, and other insurable events. A ***deductible clause*** usually limits recovery to a loss in excess of a specified amount, such as $100.

Insurance policies provide for recovery of loss based on the replacement cost (current fair value) of the asset destroyed. The carrying amount of an asset, although irrelevant in determining the amount of recovery from insurance companies, is used to measure the loss or gain as a result of the casualty. For example, if $10,000 is collected from an insurance company on complete destruction of an asset with a carrying amount of $7,500, a gain of $2,500 results.

The amount of insurance carried on an asset should never exceed the current fair value of the asset, because the amount recovered never exceeds the current fair value of the asset. When inadequate insurance is carried on an asset, the insured in effect becomes a ''coinsurer'' with the insurance company. For example, if an asset worth $5,000 that is insured for only $4,000 is totally destroyed, the insurance company would bear $4,000 of the loss and the owner would absorb the remaining $1,000.

11 FASB, ***FASB Interpretation No. 30:*** ''Accounting for Involuntary Conversions of Nonmonetary Assets to Monetary Assets — An Interpretation of ***APB Opinion No. 29***'' (Stamford: 1979), p. 1.

Coinsurance Clause in an Insurance Policy

If it were possible to obtain insurance coverage for only a fraction of the current fair value of an asset, the owner would benefit by receiving full reimbursement of most losses with a minimum insurance coverage and cost. However, insurance companies usually include a ***coinsurance clause*** in the insurance policy to prevent this approach to low-cost insurance protection. A coinsurance clause requires that an asset be insured for a specified minimum amount, usually 80% of current fair value, if a loss is to be absorbed fully (up to the face amount of the policy) by the insurance company. If the insurance coverage is below the specified percentage, the owner absorbs a portion of the loss, even though the loss does not exceed the face amount of the policy.

To illustrate the application of a coinsurance clause in a fire insurance policy, assume the following:

Assumptions for coinsurance illustration

Carrying amount of machinery damaged by fire (cost, $140,000)	$ 55,000
Insurance carried (face amount of policy)	60,000
Current fair value of machinery on date of fire	100,000
Coinsurance required by policy (80% of current fair value)	80,000
Amount of fire loss (based on current fair value of machinery)	40,000

The recovery from the insurance company is determined under the coinsurance formula as follows:

$$\frac{\$60{,}000 \text{ (amount of insurance)}}{\$80{,}000 \text{ (coinsurance requirement)}} \times \$40{,}000 \text{ (loss)} = \underline{\underline{\$30{,}000}}$$

It is important to note the following points regarding property insurance:

1 The amount of insurance coverage is not dependent on the cost or the carrying amount of the asset. (Cost and carrying amount are irrelevant for purposes of measuring either the amount of insurance that may be carried or the amount of recoverable loss.)

2 Recovery on the loss is dependent on the current fair value of the asset, the amount of insurance carried, and the minimum amount of insurance required by the coinsurance clause.

3 If insurance is carried equal to or in excess of the amount required by the coinsurance clause, any loss up to the face amount of the policy is fully recoverable; if less than the required amount of insurance is carried, the loss is absorbed in part by the ***insured***.

4 If the amount of insurance carried exceeds the coinsurance requirement, there is no need to apply the coinsurance formula.

A careful study of the coinsurance formula indicates that ***the recoverable portion of the loss always is the lower of (1) the amount of the loss adjusted by the coinsurance formula and (2) the face amount of the policy.***

Two or More Insurance Policies

If an asset is insured under two or more policies that do not have coinsurance clauses, any loss is shared by the insurance companies in proportion to the amount of insurance written by each company; the same procedure applies when the insurance policies contain identical coinsurance requirements. If two or more insurance policies cover the same asset, and the policies have ***different*** coinsurance clauses, ***the coinsurance formula is applied to each policy separately***. However, the loss absorbed by any insurance company will not exceed its proportion of the total insurance carried with all insurance companies. For example, assume that a building with a current fair value of $400,000 is insured under two policies as follows:

- *Policy A:* $150,000, with an 80% coinsurance clause
- *Policy B:* $150,000, with a 70% coinsurance clause

Assuming that a fire causes damage of $240,000 to the building, how much of the loss will be recovered under each policy? If neither policy had a coinsurance clause, each insurance company absorbs 50% of the loss ($120,000) because each policy represents 50% of the total insurance ($300,000). If both policies had a 70% coinsurance requirement, each insurance company absorbs $120,000 of the loss because the total insurance carried ($300,000) exceeds the minimum insurance required by the coinsurance clause ($400,000 × 0.70 = $280,000). However, because policy A has an 80% coinsurance clause in this case, the recovery under each policy is determined as follows:

Allocation of loss between two insurance companies

Policy A

$$\frac{\$150{,}000 \text{ (insurance under policy A)}}{\$320{,}000 \text{ (coinsurance req. for policy A)}} \times \$240{,}000 \text{ (loss)} = \underline{\underline{\$112{,}500}}$$

Policy B

$$\frac{\$150{,}000 \text{ (insurance under policy B)}}{\$300{,}000 \text{ (total insurance on building)}} \times \$240{,}000 \text{ (loss)} = \underline{\underline{\$120{,}000}}$$

The recovery under policy A is $\frac{15}{32}$ of the loss, which is less than the pro rata coverage of $\frac{15}{30}$, because the coinsurance requirement under this policy ***was not met***. In contrast, the recovery under policy B is $\frac{15}{30}$ of the loss, because the total insurance on the building ($300,000) exceeds the minimum required under policy B ($280,000). Thus, the coinsurance formula is not applicable to policy B.

Insurance contracts vary in form and complexity. The discussion here is brief and simplified. Although accountants need not be experts in insurance contracts, they should have a basic understanding of insurance to be able to account properly for premiums paid and proceeds received, and to help clients formulate a sound property insurance program.

REVIEW QUESTIONS

1 Define ***tangible asset, natural resource,*** and ***intangible asset***, and list a few examples of each.

2 What are the arguments in favour of using historical cost as the basis of accounting for plant assets? Might this be referred to as an asset ***valuation procedure***?

3 How is the cost of a plant asset determined for financial accounting? What three issues are involved in accounting for the cost of plant assets?

4 What is meant by the terms ***capital expenditure*** and ***revenue expenditure***? How are these terms related to the accounting principles of revenue realization and matching of costs and revenue?

5 Which of the following are capital expenditures? Indicate the appropriate accounting treatment of any item that is not a capital expenditure.

a Cost of grading land prior to construction
b Cost of installing equipment, including cost of spoiled material during test runs
c Tax assessment for street paving
d Delinquent property taxes on land acquired
e Cost of maintaining equipment in good operating condition
f Cost of moving and reinstalling equipment in another part of factory
g Cost of repairs to used equipment (The need for repair was discovered immediately after acquisition of the equipment)
h Cost of demolishing an old building in preparation for new construction (The old building was used for 24 years and was fully depreciated)
i Cost of insurance policy covering possible damages that may arise during construction of a new building
j Excess of operating expenses over revenue during first year of operations
k Cost of removing soil to build foundation for new building

6 Duke Company has constructed a special-purpose machine for its own use. Direct labour and material costs were $10,000. Variable overhead costs were 10% of direct costs, and fixed overhead costs allocable to the constructed machine were $2,400. Duke's engineers estimate that an equivalent machine would cost $15,000 if acquired for cash. At what amount should the machine be recorded? Why? Is there a profit on the self-construction? Assuming that the machine could have been acquired for $8,000, at what amount should the machine be recorded for financial accounting?

7 Capitalizing interest cost during construction is an accepted accounting procedure; adding interest on an instalment contract to the cost of the asset acquired is not. Explain the distinction between these two situations.

8 What position did the FASB in the United States take in ***Statement No. 34:*** "Capitalization of Interest Cost" on the capitalization of interest cost?

9 Discuss the accounting problem that arises in each of the following situations involving plant assets, and explain the proper accounting procedure:

a Assets are acquired under a deferred payment plan.

b A group of assets is acquired for a lump-sum price.
c Assets are acquired in exchange for common stock or bonds of the acquiring corporation.
d Assets are acquired by gift.

10 Briefly describe the accounting procedures appropriate for the following:
a Additions
b Improvements, renewals, and replacements
c Ordinary repair and maintenance costs
d Extraordinary repairs as a result of fire damage not covered by insurance
e Gain or loss on involuntary conversion of land to cash

11 The accountant for Waddell Company estimates annual repair costs on equipment and prepares a journal entry each year debiting Repairs Expense and crediting Allowance for Repairs, which sometimes shows a credit balance and sometimes a debit balance. What is the appropriate classification of the latter ledger account in the balance sheet? Why?

12 Evans Company debits the cost of major repairs of plant assets to the Accumulated Depreciation ledger account. Evaluate this procedure.

13 How are gains and losses on retirements, disposals, or exchanges of plant assets reported in the income statement?

14 *a* Describe the ***basic principle*** stated in ***APB Opinion No. 29:*** ''Accounting for Nonmonetary Transactions'' relating to accounting for exchanges of plant assets.
b List three modifications of the basic principle stated in ***APB Opinion No. 29.***

15 Describe the conditions under which exchange transactions involving plant assets require the recognition of gains and losses for financial accounting.

16 What is meant by ***coinsurance***? Describe the coinsurance formula. May the destruction of insured property result in a gain for financial accounting? Explain.

EXERCISES

Ex. 11-1 Select the best answer for each of the following multiple-choice questions:

1 On June 25, Year 7, Lino Printers, Inc., incurred the following costs for one of its printing presses:

Acquisition of collating and stapling attachment	$42,000
Installation of attachment	18,000
Replacement parts for overhaul of press	13,000
Labour and plant overhead costs applicable to overhaul of press	7,000
Total costs	$80,000

The overhaul resulted in a substantial increase in the output of the printing press. Neither the attachment nor the overhaul increased the estimated

economic life of the press. The amount of the foregoing costs that Lino Printers debits to the Printing Presses ledger account is:
a $42,000 *b* $55,000 *c* $60,000 *d* $80,000 *e* Some other amount

2 Mansfield Company acquired equipment under a deferred payment contract on December 31, Year 3. The contract required the payment of $20,000 on December 31, Year 3, and $20,000 on December 31 of each of the following five years. The amount that Mansfield debits to the Equipment ledger account is:
a The present value of an ordinary annuity of six rents of $20,000
b $120,000
c $120,000 less imputed interest
d $120,000 plus imputed interest
e Some other amount

3 In an arm's-length transaction, Lewis Company and Clark Company exchanged similar plant assets, with no cash involved in the exchange. Current fair values of both plant assets were available. Clark's accounting for the exchange is based on the:
a Current fair value of the asset surrendered by Clark
b Current fair value of the asset received by Lewis
c Carrying amount of the asset surrendered by Clark
d Carrying amount of the asset received from Lewis

4 Which of the following costs is debited to the Land ledger account?
a Landscaping of the land
b Sidewalks constructed and maintained by owner of the land
c Parking lot constructed and maintained by owner of the land
d Parking structure constructed and maintained by owner of the land

5 The ***acquisition period*** for the capitalization of interest cost incurred for a plant asset begins when all the following conditions are present, except:
a The plant asset has been placed in use.
b Interest cost is being incurred.
c Expenditures for the plant asset have been incurred.
d Activities to prepare the plant asset for use are in progress.

6 Plant assets retired from active service but kept on a standby status for use in emergency are:
a Depreciated over their remaining estimated economic lives
b Written down to residual values
c Written off in total as an extraordinary loss
d Included in the current assets section of the balance sheet

7 Corsair Company paid $7,000 cash and exchanged an old machine that had a cost of $10,000, a carrying amount of $4,000, and a current fair value of $5,000, for a similar new machine with a current fair value of $12,000. In the journal entry to record the transaction in accordance with generally accepted accounting principles, Corsair:
a Credits Gain on Exchange of Plant Assets, $1,000
b Credits Machinery (old), $4,000
c Debits Machinery (new), $11,000
d Credits Machinery (old), $5,000

Ex. 11-2 Among the Year 8 transactions involved in Grange Company's acquisition of land for the construction of a new building, so that Grange could give up leased premises, were the following:

Mar. 16 Paid billing from subcontractor for clearing trees and brush from land, $15,000.

18 Received $2,000 from firewood dealer for timber salvaged from land-clearing operation.

30 Paid billing from subcontractor for cost of razing old building acquired with land, $140,000.

Apr. 18 Paid billing from subcontractor for construction of parking lot to be maintained by Grange, $80,000.

Prepare journal entries for the foregoing transactions of Grange Company.

Ex. 11-3 On July 11, Year 8, Lupo Corporation acquired land with a current fair value of $590,000 in exchange for $200,000 face amount of bonds payable and 20,000 shares of its common stock. The stock was trading at $20 on the Toronto Stock Exchange on July 11, Year 8.

Prepare a journal entry to record Lupo Corporation's acquisition of land.

Ex. 11-4 On April 15, Year 4, Fonville Limited exchanged 10,000 shares of its no-par common stock, with a current fair value of $60 a share, for land for a future plant site. Fonville received $75,000 for scrap from the demolition of an existing building on the land that was razed at a cost of $120,000.

Compute the amount that Fonville Company should debit to the Land ledger account as the cost of the acquired land.

Ex. 11-5 The costs incurred by Armine Baeza to acquire land and construct a building were as follows:

Land (including miscellaneous acquisition costs)	$150,000
Construction insurance	3,500
Building construction contract (excluding excavation)	220,000
Architect fees	2,000
Street and sidewalk installation (maintenance by the city)	4,000
Costs of excavation for foundation	3,100
Property taxes on land (prior to construction)	1,600
Advertising costs to attract tenants	1,250
Interest cost during acquisition period on loan to pay contractor	2,600

Determine the cost for financial accounting of Armine Baeza's:
a Land *b* Building

Ex. 11-6 Lupina, Inc., replaced a used machine with a new one having a list price of $10,000, subject to a 2% cash discount if paid promptly. Net cost of removing the used machine to make room for the new one amounted to $800. Installation of the new machine cost $400. Costs of testing the new machine were $250 for operator's time and $325 in spoiled material. The cash discount was lost because of late payment of the invoice.

Compute the cost of Lupina's new machine for financial accounting.

Ex. 11-7 On January 2, Year 6, Ramirez Company contracted with Construction Specialists, Inc., for a new building at a fixed price of $4,000,000. Construction Specialists estimated a three-year construction period for the building. Also on January 2, Year 6, Ramirez borrowed $4,000,000, payable in 10 annual instalments of $400,000, plus interest at 11% a year, beginning January 2, Year 7. During Year 6, Ramirez made progress payments totalling $1,500,000 to Construction Specialists; the average amount of accumulated payments was $650,000 for Year 6. Ramirez invested unused borrowed cash in short-term securities, from which Ramirez realized interest revenue of $250,000 during Year 6.

Compute the amount of Ramirez Company's capitalized interest cost for the year ended December 31, Year 6.

Ex. 11-8 On June 30, Year 10, Silvy Company acquired equipment at a bankruptcy auction. The acquisition price consisted of the following:

Cash down payment	$ 72,150
Four non-interest-bearing promissory notes in the face amount of $50,000 each, payable annually on June 30, commencing in Year 11 ...	200,000
Total acquisition price	$272,150

Record the acquisition of the equipment in the accounting records of Silvy Company, assuming that a fair rate of interest is 10% compounded annually. Use the appropriate table in the Appendix at the end of Chapter 5 and round computations to the nearest dollar.

Ex. 11-9 On December 31, Year 1, Woodrow Company acquired equipment under a deferred payment contract requiring the payment of $100 a month for 12 months, beginning on January 31, Year 2. The interest rate implicit in the contract was 1½% a month. Compound interest tables provide the following values:

$$a_{\overline{12}|1\frac{1}{2}\%} = 1.20 \quad p_{\overline{12}|1\frac{1}{2}\%} = 0.84 \quad A_{\overline{12}|1\frac{1}{2}\%} = 13.04 \quad P_{\overline{12}|1\frac{1}{2}\%} = 10.91$$

Prepare journal entries for Woodrow Company for the deferred payment contract on December 31, Year 1; January 31, Year 2; and February 28, Year 2. Round all amounts to the nearest dollar.

Ex. 11-10 Dilworth, Inc., acquired three machines at an auction for a lump-sum cost of $14,500, and also paid $500 to have the machines delivered to its place of business. The current fair values of the three machines were as follows:

Machine X	$10,000
Machine Y	6,000
Machine Z	4,000
Total current fair value	$20,000

Determine the cost allocated to each machine acquired by Dilworth, Inc., using the relative current fair values of the machines as a basis of allocating the total cost of the machines.

Ex. 11-11 Selleck Company sold land and a building to Ackwire Company. The property had cost Selleck $39,000, including $10,000 allocated to land. Depreciation of $3,500 had been recorded on the building by Selleck. At the closing of the transaction, the following statements were submitted to Selleck and Ackwire:

	Statement to Selleck Company		*Statement to Ackwire Company*	
	Charges	*Credits*	*Charges*	*Credit*
Selling price		$40,300	$40,300	
Cash deposited in trust				$10,400
Prorated property taxes	$ 120			120
Prorated interest	70			70
Prorated insurance		200	200	
Mortgage note assumed by acquirer	30,160			30,160
Commission to broker	2,370			
Legal fee	360		150	
Cash to seller	7,420			
Cash to acquirer			100	
Totals	$40,500	$40,500	$40,750	$40,750

a Prepare a journal entry to record the sale of the property in Selleck Company's accounting records.

b Prepare a journal entry to record the acquisition of the property in Ackwire Company's accounting records. The value assigned to land is $15,500. Ackwire had recorded the cash deposited in trust, $10,400, in a Deposit Trust ledger account. Record any accrued or deferred expenses in nominal ledger accounts.

Ex. 11-12 Alice Arnold, a sole proprietor, has been maintaining her own accounting records. At the end of Year 3, after the accounting records were adjusted but before they were closed, you were engaged to review the records. The items that require correction are listed below:

1 Installation costs for fixtures, $1,200, were debited to Maintenance Expense. The fixtures have a five-year economic life, with no net residual value, and were installed at the beginning of Year 3. Assume use of the straight-line method of depreciation.

2 A machine acquired on January 2, Year 1, at a cost of $5,500 has been depreciated on a straight-line basis over a five-year period, with no net residual value. The machine was sold on June 30, Year 3. Arnold debited Cash and credited Machinery for $2,100, the proceeds on the sale. No depreciation was recorded on this machine in Year 3, but you conclude that one-half year's depreciation should have been recorded.

Prepare a correcting journal entry for Alice Arnold on December 31, Year 3, for each of the two items described above.

Ex. 11-13 Prepare journal entries to record the exchange of Machine A for machine B in each of the following situations:

a Carlton Corporation acquired machine B by trading in machine A and paying $5,000 cash. Machine A cost $95,000 and had accumulated depreciation of $25,000 on the date of exchange. Machine B could have been acquired for $80,000 cash. The machines are similar.

b Assume the same facts as in ***a***, except that instead of paying $5,000 cash, Carlton received $20,000 cash.

c Assume the same facts as in ***a***, except that instead of paying $5,000 cash, Carlton received $5,000 cash. Machine B could have been acquired for $50,000 cash.

Ex. 11-14 On June 1, Year 7, Zane Company replaced its obsolete air conditioning system having a carrying amount of $30,000 and a current fair value of $10,000 with a new system having a current fair value of $190,000. Zane paid the air conditioning contractor $180,000 and permitted the contractor to keep the obsolete air conditioner. Accumulated depreciation on the obsolete system was $50,000.

Prepare a journal entry to record Zane Company's acquisition of the new system.

Ex. 11-15 On February 28, Year 2, Hix Company traded a machine with a cost of $60,000, a carrying amount of $20,000, and a current fair value of $25,000, to Cox Company for a similar new machine with a cost and current fair value of $23,000. In addition, Hix received $2,000 from Cox.

Prepare journal entries to record the foregoing transaction in the accounting records of:

a Hix Company ***b*** Cox Company

Ex. 11-16 In Year 2, Leah Gold sold for $55,000 a parcel of land that had cost $25,000. The contract required a down payment of $15,000 and a non-interest-bearing promissory note for $40,000 due in four years.

Record the sale of land in Gold's accounting records, assuming that the present value of the note (discounted at compound interest of 12% for four years) was $25,421, and that 12% was a fair rate of interest on this type of note. Assume that the note receivable is recorded at face amount.

Ex. 11-17 On October 15, Year 9, a fire caused $100,000 in damage to Banning Company's building that had a current fair value of $300,000 and a carrying amount of $175,000. Banning had a fire insurance policy in the amount of $120,000 with an 80% coinsurance clause for the building.

Compute the maximum amount that the insurance carrier will pay to Banning Company as a result of the fire loss.

Ex. 11-18 A machine has a carrying amount of $13,000 and a current fair value of $20,000. Determine the amount recoverable from the insurance company in each case below, assuming that each insurance policy contains an 80% coinsurance clause:

Case	*Insurance coverage*	*Loss incurred*
A	$10,000	$12,000
B	12,000	11,000
C	14,000	8,000
D	16,000	18,000
E	18,000	17,000

CASES

Case 11-1 Among the principal topics related to the accounting for the plant assets of a business enterprise are acquisition and retirement.

Instructions

a What expenditures are capitalized when equipment is acquired for cash?

b Assume that the current fair value of equipment acquired is not determinable by reference to a similar acquisition for cash. Describe how the acquiring enterprise determines the capitalizable cost of equipment acquired by exchanging for it each of the following:

1 Bonds having an established market price

2 Common stock not having an established market price

3 Similar equipment having a determinable current fair value

c Describe the factors that determine whether expenditures relating to plant assets already in use should be capitalized.

d Describe how to account for the gain or loss on the sale of plant assets for cash.

Case 11-2 Plant assets generally represent a significant portion of the total assets of most business enterprises. Accounting for the acquisition and use of such assets is therefore an important part of financial accounting.

Instructions

a Distinguish between revenue expenditures and capital expenditures and explain why this distinction is important.

b Identify six costs that should be capitalized as the cost of land. For your answer, assume that land with an existing building is acquired for cash and that the existing building is to be removed in order that a new building may be constructed on the site.

c At what amount should a business enterprise record a plant asset acquired under a deferred payment plan?

d In general, at what amount should plant assets received in exchange for other nonmonetary assets be recorded? Specifically, at what amount should a business enterprise record a new machine acquired in exchange for a similar used machine and a cash payment?

Case 11-3 Olmo Company found three suitable sites, each having certain unique advantages, for a new plant facility. In order to investigate thoroughly the advantages and disadvantages of each site, one-year options were acquired for an amount equal to 5% of the contract price of each site. The costs of the options could not be applied against the contract prices. Before the options expired, one of the sites was acquired at a price of $60,000. The option on this site had cost $3,000; the two options not exercised had cost $3,500 each.

Instructions

Present arguments in support of recording the cost of the land acquired by Olmo Company at each of the following amounts:

a $60,000 *b* $63,000 *c* $70,000

Case 11-4 Rondo Company has completed payment for a new building constructed at a cost of $2 million. After reviewing the contracts and cost data, Rondo's controller suggests using the following classifications in future accounting for this building: (1) foundation, framing, and sheathing, (2) outside finish, (3) interior finish, (4) roof, (5) electric wiring and fixtures, (6) partitions, (7) acoustical ceiling, (8) furnace and boiler, and (9) plumbing system.

Instructions

Discuss the advantages and the disadvantages of following such a system of accounting for Rondo Company's building, particularly its effect on accounting for maintenance, depreciation, and retirements.

Case 11-5 Hi-Tech Company manufactures electrical appliances, most of which are used in homes. Hi-Tech's engineers have designed a new type of blender which, through the use of a few attachments, will perform more functions than any blender currently on the market. Demand for the new blender can be projected with reasonable accuracy. In order to manufacture the blenders, Hi-Tech needs a specialized machine that is not available from outside sources. Therefore, Hi-Tech decided to construct the specialized machine in its own plant.

Instructions

a Hi-Tech Company's plant may be operating at capacity or below capacity. Compare the problems in determining the cost to be assigned to the specialized machine at these different levels of operations.

b Discuss the effect of projected demand in units for the new blenders (which may be steady, decreasing, or increasing) on the determination of a depreciation method to be used for the specialized machine.

Case 11-6 Kalish Company has two manufacturing departments, A and B. During Year 5 the manager of Department A obtained a bid of $75,000 from an outside vendor for a machine needed in the department. The manager of Department B, however, convinced management of Kalish that the machine could be manufactured in Department B more economically, and the decision was made to allow Department B to undertake the project. The machine was finished near the end of Year 5, at a cost of $16,000 for material, $24,000 for direct labour, $10,000 for variable factory overhead, and $12,000 for fixed overhead allocated on the basis of direct labour cost.

The controller of Kalish entered the equipment in the accounting records at a cost of $50,000 (excluding fixed factory overhead). The manager of Department B requested that the equipment be recorded at $75,000, stating, ''If my employees had not been working on this machine, they could have been engaged in profitable production. If you record the machine at $50,000 my department is going to look bad in the reports at the end of the year. When will I ever get credit for the $25,000 ($75,000 − $50,000) I have earned for Kalish by manufacturing the machine?''

Instructions

a What are the basic issues involved in this controversy?

b If the Department B manager's position were accepted, would the net income of Kalish Company during the current and subsequent accounting periods be changed? Explain.

c Evaluate the two positions and state which one you favour and why.

PROBLEMS

Pr. 11-1 On January 2, Year 4, Brock Corporation acquired land (Land Site No. 101) with a building for $600,000. Additionally, Brock paid a real estate broker's commission of $36,000 and legal fees and related expenses of $24,000. The closing statement indicated that the land's appraised value was $500,000 and the building's appraised value was $100,000. Shortly after acquisition, the building was razed at a cost of $75,000.

Brock entered into a $3,000,000 fixed-price construction-type contract with Barnett Builders, Inc., on March 1, Year 4, for the construction of an office building on Land Site No. 101. The building was completed and occupied on September 30, Year 5. Additional construction costs were incurred as follows:

Plans, specifications, and blueprints	$12,000
Architects' fees for design and supervision	95,000

To finance the construction cost, Brock borrowed $3,000,000 on March 1, Year 4. The loan was payable in 10 annual instalments of $300,000 plus interest at the rate of 14%. Brock's average amounts of accumulated building construction costs were as follows:

For the period March 1 to December 31, Year 4	$ 900,000
For the period January 1 to September 30, Year 5	2,300,000

Instructions

a Prepare a working paper for Brock Corporation to determine the composition of the total cost of Land Site No. 101 on September 30, Year 5.

b Prepare a working paper for Brock Corporation to determine the composition of the total cost of the office building completed on September 30, Year 5. Show supporting computations.

Pr. 11-2 On December 31, Year 1, the assets included in the plant assets section of Oliver Company's balance sheet had the following balances:

Land	$100,000
Buildings	800,000
Leasehold improvements	500,000
Machinery and equipment	700,000

During Year 2 the following transactions occurred:

1 Land site No. 20 was acquired for $1,000,000. To acquire the land, Oliver paid a $60,000 commission to a real estate agent. Costs of $16,000 were incurred to clear the land. During the course of clearing the land, timber and gravel were recovered and sold for $5,000.

2 A second tract of land (Land Site No. 21) with a building was acquired for $300,000. The closing statement indicated that the appraised value of the land was $200,000 and the appraised value of the building was $100,000. Shortly after acquisition, the building was demolished at a cost of $30,000. A new building was constructed for $150,000, plus the following costs:

Excavation fees	$11,000
Architectural design fees	8,000
Building permit fee	1,000
Imputed interest cost (not incurred) on funds used during construction	10,500

The building was completed and occupied on September 30, Year 2.

3 A third tract of land (Land Site No. 22) was acquired for $600,000 and was listed with a real estate broker for sale.

4 Extensive work was done to a building occupied by Oliver under a lease that expires on December 31, Year 11. The total cost of the work was $125,000, which consisted of the following:

Painting of ceilings (estimated economic life 1 year)	$ 10,000
Electrical work (estimated economic life 10 years)	35,000
Construction of extension to the working area (estimated economic life 20 years)	80,000
Total cost	$125,000

The lessor paid one-half the costs incurred in connection with the extension to the working area. The lease is classified as an operating lease for financial accounting.

5 During December, Year 2, costs of $65,000 were incurred to improve leased office space. The operating lease will terminate on December 31, Year 4, and is not expected to be renewed.

6 A group of new machines was acquired under a royalty contract requiring payment of royalties based on units of production for the machines. The invoice price (after a 2% cash discount) of the machines was $78,600, freight costs were $2,100, unloading costs were $1,500, and royalty payments for Year 2 were $13,000.

Instructions

a Prepare an analysis of the changes in each of the following ledger accounts of Oliver Company for the year ended December 31, Year 2 (disregard the related accumulated depreciation accounts):

- Land
- Buildings
- Leasehold Improvements
- Machinery and Equipment

b List the items that were not used to determine the answer to ***a*** above, and indicate where, or if, these items should be included in Oliver Company's financial statements.

Pr. 11-3 Four independent situations relating to plant assets are described below for Lasswell Corporation. Separate instructions are given for each situation.

a A machine was acquired for $52,000 on May 1, Year 1. At the time of acquisition, the machine was estimated to have an economic life of 10 years and a net residual value of $4,000. Monthly depreciation was recorded under the straight-line method. On March 1, Year 10, the machine was sold for $4,200.

Instructions

Compute Lasswell Corporation's gain or loss on the disposal of the machine.

b A used delivery truck was traded in for a new delivery truck. Information relating to the trucks follows:

Used delivery truck:	
Cost	$8,000
Accumulated depreciation	6,000

Estimate of current fair value made by Lasswell's accountant....	1,600
New delivery truck:	
List price	$10,000
Cash price without trade-in	9,500
Cash paid with trade-in	7,800

Instructions
Prepare a journal entry for Lasswell Corporation to record the foregoing exchange transaction in conformity with generally accepted accounting principles.

c Land, building, and equipment were acquired for $90,000 from an insolvent enterprise. At the time of acquisition, $6,000 was paid to have the assets appraised. The appraisal indicated the following current fair values of the assets:

Land	$60,000
Building	40,000
Equipment	20,000

Instructions
Determine the cost allocated to Lasswell Corporation's land, building, and equipment for financial accounting.

d A building was appraised at $100,000. A fire occurred, causing $48,600 damage to the building. The building was insured for $60,000 under a policy that included an 80% coinsurance clause.

Instructions
Compute the amount of the loss that Lasswell Corporation will recover under the insurance policy.

Pr. 11-4 This problem consists of five independent situations relating to plant assets of Larch Corporation. Each situation contains specific instructions.

a Larch Corporation has two fire insurance policies. Policy A with Ace Fidelity covers the furniture at a face amount of $108,000 and the office building at a face amount of $360,000. Policy B with Bravo Indemnity covers only the office building at a face amount of $140,000. A fire caused losses to the furniture and the office building. The relevant data are summarized below:

	Furniture	*Office building*	
Insurance policies	A	A	B
Current fair values before fire	$150,000	$700,000	$700,000
Current fair values after fire	$ 25,000	$406,000	$406,000
Face amounts of insurance policies	$108,000	$360,000	$140,000
Coinsurance requirements	80%	80%	75%

Instructions
Compute the amount to be recovered by Larch Corporation from each insurance company for the loss on each asset category. Show computations, rounded to the nearest dollar.

b A truck was inspected thoroughly when it was noticed that the diesel engine, which normally last four years, was in need of an overhaul and that the trailer needed replacement. The engine cost $2,000 new and was two and a half years old. However, with a $900 overhaul, it was expected to last two more years. The old trailer cost $5,000, had a carrying amount of $750, and was scrapped by Larch Corporation. The price of new trailers had increased by $3,000 since the old one was acquired. Larch accounts for each truck component separately and computes depreciation by the straight-line method.

Instructions
Prepare journal entries for Larch Corporation to record the overhaul of the engine and the replacement of the trailer.

c Larch Corporation exchanged a used automobile for a new automobile. The used automobile had a cost of $6,500, a carrying amount of $1,500, and a current fair value of $2,000 when exchanged. In addition, Larch paid $7,200 cash for the new automobile. The list price of the new automobile was $9,300, and the cash price was $9,200.

Instructions
Prepare a journal entry for Larch Corporation to record the exchange of the used automobile for the new automobile.

d Larch Corporation exchanged 1,000 shares of treasury stock (its common stock) for land. The treasury stock had cost $60 a share, and had a market price of $82 a share on the exchange date. Larch received $1,200 for scrap when an existing building was removed from the land at a cost of $20,000.

Instructions
Compute the cost of Larch Corporation's land for financial accounting.

e Larch Corporation received $20,000 cash and a used computer with a current fair value of $180,000 for an old computer with a current fair value of $200,000 and a carrying amount of $150,000.

Instructions
Compute the gain (if any) that Larch Corporation should recognize on this exchange transaction and the cost of the used computer for financial accounting.

Pr. 11-5 Josten Company decided to replace its old machine, which cost $16,000 and had a carrying amount of $4,000. The following offers were received:

1 May Company offered its machine for $18,000 and agreed to allow $1,000 on the old machine as a trade-in.
2 Noye Company offered its machine for $17,500, terms 2/10, n/30, but would not accept a trade-in.

Josten accepted Noye's offer and sold its old machine for $700 after incurring $220 in labour costs to remove it from the building. Additional costs incurred in placing the new machine in use were as follows:

Freight (paid in cash)	$1,190
Installation:	
Material	350
Labour	440
Travel expenses paid to Noye Company's engineer, who supervised the installation (There was no charge for the engineer's time)	210
Costs incurred in testing new machine:	
Operator's wages	160
Spoiled material	200

During the removal of the used machine, a section of the factory floor was damaged and had to be repaired at a cost of $400 paid to an independent contractor. The damage was caused by extreme carelessness of Josten's employees.

As a result of an error in the treasurer's department, the Noye Company invoice was not paid until 30 days after invoice date; therefore, the cash discount could not be taken.

Instructions

Prepare journal entries for Josten Company, together with supporting computations, to record the retirement of the used machine and the acquisition of the new machine. Credit the Material Inventory account for the cost of material used and the Payable Payroll account for labour costs incurred.

Pr. 11-6 In auditing the financial statements of Lambeth Company for the fiscal year ended December 31, Year 5, you discover the following:

1 Machine W with a cash selling price of $18,800 was acquired on April 1, Year 5, in exchange for $20,000 face amount of bonds payable trading at 94 and maturing on April 1, Year 15. The accountant recorded the acquisition by a debit to Machinery and a credit to Bonds Payable for $20,000. Straight-line depreciation was recorded based on a five-year economic life and amounted to $2,400 for nine months. In the computation of depreciation, a net residual value of $4,000 was used.
2 Machine X listed at a cash price of $6,400 was acquired on January 2, Year 5. Lambeth paid $1,000 down and $500 a month for 12 months. The last payment was made on December 30, Year 5. All cash payments were debited to Machinery. Straight-line depreciation, based on a five-year economic life and no net residual value, was recorded at $1,400 for the year. Freight of $400 on Machine X was debited to the Freight-In ledger account.
3 On December 28, Year 5, Machine Y was recorded at $5,100, which included

the carrying amount of $1,100 for an old machine accepted as a trade-in and cash of $4,000. The cash price of Machine Y was $4,500, and the trade-in allowance was $500.

4 Machine Z was acquired on January 10, Year 5, in exchange for past-due accounts receivable of $14,000 on which an allowance of 20% had been established on December 31, Year 4. The current fair value of the machine on January 10 was $11,000. The machine was recorded by a debit to Machinery and a credit to Accounts Receivable for $14,000. No depreciation was recorded on Machine Z, because it was not used in operations. In March, Machine Z was exchanged for 100 shares of Lambeth's outstanding common stock with a market price of $105 a share. The Treasury Stock ledger account was debited for $14,000, the carrying amount of Machine Z.

Instructions

Record any correcting journal entries required for Lamberth Company on December 31, Year 5, for each transaction. Assume that revenue and expense ledger accounts have not been closed for Year 5. Amortize bond discount by the straight-line method.

Pr. 11-7 On July 10, Year 5, Sayle Company sold a building to Beyer Company. The statements for the seller and the acquirer are presented below:

	Sayle Company (Seller)		*Beyer Company (Acquirer)*	
	Charges	*Credits*	*Charges*	*Credits*
Sale price		$310,000	$310,000	
First mortgage note assumed by acquirer	$120,000			$120,000
12% second mortgage note receivable	80,000			80,000
Prorations:				
Property taxes from July 1 to July 10, Year 5	250			250
Insurance		200	200	
Interest accrued	350			350
Legal fees	140		1,500	
Cash deposited in a trust account on July 10, Year 5				111,100
Items paid from the trust account:				
Commission	18,600			
Remittance to seller	90,860			
Totals	$310,200	$310,200	$311,700	$311,700

Additional Information

1 A Suspense ledger account was used by Sayle to record cash received in connection with the sale, including monthly receipts on the second mortgage. The Suspense ledger account had a credit balance of $94,450 on September 30, Year 5.

2 The second mortgage note payments are $1,000 a month, plus accrued interest on the unpaid balance. The first payment was received on August 10

and amounted to $1,800; the second payment was received on September 9 and amounted to $1,790. Both amounts were credited by Sayle to the Suspense ledger account.

3 The building and land had been acquired by Sayle on July 1, Year 1, for $270,000. The building was depreciated over a 40-year economic life under the straight-line method. Accumulated depreciation on December 31, Year 4, was $17,500. A half-year's depreciation has been consistently recorded for assets acquired or sold during the year. No depreciation had been recorded by Sayle for Year 5.

Instructions

a Determine the net proceeds to Sayle Company for the land and for the building. The sales price and expenses of sale were allocated by Sayle as follows: land 30%, building 70%.

b Prepare journal entries to record the sale and related transactions in Sayle Company's accounting records. Prepare a supporting analysis showing the gain or loss on the sale of land and the gain or loss on the sale of building. Disregard income taxes, and do not record cash received from Beyer Company on the second mortgage note because the receipts already had been recorded.

c Prepare a journal entry to record the acquisition of land and building in Beyer Company's accounting records. The acquisition price, including all fees, is allocated 30% to land and 70% to building.

Pr. 11-8 Lang Company offered More Company $200,000 cash for used machinery. More responded that the price offered was acceptable but it did not want an all-cash transaction. More then offered to sell the machinery to Lang for a $50,000 cash down payment, the balance payable in five equal annual instalments of $30,000 each with interest payable annually at 6% on the unpaid balance. In addition, Lang agreed to sign a contract to purchase merchandise from More.

Lang decided that, although More's merchandise prices were in excess of current market prices, the 6% interest rate on the promissory note was sufficiently below the 10% that Lang would have to pay to borrow elsewhere to make the contract acceptable. Accordingly, on July 2, Year 7, Lang accepted More's proposal, made the down payment, signed the 6% promissory note and the contract for the purchase of the merchandise, and accepted delivery of the used machinery.

Instructions

a Record the acquisition of the used machinery in the accounting records of Lang Company on July 1, Year 7. On that date, the discounted value of the five-year, 6% promissory note, based on an interest rate of 10%, was $135,490.

b Prepare journal entries for Lang Company on December 31, Year 7, to record the following:

1 Interest expense for six months. Use the interest method of amortization for the discount on the note payable and round to the nearest dollar.

2 Depreciation for six months. Assume a four-year economic life for the

used machinery, no net residual value, and the straight-line method of depreciation.

3 Any required adjustment to cost of goods sold. Assume that one-half of the merchandise contracted for with More had been purchased and that the merchandise purchased had been sold by Decmeber 31, Year 7.

Pr. 11-9 Bosnia Company was incorporated on January 4, Year 10, but was unable to begin manufacturing activities until July 2, Year 10, because its plant was not finished until that date.

On December 31, Year 10, Bosnia's record of the construction and accounting for the plant appeared in a Plant ledger account as follows:

Plant

Date	*Explanation*	*Debit*	*Credit*	*Balance*
Year 10				
Jan. 31	Cost of land and old building.	325,000		325,000 Dr
Feb. 28	Cost of removing old building.	7,400		332,400 Dr
Mar. 1	Proceeds from sale of salvaged material from old building.		3,000	329,400 Dr
May 1	Partial payment for new building.	175,000		504,400 Dr
1	Legal fees.	4,000		508,400 Dr
June 1	Second payment for new building.	175,000		683,400 Dr
1	Insurance premium (May 1, Year 10, to Apr. 30, Year 13).	3,600		687,000 Dr
1	Special tax assessment.	5,000		692,000 Dr
30	Expenses.	24,000		716,000 Dr
July 2	Final payment for new building.	175,000		891,000 Dr
Dec. 31	Write-up of new building per appraisal.	50,000		941,000 Dr
31	Depreciation expense for 6 months ($941,000 × 0.02).		18,820	922,180 Dr

Additional Information

1 On January 31, Bosnia paid $25,000 cash and issued 3,000 shares of 8% cumulative preferred stock, $100 par, for land and an old building. On January 30, a large block of preferred stock had been traded in the market for $105 a share. The preferred stock issued was recorded at par.

2 The demolition company charged $7,400 for removal of the old building. The salvaged material from the old building was sold for $3,000.

3 Legal fees covered: organization of Bosnia, $1,500; acquisition of land, $2,000; and construction contract for the new building, $500.

4 Insurance on the new building was acquired on May 1. The three-year premium was paid on June 1, on receipt of the invoice.

5 The special tax assessment covered street improvements.

6 The expenses were for the period from January 2 to June 30 and include: president's salary, $12,000; salary of plant superintendent who supervised construction of the new building, $10,000; and office salaries, $2,000.

7 During the six-month construction period, a new union contract for

construction workers was negotiated calling for an increase of 15% in wages, and there were increases in construction material costs. On the basis of these facts, the plant superintendent suggested that the building be written up by $50,000 to recognize the increase in the current cost of the building. The credit was recorded in the Retained Earnings ledger account.

8 The new building was to be depreciated at the rate of 4% a year, with no net residual value. Depreciation of $18,820 for six months was debited to the Depreciation Expense ledger account.

Instructions

a Prepare a working paper to classify the transactions of Bosnia Company in appropriate ledger accounts. Provide separate columns for Land and for Building; other accounts should be analyzed in a Miscellaneous column.

b Prepare a single journal entry on December 31, Year 10, to correct the accounting records of Bosnia Company. The accounting records have not been closed for the year ended December 31, Year 10.

Pr. 11-10 Coal Limited completed certain transactions in the current year to simplify its operations, to improve its competitive position, and to resolve several business disputes. Three transactions involved transfers of mining claims to shareholders of Coal Limited, and three transactions were with Olson Corporation, a competitor. The transactions are listed below:

1 Mining claim no. 1, carried in the accounting records at a cost of $5,000, was sold to a shareholder of Coal Limited for $12,000 cash.

2 Mining claim no. 2, carried in the accounting records at a cost of $3,000, was exchanged for 200 shares of Coal's outstanding common stock. The common stock was trading for $125 a share at the time of the exchange. (Record the common stock acquired in the Treasury Stock ledger account.)

3 Mining claim no. 3, carried in the accounting records at a cost of $20,000, was transferred to Betty Strong, a shareholder, in consideration of her withdrawal of a patent-infringement suit against Coal. When asked for an estimate of the current fair value of the mining claims, the president of Coal answered that it was ''anyone's guess.'' Further questioning elicited the reluctant response that ''Claim no. 1 probably was worth about $12,000 and each of the other two claims was worth about twice that.'' You have concluded that no more precise estimates of current fair values were obtainable.

4 Coal exchanged its 5% common stock investment in Belmont Corporation, carried at cost of $90,000, for a plant site owned by Olson Corporation appraised at $200,000.

5 Coal traded certain inventory items located in Calgary for similar items held by Olson Corporation in Ottawa. To equalize trading values, Olson also paid $2,000 cash to Coal. The cost of the inventory items given up by Coal was $8,200, and the current fair value was $10,000. Coal uses the perpetual inventory system.

6 Coal obtained production jigs and dies from Olson Corporation, giving in exchange a used milling machine and cash of $1,700. The milling machine, carried in Coal's accounting records at a cost of $20,000, was considered similar to jigs and dies; accumulated depreciation was $12,000. Olson was willing to pay the $10,500 appraised value of the milling machine in cash, but Coal insisted on an exchange for the jigs and dies.

Instructions

Prepare journal entries for Coal Limited to record each of the six transactions described above.

Pr. 11-11 Margo Beatty maintains her accounting records on a cash basis. On February 28, Year 10, she sold property, acquired 17 years earlier for $110,000, to Lana Conley for $161,200. The cost allocated to the building was $70,000, and the accumulated depreciation to the date of the sale was $42,500.

The statements on February 28 for the acquirer and the seller are shown below:

Acquirer's Statement

Acquisition price of property	$161,200	
Deposit of cash by acquirer on Jan. 30 (recorded in Deposit in Trust ledger account)		$ 83,100
Legal fee	445	
Fire insurance, prorated	1,430	
Mortgage note assumed by acquirer		78,460
Property taxes for period Jan. 1 to Feb. 28, Year 10, accrued and unpaid		200
Lease deposits		850
Rent, prorated		340
Interest accrued on mortgage note		185
Cash to acquirer	60	
Totals	$163,135	$163,135

Seller's Statement

Selling price of property		$161,200
Legal fee	$ 595	
Property taxes for period Jan. 1 to Feb. 28, Year 10 accrued and unpaid	200	
Interest accrued on mortgage note	185	
Lease deposits	850	
Rent, prorated	340	
Mortgage note assumed by acquirer	78,460	
Fire insurance, prorated		1,430
Real estate broker's commission	10,300	
Cash to seller	71,700	
Totals	$162,630	$162,630

Instructions

a Prepare a working paper to show how Margo Beatty should determine the gain or loss on the foregoing transaction. Disregard income taxes.

b Prepare a journal entry to record the foregoing transaction in the accounting records of Margo Beatty.

c Prepare a journal entry to record the foregoing transaction in the accounting records of Lana Conley, assuming that $100,000 of total cost is allocated to land and that items representing future expenses or revenue are recorded in nominal (expense and revenue) ledger accounts.

Pr. 11-12 Nakota Corporation manufactures auto parts. On August 31, Year 2, a fire completely destroyed Nakota's building, goods in process inventory, and machinery.

Additional Information

1 The cost of plant assets destroyed and the related accumulated depreciation ledger accounts on August 31, Year 2, were as follows:

	Cost	*Accumulated depreciation*
Building	$40,000	$17,500
Machinery	15,000	4,500

At present prices, the cost to replace the destroyed property are: building $80,000, machinery $37,500. At the time of the fire it was estimated that the building was 50% depreciated, and the destroyed machinery was one-third depreciated. Insurance companies agreed that the insurable value (current fair value) of the building and machinery was $65,000 on the date of fire.

2 After the fire, a physical inventory was taken. The inventories of material and finished goods had a cost (and current fair value) of $26,000 and $52,000 respectively.

3 The inventories on December 31, Year 1, were: material $20,000, goods in process $48,000, and finished goods $54,000.

4 The sales of the first eight months of Year 2 were $150,000, and purchases of material were $55,000. Direct labour for the eight months was $40,000; for the past five years factory overhead has been applied at the rate of 80% of direct labour cost. The gross profit for the last five years has averaged 30% of net sales.

5 Insurance is carried with two companies, each policy with an 80% coinsurance clause. The amounts of insurance carried with each company are listed below:

	Building and machinery	*Inventories*
Acme Insurance Company	$42,000	$64,800
Zenith Indemnity Company	20,000	21,600

Instructions

a Compute the estimated cost of Nakota Corporation's inventory of goods in process lost in the fire on August 31, Year 2.

b Compute Nakota Corporation's expected recovery from each insurance company, assuming that the estimated cost of inventories lost is accepted as a measure of current fair value on the date of the fire.

c Assuming that Nakota Corporation recovers the loss determined in part ***b***, what is the loss or gain from fire reported in its income statement for the year ended December 31, Year 2? Disregard the income tax effect of the loss or gain.

Pr. 11-13 On September 20, Year 8, a fire damaged the office and warehouse of Wholesalers, Inc., whose fiscal year ends on December 31. The only accounting record salvaged was the general ledger, from which the following information was obtained as of August 31, Year 8:

	Debit	*Credit*
Accounts receivable	$25,000	
Inventory, Dec. 31, Year 7	60,920	
Accounts payable		$ 27,500
Sales, Jan. 1 to Aug. 31, Year 8		100,000
Purchases, Jan. 1 to Aug. 31, Year 8	80,000	

Additional Information

1 The September bank statement and paid cheques disclosed that cheques written during the period September 1 to 20 totalled $15,000: $8,000 for accounts payable as of August 31, $2,000 for September purchases, and $5,000 for operating expenses. Deposits during the same period amounted to $11,500, which consisted of receipts from customers, with the exception of a $1,300 refund from a supplier for goods returned in September.

2 Correspondence with suppliers disclosed unrecorded obligations of $7,200 on September 20, for merchandise purchased during September.

3 Customers confirmed payables of $29,500 to Wholesalers, Inc., as of the close of business on September 20, Year 8.

4 The following insurance on inventory was in effect on the date of the fire:

	Amount of coverage	*Coinsurance requirement*
Allied Mutual	$30,000	80%
Blue Regional	20,000	70%
Claim Free	10,000	None

5 The insurance companies agreed that the fire loss claim should be based on the assumption that the overall gross profit rate of 40% of sales for the past two years was in effect during Year 8 and that the cost of inventory so determined is a reasonable estimate of the current fair value of the inventory.

6 Inventory with a cost of $22,400 was recovered in good condition. The remainder of the inventory was a total loss. The office and the warehouse building were not insured. Wholesalers, Inc., paid $4,150 to repair the damage to the office, but the warehouse was a total loss. The warehouse (excluding land) cost $50,000 to construct, was fully depreciated, and had a current fair value of $10,000 on the date of the fire.

Instructions

a Prepare a working paper for Wholesalers, Inc., to compute the approximate cost of inventory lost in the fire on September 20, Year 8.

b Prepare a working paper for Wholesalers, Inc., to compute the pro rata claim to be filed with each insurance company.

c Assuming that Wholesalers, Inc., is indemnified as determined in *b*, what is the loss or gain from fire included in its income statement for Year 8? Disregard income tax effect of the loss or gain.

Pr. 11-14 The inexperienced accountant for Watergreen Company, a service enterprise that began operations on February 1, Year 2, made a number of errors in accounting for Wintergreen's plant assets. Wintergreen's plant asset ledger accounts on December 31, Year 2, were as follows:

Land and Building

Date	*Explanation*	*Debit*	*Credit*	*Balance*
Year 2				
Feb. 1	Cheque to close trust account.	24,600		24,600 Dr
Apr. 5	Routine painting of building.	5,210		29,810 Dr
June 1	Grading and paving of new parking lot.	22,400		52,210 Dr
Sept. 30	Cost of completed new wing of building.	78,700		130,910 Dr

Automobiles

Date	*Explanation*	*Debit*	*Credit*	*Balance*
Year 2				
Feb. 1– Oct. 1	\$420 × 9 monthly rent on leased automobile.	3,780		3,780 Dr
Oct. 31	Down payment on new automobile.	5,000		8,780 Dr
Nov. 30	Monthly payment on new automobile.	392		9,172 Dr
Dec. 31	Monthly payment on new automobile.	392		9,564 Dr

Furniture and Equipment

Date	*Explanation*	*Debit*	*Credit*	*Balance*
Year 2				
Feb. 1	Furniture and equipment acquired for cash.	15,000		15,000 Dr
Sept. 26	Routine repairs to microcomputer.	720		15,720 Dr
Dec. 1	Furniture and equipment acquired for preferred stock.	4,000		19,720 Dr

Additional Information

1 On January 2, Year 2, after issuing common stock for cash, Wintergreen made a \$100,000 deposit in a trust account for the acquisition of land and a building. The accountant debited a Suspense Expense ledger account for the deposit. The statement issued to Wintergreen at the close of the transaction on February 1, Year 2, was as given in the next table.

Statement for Acquirer

Items	Date: Feb. 1, Year 2 Charges	Credits
Acquisition price of property	$369,200	
Balance of mortgage note assumed by acquirer		$240,000
Interest at 10% from Jan. 16, Year 2, to Feb. 1, Year 2		1,000
Property taxes prorated, $14,400 a year from July 1, Year 1, to Feb. 1, Year 2		8,400
Fire insurance prorated (coverage for period from Feb. 1, Year 2, to June 1, Year 2)	120	
Deposited in trust by acquirer		100,000
Legal fees	4,680	
Cheque to balance		24,600
Totals	$374,000	$374,000

2 An appraisal of the building obtained by Wintergreen on February 1, Year 2, established the current fair value of the building at $204,500.

3 On February 1, Year 2, Wintergreen leased an automobile under a one-year cancellable operating lease at $420 a month rent.

4 On October 31, Year 2, Wintergreen terminated the automobile lease dated February 1, Year 2, and acquired an automobile with a cash price of $15,000. Terms of the sale were as follows:

Cash price of automobile	$15,000
Less: Down payment	5,000
Balance payable over 36 months	$10,000
Add: Interest at 13¾% for three years on $10,000	4,125
Total contract payable (36 payments of $392 beginning Nov. 30, Year 2)	$14,125

The effective interest rate on the deferred payment contract for the automobile was 2% a month.

5 Wintergreen acquired furniture and equipment costing $15,000 on February 1, Year 2. When the invoice for the equipment was paid on February 10, Year 2, the $300 cash discount was credited to the Purchases Discounts ledger account.

6 On December 1, Year 2, Wintergreen acquired furniture and equipment with a cash price of $4,400 in exchange for 400 shares of Wintergreen's preferred stock with a par value of $10 a share.

Instructions

Prepare correcting journal entries for Wintergreen Company on December 31, Year 2, the end of its first fiscal year. Disregard depreciation and income taxes. Round all amounts to the nearest dollar and record expense prorations (from the Statement for Acquirer) in asset and liability accounts.

chapter 12

PLANT ASSETS: DEPRECIATION AND DEPLETION

In Chapter 11 we describe plant assets as a ''bundle of future services,'' and consider the problem of determining the acquisition cost of the future services embodied in such assets. In this chapter we are concerned with the problem of measuring the portion of the services of plant assets and natural resources ''withdrawn from the bundle'' and consumed in business operations.

Depreciation is the portion of the cost of plant assets that is deducted from revenue for asset services used in the operations of a business enterprise. In practice, depreciation describes the cost of the expired services of tangible plant assets. For financial accounting, ***depletion*** refers to the estimated cost of natural resources such as oil, gas, timber, and iron ore that have been removed from their source. Recording the expired service cost of intangible assets, such as patents and goodwill, is called ***amortization***, and is discussed in Chapter 13.

DEPRECIATION

The concept of depreciation is linked closely to the measurement of net income. Because part of the service potential of depreciable plant assets is exhausted in the revenue-generating process each accounting period, the cost of these services must be deducted from revenue in the measurement of net income; the expired cost must be recovered before a business enterprise is considered ''as well off'' as at the beginning of the period. Depreciation is the measurement of this expired cost.

Depreciation has been one of the most misunderstood concepts of accounting. In the early history of accounting, it was necessary to convince users of accounting information that depreciation was a cost (expense) of doing business. Business executives tended to view depreciation as a matter of "setting aside something" during profitable years for the replacement of depreciable assets. When earnings were high, large amounts of depreciation might be recorded; when earnings were low or losses were incurred, depreciation was not recorded. Today, it is universally agreed that depreciation is an expense that must be recognized regardless of the level of earnings, and that depreciation accounting does not involve "setting aside" cash or other assets in a fund to replace depreciable assets.

Accounting for depreciation is a process of ***cost allocation***, not asset valuation. The acquisition of plant assets means that asset services have been acquired in advance of their use. Between the time of acquisition and the time of use, the value of these services may change materially because of supply and demand factors or changes in price levels. Therefore, the measurement of the historical cost of plant asset services that are used may differ from the current cost of similar services. This difference is germane to a variety of managerial decisions; however, the question of revaluing depreciable assets (in effect, revaluing the remaining unused services) at some time subsequent to acquisition should not be confused with the cost allocation problem. In this chapter we deal only with the allocation of the cost of plant assets and natural resources. The revaluation of plant assets and depreciation expense in response to increases in current costs and the general price level is considered in Chapter 25.

Factors in the Estimation of Periodic Depreciation

The estimate of periodic depreciation is dependent on the following three variables:

1 *Economic life* This involves choosing the unit in which economic life of plant assets is to be measured and estimating how many units of service are embodied in each asset. The units may be measured in years, hours of operation, or number of items produced.

2 *Depreciation base* The depreciation base is the cost of asset services that will be used; it usually is less than the total cost of the asset because net residual (salvage) value is subtracted from cost to compute the depreciation base.

3 *Method of cost allocation* The problem here is to determine the amount of services that has been used in each accounting period. A corollary issue is to decide whether all units of service have an equal cost, or whether some units of service have a larger or smaller cost than others.

Estimate of Economic Life

The economic life of a plant asset is the total units of service expected to be derived from the asset. Accountants commonly measure economic life of a plant asset in terms of time units, for example, months or years. Economic life of a plant asset also may be measured in terms of output or activity, expressed in such physical units as kilometres or machine-hours. For example, the estimated economic life of a truck may be described as ***four years*** or ***200,000 kilometres***. Forces that tend to limit the economic life of a plant asset should be considered in the determination of the type of ***unit of service*** to use for a specific asset or group of assets. The causes of a decrease in economic life may be divided into ***physical deterioration*** (including casualties), and ***functional*** or ***economic*** factors.

Physical deterioration results largely from wear and tear from use and the forces of nature. These physical forces terminate the usefulness of plant assets by rendering them incapable of performing the services for which they were intended and thus set the maximum limit on economic life. Unusual events such as accidents, floods, and earthquakes also serve to terminate or reduce the economic life of plant assets.

Functional or ***economic factors*** may render a plant asset that is in good physical condition no longer useful because it is not economical to keep the asset in service, or because of legal or income tax considerations related to the use of the asset. Two primary causes of functional depreciation are obsolescence and inadequacy. ***Obsolescence*** refers to the effect of innovations and technological improvements on the economic life of plant assets. An inevitable result of research and development activities is the obsolescence of existing plant assets. Jet airliners, for example, made piston-drive aircraft uneconomical for major airlines to operate. Thus, obsolescence terminated the economic life of many piston-drive aircraft and sent them to the used-plane market even though they had a physical potential of many more years of service.

Inadequacy refers to the effect of growth and changes in the scale of a business operation in terminating the economic life of plant assets. A warehouse may be in sound condition, but if more space is required than may be provided economically by the addition of a separate building, the old warehouse has become inadequate, and its economic life, from the standpoint of the business enterprise, is terminated. In a general sense, any plant asset whose capacity is such that it cannot be operated efficiently or does not fit the requirements of the enterprise is ***inadequate***.

In a highly developed industrial society, functional factors of depreciation probably have a greater influence on economic lives of plant assets than physical deterioration, particularly with respect to special-purpose equipment. Estimates of economic life, therefore, are influenced by these factors.

The choice of an appropriate ***unit*** of economic life for a plant asset also requires a determination of the causes of depreciation. The objective is to choose the unit most closely related to the cause of service exhaustion. When the economic life of a plant asset is limited largely by the effect of physical deterioration, a unit that reflects physical use of the asset is appropriate. For example, hours of service might be chosen as the unit of economic life for an electric motor, or kilometres of service for a truck. In contrast, the physical deterioration that limits the economic life of buildings probably is related more closely to the passage of time than to usage. Thus, an estimated economic life in terms of years is more appropriate for buildings.

No estimate of economic life can be made with high precision. The best procedure is to start with an estimate of physical economic life as a maximum, modify this for the probable effects of obsolescence and inadequacy, and then be prepared to adjust these estimates in the light of actual experience. If the estimated economic life of a plant asset is revised, the undepreciated cost of the asset is allocated to the remaining units of service.

The Depreciation Base

The depreciation base (or depreciable cost) of a plant asset is the portion of its cost that is allocated to depreciation expense during its economic life. Because the owner of an asset may sell it before its serviceability is ended, the initial cost of a plant asset, as determined by the guidelines described in Chapter 11, is not necessarily its depreciation base. For example, a car rental company may pay $16,000 for a new car and sell it at the end of three years for $7,000, even though its economic life is much longer. The depreciation base is $9,000, the difference between cost and ***residual value***.

The scrapping or removal of plant assets such as buildings, structures, and heavy equipment may involve substantial costs in the year of retirement. Theoretically, removal costs should be estimated and included in the depreciation base. The inclusion of removal costs in the depreciation base means that the entire cost involved in obtaining services from plant assets will be allocated to the revenue generated by the assets, without regard to the timing of the expenditure. In practice, however, removal costs may be either disregarded or netted against the estimated residual value of the assets. The depreciation base for a plant asset thus becomes:

Depreciation base of plant asset

Depreciation base = cost − estimated residual value (net)

In some instances, net residual value (gross residual value minus estimated removal costs) is likely to be so small or uncertain that it may be disregarded in the computation of the depreciation base.

Depreciation Methods — Cost Allocation

When the economic life of a plant asset has been estimated, and its depreciation base established, there remains the problem of determining the portion of cost that will expire with each unit of economic life. There are two major variables to be considered in reaching a solution to this problem:

1 The ***quantity*** of services used may be equal or may differ during each accounting period of economic life.

2 The ***cost*** of various units of service may be equal or may differ during each accounting period of economic life.

Because of the relatively high degree of uncertainty that underlies estimates of economic life and service use, the distinction between these two variables may become blurred. We may illustrate by reference to a situation that is familiar — the depreciation of an automobile used for business purposes. Assume that the automobile cost $19,000, has an expected net residual value of $1,000, and is estimated to have an economic life of 100,000 kilometres. The average depreciation expense per unit of service (1 kilometre) is 18 cents [($19,000 − $1,000) ÷ 100,000 = $0.18]. However, the kilometres of service used in each accounting period may vary. If 20,000 kilometres are driven during the first year and 30,000 kilometres during the second year, there has been a variation in the ***quantity*** of service used, and depreciation expense of $3,600 for the first year and $5,400 for the second recognizes this fact.

However, even if the automobile is driven 20,000 kilometres each year for five years, there may be a difference in the ***cost*** of the kilometres of service in each of these five accounting periods. The kilometres of service when the automobile is new and operating efficiently may be more valuable (and thus presumably more costly) than the kilometres of service during later years. Therefore, the assumption that each kilometre bears the same depreciation expense may not be reasonable, and we might compute depreciation on the assumption that early kilometres cost more than later kilometres. For example, depreciation might be computed at 24 cents a kilometre for the first 20,000 kilometres, 20 cents for the next 20,000 kilometres, and so forth.

There are several depreciation methods that attempt to recognize these factors in varying degrees. They may be classified as follows:

1 Straight-line method (based on expiration of time)

2 Accelerated methods (based on expiration of time)
 a Fixed-percentage-of-declining-balance
 b Double-declining-balance and other arbitrary fixed-percentage methods
 c Sum-of-the-years'-digits

3 Output (or units-of-production) method (based on physical service or production)

4 Retirement-replacement-betterment method

5 Interest methods

Depreciation under the straight-line and accelerated methods is a function of time rather than use. In contrast, depreciation under the output method is a function of actual usage rather than the passage of time.

Depreciation that is a function of time generally is computed to the nearest month, although other procedures consistently applied may be acceptable. For example, one-half of a full year's depreciation may be recognized in both the year of acquisition and the year of disposal of a plant asset. Descriptions of the most widely used depreciation methods follow.

Straight-Line Method

The distinguishing characteristic of the straight-line method of depreciation is that each full year of service absorbs an equal portion of cost. Depreciation per year is computed as follows:

Straight-line method means equal periodic expense

$$\text{Depreciation per year} = \frac{\text{cost} - \text{estimated net residual value}}{\text{years of economic life}}$$

To illustrate the straight-line method of depreciation, assume that a machine is acquired on January 2, Year 1, for $7,000 and that the net residual value of the machine at the end of four years of economic life is estimated at $1,000. The depreciation expense, accumulated depreciation, and ***carrying amount*** (cost less accumulated depreciation) of the machine over its economic life are presented in the table below.

Carrying amount of machine decreases by $1,500 each year of its economic life

Date	*Depreciation expense for year*	*Accumulated depreciation*	*Carrying amount*
Jan. 2, Year 1			$7,000
Dec. 31, Year 1	$1,500	$1,500	5,500
Dec. 31, Year 2	1,500	3,000	4,000
Dec. 31, Year 3	1,500	4,500	2,500
Dec. 31, Year 4	1,500	6,000	1,000*

*Net residual value.

At the end of each year, depreciation expense on this machine is recorded as follows:

Journal entry to record depreciation

Depreciation Expense	1,500	
Accumulated Depreciation of Machinery		1,500
To record depreciation for year.		

Accelerated Methods

The assumption that plant assets yield either a greater quantity of service or more valuable service in early years of their economic life has led accountants to devise methods of depreciation that result in larger amounts of depreciation in early years of economic life, and smaller amounts in later years. These methods are known as ***accelerated methods*** of depreciation. The three most widely used accelerated methods of depreciation are described in the following subsections.

1 Fixed-Percentage-of-Declining-Balance Method Under this method (frequently called the ***declining-balance*** or ***diminishing-balance method***), a percentage depreciation rate is computed that, when applied to the carrying amount of the asset at the beginning of each accounting period, results in reducing the carrying amount of the asset to estimated net residual value at the end of its economic life. Because the rate computed is applied on a constantly declining carrying amount, the depreciation expense decreases each year. The formula for the computation of the required rate per year (when n = years of economic life) is:

Formula to compute fixed percentage

$$\text{Depreciation rate} = 1 - \sqrt[n]{\frac{\text{net residual value}}{\text{cost}}}$$

In the application of this formula a net residual value of at least $1 must be used, because it is impossible to reduce any amount to zero by applying a constant percentage to the successively declining carrying amount. The depreciation rate for a plant asset that cost $10,000, has a net residual value of $1,296, and has an economic life of four years, is computed below:

Formula solved

$$\text{Depreciation rate} = 1 - \sqrt[4]{\frac{\$1,296}{\$10,000}} = 1 - \frac{6}{10} = \underline{\underline{40\%}}$$

If this formula yields a rate of, say, 39.69%, rounding the rate to 40% would not be objectionable, because measurement of depreciation at best is only a rough estimate. This formula yields a ***precise rate*** that depreciates a plant asset to a carrying amount equal to its net residual value. The tabulation below shows depreciation expense for the four-year economic life for a fixed percentage of 40% on the declining carrying amount of the plant asset:

Amount of depreciation decreases each year under declining-balance method

		Depreciation expense		
Year of economic life	*Carrying amount at beginning of year*	*Amount (40% of carrying amount at beginning of year)*	*Percentage of total*	*Accumulated depreciation*
1	$10,000	$4,000	46.0	$4,000
2	6,000	2,400	27.6	6,400
3	3,600	1,440	16.5	7,840
4	2,160	864	9.9	8,704
Balance	1,296*			
		$8,704	100.0	

*Net residual value.

It should be noted that the carrying amount at the end of the fourth year is equal to the estimated net residual value, $1,296, and that annual depreciation expense decreases rapidly. (In this example, because the depreciation rate is 40%, the depreciation expense in the second year and each of the succeeding years of economic life is only 60% of the expense reported a year earlier.)

2 Double-Declining-Balance Method In some cases, the fixed percentage for certain assets may be as high as twice the applicable straight-line rate. For example, the straight-line rate for an asset with an estimated economic life of four years is 25%, and the fixed-percentage rate is 50% (25% × 2). This approach is referred to as the ***double-declining-balance*** (or ***200%-declining-balance***) ***method***.

To illustrate the double-declining-balance method of depreciation, let's use the example of a plant asset costing $22,000, having a net residual value of $2,000, and an economic life of four years. The depreciation percentage is 50% (¼ = 25%; 25% × 2 = 50%).

In the next tabulation, depreciation for Year 2 and Year 3 is 50% of the prior-year depreciation. However, depreciation for Year 4 has no such relationship to the Year 3 depreciation; it is merely the amount required to reduce the carrying amount of the plant asset to its net residual value at the end of its economic life of four years.

Double-declining-balance method of depreciation

Year of economic life	*Carrying amount at beginning of year*	*Depreciation expense*		*Accumulated depreciation*
		Amount (50% of carrying amount at beginning of year)	*Percentage of total*	
1	$22,000	$11,000	55.0	$11,000
2	11,000	5,500	27.5	16,500
3	5,500	2,750	13.8	19,250
4	2,750	750*	3.7	20,000
Balance	2,000†			
		$20,000	100.0	

*Amount required to reduce carrying amount to net residual value.
†Net residual value.

Fractional-Period Depreciation Under Double-Declining-Balance Method The acquisition during the year of a plant asset that is to be depreciated under the double-declining-balance method does not require the allocation of each full year's depreciation between two fiscal years because the fixed percentage is applied to the carrying amount (undepreciated cost) of the plant asset at the beginning of each year. However, in the last full year of asset life, depreciation is computed for a fraction of a year (or an amount that reduces the beginning-of-year carrying amount of the asset to net residual value).

For example, depreciation expense under the double-declining-balance method of depreciation for a plant asset having an economic life of five years, residual value of $500, and a cost of $8,000 on April 1, Year 4, is computed for the six years ended December 31, Year 9, as illustrated in the next table.

If, instead of the foregoing method, double-declining-balance depreciation had been computed by the allocation of each full year's depreciation between two

Double-declining-balance depreciation involving fractional periods, *with no allocation* of each full year's depreciation between two fiscal years

Period ended	Carrying amount at beginning of period	Depreciation expense: Amount (40% of carrying amount at beginning of period times fraction of period)	Depreciation expense: Percentage of total	Accumulated depreciation
Dec. 31/4	$8,000	$2,400*	32.0	$2,400
Dec. 31/5	5,600	2,240	29.9	4,640
Dec. 31/6	3,360	1,344	17.9	5,984
Dec. 31/7	2,016	806	10.7	6,790
Dec. 31/8	1,210	484	6.5	7,274
Dec. 31/9	726	226†	3.0	7,500
Balance	500‡			
		$7,500	100.0	

*($8,000 × 0.40) × $\frac{9}{12}$ = $2,400.
†Amount required to reduce carrying amount to net residual value.
‡Net residual value.

fiscal years, only the depreciation for the last two years would be different, as demonstrated below:

Double-declining-balance depreciation involving fractional periods *with allocation* of each full year's depreciation between two fiscal years

Period ended	Computation of depreciation	Depreciation expense	Accumulated depreciation	Carrying amount
Dec. 31/4	[($8,000 × 0.40) × $\frac{9}{12}$] (Apr. 1/4 to Dec. 31/4)	$2,400	$2,400	$5,600
Dec. 31/5	[($8,000 × 0.40) × $\frac{3}{12}$] + [($4,800 × 0.40) × $\frac{9}{12}$]	2,240	4,640	3,360
Dec. 31/6	[($4,800 × 0.40) × $\frac{3}{12}$] + [($2,880 ×0.40) × $\frac{9}{12}$]	1,344	5,984	2,016
Dec. 31/7	[($2,880 × 0.40) × $\frac{3}{12}$] + [($1,728 × 0.40) × $\frac{9}{12}$]	806	6,790	1,210
Dec. 31/8	[($1,728 × 0.40) × $\frac{3}{12}$] + ($537* × $\frac{9}{12}$)	576	7,366	634
Dec. 31/9	($537* × $\frac{3}{12}$) (Jan. 1/9 to Mar. 31/9)	134	7,500	500†
		$7,500		

*Amount required to reduce carrying amount to net residual value.
†Net residual value.

Depreciation for Year 8 in the foregoing computation is $92 larger ($576 − $484 = $92) than in the first computation on this page; conversely, depreciation for Year 9 above is $92 less ($226 − $134 = $92) than in that computation. This is because the depreciation of $710 ($1,210 – $500 = $710) for the final year of asset life is allocated to two fiscal years under the ***allocation method***.

3 Sum-of-the-Years'-Digits Method Under this method, a decreasing depreciation expense is computed by a simple mathematical procedure relating to arithmetic progressions. The sum of a series of digits representing the years of economic life of a plant asset becomes the denominator of the depreciation fraction in any year.[1] The numerator of the depreciation fraction for each year is the remaining number of years of economic life ***at the beginning of the year***. Because the denominator remains constant and the numerator declines each year, the result is a decreasing depreciation expense. Furthermore, because the total of the numerators of the depreciation fractions is equal to the denominator, the sum of all the fractions is 1, and 100% of the depreciation base ultimately is allocated to depreciation expense.

The tabulation below illustrates the application of the sum-of-the-years'-digits method to a plant asset costing $22,000, having a net residual value of $2,000, and an economic life of four years:

Sum-of-years'-digits method of depreciation

Year of economic life	*Depreciation fraction*	*Depreciation base ($22,000 – $2,000)*	*Depreciation expense*	*Accumulated depreciation*	*Carrying Amount*
					$22,000
1	4/10	$20,000	$8,000	$ 8,000	14,000
2	3/10	20,000	6,000	14,000	8,000
3	2/10	20,000	4,000	18,000	4,000
4	1/10	20,000	2,000	20,000	2,000*
Sum 10					

*Net residual value.

Fractional-Period Depreciation Under the Sum-of-the-Years'-Digits Method Under accelerated methods, depreciation is determined for each full unit of economic life. A question of mechanics arises when plant assets are acquired during the year and less than a full year's depreciation is to be recorded during the first and last fiscal years of economic life. A logical solution to this problem for the sum-of-the-years'-digits method of depreciation is to compute the depreciation for each full year of economic life, and then allocate each full year's depreciation between two different fiscal years.

To illustrate, assume the following data for a plant asset for which the sum-of-the-years' digits method of depreciation is used:

1 The formula for determining the sum of any arithmetic progression of n consecutive digits is $n\left(\frac{n+1}{2}\right)$. Thus, the sum of all digits from 1 to 15 is $15\left(\frac{16}{2}\right)$, or 120. Tables are available that provide the decimal equivalent of the depreciation rate for each year of economic life.

Data for illustration of fractional-period depreciation

Cost of plant asset, acquired Apr. 1, Year 4	$8,000
Estimated economic life	5 years
Sum of the years' digits $\left[5\left(\frac{5+1}{2}\right)\right]$	15
Estimated net residual value	$500

The computation of depreciation for the first partial year (Year 4) and the remaining years ended December 31 under the sum-of-the-year's-digits method is demonstrated below.

Computation of depreciation under sum-of-the-years' digits method for fractional periods

Period ended	*Computation of depreciation*	*Depreciation expense*	*Accumulated depreciation*	*Carrying amount*
Dec. 31/4	[($7,500 × 5/15) × 9/12] (Apr. 1/4 to Dec. 31/4)	$1,875	$1,875	$6,125
Dec. 31/5	[($7,500 × 5/15) × 3/12] + [($7,500 × 4/15) × 9/12]	2,125	4,000	4,000
Dec. 31/6	[($7,500 × 4/15) × 3/12] + [($7,500 × 3/15) × 9/12]	1,625	5,625	2,375
Dec. 31/7	[($7,500 × 3/15) × 3/12] + [($7,500 × 2/15) × 9/12]	1,125	6,750	1,250
Dec. 31/8	[($7,500 × 2/15) × 3/12] + [($7,500 × 1/15) × 9/12]	625	7,375	625
Dec. 31/9	[($7,500 × 1/15) × 3/12] (Jan. 1/9 to Mar. 31/9)	125	7,500	500*

*Net residual value.

Output Method

A more realistic allocation of the cost of some plant assets may be obtained by dividing the depreciation base by the estimated units of use or production (machine-hours, units of product produced, or kilometres driven) rather than by the years of economic life. For example, a bus company might compute depreciation on its vehicles under a kilometrage basis. If a bus cost $60,000 and is estimated to have an economic life of 200,000 kilometres and no residual value, the depreciation rate per kilometre of operation is 30 cents ($60,000 ÷ 200,000 = $0.30). At the end of each year, the amount of depreciation is determined by multiplying the number of kilometres the bus was driven during the year by the 30-cent rate.

The estimated economic life of a plant asset under the output method is measured in terms of potential physical services or units of output, and periodic depreciation is based on the actual use of the asset. As a result, ***total depreciation expense*** for each fiscal year varies if use varies, but the ***depreciation per unit of output is constant***. The output method of depreciation is particularly appropriate when plant asset use fluctuates widely from year to year, and depreciation is more closely related to actual use than to functional obsolescence.

Some accountants have suggested that certain plant assets should be depreciated on the basis of periodic appraisals. This method may result in periodic depreciation expense to certain plant assets that closely parallels the output method, because the current fair value of a plant asset depends to a considerable extent on the amount of its usage. The ***appraisal method*** requires a determination of the value of services that ***remain in the asset*** at the end of each accounting period. Depreciation is estimated by appraising each plant asset at the end of an accounting period, and expensing an amount sufficient to reduce the carrying amount of the asset to its appraised value. Thus, the depreciation is affected by the change in the value of the asset and is not necessarily a cost allocation process. The appraisal method of depreciation is appropriate for short-lived plant assets such as small tools, dies, dishes, and kitchen utensils.

Retirement-Replacement-Betterment Method

The methods of depreciation discussed thus far represent an attempt to measure the expiration of a plant asset's cost as it occurs. An alternative approach, advocated in the past by some regulated industries, is to recognize depreciation only at the time assets reach the end of their economic lives. Under the ***retirement-replacement-betterment*** method, plant asset ledger accounts include the full cost of all plant assets currently in use. Costs of replacing plant assets are recognized as expense unless the replacement represents a betterment. For a betterment, the current fair value of the plant asset replaced is recognized as expense, and the amount by which the cost of the betterment exceeds such current fair value is debited to the plant asset ledger account. When a plant asset is retired, its cost is recognized as expense and removed from the plant asset ledger account.

There are two objections to the retirement-replacement-betterment method. The first is that no depreciation is recorded until retirement of plant assets occurs. Not only is net income overstated in the early years of economic life, but also the original plant asset cost appears in the balance sheet, despite the fact that a portion of this cost has expired. The second objection is that depreciation expense is determined by the number of plant assets replaced and the cost of the new assets. The probability that the cost of replacements or retirements in a fiscal year will coincide with the cost of asset services used during that year is rather slim. The force of this objection is increased when it is noted that the plant asset replacement policy of a business enterprise is likely to vary in response to the availability of funds for capital expenditures, the stage of the business cycle, the earnings prospects of the enterprise, and the income tax incentives available. Consequently, the retirement-replacement-betterment method is seldom used today.

Interest Methods

The ***annuity*** and ***sinking-fund*** methods of depreciation involve the application of compound-interest concepts in the measurement of periodic depreciation. These methods are illustrated in the Appendix at the end of this chapter.

Composite Depreciation Method

Many business enterprises find it expedient to account for depreciation of certain kinds of plant assets on a ***composite*** or ***group basis***, to minimize the record keeping for individual assets. Composite or group depreciation is a process of averaging the economic lives of a number of plant assets and computing depreciation on the entire class of assets as if it were an operating unit. The term ***composite*** generally refers to a collection of somewhat dissimilar plant assets; the term ***group*** usually refers to a collection of similar assets. The procedures for the computation of periodic depreciation are essentially the same in either case.

Several methods may be used to develop a composite or group depreciation rate to be applied to the total cost of a group of plant assets. The computation of a ***straight-line composite depreciation rate*** for a group of machines owned by Wilbur Company is illustrated below.

Straight-line composite depreciation rate

WILBUR COMPANY
Computation of Straight-Line Composite Depreciation Rate for Machinery

Machine	*Cost*	*Net residual value*	*Depreciation base*	*Economic life (years)*	*Annual depreciation expense*
W	$ 6,000	$ -0-	$ 6,000	5	$1,200
X	10,000	1,200	8,800	8	1,100
Y	15,000	1,000	14,000	10	1,400
Z	19,000	1,000	18,000	12	1,500
Totals	$50,000	$3,200	$46,800		$5,200

Composite depreciation rate based on cost: $5,200 ÷ $50,000 = 10.4%.
Composite economic life of machines: $46,800 ÷ $5,200 = 9 years.

The composite depreciation rate is 10.4%, and the composite economic life of the machines is nine years. Thus, the application of the 10.4% composite rate to the cost of $50,000 will reduce the composite net residual value of the machines to $3,200 in exactly nine years [$50,000 – ($5,200 × 9) = $3,200].

Once the composite depreciation rate is computed, ***it is continued in use until a material change occurs in the composition of plant assets or in the estimate of their economic lives.*** The assumptions underlying the use of composite depreciation methods are that (1) plant assets are regularly retired near the end of their economic lives, (2) retired plant assets are regularly replaced with similar assets, and (3) proceeds on retirement are approximately equal to the net residual value used for the computation of the composite depreciation rate. If assets are not replaced, for example, the use of the 10.4% rate computed above eventually would result in the recording of excessive depreciation.

In the determination of yearly depreciation, the 10.4% rate is applied to the balance of the Machinery ledger account at the beginning of the year, which balance excludes the original cost of all machines retired prior to the beginning of the year. Thus, for each of the first five years, annual depreciation is $5,200; and in the sixth year (assuming machine W was replaced at the end of the fifth year with a similar machine costing $9,000), depreciation would be $5,512 [($50,000 – $6,000 + $9,000) × 10.4% = $5,512]. The composite depreciation rate is not revised when plant assets are replaced with comparable assets, and the asset group should not be depreciated below net residual value at any time.

When composite depreciation procedures are employed, a record is not maintained for accumulated depreciation on individual plant assets. When an asset is retired from use or sold, a journal entry is required to remove the original cost from the plant asset account, and any difference between original cost and the proceeds received is debited to Accumulated Depreciation; a gain or loss is not recognized because gains and losses are assumed to offset over time. To illustrate, if machine W were sold at the end of the fourth year for $1,500, the journal entry to record the sale would be as follows:

No gain or loss is recognized

Cash	1,500	
Accumulated Depreciation of Machinery	4,500	
Machinery		6,000
To record sale of machine W. Composite depreciation method is used; therefore, no gain or loss is recognized.		

The primary disadvantage of the composite depreciation method is that the averaging procedure may obscure significant variations from average. The accuracy of the straight-line composite depreciation rate may be verified by recomputing depreciation on the straight-line basis for individual plant assets. Any significant discrepancies between the two results require a change in the composite depreciation rate.

The advantages claimed for the composite method are simplicity, convenience, and a reduction in the amount of detail involved in plant asset records and depreciation computations. The availability of computers has reduced the force of this argument. In many cases unit plant asset records are now feasible, although composite methods previously were considered a necessity.

The requisites for the successful operation of composite depreciation procedures are that there be a large number of homogeneous plant assets, of relatively small individual value, with similar economic lives. Telephone and electric transmission poles, underground cables, railroad tracks, and hotel furniture are examples of plant assets for which composite depreciation methods may give satisfactory results.

DEPRECIATION METHODS AND MANAGEMENT DECISIONS

In highly industrialized nations, plant assets play a large part in the productive process. It is easy to see that the cost of direct material and direct labour becomes a part of finished product. It is not always so clearly recognized, however, that a business enterprise also sells to its customers the services of the plant assets used to manufacture and market its products.

The importance of depreciation stems from the various management decisions that are affected by it. To the extent that depreciation is a significant part of operating costs, and that operating costs are relevant in business decisions, the relative merits of various depreciation methods are significant in decisions relating to the following areas:

1 Measurement of net income and the impact of inflation

2 Computation of income taxes

3 Investment of capital

The effect of different depreciation methods in relation to each of these decision areas is discussed in the following sections.

Depreciation, Net Income Measurement, and Inflation

The purpose of depreciation accounting is to measure the amount that must be recovered from revenue to compensate for the portion of plant asset cost that has been used up. This idea is embodied in the phrase ***maintenance of capital***, which often is used in relation to income measurement.

The widespread use of the straight-line method of depreciation results from its simplicity and convenience. Two objections may be levelled against the straight-line method, each of which becomes a supporting argument for some other method of depreciation.

1 It does not allow for the fact that productivity of plant assets may decline with age.

2 It does not take into account variations in the rate of plant asset use.

Some business executives suggest that the decline in productivity of many plant assets is so pronounced that the value (and thus the cost) of asset services in the early stages of economic life is materially greater than in later years. If this is true, accelerated methods of depreciation may achieve a better matching of costs and revenue than the straight-line method. Originally, the declining productivity argument centred on a rising curve of repair and maintenance costs as assets aged. In recent years, greater weight has been given to the effects of obsolescence. Often, the period of high earnings on new plant assets is short because of the inroads of innovation and competition.

The use of the straight-line depreciation method makes depreciation a fixed period cost by assumption, and thereby fails to allow for the loss of service potential related to wear and tear through usage. If a plant asset is used twice as much in one year as another, it would be unrealistic to assume that the amount and cost of asset services consumed is the same in both years. This objection to straight-line depreciation becomes an argument for the use of a measure of output as the unit of economic life, which would tend to make depreciation a variable cost rather than a fixed cost.

During an inflationary period, any depreciation method based on historical cost tends to understate the amount of capital consumed (depreciation). Thus, a part of reported net income essentially represents ***return of capital***. Users of financial statements should consider this shortcoming in the traditional income measurement model and should make appropriate adjustments to restate depreciation and net income in terms of current cost of plant assets. A more detailed discussion of the impact of inflation on depreciation accounting appears in Chapter 25.

Depreciation Policy and Income Taxes[2]

Probably the strongest influence on depreciation policy is the federal income tax law. The direction of the influence is toward rapid depreciation deductions. Depreciation expense reduces taxable income and income taxes expense. Taxpayers generally may not deduct more than the actual cost of a depreciable asset over its economic life, but income taxes may be postponed by maximizing depreciation deductions, and deferred taxes represent an interest-free loan for the period of the postponement. The only possible tax disadvantage of large initial depreciation deductions is that income tax rates might increase sufficiently during the economic life of a plant asset to more than offset the interest savings.

Federal income tax provisions generally do not require estimates of economic lives or net residual value of plant assets. In certain cases, the accelerated methods of depreciation are implemented without regard to issues of accounting theory or economic reality. If such practices applied only to the computation of taxable income, no damage would be done to the validity of financial statements. For many business enterprises, however, the convenience of keeping only one set of depreciation records is such that the accounting records often are made to conform to federal income tax requirements.

If income tax depreciation (capital cost allowance) and financial accounting depreciation substantially are equivalent, there are practical advantages to maintaining the accounting records on a tax basis. Tax deductions, however, are shaped by matters of public policy and the need for revenue by the federal and provincial governments, and are in no way related to the objectives of financial accounting. Material divergence between income tax and financial accounting data is possible. For example, many business enterprises use accelerated depreciation methods for federal income tax purposes but use the straight-line method for financial accounting.

Allowing relatively large depreciation deductions for income tax purposes is a means of subsidizing business investment. As a result, tax proposals for speeding up depreciation allowances as a means of stimulating investment or encouraging certain kinds of investment frequently are made. Therefore, the continued usefulness of accounting data for managerial and investment purposes may depend on maintaining a state of independence between financial accounting and income tax rules.

Depreciation and Capital Investment Decisions

The two most important questions relating to the role of depreciation in a capital investment decision are: (1) Is depreciation a relevant cost in the decision? (2) How does depreciation affect the cash flows from the investment?

Depreciation Expense May Be Either an Incremental Cost or a Sunk Cost

In essence, two kinds of costs are relevant to the decision to invest capital in productive assets: (1) ***future costs***, that is, costs that will be incurred as the result

2 Depreciation under the Income Tax Act is essentially on an accelerated basis and is called "capital cost allowance."

of the decision, and (2) ***incremental costs***, that is, costs that will change as the result of the decision. The expense represented by depreciation on existing plant assets is attributable to an investment made at some time in the past. Except to the extent that an existing plant asset may be sold and some portion of the past investment recovered, no present decision can change the amount of cost that has been sunk into that asset. Thus, depreciation often has been referred to as a ***sunk cost***.

A decision to invest in productive facilities should be based on an analysis of incremental costs and revenue. The carrying amount of existing plant assets (a sunk cost that cannot be changed in the short run) is an irrelevant factor and may be disregarded (except for income tax considerations). Most managerial decisions as to alternative actions such as acquiring or leasing, acquiring or making, or accepting or not accepting a special order, depend on an analysis of incremental costs and revenue. Depreciation may or may not represent a relevant cost in comparing such alternative courses of action. Depreciation on special equipment acquired for a specific activity is always an incremental cost to that activity, but depreciation on existing plant assets is an incremental cost only if the use of the assets for the specific activity reduces their economic life or residual value.

We have oversimplified the problem in this discussion, but a valid generalization may be drawn. Whether or not depreciation should be regarded as an incremental cost depends on whether the limiting factor in plant asset life is obsolescence or use, and whether the asset in question is being used to capacity. For this reason, depreciation expense computed for purposes of income determination generally has a low level of relevance for capital investment decision.

Effect of Depreciation on Cash Flows

Investment decisions frequently are made on the basis of the expected rate of return on the investment. In the computation of the rate of return, ***net cash flow*** from the investment generally is a more useful concept than ***net income*** from the investment. Depreciation expense does not generate cash directly; it is an expense that does not reduce cash, but is deducted to compute taxable income. Thus, depreciation expense indirectly generates larger cash flows from operations by reducing income taxes. For this reason, depreciation is viewed as a powerful instrument for increasing cash flows and reducing the ***payback period*** (the number of years required to recover an investment in a plant asset) on new investments in plant assets.

To illustrate the relationships between depreciation and cash flows, assume the following annual results for an asset that is rented to others:

Depreciation does not require a cash outflow in the current accounting period

Amount of cash received as rental revenue	$5,000
Less: All expenses (except income taxes and depreciation of $2,000)	1,200
Net cash received	$3,800
Income taxes, 45% of income after depreciation [($3,800 – $2,000) × 0.45]	810
Net cash flow each year	$2,990

The annual net cash flow of $2,990 also may be determined by adding the depreciation expense of $2,000 to the net income of $990 ($3,800 − $2,000 − $810 = $990). Determination of the present value of net cash flows from an investment is a critical procedure in the evaluation of investment alternatives under ***capital budgeting*** techniques.

Depreciation Procedures and Records

Property Records

The typical business enterprise employs many different kinds of plant assets having varying characteristics and economic lives. Precision in accounting for the use of such assets is facilitated by detailed and complete property records. Property records may be maintained on ledger cards, punched cards, magnetic tapes or disks, or in a computer storage.

An ideal system is to maintain a record for each plant asset. The record should show, for each asset, its cost, additions, economic life, net residual value, date of installation, location, basis and amount of periodic depreciation, and other information such as the serial number. In addition to providing thorough support for depreciation and retirement journal entries, such property records are useful for maintaining internal control for plant assets.

Accumulated Depreciation Ledger Account

In theory, depreciation could be recorded as a credit to the plant asset ledger accounts because depreciable plant assets basically are long-term deferred charges. The direct write-off procedure often is used for large numbers of small-value plant assets when periodic inventories are taken to determine the portion of asset cost remaining on hand. For larger assets, the usual practice is to credit a contra-asset ledger account titled Accumulated Depreciation. The primary argument for the use of a separate ledger account is to preserve information about the cost of plant assets and the proportion of cost that has expired. Also, in an analysis of account balances, it is convenient to be able to distinguish plant additions and retirements from adjustments in accumulated depreciation.

The Accumulated Depreciation ledger account is frequently, but improperly, referred to as a ***valuation account***. The Accumulated Depreciation account represents the portion of the acquisition cost of a plant asset that has been allocated to expense through the process of depreciation. Its purpose is not to value a plant asset in terms of current prices, but rather to determine the unallocated cost (or carrying amount) of a plant asset on a specific date.

Depreciation Schedules

When the number of individual items within each class of plant assets is not large, a ***depreciation schedule*** (sometimes known as a ***lapsing schedule***) may be used. These schedules may take many forms and often are prepared by the use of computer spreadsheets if the number of assets is large. A depreciation schedule is a means of maintaining unit property records with a minimum of effort. Its purposes are to facilitate the computation of periodic depreciation and to provide a continuing record of asset costs and the related accumulated depreciation.

A typical depreciation schedule includes columns for cost, estimated net residual value, accumulated depreciation, and ***prospective depreciation charges*** throughout the economic life for each plant asset. If a plant asset is retired at the end of its economic life, its cost is deducted from the cost column, and its accumulated depreciation to date is deducted from the accumulated depreciation column. The retirement is recorded in the general journal or the cash receipts journal, together with any gain or loss. If a plant asset is retired prematurely, it is not necessary to erase or change the originally scheduled depreciation amounts. It is more convenient to cancel the future depreciation charges by recording appropriate ***deductions*** on the line used to record the retirement.

Disclosure of Depreciation in Financial Statements

Because of the significant effects on financial position and results of operations that stem from depreciation expense and the depreciation methods used, the following disclosures are made in the financial statements or in notes to the financial statements:

1 Depreciation expense for the accounting period

2 Balances of major classes of depreciable plant assets, by nature or function

3 Accumulated depreciation, either by major classes of depreciable plant assets or in total

4 A general description of the method or methods used in the computation of depreciation with respect to major classes of depreciable plant assets

According to a recent edition of the CICA's ***Financial Reporting in Canada***, the straight-line method is by far the most common method used by companies, the output method ranks a distant second, and the accelerated depreciation (diminishing-balance) methods came in third.[3] If a change in the method of computing depreciation is made, the effect of the change on the current year's net income should be disclosed. Similarly, the effect of any unusual depreciation charges should be disclosed. Accounting for changes in depreciation methods, changes in economic lives of depreciable assets, and corrections of errors in the recording of depreciation are discussed in Chapter 22.

DEPLETION OF NATURAL RESOURCES

Depreciable plant assets usually retain their physical characteristics as they are used in operations. In contrast, ***natural resources*** in essence are long-term inventories of material that will be removed physically from their source. In either case — whether accountants are dealing with a ''bundle of services'' or a ''store of material'' — the basic problem is to determine the cost of the units of services or material that are consumed during each accounting period. The portion of the

3 CICA, ***Financial Reporting in Canada*** (Toronto, 1985), 16th ed., p. 177.

cost (or other valuation) assigned to property containing natural resources that is applicable to the units removed from the property is known as ***depletion***.

The Depletion Base

The ***depletion base*** of property containing natural resources is the acquisition cost less the estimated net residual value of the property after the resources have been removed. The estimated cost of dismantling, abandoning, or restoring the property is taken into account in the determination of the net residual value of the property.

Acquisition cost of a natural resource includes the price paid for the property and legal fees, broker's fees, and other fees incurred to acquire the property.

In the lumber industry, substantial costs are incurred for fire protection, insect and disease control, property taxes, and other maintenance costs applicable to standing timber that will not be harvested for a considerable length of time. These costs, known as ***carrying costs***, are capitalized (added to the cost of the property) while the property is being developed. For example, if carrying costs of $400,000 are applicable to a tract of timber, and during an accounting period 20% of the timber is cut, 80%, or $320,000, is applicable to uncut timber and is capitalized.

Exploration and Development Costs

In the production of natural resources such as petroleum, considerable exploration costs, and development costs such as preparation of sites, drilling and equipping wells, and construction of production facilities, are incurred. These costs are capitalized as part of the petroleum enterprise's wells and related equipment and facilities.[4]

The Problem of "Dry Holes"

What if the expenditures made to acquire, explore, and develop natural resources prove unproductive? Under one view, termed the ***successful efforts method***, if each specific property is considered a separate venture, the logical interpretation is that no asset exists, and a loss therefore has occurred. A contrasting theory, termed the ***full cost method***, holds that from the viewpoint of the enterprise as a whole, particularly if it is seeking constantly to maintain its natural resource base by exploration and acquisition of new deposits, a certain amount of unproductive effort may be treated as a normal cost of discovering new natural resource deposits. If, for example, 10 dry wells are drilled for each producing oil well brought in, the argument that 11 drillings are necessary to bring in a producing well and that the cost of a producing well includes the cost of 10 unsuccessful efforts has some merit. The problem is analogous to that of accounting for spoilage in manufacturing. If a certain amount of spoilage is considered normal, it is treated as a part of the cost of the good units produced; if the amount of spoilage is abnormal, it is

4 FASB, ***FASB Statement No. 19***: "Financial Accounting and Reporting by Oil and Gas Producing Companies" (Stamford: 1977), pp. 6–7.

recognized as a loss.

In ***FASB Statement No. 19***: ''Financial Accounting and Reporting for Oil and Gas Producing Companies,'' the Financial Accounting Standards Board expressed a preference for the successful efforts method of accounting.[5] However, the Securities and Exchange Commission in the United States permits use of the full cost method by companies that report to it.[6] In Canada, the CICA has no official recommendations in this area.[7]

Estimate of Recoverable Units

The estimate of economic lives for plant assets is a relatively simple undertaking compared with the estimate of recoverable units of natural resources. The quantity of ore in a vein and the recoverable deposit in petroleum-producing property often are difficult to determine, and revisions may be necessary as production takes place and new evidence becomes available. Adding to the problem is the fact that changes in the method of extraction may make it possible to work deposits of natural resources that originally were deemed uneconomical.

Ideally, the recoverable deposit of a natural resource should be measured in units of ***desired*** product, such as one gram of silver or a kilogram of copper, rather than in units of ***mined*** product, such as a tonne of raw ore. If depletion is based on tonnes of mined ore, the same charge will be applied to a tonne of high-grade ore as to a tonne of low-grade ore. This treatment is hardly logical in terms of the way mining property is valued and in terms of efforts by accountants to match costs and revenue.

Cost Depletion

Conceptually, any of the methods of depreciation previously discussed might be applied in a comparable manner to the computation of depletion. However, the straight-line method is of doubtful applicability because the exhaustion of natural resources is a matter of physical output rather than the passage of time. Accelerated methods have not been widely used to measure depletion, despite the fact that the productivity of natural resources may decline rapidly when the unit cost of recovery increases as production moves from richer to poorer deposits.

By far the most widely used method of depletion for financial accounting is the output (units-of-production) method, which produces a constant depletion charge per unit of the natural resource removed. To illustrate, assume that early in Year 7 Lowell Corporation acquired mining property for $720,000. It is estimated that there are 1.2 million recoverable units of the natural resource, and that the land will have a net residual value (after restoration costs) of $60,000 when the resource is exhausted. The depletion per unit of output is computed as follows:

5 FASB, ***FASB Statement No. 19***, p. 5.

6 Securities and Exchange Commission, ***Codification of Financial Reporting Policies*** (Washington: 1982), sec. 406.

7 The accounting guideline issued by the CICA in September 1986 is concerned only with the application of the full cost method; it does not express preference for the full cost, the successful efforts, or any other method.

Formula to compute depletion per unit

$$\text{Depletion} = \frac{\text{cost} - \text{net residual value}}{\text{estimated total recoverable units}}$$

$$= \frac{\$720{,}000 - \$60{,}000}{1{,}200{,}000 \text{ units}} = \$0.55 \text{ per unit}$$

If Lowell removed 300,000 units of the natural resource from the ground in Year 7, the journal entry to record depletion is as follows:

Journal entry to record depletion

Depletion (300,000 × $0.55)	165,000	
Accumulated Depletion of Mining Property		165,000
To record depletion for Year 7.		

The amount of cost depletion is included in the cost of the inventory of the natural resource and is recognized as an expense (cost of goods sold) only when the inventory is sold. For example, if in Year 7 Lowell sold 200,000 of 300,000 units extracted, the cost of goods sold for Lowell for Year 7 is determined as follows (costs other than depletion are assumed):

Depletion is included in total cost and unit cost

	Total	*Unit cost*
Cost of goods sold:		
Depletion	$165,000	$0.55
Material, labour, and overhead (other than depletion and depreciation)	237,000	0.79
Depreciation of equipment	15,000	0.05
Total cost of production (300,000 units)	$417,000	$1.39
Less: Ending inventory (100,000 units × $1.39)	139,000	
Cost of goods sold (200,000 units × $1.39)	$278,000	

When additional costs are incurred in the development of mining properties or estimates of recoverable units are revised, the depletion rate should be recomputed. Depletion previously recorded should not be revised. The new depletion rate is computed by dividing the carrying amount (cost less accumulated depletion, less net residual value) of the mining property (including any additional development costs) by the new estimate of recoverable units.

Depreciation of Plant Assets Associated with Natural Resources

Buildings and equipment used to remove natural resources may have an economic life shorter than the time required to complete the removal, in which case the depreciation of these assets should be recorded over their economic lives. Otherwise, depreciation is computed by the output method, similarly to the computation of depletion.

APPENDIX: INTEREST METHODS OF DEPRECIATION

For many years the ***annuity*** and ***sinking-fund*** methods of depreciation have received attention from accounting theorists because of their focus on cost recovery and rate of return on the investment in depreciable plant assets. A depreciable plant asset represents a bundle of future services to be received periodically over the economic life of the asset. The cost of such an asset may be viewed as the present value of the equal periodic rents (services) discounted at a rate of interest consistent with the risk factors identified with the investment in the plant asset.

Annuity Method

The annuity method of depreciation is appropriate when the periodic cost (depreciation) of using a long-lived plant asset is considered to be equal to the total of the expired cost of the asset and the implicit interest on the unrecovered investment in the asset. Depreciation Expense is debited and Accumulated Depreciation and Interest Revenue are credited periodically, as explained in the example below.

Assume that a computer with an economic life of five years and a net residual value of $67,388 is acquired by Dorsey, Inc., for $800,000. If the fair rate of interest for this type of investment is 10% compounded annually, the yearly depreciation expense is computed as illustrated below:

Computation of annual depreciation expense under annuity method

$$\text{Depreciation} = \frac{\text{cost of asset less present value of net residual value}}{\text{present value of ordinary annuity of 5 rents of 1 at 10\%}}$$

$$= \frac{\$800{,}000 - (\$67{,}388 \times 0.620921^{*})}{3.790787^{\dagger}}$$

$$= \frac{\$800{,}000 - \$41{,}843}{3.790787}$$

$$= \underline{\underline{\$200{,}000}}$$

*Present value of 1 for five periods at 10% (Table 2 in the Appendix at the end of Chapter 5).
†See Table 4 in the Appendix at the end of Chapter 5.

A summary of the results of the annuity method of depreciation, and the journal entries to record depreciation for the first two years, are shown on page 580.

The summary shows that: (1) depreciation expense computed by the annuity method is debited for $200,000 each year; (2) interest revenue is credited each year with 10% of the unrecovered investment (carrying amount of the computer); (3) the difference between annual depreciation expense and interest revenue is credited to Accumulated Depreciation; and (4) the carrying amount of the computer at the end of Year 5 is $67,388, the net residual value at the end of its economic life. The total depreciation expense over the economic life of the computer exceeds its depreciable cost by $267,388 ($1,000,000 – $732,612 = $267,388), an amount equal to the implicit interest revenue recognized during the economic life of the computer. The net charge to income over the five-year period is equal to the depreciation base of the computer and *increases* each year. The annuity method of depreciation thus tends to produce a more constant rate of return on investment than, say, the straight-line method of depreciation. Consequently, the use of the annuity method of depreciation for assets acquired under capital leases has been advocated by some accountants in recent years.

DORSEY, INC.
Summary of Annuity Method of Depreciation

Year	*Depreciation expense*	*Implicit interest revenue (10% of carrying amount)*	*Credit to Accumulated Depreciation ledger account*	*Balance of Accumulated Depreciation ledger account*	*Carrying amount of computer*
0					$800,000
1	$ 200,000	$ 80,000	$120,000	$120,000	680,000
2	200,000	68,000	132,000	252,000	548,000
3	200,000	54,800	145,200	397,200	402,800
4	200,000	40,280	159,720	556,920	243,080
5	200,000	24,308	175,692	732,612	67,388
	$1,000,000	$267,388	$732,612		

Journal Entries

	Year 1		*Year 2*	
Depreciation Expense	200,000		200,000	
Interest Revenue		80,000		68,000
Accumulated Depreciation		120,000		132,000
To record depreciation by annuity method.				

Sinking-Fund Method

The sinking-fund method of depreciation might be used when a fund is to be accumulated to replace a plant asset at the end of its economic life. Under the sinking-fund method, the amount of annual depreciation expense is equal to the increase in the asset replacement fund. The increase in the fund consists of the equal periodic deposits (rents) plus the interest revenue realized at the assumed rate on the sinking-fund balance.

Computation of annual sinking-fund deposits under sinking-fund method of depreciation

$$\text{Sinking-fund deposits} = \frac{\text{cost of asset less net residual value}}{\text{amount of ordinary annuity of 5 rents of 1 at 10\%}}$$

$$= \frac{\$800{,}000 - \$67{,}388}{6.1051^*}$$

$$= \underline{\underline{\$120{,}000}}$$

*See Table 3 in the Appendix at the end of Chapter 5.

We shall illustrate the sinking-fund method of depreciation with the same example as we used to illustrate the annuity method, that is, a computer acquired by Dorsey, Inc., for $800,000 with an economic life of five years and a net residual value of $67,388 at the end of five years. If we again assume a 10% annual compound rate of interest, the annual deposits to the sinking fund are determined as shown at the bottom of page 580.

Here are a summary of the results of the sinking-fund method of depreciation and the journal entries to record depreciation for the first two years:

DORSEY, INC.
Summary of Sinking-Fund Method of Depreciation

	Sinking fund				*Depreciation and carrying amount*		
Year	*Annual deposit*	*Realized interest revenue (10% of fund balance)*	*Total fund increase*	*Fund balance*	*Depreciation expense*	*Balance of Accumulated Depreciation ledger account*	*Carrying amount of computer*
0							$800,000
1	$120,000		$120,000	$120,000	$120,000	$120,000	680,000
2	120,000	$ 12,000	132,000	252,000	132,000	252,000	548,000
3	120,000	25,200	145,200	397,200	145,200	397,200	402,800
4	120,000	39,720	159,720	556,920	159,720	556,920	243,080
5	120,000	55,692	175,692	732,612	175,692	732,612	67,388
	$600,000	$132,612	$732,612		$732,612		

Journal Entries

	Year 1		*Year 2*	
Sinking Fund	120,000		132,000	
Depreciation Expense	120,000		132,000	
Cash		120,000		120,000
Interest Revenue				12,000
Accumulated Depreciation		120,000		132,000
To record depreciation by sinking-fund method.				

The foregoing summary and journal entries show that: (1) depreciation expense computed by the sinking-fund method is debited each year for ***increasing*** amounts equal to the total increase in the sinking fund; (2) interest revenue is credited each year with earnings at 10% on the fund balance; (3) the net charge to income (depreciation expense less interest revenue) each year remains constant at $120,000; and (4) the carrying amount of the computer at the end of Year 5 is $67,388, the net residual value at the end of its economic life.

The sinking-fund method of depreciation may be used without the accumulation of a sinking fund. However, depreciation expense still would be recorded equal to the hypothetical fund increases, as illustrated. The sinking-fund method of depreciation is used only by a few utility companies.

REVIEW QUESTIONS

1 Distinguish between the terms ***depreciation, amortization,*** and ***depletion.*** How is depreciation accounting related to the replacement of a plant asset at the end of its economic life?

2 What are the three variables used in the computation of periodic depreciation expense? Is depreciation a valuation procedure or a cost allocation procedure?

3 The manager of an electric utility stated, ''Our transmission lines are kept in good operating condition by regular repairs and maintenance, and their efficiency is relatively constant—they just don't depreciate!'' Do you agree with this statement? Explain.

4 What is meant by the term ***estimated economic life*** of a plant asset, and how is it measured?

5 What are the major causes of a decrease in the economic life of a plant asset? How accurately may the causes be identified for a specific asset?

6 Jordan Company acquires delivery trucks for $18,000. These trucks have an economic life of six years based on physical deterioration and a net residual value of $3,000. Jordan typically sells a truck for $7,000 after operating it 100,000 kilometres. What is the depreciation base for a delivery truck? What is its estimated economic life to Jordan?

7 Both the quantity of plant asset services used each accounting period and the relative value of the asset services are factors in the choice of a method of depreciation. Explain.

8 *a* List the methods that may be used to compute depreciation.
b State two objections to the straight-line method of depeciation.
c List some advantages of the straight-line method of depreciation.

9 During Year 5, a strike halted manufacturing operations of Arcadia, Inc., for four months. Depreciation of its spinning and weaving machines for the full year under the straight-line method is $216,000. Arcadia's operations for Year 5 resulted in a net loss of $132,000 (after deduction of depreciation expense). The president of Arcadia suggests that the depreciation expense for Year 5 should be reduced because of the low volume of operations. Do you agree?

10 Describe a situation in which the use of the ***output method*** of depreciation is appropriate.

11 What is meant by a ***composite*** or ***group basis method of depreciation***? What are the advantages and limitations of this method?

12 Explain why the use of accelerated depreciation methods is advantageous for income tax purposes.

13 What principle should be applied to determine whether depreciation is a fixed or a variable expense? Why is depreciation called a ''noncash expense''?

14 What disclosures relating to depreciation and depreciation methods are made in the financial statements or in notes to the financial statements?

15 Bronze Corporation acquired for $800,000 land from which it expects to extract 1 million tonnes of Grade A ore and 2 million tonnes of Grade B ore. Grade A ore is three times as valuable as Grade B ore. Compute depletion per tonne of each grade of ore extracted.

16 Plant assets or natural resources donated to a business enterprise generally are recorded by the enterprise, and depreciation or depletion on such assets is allocated to expense. Justify this practice.

EXERCISES

Ex. 12-1 Select the best answer for each of the following multiple-choice questions:

1 If a plant asset with a five-year economic life is sold during the second year, how would use of the sum-of-the-years'-digits method of depreciation instead of the straight-line method of depreciation affect the gain or loss on disposal of the asset? Answer ***a, b, c,*** or ***d*** according to the following table.

	Gain	*Loss*
a	Decrease	Increase
b	Increase	Decrease
c	No effect	No effect
d	No effect	Decrease

2 Which of the following depreciation methods involves the same computational techniques as those used for depletion?
a Straight-line *b* Sum-of-the-years'-digits *c* Double-declining-balance *d* Output *e* None of the foregoing

3 The composite depreciation method:
a Is applied to a group of homogeneous plant assets
b Is an accelerated method of depreciation
c Does not involve the recognition of a gain or loss on the retirement of an individual plant asset of the group
d Disregards net residual value in the computation of the depreciation base

4 On November 1, Year 1, Platte Company acquired for $50,000 equipment having an economic life of 10 years and a net residual value of $2,000. Platte adopted the double-declining-balance method of depreciation for the equipment. If Platte computes depreciation to the nearest month, depreciation expense for the equipment for the year ended April 30, Year 3, is:
a $7,680 *b* $9,000 *c* $9,600 *d* $10,000 *e* Some other amount

5 The effect of growth and changes in the scale of a business enterprise's operations in terminating the economic life of plant assets is termed:
a Depreciation *b* Obsolescence *c* Inadequacy *d* Economies of scale

6 The formula for determining the sum of an arithmetic progression, used in the sum-of-the-years'-digits method of depreciation, is:

a $2n(n + 1)$ *b* $\frac{n + 1}{2n}$ *c* $n(n + 1)$ *d* $n\left(\frac{n + 1}{2}\right)$

e None of the foregoing

7 On January 2, Year 6, Dragoon Company acquired for $120,000 equipment with an economic life of eight years and a net residual value of $12,000. Dragoon adopted the sum-of-the-years'-digits method of depreciation for the equipment. On December 31, Year 7, accumulated depreciation on the equipment totals:

a $15,000 less than under the straight-line method of depreciation
b $15,000 less than under the double-declining-balance method of depreciation
c $18,000 more than under the straight-line method of depreciation
d $18,000 more than under the double-declining-balance method of depreciation

Ex. 12-2 Yazoo Company leased a building under an operating lease and immediately acquired equipment for $430,000 and spent $45,000 to have special platforms and supporting encasements built. The lease contract provides that when the lease expires Yazoo must remove the equipment, demolish the platforms and encasements, and restore the building to its original condition, an operation that is expected to cost $20,000.

Compute the depreciation base of Yazoo Company's equipment, including platforms and encasements.

Ex. 12-3 Determine the fractions to be used in the computation of depreciation expense under the sum-of-the-years'-digits method for each of the following:

a The third year of a six-year economic life
b The sixth year of a 10-year economic life
c The seventh year of an eight-year economic life

Ex. 12-4 A plant asset cost $56,000, had an economic life of eight years, and an estimated net residual value of $2,000.

a Compute depreciation expense for the first year of economic life under the sum-of-the-years'-digits method of depreciation.
b Assume that this asset was acquired on April 1, Year 1. Compute depreciation expense for the full year ended December 31, Year 2, under the sum-of-the-years'-digits method of depreciation.

Ex. 12-5 On October 1, Year 1, Lessing Company, whose fiscal year is the calendar year, acquired for $4,000 a machine with an economic life of four years and a net residual value of $250. Lessing adopted the double-declining-balance method of depreciation for the machine.

Compute depreciation expense for Lessing Company for Year 1 through Year 5, using two methods to determine depreciation expense for fractional years. Round all amounts to the nearest dollar.

Ex. 12-6 On January 2, Year 3, Lucas Company acquired for $1,000,000 a machine with an economic life of eight years and a net residual value of $100,000. Lucas adopted the sum-of-the-years'-digits method of depreciation for the machine.

Compute the carrying amount of the machine on December 31, Year 4.

Ex. 12-7 Deluxe Corporation has three machines, each with an economic life of five years. Deluxe records a full-year's depreciation expense in the year in which plant assets are acquired, and no depreciation expense in the year of disposal of plant assets. Details of Deluxe's three machines on December 31, Year 3, are as follows:

Machine	*Year acquired*	*Cost*	*Net residual value*	*Accumulated depreciation*
No. 1	Year 2	$100,000	$20,000	$64,000
No. 2	Year 1	55,000	10,000	36,000
No. 3	Year 1	70,000	14,000	33,600

a Compute Deluxe Corporation's depreciation expense for machine No. 1 for Year 4, under the double-declining-balance method used by Deluxe Corporation for the machine.

b Compute Deluxe Corporation's depreciation expense for machine No. 2 for Year 4, under the same method used by Deluxe Corporation for the machine for Year 1 through Year 3.

c Compute the gain or loss realized by Deluxe Corporation on June 30, Year 4, when it sold machine No. 3, which it had been depreciating under the straight-line method, for $28,000.

Ex. 12-8 A machine with an estimated economic life of five years, or 100,000 units of output, was acquired by Webb Company on October 4, Year 1. The cash price of the machine was $9,000, which was to be paid for as follows:

Cash	$ 1,500
Old machine accepted as trade-in (carrying amount is equal to current fair value)	500
Four instalments payable at the rate of $2,000 every six months (includes $1,000 interest and financing charges)	8,000
Total	$10,000

Compute Webb Company's depreciation expense for the three months ended December 31, Year 1, and for Year 2, assuming that the net residual value of the machine is $1,500, under each of the following methods:

a Straight-line

b Sum-of-the-years'-digits

c Double-declining-balance
d Output (8,000 units were produced in Year 1 and 33,000 units in Year 2)

Ex. 12-9 Romero Company acquired a plant asset at the beginning of Year 1 for $16,000. The asset has an economic life of four years and a net residual value of $1,000.
Compute the depreciation on Romero Company's asset for Year 1, under each of the following methods:
a Straight-line
b Sum-of-the-years'-digits
c Fixed-percentage-of-declining-balance
For *c* compute the theoretically correct rate and prove that it yields a net residual value of $1,000 at the end of four years.

Ex. 12-10 On January 3, Year 1, Lund Company acquired equipment that had an estimated economic life of 10 years and a net residual value of $20,000. The depreciation expense for Year 5 was $12,000 under the sum-of-the-years'-digits method.
Compute the cost of the equipment acquired by Lund Company.

Ex. 12-11 The controller of Producto Company maintains records of plant assets under the composite method. A list of plant assets acquired to January 2, Year 1, follows:

Plant assets	*Cost*	*Net residual value*	*Economic life (years)*
A-101	$4,000	$400	3
A-102	1,500	300	4
A-103	7,000	750	5

a Compute Producto Company's straight-line composite depreciation rate based on cost.
b Assuming that on December 31, Year 3, asset A-101 was sold for $1,200, prepare a journal entry for Producto Company to record the sale.

Ex. 12-12 At the beginning of Year 1, Tangiers Company acquired 20 similar machines for $4,000 each and developed a straight-line group depreciation rate of 30% based on the following expectations:

	Year 2	*Year 3*	*Year 4*
Number of machines to be retired at end of year	5	10	5
Net residual value of machines to be retired	$6,000	$4,000	None

The retirements and proceeds realized were exactly as expected. The 30% depreciation rate is correct.
Record all transactions of Tangiers Company for the four-year period in the form of T accounts and explain the balance in the Accumulated Depreciation of

Machinery ledger account at the end of Year 4.

Ex. 12-13 An analysis of the Machinery ledger account of Locado Corporation for Year 8 appears below:

Jan. 2	Acquisition of four machines with an economic life of five years	$24,000
6	Installation cost for the four machines	800
	Total debits	$24,800
Dec. 28	Less: Credit representing proceeds on disposal of one machine (debit was recorded in the Cash ledger account)	4,200
31	Balance of Machinery ledger account	$20,600

a Prepare a journal entry for Locado Corporation to record depreciation expense for Year 8 for the four machines. The estimated net residual value of each machine is $700. Use the straight-line method of depreciation.

b Prepare a journal entry for Locado Corporation to correct the accounting records on December 31, Year 8, including the gain or loss (which was not recognized on December 28) on the disposal of one machine. The accounting records have not been closed for Year 8.

Ex. 12-14 Elezar Company acquired land containing a natural resource. Elezar is required by its acquisition contract to restore the land to a condition suitable for recreational use after it extracts the natural resource. Geological surveys indicate that the recoverable amount of the natural resource is estimated at 3 million tonnes, and that the land will have a value of $600,000 after restoration. Relevant cost information follows:

Land	$6,000,000
Restoration of land	920,000
Geological surveys	400,000

Assuming that Elezar Company maintains no inventories of the extracted natural resource, compute the depletion per tonne of the natural resource extracted.

Ex. 12-15 Data regarding Copper Company for the year ended April 30, Year 2, follow:

Sales of copper ore (100,000 tonnes)	$8,000,000
Expenses (excluding depletion)	$3,100,000
Depletion base, May 1, Year 1	$6,000,000
Estimated tonnes of copper ore recoverable, May 1, Year 1	1,200,000

Compute the cost depletion for Copper Company for the year ended April 30, Year 2. (There was no beginning or ending inventory of copper ore.)

Ex. 12-16 Colorado Ore Limited acquired mining property for $1.2 million. The property was expected to yield 800,000 tonnes of ore, after which the property would have a net residual value of $200,000. During the first year of operations, 60,000 tonnes of ore were mined and sold for $800,000. Operating expenses other than cost depletion amounted to $350,000. Income taxes are 45% of taxable income.

Compute for Colorado Ore Company's first year of operations the amount of ***a*** cost depletion on the mining property and ***b*** net income for financial accounting.

CASES

Case 12-1 Proponents of the ***successful efforts method*** and the ***full cost method*** of accounting for natural resources acquisition, exploration, and development costs have argued the relative merits of the two methods for many years. Presently, in the United States, the Financial Accounting Standards Board prefers the successful efforts method, but the Securities and Exchange Commission permits use of the full cost method in reports filed by companies subject to its jurisdiction.

Instructions

a Present arguments in support of the successful efforts method of accounting.
b Present arguments in support of the full cost method of accounting.
c Which is more consistent with the conceptual framework of financial accounting theory, the successful efforts method or the full cost method? Explain.

Case 12-2 The controller of Dublin Corporation is preparing accounting policies for Dublin in its first month of operations. Dublin has a variety of plant assets, including a significant investment in highly specialized equipment. You have been asked to assist the controller with this project.

Instructions

a Define ***depreciation*** as the term is used in financial accounting.
b Identify the factors that are relevant in the measurement of annual depreciation expense on plant assets and explain whether these factors are determined objectively or whether they are based on judgement.
c Explain why depreciation is shown in the ''Cash Provided by Operating Activities'' section of the statement of changes in financial position.

Case 12-3 Arlo Steel Corporation computes depreciation based on the level of its production activity. In the third quarter of Year 7, Arlo Steel, according to a financial news story, ''returned to profit a sum equal to $0.25 a share that had been recognized as depreciation in the previous six months but that it determined had not been needed.''

Instructions

a Evaluate Arlo Steel Corporation's depreciation policy.

b Do you believe that Arlo Steel Corporation is smoothing its net income by means of its depreciation policy or trying to match the service potential (cost) of its assets with the economic benefits derived (tonnes of steel produced)?

Case 12-4 Luna Company owned an old factory building that had a carrying amount of $200,000. Machinery and equipment in the building had a carrying amount of $300,000. In Year 5, Luna built a new building at a cost of $1.2 million and installed new equipment costing $650,000. Some of the equipment in the old building was replaced, and both plants were operated at near-capacity from Year 5 to Year 10. Depreciation was recorded under the straight-line method.

In Year 10, Luna shut down the old plant because of a decline in sales. The controller of Luna proposes to stop recording depreciation on the old building and machinery, stating that while the old plant is useful, it is not wearing out; furthermore, depreciating the old plant increases costs, overstates inventories, and places Luna in a poor position to bid for new orders because its production costs are high.

Instructions

Discuss and evaluate the controller's position. What recommendation would you make to Luna Company?

Case 12-5 An article in a financial journal stated that the net income for Cann Oil Corporation has decreased from $5 million in Year 3 to only $2 million in Year 4, largely because of increases in depletion and depreciation. These increases were necessary because an independent consultant prepared revised estimates of oil and gas reserves that were substantially less than Cann's previous estimates. The article further stated that the revised estimates do not affect Cann's revenue or cash flow, and that revisions in estimates of oil and gas reserves are not unusual in the oil and gas industry. The president of Cann was quoted as saying, "Because we are a relatively small oil and gas company, these revisions affect us more seriously than they do large companies."

Instructions

a How do you suppose the revised depletion and depreciation amount was determined? Should understatements of depletion and depreciation in prior years result in understatements of net income in subsequent years?

b How can independent auditors verify the estimates of deposits of natural resources?

c Explain why an increase in depletion and depreciation does not affect Cann Oil's revenue or cash flow.

d Why do revisions in estimates of oil and gas reserves affect a small company "more seriously" than they do large companies?

PROBLEMS

Pr. 12-1 Kase Corporation made a study of its five-year experience with a group of trucks. The appraised values of the trucks at the end of each year and average kilometres driven each year for each truck during a typical five-year period are shown in the following table:

Year	*Kilometres driven*	*Appraised value (% of cost)*
1	40,000	80%
2	60,000	55
3	40,000	40
4	30,000	30
5	30,000	25

Instructions

Using the foregoing information, compute Kase Corporation's depreciation expense each year during the five-year economic life of a truck that cost $36,000 and is expected to have a net residual value of $9,000, under each of the following depreciation methods (round all computations to the nearest dollar):

a Appraisal
b Straight-line
c Output
d Sum-of-the-years'-digits
e Double-declining-balance

Pr. 12-2 On January 2, Year 2, Lokey Company, a machine-tool manufacturer, acquired new equipment for $1,000,000. The equipment had an estimated economic life of five years, and the net residual value was estimated to be $100,000. Lokey estimated that the equipment would produce 10,000 units in its first year. Production was expected to decline by 1,000 units a year over the remaining four years of economic life of the equipment.

The following depreciation methods may be used for financial accounting:

1 Double-declining-balance
2 Straight-line
3 Sum-of-the-years'-digits
4 Output

Instructions

a Which depreciation method would result in the maximization of net income for financial accounting purposes for the three-year period ended December 31, Year 4? Prepare a working paper to show the amount of accumulated depreciation on December 31, Year 4, under the method selected. Show supporting computations. Ignore present value, income tax, and deferred income tax considerations in your answer.

b Assuming that all the four methods are acceptable for income tax purposes, which depreciation method would result in the minimization of taxable income for the three-year period ended December 31, Year 4?

Pr. 12-3 The cash price of a machine acquired by Mosby Manufacturing Corporation on September 30, Year 1, was $62,400, including sales taxes. It was paid for as follows:

Cash down payment	$ 7,800
Common stock, 600 shares with a current fair value of $42 a share	25,200
Promissory note payable in 24 monthly instalments of $1,500 each, including interest, beginning Oct. 31, Year 1	36,000
Total (paid or payable)	$69,000

The following additional costs were incurred before the machine was ready to be used in operations:

Installation costs	$2,400
Direct costs of trial runs	1,200

The machine was expected to produce 100,000 units during its economic life. It was placed in service on October 4, Year 1.

Instructions

a Determine the cost of Mosby Manufacturing Company's machine for financial accounting. Assume that the discount on the promissory note is equal to the difference between the total payments to be made and the cash price of the machine.

b Assuming that the net residual value of the machine is $6,000 and that the economic life is five years, compute Mosby Manufacturing Corporation's depreciation expense for Year 1 (three months) and Year 2 under each of the following methods:

1 Straight-line method
2 Sum-of-the-years'-digits method
3 Double-declining-balance method
4 Output method (The machine produced 5,000 units in Year 1 and 21,000 units in Year 2)

Pr. 12-4 In auditing the financial statements of Vista Corporation, you note that the journal entries in the Machinery ledger account are as given in the next table.

Depreciation expense was recorded at the end of each year at 20% of the balance of the Machinery ledger account. The economic life of the machines was five years, and the net residual value of each machine was 10% of invoice cost.

Instructions

a Prepare a working paper to compute the correct balances of the Machinery and Accumulated Depreciation of Machinery ledger accounts of Vista

Debits:			
Jan. 2, Year 3	Acquisition of machine A (invoice cost)	$22,000	
2, Year 3	Installation of machine A	2,000	
Sept. 30, Year 3	Acquisition of machine B (invoice cost)	30,000	
Mar. 31, Year 4	Acquisition of machine C (invoice cost)	16,000	
July 1, Year 5	Repairs as a result of flooding	4,500	$74,500
Credits:			
Dec. 31, Year 3	Depreciation for Year 3	$10,800	
Dec. 31, Year 4	Depreciation for Year 4	11,840	
Apr. 1, Year 5	Proceeds on sale of machine A	8,560	
Dec. 31, Year 5	Depreciation for Year 5	7,460	38,660
31, Year 5	Balance		$35,840

Corporation on December 31, Year 5. Use the straight-line method of depreciation.

b Using the information in ***a***, prepare a single correcting journal entry to restate the accounting records of Vista Corporation to conform with generally accepted accounting principles on December 31, Year 5. The revenue and expense ledger accounts for Year 5 are still open. Record the correction of any errors in depreciation expense for Years 3 and 4 in the Retained Earnings ledger account as adjustment to prior years. Disregard income taxes.

Pr. 12-5 The following entries were in an improperly established Property ledger account in the accounting records of Scoville Company at the end of Year 1:

Debit entries:			
Feb. 1	Amount paid to acquire building site		$ 45,000
12	Cost of removing old building from site		10,000
15	Contract price for new building, which was completed on Apr. 1		159,000
Apr. 1	Insurance and other costs directly connected with construction of new building		9,000
	Total debits		$223,000
Credit entries:			
Feb. 12	Proceeds from sale of material obtained from dismantling of old building	$ 6,000	
Dec. 31	Depreciation expense for Year 1—5% of balance of Property ledger account, $217,000 (Debit was recorded in the Depreciation Expense ledger account)	10,850	
	Total credits		16,850
31	Balance		$206,150

Instructions

a Prepare a correcting journal entry for Scoville Company on December 31, Year 1, assuming that the economic life of the new building is 20 years, that no net residual value is anticipated, and that depreciation expense under the straight-line method is to be recognized for nine months in Year 1. The accounting records have not been closed for Year 1.

b Compute depreciation expense for Scoville Company's building for Year 1, Year 2, and Year 3 under the following methods: (1) straight-line, (2) double-declining-balance, and (3) sum-of-the-years'-digits.

Pr. 12-6 Cable Products Company acquired 15 used machines on January 2, Year 1, for $60,000. The machines are not identical, but they perform similar functions. The machines have an average economic life of four years, and the residual value for each will approximately equal the removal costs. A composite depreciation method (straight-line) is used to allocate the cost of the machines to expense. Depreciation expense on assets retired or sold is computed for a full year.

Machines retired or sold and the proceeds on sale are summarized below:

End of:	*Machines retired or sold*	*Proceeds on sale*
Year 3	3	$ 700
Year 4	10	1,200
Year 5	2	100

New machines of this type were not acquired as replacements.

Instructions

a Prepare a cost allocation working paper for Cable Products Company under the composite depreciation method for the five-year period ended December 31, Year 5, during which the assets were used. Use these working paper headings:

		Machinery ledger account		*Accum. Dep. ledger account*		
End of year	*Depreciation expense*	*Debit (Credit)*	*Balance*	*Debit (Credit)*	*Balance*	*Carrying amount*

b Prepare a similar working paper for Cable Products Company, but assume (1) that nothing was received on the sale of the machines and (2) that two machines were retired at the end of Year 3, eleven machines were retired at the end of Year 4, and two machines were retired at the end of Year 5.

c Comment on differences between the results obtained in ***a*** and ***b***.

Pr. 12-7 Selected ledger accounts included in the plant assets section of Lopez Corporation's balance sheet on December 31, Year 8, had the following balances:

Land	$175,000
Land improvements	90,000
Buildings	900,000
Machinery and equipment	850,000

During Year 9, the following transactions were completed:

1 Land was acquired for $125,000 as a potential future building site.

2 A facility consisting of land and buildings was acquired from Chu Company in exchange for 10,000 shares of Lopez's common stock. On the exchange date, Lopez's common stock had a current fair value of $48 a share. The facility was carried in Chu's accounting records on the exchange date at $89,000 for land and $130,000 for buildings. Appraised value on the exchange date for property tax purposes was $120,000 for land and $240,000 for buildings.

3 Machinery and equipment were acquired at a cost of $300,000. Additional costs were incurred as follows:

Freight and unloading	$15,000
Sales taxes	12,000
Installation	25,000

4 Expenditures totalling $80,000 were made for new parking lots, streets, and sidewalks at Lopez's various plant locations. These expenditures had an economic life of 15 years.

5 Machine Q, which had been acquired for $50,000 on January 2, Year 1, was scrapped on June 30, Year 9. Double-declining-balance depreciation based on a 10-year economic life had been recorded.

6 Machine R was sold for $20,000 on July 2, Year 9. The cost of the machine was $36,000 on January 2, Year 6, and it was depreciated under the straight-line method over an economic life of seven years and a net residual value of $1,000.

Instructions

a Prepare an analysis of the changes in each of the following ledger accounts of Lopez Corporation for Year 9:
   1 Land
   2 Land improvements
   3 Buildings
   4 Machinery and equipment
   (Disregard the related accumulated depreciation ledger accounts.)

b List and compute the items in the fact situations that were not used to determine the answer to ***a*** above, showing the pertinent amounts and supporting computations for each item. In addition, indicate where, or if, these items should be included in the financial statements.

Pr. 12-8 On January 2, Year 1, Diggers, Inc., acquired for cash the following:

1 Land costing $1,800,000 with a net residual value of $200,000 and an estimated total mineral ore content of 400,000 tonnes

2 A building on the land costing $600,000 with a net residual value of $100,000 and an economic life of 10 years (disregarding the mineral content of the land)

3 Mining machinery and equipment costing $200,000 with a net residual value of $50,000 and an economic life of five years

Diggers estimated that eight years of mining would exhaust the mineral content of the land. Diggers uses the straight-line method of depreciation, where appropriate, for plant assets.

During Year 1, Diggers mined 22,000 tonnes of ore. On January 2, Year 2, the remaining ore content was estimated at 360,000 tonnes. During Year 2, Diggers mined 42,000 tonnes of ore.

Instructions

Compute the depletion and the depreciation amounts to be included in the cost of ore inventory for Diggers, Inc., for both Year 1 and Year 2. Show supporting computations. Round all amounts to the nearest dollar.

Pr. 12-9 A two-year record of the Equipment ledger account in the accounting records of Stowe Company, which began operations January 2, Year 1, is shown below. Stowe has a policy of taking a full year's depreciation in the year of acquisition and no depreciation in the year of disposal of plant assets.

				Disposals	
Year	*Cost of equipment*	*Economic life (years)*	*Net residual value*	*Year acquired*	*Cost*
1	$110,000	10	20% of cost		
2	84,000	6	20% of cost	1	$20,000

Instructions

Prepare a working paper for Stowe Company showing for the two-year period the additions, disposals, and ending balances for the Equipment ledger account, and for the related Accumulated Depreciation of Equipment account, using the following depreciation methods:

a Straight-line
b Sum-of-the-years'-digits
c Double-declining-balance

Pr. 12-10 On July 2, Year 5, Bayless Company, which has a December 31 fiscal year, established a new manufacturing department that requires several different types of machinery. Bayless uses the sum-of-the-years'-digits method of depreciation and takes a full year's depreciation in the year of acquisition, but no depreciation in the year of disposal, of plant assets. The transactions involving the machines in the new department for a period of three years are as follows.

Year 5

July 2 Acquired the following machines:

Machine No.	*Cost*	*Net residual value*	*Economic life (years)*
100	$40,000	$8,500	6
101	15,300	1,300	7
102	47,500	2,500	5

Year 6

Jan. 2 Acquired machine No. 103 for $60,000. Economic life 10 years; net residual value $5,000.

Year 7

May 1 Sold machine No. 100 for $20,000 and replaced it with machine No. 104, which was acquired for $54,000 and has a net residual value of $10,800 at the end of eight years of economic life.

Year 8

Oct. 1 Exchanged machine No. 102 for a similar new machine (No. 105), paying $43,500 in cash and receiving a trade-in allowance (equal to current fair value) of $15,000. Machine No. 105 has an economic life of 10 years and no net residual value.

Instructions

a Prepare a working paper for Bayless Company showing the computation of depreciation expense for each of the years ended December 31, Years 5, 6, 7, and 8, and the balances in the Machinery ledger account and Accumulated Depreciation of Machinery account on December 31, Year 8.

b Prepare journal entries for Bayless Company to record the sale of machine No. 100 and the trade-in of machine No. 102. Show computation of the carrying amount of these machines at the time of sale or exchange. Any gain or loss is to be recognized consistent with the provisions of ***APB Opinion No. 29***: ''Accounting for Nonmonetary Transactions,'' as summarized in Chapter 11.

Pr. 12-11 Dakota Mining Limited paid $1,850,000 for land containing valuable ore and spent $450,000 in developing the property during Year 1, preparatory to beginning mining activities on January 2, Year 2. Dakota's geologists estimated that the mineral deposit would produce 8 million tonnes of ore over a 15-year period, and it was estimated that the land will have a net residual value of $300,000 after the ore deposit is exhausted.

A record of plant asset expenditures during the last half of Year 1, exclusive of the development costs previously mentioned, follows:

Asset	*Economic life (years)*	*Cost*
Mine buildings	30	$200,000
Railroad and hoisting equipment	20	600,000
Miscellaneous mining equipment	10	250,000

The buildings, railroad, and hoisting equipment could not be removed economically from the mine location, but the miscellaneous mining equipment was moveable and had alternative uses.

Operations during Year 2 are summarized below:

Tonnes of ore mined	1,000,000
Tonnes of ore sold at $5.10 a tonne (FOB at the mine)	950,000
Mining labour and other operating costs (exclusive of depreciation and depletion)	$2,400,000
Selling and administrative expenses	$625,750

Income taxes expense for the year was $492,000.

Instructions

a Prepare an income statement for Dakota Mining Limited for Year 2, showing the computation of depletion and depreciation per tonne of ore mined in a supporting exhibit. Use the straight-line method of depreciation, with no net residual value for the miscellaneous mine equipment. Dakota had 200,000 shares of common stock outstanding during Year 2.

b Early in Year 3, Dakota Mining Limited received an offer from an Indonesian company to purchase 500,000 tonnes of ore at a price of $3.90 a tonne delivered in Indonesia. Dakota estimated that it would cost $1.40 a tonne to ship the ore to Indonesia, and believed that accepting this offer would not affect the domestic price. It was estimated that the cost of acquiring and developing additional ore property had not increased. One-fourth of Dakota's "mining labour and other operating costs" are fixed as long as at least 600,000 tonnes of ore are produced annually. Would you recommend that Dakota Mining accept the offer from the Indonesian company? Present computations to support your conclusion.

Pr. 12-12 City Trucking Company acquired 100 trucks on January 2, Year 1, for $600,000. The controller of City decided to use the group depreciation method for these trucks, and estimated the composite rate at 21% ($126,000 ÷ $600,000 = 0.21) as follows:

Year	*Number of trucks to be retired*	*Cost*	*Net residual value*	*Depreciation base*	*Economic life, years*	*Annual depreciation expense*
1	5	$ 30,000	$ 21,000	$ 9,000	1	$ 9,000
2	20	120,000	72,000	48,000	2	24,000
3	30	180,000	59,400	120,600	3	40,200
4	30	180,000	36,000	144,000	4	36,000
5	15	90,000	6,000	84,000	5	16,800
	100	$600,000	$194,400	$405,600		$126,000

At the end of Year 7, when the last truck had been retired, the controller prepared the following summary of City's actual experience:

Year	*Number of trucks retired*	*Proceeds received on retirement*
1	4	$ 17,200
2	11	32,800
3	28	74,700
4	42	49,600
5	8	5,000
6	5	1,800
7	2	800
	100	$181,900

City had followed group depreciation procedures and recognized no gain or loss when the trucks were retired.

Instructions

a Reconstruct City Trucking Company's Trucks and Accumulated Depreciation of Trucks ledger accounts as they would have appeared had the controller's estimates been realized, and the computed rate of 21% had been used as a basis for recording depreciation. Would the controller's rate have produced accurate results if the assumptions had been correct? Why?

b On the basis of hindsight, that is, the actual record of experience with the 100 trucks, compute the group depreciation rate that should have been used by City Trucking Company. Also determine the group economic life of the trucks.

c Using the rate computed in ***b***, reconstruct City Trucking Company's Trucks and Accumulated Depreciation of Trucks ledger accounts. Explain any balance of the Accumulated Depreciation of Trucks account at the end of Year 7 and state why this balance, if any, differs from the balance of the Accumulated Depreciation of Trucks account obtained in ***a***.

Pr. 12-13 Lido Corporation, a manufacturer of steel products, began operations on October 1, Year 2. Lido's accounting department has begun the depreciation analysis shown on the next page.

You have been asked to assist in completing the foregoing analysis. In addition to ascertaining that the data already in the analysis were correct, you have obtained the following information from Lido's accounting records:

1 Depreciation is computed from the first of the month of acquisition to the first of the month of disposal.

2 Land L and building B were acquired from a predecessor corporation. Lido paid a total of $830,500 for the land and building. At the time of acquisition, the land had an appraised value of $72,000 and the building had an appraised value of $828,000.

3 Land LL was acquired on October 2, Year 2, in exchange for 3,000 shares of

LIDO CORPORATION
Depreciation Analysis
For Years Ended September 30, Year 3 and 4

Assets	*Acquisition date*	*Cost*	*Net residual value*	*Depreciation method*	*Estimated life (years)*	*Depreciation for year ended Sept. 30:*	
						Year 3	*Year 4*
Land L	Oct. 1, Year 2	$ (a)	*	*	*	*	*
Building B	Oct. 1, Year 2	(b)	$64,060	Straight-line	(c)	$14,000	$ (d)
Land LL	Oct. 2, Year 2	(e)	*	*	*	*	*
Building BB	(Under construction)	210,000 to date	None	Straight-line	30	None	(f)
Donated equipment	Oct. 2, Year 2	(g)	2,000	150%-declining-balance	10	(h)	(i)
Machine M	Oct. 2, Year 2	(j)	5,500	Sum-of-the-years'-digits	10	(k)	(l)
Machine MM	Oct. 1, Year 3	(m)	None	Straight-line	12	None	(n)

*Not applicable.

Lido's common stock. On the date of acquisition, the common stock had a book value of $5 a share and a current fair value of $25 a share. During October, Year 2, Lido paid $10,400 to demolish an existing building on this land to construct a new building (building BB).

4 Construction of building BB began on October 1, Year 3. By September 30, Year 4, Lido had paid $210,000 of the estimated total construction costs of $300,000. Estimated completion and occupancy date was July, Year 5.

5 Equipment was donated to Lido by the shareholders. An independent appraisal of the equipment on the date of donation placed the current fair value at $16,000.

6 The total cost of $110,000 for machine M included installation costs of $550 and normal repairs and maintenance of $11,000 incurred through January 31, Year 4. Machine M was sold on February 1, Year 4.

7 On October 1, Year 3, machine MM was acquired under a deferred payment contract requiring a down payment of $3,760 and 10 annual instalments of $4,000 each beginning October 1, Year 4. The current fair rate of interest was 8%. The following data are available from present-value tables:

Present value of 1 at 8%	
10 periods	0.463
11 periods	0.429
15 periods	0.315

Present value of ordinary annuity of 1 at 8%	
10 rents	6.710
11 rents	7.139
15 rents	8.559

Instructions

For each lettered item in the foregoing analysis for Lido Corporation, supply the correct amount. Round each amount to the nearest dollar. Do not recopy the analysis, but show supporting computations.

c h a p t e r 1 3

INTANGIBLE ASSETS

NATURE OF INTANGIBLE ASSETS

The basic characteristic that distinguishes intangible assets from tangible assets is that the former are not physical in nature. In legal terminology this distinction is maintained consistently, the term ***intangibles*** being applied to all nonphysical properties, including cash, accounts and notes receivable, and investments in corporate securities. Intangible assets for financial accounting include patents, copyrights, trademarks, trade names, secret formulas, organization costs, franchises, licences, and goodwill (the excess of cost of an acquired business enterprise over the current fair value of identifiable net assets acquired).

One reason for distinguishing between tangible and intangible assets is that it often is difficult to identify intangible assets. Because one can ''stub a toe'' on a tangible asset, it is relatively easy to know when a tangible asset exists. Evidence of the existence of intangible assets may be vague, and the relationship between costs incurred and the emergence of an asset may be difficult to establish objectively. The economic value of both tangible and intangible assets is dependent on their ability to generate future revenue and earnings, and this often is as difficult to measure for tangible assets as it is for intangibles. However, physical existence is not a guarantee of economic value (obsolete machinery, for example), nor does the absence of physical existence preclude economic value (the Listerine formula, for example). For some business enterprises, the value of intangible assets may exceed the value of their tangible assets.

Cost of Intangible Assets

A business enterprise may acquire intangible assets from others, or it may develop internally certain types of intangible assets. The general objectives in accounting for intangible assets are comparable with those for tangible assets; the initial cost is determined and deducted from the revenue that the assets help to generate. A significant and permanent decline in the value of an intangible asset is written off as an expense in the year the decline occurs. Generally, such write-offs are not considered extraordinary items.[1]

When an intangible asset is acquired from others, its cost may be measured with little difficulty. It may be necessary to estimate the value of nonmonetary assets given in exchange for intangible assets, or to allocate the total cost among various assets acquired as a group. The principles used in dealing with these problems, described in Chapter 11 for plant assets, also are applicable to intangible assets. Accounting for intangible assets ***developed*** by business enterprises, however, is still a rather complex task because of the difficulty of identifying the development costs to be capitalized, as required by section 3450.21 of the ***CICA Handbook***. The discussion on research and development costs is presented in a later section of this chapter.

In the United States, the accounting profession requires that costs incurred in the in-house development of most intangible assets be immediately recognized as expenses. In 1970, the Accounting Principles Board of the AICPA required the costs of developing, maintaining, or restoring intangible assets that are not specifically identifiable (such as goodwill) to be expensed when incurred.[2] Four years later, the Financial Accounting Standards Board wrestled with one of the most difficult problems related to intangible assets, namely, the accounting for research and development costs, and reached the conclusion that "all research and development costs... shall be charged to expense when incurred."[3]

Amortization of Intangible Assets

The process of systematically writing off the cost of intangible assets is called ***amortization***. For many years, accountants approached the question of amortization by classifying intangible assets into two categories: (1) those having a ***limited*** term of existence, such as patents, and (2) those with an ***indefinite*** or ***unlimited*** term of existence, such as goodwill. Those with a limited economic life were amortized; those with an indefinite or unlimited economic life were maintained intact until they became worthless, at which time they were written off. This gave management of business enterprises considerable leeway in accounting for intangible assets.

In Canada, with the exception of the areas of goodwill and of capitalized development costs, the management of a business enterprise has the sole responsibility for deciding whether or not amortization should be taken. Section 3080 of the ***CICA Handbook*** only requires that, ***if*** amortization is taken for the period, then that amount should be disclosed, and if amortization has been deducted in arriving at the carrying value of the intangible asset, then this deduction should be

1 CICA, ***CICA Handbook*** (Toronto), sec. 3450.32.

2 AICPA, ***APB Opinion No. 17:*** "Intangible Assets" (New York: 1970), p. 339.

3 FASB, ***FASB Statement No. 2:*** "Accounting for Research and Development Costs" (Stamford: 1974), p. 6.

disclosed.[4] But even when amortization is required, management still has a great deal of flexibility over the length of the amortization period. In the case of goodwill, the period of amortization is its estimated useful life or 40 years, whichever is shorter.[5] For capitalized development cost, no maximum period for amortization is stipulated.[6]

In the United States, the Accounting Principles Board concluded "that the value of intangible assets at any one date eventually disappears and that the recorded costs of intangible assets should be amortized by systematic charges to income over the periods estimated to be benefited."[7] Factors that should be considered in estimating the economic life of an intangible asset include:[8]

1 Legal, regulatory, or contractual provisions when they place a limit on the maximum economic life

2 Provisions for renewal or extension of rights or privileges covered by specific intangible assets

3 Effects of obsolescence, customer demand, competition, rate of technological change, and other economic factors

4 Possibility that economic life of intangible assets may be related to life expectancies of certain groups of employees

5 Expected actions of competitors, regulatory bodies, and others

6 An apparently unlimited economic life of an intangible asset may in fact be only indefinite, and future benefits cannot be reasonably projected

7 An intangible asset may be a composite of many individual factors with diverse economic lives

The period of amortization for intangible assets is determined after a careful review of all relevant factors. This review enables management of a business enterprise to make a reasonable estimate of the economic life of most intangible assets. According to ***APB Opinion No. 17***, the period of amortization for ***any*** intangible asset ***should not exceed 40 years***, and if a longer economic life is expected, the amortization period should be 40 years. No minimum period for amortization was specified in ***APB Opinion No. 17***.

In our opinion the maximum period of amortization of 40 years is much too long for most intangible assets. During the current era of rapid technological innovations and changes in consumer tastes, few intangible assets retain their usefulness for 40 years. Consequently, many business enterprises probably overstate their net income by amortizing intangible assets over the maximum period

4 CICA, ***CICA Handbook***, sec. 3080.03–.04.

5 CICA, ***CICA Handbook***, sec. 1580.58.

6 CICA, ***CICA Handbook***, sec. 3450.28 and .32.

7 AICPA, ***APB Opinion No. 17***, pp. 339–340.

8 AICPA, ***APB Opinion No. 17***, p. 340.

allowed. Conversely, mandatory amortization of some types of intangible assets that tend to increase in value over time (such as licences to operate radio or television stations) may be unrealistic. Amortization of these intangible assets (even over a 40-year period) may result in an understatement of total assets, shareholders' equity, and net income.

The accounting procedures for the amortization of intangible assets are comparable to those employed for depreciable plant assets. The cost of intangible assets should be amortized in a systematic manner over their estimated economic lives. Common practice is to use the ***straight-line*** method of amortization, unless management of the business enterprise presents a convincing case that some other systematic method is more appropriate. For example, if there is evidence that the value of services provided by an intangible asset in early accounting periods of its economic life is significantly higher than the value in later years, an appropriate accelerated method of amortization may be used.

The amortization of intangible assets may be credited directly to the asset ledger account, leaving a balance representing the unamortized cost. This is a matter of custom rather than accounting logic. For example, the journal entry to record the amortization of patents in the amount of $4,200 is illustrated below:

Recording periodic amortization

Patent Amortization Expense	4,200	
Patents (or Accumulated Amortization of Patents)		4,200
To record amortization of patents.		

The amortization of intangible assets may be either a factory overhead cost or an operating expense, depending on the nature and use of the assets. For example, the amortization of a patent on a manufacturing process is included in factory overhead costs, and the amortization of a trademark used to promote products is a selling expense.

Disclosure of the method and the period of amortization for intangible assets, as well as the amount of amortization for the accounting period, is required, usually in a note to the financial statements. The period used to amortize intangible assets is reviewed continually to determine whether changing circumstances require a change in the estimate of economic life. When a change is made in the estimated economic life of an intangible asset, the unamortized cost is allocated over the ***remaining economic life*** of the asset. The remaining economic life may be longer or shorter than the original estimate. A review of the amortization policy also may indicate that a material amount of unamortized cost of intangible assets should be written off. However, a single loss year or even several loss years do not necessarily justify a write-off of all or a large part of the unamortized cost of an intangible asset.

IDENTIFIABLE INTANGIBLE ASSETS

Certain intangible assets, such as patents, copyrights, and franchises, are identifiable as distinct and separable property rights; others, such as goodwill, are difficult to identify. The more common identifiable intangible assets are discussed in the following sections.

Patents

A patent is a grant by the federal government giving the owner the exclusive right to manufacture and sell a particular invention for a period of 17 years. Patent rights may be assigned in part or in their entirety. Frequently, licensing contracts require payments of royalties to the owner of a patent for the right to use a patented innovation or to manufacture a patented product. Legally, patents may not be renewed, but in practice their economic lives often are extended by obtaining patents on slight variations and improvements near the end of the legal life of the original patent.

A patent has economic value only if the protection it affords against competition results in increased earnings through an ability to operate at a lower cost, to manufacture and sell a product, or to obtain a higher price for goods and services. The economic life of a patent generally is much shorter than its legal life; therefore, amortization should be recognized over the period of usefulness.

If a patent is acquired from others, its cost is measured by the acquisition price plus any incidental costs. The acquisition of a patent from another party is recorded as follows:

Journal entry to record acquisition of an intangible asset

Patents	60,000	
Cash		60,000
To record acquisition of patent.		

If a patent is developed as a result of a business enterprise's research and development efforts, the cost assigned to the patent includes the direct legal costs and fees incurred in obtaining the patent and those development costs of the patent that meet the specific criterion established by Section 3450.21 of the ***CICA Handbook***. Any research cost applicable to a patent (or patentable) product are expensed when incurred, as are most of the development costs.

A patent does not include automatic protection against infringement; patent owners must prosecute those who attempt to infringe their patents and defend against infringement suits brought by owners of similar patents. The cost of successfully establishing the legal validity of a patent should be capitalized (added to the carrying amount of the patent), because such cost will benefit revenue over the remaining economic life of the patent. If the legal decision is favourable, legal costs may be paid by the losing party; if the legal decision is adverse, both the amount of damages paid and the unamortized cost of the patent should be written off, because no further economic benefits can be expected to result from the patent.

The right to use a patent owned by others under a licensing contract is not recorded as an intangible asset, unless a lump-sum payment is made at the outset of such a contract. The periodic royalty payments are recorded as factory overhead costs or as operating expense, depending on the use made of the patent.

Copyrights

A copyright is a grant by the federal government giving an author, creator, or artist the exclusive right to publish, sell, or otherwise control literary or artistic products for the life of the author plus 50 years. A business enterprise may obtain the rights granted under copyrights by paying royalties, by acquisition of the copyright from the author, or by obtaining a copyright on a literary or artistic product developed by the enterprise. The problems that arise in measuring the cost of copyrights are comparable with those discussed in connection with patents.

Although a copyright has a long legal life, its economic life is limited to the period for which a commercial market exists for the publication. In order to achieve a proper matching of costs and revenue, copyright costs are amortized against the total revenue that is anticipated from the copyright. Because of the difficulty encountered in estimating copyright revenue and because experience indicates that such revenue generally results over only a few years, copyrights typically are amortized over a relatively short period of time. On occasion, copyrights thought to be worthless may bounce back to life with renewed vigour. An outstanding example is old movies: Their production and copyright costs previously had been fully amortized, but these films became extremely valuable with the development of television. However, this increase in the value of copyrights was not reflected in the balance sheets of motion picture producers.

Licences and Contracts

Many business enterprises expend considerable amounts to obtain licences to engage in certain types of business activities or to acquire rights to use copyrighted materials owned by others. For example, network-affiliation contracts and film rights probably are the most valuable assets of an enterprise engaged in the broadcasting industry. A network-affiliated station is more valuable than an independent station because of network-supplied programming. The rights to show old movies are an important source of revenue for television broadcasters.

The cost of a licence or a contract is amortized over the accounting periods expected to benefit. A network-affiliation contract is amortized over the period specified in the contract and film rights acquired by a televison station generally are amortized on an accelerated basis, because first showings generate more advertising revenue than reruns.[9] If a licence or a contract is cancelled or for any reason becomes worthless, any unamortized cost is recognized as an expense.

Trademarks, Trade Names, and Secret Formulas

Trademarks, trade names, secret formulas, and various distinctive labels are important means of building and maintaining customer acceptance for many products. The value of such product identification and differentiation stems from the ability of the business enterprise to sell products in large volume and at prices higher than those for unbranded products.

9 FASB, *FASB Statement No. 63:* ''Financial Reporting by Broadcasters'' (Stamford: 1982), pp. 2–3.

Trademarks, trade names, secret formulas, and labels are property rights that may be licensed, assigned, or sold. Their economic lives continue as long as they are used, and their cost should be amortized over their economic lives.

The value of trademarks, trade names, or secret formulas often is enhanced as the enterprise succeeds in building consumer confidence in the quality of products distributed under a particular brand name. Presumably this growth in value is not without cost, because enterprises spend large sums for advertising and otherwise promoting trade names. The relationship between promotional expenditures and the increase in the value of a trade name is nebulous; therefore, accountants do not assign a cost to this intangible asset, except when it is acquired from another party.

Organization Costs

The organization of a corporate business enterprise usually requires a considerable amount of time, effort, and cost. Compensation must be paid to those who conceive, investigate, and promote the idea; legal fees relating to drafting of the corporate charter, article of incorporation, and bylaws, accounting fees, and incorporation fees are incurred; and costs may be incurred in conducting initial meetings of shareholders and directors. All these expenditures are made with the expectation that they will contribute to future revenue. Therefore, the cost of organizing a corporate enterprise logically should be treated as an asset and not as an expense. However, items such as operating losses incurred by a corporation in the early years, bond discount and issuance costs, large initial advertising expenditures, or issuance costs on common stock, should not be included in organization costs. Expenditures incurred in connection with the issuance of shares of common stock, such as professional fees and printing costs, generally should be deducted from the proceeds received for the stock. However, although this method is theoretically correct, such share issue costs are usually included in organization costs. One possible reason for this practice may be the fact that the income tax department permits a corporation to amortize 50% of organization costs at an annual rate of 10% on the declining balance. Similar expenditures relating to the issuance of bonds or other debt instruments are deferred and amortized over the term of the debt.

Theoretically, the costs of organization have an economic life as long as the corporate enterprise remains a going concern. Because the life of most large corporations is unlimited, organization costs may be viewed as a permanent asset that will continue in existence until the corporation goes out of business. Despite the logic of this position, organization costs generally are amortized over an arbitrary short period.

Franchises

A *franchise* is a right or privilege received by a business enterprise for the exclusive right to engage in business in a specified geographic area, as in the case of Kentucky Fried Chicken and McDonald's restaurants. The franchise may be acquired from a governmental unit or from another enterprise. For example, public utilities generally receive a franchise from provincial or federal agencies and are subject to specific regulations; a retailer may obtain an exclusive right from a manufacturer to sell certain products in a specified territory; an operator of a restaurant may obtain the right to utilize trade names and recipes developed by another enterprise; and a cable television company may obtain exclusive rights for television programming in one or more communities.

Some franchises granted by manufacturers or retail chains (***franchisors***) may cost substantial amounts. The amount paid for such a franchise is recorded by the ***franchisee*** as an intangible asset and amortized over its expected economic life. The proceeds received by franchisors are recognized as revenue when the contractual commitments to franchisees are fulfilled.[10] If the right to operate under a franchise is limited to 10 years, for example, the amortization period should not exceed 10 years. Although some franchises prove to be worthless in a short period of time, others may increase substantially in value if the location and product (or service) prove successful.

Leasehold Costs

An existing lease right and a lump-sum payment to acquire rights to explore for oil and minerals on land are valuable property rights that may be included with intangible assets in the balance sheet. However, because such assets represent rights to use tangible assets, they may be included under plant assets in the balance sheet.

UNIDENTIFIABLE INTANGIBLE ASSETS: GOODWILL

Thus far we have discussed the major types of identifiable intangible assets. However, the earning power of most prosperous business enterprises is attributable to a variety of intangible factors that cannot be specifically identified. Accountants, business executives, and laywers often refer to these factors collectively as goodwill.

In ordinary usage the term ***goodwill*** is associated with kindly feeling or benevolence. However, in business and law goodwill has a different meaning. The most acceptable evidence of goodwill is the ability of a business enterprise to earn a rate of return on net assets (owners' investment) in excess of a normal rate for the industry in which the enterprise operates. ***Goodwill is the difference between the value of a business enterprise as a whole and the sum of the current fair values of its identifiable tangible and intangible net assets.*** Goodwill is in essence a ''master valuation account'' — the missing link that reconciles the current fair value of an enterprise as a going concern with the current fair value of the sum of its identifiable parts.

10 For a complete discussion on this topic, see the ***CICA Handbook***'s accounting guideline ''Franchise Fee Revenue'' and ***FASB Statement No. 45:*** ''Accounting for Franchise Fee Revenue'' (Stamford: 1981).

Nature of Goodwill

The first procedure toward an understanding of goodwill is to estimate the current fair value of a business enterprise as a going concern. The current fair value of the enterprise may be greater than the amount of identifiable tangible and intangible net assets, because of the presence of unidentifiable intangible assets. A simple example may help to clarify this point. Assume that Parke Limited is offered for sale and that the balance sheet below is used as a basis for negotiating a fair price:

Net assets (shareholders' equity) is $400,000

PARKE LIMITED
Balance Sheet
December 31, Year 10

Cash and receivables	$130,000	Liabilities	$100,000
Inventories	90,000	Common stock, no par	250,000
Plant assets (net)	280,000	Retained earnings	150,000
Total assets	$500,000	Total liabilities & shareholders' equity	$500,000

We shall assume that Parke Limited is expected to earn an average net income of $60,000 a year indefinitely in the future. Because the current fair value of net assets depends directly on the earning power of the assets, we may value Parke as a going concern, without reference to its balance sheet, by determining the present value of future earnings of $60,000 a year. A logical way of appraising this is in terms of the rate of return on alternative investment opportunities of comparable risk. We shall assume this rate to be 10%. If it is possible to earn a 10% return on similar investments, the current value of the prospect of receiving $60,000 a year ***in perpetuity*** may be computed by determining the amount which must be invested at 10% to earn an annual return of $60,000. This procedure is called ***capitalization of income***, and the result in this case is a value for the net assets of Parke of $600,000 ($60,000 ÷ 0.10 = $600,000), compared with a carrying amount of only $400,000 ($500,000 − $100,000 = $400,000).

If the net assets of Parke are worth $600,000, why are they reported in the balance sheet at only $400,000? One reason is that Parke's accounting records do not reflect the current fair value of identifiable net assets. Inventories and plant assets, for example, might be worth considerably more than their carrying amounts, and liabilities might be overstated. If these discrepancies are identified during the negotiations, appropriate adjustments should be made.

It is possible, however, that the carrying amount of each asset and liability included in the balance sheet closely approximates its current fair value, but still Parke's net assets are worth $200,000 more than their carrying amount. Is this an accounting exception to the principle that the whole must equal the sum of its parts, or is it possible that some of the parts are not included in the balance sheet? The latter is the more likely explanation, and it is apparent that the missing parts are those characteristics of Parke Limited that enable it to earn $60,000 a year (10%

of $600,000) rather than $40,000 a year (10% of $400,000). Parke apparently has intangible assets not included in its balance sheet. Any of the identifiable intangible assets previously discussed in this chapter are possible sources of the unexplained $200,000 in the current fair value of Parke as a going concern.

For purposes of this illustration, we assume that Parke has a patent worth $50,000 that is not included in the balance sheet, because it was developed internally or because it had been fully amortized. After all identifiable assets, both tangible and intangible, have been appraised, only $150,000 ($200,000 – $50,000) remains unexplained, and we have isolated the ***imputed value*** of all unidentifiable intangible assets, that is, ***goodwill***. Goodwill exists as an asset only because it is impossible to identify separately all sources of the prospective earning power of a business enterprise. This analysis may be summarized as follows for Parke Limited:

Imputed value of goodwill

Current fair value of total assets		$700,000*
Less: Current fair value of tangible net assets	$400,000	
Current fair value of patent not included in the accounting records	50,000	
Liabilities	100,000	550,000
Unidentifiable intangible asset (goodwill)		$150,000

*$600,000 net assets + $100,000 liabilities = $700,000.

If patents of $50,000 and goodwill of $150,000 were added to the assets of Parke Limited, the carrying amount of its ***net assets*** would be $600,000 (assets of $700,000 less liabilities of $100,000). Therefore, if Parke earned $60,000, its earnings no longer would be large in relation to the carrying amount of its net assets. Thus, the ability to earn a ***superior rate of return*** on net assets that ***do not include*** goodwill is evidence that goodwill exists; the ability to earn a normal rate of return on assets that ***include*** the goodwill and all identifiable intangible assets is evidence of the existence of goodwill in the amount computed.

Negative Goodwill

Goodwill, as we have defined it, may be either positive or negative in amount. Suppose, for example, that the prospective earnings of Parke Limited had been estimated at only $36,000 a year indefinitely into the future and that its identifiable net assets are fairly stated at $400,000. On a 10% yield basis, the capitalized value of these earnings is $360,000 ($36,000 ÷ 0.10 = $360,000), and it is evident that the carrying amount of the net assets exceeds the current fair value of Parke as a whole by $40,000 ($400,000 – $360,000 = $40,000). This $40,000 is termed ***negative goodwill***.

When the earning potential of a business enterprise is such that the enterprise as a whole is worth less than its net assets, the owners would be better off to dispose of the assets piecemeal, pay the liabilities, and terminate the enterprise. In reality this may not be done because of concern for the welfare of employees, willingness of the owners to continue operating an unprofitable enterprise, optimism about future prospects, or other considerations. Because the presence of negative goodwill suggests that liquidation is the best course of action, positive goodwill is more likely to be found in going concerns than negative goodwill. Although negative goodwill exists in many unprofitable enterprises, it is not isolated and reported in the balance sheet; the only evidence of its existence is a ***low rate of earnings*** on the net assets of the enterprises.

If an enterprise with negative goodwill is sold as a going concern, the value assigned to the net assets acquired by the acquirer should not exceed the ***cost actually paid***. The total current fair value of identifiable assets acquired less the liabilities assumed occasionally may exceed the price paid for the acquired enterprise. According to the ***CICA Handbook*** section 1580, such an excess over cost should be allocated to reduce the values assigned to identifiable nonmonetary assets in determining their ''fair values.''[11]

Recording of Goodwill (Excess of Cost over Net Assets Acquired)

The high degree of certainty about the future assumed in the measurement of goodwill of Parke Limited in the foregoing example does not exist in the real world. Assessing the earnings potential of a business enterprise is an uncertain process, and any resulting estimate of goodwill is a matter of judgement and opinion.

In the face of this uncertainty, accountants have adopted a conservative stance with respect to goodwill. It is generally accepted that goodwill should be recorded in the accounting records only when its amount is substantiated by an arm's-length transaction. Because goodwill cannot be either sold or acquired separately, accounting recognition of goodwill is restricted to those occasions in which the entire net assets of a business enterprise, or a substantial interest in the net assets representing a clearly defined segment of a business enterprise, are acquired and goodwill may be established with reasonable objectivity.[12] In such cases goodwill frequently is labelled as ***Excess of Cost over Fair Value Net Assets Acquired***.

Limiting the recording of goodwill to ***purchased goodwill*** is admittedly not an ideal solution to the problem. Internally developed goodwill actually may exist in a business enterprise and not be recorded; conversely, goodwill acquired in the past may appear in the accounting records when there is no current evidence (in terms of earning power) that it actually exists. The financial statements of business enterprises that have changed ownership will appear to be inconsistent with those of enterprises that have had a continuing existence. For example, assume that Parke Limited, discussed earlier, has identifiable net assets of $450,000 and that a new company is formed to acquire its net assets for $600,000 cash. The

11 CICA, ***CICA Handbook***, sec. 1580.44.

12 Cases in which goodwill is recorded in connection with changes in owners of partnerships and in the preparation of consolidated financial statements are presented in advanced accounting courses. Our discussion at this point is limited to goodwill arising out of the ***purchase*** of the entire business enterprise for cash. When a going business enterprise is acquired in exchange for shares of common stock, the transaction may be accounted for as a ***pooling of interests***. Goodwill may be recorded in a purchase-type transaction, but not in a pooling of interests.

beginning balance sheet of the new company would include goodwill of $150,000. Is there any justification for a rule that prohibits the recording of $150,000 goodwill in the accounting records of Parke but permits the inclusion of this amount in the balance sheet of the new company?

On balance, an affirmative answer is warranted. Specific assets represent resources in which the capital of a business enterprise is invested, to the extent that it has been possible to determine them. The periodic adjustment of these asset valuations by a variable amount labelled ''goodwill'' to a level consistent with the present value of future earnings not only would be highly subjective but also would obscure the significant relationship between actual investment and earning power. If $150,000 of goodwill had been recorded by Parke, not only would there be a serious question as to the validity of this amount, but also the high level of earnings on investment that Parke had been able to attain would be concealed. The investment of the new owners, however, was not $450,000, but $600,000. The new owners paid $150,000 for future superior earnings, and if only $150,000 of superior earnings should materialize, this amount will not represent income to the new owners but a ***recovery of their investment***. The position that goodwill should be recorded only when it is evidenced by an acquisition appears to be consistent with the accounting concept of reliability and the valuation principle.

Estimate of Goodwill

The price to be paid for a business enterprise is established as the result of bargaining between independent parties. The bargaining process includes the possible existence of goodwill. The amount of goodwill ***to be recorded***, however, is determined after the terms of the contract are set by deducting the current fair value of all identifiable net assets from the total acquisition price. Accountants are interested in the process of estimating goodwill because they often are called upon to aid in establishing the current fair value of an enterprise at the time of negotiations for the acquisition or sale of an enterprise and in court cases.

Procedures generally required to estimate the current fair value of a business enterprise, and thus the amount of goodwill, are listed below:

1. Estimate the current fair value of all identifiable tangible and intangible assets of the enterprise, and deduct from this total the amount of all liabilities. The difference is the current fair value of the ***identifiable net assets*** of the enterprise.
2. Forecast the average annual earnings that the enterprise ***expects to earn*** in future years with the use of its present resources.
3. Choose an appropriate rate of return to estimate the normal annual earnings the enterprise ***should earn*** on its identifiable net assets.
4. Compute the amount of expected annual ***superior earnings***, if any.
5. Capitalize the expected annual superior earnings, if any, at an appropriate rate (or rates) of return to estimate the present value of such earnings. ***The present capitalized value of any expected annual superior earnings is the estimated value of goodwill for the enterprise.***

In the following sections, an estimate of goodwill is developed for Reed Corporation (which is for sale) to serve as a basis for a discussion of the problems that arise in connection with each of the foregoing procedures.

Estimate of the Current Fair Value of Identifiable Net Assets

Because carrying amounts and current fair values of assets seldom correspond, an appraisal of identifiable assets is necessary to establish the current fair value of the business enterprise (excluding goodwill) and to identify the assets that generate the earnings of the enterprise.

The fair values of current assets, such as cash and accounts receivable, usually approximate their carrying amounts. Inventories, if verified by a physical inventory and priced on a first-in, first-out or average-cost basis, also may be reasonably stated. Last-in, first-out inventories, however, probably are stated in terms of costs incurred many years earlier and should be adjusted to current fair value. The carrying amounts of plant assets are not likely to approximate current fair values. Various methods of indirect valuation may be employed to appraise such assets on a going-concern basis. The current fair value of all identifiable intangible assets should be estimated, even if these assets do not appear in the accounting records. The liabilities of the business enterprise should be reviewed and measured at present value, and any unrecorded liabilities should be estimated and recorded. Liabilities that will not be assumed by the new owners are disregarded unless payment from present assets is contemplated before the enterprise changes ownership. Identifiable assets at current fair values, less the present or current fair value of liabilities to be assumed by the new owners, is the adjusted amount (estimated current fair value) of identifiable net assets for purposes of estimating the value of goodwill.

The assumed data for Reed Company shown in the following table illustrate the process of estimating the current fair value of identifiable net assets of a business enterprise.

Data for estimates of goodwill

REED CORPORATION
Carrying Amount and Current Fair Value of Identifiable Net Assets
December 31, Year 10

Items	*Carrying amount*	*Adjustments*	*Estimated current fair value*
Cash, accounts receivable, and short-term prepayments	$142,000	$ (2,000)	$140,000
Inventories (last-in, first-out)	178,000	42,000	220,000
Plant assets (net)	480,000	120,000	600,000
Patents and secret formulas		30,000	30,000
Total identifiable assets	$800,000	$190,000	$990,000
Less: Liabilities	160,000	10,000	170,000
Identifiable net assets	$640,000	$180,000	$820,000

Forecast of Expected Average Annual Earnings

The aggregate value of a business enterprise depends on its future earnings, not on its past earnings. Thus, the key procedure in an estimate of the current fair value of an enterprise is a forecast of its future earnings, a process which, unfortunately, is never more than an intelligent guess. Because the immediate past history of an enterprise ordinarily provides the best available evidence and is most relevant, the usual procedure is to compute the average annual earnings of an enterprise during the past three to six years and to project them into the future, adjusting for any changing conditions that may be foreseen. The estimate of future conditions and earnings generally is made by the parties to the transaction and not by accountants. A single year's performance clearly is not a sufficient basis for judgement; however, little may be gained by reaching too far into the past, because both the internal and the external conditions influencing business operations may have changed significantly.

In the compilation of the past earnings record suitable for estimating future earnings, two points should be considered:

1 We are not interested in establishing what past earnings were, but in learning what past experience tells us about probable future earnings.

2 Our objective is to obtain an estimate of future earnings that is consistent with the adjusted current fair values of specific identifiable tangible and intangible assets and liabilities.

It seldom is possible to obtain satisfactory data by computing an average of past reported earnings. A more reasonable approach is to work from actual revenue and expense amounts, because changes in revenue and expenses are likely to be related to projected economic and operating conditions. The effect on earnings of a 10% increase in revenue and a 15% increase in operating expenses, for example, may have to be determined. Past data should be adjusted for changes in the value of assets. For example, if inventories and equipment are understated in terms of current fair values, adjustments of past cost of goods sold and depreciation expense must be made. Extraordinary items generally are omitted from past earnings. In view of the subjectivity of estimates and income measurement, immaterial adjustments may be disregarded.

In the evaluation of an average of past data, particular attention must be given to ***significant trends***. For example, two business enterprises may have the same five-year average sales, but if the sales of one enterprise have increased in each of the past five years, while the sales of the other have declined steadily, the average sales amounts of the two enterprises should be interpreted differently.

An important point, often overlooked in the adjustment of past earnings in the light of future expectations, is that improvements in earnings expected as a result of the efforts of new owners and management should be distinguished carefully from prospective improvements that are related to existing conditions. If the acquirer of a business enterprise expects to make changes in management, production methods, products, and marketing techniques to increase earnings in the future, these changes should not be considered in the valuation of the enterprise because they will flow from the efforts of the new owners. However, the final price paid for goodwill in any transaction is a matter of bargaining between the acquirer and the seller.

The working paper below is a continuation of the Reed Corporation example. It represents an assumed computation on December 31, Year 10, of estimated future earnings, based upon an average of the results experienced over the past five years. This estimate might be interpreted by the prospective acquirer to indicate a probable range of future annual earnings for Reed of, say, between $90,000 and $120,000 a year. However, for illustrative purposes, we use the amount of $116,000.

Computation of estimated average future earnings

REED CORPORATION
Estimate of Average Future Earnings
December 31, Year 10

Revenue:		
Average annual revenue for past five years, which is expected to be typical of future years (extraordinary items have been excluded)		$920,000
Expenses:		
Average cost of goods sold and operating expenses for past five years, excluding depreciation expense and income taxes expense	$635,600	
Add: Anticipated annual increase in wages and fringe benefits expense as a result of a new union contract	45,800	
Less: Average of the five-year increase in inventory valuation not included in the last-in, first-out basis of pricing inventories ($42,000 ÷ 5)	(8,400)	
Depreciation and amortization:		
Average depreciation expense on carrying amounts of assets	24,000	
Add: Increase in depreciation expense on the basis of current fair value (25% increase in value)	6,000	
Amortization expense of patents and secret formulas, not previously carried in the accounting records ($30,000 divided by the economic life of 6 years)	5,000	708,000
Expected average future earnings before income taxes		$212,000
Less: Estimated income taxes expense		96,000
Estimated average future earnings		$116,000

Normal Rate of Return

The rate of return used to capitalize future earnings and to separate superior earnings from ordinary earnings is determined by the risks and investment alternatives involved. The objective is to approximate the rate necessary to attract capital to the business enterprise under review, given the existing risk conditions. The cost of capital, as other costs, varies in relation to a variety of factors. The primary cause of differences in the rate of return necessary to attract capital to a specific investment is the amount of risk involved.

Data on average earnings rates for enterprises in particular industries are available in financial services, trade association studies, and government publications. Care should be exercised in the use of such data to be sure that they are applied to comparable situations; for example, that the earnings rate consistently is assumed to be either before or after income taxes. We assume for purposes of illustration that a reasonable normal rate of return for Reed Corporation is 10% ***after income taxes***.

Estimate of Future Superior Earnings

The amount of estimated future superior earnings may be defined as the amount of earnings expected in excess of normal earnings on the current fair value of identifiable tangible and intangible net assets.

All variables necessary to compute the estimated future superior earnings of Reed Corporation have been discussed and now may be illustrated. The current fair value of Reed's identifiable net assets is $820,000 (see data on page 613), and its average future earnings are estimated at $116,000. Because a 10% after-tax rate of return is sufficient to attract an investment in Reed, its estimated future superior earnings may be computed as follows:

Superior earnings: the ultimate source of goodwill

Estimated average future earnings	$116,000
Less: 10% return on current fair value of identifiable net assets ($820,000 × 0.10)	82,000
Estimated future superior earnings	$ 34,000

This computation shows that $82,000 ($820,000 × 0.10 = $82,000) a year is necessary to support a valuation of $820,000 for the identifiable net assets of Reed Corporation. Because Reed's prospects are for earnings in excess of $82,000, the source of this excess earning power must be the unidentifiable intangible assets (goodwill) that enable Reed to earn a higher-than-normal rate of return.

Estimate of Present Value of Superior Earnings—The Final Procedure

A number of different methods may be used to value the estimated future superior earnings, and thus determine an estimate of goodwill. We will illustrate four of them.

Method 1: Estimated future superior earnings are capitalized at the normal rate of return. One assumption is that the superior earnings of $34,000 a year, as determined above, will continue unimpaired into the future and that this prospect is attributable entirely to the existing resources of Reed Corporation. The annual superior earnings are ***capitalized*** to answer the following question: How much capital should be invested if the annual superior return on the investment is $34,000 in perpetuity, and the desired rate of return is 10% a year? Under this approach, goodwill is estimated at $340,000 as follows:

What objection do you see to this approach?

Value of estimated annual average earnings of $116,000 capitalized at 10% in perpetuity ($116,000 ÷ 0.10)	$1,160,000
Less: Estimated current fair value of identifiable net assets	820,000
Estimated amount of goodwill	$ 340,000
Alternative computation:	
Value of estimated future superior earnings capitalized at 10% in perpetuity (goodwill) ($34,000 ÷ 0.10)	$ 340,000

There are serious flaws in the assumptions on which this method rests. It may be reasonable to forecast that a business enterprise will earn a 10% return on its net assets over a long period of time, but the assumption that superior earning power will persist in perpetuity in the face of competitive pressures and the hazards of free enterprise is optimistic, to say the least. Furthermore, even if superior earnings do continue for a business enterprise, it seldom is possible to trace their origin to conditions that existed at the time of acquisition of the enterprise. The forces that erode superior earnings are such that a persistent ability to earn a higher-than-normal rate of return ultimately will be due to some additional propellant in the form of research, innovations, efficiency, and strategy on the part of the new owners and management.

Method 2: Estimated future superior earnings are discounted for a limited number of years to determine the present value of such earnings. The estimate of goodwill may be modified in several ways to allow for the uncertain nature of superior earnings. One approach is to assume that any estimated future superior earnings will continue for a ***limited period***—for example, three or five years. The ***present value*** of a series of superior earnings at a specified rate of return may be computed by the use of present value concepts described in Chapter 5. In the Reed Corporation example, if estimated future superior earnings of $34,000 a year will continue for a five-year period, the present value of this prospect at 10% is approximately $129,000, determined as follows:

A conceptually sound approach for estimating goodwill

Estimated future superior earnings (assume receipt at end of each year)	$34,000
Present value of ordinary annuity of five rents of 1 each, discounted at 10%	3.790787
Present value of estimated future superior earnings (goodwill) ($34,000 × 3.790787)	$128,887

Method 3: Estimated future superior earnings are capitalized at a higher-than-normal rate of return. A variation of method 1 is to capitalize estimated future superior earnings at a higher discount rate than is used to capitalize normal earnings. For example, if the normal rate of return is considered to be 10%, a rate of 20% or 30% may be used to capitalize superior earnings. The higher assumed rates of return allow for higher risk, because the prospect that superior earnings will continue unimpaired into the future is ***much more uncertain*** than the prospect of continued normal earnings. Referring once more to the Reed Corporation illustration, if superior earnings of $34,000 a year are capitalized at 30%, for example, goodwill is estimated at approximately $113,000 as follows:

Higher capitalization rate recognizes that superior earnings are subject to erosion

Estimated future superior earnings	$34,000
Capitalization rate	0.30
Capitalized value of estimated future superior earnings discounted at 30% in perpetuity (goodwill) ($34,000 ÷ 0.30)	$113,333

Under this approach, the earnings prospects of Reed have been divided into two layers — $82,000 of normal earnings and $34,000 ($116,000 − $82,000 = $34,000) of superior earnings — and a different discount rate has been used to value each layer. Any number of different layers and any number of different discount rates might be used to estimate goodwill.

Method 4: Estimated future superior earnings for a stated number of years are acquired. Another approach to the estimate of goodwill is to multiply estimated future superior earnings by a number of years and to refer to the result as a "number of years of estimated future superior earnings acquired." For example, a goodwill estimate of $170,000 may be described as "the acquisition of five years of estimated future superior earnings of $34,000 a year." Such loose statements may obscure the real issues involved. As noted previously, the present value of five years of estimated future superior earnings of $34,000 discounted at 10% is approximately $129,000, not $170,000. Therefore, no reason exists for paying $170,000 for superior earnings of $170,000 to be received over a five-year period if money is worth 10% compounded annually.

Summary of Methods Uncertainty and subjectivity surround each of the variables involved in an estimate of goodwill. The probable amount of future earnings, the portion that represents superior earnings, the length of time, and the appropriate rate of return to be used in the valuation of superior earnings—all are variables not subject to objective verification. They may be estimated only within a ***reasonable*** range. The illustrated methods indicate the following possible range (from highest to lowest) in the estimated value of goodwill for Reed Corporation:

Results of preceding four approaches compared

Estimated future superior earnings of $34,000 are capitalized at 10% in perpetuity	$340,000
Estimated future superior earnings of $34,000 for five years are acquired	170,000
Estimated future superior earnings of $34,000 for five years are discounted at 10% (rounded)	129,000
Estimated future superior earnings of $34,000 are capitalized at 30% (to recognize a higher risk factor) in perpetuity (rounded)	113,000

In a transaction involving the acquisition of Reed Corporation, the value established for goodwill probably would be somewhere between $340,000 and $113,000, depending on the relative bargaining power of the acquirer and the seller. Inability to agree on a specific value for goodwill frequently results in an agreement to pay a minimum amount for goodwill, to be supplemented by additional payments ***contingent*** on future superior earnings of the acquired enterprise. Such agreements may raise numerous accounting questions. For example: (1) How should the future payments be recorded? (2) How should the earnings on which the contingent payments are based be measured? (3) How should future contingent payments be disclosed by the acquirer?

It sometimes is suggested that the market value of a corporation's common stock provides a basis for estimating the current fair value of the corporation. Thus, if Reed Corporation, whose net assets have a current fair value of $820,000, has 200,000 shares of common stock outstanding, quoted on the market at $6 a share, this suggests that Reed is worth $1,200,000 (200,000 × $6 = $1,200,000), and that goodwill is $380,000 ($1,200,000 – $820,000 = $380,000). This conclusion would have some merit if the market price of $6 a share applied to the entire issue of 200,000 shares, or to a block representing a substantial and controlling interest in Reed Corporation. However, only a small fraction of the total shares outstanding normally is offered for sale on the market at any one time. The market prices of this small ***floating supply*** of common stock may fluctuate widely, and are influenced by short-term factors that may be unrelated to Reed's long-term prospects. Furthermore, there is no quoted market price for the common stock of most small corporations. Stock prices may be useful as evidence of ***relative*** values in the negotiation of a business combination involving an exchange of common stock, and they also may substantiate or invalidate the estimates of goodwill reached independently. However, common stock prices seldom are useful in the direct valuation of goodwill.

Non-Compete Agreements

When a business enterprise is acquired, the acquirer may pay an amount in excess of the current fair value of the identifiable net assets acquired. Typically, the excess is recorded as goodwill. However, there are situations in which a part of the acquisition price may be attributable to an agreement by the seller not to engage in a competing enterprise for a specified period of time. The acquirer of a retail store or a restaurant, for example, would not want the former owner to establish a competing enterprise in the same geographic area.

A ***non-compete agreement*** is incorporated in the contract for the sale of a business enterprise, in words such as ''the seller agrees not to engage in the restaurant business in the City of Ames for a period of five years.'' Such an agreement obviously has value to the acquirer, and a reasonable portion of the acquisition price should be assigned to it in the contract. Although the value of a non-compete agreement is difficult to determine, the acquirer and seller should be able to agree on a fair price. The value assigned to goodwill does not include the value assigned to the non-compete agreement, because the latter represents an ***identifiable*** intangible asset. For example, if Bates Limited, with identifiable net assets of $100,000 at current fair value, is acquired for $150,000, it appears that the acquirer paid $50,000 for goodwill. However, if the parties assign a value of $30,000 to a non-compete agreement for five years, the acquisition of Bates is recorded as follows:

Entry to record a non-compete agreement

Net Assets	100,000	
Non-Compete Agreement	30,000	
Goodwill	20,000	
Cash		150,000
To record the acquisition of Bates Limited, with non-compete agreement and goodwill valued separately.		

Controversy over Amortization of Goodwill

Whether goodwill arising out of the acquisition of a business enterprise should be amortized has been a controversial issue for many years. After the issuance of section 1580 of the ***CICA Handbook***, many business executives and accountants disagreed with the mandatory amortization of acquired goodwill.

It has been argued that goodwill has an indefinite economic life and, therefore, should not be amortized until there is evidence that it no longer exists. Supporters of this view maintain that as long as earnings are sufficient to indicate that goodwill is unimpaired, it is a permanent asset. To amortize goodwill in the absence of a decline in earnings, it is argued, would obliterate the superior earnings that supported the recording of the goodwill in the first place.

The argument against the amortization of acquired goodwill is particularly strong when earnings are at a level that indicates that goodwill continues to exist. It is doubtful that continuing goodwill stems solely from conditions existing at the time of acquisition. A more likely situation is that goodwill is maintained through the successful efforts of the new owners and management of the business enterprise to stay ahead of competition. It is unlikely that the exact amount of original goodwill that has dissipated will be replaced by internally developed goodwill. Retaining acquired goodwill intact in the accounting records would be an attempt to compensate for the accounting inconsistency of recording acquired goodwill and not recording internally developed goodwill. Expenditures for research and advertising necessary to maintain superior earning power are recorded as expenses. If acquired goodwill is amortized, there would be a duplication of expenses — the current expenditures incurred to build and maintain goodwill, and the periodic amortization of previously acquired goodwill.

The opposing view is that the amount paid for goodwill represents the acquisition of an unidentifiable intangible asset and superior earnings for a limited number of years. It is argued that goodwill does not last forever and that the realization of superior earnings is not income to the new owners but rather a recovery of capital. Amortization of acquired goodwill is supported on practical grounds, because the value of the goodwill is likely to become zero at some future date. Thus, the investment in goodwill should be accounted for in the same manner as other productive assets having a limited economic life. If expectations were realized, that is, if earnings continued unchanged for the period of years used to estimate and amortize acquired goodwill, the amortization will result in less-than-normal earnings on the investment of the new owners during the amortization period. This squares with reality, because the payment for superior earnings makes their ultimate emergence a ***return of investment***, not income.

Both sides in this controversy agree that goodwill should be written down when there is clear evidence that is overstated. If superior earnings are eroded by competition and other economic conditions, the disappearance of goodwill is recognized as a loss.

ACCOUNTING FOR RESEARCH AND DEVELOPMENT (R&D) COSTS

Many business enterprises spend large amounts of money on research aimed at the discovery and development of improved processes and products. Some research expenditures result in patentable discoveries and some produce non-patentable benefits in the form of better production methods and techniques. However, significant amounts of research and development ***(R&D)*** costs produce no measurable benefits to future revenue.

Corporate managements had almost complete discretion to defer or to expense R&D costs until July, 1978, when section 3450 of the ***CICA Handbook*** was issued. The basic premise in this pronouncement is that all R&D costs will be expensed as incurred ***unless*** certain ***development costs*** conform to some specified criteria, in which case these costs will be capitalized and amortized. This capitalization of certain development costs differs from the United States' ***FASB Statement No. 2*** requirement that ***all*** R&D costs be expensed.

Development costs should be deferred to future periods (capitalized) if ***all*** of the following criteria are satisfied:[13]

1 The product or process is clearly defined and the costs attributable thereto can be identified.

2 The technical feasibility of the product or process has been established.

3 The management of the enterprise has indicated its intention to produce and market, or use, the product or process.

4 The future market for the product or process is clearly defined or, if it is to be used internally rather than sold, its usefulness to the enterprise has been established.

5 Adequate resources exist, or are expected to be available, to complete the project.

The rationale for this ***CICA Handbook*** recommendation is that the fulfillment of these five criteria would ensure a reasonable certainty of recovering such developmental costs in future revenues.

Research costs are costs incurred to conduct a ''planned investigation undertaken with the hope of gaining new scientific or technical knowledge and understanding. Such investigation may or may not be directed towards a specific

13 CICA, ***CICA Handbook***, sec. 3450.21.

practical aim or application.''[14] Some examples of typical research activities are:[15]

1 Laboratory research aimed at the discovery of new knowledge

2 Searching for applications of new research findings or other knowledge

3 Conceptual formulation and design of possible product or process alternatives

As can be seen from the definition and examples above, there is no reasonable certainty of future revenue from these research activities, and therefore the expensing of all research costs is necessary.

Development costs are costs incurred to translate ''research findings or other knowledge into a plan or design for new or substantially improved materials, devices, products, processes, systems or services prior to the commencement of commercial production or use.''[16] Some examples of activities that typically would be included in development are:[17]

1 Testing in search for, or evaluation of, product or process alternatives

2 Design, construction and testing of preproduction prototypes and models

3 Design of tools, jigs, moulds and dies involving new technology

In most cases, such development costs will result in items with uncertain future potential, and the expensing of all development costs is required. However, in other cases a new or substantially improved product may emerge, with reasonable certainty of future revenues, and the business entity should capitalize such development costs and amortize these costs against future revenues.

The capitalization recommendation does not include a retroactive provision. Thus, development costs that have been expensed in prior periods should not be reinstated as an asset, even though the uncertainties present at the time of expensing are now resolved and future benefits are apparent.

When the future benefits can be estimated with reasonable certainty, the amortization pattern should match the expected flow of benefits in both timing and pattern. If the specific criteria which permitted the development costs to be capitalized are no longer met, the development costs should be written off. Also, if the unamortized balance of development costs exceeds the future benefits, then the excess should be written off.

In summary, the main provisions of section 3450 recommend that R&D costs should be expensed as incurred unless specific criteria are met so as to provide reasonable assurance that measurable future benefits will be derived from the development costs. This was a compromise solution to a very difficult financial accounting problem. Those who opposed the deferral of R&D were, for the most part, pleased with this pronouncement. On the other hand, some accountants

14 CICA, ***CICA Handbook***, sec. 3450.02.

15 CICA, ***CICA Handbook***, sec. 3450.04.

16 CICA, ***CICA Handbook***, sec. 3450.02.

17 CICA, ***CICA Handbook***, sec. 3450.05.

and corporate executives have questioned the logic of immediately writing off those R&D costs that have some probability of contributing to future revenue.

Admittedly, there is a considerable degree of uncertainty about the future benefits on individual R&D projects or generalized research carried out on an ongoing basis. Because a direct relationship between costs and specific future revenues generally is difficult to establish, the recognition of such costs as expenses is a conservative application of the matching principle.

In the United States, corporate managements had almost complete discretion to defer or to expense R&D costs until 1970, when the Accounting Principles Board stated that "a company should record as expenses the costs to develop intangible assets which are not specifically identifiable."[18] However, this accounting principle was vague and did not prevent the accumulation of vast sums of R&D costs in the balance sheets of many enterprises. In some instances such costs could not be related to specific future revenue and were often written off in a "year of the big bath," because of deterioration in demand for the enterprise's products or for other economic reasons.

The AICPA recognized the need to develop sharper accounting standards for R&D costs, and in 1973 published ***Accounting Research Study No. 14:*** "Accounting for Research and Development Expenditures." ***ARS No. 14*** recommended, among other things, that costs incurred in continuing research programs be recorded as expenses immediately, and that costs of any substantial development projects be deferred and amortized over the future accounting periods that they are intended to benefit.[19] This study provided background material for the Financial Accounting Standards Board in the development of ***FASB Statement No. 2***, the current accounting standard for R&D costs, which requires the expensing of all R&D costs.

Deferred Charges

The term ***deferred charges*** frequently is used to describe long-term prepayments subject to amortization. For example, the costs of issuing bonds produce benefits by providing funds for use by a business enterprise; however, the funds provided contribute to revenue over the entire term of the bonds. Similarly, the cost of machinery rearrangements presumably results in a more efficient and valuable plant and, therefore, should be allocated to revenue over an appropriate number of years. Other examples of deferred charges are noncurrent prepaid income taxes (or deferred income tax debit balances), preoperating (or start-up) costs, and certain pension costs.

The use of the term ***deferred charges*** may be criticized, because all assets other than cash, receivables, investments, and land are forms of deferred charges to revenue. Most deferred charges may be classified either as plant assets (machinery rearrangement) or as intangible assets (oil exploration costs). If a deferrable cost is

18 AICPA, ***APB Opinion No. 17***, p. 334.

19 Oscar S. Gellein and Maurice S. Newman, ***Accounting Research Study No. 14:*** "Accounting for Research and Development Expenditures" (New York: AICPA, 1973), pp. 6–8.

not classified under plant assets or intangible assets, it should be included under "Other Noncurrent Assets" in the balance sheet to avoid a separate category for deferred charges.

The deferral of an expenditure may be justified only if an asset with future service potential has resulted. If the future service potential of any cost incurred is obscure, it should be recognized as an expense.

Accounting for Development-Stage Enterprises

In the 1970s, a special category of deferred charges received considerable attention. Costs incurred by business enterprises in the development stage were designated as ***preoperating*** or ***start-up costs***. Such costs generally were deferred and amortized over a relatively short period after the enterprise emerged from the development stage and started generating revenue. Preoperating costs that were applicable to abandoned projects and other costs that were not expected to contribute to revenue in future accounting periods were written off in the accounting period in which the loss of service potential became apparent.

Accounting practices for enterprises in the development stage varied considerably. However, there is no pronouncement by the CICA in this area. On the other hand, in the United States, the FASB issued ***Statement No. 7:*** "Accounting and Reporting by Development Stage Enterprises," which specified guidelines for identifying enterprises in the development stage and the standards of accounting and reporting applicable to such enterprises. An enterprise is considered to be in a development stage if it is devoting most of its efforts to establishing a new business and planned principal operations have not begun, or, if they have begun, no significant revenue has been realized. A development-stage enterprise typically devotes most of its efforts to financial planning, raising capital, exploring for and developing natural resources, research and development, establishing sources of supply, acquiring plant assets, and gearing up for production.[20] A summary of the accounting and disclosure requirements of ***FASB Statement No. 7*** follows:[21]

1 Financial statements issued by development-stage enterprises should present financial position, changes in financial position, and results of operations ***in conformity with generally accepted accounting principles that apply to established operating enterprises***.

2 In issuing the same basic financial statements as an established operating enterprise, development-stage enterprises also should disclose the following information:

20 FASB, ***FASB Statement No. 7:*** "Accounting and Reporting by Development Stage Enterprises" (Stamford: 1975), pp. 3–4.

21 FASB, ***FASB Statement No. 7***, pp. 5–6.

a A balance sheet, including any cumulative net losses reported with a descriptive caption, such as "deficit accumulated during the development stage," in the owners' equity section.
b An income statement, showing amounts of revenue and expenses for each accounting period covered by the income statement and, in addition, cumulative amounts from the enterprise's inception.
c A statement of changes in financial position, showing the sources and uses of financial resources for each accounting period for which an income statement is presented and, in addition, cumulative amounts from the enterprise's inception.

3 A statement of owners' equity, showing for a corporation, for example, for each issuance of securities from the enterprise's inception: ***a*** the date and number of shares of capital stock, stock warrants, or other securities issued for cash and for other consideration; ***b*** the dollar amounts assigned to the consideration received; and ***c*** the nature of the noncash consideration and the basis for assigning current fair values to the noncash consideration.

In addition, the financial statements must be identified as those of a development-stage enterprise and must include a description of the nature of the development-stage activities. The financial statements for the first fiscal year in which an enterprise no longer is considered to be in the development stage should disclose that in prior years ***it had been in the development stage***.

Plant and Intangible Assets in the Balance Sheet

There is a noticeable trend in financial reporting toward including all noncurrent assets (other than investments) under a single major heading labelled "plant assets," "plant and equipment," or "property, plant, and equipment." Tangible and intangible assets are reported separately, and plant assets held for sale are included under Other Noncurrent Assets. The methods of depreciation and amortization used, as well as the amounts of depreciation and amortization expense for the latest accounting period, should be disclosed.

In a recent survey of 325 public companies, 147 reported intangible assets in their balance sheet, and 129 of the 147 companies showed that the intangible assets were amortized[22] The most common types of intangible assets reported were goodwill (excess of cost over net assets acquired in business combinations), patents, franchises, licences, and trademarks.[23] The following example illustrates the presentation of plant assets and intangible assets in the balance sheet.

22 CICA, *Financial Reporting in Canada*, 16th ed. (Toronto, 1985), p. 138.

23 CICA, *Financial Reporting in Canada*, p. 138.

Presentation of plant assets and intangible assets in the balance sheet

Plant assets:		
Land, at cost	$ 350,000	
Buildings (cost $1,640,000, less accumulated depreciation of $185,000)	1,455,000	
Equipment (cost $870,000, less accumulated depreciation of $150,000)	720,000	
Tools and patterns (at unamortized cost)	25,000	
Total plant assets (net)		$2,550,000
Intangible assets:		
Patents (amortized over 12 years)	$ 85,000	
Trademarks (amortized over 20 years)	100,000	
Organization costs (amortized over 10 years)	15,000	
Goodwill (amortized over 40 years)	180,000	
Total intangible assets (net)		380,000

NOTE: Depreciation and amortization expense amounted to $310,000 for the last accounting period. The straight-line method is used to compute depreciation and amortization.

REVIEW QUESTIONS

1 Accountants use the term ***intangible assets*** in a more limited sense than the legal meaning of this term. Explain why this is so.

2 Why is the identification and measurement of the cost of intangible assets more difficult than it is for tangible assets? What are some similarities between tangible assets and intangible assets?

3 Lennox Corporation has just been organized. The costs of forming Lennox and issuing its common stock amounted to $85,000. One officer of Lennox suggests that this amount be charged immediately against the amount invested by shareholders of common stock. Another officer suggests that the amount be amortized over a period of a few years by direct charges to retained earnings. Evaluate these two proposals.

4 In the computation of the equity (book value) per share of common stock, security analysts generally disregard intangible assets. Evaluate this practice.

5 Roe Limited applied for and received a patent on a manufacturing process. The legal fees and patent application fees totalled $10,000. Research costs related to the patent were estimated at $60,000. Shortly after the patent was issued, Roe spent $25,000 in legal fees in a successful defence against a suit in which it was claimed that Roe's patent infringed a patent owned by a competitor.

a At what amount should the patent be recorded?

b What is the legal life of the patent?

c What factors should be considered in the determination of the patent's economic life?

6 What amortization policy should be followed for ***copyrights, trademarks, secret formulas***, and ***licences and contracts***?

7 It has been argued, on the grounds of conservatism, that all intangible assets should be written off immediately on acquisition. Present arguments against this position.

8 What expenditures generally are included in ***organization costs***?

9 What is meant by the term ***goodwill***? What are the tests of the existence of goodwill? What is meant by the term ***negative goodwill***? Is negative goodwill reported in the balance sheet?

10 In negotiations for the sale of a going-concern business enterprise, an intangible factor called ***goodwill*** sometimes is estimated by capitalizing average superior earnings, that is, by dividing average superior earnings by an assumed earnings-rate factor. Explain how the average superior earnings are determined, and justify the capitalization of superior earnings in the estimation of the amount of goodwill.

11 What is the distinction between ***capitalizing*** estimated future earnings and ***computing the present value*** of estimated future earnings?

12 "If all individual assets and liabilities of a business enterprise are identified and valued properly, goodwill will not exist." Do you agree with this quotation?

13 Acquired goodwill usually is recorded and included in the balance sheet; internally developed goodwill is not. Explain the reason for this accounting practice.

14 List five procedures that may be followed to estimate the amount of goodwill of a business enterprise. May the market value of its outstanding common stock be used to estimate the amount of goodwill of a publicly owned corporation?

15 Lento Company has identifiable net assets with an estimated current fair value of $1 million. Lento has an indicated ability to earn $160,000 a year, and the normal earnings rate in its industry is 10%. Describe three methods that might be used to estimate the amount of goodwill of Lento Company.

16 List the five criteria established by section 3450 of the ***CICA Handbook*** to determine whether development costs should be capitalized or expensed.

17 What are the requirements under section 3450 of the ***CICA Handbook*** with respect to accounting for research costs?

18 Iowa Limited incurs development costs in the early exploratory stage of the development of new products, in the improvement of existing products, and in the improvement of its manufacturing process. How should these development costs be recorded for financial accounting?

EXERCISES

Ex. 13-1 Select the best answer for each of the following multiple-choice questions:

1 During the year ended April 30, Year 3, Keene Limited incurred $176,000 in research costs for an invention that was eventually patented on May 1, Year 3. Legal costs incurred for the patent were immaterial and were expensed during the year ended April 30, Year 4. The patent had a legal life of 17 years and an economic life of eight years on May 1, Year 3. On May 1, Year 7, Keene incurred legal fees of $16,000 in a successful defence of the patent. Keene's patent amortization expense for the year ended April 30, Year 8, is:

a $0 *b* $1,231 *c* $4,000 *d* $26,000 *e* Some other amount

2 Which of the following is not a consideration in the determination of economic life of an intangible asset?

a Legal, regulatory, or contractual provisions
b Provisions for renewal or extension
c Expected actions of competitors
d Cost of the intangible asset
e None of the foregoing

3 Goodwill represents the excess of the cost of an acquired business enterprise over the:

a Total of the current fair values of the enterprise's identifiable assets less its liabilities
b Total of the current fair values of the enterprise's tangible assets less its liabilities
c Total of the current fair values of the enterprise's intangible assets less its liabilities
d Carrying amount of the net assets of the enterprise

4 On May 1, Year 6, newly organized Nolan Corporation incurred organization costs of $240,000. Nolan decided to amortize the organization costs over a period of five years. The unamortized balance of Nolan's Organization Costs ledger account on April 30, Year 7, is:

a $0 *b* $48,000 *c* $192,000 *d* $240,000 *e* Some other amount

5 In the negotiations for the acquisition of Fargo Company's net assets by Dover Limited, it was agreed that the amount to be paid by Dover for Fargo's goodwill would be determined by capitalizing the $60,000 estimated future superior earnings of Fargo's identifiable net assets at a 10% normal rate of return. The carrying amount and current fair value of Fargo's identifiable net assets were $1,800,000 and $2,500,000 respectively. The amount that Dover will pay for Fargo's goodwill is:

a $180,000 *b* $240,000 *c* $600,000 *d* $700,000 *e* Some other amount

6 On July 2, Year 4, Todd Company acquired for $89,250 a patent with a remaining economic and legal life of 15 years, expiring on June 30, Year 19. During the year ended June 30, Year 8, Todd determined that the remaining economic life on July 2, Year 4, should have been 10 years rather than 15 years. Todd's patent amortization expense for the year ended June 30, Year 8, is:

a $5,250 *b* $8,925 *c* $10,200 *d* $17,850 *e* Some other amount

Ex. 13-2 On January 2, Year 5, Keko Company acquired for $192,000 a patent with a remaining legal life of 12 years and an estimated economic life of eight years. On January 2, Year 9, Keko paid legal fees of $12,000 in a successful defence of the patent.

Compute Keko Company's patent amortization expense for Year 9.

Ex. 13-3 On January 2, Year 2, Adam Corporation acquired a patent with a remaining legal life of 15 years and an estimated economic life of eight years. The cost of the patent was $124,000. On January 2, Year 6, Adam paid $48,000, as an out-of-court settlement, to Ted Dale, who had claimed in a Year 5 lawsuit that the patent acquired in Year 2 infringed on one of his inventions.

Prepare journal entries for Adam Corporation to record the acquisition of the patent, the payment on the patent infringement settlement, and the amortization for Year 6. Amortization is recorded as a credit in the Patents ledger account.

Ex. 13-4 On January 2, Year 1, Loy Company acquired for $85,000 a patent for a new consumer product. At the time of acquisition, the legal life of the patent was 17 years. Because of the competitive nature of the product, the patent was estimated to have an economic life of five years. On January 5, Year 4, the product was removed from the market under governmental order because of a potential health hazard present in the product.

Compute the amount that Loy Company should recognize as a loss in Year 4, assuming amortization is recorded at the end of each year.

Ex. 13-5 On January 2, Year 1, Carlo Corporation sold to Dow Company a patent that had a carrying amount of $23,000 in Carlo's accounting records. Dow gave Carlo an $80,000 non-interest-bearing note payable in five equal annual instalments of $16,000, with the first payment due and paid on January 2, Year 2. There was no established market price for the patent, and the note payable had no ready market. The prevailing rate of interest for a note of this type on January 2, Year 1, was 12%. Information on present value and future amount factors is shown below:

	Periods				
	1	*2*	*3*	*4*	*5*
Present value of 1 at 12%	0.893	0.797	0.712	0.636	0.567
Present value of an ordinary annuity of 1 at 12%	0.893	1.690	2.402	3.037	3.605
Future amount of 1 at 12%	1.120	1.254	1.405	1.574	1.762
Future amount of an ordinary annuity of 1 at 12%	1.000	2.120	3.374	4.779	6.353

Compute the income or loss before income taxes (rounded to the nearest dollar) of Carlo Corporation for Years 1 and 2 ended December 31 as a result of the foregoing information.

Ex. 13-6 On May 1, Year 7, Willard Music Limited acquired from a composer for $80,000 the copyright for a popular song written by the composer. For the year ended April 30, Year 8, Willard amortized the copyright over the maximum economic life of 40 years. On May 1, Year 8, because of an unexpected decline in popularity of the composer's works, the company concluded that the economic life of the copyright would not exceed five more years.

Prepare journal entries for Willard Music Limited for the acquisition of the copyright on May 1, Year 7, and for amortization of the copyright for the years ended April 30, Year 8 and Year 9.

Ex. 13-7 The Organization Costs ledger account for Vista Limited appeared as follows on April 30, Year 4, the date Vista began operations:

Organization Costs

Date	*Explanation*	*Debit*	*Credit*	*Balance*
Year 4				
Mar. 1	Fees paid to promoters.	10,000		10,000 Dr
4	Fees paid to lawyers for drafting corporate documents.	5,000		15,000 Dr
5	Incorporation fee.	500		15,500 Dr
31	Discount on $100,000 bond issued at 99.	1,000		16,500 Dr
31	Bond issue costs paid.	1,500		18,000 Dr
Apr. 15	Payment of costs incurred in issuing 10,000 shares of common stock at $15 a share.	2,500		20,500 Dr

Prepare a single correcting journal entry for Vista Limited's Organization Costs ledger account on April 30, Year 4. Disregard amortization.

Ex. 13-8 The income before income taxes of Leslie Corporation for Year 1 was $330,000, and included the following:

Extraordinary gains	$80,000
Extraordinary losses	35,000
Profit-sharing payments to employees	25,000
Amortization of goodwill	15,000
Amortization of identifiable intangible assets	17,500
Depreciation of building (straight-line method)	44,000

The building is worth three times as much as carrying amount, and the remaining economic life will be increased by 100% by the new owner of Leslie. The new owner will continue the profit-sharing payments to employees. These payments are based on income before depreciation and amortization.

Compute the normal earnings of Leslie Corporation for Year 1 for purposes of measuring the possible existence of superior earnings and goodwill.

Ex. 13-9 On April 1, Year 10, Oliver Corporation acquired the assets and assumed the liabilities of Wong Company, a sole proprietorship, for $400,000 cash. The condensed balance sheet of Wong Company on the date of acquisition is shown on the next page.

Oliver valued the tangible and identifiable assets of Wong Company at $515,000, and restated the liabilities at $162,500. Included in the acquisition contract was a provision that James Wong could not operate a competing business enterprise for three years; the acquisition price of $400,000 included

WONG COMPANY
Condensed Balance Sheet
April 1, Year 10

Assets	$480,000	Liabilities	$150,000
		James Wong, capital	330,000
Total assets	$480,000	Total liabilities & capital	$480,000

$25,000 for the non-compete agreement.

Prepare a journal entry to record the acquisition of Wong Company on April 1, Year 10, in the accounting records of Oliver Corporation.

Ex. 13-10 Net income and shareholders' equity of Nell's Restaurant for a three-year period are shown below:

Year	*Net income*	*Shareholders' equity at end of year*
1	$62,000	$180,000
2	75,000	230,000
3	91,000	220,000

At the end of Year 3, James Lu acquired Nell's Restaurant on the following basis:

1 20% is considered a normal return on restaurant investments.
2 Payment for goodwill is to be determined by capitalizing at 40% the average annual net income that is in excess of 20% of average shareholders' equity for the past three years.
3 Net assets, which do not include any goodwill, will be recorded by Lu at the carrying amounts reported by Nell's Restaurant.

Prepare a journal entry in the accounting records of James Lu to record the acquisitions of Nell's Restaurant at the end of Year 3.

Ex. 13-11 Western Company is planning to acquire Eastern Company. The past earnings of Eastern have averaged $40,000 a year. It is estimated that Eastern's earnings will be 20% larger in the future. Normal earnings for Eastern are $19,000 a year.

Compute the amount that Western Company should pay for Eastern Company's goodwill, assuming that:

a Goodwill is equal to the total of superior earnings for five years.
b Goodwill is estimated by capitalization of superior earnings at 25%.

Ex. 13-12 San Company acquired the net assets of Paulo Company for $100,000. In acquiring the net assets, the owners of San determined that Paulo had unrecorded goodwill. They decided to capitalize the estimated annual superior earnings of Paulo at 20% to determine the amount of goodwill. This computation resulted in an estimate of goodwill at $20,000. A rate of 10% on net assets before recognition of goodwill was used to determine normal annual earnings of Paulo because it was the rate that is earned on net assets in the industry in which Paulo operates. All other assets of Paulo were recorded properly.

Compute the estimated annual earnings of Paulo Company.

Ex. 13-13 Nimoy Corporation incurred research and development (R&D) costs in Year 10 as follows:

Material used in R&D projects	$160,000
Equipment acquired that will be used in future R&D projects	800,000
Depreciation for Year 10 on foregoing equipment	200,000
Labour costs of employees involved in R&D projects	400,000
Consulting fees paid to outsiders for R&D projects	50,000
Indirect costs reasonably allocable to R&D projects	80,000
Fully reimbursable R&D costs	77,200

Compute the amount of R&D costs that should be reported as research and development expense in the income statement of Nimoy Corporation for Year 10, assuming that the development costs included above, which will result in revenue estimated at $60,000, are $126,000.

Ex. 13-14 From the following amounts, prepare the intangible assets section of Earley Corporation's balance sheet:

Deposits with advertising agency that will be used to promote sales	$ 4,500
Organization costs	25,000
Discount on bonds payable	15,500
Excess of cost over fair value of net assets of acquired enterprise	40,000
Patents	24,400
Franchise to operate in British Columbia	10,000
Marketing costs of introducing new products	15,000
Development costs expected to benefit future accounting periods	42,000

CASES

Case 13-1 On June 30, Year 1, your client, Hight Corporation, was granted two patents covering plastic cartons that it had been producing and marketing profitably for the past three years. One patent covered the manufacturing process, and the other covered the related products.

Executives of Hight informed you that the patents represent the most significant breakthrough in the industry in the past 30 years. The products had been marketed under the following registered trademarks: Safetainer, Duratainer, and Sealrite. Licences under the patents already had been granted by Hight to manufacturers in the United States and abroad and were producing substantial royalties.

On July 2, Year 2, Hight commenced patent infringement suits against several companies whose names you recognize as those of substantial and prominent competitors. Management of Hight is optimistic that these suits will result in a permanent injunction against the manufacture and sale of the infringing products, and in the collection of damages for lost profits caused by the alleged infringements.

The financial vice president of Hight has suggested that the patents be recorded at the discounted value of expected net royalty receipts.

Instructions

a Explain the meaning of ***intangible assets*** and ***discounted value of expected net royalty receipts***. How is discounted value of royalty receipts computed?

b What basis of valuation for Hight Corporation's patents is in accordance with generally accepted accounting principles? Give supporting reasons for this basis.

c Assuming no problems of implementation and disregarding generally accepted accounting principles, what is the preferable basis of valuation and amortization for patents?

d What disclosure, if any, should be made regarding the infringement suits in a note to the financial statements of Hight for the year ended September 30, Year 2?

Case 13-2 Litchy Corporation, a retail fuel distributor, has increased its annual sales volume to a level three times the annual sales of the dealership that it acquired in Year 1 to begin operations.

In Year 6, the board of directors of Litchy received an offer to negotiate the sale of Litchy. The majority of the board want to increase the carrying amount of goodwill in the balance sheet to reflect the larger sales volume developed through intensive promotion and the favourable market price of fuel. However, some board members prefer to eliminate goodwill from the balance sheet "to prevent possible misinterpretations." Goodwill had been recorded in Year 1 in conformity with generally accepted accounting principles.

Instructions

a Define ***goodwill*** and list the techniques used to estimate its value in negotiations to acquire a business enterprise. To what extent does the value of goodwill depend on sales volume?

b Why are the carrying amount and current fair value for goodwill of Litchy Corporation different?

c Discuss the propriety of increasing or eliminating the carrying amount of goodwill prior to negotiations for the sale of a business enterprise.

Case 13-3 Some years ago the annual report of Canna Communications Corporation (CCC) included the following message to shareholders:

> Because amortization of goodwill as required by section 1580 of the ***CICA Handbook*** is significant to CCC's earnings and because management of CCC does not agree with this amortization requirement, we hereby make our views known in the hopes

you will then be in a better position to analyze our financial statements and the performance of CCC.

Goodwill represents the difference between the total amount paid in a purchase-type business combination and the fair market value of the identifiable net assets acquired. The CICA's Accounting Standards Committee, in issuing its pronouncement requiring the amortization of goodwill acquired after March 31, 1974, apparently made the assumption that goodwill gradually loses its value over a period of years and established an arbitrary maximum economic life of 40 years.

Management is in absolute disagreement with the required amortization of the goodwill related to broadcast stations and newspapers where the goodwill retains its value and, in many instances, increases in value over the years. We believe there is a sufficient number of business combinations each year in the broadcast and newspaper fields to demonstrate this fact. We simply do not accept a conclusion that one rule for the amortization of goodwill fits all business enterprises.

It is management's opinion that goodwill should not be expensed (in whole or in part) until it becomes apparent that there has been or will be a measurable diminution in its value. Should it become apparent in years subsequent to the acquisition that a downward adjustment is necessary, it should be the responsibility of management to determine the amount of the adjustment and the accounting period or periods to which such adjustment should be applied. Such a determination should, of course, be subject to the approval of the independent auditors of the business enterprise.

Instructions

Do you agree with the management of Canna Communications Corporation? Explain your position.

Case 13-4 Niles Limited was in the process of developing Novo, a revolutionary new product. A new division of Niles was formed to develop, manufacture, and market Novo. As of December 31, Year 7, Novo had not been manufactured for resale; however, a prototype unit of Novo had been built and was in operation.

Throughout Year 7 the new division incurred certain costs. These costs included design and engineering studies of the preproduction prototype, administrative costs (including salaries of administrative personnel), and market research costs. In addition, approximately $500,000 in equipment (estimated economic life of 10 years) was acquired for use in developing and manufacturing Novo. Approximately $200,000 of this equipment was built specifically for the design development of Novo. The remaining $300,000 of equipment was used to manufacture the preproduction prototype, and will be used to manufacture Novo once it is in commercial production.

Instructions

a What are the definitions of ***research*** and of ***development*** according to section 3450 of the ***CICA Handbook***?

b Briefly indicate the reasons for the conclusion reached by the CICA's Accounting Standards Committee on accounting for research and development costs.

c In accordance with section 3450, how are the various costs of Niles Limited described above reported in the financial statements for the year ended December 31, Year 7?

PROBLEMS

Pr. 13-1 Lambert Corporation began operations on January 2, Year 1. On December 31, Year 1, its accounting records included the asset ledger account reproduced below. (Lambert posts journal entries at month-end only.)

Research and Development

Date	*Explanation*	*Debit*	*Credit*	*Balance*
Year 1				
Jan. 31	Material, salaries, and indirect costs related to general research activities.	14,000		14,000 Dr
Feb. 28	Engineering salaries and indirect costs related to production troubleshooting.	3,500		17,500 Dr
Mar. 31	Material, salaries, and indirect costs incurred for customer, Raymond Company.	6,300		28,800 Dr
Apr. 30	Fee of Leslie Engineering Company regarding testing in search for a product alternative.	1,700		25,500 Dr
June 30	Fee from Raymond Company.		8,400	17,100 Dr
July 31	Engineering salaries and indirect costs related to design of preproduction models.	2,400		19,500 Dr
Aug. 31	Legal fee for patent acquired on product developed through general R&D activities.	3,600		23,100 Dr
Dec. 31	Allocation of Year 1 salaries of officers, none of whom were engaged in R&D (credit was to Officers' Salaries Expense ledger account).	14,400		37,500 Dr

Instructions

a Prepare a working paper to allocate the items in Lambert Corporation's Research and Development ledger account on December 31, Year 1, to the correct ledger accounts. Use the following columnar headings:

1 Date
2 Description
3 Amount
4 Research Expense
5 Engineering Expense
6 Research and Development Fee Revenue (net)
7 Development Expense
8 Patents
9 Officers' Salaries Expense

b Prepare a single journal entry to correct Lambert Corporation's accounting records on December 31, Year 1. The patent acquired on August 31, Year 1, had an estimated economic life of six years.

Pr. 13-2 Stratton Limited has provided information on intangible assets as follows:

1 A patent was acquired from Cobb Company for $1,500,000 on January 2, Year 7. Stratton estimated the remaining economic life of the patent to be 10 years. The patent was carried in the accounting records of Cobb at $1,250,000 when it was sold to Stratton. On January 3, Year 8, Stratton management, on the basis of developments in the industry, estimated that the remaining economic life of the patent acquired on January 2, Year 7, was only six years from January 1, Year 8.

2 In Year 8, a franchise was acquired from Wok Company for $600,000. In addition, 3% of revenue from the franchise must be paid to Wok as a royalty. Revenue from the franchise for Year 8 was $2,000,000. Stratton's management estimated the economic life of the franchise to be eight years, and decided to take a full year's amortization in the year of acquisition.

3 Stratton incurred development costs in Year 8 as follows:

Material	$ 80,000
Salaries and wages	140,000
Indirect costs	60,000
Total research and development costs	$280,000

Stratton's management expected that these efforts would lead to a development of new products by December 31, Year 16, even though the market potential for these products was not quite clear at the end of Year 8.

Instructions

Prepare a working paper for the computation of the amount of (1) intangible assets to be included in Stratton Limited's balance sheet on December 31, Year 8, and (2) all expenses related to research and development and intangible assets to be included in Stratton's income statement for the year ended December 31, Year 8. Assume that amortization is recorded as a credit to each intangible asset ledger account.

Pr. 13-3 The following information was obtained from the accounting records of Logan Corporation and Cabot, Inc., on January 2, Year 6, in connection with the proposed merger of the two companies:

	Logan Corporation	*Cabot, Inc.*
Assets other than goodwill	$2,625,000	$1,593,000
Liabilities	975,000	720,000
Average income before income taxes for Year 1 through Year 5	408,000	281,400

The current fair values of assets, including goodwill, are to be determined as follows: 20% is considered a reasonable pre-tax return on net assets, excluding goodwill; average pre-tax income for Years 1 through 5 in excess of 20% on such net assets on January 2, Year 6, is to be capitalized at 25% to determine goodwill. The following adjustments to average pre-tax income are required before determination of the going-concern value of each company:

1 Equipment of Logan has a current fair value that is $150,000 in excess of its carrying amount; the equipment has a remaining economic life of 10 years.

2 At the beginning of Year 1, Cabot debited the cost of a franchise to expense.

The franchise cost $54,000 and had an estimated economic life of 10 years. The current fair value of the franchise on January 2, Year 6, was $27,000.

3 Included in the net income of Cabot for Years 1 through 5 are extraordinary gains of $46,500 and extraordinary losses of $99,000.

Instructions

Prepare a working paper showing for both Logan Corporation and Cabot, Inc., the valuation of:

a Net assets other than goodwill
b Goodwill
c The company as a whole

Pr. 13-4 Clovis Corporation performs subcontracting work for several major aircraft manufacturers. On January 2, Year 3, Clovis acquired from Researchers, Inc., a patent for a new type of navigational instrument. The economic life of the patent was equal to its legal life, which expires on January 2, Year 18. Clovis planned to incorporate the technology covered by the patent in one of its major projects after addition of several new features to the patent.

In January, Year 4, while auditing the financial statements of Clovis Corporation for Year 3, you reviewed the ledger account below that summarizes costs incurred in the development of the new and improved patent for the navigational instrument.

Navigational Instrument Project

Date	*Explanation*	*Debit*	*Credit*	*Balance*
Year 3				
Jan. 2	Cost of patent acquired from Researchers, Inc.	60,000		60,000 Dr
30	Legal costs incurred in connection with acquisition of patent from Researchers, Inc.	4,000		64,000 Dr
June 30	Costs of improving patent:			
	Blueprints for improvements	300		64,300 Dr
	Assembly and testing of preproduction prototypes and models	25,400		89,700 Dr
	Other development costs incurred	19,300		109,000 Dr
July 5	Cost of settlement of a threatened infringement suit on patent acquired from Researchers, Inc.	5,000		114,000 Dr
Dec. 31	Proceeds on sale of data developed in June 30, Year 3 (at related costs).		7,500	106,500 Dr

The improved patent was ready for use on July 2, Year 3, but the new navigational instrument was not sold to aircraft manufacturers until Year 4.

Instructions

a Prepare a working paper to summarize the costs that should be included in Clovis Corporation's Patents ledger account in accordance with generally accepted accounting principles.
b Prepare a single journal entry to eliminate Clovis Corporation's Navigational

Instrument Project ledger account and to record the items in this account in conformity with generally accepted accounting principles.

c Prepare a journal entry for Clovis Corporation, if required, to record the amortization of the patent for Year 3. If no entry is required, explain why.

Pr. 13-5 Telecom Company operates two television stations. On August 31, Year 10, Telecom contracted with a film distributor for a series of films. The contract gave Telecom an option to telecast the films as follows:

- 40 initial weekly telecasts starting on September 1, Year 10
- 12 reruns of the best films during the summer of Year 11
- 50 more reruns from September of Year 11 to August of Year 12

Telecom plans to telecast the original series during prime viewing hours, the summer reruns as a late show, and second-year reruns as a late-late show. The expected revenue from advertisers on both stations is estimated by Telecast management as follows:

Revenue from original 40 weeks	$420,000
Revenue from 12 summer reruns	108,000
Revenue from 50 second-year reruns (late-late shows)	72,000

The cost of the film rental rights is $240,000, which Telecom will pay in instalments over a two-year period at the rate of $18,000 a month during the first year (starting on September 30, Year 10) and $3,745 a month during the second year. These payments include interest at 1% a month on the carrying amount of the outstanding liability.

Instructions

a Prepare a journal entry for Telecom Company to record the film rental contract on August 31, Year 10, assuming that Telecom elects to make payments on the instalment basis. Use a Discount on Contract Payable ledger account.

b Prepare a working paper for Telecom Company showing amortization of cost of the film rental rights for each telecast over the two-year period.

c Prepare journal entries for Telecom Company to record:

1 The first payment on the contract on September 30, Year 10

2 Amortization of the cost of the film rental rights for the year ended December 31, Year 10 (after 17 telecasts have been run)

d If Telecom Company decided in August, Year 11, not to rerun the films during the second year, what journal entry should be made at that time to write off the unamortized film rental rights?

Pr. 13-6 Linager Limited is being audited at the end of Year 1, its first year of operations. The accountant for Linager recorded numerous transactions in the Intangible Assets ledger account. You have been assigned to audit this account, which included the following entries for Year 1:

Debit entries in Intangible Assets ledger account:			
Jan. 2	Incorporation fees		$ 6,500
2	Cost of common and preferred stock certificates (engraving, etc.)		2,100
10	Legal fees in connection with organization of company		15,000
Mar. 1	Costs of advertising campaign during Year 1		20,000
July 2	Operating loss for first six months of Year 1		22,200
7	Development costs on abandoned projects		45,000
Aug. 1	Goodwill recorded by credit to Retained Earnings ledger account based on estimate of future earnings		50,000
Oct. 10	General research and development costs		48,400
Nov. 1	Acquisition of patent (remaining economic life of five years from Nov. 1, Year 1)		25,200
Dec. 30	Bonus to design supervisor for "creative contribution to the product lines for Year 1"		4,800
Total debits			$239,200
Credit entries in Intangible Assets ledger account:			
Jan. 15	Proceeds on issuance of preferred stock in excess of par	$80,500	
Oct. 1	Proceeds from sale of potentially patentable design of new product. The costs of developing this design were debited to R&D expense in Year 1 and exceeded $15,000	6,000	86,500
Dec. 31	Balance		$152,700

Instructions

a Prepare journal entries to correct Linager Limited's ledger accounts, assuming that the nominal (revenue and expense) accounts have not been closed for Year 1. Any amount allocated to organization costs is amortized over five years.

b Prepare the intangible assets section of Linager Limited's balance sheet on December 31, Year 1.

Pr. 13-7 Petrol Corporation is considering the acquisition of Calgary Drillers, Inc., on March 31, Year 4. Relevant data for Calgary Drillers, Inc., follow:

Net assets (shareholders' equity)	$ 749,000
Total assets	1,200,000
Pre-tax earnings for three most recent fiscal years ($141,000 + $140,000 + $115,000)	396,000
Cash dividends paid during three most recent years	135,000

Calgary Drillers has a valuable patent that is fully amortized and will be transferred to Petrol at a valuation of $126,000. Other assets of Calgary Drillers have a current fair value equal to carrying amount. The estimated remaining economic life of the patent is five years. The earnings of Calgary Drillers during the next four fiscal years are expected to average 20% more than the average earnings of the past three fiscal years (before patent amortization).

Instructions

Estimate the amount of goodwill of Calgary Drillers, Inc., under each of the following independent assumptions:

a Average estimated future pre-tax earnings are capitalized at 15% to compute the total value of net assets of Calgary Drillers, Inc.

b Pre-tax earnings at the rate of 14%, based on identifiable net assets at current fair value, are considered normal for Calgary's type of business. Goodwill is estimated to be equal to average superior earnings capitalized at 20%.

c Normal pre-tax earnings rate on identifiable net assets at current fair value is considered to be 12½%, and goodwill is estimated at an amount equal to estimated superior earnings for three years.

d Pre-tax earnings of $120,700 are considered normal. Goodwill is estimated to be equal to the present value of average superior earnings (before income taxes) for four years, discounted at 20%. The present value of an ordinary annuity of four rents of 1 at 20% is 2.5887.

Pr. 13-8 Ludwig Corporation, a closely owned business enterprise, has not issued financial statements since it was incorporated in Year 1. You have been engaged in April, Year 16, to audit the financial statements of Ludwig for the year ended December 31, Year 15. Management of Ludwig plans to present financial statements to an investment banker in conjunction with a preliminary discussion of the possibility of issuing common stock to the public. Management desires to report the maximum net income for Year 15 under generally accepted accounting principles.

This problem relates solely to your audit of the Intangible Assets ledger account, summarized below:

Debit entries in Intangible Assets ledger account:		
Feb. 1/1	Organization costs	$ 18,000
Dec. 31/1	Goodwill acquired in business combination	40,000
Dec. 31/1	Net loss incurred in development stage of the corporation	55,500
July 1/5	Patent (estimated remaining economic life 15 years)	25,200
Dec. 31/9	Goodwill acquired in business combination	66,000
Dec. 31/10	Non-compete agreement covering six-year period	12,000
Dec. 31/10	Research costs eventually resulting in new and improved products and processes in Year 16	32,500
Dec. 31/12	Financing costs related to five-year loan of $2 million from Local Insurance Company, arranged on Dec. 31/12	33,000
Dec. 31/14	Development costs—new products in Year 16	45,000
Dec. 31/15	Development costs—new processes in Year 16	85,000
Dec. 31/15	Balance	$412,200

No credit entries have been made in the Intangible Assets ledger account since Ludwig was organized, and no amortization has been recorded for any of the items included in the account. You ascertain that the dollar amounts for all debits to the Intangible Assets ledger account were determined correctly. Management agreed with your suggestion that the organization costs should have been amortized over a five-year period, and that there has been no decline in the economic value of any goodwill acquired.

Instructions

(Disregard income tax considerations.)

a Observing management's desire to report the maximum net income for Year 15 in conformity with generally accepted accounting principles, prepare a working paper analysis of Ludwig Corporation's Intangible Assets ledger account. Any unamortized balance of an intangible asset as of December 31, Year 15, should be recorded in a separate ledger account. Use the following format (disposition of organization costs is given as an example):

Description of item	*Amount recorded in Intangible Assets ledger account*	*Adjustment to Retained Earnings (debit)*	*Expense (or factory overhead) for Year 15*	*Other ledger accounts debited*	
				Amounts	*Accounts*
Organization costs — should have been fully amortized prior to Year 15	$ 18,000	$ 18,000			

b Prepare a single journal entry for Ludwig Corporation to eliminate the Intangible Assets ledger account and to correct the accounting records on December 31, Year 15. The accounting records have not been closed for Year 15.

c What change or changes would be made to ***b*** if ***FASB Statement No. 2*** were followed?

Pr. 13-9 Lon Webb is investigating the possibility of acquiring Peg's Place, a sole proprietorship owned by Peggy Price. The condensed balance sheet of Peg's Place on December 31, Year 5, follows:

PEG'S PLACE
Condensed Balance Sheet
December 31, Year 5

Assets		*Liabilities & Proprietor's Capital*	
Current assets	$191,500	Current liabilities	$160,000
Land	115,000	12% mortgage note payable	400,000
Buildings	540,000	Total liabilities	$560,000
Less: Accumulated depreciation	(50,000)		
Equipment	186,000		
Less: Accumulated depreciation	(42,500)	Peggy Price, capital	380,000
Total assets	$940,000	Total liabilities & proprietor's capital	$940,000

Webb examined the foregoing balance sheet and determined that all assets were fairly stated, except that land was worth at least $195,000. An independent auditor had examined the income statements of Peg's Place for each of the five years ended December 31, Year 5, and reported that income, before interest on the mortgage note payable and income taxes, amounted to $100,000 for Year 5. The average unpaid balance of the mortgage note payable during the next four years will be $370,000. Because of an expected increase in sales volume, the income before interest and income taxes for each of the next four years is expected to increase at a compound rate of 10% a year. The present facilities of Peg's Place are sufficient to handle the expected increase in volume. Price is asking $525,000 cash for Peg's Place. Webb considers 15% a normal rate of return (before income taxes) for a business enterprise of this type.

Instructions

a Prepare an estimate of the goodwill of Peg's Place on December 31, Year 5, under each of the following methods. Round estimates of expected average income before income taxes and goodwill to the ***nearest hundred dollars***.

1 Capitalization of the average expected superior income before income taxes over the next four years at 15%.

2 Acquisition of expected superior income before income taxes for the next four years.

3 Present value of average superior income before income taxes expected to be realized at the end of each of the next four years, discounted at 15%. (The present value of an ordinary annuity of four rents of 1 at 15% a year is 2.855.)

4 Capitalization of the first $5,000 of expected average superior income before income taxes at 12½%, the next $5,000 at 20%, and the remainder at 25%.

b Should Lon Webb pay the amount Peggy Price is asking? Explain.

c Assume that Lon Webb's investigation indicates that Peg's Place will earn an average income before income taxes of $72,000 a year for an indefinite period. What maximum amount should Webb be willing to pay for Peg's Place? Prepare a journal entry to record the acquisition in Lon Webb's accounting records (assume a sole proprietorship), under the assumption that Webb acquired Peg's Place for the maximum price you computed.

chapter 14

LONG-TERM INVESTMENTS

In Chapter 6 we discussed short-term investments which can be converted quickly to cash and are classified as current assets. Many business enterprises (termed ***investors***) also make long-term investments in corporate securities (stocks, bonds, mortgage notes, long-term receivables, etc.) to create close business ties with other companies (termed ***investees***). These long-term investments are not current assets because they do not represent resources available to meet working capital needs.

The basis of distinction between short-term investments and long-term investments lies in the nature and purpose of the investment. Investments that are readily marketable and that may be sold without disrupting business relationships or impairing the operations of the business enterprise are classified as current assets. Investments made to foster business relationships with other enterprises are classified as long-term investments. Also, investments that do not meet the test of ready marketability are considered long-term, even if these investments do not promote business relationships. Long-term investments are listed immediately below the current assets section of the balance sheet.

Objectives of Long-Term Investments

A business enterprise may make long-term investments in the preferred and common stocks of other corporations for many reasons. For example, these investments may be used to create close ties to major suppliers or to retail outlets. The rights of ownership inherent in common stock investments give an investor in such securities a degree of influence or control over the management of the investee. Thus, many enterprises use investments in common stock as a means of gaining control of a competitor, acquiring ownership of a corporation with a strong cash position, or diversifying by acquiring an ownership interest in investees in order to obtain dividend revenue and capital appreciation.

Consolidated Financial Statements

A company that acquires a controlling interest in the common stock of another company is termed the ***parent company***, and the controlled company is the ***subsidiary***. The investment in the common stock of the subsidiary is a long-term investment for the parent company. In addition to the separate financial statements prepared for the parent company and for the subsidiary, ***consolidated financial statements*** also are prepared. Consolidated financial statements disregard the legal fact that each enterprise is a separate legal entity and treat the parent company and its subsidiaries as a single economic entity.

Viewing both parent company and subsidiary as a single economic entity is an alternative to treating the subsidiary as an investment owned by the parent company.

Acquisition Cost

The cost of an investment in securities includes the acquisition price plus brokerage fees and any other expenditures incurred in the transaction. If assets other than cash are given in payment for the securities and the current fair value of such noncash assets is unknown, the current market price of the securities may be used to establish the cost of the securities acquired and the value of the noncash assets given in exchange. When neither a market price for the securities nor the current fair value of the assets given in exchange is known, accountants must rely on independent appraisals to establish values for recording the transaction.

If two or more securities are acquired for a lump sum, the total cost should be allocated among the various securities. If the various securities acquired are publicly traded, the existing market prices serve as the basis for apportionment of the total cost. This type of cost apportionment is termed ***relative market value allocation***.

For example, assume that X Limited acquires from Y Corporation 100 units of five shares of common stock and one share of preferred stock each, at a price of $240 a unit, when the common stock is trading at $30 and the preferred stock at $100 a share. The portion of the cost allocated to the common stock is $\$24,000 \times {}^{150}/_{250}$, or $14,400, and the portion allocated to the preferred stock is $\$24,000 \times {}^{100}/_{250}$, or $9,600. If only one class of the stock is publicly traded, that class usually is recorded at its market value, and the remaining portion of the cost is considered the cost of the other class. When neither class of stock trades in the open market, the apportionment of the cost may have to be delayed until current fair values or market values of the shares are established.

ACCOUNTING FOR LONG-TERM INVESTMENTS IN COMMON STOCK

Measuring Return on Investment

What is the "return" on an investment in common stock? One point of view is that the investor's return consists of the stream of dividends received from the investment. A second point of view is that the investor's return consists of a proportionate share of the net income (minus preferred dividends, if any) of the investee, without regard to whether this income is distributed in the form of dividends during the accounting period. Supporting the latter point of view is the fact that the earnings of the investee that are not distributed as dividends are retained by the investee, with a resultant increase in the investee's shareholders' equity. A third interpretation of the investor's return consists of the dividends received plus (or minus) the change in the market value of the investment.

Three different accounting methods exist, depending on which return an investor wishes to measure. These methods are:

1 ***Cost method*** Investment income consists only of dividends received.

2 ***Equity method*** Investment income consists of the investor's proportionate share of the investee's net income.

3 ***Market value method*** Investment income includes dividends received and changes in the market value of the investment.

The market value method (as an alternative to the cost method) is illustrated for short-term investments in Chapter 6. However, the market value method is much less appropriate for long-term investments. By definition, long-term investments are not held to take advantage of short-term fluctuations in market prices. When an investor intends to hold investments in shares for long periods of time, the daily changes in market price lose significance. Therefore, either the cost method or the equity method generally is used to account for long-term investments in common stock. Usually, the accounting method required ***for reporting purposes*** may be determined as shown in the decision chart on page 646.[1]

Accounting for Dividends Received

The payment of dividends on capital stock (both preferred and common) is a discretionary act, requiring that the board of directors first declare the dividend. For this reason, investors should not accrue dividend revenue over a period of time as they do interest revenue on a bond. There are three acceptable alternatives for the recognition of dividend revenue under the cost method of accounting: (1) when the dividend is declared (***declaration date***), (2) when the dividend "accrues" to the current shareholder even if the stock is subsequently sold (***ex-dividend date***), or (3) when the dividend is received (***payment date***). Most investors record dividend revenue on the date of receipt. For purpose of consistency, all illustrations in this chapter recognize dividend revenue on the date the dividend is received.

Not all dividends received represent revenue to the investor. Sometimes corporations may pay dividends in excess of net income. In such cases the amount by which the cash distribution ***exceeds total earnings to date*** is considered a ***return of capital***, termed a ***liquidating dividend***, rather than dividend revenue.

Some accountants have suggested that, from the viewpoint of any shareholder,

1 Adapted from a chart used in 1982 by the School of Accountancy of the Institute of Chartered Accountants of Ontario (ICAO).

Decision chart for choice of accounting method

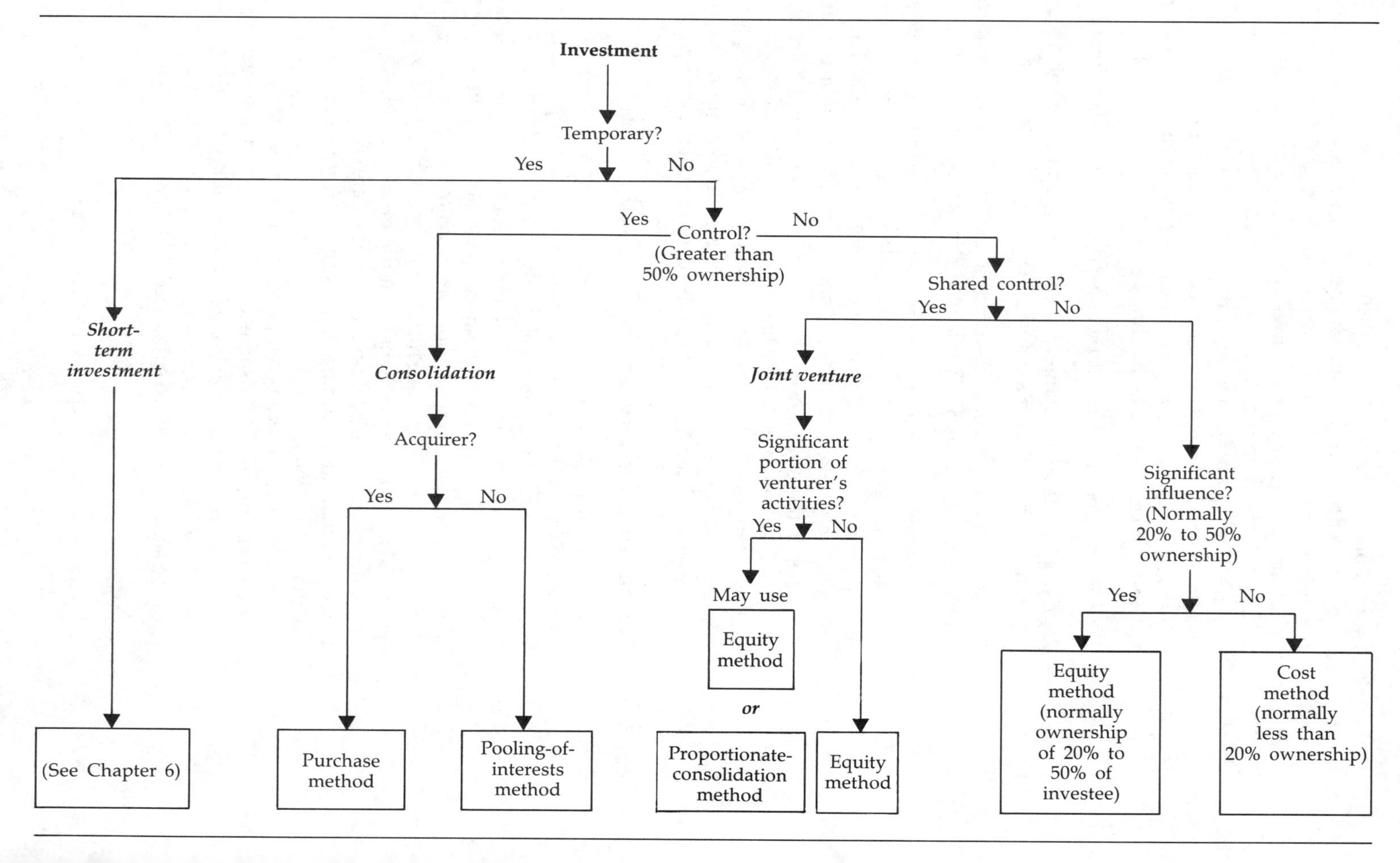

a liquidating dividend may be deemed to have occurred if dividends received exceed total net income of the investee after the date the investment was acquired. Practical application of such a concept may be difficult, beause corporations do not measure net income on a daily basis, whereas the acquisition of shares of common stock by individual investors occurs throughout the year. Moreover, some large investors make a series of acquisitions of an investee's common stock without disrupting the market price of the stock. Only in special circumstances would an investor be able to determine that a dividend received represented net income earned prior to the date of a specific acquisition of common stock.

It should be noted that the method of accounting which may be used by the investor during the year may be the cost or the equity method for long-term investments. If the cost method is used but the investment is other than one without significant influence, adjustments will have to be made at the year-end to reflect the equity method of accounting or for consolidation purposes depending on whether control exists and, if so, whether consolidation is appropriate.

The Cost Method of Accounting for Long-Term Investments in Common Stocks

When an investor owns only a small portion (for example, less than 20%) of the total outstanding common stock of an investee, the investor has little or no influence over the investee. ***CICA Handbook*** section 3050.19 states: "If the investor holds less than 20% of the voting interest in the investee, it should be presumed that the investor does not have the ability to exercise significant influence, unless such influence is clearly demonstrated."[2] In this case, the investor cannot influence the investee's dividend policy, and the only portion of the investee's income that reaches the investor is the dividends paid by the investee. Thus, when the investor has little or no influence over the investee, the dividends received represent the only return realized by the investor. Under these circumstances, the ***cost method*** of accounting for the investment in common stock is appropriate.

When the cost method of accounting is used, the investment ledger account is maintained in terms of the cost of the common stock acquired. Revenue is recognized by the investor only to the extent of dividends received. However, if a material portion of the dividends received represents a distribution of investee's earnings realized prior to the time the stock was acquired, that portion of the dividends is a ***return of capital*** (a ***liquidating dividend***), not revenue. Changes in the net assets of the investee are disregarded unless a liquidating dividend occurs or a ***significant*** and ***permanent*** impairment of value of the investment occurs. The above two events that may cause a departure from the cost basis are discussed below.

Liquidating Dividends

Because liquidating dividends represent a return of capital, receipt of such dividends by the investor is recorded by a credit to the investment ledger account. To

2 CICA, ***CICA Handbook*** (Toronto), sec. 3050.19.

illustrate the accounting for a liquidating dividend, assume that Toko Limited acquired 15% of the outstanding common stock of Duran Limited early in Year 1. During Year 1, Duran reported net income of $100,000 and paid a cash dividend of $150,000. Because the dividend exceeded by a material amount the net income of Duran for the period Toko owned Duran common stock and Toko is aware of this, Toko records the dividend as follows:

Journal entry for liquidating dividend

Cash ($150,000 × 0.15)	22,500	
Dividend Revenue ($100,00 × 0.15)		15,000
Investment in Duran Limited Common Stock...		7,500
To record receipt of dividend, including distribution of $7,500 in excess of net income since the investment was acquired.		

Permanent Decline in Value of Investment

Operating losses of the investee that reduce the investee's net assets substantially and seriously impair its future prospects are recorded as losses by the investor. A portion of the long-term investment has been lost, and this fact is recorded by reducing the carrying amount of the investment. Section 3050.33 of the ***CICA Handbook*** endorsed this approach with the following recommendation:[3]

> ***When there has been a loss in value of an investment that is other than a temporary decline, the investment should be written down to recognize the loss.*** The write-down would be included in the determination of income and may or may not be an extraordinary item.

For example, the journal entry to record a permanent decline of $210,000 in the value of long-term investments in Gray Limited common stock is as follows:

Journal entry for permanent decline in value of long-term investments

Loss in Value of Long-Term Investments	210,000	
Investments in Gray Limited Common Stock ...		210,000
To record a permanent decline in value of long-term investments in common stock.		

Section 3050.35 of the ***CICA Handbook*** states, in a recommendation, that such a loss "should not be reversed if there is a subsequent increase in value" of the investment.[4]

In some cases, a permanent loss in value of an investment is obvious, such as bankruptcy of the investee or an agreement to sell the investment at an amount below its carrying value. In other cases, a permanent loss may be indicated by the following conditions:[5]

1 A prolonged period during which the quoted market value of the investment is less than its carrying value

3 CICA, ***CICA Handbook***, sec. 3050.33.

4 CICA, ***CICA Handbook***, sec. 3050.35.

5 CICA, ***CICA Handbook***, sec. 3050.31.

2 Severe losses by the investee in the current year or current and prior years
3 Continued losses by the investee for a period of years
4 Suspension of trading in the securities
5 Liquidity or going-concern problems of the investee
6 The current fair value of the investment (an appraisal) being less than its carrying value

Gains and Losses on Sales of Investments

When part of a holding of securities is sold, the cost thereof is to be calculated on the basis of the average carrying value of that investment.

The Equity Method of Accounting for Long-Term Investments in Common Stocks

When an investor owns enough common stock of an investee to exercise significant influence over the investee's management, the dividends paid by the investee no longer may be an appropriate measure of the return on the investment. This is because the investor may influence the investee's dividend policy. In such a case, dividends paid by the investee may reflect the ***investor's*** income tax considerations and cash needs, rather than the profitability of the investment in common stock.

For example, assume that an investor owns 100% of the common stock of an investee. For two years the investee had significant net income but paid no dividends, because the investor had no need for additional cash and no need to increase income. In the third year, the investee has a net loss but pays a large cash dividend because the investor needs additional cash or wishes to report higher net income. It would be misleading for the investor to report no investment income while the investee was operating profitably, and then to show large investment income in a year when the investee operated at a loss.

The investee need not be 100% owned for the investor to have significant influence over its operating and financial policies. When the common stock of the investee is widely held, an investor owning much less than 50% of the common stock may have significant influence over the investee, because it is doubtful that the remaining outstanding shares will vote as an organized block.

When the investor has a significant degree of influence over the operating and financial policies of the investee, the equity method of accounting more fairly presents the benefits accruing to the investor than does the cost method. When the investor has little or no influence over the operating and financial policies of the investee, the benefits received by the investor may be limited to the dividends received, indicating the cost method of accounting to be more appropriate. The key criterion in selecting between the methods is the ***degree of influence*** the investor is able to exercise over the investee.

To achieve uniformity in accounting practice, the ***CICA Handbook***, as stated earlier, has suggested that less than 20% ownership indicates the use of the cost basis of accounting for the investment. This would seem to imply that ownership of 20% or more of the common stock of the investee would make the degree of influence significant, so that the use of the equity basis would be appropriate. However, the ***CICA Handbook*** further states that "the holding of 20% or more of the voting interest in the investee does not in itself confirm the ability to exercise significant influence."[6] Thus, while investments representing 20% or more of the voting stock of an investee usually are accounted for by the equity method of accounting, if the investor owns 20% or more but is unable to exercise significant influence over the investee, use of the cost method is required. On the other hand investments of less than 20% usually are accounted for by the cost method of accounting, unless clear-cut ability to influence the operating and financial policies of the investee may be demonstrated. Investments in preferred stock are accounted for by the cost method, because preferred shareholders usually do not have either voting rights or a residual equity in net income.

When the equity method of accounting is used, an investment in common stock initially is recorded at the cost of the stock acquired, but is adjusted for changes in the net assets of the investee subsequent to acquisition. The investor's proportionate share of the investee's net income is recorded as ***investment income***, causing an increase in the investment ledger account. If the investee's net income includes extraordinary items, the investor records its share of such items as extraordinary (if material in amount to the investor), rather than as ordinary investment income. Dividends paid by the investee are recorded by the investor as a conversion of the investment to cash, causing the investment ledger account to decrease.

Illustration of Equity Method of Accounting

To illustrate the equity method of accounting, assume that on January 2, Year 1, Investor Limited acquired 40% of the common stock of Lee Inc. for $300,000, which corresponded with the carrying amount of Lee's net assets. On December 31, Year 1, Lee reported net income of $70,000 (including a $10,000 extraordinary gain) and declared and paid dividends of $30,000. Investor Limited accounts for its investment in Lee Inc. as follows (disregarding income tax effects):

Journal entries for equity method of accounting — first year of affiliation

Date	Account	Debit	Credit
Year 1			
Jan. 2	Investment in Lee Inc. Common Stock	300,000	
	Cash		300,000
	To record acquisition of 40% of common stock of Lee Inc. at carrying amount of Lee's net assets.		
Dec. 31	Investment in Lee Inc. Common Stock	28,000	
	Investment Income (ordinary)		24,000
	Investment Income (extraordinary)		4,000
	To record 40% of net income of Lee Inc. for Year 1 ($60,000 × 0.40 = $24,000; $10,000 × 0.40 = $4,000).		
31	Cash	12,000	
	Investment in Lee Inc. Common stock		12,000
	To record dividends received from Lee Inc. ($30,000 × 0.40 = $12,000).		

6 CICA, ***CICA Handbook***, sec. 3050.19.

After the foregoing journal entries have been posted, the investment and investment income ledger accounts appear as follows (before closing entries for the investment income accounts):

Investor's ledger accounts under equity method of accounting

Investment in Lee Inc. Common Stock

Date	*Explanation*	*Debit*	*Credit*	*Balance*
Year 1				
Jan. 2	Cost of investment.	300,000		300,000 Dr
Dec. 31	Share of net income ($70,000 × 0.40).	28,000		328,000 Dr
31	Dividends received ($30,000 × 0.40).		12,000	316,000 Dr

Investment Income (Ordinary)

Date	*Explanation*	*Debit*	*Credit*	*Balance*
Year 1				
Dec. 31	Share of net income ($60,000 × 0.40).		24,000	24,000 Cr

Investment Income (Extraordinary)

Date	*Explanation*	*Debit*	*Credit*	*Balance*
Year 1				
Dec. 31	Share of net income ($10,000 × 0.40).		4,000	4,000 Cr

Note that the net effect of Investor's accounting for Lee's net income and dividends was to increase the balance of the investment ledger account by $16,000. This corresponds with 40% of the increase in Lee's net assets as a result of undistributed earnings during Year 1 [($70,000 − $30,000) × 0.40 = $16,000].

Problems in the Application of the Equity Method

Two problems may arise in the application of the equity method of accounting. First, intercompany profits (gains) and losses resulting from transactions between the investor and the investee must be eliminated until realized by a transaction with an unaffiliated entity. Second, when the acquisition cost of an investment differs from the carrying value of the investee's identifiable net assets, adjustments may have to be made to the investment income recorded by the investor.

Intercompany Profits (Gains) or Losses

An investor or an investee may sell merchandise or, less frequently, plant or intangible assets to its affiliate. If so, any unrealized profit (gain) or loss must be excluded from the net income of the investor.

To illustrate, assume that on November 30, Year 2, Investor sold merchandise costing $50,000 to Lee Inc. for $80,000, or a gross profit rate of 37½% ($30,000 ÷ $80,000 = 0.375). On December 31, Year 2, the inventories of Lee included $60,000 (at billed price) of this merchandise. In addition, on December 31, Year 2, Lee sold merchandise that cost $30,000 to Investor for $50,000; none of this merchandise was sold by Investor to its customers on that date. If Lee reported net income of

$95,000 (none of which was an extraordinary item) for Year 2, but did not declare or pay dividends for that year, Investor prepares the following journal entries on December 31, Year 2, under the equity method of accounting (disregarding income tax effects):

Journal entries for equity method of accounting — second year of affiliation

Investment in Lee Inc. Common Stock [($95,000 − $20,000) × 0.40]	30,000	
Investment Income (ordinary)		30,000
To record 40% of net income of Lee Inc. for Year 2 after elimination of $20,000 unrealized gross profit ($50,000 − $30,000 = $20,000) remaining in Investor's inventories on Dec. 31, Year 2.		
Investment Income (ordinary)	22,500	
Investment in Lee Inc. Common Stock		22,500
To eliminate unrealized gross profit attributable to merchandise in Lee Inc.'s inventories on Dec. 31, Year 2.		

The net effect of the two foregoing journal entries is to reduce Investor's net income (disregarding income tax effects) by $30,500, computed as follows:

Composition of reduction of Investor Company's net income

Investor's share of unrealized gross profit of Lee Inc. ($20,000 × 0.40)	$ 8,000
Investor's unrealized gross profit on sales to Lee Inc. ($60,000 × 0.375)	22,500
Total reduction of Investor's net income	$30,500

A review of the foregoing illustration of intercompany profits emphasizes the necessity of excluding unrealized intercompany profits (gains) and losses from an investor's net income. The investor's ability to influence the operating and financial policies of an investee enables the investor to determine to a large degree the quantity and unit price of merchandise sold by investor to investee, and vice versa. Obviously, if unrealized intercompany profits were not eliminated from the investor's net income, the investor might reach a desired net income and earnings-per-share amount merely by selling merchandise to, or purchasing merchandise from, an investee.

Cost in Excess of Carrying Value (Equity) Acquired

Often an investor will pay more than the ***carrying value*** of an investment because current fair values of the investee's identifiable assets may be larger than their carrying values, or because the investee has unrecorded goodwill. In either case, this excess of cost over the carrying value will benefit the investor only over the economic lives of the understated (or unrecorded) assets.

To the extent that the excess of cost over the carrying value was paid to acquire an interest in specific understated assets, this amount should be amortized over the economic lives of those assets. The journal entry to reflect the amortization is as shown at the top of page 653.

To the extent that the excess cost was incurred because of implied goodwill, the excess is amortized over the estimated economic life of the goodwill. The *CICA*

Journal entry for amortization of excess of cost over carrying value acquired

Investment Income (ordinary)	XXX	
Investment in Investee's Common Stock		XXX
To adjust investment income for amortizaton of excess of cost over carrying value of Investee's net assets.		

Handbook states that amounts paid for goodwill should be amortized by the straight-line method over a period of not more than 40 years.[7] Accounting for goodwill is discussed in Chapter 13.

Cost Less than Carrying Value (Equity) Acquired

When an investor acquires an investment in common stock at a cost less than the carrying value, it is assumed that specific identifiable assets of the investee are overstated. If these assets have limited economic lives, the investor allocates the excess of the carrying value over cost to investment income over the economic lives of the assets. The journal entry to record this amortization is shown below:

Journal entry for amortization of excess of carrying value acquired over cost

Investment in Investee's Common Stock	XXX	
Investment Income (ordinary)		XXX
To adjust investment income for amortization of excess of carrying value of Investee's net assets over cost.		

Note that this adjustment ***increases*** investment income. The rationale for this action is that the investee's reported net income is understated because the investee has based recorded depreciation or amortization on overstated carrying amounts of assets.

It is possible for the ***fair value*** of the investee's net assets to exceed book value and for the cost to still be less than book value. This situation signifies a credit or negative goodwill occurring on the acquisition. This is often referred to as a bargain purchase. The negative goodwill is credited to the identifiable nonmonetary assets of the investee company.[8] This credit will be added to net income over the economic lives of the nonmonetary assets to which the negative goodwill was applied and will increase investment income of the investor accordingly.

Summary of Procedures Under the Equity Method of Accounting

Accounting procedures under the equity method may be summarized as follows:

1. The investment initially is recorded at cost.
2. The investor subsequently recognizes its proportionate share of the investee's net income (after elimination of intercompany profits) by a debit to the investment ledger account and a credit to Investment Income. In event of a loss, Investment Loss is debited and the investment account is credited.
3. The investor views its share of dividends declared and paid by the investee as

7 CICA, *CICA Handbook*, sec. 1580.59.

8 CICA, *CICA Handbook*, sec. 1580.44.

a conversion of the investment to cash. Thus, the investor debits Cash and credits the investment ledger account.

4 The investor adjusts the recorded amount of investment income or loss by the amortization of any excess of cost of its investment over the carrying value associated with the investee's depreciable assets or goodwill. This adjustment consists of a debit to Investment Income (or Loss) and a credit to the investment ledger account.

5 The investor adjusts the recorded amount of investment income or loss by the amortization of any excess of the carrying value over cost by a debit to the investment ledger account and a credit to Investment Income (or Loss).

Comparative Illustration of the Cost and Equity Methods of Accounting for Long-Term Investments in Common Stocks

To illustrate the differences in the cost and equity methods, assume that on January 2, Year 1, Investor Limited acquired 4,000 shares (20%) of the outstanding common stock of Investee Inc. for $1,000,000. On the date of acquisition, the carrying value of Investee's identifiable net assets was $4,550,000. Investor was willing to pay more than the carrying value for the investment because it was estimated that Investee owned land worth $100,000 more than its carrying value, depreciable plant assets worth $150,000 more than their carrying value, and enough goodwill to make a 20% interest in Investee worth the $1,000,000 cost.

The excess of the cost of the investment over the carrying value is analyzed below:

Analysis of excess of cost of investment over carrying value

Cost of investment	$1,000,000
Less: carrying value ($4,550,000 × 0.20)	910,000
Excess of cost over carrying value acquired	$ 90,000
Composition of excess:	
20% interest in understated land ($100,000 × 0.20)	$ 20,000
20% interest in understated depreciable plant assets ($150,000 × 0.20)	30,000
Implied goodwill ($90,000 − $20,000 − $30,000)	40,000
Excess of cost over carrying value acquired	$ 90,000

The understated depreciable plant assets have an average remaining economic life of 10 years, and Investor's policy with respect to goodwill is to amortize it over 40 years.

During Year 1, Investee reported net income of $430,000, after an extraordinary loss of $50,000, and declared and paid dividends of $200,000 at year-end. Investor's accounting for its investment in Investee during Year 1 is illustrated on page 655 under the cost and the equity methods of accounting.

Note that no adjustment is made under either the cost or the equity method for the $20,000 excess of cost over the carrying value representing Investor's 20%

INVESTOR LIMITED
Comparison of Cost and Equity Methods of Accounting
For Year 1

Date	*Explanation*		*Cost method (Investor assumed to have no significant influence over Investee)*			*Equity method (Investor assumed to have significant influence over Investee)*		
Year 1 Jan. 2	To record acquisition of 4,000 shares of Investee Inc.'s common stock.		Investment in Investee Inc. Common Stock..	1,000,000		Investment in Investee Inc. Common Stock....	1,000,000	
			Cash		1,000,000	Cash		1,000,000
Dec. 31	To record receipt of dividend of $40,000 from Investee Inc. ($200,000 × 0.20 = $40,000).		Cash	40,000		Cash	40,000	
			Dividend Revenue		40,000	Investment in Investee Inc. Common Stock...		40,000
31	To record $86,000 share of Investee Inc's net income ($430,000 × 0.20 = $86,000) including $10,000 share of extraordinary loss ($50,000 × 0.20 = $10,000).		(No journal entry)			Investment Loss (extraordinary)	10,000	
						Investment in Investee Inc. Common Stock	86,000	
						Investment Income (ordinary)		96,000
31	To amortize a portion of the excess of investment cost over the carrying value, as follows:		(No journal entry)			Investment Income (ordinary)	4,000	
	Depreciable plant assets ($30,000 ÷ 10 years)	$3,000				Investment in Investee Inc. Common Stock ...		4,000
	Goodwill ($40,000 ÷ 40 years)	1,000						
	Total amortization................	$4,000						

interest in Investee's understated land. This is because land is not depreciated. The results for Year 1 are illustrated below for the two methods of accounting:

Comparison of results of equity method and cost method

	Cost method of accounting	*Equity method of accounting*
Investment in common stock of Investee Inc. (ending balance)	$1,000,000	$1,042,000
Investment income (loss) recognized by Investor Limited:		
Ordinary income	$ 40,000	$ 92,000
Extraordinary loss		(10,000)

Joint Ventures and Consolidations

Two other areas of interest are depicted in the decision chart on page 646. ***Joint ventures*** are shared-control enterprises and ***consolidations*** relate to those long-term investments where greater than 50% of the shares are purchased or exchanged and where, therefore, control exists.

Joint ventures represent a special area of accounting, because usually the investors are participants in a venture with limited life. For example, there are many joint ventures in the extractive industries, where the project ends when a natural resource has been exhausted in a particular location; at that time, the joint venture too is completed. As depicted in the chart, participants in a joint venture are required normally to account for their investment in the joint venture on the equity basis for reporting purposes. There may be cases in which it would be more informative to the users of the venturer's financial statements to see a number of individual joint ventures accumulated in what is known as a proportionate consolidation. It is the venturer's prerogative to use the proportionate-consolidation method or the equity method to account for joint venture investments for reporting purposes.

Consolidated financial statements will differ according to whether one of the participants is an acquirer of the other(s), or two or more companies simply join for their common benefit. A company that acquires a controlling interest in the issued common stock of another company is termed the ***parent company***, and the controlled company the ***subsidiary***. The investment in the common stock of the subsidiary is a long-term investment for the parent company. In addition to the separate financial statements prepared by the parent company and by the subsidiary, ***consolidated financial statements*** also are prepared. Consolidated financial statements ignore the legal concept that each enterprise is a separate entity and treat the parent company and its subsidiaries as a single economic entity. Viewing both enterprises as a single economic entity is an alternative to treating the subsidiary as an investment owned by the parent company.

When two or more companies join together such that it is not possible to identify an acquirer in the group, a different method of consolidation exists. This method is called the ***pooling-of-interests method***.

When an acquirer is identified, the purchase is treated the same as previously explained under equity accounting. That is, fair values must be determined and goodwill ascertained at the purchase date. In addition, gains, profits and losses on intercompany transactions, which have not been completed with an outside entity, must be removed.

In pooling-of-interests reporting, the net assets of the companies involved are combined at book values at the combination date. As a result, there is no fair value or goodwill involved in such a combination. Business combinations treated as a pooling of interests for reporting purposes are rare occurrences as usually an acquirer can be identified.

The purchase transaction, as previously shown under the equity method of accounting for the investee company, includes the purchased carrying value of the net assets of the subsidiary plus or minus the purchased share of the difference between the sum of the fair values of the individual net assets and the sum of their individual carrying values, plus or minus the residual, known as goodwill. The entire cost therefore may be broken down into the three components: carrying value, fair value increment (decrement), and goodwill.

When the parent company purchases 100% of the subsidiary company, it is purchasing 100% of each of the three components. The situation is as shown in the following chart:

Three components in a purchase transaction when 100% of subsidiary is acquired

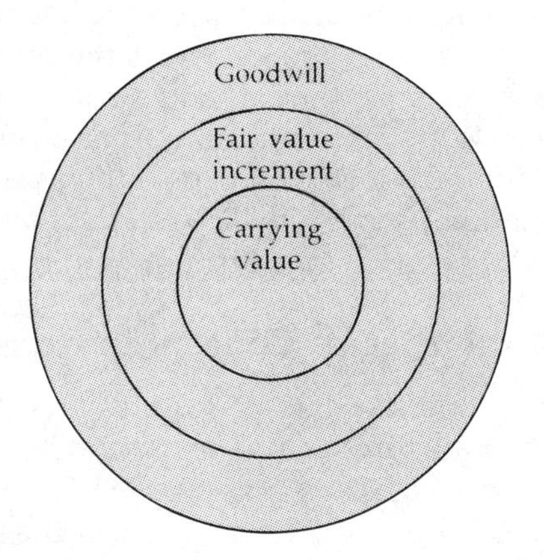

The 100% carrying value plus the 100% fair value increment is equal to the fair value of the subsidiary company's net assets. That total, together with the 100% goodwill cost, will equal the purchase price to the parent company for its 100% interest in the subsidiary company. The shaded area (all of this pie, as parent purchased 100% of subsidiary company) will be included in the consolidated balance sheet.

When the parent company purchases less than 100% of the subsidiary company, a portion of each of the three components belongs to other than the parent company. This portion is called ***minority interest***. The situation wherein the parent owns less than 100% of the subsidiary company is as depicted in the following pie chart.

Three components in a purchase transaction when less than 100% of the subsidiary is acquired

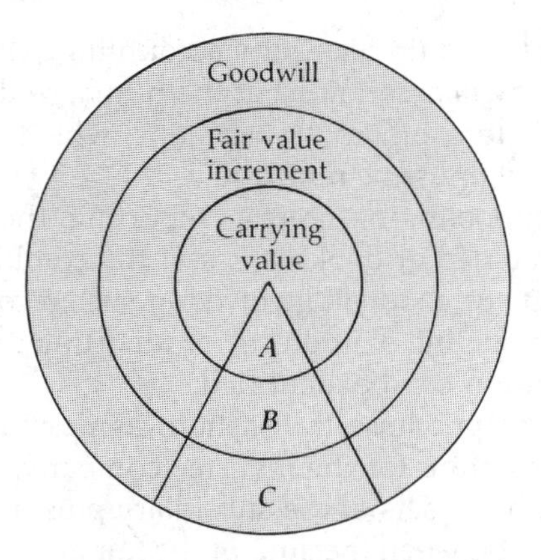

This small slice of the pie represents the minority-interest share of the subsidiary company. That share may be further broken down into the three components as follows:

- *A* Minority-interest share of subsidiary company's carrying value
- *B* Minority-interest share of subsidiary company's fair value increment
- *C* Minority-interest share of subsidiary company's goodwill

There are four concepts underlying acquirer-identified consolidated financial statements. They are known as the ***proprietary concept***, the ***entity concept***, the ***parent company concept***, and the ***parent company extension concept***. They have relevance for consolidation purposes when the parent company owns less than 100% of the issued common (voting) stock of the subsidiary company. When the parent company has a 100% interest in the subsidiary company the four concepts will have identical results for reporting purposes.

The Proprietary Concept in Consolidating

The proprietary concept requires that the parent company consolidate only its share of the three components with its own financial statements. For example, if the parent company (P) owns 75% of the subsidiary company (S), the minority-interest portion is 25% of S. Under the proprietary concept the breakdown of S for the three components would be as shown below:

Three components in a purchase transaction when less than 100% of subsidiary is acquired and parent uses the proprietary concept when consolidating

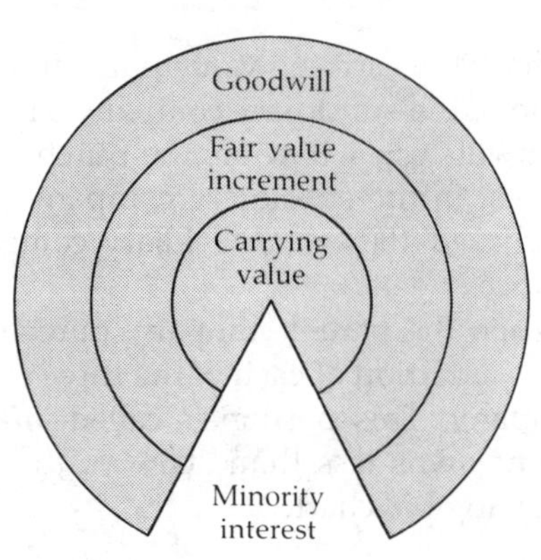

The shaded portion of the pie represents the portion of S's net assets that will be included in the consolidated balance sheet.

In this example, the parent company would consolidate with all but the unshaded (minority-interest) area of the subsidiary company, namely 75% of S's carrying value plus 75% of the fair value increment of S's net assets, plus 75% of the total goodwill inherent in the subsidiary company as evidenced by (extrapolated from) the price P has paid for 75% thereof.

Assume the carrying value of the net assets of S to be $800,000 and their fair value to be $1,000,000, and further assume P paid $1,050,000 for its 75% interest in S. The purchase price of $1,050,000 may be broken down into the three components as follows:

Determination of amounts for three components — proprietary concept

75% of carrying value of S's net assets purchased	$ 600,000
75% of fair value increment purchased [($1,000,000 − $800,000) × 75%]	150,000
75% of total goodwill (equals goodwill purchased) [$1,050,000 − ($600,000 + $150,000)]	300,000
	$1,050,000

The consolidation of P with S would entail the including of $600,000 of S's net assets' carrying values, $150,000 of S's net assets' fair value increments and $300,000 of goodwill, in the consolidated entity.

As a result, the proprietary concept includes in the consolidated statements the total of S "*owned*" by P.

The Entity Concept in Consolidating

The entity concept requires the parent company to consolidate 100% of the three components with its own financial statements, even though it may have purchased less than 100% of the subsidiary company in the acquisition. The first pie chart shown on page 658 depicts this situation, as the entire pie is shaded and therefore is included in the consolidated balance sheet. In this situation, the minority-interest portion of the pie would be included in the consolidation and an offsetting account titled Minority Interest would be included in the financial statements for the minority interest's 25% share of the subsidiary company. That is, the consolidated financial statements would include 100% of the carrying value of S's net assets plus 100% of the fair value increment of S's net assets plus 100% of S's extrapolated goodwill, all offset by a ***credit*** to minority interest, representing 25% of each of the above three components.

Using the information in the previous example, the consolidation of P with S would entail the adding of $800,000 of S's carrying value of net assets, $200,000 ($1,000,000 − $800,000) of S's net assets fair value increments and $400,000 ($300,000 ÷ 0.75) of goodwill, together with a minority interest ***credit*** of 25% of ($800,000 + $200,000 + $400,000) or $350,000. As a result, the entity concept includes in the consolidated statements the total of S "***controlled***" by P.

The ***net*** result is the same for both the proprietary concept and the entity concept, as follows:

Total addition to the consolidation of S:	
Proprietary concept:	
75% carrying value plus 75% fair value increment plus 75% goodwill equals	$1,050,000
Entity concept:	
$1,400,000 ($800,000 + $200,000 + $400,000) – $350,000 minority interest equals	$1,050,000

However, the disclosure for consolidation purposes is entirely different for the two concepts. The minority interest is not disclosed under the proprietary concept, whereas under the entity concept it will be disclosed in the amount of $350,000. The total consolidated assets will be larger by $350,000 under the entity concept.

Parent Company and Parent Company Extension Concepts

It is possible to add two additional concepts when moving from the proprietary concept to the entity concept. These two concepts are called the ***parent company concept*** and ***parent company extension concept*** respectively, and are as depicted in the following charts:

Three components in a 75% purchase for each of four concepts

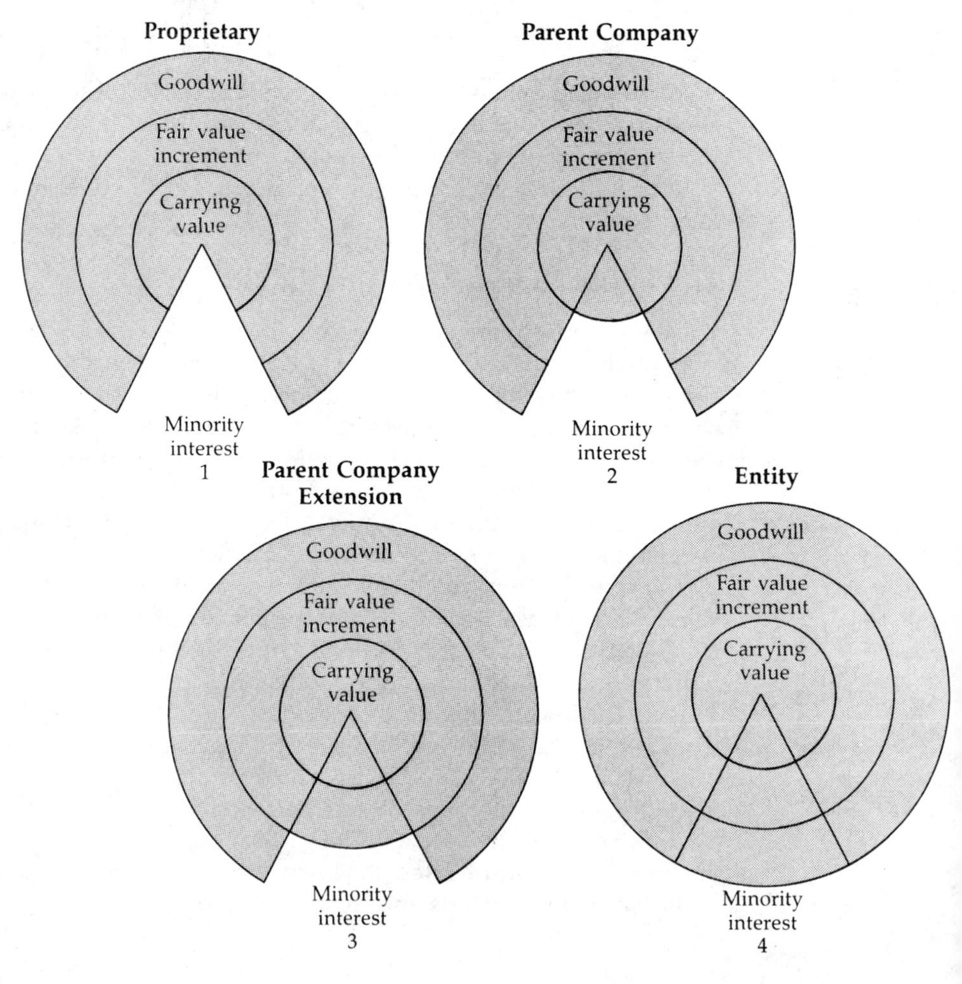

The portion of each pie that is included in the consolidated balance sheet is the ***shaded portion***. The first chart is the proprietary concept where no minority-interest share is included. That is, the 25% of the carrying value of S, the 25% of fair value increment of S, and the 25% of goodwill inherent in S are excluded from the consolidation.

The second chart, the parent company concept, includes minority interests' share of the carrying value of S's net assets. Therefore, the consolidation includes 100% of the carrying value of S's net assets plus 75% of the fair value increment of S and 75% of the extrapolated goodwill of S and, as a result, a ***credit*** for minority interest representing 25% of the carrying value of S's net assets. Therefore, the only difference between chart 1 and chart 2 is the additional 25% of carrying value of S's net assets added to net assets in the consolidation and offset by a credit of the same amount to minority interest in the consolidation.

The third chart, the parent company extension concept, adds to the second chart 25% more of the fair value increment, increasing it to 100% with a corresponding increase to the minority-interest account. As a result, the consolidation will include 100% each of S's carrying value of net assets and fair value increment of net assets (the sum of the two represents 100% of the fair value of S's net assets), plus 75% of S's extrapolated goodwill, with an offsetting credit to minority interests representing 25% of each of the carrying value and the fair value increment of S's net assets (representing 25% of the fair value of S's net assets).

The fourth chart is the entity concept, in which 100% of each element is included in the net assets and 25% of each element is credited to minority interest for consolidation purposes.

Using the earlier example to illustrate the parent company concept and the parent company extension concept, the consolidation of P with S would include the following:

Components included in *consolidation under parent company* and *parent company extension* concepts

	Parent Company Concept 2	*Parent Company Extension Concept 3*
100% of carrying value of S's net assets	$ 800,000	$ 800,000
75% of fair value increment	150,000	-0-
100% of fair value increment	-0-	200,000
75% of extrapolated purchased goodwill	300,000	300,000
	$1,250,000	$1,300,000
Minority interest:		
25% of carrying value of S's net assets	$ 200,000	$ 200,000
25% of fair value increment	-0-	50,000
Total Minority Interest	$ 200,000	$ 250,000
Net amount	$1,050,000	$1,050,000

To clarify the distinction among the four concepts a summary using the example follows.

Example: Summary of Four Methods at Acquisition Date

Subsidiary Amounts Included in Consolidation	*Proprietary Concept*	*Parent Company Concept*	*Parent Company Extension Concept*	*Entity Concept*
75% carrying value of S's net assets	$ 600,000	-0-	-0-	-0-
100% carrying value of S's net assets	-0-	$ 800,000	$ 800,000	$ 800,000
75% fair value increment of S's net assets	150,000	150,000	-0-	-0-
100% fair value increment of S's net assets	-0-	-0-	200,000	200,000
75% goodwill purchased	300,000	300,000	300,000	-0-
100% extrapolated goodwill purchased	-0-	-0-	-0-	400,000
	$1,050,000	$1,250,000	$1,300,000	$1,400,000
Minority interest credit:				
25% carrying value of S's net assets		$ -0-	$ 200,000	$ 200,000
25% fair value increment of S's net assets	-0-	-0-	50,000	50,000
25% extrapolated goodwill purchased	-0-	-0-	-0-	100,000
Total minority interest credit	$ -0-	$ 200,000	$ 250,000	$ 350,000
Net amount	$1,050,000	$1,050,000	$1,050,000	$1,050,000

The purpose of preparing financial statements is to provide shareholders of the parent company with information to aid them in their economic decison-making processes. The consolidated financial statements show all the assets, liabilities, and incomes of the parent and subsidiaries as a single economic entity. It is a quantitative portrayal of the resources and results of operations of the group as a whole.

Each of the four concepts above represents a ***detailed*** quantitative portrayal which differs from each of the others. However, in the ***aggregate***, the final amount (net amount of $1,050,000 above) is the same. The magnitude of the detailed quantitative differences will depend upon the percentage of minority interest, the size of the fair value increment, and the amount of purchased goodwill at the date the parent company purchased its controlling interest in the subsidiary company.

The proprietary concept portrays what is ***owned*** by the parent company, whereas the entity concept portrays what is ***controlled*** by the parent company. Each of the other concepts falls in between these two. If the consolidated financials are to provide information to aid shareholders of the parent company in their decision making, it would seem reasonable to consider the entity concept the preferred one. It depicts the fair value of the net assets of the subsidiary company at the acquisition date. This is the value of the subsidiary's net assets controlled by the parent company at that date.

However, the 100% goodwill amount may not represent the fair value of goodwill. If the parent company paid the excess amount in order to further its own ends such as to expand into a new geographical area or to acquire specific management talent, it would probably pay an additional amount for its share. An increase of this amount to 100% would not reflect the fair value of goodwill to others.

It may not be reasonable to set up only the purchased amount of goodwill, where, in fact, that amount does represent that share of the total goodwill truly attributable to the subsidiary company itself. It would be theoretically correct to do one or the other, depending on the reason for the excess cost.

A further attribute of the entity concept is that it increases the carrying value of the net assets to their fair value at the purchase date. This certainly would appear to be the more informative amount for reporting purposes with respect to portraying the resources of the consolidated group.

The act of not increasing the net assets of the subsidiary company above that amount representing the fair value of the net assets of the subsidiary multiplied by the percent of ownership results in the net assets of the subsidiary being consolidated at somewhere between carrying value and fair value, the amount depending on the percentage of ownership of the subsidiary company by the parent company.

The Accounting Standards Committee of the CICA agonized over which of these concepts should be required for consolidation purposes. An exposure draft for consolidated financial statements was issued in which the parent company extension concept was espoused. The fair value of the net assets was to be set up and ***only*** purchased goodwill (P's share) was to be set up. However, a re-exposure draft was later issued in which the carrying value of the net assets of S was set up and ***only*** the purchased share of the fair value increment of S's net assets and of goodwill was set up. This is the parent company concept that was eventually incorporated into the ***CICA Handbook***.

ACCOUNTING FOR LONG-TERM INVESTMENTS IN BONDS

A bond contract represents a promise to pay an amount of money at maturity and a series of interest payments (usually every six months) during the term of the contract. Investors acquire corporate bonds to earn a ***return on investment***. The effective rate of return (***yield***) on bonds to investors is determined by the price investors pay for the bonds (because the terms of the contract are fixed). The yield on the bonds to investors generally will differ from the effective interest cost to the borrower when the bonds are acquired by investors subsequent to the issuance date.

Computation of Acquisition Price of Long-Term Investment in Bonds

The cost of an investment in bonds is the present value of the future cash receipts pursuant to the bond contract, measured in terms of the ***market rate of interest*** at the time of investment. The ***stated*** (***nominal***) ***annual rate of interest*** in the bond contract measures the cash to be received periodically by the investor. If the rate of return demanded by investors is exactly equal to the nominal rate, the bonds may be acquired at the face amount. If the market rate of interest exceeds the nominal rate, the bonds may be acquired at a ***discount***, because the investor is demanding a higher return than the bond contract offers; therefore, to equate the yield on the bond with the market rate of interest, the bond is acquired at a price below face amount. If the market rate of interest is ***below*** the nominal rate, the investor will be willing to pay a ***premium*** for the bond, that is, a price above face amount.

To illustrate the computation of the acquisition price of bonds (using the present-value concepts described in Chapter 5), assume that $200,000 of 7% bonds of Villa Ltd. maturing in 15 years are acquired by Kane Limited to yield 8% compounded semiannually. The bonds pay interest semiannually starting six months from date of acquisition. Because the market rate of interest exceeds the nominal rate, the bonds are acquired at a discount, as shown below (using the Appendix at the end of Chapter 5):

Computation of acquisition price of bonds issued at a *discount*

Present value of $200,000 discounted at 4% for 30 six-month periods ($200,000 × 0.308319)	$ 61,664
Add: Present value of ordinary annuity of 30 rents of $7,000 (semiannual interest payments) discounted at 4% ($7,000 × 17.292033)	121,044
Acquisition price of bonds (discount of $17,292)	$182,708*

*Alternative computation: [$200,000 − ($1,000 semiannual interest "deficiency" × 17.292033) = $182,708]

If the market rate of interest was only 6% compounded semiannually, the bonds paying semiannual interest at 7% a year would be acquired at a premium, as shown below.

Computation of acquisition price of bonds issued at a *premium*

Present value of $200,000 discounted at 3% for 30 six-month periods ($200,000 × 0.411987)	$ 82,397
Add: Present value of ordinary annuity of 30 rents of $7,000 discounted at 3% ($7,000 × 19.600441)..........	137,203
Acquisition price of bonds (premium of $19,600)	$219,600*

*Alternative computation: [$200,000 + ($1,000 semiannual "extra" interest × 19.600441) = $219,600]

Acquisition of Bonds Between Interest Dates

Interest on a bond contract accrues with the passage of time in accordance with the provisions of the contract. The issuer pays the contractual rate of interest on the stated date to the investor owning the bond on that date. The investor who acquires a bond between interest dates must pay the previous owner the market price of the bond plus the interest accrued since the last interest payment. The investor is paying the previous owner of the bond the interest applicable to the first portion of the interest period and will in turn collect that portion plus the additional interest earned by holding the bond until the next interest payment date.

Illustration

On July 1, an investor acquired 10 bonds ($1,000 face amount each) of Ray Limited, which had been issued several years ago. The bond contract provides for interest at 8% a year, payable semiannually on April 1 and October 1. The market rate of interest is higher than 8% at the present time, and the bonds are currently quoted at 97¾ plus accrued interest for three months. The journal entry for the investor to record the acquisition of the 10 bonds is:

Investor's journal entry to record acquisiton of bonds between interest dates

Investment in Ray Limited Bonds ($10,000 × 0.9775)	9,775	
Interest Receivable ($10,000 × 0.08 × 3/12)	200	
Cash		9,975
To record acquisition of 10 bonds plus accrued interest of $200 for three months.		

The $200 paid by the investor for accrued interest may be debited to Interest Revenue; if so, when the first $400 interest payment ($10,000 × 0.08 × 6/12 = $400) is received on October 1, the entire amount is credited to Interest Revenue.

Discount and Premium on Long-Term Investments in Bonds

On the date of acquisition of bonds, the investment ledger account is debited for the cost of acquiring the bonds, including brokerage and other fees, but excluding any accrued interest. A separate discount or premium ledger account as a valuation account is seldom used. The subsequent treatment of the investment might be handled in one of three ways: (1) The investment might be carried at cost, ignoring the ***accumulation*** of discount or ***amortization*** of premium; (2) the investment ledger account balance might be revalued periodically to reflect market value changes; or (3) the discount or premium might be accumulated or amortized to reflect the change in the carrying amount of the bonds based on the effective rate of interest prevailing at the time of acquisition.

The first alternative (the cost basis) is used primarily in accounting for short-term bond investments, as discussed in Chapter 6 (see page 287), for convertible bonds and for other bonds for which the discount or premium is insignificant. The discount or premium on convertible bonds seldom is related to the level of interest rates, but rather reflects the effect of the price of the common stock to which the bond is convertible. These securities are subject to wide price movements related to changes in the market price of common stocks; therefore, the amortization of premium or accumulation of discount by investors does not seem appropriate for convertible bonds.

The second alternative (valuation at market) is not in accord with the present interpretation of the realization principle or the concept of conservatism, especially during periods of rising bond prices. Changes in market prices of bonds held as long-term investments may be of less significance to the investor than changes in prices of short-term investments, because the long-term investments frequently are held to maturity, at which time market price and face amount of the bonds are equal. When the investment in bonds is in jeopardy because of serious cash shortages of the issuer, it generally is acceptable to write the investment down to its expected net realizable value and to recognize a loss.

The third alternative (systematic accumulation or amortization) is the preferred treatment for long-term investments in bonds. This approach recognizes that the interest revenue represented by the discount, or the reduction in interest revenue represented by the premium, accrues over the term of the bonds. This method is consistent with the principle that requires that assets other than cash and receivables be recorded at cost.

Interest Revenue

The periodic interest payments provided for in a bond contract represent the total interest revenue to an investor holding a bond to maturity only if the investor acquired the bond at its face amount. If an investor acquires a bond at a premium, the amount received on maturity of the bond will be less than the amount of the initial investment, thus reducing the cumulative interest revenue by the amount of the premium. Similarly, if the bond is acquired at a discount, the amount received at maturity will be larger than the initial investment, thereby increasing the cumulative interest revenue by the amount of the discount.

When an investor intends to hold bonds to maturity, there is little logic in treating the discount or premium as a gain or loss occurring on the maturity date. Rather, the increase in the carrying amount of the bonds, as a discount disappears, should be viewed as part of the revenue accruing to the investor over the entire period the bonds are owned. Similarly, the decrease in value when a premium disappears is a cost the investor is willing to incur during the holding period to receive periodic interest payments higher than the market rate at the time the bonds were acquired. Thus, the amount of the discount or premium is viewed as an integral part of the periodic interest revenue earned by the investor. The accumulation of a discount increases periodic interest revenue, and the amortization of a premium decreases periodic interest revenue.

Methods of Discount Accumulation or Premium Amortization

The methods of amortization for bond discount and bond premium by the issuer are discussed in Chapter 15. These methods present precisely the same problem for the investor as for the issuer. The purpose of ***accumulating the discount*** or ***amortizing the premium*** is to reflect accurately the interest revenue derived from the investment in bonds.

Interest Method

The ***interest method*** (***effective interest method***) produces a constant rate of return on the investment in bonds. That is, the periodic interest revenue always represents the same percentage return on the carrying amount of the investment. Thus, when a discount is being accumulated and the investment account is increasing, the interest revenue recognized each interest period also ***increases***; this is accomplished by accumulating an ever-increasing portion of the discount each period. When the premium on a long-term investment in bonds is being amortized and the balance in the investment account is decreasing, the interest revenue recorded each period also ***decreases***. Under the interest method, the interest revenue is computed for each interest period by multiplying the balance of the investment account by the effective interest rate at the time the investment was made. The accumulation of the discount (or amortization of the premium) thus is the difference between the periodic cash receipt and the interest revenue for the period computed by the effective rate of interest.

Straight-Line Method

Under the ***straight-line method***, the discount or premium is spread uniformly over the term of the bonds. Although the bonds may be sold by the investor or redeemed by the issuer prior to maturity, the accumulation or amortization always ***is based on the years remaining to maturity***. The straight-line method is simple to apply and avoids the necessity for determining the yield rate. ***The primary objection to the straight-line method is that it produces a constant amount of interest revenue each accounting period, which results in an uneven rate of return on the investment***. For this reason, the interest method is conceptually superior to the straight-line method.

Illustration

The computation of periodic discount to be accumulated or premium to be amortized and the related journal entries will be illustrated with the examples for Kane Limited given on page 664. The Kane Limited examples involved (1) the acquisition of $200,000 face amount of 7% bonds maturing in 15 years (or 30 semiannual periods) to yield 8% compounded semiannually and (2) the acquisition of the same bonds to yield 6% compounded semiannually. The journal entries to record the investment, receipt of interest for the first year, and the related accumulation or amortization under the interest method and the straight-line method are presented on pages 668 and 669. (All computations are rounded to the nearest dollar.)

Interest revenue on long-term bond investments, like interest revenue on any other investment, is accrued only on significant dates. The significant dates are: (1) interest payment dates, (2) the end of the investor's accounting period, and (3) the time of any transaction (such as the sale of any portion of the investment) involving the particular investment that does not coincide with a regular interest payment date. The discount also is accumulated or the premium amortized in accordance with whatever method of accumulation or amortization is used.

When the bonds are acquired at a discount and the interest method of accumulation is used, the investment account is increased to $183,016 at the end of the first six-month period; therefore, interest revenue for the second six-month period is $7,321 ($183,016 × 4% = $7,321), which required $321 of the discount to be accumulated.

Journal entries for acquisition of bonds on the date in the bond indenture and accumulation of discount

KANE LIMITED
Journal Entries

	Interest method		*Straight-line method*	
1 *Bonds acquired to yield 8% compounded semiannually:*				
Investment in Villa Ltd. Bonds	182,708		182,708	
Cash		182,708		182,708
To record acquisition of 7% bonds at a discount of $17,292 to be accumulated over 30 six-month periods.				
Cash	7,000		7,000	
Investment in Villa Ltd. Bonds	308		576	
Interest Revenue		7,308		7,576
To record receipt of interest at the end of the first six-month period: $200,000 × 7% × ½ = $7,000. Accumulation of discount: Interest method: ($182,708 × 4%) − $7,000 = $308. Straight-line method: $17,292 ÷ 30 = $576.				
Cash	7,000		7,000	
Investment in Villa Ltd. Bonds	321		576	
Interest Revenue		7,321		7,576
To record receipt of interest at the end of the second six-month period: $200,000 × 7% × ½ = $7,000. Accumulation of discount: Interest method: [($182,708 + $308) × 4%] − $7,000 = $321. Straight-line method: $17,292 ÷ 30 = $576.				

Journal entries for acquisition of bonds on the date in the bond indenture and amortization of premium

KANE LIMITED
Journal Entries

	Interest method		*Straight-line method*	
2 *Bonds acquired to yield 6% compounded semiannually:*				
Investment in Villa Ltd. Bonds	219,600		219,600	
Cash		219,600		219,600
To record acquisition of 7% bonds at a premium of $19,600 to be amortized over 30 six-month periods.				
Cash	7,000		7,000	
Investment in Villa Ltd. Bonds		412		653
Interest Revenue		6,588		6,347
To record receipt of interest at the end of				

	Interest method		Straight-line method	
the first six-month period: $200,000 × 7% × ½ = $7,000. Amortization of premium: Interest method: $7,000 − ($219,600 × 3%) = $412. Straight-line method: $19,600 ÷ 30 = $653.				
Cash	7,000		7,000	
Investment in Villa Ltd. Bonds		424		653
Interest Revenue		6,576		6,347
To record receipt of interest at the end of the second six-month period: $200,000 × 7% × ½ = $7,000. Amortization of premium: Interest method: $7,000 − [($219,600 − $412) × 3%] = $424. Straight-line method: $19,600 ÷ 30 = $653.				

When the bonds are acquired at a premium and the interest method of amortization is used, the investment account is reduced to $219,188 at the end of the first six-month period; therefore, interest revenue for the second six-month period is $6,576 ($219,188 × 3% = $6,576), which required $424 of the premium to be amortized.

When bonds are issued subsequent to the date specified in the bond indenture, the lifetime of the bond issue becomes less than that stated in the bond indenture. ***This will affect the amortization of premium or accumulation of discount if the straight-line method is used and will incorporate accrued interest if the original issue date is between interest dates.*** Many issues are delayed beyond the date stipulated in the bond indenture due to unfavourable market conditions prevailing at the bond indenture date. It is not unusual for the actual issue to be more than six months after the date stipulated in the bond indenture. The journal entries to record the investment, receipt of interest for the first year, and the related accumulation or amortization under the ***effective interest method*** and under the ***straight-line method*** are presented below and on pages 670–672. (All computations are rounded to the nearest dollar.)

Journal entries for acquisition of bonds after the date in the bond indenture and accumulation of discount

KANE LIMITED
Journal Entries

			Interest method		*Straight-line method*	
1		***Bonds acquired to yield 8% compounded semiannually:***				
	a	Investment in Villa Ltd. Bonds	182,862		182,862	
		Interest Receivable	3,500		3,500	
		Cash		186,362		186,362
		To record acquisition of 7% bonds at a discount of $17,138 to be accumulated over a period of 29½ six-month periods.				

b	Cash	7,000		7,000	
	Investment in Villa Ltd. Bonds	154		290	
	Interest Revenue		3,654		3,790
	Interest Receivable		3,500		3,500
	To record receipt of interest and accumulation of discount at the end of the first six-month period.				
c	Cash	7,000		7,000	
	Investment in Villa Ltd. Bonds	321		581	
	Interest Revenue		7,321		7,581
	To record receipt of interest and accumulation of discount at the end of the second six-month period.				

Computations:

1 a Present value of $200,000 discounted at 4% for 29 six-month periods:

$200,000 × 0.320651	$ 64,130
Add: Present value of ordinary annuity of 29 rents of $7,000 discounted at 4%: $7,000 × 16.983715	118,886
Total purchase price if purchased six months after bond indenture date	$183,016
Total purchase price if purchased on bond indenture date (page 664)	$182,708

Difference: $183,016 − $182,708 = $308 for six months. Since the issue date is three months after the indenture date, $\frac{3}{6}$ × $308 is used up. This equals $154.

(The use of this straight-line method results in an approximation of the "true" accumulation.)

Therefore the purchase price is $183,016 minus $154 or $182,708 plus $154 = $182,862.

Therefore the discount is $200,000 − $182,862 = $17,138.

The accrued interest is $\frac{3}{12}$ × $200,000 × 7% = $3,500.

For effective interest method accumulation:

1 b This will be $154 as computed in **1 a** above.

1 c This will be $321, computed as follows:

[($182,862 + $154) × 4%] − $7,000 = $321 (rounded)

For straight-line accumulation:

1 b $\frac{\$17{,}138 \text{ discount}}{177 \text{ months}} \times 3 \text{ months} = \$290$ (rounded)

1 c $\frac{\$17{,}138 \text{ discount}}{177 \text{ months}} \times 6 \text{ months} = \$581$ (rounded)

Journal entries for acquisition of bonds after the date in the bond indenture and amortization of premium

KANE LIMITED
Journal Entries

	Interest method		Straight-line method	
2 *Bonds acquired to yield 6% compounded semiannually:*				
a Investment in Villa Ltd. Bonds	219,394		219,394	
Interest Receivable	3,500		3,500	
Cash		222,894		222,894
To record acquisition of 7% bonds at a premium of $19,394 to be amortized over 29½ six-month periods.				
b Cash	7,000		7,000	
Investment in Villa Ltd. Bonds		206		329
Interest Revenue		3,294		3,171
Interest Receivable		3,500		3,500
To record receipt of interest and amortization of premium at the end of the first six-month period, 3 months after issue date.				
c Cash	7,000		7,000	
Investment in Villa Ltd. Bonds		424		657
Interest Revenue		6,576		6,343
To record receipt of interest and amortization of premium at the end of the second six-month period.				

Computations:

2 a Present value of $200,000 discounted at 3% for 29 six-month periods:

$200,000 × 0.424346	$ 84,869
Add: Present value of ordinary annuity of 29 rents of $7,000 discounted at 3%: $7,000 × 19.188455	134,319
Total purchase price if purchased six months after bond indenture date...	$219,188
Total purchase price if purchased on bond indenture date (page 664)	$219,600

Difference: $219,600 − $219,188 = $412 for six months. Since the issue date is three months after the indenture date, $\frac{3}{6}$ × $412 is used up. This equals $206.

(The use of this straight-line method results in an approximation of the ''true'' amortization.)

Therefore the purchase price is $219,188 plus $206 or $219,600 minus $206 = $219,394.

Therefore the premium is $200,000 − $219,394 = $19,394.

The accrued interest is $\frac{3}{12}$ × $200,000 × 7% = $3,500.

For effective interest method amortization:

2 b This will be $206 as computed in **2 a** above.

2 c This will be $424, computed as follows:

$$\$7{,}000 - [(\$219{,}394 - \$206) \times 3\%] = \$424 \text{ (rounded)}$$

For straight-line amortization:

2 b $\frac{\$19{,}394 \text{ premium}}{177 \text{ months}} \times 3 \text{ months} = \$329$ (rounded)

2 c $\frac{\$19{,}394 \text{ premium}}{177 \text{ months}} \times 6 \text{ months} = \$657$ (rounded)

SPECIAL PROBLEMS IN ACCOUNTING FOR INVESTMENTS IN SECURITIES

Cost Identification

Investments in securities may pose a problem as to which costs should be offset against revenue in the period of sale. For example, assume that an investor acquires 1,000 shares of Z Limited common stock at a price of $80 a share, and 1,000 shares at $90 a share. Several years later, the investor sells 1,000 shares of Z Limited common stock for $84 a share. Should the investor recognize a $4,000 gain or a $6,000 loss?

The answer to this question requires making a ***cost flow assumption***, as with inventories. Because securities usually are identified by a certificate number, it would be possible to use specific identification of stock certificates to establish the cost of the 1,000 shares sold. However, an alternative cost flow assumption might be adopted. The alternative methods of cost flow include: (1) fifo — the first shares acquired are assumed to be the first ones sold; (2) lifo — the last shares acquired are assumed to be the first ones sold; and (3) weighted-average cost — each share is assigned the same cost basis.

From a theoretical viewpoint, weighted average is the only cost flow assumption that recognizes the economic equivalence of identical securities. In our illustration of successive purchases of the common stock of Z Limited at different prices, it is undeniable that each share of Z Limited common stock owned has exactly the same economic value regardless of the price paid to acquire it. The weighted-average cost flow assumption recognizes the economic reality that it makes no difference which 1,000-share certificate is sold and which is retained. According to the ***CICA Handbook***, the cost of investments sold should be calculated on the weighted-average basis for the purpose of calculating a gain or loss on the disposal.[9]

Accounting for Stock Dividends and Stock Splits

Stock dividends and stock splits do not result in revenue to investors. Thus, the total cost of the shares purchased should be adjusted to reflect the increase of the number of shares as a result of stock dividends and stock splits. While there are no official pronouncements by the accounting profession in Canada in this area, the accounting profession in the United States has supported this position.[10]

9 CICA, *CICA Handbook*, sec. 3050.35.

10 AICPA, *Accounting Research and Terminology Bulletins — Final Edition* (New York: 1961), chap. 7b, p. 51.

> Since a shareholder's interest in the corporation remains unchanged by a stock dividend or split-up except as to the number of share units constituting such interest, the cost of the shares previously held should be allocated equitably to the total shares held after receipt of the stock dividend or split-up. When any shares are later disposed of, a gain or loss should be determined on the basis of the adjusted cost per share.

The investor's accounting procedure to record the receipt of additional shares from a stock dividend or stock split usually is confined to a memorandum entry that indicates the number of shares of stock received and the new cost per share.

Property Dividends

When a corporation distributes a dividend in the form of merchandise, securities of other corporations, or other noncash assets, the investor records the property received at its current fair value.

Stock Purchase Warrants and Stock Rights

A ***stock warrant*** is a certificate issued by a corporation conveying to the holder ***rights*** to purchase shares of its common stock at a specified price within a specified time period. A single right attaches to each share of outstanding stock, and two or more rights usually are required to acquire one new share at the specified price. For example, when rights are issued, the owner of 100 shares of common stock will receive a warrant representing 100 rights and specifying the number of rights required to acquire one new share of common stock. The term of these rights usually is limited to a few weeks. The rights must be exercised or sold before the expiration date or they become worthless.

Accounting for Stock Warrants Acquired for Cash

The accounting problems involved when an investor acquires warrants in the open market are similar to those relating to the acquisition of any security. The acquisition price, plus brokerage fees and other acquisition costs, is debited to Investment in Stock Warrants, and Cash is credited. When warrants are acquired in conjunction with the acquisition of other securities, the total cost must be allocated to the various securities included in the package, on the basis of relative market values.

When the warrants are used to acquire common stock, the initial cost of the warrants used plus the cash paid is the cost of the stock. The Investment in Common Stock ledger account is debited; Cash and Investment in Stock Warrants are credited. If the market price of the common stock differs from this combined cost, this fact is disregarded until the stock is sold, at which time a gain or loss is recognized.

Accounting for Stock Warrants Acquired from Issuer

Stock warrants for rights are distributed to the shareholders of a corporation in proportion to their holdings of common stock. The receipt of stock warrants for rights may be compared with the receipt of a stock dividend. The issuer distributes no assets; instead, a method has been provided for an additional investment by the present shareholders. Until the shareholders elect to exercise or sell their warrants, their investment in the corporation is represented by (1) shares of common stock that have been acquired, and (2) stock warrants for rights to acquire additional shares of common stock at a price below the current market price. The cost of the original common stock investment consists now of the cost of the common stock and the warrants; therefore, the cost of the original investment is apportioned between these two parts of the investment on the basis of relative market values. The common stock will trade in the market on a ''rights-on'' basis until the ex-rights date, at which time the stock sells ''ex-rights,'' and the stock warrants have a market of their own. Relative market value allocation may be used to apportion the cost between the common stock and the stock warrants as follows:

Allocation of cost of common stock investment to stock warrants

$$\text{Cost assigned to stock warrants} = \text{Cost of original investment in common stock} \times \left(\frac{\text{market value of one right}}{\text{market value of one share of stock ex-rights} + \text{market value of one right}} \right)$$

To illustrate, assume that on June 1, Year 7, Lott Limited received warrants from Anne Ltd. for 10,000 rights to acquire one additional share of Anne's common stock for four rights plus $80. On that date, Lott's Investment in Anne Ltd.'s Common Stock ledger account (10,000 shares) had a balance of $432,000. On the ''ex-rights'' date, market values of Anne's securities were as follows: common stock, $95 a share; stock warrants, $5 a right.

Lott Limited prepares the following journal entry to record the receipt of the stock warrants:

Journal entry for allocation of cost to stock warrants

Investment in Anne Ltd. Stock Warrants ($432,000 × $5/$100)	21,600	
Investment in Anne Ltd. Common Stock		21,600
To allocate cost of Anne Ltd. investment to stock warrants received June 1, Year 7, on basis of relative market values of Anne's common stock and stock warrants.		

If Lott subsequently exercised all the rights to acquire 2,500 shares of Anne's common stock, the following journal entry would be appropriate:

Journal entry for exercise of stock rights

Investment in Anne Ltd. Common Stock [(2,500 × $80) + $21,600]	221,600	
Cash (2,500 × $80)		200,000
Investment in Anne Ltd. Stock Warrants		21,600
To record acquisition of 2,500 shares of Anne Ltd. common stock at $80 a share plus rights.		

If Lott allowed the warrants to lapse without exercising the rights, it would debit a realized loss ledger account and credit Investment in Anne Ltd. Stock Warrants in the amount of $21,600.

Convertible Securities

An investor may invest in bonds or preferred stocks that are convertible to the common stock of the investee at the option of the investor. The characteristics of convertible securities are discussed in Chapters 15 and 17. At this point, we consider the action to be taken by investors who exercise the ***conversion option*** (***feature***) and receive common stock in exchange for convertible bonds or convertible preferred stock.

The market value of the common stock received may differ materially from the carrying value of the converted securities. However, it is virtually universal practice to assign the carrying value of the convertible security to the common stock acquired in exchange. Thus, ***no gain or loss is recorded at the time of conversion***. This treatment is supported by the theoretical argument that investors contemplate conversion when they acquire a convertible security. Thus, no gain or loss is recognized until the common stock acquired by conversion is sold.

The following journal entry illustrates the ***carrying value*** (or ***book value***) ***method*** for the conversion of an investment in Quincy Limited bonds with a carrying value of $96,720 to Quincy's common stock with a current market value of $120,000:

Journal entry for conversion of bonds to common stock—*carrying value* (or *book value*) *method*

Investment in Quincy Limited Common Stock	96,720	
Investment in Quincy Limited Convertible Bonds		96,720
To record conversion of bonds to common stock.		

Some accountants have proposed recording the common stock acquired by conversion of bonds at the market value of the stock. Under this ***market value method***, the journal entry to record the conversion would be as follows:

Journal entry to record conversion of bonds to common stock—*market value method*

Investment in Quincy Limited Common Stock	120,000	
Investment in Quincy Limited Convertible Bonds		96,720
Gain on Conversion of Bonds ($120,000 – $96,720)		23,280
To record conversion of bonds to common stock.		

The difficulty with the market value method is the financial statement presentation of the Gain on Conversion of Bonds Ledger account. The realization principle precludes inclusion of the unrealized gain in the income statement; and the gain does not fit the definition of a liability or shareholders' equity.

OTHER LONG-TERM INVESTMENTS

Long-Term Receivables

As indicated in Chapter 4 (page 165) and Chapter 7 (page 318), receivables not collectible during the next year or operating cycle, whichever is longer, are excluded from current assets and may be reported with other long-term investments in the balance sheet. Among such receivables are long-term notes and instalment contracts receivable and notes receivable from officers, employees, or affiliated companies not collectible in the next year or operating cycle. The current portion of instalment contracts receivable and other notes receivable collectible in installments is reported with other current assets in the balance sheet. Adequate allowances for doubtful amounts are required for long-term receivables as they are for current accounts and notes receivable. If a long-term receivable acquired in exchange for goods or services is non-interest-bearing or pays an interest rate that is materially different from the current market rate, the receivable is valued in accordance with the standards described in Chapter 7 (pages 317–318).

Investments in Special-Purpose Funds

Occasionally, a business enterprise accumulates a fund of cash, usually invested temporarily in securities, for a special purpose. Funds generally are created to pay a liability or to acquire specific assets. In general, funds are treated as long-term investments only when they are established by contract and the resources of the funds are not available to management for general operating needs. A fund is classified as a current asset if it is created voluntarily and may be used for operating purposes.

The transactions that must be accounted for in connection with fund accumulation and administration are: (1) the transfer of assets to the fund, (2) the investment of the assets in internally managed funds, (3) the collection of revenue and payment of expenses if the fund is managed internally, and (4) the use of fund assets for the intended purpose.

There are two methods of handling funds: (1) The fund may be established and operated internally or (2) the assets may be deposited with a ***trustee*** (a bank, for example) who receives deposits, invests cash, collects revenue, pays expenses, and renders an appropriate accounting to the responsible officials.

Typically, funds that are created voluntarily are operated internally, whereas those created by contract are handled by a trustee. The periodic deposit in the fund generally is set in advance. It may be related to the level of operations, or it may be set either as a stated amount each period or as a stated amount less earnings on fund assets for the period. The method of determining the amount and time for the deposit generally may be found by referring to the document authorizing the establishment of the fund. In cases when the fund is committed irrevocably for the purpose designated, and cash actually is deposited with a trustee, the fund itself may not appear among the assets of the business enterprise, and the liability that is to be paid from fund assets may be excluded from the liabilities. This procedure is used most often when the liability does not exceed the fund balance, which means that the enterprise has no liability other than that for the periodic deposits stipulated in the contract. Some of the employee pension plans discussed in Chapter 19 are of this type.

Bond sinking funds usually are included under long-term investments, and bonds outstanding are shown as a long-term liability. The sinking fund should not be offset against the bond liability. A sinking fund and other similar funds usually are included in the balance sheet as an asset even though they are held by trustees.

One of the most common methods of accumulating a sinking fund is to deposit fixed amounts at periodic intervals. The periodic deposit is computed by use of an amount of annuity formula described in Chapter 5.

The transactions relating to the acquisition and sale of securities, and the accrual and collection of revenue for the sinking fund, are accounted for in the same manner in which transactions relating to regular investments are recorded.

Cash Surrender Value of Life Insurance Policies

When a business enterprise is dependent on certain officers for direction and management, life insurance policies may be acquired on the lives of these officers, with the enterprise named as the beneficiary. Certain types of insurance policies combine a savings program and an insurance plan. When these are acquired, the accumulated amount of the savings portion of the insurance premium is reported in the balance sheet as a long-term investment.

The savings part of a life insurance policy is referred to as the ***cash surrender value*** of the policy. This is the amount the enterprise would receive in the event that the policy were cancelled; this same amount also may be used as collateral for a loan.

The following data represent the first four years' experience of White Limited, which has a $100,000 life insurance policy on one of its officers:

Breakdown of gross life insurance premium

Year	*Gross premium*	*Cash value increase*	*Insurance expense*
1	$3,040	$ 30	$3,010
2	3,040	250	2,790
3	3,040	260	2,780
4	3,040	280	2,760

From these limited data, we can readily see the increase in the asset and the decreasing annual cost of life insurance. The journal entries for the first two years are as follows:

Journal entries for payment of life insurance premiums for first two years

Year 1	Insurance Expense	3,010	
	Cash Surrender Value of Life Insurance Policy	30	
	Cash		3,040
	To record the payment of life insurance premium.		
Year 2	Insurance Expense	2,790	
	Cash Surrender Value of Life Insurance Policy	250	
	Cash		3,040
	To record the payment of life insurance premium.		

In the event of death of the insured officer, White Limited would collect the face amount of the insurance policy. The journal entry to record this event, assuming death occurred early in Year 3, would be as follows:

Journal entry for receipt of proceeds of life insurance policy

Year 3	Cash	100,000	
	Gain on Settlement of Life Insurance Policy		99,720
	Cash Surrender Value of Life Insurance Policy		280
	To record collection of life insurance proceeds.		

For financial accounting, the gain is included in income (as a separate item if abnormal in size) before extraordinary items in the income statement.

Presentation in Financial Statements

Long-term investments that cannot be sold without impairing business relationships are classified as noncurrent assets.

The following illustration is indicative of the features of the investments section of a balance sheet, including the required disclosures for significant investments accounted for under the equity method of accounting:

Illustration of long-term investment section of balance sheet

Investments:	
Common stock of Arletz Limited, at cost	$ 60,450
Common stock of Fenby, Inc., at underlying equity (**NOTE**)	286,200
12% bonds of Jardine Ltd. due December 31, Year 9, at cost less unamortized discount of $5,971	94,029
Sinking fund for 10% bonds due June 30, Year 14	348,721
Receivable from affiliated company	50,000
Cash surrender value of life insurance policies	283,400
Total investments	$1,122,800

NOTE: The 35% investment in the outstanding common stock of Fenby, Inc., is accounted for by the equity method of accounting. The difference of $60,000 between the cost of the investment and the underlying equity on the date of acquisition is attributable to goodwill and is being amortized over a 20-year economic life. Aggregate market value of the investment was $320,000 on December 31, Year 5.

Dividends and interest revenue normally are listed under the caption "Other Revenue" and are included in the determination of income before extraordinary items. When the equity method of accounting is used, ordinary investment income (or loss) is separately disclosed in the income statement before extraordinary items. The investor's share of any extraordinary item of the investee retains its extraordinary nature and is classified as an extraordinary item if it is material to the investor. Because of the nature of long-term investments, gains and losses from sales occur relatively infrequently. A business enterprise with numerous long-term investments may expect occasional gains and losses from sales of these investments and should record such gains and losses as extraordinary items, provided they meet the criteria for being so classified.[11]

REVIEW QUESTIONS

1 Distinguish between the asset categories of short-term investments and long-term investments. Might the same securities constitute short-term investments for one business enterprise and long-term investments for another? Explain.

2 What is the ***cost*** of a security acquired for cash? Acquired in exchange for

11 CICA, *CICA Handbook*, sec. 3480.04(a).

assets for which current fair value is not readily determinable? Acquired as part of a group acquisition?

3 Explain three concepts of the "return on investment" to an investor in common stock and identify the appropriate accounting method for each concept.

4 Why should dividend revenue not be accrued over time by an investor as is interest revenue? What are the alternatives for the recognition of dividend revenue?

5 An investor acquired 1,000 shares of Anne Limited common stock on May 15 for $75 a share when the carrying amount of Anne's common stock was composed of the following:

Common stock, no par value	$3,000,000
Retained earnings	4,500,000
Total shareholders' equity	$7,500,000

On May 16, Anne declared a dividend of $3 a share. What was the nature of this distribution from the point of view of the investor? Of Anne? What was the legal interpretation of this distribution to the investor?

6 Distinguish between the ***cost*** and the ***equity*** methods of accounting for a long-term investment in common stock. When is each appropriate?

7 Identify three events that necessitate a write-down of a long-term investment under the cost method of accounting.

8 Compare the accounting for dividends from an investee under the cost and equity methods of accounting for a long-term investment in common stock. How is the difference in accounting for dividends justified?

9 Is the elimination of unrealized intercompany profits on merchandise shipments by an investor to an investee different from the reverse situation? Explain.

10 How may the acquisition price of a long-term investment in common stock affect the subsequent measurement of investment income or loss under the equity method of accounting?

11 P Ltd. acquired 80% of S Ltd. on December 31, 19X1. At that date, the fair values of S Ltd.'s net assets exceeded their book values. P Ltd. also paid an additional amount for goodwill. The two companies will consolidate on December 31, 19X1. Describe in general terms how such a consolidation would be treated under:

a The proprietary concept
b The entity concept
c The parent company concept
d The parent company extension concept

12 Describe the differences between the accounting for an "acquisition date" consolidation treated as a purchase and the accounting for such a consolidation treated as a pooling of interests. Assume no minority interest.

13 Why does the effective yield of a long-term investment in bonds often differ from the interest rate stated in the bond contract? Explain the effect of interest rate fluctuations on bond prices.

14 Why is the discount or premium on long-term bond investments treated as an adjustment of interest revenue rather than as a gain or loss on sale, redemption, or maturity of the bonds?

15 Distinguish between the ***interest method*** and the ***straight-line method*** of accumulating a discount and amortizing a premium on a long-term investment in bonds.

16 What is the theoretical support for the use of a weighted average as a basis for determining cost when units of the same equity security are acquired on different dates and at different prices?

17 From an investor's point of view, is there any significant difference between a stock dividend and a stock split? Does either represent revenue to an investor?

18 What are ***stock warrants for rights***? How are they accounted for by an investor?

19 When a convertible bond is converted to common stock, what journal entry does the investor make? Would your answer be different if the market price of the common stock were known? If the market price were not known? Explain.

20 Why is the ***cash surrender value*** of an insurance policy on the life of an officer of a business enterprise included as a long-term investment in the balance sheet of the enterprise?

EXERCISES

Ex. 14-1 Select the best answer for each of the following multiple-choice questions:

1 On January 2, Year 6, Lido Limited acquired (as a long-term investment) 5,000 shares of DeKalb Ltd.'s common stock at $60 a share. The 5,000 shares were less than 10% of DeKalb's outstanding common stock. On December 15, Year 6, when the market value of DeKalb common stock was $47 a share, Lido determined that the market value decline was permanent. The market value of DeKalb common stock was $46 a share on December 31, Year 6.

The Investment in Common Stock of DeKalb Ltd. ledger account balance for Lido Limited on December 31, Year 6 is:

a $0 ***b*** $300,000 ***c*** $235,000 ***d*** $230,000 ***e*** Some other amount

2 An investor that uses the equity method of accounting for a 40%-owned investee, which had net income of $20,000 and declared and paid dividends of $5,000 during Year 6, prepared the following journal entries (explanations omitted) on December 31, Year 6:

Investment in Investee Common Stock	8,000	
Investment Income		8,000
Cash	2,000	
Dividend Revenue		2,000

The effect of the foregoing journal entries on the balance sheet of the investor on December 31, Year 6, is to:

a Understate the investment ledger account and retained earnings
b Overstate the investment ledger account and retained earnings
c Overstate the investment ledger account and understate retained earnings
d State financial position correctly

3 Investor Limited received stock warrants for 10,000 rights to acquire one additional share of Investee Ltd. common stock for one right plus $100 cash. The cost of Investor's 10,000 shares of Investee common stock on which the rights were received was $240,000. On the ''ex-rights'' date, the market value of one right was $8 and the market value of one share of Investee common stock was $112. In the journal entry to record receipt of the stock warrants, Investor debits the Investment in Investee Ltd. Stock Warrants ledger account for:

a $12,000 *b* $16,000 *c* $80,000 *d* $92,000 *e* Some other amount

4 On January 2, Year 5, Margold Limited established a sinking fund for a bond issue due on January 2, Year 15. On December 31, Year 7, the bank serving as independent trustee for the sinking fund reported a fund balance of $364,000, representing $300,000 of Margold's annual deposits to the fund and earnings of $64,000. How is the sinking fund reported in Margold's December 31, Year 7, balance sheet?

a No part of the sinking fund is included in the balance sheet
b $64,000 is included with current assets
c $364,000 is included with current assets
d $364,000 is included with long-term investments

5 The following journal entry (explanation omitted) appeared in the accounting records of Jax Limited on April 30, Year 7, the end of its fiscal year:

Loss in Value of Long-Term Investments	60,000	
Investments in Common Stocks		60,000

A possible explanation for the foregoing journal entry is:

a To record dividends received from long-term investments in common stocks
b To record loss on sale of common stocks
c To record a permanent decline in value of long-term investments in common stocks
d None of the foregoing

6 Liquidating dividends received from an investee are credited to the Investment in Investee Ltd. Common Stock ledger account under:

a The equity method of accounting only
b The cost method of accounting only
c Both the equity method and the cost method of accounting
d Neither the equity method nor the cost method of accounting

7 The method of premium amortization or discount accumulation on long-term investments in bonds that produces a constant rate of return on the investment is the:
a Equity method
b Interest method
c Constant-rate method
d Straight-line method

Ex. 14-2 The following transactions or events relate to Bowen Limited's long-term investment in Weber Inc. common stock (1,500,000 shares outstanding):

Apr. 10 Acquired 500 shares of common stock at $22 a share, plus brokerage commission of $400.
June 15 Acquired 1,000 shares of common stock at $29 a share, plus brokerage commission of $712.
Aug. 31 Weber distributed a 20% stock dividend.

a Prepare journal entries for Bowen Limited to record the foregoing transactions.
b Compute the cost per share of Bowen Limited's investment in Weber Inc. common stock, assuming (1) the two acquisitions are treated as separate lots (to permit the use of fifo) and (2) a weighted average is computed for the investment as a whole.
c Prepare a journal entry for Bowen Limited to record the sale of 800 shares of Weber Inc. common stock at $25 a share, assuming the cost of the shares sold is determined by (1) fifo and (2) weighted average.

Ex. 14-3 On January 2, Year 9, Clarence Limited acquired for $500,000 as a long-term investment a 30% interest in the outstanding common stock of Foley, Inc. On that date, Foley had identifiable net assets with a carrying value and current fair value of $1,600,000. During Year 9, Foley declared and paid dividends of $40,000 and reported net income of $180,000.

Compute the maximum amount of investment income that Clarence Limited may recognize under the equity method of accounting for its investment in Foley, Inc., common stock for Year 9, disregarding income taxes.

Ex. 14-4 On January 2, Year 5, Luna Incorporated acquired for $800,000 a 20% interest in the outstanding common stock of Jewel Ltd. Luna's long-term investment enabled it to exercise significant influence over Jewel's operating and financial policies. Jewel's shareholders' equity attributable to the common stock acquired by Luna was $600,000; the $200,000 excess paid by Luna was attributable to Jewel's patent, which had a remaining economic life of 10 years on January 2, Year 5. Jewel reported net income of $220,000 and declared and paid dividends of $80,000 during Year 5.

Compute the balance of Luna Incorporated's Investment in Jewel Ltd. Common Stock ledger account on December 31, Year 5. Disregard income taxes.

Ex. 14-5 On January 2, Year 7, Dobb Limited acquired 40% of the 300,000 outstanding shares of common stock of Lidden Inc. for $1,800,000, when 40% of the carrying vaue of Lidden was $1,400,000. The excess of cost over the carrying value was assigned to goodwill. Dobb amortizes goodwill over a 20-year period, with a full year's amortization taken in the year of acquistion. As a result of this transaction, Dobb had the ability to exercise significant influence over Lidden's operating and financial policies. Lidden's net income for the year ended December 31, Year 7, was $500,000. During Year 7, Lidden declared and paid $325,000 in dividends.

Compute the investment income to be recognized by Dobb Limited for its long-term investment in Lidden Inc. common stock for the year ended December 31, Year 7. Disregard income taxes.

Ex. 14-6 On May 1, Year 2, the beginning of a fiscal year, Lindell Incorporated acquired 40% of the outstanding shares of common stock of Madison Ltd. for $440,000, including implicit goodwill of $40,000 that had a 10-year economic life. For the year ended April 30, Year 3, Madison had net income of $100,000, and on April 1, Year 3, Madison declared common stock dividends totalling $30,000, payable April 30, Year 3, to shareholders of record on April 15, Year 3.

Prepare Lindell Incorporated's journal entries for its investment in Madison Ltd. common stock on May 1, Year 2, April 1, Year 3, and April 30, Year 3, under the equity method of accounting. Disregard income taxes.

Ex. 14-7 Norman Inc. owns 40% of the outstanding common stock of Saxon Limited; this long-term investment enables Norman to exercise significant influence over the operating and financial policies of Saxon. Norman acquired its investment at a price equal to 40% of Saxon's shareholders equity on the date of acquisition. For the year ended December 31, Year 6, Saxon reported net income of $180,000, but did not declare or pay dividends. Included in Norman's December 31, Year 6, inventories is merchandise billed at $160,000 by Saxon, at a 30% gross profit rate. Included in Saxon's December 31, Year 6, inventories is merchandise billed at $550,000 by Norman, at a gross profit rate of 20%.

Prepare journal entries for Norman Inc. on December 31, Year 6, to account for its investment in Saxon Limited common stock under the equity method of accounting and to eliminate unrealized intercompany profits in inventories. Disregard income taxes.

Ex. 14-8 On January 2, Year 5, Investor Limited acquired 20% of the 100,000 outstanding shares of Investee Ltd. common stock. During Year 5, Investee reported net income of $140,000.

Compute the equity per share of Investee Ltd. stock and the carrying amount per share of Investor Limited's long-term investment in Investee's common stock under each of the following independent assumptions (disregarding income taxes):

a Investor acquired Investee's common at the carrying value of $12 a share, and correctly accounted for the investment by the cost method of accounting.

Investee declared and paid dividends of $80,000 during Year 5.

b Same facts as case *a*, except that Investee declared and paid dividends of $160,000 during Year 5.

c Same facts as case *a*, except that Investor correctly used the equity method of accounting to account for the investment.

d Same facts as case *c*, except that Investor acquired the Investee common stock at a price of $15 a share, although the carrying value was only $12 a share. The excess of cost over carrying value was paid because a patent with a remaining economic life of six years was understated in Investee's accounting records.

Ex. 14-9 On January 2, Year 3, Olive Limited acquired as a long-term investment at a 10% yield rate 100 of the $1,000 face amount, 8% bonds of Edgar Ltd. maturing on January 2, Year 13. Interest on the bonds is paid annually on each January 2, beginning Year 4. Information on present-value factors is as follows:

$$p_{\overline{10}|8\%} = 0.4632 \qquad p_{\overline{10}|10\%} = 0.3855 \qquad P_{\overline{10}|8\%} = 6.7701 \qquad P_{\overline{10}|10\%} = 6.1446$$

Prepare journal entries for Olive Limited on January 2, Year 3, to record the acquisition of the Edgar Ltd. bonds and on December 31, Year 3, to accrue interest on the bonds for a full year. Use the interest method to accumulate bond discount and round computations to the nearest dollar.

Ex. 14-10 On July 1, Year 8, Ford Limited acquired 500 of the $1,000 face amount, 14% bonds of Nixon Ltd. for $460,481, at a yield rate of 16% a year. The bonds, which mature on January 1, Year 15, pay interest semiannually on January 1 and July 1. Ford recorded the bonds as a long-term investment and adopted the interest method for accumulating the discount on the bonds.

Compute the carrying amount, rounded to the nearest dollar, of the Nixon Ltd. 14% bonds in Ford Limited's balance sheet on December 31, Year 8.

Ex. 14-11 The following data (rounded to the nearest dollar) are the beginning of an amortization table prepared by Hogan Inc. to account for its long-term investment in $80,000 face amount bonds of Popp Ltd., maturing in 17 years, which pay interest annually:

Year	*Payment received*	*Interest revenue*	*Accumulation of discount*	*Carrying amount of investment*
				$61,132
1	$4,000	$4,585	$585	61,717
2	4,000	4,629	629	62,346
3				

a Is the discount being accumulated by the straight-line method or the interest method? Explain.

b What is the nominal rate of interest on the bonds?

c What is the effective yield on the long-term investment in bonds?

d Prepare a journal entry to record Hogan Inc.'s interest revenue in Year 2.
e Compute the amounts to be entered in each column of the table for Year 3.
f What would be the interest revenue recognized each year if the discount were accumulated by the straight-line method?
g Compute the percentage return (to the nearest tenth of one percent) on the carrying value of the investment in years 1 and 3, assuming that the discount was accumulated by the straight-line method.

Ex. 14-12 Lew Limited owns 300 shares of the outstanding common stock of Parke Inc., which has several hundred thousand shares of common stock publicly traded. The 300 shares were acquired as a long-term investment by Lew in Year 3 for $105 a share. On June 20, Year 5, Parke distributed stock warrants for rights to its shareholders to acquire one new share of Parke common stock for $120 cash and three rights. On June 20, Year 5, each share of Parke common stock had a market value of $134 ex-rights, and each right had a market value of $6.

Compute the cost of each new share of Parke Inc. common stock that Lew Limited acquired by exercising the rights on July 18, Year 5.

Ex. 14-13 Prepare journal entries for Nebitt Incorporated to record the following transactions for long-term investments:

Feb. 10	Nebbitt acquired 1,000 shares of Nobe Inc. common stock at $88 a share.
Mar. 31	Nobe issued a 10% stock dividend to common shareholders.
June 30	Nobe issued stock warrants for rights to common shareholders, enabling the acquisition of one additional share of Nobe common stock at $90 for every five shares held. Nobe common stock was trading ex-rights at $114 a share, and the rights had a market value of $6 each.
July 18	Nebbitt exercised 1,000 rights to acquire new shares of Nobe common stock.
20	Nebitt sold the remaining stock warrants for 100 rights for $6.50 each.
Oct. 12	Nebitt sold 400 shares of Nobe common stock for $48,000. Nebbitt used the average cost basis to determine the cost of the sale.

Ex. 14-14 Prepare a single journal entry for Roxy Ltd. on December 31, Year 4, to correct the following ledger account. Include supporting computations in the explanation for the journal entry. The accounting records have not been closed for Year 4. *Note:* Credits to the account represent ***net cash*** received.

Investment in Tupp Limited Common Stock (Long-Term)

Date	*Explanation*	*Debit*	*Credit*	*Balance*
Year 4				
Jan. 18	Acquired 200 shares (½% interest).	24,000		24,000 Dr
Mar. 6	Sold 40 shares received as a 20% stock dividend on this date.		3,800	20,200 Dr

July 26	Received cash dividend of $1.50 a share.		300	19,900 Dr
Aug. 21	Sold stock warrants for 200 rights received on this date (3% of adjusted cost is allocable to rights).		700	19,200 Dr
Dec. 20	Sold 100 shares after a 2-for-1 stock split effective Oct. 10, Year 4.		5,350	13,850 Dr

Ex. 14-15 This exercise, and exercises ***14-16***, ***14-17***, and ***14-18***, are based on the following information:

On January 2, 1987, Port Ltd. purchased 30% of the outstanding common shares of Sail Inc. At that date, Sail's shareholders' equity comprised:

Common stock, no par value	$100,000
Retained earnings	$ 50,000

Subsequent to January 2, 1987, the following information relevant to this investment was obtained:

1 Sail Inc. reported net income of $80,000 for the 1987 year.
2 Sail Inc. paid a cash dividend to common shareholders, at December 31, 1987, in the amount of $25,000.
3 On July 1, 1987, Sail Inc. sold land to Port Ltd. for $100,000 cash. The land cost Sail Inc. $50,000 early in 1981.
4 On August 1, 1987, Port Ltd. sold land to Sail Inc. for $80,000. This land had been purchased by Port Ltd. for $50,000 on January 1, 1983.

Prepare the journal entry in Port Ltd.'s books to record Port Ltd.'s purchase of 30% of Sail Inc.'s outstanding shares January 2, 1987 under ***each*** of the following conditions (omit narratives):

a Cost of the investment was $45,000 cash and the fair value of Sail Inc.'s net assets was $150,000 on January 2, 1987.
b Cost of the investment was $60,000 cash and the fair value of Sail Inc.'s net assets was $200,000 on January 2, 1987. The excess of fair value over book value was attributable to undervalued land.
c Cost of the investment was $75,000 cash and the fair value of Sail Inc.'s net assets was $200,000 on January 2, 1987. The excess of fair value over book value was attributable to undervalued land. Any goodwill is amortized over 40 years.
d Cost of the investment was $75,000 cash and the fair value of Sail Inc.'s net assets was $200,000 on January 2, 1987. The excess of fair value over book value represented depreciable fixed assets which are being depreciated on the straight-line basis and have 20 years' remaining economic life at January 2, 1987. Any goodwill is amortized over 40 years.

Ex. 14-16 For ***each*** of the conditions ***a***, ***b***, ***c***, and ***d*** above, prepare the journal entries in Port Ltd.'s books for transactions subsequent to the date Port Ltd. acquired 30%

of Sail Inc.'s outstanding shares to the common year-end for the two companies, December 31, 1987, assuming Port Ltd. uses the ***cost*** basis for recording information with respect to its investment in Sail Inc.

Ex. 14-17 For ***each*** of the conditions ***a***, ***b***, ***c***, and ***d*** above, prepare the journal entries Port Ltd. would make in its books for the 1987 transactions subsequent to January 2, 1987, up to December 31, 1987, the two companies' year-ends, under the assumption that Port Ltd. records such entries on the ***equity*** basis.

Ex. 14-18 For ***each*** of the conditions ***a***, ***b***, ***c***, and ***d*** above, prepare the adjusting entries necessary at Port Ltd.'s year-end assuming Port Ltd. has significant influence over Sail Inc. but has accounted for its investment in Sail Inc. for the 1987 year on the cost basis.

CASES

Case 14-1 On July 1, Year 5, Drosser Limited acquired for cash 40% of the outstanding common stock of Furman, Inc. Both Drosser and Furman have a December 31 fiscal year. Furman reported its net income for Year 5 to Drosser, and also declared and paid cash dividends in Year 5 to its shareholders.

Instructions
How should Drosser Limited report the foregoing facts in its balance sheet on December 31, Year 5, and its income statement for the year then ended? Explain. (Disregard income taxes.)

Case 14-2 During your examination of the financial statements of Lure Limited, which has never before been audited, you discover that the cash surrender value of a $250,000 life insurance policy on the president, for which Lure was the beneficiary, had not been entered in the accounting records. The president stated that the total premium on the policy was debited to the Insurance Expense ledger account each year because Lure had no intention to ''cash in'' the policy or to use the cash surrender value as collateral for a loan from the insurance company or a bank. Therefore, asserted the president, it would be misleading for Lure to record as an asset an amount never expected to be realized or used by Lure.

Instructions
Evaluate the position of the president of Lure Limited.

Case 14-3 For the past five years Root Inc. has maintained a long-term investment (accounted for and reported correctly) in Koler Ltd. amounting to a 10% interest in the common stock of Koler. The cost of the investment was $700,000, and the net carrying value in Koler on the date of acquisition was $620,000. On January 2, Year 7, Root acquired an additional 15% of the common stock of Koler for $1,200,000; the carrying value of the additional investment on January 2 was

$1,000,000. Koler has been profitable and has paid dividends annually since Root's initial acquisition.

Instructions

Discuss how the increase in Root Inc.'s ownership of Koler Ltd. common stock affects the accounting for and reporting of the investment in Koler. Also indicate how the investment in Koler Ltd. common stock is reported in Root's financial statements of Year 7 and subsequent accounting periods.

Case 14-4 Null Ltd. has been operating profitably for many years. On March 1, Year 4, Null acquired 50,000 shares of Tulak Inc. common stock for $2,000,000. The 50,000 shares represented 25% of Tulak's outstanding common stock. Both Null and Tulak have a fiscal year ending August 31.

For the year ended August 31, Year 4, Tulak reported net income of $800,000, earned ratably throughout the year. During November, Year 3, and February, May, and August, Year 4, Tulak declared and paid regular quarterly cash dividends of $125,000.

Instructions

a What criteria should Null Ltd. consider in determining whether its investment in Tulak Inc. should be classified as a current asset or a noncurrent asset in Null's August 31, Year 4, balance sheet? Confine your discussion to the decision criteria for determining the balance sheet classification of the investment.

b Assume that the investment is classified as a long-term investment in Null Ltd.'s balance sheet. The cost of the investment equalled Null's equity in Tulak Company's net assets; carrying values were not materially different from current fair values (individually or collectively). How much investment income does Null recognize as a result of its investment in Tulak common stock for the year ended August 31, Year 4? Explain.

Case 14-5 Nickleby Inc. acquired 45,000 of 150,000 outstanding shares of common stock of Zane Ltd. on January 2, year 6, at $30 a share. The carrying value of Zane's common stock on December 31, Year 5, was $22.75 a share. During the year following the acquisition of the stock by Nickleby, Zane earned $325,000 and declared and paid dividends of $1.10 a share. The management of Nickleby is concerned about the appropriate method of presenting the investment in Zane in the financial statements. The controller argues that Nickleby had earned 30% of Zane's net income, because it owns 30% of Zane's common stock. The financial vice president argues that the investment must be carried at cost as are all other nonmonetary assets, and that the net income of Nickleby should include only the dividends received from Zane.

Instructions

a Attempt to resolve this debate by pointing out the relevant issues on both sides of the argument.

b The vice president counters your points in favour of the controller's position with the statement that, "What you say makes sense until you try to explain what the dollar amount of the investment represents. It is not market value of the common stock, because the current market price is $29 a share, and it most certainly is not cost.'' Present your answer to the vice president.

Case 14-6 Investor Limited purchased 75% of Investee Limited, paying $900,000 in excess of the carrying value of Investee's net assets, which amounted to $5,000,000. The $900,000 has been distributed as follows: $600,000 as fair value increments on depreciable fixed assets and the remainder to goodwill. The management of Investor Limited has been told there are two major concepts which may be applicable to the consolidation numbers which will be used for the above purchase difference. The two concepts are the proprietary concept and the entity concept. However, in Canada the accounting profession has chosen a third concept which is a combination of these two concepts. They have requested a meeting with you. The president, in particular, is confused and has asked you to describe the numerical effects on the consolidated balance sheet of ***each*** of the two major concepts and also of the profession's recommended concept. He also requests you to discuss the individual attributes and shortcomings of these three concepts. Set out your thoughts on paper for review immediately before your meeting with management, in the near future.

PROBLEMS

Pr. 14-1 On June 1, Year 9, Liston Limited acquired as a long-term investment 800 of the 8% bonds with a $1,000 face amount of Welsh Corporation for $738,300. The bonds were acquired to yield 10% interest. They pay interest on June 1 and December 1 and mature on June 1, Year 14. Liston uses the interest method to accumulate bond discount. On November 1, Year 10, Liston sold the bonds for $785,000, including accrued interest of $26,667.

Instructions

Prepare a working paper to compute the pre-tax income or loss from the bond investment recorded by Liston Limited for the years ended December 31, Year 9 and Year 10. Show supporting computations and round all amounts to the nearest dollar.

Pr. 14-2 On April 1, Year 9, Chatt Inc. acquired 6% convertible bonds of Curtin, Inc., with face amount of $1,500,000 for $1,818,000 plus accrued interest for two months. The bonds pay interest semiannually on February 1 and August 1 and mature in eight years and 10 months from date of acquisition. Each $1,000 bond is convertible on any interest date to 40 shares of common stock.

On August 1, Year 9, 500 bonds were converted to Curtin common stock. On the date of conversion the Curtin common stock was selling for $40 a share. On Sepember 1, Year 9, a 10% stock dividend was declared on the common stock, to be distributed on October 10 to shareholders of record on September 20. On December 1, Year 9, 5,500 shares of Curtin common stock were sold for $35 a share.

Instructions

a Prepare journal entries for Chatt Inc. for the foregoing transactions or events, including receipt of interest on August 1, Year 9, and the accrual of interest on December 31, Year 9, assuming that the conversion of the bonds is recorded by the carrying value (book value) method.

b Justify your reason for amortizing or not amortizing the premium on Chatt Inc.'s investment in convertible bonds.

Pr. 14-3 On January 2, Year 3, Kirby Limited paid $700,000 for 10,000 shares (a 10% interest) of Lude Ltd. outstanding common stock. On that date the carrying amount of Lude's identifiable net assets was equal to the current fair value of $6,000,000. Kirby did not have the ability to exercise significant influence over the operating and financial policies of Lude. Kirby received dividends of $0.90 a share from Lude on October 1, Year 3, and Lude reported net income of $400,000 for the year ended December 31, Year 3.

On July 1, Year 4, Kirby paid $2,300,000 for 30,000 additional shares of Lude's outstanding common stock, for an additional 30% interest. The current fair value of Lude's identifiable net assets equalled the carrying amount of $6,500,000 on July 1, Year 4. As a result of this transaction, Kirby had the ability to exercise significant influence over the operating and financial policies of Lude. Kirby received dividends from Lude during Year 4 of $1.10 a share on April 1 and $1.35 a share on October 1. Lude reported net income of $300,000 for the six months ended June 30, Year 4, and $200,000 for the six months ended December 31, Year 4. Kirby amortizes goodwill over an economic life of 40 years.

Instructions

a Prepare a working paper to show the pre-tax income or loss reported by Kirby Limited from its investment in Lude Ltd. for the year ended December 31, Year 3.

b Prepare a working paper to compute the balance of Kirby Limited's investment in Lude Ltd. common stock on December 31, Year 3 and Year 4, for inclusion in comparative balance sheets to be issued by Lude in its annual report for Year 4.

Pr. 14-4 On October 1, Year 7, Linfield Ltd. acquired for cash 200,000 shares, representing 45% of the outstanding common stock of Berst Inc. As a result of the acquisition, Linfield had the ability to exercise significant influence over the operating and financial policies of Berst. Goodwill of $500,000 was appropriately computed by Linfield on the date of the acquisition.

On January 2, Year 8, Linfield also acquired 300,000 shares, representing 30% of the outstanding common stock of Ansel Limited. The amount of cash paid for the Ansel common stock was $2,500,000. The shareholders' equity section of Ansel's balance sheet on January 2, Year 8, was as shown on page 691. Furthermore, on January 2, Year 8, the current fair value of Ansel's plant assets was $4,000,000, and the carrying value was $3,600,000. For all other assets and liabilities of Ansel the current fair values and carrying values were equal. As a

Common stock, no par	$3,000,000
Retained earnings	3,500,000
Total shareholders equity	$6,500,000

result of the acquisition, Linfield had the ability to excercise significant influence over the operating and financial policies of Ansel.

Assume that Linfield amortizes goodwill to the nearest month over the maximum period allowed by generally accepted accounting principles.

Instructions

Prepare a working paper for computation of the amount of goodwill and accumulated amortization for Linfield Ltd. on December 31, Year 8, and the goodwill amortization for the year ended December 31, Year 8. Show supporting computations.

Pr. 14-5 Coco Corporation has supplied you with the following information regarding two long-term investments that were made during Year 4. Coco uses a single Investments ledger account.

1 On January 2, Year 4, Coco acquired 40% of the 500,000 shares of outstanding common stock of Filbert Limited for $2,400,000, equal to 40% of the carrying value of the net assets of Filbert. Net income of Filbert for Year 4 was $750,000, including $80,000 unrealized intercompany profit on sales of merchandise to Coco. Filbert declared and paid dividends of $0.50 a share in Year 4. The market price of Filbert's common stock was $14 a share on December 31, Year 4. Coco exercised significant influence over the operating and financial policies of Filbert.

2 On July 1, Year 4, Coco acquired 15,000 shares, representing 5% of the outstanding common stock of Leach Ltd., for $450,000. Leach's net income for the six months ended December 31, Year 4, was $350,000; for the year ended December 31, Year 4, net income was $600,000. Leach declared and paid dividends of $0.30 a share each quarter during Year 4 to shareholders of record on the last day of each quarter. The market price of Leach's common stock was $34 a share on December 31, Year 4.

Instructions

a Prepare a working paper to compute the balance in Coco Corporation's Investments ledger account on December 31, Year 4. Show supporting computations. Disregard income taxes.

b Compute the investment income, under the accrual basis of accounting for dividends, reported by Coco Corporation for the year ended December 31, Year 4. Show supporting computations. Disregard income taxes.

Pr. 14-6 In Year 5, Liggett Limited acquired 1% of the outstanding common stock of Yorba Ltd. as a long-term investment. The accountant for Liggett was inexperienced and made the following errors in recording the transactions relating to the investment in the common stock of Yorba: (1) Shares received as a

10% stock dividend were valued at the current market price and recorded by a debit to the investment ledger account and a credit to Dividend Revenue; (2) the net cash proceeds on the sales of shares of Yorba common stock and stock warrants for rights were credited to the investment ledger account; and (3) a cash dividend was credited to the investment ledger account.

On June 9, Year 5, the common stock of Yorba was trading ex-rights at $98, and the rights were trading at $2. The activity in the investment ledger account during Year 5 is presented below:

Investment in Yorba Ltd. Common Stock (Long-Term)

Date	*Explanation*	*Debit*	*Credit*	*Balance*
Year 5				
Jan. 18	Acquired 4,000 shares (1% interest).	374,000		374,000 Dr
Feb. 28	Received 400 shares as 10% stock dividend (400 × $100).	40,000		414,000 Dr
Mar. 6	Sold 400 shares received Feb. 28.		38,000	376,000 Dr
May 25	Received cash dividend (4,000 × $1.10).		4,400	371,600 Dr
June 27	Sold stock warrants for 4,000 rights received June 9.		7,850	363,750 Dr
Dec. 20	Sold 3,200 shares (20%) after a 4-for-1 split effective Oct. 10.		98,800	264,950 Dr

Instructions

a Prepare a working paper to summarize the transactions in Liggett Limited's investment in Yorba Ltd. Common Stock ledger account as the transactions should have been recorded. Use the following column headings:

Date	*Transactions*	*Number of shares*	*Cost*	*Proceeds on sale*	*Gain or (loss)*
Year 5 Jan. 18					

b Prepare a single journal entry to correct the accounting records of Liggett Limited as of December 31, Year 5. Assume that the accounting records have not been closed for Year 5.

Pr. 14-7 On January 1, 19X1, Joe Spid, Inc., made the following long-term investments:

1 Purchased 30% of the 200,000 outstanding shares of common stock of Womack Ltd. for $2,000,000 cash. At that date, the fair value of Womack's net assets approximated their carrying value of $5,000,000 except for the following:

a The fair value of depreciable assets, with a remaining useful life of 10 years, exceeded their carrying value by $400,000. Womack Ltd. depreciates such assets on the straight-line basis.

b The fair value of inventory on December 31, 19X0, exceeded its carrying value by $100,000.

2 Purchased 10% of the 500,000 outstanding shares of Sandy Limited for $200,000 cash. At that date, the fair value of Sandy's net assets approximated their carrying value of $1,800,000.

Inventory of Womack Ltd. turns over five times per year. Goodwill, if any, arising from Sandy Limited investments, is amortized in the appropriate manner over the maximum period allowed by generally accepted accounting principles.

During 19X1, Womack Ltd. reported net income of $500,000 and paid cash dividends totalling $200,000. For the same period, Sandy Limited earned $300,000 and paid out dividends totalling $1 per share.

Instructions

a As a result of these two investments, what should be the balance in the investment account of Joe Spid, Inc., at December 31, 19X1?

b As a result of these two investments, what should be the investment income reported by Joe Spid, Inc., for the year ended December 31, 19X1?

Pr. 14-8 The following transactions and adjustments relate to long-term investments of Logan Limited during Year 6:

Apr. 30 Acquired $60,000 face amount 16% bonds of March Limited at a cost of $63,760 plus accrued interest. The bonds pay interest semiannually on March 1 and September 1, and mature 94 months from the date of acquisition.

July 10 Acquired for a total of $155,000 a package of 500 shares of 12%, $100 par, preferred stock and 1,000 shares of common stock of Niles Inc. The preferred and common stock were trading at $80 a share and $120 a share, respectively.

Sept. 1 Received semiannual interest payment on the March Limited bonds. Premium is amortized by the straight-line method when interest is received and at the end of the fiscal year.

Oct. 15 Received the quarterly dividend on the Niles Inc. preferred stock.

25 Received new shares from a 2-for-1 stock split of the Niles Inc. common stock.

Dec. 31 Prepared appropriate adjusting entry (or entries), including amortization of premium, for the end of the fiscal year.

Instructions

Prepare journal entries for Logan Limited to record the foregoing transactions and adjustments.

Pr. 14-9 On July 1, Year 5, Lubell Limited acquired 25% of the outstanding shares of common stock of Slocum Limited at a total cost of $720,000. The carrying value of the stock acquired by Lubell was only $600,000. Lubell was willing to pay more than the carrying value for the Slocum common stock for the following reasons:

1 Slocum owned depreciable plant assets (10-year remaining economic life) with a current fair value $60,000 more than their carrying value.

2 Slocum owned land with a current fair value $300,000 more than its carrying value.

3 Lubell believed that Slocum possessed enough goodwill to justify the remainder of the cost. Lubell's accounting policy with respect to goodwill is to amortize it over 10 years.

Slocum earned net income of $540,000 uniformly over the year ended December 31, Year 5. On December 31, Year 5, Slocum declared and paid a cash dividend of $360,000. Both Lubell and Slocum close their accounting records on December 31.

Instructions

a Compute the total imputed amount of goodwill of Slocum Limited, based on the price paid by Lubell Limited for Slocum's common stock.

b Assuming that Lubell Limited's investment does not enable it to exercise significant influence over Slocum Company, prepare all journal entries for Lubell relating to the investment for the year ended December 31, under the cost method of accounting.

c Assuming that Lubell Limited's investment enables it to exercise significant influence over Slocum Limited, prepare all journal entries for Lubell Limited relating to the investment for the year ended December 31, under the equity method of accounting.

Pr. 14-10 Noria Inc. acquired as a long-term investment $500,000 face amount of Tork Corporation bonds on September 30, Year 2. The bonds have a 14% nominal rate with interest payable semiannually on March 31 and September 30. The remaining term of the bonds is 10 years, and the bonds have an effective yield to maturity of 16% compounded semiannually.

Instructions

(Round all computations to the nearest dollar.)

√*a* Using the tables in the Appendix at the end of Chapter 5, compute the amount that Noria Inc. paid for the Tork Corporation bonds.

√*b* Prepare tables for Noria Inc. for the first two years to show the accumulation of the discount and the computation of interest revenue on the Tork Corporation bonds, under both the interest method and the straight-line method.

√*c* Prepare journal entries for Noria Inc. to record the first year's transactions, excluding the acquisition of the bonds and closing entries, under both the interest method and the straight-line method. Noria's fiscal year ends on September 30.

Pr. 14-11 On June 30, Year 2, Alber Ltd. acquired as a long-term investment 20% of the 100,000 outstanding shares of common stock of Nemo Inc. The shareholders' equity of Nemo on June 30, Year 2, was as follows:

Common stock, no par value	$2,750,000
Retained earnings	2,350,000
Total shareholders' equity	$5,100,000

Alber paid $1,410,000 cash for the common stock of Nemo. The excess of the cost over the carrying value was paid because (1) the land owned by Nemo had a current fair value $550,000 more than its carrying value; (2) the depreciable plant assets of Nemo were worth $450,000 more than their carrying value; (3) Nemo had at least the amount of goodwill imputed by the cost of Alber's 20% interest. The accounting policy of Alber with respect to goodwill is to amortize over 40 years. The depreciable plant assets of Nemo had a remaining economic life of 12 years on June 30, Year 2.

During the last six months of Year 2, Nemo earned net income of $270,000, after an extraordinary loss of $45,000, and declared and paid dividends of $1 a share. In Year 3, Nemo reported a net loss of $90,000 and declared and paid dividends of $2 a share. Both Alber and Nemo end their fiscal year on December 31.

Instructions

a Compute the total imputed amount of Nemo Inc.'s goodwill based on the cost of Alber Ltd.'s 20% interest in Nemo.

b Prepare Alber Ltd.'s journal entries for Year 2 and Year 3 relating to the investment in Nemo under the cost method of accounting. Assume that all end-of-period adjustments are made and that dividends are received at the end of each year.

c Prepare Alber Ltd.'s journal entries for Year 2 and Year 3 relating to the investment in Nemo under the equity method of accounting.

d On January 2, Year 4, Alber Ltd. decided that Nemo Inc.'s goodwill no longer had any value and that the investment ledger account balance should be reduced by Alber's portion of unamortized goodwill. Prepare a journal entry to record Alber Ltd.'s write-off of goodwill, assuming that the equity method of accounting had been in use.

Pr. 14-12 Quarry Company acquired three lots of Moto Limited common stock as follows:

Lot No.:	*Number of shares*	*Cost of each share*	*Brokerage and other costs*
1	2,000	$28	$600
2	800	36	300
3	1,200	30	400

Moto issued a 10% stock dividend on May 10 and stock warrants for rights on August 15 entitling common shareholders to acquire for $40 one new share for every 10 shares held. Shortly after the stock warrants for rights were issued, the common stock was trading ex-rights at $49 a share, and the rights at $1 a right. Quarry sold 1,000 rights at $1.125 a right, less brokerage commission of $45. The remaining rights were exercised. Moto has 5,000,000 shares of common stock outstanding.

Instructions

a Compute Quarry Company's gain or loss on the sale of rights under (1) fifo, (2) lifo, and (3) average cost of the common stock to determine the cost of the rights sold. Round cost of each right to the nearest tenth of a cent.

b Prepare a working paper for Quarry Company to show the number of shares of Moto Company common stock in each lot, the total cost of each lot, and the unit cost of each lot (to the nearest cent), assuming the use of average cost in part *a* and considering the shares acquired through the exercise of rights as Lot No. 4.

Pr. 14-13 At the beginning of Year 1, Galber Ltd. issued at face amount $500,000 of 15%, 10-year bonds, interest to be payable annually. A sinking fund was established at the same time to accumulate the $500,000 at the end of 10 years. Galber was to make payments of $28,492 to the fund at the end of each year. The fund balance was to be invested to earn 12% a year.

In addition to the sinking fund, Galber acquired at the beginning of Year 1 a $100,000 life insurance policy on Lois Hatch, Galber's president. The terms of the insurance policy were as follows:

Year	*Gross premium*	*Cash surrender value at end of year*
1	$7,770	$ 1,340
2	7,770	7,460
3	7,770	13,780
4	7,770	20,290
5	7,770	27,030
6	7,770	34,020
7	7,770	41,290
8	7,770	48,880
9	7,770	56,830
10	7,770	65,210

Instructions

a Prepare for Galber Ltd. a fund accumulation table for the sinking fund for the first three years. Round all computations to the nearest dollar.

b Prepare for Galber Ltd. a table to determine the effect on net income of the life insurance policy for each of the first three years.

c Prepare journal entries for Galber Ltd. for all transactions involving the bonds, the sinking fund, and the life insurance policy for each of the first three years.

Pr. 14-14 The following transactions and events relate to the long-term investments of Marquez Inc. for the year ended December 31, Year 2:

Jan. 2	Acquired 30,000 of 100,000 outstanding shares of Garth Ltd. common stock for $15 a share. Underlying equity was $12 a share; Marquez attributed the excess of cost over equity acquired to goodwill, to be amortized over 30 years. The acquisition gave Marquez a significant degree of influence over Garth.
Jan. 6	Acquired $100,000 of Haggis Limited first mortgage 18% bonds at face amount plus accrued interest for 36 days. Interest was payable semiannually on December 1 and June 1, with maturity on December 1, Year 11. The bonds were callable at 106 (106% of face amount). (Use a 360-day year.)
Feb. 15	Acquired 1,000 shares of Ingle Corporation $10-par common stock for $65,280. Ingle had 200,000 shares of common stock outstanding.
May 5	Received cash dividend of 65 cents a share on Ingle Corporation common stock.
June 1	Received semiannual interest on Haggis Limited bonds.
Aug. 5	Received cash dividend of 65 cents a share and a 2% stock dividend on Ingle Corporation common stock.
Sept. 30	Sold the shares of Ingle Corporation common received as a stock dividend for $70 a share and acquired 50, $1,000 16% subordinated denbenture bonds of James Incorporated at 94 (94% of face amount), with interest payable semiannually on March 31 and September 30, and with maturity 10 years from date of acquisition. The bonds were callable at 102 (102% of face amount).
Oct. 1	Received cash dividend of 75 cents a share from Garth Ltd. (The dividend was paid from earnings.)
Nov. 5	Received cash dividend of 70 cents a share on Ingle Corporation common stock.
Dec. 1	Received semiannual interest on Haggis Limited bonds and surrendered to Haggis 60 of the $1,000 bonds at the call price of 106, in accordance with the provisions of the bond indenture.
31	Garth Ltd. reported net income of $164,000 for Year 2, including an extraordinary gain of $44,000.

Instructions

a Prepare journal entries for Marquez Inc. for the foregoing transactions and events and record any adjustments required on December 31, Year 2. Accumulate the discount on the bonds of James Incorporated to the nearest month, under the straight-line method. The market value of Ingle Corporation common stock on December 31, Year 2, was $75,000.

b Prepare a listing of long-term investments to appear in the balance sheet of Marquez Inc. on December 31, Year 2.

Pr. 14-15 Rampe, Inc., had the following long-term receivables on December 31, Year 3:

Note receivable from sale of electronics division	$1,500,000
Note receivable from officer	400,000

Additional Information

1 The $1,500,000 note receivable is dated May 1, Year 3, bears interest at 9%, and represents the balance of the consideration received from the sale of Rampe's electronics division to Carlin Limited. Principal payments of $500,000 plus appropriate interest are due on May 1 of Year 4, Year 5, and Year 6. The first principal and interest payment was made on May 1, Year 4. Collection of the note instalments from Carlin is reasonably assured.

2 The $400,000 note receivable is dated December 31, Year 1, bears interest at 8%, and is due on December 31, Year 6. The note is due from Robert Finley, president of Rampe, and is secured by 10,000 shares of Rampe common stock. Interest is payable annually on December 31, and all interest payments were paid on their due dates through December 31, Year 4. The market price of Rampe common stock was $45 a share on December 31, Year 4.

3 On April 1, Year 4, Rampe sold a patent to Bell Limited for a $100,000 non-interest-bearing note due on April 1, Year 6. There was no market price for the patent, and the note had no ready market. The prevailing rate of interest for a note of this type on April 1, Year 4, was 15%. The present value of 1 discounted for two periods at 15% is 0.756. The patent had a carrying amount of $40,000 on January 1, Year 4, and the amortization for the year ended December 31, Year 4, would have been $8,000. Collection of the note receivable from Bell is reasonably assured.

4 On July 1, Year 4, Rampe sold a parcel of land to Carr Corporation for $200,000 under an instalment sale contract. Carr made a $60,000 cash down payment on July 1, Year 4, and signed a four-year promissory note with an effective interest rate of 16% for the $140,000 balance. The equal annual payments of principal and interest on the note are $50,000, payable on July 1, Year 5, through July 1, Year 8. The land could have been sold for $200,000 cash. The cost of the land to Rampe was $150,000. Collection of the note instalments from Carr is reasonably assured.

Instructions

a Prepare the long-term receivables section of the investments section of Rampe's balance sheet on December 31, Year 4.

b Prepare a working paper to compute the current portion of the long-term receivables and interest receivable for presentation in Rampe's balance sheet on December 31, Year 4.

c Prepare a working paper to compute interest revenue from the long-term receivables and gains on sales of assets for presentation in the income statement of Rampe, Inc. for the year ended December 31, Year 4.

APPENDIX: CONSOLIDATION ACCOUNTING

This appendix to Chapter 14 is for the use of those colleges and universities which do *not* offer an advanced course in consolidation accounting.

In Chapter 14, four concepts were used to illustrate consolidation accounting. However, in this appendix only the ***parent company concept*** will be used. As discussed earlier, it has certain flaws, but it is the one recommended by the ***CICA Handbook*** and is the one used in practice.

Consolidation at the Acquisition Date

At the acquisition date, since no time has passed subsequent to the parent company's purchase of a controlling interest in the subsidiary, only the balance sheets are consolidated. The parent company's balance sheet will include a line "Investment in common stock of (subsidiary)" and the amount of the purchase. Consolidation entails the removal of this "one-line" amount and in its place adding the individual line-by-line amounts appearing in the balance sheet of the subsidiary. The sum of the line-by-line amounts must equal that in "Investment in common stock of (subsidiary)." However, consolidation practice requires that 100% of the carrying value of the subsidiary's net assets be included in the line-by-line consolidation. As a result, when the parent company has acquired less than 100% of the subsidiary, a credit must be set up in the balance sheet for the amount not owned by the parent company. That amount is shown in one line and is captioned, appropriately, "Minority interest."

To illustrate, assume P Limited acquired 80% of the outstanding shares of S Limited on December 31, Year 1, for $1,200,000 cash. At that date the fixed assets (net) of S Limited had a fair value of $1,200,000. All other carrying values of assets and liabilities approximated their fair values. Assume the fixed assets will be depreciated on the straight-line basis over the next 16 years. Any goodwill arising at the acquisition date will be amortized on the straight-line basis over the next 40 years. The balance sheets for the two companies, immediately after the acquisition, are as follows:

	P Limited balance sheet December 31, Year 1	*S Limited balance sheet December 31, Year 1*
Current assets	$ 400,000	$ 500,000
Fixed assets (net)	1,600,000	900,000
Investment in common stock of S Limited	1,200,000	
Other assets	300,000	100,000
	$3,500,000	$1,500,000
Current liabilities	$ 200,000	$ 200,000
Long term debt	1,500,000	300,000
Common stock, no par	800,000	100,000
Retained earnings	1,000,000	900,000
	$3,500,000	$1,500,000

Under the parent company concept the $1,200,000 investment is composed of:

1 100% of the carrying value of S's net assets, ***minus***

2 20% of the carrying value of S's net assets representing minority interest, ***plus***

3 80% of the fair value increment in S's net assets, ***plus***

4 80% of the extrapolated goodwill at acquisition

The following computations reflect these four items:

1 100% of the carrying value of S's net assets (assets − liabilities) ..	$1,000,000
2 20% of the carrying value of S's net assets	(200,000)
80% of the carrying value of S's net assets	$ 800,000
3 80% of the fair value increment in S's net assets	
= ($1,200,000 − $900,000) × 80%	240,000
4 80% of extrapolated goodwill	160,000*
Total of investment at acquisition date	$1,200,000

*Goodwill acquired by P Limited (which is 80% of extrapolated goodwill) will be:

Cost of investment	$1,200,000
80% of carrying value (above)	800,000
	$ 400,000
80% of fair value (above)	240,000
Balance equals goodwill	$ 160,000

In the move from the one-line balance sheet presentation to the line-by-line balance sheet presentation, it is necessary to remove the investment and in its place add S's line-by-line net assets (at carrying value) to P's line-by-line net assets (at carrying value) and to adjust those line-by-line carrying value amounts by applicable fair value increments of S's net assets as well as add purchased goodwill and minority interest to the consolidated balance sheet. Since the net assets of S are consolidated with those of P, the shareholders' equity section of S must be removed as it cannot be included in the consolidated balance sheet under the acquirer-method consolidation. The entry (commonly called the ***investment elimination entry***) necessary to accomplish this for the parent company concept at the acquisition date is at top of page 701.

All journal entries, except those necessary to record intercompany transactions in the accounting records of each company being consolidated, are made for consolidation purposes only. That is, ***they are not entered into the accounting records of any of the companies involved in the consolidation***. Work sheets for consolidations, together with supporting journal entries, are maintained ***independently*** of the companies affiliated with the consolidation. Thus, similar entries necessary for consolidation purposes are made each time consolidated financial statements are prepared.

The minority interest will always represent the carrying value of S's net assets multiplied by the minority-interest percent ownership of S, under the parent company concept. For example, in the above case, the carrying value of S's net

Common Stock — S	100,000	
Retained Earnings — S	900,000	
Fixed Assets (net)	240,000	
Goodwill	160,000	
Investment in Limited Common Stock		1,200,000
Minority Interest		200,000
To eliminate the investment account and to set up the fair value increments and goodwill upon consolidation at the acquisition date.		

assets = shareholders equity or $100,000 common stock plus $900,000 retained earnings = $1,000,000. The minority-interest percent ownership of S is 20% (P owns 80%), and as a result, $1,000,000 × 20% = $200,000 minority interest.

The use of a work sheet facilitates the process of arriving at the consolidated balance sheet, at the consolidation date, as follows:

Work Sheet for P Limited Consolidated Balance Sheet
December 31, Year 1

Accounts	*P Limited balance sheet*	*S Limited balance sheet*	*Adjustments*		*P Limited consolidated balance sheet*
			Dr	*Cr*	
Current assets	400,000	500,000			900,000
Fixed assets (net)	1,600,000	900,000	240,000		2,740,000
Investment in S Limited common stock	1,200,000			1,200,000	-0-
Other assets	300,000	100,000			400,000
Goodwill			160,000		160,000
	3,500,000	1,500,000			4,200,000
Current liabilities	200,000	200,000			400,000
Long-term debt	1,500,000	300,000			1,800,000
Minority interest				200,000	200,000
Common stock, no par	800,000	100,000	100,000		800,000
Retained earnings	1,000,000	900,000	900,000		1,000,000
	3,500,000	1,500,000	1,400,000	1,400,000	4,200,000

An examination of the "Consolidated Balance Sheet" column of the work sheet shows that:

1 The investment in S account in the amount of $1,200,000 has been removed, as it has been replaced by the line-by-line addition of the carrying value of S's net assets, the fair value increments, and the goodwill.

2 Minority interest representing 20% of the carrying value of S's net assets has

been set up as a credit. This credit is to be placed ***outside*** of shareholders' equity.

3 Shareholders' equity accounts, represented here by no-par-value common stock and retained earnings in the consolidated balance sheet, are those of P Limited only. This will always be the case for consolidations where an acquirer is identified.

When one company purchases control of another, it purchases the fair value of that company's net assets. The fair value of depreciable assets represents the value of those assets in their present condition. Accordingly, cost and accumulated depreciation are not applicable. It is necessary to remove 100% of accumulated depreciation at its acquisition-date amount. If we assume the fixed assets (net) of $1,200,000 represented cost of $2,000,000 and accumulated depreciation of $800,000, the entry to adjust at the consolidation date would be:

Accumulated Depreciation—Fixed Assets	800,000	
Fixed Assets, at Cost		800,000
To remove 100% of accumulated depreciation at acquisition date.		

Consolidation Subsequent to the Acquisition Date

Subsequent to the date of acquisition it is necessary to include profits and gains or losses, as well as cash dividend declarations made by the subsidiary company since acquisition, in the consolidated financial statements. It is possible the parent company has recorded events subsequent to the acquisition date on either the cost basis or the equity basis. It therefore is of paramount importance to determine the basis of accounting the parent company is using ***in its accounting recording system*** for the investment in its subsidiary; the investment elimination entry for balance sheet adjustments and for income statement adjustments differs according to the basis used.

For example, assume that, except for P Limited's accounts Investment in Common Stock and Retained Earnings, the balance sheets for the two companies at December 31, Year 2, are as shown below:

	P Limited balance sheet December 31, Year 2	*S Limited balance sheet December 31, Year 2*
Current assets	$ 900,000	$ 600,000
Fixed assets (net)	2,400,000	1,200,000
Investment in S Limited common stock ..	?	
Other assets	500,000	200,000
	$?	$2,000,000
Current liabilities	$ 300,000	$ 400,000
Long-term debt	2,000,000	500,000
Common stock, no par	1,300,000	100,000
Retained earnings	?	1,000,000
	$?	$2,000,000

Additional Information

1 The net income reported for Year 2 and the dividend declared on December 31, Year 2, for S Limited are $200,000 and $100,000 respectively.

2 P Limited reported net income from all operations, except from its holdings in S Limited, of $620,000 and declared a dividend in the amount of $300,000 at December 31, Year 2.

In order to complete P Limited's balance sheet at December 31, Year 2, it will be necessary to determine the income to be recorded from the investment in S Limited.

If P Limited accounted for its investment in S Limited on the ***cost*** basis, it would have made the following accounting entry at December 31, Year 2:

Dividend Receivable	80,000	
Dividend Income		80,000
To record investment (dividend) income from S Limited in current year.		

As a result, total net income reported by P Limited would be P's own net income plus the $80,000 recorded above from S Limited or ($620,000 + $80,000) = $700,000. The completed balance sheet would appear as follows:

	P Limited balance sheet December 31, Year 2
Current assets	$ 900,000
Fixed assets (net)	2,400,000
Investment in S Limited common stock	1,200,000
Other assets	500,000
	$5,000,000
Current liabilities	$ 300,000
Long-term debt	2,000,000
Common stock, no par	1,300,000
Retained earnings	1,400,000*
	$5,000,000

*($1,000,000 + $700,000 − $300,000) = $1,400,000.

If P Limited accounted for its investment in S Limited on the ***equity*** basis, it would have made the following accounting entries on December 31, Year 2:

Investment in Common Stock	160,000	
Investment Income		160,000
To record 80% of S Limited's reported net income for Year 2.		
Dividend Receivable	80,000	
Investment in S Limited Common Stock		80,000
To record dividend receivable from S Limited at December 31, Year 2.		

	Dr.	Cr.
Investment Income	19,000	
Investment in S Limited Common Stock		19,000
To record depreciation on 80% of the difference between fair value and carrying value of fixed assets (net) at December 31, Year 1 = [80% × ($1,200,000 − $900,000) ÷ 16], plus amortization of the purchased goodwill at December 31, Year 1 = ($160,000 ÷ 40).		

As a result, total net income reported by P Limited for Year 2 would be ($620,000 + $160,000 − $19,000) = $761,000. The completed balance sheet would appear as follows:

	P Limited balance sheet December 31, Year 2
Current assets	$ 900,000
Fixed assets (net)	2,400,000
Investment in common stock*	1,261,000
Other assets	500,000
	$5,061,000
Current liabilities	$ 300,000
Long-term debt	2,000,000
Common stock, no par	1,300,000
Retained earnings †	1,461,000
	$5,061,000

* ($1,200,000 + $160,000 − $80,000 − $19,000) = $1,261,000.
†($1,000,000 + $620,000 + $160,000 − $19,000 − $300,000) = $1,461,000.

Under the assumption P Limited accounts for its investment in 80% of S Limited on the ***cost*** basis, the investment elimination entries will be as shown below.

	Dr.	Cr.
Common Stock—S Limited	100,000	
Retained Earnings—S Limited (Dec. 31, Year 1)	900,000	
Fixed Assets (net) (80% of $300,000)	240,000	
Goodwill	160,000	
Minority Interest (20% of $1,000,000)		200,000
Investment in S Limited Common Stock		1,200,000
To eliminate the investment in 80% of S Limited at December 31, Year 1.		
Retained Earnings—S Limited	100,000	
Minority Interest (20%)		20,000
Retained Earnings—P Limited		80,000
To record the change in equity of S Limited from the acquisition date to December 31, Year 2, for P Limited's share and minority-interest share [($900,000 + $200,000 − $100,000) − $900,000].		
Retained Earnings—P Limited	19,000	
Fixed Assets (net)		15,000
Goodwill		4,000

To record depreciation of 1/16 of 80% of fixed assets increase from carrying value to fair value at December 31, Year 1, and to record amortization of goodwill at 1/40 of $160,000.

The work sheet for the consolidated balance sheet of P Limited and S Limited at December 31, Year 2, when S Limited was accounted for on the *cost* basis is shown below.

Accounts	*P Limited balance sheet*	*S Limited balance sheet*	*Adjustment* *Dr*	*Adjustment* *Cr*	*P Limited consolidated balance sheet*
Current assets	900,000	600,000			1,500,000
Fixed assets (net)	2,400,000	1,200,000	(1) 240,000	(3) 15,000	3,825,000
Investment in S Limited common stock	1,200,000			(1) 1,200,000	
Other assets	500,000	200,000			700,000
Goodwill			(1) 160,000	(3) 4,000	156,000
	5,000,000	2,000,000			6,181,000
Current liabilities	300,000	400,000			700,000
Long-term debt ..	2,000,000	500,000			2,500,000
Minority interest				(2) 20,000 (1) 200,000	220,000
Common stock, no par	1,300,000	100,000	(1) 100,000 (2) 100,000		1,300,000
Retained earnings	1,400,000	1,000,000	(1) 900,000 (3) 19,000	(2) 80,000	1,461,000
	5,000,000	2,000,000	1,519,000	1,519,000	6,181,000

Under the assumption P Limited accounts for its investment in S Limited on the *equity* basis, the investment elimination entry will be as follows:

		Dr	Cr
1	Common Stock—S Limited	100,000	
	Retained Earnings — S Limited (Dec. 31, Year 2)	1,000,000	
	Fixed Assets (net) ($240,000 – $15,000)	225,000	
	Goodwill ($160,000 – $4,000)	156,000	
	Minority Interest (20% of $1,100,000)		220,000
	Investment in S Limited Common Stock		1,261,000
	To eliminate the investment in 80% of S Limited account on consolidation.		

Here is the work sheet for consolidated balance sheet of P Limited and S Limited at December 31, Year 2, when S Limited was accounted for on the *equity* basis:

Accounts	P Limited balance sheet	S Limited balance sheet	Adjustments Dr	Adjustments Cr	P Limited consolidated balance sheet
Current assets......	900,000	600,000			1,500,000
Fixed assets (net) ..	2,400,000	1,200,000	(1) 225,000		3,825,000
Investment in S Limited common stock....	1,261,000			(1) 1,261,000	
Other assets	500,000	200,000			700,000
Goodwill			(1) 156,000		156,000
	5,061,000	2,000,000			6,181,000
Current liabilities..	300,000	400,000			700,000
Long-term debt	2,000,000	500,000			2,500,000
Minority interest ..				(1) 220,000	220,000
Common stock, no par	1,300,000	100,000	(1) 100,000		1,300,000
Retained earnings*	1,461,000	1,000,000	(1) 1,000,000		1,461,000*
	5,061,000	2,000,000	1,481,000	1,481,000	6,181,000

*Note that the retained earnings reported by P Limited when that company accounts for its investment in S Limited on the ***equity*** basis is identical to the consolidated retained earnings figure of $1,461,000. This must be the case, because by definition the resulting retained earnings figure ***and*** the resulting net income figure reported by the parent company when using the ***equity*** basis of accounting must be the same as those in the consolidated statements.

The consolidated balance sheet does ***not*** differ according to the basis of accounting followed by P Limited. There is only ***one correct*** consolidated balance sheet. As a result, the investment elimination entry or entries required will be such as to arrive at the ***one*** consolidated balance sheet.

Intercompany Transactions After the Acquisition Date

Intercompany transactions entered into by the parent and subsidiary companies prior to the acquisition date are bona fide transactions unless they were entered into in contemplation of the acquisition. As a result, these pre-acquisition transactions need not be a concern when consolidation occurs. However, intercompany transactions between parent and subsidiary subsequent to acquisition (or made in contemplation of the acquisition) must not be included in the consolidated financial statements. The transactions included in the financial statements of the consolidated entity ***must*** be those occurring between the consolidated group and entities outside that group.

There are two categories of intercompany transactions to be taken into consideration. One is categorized as ***intrastatement*** and the other as ***interstatement***. Intrastatement transactions represent those transactions that affect the same financial statement in each company. For example, a sale of merchandise by the parent to a subsidiary would be recorded as a sale by the parent and a purchase by the subsidiary. Another example would be when a subsidiary rents building space to its parent. The subsidiary records rental income and the parent records rent expense. Both of the above examples affect the income statement of each company. A third example would be where one affiliate owes money to the other at the balance sheet date. In this case the one affiliate shows a receivable and the other a payable. The balance sheets of both companies are affected in equal amounts but in opposite sign (one a debit and the other a credit). If the parent and subsidiary companies have intrastatement balance sheet accounts at the acquisition date, and if consolidated balance sheets are required at that date, then these intrastatement ***balance sheet*** accounts must be removed.

The consolidated financial statements represent a combination of the line-by-line accounts of the parent company and of its subsidiary. Unless the intrastatement items are removed, they will apear as ***both*** debits and credits in the consolidation. The economic entity resulting from the consolidation would in effect be doing business with itself, or in the case of the balance sheet example, have a receivable and a payable for the same item, in the same amount and in the same balance sheet. Since the consolidated financial statements are for the use of the parent company's shareholders, the removal of the intrastatement amounts has no ***minority-interest*** effect. As a result the effect on the consolidated net income is zero, as the debit removal equals the credit removal, in that statement. Similarly, the debit entry and credit entry to balance sheet accounts, for the removal of intrastatement balances, are equal.

If the intrastatement transactions and balances are not removed for consolidation purposes, the individual accounts will include both transactions with outsiders and transactions with parent and subsidiary companies. This would result in distorted totals for all accounts affected. One of the basic criteria for consolidation is that the consolidated financial statements must depict transactions with outsiders. Statistical analysis of data in a financial statement may be very misleading if intrastatement transactions are not removed. For example, assume that 40% of total sales by the parent company are purchased by the subsidiary company, and that the markup for each company is 100% on cost. Assume total sales by the parent in the current year were $100,000. This means the subsidiary purchased $40,000 of this merchandise and marked it up to sell for a total of $80,000. Assume the subsidiary sold all the merchandise it purchased from the parent in the current year.

	Parent	*Subsidiary*	*Total*
Sales	$100,000	$80,000	$180,000
Cost of sales	50,000	40,000	90,000
Gross profit	$ 50,000	$40,000	$ 90,000

If the intercompany transactions were not removed, the ratio of sales to cost of sales and to gross profit expressed as a percent would be ($90,000 ÷ $180,000) × 100% = 50%. When the intercompany sales are removed by debiting sales $40,000 and crediting cost of sales (purchases) $40,000 the following is the result:

	Parent	*Subsidiary*	*Adjustment Dr or (Cr)*	*Consolidated*
Sales	$100,000	$80,000	40,000	$140,000
Cost of Sales	50,000	40,000	(40,000)	50,000
Gross profit	$ 50,000	$40,000		$ 90,000

Now the ratio of sales to cost of goods sold expressed as a percentage is ($50,000 ÷ $140,000) × 100% = 36% and the ratio of sales to gross profit expressed as a percentage becomes 64%.

The second category of intercompany transactions, called interstatement transactions, are transactions affecting more than one financial statement. As a consequence, each statement's ***net*** balance is ***changed*** by such transactions. For example, recording, for consolidation purposes, the amortization of goodwill arising at the acquisition date requires an expense account be debited and a balance sheet account be credited. Each statement balance has now been changed. Also, this type of transaction may ***affect minority interest*** if the entry is to adjust subsidiary accounts.

Interstatement entries usually involve profits, losses, and/or gains arising from intercompany transactions which must be removed in whole or in part when consolidation occurs. In the preparation of consolidated financial statements at the date of acquisition an investment elimination entry is required and an intrastatement entry for reciprocal balance sheet accounts balances may be required. However, interstatement entries are only applicable when income is affected and therefore, for acquisition-type consolidations, cannot occur at that date as no income for the subsidiary is reported at the acquisition date.

In the preparation of consolidated financial statements the removal of both intrastatement and interstatement items requires the use of elimination entries, in addition to the investment elimination entry itself. It should be noted that the interstatement entries subsequent to acquisition for amortizing and depreciating goodwill and fair value increments occurring at acquisition are included in the investment elimination entry when the parent is accounting for its investment in the subsidiary under the ***equity*** basis, but are separately journalized for consolidation purposes when the ***cost*** basis is used.

Computation of Consolidated Retained Earnings

If the ***equity*** basis of accounting is not followed completely by the parent subsequent to the acquisition date, the retained earnings shown in the books of the parent at the consolidation date will in all probability not be the same amount as that for consolidated retained earnings. In such cases it will be necessary to prepare a detailed computation of consolidated retained earnings wherein adjustments necessary to arrive at the consolidated retained earnings figure would be included. Also, when minority interest, representing minority shareholders' share of the carrying value of subsidiary's net assets, must be altered because the carrying value of the net assets of subsidiary is being adjusted, a schedule detailing such adjustments is sometimes necessary so as to arrive at the proper figure on the balance sheet (and on the income statement) for minority interest. Usually, the schedule depicting the final consolidated retained earnings figure is used to also depict the minority-interest figure for the retained earnings portion of the total amount for minority interest in the consolidated balance sheet.

To illustrate, assume the parent used the ***cost*** basis for recording purposes with respect to its subsidiary and the additional information on page 703 and work sheet for P Limited on page 704 are applicable.

There are two methods commonly used to carry out the detailed computation of consolidated retained earnings when the investment in the subsidiary is carried on the cost basis by the parent company. The first commences with the parent's retained earnings figure from its own operations at the consolidation date and adjusts that figure to reflect its share of reported net incomes of subsidiary from the acquisition date up to the consolidation date together with intercompany adjustments required since acquisition. The second commences with the closing retained earnings of parent and subsidiary at the current consolidation date and adjusts the total of the two such that the ending result is the consolidated retained earnings amount. The first method, incidentally, follows the definition of consolidated retained earnings as being the parent's own retained earnings plus its share of reported net incomes of the subsidiary since acquisition plus and minus adjustments required. This method is illustrated below, using the information relating to P Limited and S Limited presented earlier.

Parent's *own* retained earnings at consolidation date (reported retained earnings, less dividends recorded from subsidiary since acquisition date) ($1,400,000 – $80,000)		$1,320,000
Add: Parent's share of net incomes reported by subsidiary between acquisition date and current consolidation date (80% × $200,000)		160,000
		$1,480,000
Adjustments — Dr or (Cr):		
(a) Purchase date differentials:		
(i) Depreciation of fair value increment for fixed assets $\left(\frac{80\% \times \$300,000}{16 \text{ years}}\right)$	$15,000	
(ii) Amortization of goodwill ($\frac{1}{40}$ of $160,000)	4,000	
(b) Interstatement intercompany transactions	-0-	19,000
Consolidated retained earnings		$1,461,000
20% of subsidiary's net assets available to common shareholders or 20% of common stock and retained earnings (20% of $1,100,000)		$ 220,000
Adjustments above affecting minority-interest shareholders		-0-
Minority interest in consolidated balance sheet		$ 220,000

The illustration for the second method, using the same information for P Limited and S Limited, is presented on page 710.

In some cases, the parent will have accounted for its investment in the subsidiary on a ***partial equity*** basis. That is, some of the entries will have been made by the parent in its accounting records. For example, the parent may have recorded its share of the subsidiary's net income only. This would be as depicted at the point where the asterisk appears on the illustration. The parent also may have recorded the reductions in purchase differences to the consolidation date but not any interstatement adjustments required. Therefore, it is necessary to set up the calculation of consolidated retained earnings in such a way that you are able to commence the schedule at the level reached by the parent in its accounting for the subsidiary.

Minority interest			*Consolidated retained earnings*
	Parents' reported retained earnings at consolidation date (Dec. 31, Year 2)		$1,400,000
	Subsidiary's reported retained earnings at consolidation date (Dec. 31, Year 2)		1,000,000
			$2,400,000
	Deduct: Parent's portion of subsidiary retained earnings purchased at acquisition date (Dec. 31, Year 1) (80% of $900,000)	$720,000	
$200,000	Minority-interest share of subsidiary's reported retained earnings at consolidation date (Dec. 31, Year 2) (20% of $1,000,000)	200,000	920,000
			$1,480,000*
	Adjustments — Dr or (Cr):		
	Purchase date differentials:		
	Depreciation of fair value increment	$ 15,000	
	Amortization of goodwill	4,000	19,000
	Consolidated retained earnings		$1,461,000
$200,000	Minority interest in subsidiary's adjusted retained earnings		
	Add minority interest in other common-stock-owned shareholders' equity accounts of subsidiary:		
20,000	Common stock — (20% of $100,000)		
$220,000	***Minority interest in consolidated balance sheet***		

*This figure and all those that follow it are ***the same for both methods*** in the determination of consolidated retained earnings. Also, this figure represents the consolidated retained earnings as a result of adding all ***reported*** net incomes of subsidiary to the retained earnings of the parent. All that remains to be done after this total is reached is to add and/or deduct adjustments for:

- Purchase differential amounts used up since acquisition date.
- Interstatement transactions adjustments required since acquisition date.

In this example, had the parent accounted for the subsidiary on the ***equity*** basis, as the original example on pages 703–704 depicts, no calculation of retained earnings would be necessary, as the retained earnings of the parent ***equals*** the consolidated retained earnings. However, in many cases, as stated above, a ***partial equity*** basis is used and some calculations are required. Of course, if the ***cost*** basis of accounting for the subsidiary is used by the parent, the entire calculation of consolidated retained earnings is necessary.

Intrastatement adjustments are not included in the calculation of consolidated retained earnings since they have no net effect on income and consequently on retained earnings.

Intercompany Transactions — Intrastatement and Interstatement Adjustments

As was previously stated, intrastatement transactions between parent and subsidiary must be removed from the income statements of the affiliates for the entire period over which income is being reported and from the affiliate balance sheets for balances outstanding at the consolidation date. The intrastatement adjustments affect the individual accounts within the statements concerned but have no effect on either the net income or the retained earnings figure. Interstatement adjustments do affect the net income and the retained earnings figure. This is as a result of intercompany profits, gains, and losses' not being realized at the consolidation date because the intercompany transaction has not as yet been completed with an outside entity. Accordingly, the profit, gain, or loss cannot be recognized and must be removed at the consolidation date. A very common example of such a situation results when one affiliate sells merchandise to the other at a price in excess of its cost, and some or all of that merchandise is in the purchasing affiliate's closing inventory at the consolidation date. In such a case profit made by the selling affiliate and included in that affiliate's income is in the inventory figure in the balance sheet of the other affiliate at the consolidation date. It is therefore necessary to reduce the inventory figure to the amount of the cost to the economic entity (the consolidated group of affiliates) and to remove the profit from the income of the selling affiliate. A second, less common example occurs when one affiliate sells a fixed asset, land, machinery, building, etc., to another affiliate at a gain or a loss. If the fixed asset remains within the group at the consolidation date, it will be set up as an asset at a cost to the purchasing affiliate different from the cost the selling affiliate would have reported had the asset not been sold. The difference has been reported in the income of the selling affiliate in the year of its sale to the buying affiliate. This type of intercompany transaction may become more complex if the fixed asset is a service asset and is depreciated as it is used by the buying affiliate. Depreciation is considered a partial sale of a service asset as it offsets revenue from products sold. Accordingly, since part of the asset is considered sold, through depreciation, that part of any gain or loss on the intercompany sale has been realized (sold to outside entities). In such situations, the unrealized portion of the gain or loss on intercompany sale of the fixed asset is removed from income (or from retained earnings if the accounting is subsequent to the year of the sale) by means of an interstatement adjusting entry at the consolidation date.

Intercompany sales may be regarded as of two types. Sales from the parent to one or more subsidiaries are known as ***downstream*** sales. In such cases the parent has recorded 100% of the profit, gain, or loss on the sale in its income statement. Since 100% of the profit, gain, or loss has been included in the parent's income, 100% must be removed from current income or from retained earnings. If part of the profit, gain, or loss has been realized through subsequent depreciation, as in the fixed-asset case above, then the amount of the balance remaining to be depreciated is removed. Sales from the subsidiary to the parent, on the other hand, are known as ***upstream*** sales. In upstream sales the subsidiary has recorded 100% of the profit, gain, or loss on the sale in its income statement. If the parent does not own 100% of the subsidiary, minority interest shares in the income of the subsidiary. In such a case, the parent only owns a share of the subsidiary's profit, gain, or loss on the intercompany sale. As a result, the parent's adjustment is for its proportionate share, and minority interest is adjusted for its proportionate share. If the subsidiary's sale to the parent is depreciated over time, the share the parent will adjust will be further reduced by its proportionate share of the depreciation taken. The minority-interest share adujstment will also be reduced by its proportionate share of the depreciation taken.

To illustrate a ***downstream sale*** let us assume that a parent which owns 80% of a subsidiary sold land and a building to the subsidiary for $100,000 cash and $600,000 cash respectively. The parent had carried the land and the building, at cost, in its records at $50,000 and $800,000 respectively. The accumulated depreciation recorded on the building in the parent's records at the sale date was $400,000. The parent depreciated the building on the straight-line basis at $40,000 per year and it considered the building would have no salvage value at the end of its economic life. The calculation of gains on sale of the land and the building would be:

	Land	*Building*
Selling price to buying affiliate	$100,000	$600,000
Carrying amount in selling affiliate's books at sale date	50,000	400,000
Gain on intercompany sale	$ 50,000	$200,000

The entries to be recorded by the parent and the subsidiary are shown below.

Parent (selling) company:		
Cash	700,000	
Accumulated Depreciation	400,000	
Land		50,000
Building, at Cost		800,000
Gain on Sale of Land		50,000
Gain on Sale of Building		200,000
To record sale of land and building to affiliate.		
Subsidiary (buying) company:		
Land	100,000	
Building, at Cost	600,000	
Cash		700,000
To record purchase of land and building from affiliate.		

This was a downstream transaction, as parent sold to subsidiary. Therefore, 100% of the gain belongs to the parent and must be removed on the consolidation date. If we assume the consolidation date is 12 months after the above intercompany sale and that the subsidiary agrees with the parent as to the remaining life of the building and as to its salvage value, then the subsidiary will depreciate the building for one year of its remaining 10-year life or ($1/10 \times \$600,000$) = \$60,000. Had the building not been sold to the affiliate, depreciation would have been \$40,000. The "excess depreciation" of \$20,000 is considered to be the amount of the unrealized gain of \$200,000 realized through depreciation. Each year hereafter, for the remaining nine years, \$20,000 of the gain will be realized through "excess depreciation." In this way the gain of \$200,000 on the sale of the building will be realized for consolidation purposes over the 10-year period. The \$50,000 gain on the sale of the land will not be realized until the land is sold to an outside entity. This may not occur for a long time.

The entry to be recorded by the subsidiary would be:

	Debit	Credit
Depreciation Expense	60,000	
Accumulated Depreciation		60,000
To record depreciation on building for six months.		

When the parent accounts for its investment in the subsidiary on the ***cost*** basis, the interstatement adjustment for consolidation purposes would be reflected in the entries below.

	Debit	Credit
Building, at Cost	200,000	
Gain on Sale of Land	50,000	
Gain on Sale of Building	200,000	
Land		50,000
Accumulated depreciation		400,000
To eliminate gain on sale of land and building in current year.		
Accumulated Depreciation	20,000	
Depreciation Expense		20,000
To remove "excess depreciation" taken on building for current year.		

The credit to depreciation expense above is given 100% to the parent as the portion of the gain allowed. The net effect of the above two entries on the parent's net income (and retained earnings) is to adjust it downward (\$50,000 + \$200,000 − \$20,000) = \$230,000, thus allowing 100% of the "excess depreciation" to remain as a credit in the parent's net income (and therefore retained earnings). If we now assume the identical sale facts, except the sale is from the subsidiary to the parent, the "excess depreciation" credit of \$20,000 is given to the seller, the subsidiary. As a result, the parent's share thereof is 80% or \$16,000 and minority interest has a 20% or \$4,000 share.

If the parent accounts for its investment on the cost basis, the \$20,000 "excess depreciation" is credited to the subsidiary's depreciation expense, thereby reducing depreciation expense \$20,000 and increasing income \$20,000. The increased net income is shared by the parent and minority interests 80% and 20% respectively. Also, the elimination of the gains on the sale of land of \$50,000 and on the sale of building of $200,000 are included in the subsidiary's income determination. As a result the net reversal is a $230,000 reduction in subsidiary net income, which will be shared by the parent and minority interest in an 80%-to-20% ratio.

When the parent accounts for its investment in the affiliate on the ***equity*** basis, its entries at the consolidation date, where the parent sells to the subsidiary, will be as follows:

Investment Income*	250,000	
Investment in Subsidiary Common Stock		250,000
To eliminate gain on sale through investment income account.		
Investment in Subsidiary Common Stock	20,000	
Investment Income		20,000
To record 100% of ''excess depreciation'' as investment income.		

*Could have been made to a separate account.

The distribution to individual accounts of the charges to investment income totalling $230,000 will be made in the investment elimination entry.

Where the subsidiary sells to the parent, the entries at the consolidation date will be as follows:

Investment Income (80% × 250,000)	200,000	
Investment in Subsidiary Common Stock		200,000
To record elimination of parent's share of gain to subsidiary on sale to parent of land and building in current year.		
Investment in Subsidiary Common Stock	16,000	
Investment Income		16,000
To record 80% of ''excess depreciation'' as investment income.		

The distribution to individual accounts of the charges to investment income totalling $184,000, above, will be made in the investment elimination entry, which will also include minority interest's 20% share totalling $46,000.

The above example will be included in the problem at the end of this appendix.

Intercompany Sales of Merchandise of Which a Portion Remains in Inventory at the Consolidation Date An intrastatement entry is required to reverse the intercompany sale and purchase and an interstatement entry is required to remove the profit or loss earned by the seller of the intercompany-sold merchandise which remains in the inventory of the buying affiliate at the consolidation date. It is therefore necessary to determine the amount of the profit or loss earned on the intercompany sales of merchandise remaining in inventory at the consolidation date. Companies usually relate the profit (or loss) to markup (or markdown) on either cost or sales. Our interest is in the markup on sales because we are aware of the sales amount (the purchase amount in the buying affiliate's records) included in the buyer's closing inventory. Therefore, markups on cost in the seller's records must be adjusted to their equivalent markup on sales. To illustrate, assume a parent (P) sells to a subsidiary (S) merchandise costing P $100,000. At the same time S sells to P merchandise at a selling price of $150,000. P sells all its merchandise at a markup of 100% on cost, whereas S sells all merchandise at a markup of 40% on selling price. At the consolidation date P has 20% of its purchases from S in its inventory, and S has 25% of its purchases from P in its inventory. Assume this is the first year of operations subsequent to the acquisition by P of 75% of S's outstanding common shares and intercompany sales are as shown below:

Total sales by P to S ($100,000 cost marked up 100%)	$200,000
Total sales by S to P	150,000
Total intercompany sales	$350,000

The entry to adjust the sales and cost of goods sold on consolidation would be:

Sales	350,000	
Cost of Sales (Purchases)*		350,000
To adjust the intercompany sales.		

*A detailed income statement, including purchases in the calculation of cost of sales, would require purchases be reduced by $350,000. An income statement using a one-line cost of sales would require that account to be reduced $350,000.

The intercompany profit in ending inventory as a result of the intercompany sale is explained as follows:

P's sales to S result in S's inventory being overstated and P's income being overstated. Each would be overstated by:

Profit in sales × % of sales in closing inventory = profit in closing inventory

$$\$200{,}000 \times \left(\frac{1}{1+1}\right)^{*} \times 25\% = \underline{\underline{\$25{,}000}}$$

*The formula for changing markup on cost (MC) to markup on sales (MS) is:

$$MS = \frac{MC}{MC + 1} \text{ meaning } MS = \frac{\text{MC numerator}}{\text{MC numerator + MC denominator}}$$

The entry to adjust inventory at the date of consolidation for a consolidated balance sheet when the investment is carried on the cost basis would be:

Retained earnings	25,000	
Inventory		25,000
To remove intercompany profit in closing inventory.		

The entry to adjust inventory at the date of consolidation for a consolidated balance sheet when the investment is carried on the equity basis would be ***included*** in the balance sheet consolidation entries. Its effect would be to increase the

Investment in Subsidiary Common Stock account by $25,000 and to decrease the Inventory account by $25,000.

S's sales to P result in both P's inventory and S's income being overstated by $150,000 × 40% × 20% = $12,000.

The entry to adjust inventory at the date of consolidation for a consolidated balance sheet when P carries its investment in S on the cost basis would be:

Retained Earnings (80% × $12,000)	9,600	
Minority Interest (20% × $12,000)	2,400	
Inventory		12,000
To remove intercompany profit in closing inventory.		

The entry to adjust closing inventory at the date of consolidation for a consolidated balance sheet when P carries its investment in S on the equity basis would be ***included*** in the balance sheet consolidation entries. Its effect would be to increase the Investment in Subsidiary Common Stock by $9,600, to decrease Minority Interest by $2,400, and to decrease Inventory by $12,000.

Another example will be included in the demonstration problem at the end of this appendix.

Consolidated Income Statement

The consolidated income statement replaces a ***one-line amount*** showing investment income from the subsidiary with the ***line-by-line income statement of the subsidiary***. The line-by-line amounts represent 100% of the balance in each individual classification. (Both the balance sheet and the income statement combine 100% of the subsidiary line-by-line amounts.) This requires minority interest to be shown in one amount at the bottom of the income statement as an adjustment so that the consolidated net income shows ''the parent's own net income plus its share of S's net income.''

Entries in the balance sheet consolidation to retained earnings represent entries necessary to adjust the income statement and its minority interest share, where applicable.

The procedure followed wherein the consolidated balance sheet entries reflect entries to the balance sheet only will be extended to include entries which adjust the income statement line-by-line accounts, including the income statement minority-interest amount.

To illustrate, assume for the example on pages 702 and 703 that the income reported by each company resulted from income statement data shown at the top of page 717.

	Parent	*Subsidiary*
Sales	$2,000,000	$800,000
Cost of sales	800,000	300,000
Gross profit	$1,200,000	$500,000
Investment income	?	
	$?	$500,000
Other expenses:		
General and administrative*	$ 300,000	$200,000
Selling	280,000	100,000
	$ 580,000	$300,000
Net income	$?	$200,000

*Depreciation and amortization are included in general and administrative expenses.

If the parent accounted for its investment on the **cost** basis, the investment (dividend) income would have been 80% of the dividend of $100,000 declared by the subsidiary or $80,000, and the net income of the parent would be $700,000.

If the parent accounted for its investment on the ***equity*** basis, the investment income would have been 80% of the reported income of the subsidiary of $200,000 minus the adjustment for the purchase differences of $19,000 or $141,000 [($200,000 × 80%) – $19,000], and the net income of the parent would be $761,000.

	Cost basis	*Equity basis*
Gross profit (above)	$1,200,000	$1,200,000
Investment income	80,000	141,000
	$1,280,000	$1,341,000
Other expenses:		
General and administrative	$ 300,000	$ 300,000
Selling	280,000	280,000
	580,000	580,000
Net income	$ 700,000	$ 761,000

The consolidated income statement work sheets, when the cost basis is used and when the equity basis is used, are as shown on page 718.

The consolidated net income figure can be calculated in the same manner as consolidated retained earnings is calculated, as shown on page 719, for the parent's net income determined on a **cost** basis.

Work Sheet for Consolidated Income Statement When Parent Accounts for Investment in Subsidiary on Cost Basis

Accounts	*Parent income statement*	*Subsidiary income statement*	*Adjustments*		*Consolidated income statement*
			Dr	*Cr*	
Sales	$2,000,000	$800,000			$2,800,000
Cost of sales	800,000	300,000			1,100,000
Gross profit	$1,200,000	$500,000			$1,700,000
Investment income	80,000		$80,000*		
	$1,280,000	$500,000			$1,700,000
Other expenses:					
General and administrative	$ 300,000	$200,000	19,000		$ 519,000
Selling	280,000	100,000			380,000
	$ 580,000	$300,000			$ 899,000
Combined net income	$ 700,000	$200,000			$ 801,000
Minority interest (20% of $200,000)					40,000
Consolidated net income					$ 761,000

*Single-line amount replaced by line-by-line accounts.

Work Sheet for Consolidated Income Statement When Parent Accounts for Investment in Subsidiary on Equity Basis

Accounts	*Parent income statement*	*Subsidiary income statement*	*Adjustments*		*Consolidated income statement*
			Dr	*Cr*	
Sales	$2,000,000	$800,000			$2,800,000
Cost of sales	800,000	300,000			1,100,000
Gross profit	$1,200,000	$500,000			$1,700,000
Investment income	216,000		$216,000*		
	$1,416,000	$500,000			$1,700,000
Other expenses:					
General and administrative	$ 300,000	$200,000	19,000		$ 519,000
Selling	280,000	100,000			380,000
	$ 580,000	$300,000			$ 899,000
Combined net income	$ 836,000	$200,000			$ 801,000
Minority interest (20% of $200,000)					40,000
Consolidated net income					$ 761,000

*Single-line amount replaced by line-by-line accounts.

Minority interest			*Consolidated net income*
	Net income of parent without dividend income from subsidiary ($700,000 − $80,000)		$620,000
$40,000........	Add: Parent's share of subsidiary's reported net income (80% of $200,000)		160,000
			$780,000
	Adjustments — Dr or (Cr):		
	Amortization of purchased goodwill: ($\frac{1}{40}$ of $160,000)	$ 4,000	
	Depreciation of fair value increment for fixed assets (net) ($\frac{1}{16}$ × 80% × $300,000)	15,000	19,000
	Consolidated net income		$761,000
$40,000........	***Minority-interest share of subsidiary net income***		

or

Minority interest			*Consolidated net income*
	Net income reported by parent (*cost* basis)		$700,000
	Net income reported by subsidiary		200,000
			$900,000
	Deduct: Parent's share of current-year dividends declared by subsidiary (80% × $100,000)	$80,000	
$40,000.......	Minority-interest share of subsidiary's reported net income (20% of $200,000)	40,000	120,000
			$761,000
	Adjustments — Dr or (Cr):		
	Amortization of purchased goodwill ..	4,000	
	Depreciation of fixed-assets fair value increment	15,000	19,000
	Consolidated net income		$761,000
$40,000.......	***Minority-interest share of subsidiary net income***		

This calculation is not required when the parent accounts for its investment in 80% of the subsidiary on the equity basis, as the income reported by the parent is the same as consolidated net income. However, the parent may account for its investment in a partial equity way which would require commencing the calculation part-way down the schedules above.

There remain a number of consolidation topics to be covered, but these are normally dealt with in an advanced text. An understanding of the consolidation processes and procedures covered herein should be satisfactory for a basic understanding of the consolidation process.

SUPPLEMENTARY PROBLEM ON CONSOLIDATION ACCOUNTING

The individual balance sheets of Port Limited and Starboard Limited on December 31, Year 5, immediately ***before*** Port acquired 60% of the outstanding shares of Starboard for a cash consideration of $1,000,000, were as follows:

		Port Limited		*Starboard Limited*
Assets				
Current:				
Cash		$1,200,000		$ 100,000
Accounts receivable (net)		800,000		400,000
Merchandise inventory		1,000,000		500,000
		$3,000,000		$1,000,000
Fixed:				
Land		$ 800,000		$ 300,000
Buildings — at cost	$1,500,000		$1,500,000	
Less accumulated depreciation	400,000	1,100,000	600,000	900,000
Machinery — at cost	$1,800,000		$ 800,000	
Less accumulated depreciation	700,000	1,100,000	200,000	600,000
		$3,000,000		$1,800,000
Total assets		$6,000,000		$2,800,000
Liabilities				
Current:				
Accounts payable		$ 200,000		$ 100,000
Other payables		800,000		50,000
		$1,000,000		$ 150,000
10% bonds payable (net)		1,900,000		1,650,000
Total liabilities		$2,900,000		$1,800,000
Shareholders' Equity				
Capital stock, no par		$1,000,000		$ 800,000
Retained earnings		2,100,000		200,000
Total shareholders' equity		$3,100,000		$1,000,000
Total liabilities and shareholders' equity		$6,000,000		$2,800,000

Additional Information — Acquisition Date

At the date of acquisition, January 1, Year 6, the fair value of Starboard Limited's net assets approximated their carrying values except for the following: Starboard's inventory had a fair value of $700,000, its building a fair value of $1,200,000, and its land a fair value of $200,000. Inventory is expected to turn over three times a year and the building is depreciated on the straight-line basis, is expected to have no salvage value, and has 20 years of remaining economic life. Goodwill, if any, is to be amortized over 40 years on the straight-line basis.

At December 31, Year 6, the balance sheets of Port Limited and Starboard Limited were as follows:

		Port Limited		Starboard Limited
Assets				
Current:				
Cash		$ 800,500		$ 399,500
Accounts receivable (net)		1,000,000		500,000
Merchandise inventory		1,200,000		700,000
Prepaid rent				500
		$3,000,500		$1,600,000
Fixed:				
Land		$ 900,000		$ 250,000
Buildings — at cost	$2,300,000		$ 700,000	
Less accumulated depreciation	591,000	1,709,000	300,000	400,000
Machinery — at cost	$2,000,000		$ 700,000	
Less accumulated depreciation	800,000	1,200,000	250,000	450,000
		$3,809,000		$1,100,000
Investment in Starboard Limited		$1,090,500		
Total assets		$7,900,000		$2,700,000
Liabilities				
Current:				
Accounts payable		$ 100,000		$ 200,000
Other payables		850,000		100,000
		$ 950,000		$ 300,000
10% bonds payable (net)		1,950,000		700,000
		$2,900,000		$1,000,000
Shareholders' Equity				
Capital stock, no par		$1,000,000		$ 800,000
Retained earnings		4,000,000		900,000
Total shareholders' equity		$5,000,000		$1,700,000
Total liabilities and shareholders' equity		$7,900,000		$2,700,000

The income statements for the two affiliated companies for the current year ended December 31, Year 6, were as follows:

	Port Limited	Starboard Limited
Sales	$16,000,000	$6,000,000
Cost of sales	12,000,000	4,000,000
Gross profit	$ 4,000,000	$2,000,000
Rental income	3,000	
Investment income	126,500	
Gain on sale of land		50,000
Gain on sale of building		200,000
	$ 4,129,500	$2,250,000

Other expenses:		
Selling	$ 1,000,000	$ 700,000
Rent		3,000
Professional fees	200,000	100,000
General	280,000	300,000
Depreciation	300,000	150,000
Administrative	380,000	230,000
Sundry	9,500	7,000
	$ 2,169,500	$1,490,000
Net income	$ 1,960,000	$ 760,000

Additional Information — Consolidation Date

1 Both Port Limited and Starboard Limited paid three quarterly dividends of $15,000 each and declared the fourth-quarter dividend in the same amount. Dividends payable are in other payables and dividends receivable are in accounts receivable.

2 Port Limited accounts for its investment in Starboard Limited on the equity basis.

3 Starboard Limited rents machinery from Port Limited. The rent paid in the current year was $3,500, of which two months' rent at $250 each was prepaid at December 31, 1986. The amount prepaid is in Port Limited's accounts payable at year-end.

4 During the current year each affiliate has sold merchandise to the other. Details of these sales are as follows:

	Sales amount, $	*Amount in closing inventory,* $	*Markup percent on cost,* %
Port sales to Starboard	300,000	150,000	33⅓
Starboard sales to Port	200,000	75,000	50%

5 Starboard Limited sold land and a building to Port Limited on July 1, Year 6. Details of the sale are as follows:

- ***Land:*** Cost to Starboard was $50,000 and selling price to Port was $100,000. Port has the land recorded in its balance sheet on December 31, Year 6.
- ***Building:*** Cost to Starboard was $800,000. Accumulated depreciation to June 30, Year 6, was $400,000. Starboard depreciated the building on the straight-line basis at $40,000 per year. Starboard considered that the building would be worthless at the end of its economic life. Selling price to Port was $600,000. Port agreed with Starboard as to the length of the building's remaining economic life and as to its worth at that time. Port paid Starboard $700,000 cash on July 1, Year 6, for the two assets.

Solution to Supplementary Problem

Since December 31, Year 6, is the first consolidation date subsequent to the acquisition of a 60% interest in Starboard Limited by Port Limited on January 1, Year 6, and since Port Limited accounts for its investment in Starboard Limited on the ***equity*** basis, the investment elimination entry will be made as at December 31, Year 6. First, the components of the purchase must be determined:

Port purchased 60% of Starboard at a cost of	$1,000,000
60% of the carrying value of Starboard's net assets at the acquisition date, January 1, Year 6 was 60% × ($800,000 + $200,000)	600,000
Purchase difference	$ 400,000
Fair value increments:	
Inventory (60% × $700,000 − $500,000)	$ 120,000
Building (60% × $1,200,000 − $900,000)	180,000
Land (60% × $200,000 − $300,000)	(60,000)
	$ 240,000
Goodwill ($400,000 − $240,000)	160,000
Purchase difference	$ 400,000

Since inventory turns over three times a year, the ***$120,000*** fair value increment will be used up 100% in Year 6.

The building fair value increment of $180,000 is to be depreciated over 20 years on the straight-line basis. Therefore, annual depreciation is ***$9,000***. The land does not depreciate.

The accumulated depreciation for the buildings and the machinery, at January 1, Year 6, must be removed 100%, against the applicable fixed assets. (A purchaser does not purchase accumulated depreciation.)

The goodwill of $160,000 is to be amortized on the straight-line basis over 40 years. Therefore, annual amortization is ***$4,000***. This would be considered a general expense by the company. As a result the portion of the investment elimination entry related to the purchase difference already adjusted to investment account because Port accounts on the ***equity*** basis will be:

		Dr.	Cr.
1	Building, at Cost	180,000	
	Goodwill (net) ($160,000 − $4,000)	156,000	
	Land		60,000
	Accumulated Depreciation—Building		9,000
	Investment in Common Stock		267,000
	To set up the purchase differences at consolidation date inclusive of depreciation and amortization thereon.		
2	Accumulated Depreciation—Building	600,000	
	Accumulated Depreciation—Machinery	200,000	
	Buildings		600,000
	Machinery		200,000

To remove accumulated depreciation accounts of Starboard Limited, as they appeared on January 1, Year 6, the acquisition date.

Note: The inventory would have originally been set up as an asset if consolidation were to occur at acquisition date, but then would have been written off 100% in the first year.

The adjustments regarding interstatement profits in closing inventories which will become part of the investment elimination entry because Port carries its investment in Starboard on the ***equity*** basis are determined as follows:

- Year-end profit in Port's income, a downstream transaction (and therefore in Starboard's inventory):

$$\mathbf{MS} = \frac{\mathbf{MC}}{\mathbf{MC}+1} = \frac{\frac{1}{3}}{\frac{1}{3}+1} = \frac{\frac{1}{3}}{\frac{4}{3}} = \tfrac{1}{4} \text{ or } \underline{\underline{25\%}}.$$

- Therefore ($150,000 × 25%) = ***$37,500*** of profit in Port's net income is included in Starboard's $150,000 closing inventory. One hundred percent of this profit must be removed from Port's net income (and therefore retained earnings).
- Year-end profit in Starboard's income, an upstream transaction (and therefore in Port's inventory):

$$\mathbf{MS} = \frac{\frac{1}{2}}{\frac{1}{2}+1} = \frac{\frac{1}{2}}{1.5} = \tfrac{1}{3} = \underline{\underline{33\tfrac{1}{3}\%}}.$$

- Therefore ($75,000 × $33\frac{1}{3}$%) = ***$25,000*** profit in Starboard's net income is included in Port's closing inventory. This profit will include a minority-interest share. All of this profit must be removed from Starboard's net income (and therefore from Port's retained earnings and minority interest — 60% and 40% respectively).

As a result of the above inventory transactions, the portion of the investment elimination entry related to the removal of the unrealized profits on the intercompany sales will be adjusted on the equity basis through the investment account as follows:

3	Investment in Starboard Common Stock [(100 % × $37,500) + (60% × $25,000)]	52,500	
	Minority Interest (40% × $25,000)	10,000	
	Merchandise Inventory		62,500
	To eliminate the intercompany profit in inventory [(100% × $37,500) + (60% × $25,000)].		

Adjustments regarding interstatement gains on intercompany sale of land and building, and the adjustment for ''excess depreciation'' on the building, have also been made to the investment account because Port accounts for its investment in Starboard on the equity basis.

This transaction increases Starboard's net income, because this is an upstream transaction and the subsidiary sold to the parent at a gain. As a result, minority interest will have a share of the elimination of the sale and of the ''excess depreciation'' adjustment.

Computation of gain on transaction:			
Gain on sale of land:			
Selling price		$100,000	
Cost to Starboard		50,000	
Gain			$ 50,000
Gain on sale of building:			
Selling price		$600,000	
Carrying amount:			
Cost	$800,000		
Accumulated depreciation	400,000	400,000	
Gain			200,000
Total gain on transaction			$250,000
Computation of excess depreciation:			
Depreciation on building after sale to Port ($600,000 ÷ 10 years × ½ year)			$ 30,000
Depreciation on building had the sale not been made ($40,000 × ½ year)			20,000
Excess depreciation allowed to Starboard			$ 10,000

As a result of the above intercompany land and building sale, Port would have made the same entry as was made for the ***parent (selling) company*** on page 712. (In that illustration, the sale of land and building was a ***downstream*** sale; whereas the same sale is an ***upstream*** sale in this demonstration problem.)

On consolidation, therefore, part of the investment elimination entry relating to this transaction, required because Port accounts for its investment in Starboard on the ***equity*** basis, will be:

4	Building ($800,000 − $600,000)	200,000	
	Investment in Common Stock [($50,000 + $200,000 − $10,000) × 60%]	144,000	
	Minority Interest ($240,000 × 40%)	96,000	
	Land		50,000
	Accumulated Depreciation ($400,000 − $10,000)		390,000
	To adjust the accounts affected by the sale to balance had the sale not been made.		

Finally, that portion of the investment elimination entry which removes the shareholders' equity section of Starboard Limited will be:

5	Capital Stock, No Par	800,000	
	Retained Earnings	900,000	
	Investment in Common Stock [60% of ($800,000 + $900,000)]		1,020,000
	Minority Interest (40% of $1,700,000)		680,000
	To remove 100% of subsidiary's shareholders' equity, crediting minority interest with their share thereof.		

Combining entries **1**, **2**, **3**, **4**, and **5**, we arrive at the compound journal entry to eliminate the investment in Starboard Limited when Port accounts for its investment in Starboard on the ***equity basis***:

		Debit	Credit
1	Accumulated Depreciation — Building [$600,000 – ($390,000 + $9,000)]	201,000	
	Accumulated Depreciation — Machinery	200,000	
	Goodwill	156,000	
	Capital Stock, No Par	800,000	
	Retained Earnings (Dec. 31, Year 6)	900,000	
	Land ($60,000 + $50,000)		110,000
	Buildings [$600,000 – ($180,000 + $200,000)]		220,000
	Machinery		200,000
	Merchandise Inventory		62,500
	Investment in Starboard Limited [($267,000 + $1,020,000) – ($52,500 + $144,000)]		1,090,500
	Minority Interest [$680,000 – ($10,000 + $96,000)]		574,000
	To eliminate the Investment in Starboard Limited account at December 31, Year 6.		

Now the purchase difference entry and the interstatement entries have been made. The intrastatement entries are next.

Sixty percent of Starboard Limited's dividend payable is in Port Limited's accounts payable. This will be eliminated, as follows:

		Debit	Credit
2	Other Payables	9,000	
	Accounts Receivable		9,000
	To remove intrastatement dividend payable at 60% of $15,000.		

As both the income statement and the balance sheet are affected by this item, the rental of machinery will require two entries:

		Debit	Credit
3	Rental Income	3,000	
	Rent Expense		3,000
	To eliminate reciprocal income accounts between affiliates.		
4	Accounts Payable	500	
	Prepaid Rent		500
	To eliminate reciprocal balance sheet accounts between affiliates.		

The intercompany sales must be removed as follows:

		Debit	Credit
5	Sales	500,000	
	Cost of Sales		500,000
	To remove intercompany sales of $300,000 and $200,000 between affiliates.		

NOTE: Had the companies provided detailed cost of goods sold sections in their income statements, the credit would have been to Purchases.

This completes the presentation of journal entries required for consolidation purposes. As stated earlier, the five journal entries above are made for consolidation purposes only and are ***not*** entered into the books of either affiliate.

A work sheet for the preparation of the consolidated balance sheet, which incorporates the balance sheets of each affiliate and the above five journal entries, is shown below.

PORT LIMITED AND STARBOARD LIMITED
Balance Sheet Consolidation Worksheet
December 31, Year 6

Accounts	*Port Limited balance sheet*	*Starboard Limited balance sheet*	*Adjustment Dr*	*Adjustment Cr*	*Port Limited consolidated balance sheet*
Cash	800,500	399,500			1,200,000
Accounts receivable (net)	1,000,000	500,000		(2) 9,000	1,491,000
Merchandise inventory	1,200,000	700,000		(1) 62,500	1,837,500
Prepaid rent		500		(4) 500	·
Land		250,000		(1) 110,000	1,040,000
Building — at cost ...	2,300,000	700,000		(1) 220,000	2,780,000
Accumulated depreciation	(591,000)	(300,000)	(1) 201,000		(690,000)
Machinery	2,000,000	700,000		(1) 200,000	2,500,000
Accumulated depreciation	(800,000)	(250,000)	(1) 200,000		(850,000)
Investment in Starboard Limited	1,090,500			(1) 1,090,500	
Goodwill			(1) 156,000		156,000
	7,900,000	2,700,000			9,464,500
Accounts payable....	100,000	200,000	(4) 500		299,500
Other payables.......	850,000	100,000	(2) 9,000		941,000
10% bonds payable..	1,950,000	700,000			2,650,000
Minority interest.....				(1) 574,000	574,000
Capital stock, no par................	1,000,000	800,000	(1) 800,000		1,000,000
Retained earnings...	4,000,000	900,000	(1) 900,000		4,000,000
	7,900,000	2,700,000	2,265,500	2,265,500	9,464,500

The consolidated balance sheet assembled from this work sheet would be as follows:

PORT LIMITED AND CONSOLIDATED SUBSIDIARY
Consolidated Balance Sheet
December 31, Year 6

Assets

Current:	
Cash	$1,200,000
Accounts receivable (net)	1,491,000

Merchandise inventory			1,837,500
			$4,528,500
Fixed:			
Land, at cost		$1,040,000	
Buildings, at cost	$2,780,000		
Less accumulated depreciation	690,000	2,090,000	
Machinery, at cost	$2,500,000		
Less accumulated depreciation	850,000	1,650,000	4,780,000
Goodwill (net)			156,000
Total assets			$9,464,500
Liabilities			
Current:			
Accounts payable			$ 299,500
Other payables			941,000
			$1,240,500
10% bonds payable			2,650,000
Minority interest			574,000
Total liabilities			$4,464,500
Shareholders' Equity			
Capital stock, no par		$1,000,000	
Retained earnings		4,000,000	
Total shareholders' equity			5,000,000
Total liabilities and shareholders' equity			$9,464,500

Consolidated Income Statement

In the preparation of the consolidated income statement for Year 6, it is necessary to determine the income-statement impact of the five consolidation journal entries shown on page 726, as follows.

Journal entry **1** is a comprehensive entry, especially when the parent company accounts for its investment in the subsidiary on the ***equity*** basis.

The purchase differential accounts and amounts determined at the acquisition date have no effect on income at that point in time. However, any amounts expensed in Year 6 representing the fair value increments and/or goodwill must be included in consolidated net income. In this case, 100% of the inventory adjustment at acquisition date in the amount of $120,000, is expensed, the depreciation on the increase in the building in the amount of $9,000 is expensed, and the amortization of goodwill in the amount of $4,000 is expensed. The individual income statement accounts will be adjusted for the above three items as follows. ***Note***: The "P" means that the parent's income is adjusted and the "S" that the subsidiary's income is adjusted which includes a minority-interest share. Also, the adjustment would have been to closing inventory in the cost of goods sold section of the income statement had a detailed cost of goods sold section been included in the income statement.

Debit Cost of Sales	120,000 (P)
Debit Depreciation Expense	9,000 (P)
Debit General Expense	4,000 (P)

The adjustments regarding the income effects of interstatement profits in closing inventories, are as follows:

Debit Cost of Sales [37,500 (P) + 25,000 (S)]	62,500

The $25,000 intercompany profit elimination is to be shared by Port and minority interest in a 60-to-40 ratio. The adjustments regarding the income effects of interstatement profits from the intercompany sale of land and building are as follows:

Debit Gain on Sale of Land	50,000 (S)
Debit Gain on Sale of Building	250,000 (S)
Credit Depreciation Expense	10,000 (S)

The three sets of adjustments above represent the income-statement effect of journal entry **1**, the investment elimination entry. Journal entry **2** has no effect on the income statement. Entry **3** is an income-statement journal entry, as is journal entry **5**. (Entries **3** and **5** are intrastatement adjusting entries.) Journal entry **4** has no effect on the income statement.

A work sheet for the determination of the consolidated income statement is illustrated below. It incorporates the above adjustments and replaces the one-line investment income account with the line-by-line Starboard Limited income accounts.

PORT LIMITED AND STARBOARD LIMITED
Income Statement Consolidation Work Sheet
For the Year Ended December 31, Year 6

Accounts	*Port Limited income statement*	*Starboard Limited income statement*	*Adjustments*		*Port Limited consolidated income statement*
			Dr	*Cr*	
Sales	16,000,000	6,000,000	(5) 500,000		21,500,000
Cost of sales	12,000,000	4,000,000	(a) 120,000(P)		15,682,500
Gross profit	4,000,000	2,000,000	(b) 37,500(P)	(5) 500,000	5,817,500
			(b) 25,000(S)		
Rental income	3,000		(3) 3,000		
Investment income	126,500		126,500*		
Gain on sale land		50,000	(c) 50,000(S)		
Gain on sale building		200,000	(c) 200,000(S)		
	4,129,500	2,250,000			5,817,500
Selling expenses	1,000,000	700,000			1,700,000
Rent		3,000		(3) 3,000	
Professional fees	200,000	100,000			300,000
General expense	280,000	300,000	(a) 4,000		584,000
Depreciation	300,000	150,000	(a) 9,000	(c) 10,000(S)	449,000
Administrative expense ..	380,000	230,000			610,000

Sundry	9,500	7,000			16,500
	2,169,500	1,490,000			3,659,500
Net income reported	1,960,000	760,000			
Combined net income					2,158,000
Minority interests [40% × (760,000 − 25,000 − 50,000 − 200,000 + 10,000)]					198,000
Consolidated net income					$ 1,960,000

*The one-line item has been replaced by line-by-line amounts.

Note that the amount of the net income reported by Port Limited is the same as that of the consolidated net income. This is because Port is accounting for its investment in Starboard on the *equity* basis.

The consolidated income statement for Port Limited and its subsidiary company will be as shown in the right-hand column of the work sheet.

SUPPLEMENTARY QUESTIONS ON CONSOLIDATION ACCOUNTING

Note: The answers to these questions are given in the ***Solutions Manual***.

A14-1 Identify two transactions that require the adjustment for unrealized gains, profits, or losses when consolidating affiliates.

A14-2 Distinguish between ***interstatement*** and ***intrastatement*** adjusting entries.

A14-3 Describe why it is necessary to remove unrealized gains, profits, or losses in the consolidation process.

A14-4 Briefly explain the reason for eliminating intercompany sales in the consolidation process.

A14-5 What is ***equity pickup*** and under what circumstances is it used?

A14-6 Distinguish between ***downstream*** and ***upstream*** transactions.

A14-7 Explain the term ***excess depreciation*** in connection with the intercompany sale of a depreciable asset. Why is it important?

A14-8 The following information is needed for this question and questions ***A14-9***, ***A14-10***, and ***A14-11***.

The balance sheets of Peach Limited and Sweet Limited, immediately after Peach acquired 80% of Sweet in the open market, are as follows:

	Peach Limited, $	*Sweet Limited, $*
Current assets	100,000	50,000
Noncurrent assets	500,000	100,000
	600,000	150,000
Liabilities	100,000	50,000
Common stock	300,000	100,000
Contributed surplus		50,000
Retained earnings (deficit)	200,000	(50,000)
	600,000	150,000

Using the information above, calculate the investment elimination entry (omit explanation) at the acquisition date, assuming: The cost of the investment in Sweet Limited common stock was $80,000 and the fair values of Sweet's net assets approximated their carrying values.

A14-9 Using the *A14-8* information, calculate the same entry, this time assuming: The cost of the investment in Sweet Limited common stock was $150,000. The fair values of Sweet's net assets approximated their fair values with the exception of the land on which the plant was built. This land had a fair value in excess of carrying value of $50,000.

A14-10 Using the *A14-8* information, calculate the same entry, this time assuming: The cost of the investment in Sweet Limited common stock was $80,000. The fair values of Sweet's net assets approximated their carrying values except for the plant which has a carrying value in excess of fair value of $20,000.

A14-11 Using the *A14-8* information, calculate the same entry, this time assuming: The cost of the investment in Sweet Limited common stock was $80,000. The fair values of Sweet's net assets approximated their carrying values except for the land which had a fair value in excess of carrying value of $10,000 and equipment which had a fair value in excess of carrying value of $10,000, also. Negative goodwill, if any, is attributable to the plant building as it does not fit in well with the surrounding area and the shareholders who sold their shares to Peach Limited felt the future of this operation was in doubt.

A14-12 The following information is needed for this question and questions ***A14-13***, ***A14-14***, and ***A14-15***.

On July 1, Year 4, Pear Corporation purchased 60% of the outstanding common stock of Sipco Limited for $180,000 cash. At the acquisition date, the fair value of Sipco Limited's net assets approximated their carrying value, except for the building, which had a fair value approximating $275,000.

Immediately prior to the acquisition, the condensed balance sheets of the two companies were as follows:

	Pear Corporation	*Sipco Limited*
Current assets	$300,000	$ 50,000
Land	100,000	50,000
Buildings, at cost	700,000	500,000
Accumulated depreciation	(300,000)	(250,000)
	$800,000	$350,000
Current liabilities	$ 40,000	$ 50,000
Long-term debt	60,000	100,000
Common stock, no par	300,000	100,000
Retained earnings	400,000	100,000
	$800,000	$350,000

Using the information above, prepare the investment elimination entry and the working paper for the consolidated balance sheet immediately after the acquisition, assuming Pear Corporation follows the proprietary concept for consolidation purposes.

A14-13 Using the *A14-12* information, prepare the investment elimination entry and the working paper for the consolidated balance sheet immediately after the acquisition, assuming Pear Corporation follows the parent company concept for consolidation purposes.

A14-14 Using the *A14-12* information, prepare the investment elimination entry and the working paper for the consolidated balance sheet immediately after the acquisition, assuming Pear Corporation follows the parent company extension concept for consolidation purposes.

A14-15 Using the *A14-12* information, prepare the investment elimination entry and the working paper for the consolidated balance sheet immediately after the acquisition, assuming Pear Corporation follows the entity concept for consolidation purposes.

A14-16 Using the assumptions for ***A14-13*** and the additional information below, prepare the working paper for a consolidated balance sheet on June 30, Year 5, for Pear Corporation and Sipco Limited, together with supporting journal entries. Assume Pear Corporation accounted for its investment in Sipco Limited on the ***equity*** basis for the year ended June 30, Year 5. Use the parent company concept for your calculations and journal entries.

Additional Information

1. During this first year since acquisition, Pear Corporation reported net income of $100,000 and paid dividends totalling $30,000. Sipco Limited reported net income of $50,000 and paid dividends totalling $25,000.
2. All sales and expenses were to and from current assets, and all other balance sheet accounts, except for retained earnings and investment in Sipco Limited, remained at the same balances in the books of the two affiliates.
3. The building fair value increment is depreciated over 15 years on the straight-line basis.
4. Any goodwill is amortized on the straight-line basis over 40 years.

A14-17 On January 1, 19X1, E purchased 80% of the capital stock of Z for $59,600. On December 31, 19X1, you are given the following information:

	E		Z	
	Dr	*Cr*	*Dr*	*Cr*
Cash	12,000		12,500	
Accounts receivable	5,000		2,000	
Inventory, Jan. 1, 19X1	28,000		11,000	
Investment in Z	77,150			
Other assets (net)	59,400		80,500	
Accounts payable		18,000		12,000
Other liabilities		3,000		16,000
Capital stock, no par		100,000		50,000
Retained earnings		31,000		12,000
Dividends declared	8,500		5,000	
Sales		205,000		121,000
Investment income		21,550		
Interest income		800		
Purchases	161,000		83,000	
Freight-in	1,000		200	
Selling expenses	18,000		11,100	
Administration expenses	9,300		5,700	
	379,350	379,350	211,000	211,000
Inventory, Dec. 31, 19X1	41,000		18,000	

Also, the fair value of other assets (net) exceeded carrying value by $10,000. These assets are depreciated 10% per year and have nine years of remaining life on December 31, 19X1. The accounts payable of Z includes $3,000 payable to E, at December 31, 19X1. At January 1, 19X1, this amounted to $5,000.

Instructions

1 Prepare a consolidated income statement for the 19X1 year.
2 Prepare a consolidated balance sheet as at December 31, 19X1.

A14-18 Patterson Limited has owned 75% of Somerville, Inc., for a number of years. On July 1, Year 5, the parent company purchased from Somerville a building for $500,000 and the land on which it was situated for $100,000. On December 31, Year 4, the management of Somerville, Inc., had considered the building had a remaining economic life of 25 years, and that it would have a salvage value of $10,000 at the end of its economic life. The management of Patterson Limited concur with these estimates. The original costs of the land and of the building to Somerville, Inc., were $150,000 and $310,000 respectively. Somerville, Inc., has been depreciating the building at $10,000 per year. The accumulated depreciation balance for the building was $50,000 at December 31, Year 4.

Instructions

1 Prepare the adjusting consolidated balance sheet journal entry for the intercompany land and building sale. The consolidation date is December 31, Year 5.
2 Determine the effect the intercompany fixed-asset transaction will have on minority interest in Somerville's Year 5 net income.

A14-19 P and S have been affiliated for a number of years. P owns 60% of S's outstanding common stock. On July 1 of the current calendar year (Year 5), P purchased land and buildings from S for a $500,000 lump-sum payment. P has agreed to separate the land and building costs using the Year 5 assessment notice, which showed:

Land — assessment value	$ 1,000
Plant — assessment value	49,000
Total assessment value	$50,000

At the date of the sale S's books revealed the following:

Land — cost	$ 40,000
Plant — cost	$ 500,000
Accumulated depreciation — plant	$(255,000)
Original life of plant	50 years
Depreciation method	Straight-line

P agreed with S as to the ''years of life'' of the plant and with the depreciation method used by S.

Instructions

1 Prepare the adjusting entry for balance sheet consolidation purposes at December 31, Year 5.

2 Determine the effect on minority interest of the adjustment required for the consolidated balance sheet at December 31, Year 5.

A14-20 Parentco Limited purchased 80% of the outstanding common stock of Subco Limited on July 1, Year 6, for $240,000 cash. At that date the carrying values of Subco Limited's net assets were $200,000, and they approximated the fair values with the exception of a building which had a fair value in excess of its carrying value of $50,000. This building was being depreciated on the straight-line basis and had an expected remaining life of 20 years at July 1, Year 6. Any goodwill is to be amortized over 40 years. During the six months ending December 31, Year 6, Parentco sold $500,000 of merchandise to Subco and purchased $300,000 of merchandise from Subco.

At December 31, Year 6, each company had 20% of its intercompany purchases in ending inventory and marked up its intercompany sales merchandise 25% on cost. Parentco Limited commenced business July 1, Year 6. Net incomes reported and dividends paid by the affiliates for the six months ending December 31, Year 6, were as follows:

	Parentco Limited	*Subco Limited*
Net income reported	$800,000	$200,000
Dividends declared and paid	200,000	100,000

Subco Limited had a retained earnings balance of $100,000 on July 1, Year 6. The only other shareholders' equity account represented no-par-value common stock.

Instructions

Under the assumption that Parentco Limited accounts for its investment in Subco Limited on the ***cost*** basis, prepare entries for the consolidated balance sheet as at December 31, Year 6, and calculate the figure for each of (1) consolidated net income and minority interest in Subco Limited, (2) net income for the six months ended December 31, Year 6, (3) the minority-interest balance in the balance sheet at December 31, Year 6, and (4) consolidated retained earnings and minority interest in Subco Limited's retained earnings at December 31, Year 6.

c h a p t e r 1 5

LONG-TERM DEBT

Liabilities that do not require the payment of cash, the shipment of goods, or the rendering of services in one year (or the next operating cycle, whichever is longer) for their liquidation are designated ***long-term liabilities***, or ***long-term debt***. Examples of long-term debt are: bonds, mortgage notes, promissory notes, deposits received for utilities service, some obligations under pension and deferred compensation plans, certain types of lease obligations, deferred income tax credits, and some deferred revenue items.

Long-term debt may be ***collateralized*** (secured) by liens on business property of various kinds, for example, equipment (equipment notes), real property (mortgages), or securities (collateral trust bonds). Many companies issue ***debenture bonds*** that are backed only by the general credit standing of the issuer, and some companies have issued ***commodity backed bonds*** that are redeemable at prices linked to the prices of specified products such as gold and silver. The title of a long-term debt obligation, such as "First Mortgage Bonds Payable," may indicate the nature of collateral for the debt. Bonds may be issued that pay an exceptionally low rate of interest (***deep-discount bonds***).

As noted in Chapter 10, some current liabilities involve no specific mention of interest payments. Because money has a time value, some amount of interest probably is included in the face amount of such liabilities, but often it is disregarded because of the relatively small amounts involved. However, the interest factor in long-term debt is significant and must be given accounting consideration. Accounting for bonds is covered in this chapter, pensions and leases are discussed in Chapters 19 and 20 respectively, and deferred income tax credits are covered in Chapter 21.

Types of Bonds

Bonds are a means of dividing long-term debt into a number of small units. Usually, bonds are issued in $1,000 denominations, or in multiples of $1,000. Occasionally, additional denominations of $100 or $500 are used. In this way, amounts of money larger than that which could be borrowed from a single source may be obtained from a large number of investors. The specific conditions of the borrowing and any restrictions on the issuer (such as limitations on dividend payments and additional borrowing) are contained in a contract between the issuer of the bonds and the bondholders, which is known as the ***bond indenture***. This contract usually is held by a ***trustee***, such as a bank or a trust company, who acts as an independent third party to protect the interests of both the issuer and the bondholders.

Bonds may be issued by corporations, by federal, provincial, and municipal governments, and by governmental agencies. They may be ***registered bonds*** or ***coupon bonds***. Interest on registered bonds is paid only to the owner of record, but interest on coupon bonds is paid to persons presenting the periodic interest coupons. ***Serial bonds*** mature in predetermined instalments; ***term bonds*** mature on a single fixed maturity date.

A bond issue may rank behind previously issued ***senior bonds*** and thus may be described as ***subordinated debentures*** or ***second mortgage bonds***. Some bonds are ***callable***[1] at the option of the issuer. Some bond issues are ***convertible*** to common stock of the issuer at the option of the bondholder. Occasionally, bonds are ***guaranteed*** by a business enterprise or governmental unit other than the issuer. High-risk bonds issued by companies with a weak financial position are termed ***junk bonds***.

Bonds may be privately placed with a single institution or issued to investment dealers who in turn reissue the bonds in smaller lots to individual investors. Investment dealers may ***underwrite*** the bond issue, thus guaranteeing a fixed price to the issuer and assuming the risk in selling the issue to the public. If a bond issue is underwritten, the entire issue is recorded in the accounting records of the issuer at the time of sale to underwriters. Unissued bonds represent potential indebtedness that may be incurred without further authorization from the board of directors or additional pledge of properties. Authorized and unissued bonds are reported in the balance sheet parenthetically or in a note to the financial statements.

1 The call provision protects the issuer, which may wish to retire the debt in advance, particularly when interest rates have fallen and it may secure more favourable financing. Bondholders who are repaid at this time must reinvest their funds at a lower rate of interest, and therefore insist on a call premium as compensation for the reduced interest rate. Call premiums generally are established on a decreasing scale as the bonds approach maturity.

Financial Management Considerations

When financial managers decide to borrow money by issuing bonds, they must first resolve a number of questions. For example, they must relate the need for funds to the amount of long-term debt that may be undertaken safely by studying the financial position and earning prospects of the company; they must forecast the ability of the company to meet bond sinking fund requirements or periodic maturities of serial bonds; and a decision must be made regarding the features of the bonds, such as collateral to be offered, call provisions, convertibility, etc. It is apparent that a great deal of preparation precedes the issuance of bonds.

ACCOUNTING FOR ISSUANCE OF BONDS AND INTEREST EXPENSE

Issuance of Term Bonds

In a typical term bond contract, the issuer promises two essentially different kinds of future payments: (1) the payment of a fixed amount (***face amount*** or ***principal***) on a specified date and (2) the periodic payment of interest, usually at six-month intervals, in an amount expressed as an annual percentage of the face amount of the bonds. In the light of expectations as to what interest rate is necessary to attract the required funds, a rate of interest is set. The interest expense actually incurred on the bonds is determined by the price at which the bonds are sold; thus, the ***effective interest rate*** (sometimes called the ***yield rate***) is set by the money market.

Interest on bonds expressed as a percentage of the face amount is referred to as the ***nominal*** or ***contract rate***. If the effective interest rate is identical to the nominal rate, the bonds will sell at face amount. If the effective interest rate is higher than the nominal rate, the bonds will sell at a ***discount***. Conversely, if the effective interest rate is less than the nominal rate, the bonds will sell at a ***premium***. Differences between the nominal rate and the yield rate thus are adjusted by changes in the price at which the bonds are issued.

To illustrate, assume that $100,000 of five-year, 7% term bonds are authorized by a corporation's board of directors.[2] The bonds, which promise $100,000 at the end of five years and $7,000 annual interest, are offered to a group of investment dealers comprising an ***underwriting syndicate*** of dealers. The prices bid by the underwriters will depend on their expectations as to the effective rate of interest for this type of bonds. Under two different assumptions as to the effective annual interest rate, the proceeds are determined as follows, using the present-value tables in the Appendix at the end of Chapter 5:

2 Although bonds issued in amounts as small as $100,000, paying interest annually and maturing in five years, are not found in real life, these amounts are used to simplify the illustration.

Computation of proceeds of 7% bonds issued at a *discount* (8% effective rate) and at a *premium* (6% effective rate)

Amount bid for 7% term bonds, assuming an effective rate of 8%		*Amount bid for 7% term bonds, assuming an effective rate of 6%*	
Present value of $100,000 due in 5 years at 8%, with interest paid *annually** ($100,000 × 0.680583)	$68,058	Present value of $100,000 due in 5 years at 5%, with interest paid *annually** ($100,000 × 0.747258)	$ 74,726
Present value of $7,000 every year for 5 years at 8% ($7,000 × 3.992710).............	27,949	Present value of $7,000 every year for 5 years at 6% ($7,000 × 4.212364)............	29,487
Proceeds of bond issue	$96,007	Proceeds of bond issue	$104,213

*Had interest been paid semiannually on these bonds, the number of periods would have doubled and the interest rate halved. For example, assuming an effective annual rate of 6% and semiannual interest payments under the assumption in the right-hand column above, the amount bid for the 7% bonds would be calculated as follows:

Present value of $100,000 due in 10 periods at 3% with interest paid *semiannually*: ($100,000 × 0.744094)	$ 74,409
Present value of $3,500 every *six months* for 10 periods at 3%: ($3,500 × 8.530203)	29,856
Proceeds of bond issue	$104,265

The underwriters would expect to resell these bonds to investors at a higher price and thus a lower effective interest rate, to give them a margin to cover their costs and earn a profit. However, the yield rate to the issuer is determined by the price it receives from the underwriters. The journal entries to record the issuance of 7% term bonds, paying interest annually, at a discount and at a premium on December 31, Year 1, are shown below:

Journal entries to record the issuance of 7% term bonds paying interest annually at a *discount* (8% effective rate) and at a *premium* (6% effective rate)

Issued at effective rate of 8%			*Issued at effective rate of 6%*		
Cash	96,007		Cash	104,213	
Discount on Bonds Payable	3,993		Premium on Bonds Payable		4,213
Bonds Payable		100,000	Bonds Payable		100,000
To record issuance of bonds at a discount.			To record issuance of bonds at a premium.		

Bond Discount and Premium in the Balance Sheet

At the time of issue, the amount of bonds payable is equal to the present value of all future payments at the yield rate set by the market. However, bond discount and bond premium are valuation accounts relating to bonds payable and may or may not be set up in separate accounts in the company's general ledger. In the former case, the bond payable liability will be carried at the face value of the bonds. In the latter case, the bond payable liability will include unamortized bond discount or premium.

In practice in Canada, bonds payable may be shown in the balance sheet in one of the following three ways:

1 The face amount of the bonds payable is shown and any unamortized discount or premium is included in deferred charges or deferred credits respectively.

2 The face amount of the bond payable is shown in the balance sheet together with the unamortized discount or premium deducted therefrom or added thereto respectively.

3 The balance of the bond payable at face value less unamortized discount, or plus unamortized premium, is shown in one figure in the balance sheet.

Therefore, using the figures from the previous illustration, bonds payable on the date of issue could be reported in the balance sheet in any one of the three ways shown in the following illustrations.

1 Long-term debt:		Long-term debt:	
7% bonds payable, due in 5 years (face amount) ...	$100,000	7% bonds payable, due in 5 years (face amount)	$100,000
Deferred credit:		Deferred charge:	
Unamortized bond premium....................	$ 3,993	Unamortized bond discount	$ 4,213

2 Bonds issued at a discount:		Bonds issued at a premium:	
Long-term debt:		Long-term debt:	
7% bonds payable, due in 5 years (face amount) ...	$100,000	7% bond payable, due in 5 years	$100,000
Less: Discount	3,993	Add: Premium	4,213
Net liability (carrying amount)........	$ 96,007	Net liability (carrying amount)	$104,213

3 Long-term debt:		Long-term debt:	
7% bond payable, due in 5 years	$ 96,007	7% bond payable, due in 5 years	$104,213

At issue date these bonds have a present value below or above face amount because the market rate of interest is higher or lower than the periodic interest payments provided for in the bond contract. Therefore, the process of amortizing the bond discount or premium is a means of recording the increase or decrease ***in the carrying amount of the debt obligation as it approaches maturity***. In the bond discount case, the increase in the carrying amount of the debt is caused indirectly through the decrease in bond discount. Similarly, in the bond premium case, the decrease in the carrying amount of the debt is caused indirectly through the decrease in bond premium. In either case, the carrying amount of bonds payable will be $100,000 at maturity.

In the United States, companies are required to present long-term bonds payable in the balance sheet according to either illustration *2* or illustration *3* above. Discount or premium should not be classified as a deferred charge or deferred credit. On the other hand, ***CICA Handbook*** section 3070.02 states that major items of deferred charges should be shown separately and includes in its examples debt discount and expense; this process is depicted in illustration *1* above. However, in Canada all three methods are being used.

Term Bond Interest Expense

Because differences between the effective rate and the nominal rate of interest are reflected in bond prices, the amount of premium or discount affects the periodic interest expense of the issuer. This is illustrated by a comparison of the five-year interest expense under each of the two assumptions in the foregoing sections as to effect interest rates:

Comparison of five-year interest expense on bonds issued at a *discount* (8% effective rate) and at a *premium* (6% effective rate)

Assuming an effective rate of 8%		*Assuming an effective rate of 6%*	
Nominal interest ($7,000 × 5 *annual* payments)	$35,000	Nominal interest ($7,000 × 5 *annual* payments)	$35,000
Add: Discount ($100,000 − $96,007)	3,993	Less: Premium ($104,213 − $100,000)	4,213
Five-year interest expense	$38,993	Five-year interest expense	$30,787

If the bonds are issued to yield 8%, the discount of $3,993 represents an additional amount of interest that will be paid by the issuer at maturity. Similarly, if the bonds are issued to yield 6%, the premium of $4,213 represents an advance paid by bondholders for the right to receive larger annual interest cheques and is viewed as a reduction in the effective interest expense. The premium in effect is returned to bondholders in the form of larger periodic interest payments.

The present value of the bonds on the date of issuance differs from their face amount because the market rate of interest differs from the periodic interest payments provided for in the bond contract. Therefore, the process of ***amortizing*** the bond discount or premium in conjunction with the computation of periodic interest expense is a means of recording the ***change in the carrying amount of the bonds as they approach maturity***. In the bond discount case, the increase in the carrying amount of the bonds is caused by the decrease in bond discount through amortization. Similarly, in the bond premium case, the decrease in the carrying amount of the bonds is caused by the decrease in bond premium through amortization. In either case, the carrying amount of the bonds payable will be $100,000 on the maturity date.

Effective Interest Method of Amortization for Term Bonds

In theory, the bond interest expense in each accounting period should equal the effective interest expense, that is, the effective rate of interest applied to the ***carrying amount*** of the bonds at the beginning of that period. This approach to the computation of interest expense is known as the ***effective interest method of***

amortization. A ***constant rate*** of interest (the effective rate) is applied to the amount outstanding at the beginning of any given period. The ***amount***, of amortization of discount or premium, ***changes*** each period.

Term Bonds Issued at a Discount

When term bonds are issued at a discount, the carrying amount of the bonds increases as they approach maturity; thus, interest expense ***increases*** in each period. Annual and semiannual interest expense over the term of the bonds, journal entries to record interest expense for the first two years, and ledger accounts for Bond Interest Expense and Discount on Bonds Payable are shown below and on the next page.

Discount amortization for term bonds under effective interest method and annual interest payments

Term Bonds Issued at a Discount
Annual Interest Expense Determined by Effective Interest Method of Amortization
($100,000, 5-year bonds, interest at 7% payable annually, issued for $96,007, to yield 8% compounded annually)

Date	*(A) Interest paid (7% of face amount)*	*(B) Interest expense (8% of bonds' carrying amount)*	*(C) Discount amortization (B − A)*	*(D) Bond discount balance (D − C)*	*(E) Carrying amount, end of year ($100,000 − D)*
Dec.31/X1				$3,993	$ 96,007
Dec. 31/X2	$7,000	$7,681	$681	3,312	96,688
Dec. 31/X3	7,000	7,735	735	2,577	97,423
Dec. 31/X4	7,000	7,794	794	1,783	98,217
Dec. 31/X5	7,000	7,857	857	926	99,074
Dec. 31/X6	7,000	7,926	926		100,000

Journal entries:

	Dec. 31, Year 2		*Dec. 31, Year 3*	
Bond Interest Expense	7,681		7,735	
Cash		7,000		7,000
Discount on Bonds Payable		681		735
To record interest expense, including amortization of discount.				

Ledger accounts:

Bond Interest Expense

Date	*Explanation*	*Debit*	*Credit*	*Balance*
Dec. 31/X2	($96,007 × 0.08.)	7,681		7,681 Dr
Dec. 31/X2	Closing entry.		7,681	-0-
Dec. 31/X3	($96,688 × 0.08.)	7,735		7,735 Dr
Dec. 31/X3	Closing entry.		7,735	-0-

Discount on Bonds Payable

Date	*Explanation*	*Debit*	*Credit*	*Balance*
Dec. 31/X1	Date of issuance.	3,993		3,993 Dr
Dec. 31/X2	Amortization ($7,681 − $7,000).		681	3,312 Dr
Dec. 31/X3	Amortization ($7,735 − $7,000).		735	2,577 Dr

Discount amortization for term bonds under effective interest method and semiannual interest payments

Term Bonds Issued at a Discount
Annual Interest Expense Determined by Effective Interest Method of Amortization
($100,000, 5-year bonds, interest at 7% payable semiannually, issued for $95,944, to yield 8% compounded semiannually)

Year	*(A) Interest paid (3½% of face amount)*	*(B) "Effective" interest expense (4% of bonds' carrying amount)*	*(C) Discount amortization (B − A)*	*(D) Bond discount balance (D − C)*	*(E) Carrying amount, end of six-month period ($100,000 − D)*
0				$4,056	$ 95,944
½	$3,500	$3,838	$338	3,718	96,282
1	3,500	3,851	351	3,367	96,633
1½	3,500	3,865	365	3,002	96,998
2	3,500	3,880	380	2,622	97,378
2½	3,500	3,895	395	2,227	97,773
3	3,500	3,911	411	1,816	98,184
3½	3,500	3,927	427	1,389	98,611
4	3,500	3,945	445	944	99,056
4¼	3,500	3,962	462	482	99,518
5	3,500	3,982	482	-0-	100,000

Journal entries, first half of year:

	June 30, Year 2		*June 30, Year 3*	
Bond Interest Expense	3,838		3,865	
Cash		3,500		3,500
Discount on Bonds Payable		338		365
To record interest expense, including amortization of discount for half-year.				

Journal entries, second half of year:

	Dec. 31, Year 2		*Dec. 31, Year 3*	
Bond Interest Expense	3,851		3,880	
Cash		3,500		3,500
Discount on Bonds Payable		351		380
To record interest expense, including amortization of discount for half-year.				

Ledger accounts:

Bond Interest Expense

Date	*Explanation*	*Debit*	*Credit*	*Balance*
June 30/X2	($95,944 × 0.04.)	3,838		3,838 Dr
Dec. 31/X2	($96,282 × 0.04.)	3,851		7,689 Dr
Dec. 31/X2	Closing entry.		7,689	-0-
June 30/X3	($96,663 × 0.04.)	3,865		3,865 Dr
Dec. 31/X3	($96,998 × 0.04.)	3,880		7,745 Dr
Dec. 31/X3	Closing entry.		7,745	-0-

Discount on Bonds Payable

Date	*Explanation*	*Debit*	*Credit*	*Balance*
Dec. 31/X1	Date of issuance.	4,056		4,056 Dr
June 30/X2	Amortization ($3,838 − $3,500).		338	3,718 Dr
Dec. 31/X2	Amortization ($3,851 − $3,500).		351	3,367 Dr
June 30/X3	Amortization ($3,865 − $3,500).		365	3,002 Dr
Dec. 31/X3	Amortization ($3,880 − $3,500).		380	2,622 Dr

Term Bonds Issued at a Premium

When term bonds are issued at a premium, the carrying amount of the bonds decreases as they approach maturity, and the amount of periodic interest expense *decreases* over the term of the bonds. Annual and semiannual interest expense, journal entries to record interest expense for the first two years, and ledger accounts for Bond Interest Expense and Premium on Bonds Payable are illustrated below and on page 745.

Premium amortization for term bonds under effective interest method and annual interest payments

Term Bonds Issued at a Premium
Annual Interest Expense Determined by Effective Interest Method of Amortization
($100,000, 5-year bonds, interest at 7% payable annually, issued for $104,213, to yield 6% compounded annually)

Date	*(A) Interest paid (7% of face amount)*	*(B) Interest expense (6% of bonds' carrying amount)*	*(C) Premium amortization (A − B)*	*(D) Bond premium balance (D − C)*	*(E) Carrying amount, end of year ($100,000 + D)*
Dec. 31/X1				$4,213	$104,213
Dec. 31/X2	$7,000	$6,253	$747	3,466	103,466
Dec. 31/X3	7,000	6,208	792	2,674	102,674
Dec. 31/X4	7,000	6,160	840	1,834	101,834
Dec. 31/X5	7,000	6,110	890	944	100,944
Dec. 31/X6	7,000	6,056*	944		100,000

*Adjusted $1 for rounding.

Journal entries:

	Dec. 31, Year 2		*Dec. 31, Year 3*	
Bond Interest Expense	6,253		6,208	
Premium on Bonds Payable	747		792	
Cash		7,000		7,000
To record interest expense, including amortization of premium.				

Ledger accounts:

Bond Interest Expense

Date	*Explanation*	*Debit*	*Credit*	*Balance*
Dec. 31/X2	($104,213 × 0.06.)	6,253		6,253 Dr
Dec. 31/X2	Closing entry.		6,253	-0-
Dec. 31/X3	($103,466 × 0.06.)	6,208		6,208 Dr
Dec. 31/X3	Closing entry.		6,208	-0-

Premium on Bonds Payable

Date	*Explanation*	*Debit*	*Credit*	*Balance*
Dec. 31/X1	Date of issuance.		4,213	4,213 Cr
Dec. 31/X2	Amortization ($7,000 − $6,253).	747		3,466 Cr
Dec. 31/X3	Amortization ($7,000 − $6,208).	792		2,674 Cr

Premium amortization for term bonds under effective interest method and semiannual interest payments

Term Bonds Issued at a Premium
Annual Interest Expense Determined by Effective Interest Method of Amortization
($100,000, 5-year bonds, interest at 7% payable semiannually, issued for $104,265, to yield 6% compounded semiannually)

Year	*(A) Interest paid (3½% of face amount)*	*(B) "Effective" interest expense (3% of bonds' carrying amount)*	*(C) Premium amortization (A − B)*	*(D) Bond premium balance (D − C)*	*(E) Carrying amount, end of six-month period ($100,000 + D)*
0				$4,265	$104,265
½	$3,500	$3,128	$372	3,893	103,893
1	3,500	3,117	383	3,510	103,510
1½	3,500	3,105	395	3,115	103,115
2	3,500	3,093	407	2,708	102,708
2½	3,500	3,081	419	2,289	102,289
3	3,500	3,069	431	1,858	101,858
3½	3,500	3,056	444	1,414	101,414
4	3,500	3,042	458	956	100,956
4½	3,500	3,029	471	485	100,485
5	3,500	3,015	485	-0-	100,000

Journal entries, first half of year:

	Year 1		*Year 2*	
Bond Interest Expense	3,128		3,105	
Premium on Bonds Payable	372		395	
Cash		3,500		3,500
To record interest expense, including amortization of premium for half-year.				

Journal entries, second half of year:

	Year 1		*Year 2*	
Bond Interest Expense	3,117		3,093	
Premium on Bonds Payable	383		407	
Cash		3,500		3,500
To record interest expense, including amortization of premium for half-year.				

Ledger accounts:

Bond Interest Expense

Date	*Explanation*	*Debit*	*Credit*	*Balance*
June 30/X2	($104,265 × 0.03.)	3,128		3,128 Dr
Dec. 31/X2	($103,893 × 0.03.)	3,117		6,245 Dr
Dec. 31/X2	Closing entry.		6,245	-0-
June 30/X3	($103,510 × 0.03.)	3,105		3,105 Dr
Dec. 31/X3	($103,115 × 0.03.)	3,093		6,198 Dr
Dec. 31/X3	Closing entry.		6,198	-0-

Premium on Bonds Payable

Date	*Explanation*	*Debit*	*Credit*	*Balance*
Dec. 31/X1	Date of issuance.		4,265	4,265 Cr
June 30/X2	Amortization ($3,500 − $3,128).	372		3,893 Cr
Dec. 31/X2	Amortization ($3,500 − $3,117).	383		3,510 Cr
June 30/X3	Amortization ($3,500 − $3,105).	395		3,115 Cr
Dec. 31/X3	Amortization ($3,500 − $3,093).	407		2,708 Cr

Straight-Line Method of Amortization for Term Bonds

The additional interest expense (discount) or reduction of interest expense (premium) may be allocated evenly over the term of the bonds. This method, known as the ***straight-line method of amortization***, results in a uniform periodic interest expense. Although this method does not give the accurate results obtained by use of the interest method of amortization, it frequently is encountered in practice.

Term Bonds Issued at a Discount

When term bonds are issued at a discount, the carrying amount of the bonds increases as they approach maturity, and periodic interest expense remains constant over the term of the bonds. Annual interest expense over the term of the bonds and journal entries to record interest expense for the first two years are shown below:

Discount amortization for term bonds under straight-line method and annual interest payments

Term Bonds Issued at a Discount
Annual Interest Expense Determined by Straight-Line Method of Amortization
($100,000, 5-year bonds, interest at 7% payable annually, issued for $96,007, to yield 8% compounded annually)

Date	*(A) Interest paid (7% of face amount)*	*(B) Discount amortization (⅕ of $3,993)*	*(C) Interest expense (A + B)*	*(D) Bond discount balance (D − B)*	*(E) Carrying amount, end of year ($100,000 − D)*
Dec. 31/X1				$3,993	$ 96,007
Dec. 31/X2	$7,000	$799	$7,799	3,194	96,806
Dec. 31/X3	7,000	799	7,799	2,395	97,605
Dec. 31/X4	7,000	799	7,799	1,596	98,404
Dec. 31/X5	7,000	799	7,799	797	99,203
Dec. 31/X6	7,000	797*	7,797*		100,000

*$2 adjustment to compensate for rounding average interest expense to the nearest dollar.

Journal entries:

	Dec. 31, Year 2		*Dec. 31, Year 3*	
Bond Interest Expense	7,799		7,799	
Cash		7,000		7,000
Discount on Bonds Payable		799		799
To record interest expense, including amortization of discount.				

Term Bonds Issued at a Premium

When term bonds are issued at a premium, the carrying amount of the bonds decreases as they approach maturity, and periodic interest expense remains constant over the term of the bonds. Annual interest expense and journal entries to record interest expense for the first two years are shown on the next page.

Premium amortization for term bonds under straight-line method and annual interest payments

Term Bonds Issued at a Premium
Annual Interest Expense Determined by Straight-Line Method of Amortization
($100,000, 5-year bonds, interest at 7% payable annually, issued for $104,213, to yield 6% compounded annually)

Date	*(A) Interest paid (7% of face amount)*	*(B) Premium amortization (1/5 of $4,213)*	*(C) Interest expense (A − B)*	*(D) Bond premium balance (D − B)*	*(E) Carrying amount, end of year ($100,000 + D)*
Dec. 31/X1				$4,213	$104,213
Dec. 31/X2	$7,000	$843	$6,157	3,370	103,370
Dec. 31/X3	7,000	843	6,157	2,527	102,527
Dec. 31/X4	7,000	843	6,157	1,684	101,684
Dec. 31/X5	7,000	843	6,157	841	100,841
Dec. 31/X6	7,000	841*	6,159*		100,000

*$2 adjustment to compensate for rounding average interest expense to the nearest dollar.

Journal entries:

	Dec. 31, Year 2		*Dec. 31, Year 3*	
Bond Interest Expense	6,157		6,157	
Premium on Bonds Payable	843		843	
Cash		7,000		7,000
To record interest expense, including amortization of premium.				

Comparison of Interest and Straight-Line Methods of Amortization

A comparison of periodic interest expense when annual payments of interest are made under the interest method shown on pages 742 and 744 with the straight-line method shown on page 746 and above reveals the extent of the error involved in the use of a simple average in the straight-line method. For example, if the bonds payable were issued at a discount, the interest expense for each year ranges from $7,681 to $7,926; the use of the straight-line method results in a constant annual interest expense of $7,799. In the first year, for example, interest expense on a $100-million bond issue would be approximately $118,000 more under the straight-line method. In choosing the method to use, accountants should balance the simplicity of the straight-line method against the materiality of the difference involved. The longer the term of the bond issue and the larger the discount or premium relative to the face amount of the bonds, the larger the difference will be between straight-line interest expense and the interest expense determined by the interest method of amortization.

Another advantage of the interest method of amortization of bond discount or premium is that the carrying amount of the bonds at the end of each accounting period equals the present value of the bonds at the yield rate. For example, the table on page 748 shows the carrying amount of the bonds on December 31, Year 3, three years prior to maturity, to be $97,423. This amount equals the present value of the bonds at the original 8% yield rate, computed by reference to the tables in the Appendix at the end of Chapter 5, as follows:

Carrying amount of bonds issued at a discount amortized by interest method is equal to present value of bonds at yield rate

Present value of $100,000 due in 3 years at 8% with ***interest payable annually*** ($100,000 × 0.793832)	$79,383
Add: Present value of $7,000 every year for 3 years at 8% ($7,000 × 2.577097)	18,040
Present value of bonds (equal to carrying amount)	$97,423

When interest is paid semiannually or when interest payment dates do not coincide with the end of the fiscal year, a policy of amortizing the discount or the premium only at the end of the fiscal year may be adopted to minimize the routine work involved when the straight-line method of amortization is used.

Bond Issue Costs

A number of costs are incurred in connection with a bond issue: fees paid to accountants, lawyers, and other experts in connection with the preparation of the bond contract and prospectus; printing and engraving costs; fees of the provincial securities commissions; and costs incurred in advertising the issue. These are costs for the use of the funds borrowed and are allocated to the years that the bonds are outstanding. Amortization of bond issue costs is recorded by a debit to Bond Issue Expense, as illustrated in the Electronics Limited example on page 749.

Bond issue costs may be classified as an asset (deferred charges) and are amortized on a straight-line basis over the term of the bonds because revenue benefits from the use of the bond proceeds over this period. An alternative procedure advocated by some accountants is to add bond issue costs to bond discount or deduct them from bond premium. This procedure implies that the amount of the funds made available to the borrower is equal to the net proceeds of the bond issue after deduction of all costs of borrowing. Under this procedure, bond issue costs increase the interest expense during the term of the bonds.

Bonds Issued Between Interest Dates

Bond interest payments usually are made semiannually on dates specified in the bond contract. When term bonds are issued on a date other than an interest payment date, an adjustment for this factor may be made by reducing the amount of the interest payment for the first "short" interest period. However, it is more convenient to add to the price of bonds the amount of interest that has accrued since the last interest-payment date. Investors, in effect, prepay the issuer of the bonds for the portion of the full six-month interest payment to which they are not entitled. Thus, investors will receive the full six-month interest payment on the next semiannual interest-payment date.

Assume that Electronics Limited issued $100,000 of 10-year, 12% term bonds, with interest payable semiannually on April 1 and October 1 of each year. The bonds were issued on June 1, Year 1, for $107,080 plus accrued interest of $2,000 ($100,000 × 0.12 × $\frac{2}{12}$ = $2,000) for two months. The bonds were dated April 1, Year 1, and bond issue costs amounted to $2,360. Note that this borrowing actually runs for nine years and 10 months, or 118 months, and the accounting for the bonds and the related bond issue costs should reflect this fact. Assuming that the straight-line method of amortization is used for the bond premium, the monthly interest expense is determined below:

Computation of interest expense for each month for term bonds issued at a premium

Actual interest paid to investors over 10-year period ($12,000 × 10)	$120,000
Less: Premium received on issuance of bonds	(7,080)
Accrued interest received from investors (Apr. 1–June 1, Year 1) ..	(2,000)
Total interest expense (9 years and 10 months)	$110,920
Monthly interest expense ($110,920 ÷ 118 months)	$ 940

Because the monthly interest accrual is $1,000 ($12,000 ÷ 12 months = $1,000) and the monthly interest expense is $940, the monthly premium amortization is the difference, or $60 ($7,080 ÷ 118 = $60). Monthly amortization of bond issue costs is $20 ($2,360 ÷ 118 = $20). Assuming that amortization of the bond issue

ELECTRONICS LIMITED

Journal Entries for Term Bonds Issued Between Interest Dates

Year 1				
June 1	Bond Issue Costs		2,360	
	Cash			2,360
	To record costs of issuing bonds.			
1	Cash		109,080	
	Bonds Payable			100,000
	Bond Interest Payable			2,000
	Premium on Bonds Payable			7,080
	To record issuance of bonds and accrued interest for 2 months ($100,000 × 0.12 × 2/12 = $2,000).			
Oct. 1	Bond Interest Payable		2,000	
	Bond Interest Expense		4,000	
	Cash ($100,000 × 0.12 × 6/12)			6,000
	To record interest payment for first 6 months.			
Dec. 31	Bond Interest Expense		2,580	
	Premium on Bonds Payable		420	
	Bond Issue Expense		140	
	Bond Issue Costs			140
	Bond Interest Payable			3,000
	To accrue interest expense for 3 months and record amortization of bond issue costs and premium for 7 months. Amounts determined as follows:			
	Bond interest payable ($100,000 × 0.12 × 3/12)	$3,000		
	Less: Amortization of premium ($7,080 × 7/118)	420		
	Bond interest expense (net)	$2,580		
	Amortization of bond issue costs ($2,360 × 7/118)	$ 140		

costs and the premium is recorded only at the end of the year, the journal entries for Electronics Limited relating to the bond issue during Year 1 are as shown on page 749.

It would be possible to ***credit*** Bond Interest Expense (rather than Bond Interest Payable on June 1 for $2,000, the amount of the accrued interest for two months acquired by bondholders. On October 1, Bond Interest Expense would be debited for $6,000, thus leaving a balance of $4,000 in Bond Interest Expense representing interest incurred from June 1 to October 1. It also would be possible to amortize the premium and bond issue costs at the time interest is paid, as well as at the end of the fiscal year, but there is little point in following such an inefficient procedure when the straight-line method of amortization is used.

Serial Bonds

Thus far we have considered term bonds having a single fixed maturity date. Another type of bond contract, known as a ***serial bond***, provides for payment of the principal in periodic instalments. Serial bonds have the advantage of gearing the issuer's debt repayment to its periodic cash inflow from operations.

As in the case of term bonds, serial bonds may be issued at a premium or a discount in response to the difference between the nominal and the effective interest rate. The proceeds of a serial bond issue are somewhat more difficult to compute because of the varying maturities, but the approach is the same: The present value of the series of principal payments plus the present value of the interest payments, all at the effective interest rate, equals the proceeds received for the bonds.

At this point the question arises: Is there any single interest rate applicable to a serial bond issue? We often refer loosely to ***the rate*** of interest, when in fact in the market at any one time there are several interest rates, their amounts depending on the terms, nature, and length of the bond contract offered. In a specific serial bond issue, the terms of all bonds in the issue are the same except for the differences in maturity. However, because short-term interest rates often differ from long-term rates, it is likely that each maturity will sell at a different yield rate, so that there will be a different discount or premium relating to each maturity.

In accounting for an issue of serial bonds under these conditions, each maturity may be treated as a separate bond issue. Thus, if $500,000 of five-year, 10% serial bonds are issued, to be repaid in the amount of $100,000 each year, and each maturity sells at a price reflecting a different yield rate, the problem would be treated as a summarized accounting for five separate bond issues of $100,000 each, maturing in one, two, three, four, and five years respectively. Each maturity would have a related discount or premium, and interest expense on each maturity would be computed as previously illustrated for term bonds.

In many cases, however, this degree of precision in accounting for serial bond issues is not possible because the yield rate for each maturity is not known. Underwriters may bid on an entire serial bond issue on the basis of an average yield rate and may not disclose the particular yield rate for each maturity that was used to determine the bid price. In this situation we may have to assume that the same yield rate applies to all maturities in the issue, and proceed accordingly.

If the interest method is to be used in accounting for serial bond interest expense, the procedure is similar to that illustrated in connection with term bonds. The interest expense for each accounting period is an amount equal to the effective interest rate applied to the carrying amount of the serial bonds outstanding during that period, and the difference between this amount of interest expense and the actual interest payments represents the amortization of the bond discount or premium. The result is a constant rate of interest expense in relation to the carrying amount of the serial bonds outstanding.

A variation of the straight-line method, known as the ***bonds outstanding method***, results in a decreasing amount of premium or discount amortization each accounting period proportionate to the decrease in the amount of outstanding serial bonds.

Accounting for Serial Bonds Illustrated

To illustrate the variation in the pattern of interest expense under each of these methods, assume that at the beginning of Year 1 James Limited issued $100,000 of five-year, 5% serial bonds, to be repaid in the amount of $20,000 each year. To simplify the illustration, assume that interest payments are made annually and that no bond issue costs were incurred. If the bonds are issued to yield 6% a year, the proceeds total $97,375, as determined in the next illustration by means of the 6% column in Table 2 in the Appendix at the end of Chapter 5.

Computation of proceeds (present value) of serial bonds issued at a single effective interest rate

JAMES LIMITED
Computation of Proceeds of Serial Bond Issue
Beginning of Year 1

Principal and interest due at end of Year 1:	
($20,000 + $5,000) × 0.943396	$23,585
Principal and interest due at end of Year 2:	
($20,000 + $4,000) × 0.889996	21,360
Principal and interest due at end of Year 3:	
($20,000 + $3,000) × 0.839619	19,311
Principal and interest due at end of Year 4:	
($20,000 + $2,000) × 0.792094	17,426
Principal and interest due at end of Year 5:	
($20,000 + $1,000) × 0.747258	15,693
Proceeds of serial bond issue at 6% yield basis	$97,375

The accounting problem is to determine how the discount of $2,625 ($100,000 − $97,375 = $2,625) should be amortized over the term of the serial bond issue. Tables to determine periodic discount amortization and interest expense under the ***interest*** and the ***bonds outstanding*** methods are given on the next page.

Discount amortization table for serial bonds: interest method

JAMES LIMITED
Amortization of Discount on Serial Bonds by Interest Method

Year	(A) *Carrying amount of bonds ($100,000 − E − F)*	(B) *Interest expense (6% of A)*	(C) *Interest payment*	(D) *Discount amortization (B − C)*	(E) *Bond discount balance (E − D)*	(F) *Cumulative principal payment*
Issue	$97,375				$2,625	
1	78,217	$ 5,842	$ 5,000	$ 842	1,783	$ 20,000
2	58,910	4,693	4,000	693	1,090	40,000
3	39,444	3,534	3,000	534	556	60,000
4	19,811	2,367	2,000	367	189	80,000
5		1,189	1,000	189		100,000
Totals		$17,625	$15,000	$2,625		

The bonds outstanding method in this case produces results that are a close approximation of the interest method because of the short term of the issue and the relatively small discount. The longer the term of the bonds and the larger the discount or premium, the larger would be the discrepancy between the two methods.

Under the straight-line method, discount amortization is $525 a year ($2,625 ÷ 5 = $525). The bonds outstanding method is essentially a straight-line method because it results in a constant periodic amortization of discount or premium ***per $1,000 face amount of bonds outstanding***. In this example, the amount of annual discount amortization for each $1,000 bond outstanding is computed by dividing the total discount by the sum of the bonds outstanding over the term of the serial bond issue ($2,625 ÷ $300,000 = $8.75 per $1,000 bond). If the discount amortization for each $1,000 bond is determined at the time of issuance, it is a simple

Discount amortization table for serial bonds: bonds outstanding method

JAMES LIMITED
Amortization of Discount on Serial Bonds by Bonds Outstanding Method

Year	*Bonds outstanding (face amount)*	*Fraction of total of bonds outstanding*	(A) *Amortization of discount ($2,625 × fraction)*	(B) *Interest payments (5% of bonds outstanding*	*Interest expense (A + B)*
1	$100,000	10/30	$ 875	$ 5,000	$ 5,875
2	80,000	8/30	700	4,000	4,700
3	60,000	6/30	525	3,000	3,525
4	40,000	4/30	350	2,000	2,350
5	20,000	2/30	175	1,000	1,175
Totals	$300,000	30/30	$2,625	$15,000	$17,625

process to compute the appropriate amount of discount applicable to any amount of bonds in a given year throughout the term of a serial bond issue. Thus, in the fourth year, when $40,000 of bonds were outstanding, the discount to be amortized is computed as follows: $40,000 of bonds times $8.75 per $1,000 face amount of bonds equals $350 ($8.75 × 40 = $350).

Bond Sinking Funds

Some bond indentures require that a sinking fund be established for the retirement of the bonds. Ordinarily, a sinking fund would not be created in connection with the issuance of serial bonds; such bonds are retired periodically in lieu of making sinking fund deposits. A disadvantage inherent in bond sinking funds is that a portion of the money borrowed for planned business purposes is not being used in this manner if cash must be deposited periodically into a sinking fund. Accounting for sinking funds and their balance sheet presentation are discussed in Chapter 14 (pages 676–677).

EXTINGUISHMENT OF LONG-TERM DEBT

If the principal of term bonds or serial bonds is paid on the maturity date, no gain or loss results because the carrying amount and face amount of the bonds, and the cash paid, are the same. The journal entry to record the payment of the bonds at maturity is a debit to Bonds Payable and a credit to Cash.

Occasionally, because of favourable interest rates or other considerations, the issuer of bonds may retire them before maturity by exercising the call provision, by acquiring the bonds in the open market, in a ***debt-equity swap***, in a ***refunding***, or by means of an ***in-substance defeasance***. These ***extinguishments*** of long-term debt are discussed in the following sections. Typically, a gain or loss (before income tax effect) on the extinguishment of term or serial bonds prior to maturity is recorded equal to the difference between the amount paid to retire the bonds and their carrying amount, including any unamortized bond issue costs. In all examples in this chapter, the income tax effect on the gains or losses from extinguishment of bonds payable is disregarded. The amortization of any bond discount or premium and bond issue costs should be adjusted to the date of extinguishment ***before*** the journal entry to record the extinguishment is prepared.

Extinguishment by Calling Bonds

When an entire bond issue is ***called for redemption***, the entire unamortized premium or discount and bond issue costs are written off. Losses generally result on such redemptions because the sliding call prices ordinarily are in excess of bond carrying amounts on corresponding call dates.

If bonds are called but not formally retired, a Treasury Bonds ledger account may be debited for the face amount of the ***treasury bonds*** held, but a gain or loss still should be recognized. The Treasury Bonds account is not an asset; it is deducted from bonds payable in the balance sheet. Interest is not paid on treasury bonds unless they are held as an investment by a company-sponsored fund, such as an employee pension fund.

ELECTRONICS LIMITED
Journal Entries to Record Extinguishment of Term Bonds Through Call

Date	Account	Debit	Credit
Year 2			
Dec. 1	Premium on Bonds Payable	132	
	Bond Issue Expense	44	
	Bond Interest Expense		132
	Bond Issue Costs		44
	To record amortization on $20,000 (or 20%) of bonds for period Jan. 1 to Dec. 1, Year 2 (the date of extinguishment) as follows:		
	Amortization of bond premium:		
	$7,080 × 0.20 × 11/18 = $132.		
	Amortization of bond issue costs:		
	$2,360 × 0.20 × 11/18 = $44.		
1	Bonds Payable	20,000	
	Premium on Bonds Payable ($1,416 − $216)	1,200	
	Bond Interest Expense ($20,000 × 0.12 × 2/12)	400	
	Cash ($20,600 + $400)		21,000
	Bond Issue Costs ($472 − $72)		400
	Gain on Exinguishment of Bonds		200
	To record extinguishment of bonds at 103, plus accrued interest of $400 for 2 months. The gain is determined as follows:		
	Original issuance proceeds ($107,080 × 0.20)	$21,416	
	Less: Original bond issue costs ($2,360 × 0.20)	472	
	Subtotal	$20,944	
	Amortization for 18 months:		
	Premium ($60 × 0.20 × 18)	(216)	
	Bond issue costs ($20 × 0.20 × 18)	72	
	Carrying amount less unamortized bond issue costs on extinguishment	$20,800	
	Amount paid to extinguish bonds ($20,000 × 1.03)	20,600	
	Gain on extinguishment of bonds	$ 200	

Gains and losses on extinguishment of bonds reflect the changes in interest rates since the bonds were issued. These gains and losses are included in income before extraordinary items, and if unusual in size may be separately disclosed.

To illustrate the accounting for extinguishment of long-term debt by exercise of the call provision of term bonds, assume that $20,000 (20%) of the Electronics Limited term bonds described on page 748 were called on December 1, Year 2, or 18 months after the bonds were issued. If the bonds were redeemed at the call price of 103 (103% of face amount), plus accrued interest of $400 ($20,000 × 0.12 × 2/12 = $400) for two months, the above journal entries would be required.

Extinguishment by Open-Market Acquisition

If interest rates are rising and bond prices are falling, it may be appropriate for the issuer to realize a substantial gain by acquiring its bonds in the open market from present bondholders at a substantial discount.

To illustrate the extinguishment of serial bonds by open-market acquisition, assume that $10,000 of James Limited bonds (see pages 751–752) are acquired at 85 (85% of face amount) at the end of Year 2, two years prior to the scheduled retirement date. The bond interest had been paid for Year 2. The discount applicable to the bonds acquired is determined by the bonds outstanding method as shown below.

Computation of discount applicable to serial bonds acquired in open market

Discount applicable to Year 3: $525* × $\frac{10,000}{60,000}$	$ 87.50
Discount applicable to Year 4: $350* × $\frac{10,000}{40,000}$	87.50
Total discount applicable to acquired bonds	$175.00†

*From Column A in bottom table on page 752.
†Because the discount amortization amounts to $8.75 per $1,000 per year, this amount may be determined as follows: $8.75 × 10 × 2 = $175. Similar procedures may be used to compute amortization of discount on serial bonds when the "bond year" and the fiscal year of the issuer do not coincide.

The journal entry to record the extinguishment follows:

Journal entry for extinguishment of serial bonds

Bonds Payable	10,000	
Discount on Bonds Payable		175
Cash ($10,000 × 0.85)		8,500
Gain on Extinguishment of Bonds		1,325
To record extinguishment of serial bonds, two years prior to scheduled maturity date.		

Extinguishment Through Debt-Equity Swap

Instead of using cash to acquire its outstanding bonds in the open market, the issuer may enter into a ***debt-equity swap*** arrangement with an investment broker. The broker acquires the issuer's bonds over a period of time in the open market and exchanges the bonds for shares of the issuer's common stock, which may be unissued or in the treasury. The issuer thus retires the bonds acquired in the ***swap*** with the broker. By this means, the issuer extinguishes long-term debt without using cash, and improves its ***debt-to-equity ratio*** (the ratio of total liabilities to total shareholders' equity).

To illustrate, assume that a broker acquired in the open market $500,000 face amount of Casper Corporation's 10% bonds for a total cost of $450,000. The bonds had a carrying amount of $505,000 in Casper's accounting records ($500,000 face amount, plus $12,000 premium, and less $7,000 bond issue costs) on December 31, Year 4. On that date, Casper issued to the broker 10,000 shares of its no-par common stock with a current fair value of $48 a share in exchange for the bonds.

The journal entry to record Casper Corporation's debt-equity swap is as follows:

Journal entry for debt-equity swap

Bonds Payable	500,000	
Premium on Bonds Payable	12,000	
Bond Issue Costs		7,000
Common Stock, No Par (10,000 × $48)		480,000
Gain on Extinguishment of Bonds [($512,000 − $7,000) − $480,000]		25,000
To record extinguishment of bonds in a debt-equity swap with broker.		

Extinguishment Through Refunding

Refunding is the process of retiring a bond issue with the proceeds of a new bond issue. When refunding occurs at the time the old bonds mature, the carrying amount of such bonds is equal to face amount; no gain or loss arises from the retirement of the old bonds, and the issuance of the new bonds is recorded in the usual manner.

A problem arises when refunding occurs prior to the maturity of the old bonds. This usually happens when interest rates have declined and the issuer decides to reduce its interest expense by calling the old bonds (paying the required penalty in the form of a call premium) and issuing new bonds at a lower yield rate. If the two transactions (calling the old bonds and issuing new ones) are viewed as separate and unrelated transactions, no issues are raised that have not already been discussed. Calling and retiring the old bonds results in a gain or loss equal to the difference between carrying amount and call price; the new bonds are recorded in the usual manner. However, some accountants have argued that the loss on the refunding prior to maturity should be deferred and amortized over part of, or the entire, term of the new bond issue.

For example, assume that Cleve Corporation has outstanding $1,000,000 of 12% bonds having 10 years to maturity and a carrying amount of $960,000 (face amount of $1,000,000, less unamortized discount of $40,000). Cleve calls the bonds at 105, using the proceeds of a new 20-year issue of 10% bonds (which we assume were issued at face amount). Bonds having a carrying amount of $960,000 thus are refunded at a cost of $1,050,000, and a question arises as to the treatment of the $90,000 difference ($1,050,000 − $960,000 = $90,000). Three solutions have been proposed:

1 Recognize $90,000 as a loss at the time of refunding.

2 Record the $90,000 as a deferred charge and amortize it over the remaining term of the retired bonds (in this case 10 years).

3 Record the $90,000 as a deferred charge and amortize it over the term of the new bonds (in this case 20 years).

The first alternative has the weight of logic in its favour. The amount of unamortized bond discount at any time measures the liability for additional interest that will accrue during the remaining term of bonds to compensate for the fact that the nominal rate of interest is less than the effective rate of interest. In order to eliminate the old bond contract, the issuer is required to pay this $40,000 of interest now, and, in addition, a $50,000 call premium. These costs are ***related*** to past periods but are ***caused*** by the current decline in the interest rate and management's decision to refund. Deferral of these costs would penalize future accounting periods, because the new 10% bonds could have been issued even if the 12% bonds had not been outstanding.

Arguments for the amortization over the remaining term of old bonds are based on the principle that when a cost is incurred, the benefits of which are expected to be realized over a period of years, the cost should be recognized as an expense over those years. It may be argued that the unamortized bond discount and the call premium paid to refund the old bonds are costs incurred to obtain the benefit of lower interest expense during the remaining term of the old bonds. The payment of a call premium necessary to cancel an unfavourable bond contract and the write-off of unamortized discount on the contract may be viewed as events relating to the old bond contract and not as benefits to be derived from the new bond contract. For example, if a higher nominal rate of interest had been set on the old bonds, they would have been issued at face amount, and there would be no unamortized discount to write off on the refunding date.

The third method rests on the premise that because the new bonds are a continuation of the old, the costs of both the old and new borrowings should be expensed over the term of the new bonds. The term of the new bonds generally is longer than the unexpired term of the old bonds. It was suggested that deferral of the "loss" was appropriate when the refunding takes place because of currently lower interest rates or anticipated higher rates in the future. This position assumes that the key reason for the refunding is to obtain a lower interest cost over the term of the new bonds.

In the United States, only the first method (immediate recognition of losses or gains) is sanctioned by generally accepted accounting principles; whereas in Canada, because the ***CICA Handbook*** is silent in this area, any of the three methods may be used.

Deciding When to Refund a Bond Issue

A decline in interest rates is not in itself a sufficient basis for a decision to refund a bond issue. The out-of-pocket costs of refunding must be compared with the present value of future interest savings. In addition, the income tax impact of refunding and bond indenture features on both the old and new bonds must be considered. Future interest rates also should be considered, because a further decline in rates may mean that refunding may be made under even more favourable conditions on a later date.

Extinguishment by In-Substance Defeasance

The conventional method of extinguishing long-term debt such as bonds payable is payment of cash or the issuance of common stock pursuant to the conversion of convertible bonds. Common stock also is issued to extinguish bonds payable in a debt-equity swap.

In FASB Statement No. 76: "Extinguishment of Debt" the Financial Accounting Standards Board in the United States addressed another method of debt extinguishment, ***in-substance defeasance***. The term ***defeasance*** indicates that the debtor is released from legal liability for bonds payable or other debt. ***In-substance*** means that the *legal form* of defeasance is not present, but that *substantively* the debt has been extinguished by action of the debtor.

The Financial Accounting Standards Board provided the following criteria for in-substance defeasance of debt:[3]

> A debtor shall consider debt to be extinguished for financial reporting purposes in the following circumstances: ...
> The debtor irrevocably places cash or other assets in a trust to be used solely for satisfying scheduled payments of both interest and principal of a specific obligation and the possibility that the debtor will be required to make future payments with respect to the debt is remote. In this circumstance, debt is extinguished even though the debtor is not legally released from being the primary obligor under the debt obligation.
>
> The following requirements regarding the nature of the assets held by the trust shall be met to effect an extinguishment of debt... :
>
> **a** The trust shall be restricted to owning only monetary assets (money or a claim to receive a sum of money that is fixed or determinable without reference to future prices of specific goods and services) that are ***essentially risk-free*** as to the amount, timing, and collection of interest and principal.... For debt denominated in U.S. dollars, essentially risk-free monetary assets shall be limited to:
>
> 1 Direct obligations of the U.S. government
>
> 2 Obligations guaranteed by the U.S. government
>
> 3 Securities that are backed by U.S. government obligations as collateral...
>
> **b** The monetary assets held by the trust shall provide cash flows (from interest and maturity of those assets) that approximately coincide, as to timing and amount, with the scheduled interest and principal payments on the debt that is being extinguished.

Illustration of In-Substance Defeasance of Bonds Payable

To illustrate the in-substance defeasance of debt, assume that Magno, Inc., had the following ledger account balances related to bonds payable on May 31, Year 4, the end of a fiscal year:

Data for illustration

8% bonds payable, due May 31, Year 13, interest payable May 31 and Nov. 30, callable at 102	$8,000,000
Discount on bonds payable (based on 10% yield rate)	935,167
Bond issue costs	72,000

Because 9% government Treasury bills due May 31, Year 13, were trading at a yield rate of 16% on May 31, Year 4, Magno was able to acquire $8,000,000 face amount of the Treasury bills for $5,375,872, computed as follows:

3 FASB, ***FASB Statement No. 76***: "Extinguishment of Debt" (Stamford: 1983), pp. 1–3.

Computation of cost of 9% U.S. Treasury bonds

\$8,000,000 × 0.250249*	\$2,001,992
\$360,000 × 9.371887†	3,373,880
Total cost of government Treasury bills	\$5,375,872

*From Table 2 of the Appendix at the end of Chapter 5.
†From Table 4 of the Appendix at the end of Chapter 5.

Magno then transferred the 9% government Treasury bills to an irrevocable trust for servicing Magno's 8% bonds payable, which had the same interest payment dates (May 31 and November 30) and same maturity date (May 31, Year 13) as the Treasury bills. The trustee would use the \$360,000 (\$8,000,000 × 0.045 = \$360,000) semiannual interest received on the 9% Treasury bills to pay the semiannual interest of \$320,000 (\$8,000,000 × 0.04 = \$320,000) on Magno's bonds and the trustee's fee of \$40,000 semiannually. Further, the trustee would use the \$8,000,000 proceeds received for the 9% Treasury bills on May 31, Year 13, to extinguish the \$8,000,000 principal of the 8% Magno bonds that mature on the same date. (If the \$40,000 interest differential were insufficient to cover the trustee's fee for servicing the bonds, Magno would have to accrue the ***present value*** of the deficiency in full on May 31, Year 4; the trustee would refund to Magno any excess of the \$40,000 over the semiannual trustee's fee.)

Because the acquisition of the 9% federal Treasury bills and transfer of the bonds to the irrevocable trust comply with the provisions of ***FASB Statement No. 76***, the following journal entries are appropriate for Magno, Inc., on May 31, Year 4:

Journal entries for in-substance defeasance of bonds payable

MAGNO, INC.
Journal Entries for In-Substance Defeasance of Bonds Payable

Investment in 9% Federal Treasury Bills	5,375,872	
Cash		5,375,872
To record acquisition of \$8,000,000 face amount of 9% federal Treasury bills due May 31, Year 13, at a 16% yield rate.		
Bonds Payable	8,000,000	
Discount on Bonds Payable		935,167
Bond Issue Costs		72,000
Investment in 9% Federal Treasury Bills		5,375,872
Gain on Extinguishment of Bills		1,616,961
To record transfer of 9% federal Treasury bills to irrevocable trust for servicing of 8% bonds payable. The transaction constitutes an in-substance defeasance of bonds, with a resultant gain on extinguishment.		

As a result of the foregoing transactions, Magno, Inc., has realized a pre-tax extraordinary gain (assuming the amount is material) of \$1,616,961 for the year ended May 31, Year 4. In contrast, Magno would have incurred an extraordinary loss (if material) of \$1,167,167 if it had called the bonds at 102 on May 31, Year 4. The \$1,167,167 loss would have been computed as follows:

Computation of loss if bonds had been called

Call price of bonds ($8,000,000 × 1.02)	$8,160,000
Less: Carrying amount of bonds, May 31, Year 4 ($8,000,000 − $935,167 − $72,000)	6,992,833
Loss if bonds had been called	$1,167,167

Thus, by using the in-substance defeasance technique to extinguish bonds payable, a business enterprise may realize a gain, rather than the loss that typically results from calling the bonds. Further, an in-substance defeasance may be accomplished more quickly and efficiently than a debt-equity swap, in which the broker must acquire bonds in the open market over a substantial period of time to avoid undue upward pressure on prices of the bonds (and accompanying downward pressure on the yield rate for the bonds).

Evaluation of Accounting Principles for In-Substance Defeasance of Debt

The accounting principles for in-substance defeasance of debt enacted in the United States by the Financial Accounting Standards Board are highly controversial. Critics claim that the setting aside of assets in trust does not constitute a disposal of the assets or the extinguishment of a liability, with resultant gain or loss. The assets continue to exist in the possession of a trustee, and the liability is still outstanding. In our opinion, although financial accounting emphasizes economic substance over legal form in most business transactions, the accounting for in-substance defeasance of debt borders on being ''cute accounting,'' a term given by the Securities and Exchange Commission in the United States to accounting techniques that stretch financial accounting concepts to the limits of credibility. Nonetheless, the SEC has sanctioned the accounting principles for in-substance defeasance of debt established in ***FASB Statement No. 76***.

OTHER TOPICS RELATING TO LONG-TERM DEBT

Convertible Bonds

Current Practice

A ***convertible bond*** may be exchanged at the holder's option for a stipulated number of shares of common stock. The conversion feature of a convertible bond enables the holders of such a security to enjoy the status of a creditor and at the same time participate in the price appreciation of the common stock.

When common stock is issued in exchange for convertible bonds, the carrying amount of the bonds is assigned to the common stock. Thus, no gain or loss is recognized on a conversion of bonds to common stock under this ***carrying value*** (or ***book value***) ***method.*** Accordingly, the accounting for the issuance and conversion of bonds is illustrated in the next example.

Assume that Lucien Limited issued at face amount $10 million of 10-year, 12% convertible bonds. Interest on the bonds is payable semiannually. Each $1,000 bond is convertible to 30 shares of Lucien's no-par value common stock. The journal entries to record the issuance and subsequent conversion of the bonds (immediately after the periodic interest had been paid) are illustrated below:

Journal entries for issuance and conversion of bonds

Cash	10,000,000	
Convertible Bonds Payable		10,000,000
To record issuance of 10-year, 12% convertible bonds at face amount.		
Convertible Bonds Payable	10,000,000	
Common Stock, No Par		10,000,000
To record conversion of 10-year 12% convertible bonds to 300,000 shares of no-par common stock.		

Evaluation of Current Practice

Current practice for recording the issuance of convertible bonds ***does not***, in our opinion, recognize the economic substance of such transactions. When convertible bonds are issued, a portion of the proceeds logically is attributable to the conversion feature, a factor that is reflected in a lower nominal rate of interest. Because the bondholder receives a ''call'' on the issuer's common stock, a portion of the proceeds attributable to the conversion feature should be recorded as contributed surplus, and a bond discount (or a reduced bond premium) should be recorded. The discount (or reduced premium) is equal to the difference between the amount at which the bonds were issued and the estimated amount for which they would have been issued ***in the absence of the conversion feature***.

To illustrate, assume that the $10 million of 10-year, 12% convertible bonds were issued at face amount by Lucien Limited (see page 760) when similar nonconvertible bonds were yielding 14% compounded semiannually. Present value tables indicate that 12% nonconvertible bonds would be issued for $8,940,599 to yield 14% compounded semiannually. The journal entry to record the issuance of the bonds by Lucien Limited, ***if a value is assigned to the conversion feature***, follows:

Journal entry for issuance of convertible bonds, ***assuming a value is assigned to the conversion feature***

Cash	10,000,000	
Discount on Convertible Bonds Payable	1,059,401	
Convertible Bonds Payable		10,000,000
Contributed Surplus — Conversion Feature of Bonds Payable		1,059,401
To record issuance of 10-year, 12% convertible bonds valued at $8,940,599 (excluding value of conversion feature).		

The discount would be amortized over the term of the bonds, thus increasing the amount of interest expense. If the bonds were converted prior to maturity, the carrying amount of the bonds and the Contributed Surplus — Conversion Feature of Bonds Payable account would be transferred to the Common Stock ledger account.

Extinguishment of Convertible Bonds

Should a gain or loss be recorded on the extinguishment of convertible bonds before maturity or conversion? A convertible bond is a hybrid security; thus, a simple answer to this question is difficult. When convertible bonds are trading at a large premium because of their conversion feature, and management of the issuer decides to retire the entire issue of bonds, it may call the bonds to force bondholders to convert. However, if management plans to retire only a portion of the bond issue, it could not exercise the call privilege and would have to pay the going market price for the bonds or initiate a debt-equity swap.

Because convertible bonds that are trading at a large premium are, in effect, an equity security, accounting theory suggests that the difference between the carrying amount of the bonds and the amount paid to retire them should be debited to contributed surplus, and not recognized as a loss. Under these circumstances the extinguishment of the convertible bonds may be viewed as equivalent to an acquisition of common stock for retirement. When convertible bonds are trading at a substantial discount, not because of high market rates of interest but because the issuer's common stock is trading at a low market price, extinguishment of such bonds may be viewed as giving rise to contributed surplus. This line of reasoning is based on the fact that the intent of issuing convertible bonds is to raise equity capital, and the low market price of the bonds is caused by the fact that the value of the bonds as an equity security has decreased. However, in the United States, such differences must be treated as losses and gains.

In our opinion, this principle in some cases may result in material gains or losses being reported in the income statement that are in substance increases or decreases in contributed surplus. The ***CICA Handbook*** is silent in this area.

Additional discussion of convertible bonds appears in Chapter 17.

Bonds Issued With Common Stock Warrants Attached

When bonds are issued that are not convertible to common stock but, instead, include ***detachable common stock warrants*** giving the bondholder the right to acquire a certain number of shares of the issuer's common stock at a fixed price, a separate value is assigned to the warrants, based on the relative market values of the two securities, because the securities usually are traded separately in the market. If only one security has a market value, such value is assigned to the one security, and the remainder of the proceeds is assigned to the other security. Thus, if $10 million of bonds, with common stock warrants attached that have a market value of $500,000, are issued for $10 million, the issuance would be recorded as shown below. Because the warrants are valued at $500,000, the bonds in effect were issued at 95.

Journal entry for issuance of bonds with common stock warrants attached

Account	Debit	Credit
Cash	10,000,000	
Discount on Bonds Payable	500,000	
Bonds Payable		10,000,000
Contributed Surplus — Common Stock Warrants		500,000
To record issuance of bonds with common stock warrants attached.		

When the common stock warrants are exercised, the carrying amount of the warrants is treated as part of the proceeds from the issuance of common stock. This topic is discussed in more detail in Chapter 17.

Miscellaneous Long-Term Debt

Other long-term debt is often found in the balance sheets of business enterprises — for example, notes payable to banks, equipment contracts payable, purchase-money obligations, and mortgage notes payable. The essential accounting problems related to these liabilities are similar to those applicable to bonds payable. The important point is that all long-term debt initially should be recorded at the present value of the amounts to be paid. This is particularly important when debts are incurred in connection with acquisition of noncash assets or are assumed by the combinor (acquiring company) in a business combination. In the acquisition of a business enterprise, if liabilities are not fairly valued, the amount of unidentifiable intangibles (goodwill) and the periodic amortization of such intangibles will be misstated.

As was pointed out in Chapter 4, a variety of other ''deferred credit'' or ''quasi-liability'' items sometimes are included under long-term debt in balance sheets of business enterprises. These may range from unearned revenue items to items such as ''excess of equity in net assets of subsidiary over cost,'' deferred investment tax credits, and deferred income tax credits.

Distinguishing Between Long-Term Debt and Equity

Because interest is deductible in the computation of taxable income, and a payment designated as a dividend is not, it is inevitable that creative financial managers will devise liability contracts that bestow on the securities as many of the characteristics of ownership as possible without destroying their income tax status as debt. As a result, the dividing line between long-term debt and equity (shareholders' equity) often is blurred. An example on the liability side is ***subordinated income bonds***. Such bonds are secured only by the general credit standing of the issuer, and the bond contract provides that interest will be paid only when and if earnings are sufficient. Interest payments on such a bond usually are cumulative, but failure to pay interest does not give bondholders the right to interfere in corporate affairs. It is clear that a substantial amount of risk, comparable to that borne by shareholders, attaches to such bonds. The basic characteristic distinguishing subordinated income bonds from preferred stock is that the bonds have a maturity date.

On the shareholders' equity side of the dividing line, some forms of preferred stock are similar to debt. A preferred stock issue that has no voting rights, provides a stated cumulative dividend, and requires redemption on specified dates represents only a limited form of ownership equity. Such preferred stock, in effect, represents ''a liability masquerading as shareholders' equity,'' and requires special reporting in the balance sheet. This type of redeemable preferred stock is discussed in Chapter 16.

The question arises, in dealing with such cases, whether a distinction may be drawn with sufficient clarity to make a clear-cut division in accounting between long-term liabilities and shareholders' equity. Some accountants have argued that the entire right side of the balance sheet should be labelled "Equities," and that the distinction between liabilities and shareholders' equity may not be important. This is an extreme position, however, and is not consistent with the definitions of ***liabilities*** and ***equities*** on page 19 of Chapter 1.

Long-Term Debt in the Balance Sheet

All long-term debt should be described in the balance sheet or in a note to the financial statements. Business enterprises having large amounts of long-term debt in the form of numerous issues often show only one amount in the balance sheet and support this with a note to the financial statements that presents the details of maturity dates, interest rates, call provisions, conversion features, assets pledged as collateral, and limitations on dividends or other restrictions imposed on the issuer.

In the event the company has purchased its own securities that have not been cancelled at the balance sheet date, such purchases must be deducted from the related liability and must therefore not be shown as an asset.

Disclosure of the combined aggregate amount of maturities and any sinking fund requirements of all long-term borrowings for each of the five years following the balance sheet date is necessary according to generally accepted accounting principles.

Any portion of long-term debt that matures in one year is listed as a current liability, unless the retirement of the debt will not require the use of current assets. If, during the ensuing year, long-term debt is expected to be converted to common stock, refunded, or repaid from a sinking fund, there is no reason to reclassify it as a current liability. However, the expected method of retirement should be disclosed.

Interest in the Income Statement

Interest on obligations initially incurred for a period of a year or less should be shown separately from interest initially incurred for a term of more than a year. The amortization of debt discount or premium, together with the amortization of issue costs, should be included in the interest on obligations initially incurred for more than one year.

REVIEW QUESTIONS

1 Define the following: ***debenture bonds, term bonds, serial bonds, convertible bonds, bond indenture, nominal (contract) rate, effective (yield) rate,*** and ***call premium***.

2 Bonds with a nominal rate of interest of 10% are issued to yield 12%. Will the bond sell at a premium or a discount? Explain.

3 A $1-million bond issue is issued for $990,000 and callable at 105. A few months later the bonds are trading at 106. List possible reasons for the

increase in the market price of the bonds and explain the significance of the increase to the issuer.

4 Viking Limited plans to issue $1 million 12%, 10-year bonds. What will be the average annual interest expense if the bonds are issued at 104? At 97?

5 If bonds are issued at a premium and the ***effective interest method*** is used to amortize the premium, will the annual interest expense increase or decline over the term of the bonds? Explain.

6 Canton Limited has just issued $100 million of 15-year debenture bonds at a discount. At an annual shareholders' meeting, a shareholder asks the controller to explain the nature of bond discount and issue costs, which are included among Canton's assets at $4,829,000. The controller answers, "This represents prepaid interest of $4.7 million and bond issue costs of $129,000 on our bonds, which are being amortized over the term of the debt." Evaluate the controller's answer.

7 Explain the appropriate balance sheet classification of:
   a Premium on bonds payable
   b Discount on bonds payable
   c Bond issue costs

8 Why is the ***effective interest method*** of amortization of premium or discount on bonds payable considered conceptually superior to the ***straight-line method***? Explain.

9 Explain how the interest accrued on bonds may be accounted for when bonds are issued between interest dates.

10 Describe the accounting for the difference between the carrying amount of bonds payable and the amount paid to extinguish the bonds. How is the difference entered in the accounting records and reported in the financial statements when bonds are refunded?

11 List some factors that management of a business enterprise should consider in deciding when to refund a bond issue.

12 Explain the following techniques for extinguishment of long-term bonds:
   a ***Debt-equity swap***
   b ***In-substance defeasance***

13 What are the advantages to a growing corporation of issuing convertible bonds?

14 What is the generally accepted practice in regard to the assignment of a value to the conversion feature of convertible bonds? Present an argument in favour of assigning to the conversion feature a part of the proceeds received on the issuance of convertible bonds.

15 Briefly describe the accounting for bonds that include detachable common stock warrants to acquire the issuer's common stock.

16 An executive of a railroad was quoted as saying, "Debt management is a continuous process that is essential to good operations. I shall never take on debt without a sinking fund." Comment on the executive's position.

17 Pardee Limited has outstanding an issue of ***10% subordinated debentures*** and an issue of ***10% cumulative preferred stock***, both callable at face amount or par. What basic distinction between these two securities determines their balance sheet classification?

18 What disclosures regarding long-term debt are typically included in a note to the financial statements?

EXERCISES

Ex. 15-1 Select the best answer for each of the following multiple-choice questions:

1 Lemon Limited borrowed $200,000 from Commercial Bank under a 16%, three-year promissory note dated December 31, Year 1, with interest payable annually on December 31 of Year 2 through Year 4. The December 31, Year 2, interest payment was made on time by Lemon. During Year 3, Lemon experienced financial difficulties that made default on the note payable likely unless Commercial made concessions. On December 31, Year 3, Commercial agreed to accept $10,000 cash and land with a current fair value of $140,000 and a carrying amount of $100,000 from Lemon in full settlement of the note and accrued interest payable. Disregarding income taxes, the amount of Lemon Limited's gain attributable to payment of the indebtedness is:
a $0 *b* $50,000 *c* $82,000 *d* $122,000 *e* Some other amount

2 On July 1, Year 2, Ramon Corporation issued $1,000,000 face amount of 10%, 20-year bonds, with detachable common stock warrants attached, for $1,060,000. Each $1,000 bond had a detachable common stock warrant enabling the acquisition of one share of Ramon's no-par common stock for $60. Immediately after issuance of the bonds, market values of Ramon's securities were as follows:

10% bonds (ex-warrants)	$1,040
Common stock warrants	20
No-par common stock	56

In the journal entry to record issuance of the bonds, Ramon Corporation credits Premium on Bonds Payable for:
a $0 *b* $20,000 *c* $40,000 *d* $60,000 *e* Some other amount

3 If the cash received for bonds issued with detachable common stock warrants attached exceeds the total of the face amount of the bonds and the current fair value of the common stock warrants, the excess is credited to:
a Contributed Surplus in Excess of Stated Value
b Retained Earnings
c Premium on Bonds Payable
d Contributed Surplus — Stock Warrants

4 How is the current fair value of detachable common stock warrants on issued bonds accounted for?
a No value is accounted for
b The value is credited to a contributed surplus ledger account
c The value is credited to a retained earnings reserve ledger account
d The value is credited to a liability ledger account

5 On January 2, Year 2, Ludwig Limited issued $500,000 face amount of 9%, 10-year bonds at 95. Interest on the bonds is payable on January 1 and July 1. Bond issue costs paid by Ludwig on January 2, Year 2, totalled $20,000. If Ludwig uses the straight-line method of amortization for bond discount and issue costs, the carrying amount of the bonds payable in Ludwig Limited's December 31, Year 2, balance sheet is:
a $459,500 *b* $477,500 *c* $495,500 *d* $522,500 *e* Some other amount

6 The yield rate of interest for bonds that are issued for more than face amount is:
a Less than the nominal rate
b Equal to the nominal rate
c Larger than the nominal rate
d Independent of the nominal rate

7 On May 1, Year 7, Quando Limited issued $1,000,000 face amount of 10% debenture bonds dated March 1, Year 7, with interest payable March 1 and September 1. The debenture bonds were issued at face amount plus accrued interest. Quando Limited's debit to the Cash ledger account on May 1, Year 7, is:
a $966,667 *b* $983,333 *c* $1,016,667 *d* $1,033,333 *e* Some other amount

8 On April 1, Year 4, when the market rate of interest for comparable bonds was 14%, Wiley Corporation issued $500,000 face amount of 12%, 10-year bonds with interest payable semiannually. The discount of $52,970 on the bonds was amortized under the effective interest method. Discount amortization on October 1, Year 4, is:
a $1,277 *b* $2,659 *c* $3,191 *d* $3,723 *e* Some other amount

Ex. 15-2 Leach Limited plans to issue $5 million of 12% bonds, due 20 years from date of issue. Interest is payable semiannually.

Compute the proceeds of Leach Limited's bond issue if the effective rate of interest compounded semianually is *a* 10%, and *b* 14%. Use the present-value tables in the Appendix at the end of Chapter 5.

Ex. 15-3 On September 30, Year 2, the end of a fiscal year, Loman Limited issued $1,000,000 face amount of 20-year, 24% ''junk bonds'' for $1,195,581, a 20% yield. Interest on the bonds was payable each March 31 and September 30. Loman uses the effective interest method of amortizing bond discount and bond premium.

Prepare journal entries for Loman Limited to record the issuance of the bonds on September 30, Year 2, and the payment of interest on March 31 and September 30, Year 3. Disregard bond issue costs.

Ex. 15-4 On January 2, Year 5, Gayle Inc. issued 12% bonds with a face amount of $1,000,000. The bonds mature in 10 years, and interest is paid semiannually on June 30 and December 31. The bonds were issued for $894,060 to yield 14% compounded semiannually.

Using the effective interest method, compute the amount that should be debited by Gayle Inc. to Bond Interest Expense in Year 5. Round all amounts to the nearest dollar.

Ex. 15-5 Lazar Limited plans to finance the acquisition of plant assets by issuing 10% bonds. Management projects earnings, ***before*** deduction of bond interest expense and income taxes expense, at $4,664,000 a year. Lazar's income tax rate is 40%. Management wants its net earnings ***after*** deduction of bond interest and income taxes to be 10 times the bond interest expense.

Assuming that the bonds may be issued to yield 10%, compute the face amount of bonds that should be issued by Lazar Limited.

Ex. 15-6 Landau Corporation uses the effective interest method to amortize at a 10% yield rate the premium on its 11%, 20-year bonds with a face amount of $1,000,000 and a carrying amount of $1,017,729 on June 30, Year 23, two years prior to maturity of the bonds. Interest on the bonds is payable on June 30 and December 31.

Prepare a three-column Premium on Bonds Payable ledger account for Landau Corporation and post thereto journal entries for December 31, Year 23, June 30 and December 31, Year 24, and June 30, Year 25. Round all amounts to the nearest dollar.

Ex. 15-7 On October 1, Year 8, Likert Limited issued $6 million of serial bonds requiring the payment of $1.2 million principal each year, beginning October 1, Year 9.

a Explain how a $270,000 discount on Likert Limited's bond issue would be amortized if the bonds outstanding method were used.

b How much of the discount would be amortized for the year ended December 31, Year 10, under the bonds outstanding method?

c Assuming, as a separate case, that Likert Limited's bonds required the payment of $1.2 million at the end of each of five years, starting at the end of the third year after issue date, prepare a schedule of discount amortization computed under the bonds outstanding method.

Ex. 15-8 On September 30, Year 13, the accounting records of Losswell Limited had the following ledger account balances related to $500,000 face amount of 16%, 10-year bonds payable that had been issued October 1, Year 5, to yield 18%. Interest on the bonds was payable April 1 and October 1. All end-of-period adjustment had been made as of September 30, Year 13.

Bond interest payable	$ 40,000
Bond issue costs	10,000
Discount on bonds payable	16,199
16% bonds payable	500,000

On September 30, Year 13, Losswell called the entire bond issue at the call price of 102.

Prepare a journal entry for Losswell Limited to record the call (and extinguishment) of the bonds on September 30, Year 13. Disregard income taxes.

Ex. 15-9 On December 31, Year 12, Beale Inc. had outstanding 10 million of 12%, 20-year bonds due in seven years and nine months. The premium on the bonds on October 1, Year 12, was $840,000.

Prepare journal entries for Beale Inc. ***a*** to record the accrual of interest and amortization of the premium for the three months ended December 31, Year 12, and ***b*** to record the call of $1 million of the bonds on January 2, Year 13, at 102 plus accrued interest for three months, assuming that premium is amortized on a straight-line basis and that reversing entries are not used. Disregard bond issue costs and income taxes.

Ex. 15-10 On December 1, Year 6, Kier Corporation issued $2,000,000 face amount of 13% bonds for $2,200,000, plus accrued interest. Interest is payable on February 1 and August 1. Bond issue costs may be disregarded. On December 31, Year 8, the carrying amount of the bonds, inclusive of the unamortized premium, was $2,100,000. On July 1, Year 9, Kier acquired the bonds in the open market at 98, plus accrued interest. Kier uses the straight-line method for the amortization of bond premium—appropriately, because the results do not differ materially from the effective interest method.

Compute the gain or loss on the extinguishment of Kier Corporation's bonds. Show supporting computations and disregard income taxes.

Ex. 15-11 On November 30, Year 4, Ginger Ltd. issued 10,000 shares of its no-par common stock (current fair value $38 a share) to an investment broker in a debt-equity swap for $500,000 face amount of Ginger's 10% bonds maturing November 30, Year 8, which had been issued to yield 14%. The bonds paid interest on May 31 and November 30. Bond issue costs amounted to $20,000 on November 30, Year 4. Ginger amortized bond discount under the effective interest method.

Prepare a journal entry to record Ginger Ltd.'s debt-equity swap on November 30, Year 4. Disregard income taxes.

Ex. 15-12 On March 31, Year 7, Newland Corporation completed an in-substance defeasance of its $600,000-face-amount, 10% bonds due March 31, Year 15, which had been issued on March 31, Year 5, to yield 12%. The bonds, which paid interest March 31 and September 30, had a call price of 103 on March 31, Year 7. Newland amortizes bond discount under the effective interest method. Newland accomplished the in-substance defeasance by acquiring and placing in an irrevocable trust $600,000 face amount of riskless government bonds due March 31, Year 15, which had a nominal interest rate of 12% and a yield rate of 16% on March 31, Year 7. Interest payment dates for the 12% bonds were the same as those for Newland's 10% bonds. The trustee agreed to accept the semiannual interest differential of $6,000 as a fee for servicing Newland's 10% bonds. Bond issue costs may be disregarded.

a Compute Newland Corporation's gain on the in-substance defeasance of its 10% bonds on March 31, Year 7. Disregard income taxes.

b Compute the loss that Newland Corporation would have incurred had it called the 10% bonds at 103 on March 31, Year 7.

Ex. 15-13 On April 1, Year 8, Ardell Limited issued $1 million face amount of 10%, 10-year convertible bonds to yield 12% compounded semiannually. Ardell's investment brokers estimated that a 14% yield rate, compounded semiannually, would have applied had Ardell's bonds been nonconvertible. Bond issue costs may be disregarded.

a Prepare a journal entry to record Ardell Limited's issuance of 10% convertible bonds on April 1, Year 8, in accordance with generally accepted accounting principles, that is, with no value assigned to the conversion feature.

b Prepare a journal entry to record Ardell Limited's issuance of 10% convertible bonds on April 1, Year 8, assuming a value had been assigned to the conversion feature.

Ex. 15-14 On September 1, Year 1, Crosby Corporation issued for $198,000, $200,000 face amount of 12%, 20-year bonds, with interest payable March 1 and September 1. Each $1,000 bond had 10 detachable common stock warrants attached entitling the owner to acquire one share of Crosby's $10-par common stock for each warrant plus $20 cash. Shortly after issuance of the bonds, they were trading at 100 ex-warrants, and the warrants were trading at $10 each. Bond issue costs may be disregarded.

Prepare a journal entry to record Crosby Corporation's issuance of 12% bonds with detachable common stock warrants attached on September 1, Year 1.

Ex. 15-15 Cagle Corporation issued $1 million face amount, 9% bonds with detachable common stock warrants attached. The bonds were issued for $1,015,000. Immediately after issuance, the bonds were quoted ex-warrants at 96, and the warrants had a total market value of $90,000.

Prepare a journal entry to record Cagle Corporation's issuance of the bonds, assuming that no accrued interest was charged to acquirers of the bonds and that total proceeds were allocated on the basis of the relative market values of the bond and common stock warrants. Disregard bond issue costs.

CASES

Case 15-1 One method for a corporation to accomplish long-term debt financing is through the issuance of bonds.

Instructions

a Describe the accounting for the proceeds from bonds issued with detachable common stock warrants attached.

b Explain the differences between a serial bond and a term bond.

c For a five-year term bond issued at a premium, why does amortiation of the premium for the first year under the interest method differ from amortization under the straight-line method? Include in your discussion a statement as to whether premium amortization under the effective interest method is greater or less than amortization under the straight-line method for the first year.

d When bonds are issued at a discount between interest dates, what journal entry is prepared and how is the subsequent amortization of the discount affected? Include in your discussion an explanation of how the amount of each debit and credit item in the journal entry for issuance of the bonds is computed.

e Describe the presentation in the financial statement of a gain or loss from extinguishment of bonds payable.

Case 15-2 *a* One method of amortizing a premium or discount on bonds payable is the effective interest method.

Instructions

1 What is the effective interest method of amortization, and how is it different from and similar to the straight-line method of amortization?

2 How is amortization computed under the effective interest method, and why and how do amounts computed under the effective interest method differ from amounts computed under the straight-line method?

b Gains or losses from the extinguishment of bonds that are refunded may be accounted for in three ways:

- Amortized over the remaining term of the old bonds
- Amortized over the term of the new bonds
- Recognized in full in the accounting period of the refunding

Instructions

1 Discuss the supporting arguments for each of the three methods of accounting for gains and losses from the extinguishment of debt that is refunded.

2 How should the appropriate amount of gain or loss be reported in the income statement?

Case 15-3 The balance sheet of Noland Limited on December 31, Year 5, is shown on the next page.

The president of Noland believes that Noland is facing a serious financing problem, which she outlines for you as follows:

> We must raise approximately $50 million dollars over the next two years in order to finance the expansion of our product lines and sales territories. My banker friends tell me that our balance sheet is not in good shape. They have pointed out repeatedly that our current ratio (current assets divided by current liabilities) is significantly below the industry standard of 2 to 1 and that approximately 75% of our assets are financed by borrowed capital. They feel this is much too high, considering the type of industry we are in. We don't want to issue more common stock to the public, and apparently we can't issue additional bonds unless our balance sheet can be cleaned up. I wish we had paid more attention to the management of our assets: We have $15 million invested in low-yielding securities, our accounts receivable and inventories are twice as large as they ought to be, and we have been paying out too much in dividends. Our profits have been growing steadily, and we pay a dividend of $3 a share on our stock. As a result, our stock is trading at $55 a share and our bonds at 140 on the open market. I would appreciate your advice on this matter.

NOLAND LIMITED
Balance Sheet
December 31, Year 5
(In thousands of dollars)

Assets		
Current assets:		
Cash		$ 5,000
Short-term investments (at cost, market value $15.2 million)		15,000
Accounts receivable (net)		10,000
Inventories		24,000
Short-term prepayments		1,000
Total current assets		$ 55,000
Plant assets (net)		40,000
Other noncurrent assets		5,000
Total assets		$100,000
Liabilities & Shareholders' Equity		
Current liabilities		$ 35,000
12% bonds payable, callable at 105, each $1,000 bond convertible to 25 shares of common stock		40,000
Total liabilities		$ 75,000
Shareholders' equity:		
Common stock, no par value, 2,000,000 shares authorized, 1,000,000 shares issued and outstanding	$ 5,000	
Retained earnings	20,000	
Total shareholders' equity		25,000
Total liabilities & shareholders' equity		$100,000

Instructions

Briefly outline a course of action the president should follow in ''cleaning up'' the balance sheet of Noland Limited and raising the $50 million needed for expansion. Disregard the effects of income taxes in your answer.

Case 15-4 Olmo Limited was organized two years ago by two experienced business executives and several members of the faculty at a local university. The main product line of Olmo consists of medium-size computers and software for all types of data-processing and information systems. Olmo's assets total $15 million and the liabilities amount to $10.5 million, consisting of $3 million of short-term debt and $7.5 million of long-term notes payable to an insurance company. There are 100,000 shares of common stock issued and outstanding. In order to expand its activities, Olmo needs $5 million in long-term capital. Members of the board of directors have discussed various proposals for raising the capital and have asked for your advice regarding the following alternatives:

1 Issue bonds bearing interest at 13% with a sinking-fund provision.
2 Issue 10% bonds at face amount. The bonds would be convertible to 40,000 shares of Olmo's common stock at $125 a share. The current market price of the common stock is $96 a share.

3 Issue $9 preferred stock at $100 per share. The preferred stock would be callable at $105 a share and convertible to three-fourths of one share of common stock for one share of preferred.
4 Issue 60,000 shares of common stock at $85 a share through a rights offering. Shareholders would be given stock warrants for rights to acquire one additional share of common stock for every 10 shares held.

Instructions
Evaluate the advantages and disadvantages of each of the four alternatives proposed by Olmo Limited's board of directors.

Case 15-5 The directors of Miller Limited are considering the issuance of $15 million of bonds. Miller does not need the money immediately, but Director Alan, a former banker, has convinced the board that the bonds should be issued ''while interest rates are low and money is readily available.''

Director Krueger, partner of a leading investment firm, also recommended that bonds should be issued because interest rates are beginning to rise and a nominal rate of 12% probably would command a modest premium. However, Krueger believes that the directors are making a mistake in not considering the issuance of convertible debentures for the following reasons:
1 It would be cheaper for Miller (a rate of about 9% probably would be sufficient).
2 Miller's shareholders' equity will need ''beefing up'' as Miller continues to expand its operations.
3 It is essentially a means of issuing common stock at about 20% above the current market price.

Director Barney, vice president of finance, suggested that a 13% rate be assigned to nonconvertible bonds stating, ''A large premium is a sign of financial strength of our company; if interest rates continue to advance, 12% bonds will sell at a discount, and I don't want people thinking that our credit is so poor that we have to give a discount in order to sell our bonds.''

Director Carla, a public relations executive, disagreed with Director Barney. She stated that investors are ''bargain hunters'' who would be more willing to invest in bonds at a discount that at a premium. She would assign an 11% interest rate to the bonds, stating ''discount on bonds payable is prepaid interest, and it will not hurt us to get a jump on our interest payments to bondholders.''

Instructions
Evaluate the view expressed by each of the four directors of Miller Limited.

Case 15-6 Crowe Inc. recently issued $1 million face amount of 14%, 30-year subordinated debentures at 97. The debentures are callable at 103 on any date on 30 days notice, beginning 10 years after issuance. The debentures are convertible to no-par-value common stock of Crowe at the conversion price of $12.50 a share for each $500 (or multiple thereof) of the face amount of the debentures. Debenture issue costs may be disregarded.

Instructions

a Explain how the conversion feature of convertible debentures has a value (1) to the issuer, and (2) to the investor.

b Management of Crowe Inc. has suggested that in recording the issuance of the debentures a portion of the proceeds should be assigned to the conversion feature.

1 What are the financial accounting arguments for assigning a value to the conversion feature of the debentures?

2 What are the financial accounting arguments supporting accounting for the convertible debentures as a single element?

PROBLEMS

Pr. 15-1 On September 1, Year 1, Lingo Limited issued $1,000,000 face amount of 18%, 20-year bonds for $1,119,246, a 16% yield rate. Interest on the bonds was payable each March 1 and September 1. Bond issue costs of $50,000 were paid on September 1, Year 1. Lingo uses the effective interest method of amortization for bond premium.

Instructions

Prepare journal entries for Lingo Limited to record the issuance of the bonds and the payment of bond issue costs on September 1, Year 1, the payment of interest on March 1, Year 2, and the accrual of interest on August 31, Year 2, the end of the fiscal year. Lingo prepares adjusting entries only at the end of the fiscal year.

Pr. 15-2 The balance sheet of Wolfram Corporation on September 30, Year 11, included the following items:

14% bonds payable, due Sept. 30, Year 26, interest payable Mar. 31 and Sept. 30	$2,500,000
Discount on bonds payable, at 16% yield rate	281,445
Bond issue costs	36,000

Instructions

a Prepare journal entries to record the payment of bond interest by Wolfram Corporation on March 31, Year 12, and September 30, Year 12, assuming bond discount is amortized by the effective interest method. Amortization of bond issue costs is recorded on each interest payment date by the straight-line method.

b Prepare a working paper to compute the gain or loss on Wolfram Corporation's call (and extinguishment) of the 14% bonds at 102 on September 30, Year 12, the end of a fiscal year.

Pr. 15-3 On January 2, Year 4, Ruiz Inc. issued $1,000,000 of five-year, 9% serial bonds to be repaid in the amount of $200,000 on January 2, Year 5 through Year 9. Interest is payable at the end of each year. The bonds were issued to yield an annual rate of 10%. Bond issue costs may be disregarded.

Instructions

a Prepare a working paper to compute the proceeds received by Ruiz Inc. from the issuance of the serial bonds. Show supporting computations (rounded to the nearest dollar) and use the Appendix at the end of Chapter 5.

b Prepare a working paper for Ruiz Inc. for the amortization of the bond discount by the effective interest method for the full term of the bond issue. Show supporting computations, rounded to the nearest dollar.

Pr. 15-4 On December 1, Year 5, Windsor, Inc., issued 10-year bonds of $2 million at 102. Interest is payable on June 1 and December 1 at the rate of 12%. On April 1, Year 7, Windsor acquired in the open market 600 of these bonds at 96, plus accrued interest. The accounting period for Windsor ends on December 31. Bond issue costs may be disregarded.

Instructions

Prepare journal entries for Windsor, Inc., to record the following. (Round all amounts to the nearest dollar and disregard the effects of income taxes.)

a The issuance of the bonds on December 1, Year 5.

b Interest payments and amortization in Year 6. Amortization is recorded by the straight-line method at the time of interest payments and at the end of the calendar year. Windsor Inc., does not prepare reversing entries for the accrual of bond interest at the end of the calendar year.

c The extinguishment of $600,000 face amount of bonds on April 1, Year 7. ***Hint:*** First amortize premium for three months on the bonds retired, with a credit to Bond Interest Expense.

Pr. 15-5 On July 1, Year 1, Crimson Limited issued bonds with a face amount of $1,000,000 maturing in 10 years. The nominal interest rate was 10%, payable semiannually on June 30 and December 31. The bonds were issued to yield 12% compounded semiannually. Disregard bond issue costs.

On June 30, Year 2, Crimson issued $500,000 face amount of bonds with common stock warrants attached. These bonds had a nominal interest rate of 8%, payable semianually, and were issued at 105. One detachable warrant to acquire common stock was attached to each $1,000 bond. The current fair value of each bond without the warrant was $966. Disregard bond issue costs.

Instructions

a Using the Appendix at the end of Chapter 5, compute the amount of cash received by Crimson Limited for the 10% bonds issued on July 1, Year 1.

b Prepare journal entries for Crimson Limited to record the following:

1 Issuance of 10% bonds on July 1, Year 1

2 Payment of interest and amortization (under the effective interest method) on December 31, Year 1
3 Payment of interest and amortization (under the effective interest method) on June 30, Year 2

c Prepare a journal entry for Crimson Limited to record the issuance of the 8% bonds on June 30, Year 2.

Pr. 15-6 The balance sheet of Ergo Corporation on June 30, Year 5, included the following:

12% first mortgage bonds payable, maturing on June 30, Year 20	$20,000,000
Discount on bonds payable	600,000
Bond issue costs	132,000

Instructions

a Compute the annual interest expense for Ergo Corporation's first mortgage bonds payable. Interest expense includes amortization of bond issue costs. Straight-line amortization is used.

b Prepare a journal entry for Ergo Corporation to record the open market acquisition of $4 million of bonds at 105 on July 1, Year 10. Ergo's fiscal year ends on June 30. Disregard income taxes.

c Show three possible ways that the amounts relating to bonds payable can be presented in the balance sheet of Ergo Corporation on June 30, Year 15.

Pr. 15-7 On July 2, Year 5, Pons Limited issued $5 million of 9%, 20-year bonds with interest payable on March 1 and Septmber 1. Pons received proceeds of $5,120,500, including accrued interest from March 1, Year 5. Bond issue costs may be disregarded. The bonds mature on March 1, Year 25. On December 31, Year 5, Pons completed a debt-equity swap with an investment firm by issuing 100,000 shares of no-par common stock with a current fair value of $45 a share in exchange for the entire bond issue. The accrued interest was paid in cash.

Instructions

Prepare journal entries for Pons Limited on the following dates (disregard income taxes):

a July 2, Year 5 (issuance of bonds)

b September 1, Year 5 (payment of interest and amortization of discount for two months under the straight-line method)

c December 31, Year 5 (accrual of interest and amortization of discount from September 1 to December 31 and issuance of common stock in debt-equity swap)

Pr. 15-8 In July, Year 1, the board of directors of Noble Arms, Inc., authorized the issuance of $50 million of 10%, 20-year bonds payable. The bonds were dated September 1, Year 1, and interest was payable semiannually on March 1 and September 1. The bonds were issued to underwriters on September 1, Year 1. Noble Arms amortizes discount and premium under the effective interest method on each interest payment date and at the end of the accounting period. Bond issue costs may be disregarded.

Instructions

Prepare journal entries for Noble Arms, Inc., to record the issuance of the bonds, the adjusting entry on December 31, Year 1 (the close of the fiscal year), the journal entries to record the first two semiannual interest payments in Year 2, and the adjusting entry on December 31, Year 2, assuming that:

a The bonds were issued to the underwriters to yield 9%. (Use the Appendix at the end of Chapter 5 and round all computations to the nearest dollar.)

b The bonds were issued to the underwriters to yield 11%.

Pr. 15-9 Loredo Limited was authorized to issue $10 million of 10-year, 12% convertible bonds due December 31, Year 15. Each $1,000 bond is convertible to 40 shares of Loredo's no-par common stock, and the bond indenture contained an antidilution provision. The bonds were issued to underwriters on March 1, Year 6, for net proceeds of $10,129,200, including accrued interest. Interest is payable semiannually on June 30 and December 31. Discount is amortized by the straight-line method. Bond issue costs may be disregarded.

Late in Year 6, Loredo declared a 10% stock dividend on the common stock, and in Year 7 the common stock was split 2 for 1. The interest payments and the amortization of discount by the straight-line method were correctly recorded through December 31, Year 7. On May 1, Year 8, bonds with a face amount of $1,000,000 were converted, and the accrued interest on these bonds was paid.

Instructions

a Prepare a journal entry for Loredo Limited to record the issuance of bonds on March 1, Year 6. No value was assigned to the conversion feature of the bonds.

b Prepare a journal entry for Loredo Limited to record, for the first four months of Year 8, the payment of interest and the amortization of discount on the bonds converted on May 1, Year 8.

c Prepare a journal entry for Loredo Limited to record the conversion of $1,000,000 face amount of bonds on May 1, Year 8. (An antidilution provision in the bond indenture provides for a proportionate adjustment in the number of shares to which each bond may be converted if the common stock is split or if stock dividends are distributed.)

Pr. 15-10 Crosby Corporation issued $2 million of 11% serial bonds for $2,072,000 on January 2, Year 1. The bonds mature at the rate of $400,000 a year starting on December 31, Year 1. Interest is payable on June 30 and December 31. Bond issue costs may be disregarded.

Instructions

a Prepare a working paper for Crosby Corporation showing the amortization of the premium and total interest expense for each year through Year 5. Amortization is computed by the bonds outstanding method.

b On July 1, Year 2, $200,000 face amount of the bonds, which were ***scheduled***

to be retired on December 31, Year 4, were acquired by Crosby Corporation in the open market at 101. Prepare a journal entry for Crosby to record the extinguishment of the bonds, assuming that the amortization of the premium was recorded through June 30, Year 2, when the semiannual interest was paid.

Pr. 15-11 Rickert, Inc., issued $4 million face amount of three-year, 9% bonds. Interest is payable semiannually on June 30 and December 31. The bonds were issued on January 2, Year 1, at a price that gave Rickert an effective interest cost of 5% semiannually. Bond issue costs may be disregarded.

Instructions

a Compute the proceeds of Rickert's bond issue and prepare an amortization table, similar to that illustrated on page 742, showing the interest expense for each six-month period by the interest method. (Use the Appendix at the end of Chapter 5 and round all computations to the nearest dollar.)

b Using the data in the amortization table prepared in ***a*** prepare journal entries for Rickert, Inc., to record the issuance of the bonds, the interest payments at the end of the first six months and at the end of the last six months of the bond issue, and the extinguishment of the bonds at maturity on December 31, Year 3.

Pr. 15-12 Norbert Corporation issued $10 million of 10-year, 12% convertible bonds on September 30, Year 1, for $9,064,000, plus interest for three months. Bond issue costs of $23,400 were incurred and recorded in a separate ledger account. No value was assigned to the conversion feature. Interest is payable semiannually on June 30 and December 31. The bonds were callable after June 30, Year 6, and until June 30, Year 8, at 104, thereafter until maturity, at 102; and were convertible to no-par common stock as follows:

1 Until June 30, Year 6, at the rate of six shares for each $1,000 bond

2 From July 1, Year 6, to June 30, Year 9, at the rate of five shares for each $1,000 bond

3 After June 30, Year 9, at the rate of four shares for each $1,000 bond

The bonds mature on June 30, Year 11. Norbert prepares adjusting entries monthly and closes its accounting records yearly on December 31. Bond discount and bond issue costs are amortized on a straight-line basis.

The following transactions occurred in connection with the bonds:

Year 7

July 1 $2 million of bonds were converted to common stock.

Year 9

Jan. 1 $1 million of bonds were acquired in the open market at 98 and were extinguished.

June 30 The remaining $7 million of bonds were called for redemption. In order to obtain the necessary funds for redemption and business expansion, Norbert issued $12 million of 10% bonds at face amount. These bonds were dated May 31, Year 9, and were due on May 31, Year 29. Bond issue costs of $40,600 were paid.

Instructions

Prepare journal entries for Norbert Corporation to record the foregoing transactions, including monthly adjustments where appropriate, on each of the following dates. (Do not prepare closing entries, and include supporting computations as part of journal entry explanations.)

√*a* September 30, Year 1 (Record bond issue costs in a separate journal entry.)
b December 31, Year 1 (Record one month's interest and amortization in a separate journal entry before recording the payment of interest.)
c July 1, Year 7
d January 1, Year 9
e June 30, Year 9 (Record the accrual of interest and related amortization of discount and issue costs, the payment of interest, the redemption of $7 million of 12%, convertible bonds, and the issuance of $12 million of 10% bonds and payment of bond issue costs in separate journal entries.)

part four

SHAREHOLDERS' EQUITY

The accounting for assets and liabilities has a direct impact on the measurement of net income. In contrast, the accounting for shareholders' equity generally does not affect revenue and expense measurements.

Invested capital for a corporation is differentiated from earned capital, legal capital is differentiated from other sources of contributed surplus, and the portion of capital legally available for the declaration of dividends must be clearly identified. Legal requirements have a strong influence on generally accepted accounting principles for shareholders' equity.

Numerous forms of stock warrants, convertible securities, and employee capital accumulation plans currently are used by business corporations. Contraction of shareholders' equity through treasury stock acquisitions has become an important financial strategy in recent years. The accounting for treasury stock transactions and the computation of earnings per share also are included in Part Four.

c h a p t e r **16**

CAPITAL STOCK, CONTRIBUTED SURPLUS, RETAINED EARNINGS, AND DIVIDENDS

One of the striking features of our economy is the dominant role played by corporations. Corporations are responsible for the bulk of the national output of goods and services; they also are the principal source of employment, a major medium for the investment of capital, and a leading factor in the research and development activities that are so vital in keeping the economy growing and competitive in the world markets.

Efficiency of production and distribution in many industries requires more capital than can be obtained by a single proprietor or a partnership. The large amounts of capital needed for successful entry into many fields of business are most easily acquired by issuing shares of common stock to the public. Corporations have reached their dominant role largely because of their efficiency for the concentration of capital. Because most corporations have numerous shareholders who do not participate directly in management, complete accounting and internal control systems are of critical importance as a means of protecting the interests of absentee owners of corporate securities.

Several specific advantages of the corporate form of organization help explain why corporations are so successful in attracting capital. Among these advantages are the following:

1 ***Limited liability*** A shareholder has no personal liability for debts of the corporation. Creditors must look for payment only to the corporation itself and not to the personal resources of the owners. Freedom from personal liability is an important factor in encouraging investors to acquire common stock of corporations.

2 *Liquidity of investments in corporate securities* The owners of corporate securities (especially securities listed on stock exchanges) may sell all or part of their investment for cash at any time. The liquidity of corporate securities is a major reason for their popularity.

3 *Continuity of existence* A corporation is a separate legal entity with unlimited life, whereas a partnership may be terminated by the death or retirement of any partner.

4 *Separation of the functions of management and ownership* By attracting capital from a large number of investors and selecting management on a basis of executive ability, a corporation achieves expert direction of large amounts of economic and human resources.

Structure of the Corporation

Each of the 10 provinces has an act that governs the incorporation, the powers, and the dissolution of a business corporation. Usually, an organization that intends to conduct the majority of its business in one province will incorporate under the act of that province. Some provincial statutes use the letters patent system, supplemented by bylaws; other statutes use the memorandum of association process, which is supplemented by articles of association; and still others use the system required under federal incorporation involving articles of incorporation.

Organizations may be federally incorporated under the Canada Business Corporations Act (CBCA). Organizations that wish to carry on business in a number of provinces usually become federally incorporated. However, it should be noted that provincially incorporated companies may carry on business in other provinces, depending on licensing requirements in some instances.

There may be a number of instances in which provincial statutes differ from federal statutes. However, since the enactment of the CBCA in 1975, many provinces have begun to pattern their corporation legislation after the CBCA. Accordingly, in this book we will follow the CBCA, together with explanations of any major differences in a province's legislation, where applicable.

The CBCA requires that articles of incorporation be submitted to the Director of the Department of Consumer and Corporate Affairs. The CBCA stipulates what must be included in and with the articles of incorporation and, if the documentation is correct and complete, the Director ***must*** issue a certificate of incorporation. The Director has no discretionary powers as to whether to grant a certificate of incorporation. Incorporation under federal jurisdiction, and for some provinces, is a ***right***, not a privilege. When the certificate of incorporation is issued, the corporation becomes a legal entity, separate from its owners, and is treated in law as though it were a person. The shareholders' control over the corporation rests with their right to elect a board of directors, who in turn elect or appoint officers to manage the day-to-day affairs of the corporation. The shareholders meet at least annually to, among other things, review the activities of the corporation for the past year and elect the board of directors for the coming year.

The CBCA distinguishes among different share securities by class, for example, class A, B, or C. However, traditionally there have been two major classes of shares distinguished, namely common (residual ownership) shares and preferred (having some preference over common) shares. In this book the traditional nomenclature of common and preferred shares will be followed, as this practice is still embodied in provincial legislation.

In order to differentiate incorporated businesses from unincorporated businesses, the word ***Limited, Incorporated,*** or ***Corporation*** is used following the name of the business; the abbreviated forms and the French version of these words are also acceptable.

Elements of Corporate Capital

The word ***capital*** is used with a variety of meanings. Consequently, accountants have developed the following, more specific terms to describe important elements of corporate capital.

1 ***Contributed capital*** Contributed capital is that portion of the shareholders' equity that was invested or paid in by the shareholders, as opposed to capital arising from profitable operations. It includes legal capital and also contributed surplus where appropriate.

2 ***Legal capital*** Legal capital is that portion of the shareholders' equity that the statutes require to be held in the business for the protection of creditors, as opposed to capital that is available for the declaration of dividends to owners. It is the par value times the number of shares issued for shares with a par value. For no-par-value shares, it represents the proceeds from the issue.

3 ***Contributed surplus*** Contributed surplus represents amounts received from shareholders that are not a part of legal capital. It also represents capital received from others.

Shareholders' Equity of the Corporation

In the balance sheet of a single proprietorship, the owner's equity is shown as a single amount. For a partnership, the owner's equity of each partner is presented as a single amount, without any distinction between contributed capital and accumulated earnings. However, in the balance sheet of a corporation, a basic objective in reporting the shareholders' equity is to distinguish clearly between contributed capital and retained earnings.

Why should the shareholders' equity be subdivided? One reason is that shareholders and creditors need to know whether a corporation that pays dividends is distributing earnings or is returning invested capital. The owners of single proprietorships and partnerships may withdraw capital in any amounts they choose, even though such withdrawals may exceed earnings. In a corporation, however, only the accumulated earnings ordinarily are regarded as available for dividends. This view reflects corporate policy and desire for continuity of existence, as well as legal considerations. Consequently, accountants keep a clear distinction between contributed capital and retained earnings. The maintenance of these two separate categories of capital also is desirable because shareholders are absentee owners who do not participate directly in management. They may regard the active management of the corporation as custodians of the contributed capital and may judge the efficiency of management to some extent by the amount of earnings accumulated by the corporation.

Therefore, from the standpoint of accounting theory, it is necessary to distinguish total contributed capital from retained earnings. Any further classification of shareholders' equity usually rests on legal requirements rather than on accounting principles. The framers of corporation laws have attempted to protect creditors by creating the concept of ***legal capital***—an amount of shareholders' equity not subject to withdrawal. In recognition of these legal requirements, accountants customarily make a further classification of shareholders' equity by subdividing contributed capital between legal capital (capital stock) and other contributed capital (contributed surplus). Legal capital generally is not subject to withdrawal; contributed surplus may legally be available for dividends in some provinces, provided that shareholders are notified of the source of the dividends. Corporate financial policy is usually very cautious, and dividends from any source other than retained earnings are rare.

Components of Shareholders' Equity

The following components of shareholders' equity generally are used in the balance sheet:

1 Capital stock (legal capital)

2 Contributed surplus

3 Retained earnings (or deficit)

A subtotal titled ''contributed capital'' may be inserted in the shareholders' equity section of the balance sheet to show the aggregate of the capital stock and contributed surplus.

The question of ''appraisal capital'' has little practical importance because corporations generally have adhered to the cost principle of asset valuation. If any appreciation in the value of assets is included in the shareholders' equity, it should be shown separately and given a title such as ***unrealized appreciation from revaluation of assets*** or simply ***appraisal capital***.

Contributed Surplus

Contributed surplus comes principally from the following sources:[1]

1 Excess of proceeds from reissuance of treasury stock over the cost of the treasury stock

2 Reacquisition and cancellation, or redemption, of company stock at less than its issue price

1 Companies incorporated federally under the Canada Business Corporation Act subsequent to December 15, 1975, under the Ontario Business Corporation Act subsequent to July 29, 1983, and under the Corporation Acts of other provinces, have only no-par-value shares. Accordingly, items 5, 6, and 7 cannot arise from the issuance of such companies' common stock.

3 Donations of assets to the corporation by shareholders or others

4 Gain on forfeited shares

5 Excess of issuance proceeds over the par value of capital stock

6 Conversion of convertible bonds or preferred stock to common stock

7 Reduction of par value of capital stock

Although capital from all these sources may be combined into the single balance sheet item of contributed surplus, a separate ledger account is needed for each in order to carry out the principle of classifying shareholders' equity by source.[2]

Neither operating losses nor extraordinary losses should be debited to contributed surplus accounts. Examples of improper debits to contributed surplus accounts are the following:

1 Write-off of purchased goodwill

2 Write-down of plant assets that have lost usefulness because of obsolescence or unexpectedly rapid deterioration

3 Write-off of bond discount at the time of issuance of the bonds

4 Loss on sale of investments

The impropriety in all these situations is that contributed surplus is being used to absorb losses that should have been included in the income statement as deductions from revenue. If contributed surplus were to be debited for such losses, net income and retained earnings would be overstated.

Although acceptable debits to contributed surplus accounts are infrequent, they are warranted in such situations as the following:

1 Declaration of a liquidating dividend

2 Redemption of capital stock, originally issued for more than par, at a price in excess of par (For example, X Corporation redeemed at a call price of $104 a portion of its $100-par preferred stock originally issued at a price of $105. The $4-a-share ***redemption premium*** may be debited to premium on preferred shares in those jurisdictions where par-value stock issues are allowed.)

3 Absorption of a deficit as part of a reorganization

Retained Earnings

Retained earnings represents the accumulated net income of a corporation, minus amounts distributed to shareholders, amounts transferred to contributed capital accounts as a result of stock dividends, prior period adjustments, the cumulative effect of a change in accounting policy, and amounts for corrections of errors made in prior periods. Extraordinary gains and losses and operating revenue and

2 CICA, ***CICA Handbook*** (Toronto), sec. 3250.04.

expenses are included in the determination of net income, which is transferred to the Retained Earnings account. A negative amount (debit balance) in the Retained Earnings account is termed a *deficit*.

CONTRIBUTED CAPITAL

Rights Associated with Ownership of Capital Stock

If a corporation has only one class of capital stock, shareholders usually have certain basic rights to be exercised in proportion to the number of shares of capital stock they own. These rights include: (1) the right to vote for directors and thus to be represented by management, (2) the right to receive dividends declared by the board of directors, and (3) the right to share in the distribution of cash or other assets if the corporation is liquidated. Another right, which may be included in the incorporation documentation and which, therefore, is ***not*** a basic right, is the preemptive right to acquire additional shares of capital stock in proportion to present holdings in the event that the corporation increases the amount of capital stock outstanding.

Common Stock and Preferred Stock

When only one type of capital stock is issued, it has the basic rights described above and is called *common stock*. However, many corporations, in an effort to appeal to all types of investors, offer two or more classes of capital stock with different rights or priorities attached to each class. Stock that carries certain preferences over the common stock, such as a prior claim on dividends, is called *preferred stock*. Often a preferred stock has no voting rights, or only limited voting rights. The characteristics of preferred stocks vary widely among corporations; it is unwise, therefore, to assume that a preferred stock has any particular rights or priorities without positive determination of its status. The special rights of a particular preferred stock are set forth in the incorporation documentation and in the preferred stock certificates issued by the corporation.

When only one class of stock, that is, common stock, is issued by a corporation, it may be labelled "Capital Stock" in the ledger and in the balance sheet.

Class A and Class B Stock

Corporations that issue more than one class of capital stock may designate the various issues by letter, such as "Class A stock" and "Class B stock." In such cases one of the issues is common stock and the other issue has some preference or restriction of basic rights. To determine the significant characteristics of such capital stock, it is necessary to examine the incorporation documentation and stock certificates.

Characteristics of Preferred Stock

The following features are associated with most preferred stock issues:

1 Preference as to dividends at a stated amount or rate

2 Preference as to assets in the event of liquidation of the corporation

3 Callable at the option of the corporation

4 Absence of voting rights

A preference as to dividends does not give assurance that dividends will be paid; it signifies only that the stated dividend amount or rate applicable to the preferred stock must be paid before any dividends are paid on the common stock. Unlike interest on bonds and notes payable, dividends do not accrue. A liability to pay a dividend arises only when the board of directors declares a dividend. Any dividend action by the board must take into consideration (1) whether the corporation legally may pay a dividend and (2) whether the present cash position and future cash needs make it advisable to pay a dividend.

The annual dividend on no-par preferred stock is stated at a fixed dollar amount, such as ''$4.50 Cumulative Preferred Stock.'' For preferred stocks having a par value, the dividend rate can be stated either as a percentage of par value or as a fixed dollar amount.

Cumulative and Noncumulative Preferred Stock

Most preferred stocks have a cumulative provision as to dividends. If all or any part of the stated dividend on a cumulative preferred stock is not paid in a year, the unpaid portion ***accumulates*** and must be paid in a subsequent year ***before any dividend is paid on the common stock***.

A dividend is said to have been ***passed*** if the directors fail to declare a dividend on the established date for dividend action. Any omitted dividends on cumulative preferred stock constitute ***dividends in arrears***. The amount of preferred dividends in arrears is not a liability of the corporation, because no liability exists until the board of directors declares a dividend. However, no dividends may be declared on common stock until any dividends in arrears on preferred stock, as well as the current period's preferred dividend, have been paid. Thus, the amount of any dividends in arrears on preferred stock is important to investors and always is disclosed, usually in a note to the financial statements.

In the case of noncumulative preferred stocks, a dividend omitted or passed in one year is lost forever to shareholders. Because most investors refuse to acquire noncumulative preferred stocks, they seldom are issued.

As an illustration of the significance of dividends in arrears and the inherent weakness of a noncumulative preferred stock, assume that Garwood Corporation has three classes of capital stock as follows:

Three classes of capital stock issued by a corporation

$6 cumulative preferred stock, $100 stated value, issued and outstanding 20,000 shares	$2,000,000
$7 noncumulative second preferred stock, $100 stated value, issued and outstanding 20,000 shares	2,000,000
Common stock, no par value, issued and outstanding 200,000 shares	2,000,000

Assume also that operations of Garwood Corporation were unprofitable in Years 1, 2, and 3 and no dividends were declared during those three years.

In Year 4, however, a large net income was earned, and Garwood's directors decided on December 31, Year 4, that $900,000 should be distributed as dividends. Despite the equal amounts of capital represented by the three capital stock issues, the dividend payments favour the cumulative preferred stock and the common stock. The holders of the noncumulative second preferred stock receive relatively little, as illustrated below:

Distribution of dividends totalling $900,000 to three classes of capital stock

	$6 cumulative preferred stock	*$7 noncumulative second preferred stock*	*Common stock*
Dividends in arrears	$360,000 (1)		
Preferred dividends, current year	120,000 (2)	$140,000 (3)	
Remainder, to common stock			$280,000 (4)
Total dividends paid	$480,000	$140,000	$280,000

(1) (20,000 × $6) × 3 = $360,000
(2) (20,000 × $6) = $120,000
(3) (20,000 × $7) = $140,000
(4) $900,000 − ($480,000 + $140,000) = $280,000

Participating and Nonparticipating Preferred Stock

A preferred stock is ***nonparticipating*** unless the share certificate specifically provides for participation. Participating preferred stocks are rare. A ***fully participating*** preferred stock shares equally with the common stock in any dividends paid after the common stock has received a dividend at a rate (percentage or dollar amount per stated value amount) equal to the preference rate on the preferred stock. For example, assume that in the current year Lude Corporation declared the usual $10 dividend on its fully participating $100 stated value, no-par preferred stock and also declared a dividend of $10 a share on the $100 stated value, no-par common stock. If any additional dividend is declared on the common stock, a corresponding additional amount must be declared on the preferred stock. A ***partially participating*** preferred stock is one with a ceiling established limiting the extent to which it participates in dividends with the common stock.

Convertible Preferred Stock

Many corporations make their preferred stock attractive to investors by including a ***conversion option*** that entitles the shareholders to exchange their preferred stock for common stock in a stated ratio. The holders of convertible preferred stock have the advantage of a preferred claim on dividends and also the option of switching to common stock, which enjoys unlimited participation in dividends.

Preferred stock usually will be converted to common if the dividend rate on the common stock is increased. As long as the conversion option is open, the preferred shareholder gains the benefit of any increase in market price of the common stock without actual conversion, because market price of the preferred increases in proportion to any increase in the price of the common stock. It is sometimes said that the market prices of a common stock and the related convertible preferred stock are "in gear." The primary determinant of when to convert is the relative yields of the common and preferred stock at the prevailing market prices. In addition, consideration may be given to the greater assurance of continued dividend payments on the preferred stock. For some preferred stocks the conversion option expires after a specified number of years; for others the conversion period is unlimited; and in some cases the conversion terms are subject to change on specified future dates.

Redeemable Preferred Stock

Most preferred stock can be redeemed (called) ***at the option of the corporation***. The redemption (call) feature is advantageous to the corporation because the capital obtained through issuance of redeemable preferred stock is available as long as needed and can be repaid whenever the corporation desires. The ***redemption (call) price*** is specified in the preferred stock contract, and usually any dividends in arrears are paid when a cumulative preferred stock is redeemed.

If a convertible preferred stock is called for redemption, the holders of the stock have the option of converting to common stock rather than surrendering their investment in the corporation. As a result, the market price of outstanding convertible preferred stock tends to move with the price of the common stock even though this amount is well above the redemption price.

Retractable Preferred Stock

The holder of the preferred stock may require the issuing company to buy back its preferred stock, ***at the holder's option***. There is usually a specified price and a specified time at which this can be done.

Term-Preferred Shares

Shares that have the legal form of a preferred share, while at the same time also having many of the attributes of a debt security, are term-preferred shares. The combination of equity features and debt features raises the question as to whether such securities should be treated as debt or as equity for financial statement purposes. In July 1977 the Ontario Securities Commission issued ***Policy No. 3-35: Term-Preferred Shares: Disclosure in Financial Statements***. This policy required that such issues be clearly reported in financial statements pending CICA pronouncements in this area.

Subsequently, in December 1977, the Accounting Research Steering Committee issued ***Accounting Guideline on Term-Preferred Shares***, dealing with the appropriate classification and disclosure of such securities. The conclusion of the committee was that clear disclosure of the unique characteristics of the ***term-preferred shares*** ought to be made in the financial statements. Also, such shares would normally be included in the shareholders' equity, set out separately from other classes of share capital. In 1984, of 57 companies that disclosed the existence of term-preferred shares, 46 showed these shares separately under the shareholders' equity caption.[3]

3 CICA, ***Financial Reporting in Canada***, 16th ed. (Toronto: 1985), p. 165.

Liquidation Preference

Most preferred stocks have preference over common stocks as to assets in the event of liquidation of the corporation. The claims of creditors take preference over both preferred and common shareholders. The preference of a cumulative preferred stock as to assets usually includes any dividends in arrears in addition to the stated liquidation value. Not every preferred stock has a prior claim on assets; the status of the stock in the event of liquidation depends on the specific provisions of the preferred stock contract.

Is Preferred Stock Debt or Equity?

The preferred shareholder is in some respects more a creditor than an owner. Typically, the preferred shareholder provides capital to the corporation for an agreed rate of return and has no voice in management. If the corporation prospers, it probably will increase the dividend rate on its common stock, but it cannot consider increasing the dividend on preferred stock. Preferred stock generally has no maturity date, but the preferred shareholder's relationship with the corporation may be terminated if the corporation chooses to redeem the preferred stock.

Par-Value and No-Par-Value Stock

In the early history of Canadian companies all capital stock was required to have a par value, but now most provincial laws either require corporations to issue no-par-value stock or permit them to choose between par and no-par stock. Federally incorporated companies are required to have no-par capital stock.[4] A corporation which chooses to issue par-value capital stock can set the par at any amount desired, such as $1, $5, or $100 a share. If a corporation subsequently splits its stock, the par value of each share is reduced accordingly. In some instances, corporations have changed their authorized and issued capital stock from par-value to no-par-value.[5]

The par value of capital stock is the amount per share to be entered in the Capital Stock account. This portion of the value of assets originally invested in the corporation must be kept permanently in the enterprise. The par value thus signifies a ***cushion*** of ownership equity for the protection of creditors.

The par-value device originally was introduced for the protection of creditors, but it proved less effective than anticipated because the intent of the law could be circumvented by the issuance of capital stock in exchange for assets other than cash. In the era before rigorous security laws, large amounts of capital stock sometimes were issued for mining claims, patents, goodwill, and other assets of unproved value. These assets usually were recorded at the par value of the stock issued in exchange. This resulted in a gross overvaluation of assets and overstatement of shareholders' equity.

4 Canada Business Corporations Act, December 15, 1975, sec. 24(1).

5 Companies incorporated under federal jurisdiction prior to December 15, 1975, with par-value capital stock, were given until December 15, 1980, to change their shares to no-par shares. Consequently, federally incorporated companies do not now have par-value capital stock. Many provinces have subsequently enacted similar legislation.

To avoid this abuse of the par-value concept, most jurisdictions have enacted legislation either requiring or permitting corporations to issue capital stock without par value. It was argued that many investors had incorrectly assumed that any capital stock was worth as much as its par value, and that the use of no-par stock would force investors to consider more fundamental factors such as earnings, dividends, and current fair value of assets owned by the corporation.

The trend for corporations to set par values at quite low amounts, such as $1 or $5 a share, has lessened the effectiveness of the arguments against no-par stock and has reduced some of the significance attached to the term ***par value***. Further, the 1975 Canada Business Corporations Act, which did away with the concept of par value for capital stock, has significantly influenced many of the provinces.

When no-par stock is issued by federally incorporated companies, the credit to capital stock must be equal to the ***total*** of the proceeds of the issue. The act states:[6] ''a corporation shall add to the appropriate stated capital account the full amount of any consideration it receives for any shares it issues.'' This is regarded as the legal capital for such corporations. However, many other jurisdictions, and the federal jurisdiction prior to July 1, 1965, allowed the corporation's directors the opportunity to set aside, as ***distributable surplus***, up to 25% of the proceeds received on the issue of no-par shares. Such contributed surplus was not part of the legal capital (the cushion for creditors). Many federally incorporated companies still have an account ''Distributable Surplus'' in the shareholders' equity section of their published financial statements.

In some provinces, a form of no-par-value shares with a board of director's determined stated value on issue has been common in the past. The excess of proceeds over stated value (stated value going to the legal or stated capital account) formed a part of contributed surplus. The nomenclature of this contributed surplus account has been ''excess of issue price over stated value of common shares.''

In summary, common stock may be par-value or no-par-value stock. The issue of par-value stock at a price above par value results in a contributed surplus account — ''premium on common stock.'' The issue of no-par-value stock has in the past resulted in the addition of up to two contributed surplus accounts, namely:

1 ***Distributable Surplus*** This arose when directors were able to segregate up to 25% of the proceeds of the issue in this account, thereby resulting in legal capital 75% or more of the proceeds of the issue.

2 ***Excess of Issue Price over Stated Value of Common Stock*** This arose where directors were able to set a stated value on no-par-value stock.

Finally, under the CBCA and in many of the provinces currently, with the exception of non-arm's-length transactions, the entire proceeds of the issue must be included in legal or stated capital and, as a result, no contributed surplus account arises.

6 Canada Business Corporations Act, December 15, 1975, sec. 26(1.1).

Accounting for Capital Stock Transactions

A clear understanding of the following terms is necessary in accounting for capital stock transactions:

1 *Authorized capital stock* is the number of shares of capital stock which the company is authorized to issue. Typically, a company will obtain authorization for a much larger number of shares than it plans to issue in the foreseeable future. The securing of authority to issue shares of stock does not bring an asset into existence, nor does it give the corporation any capital. Authorization simply affords a legal opportunity to obtain assets through the issuance of stock. Consequently, authorization of capital stock does not constitute a transaction to be recorded in the accounting records. A notation of the event in the general journal and in the ledger account for capital stock is appropriate. The CBCA and many of the provinces require that the incorporation documentation shall set out "the classes and any maximum number of shares that the corporation is authorized to issue. . . . " As a result, many companies' authorized share capital consists of an unlimited number of both common and preferred shares.

2 *Issued capital stock* is the number of shares of authorized capital stock that have been issued to date. Issued capital stock includes treasury stock, as defined in **5** below.

3 *Unissued capital stock* describes the authorized shares of capital stock that have not been issued to investors.

4 *Outstanding capital stock* is the number of shares of authorized capital stock that have been issued and presently are held by shareholders.

5 *Treasury stock* is the corporation's own capital stock that had been issued, fully paid, and reacquired by the corporation but not cancelled. Treasury stock is included in issued capital stock as defined in **2** above, but is not part of outstanding capital stock as defined in **4** above.

6 *Subscriptions to capital stock* represent an asset, in the form of a receivable from investors who have promised to pay the subscription price at a future date.

7 *Subscribed capital stock* refers to authorized but unissued shares of capital stock that are earmarked for issuance under existing contracts with subscribers. The subscribed capital stock is issued when a subscription contract is collected in full. If financial statements are prepared between the date of obtaining capital stock subscriptions and the date of issuing the stock, the subscribed stock is included in the shareholders' equity section of the balance sheet.

Ledger Accounts for Capital Stock and Contributed Surplus

Investments of capital by shareholders usually require the use of two types of shareholders' equity accounts: (1) capital stock accounts and (2) contributed surplus accounts.

Capital Stock Accounts

A separate ledger account is used for each class of capital stock. The number of shares authorized may be recorded by a memorandum entry in the general journal and also may be indicated in the ledger accounts as shown below.

Capital stock accounts illustrated

8% Cumulative Preferred, $100 Par

Date	*Explanation*	*Debit*	*Credit*	*Balance*
Year 7 Oct. 1	Authorized 10,000 redeemable at $105 a share.			

Common Stock, No Par Value

Date	*Explanation*	*Debit*	*Credit*	*Balance*
Year 7 Oct. 1	Authorized 1,000,000 shares.			

Accounts for Contributed Surplus

Par-value capital stock often is issued at a price in excess of the par value. This excess is treated as contributed surplus and is credited to an account with a descriptive title indicating its source such as ''Premium on Preferred Stock'' or ''Premium on Common Stock.'' In the preparation of financial statements, it is not necessary to use the exact titles of the ledger accounts as long as the sources of capital are disclosed. For example, the contributed surplus indicated by the preceding account titles might appear in the balance sheet as shown below (amounts are assumed).

Contributed surplus in the balance sheet

Shareholders' equity:	
8% cumulative preferred stock $100 par (redeemable at $105 a share) authorized 10,000 shares, issued and outstanding 9,000 shares	$ 900,000
Common stock, no par value, authorized 1 million shares, issued and outstanding 600,000 shares	3,122,000
Contributed surplus:	
Premium on preferred shares	18,000
Total contributed capital	$4,040,000

Some accountants prefer to list the contributed surplus applicable to the preferred stock with the listing of preferred stock. Other accountants combine the various sources of contributed surplus under that name as a single caption. Other sources of contributed surplus (such as from treasury stock transactions) are discussed elsewhere in this chapter and in Chapters 17 and 18.

Journal Entries for Issuance of Capital Stock for Cash

The following journal entries illustrate issuance of the capital stocks summarized in the foregoing balance sheet:

Journal entries for issuance of preferred and common stock

Cash	918,000	
8% Cumulative Preferred Stock		900,000
Premium on Preferred Stock		18,000
To record issuance of 9,000 shares of $100-par cumulative preferred stock for $102 a share.		
Cash	3,122,000	
Common Stock		3,122,000
To record proceeds of issuance of 600,000 shares of no-par common stock.		

Discount on Par-Value Capital Stock

Most jurisdictions in Canada prohibit the issuance of capital stock at less than par value. In planning a par-value capital stock issue, a corporation can set the par value as low as it pleases. Because par value usually is set at an amount considerably below the issuance price, the question of discount on capital stock is no longer of much practical importance. The topic deserves brief consideration, however, because of its theoretical implications.

If par-value capital stock is issued at a price below par, the amount of the discount is debited to an account entitled ''Discount on Capital Stock,'' which would appear as a deduction (or negative element of contributed surplus) in the shareholders' equity section of the balance sheet. The discount on capital stock is carried in the accounting records as long as the related stock issue is outstanding, so that an accurate record of the original investment by shareholders is maintained, as shown on page 794 for preferred stock issued at a premium.

Issuance Price and Subsequent Market Price of Capital Stock

The preceding discussion of the issuance of par-value capital stock at prices above and below par raises a question as to how a corporation decides on the issuance price. For a new issue of capital stock, whether par-value or no-par value, the issuer usually sets an issuance price based on factors such as (1) the expected future earnings and dividends, (2) the financial condition and reputation of the issuer, and (3) the current conditions in the security markets. After capital stock has been issued, the subsequent market price at which it is traded among investors tends to reflect the progress and prospects of the issuer and factors such as the state of investor confidence and the general trend of the economy. The current market prices of capital stock generally bear no discernible relationship to par value or to original issuance price.

Subscriptions for Capital Stock

The preceding sections have illustrated the issuance of capital stock for cash. Sometimes capital stock is issued under a subscription contract requiring payment by subscribers on a later date. Generally, the stock certificates are not issued until the subscription price is collected in full.

The increase in assets caused by obtaining a stock subcription receivable is offset by an increase in shareholders' equity. The ledger acounts to be credited (in the case of par-value common stock) are Common Stock Subscribed and Premium on Common Stock. On a later date when the stock is issued, the Common Stock Subscribed ledger account is debited and the Common Stock account is credited. If financial statements are prepared between the obtaining of subscriptions and the issuance of the common stock, the Common Stock Subscribed account appears in the shareholders' equity section of the balance sheet.

Journal Entries

Assume that subscriptions are received for 10,000 shares of $10-par common stock at a price of $50 a share. The journal entry to record the subscriptions follows:

Journal entry to record subscriptions for common stock

Subscriptions Receivable: Common Stock (10,000 × $50)	500,000	
Common Stock Subscribed (10,000 × $10)		100,000
Premium on Common Stock		400,000
To record subscriptions for 10,000 shares of $10-par common stock at $50 a share.		

All subscribers paid one-half of the amounts due on their subscriptions. The journal entry to record the collection of the subscription is:

Collection of subscriptions

Cash ($500,000 × ½)	250,000	
Subscriptions Receivable: Common Stock		250,000
To record collection of one-half of subscriptions receivable.		

Subscribers paid the balance due on their subscriptions with the exception of one subscriber who had subscribed for 100 shares. The journal entries to record the collection of the subscriptions and the issuance of common stock are illustrated below:

Collection of subscriptions and issuance of common stock

Cash (9,900 × $25)	247,500	
Subscriptions Receivable: Common Stock		247,500
To record collection of balance due on subscriptions for 9,900 shares.		
Common Stock Subscribed (9,900 × $10)	99,000	
Common Stock, $10 par		99,000
To record issuance of 9,900 shares after collection of subscriptions in full.		

Defaults by Subscribers

If subscribers fail to pay all or part of their subscriptions, the disposition of the subscription contracts and of any amounts paid by the subscribers depends on the laws of the jurisdiction and the policies of the corporation. If no payment has been made by the subscribers and nothing can be collected from them, the corporation should reverse the journal entries that recorded the subscriptions. If the subscribers have made one or more partial payments prior to default, the entire amount paid in prior to default may be refunded. As an alternative, the amount refunded may be the amount paid in minus any costs and "loss" incurred by the corporation in reissuing the subscribed stock. Another possible alternative calls for amending the subscription contracts to permit the issuance of a reduced number of shares corresponding to the cash collected. Still another alternative calls for forfeiture by the subscribers of the amount paid prior to the default.

Default by a subscriber requires the writing-off of the outstanding subscription receivable; the journal entry also includes a debit to the Common Stock Subscribed ledger account and usually a debit to a contributed surplus account. If the corporation retains any amounts paid in on defaulted subscriptions without issuing common stock, this increase in contributed surplus may be credited to a separate ledger account with a title such as "Contributed Surplus from Defaults on Stock Subscriptions." For example, if the $2,500 (100 × $50 × ½ = $2,500) paid by the defaulting subscriber for 100 shares in the foregoing example is forfeited, the journal entry to record the forfeiture might be as follows:

Journal entry to record forfeiture by defaulting subscriber

Common Stock Subscribed (100 × $10)	1,000	
Premium on Common Stock (100 × $40)	4,000	
Subscriptions Receivable: Common Stock		2,500
Contributed Surplus from Defaults on Stock Subscriptions		2,500
To record forfeiture of $2,500 paid by subscriber for 100 shares of common stock.		

Nature of Stock Subscriptions Receivable

From the corporation's viewpoint, an amount receivable under a stock subscription contract generally is regarded as an asset (a special type of receivable). When there are many subscribers, the subscriptions receivable ledger account is a controlling account supported by a subsidiary ledger containing an account with each subscriber. In the balance sheet, the subscriptions receivable ledger account balance is included with the current assets, provided that early collection is anticipated.

Some accountants argue that stock subscriptions do not represent assets, and that they should be shown as contra items in the shareholders' equity section of the balance sheet. Under this view, stock subscriptions receivable are contrasted with ordinary trade receivables; and it is argued that the stock subscriptions are a dubious claim against the subscribers because the corporation has not delivered merchandise or rendered services to them. As a practical matter, stock subscriptions constitute valid legal claims and usually are collected in full.

Shareholders' Ledger and Stock Certificate Book

In addition to maintaining a ledger account for each class of capital stock, a corporation must maintain detailed subsidiary records showing the identity of shareholders. A ***shareholders' ledger*** contains a separate account for each shareholder showing the number of shares owned. The shareholders' ledger is maintained in number of shares of stock rather than in dollars. When a shareholder sells capital stock to another investor, no entry is necessary in the general journal, because the amount of capital stock outstanding remains unchanged. However, each of the shareholder's ledger accounts in the ***shareholders' ledger*** will be adjusted to reflect the sale and the purchase.

A ***stock certificate book*** also is needed to control the amount of capital stock outstanding. When a stock certificate is issued, the name of the owner and number of shares are listed on the certificate stub. When a shareholder sells capital stock, the original certificate is cancelled and attached to the stub, and a new certificate is issued to the new shareholder. The open stubs in the stock certificate book indicate the number of shares of capital stock outstanding. Most large corporations retain an independent ***stock registrar*** and ***transfer agent*** to control stock certificates and to maintain shareholders' ledgers. Such records are maintained by computers when the volume of transactions is large.

Issuance of Two Types of Securities as a Unit

Corporations sometimes offer preferred and common stock as a unit, with no indication of the issuance price of either security considered separately. Such unit offerings raise a question as to how the proceeds should be allocated between the two securities. The same question arises when a corporation issues two or more kinds of securities to acquire another business enterprise. For par-value shares the aggregate par value of preferred and common stock issued as a unit usually is less than the proceeds received. How should the proceeds received be allocated to the two securities? If either security is issued concurrently for cash, the market price of that security may be used as evidence of its value; the remainder of the proceeds is applicable to the other security. If both securities have market values, the proceeds received are allocated to the two securities based on the ***relative market values*** of the securities.

Capital Stock Issued in Exchange for Assets or Services

When capital stock is issued for assets other than cash, the current fair value of the assets or the current fair value of the stock, ***whichever is more clearly evident***, is used to record the assets received and the related amount of contributed capital. In the absence of an arm's-length sale of assets for cash, opinions may differ as to the current fair value of the assets received. Consequently, it is appropriate to consider how much the capital stock would have been issued for if offered for cash. The underlying reasoning is that the exchange of capital stock for assets essentially is the equivalent of issuing the stock for cash and using the cash to acquire the assets.

If the corporation's capital stock is actively traded, the price of the stock on the date of the exchange constitutes reliable evidence as to the values exchanged.

However, if stock sales are infrequent and small in amount, there is no assurance that the corporation could have issued a large block of stock for cash without forcing the price down.

Either treasury stock or previously unissued capital stock may be exchanged for assets. However, the cost of treasury stock used for this purpose does not constitute a proper basis of valuation for the exchange unless by chance the cost is equal to the current fair value of the stock.

The establishing of valuations for assets acquired in exchange for capital stock is the responsibility of the corporation's board of directors. The decisions of the board and the use of appraisals or other valuation techniques should be set forth in the corporate minutes. Under no circumstances should the recorded value of the capital stock issued in exchange for assets be regarded as the decisive factor in establishing the current fair value of the assets acquired by a corporation.

The valuation problem when a corporation issues capital stock for personal services parallels that described in Chapter 11 for the issuance of capital stock for plant assets. The current fair value of the services received is a proper basis of valuation, but the current fair value of the stock often is more clearly evident and also is acceptable for establishing the accounting basis for the transaction.

The *CICA Handbook* requires the disclosure of the details of shares issued directly or indirectly for services and for assets other than cash.[7]

Watered Stock and Secret Reserves

A corporation's common stock is said to be ***watered*** if the shareholders' equity is ***overstated*** because of an overstatement of assets or an understatement of liabilities. ***Watered stock*** usually relates to inflated asset values, and the most direct approach to eliminating ''water'' from a corporation's balance sheet is through writing down the overstated assets.

The existence of ***secret reserves*** in a corporation's balance sheet means that shareholders' equity is ***understated*** because assets are understated or liabilities are overstated. An understatement of shareholders' equity may be achieved by using inappropriate depreciation rates, by excessive provision for doubtful accounts, by recognizing capital expenditures as expenses, or by any similar action that understates assets or overstates liabilities. The deliberate creation of secret reserves is inconsistent with the maintenance of integrity in financial accounting.

Stock Splits

When the market price of a corporation's common stock reaches a high trading range such as $100 a share or more, the corporation may decide to split the stock. A stock split of, say, 3 for 1 of a stock trading at $150 a share causes the number of shares held by each shareholder to triple and should cause the market price to drop to approximately $50 a share.

A stock split causes no change in the total shareholders' equity and no change in contributed capital or retained earnings. The par value per share, or average

7 CICA, *CICA Handbook*, sec. 3240.04.

value per share for no-par-value shares, of common stock is reduced in proportion to the increase in number of shares. For example, in a 4-for-1 split of $10-par common stock, the new stock has a par value of $2.50. For no-par-value common stock issued at an average price of $10 per share, the new stock will have an average price of $2.50 per share.

Because the only ledger account affected by a stock split is the Common Stock account, the stock split may be recorded in a memorandum entry. Alternatively, a journal entry such as the following may be made to record the reduction in par value per share and the increase in the number of outstanding shares:

Journal entry for a stock split

Common Stock, $10 par	10,000,000	
Common Stock, $2.50 par		10,000,000
To record a 4-for-1 stock split carried out by reducing par value from $10 to $2.50 a share.		

A ***reverse stock split***, as the name suggests, is the opposite of a stock split. The number of outstanding shares of common stock is reduced proportionately for all shareholders. For example, the outstanding common stock might be reduced from 3 million shares to 300,000 shares in a 1-for-10 reverse stock split. All shareholders would surrender their stock certificates in exchange for one-tenth as many new shares. A reverse stock split does not affect the assets or liabilities of the corporation and, therefore, does not change the shareholders' equity. Reverse stock splits are rare and usually are effected only by corporations with common stock that has dropped in market price to an extremely low level. A reverse stock split tends to increase the market price per share in inverse proportion to the reduction in number of shares outstanding.

RETAINED EARNINGS

The illustration below indicates the debits and credits entered in the Retained Earnings ledger account:

Composition of typical Retained Earnings ledger account

Retained Earnings	
Net loss	Net income
Dividends declared	Prior period adjustments
Prior period adjustments	

As explained in Chapter 3 (pages 129–130), generally accepted accounting principles require that extraordinary items be included in the determination of net income rather than being entered directly in retained earnings. ***Prior period adjustments*** are entered directly in the Retained Earnings ledger account and are not included in the determination of net income.

Prior period adjustments do not include normal recurring corrections and adjustments arising from the use of estimates in the accounting process. Thus, changes in depreciation rates because of revised estimates of economic lives of plant assets are not prior period adjustments; they are reflected in operations of the current and future accounting periods.

After listing the principal components of retained earnings, it may be useful to mention a few items that ***do not*** belong in retained earnings. These are:

1 Treasury stock transactions that result in a ''gain''

2 Donations of assets

3 Increases in shareholders' equity resulting from write-ups of plant assets to current fair values in excess of carrying amounts.

Let us consider briefly why each of these items does not belong in retained earnings. The reissuance of treasury stock at an amount in excess of cost increases contributed surplus. The receipt of donated assets is not a source of earnings and is recorded in a separate contributed surplus account such as Donated Capital. Increases in the carrying amounts of plant assets, if recorded at all, produce unrealized increases in shareholders' equity and require separate classification; to include such increases in retained earnings would suggest that they are realized and available for dividends.

Restrictions on Retained Earnings

The board of directors of a corporation may restrict or appropriate a portion of the retained earnings by transfer to a separate ledger account. For example, appropriations of retained earnings (sometimes called ***reserves***) may be made for expansion of plant, retirements of bonds, redemption of preferred stock, and general business contingencies. Although the practice of appropriating retained earnings is not widely followed, the CICA sanctions it in ***Section 3260*** of the ***Handbook***.[8] An appropriation of retained earnings is recorded as follows (amount is assumed):

Retained Earnings	100,000	
Retained Earnings Appropriated for Plant Expansion		100,000
To record appropriation of retained earnings under resolution of board of directors.		

A portion of retained earnings may be restricted and thus not available as a basis for dividend declaration for a variety of legal, contractual, or discretionary reasons. Disclosure of such a restriction may be made in a note to the financial statements, or by establishing an appropriation of retained earnings. An example of a note disclosure follows:

> The company's articles of incorporation and credit agreements with commercial banks contain restrictions limiting the payment of cash dividends. Retained earnings of $30 million dollars on December 31, 19—, are free of such restrictions.

8 CICA, ***CICA Handbook***, sec. 3260.01.

DIVIDENDS

Cash Dividends

The usual meaning of ***dividend*** is a distribution of assets to shareholders in proportion to the number of shares of capital stock owned. The term ***dividend,*** when used by itself, generally means a cash dividend; this usage is followed throughout this book. The ratio of cash dividends declared to current net income is termed the ***dividend payout ratio***. Corporations frequently distribute additional shares of their common stock to shareholders as ***stock dividends***. Strictly speaking, a stock dividend is not a dividend at all because no assets are distributed to shareholders. However, stock dividends are of considerable practical importance and raise some challenging accounting questions that are discussed in a later section of this chapter.

No obligation to pay a dividend exists until the board of directors formally declares a dividend. Dividend action by the board consists of a resolution specifying the following information:

1 Date of declaration

2 Date of record

3 Date of payment

4 Amount per share

On the ***date of declaration*** of a cash dividend, the appropriate journal entry is a debit to Dividends (or directly to the Retained Earnings ledger account) and a credit to Dividends Payable, a current liability. When the Dividends ledger account is used, it is closed to Retained Earnings at the end of the accounting period. If the corporation has both common and preferred stock, a separate Dividends ledger account may be used for each (for example, Dividends: Common Stock and Dividends: Preferred Stock).

The ***date of record*** is specified in the dividend declaration and usually follows the date of declaration by a few weeks. To qualify for the dividend, a person must be listed as a shareholder in the corporation's shareholders' ledger on the date of record. Capital stocks of corporations listed on the stock exchanges trade ***ex-dividend*** five business days before the date of record, thus facilitating compilation of the list of owners on the record date. An investor who acquires capital stock before the ex-dividend date is entitled to receive the dividend; conversely, a shareholder who sells capital stock before the ex-dividend date is selling the right to receive the dividend that has been declared as well as the shares of stock.

The ***date of payment*** of a dividend usually is set for a few weeks after the date of record. Payment is recorded by a debit to Dividends Payable and a credit to Cash.

The ***amount per share*** may be stated as, for example, ''regular quarterly dividend of $0.25 a share,'' or as an ''extra year-end dividend of $1 a share.''

As indicated in the preceding discussion, general requirements for declaration and payment of a cash dividend include (1) existence of retained earnings, (2) an adequate cash position, and (3) action by the board of directors. As protection for creditors, corporation laws generally place various other restrictions on the declaration of dividends.

Dividends Paid in the Form of Nonmonetary Assets

Most dividends are in cash, but occasionally a corporation may declare a dividend in the form of merchandise or other nonmonetary assets, such as securities of another corporation held as a short-term or long-term investment. When such ***nonmonetary*** dividends are declared, the ***current fair value*** (not the ***carrying amount***) of the nonmonetary asset distributed is the appropriate amount to be recorded as a dividend. Similarly, shareholders record the receipt of the nonmonetary dividend at the current fair value of the asset received.

If the current fair value of the nonmonetary asset distributed is not objectively measurable at the time of the distribution, the only feasible alternative may be to record the dividend at the carrying amount of the nonmonetary asset.

To illustrate the accounting for a dividend paid in the form of a nonmonetary asset, assume that Dover Corporation owns 10% of the common stock of Lange Limited with a carrying amount of $400,000 in the accounting records of Dover. On December 31, Year 10, when the current fair value of this long-term investment is $750,000, the board of directors of Dover authorizes the distribution of the Lange common stock as a dividend to the shareholders of Dover. The journal entries for Dover to record the declaration and distribution of this nonmonetary dividend are as follows:

Journal entries for nonmonetary dividend

Dividends (or Retained Earnings)	750,000	
Dividend Payable in Common Stock of Lange Limited		750,000
To record declaration of nonmonetary dividend.		
Dividend Payable in Common Stock of Lange Limited	750,000	
Investment in Lange Limited Common Stock ...		400,000
Gain on Disposal of Investments		350,000
To record payment of nonmonetary dividend.		

It would be possible for Dover to record the gain on the investment in common stock of Lange before the declaration of the nonmonetary dividend is recorded. This procedure might be followed to avoid recording a liability in excess of the carrying amount of the asset that will be used to liquidate the dividend liability. If a balance sheet is prepared for Dover after the declaration but before the distribution of the nonmonetary dividend, the asset to be distributed is classified as a current asset because the dividend payable is a current liability.

Liquidating Dividends

The term ***liquidating dividend*** may be used in the following situations:

1 A pro rata distribution of assets to shareholders that reduces contributed surplus rather than retained earnings

2 A pro rata distribution to shareholders by a corporation having wasting assets such as mineral deposits or timberlands, representing a return of invested capital

3 A pro rata distribution to shareholders when a corporation is liquidated

A liquidating dividend may be recorded as a debit to a specific contributed surplus ledger account or to a separate account such as Liquidating Dividend Distributed. Any balance in this account is deducted from total contributed surplus in the balance sheet.

Corporations generally must inform their shareholders when a dividend, or a portion of a dividend, represents a return of invested capital. Liquidation dividends are recorded by shareholders as reductions in the cost of their investment rather than as revenue, as illustrated on pages 647–648 in Chapter 14.

A spin-off is closely related to a liquidating dividend, except that a spin-off may involve a reduction in retained earnings. A ***spin-off*** is a transfer by a corporation of selected assets to a new corporation in exchange for its capital stock, which then is distributed pro rata to shareholders of the first corporation.

Generally, ***a gain is not recognized on a distribution of a liquidating dividend or on a transfer of assets to a new corporation in a spin-off, but a loss is recognized.*** This is so because ***the recorded amount (after reduction, if appropriate, for an indicated impairment of value)*** of the nonmonetary assets distributed is used in accounting for the liquidating dividend.

A distribution to shareholders of common stock of an investee that has been accounted for under the equity method is considered a spin-off. Thus, no gain is recognized pursuant to such a distribution.

Stock Dividends

Many corporations distribute stock dividends to their shareholders. A ***stock dividend*** is a distribution of additional shares of capital stock, called ***dividend shares***, to shareholders in proportion to their existing holdings. ''Common on common'' is the usual type of stock dividend; such a distribution is known as an ***ordinary stock dividend***, and is assumed in the discussion that follows. When a stock dividend is declared, Retained Earnings (or Stock Dividends) is debited and Common Stock — and possibly a contributed surplus account — is credited.

Distribution of a stock dividend causes no change in the assets or liabilities of a corporation; the only effect is a transfer between shareholders' equity ledger accounts. Because there is no decrease in the net assets of the corporation, a stock dividend does not give shareholders anything they did not have before. The number of shares of common stock held by each shareholder is increased, but each share represents a smaller equity in the corporation.

The principal argument for stock dividends is that they enable a ''growth company'' to retain accumulated earnings, yet provide the shareholders with additional shares of common stock as evidence of the growth in the net assets of the corporation. Most shareholders view stock dividends as distributions of corporate earnings in an amount equal to the market value of the dividend shares received. Such a view is strengthened by the fact that small stock dividends often do not cause a decline in the market price of the common stock, and the ***total*** market value of the original common stock often remains unchanged.

Securities that are convertible to common stock (such as convertible bonds and convertible preferred stock) contain an ***antidilution clause*** that requires ***adjustment of the conversion ratio*** to compensate for the ''reduced size'' of a share of

common stock after a stock dividend or a stock split. If, for example, a preferred stock is convertible to three shares of common stock, the conversion ratio is increased to 3.3 shares after a 10% stock dividend on the common stock, and to 6.6 shares after a 10% stock dividend that is followed by a 2-for-1 split.

Accounting for Stock Dividends

What amount of retained earnings should be transferred to Common Stock and possibly a contributed surplus ledger account for each share of common stock issued as a stock dividend? Although the *CICA Handbook* is silent in this area, in the United States generally accepted accounting principles for small stock dividends require the transfer of an amount equal to the *market price per share* prior to the dividend. Both the SEC and the AICPA support the use of market price as a measure of the amount of retained earnings transferred to contributed capital (the combination of capital stock and contributed surplus accounts) for all stock dividends that increase the number of outstanding shares of common stock by less than 20 or 25%. For larger stock dividends, only the par or average value per share is transferred from retained earnings to contributed capital. The reasons underlying this difference in treatment of small and large stock dividends in the United States are explained in the following sections.

Small Stock Dividends

The AICPA has suggested 20 or 25% as a dividing line between *large* and *small* stock dividends. Above this amount it may be assumed that the purpose of the common stock distribution is to reduce the market price of the common stock, as in the case of a stock split. Below this level it may be assumed that the dividend shares will be regarded by most shareholders as a distribution of earnings.

Large Stock Dividends

A large stock dividend, such as one increasing the number of outstanding shares of common stock by 25% or more, may cause a material decrease in the market price per share of common stock. Such dividends are in the nature of stock splits. In other words, the amount of retained earnings transferred to contributed capital pursuant to a large stock dividend is an amount equal to the aggregate par or average value of the dividend shares. The following somewhat extreme example illustrates the probable reaction to a large stock dividend by a shareholder. Assume that shareholder A owns 10 shares of $10-par common stock of Bragg Limited, with a current market price of $150 a share. Bragg distributed a 100% stock dividend, and the market price of its common stock promptly dropped to approximately $75 a share. Shareholder A no doubt will recognize that the so-called ''stock dividend'' is not a distribution of earnings but is similar to a 2-for-1 split.

Corporations should avoid the use of the word ''dividend'' in notices relating to large stock dividends that reduce materially the market price per share of outstanding common stock. If legal considerations require use of the word ''dividend,'' the transaction might be described as a ***stock split effected in the form of a stock dividend***.

Illustrative Journal Entries for Stock Dividends on Par-Value Common Stock
Assume that Rosen Limited has 1 million authorized shares of $5-par common stock, of which 500,000 shares are outstanding. The market price is $80 a share, and a quarterly cash dividend of 50 cents has been paid for several years. Current earnings are large and increasing annually, but Rosen plans to conserve cash for expansion of plant assets. Thus, the board of directors decides to issue a 2% stock dividend rather than to increase the current annual cash dividend of $2 a share. A journal entry ***summarizing both the declaration and the distribution*** of the 2% stock dividend is presented below to emphasize the end results of the stock dividend:

Condensed journal entry for declaration and distribution of small stock dividend for par value common stock

Retained Earnings [(500,000 × 0.02) × $80]	800,000	
Common Stock, $5 par (10,000 × $5)		50,000
Premium on Common Stock from Common Stock Dividends		750,000
To record the declaration and distribution of a 2% common stock dividend consisting of 10,000 shares of $5-par common stock with a market price of $80 a share on the declaration date.		

The foregoing illustration of a journal entry for a small stock dividend could appear as ***three separate journal entries***. The first entry would record declaration of the stock dividend by a debit to Common Stock Dividends for the market value of the shares to be issued, a credit to Common Stock Dividends to Be Distributed for the par value of the dividend shares, and a credit to Premium on Common Stock from Common Stock Dividends for the excess of the market value over the par value of the shares to be issued. The second journal entry would record issuance of the shares by a debit to Common Stock Dividends to Be Distributed and a credit to Common Stock. At the end of the year, the Common Stock Dividends ledger account is closed to Retained Earnings. If a balance sheet is prepared between the date of declaration of the stock dividend and the date of distribution, the account Common Stock Dividends to Be Distributed is included in shareholders' equity below common stock.

Illustrative Journal Entries for Stock Dividends on No-Par Common Stock
In this case, Rosen Limited has 1 million authorized no-par shares of common stock. All other data, presented above, are unchanged. The journal entry summarizing the declaration and the distribution of the 2% stock dividend follows:

Condensed journal entry for declaration and distribution of small stock dividend for no-par common stock

Retained Earnings	800,000	
Common Stock, no par value		800,000
To record the declaration and distribution of a 2% common stock dividend consisting of 10,000 shares of no-par common stock with a market price of $80 a share on the declaration date.		

In the no-par example, the first entry (of the three separate journal entries) would record the declaration of the stock dividend by a debit to Common Stock Dividends for the market value of the shares to be issued, and a credit to Common Stock Dividends to be Distributed for the market value of the shares to be issued. The second and third journal entries would be to the same accounts as in the par example. However, the amount credited to Common Stock in the second journal entry would be $800,000 [(500,000 × 0.02) × $80] instead of $50,000 [(500,000 × 0.02) × $5 par value].

If Rosen Company had declared and distributed a large stock dividend, say 50%, for the $5-par-value common stock example the following journal entry would be required:

Condensed journal entry for declaration and distribution of large stock dividend for par-value common stock

Retained Earnings [(500,000 × 0.50) × $5]	1,250,000	
Common Stock, $5 par		1,250,000
To record the declaration and distribution of a 50% common stock dividend consisting of 250,000 shares of $5-par common stock.		

Assume the common stock was no-par-value common shares and that the 500,000 outstanding shares had been issued for an aggregate amount of $4,800,000. The average value per common share would be $9.60 ($4,800,000 ÷ 500,000). The 50% stock dividend would require the following journal entry:

Condensed journal entry for declaration and distribution of large stock dividend for no-par common stock

Retained Earnings (500,000 × 0.50) × $9.60	2,400,000	
Common Stock, no par value		2,400,000
To record the declaration of a 50% common stock dividend consisting of 250,000 shares of no-par common stock with an average value of $9.60 per share.		

Fractional Shares

When a small stock dividend is declared, shareholders owning only a few shares of common stock are entitled to receive only a fraction of a share. For example, in the foregoing illustration of a 2% stock dividend declared by Rosen Limited, the holder of less than 50 shares of common stock is entitled to only a fraction of a share. To avoid the inconvenience of issuing fractional shares, most corporations offer shareholders the alternative of receiving in cash the market value of the fraction of a share due, or of paying sufficient cash to the corporation to qualify for a full share of common stock.

Business Combinations — Purchase Versus Pooling of Interests

In recent years many corporations have been combined to obtain the economies of large-scale operation and the financial strength arising from diversification in various industries. Business combinations may be accounted for by the purchase method or by the pooling-of-interest method, according to the circumstances. Our purpose at this point is to call attention to the difference in impact on shareholders' equity of the ***purchase method*** and the ***pooling-of-interests method*** of accounting for business combinations. In a ***purchase***, the outstanding common stock of the acquired corporation usually is paid for in cash or through issuance of debt securities; in a ***pooling***, the outstanding common stock of another corporation is acquired by issuance of common stock.

When a business combination is accounted for as a ***purchase***, the acquiring corporation records its investment at the cost established by cash paid or current fair value of shares issued in exchange for outstanding common stock of the acquired corporation. ***The shareholders' equity of the corporation acquired does not become part of combined shareholders' equity***. Revenue and expenses of the two corporations are combined only from the date of the business combination.

In contrast, when a business combination is accounted for as a ***pooling of interests***, the net assets of the two corporations are combined at their carrying amounts. The current fair values of the common stock issued and of net assets acquired are disregarded. The pooling-of-interests method of accounting rests on an assumption of continuity of ownership, and the ***shareholders' equity of the two corporations generally are added together to measure the amount of shareholders' equity of the combined enterprise***. The net income of the combined enterprise includes revenue and expenses of both corporations for the entire year in which the business combination occurred.

Reorganizations of Financial Structure

A reorganization (***quasi-reorganization***) occurs when a corporation in financial difficulties modifies its capital structure without being forced to do so by creditors and without coming under the supervision of a bankruptcy court.[9]

Typically, such a reorganization involves writing off a deficit against additional contributed capital; sometimes there is a reduction in the par or average value of common stock and a write-down of overvalued assets. Following a quasi-reorganization, the corporation is considered from an accounting standpoint to have a ***fresh start***, and the way is cleared for reporting net income and declaring dividends in future years. Although the write-down of assets and the elimination of a deficit obscure historically significant data, the procedure is generally accepted because it results in more relevant asset values. Furthermore, a quasi-reorganization may help a corporation to regain its place as a profitable business enterprise without the stigma that attaches to a large deficit, continuous operating losses, and inability to declare cash dividends.

Sequence of Procedures in a Reorganization

A reorganization (quasi-reorganization) typically involves the following procedures:

1 After shareholders approve the reorganization, assets that are considered to be overstated are written down to current fair value by a debit to Retained

9 The prefix *quasi-* means resembling or seemingly, but not actually. Thus, a quasi-reorganization resembles, but is not, a formal type of corporate reorganization.

Earnings. If the current fair value of any asset exceeds its carrying amount, the carrying amount of such an asset is increased with a corresponding amount being credited to an appraisal increase credit account.[10]

2 The deficit in retained earnings following the asset write-downs is eliminated against contributed surplus. Gains or losses realized subsequent to the quasi-reorganization that are attributable to the period prior to the quasi-reorganization are recorded as increases or decreases in contributed surplus.

3 If contributed surplus at the time of the quasi-reorganization is insufficient to absorb the deficit, the par or average value of common stock is reduced accordingly.

4 Retained earnings following a quasi-reorganization must be identified (dated), for a period of at least three years.[11] In subsequent balance sheets, this disclosure, called ***dating the retained earnings***, may appear as follows:

"Dating retained earnings" subsequent to a reorganization

Retained earnings accumulated since June 30, Year 8, when a deficit of $4,202,000 was written off against contributed surplus as part of a reorganization	$1,917,400

Illustration of a Reorganization

To illustrate the accounting for a reorganization (quasi-reorganization) assume that Lumen Corporation acquired another enterprise's identifiable net assets and goodwill at substantial costs, and that several years of unprofitable operations resulted in the balance sheet at the top of page 810.

The existence of the $1,600,000 deficit and the substantial carrying amount of plant assets and goodwill make it impossible for Lumen to report earnings or to pay dividends. To overcome these obstacles, let us assume that management proposes to effect a quasi-reorganization on December 31, Year 15, as follows:

1 The carrying amount of plant assets is to be reduced by $2,100,000, consisting of a $4,000,000 reduction in cost and a $1,900,000 reduction in accumulated depreciation; in addition, the entire goodwill of $1,000,000 is to be written off, thus increasing the amount of the deficit from $1,600,000 to $4,700,000 ($1,600,000 + $2,100,000 + $1,000,000 = $4,700,000).

2 The contributed surplus is to be reduced from $200,000 to zero, and the deficit is to be reduced by a like amount.

3 The balance of the deficit of $4,500,000 is to be written off against common stock, resulting in a zero balance in the Retained Earnings ledger account and a $6,500,000 balance in the common stock account.

10 CICA, *CICA Handbook*, secs. 3060.01 and 3270.01.

11 CICA, *CICA Handbook*, sec. 3250.12.

LUMEN CORPORATION
Balance Sheet
December 31, Year 15

Assets		
Current assets		$ 6,200,000
Plant assets	$12,500,000	
Less: Accumulated depreciation	5,700,000	6,800,000
Goodwill (net)		1,000,000
Total assets		$14,000,000
Liabilities & Shareholders' Equity		
Liabilities:		
Current liabilities		$ 3,900,000
Long-term debt		500,000
Total liabilities		$ 4,400,000
Shareholders' equity:		
Common stock, no par value	$11,000,000	
Contributed surplus	200,000	
Total contributed capital	$11,200,000	
Retained earnings (deficit)	(1,600,000)	9,600,000
Total liabilities & shareholders' equity		$14,000,000

The journal entries to record the reorganization of Lumen Corporation on December 31, Year 15, are as follows:

Journal entries for reorganization

Retained Earnings	3,100,000	
Accumulated Depreciation	1,900,000	
Plant Assets		4,000,000
Goodwill (net)		1,000,000
To write down carrying amount of plant assets and goodwill as part of reorganization.		
Contributed Surplus	200,000	
Common Stock	4,500,000	
Retained Earnings		4,700,000
To eliminate deficit as part of reorganization.		

Any retained earnings accumulated after December 31, Year 15, are available as a basis for dividend declaration and are dated in balance sheets following the reorganization. For example, assume that Lumen Corporation reported net income of $375,000 and declared cash dividends of $125,000 in Year 16: the shareholders' equity section of Lumen's balance sheet on December 31, Year 16, would be as follows:

Shareholders' equity one year after reorganization

Shareholders' equity:	
Common stock, no par value	$6,500,000
Retained earnings, accumulated since Dec. 31, Year 15, at which time a deficit of $4,700,000 was written off against common stock	

in the amount of $4,500,000 and contributed surplus in the amount of $200,000 as part of a reorganization	250,000
Total shareholders' equity	$6,750,000

REVIEW QUESTIONS

1 Why do corporations often issue two or more types of capital stock?

2 What are the basic rights inherent in the ownership of capital stock? What modification of these basic rights usually is found in preferred stock?

3 If a corporation with cumulative preferred stock outstanding fails to declare any dividend during a year, what disclosure is made in a note to the financial statements?

4 What is ***redeemable preferred stock***?

5 Distinguish between a ***conversion provision*** in a preferred stock and a ***call provision***. May a preferred stock be both convertible and callable? If so, may both provisions be exercised?

6 In what respects does the status of preferred shareholders resemble that of bondholders rather than common shareholders? How does preferred stock differ from bonds payable?

7 For what purpose was the par-value concept originally required for capital stock?

8 State briefly the accounting principle to be followed in recording the issuance of capital stock in exchange for nonmonetary assets or services.

9 Answer for each of *a*, *b*, and *c*. Are most preferred stocks:

a Voting or nonvoting?

b Cumulative or noncumulative?

c Participating or nonparticipating?

10 May a corporation have both ***watered stock*** and ***secret reserves***? Explain.

11 How is a ***nonmonetary dividend*** recorded by the issuer?

12 Distinguish between a ***stock split*** and a ***stock dividend***.

13 Weeks Corporation distributes a 3% common stock dividend each year, in addition to paying an annual cash dividend of $2 a share to common shareholders. How is the amount of the debit to the Retained Earnings ledger account for the stock dividend determined?

14 Stock splits and stock dividends may be used by a corporation to increase the number of shares of its common stock outstanding.

a What is meant by a ***stock split effected in the form of a stock dividend***?

b How is a common stock dividend that has been declared but not distributed classified in a balance sheet? Why?

15 In what ways might a corporation offer creditors protection against excessive cash dividend payments to shareholders?

16 To eliminate a deficit of $700,000, Coker Corporation obtained approval from its shareholders for a "reorganization and a reverse split." One new share of $5-par common stock was issued for each two old shares of $10-par common stock. The entire issue of 100,000 old shares was retired. Prepare

the journal entries to record the exchange of shares of common stock and the elimination of the deficit.

17 Under what circumstances is a corporation's retained earnings "dated"? Does dating of retained earnings refer to an item in the balance sheet or to a ledger account?

EXERCISES

Ex. 16-1 Select the best answer for each of the following multiple-choice questions:

1 DeFoe Corporation has 1,000,000 authorized shares of $3-par common stock of which 600,000 shares are issued and outstanding. When the market value of its common stock was $8 a share, DeFoe declared a 16⅔% common stock dividend. The journal entry (explanation omitted) summarizing ***both the declaration and the distribution*** of the common stock dividend is:

a Retained Earnings	300,000	
Common Stock		300,000
b Premium on Common Stock from Common Stock Dividends	300,000	
Common Stock		300,000
c Retained Earnings	800,000	
Common Stock		300,000
Premium on Common Stock from Common Stock Dividends		500,000
d Premium on Common Stock from Common Stock Dividends	800,000	
Common Stock		300,000
Retained Earnings		500,000

2 The following increases in aggregate or individual ledger account balances of Lindsay Limited during Year 9 were as follows:

Total assets	$356,000
Total liabilities	132,000
Common stock	240,000

If the only debit to the Retained Earnings ledger account for Year 9 was for cash dividends of $52,000, Lindsay Company's net income for Year 9 was:
a $16,000 *b* $36,000 *c* $52,000 *d* $68,000 *e* Some other amount

3 Authorized common stock is issued on a subscription basis at a price in excess of par. Additional contributed surplus is recorded when the subscribed common stock is:
a Contracted for *b* Paid for *c* Issued *d* Authorized

4 The Subscriptions Receivable: Common Stock and Common Stock Subscribed ledger accounts used in connection with common stock subscriptions are, respectively:

a Asset and liability accounts
b Asset and shareholders' equity accounts
c Asset and contra-asset accounts
d Contra-shareholders' equity and shareholders' equity accounts

5 Which of the following is not an acceptable debit to an additional contributed surplus ledger account?
a Write-off of bond discount at the time of issuance of the bonds
b Out-of-pocket costs of issuing capital stock
c Declaration of a liquidating dividend
d Redemption premium on preferred stock
e All of the foregoing

6 Outstanding common stock is always equal to:
a Authorized common stock less unissued common stock
b Issued common stock plus subscribed common stock
c Unissued common stock less issued common stock
d Issued common stock less treasury stock: common

7 With respect to subscriptions for capital stock, an additional contributed surplus ledger account is credited when:
a Capital stock is subscribed at a price in excess of par value
b Subscribed capital stock is issued after subscribers pay the subscription price, which exceeded par value
c A subscriber defaults and the corporation retains the amount paid on the defaulted subscription
d Either *a*, *b*, or *c* occurs
e Either *a* or *c* occurs

8 On July 14, Year 4, Lucerne Limited exchanged 1,000 shares of its no-par-value common stock for land with an appraised value of $23,000. The closing market price of Lucerne's common stock on the Montreal Stock Exchange was $21 a share on July 14, Year 4. As a result of the exchange, Lucerne's contributed surplus was increased by:
a $0 *b* $8,000 *c* $13,000 *d* $15,000 *e* Some other amount

Ex. 16-2 Wisely Corporation was incorporated on January 2, Year 8, with the following authorized capitalization:
1 5,000 shares of 8% cumulative preferred stock, $10 par
2 20,000 shares of no-par-value common stock
During Year 8, Wisely issued 12,000 shares of common stock for a total of $600,000 and 3,000 shares of preferred stock at $16 a share. In addition, on December 20, Year 8, subscriptions for 1,000 shares of preferred stock were received at a price of $18 a share. The subscribed shares were paid for on January 2, Year 9.

Compute the amount that Wisely Corporation reports as total contributed capital in its December 31, Year 8, balance sheet.

Ex. 16-3 Polar Corporation received authorization to issue an additional 100,000 shares of no-par-value common stock. The stock was offered to subscribers at a subscription price of $50 a share. Subscriptions were recorded by a debit to

Subscriptions Receivable: Common Stock and a credit to Common Stock Subscribed. A short time later, subscribers who had contracted to acquire 100 shares defaulted on their contracts after paying 40% of the subscription price. Costs of issuing the 100 shares totalled $200. The method used by Polar to record the default depends on the contractual and legal rights of the defaulting subscribers.

Identify four methods of accounting at the time of the default for the amount paid in by subscribers prior to the default. Prepare a journal entry for Polar Corporation for each method to show how the default would be recorded. Omit explanations for the journal entries.

Ex. 16-4 The condensed balance sheet of Ollie's, a single proprietorship, on December 31, Year 2, was as follows:

OLLIE'S
Balance Sheet
December 31, Year 2

Assets	
Current assets	$100,000
Plant assets (net of $120,000 accumulated depreciation)	80,000
Total assets	$180,000
Liabilities & Proprietor's Capital	
Liabilities	$ 40,000
Oliver Miller, capital	140,000
Total liabilities & proprietor's capital	$180,000

Current fair values of Ollie's current assets and plant assets (net) were $110,000 and $290,000 respectively on December 31, Year 2; current fair values of liabilities on that date equalled their carrying amounts. On January 2, Year 3, Ollie's was incorporated as Ollie's, Inc., with 2,000 shares of $20 par common stock issued to Oliver Miller.

Compute the credit to the Premium on Common Stock ledger account of Ollie's, Inc., on January 2, Year 3.

Ex. 16-5 Loco Limited had net income for Year 4 of $10,600,000 and earnings per share of common stock of $5.00. Included in the measurement of net income was $1,000,000 of bond interest expense on Loco's long-term debt. The income tax rate for Year 4 was 45%. Dividends declared on preferred stock were $600,000. Forty percent of the net income available for common stock was declared as dividends.

Compute the dividends declared on common stock by Loco Limited for Year 4.

Ex. 16-6 Kendall, Inc., was organized on January 2, Year 4, and issued the following capital stock:

1 5,000 shares of no-par-value, $10-dividend, cumulative preferred stock, at $125 a share (authorized 150,000 shares)

2 200,000 shares of no-par-value common stock at $12 a share (authorized 500,000 shares)

The total net income for Years 4 and 5 was $420,000, and although no dividends were declared in Year 4, cash dividends of $234,000 were declared in Year 5.

Compute the dividends declared by Kendall, Inc., on the preferred stock and common stock during Year 5.

Ex. 16-7 On September 15, Year 8, Nillo Corporation declared a nonmonetary dividend of 1,000 shares of Wimble, Inc., appropriately carried at cost of $9,000 as a long-term investment. The market price of Wimble's outstanding common stock on September 15, Year 8, was $14 a share.

Compute the debit to Retained Earnings and the credit to Realized Gain on Disposal of Investments ledger accounts resulting from Nillo Corporation's dividend declaration on September 15, Year 8.

Ex. 16-8 Suffolk Limited declared and distributed dividends as follows:

1 The entire long-term investment in the common stock of Ney, Inc., a wholly owned subsidiary accounted for by the equity method of accounting, was distributed to Suffolk's shareholders. The carrying amount of this investment on the date of distribution was $725,000; Suffolk made the distribution instead of accepting a cash offer of $2,000,000 for the common stock of Ney from an independent investor. This distribution is considered a spin-off for financial accounting.

2 Suffolk's 5% common stock interest in Haig Limited was distributed to shareholders. The long-term investment in Haig was carried at cost of $62,000; the current fair value of this investment was $92,000.

Prepare single journal entries for Suffolk Limited for the declaration and distribution of each of the two dividends described above.

Ex. 16-9 The shareholders' equity of Nako Limited on July 31, Year 6, is presented below:

Shareholders' equity:	
Common stock, no par value, authorized 400,000 shares, issued and outstanding 150,000 shares	$3,140,000
Retained earnings	390,000
Total shareholders' equity	$3,530,000

On August 1, Year 6, the board of directors of Nako declared a 5% stock dividend on common stock, to be distributed on September 15. The market price of Nako's common stock was $35 a share on August 1, Year 6, and $40 a share on September 15, Year 6.

Compute the amount of Nako Limited's debit to the Retained Earnings ledger account as a result of the declaration and distribution of the stock dividend.

Ex. 16-10 Golan Limited had substantial retained earnings but was short of cash. Accordingly, on September 20, Year 3, the board of directors of Golan declared the following dividends, distributable October 19, Year 3, to shareholders of record October 5, Year 3:

1 2,000 shares of Harold Ltd. $1-par common stock, with a cost and carrying amount of $20,000. Golan's investment in Harold did not enable it to influence Harold's operating or financial policies.

2 A 15% stock dividend on the 100,000 outstanding shares of Golan's no-par-value common stock.

Per-share market values of the common stock of Goland and Harold on September 20, Year 3, were $14 and $23 respectively.

Prepare journal entries for Golan Limited to record the declaration of the dividends on September 20, Year 3.

Ex. 16-11 The shareholders' equity section of the balance sheet of Norwalk Limited at the beginning of Year 5 contained the following items:

Shareholders' equity:	
$12 convertible preferred stock, no par value, authorized, issued, and outstanding 10,000 shares (**NOTE 1**)	$1,000,000
Common stock, no par value, authorized 1,000,000 shares, issued and outstanding 400,000 shares	2,000,000
Retained earnings	6,000,000
Total shareholders' equity	$9,000,000

NOTE 1: The preferred stock is convertible at any time to common stock at a conversion ratio of four common shares for each preferred share, with the conversion ratio subject to adjustment for any dilution of the common stock.

On January 10, Year 5, a 5% common stock dividend was declared, to be distributed January 30 to shareholders of record January 15. On March 1, Year 5, all the preferred stock was converted to common stock. Market price a share for the common stock was as follows: January 10, $41; January 15, $42; January 30, $43; March 1, $45.

Post the transactions and events of Norwalk Limited described above in appropriate ledger accounts and determine the balances of the ledger accounts after giving consideration to all the listed transactions. Also compute Norwalk's total shareholders' equity after giving effect to these transactions.

Ex. 16-12 The shareholders' equity of Farber Limited on December 31, Year 9, prior to a reorganization completed on that date was as follows:

Shareholders' equity:	
Common stock, no par value, authorized, issued, and outstanding 700,000 shares	$8,600,000
Retained earnings (deficit)	(900,000)
Total shareholders' equity	$7,700,000

Inventories were carried in Farber's accounting records on December 31, Year 9, at market value of $6,000,000, which was $500,000 less than cost. Farber's plant assets, carried at $12,000,000 net of accumulated depreciation, had a current fair value of $8,000,000 on December 31, Year 9. Under the provisions of the reorganization, the deficit was to be reduced to zero and the plant assets were to be reduced to their fair value.

Prepare the shareholders' equity section of Farber Company's balance sheet on December 31, Year 9, following completion of the reorganization. Show supporting computations.

Ex. 16-13 The condensed balance sheet of Noro Corporation on June 30, Year 6, prior to a reorganization, was as follows:

NORO CORPORATION
Balance Sheet
June 30, Year 6

Assets	
Current assets	$ 550,000
Plant assets (net of $650,000 accumulated depreciation)	1,350,000
Other assets	200,000
Total assets	$2,100,000
Liabilities & Shareholders' Equity	
Liabilities	$ 600,000
Common stock, no par value, 32,000 shares issued and outstanding	$1,900,000
Retained earnings (deficit)	(400,000)
Total liabilities & shareholders' equity	$2,100,000

The reorganization was to be implemented by erasing the deficit, an increase of $350,000 in accumulated depreciation, a $150,000 write-down of other assets, and an appropriate reduction in the common stock.

Compute the revised average value, per share and total, of Noro Corporation's common stock on June 30, Year 6, following the reorganization.

Ex. 16-14 From the following information, prepare the shareholders' equity section of the balance sheet of Goth Corporation on October 31, Year 6:

Subscriptions receivable: common stock	$ 55,000
Premium on preferred stock	50,000
Common stock, $5 par, authorized 40,000 shares, issued and outstanding 20,000 shares	100,000
Premium on common stock	150,000
Retained earnings, unappropriated	327,000
Retained earnings appropriated for general contingencies	125,000
Common stock subscribed	25,000
12% cumulative preferred stock, $50 par, authorized 20,000 shares, issued and outstanding 10,000 shares	500,000
Contributed surplus from donation of plant site by city of Prado	140,000

CASES

Case 16-1 Problems may be encountered in accounting for transactions involving the shareholders' equity section of the balance sheet.

Instructions

Assuming that only one class of capital stock, common stock, is authorized:

a Describe the accounting for the subscription of common stock at a price in excess of the par value of the common stock.

b Describe the accounting for the issuance of no-par common stock for cash at a price per share in excess of the average book value per share.

c Explain the significance of the three dates that are important in accounting for cash dividends to shareholders. Describe the journal entry, if any, prepared on each date.

d Assume retained earnings are available for the declaration of stock dividends. What is the effect of a 10% common stock dividend on retained earnings and total shareholders' equity when the common shares are no-par-value shares?

Case 16-2 Obsolescence has become a major problem in the inventories of Robin, Inc. Lack of attention to inventory turnover rates, combined with a change in product design to permit use of lighter-weight materials, has caused much of the existing inventories to become obsolete. An analysis of the inventories on December 31, Year 5, indicated that the carrying amount of inventories should be reduced by $1,100,000 because of obsolescence.

The income of Year 5 before the obsolescence loss and income taxes was estimated at $210,000. The shareholders' equity before year-end adjusting entries for Year 5 was as follows:

Shareholders' equity:	
Common stock, no par value	$1,600,000
Retained earnings	400,000
Total shareholders' equity	$2,000,000

The board of directors informs you that it regards obsolescence as an extraordinary item and that a decision has been made to write down inventories by the full amount of the obsolescence loss; to debit $400,000 to retained earnings and $600,000 to the common stock account; and to recognize a loss of only $100,000 in Year 5.

Instructions

Evaluate the proposed treatment of the obsolescence loss in the light of generally accepted accounting principles. Disregard income tax considerations. Compute the amount of Robin's income or loss before income taxes for Year 5 and explain how the obsolescence loss should be reported. Disregard other adjustments that may be required in the computation of income or loss before income taxes.

Case 16-3 You are engaged in an audit of the financial statements of Mickelson Limited on March 31, Year 1, the end of its first year of operations. During your examination of the shareholders' equity accounts, you discover that Mickelson issued common stock to three customers at a price substantially below the market prices of the stock on the dates of issuance.

Mickelson's controller proposes to present the difference between market value of the common stock and the proceeds received from the customers as an extraordinary loss in Mickelson's income statement for the year ended March 31, Year 1. The controller points out that all other common stock issuances were for proceeds equal to current market value, and that the ''discount'' allowed to the customers who acquired Mickelson's common stock was for the purpose of encouraging future purchases of merchandise by those customers. The controller acknowledged, however, that the customers acquiring Mickelson's common stock at a discount from market value had no long-term contractual commitment to purchase merchandise from Mickelson.

Instructions

Do you concur with the controller's proposal for the accounting for Mickelson Limited's discount from market value on common stock? Explain.

Case 16-4 The independent auditor of Neeham Limited explained to its president that the use of the last-in, first-out inventory method during an extended period of rising prices and the expensing of research and development costs are examples of accounting practices that may create ***secret reserves***. The auditor also pointed out that ***watered stock*** is the opposite of secret reserves.

Instructions

a What are ***secret reserves***? How may secret reserves be created or enlarged?
b What is the basis for the statement that the two specific practices cited above would tend to create secret reserves?
c Is it possible to create secret reserves in connection with accounting for liabilities? If so, explain or give an example.
d What are the objections to the creation of secret reserves?
e What is ***watered stock***?
f Describe the general circumstances in which watered stock may arise.
g What actions may be taken to eliminate ''water'' from a balance sheet?

Case 16-5 After the cancellation of some of its government contracts, Ludwig Limited began production under a new long-term government contract. During the period of operating losses resulting from the contract cancellations, Ludwig had suspended dividend payments on all four capital stock issues. These four issues consisted of a $7 cumulative, no-par-value, first preferred stock; a $2.50 noncumulative, convertible, no-par-value, preferred stock; an $8, no-par-value, noncumulative preferred stock; and common stock. Ten thousand shares of each issue of capital stock were outstanding. All dividends had been paid through Year 3, but Ludwig had been unable to pay any dividends in Year 4 or Year 5. During Year 6, Ludwig's financial position improved, and at a director's meeting near the end of Year 6, a proposal was made to pay a dividend of $2.25 a share on the common stock to shareholders of record December 31, Year 6.

Edward Cobb, who owned 100 shares of the $2.50 noncumulative, convertible, no-par-value, preferred stock, had been considering converting those 100 shares to common stock at the existing conversion ratio of four shares of common stock for each share of the convertible preferred stock. The conversion ratio was scheduled to drop to 3½ to one at the end of Year 6. Observing that the market price of the common stock was rising rapidly, Cobb explained that he was "torn between a desire to retain his preferred stock until the dividend of $2.50 a share was received and a desire to convert promptly before the price of the common stock went higher and the conversion ratio was reduced."

Instructions

a Determine the amount of cash needed by Ludwig Limited for dividend payments if the proposal to pay a $2.25 dividend on the common stock is adopted. (Assume that there is no conversion of preferred stock.)

b Advise Edward Cobb on the merits of converting the Ludwig Limited preferred stock at this time as opposed to converting after the dividends have been paid and the conversion ratio decreased. Explain the issues involved.

Case 16-6 A few months after the organization of Lund Corporation, one of the principal shareholders, Norman Chow, offered to transfer land and a factory to Lund in exchange for 11,000 shares of Lund's no-par-value common stock. Under the terms of the offer, an existing mortgage note payable of $28,000 on the factory was to be assumed by Lund.

The board of directors of Lund determined that the factory was well-suited to Lund's needs. The board was informed by the secretary of Lund that 15,000 authorized but unissued shares of common stock were available. The secretary also advised the board that the average book value of the issued common stock was $10 per share.

One member of the board, Rita Worth, opposed the idea of assuming the mortage note payable, on the grounds that long-term debt could prove burdensome for a new company without established earning power, and suggested making a counteroffer of 13,800 shares with the understanding that Chow pay the mortgage note in full on the date title to the land and factory was received.

A second director, Carl Lope, argued against further issuance of common stock, pointing out that Lund had just obtained $325,000 cash from issuance of 26,000 shares of common stock and that this cash should be used to acquire plant assets. Lope proposed that Lund offer Chow $110,000 cash, assume the mortgage note, and pay it in full immediately.

A third director, Mary Fine, urged prompt acceptance of Chow's offer without modification. Fine produced documents showing that the land and factory had been acquired by Chow 10 years previously for $206,000 and that Chow's accounting records indicated depreciation to date of $36,000. In conclusion, Fine stated that these facts showed that Lund would be saving $32,000 by accepting Chow's offer.

Instructions

a Comment on the logic and reasonableness of the views expressed by each of the three directors. Explain how each computed the amounts mentioned.

b Indicate which deal you believe would be most advantageous to Lund Corporation, assuming that it was acceptable to Norman Chow.

c Assuming that Lund Corporation accepted the original offer by Norman Chow, prepare the journal entry to record the transaction, and explain the reasoning underlying the entry. Assume that the land is worth 25% as much as the factory building.

Case 16-7 After receiving a share certificate for three common shares, Ruth Ross, a shareholder of Tillman Corporation, expressed this reaction:

''Tillman Corporation has just declared another stock dividend despite that letter of protest I wrote to the president last year. I wrote that I hate to see a company declare a stock dividend because it causes a transfer of retained earnings to contributed capital. Such a transfer obviously reduces the amount available for cash dividends.''

''You are absolutely right,'' said Wilma Wade. ''When I acquired Tillman common stock I was hoping for an increase in cash dividends over a period of time, but the declaration of stock dividends certainly reduces my expectations for cash dividends. Let's write the president another letter.''

Instructions

Evaluate the opinions expressed by Ruth Ross and Wilma Wade from the standpoint of accounting principles, and also in the light of customary dividend practices. Identify any elements of truth in the statements by Ross and Wade and any lack of logic in the conclusions they reached.

PROBLEMS

Pr. 16-1 Tinsel Limited began operations in January, Year 1, and had the following net income or (loss) for each of its first five years of operations:

Year 1	$ (150,000)
Year 2	(130,000)
Year 3	(120,000)
Year 4	260,000
Year 5	1,022,000

On December 31, Year 5, Tinsel's capital stock ledger accounts were as shown on page 822.

Tinsel has never paid a cash dividend or distributed a stock dividend. There has been no change in the capital stock ledger accounts since Tinsel began operations.

1 $10 nonparticipating, noncumulative preferred stock, no par value, authorized, issued, and outstanding 1,000 shares	$ 100,000
2 $8 nonparticipating, cumulative preferred stock, no par value, authorized, issued, and outstanding 10,000 shares	1,000,000
3 Common stock, no par value, authorized 100,000 shares, issued and outstanding 50,000 shares	500,000

Instructions

Prepare a working paper to show the maximum amount available for cash dividends to Tinsel Limited's shareholders on December 31, Year 5, and how it would be distributed to the holders of the common stock and each of the preferred stock issues. Show supporting computations.

Pr. 16-2 On January 4, Year 1, Kelly Limited was organized and issued capital stock as follows:

1 $5 preferred stock, no par value, 250,000 shares
2 Common stock, no par value, 1,000,000 shares

After this authorization to issue capital stock, the following transactions affecting shareholders' equity occurred during the first quarter of Year 1:

Jan. 15 Received subscriptions for 25,000 shares of preferred stock at $105 a share. A payment of 40% of the subscription price accompanied each subscription; the balance was to be paid on March 15. (Record the full amount subscribed and then, in a separate journal entry, record the cash collections for 40% of this amount.)

17 Received subscriptions for 125,000 shares of common stock at $20 a share, payable March 1.

30 Issued 1,500 shares of common stock in payment for legal and accounting services reasonably valued at $30,000 relating to the organization of Kelly Limited

Mar. 1 Received payment in full of the amount due on common stock subscriptions and issued the stock certificates.

15 Received payment in full of the balance due on preferred stock subscriptions and issued the stock certificates.

30 Issued 5,000 shares of preferred stock for $520,000.

30 Issued 6,000 shares of common stock and 2,500 shares of preferred stock in exchange for assets for which the board of directors established the following current fair values:

Land	$154,000
Building	190,000
Delivery equipment	20,000
Inventories	15,000

Mar. 31 Net income earned to March 31 amounted to $176,000. No dividends had been declared.

Instructions

a Prepare journal entries to record the foregoing transactions of Kelly Limited.

b Prepare the shareholders' equity section of Kelly Limited's balance sheet on March 31, Year 1.

Pr. 16-3 The board of directors of Hobb Corporation declared a 6% common stock dividend on October 1, Year 8, to be distributed on October 25 to shareholders of record October 15. The market price of Hobb's common stock was as follows on those dates: October 1, $63; October 15, $66; and October 25, $70. The accounting records of Hobb are maintained on the basis of a fiscal year ended September 30.

On October 28, Year 8, the board of directors declared a cash dividend of $0.90 a share on the common stock. The dividend was payable December 1 to shareholders of record November 18.

The shareholders' equity section of Hobb's balance sheet on September 30, Year 8, is shown below. For October, Year 8, Hobb's net income was $41,750.

Shareholders' equity:	
Common stock, no par value, authorized 200,000 shares, issued and outstanding 60,000 shares	$2,150,000
Retained earnings	2,380,000
Total shareholders' equity	$4,530,000

Instructions

a Prepare journal entries for Hobb Corporation for the declaration and the distribution of the dividends during the month of October, Year 8. Also prepare a journal entry to record the net income for October (debit Income Summary).

b Prepare the shareholders' equity section of Hobb Corporation's balance sheet on October 31, Year 8.

Pr. 16-4 Crosby Corporation was organized on September 5, Year 2, with authorization to issue 600,000 shares of no-par-value common stock and 22,500 shares of no par value, $4 cumulative preferred stock. On September 15, Year 2, the assets of a single proprietorship were acquired in exchange for 12,000 shares of preferred stock, plus the assumption of a mortgage note payable of $276,000. The assets acquired were valued by a firm of independent appraisers at $900,000. On September 20, subscriptions were obtained for 30,000 shares of common at a price of $15 a share.

All subscriptions were collected and recorded on October 5, except for a subscription by Carol Willan for 300 shares. Willan paid $1,500 but defaulted on the balance of the contract. On October 10, the 300 shares were issued for cash by Crosby at a price of $13 a share. Crosby refunded the amount paid by Willan after deducting the ''loss'' realized on the issuance of the 300 shares.

No dividends were declared on the common stock. A quarterly dividend of $1 a share on the preferred stock was declared on November 9, payable on

December 15, to shareholders of record on December 1. Operations for the period ended December 31, Year 2, resulted in net income of $72,500.

Instructions

a Prepare journal entries for the capital stock transactions of Crosby Corporation and the dividend declaration and payment.

b Prepare the shareholders' equity section of Crosby Corporation's balance sheet on December 31, Year 2.

Pr. 16-5 Oliver Corporation maintains its accounting records on the basis of a fiscal year ending March 31. The shareholders' equity section of the balance sheet on March 31, Year 6, appears below:

Shareholders' equity:	
Common stock, no par value, authorized 250,000 shares, issued and outstanding 100,000 shares	$3,675,000
Retained earnings	2,420,000
Total shareholders' equity	$6,095,000

On April 1, Year 6, the board of directors of Oliver declared a cash dividend of $1 a share payable on April 29 to common shareholders of record April 15.

On April 10, Year 6, the board of directors of Oliver also declared a 3% stock dividend distributable on May 31 to common shareholders of record May 15. The market price of the common stock on April 10 was $50 a share. The net income for April amounted to $78,500.

Instructions

a Prepare journal entries for Oliver Corporation for the declaration and the distribution of the dividends and to record net income for April. Debit Income Summary to record the net income.

b Prepare the shareholders' equity section of Oliver Corporation's balance sheet on April 30, Year 6, and a statement of retained earnings for the month ended April 30, Year 6.

Pr. 16-6 The market price of Kantor Corporation's common stock on June 30, Year 1, was $52 a share. The shareholders' equity on that date included substantial retained earnings, in addition to 250,000 shares of no-par-value common stock that had been issued at a price of $12 a share. A total of 500,000 shares was authorized to be issued.

A nonmonetary dividend (short-term investments) of $1.10 a share was declared on March 10, Year 2, payable April 25, Year 2, to shareholders of record March 31, Year 2. The carrying amount of the short-term investments distributed as the nonmonetary dividend was $180,000.

A cash dividend of $1.50 a share was declared on June 1, Year 2, payable July 20, Year 2, to shareholders of record July 1, Year 2; a 5% stock dividend was declared at the same time and with the same dates of record and distribution. The cash dividend was not applicable to the shares of common stock issued as a stock dividend. The market price per share of the common stock was $55 on June 1, Year 2, and $56 on June 30, Year 2.

For the year ended June 30, Year 2, net income amounted to $1,643,700 (including the effect, if any, of the nonmonetary dividend), which represented an earnings rate of 10% on total shareholders' equity as of June 30, Year 1.

Instructions

a Record Kantor Corporation's transactions and events affecting shareholders' equity during Year 2 in the general journal. Debit Income Summary to record the net income for the year ended June 30, Year 2.

b Prepare a statement of retained earnings for Kantor Corporation for the year ended June 30, Year 2.

c Prepare the shareholders' equity section of Kantor Corporation's balance sheet on June 30, Year 2.

Pr. 16-7 Current conditions require that Vance Limited carry out a reorganization on December 31, Year 6. Selected balance sheet items prior to the reorganization were as follows:

1. Inventories were carried in the accounting records on December 31, Year 6, at market value of $3,000,000. The cost of the inventories was $3,250,000.
2. Plant assets were carried in the accounting records on December 31, Year 6, at $6,000,000 net of accumulated depreciation. Plant assets had a current fair value of $5,000,000, and were to be written down to that amount by a credit to Accumulated Depreciation.
3. Shareholders' equity on December 31, Year 6, consisted of the following:

Shareholders' equity:	
Common stock, no par value, authorized, issued, and outstanding 350,000 shares	$4,300,000
Retained earnings (deficit)	(450,000)
Total shareholders' equity	$3,850,000

The average value of the common stock was to be reduced to $5 a share with a corresponding credit to Retained Earnings.

Instructions

a Prepare journal entries to record the reorganization of Vance Limited on December 31, Year 6.

b Prepare the shareholders' equity section of Vance Limited's balance sheet on December 31, Year 6, after the reorganization had been effected. Show supporting computations. Disregard income tax and deferred tax considerations.

Pr. 16-8 Farley Corporation was authorized to issue 500,000 shares of $25 par, 8% cumulative preferred stock, and 1,500,000 shares of no-par-value common stock.

Early operations of Farley were profitable, but a prolonged strike caused a net loss of $910,000 for the fiscal year ended June 30, Year 6. Because of the loss,

Farley declared no dividends on its common stock during the year ended June 30, Year 6. Dividends on preferred stock were declared and paid earlier in Year 6 in the amount of $120,000, but dividends were in arrears on the preferred stock on June 30, Year 6, in the amount of $360,000.

A trial balance of the ledger on May 31, Year 6, included the following:

8% cumulative preferred stock, $25 par	$6,000,000
Common stock, no par value, 400,000 shares issued	2,100,000
Subscriptions receivable: preferred stock	618,000
Retained earnings (June 30, Year 5)	1,476,000
Premium on preferred stock	198,000
Preferred stock subscribed	600,000
Subscriptions receivable: common stock	525,000
Common stock subscribed	525,000
Dividends: preferred stock	120,000

Transactions during June, Year 6, relating to capital stock included the issuance on June 5 of 4,200 shares of common stock in exchange for a patent. An additional 30,000 shares of common stock were issued for cash on June 5 at a price of $6.50 a share. Cash was collected on June 21 representing payment in full for common stock subscriptions covering 20,000 shares. These subscriptions had been received and recorded prior to May 31. All common stock offerings by Farley prior to May 31, Year 6, had been at the same price.

Instructions

a Compute the average price at which the preferred stock was issued by Farley Corporation.

b Compute the price at which the common stock was issued by Farley Corporation prior to June, Year 6.

c Prepare journal entries to record Farley Corporation's transactions and events (including closing entries for the net loss and dividends) during June that affected the shareholders' equity ledger accounts.

d Prepare the shareholders' equity section of Farley Corporation's balance sheet on June 30, Year 6, including any applicable notes to the financial statements.

Pr. 16-9 The shareholders of Putney Corporation have voted approval for Putney to carry out a reorganization effective October 1, Year 3. Putney's balance sheet on September 30, Year 3, is shown on page 827.

Putney is engaged in the manufacture of space exploration equipment and has acquired several small business enterprises at prices in excess of the current fair value of their identifiable net assets. The acquisition prices included, among other things, payment for research work and for the services of technically trained personnel. The value assigned to the acquired assets was based on the par value of common stock issued in the purchase-type business combinations. The market value of Putney's common stock was approximately equal to its par value.

PUTNEY CORPORATION
Balance Sheet
September 30, Year 3

Assets		
Current assets		$1,080,000
Plant assets	$800,000	
Less: Accumulated depreciation	395,000	405,000
Goodwill (net)		1,520,000
Total assets		$3,005,000
Liabilities & Shareholders' Equity		
Liabilities:		
Current liabilities		$ 305,000
12% bonds payable		250,000
Total liabilities		$ 555,000
Shareholders' equity:		
10.5% preferred stock, $100 par (dividends in arrears, $42,000)	$ 200,000	
Common stock, $10 par	2,200,000	
Retained earnings	50,000	2,450,000
Total liabilities & shareholders' equity		$3,005,000

In recent months, several major research projects were abandoned, and some key employees left Putney. As a result, many contracts were lost, and the goodwill was deemed to be worthless. In order to get a "fresh start" for financial accounting, the following actions were taken to carry out a reorganization effective October 1, Year 3, approved by shareholders:

1 Inventories were written down by $140,000 and the allowance for doubtful accounts was increased by $10,000.
2 The carrying amount of plant assets was reduced to $250,000 by an increase in accumulated depreciation.
3 The goodwill was written off.
4 The par value of common stock was reduced to $1 a share.
5 The dividends in arrears on the preferred stock were paid in cash, and 80,000 shares of $1-par common stock were issued to the preferred shareholders in exchange for their stock.
6 Following the asset write-offs, the deficit was eliminated against premium on common stock.
7 During the last quarter of Year 3, Putney earned net income of $85,000, and as a result, current assets increased by $120,000, current liabilities increased by $10,000, and accumulated depreciation increased by $25,000. Current liabilities also increased by $7,000 as a result of additional income taxes assessed for Year 1 because of an error in the computation of income taxes payable.

Instructions

a Prepare journal entries for Putney Corporation to record the reorganization on October 1, Year 3, and to summarize the transactions and events for the last quarter of Year 3.

b Compute the balance of Putney Corporation's retained earnings on December 31, Year 3.

Pr. 16-10 On January 1, Year 9, the shareholders' equity of Albert Limited was as follows:

Shareholders' equity:	
$12 convertible preferred stock, no par value, authorized 10,000 shares, issued and outstanding 5,000 shares (**NOTE 1**)	$ 500,000
Common stock, no par value, authorized 1,000,000 shares, issued and outstanding 350,000 shares	3,906,000
Common stock subscribed, 8,000 shares	310,000
Total contributed capital	$4,716,000
Retained earnings	5,262,000
Total shareholders' equity	$9,978,600

NOTE 1: Preferred stock is callable at $105, and is convertible to common stock at a rate of 3 for 1, subject to an antidilution provision.

During the quarter ended March 31, Year 9, the following transactions were completed:

Jan. 7	Collected $310,000 representing payment in full for all outstanding common stock subscriptions; issued the common stock.
31	Declared the regular quarterly dividend on the preferred stock to be paid March 3 to shareholders of record February 19.
Feb. 1	Declared a 10% common stock dividend to be distributed March 4 to shareholders of record February 20.
Mar. 3	Paid quarterly dividend on the preferred stock.
4	Distributed the 10% common stock dividend.
15	Issued 11,000 shares of common stock for cash at $44 a share.
30	All preferred stock was converted to common stock.
31	Issued 100,000 shares of common stock in exchange for the net assets of Raye Corporation (appraised at $4.5 million) in a purchase-type business combination.
31	Net income for the quarter ended March 31, Year 9, was $877,700. (Debit the Income Summary ledger account.)

Market prices of Albert Limited's common stock during Year 9 were as follows: January 7, $40; February 1, $38; February 20, $40; March 4, $42; March 15, $44; March 31, $45.

Instructions

a Prepare journal entries for the transactions and events of Albert Limited described above.

b Prepare a statement of shareholders' equity (including retained earnings) for Albert Limited for the quarter ended March 31, Year 9.

Pr. 16-11 On December 31, Year 1, the end of its first year of operations, Watson Inc. prepared a balance sheet containing the following items, among others:

Subscriptions receivable: preferred stock		$ 208,000
Subscriptions receivable: common stock		720,000
8% cumulative preferred stock, $100 par, authorized 200,000 shares, issued and outstanding 44,000 shares	$4,400,000	
8% cumulative preferred stock subscribed 4,000 shares	400,000	4,800,000
Common stock, $10 par, authorized 400,000 shares, issued and outstanding 47,000 shares	$ 470,000	
Common stock subscribed 48,000 shares	480,000	950,000
Contributed surplus:		
Premium on preferred stock		32,000
Premium on common stock		1,930,000

Watson had been organized on January 2, Year 1, and had immediately received subscriptions for 40,000 shares of 8% cumulative preferred stock. Subscriptions for common stock were received on the same date. (The number of common shares subscribed and the subscription price can be determined from information given in the problem.) On May 5 subscriptions were received for an additional 8,000 shares of 8% cumulative preferred stock at a price of $104 a share.

Cash payments were received from subscribers at frequent intervals for several months after subscription. Watson issued shares only when subscribers had paid in full. On December 22, Year 1, Watson issued 15,000 shares of its common stock in exchange for a tract of land with a current fair value of $480,000. (Subscriptions were not used in this transaction.)

Instructions

Prepare journal entries for all the transactions completed during Year 1 by Watson, Inc., as indicated by the December 31, Year 1, account balances. Assume that collections on the preferred stock subscriptions were made on a first-in, first-out basis.

c h a p t e r 1 7

WARRANTS, CONVERTIBLE SECURITIES, AND EMPLOYEE CAPITAL ACCUMULATION PLANS

In this chapter we consider stock warrants, convertible securities, and employee capital accumulation plans such as stock option and stock purchase plans. A common characteristic of these securities or plans it that they provide for ***contingent*** issuances of common stock and (less frequently) preferred stock and convertible bonds payable, at the election of the holder prior to the expiration of a specified time period.

STOCK WARRANTS AND WARRANTS TO ACQUIRE BONDS

As explained in Chapter 14, a ***stock warrant*** is a certificate issued by a corporation conveying to the owner rights to acquire shares of the issuer's common stock at a specified price in a specified time period. The term ***right*** means the privilege attaching to each outstanding stock warrant to acquire a specified number of shares of common stock. For example, the owner of 100 shares of common stock might receive a stock warrant for 100 rights, which would permit the owner to acquire 10 shares of common stock (because 10 rights are needed to acquire one additional share of common stock) at a price (the ***exercise price***) below the current market price.

The use of rights is not limited to the acquisition of additional shares of common stock. Some corporations have issued warrants for rights to their common shareholders entitling them to acquire convertible bonds at a specified price. The use of rights in the acquisition of bonds is considered later in this chapter. At this point we are concerned only with rights that entitle the owner to acquire common stock at a specified price and in a specified time period.

When stock warrants are outstanding, the issuer should disclose the number of shares of common stock held in reserve to meet the contractual commitments to issue additional shares of common stock. This disclosure may be made in the shareholders' equity section of the balance sheet or in a note to the financial statements.

Stock Warrants to Existing Shareholders

When stock warrants are issued to existing shareholders as a preliminary step to raise capital through the issuance of additional shares of common stock, the issuer receives nothing in exchange for the warrants when they are ***issued***. Only when the warrants are ***exercised*** does the issuer receive cash.

Stock warrants granted to existing shareholders as a preliminary step to raising capital through the issuance of additional common stock usually expire in a few weeks. The issuer thus may complete rapidly its program of raising capital through the issuance of additional common stock to present shareholders before offering stock to other investors. Stock warrants of this type are transferable, and some investors obtain warrants by acquisition from other investors. When investors who have acquired warrants from other investors exercise the warrants, the cost of the warrants is combined with the amount paid to the issuer to measure the cost of the shares of common stock acquired, as explained on page 673. The acquisition price specified in stock warrants granted to existing shareholders always is set below the current market price of the common stock, thus giving a market value to the stock warrants.

The issuance of stock warrants to shareholders does not require debits or credits to any ledger accounts of the issuer, although a memorandum entry stating the number of warrants issued and the terms involved may be used. When the warrants are exercised by the owners, they receive shares of common stock at the specified price. This transaction requires the usual journal entry for issuances of common stock.

Warrants to Acquire Convertible Bonds

As stated on page 787, the common shareholders may have the preemptive right to acquire additional shares of common stock in proportion to their present holdings in the event that a corporation increases the amount of stock outstanding. This preemptive right logically applies also to any new issues of convertible bonds or convertible preferred stock because these securities eventually may be converted to common stock.

During periods of high stock prices, convertible bonds are a popular form of financing. Warrants may be issued to common shareholders entitling them to acquire convertible bonds at a specified price, and usually with the provision that the warrants will expire if not exercised within a month or two. For example, National Cash Register issued to its common shareholders warrants for rights to acquire convertible bonds maturing in 20 years. Ten rights and $100 cash were required to acquire $100 face amount of bonds. The warrants traded for several weeks on the stock exchange at prices varying between $1 and $2 a right; concurrently, the convertible bonds were trading on a ***when-issued*** basis at prices ranging from $108 to $116 for each $100 face amount. (Securities distributed on a "when-issued" basis do not require delivery until after the scheduled date of issuance.)

The accounting procedures for warrants to acquire convertible bonds are similar to the procedures described for warrants to acquire common stock. The issuer prepares no journal entry when the warrants are issued but must maintain memorandum records of the number of warrants issued, exercised, and outstanding. When the warrants are exercised, the appropriate journal entry is a debit to Cash and a credit to the liability account for the convertible bonds. Usually, the exercise price for the bonds is face amount; thus, no discount or premium is involved when the convertible bonds are issued.

Stock Warrants Issued in Combination With Bonds or Preferred Stock

A corporation may add to the attractiveness of its bonds or preferred stock by including a detachable stock warrant to acquire its common stock at a specified price. The longer the term of the warrant, the greater its speculative appeal; detachable stock warrants issued with bonds or preferred stock often run for several years, and some have no expiration date.

When bonds are issued with detachable stock warrants, the interest rate on the bonds usually is less than if the bonds were offered alone. Similarly, preferred stock accompanied by detachable stock warrants for the acquisition of common stock may attract investors even though the dividend rate on the preferred stock is less than would otherwise be necessary. In other words, a part of the proceeds to the corporation from issuing bonds or preferred stock with detachable stock warrants attached represents payment by investors for the warrants. Therefore, the accounting for these "combination packages" of securities ***should show that part of the proceeds is attributable to the warrants***.

Accounting for bonds payable issued with detachable stock warrants is illustrated in Chapter 15. Therefore, our discussion here is focussed on the issuance of detachable stock warrants in combination with preferred stock.

Warrants giving the owner the right to acquire common stock at a specified price at any time during a span of years have an economic value regardless of whether the specified exercise price is higher than, lower than, or equal to the market price of the common stock when the warrants are issued. Because the detachable stock warrants often are traded separately from the preferred stock or bond with which they were originally issued, objective evidence (the relative fair values of the two securities at the time of issuance) is available for the allocation of the proceeds between the two types of securities.

Assume, for example, that Meeker, Inc., issued 1 million shares of no-par preferred stock at $26½ and included with each share a detachable stock warrant to acquire one share of no-par common stock at $30 at any time during the next 10 years. The common stock had a current market price of $26. The warrants had a value because of the likelihood that the market price of the common stock would increase above $30 a share during the next 10 years. Assume also that immediately after issuance the warrants had a market price of $1 each and the preferred stock had a market price of $25.50 a share. The journal entry to record the proceeds of the preferred stock offering is as follows:

Journal entry to record issuance of preferred stock and detachable stock warrants

Cash (1,000,000 × $26.50)	26,500,000	
Preferred Stock (1,000,000 × $25.50)		25,500,000
Common Stock Warrants (1,000,000 × $1)		1,000,000
To record issuance of 1 million shares of no-par-value preferred stock at $25½ and 1 million detachable stock warrants with market price of $1 each.		

The Common Stock Warrants ledger account is included in the shareholders' equity section of the balance sheet with other types of additional contributed capital. If the warrants are exercised and the common stock issued at $30 a share, the journal entry is as follows:

Journal entry for exercise of warrants for common stock

Cash (1,000,000 × $30)	30,000,000	
Common Stock Warrants	1,000,000	
Common Stock		31,000,000
To record issuance of 1 million shares of no-par-value common stock in exchange for 1 million warrants and cash of $30 a share.		

If a part of the detachable stock warrants is not exercised and expires, the balance of the Common Stock Warrants ledger account remains a part of the contributed capital of Meeker, Inc.

The *CICA Handbook* provides no specific guidelines as to whether the value of the stock warrants should be recognized and recorded. Companies in Canada may follow either the above method or make no recognition of the value of the stock warrants. In the latter case, in the journal entry to record issuance of preferred stock and detachable stock warrants, the preferred stock would total $26,500,000 (including the Common Stock Warrants amount above). In the journal entry for exercise of the warrants for common stock, the Common Stock ledger account would total $30,000,000 (excluding the Common Stock Warrants amount above). As a result, preferred stock would be $1,000,000 higher, and common stock would be $1,000,000 lower, if there was no recognition of the value of the stock warrants. The recognition of the common stock warrants is more logical because it distinguishes clearly the source of the contributed capital.

CONVERTIBLE SECURITIES

Conversion of Bonds to Common Stock

As explained in Chapter 15, bonds that allow investors to exchange their bonds for common stock are known as ***convertible bonds***, and this feature is called a ***conversion option***. Inclusion of the conversion option makes bonds more attractive to investors and enables the issuer to obtain funds at an interest rate below the rate that would be paid on nonconvertible bonds. The conversion feature also may have the effect of providing for a gradual retirement of debt as the bondholders elect to exchange their bonds for common stock. Thus, by issuing convertible bonds, a corporation in effect issues common stock at a price substantially in excess of the market price of the common stock at the time the bonds are issued.

When convertible bonds are converted, the retirement of the debt and the issuance of common stock are recorded. To illustrate, assume that Skagg Corporation had outstanding $10,000,000 of 12% convertible bonds, carried in its accounting records at $10,400,000, including $400,000 unamortized bond premium. The bonds were convertible to no-par-value common stock with a market price of $125 a share, at a ***conversion ratio*** of 10 shares of common stock for each $1,000 bond. Assume that Skagg called the bonds and that all bondholders presented their bonds for conversion.

In effect, Skagg has exchanged common stock with a total market value of $12,500,000 (10,000 × 10 × $125 = $12,500,000) for bonds payable with a carrying amount of $10,400,000. Two alternative methods have been suggested for accounting for the conversion—the ***carrying amount method*** (or ***book value method***) and the ***market value method***.

Carrying Amount (Book Value) Method

The carrying amount (book value) method of accounting for the conversion of convertible bonds is based on the view that on the issuance date of the convertible bonds, the proceeds received reflected the prospect that the bonds might be exchanged for common stock at some later time. Thus, the proceeds represented the market value of the bonds *and* the conversion option. When conversion takes place, ***the carrying amount of the bonds measures the increase in contributed capital from the issuance of common stock***, as illustrated in the following journal entry for Skagg Corporation:

Journal entry to record conversion of bonds, ***carrying amount (book value) method***

12% Convertible Bonds Payable	10,000,000	
Premium on Bonds Payable	400,000	
Common Stock, no par value		10,400,000
To record conversion of bonds to 100,000 shares of common stock.		

Market Value Method

Adherents of the market value method of accounting for convertible bonds maintain that the issuance of common stock in the conversion of bonds should reflect the market value of the stock, just as issuances of common stock for cash or in nonmonetary transactions do. In their view, the issuance of common stock with a market value of $12,500,000 to liquidate long-term debt with a carrying amount of $10,400,000 results in a $2,100,000 loss ($12,500,000 − $10,400,000 = $2,100,000) to Skagg Corporation, in the same manner as though Skagg had issued the common stock for $12,500,000 cash and paid the cash to the holders of the convertible bonds to extinguish the debt. Under the market value method, Skagg would prepare the following journal entry:

Journal entry to record conversion of bonds, *market value method*

12% Convertible Bonds Payable	10,000,000	
Premium on Bonds Payable	400,000	
Loss on Conversion of Bonds Payable	2,100,000	
Common Stock, no par value		12,500,000
To record conversion of bonds to 100,000 shares of common stock with a market price of $125 a share.		

Evaluation of the Two Methods

The carrying amount (book value) method of accounting for the conversion of convertible bonds appears to be more in accordance with generally accepted accounting principles than does the market value method. The latter method presumes that the current market price for the issuer's common stock is an appropriate measure of the value of the common stock issued in the conversion of bonds. However, this presumption disregards the fact that large blocks of stock often may not be traded at the market price for smaller lots. Further, the issuer has not entered the stock market when it issues common stock to bondholders; the entry into the market took place ***when the bonds were issued***. To assign current market value of the common stock to the stock issued to bondholders implies that a ***bargained exchange transaction*** had taken place when none did.

When preferred stock or common stock is issued to extinguish convertible bonds in an ***exchange offer*** designed to improve the issuer's debt-to-equity ratio, a gain or loss always is recognized. Such exchanges are not made pursuant to the conversion option; thus, the current fair value of the securities issued measures the consideration paid to extinguish the bonds, and a gain or loss is recognized.

Induced Conversion of Convertible Bonds

In order to reduce the cash outflow from interest payments or to improve its ***debt ratio*** (total liabilities divided by total assets), a business enterprise having outstanding convertible bonds may attempt to induce conversion of the bonds. One method would be to call the bonds at a time when the conversion ratio was favourable (that is, the market price of the enterprise's common stock exceeded the conversion price). However, there is no assurance that ***all*** bondholders would respond to a call by converting their bonds to common stock; thus, the enterprise might have to pay substantial amounts of cash for called bonds that were not converted. Thus, another method to induce conversion of convertible bonds is to "sweeten" the conversion feature by either reducing the conversion price or paying cash or other consideration to bondholders who convert.

In ***FASB Statement No. 84***, the U.S. Financial Accounting Standards Board required recognition of an expense equal to the current fair value of consideration issued or paid by a business enterprise to induce conversion of convertible bonds.[1] (Alternative treatments of such consideration might have been as a loss on extinguishment of the bonds or as a reduction of contributed capital attributable to the common stock issued for the bonds converted.) For example, assume that Lacey Limited had 9% convertible bonds outstanding on May 31, Year 6, at face amount

1 FASB, ***FASB Statement No. 84***: "Induced Conversions of Convertible Debt" (Stamford: 1985), p. 2.

and carrying amount of $10 million, which were convertible to 200,000 shares of Lacey's no-par common stock with a market price of $45 a share on May 31. Because the conversion price of $50 a share ($10,000,000 ÷ 200,000 = $50) exceeded the $45 market price of the common stock, Lacey "sweetened" the conversion feature by reducing the conversion price to $40 a share. Assuming all bondholders converted their bonds on May 31, Year 6, and disregarding bond issue costs, Lacey recognized bond conversion expense of $2,250,000, computed as follows:

Computation of bond conversion expense

Market value of common stock issued in induced conversion [($10,000,000 ÷ $40) × $45]	$11,250,000
Less: Market value of common stock that would have been issued under original conversion price (200,000 × $45)	9,000,000
Bond conversion expense	$ 2,250,000

Lacey Limited's journal entry on May 31, Year 6, for the induced conversion of the bonds is as follows:

Journal entry for induced conversion of bonds

9% Convertible Bonds Payable	10,000,000	
Bond Conversion Expense	2,250,000	
Common Stock		12,250,000
To record induced conversion of 9% convertible bonds.		

The result of the foregoing journal entry (disregarding any income tax effect) is a ***net*** increase in Lacey Limited's shareholders' equity of $10,000,000 ($12,250,000 total contributed capital less $2,250,000 bond conversion expense equals $10,000,000), which is equal to the carrying amount of the bonds converted. In Canada, there is no recommendation with respect to induced conversion of bonds. Accordingly, the journal entry would in all likelihood follow that for the example on page 834, wherein no recognition is made of the induced conversion of the convertible bonds.

Characteristics of Convertible Preferred Stock

Many preferred stocks are convertible to common stock at the option of the preferred shareholders. The appeal of convertible preferred stock lies in the fact that it combines certain attributes of both common stock and preferred stock in a single security. Because convertible preferred stock may be exchanged for common stock in a fixed ratio (the ***conversion ratio***), it has the same appreciation potential as the related common stock. The status of convertible preferred stock as a ***senior security*** with a stated annual dividend rate gives it the same reduced risk inherent in nonconvertible preferred stock.

The conversion ratio is set when the convertible preferred stock is issued, but the ratio is subject to adjustment in the event a stock split or a stock dividend is distributed on the common stock. For example, assume that each share of Lansberry

Corporation's $2 cumulative convertible preferred stock was convertible to 1½ shares of its common stock. When the common stock was split 3 for 1, the conversion ratio increased to 4½ (1½ × 3 = 4½) shares of common stock for each share of the convertible preferred stock.

Conversion of Preferred Stock to Common Stock

Investors who acquire convertible preferred stock are influenced by the possibility that conversion would be advantageous on some future date. Therefore, the proceeds received by the issuer for convertible preferred stock may be regarded as the appropriate amount of contributed capital applicable to the common stock that investors receive on exercise of their conversion option, in accordance with the carrying value (book value) method of accounting. Accordingly, when preferred stock conversions are recorded, any additional contributed capital applicable to the preferred stock is eliminated by transfer to the contributed capital ledger accounts representing the common stock being issued. Assume, for example, that Wilkie, Inc., had a $100-par preferred stock convertible at the option of the preferred shareholders to four shares of $10-par common stock. The preferred stock had been issued at a price of $105 a share, resulting in the following ledger account balances:

Ledger account balances related to convertible preferred stock

Convertible preferred stock, $100 par	$1,000,000
Premium on preferred stock	50,000

If 100 shares of preferred stock are presented for conversion, the journal entry is as follows under the carrying amount (book value) method:

Journal entry to record conversion of preferred stock, *carrying amount (book value) method*

Convertible Preferred Stock (100 × $100)	10,000	
Premium on Preferred Stock (100 × $5)	500	
Common Stock (100 × 4 × $10)		4,000
Premium on Common Stock		6,500
To record issuance of 400 shares of $10-par common stock in exchange for 100 shares of $100-par convertible preferred stock.		

In the rare situation in which the par value of the common stock in a conversion transaction exceeds the par value of the preferred stock being converted and the preferred stock was issued at par value, a debit to the Retained Earnings ledger account would be necessary. Note, however, that the amount of retained earnings ***is not increased*** by a conversion of preferred stock to common stock.

Had the preferred and common shares of Wilkie, Inc., been no-par-value shares, the ledger account for the convertible preferred stock of no par value would have a balance of $1,050,000 in it prior to the partial conversion. The conversion of the 100 shares would require a debit to Preferred Stock, and a credit to Common Stock, in the amount of $10,500.

EMPLOYEE CAPITAL ACCUMULATION PLANS

Stock option and stock purchase plans represent an important element of executive compensation. Collectively, plans such as employee stock ownership plans, stock appreciation rights plans, and comparable plans often are referred to as ***employee capital accumulation plans*** because they enable employees to obtain compensation in the form of common stock or cash, in addition to salaries and wages.

Stock Option and Stock Purchase Plans

A ***stock option plan*** gives officers and key employees of a corporation who are granted stock options the opportunity to acquire the corporation's common stock at the ***exercise price*** (or ***option price***) in a specified time period. Thus, a stock option is in essence a ***call*** on the issuer's common stock at a fixed price over a period of years with no risk to the owner. The opportunity for gain is high, and the chance of loss is zero. For example, assume that an executive of Wylie Corporation received an option on January 2, Year 3, to acquire 1,000 shares of Wylie's common stock at $20 a share (the current market price) at any time from January 2, Year 5 (the ***vesting date***), until December 31, Year 12 (the ***expiration date***). If, during the period the stock option is exercisable, the market price of Wylie's common stock increased to, for example, $70 a share, the executive could exercise the stock option and acquire for $20,000 (1,000 × $20 = $20,000) common stock with a market value of $70,000 (1,000 × $70 = $70,000). If Wylie split its common stock or issued a stock dividend during the term of the stock option, the exercise price and the number of shares under option would be adjusted accordingly, under an ***antidilution*** provision of the stock option plan. Thus, the recipients of stock options are rewarded by increases in the market price of the issuer's common stock — a fact that is intended to motivate the recipients to remain in the issuer's employ and to be more productive.

A ***stock purchase plan*** is similar to a stock option plan, except that employees typically may elect to participate in such a plan by authorizing the corporation to deduct specified amounts from the employees' salaries or wages for use in acquiring the corporation's common stock (which may be treasury stock) at a price which may be less than the market price of the stock. Thus, an employee may choose to participate or not to participate in a stock purchase plan; in contrast, the employer selects recipients of stock options under a stock option plan.

Theoretical Issues Involved in Stock Option Plans

From a theoretical viewpoint, the valuation of the compensation expense inherent in stock options is a difficult and challenging problem. In current practice, however, the difficult problem of determining the current fair value of stock options generally is avoided ***by assuming that the options have no value***.

Although this treatment of stock options may be convenient for administration purposes, the current practice clearly has little theoretical support. Because stock options generally represent an important part of the total compensation cost of a corporation, it has been suggested that the options be valued at the amount for

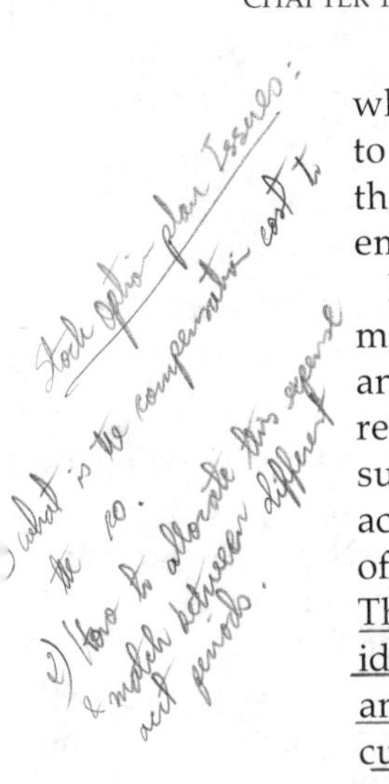

which options could be issued to the public at the time similar options are granted to employees. However, those who frame accounting standards have not found this line of reasoning persuasive, because stock options are designed to give employees additional compensation and are not available for public issuance.

In our opinion, the current practice of not recording compensation expense for many stock option plans results in an understatement of compensation expense and contributed capital, and a corresponding overstatement of net income and retained earnings. The basic accounting principle of matching costs with revenue suggests that the compensation expense implicit in stock option plans should be accrued throughout the term of the option. Such accruals would require the use of estimates (perhaps based on market prices of common stock from year to year). Thus, the two major accounting problems relating to stock option plans may be identified as (1) the measurement of any compensation cost implicit in stock options and (2) the allocation of such compensation cost among accounting periods. The current generally accepted accounting principles addressing these two problems are found, in the United States, in *APB Opinion No. 25*: "Accounting for Stock Issued to Employees."[2] There is no comparable pronouncement in Canada.

APB Opinion No. 25: "Accounting for Stock Issued to Employees"

APB Opinion No. 25 provided a historical summary of the problems encountered in accounting for stock options and set forth the current accounting and disclosure requirements for stock option plans. Generally, such accounting and disclosure requirements depend essentially on whether the stock options are viewed as ***noncompensatory*** or ***compensatory***.

Noncompensatory Stock Option Plan

A stock option plan that is designed to raise capital or induce widespread ownership of the issuer's common stock among officers and employees is classified for financial accounting as a ***noncompensatory plan***. Essential characteristics of a noncompensatory plan listed in ***APB Opinion No. 25*** are: (1) participation of all full-time employees; (2) offering of common stock on an equal basis or as a uniform percentage of salary to all employees; (3) a limited time for exercise of the option; and (4) a discount from market price no greater than would be reasonable in an offering of common stock to existing shareholders. In such noncompensatory plans, no compensation is presumed to be involved. Consequently, the issuer recognizes no compensation expense in its accounting records.

The exercise of noncompensatory stock options is recorded as is any issuance of common stock, as illustrated on page 840 for the issuance of 1,000 shares of no-par-value common stock to employees at $40 a share.

The noncompensatory type of stock option plan was summarized in ***APB Opinion No. 25*** to clear the way for consideration of the more controversial issues of accounting for compensatory stock option plans.

2 AICPA, ***APB Opinion No. 25***: "Accounting for Stock Issued to Employees" (New York: 1972).

Journal entry for exercise of noncompensatory stock options

Cash (1,000 × $40)	40,000	
Common Stock		40,000
To record issuance of 1,000 shares of common stock at $40 a share pursuant to exercise of noncompensatory stock options by employees.		

Compensatory Stock Option Plan

Any stock option plan not possessing the four specified characteristics of a noncompensatory plan is classified as a ***compensatory plan*** even though compensation cost may not be recognized. The features of a compensatory plan may vary in an almost endless number of respects. For example, the ***grantee*** (employee granted the stock option) may be obligated to continue in the employment of the issuer or of its subsidiaries. The number of shares of common stock specified in the stock option plan may be acquired at one time or in instalments during each year of the plan's term. The consideration received by the issuer for common stock issued under a compensatory stock option plan may include cash, notes receivable, or other assets, as well as services from the employee. In compensatory plans, services from the grantee always represent part of the consideration for the common stock issued.

A key provision of ***APB Opinion No. 25*** is that compensation for services received as consideration for the stock options granted is measured by the difference (''***spread***'') between ***the market price of the stock on the measurement date*** (defined below) ***and the amount that the employee is required to pay*** (exercise price). In the application of this principle, determination of the measurement date for ascertaining compensation cost touches the theoretical core of the problem. The ***measurement date*** is the ***first date on which are known both the number of shares of common stock to be received by each grantee and the exercise price***. On the measurement date the issuer of the stock options and the grantees presumably reach agreement as to the amount of total compensation to be paid, and the issuer forgoes any alternative uses of the common stock reserved for the exercise of the options. For most stock option plans, the measurement date is the date that the options are granted.

APB Opinion No. 25 required that an issuer should recognize compensation cost under compensatory stock option plans when the exercise price is less than the market price of the common stock on the measurement date. Because the exercise price in many stock option plans is set at or above the market price of the common stock on the date of grant, no compensation cost is recognized for such plans. When compensation cost is recognized, it should be allocated to the accounting periods subsequent to the adoption of a stock option plan that benefit from the services provided by the grantees. The following guidelines for accruing compensation cost under compensatory stock option plans are presented in ***APB Opinion No. 25***:[3]

3 AICPA, ***APB Opinion No. 25***, pp. 474–475.

> Compensation cost in stock option, purchase, and award plans should be recognized as an expense of one or more periods in which an employee performs services and also as part or all of the consideration received for stock issued to the employee through a plan. The grant or award may specify the period or periods during which the employee performs services, or the period or periods may be inferred from the terms or from the past pattern of grants or awards....
>
> An employee may perform services in several periods before an employer corporation issues stock... for those services. The employer corporation should accrue compensation expense in each period in which the services are performed. If the measurement date is later than the date of grant or award, an employer corporation should record the compensation expense each period from date of grant or award to date of measurement based on the quoted market price of the stock at the end of each period....
>
> If stock is issued in a plan before some or all of the services are performed, part of the consideration recorded for the stock issued is unearned compensation and should be shown as a separate reduction of stockholders' equity. The unearned compensation should be accounted for as expense of the period or periods in which the employee performs service....
>
> Accruing compensation expense may require estimates, and adjustment of those estimates in later periods may be necessary.... For example, if a stock option is not exercised (or awarded stock is returned to the corporation) because an employee fails to fulfill an obligation, the estimate of compensation expense recorded in previous periods should be adjusted by decreasing compensation expense in the period of forfeiture.

The reporting of unearned (deferred) compensation cost as a reduction of shareholders' equity is appropriate because the entire recorded consideration relating to issuance of common stock has not been received. When the services are performed, the debit balance in the Deferred Compensation Cost ledger account is recognized as compensation expense.

Illustrations of a Compensatory Stock Option Plan

When Measurement Date Is Grant Date and Exercise Price Equals Market Price To illustrate the accounting for a compensatory stock option plan when the measurement date is the grant date, assume the following facts: On January 2, Year 1, Clark Corporation granted to key employees options to acquire 10,000 shares of its no-par common stock at $20 a share in exchange for services to be performed over the next three years. The market price of the common stock on that date was $20 a share. The options were exercised on December 31, Year 3, when the market price of the common stock was $31 a share.

Journal entry for compensatory stock options: measurement date is grant date; exercise price equals market price

Cash (10,000 × $20)	200,000	
Common Stock		200,000
To record issuance of 10,000 shares of common stock at $20 a share pursuant to compensatory stock option plan.		

Although Clark Corporation's stock option plan is a compensatory one, no compensation cost is recognized because the exercise price is equal to the market price on the measurement date, which is January 2, Year 1, the grant date. Accordingly, the ***only*** journal entry prepared by Clark for its stock options is on December 31, Year 3, the ***exercise date***, as shown at the bottom of page 841.

Thus, although Clark's employees received common stock with a market value of $310,000 (10,000 × $31 = $310,000) for cash of only $200,000, no compensation expense is recognized by Clark under the provisions of ***APB Opinion No. 25***.

When Measurement Date Is Grant Date and Exercise Price Is Less Than Market Price Let us change the assumptions in the foregoing illustration to provide that the market price of Clark Corporation's common stock on January 2, Year 1, the measurement (and grant) date, was $23, rather than $20, a share. In such circumstances, the following journal entries are prepared by Clark (income tax effects are disregarded):

Journal entries for compensatory stock options: measurement date is grant date; exercise price less than market price

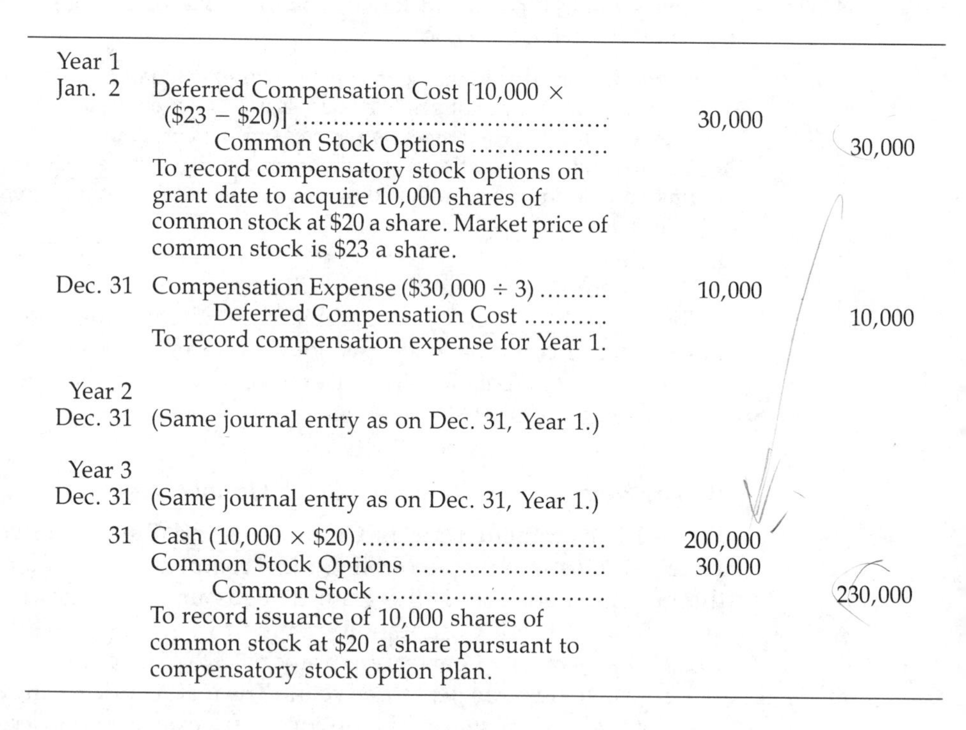

Date	Account	Debit	Credit
Year 1			
Jan. 2	Deferred Compensation Cost [10,000 × ($23 – $20)]	30,000	
	Common Stock Options		30,000
	To record compensatory stock options on grant date to acquire 10,000 shares of common stock at $20 a share. Market price of common stock is $23 a share.		
Dec. 31	Compensation Expense ($30,000 ÷ 3)	10,000	
	Deferred Compensation Cost		10,000
	To record compensation expense for Year 1.		
Year 2			
Dec. 31	(Same journal entry as on Dec. 31, Year 1.)		
Year 3			
Dec. 31	(Same journal entry as on Dec. 31, Year 1.)		
31	Cash (10,000 × $20)	200,000	
	Common Stock Options	30,000	
	Common Stock		230,000
	To record issuance of 10,000 shares of common stock at $20 a share pursuant to compensatory stock option plan.		

In the foregoing situation compensation expense of only $30,000 is recognized, despite the employees' having received common stock with a market value of $110,000 ($310,000 – $200,000 = $110,000) in excess of the amount of cash they paid for the common stock.

The common stock options and deferred compensation cost are included in the contributed capital section of the balance sheet on December 31, Year 1, as follows:

Balance sheet presentation of stock options and related deferred compensation

Common stock options	$30,000	
Less: Deferred compensation cost	20,000	$10,000

Illustration of Variable Compensatory Stock Option Plan

When Measurement Date Is Two Years After Grant Date and Market Price Ultimately Exceeds Exercise Price To illustrate the accounting for a ***variable*** compensatory stock option plan when the measurement date is ***subsequent*** to the grant date (because the exercise price and the number of shares of common stock that may be acquired by employees have not been determined), assume the following facts: On January 2, Year 1, Dome Corporation adopted a compensatory stock option plan for key employees to acquire an ***estimated*** 20,000 shares of no-par-value common stock at an exercise price estimated at $20 a share. The market price of the common stock on January 2, Year 1, is $19 a share. Both the number of shares to be issued and the exercise price are to be determined on December 31, Year 2, the measurement date. The options were granted on January 2, Year 1, in consideration for services to be performed during years 1 and 2, and may be exercised at any time starting on January 2, Year 3. The number of shares of common stock covered by the compensatory stock option plan, the exercise price, and the market price of the common stock on the relevant dates are as follows:

Data regarding compensatory stock option plan

	January 2, Year 1 (grant date)	*December 31, Year 1*	*December 31, Year 2 (measurement date)*
Number of shares optioned	20,000 (est.)	20,000 (est.)	21,000 (actual)
Exercise price	$20 (est.)	$20 (est.)	$22 (actual)
Market price of common stock	$19	$25	$33

No journal entry is required on January 2, Year 1, because the estimated exercise price exceeded the market price of the common stock and because the measurement date is December 31, Year 2. On December 31, Year 1, ***estimated compensation expense and deferred compensation cost*** are recorded as follows:

Journal entry for compensatory stock option plan prior to measurement date (which is later than grant date)

Year 1			
Dec. 31	Compensation Expense ($100,000 ÷ 2)	50,000	
	Deferred Compensation Cost	50,000	
	Common Stock Options [20,000 × ($25 − $20)]...............................		100,000
	To record estimated compensation expense for Year 1 based on market price of common stock, estimated number of shares optioned, and estimated exercise price. (Income tax effects are disregarded.)		

On the measurement date, December 31, Year 2, the journal entry below is prepared:

Journal entry for compensatory stock option plan on measurement date (which is later than grant date)

Year 2			
Dec. 31	Compensation Expense	181,000	
	Common Stock Options ($231,000 − $100,000)		131,000
	Deferred Compensation Cost		50,000
	To record compensation expense for Year 2 on the measurement date, determined as follows:		
	Total compensation cost [21,000 × ($33 − $22)]	$231,000	
	Less: Compensation expense recorded in Year 1	50,000	
	Compensation expense for Year 2	$181,000	
	(Income tax effects are disregarded.)		

In the foregoing situation, total compensation cost of $231,000 is measured by the difference between the market price of the common stock under option, $693,000 (21,000 × $33 = $693,000) and the total exercise price to be paid by employees, $462,000 (21,000 × $22 = $462,000). Thus, $693,000 − $462,000 = $231,000. Accounting standards for stock option plans therefore provide for differing measurements of compensation cost, depending on whether the measurement is ***on*** or ***subsequent to*** the grant date.

At the time the stock options are exercised by Dome Corporation's employees, a journal entry similar to the last entry illustrated on page 842 is prepared by Dome.

When compensation expense under stock option plans is reported by the issuer in an accounting period other than that in which the expense is deductible for income tax purposes, a ***timing difference*** results that requires the application of interperiod income tax allocation procedures. This topic is covered in Chapter 21.

If grantees should terminate before performing the services required for exercise of the stock options, the appropriate portions of common stock options and deferred compensation cost must be written off. For example, if on January 2, Year 2, grantees of 1,000 of Dome Corporation's common stock options terminated their employment and thus did not perform required services during Year 2, Dome would prepare the following journal entry on January 2, Year 2:

Journal entry for write-off of stock options of terminated grantees

Common Stock Options ($100,000 × 1/20)	5,000	
Deferred Compensation Cost ($50,000 × 1/20)		2,500
Compensation Expense ($50,000 × 1/20)		2,500
To write off common stock options, deferred compensation cost and Year 1 compensation expense applicable to grantees of 1,000 stock options who terminated their employment before completing the service period required for the options. (Income tax effects are disregarded.)		

The foregoing journal entry reduces compensation expense for Year 2 by the amount of compensation expense of Year 1 attributable to the terminated grantees.

Also, a decline in the market price of the issuer's common stock may require a credit to Compensation Expense. For example, ***if the market value of Dome Corporation's common stock had been $24 a share instead of $33 a share on December 31, Year 2,*** Dome would prepare the following journal entry on December 31, Year 2:

Journal entry for reduction of compensation expense related to stock options

Common Stock Options {$100,000 − [21,000 × ($24 − $22)]}		58,000	
Deferred Compensation Cost			50,000
Compensation Expense			8,000
To record reduction of compensation expense for Year 2 on the measurement date, determined as follows:			
Total compensation cost 21,000 × ($24 − $22)	$42,000		
Less: Compensation expense recorded in Year 1	50,000		
Reduction of compensation expense for Year 2	($ 8,000)		
(Income tax effects are disregarded.)			

Journal Entries for Stock Purchase Plans

The accounting for compensation cost associated with stock purchase plans is similar to that for stock option plans. However, many stock purchase plans provide for withholding from employees' salaries or wages to accumulate the total purchase price. A liability ledger account is credited for such withholdings in the journal entries for payroll; when common stock is issued under the stock purchase plan, the liability account (rather than Cash) is debited.

Accounting for Stock Appreciation Rights

In recent years, a modification of stock options known as stock appreciation rights has become popular. ***Stock appreciation rights*** are awards entitling employees to receive cash, common stock, or a combination of cash and common stock in an amount equivalent to any excess of the market value of a stated number of shares of the issuer's common stock over a stated price. Although stock appreciation rights may be granted separately, they typically are granted in conjunction with stock options, in a ***tandem*** (or ***variable***) ***plan***. Stock option plans that include stock appreciation rights typically provide that the stock options are forfeited if the stock appreciation rights are exercised, and vice versa. Since the ***CICA Handbook*** contains no information with respect to stock appreciation rights, the following discussion of such plans is adapted from ***FASB Interpretation No. 28***: "Accounting for Stock Appreciation Rights. . . .[4]

4 FASB, ***FASB Interpretation No. 28***: "Accounting for Stock Appreciation Rights and Other Variable Stock Option or Award Plans" (Stamford: 1978).

Compensation expense for a stock option plan that includes stock appreciation rights usually is measured under the presumption that grantees will exercise the stock appreciation rights, which require no cash payment, rather than the stock option, which requires a cash payment. The compensation element of stock appreciation rights is measured by the excess of the market price of the common stock over the exercise price. Changes in the market price of the common stock during the period from the grant date to the measurement date (which always is the exercise date) require changes in the measurement of compensation expense. The measurement date for stock appreciation rights is the date the rights are exercised because the number of shares of common stock to be issued is indeterminable until the exercise date. The compensation expense is accrued proportionately for each accounting period during which the grantees perform services required by the stock option plan. If no service period is specified, the vesting period is used to recognize compensation expense. Typically, the ***vesting period*** runs from the grant date to the date the stock options or stock appreciation rights become exercisable.

Compensation expense accrued in one accounting period is increased or decreased in subsequent periods for changes in the market price of the common stock, but it is never reduced below zero. If grantees elect to exercise the stock option rather than the stock appreciation rights, the compensation expense previously recognized for the stock appreciation rights becomes part of contributed capital for the common stock issued.

Illustration of Accounting for Stock Appreciation Rights

Under a tandem stock option plan that had been approved by its shareholders, Winfield Corporation granted stock options with stock appreciation rights to its employees on January 2, Year 1. The options were to expire on December 31, Year 10, cover 10,000 shares of Winfield's no-par common stock, and were exercisable beginning January 2, Year 4. No service period was specified for the grantees; therefore, ***the vesting period is three years and the measurement date is not known until grantees exercise the options***. The exercise price was $15 a share, which was equal to the market price of Winfield's common stock on January 2, Year 1. The per-share market prices of Winfield's common stock were as shown in the table below.

Jan. 2, Year 1	$15
Dec. 31, Year 1	18
Dec. 31, Year 2	21
Dec. 31, Year 3, and Jan. 2, Year 4	25

On January 2, Year 4, grantees exercised ***stock appreciation rights*** for 7,000 of the 10,000 shares of common stock covered by the stock option plan, as follows:

1 Grantees of options for 4,000 shares elected to receive cash.

2 Grantees of options for 3,000 shares elected to receive 1,200 shares of Winfield's common stock in lieu of cash.

Thus, the measurement date for 7,000 (4,000 + 3,000 = 7,000) shares covered by the stock option plan was January 2, Year 4. The measurement date for the remaining 3,000 shares under option (10,000 – 7,000 = 3,000) remains unknown until grantees of those options exercise either the stock appreciation rights or the stock options of Winfield's ***tandem plan***. Because of the existence of the two alternatives, the measurement date for tandem plans must be the exercise date.

The following journal entries are prepared for Winfield Corporation's stock option plan, under the assumptions that grantees will elect the stock appreciation rights alternative, that the vesting period is three years (January 2, Year 1, to January 2, Year 4), and that income tax effects are disregarded:

Journal entries for stock appreciation rights

Date	Account / Explanation	Computation	Debit	Credit
Year 1				
Dec. 31	Compensation Expense		10,000	
	Compensation Payable			10,000
	To record compensation expense under stock option plan for Year 1, determined as follows:			
	Total compensation cost [10,000 × ($18 – $15)]	$30,000		
	Portion vested on Dec. 31, Year 1	⅓		
	Compensation expense for Year 1	$10,000		
Year 2				
Dec. 31	Compensation Expense		30,000	
	Compensation Payable			30,000
	To record compensation expense under stock option plan for Year 2, determined as follows:			
	Total compensation cost [10,000 × ($21 – $15)	$60,000		
	Portion vested on Dec. 31, Year 2	⅔		
	Accrued compensation cost, Dec. 31, Year 2	$40,000		
	Less: Compensation expense for Year 1	10,000		
	Compensation expense for Year 2	$30,000		
Year 3				
Dec. 31	Compensation Expense		60,000	
	Compensation Payable			60,000
	To record compensation expense under stock option plan for Year 3, determined as follows:			
	Total compensation cost [10,000 × ($25 – $15)]	$100,000		
	Portion vested on Dec. 31, Year 3	3/3		
	Accrued compensation cost, Dec. 31, Year 3	$100,000		
	Less: Compensation expense for Year 1 and Year 2 ($10,000 + $30,000)	40,000		
	Compensation expense for Year 3	$ 60,000		

Year 4			
Jan. 2	Compensation Payable ($100,000 × 0.70)	70,000	
	Cash		40,000
	Common Stock		30,000
	To record exercise of stock appreciation rights as follows:		
	Cash [4,000 × ($25 – $15)] $40,000		

Note that a Compensation Payable liability ledger account is credited in the foregoing journal entries that debit Compensation Expense because until employees exercise the stock appreciation rights, there is uncertainty as to how much cash will be paid and how many shares, if any, of common stock will be issued.

For Year 4 through Year 10, or until all the stock appreciation rights are exercised, Winfield Corporation must debit or credit the Compensation Payable ledger account for the effects of annual changes in the market price of Winfield's common stock, because the stock appreciation rights were fully vested on January 2, Year 4. The offsetting credit or debit is to the Compensation Expense ledger account. However, total compensation expense is not reduced below zero. Accrued compensation applicable to any options that expire on December 31, Year 10, would be written off by a debit to Compensation Payable and a credit to Compensation Expense.

The accounting for stock appreciation rights of Winfield Corporation resulted in total compensation expense of $100,000 for Year 1 through Year 3. Note that, had Winfield accounted for the tandem stock option plan under the assumption that this was a stock option plan ***only***, Winfield would have recorded ***no compensation expense*** for Year 1 through Year 3. This outcome results because the measurement date for the stock options is January 2, Year 1 (the number of shares under option and the exercise price being known on that date), and there is no difference between the exercise price and the market price of Winfield's common stock on January 2, Year 1. This significant difference in the computation of compensation cost for a tandem stock option plan is troublesome for accountants because under a straight stock option plan benefits to grantees are essentially the same as under a tandem plan that includes stock appreciation rights.

Accounting for Stock Options Involving Junior Stock

Recently, some stock option and stock purchase plans have involved ***junior stock***, which is a specific type of capital stock issued to employees that is subordinate to the issuer's common stock in terms of voting, liquidation, and dividend rights and is convertible to common stock of the issuer if certain performance goals are achieved or if certain transactions occur. Thus, the measurement date for stock option and purchase plans involving junior stock generally is later than the grant date because the attainment of the performance goals or the occurrence of the specified transactions is after the grant date. Again, since the ***CICA Handbook*** is silent in this area, the following discussion of stock option plans involving junior stock is adapted from ***FASB Interpretation No. 38***: "Determining the Measurement Date for... Plans Involving Junior Stock."[5]

The ***measurement date for plans involving junior stock is the same as for stock option plans with variable terms***, that is, the first date on which are known both the number of shares of the issuer's common stock to be issued in exchange for the junior stock and the exercise price, if any. Compensation cost for junior stock is accrued by the issuer only if it becomes ***probable*** that the required performance goals will be achieved or the specified transactions will occur. The compensation cost, which is the difference between the market price of the issuer's common stock on the measurement date and the amount the employee paid or will pay for the junior stock, ***is accrued between the date that attainment of the requirements for conversion of the junior stock to common stock becomes probable and the measurement date***. If junior stock may not be converted to common stock until ***after*** the measurement date, the period for accrual of compensation cost ends on the date the junior stock first becomes convertible or the end of the employee's required service period, whichever occurs first. The procedure for measuring compensation expense for each accounting period during the term of accrual of compensation cost is the same as for stock appreciation rights, as discussed in the preceding section.

Illustration of Accounting for Junior Stock

On January 2, Year 1, under a plan approved by shareholders, Rebo Corporation issued to key employees stock options involving 10,000 shares of junior stock that was convertible in a 1-to-1 ratio to 10,000 shares of Rebo's no-par common stock, starting on January 2, Year 5, if the employees remained with Rebo through that date and if the amount of Rebo's earnings per share for Year 4 was at least $2 a share more than Year 1 earnings per share. The employees paid Rebo $5 a share for the junior stock. Not until December 31, Year 2, did Rebo management judge that it was ***probable*** that Year 4 earnings per share would be at least $2 a share more than the $3.18 earnings per share for Year 1. Market prices per share of Rebo's common stock were as follows:

Jan. 2, Year 1	$ 8
Dec. 31, Year 1	11
Dec. 31, Year 2	14
Dec. 31, Year 3	17
Dec. 31, Year 4	20
Dec. 31, Year 5	21

On December 31, Year 4, it was ***certain*** that Year 4 earnings per share would exceed $5.18; thus, December 31, Year 4, was the measurement date.

Following are journal entries (disregarding income tax effects) for Rebo Corporation for the junior stock:

5 FASB, ***FASB Interpretation No. 38***: "Determining the Measurement Date for Stock Option, Purchase, and Award Plans Involving Junior Stock" (Stamford: 1984).

Journal entries for stock options involving junior stock

Date	Account / Explanation		Debit	Credit
Year 1				
Jan. 2	Cash (10,000 × $5)		50,000	
	Junior Stock Issued			50,000
	To record issuance of 10,000 shares of junior stock to employees.			
Year 2				
Dec. 31	Compensation Expense		30,000	
	Compensation Payable			30,000
	To record compensation expense under stock option plan involving junior stock as follows:			
	Total compensation cost [10,000 × ($14 − $5)]	$90,000		
	Portion vested on Dec. 31, Year 2	⅓		
	Compensation expense for Year 2	$30,000		
Year 3				
Dec. 31	Compensation Expense		50,000	
	Compensation Payable			50,000
	To record compensation expense under stock option plan involving junior stock as follows:			
	Total compensation cost [10,000 × ($17 − $5)]	$120,000		
	Portion vested on Dec. 31, Year 3	⅔		
	Accrued compensation cost, Dec. 31, Year 3	$ 80,000		
	Less: Compensation expense for Year 2	30,000		
	Compensation expense for Year 3	$ 50,000		
Year 4				
Dec. 31	Compensation Expense		70,000	
	Compensation Payable			70,000
	To record compensation expense under stock option plan involving junior stock as follows:			
	Total compensation cost [10,000 × ($20 − $5)]	$150,000		
	Portion vested on Dec. 31, Year 4	3/3		
	Accrued compensation cost, Dec. 31, Year 4	$150,000		
	Less: Compensation expense for Year 2 and Year 3	80,000		
	Compensation expense for Year 4	$ 70,000		
Year 5				
Jan. 2	Compensation Payable		150,000	
	Junior Stock Issued		50,000	
	Common Stock			20,000
	To record conversion of 10,000 shares of junior stock to 10,000 shares of common stock.			

The following aspects of the foregoing journal entries should be noted:

1 The Junior Stock Issued ledger account is credited for the $50,000 paid by employees for the junior stock because such stock is not the conventional common stock of a corporation. Until the junior stock is converted to common stock, the contributed capital ledger accounts applicable to common stock are not affected.

2 There is no journal entry for compensation expense on December 31, Year 1, because Rebo Corporation's management had not determined by then that attainment of the required Year 4 earnings per share in the amount of $5.18 ($3.18 + $2.00 = $5.18) was ***probable***.

3 Once attainment of the required Year 4 earnings per share of $5.18 had been determined to be probable, on December 31, Year 2, Rebo begins accruing compensation cost over the remaining three-year period of employee service.

4 Total consideration for the common stock issued on January 2, Year 5, is $200,000, the $50,000 paid by employees for the junior stock plus the $150,000 compensation measured and recognized in Year 2 through Year 4.

If junior stock does not become convertible to common stock, and the issuer pays cash to employees to reacquire the junior stock from them, total compensation cost is measured by the difference between the cash paid to employees and the amount employees paid for the junior stock.

Disclosure of Employee Capital Accumulation Plans

Because of their significance to a business enterprise, employee capital accumulation plans are disclosed in a note to the financial statements. The disclosure may be extensive, especially if there are several such plans in effect. An important feature of the disclosure is the number of shares of authorized but unissued common stock that are reserved for exercise of stock options and for employee stock purchase plans.

An example of disclosure of employee capital accumulation plans is on page 214 of Chapter 4.

Shareholders' Equity in the Balance Sheet

The balance sheet presentation of shareholders' equity is illustrated on page 852 for Database Limited. Note that this illustration discloses the following information:

1 The fact that each class of capital stock issued and outstanding has no par value

2 The dividend preference and redemption (call) price of the convertible cumulative preferred stock (Conversion terms of preferred stock would be described in a note to the financial statements)

3 The number of shares authorized, issued, and outstanding for each class of capital stock

4 The additional contributed capital from various sources

5 The total amount of contributed capital, retained earnings, deferred compensation cost as a deduction from the value assigned to common stock options, and the total amount of shareholders' equity

Shareholders' equity section of balance sheet

DATABASE LIMITED
Shareholders' Equity Section of Balance Sheet
December 31, Year 8

$4 convertible, cumulative preferred stock, no par value, callable at $106 a share, authorized, issued, and outstanding 100,000 shares		$10,000,000
Common stock, no par value, authorized, an unlimited number of shares, issued and outstanding, 1,000,000 shares		7,500,000
Common stock options	$420,000	
Less: Deferred compensation cost	250,000	170,000
Stock warrants		500,000
Total contributed capital		$18,170,000
Retained earnings		4,100,000
Total shareholders' equity		$22,270,000

In balance sheets of large business enterprises, the need for concise presentation may require some of the information concerning contributed capital to be disclosed in a note to the financial statements rather than in the balance sheet. For example, the information concerning preferred stock preferences, conversion ratios, and sources of additional contributed capital, may be disclosed thus. In addition, the number of shares of authorized but unissued common stock reserved for conversion of convertible bonds and preferred stock and for employee capital accumulation plans is disclosed in a note to the financial statements.

Pro Forma Financial Statements

When significant new financial changes are in prospect for a business enterprise, accountants may be asked to prepare financial statements that give effect to the planned transactions. Such statements are called ***pro forma financial statements***. For example, when two or more companies are planning a business combination, the shareholders and management of each company will want pro forma financial statements for the combined enterprise to facilitate analysis of the financial position and earnings of the combined enterprise.

Another use for pro forma financial statements arises when a purchase-type business combination of two companies occurs ***during*** the current year. A pro forma income statement for a full year may be prepared to show the operating results that ***would have*** resulted for the entire year ***if*** the combination had taken place at the beginning of the current year.

Pro forma financial statements also are useful in situations other than business combinations. For example, a business enterprise might be considering the issuance of preferred stock to obtain cash with which to retire bonds outstanding. In weighing the merits of this action, management will need a pro forma balance sheet to show the financial position of the enterprise as it would have appeared if these transactions had been carried out. Because the substitution of preferred stock for bonds would eliminate interest expense and have a bearing on taxable income, it also is desirable to prepare a pro forma income statement showing how the net income and earnings per share of the past year would have been modified if the changes in the capital structure had been in effect.

Other potential uses of pro forma financial statements are in connection with the contemplated disposal of a business segment and the change in a business enterprise from a partnership to a corporation.

REVIEW QUESTIONS

1 How are outstanding common stock warrants presented in the financial statements of a business enterprise?

2 Dane Corporation issued warrants to the holders of its 600,000 shares of common stock on November 30, Year 4, entitling them to acquire one convertible $1,000 bond at face amount for each 100 shares of common stock owned. The warrants expired on January 28, Year 5. On December 31, Year 4, bonds in the face amount of $2,500,000 had been issued through the exercise of warrants. What disclosure is made of these events in Dane Corporation's balance sheet on December 31, Year 4, or in a note to the financial statements?

3 Is the ***preemptive right*** which is usually included in the Certificate of Incorporation with respect to common stock ownership logically applicable only to additional issuances of common stock, or should it also apply to additional issuances of convertible bonds and convertible preferred stock? Explain.

4 If common stock warrants are assigned a value at the time of issuance, what accounting is necessary if the warrants are not exercised and expire?

5 How are owners of convertible preferred stock or convertible bonds protected from the dilutive effects of stock dividends and stock splits on the issuer's common stock?

6 What treatment is given to the current fair value of common stock issued in exchange for convertible bonds? Explain.

7 What are the two major accounting problems relating to stock option plans?

8 Moore Corporation issued five-year stock options to its key executives on May 21, Year 6, at 100% of the market price of the common stock on that date. State arguments for and against recognizing compensation expense corresponding to the estimated current fair value of these options.

9 What are the major differences between a ***compensatory stock option plan*** and a ***noncompensatory plan***? Does the issuer recognize compensation expense applicable to either?

10 What date does ***APB Opinion No. 25***: ''Accounting for Stock Issued to Employees'' stipulate for use in the measurement of compensation for employee services relating to stock option plans? How is the amount of compensation cost measured?

11 What are ***stock appreciation rights***? How are they related to stock option plans?

12 What is the ***vesting period*** for stock appreciation rights?

13 Is a journal entry required when ***junior stock*** is issued to employees in connection with a stock option plan? Explain.

14 Define ***pro forma financial statements*** and state some examples of circumstances in which pro forma financial statements may be prepared.

EXERCISES

Ex. 17-1 Select the best answer for each of the following multiple-choice questions:

1 Compensation cost under a compensatory stock option plan for which the measurement date is the grant date is recognized in the issuer's income statement:

a On the date grantees of the stock options retire
b On each accounting period subsequent to the adoption of the plan in which grantees of the stock options are required to render services
c On the exercise date
d On the date the stock option plan is adopted

2 Under a compensatory stock option plan for which the measurement date is the grant date, what ledger account is credited on the measurement date?

a Retained Earnings
b Common Stock Options
c Deferred Compensation Cost
d Compensation Expense
e None of the foregoing

3 A company's granting to its shareholders the opportunity to acquire additional shares of common stock at a specified price during a specified time period is an example of a:

a Dividend reinvestment plan
b Stock right
c Stock dividend
d Stock option
e None of the foregoing

4 If the common stock for a compensatory stock option plan is issued before some or all of the services are performed by the grantee employees, a part of the consideration recorded for the stock issued is unearned compensation and is shown in the balance sheet as a line item in:

a Noncurrent liabilities
b Shareholders' equity
c Current assets
d Noncurrent assets
e Some other classification

5 A company issued to its shareholders warrants for rights to acquire for $25 a share 50,000 unissued shares of $10-par common stock. The Premium on Common Stock ledger account is credited when the warrants:

a Are issued
b Expire

c Become exercisable
d Are exercised

6 Stock appreciation rights are a modification of stock option plans that permit employees to receive:
a Cash only
b Common stock only
c A combination of cash and common stock
d Any of the foregoing

7 If the par value of common stock issued in a conversion transaction exceeds the par value of the converted preferred stock which had been issued at par, the excess is debited to:
a Loss on Conversion of Preferred Stock
b Premium on Common Stock
c Retained Earnings
d Conversion Expense

8 When convertible bonds are converted to common stock, the journal entry to record the conversion under the market value method includes the effect of:
a The market value of the bonds but not of the common stock
b The market value of the common stock but not of the bonds
c The market values of both the bonds and the common stock
d The market value of either the bonds or the common stock

9 On September 1, Year 3, Oak Limited issued 100,000 shares of $12, no-par preferred stock together with 100,000 warrants to acquire one share of Oak's no-par common stock for one warrant plus $20 cash. The warrants had an aggregate market value of $400,000 on September 1, Year 3. Oak records the exercise of 20,000 warrants on September 29, Year 3, with the following journal entry (explanation omitted):

		Debit	Credit
a	Cash	400,000	
	Common Stock Warrants	80,000	
	Common Stock		480,000
b	Cash	400,000	
	Common Stock		400,000
c	Cash	400,000	
	Common Stock Warrants		80,000
	Common Stock		320,000
d	Cash	400,000	
	Common Stock Warrants	400,000	
	Common Stock		800,000

Ex. 17-2 The no-par-value common stock of Hull Corporation presently is trading at $30 a share. Hull has an unlimited number of authorized shares of common stock; four million are issued and outstanding. Because of a need for additional capital, Hull issued to its common shareholders stock warrants for rights permitting the acquisition of one new share of common stock in exchange for five warrants and $28 cash. The warrants expire 30 days after the date of issuance.

a Prepare a journal entry, if any, for Hull Corporation to record the issuance of the stock warrants.

b Assuming that all the stock warrants were exercised, prepare a journal entry for Hull Corporation to record the exercise of the stock warrants.

c Assuming that only 80% of the stock warrants were exercised before the expiration date, prepare the required journal entry or entries for Hull Corporation.

Ex. 17-3 Burk Corporation issued for $8,250,000, 150,000 shares of no-par-value preferred stock, together with detachable stock warrants entitling the holders to acquire one share of common stock for each share of preferred stock on presentation of a warrant and $25 cash. At the time of issuance, the common stock was trading on the stock exchange at $23 a share. The warrants began trading on the stock exchange at a price of $4 each, and the preferred stock began trading at $51 a share. The warrants expire in six months.

Prepare a journal entry for Burk Corporation to record the issuance of the preferred stock with warrants attached.

Ex. 17-4 On July 1, Year 7, Wing Corporation issued for $525,000 a total of 5,000 shares of no-par-value, $10 noncumulative preferred stock, together with one detachable stock warrant for each share of preferred stock issued. Each warrant contained a right to acquire one share of Wing's no-par common stock for $15 a share. The market price of the warrants on July 1, Year 7, was $2.50 a warrant. On October 31, Year 7, when the market price of the common stock was $19 a share and the market price of the warrants was $3 a warrant, 4,000 rights were exercised.

Prepare a journal entry for Wing Corporation to record the exercise of the rights and the issuance of the common stock.

Ex. 17-5 Newton Corporation had two issues of securities outstanding: common stock and a 9% convertible bond issue with a face amount of $10,000,000. Interest payment dates of the bond issue were June 30 and December 31. The conversion option in the bond indenture entitled the bondholders to receive 40 shares of $10-par common stock in exchange for each $1,000 bond. On June 30, Year 9, the holders of $900,000 face amount of bonds exercised the conversion option. The market price of the bonds on that date was $1,425 a bond, and the market price of the common stock was $35 a share. The amount of the unamortized bond discount on the date of conversion was $500,000.

Compute the amount that Newton Corporation credits to the Common Stock ledger account on June 30, Year 9, as a result of the conversion, under the carrying amount (book value) method.

Ex. 17-6 On December 31, Year 11, Lyle Limited had outstanding $2,000,000 face amount of 8% convertible bonds that were to mature on December 31, Year 15, with interest payable semiannually on June 30 and December 31. The Premium on Bonds Payable ledger account had a balance of $45,000 on December 31, Year 11, which was being amortized by the straight-line method. Each $1,000 bond was convertible to 60 shares of Lyle's no-par-value common stock. On December 31, Year 12, when the market price of Lyle's common stock was $18 a share, a bondholder converted 200 of the bonds.

retire shares @ mkt value

Compute the amount that Lyle Limited credits, as a result of the conversion of the bonds, to the Common Stock ledger account on December 31, Year 12, under the market value method.

Ex. 17-7 Kopp Corporation has outstanding two issues of securities: convertible preferred stock and common stock. Both securities are traded on the Vancouver Stock Exchange. Assume that you acquired 100 shares of the $8, no-par-value convertible preferred stock at $103 a share when it was originally issued by Kopp. The preferred stock is convertible to four shares of no-par common stock at any time. When you invested in the convertible preferred stock, the common stock had a market price of $22 a share. Now, several years later, the common stock has a market price of $90 a share, and you decide to convert your preferred stock to common stock.

Prepare a journal entry for Kopp Corporation to record the conversion, under the carrying value (book value) method.

Ex. 17-8 In Year 3, Alba Corporation issued, for $105 a share, 8,000 shares of $100-par, 12% convertible preferred stock. One share of preferred stock could be exchanged for three shares of Alba's $5-par common stock at the option of the preferred shareholder. In August, Year 4, all the preferred stock was converted to common stock. The market price of the common stock on the date of the conversion was $30 a share.

Compute the total amount that Alba Corporation credits to Premium on Common Stock as a result of the issuance of the preferred stock and its subsequent conversion to common stock, under the carrying value (book value) method.

Ex. 17-9 On September 29, Year 4, grantees of options to acquire 10,000 shares of Nako Limited's no-par common stock at an exercise price of $40 a share exercised their options. On the September 1, Year 1, grant date (which was the measurement date), the market price of Nako's common stock was $50 a share. On September 29, Year 4, the market price of Nako's common stock was $60 a share. Nako had correctly recognized compensation expense related to the compensatory stock options.

Prepare a journal entry for Nako Limited to record the exercise of the stock options on September 29, Year 4. Disregard income taxes.

Ex. 17-10 On July 18, Year 4, Cortez Corporation granted stock options to certain of its key employees as additional compensation. The options permitted the acquisition of 10,000 shares of Cortez common stock at $32 a share. On the grant date, the market price of the common stock was $38 a share. The options were exercisable beginning January 2, Year 5, and expire on December 31, Year 6. On February 3, Year 5, when the common stock was trading at $45 a share, all the options were exercised.

Compute the total amount of compensation cost that Cortez Corporation should recognize for the issuance of the stock options. Disregard income taxes.

Ex. 17-11 On January 2, Year 5, Liebold, Inc., granted its president an option to acquire 1,000 shares of Liebold's no-par common stock at $40 a share beginning January 2, Year 7, after the president had completed two years of service. The market price of Liebold's common stock on December 31, Year 5, was $55 a share.

Compute the amount of Liebold's total compensation cost with respect to the stock option if the market price of Liebold's common stock on January 2, Year 5, was ***a*** $40 a share ***b*** $45 a share. Disregard income taxes.

Ex. 17-12 On July 1, Year 7, the beginning of a fiscal year, Yew Corporation granted stock options with stock appreciation rights to officers and key managers. The options covered 25,000 shares of Yew's $5-par common stock, and were exercisable beginning on July 1, Year 9, if the grantees remain employed by Yew for the entire two-year period ending on that date. The exercise price was $20 a share. Market prices of a share of Yew's common stock were as follows:

July 1, Year 7	$20
June 30, Year 8	24
June 30, Year 9	31

Prepare journal entries for Yew Corporation's stock options on June 30, Year 8, and on June 30, Year 9. Disregard income taxes.

Ex. 17-13 On September 30, Year 5, the first date on which Roman Limited's 50,000 outstanding stock options with stock appreciation rights became exercisable, Roman's Compensation Payable ledger account had a credit balance of $500,000, representing the excess of the $30 a share market price of Roman's no-par-value common stock on September 30, Year 5, over the $20 a share exercise price on the grant date (September 30, Year 1) times the 50,000 shares under option [50,000 × ($30 − $20) = $500,000]. On September 30, Year 5, grantees of options for 20,000 shares of Roman's common stock elected to receive cash, and grantees of options for 30,000 shares of common stock elected to receive 10,000 shares of common stock in lieu of cash.

Prepare a journal entry on September 30, Year 5, to record Roman Limited's distribution of cash and common stock for the exercise of stock appreciation rights by grantees.

Ex. 17-14 On January 2, Year 6, Norell, Inc., issued 5,000 shares of junior stock to selected employees for cash of $12 a share. The junior stock was convertible to Norell's no-par-value common stock on a share-for-share basis beginning January 2, Year 8, if the employees served Norell continuously during the two-year period ended on that date and if Norell's earnings per share for Year 7 was 50% larger than the earnings per share for Year 5, an outcome that Norell considered probable on December 31, Year 6. The market price of Norell's common stock was $16 a share on January 2, Year 6. As of December 31, Year 6, the anticipated market price on December 31, Year 7, was $22 a share, and the actual market price was $25 a share on December 31, Year 7.

Prepare journal entries for Norell, Inc., on January 2 and December 31, Year 6, and December 31, Year 7. Disregard income taxes.

CASES

Case 17-1 On February 1, Year 7, DeSoto Corporation issued $10,000,000 face amount of 10-year, 12% convertible bonds at a discount. Interest on the bonds was payable February 1 and August 1. Each $1,000 bond was convertible to 10 shares of DeSoto's no-par common stock. On February 1, Year 10, a bondholder converted 1,000 bonds to 10,000 shares of DeSoto's common stock, which had a market price of $110 a share on that date.

Instructions

Describe how De Soto Corporation would account for the conversion of the bonds to common stock under each of the carrying value (book value) and the market value methods. Discuss the rationale for each method.

Case 17-2 Witt Corporation issued to preferred shareholders warrants for two rights for each share of preferred stock outstanding, and to common shareholders warrants for one right for each share of common stock outstanding. The preferred stock is cumulative, but is neither convertible nor participating. The warrants provided that 10 rights and $1,000 cash would be required to acquire $1,000 face amount of 9% convertible bonds, and that the warrants would expire in 60 days. A total of two million rights was issued.

Some shareholders sold their warrants immediately, and trading in the warrants began at $30 a right. The convertible bonds, although not yet issued, traded on a "when-issued" basis, meaning that delivery would not be required until after the scheduled issuance date. All rights issued were exercised before the expiration date, and the convertible bonds were issued.

Instructions

a Was the issuance of warrants for rights by Witt Corporation typical of current practice? Explain.

b What was the approximate trading price of the convertible bonds on a "when-issued" basis?

c Would a common shareholder who sold the warrants instead of exercising them own a smaller share of the net assets of Witt corporation than before the warrants were issued? Explain.

d Prepare a journal entry for Witt Corporation to record the exercise of warrants for two million rights and the issuance of the convertible bonds.

Case 17-3 A corporation has a noncompensatory stock purchase plan for all of its employees and a compensatory stock option plan for its officers.

Instructions

a Compare and contrast the accounting on the date the no-par common stock is issued for the noncompensatory stock purchase plan and the compensatory stock option plan.

b What journal entry is prepared for the compensatory stock option plan on the grant date?

Case 17-4 Lenora Corporation granted 10-year stock options to five executives. The options for 50,000 shares of no-par-value common stock had an exercise price of $25 a share. The market price of common stock on the grant date was $28. Each of the five executives who were granted 10,000-share options under the plan was given the right to exercise the options at any time within a 10-year period and could sell the common stock acquired at any time. Lenora's common stock is listed on the Winnipeg Stock Exchange and is actively traded.

In a discussion of the plan after its adoption by the shareholders, one executive suggested that the difference between the market price and the exercise price be debited to the Retained Earnings ledger account because the cost to Lenora was attributable to the past services of the five executives. Another executive expressed the view that there was no cost to Lenora because no payment of cash or other assets would be required for Lenora.

Instructions

√ *a* In the light of ***APB Opinion No. 25***: ''Accounting for Stock Issued to Employees,'' is there a cost to Lenora Corporation that should be recognized? If so, should it be recognized at the time the options are granted, when they are exercised, or at some other time?

√ *b* Prepare the journal entry, if any, for Lenora Corporation to record issuance of the stock options, and the journal entry to record the exercise of the options for 50,000 shares of common stock. The market price on the date the options were exercised was $40. Observe the concepts set forth in ***APB Opinion No. 25*** in your solution. Disregard income taxes.

Case 17-5 On January 2, Year 10, Riesbord Corporation adopted a stock option plan to grant selected executives options for 500,000 shares of its no-par-value common stock. The options were granted on May 1, Year 10, at an exercise price of $25 a share, the market price of the common stock on that date. All options were exercisable one year later and for four years thereafter, providing that the grantee was employed by Riesbord on the exercise date.

The market price of Riesbord's common stock was $40 a share on May 1, Year 11. All options were exercised before December 31, Year 11, on dates when the market price of the common stock was between $40 and $50 a share.

Instructions

It has been said that the exercise of a stock option would dilute the equity of existing shareholders.

a How could this happen? Discuss.

b What condition could prevent a dilution of existing equities from taking place with regard to Riesbord Corporation's stock option plan? Explain.

Case 17-6 Ward Carle, president of Olav Corporation, commented during the course of a directors' meeting that Olav had achieved increases in both sales and net income during each of the past seven years. Also, the market price of both the common stock and the convertible preferred stock had been in an uptrend. Carle also stated:

"We have 50,000 shares of $12, no-par-value, convertible preferred stock outstanding, which was originally issued for $5,100,000. This stock is callable at $106 and convertible at any time to our no-par-value common stock in the ratio of three shares of common for each share of preferred. We have been paying $1 a year dividends on our common stock and do not plan any increase in the near future. Although our earnings have been increasing, we need to reinvest these earnings to take advantage of opportunities for growth. Our common stock is now trading for $70 a share, so apparently our shareholders are more interested in earnings than in dividends."

After these comments, Carle invited questions or suggestions from the directors. Director Anne Asche offered the following suggestion:

"Our convertible preferred stock is too small an issue for a corporation of our size. I propose that we call it at once and get rid of it. If everyone is forced to convert to common stock, the additional common dividend will increase by only $150,000 a year, and we shall save $600,000 a year in preferred dividends. Also, if some preferred shareholders fail to convert, we shall have a larger gain on those shares equal to the excess of the market price over the call price. And if we want convertible preferred stock in the future we shall be able to issue it at less than the $12 rate we're now paying. Consequently, calling the preferred stock will give us several benefits and cost us nothing."

Instructions

a Evaluate point by point the proposal by Director Anne Asche. For each point indicate (and explain) your agreement or disagreement.

b What is the probable market price of Olav Corporation's convertible preferred stock? Explain.

c Prepare the journal entry (or entries) for Olav corporation that would be necessary if Asche's plan to call the preferred stock is carried out.

PROBLEMS

Pr. 17-1 On January 2, Year 8, Yolo Corporation granted to officers and key employees options to acquire 20,000 shares of Yolo's no-par common stock at an exercise price of $25 a share. The options were exercisable during a four-year period beginning January 2, Year 10, by officers and key employees still employed by Yolo. The market price of Yolo's common stock was $33 a share on January 2, Year 8.

On March 31, Year 10, options for 12,000 shares of common stock were exercised when the market price of the common stock was $40 a share.

Instructions

a Prepare journal entries for Yolo Corporation to record the issuance of the stock options, debits to Compensation Expense on December 31, Year 8 and Year 9, and the exercise of the stock options. Disregard income taxes.

b Show how the balance sheet ledger accounts affected by the journal entries in *a* are presented in Yolo Corporation's balance sheets on December 31, Year 8 and Year 9.

Pr. 17-2 The shareholders' equity section of Kapper Corporation's December 31, Year 4, balance sheet was as follows:

KAPPER CORPORATION
Shareholders' Equity Section of Balance Sheet
December 31, Year 4

Common stock, no par value, authorized 500,000 shares, issued and outstanding 200,000 shares	$ 842,000
Retained earnings	348,200
Total shareholders' equity	$1,190,200

On December 31, Year 4, the market price of Kapper's common stock was $12 a share.

On January 2, Year 5, Kapper issued 200,000, 60-day stock warrants to common shareholders for rights to acquire one additional share of common stock for one warrant and $10 cash.

Additional Information

1 On January 18, Year 5, stock warrants to acquire 140,000 shares of Kapper's common stock were exercised by common shareholders.

2 On March 3, Year 5, the remaining 60,000 stock warrants issued to common shareholders expired.

Instructions

a Prepare journal entries for Kapper Corporation's stock warrants, as required, on January 2, January 18, and March 3, Year 5. If no journal entry is required, so state and explain why.

b Prepare the shareholders' equity section of Kapper Corporation's balance sheet on December 31, Year 5. Kapper had retained earnings of $562,700 on that date.

Pr. 17-3 On January 2, Year 3, under a stock option plan that had been approved by shareholders, Joyce Limited issued to key employees 20,000 shares of junior stock at $25 cash a share. The junior stock was convertible to Joyce's no-par-value common stock beginning on January 2, Year 6, on a 1-to-1 basis if the employees were still serving on that date and if Joyce's earnings per share for Year 5 had reached a specified level. Joyce's December 31, Year 2, balance sheet had the shareholders' equity as shown on the next page.

Additional Information

1 On December 31, Year 3, Joyce's management determined that it was probable that the employees who had acquired junior stock would remain

JOYCE LIMITED
Shareholders' Equity Section of Balance Sheet
December 31, Year 2

$9 convertible, cumulative preferred stock, no par value, callable at $105 a share, authorized, issued and outstanding 50,000 shares	$ 5,250,000
Common stock, no par value, authorized 10,000,000 shares, issued and outstanding 6,000,000 shares	112,800,000
Total contributed capital	$118,050,000
Retained earnings	32,700,000
Total shareholders' equity	$150,750,000

employed during the service period and that the specified level for earnings per share for Year 5 would be attained.

2 On December 31, Year 5, Joyce called the $9 convertible, cumulative preferred stock. Holders of 30,000 shares of preferred stock exercised the conversion option to obtain 60,000 shares of Joyce's common stock. Holders of the remaining shares of preferred stock accepted the cash payment from Joyce. Joyce uses the carrying value (book value) method for conversions.

3 Market prices of Joyce's common stock were as follows:

Jan. 2, Year 3	$40
Dec. 31, Year 3	46
Dec. 31, Year 4	44½
Dec. 31, Year 5	52

4 Earnings per share for Year 5 exceeded the specified level for conversion of the junior stock.

Instructions

a Prepare journal entries for Joyce Limited in connection with the stock option plan involving junior stock and for the call and conversion of the preferred stock. Disregard income taxes.

b Prepare the shareholders' equity section of Joyce Limited's balance sheet on December 31, Year 5. Joyce's retained earnings balance on that date was $46,900,000.

Pr. 17-4 On January 2, Year 6, Lindstrom Corporation issued $100,000,000 face amount of 8%, 10-year convertible bonds at 101. The bonds, which paid interest semiannually on January 2 and July 2, were convertible on the basis of 10 shares of Lindstrom's no-par common stock for each $1,000 bond. Because of the immateriality of the premium, Lindstrom adopted the straight-line method of amortization.

Additional Information

1 On January 2, Year 8, holders of $40,000,000 face amount of the bonds exercised the conversion option.

2 On January 2, Year 16 (the maturity date of the bonds), because of severe liquidity problems, Lindstrom made an offer to the remaining bondholders to issue 10 shares of $6, no-par-value convertible preferred stock with a current fair value of $55 a share in exchange for each $1,000 bond. Because Lindstrom's bonds were trading at 45 (45% of face amount) and its common stock was trading at only $40 a share on January 2, Year 16, all bondholders accepted the exchange offer rather than converting to Lindstrom's common stock. The preferred stock was convertible to Lindstrom's common stock on a share-for-share basis.

3 On January 2, Year 20, when Lindstrom's common stock was trading at $60 a share, Lindstrom called the $6 convertible preferred stock at the call price of $52 a share. All preferred shareholders converted to common stock.

Instructions

Prepare journal entries for Lindstrom Corporation on January 2, Year 6; January 2, Year 8; January 2, Year 16; and January 2, Year 20. Use the carrying value (book value) method to record the conversions of both the bonds and the preferred stock. Disregard income tax effects.

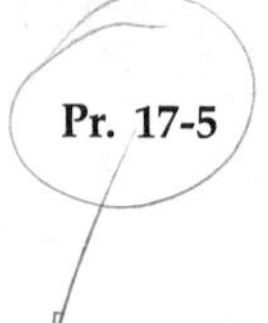

Pr. 17-5 On August 31, Year 10, the shareholders' equity section of Mercer Corporation's balance sheet was as follows:

MERCER CORPORATION
Shareholders' Equity Section of Balance Sheet
August 31, Year 10

Common stock, $2.50 par value, authorized 5,000,000 shares, issued and outstanding 3,000,000 shares	$ 7,500,000
Premium on common stock	38,400,000
Total contributed capital	$45,900,000
Retained earnings	16,600,000
Total shareholders' equity	$62,500,000

During August, Year 10, Mercer completed plans for a September public offering of 200,000 shares of $6, no-par preferred stock. Accompanying each preferred share was a detachable stock warrant entitling the holder to acquire one share of common stock of $2.50 par value at $40 a share at any time within the next 10 years. The common stock was trading at $36 a share. As soon as the terms of the preferred stock and warrants offering were announced, the warrants began trading separately on the stock exchange at $3.50 each on a "when-issued" basis.

The entire issue of 200,000 shares of preferred stock with warrants attached was issued on September 1, Year 10, at $55 a share. During the next few months the market price of the common stock increased, and on December 1, Year 10, it traded at $66 a share. On December 1, Year 10, 40,000 warrants were exercised, and Mercer issued 40,000 shares of common stock.

Instructions

a Prepare journal entries for Mercer Corporation to record the issuance of the preferred stock and detachable stock warrants on September 1, Year 10, and the issuance of common stock on December 1, Year 10. (Journal entries are not required for dividends.)

b Prepare the shareholders' equity section of Mercer Corporation's balance sheet on December 31, Year 10, assuming that net income since August 31, Year 10, was $4,500,000 and that on November 1, Year 10, a quarterly dividend of $1.50 a share was declared on the preferred stock, payable December 2, Year 10, to shareholders of record on November 20, Year 10. Dividends of $1,500,000 were declared on the common stock subsequent to August 31, Year 10.

Pr. 17-6 The fiscal year for Saldana, Inc., ends on December 31. On January 2, Year 10, Saldana established a compensatory stock option plan for its key executives who had been employed at least five years. The number of shares of common stock initially included in the plan was approximately 100,000, at an estimated exercise price of $40 a share. The final determination of the number of shares to be offered and the exercise price were to be made on December 31, Year 11, based on a predetermined formula. The formula was designed to adjust the number of shares to be optioned and the exercise price by taking into account the earnings of Saldana and the market price of its common stock during Years 10 and 11.

Options were granted for services to be performed through the end of Year 11, and were exercisable at any time after January 2, Year 12. The estimated number of shares of common stock to be included in the stock option plan, the estimated exercise price, and the market price of the common stock on January 2, Year 10, and on December 31, Year 10, were as follows:

	Jan. 2, Year 10	*Dec. 31, Year 10*
Estimated number of shares of common stock to be included in stock option plan	100,000	100,000
Estimated exercise price	$40	$40
Market price of common stock	$38	$45

The final contractual provisions of the stock option plan and the market price of Saldana's common stock were determined on December 31, Year 11, as follows:

Number of shares of common stock included in stock option plan	95,000
Exercise price	$41
Market price	$52

On April 20, Year 12, employees exercised options for 30,000 shares of common stock. Saldana had 3,500,000 shares of no-par-value common stock outstanding on December 31, Year 11.

Instructions

a What is the measurement date for Saldana's stock option plan? Explain.

b Compute the total compensation cost to be recognized by Saldana, Inc., under the stock option plan. How is total compensation cost allocated among accounting periods? Show supporting computations and disregard income taxes.

c Prepare journal entries for Saldana, Inc., to record all transactions and events relating to the stock option plan for Year 10 through Year 12. Disregard income taxes.

Pr. 17-7 Tully Corporation had the following amounts in the shareholders' equity section of its balance sheet on May 31, Year 3:

TULLY CORPORATION
Shareholders' Equity Section of Balance Sheet
May 31, Year 3

Common stock, no par value, 6,000,000 shares, issued and outstanding 2,500,000 shares	$37,500,000
Retained earnings	15,775,000
Total shareholders' equity	$53,275,000

Tully's operations had been profitable, but management had decided that additional capital was needed. Therefore, authorization was obtained for the issuance of 250,000 shares of $5, no-par-value preferred stock. To help assure success of this financing, Tully offered with each share of preferred stock a detachable stock warrant that entitled the holder to acquire one share of Tully's common stock at $40 a share at any time within the next 10 years. The common stock was trading at $35 a share. As soon as the terms of the offering were announced, the warrants began trading at a price of $6 each.

The issuance of 250,000 shares of the $5 preferred stock with detachable stock warrants attached was completed on June 1, Year 3, at $60 a share (including the stock warrant). The market price of the common stock increased during the next several months. On December 1, Year 3, when the common stock was trading at $65 a share, 25,000 warrants were exercised, and Tully issued 25,000 shares of common stock.

Instructions

a Prepare journal entries for Tully Corporation to record the issuance of the preferred stock and the detachable common stock warrants on June 1, Year 3, and the issuance of common stock on December 1, Year 3, when 25,000 warrants were exercised. (Journal entries are not required for dividends on the preferred stock.)

b Prepare the shareholders' equity section of Tully Corporation's balance sheet on December 31, Year 3, assuming that net income since May 31, Year 3, was $8,400,000, and that dividend action on the preferred stock since that date had been as follows:

Sept. 1	Declared quarterly dividend of $1.25 a share on preferred stock.
Oct. 1	Paid quarterly dividend on preferred stock.
Dec. 1	Declared quarterly dividend of $1.25 a share on preferred stock, payable January 10, Year 4, to shareholders of record December 15, Year 3.

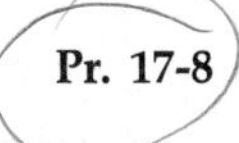

Pr. 17-8 Roper Incorporated had outstanding two issues of securities: no-par-value common stock, and 9% convertible bonds in the face amount of $20,000,000. Interest payment dates of the bond issue were April 1 and October 1. The conversion option in the bond indenture entitled the bondholders to receive 30 shares of Roper's common stock in exchange for each $1,000 bond.

On March 15, Year 4, the annual dividend rate on the common stock was increased from $1.50 to $2 a share. On April 1, Year 4, the holders of $2 million face amount of bonds exercised the conversion option. The market price of the 9% convertible bonds on that date was $122 for each $100 face amount; the market price of Roper's common stock was $40 a share. The ledger account balances pertaining to the convertible bonds and the common stock were as follows on April 1, Year 4, prior to the conversion:

9% convertible bonds payable (maturing in 10 years)	$20,000,000
Discount on 9% convertible bonds payable (amortized by interest method at 10% yield rate)	1,246,221
Common stock, no par value; authorized an unlimited number of shares, issued and outstanding 750,000 shares	15,580,500

Instructions

a Prepare a journal entry for Roper Incorporated to record the conversion of bonds on April 1, Year 4, under the carrying value (book value) method.

b Evaluate the effects of the conversion on income of Roper Incorporated for the year ended March 31, Year 5, with respect to:

1 Income before income taxes (Consider amortization of bond discount)

2 The amounts of income taxes expense and net income (Assume an income tax rate of 45%)

3 The total annual amount of payments to security holders

c What effect would the conversion have on the annual cash receipts of an investor who converted 100 bonds to common stock on April 1, Year 4?

d Prepare a journal entry for Roper Incorporated to record the conversion of bonds on April 1, Year 4, under the market value method.

Pr. 17-9 On December 31, Year 5, under a stock option plan that had been approved by shareholders in November, Year 5, Ingle Corporation granted stock options for 40,000 shares of no-par-value common stock at an exercise price of $16 a share to officers and key employees. The plan included stock appreciation rights that were exercisable only if the stock options were forfeited; exercise of the stock options required forfeiture of the stock appreciation rights. The options were exercisable in full beginning on December 31, Year 9. No service period was specified for the grantees. Market prices of Ingle's common stock were as follows:

Dec. 31, Year 5	$16
Dec. 31, Year 6	20
Dec. 31, Year 7	24
Dec. 31, Year 8	22
Dec. 31, Year 9	28

On December 31, Year 9, grantees exercised their stock appreciation rights and stock options as follows:

- ***Stock appreciation rights exercised:*** Grantees of options for 20,000 shares elected to receive cash, grantees of options for 15,400 shares elected to receive shares of Ingle's common stock.
- ***Stock options exercised:*** 4,600 shares of Ingle's common stock.

Instructions

Prepare all journal entries for Ingle Corporation's stock option plan for Year 6 through Year 9. Show supporting computations in explanations for the journal entries. Round computations to the nearest dollar and disregard income taxes.

c h a p t e r 1 8

TREASURY STOCK AND EARNINGS PER SHARE

Additional topics dealing with shareholders' equity not discussed in the preceding two chapters are (1) the acquisition and retirement or reissuance by a corporation of its capital stock, (2) the preparation of statements of retained earnings and shareholders' equity, and (3) the computation of earnings per share of common stock. A corporation's acquisition of its capital stock reduces its shareholders' equity and affects the computation of earnings per share. Earnings per share is the amount of net income earned on each share of common stock and is considered by many investors to be the most important financial measurement.

TREASURY STOCK

Treasury stock of a corporation is capital stock that has been issued, fully paid for, and subsequently acquired by the corporation ***but not formally retired***. When a corporation acquires shares of its capital stock, certain shareholders surrender their ownership interest in the corporation. Thus, the acquisition of treasury stock by a corporation may be viewed as a partial liquidation of the corporation, and the reissuance of treasury stock is a financing transaction. No gain or loss is realized from such transactions, because gains and losses result from disposals of assets and extinguishments of debt, not from issuances or acquisitions of capital stock.

Treasury stock may be acquired by corporations for a variety of reasons, including the following: (1) to buy out a particular shareholder, (2) for use in connection with stock option plans or business combinations, (3) to settle claims against debtors who are also shareholders, (4) to increase earnings per share by reducing the number of shares of common stock outstanding, and (5) to support the market price of the common stock. There is little justification for a corporation's attempting to influence the market price of its common stock through the acquisition and reissuance of treasury stock; such efforts may create a conflict of interest between the corporation and its shareholders and may be illegal in some circumstances.

Treasury Stock and Legal Capital

Legal capital, as explained in Chapter 16, is a statutory definition of the amount of capital to be retained in the corporation for protection of creditors; it is not available for withdrawal by shareholders. Legal capital generally consists of the total par value of par-value capital stock issued, or the proceeds from the issue of no-par-value capital stock issued. The acquisition of its own stock by a corporation involves an outflow of assets to shareholders, and therefore certain legal restrictions are necessary to protect the corporation's creditors. Generally, a corporation is not permitted to acquire its own capital stock if the acquisition would result in the inability of the corporation to pay its liabilities or if the realizable value of its net assets would become less than its liabilities and legal capital.

The acquisition of treasury stock is not regarded as a reduction in legal capital in those provincial jurisdictions in which it is allowed. However, such an acquisition does involve an outflow of assets to shareholders, and therefore legal restrictions, such as those detailed above, are necessary to protect the corporation's creditors. Some provincial corporation legislation (whether it is by legislation itself or by incorporation documents) allows corporations to have treasury stock, but the corporation must restrict its retained earnings by the amount representing the cost of the treasury stock.

It should be emphasized that the ***retirement of capital stock*** reduces legal capital, but the ***acquisition of treasury stock*** does not. In terms of economic significance, the retirement of capital stock and the acquisition of treasury stock are similar, because both transactions consist of a return of corporate assets to shareholders and a corresponding reduction in the amount of capital invested in the corporation.

Most provincial jurisdictions permit the acquisition of issued capital stock to be held by the corporation for future reissue or future cancellation. However, the Canada Business Corporations Act requires the following:[1]

> Shares or fractions thereof issued by a corporation and purchased, redeemed or otherwise acquired by it, shall be cancelled or, if the articles limit the number of authorized shares, may be restored to the status of authorized but unissued shares.

The above action prohibits a federally incorporated company from holding shares in itself and therefore there cannot be "treasury stock" under the CBCA.

Treasury Stock Is Not an Asset

A corporation may not own a portion of itself; for this reason, treasury stock is not considered an asset. The ownership of treasury stock does not give a corporation

1 Canada Business Corporations Act, Dec. 15, 1975, sec. 23–15la(5).

the right to receive cash dividends, to vote, to exercise preemptive rights as a shareholder, or to receive assets when the corporation is liquidated. Corporations may, and sometimes do, formally cancel treasury stock; this action would not be taken if the cancellation actually destroyed an asset. If a corporation were to dissolve, any treasury stock owned by the corporation would contribute nothing in the process of converting assets to cash for distribution to shareholders.

The view that treasury stock is not an asset is strengthened by recognition that treasury stock essentially is the same as unissued capital stock, and no one advocates that unissued stock be classified as an asset in the balance sheet.

Treasury stock sometimes is acquired for subsequent reissuance under employee stock purchase or incentive plans. A corporation may have a liability to employees under such plans. To meet this liability the corporation expends cash to acquire treasury stock and soon thereafter discharges the liability by delivery of the treasury stock to employees. Because the treasury stock will be used to liquidate the liability, it may be viewed as being similar to an investment in securities of any other corporation. In the United States, the Accounting Principles Board has given recognition to this situation as follows:[2]

> When a corporation's stock is acquired for purposes other then retirement (formal or constructive), or when ultimate disposition has not yet been decided, the cost of acquired stock may be shown separately as a deduction from the total of capital stock, capital surplus, and retained earnings, or may be accorded the accounting treatment appropriate for retired stock, or in some circumstances may be shown as an asset....

However, in Canada, section 3240.11 of the *CICA Handbook* states that treasury stock "should be carried at cost and shown as a deduction from shareholders' equity until cancelled or resold."

The reasons for refusing to view treasury stock as an asset are many and generally are recognized as valid, yet the issue is kept alive by the policy of a few corporations that continue to list treasury stock as an asset.

Alternative Accounting Methods for Treasury Stock

Two accounting methods which have been used to account for treasury stock transactions are (1) the ***single transaction*** or ***cost method*** and (2) the ***two-transaction*** or ***par-value*** or ***stated-value method***. Although the two-transaction method still receives some theoretical support in accounting literature, large corporations have turned increasingly to the single-transaction method in recent years. In Canada, ***only*** the single-transaction method is sanctioned as a generally accepted accounting principle for treasury stock by the ***CICA Handbook***. However, in the United States, ***both*** methods are sanctioned as generally accepted accounting principles.

Under the single-transaction method, the acquisition of treasury stock is regarded as a first step in a financial move which is completed by the reissuance or retirement of the treasury stock. Treasury stock thus is viewed as a "suspense" item of

2 AICPA, ***APB Opinion No. 6***: "Status of Accounting Research Bulletins" (New York; 1965), p. 40.

shareholders' equity, with the corporation acting as an intermediary between the former shareholders and new shareholders. When the single-transaction method is used, the Treasury Stock account is debited for the cost of the capital stock acquired; this account is reported in the balance sheet as a deduction from ***total*** shareholders' equity. With this arrangement of the shareholders' equity section of the balance sheet, there is no reduction in the legal capital.

Under the two-transaction method, the possibility of reissuance of the treasury stock is not given much weight. The relationship between the corporation and the former owners of shares of capital stock now held in the treasury has ended; therefore, the account showing premium on capital stock relating to the treasury stock is reduced and a treasury stock account is set up for the legal portion (the Capital Stock account amount) and, if the corporation decided to retire the capital stock, capital stock is reduced with a corresponding entry to the Treasury Stock account. Another method of accounting under the two-transaction method is to dispense with the use of a Treasury Stock account and instead to reduce the Capital Stock account itself at the time of acquisition of the stock; the reissuance of treasury stock is recorded as though the capital stock is issued for the first time.

Although the ***CICA Handbook*** sanctions only the single-transaction method, the two-transaction method will also be illustrated, because many companies in Canada are subsidiaries to United States' companies with whom they will be consolidated and because comparison enhances a better understanding of the merits of the single-transaction method.

The illustration relating to the single-transaction method follows the recommendations of section 3240 of the ***CICA Handbook***. The illustration of the two-transaction method will include a Treasury Stock account. As stated earlier, the treasury stock account could have been replaced by the Capital Stock (Legal Capital) account.

Illustration of Accounting for Treasury Stock

To illustrate the two methods of accounting for treasury stock transactions, assume that the balance sheet for Mix Corporation includes the shareholders' equity section as shown below.

Balance sheet shareholders' equity section for treasury stock illustration $100-par capital stock

MIX CORPORATION
Partial Balance Sheet

Shareholders' equity:	
Capital stock, $100 par; authorized, issued, and outstanding 10,000 shares	$1,000,000
Premium on capital stock	200,000
Total contributed capital	$1,200,000
Retained earnings	500,000
Total shareholders' equity	$1,700,000

At this time Mix Corporation acquired in the open market 300 shares of its common stock for the treasury at $115 a share. The 300 shares were issued originally at ($1,200,000 ÷ 10,000) = $120 each, or for a total of ($120 × 300) = $36,000.

The journal entry to record the acquisition for the single-transaction method is as follows:

Journal entry for acquisition of treasury stock — single-transaction method

	Debit	Credit
Treasury Stock (300 × $115)	34,500	
Cash		34,500
To record acquisition of 300 shares of treasury stock at $115 a share under the single-transaction method.		

The journal entry to record the acquisition for the two-transaction method is as follows:

Journal entry for acquisition of treasury stock — two-transaction method

	Debit	Credit
Treasury Stock	30,000	
Premium on Capital Stock	4,500	
Cash		34,500
To record acquisition of 300 shares of treasury stock at $115 a share under the two-transaction method.		

Under the single-transaction method the entire cost of acquisition of the shares is debited to the Treasury Stock account, awaiting final disposition of the acquired shares. However, under the two-transaction method, the Treasury Stock account (or Capital Stock account) is debited with an amount representing the legal capital portion of the cost to acquire the stock. The remainder is debited to the Premium on Capital Stock account, thereby reducing the credit to this account at the original issue date of the stock. In the two-transaction journal entry the reduction in the shareholders' equity amounts to $34,500, or $1,500 less than the $36,000 originally paid by shareholders. In other words, $1,500 of the capital originally invested by those shareholders who have sold their stock to the corporation remains in the corporation.[3]

3 Under the two-transaction method, if the amount paid for treasury stock is more than the amount originally invested by shareholders, the excess is recorded as a reduction of retained earnings. For example, if Mix Corporation paid $40,000 to acquire 300 shares of its capital stock originally issued for $36,000, the transaction would be recorded as follows:

	Debit	Credit
Treasury Stock	30,000	
Premium on Capital Stock	6,000	
Retained Earnings	4,000	
Cash		40,000

Under the two-transaction method, if treasury stock is acquired at a price below par value, the excess of par value over cost of treasury stock is credited to a contributed surplus account such as Excess From Acquisition of Corporation Stock. For example, if Mix Corporation paid only $25,000 for the 300 shares of capital stock, the journal entry to record the acquisition would be as follows:

	Debit	Credit
Treasury Stock	30,000	
Excess from Acquisition of Corporation Stock		5,000
Cash		25,000

The shareholders' equity portion of the balance sheet for Mix Corporation under each method is presented below.

Single-transaction method: balance sheet shareholders' equity section showing acquisition of treasury stock $100-par capital stock

MIX CORPORATION Partial Balance Sheet	
Shareholders' equity:	
Capital stock, $100 par; authorized and issued 10,000 shares, of which 300 shares are in treasury	$1,000,000
Premium on capital stock	200,000
Total contributed capital	$1,200,000
Retained earnings	500,000
Total contributed capital and retained earnings	$1,700,000
Less: Cost of 300 shares of treasury stock	34,500
Total shareholders' equity	$1,665,500

Two-transaction method: balance sheet shareholders' equity section showing acquisition of treasury stock

MIX CORPORATION Partial Balance Sheet		
Shareholders' equity:		
Capital stock, $100 par; authorized and issued 10,000 shares	$1,000,000	
Less: Treasury stock, 300 shares at par	30,000	$ 970,000
Premium on capital stock		195,500
Total contributed capital		$1,165,500
Retained earnings		500,000
Total shareholders' equity		$1,665,500

The presentation of shareholders' equity when treasury stock is recorded at cost does not show the net amount of capital invested by shareholders; thus, it does not achieve one of the more important objectives in the classification of corporate capital. However, the single-transaction approach to treasury stock does have the merit of showing as capital stock an amount equal to the legal capital of the corporation.

This form for reporting the shareholders' equity section has the merit of showing the net amount for contributed capital after the treasury stock acquisitions. However, it may be criticized on the grounds that the net amount shown for capital stock ($970,000) may be interpreted erroneously as the legal capital; the legal capital of $1,000,000 was not reduced by the acquisition of treasury stock.

Let us assume that Mix Corporation cancelled the 300 shares of treasury stock.

Under the single-transaction method, this action caused a reduction in legal capital and in the premium on Capital Stock account by the amount paid for the treasury stock cancelled. The journal entry to record the cancellation of the treasury stock is shown at the top of the next page.

The cancellation of the 300 shares of treasury stock requires a reduction of only $34,500 in the contributed capital accounts; the excess of the amount originally

Single-transaction method: journal entry for cancellation of treasury stock $100-par capital stock

Capital Stock	30,000	
Premium on Capital Stock	4,500	
Treasury Stock		34,500
To record cancellation of 300 shares of treasury stock carried at cost.		

paid in by shareholders over the cost of the treasury stock, ($36,000 − $34,500) = $1,500, remains in the Premium on Capital Stock account.

Section 3240.15 of the ***CICA Handbook*** details the steps necessary when acquired shares are cancelled and the cost of the shares was equal to or above par, stated, or assigned value, as follows:

> Where a company redeems its own shares, or cancels its own shares that it has acquired, and the cost of such shares is equal to or greater than their par, stated or assigned value, the cost should be allocated as follows:
> **a** To share capital, in an amount equal to the par, stated or assigned value of the shares;
> **b** Any excess, to contributed surplus to the extent that contributed surplus was created by a net excess of proceeds over cost on cancellation or resale of shares of the same class;
> **c** Any excess, to contributed surplus in an amount equal to the pro-rata share of the portion of contributed surplus that arose from transactions, other than those in **b** above, in the same class of shares;
> **d** Any excess, to retained earnings.

Under the two-transaction method the Premium on Capital Stock account would have already been adjusted on the date Mix Corporation acquired the capital stock. Accordingly, under the two-transaction method, the Capital Stock account and the Treasury Stock account will be debited and credited, respectively, in the amount of $30,000 to record the cancellation.

Under the two-transaction method, the cancellation causes a reduction in the legal capital which is accomplished by a debit to Capital Stock and a credit to treasury stock for $30,000.

The cancellation has reduced legal capital to $970,000 under both methods. The two balance sheet presentations would now be identical. That is, legal capital would be $970,000 and contributed capital would be $1,165,500.

If Mix Corporation, instead of cancelling the 300 shares of treasury stock, reissued the shares at a price ***above par***, say $108 each, or $2,100 ***below cost***, the journal entry for the single-transaction method would be:

Single-transaction method: journal entry for reissuance of treasury stock at a price below cost $100-par capital stock

Cash	32,400	
Retained earnings	2,100	
Treasury Stock		34,500
To record reissuance of 300 shares of treasury stock at $108 a share, or $2,100 below cost.		

Under the single-transaction method, the Treasury Stock account is credited for the cost of the shares of treasury stock which are reissued. Section 3240.20 recommends, on the reissue of treasury stock at a price below cost (or a deficiency), the following:

> Where a company resells shares that it has acquired, any excess of the proceeds over cost should be credited to contributed surplus; any deficiency should be charged to contributed surplus to the extent that a previous net excess from resale or cancellation of shares of the same class is included therein, otherwise to retained earnings.

Note that the Premium on Common Stock account remains as originally determined with respect to these particular reissued shares. Since they are again outstanding, the premium on their original issue must remain intact.

The journal entry for the two-transaction method would be:

Two-transaction method: journal entry for reissuance of treasury stock at a price above carrying amount

Cash	32,400	
Treasury Stock		30,000
Premium on Capital Stock		2,400
To record reissuance of 300 shares of treasury stock at $108 a share, or $2,400 above carrying amount (par).		

Note that the journal entry for the two transaction method for reissuance of treasury stock is similar to an entry for original issuance of capital stock. The difference between the issuance price of the treasury stock and the par of the treasury stock, as recorded in the Treasury Stock account, is credited to the Premium on Capital Stock account. Under this method, the acquisition of treasury stock is viewed as a temporary retirement of the stock; thus, the reissuance of treasury stock logically should be recorded in the same manner as an original issuance of capital stock.

In the event that the treasury stock were reissued at less than par, it would not be appropriate under the two-transaction method to debit a Discount on Capital Stock account because no ''discount liability'' attaches to treasury stock reissued below par. Instead, the deficiency is recorded by a debit to Premium on Capital Stock and/or Excess from Acquisition of Corporation Stock if such contributed surplus is available. In the absence of sufficient premium on capital stock and/or excess from acquisition of corporation stock to absorb the deficiency, it should be debited to Retained Earnings.

Under the single-transaction method, when treasury stock is reissued at a price above cost, the excess of the proceeds over cost of the treasury stock is credited to Excess from Transactions in Treasury Stock, as illustrated below:

Single transaction method: journal entry for reissuance of treasury stock at a price above cost $100-par capital stock

Cash	37,500	
Treasury Stock		34,500
Excess from Transactions in Treasury Stock		3,000
To record reissuance of 300 shares of treasury stock at $125 a share, or $3,000 above cost.		

Let us now illustrate the journal entries required when a company's shares are ***no-par-value*** shares and the single-transaction method is used. Assume Mix Corporation had originally issued no-par-value capital stock. The balance sheet for Mix Corporation would then include the shareholders' equity, shown as follows:

Balance sheet shareholders' equity section for treasury stock illustration no-par capital stock

MIX CORPORATION
Partial Balance Sheet

Shareholders' equity:	
Capital stock, no par value; authorized an unlimited number of shares; issued and outstanding 10,000 shares	$1,200,000
Retained earnings	500,000
Total shareholders' equity	$1,700,000

Journal entry for acquisition of treasury stock — single-transaction method

Treasury Stock (300 × $115)	34,500	
Cash		34,500
To record acquisition of 300 shares of treasury stock at $115 a share under the single-transaction method.		

The shareholders' equity portion of the balance sheet for Mix Corporation immediately after the above transaction is presented below.

Single transaction method: balance sheet shareholders' equity section showing acquisition of treasury stock for no-par capital stock

MIX CORPORATION
Partial Balance Sheet

Shareholders' equity:	
Capital stock, no par value; authorized an unlimited number of shares; issued 10,000 shares of which 300 shares are in treasury	$1,200,000
Retained earnings	500,000
Total contributed capital and retained earnings	$1,700,000
Less: Cost of 300 shares of treasury stock	34,500
Total shareholders' equity	$1,665,500

When no-par-value shares are ***originally issued*** by a corporation, ***the entire proceeds of the issue are credited to capital stock***. In order to determine the correct amount to be removed from the Capital Stock account ***when cancellation of treasury stock occurs***, section 3240.18 of the ***CICA Handbook*** states the following:

> ... the amount to be allocated to the share capital account should be based on the average per-share amount in such account for that class of shares at transaction date.

If Mix Corporation cancelled the 300 shares of treasury stock, under the single-transaction method the journal entry to record the cancellation would be as follows:

Single-transaction method journal entry for cancellation of treasury stock, no-par capital stock

Capital Stock [($1,200,000 ÷ 10,000) × 300]	36,000	
Excess from Transactions in Treasury Stock		1,500
Treasury Stock		34,500
To record cancellation of 300 shares of treasury stock carried at average cost of $120 per share.		

If Mix Corporation, instead of cancelling the 300 shares of treasury stock, reissued the shares at a price of $108 each, or $2,100 ***below cost***, the journal entry for the single-transaction method would be:

Single-transaction method journal entry for reissuance of treasury stock at a price below cost, no-par capital stock

Cash	32,400	
Retained Earnings	2,100	
Treasury Stock		34,500
To record reissuance of 300 shares of treasury stock at $108 a share, or $2,100 below cost.		

If an ''Excess from Transactions in Treasury Stock'' account, for the same class of capital stock, had been available, the debit would have been to that account until its balance was zero and ***then*** Retained Earnings would be debited. Note that, in the case of par-value stock, once the balance of the Excess from Transactions in Treasury Stock account became zero, if a Premium on Capital Stock account existed for that class of stock it would have to be reduced on a pro rata basis before any excess would go to retained earnings as a reduction thereof.

If Mix Corporation were to reissue the 300 shares of treasury stock, at $125 a share, or $3,000 above cost, under the single-transaction method the journal entry would be the same as for the par-value shares example, as follows:

Single-transaction method: journal entry for reissuance of treasury stock at a price above cost, no-par capital stock

Cash	37,500	
Treasury Stock		34,500
Excess from Transactions in Treasury Stock		3,000
To record reissuance of 300 shares of treasury stock at $125 a share, or $3,000 above cost.		

Summary of Accounting for Treasury Stock

The foregoing discussion suggests the following key points relative to accounting for treasury stock:

1 Treasury stock is not an asset and is not entitled to receive cash dividends, to vote, or to receive assets on liquidation of the corporation.

2 No gain or loss is recognized on treasury stock transactions.

3 The balance of retained earnings is never increased by treasury stock transactions; however, retained earnings may be reduced by such transactions.

4 Retained earnings in an amount equal to the cost of treasury stock usually is unavailable for declaration of cash dividends.

5 In some jurisdictions, transactions in treasury stock are generally prohibited.

Redemption of Preferred Stock

Most corporations that issue preferred stock include in the contract a provision that all or any part of the preferred stock may be called for redemption[4] (retirement) at any time desired by the issuer. The call price usually exceeds the issuance price; it may be an unchanging amount or it may be a series of amounts on a sliding scale relating to specified time periods and eventually decreasing to par for par-value preferred shares. When preferred stock is called for redemption, the stock is cancelled and is not available for reissuance. Redemption may be effected by a ***call*** of the stock pursuant to the call provision, by acquisition in the open market, or by a special offer to preferred shareholders to ***tender*** their stock to the corporation at a price that exceeds the current market price of the stock.

The redemption of preferred stock should not be confused with the acquisition of treasury stock, because ***redemption*** signifies ***both acquisition and cancellation*** of the stock. Preferred stock also may be acquired for subsequent reissuance and would then be held in the treasury. However, acquisitions of preferred stock generally are made with the intent to cancel the stock.

The accounting treatment of the redemption of preferred stock is the same as that of the acquisition and cancellation of common stock discussed in the preceding section. The recommendations in section 3240 of the ***CICA Handbook*** cover both common and preferred stock.

To illustrate the redemption of preferred stock and entries for no-par-value capital stock transactions, assume that Winters Corporation had issued 10,000 shares of no-par-value preferred stock at $102 a share. The call price was $105 a share. If Winters had entered into no other transactions involving this capital stock until it redeemed the entire issue at the call price of $105 a share, the journal entry to record the redemption would be as follows:

Journal entry for redemption of preferred stock at a premium

Preferred Stock, no par value (10,000 × $102)	1,020,000	
Retained Earnings	30,000	
Cash		1,050,000
To record redemption of 10,000 shares of preferred stock for $30,000 in excess of the original issuance price.		

This journal entry eliminates the Preferred Stock ledger account, because the capital invested by the preferred shareholders has been returned in full, and these investors no longer have any ownership equity in the corporation. The $30,000 paid to the preferred shareholders in excess of their original investment, referred to as ***premium paid on retirement of preferred stock***, is debited to Retained Earnings and not to any contributed capital ledger accounts applicable to ***other*** classes of capital stock.

4 The terms "call" and "redemption" and "called" and "redeemed" are used interchangeably.

When the preferred stock is selling at a market price less than redemption price, the issuer may redeem a portion of the stock by acquisition in the open market. To return to the previous example, assume that Winters Corporation acquired 1,000 shares of preferred stock in the open market at $90 a share. The journal entry to record the redemption is shown below.

Journal entry for redemption of preferred stock at a discount

Preferred Stock, no par value (1,000 × $102)	102,000	
Cash (1,000 × $90)		90,000
Contributed Surplus from Redemption of Preferred Stock		12,000
To record redemption of 1,000 shares of preferred stock at a price $12,000 below the original issuance price.		

By a payment of $90,000, Winters has eliminated 1,000 shares of preferred stock representing $102,000 of contributed capital. Recording the $12,000 excess of the original investment by preferred shareholders over the amount paid to redeem the 1,000 shares of preferred stock in the manner shown above results in a contributed surplus account available for use if later redemptions in this class of shares occur at a cost to the company greater than their par, stated, or assigned value. For example, had this redemption occurred prior to the call on page 879, the Contributed Surplus from Redemption of Preferred Stock account would have been debited in the amount of $12,000 and the Retained Earnings account would have been debited in the amount of [(9,000 × $2) − $12,000] = $6,000.

The two foregoing examples illustrate the following general rules for interpreting the redemption of preferred stock:

1 When preferred stock is redeemed for an amount less than the issuance price, the difference is recorded as a contributed surplus item and ***not*** as a gain or as an increase in retained earnings.

2 When preferred stock is redeemed at a cost in excess of the original issuance price, the excess is recorded first as a reduction in the contributed surplus account created in **1** above until that account's balance becomes zero; then, any excess is recorded as a reduction of retained earnings. The excess should ***not*** be recognized as a loss or debited to contributed surplus relating to any other class of capital stock.

STATEMENTS OF RETAINED EARNINGS AND SHAREHOLDERS' EQUITY

Because users of financial statements are interested in all changes in the various components of shareholders' equity, a complete set of financial statements includes:

1 A statement of retained earnings accompanied by a statement of contributed capital

or, alternatively,

2 A statement of shareholders' equity

Statement of Retained Earnings

As explained in Chapter 4 (pages 158–160), a ***statement of retained earnings*** shows the changes in retained earnings during an accounting period, thus reconciling the beginning and ending balances of retained earnings.

The content and relative importance of the statement of retained earnings in portraying the financial developments during an accounting period have been reduced by the movement to the all-inclusive concept of income measurement. The concept requires that all items of profit and loss recognized during a period be included in the determination of net income, except for prior period adjustments and the cumulative effect of changes in accounting policy and correction of errors of prior years that is not presented in the comparative income statement. Currently, very few transactions and events meet the rigorous requirements for classification as prior period adjustments to be recorded in the Retained Earnings account. Thus, the statement of retained earnings is relatively short and generally consists of the following:

1 The beginning balance of retained earnings (adjusted for any cumulative effect of changes in accounting policy and correction of errors of prior years not included in the income statement for comparative purposes)

2 An addition of net income (or deduction of net loss) for the accounting period

3 A deduction for any dividends declared

4 The ending balance of retained earnings

A two-year comparative statement of retained earnings for Torrance Company, Inc., that includes an adjustment for a correction of an error, is shown below.

TORRANCE COMPANY, INC.
Statements of Retained Earnings
For Years Ended June 30, Year 10 and Year 9

	Year 10	*Year 9*
Retained earnings, beginning of year, as originally reported		$850,000
Less: Adjustment for correction of error (net of income tax effect of $250,000)		280,000
Retained earnings, beginning of year (as restated for Year 9)	$675,000	$570,000
Add (deduct): Net income (loss)	(85,000)	205,000
Subtotals	$590,000	$775,000
Less: Dividends declared ($0.25 and $1.00 a share)	25,000	100,000
Retained earnings, end of year	$565,000	$675,000

Instead of a separate statement of retained earnings, some corporations prepare a ***combined statement of income and retained earnings*** such as the one for Levant Corporation below:

LEVANT CORPORATION
Combined Statements of Income and Retained Earnings
For Years Ended December 31, Year 10 and Year 9
(Dollars in thousands except per-share amounts)

	Year 10	*Year 9*
Revenue:		
Sales	$1,317,683	$1,140,485
Other revenue	18,886	15,753
Total revenue	$1,336,569	$1,156,238
Cost and expenses:		
Cost of goods sold	$ 650,275	$ 567,206
Selling and administrative expenses	416,699	362,968
Depreciation and amortization expense	41,597	35,862
Income taxes expense	103,339	83,747
Other expenses	3,953	4,634
Total costs and expenses	$1,215,863	$1,054,417
Net income (per share: Year 10, $2.15; Year 9, $1.82)	$ 120,706	$ 101,821
Add: Retained earnings, beginning of year	469,647	391,850
Less: Cash dividends declared ($0.45 and $0.43 a share)	(25,136)	(24,024)
Retained earnings, end of year	$ 565,217	$ 469,647

Reporting Changes in Capital Stock, Contributed Surplus, and Retained Earnings

The requirements for reporting changes in capital stock, contributed surplus, and retained earnings are in sections 3240, 3260, and 3270 of the *CICA Handbook*. The recommendations in these sections generally call for full disclosure of all changes which have occurred during the year with respect to capital stock, contributed surplus, and retained earnings. Disclosure may be made in the body of, or in the notes included in, the financial statements. Such disclosures include the changes in the number of shares of each class of stock issued, acquired, redeemed or cancelled, and received during the year, the changes in contributed surplus and retained earnings resulting from changes in capital stock, from net income or loss from operations, from dividend declarations, and from the changes in appropriated retained earnings, and appraisal credits. The following examples from published annual financial statements are presented to illustrate typical disclosure practices followed by Canadian corporations.

LIQUID AIR CORPORATION
CONSOLIDATED STATEMENT OF COMMON STOCK AND OTHER SHAREHOLDERS' EQUITY

(Thousands of dollars except per share amounts)
Years ended December 31, 1986, 1985 and 1984

	Common Stock		Capital	Retained	Cumulative Translation
	Shares	Amount	Surplus	Earnings	Adjustment
Balance December 31, 1983	**12,562,796**	**$40**	**$167,249**	**$100,089**	**$(11,541)**
Current year's translation adjustment					(7,180)
Net earnings				27,304	
Cash dividends:					
Common ($1.60 per share)				(20,100)	
Preferred				(1,320)	
Reimbursement of down payment for purchase of common stock			3,128		
Balance December 31, 1984	**12,562,796**	**40**	**170,377**	**105,973**	**(18,721)**
Current year's translation adjustment					(6,806)
Net earnings				31,753	
Cash dividends:					
Common ($1.60 per share)				(20,100)	
Preferred				(1,320)	
Balance December 31, 1985	**12,562,796**	**40**	**170,377**	**116,306**	**(25,527)**
Current year's translation adjustment					1,573
Net earnings				34,680	
Cash dividends:					
Common ($1.60 per share)				(20,279)	
Preferred				(4,056)	
Stock issued	116,900		2,530		
Balance December 31, 1986	**12,679,696**	**$40**	**$172,907**	**$126,651**	**$(23,954)**

See notes to consolidated financial statements.

UNICORP

UNICORP CANADA CORPORATION

ANNUAL REPORT 1985

CONSOLIDATED STATEMENT OF CHANGES IN SHAREHOLDERS' EQUITY

	Preference Shares						
	Class I		Class II				
	Series C	Employee Shares, Series 1	Series A	Series B	Class A Non-Voting Shares	Class B Voting Shares	Retained Earnings
	Expressed in thousands of dollars						
Balances, January 1, 1984	$5,520	$904	$11,368	$ —	$14,157	$5,867	$11,744
Issue of 104,141 Class II Preference Shares, Series A in exchange for 416,190 common shares of Skill Resources Ltd.	—	—	1,039	—	—	—	—
Issue of 2,331,860 Class II Preference Shares, Series A in exchange for 3,886,767 common shares of Embassy Resources Ltd.	—	—	23,321	—	—	—	—
Conversion of 1,675 Class I Employee Preference Shares, Series 1 into 6,700 Class A Non-Voting Shares	—	(34)	—	—	34	—	—
Conversion of 6,941 Class II Preference Shares, Series A into 6,941 Class A Non-Voting Shares	—	—	(69)	—	69	—	—
Acquisition for cancellation of 9,298 Class A Non-Voting Shares, 8,516 Class B Voting Shares, and 18,993 Class II Preference Shares, Series A	—	—	(190)	—	(84)	(77)	—
Net income	—	—	—	—	—	—	19,009
Cash Dividends	—	—	—	—	—	—	(4,757))
Cost of share issue	—	—	—	—	—	—	(62)
Balances, December 31, 1984	5,520	870	35,469	—	14,176	5,790	25,934

Conversion of 2,500 Class I Employee Preference Shares, Series 1 into 10,000 Class A Non-Voting Shares	—	(50)	—	—	50	—	—
Issue of 15,198,256 Class II Preference Shares, Series B and warrants to purchase 7,599,146 Class A Non-Voting Shares in exchange for 15,198,256 common shares of Union Enterprises Ltd.	—	—	—	197,577	—	—	—
Conversion of 3,546,870 Class II Preference Shares, Series A into 3,546,870 Class A Non-Voting Shares	—	—	(35,469)	—	35,469	—	—
Net income	—	—	—	—	—	—	11,614
Cash dividends	—	—	—	—	—	—	(20,918)
Balances, December 31, 1985	**$5,520**	**$820**	**$ —**	**$197,577**	**$49,695**	**$5,790**	**$16,630**

EARNINGS PER SHARE

Because of the complexities of business activities and the need for a small number of comparative measurements to highlight financial analysis, earnings per share has become perhaps the most important computation for many investors. Probably no financial statistic is cited more widely than earnings per share. In the opinion of many investors, market prices of common stocks are closely related to earnings per share.

Earnings per share is the amount of net income earned on each share of common stock during an accounting period. *Earnings per share is meaningful only with respect to common stock; it should not be computed for preferred stock because the participation in earnings by preferred shareholders is limited by contract*.

The determination of whether a share of capital stock is a common or a preferred share, with respect to earnings-per-share computations, depends on which stock issue represents the residual portion of the earnings of the corporation. That particular stock issue is referred to as the common stock, and all other issues, which must have some preference with respect to sharing in corporate earnings, are referred to as preferred stock issues. Section 3500 of the *CICA Handbook* uses the terms ***common shares*** and ***senior shares*** in all references to share capital. These terms are explicitly defined in section 3500.05, as follows:

> "Common shares" are those which represent the residual equity in the earnings of a company; they would include, for example, preferred shares whose rights to participate in the earnings have no upper limit. "Senior shares" are all other types of capital shares; they would include preferred shares which participate with common shares but whose participation rights are effectively restricted. In determining whether shares are common shares or senior shares, it is the rights and privileges of the shares in relation to the earnings of the company rather than their designation which should govern.

Assuming that ***only common stock is outstanding*** and that there was no change in the number of shares outstanding during the accounting period, earnings per share is computed as follows:

$$\frac{\text{Net income}}{\text{Number of shares of common stock outstanding}} = \text{earnings per share}$$

When cumulative, nonconvertible preferred stock also is outstanding, the current dividend requirement on the preferred stock (whether declared by the board of directors or not) is deducted from net income to compute the amount of net income available for the common stock. Dividends on noncumulative, nonconvertible preferred stock are deducted only if ***declared***.

Investors in common stocks make extensive use of earnings-per-share data in the evaluation of the profitability of corporations. By computing the ***price-earnings***

ratio (market price of a share of common stock divided by earnings per share), investors also attempt to determine whether the market price of the common stock is reasonable or whether it might be too high or too low. However, financial statements are only one part of the total information that may be used to evaluate a corporation's past earnings and to predict its future earnings performance, and the earnings-per-share amount is a small piece of the total information available in financial statements. Excessive reliance on earnings-per-share data may result in failure to consider the totality of a corporation's operations, including a wide range of nonfinancial data that may be far more important to investors.

Historical Perspective

The inclusion of earnings per share in the income statement became a generally accepted accounting principle with the issuance of section 3500 of the ***CICA Handbook***, ''Earnings per Share,'' in January 1970. This section was introduced to endorse the usefulness of earnings-per-share data and to minimize the many differences in methods of both calculating and presenting earnings-per-share figures.

In the United States, the inclusion of earnings per share in the income statement became a generally accepted accounting principle with the issuance of ***APB Opinion No. 9*** in 1966.[5] Three years later, the APB issued ***Opinion No. 15***: ''Earnings per Share'' to: (1) recognize the importance of the increasingly complex capital structures of many corporations in which the distinctions between common shareholders' equity and other forms of corporate capital were not clearly apparent; (2) provide guidelines and procedures for the computation of earnings per share in a consistent manner which would be meaningful to investors; and (3) specify procedures for reporting the potential dilution in earnings per share.[6]

Computation of Weighted-Average Number of Shares of Common Stock Outstanding; Stock Splits and Stock Dividends

The first step in the computation of earnings per share is to determine the number of shares of common stock outstanding in each accounting period for which earnings data are to be presented. Earnings per share should be based on the ***weighted-average*** number of shares of common stock outstanding during each period.

Computation of Weighted-Average Number of Shares Outstanding

The weighted-average number of shares of common stock outstanding is determined by relating the portion of time within an accounting period that a given number of shares of common stock was outstanding to the length of that period. For example, if 1,000 shares of common stock were outstanding during the first nine months of Year 1 and 1,400 shares were outstanding during the last three months of Year 1, as a result of the issuance for cash of 400 additional shares of

5 AICPA, ***APB Opinion No. 9***: ''Reporting the Results of Operations'' (New York: 1966).

6 AICPA, ***APB Opinion No. 15***: ''Earnings per Share'' (New York: 1969).

common stock, the weighted-average number of shares of common stock outstanding during Year 1 is 1,100, determined as follows:

Computation of weighted-average number of shares of common stock outstanding

1,000 shares × ¾ of a year	750
1,400 shares × ¼ of a year	350
Weighted-average number of shares of common stock outstanding during Year 1	1,100

or, alternatively:

1,000 shares × 1 year	1,000
400 shares × ¼ year	100
Weighted-average number of shares of common stock outstanding during Year 1	1,100

The use of the weighted-average number of shares outstanding is necessary when additional shares of common stock are issued for cash or other assets, in order to compute a more meaningful earnings-per-share amount. Assuming that 400 shares of common stock were issued for cash on September 30, Year 1 (in the example above), the proceeds on the issuance were available to generate earnings only during the last three months of Year 1. These 400 shares would be outstanding for one-fourth of a year, or an equivalent of 100 shares outstanding for a full year. In other words, the weighted-average number of shares of common stock outstanding consists of 1,000 shares outstanding during the entire year plus 100 full-year-equivalent shares issued on September 30, Year 1.

The computation of the weighted-average number of common shares outstanding may also be accomplished by use of the days of the year, that is, the number of days the common shares are outstanding to 365 days.

Common stock may be issued during the year under each of the following conditions:

1. For cash
2. For services rendered
3. For assets other than cash
4. Upon the exercise of stock rights, options, and warrants (in effect this is an issue for cash as in **1** above)
5. Upon conversion of senior (preferred) stock
6. Upon conversion of senior (bonds, debentures) debt
7. In a business combination
8. In payment of stock dividends or for a stock split

For **1** through **4** above, the date of issue of the common stock is used in the computation of the weighted-average number of shares of common stock outstanding. For the two conversions, **5** and **6**, the date of issue of common stock on the conversion is not necessarily the date used in the computation. For the conversion of senior shares, the conversion date to be used in the computation is the date of termination of the dividend, and for senior debt, the date at which the interest obligation on the debt was terminated.[7] Item **7** represents another circumstance wherein the date to be used for the computation of the weighted-average number of common shares differs from the actual date of their issue. In this case the common shares are considered to have been issued at the date from which the results of operations of the acquired business are included in the income statement.[8]

When the number of shares of common stock outstanding changes as a result of item **8** above, a stock split, stock dividend, or reverse split, the computation of the weighted-average number of shares of common stock outstanding should be adjusted ***retroactively***. This is necessary to report earnings per share which are fully comparable in terms of the latest capital structure. If a stock split, stock dividend, or reverse split is to become effective after the close of the latest accounting period but before financial statements are issued, the per-share computations should be made on the basis of the ***new capitalization***. When earnings-per-share data are computed on this basis, the method of computation should be disclosed in a note to the financial statements.

The computation of the weighted-average number of shares of common stock outstanding, showing retroactive adjustment for a stock dividend and a stock split, is illustrated on page 890 for Anson Corporation.

In the computation of the retroactive weighted-average number of shares of common stock outstanding in Year 1 for Anson Corporation, the 20% stock dividend declared in Year 2 is applied to the 650,000 weighted-average number of shares of common stock outstanding in Year 1; and the 3-for-1 split in Year 3 is applied to the 780,000 weighted-average number of shares of common stock after adjustment for the 20% stock dividend.

To continue the example, assume that the net income of Anson Corporation for Year 3 was $5,040,000, and that net income and earnings per share were ***originally reported*** for Year 2 and Year 1 as shown in the first illustration on page 891.

A comparative income statement at the end of Year 2 would show earnings per share for Year 1 of $3.30 ($2,574,000 ÷ 780,000 shares outstanding after giving effect to the 20% stock dividend in Year 2 = $3.30). The comparative net income and earnings-per-share amounts for Anson Corporation, giving effect to the 20% stock dividend in Year 2 and the 3-for-1 stock split in Year 3, are presented ***at the end of Year 3*** as shown at the bottom of page 891.

7 CICA, ***CICA Handbook*** (Toronto), sec. 3500.23.

8 CICA, ***CICA Handbook***, sec. 3500.21.

ANSON CORPORATION
Computation of Weighted-Average Number of Shares of Common Stock Outstanding

		Year ended Dec. 31:		
		Year 3	*Year 2*	*Year 1*
Analysis of actual changes in the number of shares of common stock outstanding:				
Year 1				
Jan. 1	Number of shares outstanding, beginning of year	840,000	700,000	500,000
Apr. 1	Issuance for cash			200,000
Year 2				
July 2	20% stock dividend		140,000	
Year 3				
Mar. 16	3-for-1 stock split (200% increase)	1,680,000		
Dec. 31	Number of shares outstanding, end of year	2,520,000	840,000	700,000
Computation of weighted-average number of shares of common stock outstanding (giving retroactive recognition to stock dividend and stock split):				
Year 1				
Jan. 1	Number of shares outstanding, beginning of year	840,000	700,000	500,000
Apr. 1	Issuance for cash (200,000 shares × ¾ yr)			150,000
	Subtotals	840,000	700,000	650,000
Year 2				
July 2	20% stock dividend (applied retroactively)		140,000	130,000
	Subtotals	840,000	840,000	780,000
Year 3				
Mar. 16	3-for-1 stock split (applied retroactively)	1,680,000	1,680,000	1,560,000
	Weighted-average number of shares outstanding	2,520,000	2,520,000	2,340,000

Earnings-per-share data thus are reported on a fully comparable basis in terms of the capital structure at the end of Year 3. For example, because one share of common stock outstanding in Year 1 is equal to 3.6 shares at the end of Year 3 as a result of the 20% stock dividend and the 3-for-1 split, the earnings for Year 1 are restated retroactively at $1.10 per share ($3.96, as originally reported in the income statement for Year 1, divided by 3.6 = $1.10).

The discussion on stock dividends to this point has been focussed on stock dividends of common stock to common stock shareholders. The weighted-average was computed by treating the stock dividend as if it were issued at the beginning

ANSON CORPORATION
Earnings per Share (as Originally Reported)
For Years Ended December 31, Year 2 and Year 1

	From income statement for Year 2	*From income statement for Year 1*
Net income	$3,780,000	$2,574,000
Earnings per share of common stock:		
Year 1: $2,574,000 ÷ 650,000 (weighted-average number of shares outstanding in Year 1, before retroactive adjustment for 20% stock dividend and 3-for-1 stock split)		$ 3.96
Year 2: $3,780,000 ÷ 840,000 (weighted-average number of shares outstanding in Year 2, before retroactive adjustment for 3-for-1 stock split)	$ 4.50	

of the year and then applied retroactively to previous years for comparative purposes. However, when common stock is issued as a dividend on preferred stock, section 3500.26 of the ***CICA Handbook*** recommends that the date of issue be used to compute the weighted-average. For example, if the 20% stock dividend of 140,000 shares of common stock used in the previous example were for preferred stock shareholders, the weighted-average would be computed from the date of issue (July 2, Year 2) and the weighted-average number of shares of common stock for Year 2 would be 70,000 shares (140,000 × $\frac{6}{12}$ = 70,000) rather than 140,000 shares.

The difficulties encountered in the computation of earnings per share do not end with the computation of the weighted-average number of shares of common stock outstanding. For example: Earnings per share must be computed for a corporation which has preferred stock (convertible or nonconvertible) or convertible bonds or stock options and warrants outstanding.

ANSON CORPORATION
Earnings per Share (Reflecting Retroactive Application of Stock Dividend and Stock Split)
For Years Ended December 31, Year 3, Year 2, and Year 1

	Year 3	*Year 2*	*Year 1*
Net income	$5,040,000	$3,780,000	$2,574,000
Earnings per share of common stock:			
Year 1: $2,574,000 ÷ 2,340,000 shares (adjusted)			$ 1.10
Year 2: $3,780,000 ÷ 2,520,000 shares (adjusted)		$ 1.50	
Year 3: $5,040,000 ÷ 2,520,000 shares (adjusted)	$ 2.00		

Single Presentation of Earnings per Share

The capital structure of a corporation may consist only of common stock; or the capital structure may include nonconvertible preferred stock, few or no potentially dilutive convertible securities, and small amounts of stock rights, options, and warrants. The potential reduction in earnings per share that would occur if convertible securities were converted or if outstanding rights, options, and warrants were exercised is called ***dilution***. If the potential dilution in earnings per share is not material,[9] potentially dilutive securities and options or warrants need not be considered in the computation of earnings per share. In such cases, a ***single presentation*** of earnings per share in the income statement is appropriate. This single presentation may include an extraordinary item, as illustrated on page 893 for Single Corporation.

The example for Single Corporation shows that the earnings per share before the extraordinary loss decreased in Year 2, despite the fact that the same number of shares of common stock was outstanding at the end of each year (400,000 shares) and that the income before the extraordinary loss actually increased in Year 2. This is attributed to the increase in the ***weighted-average*** number of shares outstanding; the 100,000 shares issued on July 1, Year 1, were outstanding for only six months in Year 1, but for all 12 months in Year 2. In the absence of extraordinary items, only a single earnings-per-share amount appears in the income statement for a corporation with a simple capital structure.

The presentation in the income statement of the earnings per share of common stock for Single Corporation disclosed three earnings-per-share figures for Year 2. Section 3500.11 of the ***CICA Handbook*** recommends that basic earnings per share be shown for the current and preceding period for income before extraordinary items and for net income for the period. In addition, it may be ***desirable*** to show the basic earnings-per-share figure for extraordinary items so as to highlight their significance. As a result, the presentation shown for Single Corporation goes beyond the recommendation, as it includes the earnings-per-share figure for the extraordinary item. The extraordinary loss of 35 cents per share is significant and therefore was included in the presentation as a ***desirable*** reporting practice.

The income statement for the preceding period may include adjustments as a result of current-period discoveries of and corrections for prior-period adjustments and prior-period errors. Also, changes in accounting policies requiring retroactive adjustment and restatement of the preceding period's income when feasible may have occurred. In such circumstances, the computation of the preceding period's basic earnings-per-share figure should be on the restated net income and restated income before extraordinary items, if applicable.

Dual Presentation of Earnings per Share

The CICA has taken the position that earnings per share should reflect potential dilution when securities which in substance are equivalent to common stock are

9 In the United States, if the potential dilution is less than 3%, it is not material. In Canada, materiality is a matter of professional judgement.

SINGLE CORPORATION
Earnings-per-Share Data and Computations
For Years Ended December 31, Year 2 and Year 1

	Year 2	*Year 1*
Data required to compute earnings per share of common stock:		
Income before extraordinary loss	$810,000	$750,000
Extraordinary loss (net of income taxes)	$140,000	
Dividend requirement on cumulative nonconvertible preferred stock	$ 50,000	$ 50,000
Shares of common stock outstanding:		
Beginning of year	400,000	300,000
Issued for cash, July 1, Year 1	-0-	100,000
End of year	400,000	400,000
Weighted-average number of shares of common stock outstanding	400,000	350,000 (1)
Presentation in the income statement:		
Earnings per share of common stock:		
Income before extraordinary loss	$ 1.90 (2)	$ 2.00 (3)
Extraordinary loss (net of income taxes)	(0.35) (4)	-0-
Net income	$ 1.55	$ 2.00

LEGEND:

(1) 300,000 shares for the full year, plus 100,000 shares for one-half year (equivalent to 50,000 for a full year) = 350,000 shares.

(2) ($810,000 − $50,000) ÷ 400,000 weighted-average number of shares = $1.90.

(3) ($750,000 − $50,000) ÷ 350,000 weighted-average number of shares = $2.00.

(4) $140,000 ÷ 400,000 weighted-average number of shares = $0.35.

outstanding. As a result, a corporation that has convertible securities, stock rights, options and warrants, or other potentially dilutive securities outstanding should report in a note to the financial statements, cross-referenced to the income statement ***basic*** earnings per share and ***fully diluted*** earnings per share; this is referred to as a ***dual presentation*** of earnings per share. (See pages 907 and 908 for two examples.) These reporting requirements for earnings per share do not change the legal rights of the various security holders or the presentation of other data in the financial statements. The computation of basic earnings per share is explained below; the explanation of fully diluted earnings per share begins on page 897.

Basic Earnings per Share

Basic earnings per share is the amount of earnings applicable to each share of common stock; the number of shares of common stock consists of a weighted-average number of common shares actually outstanding. Basic earnings per share is computed as follows:

Computation of basic earnings per share

$$\frac{\text{Net income (after preferred dividends are deducted therefrom)}}{\text{Weighted-average number of common shares outstanding}}$$

Example 1: Convertible Preferred Stock Not Converted in Year 1 and Dividends Paid on July 1, Year 1 At the beginning of Year 1, Wagner Corporation issued at $100 a share, 50,000 shares of $6 convertible preferred stock. Each share of preferred stock is convertible into two shares of common stock. A dividend of $3 per preferred share is paid on July 1 and January 1 each year. If Wagner Corporation has net income of $1,900,000 in Year 1 and 400,000 shares of common stock outstanding at the beginning of Year 1, compute the basic earnings per share for Year 1.

Solution Since no common shares were issued during Year 1, the weighted-average number of common shares outstanding would be those outstanding at the beginning of the year, or 400,000 shares. The basic earnings-per-share computation, using the above equation, would be:

$$\frac{\$1,900,000 - (50,000 \times \$3)}{400,000} = \frac{\$1,750,000}{400,000} = \$4.38$$

Example 2: Convertible Preferred Stock Converted in Year 1, and Dividends Paid at the Conversion Date At the beginning of Year 1, Wagner Corporation issued at $100 a share, 50,000 shares of $6 convertible preferred stock. On July 1, Year 1, all of the stock was converted to common stock. Each share of preferred stock was converted into two shares of common stock. A dividend of $3 per preferred share was paid on July 1. If Wagner Corporation has net income of $1,900,000 in Year 1 and 400,000 shares of common stock outstanding at the beginning of Year 1, compute the basic earnings per share for Year 1.

Solution The conversion of the preferred stock resulted in the issue of 100,000 (50,000 preferred × 2 common per preferred) shares of common stock. However, these shares would be outstanding for the period from July 1 to December 31, Year 1, only. The weighted-average number of shares outstanding from the conversion of the preferred stock would therefore be (100,000 × $\frac{6}{12}$ year) = 50,000 shares of common stock. The amount of the dividend paid on the preferred stock at the conversion date, July 1, was $150,000 (50,000 shares × $3 per share). The amount of ***basic*** earnings per share for Year 1 is computed as follows:

$$\frac{\$1,900,000 - \$150,000}{400,000 + 50,000} = \frac{\$1,750,000}{450,000} = \$3.89$$

Example 3: Convertible Preferred Stock Converted in Year 1, but Dividends Are Not Paid at the Conversion Date This is the same situation as example 2 except one quarterly dividend of $1.50 has been paid on April 1, Year 1. No dividend accompanied the common stock on the conversion date, July 1, Year 1.

Solution The conversion resulted in the issue of 100,000 shares of common stock. However, the weighted-average number of these shares outstanding would now total (100,000 × 9/12 year) = 75,000 shares of common stock. The dividend ceased April 1, Year 1, and, accordingly, the common shares are considered to have been outstanding since that date rather than since the actual conversion date.

The amount of basic earnings per share for Year 1 is computed as follows:

$$\frac{\$1{,}900{,}000 - (50{,}000 \times \$1.50)}{400{,}000 + 75{,}000} = \$3.84$$

The moving of the issue date back from the actual date to the last dividend payment date reduces the basic earnings-per-share figure. This requirement provides a consistent basis for the computation of the weighted-average number of common shares outstanding and, as a result, minimizes inconsistencies with respect to conversion dates used by corporations.

The same procedures, as in the examples above, apply to convertible senior debt. However, it is the date to which interest is paid that signifies whether the actual conversion date or an earlier date applies.

Additional Information Regarding Basic Earnings per Share When a conversion has taken place during the year, ***at other than the beginning of the year***, another computation may be required so that additional information with respect to the basic earnings-per-share figure may be available. The conversion of senior shares or debt, which has taken place, may have a significant effect on earnings per share in the future. Accordingly, the computation will be made under the assumption that the conversion had taken place ***at the beginning of the period***. In this way, the common shares are given maximum weighting, as they are assumed to be outstanding for the entire period, which will be the case in future years.

However, the net income includes, for senior shares, a reduction representing the dividends paid on the converted shares. (If no dividends had been paid on these shares, the date of issue would have been considered to be the beginning of the period, as the conversion date would have been moved back to that point.) Since, hypothetically, the common stock was issued at the beginning of the period, no dividend on the preferred stock would have been paid because it would have been converted. As a result, any dividends for this preferred stock, deducted from net income for the basic earnings-per-share computation, must now be added back so as to cancel it out.

For senior debt, the net income included the ***after-tax effect***[10] of the interest expensed with respect to this converted debt issue. The after-tax effect of this

10 Assume interest expense of $100,000, a 40% tax rate, and a net income before interest and tax of $500,000. Net income before tax would be $400,000, income tax would be (40% of $400,000) = $160,000 and net income would be ($400,000 − $160,000) = $240,000. Now assume no interest expense. The income tax would be (40% of $500,000) = $200,000 and net income would be ($500,000 − $200,000) = $300,000. The difference in net income before and after the $100,000 interest is ($300,000 − $240,000) = $60,000. This is the after-tax effect of removing the interest. By formula: Interest × (1 − tax rate) = after-tax effect.

interest expense must be removed from net income because the assumption that conversion occurred at the beginning of the period would result in no interest expense.

Example 4: The Conversion in Example 2 Assumed to Have Occurred at the Beginning of the Period In this event, the weighted-average number of shares of common stock outstanding, as determined for basic earnings per share, is increased to affect the hypothetical issue at the beginning of the period. The net income (less preferred stock dividends) figure used to determine the basic earnings-per-share figure is increased by adding back the preferred dividend deducted previously. The amount of the "adjusted" basic earnings per share for Year 1 is computed as follows:

Solution In this situation, we commence with the numerator and the denominator for the basic earnings per share (as computed in example 2 on page 894) and proceed as follows:

	Numerator		*Denominator*
Basic earnings per share from example 2 (page 894)	$1,750,000		450,000
Add back dividends paid ($3 × 50,000 shares)	150,000		
Add the weighted-average number of shares outstanding for the period January 1 to July 1, Year 1 (50,000 × 2 × 6/12 year).................................			50,000
	$1,900,000	÷	500,000

"Adjusted" basic earnings per share: $\frac{\$1,900,000}{500,000} = \$3.80$

Note: In the calculation of basic earnings per share in example 2, 50,000 weighted-average common shares represented the preferred share conversion. Those 50,000 shares were outstanding for the period July 1 to December 31, Year 1. The above 50,000 shares represents the weighted-average number for the period January 1 to June 30, Year 1. The sum of the two (one included in the 450,000 above, and the other added in this example) represents 100,000 shares which is exactly the number of common shares actually issued to effect the conversion.

In order to see the effect of income taxes, assume in examples 2 and 4 that, instead of senior shares, it had been senior debt as illustrated in example 5.

Example 5: A Conversion of Senior Debt at Other than the Beginning of the Period Requiring the Calculation of Basic Earnings per Share as Though It Had Occurred at the Beginning of the Period The corporation issued 5,000 one-thousand-dollar, 12% bonds on January 1, Year 1. On July 1, immediately after the payment of the semiannual interest in the amount of $300,000, the 5,000 bonds were converted into common stock at the rate of 20 shares of common stock for each $1,000 bond.

Solution In this situation basic earnings per share would have been computed earlier. Therefore, that figure will be computed first, and then the adjustment thereof to obtain the additional information will be made:

	Numerator		Denominator
Basic earnings per share: net income reported	\$1,900,000		
Common stock outstanding the entire year			400,000
Common stock outstanding on conversion of 12% bonds: 5,000 bonds × 20 shares per bond × $\frac{6}{12}$ year = July 1–Dec. 1.............................			50,000
	\$1,900,000	÷	450,000

Basic earnings per share: $\frac{\$1,900,000}{450,000} = \$4.22$

	Numerator		Denominator
Adjustment: The interest expense included as expense in the \$1,900,000 net income amounts to \$300,000 × (1 – 0.4)	180,000		
The additional weighted-averaged number of shares of common stock hypothetically outstanding: 100,000 × $\frac{6}{12}$ year = Jan. 1–June 30			50,000
	\$2,080,000	÷	500,000

"Adjusted" basic earnings per share: $\frac{\$2,080,000}{500,000} = \$4.16$

The "adjusted" basic earnings per share of \$4.16 would be compared to the basic earnings per share figure of \$4.22 and, if there is a material difference, the "adjusted" basic earnings-per-share figure (\$4.16) should be disclosed in a note to the financial statements cross-referenced to the income statement. In this case the difference of 6 cents is 1.42%. This is well below the 3% criterion used in the United States and probably would not be disclosed in Canada, where professional judgement is the criterion used.

It should be noted that only ***conversions*** that have occurred at other than the beginning of the year are adjusted. ***Exercises*** are not included in the calculation. Also, when the security is ***issued*** at a date later than the beginning of the current period, the common stock is still considered to have been issued at the beginning of the current period for the "adjusted" basic earnings-per-share computation.

Fully Diluted Earnings per Share

Fully diluted earnings per share would result if all potentially dilutive convertible securities had been converted into common shares at the beginning of the current period, or the issue date of the security, if later. They would also result if all outstanding stock rights, options and warrants, and other contingent issues, had been exercised at the beginning of the current period or the grant date, if later. In addition, all conversions of securities and exercises of stock options, rights, and warrants which have occurred in the current year are assumed to have occurred at the later of the beginning of the current period and the issue date. As a result, all conversions, convertibles, exercises, and exercisables (stock rights, options, and warrants outstanding at the end of the period, if exercisable within 10 years) which are potentially dilutive may enter into the computation of fully diluted earnings per share on a prospective basis. Section 3500.34 of the ***CICA Handbook*** contains the following recommendation:

> The calculation of fully diluted earnings per share should exclude any potential conversion of senior shares or debt, exercise of rights, warrants and options or other contingent issuances that would increase earnings per share or decrease a loss per share.

This, in effect, ***requires*** that the calculation result in ***maximum*** potential dilution and, as a result, some form of ranking procedure is needed to accomplish this objective. Those individual securities or rights which are not included because they do not contribute to maximum potential dilution are referred to as ***anti-dilutive*** securities or rights. Anti-dilution means the inclusion of that security will ***increase*** the earnings-per-share figure rather than ***decrease*** it (or decrease a loss per share rather than increase it). Accordingly, it is necessary to determine the earnings-per-share figure for each security or right so as to have a figure to consider with respect to the fully diluted earnings-per-share computation.

The computation of fully diluted earnings per share for each of the types of securities and rights is shown on the following pages.

Example 6: Convertible Preferred Stock Not Converted in Year 1 Assume the same information as that used in example 1 on page 894. As was the case in the calculation of adjusted basic earnings per share, the calculation of fully diluted earnings per share commences with the numerator and denominator amounts used to compute basic earnings per share, as follows:

$$\frac{\$1{,}900{,}000 - (50{,}000 \times \$3)}{400{,}000} = \frac{1{,}750{,}000}{400{,}000} = \$4.38$$

Recall that the (50,000 × \$3) was the \$150,000 dividend paid to preferred shareholders.

Solution The computation of fully diluted earnings per share requires the weighted-average number of common shares to represent the entire period (unless the preferred stock was issued in the current period). Therefore, the denominator adjustment will be 100,000 × $^{12}/_{12}$ year (representing January 1–December 31) = 100,000 shares, and the numerator ***adjustment*** will be the reversal of the \$150,000 dividends paid and deducted from net income in the basic earnings-per-share numerator calculation. Since the preferred stock is assumed to be converted on January 1, Year 1, no Year 1 dividends would have been paid thereon. The earnings per share for this ***individual*** security, for purposes of computation of maximum potential dilution, would be the ratio of the change in each of the numerator and denominator, or:

$$\frac{\$150{,}000}{100{,}000} = \$1.50 \text{ per share}$$

This figure is below the basic earnings-per-share figure of $4.38 and thus is to be ranked with others in the computation of fully diluted earnings per share. If this were the only item, fully diluted earnings per share, in the amount of $3.80, would be computed as follows:

	Numerator		*Denominator*
Basic earnings per share	$1,750,000		400,000
Convertible preferred stock	150,000		100,000
	$1,900,000	÷	500,000

Fully diluted earnings per share: $\frac{\$1,900,000}{500,000} = \$3.80$

Example 7: Convertible Preferred Stock Converted in Year 1 Assume the same information as that used in example 2 on page 894. Section 3500.17 of the ***CICA Handbook***, the basic earnings-per-share computation paragraph, is recommended as the starting point for fully diluted earnings-per-share computation. The basic calculation in example 2 was:

$$\frac{\$1,900,000 - \$150,000}{400,000 + 50,000} = \frac{\$1,750,000}{450,000} = \$3.89$$

Recall that the numerator was reduced by the $150,000 in preferred shares dividends paid, and the denominator was increased by the weighted-average number of shares of common stock issued in the preferred share conversion and represented the period from July 1 to December 31, Year 1.

Solution The computation of fully diluted earnings per share requires the weighted-average number of common shares represent the entire period (unless the preferred stock was issued in the current year). Therefore, the denominator change will be 100,000 × 6/12 year (representing January 1–June 30) = 50,000 shares. Since the preferred stock is assumed to be converted on January 1, Year 1, no Year 1 dividends would be paid. The dividend paid for these specific preferred shares (and deducted from net income in the computation of basic earnings per share) must be added back to net income in the amount of $150,000. The earnings per share for this ***individual*** security would be:

$$\frac{\$150,000}{50,000} = \$3.00$$

This amount is below the basic earnings-per-share amount of $3.89. Therefore, the security is potentially dilutive, and should be ranked with others in the computation of fully diluted earnings per share.

If this candidate were the only one, fully diluted earnings per share in the amount of $3.80 would be computed, as shown below.

	Numerator		Denominator
Basic earnings per share	$1,750,000		450,000
Preferred stock converted	150,000		50,000
	$1,900,000	÷	500,000

The "fully diluted" earnings per share becomes:

$$\frac{\$1,900,000}{500,000} = \$3.80$$

Example 8: Convertible Debt Issued in the Current Period and Not Converted During the Period Catalina Limited issued $100,000 of 10%, $1,000 convertible bonds on April 1, Year 2, at face value. Each $1,000 bond was convertible into 20 shares of common stock. The company's income tax rate was 40% in Year 2. Basic earnings per share was computed as ($74,000 ÷ 20,000 shares) = $3.70 per share for Year 2. What is the amount of fully diluted earnings per share?

Solution The period of time these bonds were outstanding and convertible was April 1 to December 31 of Year 2, or $\frac{9}{12}$ of the year. Therefore, the weighted-average number of common shares would have been 1,500 common shares:

$$\frac{9}{12} \times \left(20 \times \frac{\$100,000}{1,000}\right) = 1,500 \text{ common shares}$$

The savings in interest expense (after-tax effect), had they been converted on April 1, Year 2, would have been $4,500 [$100,000 × 10% × $\frac{9}{12}$ year × (1 – 0.4)]. Therefore, the earnings per share for this item would amount to ($4,500 ÷ 1,500) = $3.00. This is less than $3.70; therefore, the convertible bonds are potentially dilutive and should be included in the computation of fully diluted earnings per share. If this were the only one, fully diluted earnings per share would amount to $3.65, computed as follows:

	Numerator		Denominator
Basic earnings per share	$74,000		20,000
10% convertible bonds	4,500		1,500
	$78,500	÷	21,500

Fully diluted earnings per share: $78,500 ÷ 21,500 = $3.65

Example 9: Convertible Debt Issued and Converted in the Period Catalina Limited issued $100,000 of 10%, $1,000 convertible bonds on April 1, Year 2, at face value. On October 1, Year 2, all of these bonds were converted into 2,000 shares of common stock. The company's income tax rate was 40% in Year 2. In the computation of basic earnings per share, the weighted-average number of shares of common stock outstanding for this conversion were 2,000 × $\frac{3}{12}$ year (representing October 1–December 31) = 500 shares.

Solution The computation of the additional weighted-average shares of common stock for determining fully diluted earnings per share requires the assumption that the bonds were converted into common stock on the later of the beginning of Year 2 and the issue date of the bonds. Since the bonds were issued on April 1, Year 2, the period of adjustment becomes April 1, Year 2, to October 1, Year 2, or six months. Therefore, the additional weighted-average number of shares of common stock applicable to the bonds are (2,000 × $\frac{6}{12}$ year) = 1,000 shares.

The adjustment to the numerator with respect to this conversion is the interest that would not have been paid on these convertible bonds had they been converted on their issue date. Since interest expense is a reduction of net income before income taxes and therefore reduces income tax expense, the ***after-tax*** effect of this interest removal must be used. The increase in net income would be $3,000 (10% × $100,000 × [1 – 0.4] × $\frac{6}{12}$ year). The earnings per share for this individual security would be $3.00 per share ($\frac{\$3,000}{1,000}$). If we assume basic earnings per share were computed as $3.70 per share ($\frac{\$74,000}{20,000}$) and that as a result the convertible debt was not anti-dilutive, fully diluted earnings per share, assuming this is the only item, would be computed as follows:

	Numerator		*Denominator*
Basic earnings per share	$74,000		20,000
10% convertible bonds	3,000		1,000
	$77,000	÷	21,000

Fully diluted earnings per share: $77,000 ÷ 21,000 = $3.67

Example 10: Stock Option Outstanding (Exercisable) at Year-end Waterfall, Inc., granted stock options to senior executives on January 1, Year 3, as follows: 1,000 stock options containing the right to purchase two shares of common stock at $50 per share for each option. The company's current year income is taxed at a 40% rate. Management estimates the corporation's rate of return on investments at 15% ***before*** applicable income taxes.

Solution The stock options were granted at the beginning of the year. Therefore, the computation of the denominator will assume these options were exercised at the beginning of the year for 2,000 shares (1,000 × 2 × $\frac{12}{12}$ year). The numerator is also changed as follows: The assumed exercise of the options means the corporation received cash in the amount of $100,000 (2,000 × $50). It is assumed this cash would be invested in the business and would therefore have earned a return which would have increased net income. As a result, the numerator becomes $9,000 [$100,000 × 15% × (1 − 0.4) × 12/12 year]. The earnings-per-share figure for these stock options would be $\frac{\$9,000}{2,000} = \$4.50$. Assume the basic figure was $4.40, computed: $\frac{\$44,000}{10,000} = \$4.40$. Then the above item would be ***anti-dilutive***, as follows:

	Numerator		*Denominator*
Basic earnings per share	$44,000		10,000
Stock options	9,000		2,000
	$53,000	÷	12,000

Earnings per share including anti-dilutive stock option: $53,000 ÷ 12,000 = $4.42

The $4.42 figure is ***higher*** than the basic earnings-per-share figure, and the stock options are therefore ***immediately*** anti-dilutive and would not be included in the computation of fully diluted earnings per share.

Had some of these stock options been exercised during the year, the same treatment as that accorded converted stocks and bonds would have applied in the determination of the applicable weighted-average shares of common stock outstanding. The numerator change would require the calculation of the after-tax interest income that would have been earned by the company for the period from January 1 to the exercise date.

The computation of fully diluted earnings per share entails the addition to the basic earnings per share of those potentially dilutive candidates, which will result in maximum potential dilution — the lowest, most conservative, earnings per share figure. In the following example, consideration of the ranking of the dilutive effect for, and the computations of, fully diluted earnings per share are illustrated.

Example 11: Computation of Fully Diluted Earnings per Share by Ranking
Assume that the basic earnings-per-share figure for Exacto Corporation is $2.00 ($\frac{\$1,000,000}{500,000}$). The following table gives the earnings-per-share figures and the consequent ranking (low to high) of four different securities:

Security	*Earnings-per share figure*	*Rank*
a 10% convertible preferred shares	$1.60 ($\frac{\$400,000}{250,000}$)	3
b 12% convertible bonds	$1.00 ($\frac{\$500,000}{500,000}$)	1
c Stock options outstanding	$1.20 ($\frac{\$100,000}{75,000}$)	2
d Stock warrants outstanding	$2.50 ($\frac{\$300,000}{120,000}$)	4

The computation of fully diluted earnings per share by ranking requires, first, that there be potential dilution for each item considered — that is, earnings per share for each security, stock right, option, warrant, and other contingent issues must be lower than basic earnings per share. Item **d** above, the stock warrants, ranked no. 4, has an earnings per share of $2.50. This is higher than basic earnings per share of $2.00. Therefore item **d** is ***immediately anti-dilutive*** and so is not to be considered further.

The remaining three items are potentially dilutive, as each has an earnings-per-share figure lower than basic earnings per share. It is necessary, if maximum potential dilution is desired, to rank these items from lowest to highest earnings-per-share figure and then to add them to basic earnings per share one at a time in that order:

	Numerator		*Denominator*
Basic earnings per share	$1,000,000		500,000
Rank no. 1 ''candidate''	500,000		500,000
	$1,500,000	÷	1,000,000

Partially diluted earnings per share: $1,500,000 ÷ 1,000,000 = $1.50

For rank no. 2 ''candidate'' the earnings per share is $1.00. This is lower than the $1.50 above; therefore, ''candidate'' 2 is added, as follows:

	Numerator		*Denominator*
Earnings per share after rank no. 1 dilution	$1,500,000		1,000,000
Rank no. 2 ''candidate''	100,000		75,000
	$1,600,000	÷	1,075,000

Fully diluted earnings per share: $1,600,000 ÷ 1,075,000 = $1.49

The fully diluted earnings-per-share figure is $1.49 because the next ''candidate'' has a figure of $1.60, which is higher. It would be anti-dilutive to include the 10% convertible preferred shares, even though this security was potentially dilutive in that its earnings per share figure was below the basic figure of $2.00.

Although the above method of computing fully diluted earnings per share results in ***maximum*** potential dilution, in practice many companies include ***all*** securities, stock rights, options, warrants, and other contingencies which are ***potentially dilutive***. Using example 11, the fully diluted earnings per share would become $1.51, computed as follows:

	Numerator		*Denominator*
Balance from maximim potential dilution	$1,600,000		1,075,000
Rank no. 3 ''candidate''	400,000		250,000
	$2,000,000	÷	1,325,000

Fully diluted earnings per share: $2,000,000 ÷ 1,325,000 = $1.51

Only the stock warrants (ranked no. 4), with an earnings per share figure of $2.50, are excluded, as that figure is higher than ***basic*** earnings per share.

Including all potentially dilutive contingencies is unsound and violates the spirit of the ***CICA Handbook*** recommendations; however, in most cases the practice does not have a material effect on the results, and that is why it is followed.

Pro Forma Earnings per Share

Events which occur between the date of the financial statements and the date of their completion may have a material effect on the usefulness of the data reported for the year, even though the subsequent event does not require an adjustment to the financial statements themselves. When any of three types of events affecting common shares occurs in the subsequent period, and the effect is material, pro forma earnings per share must be computed. The three types of events are:[11]

1 Common shares are issued for cash in the subsequent period and some or all of that cash is used to redeem preferred shares, or retire senior debt outstanding at the end of the current year.

2 Convertible securities outstanding at the end of the current year are converted in the subsequent period.

3 A reorganization has taken place in the subsequent period.

The computation of ***pro forma basic earnings per share*** is accomplished under the assumption that the subsequent event occurred at the later of the beginning of the current period and the issue date (for event types **1** and **2** above). ***Pro forma fully diluted earnings per share*** is to be computed as well for event types **1** and **3** above. Since convertibles outstanding at the end of the period have already been converted when computing fully diluted earnings per share, the computation of pro forma fully diluted earnings per share does not include event type **2**. The information content in pro forma per-share figures is considered useful in that users of the corporation's financial statements are able currently to assess the potential impact of the subsequent event.

Example 12: Computation of Pro Forma Basic Earnings per Share and Pro Forma Fully Diluted Earnings per Share Next Year Limited reported the following capital structure at December 31, 19X5:

1 Preferred stock: authorized, issued, and outstanding 10,000 shares, 10% non-cumulative, redeemable at face value of $100 per share, issued for $1,000,000

2 Common stock: authorized an unlimited number of shares, issued 100,000 shares of no-par-value stock for a consideration of $1,300,000

3 12%, $1,000 debentures, convertible into common shares at 20 common shares per $1,000 debenture, 1,000 debentures issued for a consideration of $1,000,000

There were no common shares issued for cash, and no conversions in the current year. The company reported net income after tax of $1,500,000 for the 19X5 year. The current income tax rate is 40%. All preferred dividends have been paid for the current year.

11 CICA, ***CICA Handbook***, sec. 3500.39.

On February 15, 19X6, before the date of completion of the financial statements, the company issued 20,000 shares of common stock for $200,000 cash and used the cash to redeem 2,000 preferred shares at face value.

Solution Basic earnings per share in the amount of $14.00 is computed as follows:

$$\frac{\$1{,}500{,}000 - \$100{,}000}{100{,}000} = \frac{\$1{,}400{,}000}{100{,}000} = \$14.00$$

Fully diluted earnings per share in the amount of $12.27 is computed as follows:

	Numerator		Denominator
Basic earnings per share	$1,400,000		100,000
12% debentures:			
12% × 1,000,000 × (1 – 0.4) × 12/12 year	72,000		
1,000 × 20			20,000
	$1,472,000	÷	120,000

Fully diluted earnings per share: $1,472,000 ÷ 120,000 = $12.27

Computation of pro forma basic earnings per share The computation of pro forma basic earnings per share requires the adjustment of basic earnings per share for this subsequent event, under the assumption that the subsequent event had occurred at the beginning of the period (here January 1, 19X5) or the issue date of the preferred shares, if later. Pro forma basic earnings per share in the amount of $13.33 is computed as follows:

	Numerator		Denominator
Basic earnings per share	$1,400,000		100,000
Redemption of preferred shares:			
20,000 × $100 × 10%	200,000		20,000
	$1,600,000	÷	120,000

Pro forma basic earnings per share: $1,600,000 ÷ 120,000 = $13.33

This is dilutive, as it is lower than the $14.00 basic earnings-per-share figure. The dilutive effect is:

$$\frac{\$14.00 - \$13.33}{\$14.00} \times 100\% = 4.79\%$$

This may or may not be material, depending on the particular circumstances. If it is material, the pro forma basic earnings-per-share figure should be disclosed.

Computation of pro forma fully diluted earnings per share Pro forma fully diluted earnings per share is determined using the figures for fully diluted earnings per share and adjusting to pro forma amounts using the ***same*** figures as for the computation of pro forma basic earnings per share, as follows:

	Numerator		*Denominator*
Fully diluted earnings per share	$1,472,000		120,000
Redemption of preferred shares	200,000		20,000
	$1,672,000	÷	140,000

The pro forma fully diluted earnings-per-share figure becomes:

$$\frac{\$1,672,000}{140,000} = \$11.94$$

This is dilutive as it is lower than $12.27. The dilutive effect is 2.69%.

Disclosure of Earnings-per-Share Figures in the Financial Statements

For dual presentations, it will be necessary to disclose both basic earnings per share (as earnings per share) and fully diluted earnings per share. Although section 3500.30 of the ***CICA Handbook*** recommends dislosure of fully diluted earnings per share in a note to the financial statements, many companies include this figure on a comparable basis in the income statement alongside or under the basic figure. The figures for both earnings per share and fully diluted earnings per share are to be shown for net income and for net income before extraordinary items as described on page 892.

Material dilutive effects of earnings-per-share computations for earnings per share adjusted for current-period conversions, and for either or both of the pro forma per-share computations, will be disclosed by way of separate notes to the financial statements. All earnings-per-share note disclosures are to be cross-referenced to the income statement.

Presentation of Earnings per Share in the Income Statement

Typical presentations of earnings per share for publicly owned companies with complex capital structures are shown on pages 907 and 908.

Additional examples of presentation of earnings per share are in Chapter 4. The presentation of earnings per share following a change in accounting policy is illustrated in Chapter 22.

NORTH CANADIAN OILS LIMITED

Consolidated Statement of Earnings

(thousands of Canadian dollars)

	Years ended December 31		
	1986	1985	1984
Revenue			
Gas and oil, net	**$ 90,808**	$117,928	$59,932
Investment and other income	**21,352**	25,820	15,477
	112,160	143,748	75,409
Expenses			
Operating	**20,854**	22,514	10,259
Administrative	**7,395**	8,664	4,719
Interest on long-term debt	**26,487**	32,708	15,721
Depreciation and depletion	**33,283**	34,037	9,677
	88,019	97,923	40,376
Earnings before taxes	**24,141**	45,825	35,033
Income and resource taxes			
Deferred (Note 7)	**5,161**	10,522	6,869
Petroleum and Gas Revenue Tax	**4,580**	11,816	5,983
Alberta Royalty Tax Credit	**(4,633)**	(3,721)	(2,271)
	5,108	18,617	10,581
Earnings before minority interest	**19,033**	27,208	24,452
Minority interest	**2,208**	4,242	442
Net earnings	**16,825**	22,966	24,010
Dividends on preferred shares	**13,224**	9,881	4,458
Net earnings attributable to common shares	**$ 3,601**	$ 13,085	$19,552
Earnings per common share			
Basic	**$ 0.30**	$ 1.21	$ 2.26
Fully diluted	**$ 0.30**	$ 1.10	$ 1.59

Federal Industries Ltd.

Annual Report 1986

Consolidated Statement of Earnings

		$000	
For the year ended December 31	**1986**	1985	1984
Sales and services (Note 10)	**$1,179,814**	$719,038	$572,591
Cost of sales and operating expenses	**1,080,163**	659,879	521,874
Depreciation	**24,866**	10,642	9,584
Amortization	**1,988**	710	614
Interest on long term debt	**21,298**	17,168	17,077
Other interest expense	**7,693**	4,062	2,957
Investment income	**(4,616)**	(2,607)	(2,503)
Gain on sale of fixed assets	**(2,742)**	(1,670)	(2,907)
	1,128,650	688,184	546,696
Earnings before income taxes and extraordinary item	51,164	30,854	25,895
Provision for income taxes (Note 9)			
Current	**20,451**	3,616	1,177
Deferred	**2,469**	8,576	9,014
	22,920	12,192	10,191
Earnings before extraordinary item	**28,244**	18,662	15,704
Extraordinary item (Note 11)	—	—	15,219
Net earnings	**28,244**	18,662	485
Earnings allocated to minority shareholders	**1,017**	654	491
Net earnings (loss) for the year	**$ 27,227**	$ 18,008	$ (6)
Earnings (loss) per common share			
Before extraordinary item	**$1.28**	$1.17	$ .99
Including extraordinary item	**$1.28**	$1.17	$ (.30)
Fully diluted earnings (loss) per common share			
Before extraordinary item	**$1.19**	$1.05	$ .92
Including extraordinary item	**$1.19**	$1.05	$ (.30)

See accompanying notes to financial statements.

Evaluation of Standards for Earnings per Share

The establishment of uniform standards for the computation and presentation of earnings per share in the income statement of publicly owned corporations has achieved a degree of reliability for this important financial ratio. However, many accountants have reservations about the computational techniques established for earnings-per-share data, and other aspects of earnings per share. Among these reservations are the following:

- Accountants acknowledge that accounting is an art, not an exact science. The determination of net income involves numerous assumptions and estimates. The inclusion of net income in the computation of earnings per share brings the same imprecision to earnings-per-share data that is present in net income.
- A corporation can affect its earnings-per-share amounts by the acquisition and reissuance of treasury stock. Because treasury stock is not outstanding, it is excluded from the weighted-average number of shares of common stock outstanding in the denominator of the earnings-per-share computation.

In view of the foregoing, it is appropriate to stress once again that many factors other than earnings per share should be considered in the appraisal of a business corporation.

REVIEW QUESTIONS

1 Define ***treasury stock*** and explain how it typically is shown in the balance sheet.

2 For what reasons do corporations acquire their own outstanding capital stock?

3 The president of Lawson Corporation stated, ''We seek to acquire 8.4% of our outstanding common stock in order to secure a safe and profitable short-term investment for our excess cash.'' Comment on this quotation.

4 Does the acquisition and reissuance of its outstanding capital stock by a corporation result in a realized gain or a loss to the corporation? Explain.

5 In reviewing the Miscellaneous Revenue ledger account of Roddy Corporation, you find a credit for $200 representing a dividend of $1 a share on 200 shares of treasury stock. You determine that the dividend declaration covered the entire 10,000 shares of common stock originally issued, that the Retained Earnings ledger account was debited for $10,000, and that $9,800 cash was paid to shareholders. Discuss the propriety of Roddy Corporation's accounting for dividends.

6 *a* Discuss the propriety of declaring stock dividends on treasury stock.
b Should treasury stock be split?
c How is the issuance of treasury stock (carried at cost) pursuant to a 2% stock dividend recorded?

7 The Treasury Stock ledger account of Tipton Corporation had a debit balance of $108,000, representing the cost of 6,000 shares of its outstanding common stock acquired by Tipton. Later, Tipton exchanged the treasury stock for land that is now listed in its balance sheet as ''Land, at cost...

$108,000.'' Do you approve of this accounting treatment? Explain.

8 Corporation laws generally place some restriction on the acquisition by a corporation of its outstanding capital stock. What is the usual nature of such a restriction? What is the purpose of such a restriction?

9 The majority shareholder in Calla Limited, a closely held corporation, had an option to acquire all the common stock of a minority shareholder at equity (book value) per share at any time during the first 10 years of operation. After four years, the method of valuing inventories was changed from first-in, first-out to average. At the end of the tenth year, the majority shareholder exercised the option. The minority shareholder objected, arguing that the change in the valuation of inventories reduced the option price by thousands of dollars. Discuss.

10 What is the appropriate accounting treatment of the difference between original issuance price and the price paid to retire preferred stock?

11 Define ***earnings per share*** and indicate how this statistic is used by investors.

12 *a* How is the weighted-average number of shares of common stock outstanding during a year computed?

b What effect do stock dividends and stock splits have on the presentation of earnings per share of common stock for two or more years?

13 Differentiate between:

a ***Basic*** and ***fully diluted*** earnings per share

b ***Single*** and ***dual*** presentations of earnings per share

14 For the first six months of the current year, Sark Corporation reported basic earnings per share of $4.50 and fully diluted earnings per share of $2. What factors may cause such a large difference between the two amounts? If the common stock of Sark Corporation sells for $36 per share, what is the price-earnings ratio?

15 In an article in a business journal, an executive of a large bank observed: ''any evaluation of corporate policies in terms of their impact on earnings per share (EPS) is fraught with danger. . . . If the leverage idea is sound, management can increase EPS without making any investment whatever, merely by borrowing to retire common shares.'' Do you agree with this observation? Explain.

16 One of the earnings-per-share computations results in an adjusted basic figure. Describe why such an earnings per share is needed and how it differs from the basic earnings-per-share figure.

17 Of the three subsequent events applicable to the calculation of pro forma basic earnings per share, why are only two applicable to the calculation of pro forma fully diluted earnings per share?

18 Describe the maximum potential dilution method and the method often used in practice by which dilution is assured in calculating fully diluted earnings per share. Which of the two is preferable? Why?

19 What are the requirements with respect to the calculation of current-period and preceding-period earnings-per-share figures for the following situations?

a A stock split before the year-end

b A stock split after the year-end but before the financial statements are issued

EXERCISES

Ex. 18-1 Select the best answer for each of the following multiple-choice questions:

1 When treasury stock accounted for by the single-transaction method is reissued for more than its carrying amount, the excess is recorded as:
- *a* An extraordinary gain
- *b* Income from continuing operations
- *c* An increase in contributed surplus
- *d* An increase in retained earnings

2 Which of the following is included in the computation of basic earnings per share for a corporation?
- *a* Dividends (whether declared or not) on cumulative, nonconvertible preferred stock
- *b* Dividends on common stock
- *c* Number of shares of nonconvertible preferred stock
- *d* None of the foregoing
- *e* All of the foregoing

3 The general rule for the balance sheet presentation and disclosure of treasury stock accounted for by the single-transaction method is:
- *a* Disclosure of number of shares of treasury stock and deduction of cost of treasury stock from total contributed capital and retained earnings
- *b* Disclosure of number of shares of treasury stock and deduction of cost of treasury stock from total contributed capital
- *c* Inclusion in current assets
- *d* Both *a* and *c*
- *e* None of the foregoing

4 Riggs Ltd. had 1,000 shares of no-par-value, $8 cumulative, convertible preferred stock and 10,000 shares of no-par-value common stock outstanding throughout the year ended September 30, Year 3. Each share of preferred stock was convertible to one share of common stock. Net income of Riggs for the year ended September 30, Year 3, was $18,200. Basic earnings per share for Riggs Ltd. for the year ended September 30, Year 3, is:
a $1.10 *b* $1.02 *c* $1.00 *d* $0.93 *e* Some other amount

5 In the computation of basic earnings per share, dividends on noncumulative, nonconvertible preferred stock are:
- *a* Deducted from net income whether declared or not
- *b* Deducted from net income only if declared
- *c* Added to net income whether declared or not
- *d* Disregarded

Ex. 18-2 Elizar, Inc., which had 1,000,000 authorized shares of no-par-value common stock, completed the following common stock transactions during Year 1, its first year of operations:

Jan. 4	Issued 200,000 shares at $5 a share.
Apr. 8	Issued 100,000 shares at $7 a share.
June 9	Issued 30,000 shares at $10 a share.
July 29	Acquired in the open market for the treasury 50,000 shares at $5 a share.

Dec. 31 Reissued 50,000 treasury shares at $9 a share.

Assuming Elizar uses the single-transaction method of accounting for treasury stock transactions, compute the balances of Elizar's contributed capital accounts on December 31, Year 1.

Ex. 18-3 The shareholders' equity accounts of Winsom Ltd. on January 1, Year 4, are listed below:

Common stock, $20 par; authorized 100,000 shares, issued and outstanding 60,000 shares	$1,200,000
Premium on common stock	180,000
Retained earnings	760,000

Winsom uses the single transaction method of accounting for treasury stock, and during Year 4 completed the following transactions:

1 March 1, Year 4: acquired 1,000 shares of its common stock for $35,000.
2 July 1, Year 4: reissued 600 shares of treasury stock at $38 a share.
3 December 1, Year 4: retired the remaining 400 shares of treasury stock.

Winsom had no other shareholders' equity transactions during Year 4. Prepare the journal entry the company would make for each of the above three transactions. Omit explanations.

Ex. 18-4 The shareholders' equity accounts of Winsom Ltd. on January 1, Year 4, are listed below:

Common stock, no par value; authorized 100,000 shares, issued and outstanding 60,000 shares	$1,380,000
Retained earnings	760,000

Winsom uses the single transaction method of accounting for treasury stock, and during Year 4 completed the following transactions:

1 March 1, Year 4: acquired 1,000 shares of its common stock for $35,000.
2 July 1, Year 4: reissued 600 shares of treasury stock at $38 a share.
3 December 1, Year 4: retired the remaining 400 shares of treasury stock.

Winsom had no other shareholders' equity transactions during Year 4. Prepare the journal entry the company would make for each of the above three transactions. Omit explanations.

Ex. 18-5 Narco, Inc., began business on January 2, Year 7, by issuing 200,000 shares of its 400,000 shares of authorized no-par-value common stock at $15 a share. During the three-year period ended December 31, Year 9, Narco had total net income of $750,000 and declared dividends totalling $380,000. On January 5, Year 9, Narco acquired from a dissident shareholder 12,000 shares of its common stock for the treasury at $12 a share. On December 31, Year 9, Narco reissued 8,000 shares of treasury stock at $8 a share. Narco uses the single-transaction method of accounting for treasury stock transactions.

Compute total shareholders' equity of Narco, Inc., on December 31, Year 9.

Ex. 18-6 The shareholders' equity section of Lane Limited's balance sheet on September 30, Year 5, was as follows:

Shareholders' equity:	
Common stock, no par value, authorized 1,000,000 shares, issued and outstanding 900,000 shares	$11,700,000
Retained earnings	1,300,000
Total shareholders' equity	$13,000,000

On October 1, Year 5, Lane acquired from a shareholder and retired 100,000 shares of its common stock for $1,800,000.

Compute the balances of Lane Limited's shareholders' equity ledger accounts after the retirement of the common stock on October 1, Year 5.

Ex. 18-7 The shareholders' equity section of Edgar Corporation's balance sheet on December 31, Year 5, was as follows:

Shareholders' equity:	
Common stock, no par value, authorized 50,000 shares, issued and outstanding 10,000 shares	$1,500,000
Retained earnings	800,000
Total shareholders' equity	$2,300,000

Early in Year 6, Edgar acquired for the treasury 400 shares of its common stock for $50,000. During Year 6, it reissued 100 shares of treasury stock at $140 a share, reissued 100 shares at $110 a share, and retired the remaining 200 shares of treasury stock. Edgar records treasury stock using the single-transaction method.

Prepare journal entries for Edgar Corporation to record the acquisition, the reissuances, and the retirement of the treasury stock.

Ex. 18-8 On the retirement of a key employee, the board of directors of Burke Corporation authorized presentation to the employee of a certificate for 100 shares of Burke's no-par-value common stock "in appreciation of past services." The shares were part of Burke's holding of treasury stock, acquired and carried at cost of $75 a share. Equity (book value) per share of common stock was $140, and market value was $125 a share.

Prepare a journal entry for the foregoing transaction of Burke Corporation.

Ex. 18-9 The shareholders' equity section of Toley Limited's balance sheet on December 31, Year 2, was as follows:

Shareholders' equity:	
Common stock, no par value, authorized 500,000 shares, issued 90,000 shares, of which 1,210 shares are in treasury	$ 920,250
Retained earnings	424,680
Total contributed capital and retained earnings	$1,344,930
Less: Cost of 1,210 shares of treasury stock	36,300
Total shareholders' equity	$1,308,630

On January 5, Year 3, 650 shares of treasury stock were reissued, and on January 20, Year 3, a 5% stock dividend was declared. The dividend shares were issued on March 10. The market price of the common stock was $22 a share on January 20.

Prepare separate journal entries for Toley Limited to record the declaration and distribution of the 5% stock dividend.

Ex. 18-10 Masters Corporation decided that because its no-par-value, $10 cumulative preferred stock (which originally was issued at $98 a share) was trading in the stock market at $85 a share, it would acquire and retire as many shares of the preferred stock as possible in an effort to improve earnings per share of common stock. On March 2, Year 6, Masters acquired 5,000 shares of the preferred stock at $86 a share and immediately retired the shares.

Prepare a journal entry for Masters Corporation on March 2, Year 6, to record the acquisition and retirement of the 5,000 shares of the $10 cumulative preferred stock.

Ex. 18-11 Solo Limited had the following shareholders' equity ledger account balances on September 30, Year 7:

$10 cumulative preferred stock, no par value, authorized 10,000 shares	$500,000
Common stock, no par value, authorized 100,000 shares	200,000
Retained earnings	640,000
Treasury stock: common (6,000 shares), at cost	30,000

Prepare the shareholders' equity section of Solo Limited's September 30, Year 7, balance sheet.

Ex. 18-12 The shareholders' equity section of Neman Corporation's December 31, Year 6, balance sheet included the information on page 915.

Assuming that on May 1, Year 7, Neman issued 3,000 shares of common stock for $25 a share, compute the weighted-average number of shares of stock to be used in the computation of Neman Corporation's earnings per share for the year ended December 31, Year 7.

$9 cumulative, nonconvertible preferred stock, no par value, authorized 10,000 shares, issued and outstanding 1,000 shares	$100,000
Common stock, no par value, authorized 300,000 shares, issued and outstanding 45,000 shares	450,000

Ex. 18-13 On December 31, Year 4, Gammage, Inc., had 500,000 shares of no-par-value common stock outstanding. On October 1, Year 5, 120,000 shares of common stock were issued for cash. Throughout Year 5, Gammage had $4,000,000 face amount of 8% convertible bonds outstanding. The bonds were convertible to 100,000 shares of Gammage's common stock.

Compute the weighted-average number of shares of common stock to be used in the computation of fully diluted earnings per share for Gammage, Inc., for the year ended December 31, Year 5.

Ex. 18-14 Sybil Corporation began operations on January 2, Year 1, by issuing 2,000 shares of common stock for plant assets. On July 1, Year 2, an additional 1,000 shares of common stock were issued for cash. On April 1, Year 3, a 10% common stock dividend was distributed. On July 1, Year 4, the common stock was split 3 for 1. Earnings and dividends per share of common stock for each of the first four years of operations are to be reported on a comparable basis in the annual report to shareholders for Year 4.

Compute the weighted-average number of shares outstanding at the end of each of the four years, Year 1 through Year 4, to be used in the computation of earnings per share of common stock for Sybil Corporation.

Ex. 18-15 Mamey Corporation had 5,000,000 shares of common stock outstanding on December 31, Year 6. An additional 1,000,000 shares of common stock were issued on April 1, Year 7, and 500,000 more on July 1, Year 7. On October 1, Year 7, Mamey issued 10,000, $1,000 face amount, 10% convertible bonds. Each bond is convertible into 50 shares of common stock. No bonds were converted to common stock in Year 7.

Compute the weighted-average number of shares of common stock to be used in the computation of basic earnings per share and fully diluted earnings per share, respectively, for Mamey Corporation for Year 7. Assume that the 10% convertible bonds are dilutive.

Ex. 18-16 On December 31, Year 7, Dealey, Inc., had 20,000 shares of nonconvertible preferred stock and 100,000 shares of common stock outstanding. On July 1, Year 8, Dealey paid a cash dividend of $2 a share (the full dividend for Year 8) on the preferred stock and distributed a 10% common stock dividend. Dealey's net income for Year 8 was $777,000.

Compute Dealey's earnings per share for Year 8.

Ex. 18-17 Sandrac Limited had 10,000 shares of $6 no-par-value convertible preferred stock and 200,000 shares of no-par-value common stock outstanding on both December 31, Year 4, and December 31, Year 5. The preferred stock, each share of which was convertible to three shares of common stock, had been issued at $100 per share on July 1, Year 4. During Year 5, Sandrac declared the annual preferred stock dividend and had net income of $862,500.

Compute Sandrac Limited's basic and fully diluted earnings per share for Year 5.

Ex. 18-18 Olivera Corporation had 100,000 shares of no-par-value common stock outstanding on December 31, Year 6. On July 1, Year 7, Olivera distributed a 10% common stock dividend. Stock options to acquire 20,000 shares of common stock (adjusted for the Year 7 common stock dividend) at $20 a share were outstanding throughout Year 7. Olivera's borrowing rate was 10% after income taxes; its net income for Year 7 was $550,000.

Compute Olivera Corporation's basic and its fully diluted earnings per share for Year 7.

Ex. 18-19 On December 31, Year 6, Gross Corporation had 400,000 shares of common stock outstanding. On October 1, Year 7, an additional 100,000 shares of common stock were issued. In addition, Gross had $10,000,000 of 8% convertible bonds outstanding on December 31, Year 6, that were convertible to 225,000 shares of common stock. No bonds were converted to common stock in Year 7. The net income of Gross for the year ended December 31, Year 7, was $3,500,000. The income tax rate was 45%.

Compute the basic and the fully diluted earnings per share of Gross Corporation for the year ended December 31, Year 7.

Ex. 18-20 Information relating to the capital structure of Cortez Corporation is as follows:

	Dec. 31, Year 8	*Dec. 31, Year 9*
9% convertible bonds	$1,000,000	$1,000,000
Outstanding shares of:		
Convertible preferred stock	10,000	10,000
Common stock	90,000	90,000

During Year 9, Cortez paid the current annual dividend of $2.50 a share on its preferred stock. The preferred stock is convertible to 20,000 shares of common stock. The 9% convertible bonds are convertible to 30,000 shares of common stock. The net income of Cortez for the year ended December 31, Year 9, was $485,000. The income tax rate is 45%.

Compute basic earnings per share and fully diluted earnings per share for Cortez Corporation for Year 9.

Ex. 18-21 On January 1, Year 4, Rudolfo Limited had 10,000 shares of $4 cumulative, nonconvertible preferred stock, no-par-value, callable at $55 a share, and 100,000 shares of no-par-value common stock outstanding. There was no long-term debt outstanding. On January 2, Year 5, Rudolfo called and retired the preferred stock, and on January 2, Year 6, Rudolfo issued at face amount $1,000,000 of 12%

bonds and used the proceeds to acquire in the open market and retire 30,000 shares of common stock. Rudolfo had income before interest and income taxes expense of $800,000 for Year 4, $750,000 for Year 5, and $700,000 for Year 6.Rudolfo's income tax rate is 45%.

Compute Rudolfo Limited's earnings per share for Year 4, Year 5, and Year 6. Comment on, and explain the significance of, the trend of earnings per share compared with the decreasing income before interest and income taxes expense.

CASES

Case 18-1 For various reasons a corporation may acquire shares of its par-value or no-par-value capital stock. When a corporation acquires treasury stock in Canada, it must account for the acquisition using the single-transaction method. However, in order to better understand the differences between this method and the two-transaction method, the management of the corporation asks you to compare and contrast the single-transaction method with the two-transaction method used in the examples in the chapter, for each of the following:

a Acquisition of treasury stock at a price less than par or average value
b Acquisition of treasury stock at a price more than par or average value
c Subsequent reissuance of treasury stock at a price less than cost but more than par or average value
d Subsequent reissuance of treasury stock at a price more than either cost or par or average value
e Effect on net income

Case 18-2 Dixie Corporation acquired equipment costing $180,000 for $120,000 cash and a promise to deliver an indeterminate number of treasury shares of its no-par-value common stock, with a market value of $15,000, on January 2 of each year for the next five years. Hence, $75,000 in ''market value'' of treasury stock will be required to discharge the $60,000 balance due on the equipment note payable. All of the outstanding common shares were issued at an average price of $16 per share.

Dixie immediately acquired for the treasury 3,000 shares of its common stock in the open market for $48,000 with the expectation that the market price of the stock would increase substantially before the scheduled delivery dates. A total of 2,500 shares of the treasury stock subsequently was issued in payment of the $60,000 balance due on the equipment note payable.

Instructions

a Discuss the propriety of recording the equipment acquired by Dixie Corporation at each of the following amounts:
 1 $120,000 (the cash payment)
 2 $180,000 (the cash price of the equipment)
 3 $195,000 (the $120,000 cash payment plus the $75,000 market value of the treasury stock that must be transferred to the vendor to settle the obligation in accordance with the terms of the contract)

4 $160,000 (the $120,000 cash payment plus the $40,000 cost of the 2,500 shares of treasury stock reissued in payment for the equipment)

b Discuss the arguments for classifying the balance on the equipment note payable as:
1 A liability
2 Treasury stock subscribed

c Assuming that legal requirements do not affect the decision, discuss the arguments for classifying Dixie Corporation's treasury stock as:
1 An asset awaiting ultimate disposition
2 An element of shareholders' equity awaiting ultimate disposition

Case 18-3 Crestwood Limited was at one time quite successful, but in recent years had been operating at a loss. In reaction to these losses, the market price of the stock had dropped to an all-time low of $5 a share. The capital stock had originally been issued at an average price of $10 a share.

At this point, an investment group acquired control of the company by purchasing in small lots a total of 20,000 shares at a total cost of $130,000. Total stock outstanding was 100,000 shares, but the remaining 80% of the stock was scattered among many small owners. By an aggressive proxy campaign, the investment group was able to secure enough outside support to elect a full slate of directors.

The investment group had no hopes for profitable operation of the company; sales were in a declining trend and the principal products were gradually becoming obsolete. The attraction of the company to the investment group was its undervalued assets and strong cash position. The group planned to recover their investment rapidly through stripping the company of its most salable assets and then selling their shares for whatever they would bring. Retained earnings of the company amounted to only $200,000 but cash, receivables, and marketable securities amounted to $500,000.

At the instruction of the investment group, the new board of directors took the following actions:

1 Issued optimistic statements to the press concerning planned acquisition of several profitable companies and resumption of cash dividends.

2 Sold the receivables and securities, thus increasing cash to approximately $500,000.

3 Borrowed $200,000 secured by pledge of the inventory, thus obtaining additional cash.

4 Began purchasing the company's own stock at steadily increasing prices. After acquisition of 10,000 shares at an average cost of $9, the company offered to purchase up to 15,000 shares at $15. Shareholders sold 10,000 shares to the company at $15 per share.

5 Sold the land and building to the investment group for $450,000 more than carrying value. This gain was included in the quarterly earnings report and was widely publicized. The sale agreement called for payment partially in stock of another company controlled by the investment group and partially in mining lands owned by them. No cash was involved.

6 Purchased from the investment group its entire holdings of 20,000 shares at a price of $20 a share. This transaction consumed nearly all the available cash. All members of the board then resigned for "personal reasons."

Instructions

(Ignore income tax considerations.)

a Prepare the shareholders' equity section of the balance sheet after these transactions.

b Did the purchase of treasury stock by the company violate the concept of limiting dividends and purchases of treasury stock to the amount of retained earnings?

c Were any of the actions by the board of directors improper? Explain.

Case 18-4 Victor Corporation had the following ledger account titles in its December 31, Year 4, trial balance:

- $12 cumulative, convertible preferred stock, no par value
- Common stock, no par value
- Retained earnings

Additional Information

1. There were 2,000,000 shares of preferred stock authorized, of which 1,000,000 were outstanding. All 1,000,000 shares outstanding were issued on January 2, Year 1, for $120 a share. The preferred stock was convertible to common stock on a 1-for-1 basis until December 31, Year 10; thereafter, the preferred stock was no longer convertible and was callable at $100 by Victor. No preferred stock had been converted to common stock, and there were no dividends in arrears on December 31, Year 4.
2. Of the 5,000,000 shares of common stock authorized, there were 3,500,000 shares outstanding on January 1, Year 4. The market price of the outstanding common stock had increased consistently for the last four years.
3. Victor had an employee stock option plan under which certain employees and officers might acquire shares of common stock at 100% of the market price on the grant date. All options were exercisable in installments of one-third each year, commencing one year after the grant date, and expired if not exercised within four years of the grant date. On January 1, Year 4, options for 70,000 shares were outstanding at prices ranging from $47 to $83 a share. Options for 20,000 shares were exercised at $47 to $79 a share during Year 4. No options expired during Year 4, and additional options for 15,000 shares were granted at $86 a share during Year 4. The 65,000 options outstanding on December 31, Year 4, had option prices ranging from $54 to $86 a share; of these, 30,000 were exercisable on that date at prices ranging from $54 to $79 a share.
4. Victor also had an employee stock purchase plan under which Victor paid one-half and the employee paid one-half of the market price of the common stock on the date of the subscription. During Year 4, employees subscribed to 60,000 shares of common stock at an average price of $87 a share. All 60,000 shares were paid for and issued in September, Year 4.
5. On December 31, Year 4, there was a total of 355,000 shares of common stock set aside for the granting of future employee stock options and for future

issuances under the employee stock purchase plan. The only changes in Victor's shareholders' equity for Year 4 were those described above, net income, and cash dividends declared.

Instructions

a Prepare the shareholders' equity section of the balance sheet of Victor Corporation on December 31, Year 4; substitute, where appropriate, Xs for unknown dollar amounts. Also prepare appropriate notes to Victor's financial statements.

b Explain how the amount of the denominator should be determined to compute the earnings-per-share figures for presentation in Victor Corporation's income statement for Year 4. Be specific as to the treatment of each item. If additional information is needed to determine whether an item should be included or excluded, or the extent to which an item should be included, identify the information needed and how the item would be handled if the information were known. Assume that Victor Corporation had substantial net income for the year ended December 31, Year 4.

PROBLEMS

Pr. 18-1 The shareholders' equity section of Benjamin Corporation's balance sheet was as follows on September 30, Year 7:

Shareholders' equity:	
Common stock, no par value, authorized 200,000 shares, issued and outstanding 120,000 shares	$3,600,000
Excess from transactions in treasury stock	20,000
Retained earnings	2,600,000
Total shareholders' equity	$6,220,000

Benjamin uses the single-transaction method of accounting for treasury stock, and during the year ended September 30, Year 8, had the following transactions or events:

Jan. 6	Acquired for the treasury 2,000 shares of outstanding common stock for $70,000
14	Reissued 1,200 shares of treasury stock at $40 a share
June 18	Retired 300 shares of treasury stock
Sept. 30	Reported net income of $200,000 for the year ended Sept. 30, Year 8 (no dividends were declared)

Instructions

a Prepare journal entries for the foregoing transactions and events of Benjamin Corporation.

b Prepare the shareholders' equity section of Benjamin Corporation's balance sheet on September 30, Year 8.

Pr. 18-2 Erbert Limited had the following long-term debt and capital stock outstanding on September 30, Year 3:

8% convertible bonds payable due Sept. 30, Year 13, interest payable Mar. 30 and Sept. 30, issued at face amount, each $1,000 bond convertible to 10 shares of common stock through Sept. 30, Year 8 ...	$100,000
$6 cumulative, convertible preferred stock, no par value, 10,000 shares issued and outstanding, each share convertible to one share of common stock through Sept. 30, Year 8 ...	10,000
Common stock, no par value, 11,000 shares issued and outstanding ..	11,000

There were no changes in the 8% convertible bonds and $6 cumulative preferred stock outstanding during the year ended September 30, Year 3. The only change in common stock during that year was the issuance of 2,000 shares for cash on March 31, Year 3. Erbert had net income of $25,000 for the year ended September 30, Year 3, net of income taxes expense at a 45% rate.

Instructions

a Compute basic earnings per share and fully diluted earnings per share for Erbert Limited for the year ended September 30, Year 3.

b Prepare the bottom portion of Erbert Limited's income statement for the year ended September 30, Year 3, beginning with income before income taxes. Show supporting computations. Include disclosure of earnings-per-share figures in the income statement.

Pr. 18-3 Nolan Corporation's capital structure for the first two years of its operations was as follows:

	Dec. 31, Year 2	*Dec. 31, Year 1*
8% convertible bonds ...	$1,000,000	$1,000,000
Outstanding shares of:		
Nonconvertible $3 preferred stock ...	10,000	10,000
Common stock ...	336,000	300,000

Additional Information

1 On September 1, Year 2, Nolan issued 36,000 shares of common stock for cash.
2 Net income of Nolan for the year ended December 31, Year 2, was $750,000.
3 During Year 2 Nolan declared dividends of $3 a share on its nonconvertible preferred stock.
4 The 8% convertible bonds were convertible to 40 shares of common stock for each $1,000 bond.
5 Stock options to acquire 30,000 shares of common stock at $22.50 a share were outstanding at the beginning and end of Year 2.
6 The company's rate of return for Year 2 was 16% before income taxes.
7 Nolan's income tax rate was 45% for both Year 1 and Year 2.

Instructions

a Compute the number of shares to be used for the computation of Nolan Corporation's basic earnings per share for the year ended December 31, Year 2.

b Compute Nolan Corporation's basic earnings per share for the year ended December 31, Year 2.

c Compute the number of shares to be used for the computation of Nolan Corporation's fully diluted earnings per share for the year ended December 31, Year 2.

d Compute Nolan Corporation's fully diluted earnings per share for the year ended December 31, Year 2.

Pr. 18-4 The shareholders' equity section of Luigi Limited's balance sheet on December 31, Year 7, is shown below.

Shareholders' equity:	
$10 preferred stock, no par value, callable at $104, authorized 50,000 shares, issued and outstanding 20,000 shares	$2,040,000
Common stock, no par value, authorized 500,000 shares, issued and outstanding 300,000 shares	3,700,000
Total contributed capital	$5,740,000
Retained earnings	4,200,000
Total shareholders' equity	$9,940,000

In Year 8, Luigi acquired in the open market and retired 3,000 shares of its preferred stock at $99 a share. Shortly thereafter, the remaining 17,000 shares of preferred stock were called for redemption and retired at the call price of $104 a share. Net income for Year 8 was $863,000; cash dividends of $2 a share were declared and paid on the common stock in Year 8. No dividends were declared or paid on the preferred stock in Year 8.

Instructions

a Prepare journal entries for Luigi Limited to record the acquisition and retirement of the preferred stock.

b Prepare the shareholders' equity section of Luigi Limited's balance sheet on December 31, Year 8.

Pr. 18-5 In Year 8, Lasky Corporation issued all shares of its outstanding common stock at a price of $25 a share. On December 31, Year 11, Lasky's balance sheet included the following shareholders' equity section:

Shareholders' equity:	
Common stock, no par value, authorized an unlimited number of shares, issued and outstanding 200,000 shares	$5,000,000
Retained earnings	1,950,000
Total shareholders' equity	$6,950,000

On February 15, Year 12, Lasky acquired for the treasury 10,000 shares of its common stock at $48 a share. On December 9, Year 12, Lasky reissued 5,000 shares of treasury stock for $284,000.

Instructions

a Prepare journal entries to record Lasky Corporation's transactions on Feburary 15 and December 9, Year 12, assuming that treasury stock is recorded using the ***single-transaction method***.

b Prepare journal entries to record Lasky Corporation's transactions on February 15 and December 9, Year 12, assuming that treasury stock is recorded using the ***two-transaction method*** and a treasury stock account.

Pr. 18-6 A comparative summary of the shareholders' equity of Burbage Corporation, together with additional information, is given below:

	Dec. 31, Year 5		*Jan. 1, Year 5*
Shareholders' equity:			
Common stock, authorized 250,000 shares; issued:			
On Dec. 31, Year 5, 70,000 shares, $8 par (1,000 shares in treasury)	$560,000		
On Jan. 1, Year 5, 40,000 shares, $10 par			$ 400,000
Common stock dividend to be distributed (6,900 shares)	55,200	$ 615,200	
Contributed surplus:			
From issuance of common stock (including $8,000 on Dec. 31, Year 5, from treasury stock transactions)	$808,700		200,000
From common stock dividend (to be distributed Jan. 25, Year 6)	276,000	1,084,700	
Total contributed capital		$1,699,900	$ 600,000
Retained earnings		1,372,440	1,420,200
Total contributed capital and retained earnings		$3,072,340	$2,020,200
Less: Treasury stock, 1,000 shares at cost		37,000	
Total shareholders' equity		$3,035,340	$2,020,200

Additional Information

1 In February, Year 5, Burbage's board of directors approved a 5-for-4 stock split, which reduced the par of the common stock from $10 to $8 a share. The split was approved by shareholders on March 1 and distributed on March 25. A memorandum entry was used to record the stock split.

2 On April 1, Year 5, Burbage acquired for the treasury 2,000 shares of its common stock at $37 a share.

3 On June 30, Year 5, 1,000 shares of treasury stock were reissued at $45 a share.

4 On July 1, Year 5, 20,000 shares of $8-par common stock were issued in exchange for certain assets of Holland Company. The current fair value of the 20,000 shares issued was $760,700.

5 A cash dividend of $2 a share was declared on December 2, Year 5, payable on December 29, to shareholders of record on December 15; a 10% common stock dividend was declared on December 20, to be distributed on January 25, Year 6. The market price of the common stock on December 20 was $48 a share. (The Year 5 financial statements were issued on January 18, Year 6.)

6 The net income for Year 5 was $421,440, which included an extraordinary item (gain) of $124,490, net of income tax effect.

Instructions

a Prepare journal entries to record Burbage Corporation's transactions relating to shareholders' equity that took place during the year ended December 31, Year 5. (Debit Income Summary and credit Retained Earnings to record net income for Year 5.)

b Prepare the lower section of Burbage Corporation's income statement for the year ended December 31, Year 5, showing operating income and the extraordinary item (gain). Include earnings per share in the income statement.

c Prepare Burbage Corporation's statement of retained earnings for the year ended December 31, Year 5.

Pr. 18-7 Tucker Corporation is a publicly owned enterprise. On December 31, Year 7, Tucker had 25,000,000 shares of no-par-value common stock authorized, of which 15,000,000 shares were issued and 14,000,000 shares were outstanding.

The shareholders' equity ledger accounts on December 31, Year 7, had the following balances:

Common stock, no par value	$230,000,000
Retained earnings	50,000,000
Treasury stock, common, 1,000,000 shares	18,000,000

During Year 8, Tucker completed the following transactions:

1 On February 1, Year 8, 2,000,000 shares of common stock were issued at $18 a share, net of issuance costs.

2 On February 15, Year 8, Tucker issued at $110 a share, 100,000 shares of no-par-value, $8 cumulative preferred stock with 100,000 detachable stock warrants. Each stock warrant contained one right that with $20 could be exchanged for one share of Tucker's common stock. On February 15, Year 8, the market price for one warrant was $1.

3 On March 1, Year 8, Tucker acquired for the treasury 20,000 shares of its common stock for $18 a share. Tucker uses the single-transaction method to account for treasury stock.

4 On March 15, Year 8, when the common stock was trading for $21 a share, a shareholder donated to Tucker 10,000 shares of common stock, which, appropriately, was recorded as treasury stock.

5 On March 31, Year 8, Tucker declared a cash dividend on common stock of

$0.10 a share, payable on April 30, Year 8, to shareholders of record on April 10, Year 8.

6 On April 15, Year 8, when the market price of the stock warrants was $2 each and the market price of the common stock was $22 a share, 30,000 warrants were exercised. Tucker used unissued shares of common stock to complete this transaction.

7 On April 30, Year 8, employees exercised 100,000 options that had been granted in Year 6 under a noncompensatory stock option plan. Each option entitled the employee to acquire one share of the common stock for $20 a share. On April 30, Year 8, the market price of the common stock was $23 a share. Tucker used unissued shares of common stock to complete this transaction.

8 On May 31, Year 8, when the market price of the common stock was $20 a share, Tucker declared a 5% common stock dividend, distributable on July 1, Year 8, to shareholders of record on June 1, Year 8. (Credit the Common Stock ledger account on date of declaration of the stock dividend.)

9 On June 30, Year 8, Tucker reissued the 20,000 shares of treasury stock acquired on March 1, Year 8, and an additional 280,000 treasury shares costing $5,600,000 that were on hand at the beginning of the year. The reissuance price was $25 a share.

10 On September 30, Year 8, Tucker declared a cash dividend on common stock of $0.10 a share and the yearly dividend on preferred stock, both payable on October 30, Year 8, to shareholders of record on October 10, Year 8.

11 On December 31, Year 8, the remaining outstanding stock warrants expired.

12 Net income for Year 8 was $25,000,000.

Instructions

Prepare a working paper to summarize, for each transaction, the changes in Tucker Corporation's shareholders' equity ledger accounts for Year 8. Show supporting computations and use the following headings in the working paper:

- Date
- Preferred Stock — Number of Shares
- Preferred Stock — Amount
- Common Stock — Number of Shares
- Common Stock — Amount
- Common Stock Warrants — Number of Rights
- Common Stock Warrants — Amount
- Contributed Surplus
- Retained Earnings
- Treasury Stock: Common — Number of Shares
- Treasury Stock: Common — Amount

Pr. 18-8 Selected data summarizing the earnings performance of Johnson Corporation for a five-year period are presented on page 926 (all dollar amounts and the number of shares are in thousands).

Late in December of each of the five years, Johnson called 10,000 shares of its preferred stock, paying the call price of 102 plus the final quarter's dividends. During Year 2, Johnson split its common stock 2 for 1, and in Year 4 issued a 20%

common stock dividend. On October 1, Year 3, an additional 2,500,000 shares of common stock were issued for cash. On July 1, Year 5, Johnson acquired 5,000,000 shares of common stock from a shareholder who planned to retire. Johnson plans to use the treasury stock for business combinations.

	Year 5	*Year 4*	*Year 3*	*Year 2*	*Year 1*
Income before interest and income taxes expense	$64,120	$38,680	$84,480	$69,940	$47,200
Interest expense	5,200	5,200	9,100	10,400	10,400
Income before income taxes	$58,920	$33,480	$75,380	$59,540	$36,800
Income taxes expense	26,514	15,066	33,921	26,793	16,560
Net income	$32,406	$18,414	$41,459	$32,747	$20,240
Number of shares of common stock outstanding at end of year	13,000	18,000	15,000	12,500	6,250
Number of shares of $12, no-par-value preferred stock outstanding at end of year.....	60	70	80	90	100

Instructions

Earnings per share of common stock for the five-year period are to be reported on a comparable basis in Johnson Corporation's annual report to shareholders for Year 5. Compute the earnings-per-share data to be reported in the Year 5 annual report to shareholders for each of the five years.

Pr. 18-9 Meeker, Inc., was organized on May 1, Year 7, with 3,000,000 authorized shares of $10-par common stock, and 300,000 shares of its common stock were issued for $3,300,000 on May 15, Year 7. Net income through December 31, Year 7, was $125,000.

On July 3, Year 8, Meeker issued 500,000 shares of common stock for $6,250,000. A 5% common stock dividend was declared on October 2, Year 8, and distributed on November 6, Year 8, to shareholders of record on October 23, Year 8. The market price of the common stock was $11 a share on October 2, Year 8. Meeker's net income for the year ended December 31, Year 8, was $350,000.

During Year 9, Meeker completed the following transactions:

1. In February, Meeker acquired 30,000 shares of its common stock for the treasury for $9 a share. Meeker uses the single-transaction method to account for treasury stock.
2. In June, Meeker reissued 15,000 shares of treasury stock for $12 a share.
3. In September, common shareholders were issued stock warrants (for each share owned) for one right to acquire two additonal shares of common stock for $13 a share. The rights expire on December 31, Year 9.
4. In October, stock warrants for 250,000 rights were exercised when the market price of the common stock was $14 a share.
5. In November, stock warrants for 400,000 rights were excercised when the market price of the common stock was $15 a share.

6 On December 15, Year 9, Meeker declared its first cash dividend, $0.10 a share, payable on January 10, Year 10, to common shareholders of record on December 31, Year 9.

7 On December 21, Year 9, Meeker retired 10,000 shares of treasury stock and restored it to the status of unissued common stock. The market price of the common stock was $16 a share on that date.

Net income for Year 9 was $750,000.

Instructions

Prepare a working paper to summarize all transactions affecting the Common Stock (shares and dollar amounts), Contributed Surplus, Retained Earnings, and Treasury Stock (shares and dollar amounts) ledger accounts, and the amounts that would be included in Meeker's balance sheet on December 31, Year 9, as a result of the foregoing information. Show supporting computations.

Pr. 18-10 On February 1, Year 6, the financial vice president of Omeron Limited, a small publicly owned enterprise, requested you to compute comparative earnings-per-share data for its first two years of operations ended December 31, Year 5, for inclusion in Omeron's annual report for Year 5.

Additional Information

1 Income statements show net income as follows: Year 4, $5,760,000; Year 5, $4,800,000.

2 On January 1, Year 4, there were outstanding 200,000 shares of no-par-value common stock and 20,000 shares of no-par-value, $12 convertible preferred stock. Each share of preferred stock was initially convertible to 2.5 shares of common stock, to be adjusted for any stock dividends and stock splits. The market price of common stock has ranged from $45 to $60 a share during the past two years.

3 On December 31, Year 4, a 20% common stock dividend was distributed on the common stock. On that date, the market price of the common stock was $50 a share.

4 In June, Year 5, the common stock was split 2 for 1.

5 Cash dividends were payable on the preferred stock on June 30 and December 31. Preferred stock dividends were paid in each year; none of the preferred stock had been converted to common stock.

Instructions

a Prepare a working paper for each of the following purposes.

  1 To compute the number of shares of Omeron Limited's common stock outstanding on December 31, Year 4 and Year 5.

  2 To compute the equivalent number of shares of Omeron Limited's common stock outstanding for Year 4 and Year 5 for the computation of basic earnings per share.

  3 To compute the equivalent number of shares of Omeron Limited's common stock outstanding for Year 4 and Year 5 for the computation of fully diluted earnings per share.

b Prepare the bottom portion of Omeron Limited's income statement, showing basic and fully diluted earnings per share for Year 4 and Year 5.

Pr. 18-11 The controller of Lido Corporation has requested your assistance in the determination of net income, basic earnings per share, and fully diluted earnings per share for presentation in Lido's income statement for the year ended September 30, Year 5. As currently determined, Lido's net income was $2,100,000 for the year ended September 30, Year 5. The controller has indicated that the net income amount might be adjusted for the following transactions that were recorded directly in the Retained Earnings ledger account. (The amounts are net of applicable income taxes.)

1 The amount of $1,875,000, applicable to a breached Year 1 contract, was received as a result of a lawsuit. Prior to the award, legal counsel was uncertain as to the outcome of the suit.

2 A gain of $1,500,000 was recognized on the sale of Lido's only subsidiary.

3 A special inventory write-off of $750,000 was made, of which $625,000 applied to goods manufactured prior to October 1, Year 4.

Your working papers include the following data for the year ended September 30, Year 5:

1 Common stock (on October 1, Year 4), no par value, authorized 300,000 shares; effective December 1, Year 4 (following a 2-for-1 stock split), no par value, authorized 600,000 shares):
- ***Balance Oct. 1, Year 4:*** Issued and outstanding, 60,000 shares
- ***Dec. 1, Year 4:*** 60,000 shares issued in a 2-for-1 stock split
- ***Dec. 2, Year 4:*** 280,000 shares issued for cash at $39 a share

2 Treasury stock:
- ***Mar. 1, Year 5:*** Acquired 40,000 shares at $37 a share
- ***Apr. 1, Year 5:*** Reissued 40,000 shares at $40 a share

3 Series A stock warrants (each warrant was exchangeable at any time for $60 for one share of common stock; effective December 1, Year 4, when the stock was split 2 for 1, each stock warrant became exchangeable for two shares of common stock at $30 a share):
- ***Oct. 1, Year 4:*** 25,000 stock warrants issued at $6 each

4 Series B stock warrants (each stock warrant is exchangeable with $40 for one share of common stock):
- ***Apr. 1, Year 5:*** 20,000 stock warrants authorized and issued at $10 each

5 First mortgage bonds, 11%, due Year 20 (nonconvertible; priced to yield 10% when issued):
- ***Balance Oct. 1, Year 4:*** Authorized, issued and outstanding, face amount of $1,400,000

6 Convertible debentures, 13.6%, issued in Year 4 and due in Year 24 (each $1,000 debenture was convertible at any time until maturity to 15 shares of common stock; effective December 1, Year 4, the conversion ratio became 30 shares of common stock for each debenture as a result of the 2-for-1 stock split):
- ***Oct. 1, Year 4:*** Issued at face amount of $12,000,000.

Instructions

a Compute the correct net income to be presented in Lido Corporation's income statement for the year ended September 30, Year 5.

b Assuming that the correct net income of Lido Corporation for the year ended September 30, Year 5, was $2,800,000 and that there were no extraordinary items, prepare a working paper to compute (1) the basic earnings per share and (2) the fully diluted earnings per share to be presented in Lido's income statement for the year ended September 30, Year 5. A supporting working paper showing the numbers of shares to be used in these computations also should be prepared. The rate of return earned by the corporation in Year 5 is estimated at 20% before applicable income taxes. Assume an income tax rate of 40%.

Pr. 18-12 The shareholder's equity section of Misto Limited's balance sheet on December 31, Year 5, is presented below.

Shareholders' equity:	
$2 cumulative convertible preferred stock ($25 par; authorized 1,600,000 shares, issued 1,400,000 converted to common 750,000, and outstanding 650,000 shares. Involuntary liquidation value, $30 a share, aggregating $19,500,000)	$16,250,000
Common stock (no par value; authorized 15,000,000 shares, issued and outstanding 8,800,000 shares)	13,950,000
Premium on preferred stock	21,000,000
Total contributed capital	$51,200,000
Retained earnings	40,595,000
Total shareholders' equity	$91,795,000

Included among the liabilities of Misto were 11% convertible debentures issued at the face amount of $20,000,000 in Year 4. The debentures are due in Year 24, and until then are convertible to the common stock of Misto at the rate of 50 shares of common stock for each $1,000 debenture. To date, none of the debentures has been converted.

On April 2, Year 5, Misto issued 1,400,000 shares of convertible preferred stock at $40 a share. Quarterly dividends to December 31, Year 5, were paid on the preferred stock. The preferred stock is convertible to common stock at the rate of two shares of common for each share of preferred. On October 1, Year 5, 150,000 shares and on November 1, Year 5, 600,000 shares of the preferred stock were converted to common stock.

On July 2, Year 4, Misto granted options to its officers and key employees to acquire 500,000 shares of the corporation's common stock at a price of $20 a share.

Assume that the corporation's rate of return before income taxes was 14% throughout Year 4 and Year 5, that Misto Limited's net income for the year ended December 31, Year 5, was $48,500,000, and that the income tax rate was 40%.

Instructions

Compute, for Year 5:

a Basic earnings per share

b Adjusted basic earnings per share
c Fully diluted earnings per share
Show all computations.

Pr. 18-13 Jersey Corporation was organized on July 3, Year 4. It was authorized to issue 500,000 shares of $5-par common stock and 100,000 shares of $10-par, 10% cumulative, nonparticipating preferred stock. Jersey adopted a June 30 fiscal year.

The following information relates to the shareholders' equity ledger accounts of Jersey:

- 30,000 shares of preferred stock were issued at $10 a share on June 30, Year 5.
- Prior to the year ended June 30, Year 7, Jersey had 160,000 shares of outstanding common stock, issued as follows:
  1. 145,000 shares were issued for cash on July 5, Year 4, at $20 a share.
  2. 10,000 shares were exchanged on August 1, Year 4, for land that had cost the seller $70,000 in Year 1 and which had a current fair value of $130,000 on August 1, Year 4.
  3. 5,000 shares were issued on March 1, Year 6; the shares had been subscribed at $32 a share on October 31, Year 5.

During the year ended June 30, Year 7, the following transactions involving common stock were completed:

Year 6

Oct. 1 Subscriptions were received for 10,000 shares at $40 a share. Cash of $80,000 was received in full payment for 2,000 shares, and stock certificates were issued. The remaining subscriptions for 8,000 shares were to be paid in full by September 30, Year 7, at which time the certificates were to be issued.

Dec. 1 Jersey acquired for the treasury 5,000 shares of its common stock in the open market at $37 a share. Jersey uses the single-transaction method of accounting for treasury stock.

Dec. 15 Jersey declared a 5% common stock dividend for shareholders of record on January 10, Year 7, to be issued on January 31, Year 7. Jersey's common stock was trading at $45 a share on December 15, Year 6.

Year 7

June 24 Jersey reissued for $108,000, one-half (2,500 shares) of the treasury stock that it had acquired on December 1, Year 6.

Jersey has followed a program of declaring cash dividends in June and December, with payments being made to shareholders of record in the following month. The cash dividends that had been declared since organization of Jersey Corporation are summarized in the table on page 931.

On June 30, Year 6, Jersey's Retained Earnings ledger account had a credit balance of $1,260,000. For the year ended June 30, Year 7, Jersey had net income of $465,000.

Declaration date	Preferred stock	Common stock
Dec. 15, Year 5	$0.50 a share	$0.10 a share
June 15, Year 6	0.50 a share	0.10 a share
Dec. 15, Year 6	0.50 a share	None
June 15, Year 7	0.50 a share	None

Instructions

a Prepare journal entries to record all transactions of Jersey Corporation affecting shareholders' equity completed during the year ended June 30, Year 7.

b Prepare the shareholders' equity section of Jersey Corporation's balance sheet on June 30, Year 7. Show supporting computations.

Pr. 18-14 Electronic Limited, which has an income tax rate of 60% and estimates its return on investments at 6% after applicable income taxes, reported net income of $1,000,000 for the year ended December 31, 1987, without any extraordinary items. The company has provided you with the following additional information:

1 There were 100,000 shares of common stock issued and outstanding on January 1, 1987.

2 Stock purchase warrants for 10,000 shares of common stock were granted prior to 1987. The warrants permit the holder to purchase one common share for $80 cash and one warrant. Five thousand of these warrants were exercised on July 1, 1987.

3 On March 31, 1987, $1,000,000 of 10% noncumulative convertible preferred stock were issued at a par value of $100 per share. Each preferred share is convertible into one common share. Three quarterly dividends were paid on this preferred stock during the 1987 year.

4 The company issued $500,000 of 12% convertible bonds on July 1, 1986, at their face value of $1,000 each. Each bond is convertible into 20 shares of common stock. No bonds were converted during the current year.

5 On October 1, 1987, 5,000 shares of the 10% noncumulative convertible preferred stock were converted into shares of common stock.

6 On February 1, 1988 (before the date of completion of the financial statements), 100,000 shares of common stock were issued for $10,000,000 cash. The proceeds of the sale were used for the expansion of the company's plant and to purchase additional equipment.

Instructions

For the year ended December 31, 1987, compute:

a Basic earnings per share

b Adjusted basic earnings per share

c Fully diluted earnings per share

Pr. 18-15 Micromint Limited reported net income before income taxes and after income taxes of $7,000,000 and $2,800,000 respectively. The company reported no extraordinary items in its income statement for the current year ending December 31, 1988.

Micromint Limited is required to present earnings-per-share figures according to section 3500 of the ***CICA Handbook***. In this connection, the company has provided you with the following information:

1 As at January 1, 1988, there were 675,000 shares of common stock outstanding.

2 100,000 stock warrants, to purchase 100,000 shares of common stock at $30 per share, were outstanding at the beginning of the current year. Thirty thousand of these warrants were exercised on September 1, 1988. The company's estimated rate of return on its investments was 20% before income taxes.

3 An issue of 12% convertible debentures with a principal amount of $10,000,000 has been outstanding for a number of years. Interest payment dates are April 1 and October 1 each year. Each $1,000 debenture is convertible into 30 shares of common stock. On April 1, 1988, $8,000,000 of the outstanding debentures were converted.

4 An issue of 8% cumulative redeemable preferred stock in the amount of $5,000,000 has been outstanding for a number of years. There was no change in this preferred stock issue during 1988.

5 On July 1, 1988, 10% noncumulative convertible preferred stock in the amount of $6,000,000 was issued at a face value of $100 per share. Each share of preferred stock is convertible into five shares of common stock. Dividends totalling $5 per share were declared on this stock during 1988.

6 On January 31, 1989 (before the completion of the 1988 financial statements on February 28, 1989), the common stock was split on the basis of two new shares for each old one.

7 On February 15, 1989, 200,000 shares of common stock were issued for $4,400,000 cash. The proceeds from the sale were used to redeem $4,000,000 of the 8% cumulative redeemable preferred stock at a premium of 10%.

Instructions

For the year ended December 31, 1988, compute each of the following:

a Basic earnings per share

b Adjusted basic earnings per share

c Fully diluted earnings per share

d Pro forma basic earnings per share

e Pro forma fully diluted earnings per share

p a r t f i v e

MORE COMPLEX ACCOUNTING TOPICS

Probably the most controversial and complex topics in financial accounting deal with pension plans, long-term leases, income taxes, and accounting changes. Accountants and rule-making bodies have been searching for solutions to the measurement of periodic pension costs, the presentation of capital leases in the balance sheet, income tax allocation procedures, and the presentation of the effect of accounting changes in the income statement. Although the current body of accounting principles in these areas has been perceived as both practical and theoretically sound, considerable pressure has been mounting in recent years for major changes in such principles.

Chapter 22, the last chapter in Part Five, includes a discussion of accounting errors and the preparation of financial statements from incomplete accounting records.

c h a p t e r 1 9

ACCOUNTING FOR PENSION COSTS AND OBLIGATIONS

Most publicly owned business enterprises, and many nonpublic enterprises, have pension plans in effect for their employees. Assets of all ***private*** (nongovernmental) and public pension funds amount to billions of dollars and are expected to increase at a rapid rate. Assets of private pension funds have been increasing much more rapidly than total assets of business enterprises, and in many cases, pension expense has been increasing faster than enterprise earnings. As a result, accounting for pension costs and obligations is one of the most important topics in financial accounting.

In this chapter we discuss the nature of pension plans, the theoretical issues involved in accounting for the costs and obligations of pension plans, and accounting standards for pension plan costs and obligations.

NATURE OF PENSION PLANS

A ***pension plan*** is any arrangement (contractual or otherwise) between a business enterprise (employer) and its employees by which a program is established to provide retirement income to employees. Ordinarily, retirement income (pension benefits) consists of monthly payments to employees after their retirement. The ***pension plan*** provides ***evidence*** of the promise the employer has made to employees. In accounting for the cost of providing pension benefits, the terms and conditions of the plan determine factors to be considered in measuring the pension costs and obligations.[1] Under a ***noncontributory pension plan***, the employer assumes responsibility for the full cost of pensions; under a ***contributory pension***

1 CICA, ***CICA Handbook*** (Toronto: 1981), sec. 3460.04. Emphasis added.

plan, employees bear a portion of the cost of pensions through payroll deductions. Under a ***defined benefit pension plan***, either the benefits to be received by the employees after retirement or the method for determining those benefits, is specified. The most commonly used defined ***benefit*** pension plans are:[2]

i ***Flat benefit pension plans*** These provide a specified benefit for each year of service rendered. The benefit earned in each period is usually fixed and determinable under the terms of the plan and the amount of benefits to be received varies only with the years of service rendered.

ii ***Career average pension plans*** These base benefits on the compensation earned during an employee's entire period of service.

iii ***Final pay pension plans*** These base benefits on an employee's length of service and compensation over a specified number of years, usually the years of an employee's highest earnings.

In contrast, a defined ***contribution*** pension plan is one in which the employer's contributions are fixed,[3] usually as a percentage of compensation, and allocated to specific individuals. The pension benefit for each employee is the amount that can be provided at retirement on the basis of the accumulated contributions made on that individual's behalf and investment earnings on those contributions.

Section 3460 of the ***CICA Handbook*** is primarily concerned with ***comparable*** accounting for the costs and obligations of these two types of ***defined pension plans***. Sections 3460.08 and 3460.09 describe the risk to the employer and to the employee under each plan as follows:

> When an enterprise establishes a ***defined benefit pension plan***, it assumes economic risks. The enterprise is at risk with respect to the amount of the benefit that each employee will receive because the amount is not known with certainty until the benefits related to the employee's retirement cease. The enterprise is also at risk with respect to the returns on amounts invested in the pension fund, because any shortfall from expected returns must be funded by the employer and any excess reduces required funding.
>
> When an enterprise establishes a ***defined contribution pension plan***, it does not assume the economic risks inherent in a defined benefit pension plan. The employer agrees to contribute a certain amount to the pension fund in each period in exchange for services rendered by the employees and has no responsibility to make any further contributions. It is the employees who are at risk because the amount of the pension benefit that will be payable to an individual employee is entirely dependent upon the amount of funds accumulated for the employee's account and the economic conditions prevailing at the retirement date.

Pension plans generally are ***formal***; however, a pension plan's existence may be implied from a well-defined, although perhaps unwritten, practice of paying postretirement benefits. In order to be classified as a pension plan, the enterprise

2 CICA, ***CICA Handbook***, sec. 3460.03(b)(i)–(iii).

3 CICA, ***CICA Handbook***, sec. 3460.03(c).

must be following a ***program*** or ***plan*** for the payment of retirement benefits to employees.

Funded and Unfunded Pension Plans

A ***funded pension plan*** requires a business enterprise (employer) to make periodic payments to a ***funding agency*** (a designated trustee or an outside agency such as a trust company or an insurance company). The process of making payments to the funding agency is known as ***funding***. The employer makes periodic contributions to a trustee that invests the fund assets in, and pays benefits to retired employees from, a separate legal and accounting entity. If a plan is not administered by a funding agency, or if employer assets are informally set aside for the payment of pensions, the plan is designated as ***unfunded***. Most pension plans today are either fully or partially funded.

Actuaries' Role in Pension Plans

The amounts involved in funding and accounting for pension costs and obligations are to a considerable extent determined by actuaries. An ***actuary*** is an expert in the mathematics of insurance. By applying mortality tables, compound-interest formulas, and assumptions regarding employee turnover, years of service, and compensation rates, actuaries compute the present value of amounts required to fund ***defined benefit pension plans***; such amounts are said to be on an ***actuarial basis***. Generally, actuaries use two methods, termed ***actuarial valuation methods***, or ***actuarial cost methods***, to determine the cost of providing pension plan benefits and to allocate that cost to specific time periods. These two families of actuarial valuation methods are:[4]

i **Level contribution methods** (also known as level cost methods). Under these methods the pension cost assigned to any period is either the same dollar amount or the same percentage of compensation as any other period, and is a portion of the cost of the total prospective benefits of an employee group, either in absolute dollars or as a percentage of salary. (Entry age, attained age and aggregate actuarial cost methods are included in this family of methods.)

ii **Accrued benefit methods** (also known as unit credit or single premium actuarial cost methods). Under these methods a distinct unit of retirement benefit is associated with each year of credited service and the actuarial present value of that unit of benefit is separately computed for the period during which it is presumed to have accrued. The most commonly used accrued benefit methods are:

- **Accumulated benefit method.** Under this method benefits earned to date are based on the plan formula, employee's history of pay, service and other factors as of the date of determination.
- **Projected benefit method pro rated on salaries.** Under this method a portion of the total estimated benefit (i.e., with salary projection, when appropriate) is attributed to each period based on the percentage of total estimated career

4 CICA, *CICA Handbook*, sec. 3460.03(h).

compensation earned in that period. The actuarial present value of the accrued pension benefits is derived after the benefits are attributed to the years of service up to the date of determination.

- **Projected benefit method pro rated on services.** Under this method an equal portion of the total estimated benefit (i.e., with salary projection, when appropriate) is attributed to each year of service. The actuarial present value of the accrued pension benefits is derived after the benefits are attributed to the years of service up to the date of determination.

The Accounting Standards Committee concluded that the ***projected benefit method prorated on services*** be required for use with ***defined benefit pension plans***.[5]

Vested Benefits and Accounting for Pension Plan Costs and Obligations

Vested benefits are those earned by the employee that are ***not*** contingent on the employee's remaining in the service of the employer. Vesting may occur at some stipulated time and under certain conditions as per the pension plan agreement—for example, after the employee has been a member of the pension plan for two consecutive years. Most provinces ***require*** vesting after 2 years if the plan does not indicate earlier vesting.

In section 3460.07 of the ***CICA Handbook*** the Accounting Standards Committee indicated that the time of vesting has nothing to do with the accounting recognition of pension costs (expense):

> In many cases, pension plans include provisions for vesting. Vesting is the recognition of the employees' legal rights to receive pension benefits that are no longer conditional on the employees remaining in the service of the employer. The Committee has concluded that the timing of vesting of employees' rights to receive benefits is a matter of plan design and cannot properly serve as a basis for recognizing pension costs. For accounting purposes, the cost of providing benefits would be recognized in the periods in which the employees render the services to which those benefits relate.

Accordingly, ***vesting*** will not be addressed further in this chapter.

Terms Commonly Used Regarding Pension Costs and Obligations

The following are definitions of some of the terms commonly used in accounting literature to describe the various methods of determining pension costs and obligations:[6]

> **Actuarial present value** is the discounted value of an amount or series of amounts payable or receivable at various times, determined as of a given date by the application of a particular set of actuarial assumptions.

5 CICA, ***CICA Handbook***, sec. 3460.28.

6 CICA, ***CICA Handbook***, sec. 3460.03. Adapted.

Actuarial assumptions are made as to the occurrence of future events that will affect pension costs and obligations. These include assumptions about such matters as mortality, withdrawal, disability and retirement and about changes in compensation, interest on accrued pension benefits, investment earnings and asset appreciation or depreciation.
Best estimate assumptions, for accounting purposes, are a set of actuarial assumptions each of which reflects management's judgment of the most likely set of conditions affecting future events.
Actuarial valuation methods (also known as actuarial cost methods) are methods used to determine the cost of providing pension plan benefits and to allocate that cost to specific time periods. [The two main families of actuarial valuation methods are detailed on pages 936–937.]
Pension fund assets are assets set aside for the purpose of meeting retirement benefit payments when they become due.
The **expected average remaining service life (EARSL) of an employee group** is the total number of years of future services expected to be rendered by that group divided by the number of employees in the group. The calculation of expected future services considers population decrements based on the actuarial assumptions but is not weighted by benefits or compensation. [The EARSL is computed by the actuary in two steps. First, the total ''expected'' future working years of current plan members are computed via applying applicable assumed decrements (for example, mortality, retirement, disability, termination of employment, etc.). Second, this expected total number of years is divided by the number of members in the employee group.]
An **experience gain or loss** is the measure of the difference between the expected and actual experience of the plan.
A **pension plan settlement** occurs when an employer legally discharges the obligation for accrued pension benefits either by transferring assets directly to plan participants in exchange for their rights to pension benefits or by purchasing annuity contracts in which a third party unconditionally undertakes to pay all accrued pension benefits.
A **pension plan curtailment** occurs when the expected years of future service to be rendered by the existing employee group is reduced significantly or when benefits will not be earned by employees for some or all future periods.
Accrued pension benefits are the benefits attributed to services rendered up to the date of the financial statements.
The **cost of pension benefits**, for defined benefit pension plans, includes a benefit component, assumed interest on the actuarial present value of accrued pension benefits less assumed earnings on pension fund assets.
A **multiemployer pension plan** is a pension plan to which two or more employers contribute, pursuant to one or more collective bargaining agreements.

The Accounting Standards Committee put the onus on ***management*** to select those ***assumptions for accounting purposes*** which reflect their ***best estimate*** of the effect of future events on the ***actuarial*** present value of accrued pension benefits provided for in exchange for services rendered. Section 3460.16 of the *CICA Handbook* states:

> The assumptions selected for accounting purposes would each reflect management's **best estimate** of the effect of future events on the actuarial present value of accrued pension benefits provided in exchange for services rendered. The assumptions would

> take into account the actual experience of the plan and, in recognition of the long term nature of the plan, expected long term future events, without giving undue weight to recent experience. Periodic assessments would be made to ensure that the assumptions continue to be relevant.

Furthermore, the ***assumptions*** should be ***internally consistent***. Section 3460.15 states:

> In making assumptions about future investment returns, salary changes, withdrawals, mortality rates, etc., management would recognize that the assumptions are interrelated and therefore should be internally consistent. For example, the inflation factor underlying the assumption about future investment returns would be the same as the inflation factor underlying the assumption about future salary levels.

The requirements of section 3460 of the *CICA Handbook* reflect ***actuarial valuations for accounting purposes***. It may be that the pension plan is actuarially valued by some other method, in fact. Such a situation would require that ***the actuary carry out two separate plan valuations***, one for plan purposes and one for accounting purposes. The ***assumptions*** made in evaluating the plan for ***accounting purposes*** must be those which reflect the ***best estimates*** of ***management***, however. Accordingly, in the remainder of this chapter assumptions are understood to be those of management, even though management most certainly would require assistance from the actuary. The assumptions are understood to represent management's best estimate at that time.

Section 3460.07 of the *CICA Handbook* is very explicit with respect to the accounting for pension costs and for the funding of the pension plan:

> The employer's objective in accounting for pension costs is distinctly different from the objective in funding a pension plan. The objective of accounting is to provide a proper allocation of the cost of the plan to the years in which the related employee services are rendered. This objective is achieved by allocating that cost in a rational and systematic manner to the employees' pre-retirement years. The objective of funding a pension plan is to provide cash or other consideration to discharge pension obligations and to provide for pension security. Funding is a financing procedure that considers cash requirements and other matters such as pension or income tax legislation. Accordingly, the amount contributed to a pension fund in a period is not necessarily the appropriate amount to be recognized as pension expense of the period.

THEORETICAL ISSUES

Accountants are faced with three significant issues relating to employers' accounting for pension costs and obligations. These are listed below:

1 ***Timing*** the recognition of pension cost ***as an expense*** in the measurement of net income, particularly when a pension plan covers employees who have already worked a number of years at the time the plan is adopted by the employer

2 *Measuring the amount* of pension expense and any related deferred pension cost or accrued pension cost that is included in the balance sheet

3 *Presenting* significant information relating to pension plans in a note to the financial statements of the employer

The measurement of periodic pension cost (expense) for ***defined benefit pension plans*** involves numerous complexities, including the application of compound-interest concepts, estimation of the life expectancy of employees, determination of the age of employees at retirement, future level of interest rates, future price-level changes, probable employee turnover, gains and losses on pension fund investments, future salary levels of employees, and pension benefits to be paid under pension plans. These complexities, combined with the long-range nature of pension plans, cause significant uncertainties as to the amount of pension benefits ultimately to be paid and the amount of periodic pension expense to be recognized currently by employers under defined benefit pension plans.

Differing Views on Liability Under Defined Benefit Pension Plans

It is generally agreed that a pension plan is an ***executory contract***, under which the employer promises to pay retirement benefits to its employees in return for their services during their term of employment. However, accountants disagree on the precise nature of the employer's commitment. Some accountants believe the employer's commitment is to the ***individual employees or to a group of employees covered by the pension plan***. Other accountants consider the enterprise's obligations to be to the ***pension plan itself*** — a separate legal and accounting entity. Resolution of these contradictory views is critical for the development of a sound theoretical basis for employers' pension plan accounting because the existence of a liability for unfunded pension cost is dependent on which view prevails.

The accountants who hold that the employer enterprise's obligation is to ***individual employees or the employees as a group*** would record a liability for the present value of all unfunded pension benefits attributable to employees on a specific balance sheet date, regardless of the requirement that employees continue to render services to the employer prior to their retirement. In contrast, accountants who consider the employer enterprise's obligation to be to the ***pension plan*** would record no such liability; they insist that the employer has a liability only for unfunded amounts of pension cost not yet paid to the funding agency for the pension plan. In the view of these accountants, pension benefits accrue in much the same fashion as do salaries and wages during the periods that employees render services to the employer. The differences between these two points of view are magnified by the many actuarial estimates that underlie the computations of pension cost and by the long time periods over which services are rendered by employees.

Illustration of Differing Views

To illustrate the difference in accounting between the two opposing views, assume that Wayland Limited established a noncontributory defined benefit pension plan for its 20 employees on January 2, Year 10. The pension plan provided for annual pension benefits to each employee who retired at age 65 after at least five years of service to Wayland computed as follows: 1% of the final annual salary multiplied by the total years of service. On January 2, Year 10, ages of Wayland's employees ranged from 27 to 63, and all except six employees had served more than five years. The actuary retained by Wayland computed the present value of ***past service cost*** (the estimated cost of prospective retirement benefits earned by employees during their years of service prior to the establishment of the pension plan) at $82,500. Accountants who attribute Wayland's obligation under the pension plan to the group of 20 employees would require Wayland to record a liability for the $82,500 present value of past service cost on January 2, Year 10, regardless of Wayland's plans for funding that amount. Views on the offsetting debit vary; some accountants would debit an ***expense*** ledger account, others would debit a ***deferred charge*** account to be recognized as expense over the employees' future years of service, and others would debit a Deferred Compensation contra-shareholders' equity account similar to that illustrated in Chapter 17 for compensatory stock option plans.

Accountants who hold that Wayland is obligated to the pension plan rather than the employee group would require no journal entry on January 2, Year 10. This is because there is likely no legal obligation to fund the past service cost immediately. Accordingly, the $82,500 present value of past service cost would be allocated to pension expense in subsequent accounting periods in which the 20 employees rendered services to Wayland. Such a ***prospective*** allocation of past service cost is founded on the premise that future accounting periods benefit from increased productivity of employees motivated by the new pension plan. It is important to keep in mind the divergent views on the existence of a liability with respect to past service cost in considering accounting standards for defined benefit pension plans.

EMPLOYERS' ACCOUNTING FOR PENSION PLANS

Employer's Accounting for Defined Contribution Pension Plan

Under a ***defined contribution pension plan***, the employer's contribution to the plan typically is measured as a percentage of employer earnings or employees' salaries, and benefits to be received by retired employees depend primarily on the amount contributed by the employer and (in the case of a funded plan) the pension plan's earnings on employer contributions. Generally, the employer's periodic pension expense under a defined contribution pension plan is measured by the employer's required contributions to the plan.[7]

The employer may agree to past service costs for the defined contribution plan. The pension expense for the current year would then be the total of the current-

7 CICA, ***CICA Handbook***, sec. 3460.65.

year costs and the amount of past service costs amortized in the current year. Section 3460.69 of the ***CICA Handbook*** states:

> For defined contribution pension plans, the pension expense for a period includes:
> (a) the cost of pension benefits provided in exchange for services rendered in the period... and
> (b) the amortization of amounts arising from plan initiation or amendment....

To illustrate the employer's accounting for a defined contribution pension plan, assume that on May 31, Year 6, Regis Limited made a required $256,000 contribution to its newly adopted defined contribution pension plan for the year ended on that date. The journal entry for Regis is as follows:

Basic journal entry for defined contribution pension plan

Pension Expense	256,000	
Cash		256,000
To record amount paid to trustee for defined contribution pension plan.		

If Regis incurred costs relating to past services at the inception or amendment of the plan, such costs should be amortized over the expected average remaining service life of the employees covered by the plan. As a result, pension expense would include both the current-year costs and the amortization amount.

Employer's Accounting for Multiemployer Pension Plan

A multiemployer pension plan is one involving two or more unrelated employers in the same industry who contribute to the plan, typically in accordance with a collective-bargaining contract. Contributions to such a plan are not segregated by employer; thus, one employer's contributions to the pension plan may be used to pay benefits to retired former employees of another employer participating in the plan. Sufficient information is normally not available for the employer to quantify its obligation under the plan. In such circumstances, the plan would be accounted for on the same basis as a defined contribution plan.

Disclosure of Defined Contribution Pension Plan Information by Employers

Section 3460.74 of the ***CICA Handbook*** requires the employer to disclose the present value of unfunded future contributions with respect to past service cost. If there are no past service costs, which is usually the case with defined contribution plans, there are no ***Handbook*** requirements for any type of disclosure. However, section 3460.75 suggests additional information may be disclosed as follows:

> An enterprise may also wish to disclose additional information to assist the financial statement user in understanding the impact of pension plans on the enterprise's financial statements, such as:
> **a** the pension expense for the period;
> **b** a general description of the pension plan(s); and

c the nature and effect of significant matters affecting comparability of information presented.

Multiemployer pension plans treated as defined contribution plans would follow the above disclosure requirement and suggestions.

Employer's Accounting for Defined Benefit Pension Plan

Most of section 3460 of the *CICA Handbook* is devoted to the complex accounting standards for defined benefit pension plans, which, because of the numerous assumptions that underlie the computation of pension cost, are subjected to far more uncertainties than are defined contribution pension plans.

In establishing standards for defined benefit pension plans, one must consider the following fundamental concepts:

1 Pension expense for an accounting period is a single net amount consisting of as many as eight components (discussed below).

2 Changes in the pension obligation of an employer and in the value of assets in a funded pension plan may be recognized systematically in the computation of pension cost for accounting periods ***subsequent to the period in which the changes occur***.

3 Pension plan assets and obligations for pensions that were recognized as pension expense in past accounting periods are presented as a ***single net amount*** in the employer's balance sheet.

The following sections of this chapter discuss and illustrate the foregoing concepts.

Components of Pension Cost (Expense) for an Accounting Period

The eight possible components of pension expense under a defined benefit pension plan are:

1 ***Current service cost (accrual for service)*** This is the cost of prospective retirement benefits provided in exchange for employees' ***services rendered in the current period***. This expense is generally determined by actuaries using an acceptable actuarial valuation method for each year subsequent to the inception of the pension plan.

2 ***Expected interest on accrued benefits*** To the actuarially determined present value of accrued benefits at the opening of the period is added the current service cost, from which is deducted any benefits paid, adjusted to reflect a 12-month period. (If the benefit was for $40,000 and was paid June 30th, the amount deducted would be $20,000 if the enterprise's year-end was December 31, because the benefit payment only affected one-half of the year.) The resulting total would be multiplied by the actuarial discount rate to arrive at the expected interest amount.

3 ***Expected interest on pension fund assets*** To the market-related value of the pension fund assets at the opening of the period would be added contributions to the fund in the current year, adjusted to reflect a 12-month period.

From this total, benefit payments, adjusted to reflect a 12-month period, would be deducted. The resulting total would be multiplied by the actuarial discount rate to arrive at the expected interest amount.

4 *Amortization of past service costs* This is amortization of those costs relating to benefits calculated from services performed by employees ***prior to the initiation of the pension plan*** and also to those benefits relating to services performed by employees ***prior to the date of and because of an amendment of the pension plan***. The costs are ***amortized prospectively*** because the plan is initiated (or amended) with the expectation that future benefits will exceed its cost including the past service costs. As a result, such benefits do not relate to prior periods and must be amortized prospectively.

5 *Adjustments arising from changes in assumptions* Assumptions made at the inception of the plan may have to be revised at a later date. These revisions (changes) will result in higher or lower costs of the plan. A change in assumption is equivalent to a change in estimate, as it relates to new information with respect to the pension plan.

6 *Amortization of experience gains and losses* Short-term experience with the plan may result in gains and losses, because adjustments to assumptions are usually not made in the short term. Experience gains and losses arise from two sources:

a The difference between the ***actual value*** of the accrued pension benefits and its ***expected value***

b The difference between the ***actual*** market-related value of pension fund assets and its ***expected*** value

These differences are amortized prospectively.

The Accounting Standards Committee has concluded that periodic pension fund asset valuation would be at market-related values, which would be either market value or a value which is adjusted to market over a period not to exceed five years.[8]

7 *Write-off of plan settlement or curtailment gains or losses* Gains or losses due to plan settlement (or partial settlement) and plan curtailment are ***terminal***. Accordingly, all actual costs and unamortized amounts applicable to such plans must be recognized in income on the settlement or curtailment date.

A ***settlement*** of a defined benefit pension plan results from transactions such as lump-sum cash payments to employees in exchange for their rights to receive specified plan benefits or acquisition of nonparticipating annuity contracts to cover vested benefits under the plan. Thus, settlements are irrevocable actions that relieve the employer or the pension plan of primary responsibility for pension benefits and eliminate significant risks related to

8 CICA, *CICA Handbook*, sec. 3460.33.

the obligation and the assets used to accomplish the settlements. A ***curtailment*** of a defined benefit pension plan takes place when, for example, employee services are terminated earlier than anticipated or a pension plan is terminated or suspended so that employees do not earn benefits for future services. The outcome of a curtailment is a reduction of expected years of future services of present employees or elimination of numerous employees from the accrual of defined benefits for future services.

Both a settlement and a curtailment may occur with respect to a single employer act regarding a defined benefit pension plan. For example, the termination of a defined benefit pension plan involves a curtailment and a settlement, because the termination itself constitutes a curtailment and the employees typically receive directly or indirectly nonparticipating annuity contracts or lump-sum payments in a settlement in conjunction with the termination of the plan.

8 ***Amortization of net pension asset or net pension obligation*** Section 3460.77 of the ***CICA Handbook*** requires the amortization of the difference between the market or market-related value of the fund assets and the present value of the accrued pension benefits, each amount being determined ***at the date on which the recommendations of the section are first applied.***

Although the Accounting Standards Committee has encouraged early application of the provisions of section 3460, it has permitted a delay until years beginning on or after December 1, 1988, in some cases. Further, they have permitted an amortization period for employers having defined benefit pension plans to record a date-of-application unrecognized net gain and related excess of pension fund assets over the present value of accrued pension benefits or to record an unrecognized net loss in the converse situation. Accordingly, the amortization of the unrecognized net gain or net loss is included in the measurement of pension expense of each accounting period. Section 3460.77 states:

> The Recommendations of this Section should be applied prospectively. For defined benefit pension plans, when the Recommendations are first applied, an enterprise should determine the actuarial present value of the accrued pension benefits and the value of pension fund assets. The difference between these amounts, whether it represents a net pension asset or a net pension obligation, and to the extent it has not previously been recognized, should be amortized in a rational and systematic manner over an appropriate period of time, which normally would be the expected average remaining service life of the employee group covered by the plan.

The foregoing components of pension expense are illustrated in the sections that follow. First, we discuss and illustrate the accounting for pension expense of an ***unfunded*** defined benefit pension plan, which does not have actual return on plan assets as an element of pension expense. Next, accounting for a ***funded*** defined benefit pension plan is considered. Our discussion and illustrations in this area include the basic technique for amortization of unrecognized past service cost, accounting for an unfunded accrued benefit obligation, and disclosure of pension plan information by employers.

Pension Cost for Unfunded Defined Benefit Pension Plan

An unfunded defined benefit pension plan initiated on the date that the employer enterprise began operations would first incur only two of the foregoing components — current service cost and interest on accrued benefits. For illustration, we assume that Darien Limited established an unfunded noncontributory defined benefit pension plan for its 25 employees on January 2, Year 1, the date it began operations. Because the pension plan became effective on the date Darien began operations, there was no past service cost.

Assume that Darien's actuaries computed current service cost under the pension plan at $40,000 and $45,000 respectively for Year 1 and Year 2, at an assumed discount rate of 10%. Journal entries for Darien Limited on December 31, Year 1 and Year 2, are as follows:

Journal entries for unfunded defined benefit pension plan with current service cost and interest on accrued benefits only

Year 1				
Dec. 31	Pension Expense		40,000	
	Accrual for Pensions			40,000
	To record current service cost of unfunded defined benefit pension plan.			
Year 2				
Dec. 31	Pension Expense		49,000	
	Accrual for Pensions			49,000
	To record pension expense as follows:			
	Current service cost	$45,000		
	Interest on accrued benefits ($40,000 × 0.10)	4,000		
	Total pension expense	$49,000		

On December 31, Year 2, the balance of Darien Limited's Accrual for Pensions is $89,000 ($40,000 + $49,000 = $89,000). This amount, which is equal to the accrued pension benefits under Darien's unfunded noncontributory defined benefit pension plan, is included with long-term liabilities in Darien's balance sheet on December 31, Year 2, under the assumption that no benefits are payable because there are as yet no retired employees. (The current portion of any benefits payable to retired employees would be included with current liabilities.)

Let us now assume that, as of January 1, Year 3, because of an overall decline in interest rates, the actuaries for Darien Limited's unfunded defined benefit pension plan changed the discount rate to 9% from 10%. As pointed out in Chapter 5 (page 226), the present value of a future amount increases when the interest rate decreases. Assuming that the actuaries' revised computation of the accrued pension benefits as of January 1, Year 3, was $101,000, there is an adjustment arising from a change in an assumption of $12,000 ($101,000 − $89,000 = $12,000) for Darien Limited's unfunded noncontributory defined benefit pension plan on that date. The amortization period is to be the expected average remaining service life of employees expected to receive benefits under the pension plan and may commence in the following period. Let us assume the service period to be 15 years.

Assuming that the actuaries' computation of current service cost for Year 3 is $62,000, Darien Limited's journal entry on December 31, Year 3, is as follows:

Journal entry for unfunded defined benefit pension plan with current service cost, interest on accrued benefits, and amortized change in assumption

Year 3				
Dec. 31	Pension Expense		71,890	
	Accrual for Pensions			71,890
	To record pension expense as follows:			
	Current service cost	$62,000		
	Interest on accrued benefits ($101,000 × 0.09)	9,090		
	Amortization of assumption change ($12,000 ÷ 15)	800		
	Total pension expense	$71,890		

Following the foregoing journal entry, the balance of the Accrual for Pensions ledger account, $160,890 ($89,000 + $71,890 = $160,890) is $11,200 less than the accrued pension benefits under the unfunded defined benefit pension plan, as computed below:

Computation of excess of accrued pension benefits over accrual for pensions

Balance of accrued pension benefits, Jan. 1, Year 3 (as revised by actuaries)	$101,000
Add: Current service cost and interest cost ($62,000 + $9,090)	71,090
Subtotal	$172,090
Less: Benefits paid	0
Balance of accrued pension benefits, Dec. 31, Year 3	$172,090
Less: Balance of Accrual for Pensions ledger account, Dec. 31, Year 3	160,890
Excess of accrued pension benefits over accrual for pensions liability	$ 11,200

The difference of $11,200 is the unamortized balance on December 31, Year 3 ($12,000 − $800 = $11,200) of the unrecognized loss due to the change in assumption.

Pension Cost for Funded (Funding Agency) Defined Benefit Pension Plan

To illustrate accounting for pension cost under a funded defined benefit pension plan, assume that Rimmer Corporation, which has been operating for 10 years, adopted a funded noncontributory defined benefit pension plan on January 2, Year 11. Under provision of the plan, Rimmer's 42 employees were entitled to retroactive benefits (representing past service cost) valued on January 2, Year 11, by Rimmer's actuaries at $2,000,000, at a discount rate of 11%. Section 3460.43 of the ***CICA Handbook*** states:

> For defined benefit pension plans, adjustments arising from plan initiation or amendment should be amortized in a rational and systematic manner over an appropriate period of time, which normally would be the expected average remaining service life of the employee group covered by the plan.

The expected average remaining service life of the employees, whose past service benefits are included in the $2,000,000, is 15 years at the inception of the plan, as illustrated below. Rimmer Corporation has decided to amortize the past service costs, using the straight-line method, over this 15-year period. Rimmer funded the entire $2,000,000 past service cost on January 2, Year 11. Management assumed an 11% expected long-term rate of return on pension fund assets to be invested to provide for the ultimate payment of benefits included in the pension plan's accrued pension benefits.

Determination of expected average remaining service life of employees in pension plan of Rimmer Corporation

Employee number	*Years to retirement*	*Employee number*	*Years to retirement*	*Employee number*	*Years to retirement*	*Employee number*	*Years to retirement*
1	1	12	11	23	18	34	19
2	5	13	7	24	14	35	21
3	11	14	12	25	15	36	31
4	6	15	8	26	22	37	29
5	18	16	19	27	31	38	32
6	13	17	20	28	27	39	18
7	7	28	16	29	18	40	28
8	8	19	7	30	4	41	29
9	4	20	8	31	6	42	27
10	12	21	9	32	17		631
11	3	22	12	33	8		

NOTE: Total number of years to retirement for the 42 employees is 631 years. This, when divided by 42, equals 15 years, the expected average remaining service life of the employee group covered by the plan. (This computation assumes a zero turnover and a zero mortality rate. The *expected* remaining service life would somehow discount these years to retirement.)

In this illustration, we assume the following additional facts for Rimmer's pension plan for Year 11:

1 The actuary determined that the ***current service cost*** from rendering services in Year 11 was $213,000. Assume the accrual for these services occurs at the beginning of each year.

2 The actual contribution to the fund in Year 11 was $213,000. This payment was made on December 31, Year 11, and was in addition to the $2,000,000 past service cost contribution to the fund on January 2, Year 11. Since the $213,000 payment was made at year-end, no interest would be earned on this amount in Year 11.

3 The actuary determined that the actual closing balance of the accrued pension benefits amounted to $2,500,000.

4 The market value of the pension fund assets, at December 31, Year 11, was $2,673,000.

5 Amortization of past service costs will amount to $133,333 annually ($2,000,000 ÷ 15 = $133,333).

The ***interest on accrued benefits*** is calculated as follows:

Computation of expected interest on accrued benefits

Opening balance January 1, Year 11	$2,000,000
Accrual for current service at January 1, Year 11	213,000
	$2,213,000
Interest on accrued benefits at 11%	$ 243,430

The ***interest on pension fund assets*** is calculated as follows:

Computation of expected interest on pension fund assets

Opening balance, January 1, Year 11	$ -0-
Past service costs payment, January 2, Year 11	2,000,000
Interest on pension fund assets at 11%	$ 220,000

The actual value of accrued benefits differs from the expected value. This difference represents Year 11's ***experience loss on accrued benefits***. It is calculated as follows:

Computation of experience gain/loss on accrued benefits

Opening balance, January 1, Year 11	$2,000,000
Accrual for current services	213,000
Interest on accrued benefits	243,430
Expected value of accrued benefits	$2,456,430
Actual value of accrued benefits	2,500,000
Experience loss during Year 11	$ 43,570

The actual value of the pension fund assets, at the end of Year 11, differs from the expected value resulting in an ***experience gain on pension fund assets*** which is calculated as follows:

Computation of experience gain/loss on pension fund assets

Payment into fund January 2, Year 11	$2,000,000
Payment into fund December 31, Year 11	213,000
Expected interest on pension fund assets	220,000
Expected value of pension fund assets	$2,433,000
Actual value of pension fund assets	2,673,000
Experience gain during Year 11	$ 240,000

Section 3460.52 of the ***CICA Handbook*** states:

> For defined benefit pension plans, experience gains and losses should be amortized in a rational and systematic manner over an appropriate period of time, which normally would be the expected average remaining service life of the employee group covered by the plan.

Further, section 3460.51 states that amortization ***may*** commence in the period following that in which the amount of the experience gain or loss was determined. Such gains and losses may arise from ***both*** the accrued pension benefits and the pension fund assets. Accordingly, experience gain or loss for a particular period will reflect the aggregate (net) gain or loss ***amortized*** in that period.

In this illustration, no amortization of experience gains and losses will be taken in the year of occurrence. Amortization will commence in the year following the occurrence of the experience gain or loss.

The net experience gain of $196,430 ($240,000 − $43,570 = $196,430) will be amortized over 15 years on the straight-line basis, commencing in Year 12 under the assumption that 15 years' EARSL is applicable to Year 12. The annual amortization will amount to $13,095 ($196,430 ÷ 15 = $13,095 [rounded]).

The closing balance of the Deferred Past Service Costs account is determined as follows:

Determination of closing balance of Deferred Past Service Costs account

Deferral of past service costs payment January 2, Year 11	$2,000,000
Amortization of 1/15 thereof	133,333
Deferred Pension Costs at December 31, Year 11	$1,866,667

Rimmer Corporation's journal entries for its noncontributory defined benefit pension plan for Year 11 are as follows:

Journal entries for defined benefit pension plan with current service cost, interest on accrued benefits and on pension fund assets, accrual for pensions, and amortized past service cost

Year 11					
Jan. 2	Deferred Past Service Cost			2,000,000	
	Cash				2,000,000
	To record funding and deferral of entire past service cost of pension plan adopted this date.				
Dec. 31	Pension Expense			369,763	
	Cash				213,000
	Deferred Past Service Cost				133,333
	Accrual for Pensions				23,430
	To record pension expense as follows:				
	Current service cost			$ 213,000	
	Interest on accrued benefits	$ 243,430			
	Interest on pension fund assets	(220,000)	23,430		
	Amortization of past service cost		133,333		
	Total pension expense		$369,763		

To summarize, for Year 11:

Pension expense for Year 11	$369,763 Dr
Accrued pension benefits at end of Year 11	$2,500,000 Cr
Pension fund assets at end of Year 11	$2,673,000 Cr
Deferred past service costs at end of Year 11	$1,866,667 Dr
Accrual for pensions at end of Year 11	$23,430 Cr

At December 31, Year 11, there is an excess of pension plan assets over accrued benefits of $173,000 ($2,673,000 − $2,500,000 = $173,000).

The accrual (liability) for pensions at the end of Year 11 is calculated as follows:

Computation of balance of accrual for pensions

Opening balance	$ -0-
Expense for the year	369,763
Remove amortization of recorded deferred past service costs	133,333
	$236,430
Funding contributions	213,000
Closing balance, end of Year 11	$ 23,430

This amount represents the excess of pension expense in Year 11 over contributions to the fund in Year 11, exclusive of the January 2, Year 11, payment of $2,000,000 for the funding of the past service cost obligation, and its annual amortization amount of $133,333. The $23,430 will normally appear in the end of Year 11 balance sheet under "Other Liabilities."

Unamortized (unrecorded) experience gains and losses are calculated as follows:

Computation of unamortized experience gains and losses

Opening balance	$ -0-
Experience (gain) loss	(196,430)
Amortization current year	-0-
	$(196,430)

The unrecorded experience gains and losses are expensed periodically. A schedule showing the remaining unamortized unrecorded balance each year-end is appropriate.

To continue our illustration of Rimmer Corporation's noncontributory defined benefit pension plan for Year 12, we assume the following:

1 One employee retired on December 31, Year 11 (see page 948) and was paid an annual pension of $40,000 by the pension plan trustee on June 30, Year 12.

2 The actuaries for Rimmer's pension plan made no changes in the discount rate or other assumptions for Year 12.

3 The actuary determined that the actual closing balance of the accrued pension benefits amounted to $2,900,000.

4 The market value of the pension fund assets, at December 31, Year 12, was $3,112,000.

5 Amortization of past service costs will amount to $133,333 for Year 12.

6 The expected average remaining service life (EARSL) of the employees in the pension plan group remains at 15 years in Year 12 and Year 13.

7 Current service cost, from rendering services in Year 12, was $224,000.

8 A funding contribution of $200,000 was made on July 1, Year 12.

The ***interest on the accrued benefits*** is calculated as follows:

Computation of expected interest on accrued benefits

Opening actual accrued benefits	$2,500,000
Accrual for current service at January 1, Year 12	224,000
Benefit payments, June 30, Year 12 (6/12 × $40,000)	(20,000)
	$2,704,000
Interest on accrued benefits at 11%	$ 297,440

The ***interest on pension fund assets*** is calculated as follows:

Computation of expected interest on pension fund assets

Opening actual pension fund assets	$2,673,000
Funding contributions, July 1, Year 12	100,000
Benefit payments, June 30, Year 12 (6/12 × $40,000)	(20,000)
	$2,753,000
Interest on pension fund assets at 11%	$ 302,830

The ***experience gain on accrued benefits*** is calculated as follows:

Computation of experience gain/loss on accrued benefits

Opening (actual) balance	$2,500,000
Accrual for current service	224,000
Interest on accrued benefits	297,440
Benefit payments	(40,000)
Expected value at end of Year 12	$2,981,440
Actual value at end of Year 12	2,900,000
Experience gain	$ 81,440

The ***experience loss on pension fund assets*** is calculated as follows:

Computation of experience gain/loss on pension fund assets

Opening (actual) balance	$2,673,000
Contributions in Year 12	200,000
Expected interest on pension fund assets	302,830
Benefit payments	(40,000)
Expected value at end of Year 12	$3,135,830
Actual value at end of Year 12	3,112,000
Experience loss	$ 23,830

The net experience gain of $57,610 ($81,440 − $23,830 = $57,620) will be amortized over 15 years on the straight-line basis, commencing in Year 13. The annual amortization will amount to $3,841 ($57,610 ÷ 15 = $3,841 [rounded]).

The first year's amortization of the Year 11 net experience gain of $196,430, in the amount of $13,095, will occur in Year 12.

The closing balance of the Deferred Past Service Costs account will be $1,733,334 ($1,866,667 − $133,333 = $1,733,334).

The ***accrual for pensions*** at the end of Year 12 is calculated as follows:

Computation of closing balance of accrual for pensions

Opening balance		$ 23,430
Expense for the year	$338,848	
Less amortization of past service cost	133,333	205,515
Funding contributions		(200,000)
Closing balance		$ 28,945

Unamortized (unrecorded) experience gains and losses are calculated as follows:

Unamortized experience gains/losses

Opening balance	$(196,430)
Experience (gain) loss, Year 12	(57,610)
Amortization of Year 11 net gain	13,095
Closing balance	$(240,945)

Rimmer Corporation's journal entries for its noncontributory defined benefit plan for Year 12 is as follows:

Journal entries for defined benefit pension plan with current service cost, accrual for pensions, interest on accrued benefits and on pension fund assets, amortization of experience gains and losses and on past service cost

Year 12					
July 1	Accrual for Pensions			200,000	
	Cash				200,000
	To record payment to trustee.				
Dec. 31	Pension Expense			338,848	
	Accrual for Pensions				205,515
	Deferred Past Service Cost				133,333
	To record pension expense as follows:				
	Current service cost		$224,000		
	Interest on accrued benefits	$297,440			
	Interest on pension fund assets	(302,830)	(5,390)		
	Amortization of experience gains and losses		(13,095)		
	Amortization of deferred past service cost		133,333		
	Total pension expense		$338,848		

Rimmer Corporation's pension plan is overfunded $212,000 on December 31, Year 12, as shown below:

Computation of overfunding of funded defined benefit pension plan

Market value of pension fund assets:		
Balance, Dec. 31, Year 11		$2,673,000
Add: Expected interest on pension fund assets	$302,830	
Experience loss, Year 12	(23,830)	279,000
Employer contribution		200,000
Subtotal		$3,152,000
Less: Benefits paid to retirees		40,000
Balance, Dec. 31, Year 12		$3,112,000
Less: Present value of accrued pension benefits:		
Balance, Dec. 31, Year 11	$2,500,000	
Add: Current service cost for Year 12	224,000	
Expected interest on accrued benefits	297,440	
Experience gain, Year 12	(81,440)	
Subtotal	$2,940,000	
Less: Benefits paid to retirees	40,000	

Balance, Dec. 31, Year 12	2,900,000
Overfunding of pension plan	$ 212,000

The market value of pension fund assets and the present value of the accrued pension benefits are disclosed in a note to the December 31, Year 12, financial statements of Rimmer Corporation, as explained in a subsequent section of this chapter. Rimmer's pension expense of $338,848 is included in its income statement for Year 12, appropriately allocated among cost of goods sold, selling expenses, and general and administrative expenses. (A portion allocable to direct labour and factory overhead may be included in inventories in Rimmer's December 31, Year 12, balance sheet.)

The $1,733,334 [$2,000,000 − (2 × $133,333) = $1,733,334] Year 12 year-end balance of the Deferred Past Service Cost account is included in the "Other Noncurrent Assets" section of the balance sheet.

The $28,945 ($23,430 + $5,515 = $28,945) Year 12 year-end balance of the Accrual for Pensions account is included in the "Other Liabilities" section of the balance sheet.

The current-year change in the Accrual for Pensions account in the amount of $5,515 ($205,515 − $200,000 = $5,515) is a deduction from Funds from Operations in the Statement of Changes in Financial Position, as it represents the difference, in Year 12, between the amount expensed in pension expense and the amount contributed to the fund.

The next illustration gives a comparison of selected accounts for Years 11 and 12 for Rimmer corporation:

Comparison of selected accounts for Years 11 and 12

	Year 11, $	Year 12, $
Interest on accrued benefits:		
Opening balance — actual	2,000,000	2,500,000
Accrual for service — January 2	213,000	224,000
Benefit payments, June 30	-0-	(20,000)
	2,213,000	2,704,000
Interest at 11%	243,430	297,440
Experience (gains) losses — accrued benefits:		
Opening balance — actual	2,000,000	2,500,000
Accrual for service	213,000	224,000
Expected interest on accrued benefits	243,430	297,440
Benefit payments	-0-	(40,000)
Expected value	2,456,430	2,981,440
Actual value	2,500,000	2,900,000
Experience (gain) loss	43,570	(81,440)
Interest on pension fund assets:		
Opening balance — actual	-0-	2,673,000
Funding contributions	2,000,000	100,000
Benefit payments	-0-	(20,000)
	2,000,000	2,753,000
Interest at 11%	220,000	302,830

Experience (gains) losses — pension fund assets:		
Opening balance — actual	-0-	2,673,000
Contributions	2,213,000	200,000
Expected interest on pension fund assets	220,000	302,830
Benefit payments	-0-	(40,000)
Expected value	2,433,000	3,135,830
Actual value	2,673,000	3,112,000
Experience (gain) loss	(240,000)	23,830
Calculation of accrual for pensions:		
Opening balance	-0-	23,430
Pension expense for year	236,430*	205,515*
Funding contributions for year	(213,000)	(200,000)
Closing balance	23,430	28,945
Unamortized experience gains and losses:		
Opening balance	-0-	(196,430)
Experience (gain) loss	(196,430)	(57,610)
Amortization of Year 11 gain	-0-	13,095
Closing balance	(196,430)	(240,945)
Deferred past service costs:		
Opening balance	-0-	1,866,667
Payment, January 2, Year 11	2,000,000	
Amortization expense	(133,333)	(133,333)
Closing balance	1,866,667	1,733,334
Pension expense:		
Accrual for service	213,000	224,000
Interest accrued on benefits	243,430	297,440
Interest on pension fund assets	(220,000)	(302,830)
Amortization of past service cost	133,333	133,333
Amortization of net experience gain, Year 11	-0-	(13,095)
Total pension expense	369,763	338,848

*Excluding amortization of Deferred Past Service Cost.

Disclosure of Defined Benefit Pension Plan Information by Employers

Paragraphs 3460.60 and 3460.61 respectively set out the requirements for disclosure and suggested additional information disclosures:

> For defined benefit pension plans, an enterprise should disclose separately the actuarial present value of accrued pension benefits attributed to services rendered up to the reporting date and the value of pension fund assets.
>
> An enterprise may also wish to disclose additional information to assist the financial statement user in understanding the impact of pension plans on the enterprise's financial statements, such as:
>
> **a** the pension expense for the period;
> **b** the amount of the deferred charge or accrual for pension costs;
> **c** the basis of valuing pension fund assets;

d the salary and interest rate assumptions used in determining the pension expense and actuarial present value of accrued pension benefits;
e the method and period used to amortize adjustments arising from plan initiation or amendment, changes in assumptions, experience gains and losses and the net pension asset or net pension obligation determined when the Recommendations of this Section took effect...;
f a general description of the pension plan(s);
g the date of the most recent actuarial valuation performed for accounting purposes; and
h the nature and effect of significant matters affecting comparability of information presented.

A suitable note accompanying Rimmer Corporation's financial statements at the end of Year 12 might read as follows:

Note to the Financial Statements

Rimmer Corporation maintains a noncontributory defined benefit final average plan which covers substantially all of its employees. The plan provides pensions based on length of service and average of final five years' earnings.

Actuarial reports were prepared during Year 12 and were based on projections of employees' compensation levels to the time of retirement. The reports indicate that the present value of the accrued pension benefits, using an 11% discount, and market value of the pension fund assets available to provide the benefits, as of December 31, are as follows:

	Year 12	*Year 11*
Accrued pension benefits	$2,900,000	$2,500,000
Pension fund assets	3,112,000	2,673,000

The pension expense of $338,848 (Year 11: $369,763) includes the amortization of past service costs and experience gains and losses. These amounts are being amortized on the straight-line basis over 15 years.

The cumulative difference between the amounts expensed and the funding contributions has been reflected in the balance sheet as a long-term accrual. These amounts do not include amortizations of past service costs. The amounts recorded are: Year 12, $28,945; Year 11, $23,430.

Past service costs were fully funded on January 2, Year 11, at a cost of $2,000,000. Accordingly, a deferred past service cost is reflected in the balance sheet. Amortization of past service costs of $133,333 each year has reduced that account to $1,733,334 at December 31, Year 12.

The Rimmer Corporation illustration for Years 11 and 12 included an example wherein the past service cost of a pension plan was funded 100% at the commencement of the plan. Although this does occur from time to time, the usual practice is to make funding contributions over the maximum period allowed. In most jurisdictions this is 15 years, and in many jurisdictions there are equal annual payments over the 15-year period. The amount of each payment would therefore represent an annuity of 15 payments at a discount rate that present values the 15 payments to the amount of the past service cost at the date of initiation or amendment of the pension plan.

To illustrate, we will assume Rimmer Corporation will contribute to the fund $250,568 {$2,000,000 ÷ [$P_{\overline{n}|i} \times (1 + i)$] = $250,568, when $n = 15$ and $i = 11\%$} on January 2 each year for 15 years to clear the obligation to the fund for past service cost at January 2, Year 11.

In accordance with the foregoing, Rimmer Corporation's journal entries for the pension plan for Year 11 are as follows:

Journal entries for defined benefit pension plan with current service cost, accrual for pensions, interest on accrued benefits and on pension fund assets, and amortized past service cost

Year 11				
Jan. 2	Accrual for Pensions		250,568	
	Cash			250,568
	To record the first payment for past service costs on plan adopted this date.			
Dec. 31	Pension Expense		562,201	
	Cash			213,000
	Accrual for Pensions			349,201
	To recognize pension expense as follows:			
	Current service cost	$213,000		
	Interest on accrued benefits	243,430		
	Interest on pension fund assets	(27,562)		
	Amortization of past service cost	133,333		
	Total pension expense	$562,201		

The December 31, Year 11, entry above to recognize pension expense is the same as was made on page 950 with the exception of the ***interest on pension fund assets***, which has been calculated as follows:

Computation of expected interest on pension fund assets

Opening balance, January 1, Year 11	$ -0-
Past service cost payment January 2, Year 11	250,568
	$250,568
Interest on pension fund assets at 11%	$ 27,562

The balance of the Accrual for Pensions account, at the end of Year 11, was $98,633 ($349,201 − $250,568 = $98,633). This is the difference between pension expense for the year and payments into the fund in Year 11 [$562,201 − ($250,568 + $213,000) = $98,633].

Also, the entry on page 950 credited a Deferred Past Service Cost account for $133,333. This amount is included in the above Accrual for Pensions account, because at the inception of the plan the $2,000,000 past service cost was not set up in a deferred account. Accordingly, it represents an unamortized unrecorded item at that time and usually is included with unamortized experience gains and losses. The Accrual for Pensions account will be debited for payments on past service costs and will be credited for amortizations of past service costs. Also, the interest on the payment to the fund will replace some of the interest lost due to the smaller expected interest on pension fund assets.

If we assume the actual value of the pension fund assets at the end of Year 11 was $500,000 and at the end of Year 12 was $1,000,000, the ***experience gain on pension fund assets*** for Year 11 becomes $8,870 calculated as follows:

Computation of experience gain/loss on pension fund assets

Opening balance, January 1, Year 11	$ -0-
Payment on January 2, Year 11	250,568
Expected interest on payment	27,562
Payment on December 31, Year 11	213,000
Expected value of pension fund assets	$491,130
Actual value of pension fund assets	500,000
Experience gain during Year 11	$ 8,870

This is much lower than in the first illustration because only $250,568 of the past service cost was contributed to the fund in the current year. ($2,000,000 was contributed in the first illustration.)

The journal entries for the pension plan for Year 12 are as follows:

Journal entries for defined benefit pension plan with current service cost, accrual for pensions, interest on accrued benefits and on pension fund assets, amortization of experience loss and of past service cost

Year 12			
Jan. 2	Accrual for Pensions	250,568	
	Cash		250,568
	To record funding of 2nd instalment for past service costs.		
July 1	Accrual for Pensions	200,000	
	Cash		200,000
	To record payment to trustee.		
Dec. 31	Pension Expense	565,724	
	Accrual for Pensions		565,724
	To recognize pension expense as follows:		
	Current service cost	224,000	
	Interest on accrued benefits	297,440	
	Interest on pension fund assets	(91,362)	
	Amortization of past service cost	133,333	
	Amortization of Year 11 experience loss	2,313	
	Total pension expense	565,724	

The ***interest on pension fund assets*** of $91,362, is calculated as follows:

Computation of expected interest on pension fund assets

Opening (actual) balance	$500,000
Funding contributions:	
Jan. 1, Year 12	250,568
July 1, Year 12	100,000
Benefit payments, June 30, Year 12	(20,000)
	$830,568
Interest on pension fund assets at 11%	$ 91,362

Here is a comparison of the calculations for Years 11 and 12, which are different when considering the two illustrations.

Comparison of Years 11 and 12 for computation results, which differ in illustrations one and two

	Year 11, $	*Year 12,* $
Interest on pension fund assets:		
Opening balance, actual	-0-	500,000
Funding contributions:		
Jan. 2	250,568	250,568
July 1, Year 12	-0-	100,000
Benefit payments, June 30	-0-	(20,000)
	250,568	830,568
Interest thereon at 11%	27,562	91,362
Experience (gain) loss, pension fund assets:		
Opening balance, actual	-0-	500,000
Contributions to fund	463,568	450,568
Expected interest on pension fund assets	27,562	91,362
Benefit payments	-0-	(40,000)
Expected value	491,130	1,001,930
Actual value	500,000	1,000,000
Experience (gain) loss	(8,870)	1,930
Accrual for pensions:		
Opening balance	-0-	98,633
Pension expense	562,201	565,724
Funding contributions	(463,568)	(450,568)
Closing balance	98,633	213,789
Unamortized (unrecorded) past service cost and experience (gains) losses:		
Opening balance	-0-	1,901,367
Past service cost	2,000,000	-0-
Experience (gain) loss	34,700	(79,510)
Amortization:		
Past service cost	(133,333)	(133,333)
Experience gain (loss)	-0-	(2,313)
Closing balance	1,901,367	1,686,211
Pension expense:		
Current service cost	213,000	224,000
Interest on accrued benefits	243,430	297,440
Interest on pension fund assets	(27,562)	(91,362)
Amortization of past service cost	133,333	133,333
Amortization of (gains) losses	-0-	2,313
Total pension cost	562,201	565,724

A suitable note accompanying Rimmer Corporation's financial statements at the end of Year 12 for this illustration might read as follows:

Note to the Financial Statements

Rimmer Corporation maintains a noncontributory defined benefit final average plan which covers substantially all of its employees. The plan provides pensions based on length of service and average of final five years' earnings.

Actuarial reports were prepared during Year 12 and were based on projections of employees' compensation levels to the time of retirement. The reports indicate that the present value of the accrued pension benefits, using an 11% discount, and the market value of the pension fund assets available to provide the benefits, as of December 31, are as follows:

	Year 12	*Year 11*
Accrued pension benefits	$2,900,000	$2,500,000
Pension fund assets	1,000,000	500,000

The pension expense of $565,724 (Year 11: $562,201) includes the amortization of past service costs and experience gains and losses. These amounts are being amortized on the straight-line basis over 15 years.

The cumulative difference between the amounts expensed and the funding contributions has been reflected in the balance sheet as a long-term accrual. The amounts recorded are: Year 12, $213,789; Year 11, $98,633.

Summary of Accounting for Pension Cost of Defined Benefit Pension Plans
The principal features of accounting for the employer's pension cost of defined benefit pension plans may be summarized as follows:

1 Pension expense of both funded and unfunded defined benefit pension plans includes ***current service cost*** and ***expected interest*** on the accrued benefits, which are computed by actuaries on the basis of an assumed ***discount rate***.

2 Only funded defined benefit pension plans include ***expected interest on pension fund assets*** in the computation of pension expense.

3 ***Past service cost*** resulting from the adoption or amendment of a defined benefit pension plan is amortized as pension expense over the average service life of employees expected to receive benefits under the plan.

4 ***Gains and losses*** resulting from differences between expected and actual returns on pension fund assets and on accrued benefits, and changes in assumptions underlying actuaries' computations for the accrued benefit obligation of the pension plan may be deferred in the period that they occur and amortized to pension expense over the average remaining service life of employees, commencing in the following year, or amortization may commence in the current year.

5 The difference between the actuarial present value of the accrued pension benefits and the market-related value of the pension fund assets, at the date the recommendations of section 3460 are first applied, is to be applied prospectively. This net pension asset or net pension obligation should normally be amortized over the expected average remaining service life of the employee group covered by the plan.

6 Pension expense of an accounting period is apportioned among cost of goods sold (to the extent that it is not included in inventories) and to operating expense. The amount of deferred pension cost or accrued pension cost, representing differences between pension expense of an accounting period and

amounts funded, if any, is included with assets or liabilities, respectively, in the balance sheet. In the first illustration, because past service costs were funded in Year 11, a separate Deferred Past Service Cost account was opened for this Year 11 deferral.

Disclosure requirements of pension costs and obligations are minimal. Only the market-related value of pension fund assets and the present value of accrued benefits are required to be disclosed. (In addition section 1505, ''Disclosure of Accounting Policies,'' requires disclosure of the amortization method selected and the method used to value pension fund assets.) For many accountants this is disappointing. Unless enterprises voluntarily disclose such additional information as is suggested in section 3460.61 of the ***CICA Handbook***, there will be insufficient information available for comparison purposes both within the enterprise and between enterprises.

It is true that in the April 1986 pronouncement the Accounting Standards Committee addressed many of the previous shortcomings of section 3460: basic plan information may be shown for defined benefit pension plans and for defined contribution plans. However, it would have been more appropriate if such information were required, in addition to further disclosures with respect to such matters as:

- The basis used for determination of benefits
- Indications of investment risk with respect to the pension fund assets portfolio
- The basis used for arriving at management's ''best estimate'' for the rate of return (discount rate)
- The basis used for arriving at actuarially determined amounts, ***for accounting purposes***, for such items as employee turnover, early retirement, hirings, mortality before retirement, mortality after retirement, etc.
- An accounting by the fund trustee of pension fund asset movements in the current year

Disclosures of information considered useful to financial statement users should be made mandatory so that comparisons may be made more easily within the company over time and between companies in the same time frame. It would appear that the new recommendation has fallen short in this respect. Nevertheless, the new section 3460 is a marked improvement over the previous version.

COMPANIES' DISCLOSURES OF PENSION PLANS

Examine the pension plan section of the Provigo Inc. ''Summary of Significant Accounting Policies'' on page 211, and also item 15 on page 215 for that company's disclosures regarding pensions. Five additional examples of companies' disclosures are presented on the following pages.

AIR CANADA

ANNUAL REPORT 1986

NOTES TO CONSOLIDATED FINANCIAL STATEMENTS

1. Summary of significant accounting policies
i) *Pension costs and obligations*

The Corporation has adopted the new recommendations of the Canadian Institute of Chartered Accountants on accounting for pension costs and obligations with prospective application from January 1, 1986. Pension expense consists of the actuarially computed costs using management's best estimate assumptions of pension benefits in respect of current year's service, imputed interest on plan assets and pension obligations, and straight-line amortization of experience gains or losses and assumption and plan changes, over the average remaining service life of the employee group. The difference between the actuarial present value of the accrued pension obligation and the market value of the pension fund assets at January 1, 1986, is also being amortized into income on a straight-line basis over the expected average remaining service life of the employee group. Corporation pension contributions during the year in excess of the amounts in the income statement are recorded as a deferred charge in the balance sheet. If this change had not been made, net income for the year would have been reduced by $23.0 million and the deferred charge in the balance sheet would have been reduced by $43.9 million.

5. Deferred charges

	1986	1985
Foreign currency exchange losses on long-term debt	$158 800	$ 79 795
Employer pension plan contributions in excess of charges to income	51 152	—
Bond issue costs	22 808	11 615
Other	26 921	28 618
	$259 681	$120 028

Amortization of deferred charges for the year amounted to $33.3 million (1985 $9.6 million).

15. Pension plans
Air Canada maintains several defined benefit pension plans covering substantially all of its employees. Based on the latest actuarial reports prepared as of December 31, 1985 using management's best estimate assumptions, the present value of the accrued pension benefits as at December 31, 1986 amounted to $1,746.2 million, and the market value of the net assets available to provide these benefits was $2,260.4 million.

In accordance with generally accepted accounting principles recommended by the Canadian Institute of Chartered Accountants, the amount by which the Corporation's 1986 funding contributions exceeded the amounts recorded in the determination of its net income, has been reflected in the balance sheet as a deferred charge.

NORTH CANADIAN OILS LIMITED
1986 Annual Report

Notes to Consolidated Financial Statements

Pension Plan

Effective July 1, 1986, the Company replaced its defined benefit plan with a defined contribution pension plan. The plan, which is available to all employees, is a voluntary contribution plan whereby employees' contributions up to 4% of base salary are matched by an equivalent contribution by the Company. Company contributions made under the plans totalled $136,000 in 1986 (1985—$104,000; 1984—$164,000). There are no unfunded liabilities under either of the plans at December 31, 1986.

MacMillan Bloedel Limited — Annual Report 1986

Notes to Consolidated Financial Statements
December 31, 1986, 1985 and 1984

1. Accounting policies:

(f) Pension costs—
Pension costs charged to earnings, including applicable amortization of pension plan experience gains and losses, are determined on the basis of annual reviews of MacMillan Bloedel's various pension plans and other retirement arrangements.

15. Pension plans:

MacMillan Bloedel has a number of contributory and non-contributory pension plans, participation in which is available to substantially all employees after one or two years of continuous service. In addition, the Company has agreements with some of its officers and executives (including retirees) which call for payments to be made under certain conditions following retirement.

During 1986 MacMillan Bloedel adopted the 1983 group annuity mortality table for Canadian pension plans. The cost of this change in actuarial assumptions is estimated at $15.0 million and is being amortized commencing in 1986.

As at December 31, 1986 the estimated excess of pension fund assets and provisions over the estimated obligations for pension benefits amounted to approximately $9.0 million.

	December 31		
	1986	1985	1984
		($ millions)	
Pension fund assets at market value	**$376.3**	$353.9	$311.3
Obligations for pension benefits under all plans and agreements	**360.9**	318.5	291.3
Excess of fund assets over obligations for benefits	**15.4**	35.4	20.0
Provisions	**(6.4)**	2.8	9.8
Excess over plan obligations	**$ 9.0**	$ 38.2	$ 29.8

Indal Limited 1986 Annual Report

Significant accounting policies

Pension costs and obligations

Commencing in 1986, pension costs are calculated, pro-rated on service, using the accrued benefit method of actuarial valuation with projected earnings, where appropriate.

Pension plans are actuarially valued at least every three years. Adjustments arising on valuation are taken to earnings over the expected average remaining service life of the relevant employee group.

Pension plans are funded using a level contribution method of actuarial valuation. Funding requirements are adjusted to reflect the results of periodic plan actuarial valuations. For funding purposes, surpluses are offset against annual contributions until exhausted, while deficits are funded over periods of up to ten years.

Notes to consolidated financial statements

for the year ended December 31, 1986

8. Pension costs and obligations

The Company maintains defined benefit pension plans which provide retirement benefits for essentially all employees, based upon the length of service and, in certain cases, the final average earnings of the employee.

Accounting for pension costs:
In accordance with the Canadian Institute of Chartered Accountants' Accounting Recommendation on Pension Costs and Obligations, the Company has changed its method of determining pension costs, from a level contribution method of actuarial valuation to the accrued benefit method, on a prospective basis from January 1, 1986.

Pension plans have been actuarially valued on the new basis at December 31, 1986, using management's best estimates of the following principal assumptions:

Average return on plan assets	7.0% per annum
Average interest rate	7.0% per annum
Average increase in compensation rates	5.5% per annum

These valuations produced an aggregate net surplus at December 31, 1986 of $14.3 million, reflecting aggregate pension fund assets of $72.3 million and aggregate actuarial present values of accrued pension benefits of $58.0 million. Individual surpluses and deficits making up this net surplus will be amortized to earnings over periods of from thirteen to seventeen years, representing the expected average remaining service lives of the relevant employee groups.

Reflecting these changes, the pension cost for the year ended December 31, 1986, compared with the previous year's cost on the old basis, was as follows:

$ millions	**1986**	1985
Current service cost	**$ 5.2**	$ 4.5
Amortization of net surplus on valuation	**(1.0)**	—
Net interest income on valuation surplus	**(0.8)**	—
	$ 3.4	$ 4.5

Funding of pension obligations:
The Company funds its pension plan obligations on a level contribution method of actuarial valuation. Funding in 1986 amounted to $5.0 million (1985 — $5.7 million).

The pension cost accrual at December 31, 1986 consisted of the balance of pension account transactions of earlier years, reduced by the excess cash contributions made in 1986, as follows:

$ millions	**1986**	1985
Balance—beginning of year	**$ 2.7**	$ 2.7
Excess cash contributions for 1986	**(1.6)**	—
Balance—end of year	**$ 1.1**	$ 2.7

INTER-CITY GAS CORPORATION ANNUAL REPORT 1986

Notes to Consolidated Financial Statements

For the years ended December 31, 1986, 1985 and 1984

15. PENSION PLANS

The Company and its subsidiaries have various pension plans available to substantially all permanent full-time employees. The Company makes contributions to the plans based on salary levels. The total pension expense for 1986 was $3,824,000 (1985 – $2,608,000; 1984 – $1,932,000), including contributions in respect of unfunded past service benefits. A summary of accumulated plan benefits and plan net assets at December 31, 1986 is as follows:

	Canada ($000)	United States ($000)
Net assets available for benefits	64,410	23,038
Actuarial present value of accumulated plan benefits	57,274	20,383

The assumed rates of return used in determining the actuarial present value of accumulated plan benefits ranged from 6.5% to 8% for the Canadian plans, and from 7% to 8.5% for the U.S. plans.

REVIEW QUESTIONS

1 Distinguish between the following:
   a *Noncontributory pension plan* and *contributory pension plan*
   b *Defined benefit pension plan* and *defined contribution pension plan*
   c *Unfunded pension plan* and *funded pension plan*
   d *Actuary* and *actuarial valuation method*
2 What represents a pension plan, according to the Accounting Standards Committee?
3 Discuss the two types of defined pension plan with respect to employer risk.
4 Compare the two families of actuarial valuation methods generally used by actuaries to determine the cost of providing pension plan benefits to employees.
5 Describe the three most commonly used accrued benefit methods and state which one the Accounting Standards Committee selected.
6 *Assumptions* must be selected for accounting purposes. With respect to assumptions, define *best estimate* and *internally consistent*.
7 Is it possible for an enterprise's pension fund to require two actuarial valuations at the same time? Explain.
8 What are three significant issues related to accounting for pension costs and obligations?
9 Do accountants who maintain that an employer's obligation under a pension plan is to the plan itself advocate the recording of a liability for the present value of all unfunded benefits attributable to employees on a specific balance sheet date? Explain.
10 Describe the Accounting Standards Committee's stand on *accounting* for pension costs and on the *funding* of the pension plan.
11 What disclosure information is *required* by section 3460 of the *CICA Handbook* with respect to defined contribution pension plans? What disclosure is *suggested* as additional information for defined contribution pension plans?
12 What are the possible components of net pension expense of a defined benefit pension plan?
13 Define the following
   a *Current service cost*
   b *Expected interest on pension fund assets*
   c *Expected interest on accrued benefits*
   d *Past service cost*
   e *Market-related values*
14 Under what circumstances is the Deferred Pension Cost ledger account used in accounting for a defined benefit pension plan?
15 Does the *discount rate* differ from the *expected long-term rate of return on pension fund assets* for a defined benefit pension plan? Explain.
16 Is the current service cost the amount contributed each year to the pension plan fund? Explain.
17 What happens to the difference that would appear between expected

interest on pension fund assets and actual interest on pension fund assets for a period? Explain.

18 How do experience gains and losses arise, and where do they go?

19 What happens to actual costs and unamortized amounts applicable to a pension plan which is settled or curtailed at a specific date?

20 Define ***net pension asset or net pension obligation*** as it relates to pension plans and section 3460 of the ***CICA Handbook***.

EXERCISES

Ex. 19-1 Select the best answer for each of the following multiple-choice questions:

1 Ideally, the total pension cost relating to a particular employee is recognized as expense:

a Over the expected service lives of all employees active on the date the pension plan is adopted

b Over the specified term of the pension plan

c During the service years of the particular employee

d Over the period specified for payment of the past service cost obligation

2 Is periodic pension expense measured by the employer's required contributions to a defined contribution pension plan? A defined benefit pension plan? Answer ***a***, ***b***, ***c***, or ***d*** according to the table below.

	Defined contribution pension plan	*Defined benefit pension plan*
a	Yes	Yes
b	Yes	No
c	No	Yes
d	No	No

3 For a defined benefit pension plan, pension cost for an accounting period is a single net amount consisting of as many as:

a Eight components

b Two components

c Six components

d Four components

4 An unfunded defined benefit pension plan initiated on the date that the employer began operations would first incur:

a Current service cost only

b Current service cost and expected interest on accrued benefits only

c Current service cost and amortization of unrecognized past service cost

d Current service cost and exchange gain or loss only

5 The discount rate for a defined benefit pension plan is used to compute:

a The expected interest on the accrued pension benefits only

b The expected interest on pension fund assets only

c Both ***a*** and ***b***

d Neither ***a*** nor ***b***

6 Defined benefit pension plans are:
   a Contribution pension plans, career-average pension plans, and unfunded pension plans
   b Career-average pension plans, contribution pension plans, and flat-benefit pension plans
   c Career-average pension plans, final-pay pension plans, and flat-benefit pension plans
   d Final-pay pension plans, career-average pension plans, and contribution pension plans

7 The method wherein the pension cost assigned to any period is either the same dollar amount or the same percentage of compensation as any other period, and is a portion of the cost of the total prospective benefits of an employee group, either in absolute dollars or as a percentage of salary, is commonly known as:
   a The level contribution method
   b The projected benefit method prorated on salaries
   c The projected benefit method prorated on services
   d The accumulated benefit method

8 The total of the expected value of pension fund assets at the end of a period will include:
   a Contributions to the fund ***plus*** expected interest ***minus*** benefits paid
   b Contributions to the fund ***minus*** expected interest ***minus*** benefits paid
   c Contributions to the fund ***minus*** expected benefits ***plus*** benefits paid
   d None of the foregoing

Ex. 19-2 On January 2, Year 1, Crump Limited adopted a noncontributory, unfunded defined benefit pension plan. Actuaries computed the current service cost under the plan at $86,500 and $91,800 respectively for Year 1 and Year 2, at a discount rate of 9%.

Compute ***a*** pension expense for Year 2 and ***b*** the balance of the accrued pension benefit on December 31, Year 2, for Crump Limited's pension plan.

Ex. 19-3 On January 1, Year 4, actuaries revised the amount of Lubeck Corporation's accrued pension benefits obligation under its noncontributory, unfunded defined benefit pension plan to $347,800 from $284,600, because of a revision in the discount rate to 10% from 12%. The expected average remaining service period for Lubeck's employees on January 1, Year 4, was eight years. The straight-line method of amortization is used.

Compute the amount of unrecognized net gain or loss from change in assumptions to be amortized as part of Lubeck Corporation's pension expense for Year 4.

Ex. 19-4 On January 2, Year 1, Lapel Ltd. adopted a noncontributory defined benefit plan. Current service costs from rendering services were computed by the actuary as $300,000 for Year 1. Assume the computation was made January 2, Year 1. Lapel Ltd. contributed $270,000 to the fund on December 31, Year 1.

Management, using their best estimate, assumed a 10% discount rate for the pension plan.

Compute the expected interest on the accrued benefits for Year 1. Also state the amount of expected interest on pension fund assets for Year 1.

Ex. 19-5 The present value of accrued benefits and the market value of pension fund assets at December 31, Year 1, were $320,000 and $270,000 respectively for the pension plan of Lapel Ltd. given in Exercise 19-5 above.

Compute the experience gain and/or loss for the plan at the end of Year 1.

Ex. 19-6 Sojo Limited adopted a pension plan on January 2, Year 6. The past service cost at the initiation date amounted to $700,000. Sojo Limited decided to contribute equal annual payments to the fund over the next 12 years. The first payment will be made on December 31, Year 6. Management determined a discount rate of 10% would be adequate to discharge its responsibility to the fund. The expected average remaining service life of the employees whose past service benefits are included in the $700,000 past service cost balance at January 2, Year 6, is 12 years. Sojo Limited has decided to amortize the past service costs, using the straight-line method, over this 12-year period.

Describe the effect of this past service cost information on pension expense for Year 6.

Ex. 19-7 In addition to the information supplied in Exercise **19-6** above, Sojo Limited supplies you with the following for Year 6:

Current service cost as at January 2, Year 6	$ 200,000
Benefits paid, June 30, Year 6	20,000
Actual balance of accrued benefits at December 31, Year 6	1,000,000
Actual balance of pension fund assets at December 31, Year 6	450,000
Contribution to fund, exclusive of past service cost payment; payment made January 2, Year 6	300,000

Compute, at December 31, Year 6:

a Experience gain or loss on accrued benefits
b Experience gain or loss on pension fund assets
c Total pension expense for Year 6, assuming the experience gains and losses will not be amortized until Year 7

Ex. 19-8 Advance Ltd. adopted a pension plan on January 2, Year 3. The company contributed the $800,000 past service cost obligation and an additional $200,000 for the "current year" to its fund trustee on January 3, Year 3. Advance Ltd. advises it incurred net experience gains of $15,000 at the end of Year 3. The past service costs and the experience gains are to be amortized on the straight-line basis over 10 years, inclusive of Year 3. The actuary determined the current service cost for Year 3 to be $300,000 as at January 2, Year 3. The expected interest on pension fund assets exceeded the expected interest on accrued benefits by

$42,000 for Year 3. Assume the company set up a separate Deferred Past Service Cost account when it paid the $800,000 to the fund trustee.

Prepare the journal entry to record pension expense for Year 3.

CASES

Case 19-1 Many business enterprises have pension plans for their employees. Accounting for the costs and obligations of defined benefit pension plans is a complex subject in which many technical terms are encountered.

Instructions

a Define ***current service cost.***

b Define ***vested benefits.***

c How are net gains and losses related to the operation of a defined benefit pension plan accounted for?

d What disclosures concerning pension plans should be made in a note to the financial statements of employers according to section 3460 of the *CICA Handbook*?

Case 19-2 The board of directors of Oxford Steel Corporation is meeting to discuss the possibility of closing Oxford's outmoded plant in Clay City and concentrating production in modern facilities in Bryanville. In a discussion of costs to be incurred in such a shutdown, a director asked the controller how Oxford's defined benefit pension plan's unrecognized past service cost attributable to employees terminated as a result of the plant closing would be reported in Oxford's financial statements for the year of the plant closing. The controller replied that the unrecognized past service cost could be amortized and funded over the time periods originally established for such cost, because the same pension plan covered employees at both the Clay City and the Bryanville plants. The director commented that generally accepted accounting principles should not be so flexible that undepreciated cost of the abandoned Clay City plant assets would have to be written off as a loss, while the unrecognized past service cost for terminated employees could be recognized as expense over future years.

Instructions

Do you agree with the controller of Oxford Steel Corporation? Alternatively, do you believe that unrecognized past service cost attributable to employees terminated as a result of the plant closing should be recognized as a loss? Explain.

Case 19-3 Cleary Products, Inc., established a defined benefit pension plan on January 2, Year 1, to provide retirement benefits for all of its employees. The plan was noncontributory and was funded through a trustee, which invested all funds and paid all benefits as they became due. Past service cost of $110,000 was being amortized by the straight-line method over 15 years and funded over 10 years at a discount rate of 5%. Cleary also funded an amount equal to current service cost, net of gains and losses. There have been no amendments to the plan since inception.

The actuary's report on June 30, Year 4, follows:

CLEARY PRODUCTS, INC.
Defined Benefit Pension Plan
Actuary's Report
June 30, Year 4

Funding and pension cost for Year 4		
Current service cost (before adjustment for gains) computed by the company's actuary		$ 34,150
Net gains:		
Investment gains (losses):		
Excess of expected dividend revenue over actual dividend revenue		$ (350)
Gain on disposal of investments		4,050
Experience gains for:		
Mortality		3,400
Employee turnover		5,050
Reduction in pension cost from closing of plant		8,000
Net gains		$ 20,150
Current service cost (funded currently)	$14,000	$ 14,000
Past service cost:		
Funding	14,245	
Amortization		7,333
Total pension cost funded	$28,245	
Total pension expense in income statement		$ 21,333
Pension fund assets, June 30, Year 4		
Cash		$ 4,200
Dividends receivable		1,525
Investment in common stocks, at current fair value		162,750
Total pension fund assets		$168,475
Accrued pension benefits, June 30, Year 4		
Number of employees		46
Number of employees retired		None
Yearly earnings of employees		$598,000
Accrued pension benefits		$145,000
Actuarial assumptions		
Discount rate		5%
Mortality (Year 1 Group Annuity Tables)		
Retirement		Age 70
Expected average remaining service life of the employee group		15 years

Instructions

On the basis of generally accepted accounting principles for the cost of defined benefit pension plans, evaluate ***a*** the treatment of experience gains and losses and ***b*** the computation of pension expense for Cleary's income statement for the year ended June 30, Year 4. Disregard income tax considerations.

Case 19-4 Generally accepted accounting principles require that pension costs be measured by the accrual basis of accounting. The various components of pension expense include (but are not limited to) ***current service cost, past service cost,*** and ***experience gains and losses.***

Instructions

Define each of the three terms designated above, and discuss how each of the costs is accounted for under generally accepted accounting principles.

Case 19-5 On January 2, Year 8, the board of directors of Canadair Corporation approved the establishment of a pension plan for all employees. The pension is payable to employees when they reach age 70 if they have had three or more years of continuous service with the company. All current employees are eligible, and past service cost must be amortized over an appropriate number of years, starting in Year 8. Canadair was organized early in Year 1.

A summary of the employees on January 2, Year 8, who are eligible to participate in the pension plan is presented below:

Number of employees	*Years of service as of Jan. 2, Year 8*
20	7
18	6
32	5
25	4
40	3
45	2
20	1
200	

A partial list of benefits to be paid to retired employees on the basis of average annual earnings and the number of years of employment appears below:

Average annual earnings	*Monthly pension benefits based on years of employment*		
	3 years	*10 years*	*25 years*
$21,000	$ 60	$240	$ 720
24,000	80	320	960
27,000	100	400	1,200
32,000	120	480	1,440

Canadair plans to amortize and fund any past service cost over the expected average remaining service life of the above 200 employees.

Instructions

a List some assumptions that would have to be made by Canadair Corporation's actuary to compute the liability for past service cost on January 2, Year 8.

b List some additional facts that would be required by Canadair Corporation's actuary to compute the liability for past service cost on January 2, Year 8.

c In reference to the 200 employees on January 2, Year 8, what factors might cause current service cost of Canadair Corporation's pension plan for Year 13 to increase over the current service cost for Year 8? What factors might cause the current service cost in Year 13 to be less than the current service cost in Year 8?

PROBLEMS

Pr. 19-1 Carrie Limited adopted an unfunded noncontributory defined benefit pension plan on January 2, Year 1, the date it began operations. Current service cost for Year 1 and Year 2 was $63,000 and $68,000 respectively, at a discount rate of 8%. As of January 1, Year 3, the actuaries for Carrie's pension plan changed the discount rate to 9% from 8%, resulting in a $9,800 increase in the accrued benefit obligation as of that date. Current service cost for Year 3 was $87,000. No benefits were paid to retired employees during the three-year period ended December 31, Year 3. Amortization of costs due to the change in assumptions will commence in Year 4.

Instructions
Prepare journal entries for Carrie Limited on December 31, Year 1, Year 2, and Year 3, to record pension expense under its unfunded noncontributory defined benefit pension plan, and the unfunded accumulated benefit obligation under the pension plan on December 31, Year 3.

Pr. 19-2 Yuen Corporation adopted a noncontributory defined benefit pension plan on January 2, Year 6, with unrecognized past service costs of $813,000. The expected average remaining service life of Yuen's 100 employees covered by the pension plan was estimated by the company's actuary to be 18 years in both Year 6 and Year 7. Yuen's management's best estimate of the long-term discount rate was 10%. Current service cost, accrued January 1, Year 6, was $192,000. The actual return on plan assets for Year 6 was 10½%. Yuen funded the $813,000 past service cost in full January 1, Year 6, and funded an additional amount of $200,000 on December 31, Year 6. The actuary estimated the actual value of the accrued pension benefits to be $1,100,000 on December 31, Year 6. Amortization of past service costs is to commence January 1, Year 6, and any amortization of experience gains and losses will commence January 1, Year 7. Yuen Corporation decided that all amortizations were to be on the straight-line basis over the expected average remaining service life of the employees in the pension plan.

Instructions

a Prepare journal entries for Yeun Corporation for Year 6 with respect to the above data. (Show supporting computations.)

b Determine the net experience gain or loss for Year 6.

Pr. 19-3 Cranston Corporation initated a defined-benefit-based plan on January 2, Year 1. During the first five years of the plan, net experience gains and losses were computed as follows: Year 1, $24,000 gain; Year 2, $12,000 loss; Year 3, $16,000 gain; Year 4, $32,000 gain; Year 5, $8,000 loss.

The expected average remaining service life of the employees in the pension plan was estimated by the actuary as follows: Year 1, 15 years; Year 2, 16 years; Year 3, 16 years; Year 4, 16 years; Year 5, 15 years; Year 6, 15 years.

Cranston Corporation has adopted the policy of amortizing experience gains and losses on the straight-line basis, commencing the year following the computation of the gain or loss.

Instructions

Prepare a working paper to show the amount of gains and losses to be included in the computation of Cranston's pension expense in each of the five years ended December 31, Year 5.

Pr. 19-4 On December 31, Year 5, information regarding the noncontributory funded defined benefit pension plan of Campo Corporation included the following:

Accrual for pensions	$24,000
Actuarial value of pension fund assets	$1,587,000
Net experience gain (difference between actual value and expected value on pension fund assets and on the accrued pension benefits) ...	$245,900
Management "best estimate" discount rate	7%
Actual accrued pension benefits	$1,234,000
Deferred past service cost	$720,000
Expected average remaining service life of pension plan employees (EARSL)	20 years

For Year 6, the following were relevant for Campo's pension plan:

Benefits paid to retirees, Dec. 31, Year 6	$86,000
Actual value accrued pension benefits at Dec. 31	$1,450,000
Actual rate of return earned on pension fund assets	8%
Current service cost, Jan. 1, Year 6	$134,000
EARSL of employees in pension plan	20 Years

Additional Information

Campo Corporation contributed 100% of the past service cost at the inception of the pension plan, December 31, Year 4. The company amortizes experience gains and losses and past service cost on the straight-line basis over the expected average remaining service life of the employees in the pension plan. Experience gains and losses amortizations commence the year following their incurrence. EARSL for Year 7 is 20 years.

On December 31, Year 6, Campo Corporation contributed to the fund trustee the total of the accrual for pensions cost at December 31, Year 5, and an additional $100,000.

Instructions

a Compute the following for Campo Corporation for Year 6, or at December 31, Year 6:
  1 Actual value of pension fund assets
  2 Experience gain or loss on pension fund assets
  3 Experience gain or loss on accrued benefits
  4 Net experience gain or loss

b Prepare a journal entry for Campo Corporation on December 31, Year 6, to record its payment to the funding agency and pension expense.

c Determine the balance of ''unrecorded unamortized experience gains and losses'' at December 31, Year 6.

Pr. 19-5 Intercorp, Inc., a calendar-year corporation, adopted a noncontributory defined benefit final average pension plan at the beginning of Year 4. The plan provides pensions based on length of service and final average earnings. The independent actuaries for Intercorp used the appropriate actuarial valuation method, for accounting purposes, to determine its current service cost for Year 4 and Year 5 as $15,000 and $16,000 respectively. The amounts paid at the beginning of Years 4 and 5 were $15,000 and $16,000, respectively.

The actuarially determined past service cost was funded in full on December 31, Year 4, at an amount computed correctly at $110,000. The past service cost was to be amortized on the straight-line basis over the expected actual remaining service life (EARSL) of the employees in the pension plan at its inception. The actuary determined this to be 20 years for Year 4, 5, and 6.

Management, using its best estimate, and in conjunction with the actuary's findings, estimated the long-term discount rate at 10%.

The actuary determined the actual value of pension fund assets at $16,000 and $140,000 on December 31, Year 4 and December 31, Year 5 respectively. The actual values of the accrued pension benefits at the end of Year 4 and Year 5 were $130,000 and $145,000 respectively.

No benefits were paid in Year 4; however, in Year 5, at mid-year, $10,000 of benefits were paid to a retired employee.

Amortization of net experience gains and losses are to commence the following year, are to be over the EARSL of the employees, and are to be on the straight-line basis.

Instructions

a Prepare journal entries required in Year 4 and Year 5 for the new pension plan of Intercorp, Inc.

b Prepare schedules to compute at December 31, Year 4 and Year 5, the following:
  1 Interest on accrued benefits

2 Interest on pension fund assets
3 Experience gain or loss on accrued benefits
4 Experience gain or loss on pension fund assets
5 Accrual for pensions
6 Unamortized experience gains and losses
7 Deferred past service cost

c Set out the appropriate sections of the comparative financial statements and notes thereto for the year ended December 31, Year 5, assuming Intercorp, Inc., discloses all information suggested by section 3460.61 of the ***CICA Handbook*** (what ***may*** be disclosed in addition to what ***should*** be disclosed).

Pr. 19-6 Fundcorp Limited adopted a pension plan early in Year 4 and has regularly, on December 31 each year, funded the full amount of its current service cost. At the time the pension plan was adopted, the past service cost amounted to $1,472,020. At the end of each year the company contributes to the fund trustee an equal amount per year for 15 years, in order to comply with provincial pension legislation with respect to past service cost. Management considers 6% to be an adequate long-term interest rate for its pension plan. The expected average remaining service life (EARSL) of the employees in the plan at its initiation was 20 years. Fundcorp amortizes past service cost and net experience gains and losses on the straight-line basis. Net experience gains/losses amortization commences in the following year. Pertinent pension plan data for Year 6 and Year 7 are presented below:

	Year 6	*Year 7*
Current service cost	$376,200	$424,500
Expected interest on accrued pension benefits	110,893	139,470
Expected interest on pension fund assets	-0-	31,666
Net experience (gain) loss	51,780	63,264
Past service cost payment	151,564	151,564

The net experience loss for Years 4 and 5 was $18,000 and $26,000 respectively. The EARSL has remained at 20 years for Years 4, 5, 6, 7, and 8. No benefits have been paid to the end of Year 7.

Instructions

Prepare journal entries to record pension expense for Year 6 and Year 7.

Pr. 19-7 Radu Corporation operates a noncontributory defined benefit final average pension plan. Prior to the beginning of the current year, the company recorded pension expense equal to its funding payments. Radu Corporation carries no pension liability on its books at the beginning of Year 6.

At the beginning of Year 6, Radu Corporation had an actuarial valuation done for accounting purposes, following the ***new*** requirements of section 3460 of the ***CICA Handbook***.

The results of the valuation were:

January 1, Year 6	
Accrued benefits	$5,000,000
Pension fund assets	$3,660,000
Rate of return (discount rate)	10%
Expected average remaining service life (EARSL) of employees who will receive past service benefits is, at January 1, Year 6	10 years
EARSL of all employees in pension plan January 1, Year 6	18 years

The opening net obligation of $1,340,000 ($5,000,000 – $3,660,000) is due to the following:

Unamortized past service costs	$800,000
Underfunding at January 1, Year 6	$540,000

The following annual amounts relate to Radu Corporation's pension experience as determined by annual valuations at the end of Year 6 and Year 7. Benefit payments and funding contributions occur at June 30 each year. The accrual for service (current service cost) occurs at the beginning of each year. The company has decided to use a straight-line method of amortizing past service costs, the underfunding at the beginning of Year 6, and net experience gains and losses. The amortization of past service cost and the underfunding at January 1, Year 6, will commence January 1, Year 6. Amortization of net experience gains and losses will commence the year following that in which they were incurred. In all cases, the applicable expected average remaining service life (EARSL) of the applicable employee group will be the time period of amortization.

Additional Information

	Year 6	*Year 7*
Current service cost	$ 250,000	$ 300,000
Funding contributions	$ 380,000	$ 516,000
Benefit payments	$ 60,000	$ 60,000
Actual closing pension fund assets	$4,309,000	$5,249,500
Remaining service life	18 years	20 years
Actual closing accrued benefits obligation	$5,730,000	$6,550,000

Instructions

a For Radu Corporation compute the following for Years 6 and 7:
1. Interest on accrued benefits
2. Interest on pension fund assets
3. Experience gains or losses on accrued benefits
4. Experience gains or losses on pension fund assets
5. Accrued pension cost
6. Unamortized past service costs, unfunded obligation at January 1, Year 6, and experience gains and losses (all in one schedule).

b Prepare the journal entries for pension expense for Radu Corporation for Year 6 and for Year 7.

c Prepare partial comparative financial statements, complete with notes thereto, for Year 7. Assume Radu Corporation includes what ***may*** be disclosed in addition to ***required*** disclosures.

c h a p t e r 2 0

ACCOUNTING FOR LEASES

Accounting for leasing transactions is a challenging problem for accountants. Leasing as a means of acquiring the services of plant assets has grown in popularity and complexity as a result of capital shortages and income tax considerations.

Plant assets may be acquired outright or by rental of the assets under a lease contract. Lease contracts are an important means of obtaining the use or financing the acquisition of almost any kind of property, ranging from office machines to factory buildings.

In some cases, a business enterprise constructs or acquires property, sells it to an investor, and simultaneously leases the property from the investor in a ***sale-leaseback transaction***. In other cases, an enterprise leases existing property or property constructed to its specifications. An enterprise that leases property for use in its operations may agree to pay certain ***executory costs*** (such as property taxes, insurance, and maintenance) incident to use of the property.

In order to enable accountants to identify leases of similar economic substance so that they would be reported in a consistent and meaningful manner, section 3065 of the ***CICA Handbook***, ''Leases,'' was issued in December 1978.

Nature of Leases

A ***lease*** is a contract conveying the right to use tangible property, usually for a stated period of time, in return for rent.[1] The owner of the property for which the right is transferred is the ***lessor***, and the party to whom the right is transferred is the ***lessee***. A further transfer of the right to use an asset from a lessee to another party during the term of the lease is a ***sublease***.

The accounting for leases may be divided into two parts—accounting by lessors

1 Adapted from CICA, ***CICA Handbook*** (Toronto: 1981), sec. 3065.03(n).

and accounting by lessees. Lessors report the transfer of rights to use property that they own, and lessees account for and disclose payments for rights to use property that they do not own. If all lease contracts were identical, the accounting for leases would be simple. However, lease accounting is complicated because contracts that are in essence sales transactions may be structured as leases, and other contracts may provide for the lease to be converted to a sale transaction on a later date, usually at the option of the lessee. Although there is no simple model for identifying a specific transaction as a lease or a sale of property, guidelines have been developed for analyzing each transaction and determining the appropriate accounting for it. The remainder of this chapter is devoted to a discussion and illustration of these guidelines.

Terminology for Leases

Like many other specialized areas, leasing has its own language. The following summary of the terminology used for leases underlines the accounting and reporting issues involved in leasing transactions:[2]

1 *Bargain purchase option* A provision giving the lessee the right to acquire leased property at a price sufficiently favourable that exercise of the option appears to be reasonably assured at the inception of the lease.

2 *Bargain renewal option* A provision giving the lessee the right to renew a lease at a rental sufficiently favourable that exercise of the option appears to be reasonably assured at the inception of the lease.

3 *Contingent rentals* Increases or decreases in lease payments after the inception of a lease that result from changes in factors on which lease payments are based, other than the passage of time.

4 *Economic life of leased property* The estimated remaining period during which the leased property is expected to be economically usable for the purpose for which it was designed, with normal repairs and maintenance, without being limited by the lease term.

5 *Estimated residual value of leased property* The estimated fair value of the leased property at the end of the lease term. The portion of the estimated residual value that is not guaranteed by the lessee or by a third party unrelated to the lessor is known as the ***unguaranteed residual value.***

6 *Fair value of leased property* The normal selling price of the leased property adjusted for any unusual market conditions, when the lessor is a manufacturer or dealer. When the lessor is not a manufacturer or dealer, the cost or carrying amount of the property and the fair value should be the same at the inception of a lease, unless substantial time has passed since the lessor acquired the property.

2 Adapted from CICA, ***CICA Handbook***, sec. 3065.03.

7 *Inception of lease* Date of the lease contract (or commitment, if earlier).

8 *Lessee's rate for incremental borrowing* The rate that, at the inception of the lease, the lessee would have incurred to borrow funds necessary to acquire the leased property.

9 *Initial direct costs* The costs (such as commissions, legal fees, and costs of processing documents) incurred by a lessor that are directly associated with negotiating and completing a lease contract.

10 *Interest rate implicit in the lease (lessor's implicit interest rate)* The discount rate (applied to the minimum lease payments and any ***unguaranteed residual value***) that causes the aggregate present value to be equal to the fair value of leased property to the lessor, at the inception of the lease.

11 *Lease term* The fixed noncancellable term of a lease plus: (1) any periods covered by bargain renewal options, (2) any periods for which failure to renew a lease places a sufficiently large penalty on the lessee that renewal appears reasonably assured, (3) any periods covered by renewal options during which a guarantee by the lessee of the lessor's debt related to leased property is expected to be in effect, (4) any periods covered by renewal options that precede the exercise date of a bargain purchase option, and (5) any periods during which the lessor has a right to renew or extend a lease. However, in no case does the lease term, by this definition, extend beyond the date on which a bargain purchase option becomes exercisable. Also, a lease term is not considered cancelled if cancellation is possible only when an unlikely contingency occurs or with permission of the lessor, or when a new lease is signed by the same lessee and lessor for the same or equivalent property, or when the penalty to the lessee for cancellation is sufficiently large that the continuation of the lease appears reasonably assured, at the inception date.

12 *Minimum lease payments* The payments that the ***lessee*** is obligated to make or may be required to make. Such payments include: (1) the minimum periodic rentals up to the date of a bargain purchase option, (2) any ***guarantee by the lessee, or by a third party related to the lessee, of residual value***, (3) any payment on failure to renew or extend a lease, and (4) the payment required by a purchase option, in which case the total of (1) above and the payment for the bargain purchase option will comprise the minimum rental payments. Executory costs (such as for insurance, maintenance, and property taxes in connection with the leased property) are excluded from minimum lease payments.

As far as the ***lessor*** is concerned, minimum lease payments comprise: (1) the minimum lease payments for the lessee as per the above and (2) any additional rent payments or residual value guaranteed by a third party unrelated to the lessee or to the lessor.

13 *Operating lease* A lease in which the lessor does not transfer substantially all the risks and benefits incident to ownership. This term is used by ***both the lessor and the lessee***.

14 *Capital lease* A term used by the ***lessee*** for a lease that transfers to the lessee substantially all of the risks and benefits incident to ownership. A capital lease should be accounted for by the lessee as the acquisition of an asset and the incurrence of an obligation.

15 *Sales-type lease* A term used by the ***lessor*** for a lease in which the lessor, at the inception of the lease, transfers substantially all of the risks and benefits incident to ownership to the lessee at a fair value either ***higher*** or ***lower*** than the carrying value of the leased property. At the inception of a sales-type lease, a profit or loss is recorded by the lessor.

16 *Direct financing lease* A term used by the ***lessor*** for a lease in which the lessor at the inception of the lease transfers substantially all of the risks and benefits incident to ownership to the lessee at a fair value ***equal*** to the carrying value of the leased property. A direct financing lease results in no profit or loss since the fair value of the lease equals its carrying value.

17 *Renewal or extension of lease* The continuation of a lease contract beyond the original lease term. This idea includes the case of a new lease for the same property with the same lessee.

As a consequence of the facts referred to in definitions **14**, **15**, and **16**, section 3065 of the ***CICA Handbook*** states:

> A lease that transfers substantially all of the benefits and risks of ownership related to the leased property from the lessor to the lessee should be accounted for as a capital lease by the lessee and as a sales-type or direct financing lease by the lessor.

The term ***unguaranteed residual value*** in definitions **5** and **10** and the term ***guarantee by the lessee of residual value*** in definition **12** warrant further comment. In some leases, the lessee guarantees a stated residual value for the leased property. The purpose of such a guarantee is to assure the lessor that the leased property will be cared for adequately by the lessee and will not be worthless at the end of the lease term. All or part of a guaranteed residual value must be paid to the lessor by the lessee unless the lessor disposes of the leased property at the end of the lease term at an amount equal to or in excess of the guaranteed value.

An unguaranteed residual value is the responsibility of the lessor. In substance, the lessor does not ''sell'' the unguaranteed residual value of the leased property to the lessee. Thus, the lessor accounts for the unguaranteed residual value as part of the ***gross investment in the lease***, as illustrated in subsequent sections of this chapter.

ACCOUNTING BY LESSEES

Leases are classified for accounting purposes by lessees as either capital leases or operating leases. ***Capital leases*** have characteristics of an acquisition, and ***operating leases*** cover the use of an asset for a portion of its economic life. The concept of the capital lease is derived from the view that a lease that transfers to the lessee most of the risks and benefits of property ownership should be accounted for by the lessee as the acquisition of an asset and the incurrence of a liability. Thus, the ***economic substance*** of the leasing transaction is given greater weight than its ***legal form***.

Criteria for Capital Lease

If a lease meets any ***one*** of the following criteria at its inception, it must be capitalized by the lessee:[3]

1 There is reasonable assurance that the lessee will obtain ownership of the leased property by the end of the lease term, or the lease contains a bargain purchase option.

2 The lease term is equal to a major portion (usually 75% or more) of the economic life of the leased property.

3 The present value of the minimum lease payments, excluding executory costs, is equal to substantially all (usually 90% or more) of the fair value of the leased property.

To compute the present value of the minimum lease payments, the lessee enterprise uses its incremental borrowing rate, unless ***a*** the lessee can learn the lessor's implicit interest rate, and ***b*** the lessor's implicit interest rate is less than the lessee's incremental borrowing rate. If both these conditions are met, the lessee uses the lessor's implicit interest rate.

Computation of Amount Capitalized by Lessee

The lessee records a capital lease as both an asset and an obligation in an amount equal to the present value of the minimum lease payments during the lease term. However, if the computed present value exceeds the fair value of the leased asset at the inception of the lease, the ***amount capitalized is the fair value of the asset***. A leased asset should never be capitalized at an amount in excess of its fair value at the inception of the lease. The lease payments capitalized exclude any executory costs such as property taxes, insurance, and maintenance, which are expensed by the lessee. If the capital lease transfers ownership of the asset to the lessee or if the lease contains a bargain purchase option, the leased asset is amortized over its economic life in the same manner as other assets owned by the lessee.[4] Assets under other capital leases also are amortized, but over the lease term. At the end of the lease term, an amount equal to any residual value to the ***lessee*** (because the lessee acquired ownership of the leased property) remains in the leased asset ledger account.

Periodic payments other than contingent rentals made by the lessee are allocated between a reduction of the lease obligation and interest expense. This

3 Adapted from CICA, ***CICA Handbook***, sec. 3065.06.

4 The terms ***amortize*** and ***amortization*** are used interchangeably with ***depreciated*** and ***depreciation*** in practice. However, ***amortize*** and ***amortization*** are the terms used in section 3065 of the ***CICA Handbook***.

allocation produces a constant periodic rate of interest expense on the carrying amount of the lease obligation. Contingent rentals are included in the lessee's expenses as they accrue. Assets and obligations recorded under capital leases are reported as separate items in the lessee's balance sheet, and the obligations are segregated between current and noncurrent amounts.

Illustration of Lessee's Accounting for a Capital Lease

Data for Illustration

On January 2, Year 1, Lee Limited, the lessee, entered into an equipment lease with Lore Corporation, the lessor, having the following provisions:

1. The lease has a fixed noncancellable term of 30 months, with rent of $270, exclusive of executory costs, payable at the beginning of each month, starting January 2, Year 1. There are no contingent rental provisions.
2. The lessee guarantees a residual value of $4,000 at the end of 30 months, when the equipment is returned to Lore Corporation.
3. The lessee pays executory costs separately to the lessor, and is to receive any excess of selling price of the equipment over the guaranteed residual value at the end of the lease term.
4. The lease is renewable periodically based on a schedule of rentals and guarantees of the residual values, which decrease over time.

Other relevant information is as follows:

1. Lore Corporation's interest rate implicit in the lease is 12% a year (1% a month); Lore has informed Lee Limited of this rate. Lee's incremental borrowing rate is 15% a year (1¼% a month).
2. The lessor's cost of the leased equipment is $10,200; this is also the lessor's fair value at the inception of the lease, January 2, Year 1.
3. The economic life of the equipment is 60 months; the lessee depreciates owned equipment on a straight-line basis.
4. The residual value at the end of the lease term is estimated to be $4,000, the amount guaranteed by the lessee.
5. On July 2, Year 3, the end of the lease term, the equipment was sold by the lessor for $4,200 to an independent third party. The lessor paid the lessee the $200 excess ($4,200 − $4,000 = $200) of the proceeds over the guaranteed residual value.
6. The fiscal years for the lessee and the lessor end on December 31.

Computations and Classification of the Lease

The minimum lease payments for the lessee are computed as shown in the next table.

Minimum lease payments by lessee

Minimum rental payments over the lease term ($270 × 30)	$ 8,100
Add: Lessee's guarantee of the residual value at end of lease term	4,000
Total minimum lease payments	$12,100

The lease ***does not meet*** the first two criteria on page 983: the lease does not transfer ownership to the lessee by the end of the lease term or contain a bargain purchase option; and the lease term (30 months) is not equal to 75% or more of the estimated economic life of the equipment (60 months). However, the third criterion ***is*** met.

The present value of the minimum lease payments, computed with the lessor's implicit interest rate (because it is less than the lessee's incremental borrowing rate and is known to the lessee), exceeds 90% of the fair value of the equipment at the inception of the lease. Thus, the ***lessee classifies the lease as a capital lease***. The present-value computations by the lessee, using the lessor's implicit interest rate of 1% a month because it is ***known to the lessee and is less than the lessee's incremental borrowing rate***, are shown below:

Computation of present value of minimum lease payments: Lee Limited (lessee) lease with Lore Corporation (lessor)

Monthly lease rentals ($270 × present value of annuity due of 30 rents of 1 at 1% = $270 × 26.065785*)	$ 7,038
Add: Residual value guaranteed by lessee ($4,000 × present value of 1 discounted for 30 periods at 1% = $4,000 × 0.741923*)	2,968
Total present value of minimum lease payments	$10,006
Fair value (cost) of equipment at inception of lease	$10,200
Present value of minimum lease payments as a percentage of fair value of equipment ($10,006 ÷ $10,200)	98%

*See Appendix at end of Chapter 5.

Journal Entries of Lessee

The journal entries for Lee Limited (lessee) for the first two monthly payments, amortization expense at the end of the first year, and the disposal of the leased equipment by the lessor at the end of the lease term (July 2, Year 3) are illustrated below. The related ledger accounts (except Cash), showing all journal entries for the lease during Year 1, appear on pages 986 and 987. (The lessor records this lease as a ***direct financing lease***, which is discussed on pages 1003–1007.)

Lessee's journal entries for capital lease

LEE LIMITED (Lessee)
Journal Entries

Year 1			
Jan. 2	Leased Equipment—Capital Lease	10,006	
	Obligation Under Capital Lease		10,006
	To record capital lease at inception of lease.		
2	Obligation Under Capital Lease	270	
	Cash		270
	To record lease payment for first month.		

Feb. 2	Interest Expense [($10,006 − $270) × 0.01]	97	
	Obligation Under Capital Lease ($270 − $97)	173	
	Cash		270
	To record lease payment for second month.		
Dec. 31	Amortization Expense [($10,006 − $4,000) × 12/30] ..	2,402	
	Leased Equipment—Capital Lease		2,402
	To record amortization expense (straight-line method) for first year of lease. (Thirty-month term of lease is used for amortization expense because the lease does not transfer ownership of the equipment to the lessee and does not contain a bargain purchase option.)		
31	Interest Expense ($7,739 × 0.01)	77	
	Interest Payable		77
	To record accrued interest on lease obligation on Dec. 31, Year 1. (See below for computation of $7,739 balance in Obligation Under Capital Lease ledger account.)		
Year 3			
July 2	Cash	200	
	Obligation Under Capital Lease	4,000	
	Leased Equipment—Capital Lease		4,000
	Gain on Disposal of Leased Equipment		200
	To record lessor's sale of leased equipment at an amount $200 in excess of guaranteed residual value and liquidation of obligation under capital lease.		

Lessee's ledger accounts for capital lease

Leased Equipment—Capital Lease

Date	*Explanation*	*Debit*	*Credit*	*Balance*
Year 1				
Jan. 2	Capital lease at inception.	10,006		10,006 Dr
Dec. 31	Amortization for Year 1.		2,402	7,604 Dr

Obligation Under Capital Lease (Net)

Date	*Explanation*	*Debit*	*Credit*	*Balance*
Year 1				
Jan. 2	Capital lease at inception.		10,006	10,006 Cr
2	First lease payment.	270		9,736 Cr
Feb. 2	($270 − $97 interest.)	173		9,563 Cr
Mar. 2	($270 − $96 interest.)	174		9,389 Cr
Apr. 2	($270 − $94 interest.)	176		9,213 Cr
May 2	($270 − $92 interest.)	178		9,035 Cr
June 2	($270 − $90 interest.)	180		8,855 Cr
July 2	($270 − $89 interest.)	181		8,674 Cr
Aug. 2	($270 − $87 interest.)	183		8,491 Cr
Sept. 2	($270 − $85 interest.)	185		8,306 Cr
Oct. 2	($270 − $83 interest.)	187		8,119 Cr

Nov. 2	($270 − $81 interest.)	189		7,930 Cr
Dec. 2	($270 − $79 interest.)	191		7,739 Cr

In the January 2, Year 1, journal entry to record the lease, the Obligation Under Capital Lease ledger account was credited with the ***present value*** of the minimum lease payments during the lease term. This ***net method*** of accounting by lessees is according to the treatment given such leases in ***Appendix A*** of section 3065 of the ***CICA Handbook***. As an alternative, the Obligation Under Capital Lease account might be credited for the $12,100 total of the minimum lease payments, as follows:

Lessee's journal entry to record capital lease at *gross amount*

Year 1			
Jan. 2	Leased Equipment—Capital Lease	10,006	
	Discount on Liability Under Capital Lease	2,094	
	Liability Under Capital Lease (gross)		12,100
	To record capital lease at inception of lease.		

This ***gross method*** is consistent with the accounting for deferred payment contracts illustrated in Chapter 11 (page 516). If the lease obligation were recorded in this manner, the journal entry for the ***second month's*** lease payment would be as shown on page 988.

Interest Payable

Date	*Explanation*	*Debit*	*Credit*	*Balance*
Year 1				
Dec. 31	Accrued interest for Dec.		77	77 Cr

Amortization Expense

Date	*Explanation*	*Debit*	*Credit*	*Balance*
Year 1				
Dec. 31	[($10,006 − $4,000) × 12/30.]	2,402		2,402 Dr

Interest Expense

Date	*Explanation*	*Debit*	*Credit*	*Balance*
Year 1				
Feb. 2	($9,736 × 0.01.)	97		97 Dr
Mar. 2	($9,563 × 0.01.)	96		193 Dr
Apr. 2	($9,389 × 0.01.)	94		287 Dr
May 2	($9,213 × 0.01.)	92		379 Dr
June 2	($9,035 × 0.01.)	90		469 Dr
July 2	($8,855 × 0.01.)	89		558 Dr
Aug. 2	($8,674 × 0.01.)	87		645 Dr
Sept. 2	($8,491 × 0.01.)	85		730 Dr
Oct. 2	($8,306 × 0.01.)	83		813 Dr
Nov. 2	($8,119 × 0.01.)	81		894 Dr
Dec. 2	($7,930 × 0.01.)	79		973 Dr
31	($7,739 × 0.01.)	77		1,050 Dr

Lessee's journal entry to record lease payment under the *gross* method

Year 1			
Jan. 2	Interest Expense	97	
	Obligation Under Capital Lease (gross)	270	
	Discount on Obligation Under Capital Lease		97
	Cash		270
	To record lease payment for second month.		

The credit to the Leased Equipment — Capital Lease ledger account in the December 31, Year 1, journal entry for amortization is in accordance with the illustrations in section 3065 of the ***CICA Handbook***. Alternatively, an Accumulated Depreciation (Amortization) ledger account might be used, as for owned equipment.

Had the lessee elected on July 2, Year 3, to renew the lease, the renewal would be treated as a new lease extending to the date of the next renewal option. The lessee would compare the present value of the minimum lease payments (rent and guarantee of any residual value) over the renewal period with the $4,000 fair value of the equipment to the lessor at the inception of the new lease. Although the fair value of the equipment on July 2, Year 3, is $4,200, the proceeds from sale of the equipment, the value accruing to the lessor is limited to $4,000, the amount guaranteed by the lessee.

Lessee's Accounting for Operating Leases

Leases that do not qualify as capital leases are accounted for as ***operating leases*** by the lessee; that is, the lease is ***not capitalized***, and periodic lease payments usually are recorded by debits to the Rent Expense ledger account. If an operating lease requires rent to be paid other than in equal periodic amounts, Rent Expense is debited on a straight-line basis unless another method is considered to be more representative of the benefits derived from use of the leased property.[5] Executory costs under operating leases are recognized as expenses in the period incurred, as they are for capital leases.

Sale-Leaseback Transactions

In certain cases an owner of an asset sells it and immediately leases it back from the purchaser. Such ***sale-leaseback transactions*** give lessees use of assets without a large investment of capital and provide lessors with profitable investments. The lease should be accounted for as a capital, direct-financing, or operating lease, depending on the particular circumstances.[6]

Because the sale of the asset and the leaseback represent in effect a single transaction, neither the selling price of the asset nor the periodic rental payments can be evaluated separately from the other. Consequently, the ***CICA Handbook*** recommends that, for a capital lease, any profits on the sale be amortized in proportion to the amortization of the leased asset and, for an operating lease, in

5 CICA, ***CICA Handbook***, sec. 3065.30.

6 CICA, ***CICA Handbook***, sec. 3065.66.

proportion to the rental payments of the operating lease. Any ''profit or loss'' arising on the sale of land should be deferred and amortized by the straight-line method over the term of the lease. However, if at the inception of the sale-leaseback transaction, the fair value of the leased asset is ''less'' than its carrying value, the difference will be recorded as a loss at that time.[7]

To illustrate the accounting for a sale-leaseback transaction, assume that on May 1, Year 1, Cree Limited sold land and a building for $1,540,000, and immediately leased the property from its owner on a 10-year ***operating*** lease for monthly rent of $15,000, beginning May 1, Year 1. On that date, the carrying amounts of the land and building in Cree's accounting records were $400,000 and $900,000 respectively, and the building had a remaining economic life of 15 years. Accumulated depreciation on the building totalled $300,000 on May 1, Year 1.

Journal entries for Cree Limited for the sale-leaseback transaction are as follows for the first month:

Lessee's journal entries for sale-leaseback transaction (operating lease)

CREE LIMITED
Journal Entries

Year 1				
May 1	Cash		1,540,000	
	Accumulated Depreciation of Building		300,000	
	Land			400,000
	Building ($900,000 + $300,000)			1,200,000
	Deferred Gain on Disposal of Plant Assets			240,000
	To record sale of land and building, and deferral of gain for amortization over term of related operating lease. Deferred gain is computed as follows:			
	Proceeds on sale	$1,540,000		
	Less: Carrying amount of land and building ($400,000 + $900,000)	1,300,000		
	Deferred gain	$ 240,000		
1	Rent Expense ($15,000 − $2,000)		13,000	
	Deferred Gain on Disposal of Plant Assets ($240,000 ÷ 120)		2,000	
	Cash			15,000
	To record payment of first month's rent of land and building under operating lease, and amortization of deferred gain over the lease term.			

The journal entry to record the payment of each month's rent is the same during the lease term. As a result of the deferral of the gain and its amortization over the lease term, total rent expense over the 10-year lease term is $1,560,000, computed as follows:

7 CICA, ***CICA Handbook***, sec. 3065.66, .68–.70.

Total rent expense over the lease term

Gross rent payments over the lease term ($15,000 × 120)	$1,800,000
Less: Deferred gain amortized over the lease term	240,000
Total rent expense over the lease term ($13,000 × 120)	$1,560,000

Assume the lease was a ***capital*** lease, and that the profit of $240,000 represented $90,000 on the land and $150,000 on the building which was to be amortized at 5% of $1,200,000 (original cost) = $60,000 per year. Cree's year-end is April 30th. The journal entry for the first year-end with respect to the amortization of the deferred gain would be as follows:

Lessee's journal entries for amortization of the deferred gain on disposal of plant assets (capital lease)

CREE LIMITED
Amortization Journal Entries

Year 2			
Apr. 30	Deferred Gain on Disposal of Plant Assets	16,000	
	Gain on Sale of Land		6,000
	Depreciation Expense (or Gain on Sale of Building)		10,000
	To record amortization of land as $6,000 ($\frac{1}{15}$ × $90,000) and of building as $10,000 ($\frac{\$60,000}{\$900,000}$ × $150,000).		

Disclosure of Leases in Financial Statements of Lessee

The ***CICA Handbook*** recommends disclosure of the following information with respect to ***capital leases*** in the lessee's financial statements or in the notes thereto:[8]

a The gross amount of capital leases together with related accumulated amortization.

b Obligations for leased assets, separated from other obligations, together with the interest rates, expiration dates and any significant restrictions imposed on the lessee because of lease agreements.

c The current and long-term portions of the lease obligations with the current portion included in current liabilities.

d Future minimum lease payments in the aggregate and for each of the next five years. Executory costs and imputed interest should be deducted from the above aggregate amount so as to arrive at the balance of the unpaid obligation.

e Methods and rates of amortization. The amount of amortization should either be disclosed separately or included in depreciation and amortization expense for fixed assets.

f The interest expense on lease obligations shown either as part of interest on long-term debt or separately.

8 CICA, ***CICA Handbook***, sec. 3065.21–.26.

The *Handbook* suggests it may be "desirable" to disclose the following information in the lessee's financial statements or in the notes thereto, with respect to capital leases:[9] (1) the major categories of leased assets including their accumulated amortization, (2) the existence of and terms of renewal for leases and purchase options that are not included in the amount for minimum lease payments, and (3) the amount of and basis for determination of contingent rentals included in net income. Finally, disclosure of the amount of future minimum rentals receivable from noncancellable sub-leases would be desirable.

Examples of ***capital leases*** note disclosures to the financial statements of Canadian corporations are illustrated on pages 992–996.

The ***Handbook*** recommends that the following information with respect to ***operating leases*** be disclosed in the ***lessee's*** financial statements or in the notes thereto:[10]

a Future minimum lease payments in the aggregate and for each of the next five years.

b A description of other commitments under operating leases.

Operating leases with an initial term of one year or less may be excluded from the above disclosure requirements.

The ***CICA Handbook*** also suggests that it is desirable to disclose the following additional information for operating leases of lessees.[11]

> . . . the amount thereof in income, the method used to determine contingent rentals, the type of property leased and its remaining lease term, as well as the existence and terms of renewal options. . . . to segregate minimum rentals, contingent rentals and sub-lease revenue.

Examples of ***lessee operating leases*** note disclosures in the financial statements of Canadian corporations are shown in note 8 on page 993 and note 6 on page 995.

9 CICA, ***CICA Handbook***, sec. 3065.21–22, .27–.28.

10 CICA, ***CICA Handbook***, sec. 3065.32.

11 CICA, ***CICA Handbook***, sec. 3065.33.

The Molson Companies Limited

Annual Report 1985

7. FIXED ASSETS

	1985	1984
Land	**$ 32,404**	$ 34,323
Buildings	**217,233**	213,001
Equipment (1)	**440,893**	391,918
	690,530	639,242
Less: Accumulated depreciation (1)	**283,618**	261,400
	$406,912	$377,842

(1) Includes capital leases of $13,687 and related accumulated depreciation of $8,613 (1984—$13,716 and related accumulated depreciation of $7,254).

8. LONG-TERM DEBT

Lease obligations

The following table represents minimum rental payments due on all lease commitments. Properties leased include warehouses, retail stores and sports arenas.

Fiscal year	Capital leases	Operating leases (1)	Total
1986	$3,127	$ 10,949	$ 14,076
1987	2,348	7,924	10,272
1988	1,272	7,106	8,378
1989	638	6,132	6,770
1990	267	9,183	9,450
Thereafter	2,007	85,877	87,884
Total minimum rental payments	9,659	$127,171	$136,830
Less: Imputed interest	3,054		
Obligations under capital leases	$6,605		

(1) Certain leases entered into prior to April 1, 1979, and accounted for as operating leases, have the characteristics of capital leases. If these leases had been accounted for as capital leases, fixed assets and long-term debt would have increased by $39,590 (1984—$49,633) and $44,057 (1984—$55,232) respectively. The effect on net earnings would not be significant.

Imasco Limited
For the years ended March 31
All tabular figures are in thousands of dollars.

Notes to the Consolidated Financial Statements		1987	1986	1985
4. Fixed assets	Land	**101,496**	93,046	90,257
	Buildings	**299,262**	275,701	254,709
	Equipment	**677,002**	622,301	542,574
	Leasehold improvements	**392,282**	348,160	314,214
	Property under capital leases	**35,051**	40,135	41,610
		1,505,093	1,379,343	1,243,364
	Accumulated depreciation and amortization	**534,330**	457,837	375,746
	Net fixed assets	**970,763**	921,506	867,618

Depreciation and amortization expense on fixed assets excluding property under capital leases amounted to $123,650,000 (1968 – $116,394,000; 1985 – $93,161,000). Amortization expense on property under capital leases amounted to $2,352,000 (1986 – $2,440,000; 1985 – $2,287,000). Accumulated amortization on property under capital leases amounted to $22,565,000 (1986 – $23,735,000; 1985 – $22,406,000).

8. Operating lease commitments

The Corporation has commitments with respect to real estate operating leases, most of which are for terms of three to 20 years. The minimum annual commitments under such leases are approximately as follows:

	Rental commitment	Assumed by associates	Net rental commitment
1988	121,842	48,389	73,453
1989	116,302	46,332	69,970
1990	107,791	41,582	66,209
1991	99,149	36,923	62,226
1992	90,140	33,614	56,526

The minimum annual rental commitments as listed above do not give effect to escalation and percentage-of-sales clauses in certain of the leases. Net rentals under leases, including escalation and percentage-of-sales payments, amounted to $110,393,000 in 1987 (1986 – $101,102,000; 1985 – $77,302,000). In addition, the Corporation has operating lease commitments for equipment which are for terms of one to six years, with an annual rental of approximately $19,172,000.

9. Capital lease commitments

The Corporation has commitments with respect to property in the Restaurant and Drug Store segments recorded under capital leases expiring on various dates through the year 2007. The minimum annual commitments under such leases are approximately as follows:

1988	6,295
1989	6,090
1990	5,787
1991	5,291
1992	4,705
1993 and thereafter	12,450
Total minimum commitments	40,618
Imputed interest at 12.3%	(16,587)
Payments due within one year	(2,566)
Long term obligations under capital leases	**21,465**

Silcorp Limited

Annual Report for the Year Ended December 28, 1986

NOTES TO THE CONSOLIDATED FINANCIAL STATEMENTS

Year ended December 28, 1986
(Tabular amounts in $000's except for Notes 5 and 7)

1. Fixed assets

	1986	1985	1984
Land	**$ 879**	$ 988	$ 1,692
Buildings	**5,058**	4,943	6,221
Machinery and equipment	**9,732**	7,603	7,764
Merchandising equipment	**73,801**	63,229	49,834
Leasehold improvements	**24,479**	21,635	15,982
	113,949	98,398	81,493
Less accumulated depreciation and amortization	**45,972**	37,442	31,102
Net book value	**$67,977**	$60,956	$50,391

Included in the net book value of fixed assets are assets under capital lease amounting to $232,000 for 1986, $3,149,000 for 1985, and $3,830,000 for 1984.

3. Long-term debt and capital lease obligations

	1986	1985	1984
Capital lease obligations	**$222**	$3,852	$4,485
Less portion due within one year included in current liabilities	**108**	537	639
	$114	$3,315	$3,846

6. Operating lease agreements and commitments

(a) Operating lease agreements

Silcorp Limited and its subsidiary companies have entered into agreements to lease equipment and properties for various periods up to 2005. Certain of the leases provide for additional rent based on sales. Minimum annual net rental commitments for non-cancellable leases in effect at December 28, 1986 are as follows:

Year ended	Amount
December 27, 1987	$33,203
December 25, 1988	31,643
December 24, 1989	29,253
December 23, 1990	26,538
December 29, 1991	22,179

Net lease commitments to year 2005 aggregating $205.9 million have been reduced by payments totalling $22.4 million for which the Corporation is to be reimbursed by franchisees who are subtenants of the Corporation.

George Weston Limited

Annual Report 1986

Notes to Consolidated Financial Statements

December 31, 1986
(Narrative and Tabular amounts in millions of dollars except Share Capital note)

5. Leases

The Company and its subsidiaries have obligations under long term leases for retail outlets, warehouse facilities and equipment. Net long term lease expense for 1986 was $53.2 (1985—$53.5). Property under capital leases entered into after December 31, 1978 is:

	1986	1985	1984
Buildings	**$ 75.0**	$ 66.6	$ 60.5
Equipment	**37.6**	49.8	52.5
	112.6	116.4	113.0
Accumulated depreciation	**49.4**	52.6	46.4
	$ 63.2	$ 63.8	$ 66.6

A retroactive application of capitalization of leases entered into before January 1, 1979 would increase assets by $47.6 (1985—$60.4, 1984—$67.9) and obligations by $75.3 (1985 — $90.7, 1984 — $97.8).

Minimum lease commitments together with the present value of the obligations under capital leases entered into after December 31, 1978 are:

For the year	Capital leases entered into after December 31, 1978	Other leases		
		Gross liability	Expected sublease income	Expected net liability
1987	$17.4	$ 86.8	$ 24.3	$ 62.5
1988	14.2	79.3	21.2	58.1
1989	11.3	73.0	17.9	55.1
1990	10.9	65.9	15.5	50.4
1991	20.6	57.0	13.1	43.9
Thereafter to 2023	88.3	302.4	60.1	242.3
Total minimum lease payments	162.7	$664.4	$152.1	$512.3
Less interest at a weighted average rate of 13.4%	83.0			
Balance of obligations	79.7			
Less current portion	7.5			
Long term obligations	$ 72.2			

ACCOUNTING BY LESSORS

Leases are classified for accounting purposes by lessors as ***sales-type leases, direct financing leases***, or ***operating leases.*** Normally, sales-type leases arise when manufacturers or dealers use leasing as a means of marketing their products. Such leases give rise to a profit (or loss) to the lessor at the inception of the lease. Leases that do not give rise to a profit (or loss) to the lessor at the inception of the lease, but otherwise qualify as sales-type leases, are treated as ***direct financing leases*** by lessors. Such leases are typically financing arrangements by lessor enterprises that are not involved in the direct sale of the assets leased. In direct financing leases, the carrying amount and the fair value of the leased property are the same at the inception of the lease. If such a lease is renewed or extended, and at the renewal or extension date the carrying amount of the property does not equal the fair value, it would not be precluded from classification as a direct financing lease for the new lease term.

Sales-type leases and direct financing leases must meet ***one*** of the criteria for a capital lease (see page 983 under "Accounting by Lessees") ***and*** the following ***two additional criteria:***[12]

(b) the credit risk associated with the lease is normal when compared to the risk of collection of similar receivables; and

(c) the amounts of any unreimbursable costs that are likely to be incurred by the lessor under the lease can be reasonably estimated. If such costs are not reasonably estimable, the lessor may retain substantial risks in connection with the

12 CICA, *CICA Handbook*, sec. 3065.07.

leased property. This may occur, for example, when the lessor has a commitment to guarantee the performance of, or to effectively protect the lessee from obsolescence of, the leased property.

Leases that are not sales-type or direct financing leases are accounted for by lessors as ***operating leases***.

Sales-Type Leases

Because sales-type leases are used by manufacturers or dealers to market their products, they resemble sales of products in exchange for long-term promissory notes. Thus, the accounting for sales-type leases is similar to the accounting for a sale of merchandise under the perpetual inventory system. For example, a sale in exchange for a note receivable bearing a fair rate of interest is recorded with a debit to Notes Receivable and a credit to Sales for the face amount of the note (and selling price of the product), and a debit to Cost of Goods Sold and a credit to Inventories for the cost of the product.

The comparable journal entries for a sales-type lease are complicated by three features not found in the typical sale of merchandise in exchange for a promissory note. One feature that is always present in a sales-type lease is the interest implicit in the minimum lease payments, which are receivable by the lessor over an extended period. Two other possible features of a sales-type lease transaction are an ***unguaranteed*** residual value (a ***guaranteed*** residual value is a component of minimum lease payments) and ***initial direct costs***, such as commissions, legal fees, and document processing costs incurred by the lessor in negotiating and completing the lease contract.

To illustrate the journal entries for a sales-type lease that includes the foregoing features, we provide the following schematic:

Elements of the accounting for a sales-type lease

	Debit	Credit
Lease Receivables	(1)✓	
Cost of Goods Sold	(2)✓	
Unearned Interest Revenue		(3)✓
Sales		(4)✓
Inventories		(5)✓
To record sales-type lease at inception and cost of leased property.		
Cost of Goods Sold	(6)	
Cash		(6)
To record payment of initial direct costs incurred under sales-type lease.		

(1) ***Gross investment in the lease:*** The total of the minimum lease payments (which includes any ***guaranteed residual value*** of the property but excludes any ***executory costs***), plus any ***unguaranteed residual value***
(2) Cost (or carrying amount) of leased property, less present value of any ***unguaranteed residual value*** (which is not "sold" by the lessor)
(3) Gross investment in the lease less the ***net investment in the lease***, which is the present value (at the lessor's implicit rate) of the items comprising the gross investment in the lease
(4) Present value (at the lessor's implicit rate) of the minimum lease payments only (because any ***unguaranteed residual value*** is not "sold" by the lessor)
(5) Cost (or carrying amount) of leased property
(6) Amount of initial direct costs

The key amounts in the foregoing illustration are the ***gross investment in the lease*** and the ***net investment in the lease***. Once these amounts have been computed, completion of the two journal entries at the inception of a sales-type lease that includes initial direct costs is a matter of supplying the amounts for the components of the journal entries. Initial direct costs should be expensed at the inception of the lease as they are considered to be incurred in order to produce the sale.[13] It should be noted that the net investment in the lease (gross investment in the lease less unearned interest revenue) is the amount that appears in the lessor's balance sheet, segregated between current and noncurrent assets. The unearned interest revenue is recognized as interest revenue over the lease term at the lessor's implicit rate under the ***interest method***. Periodic cash receipts from the lease are recorded as credits to Lease Receivables.

Any estimated residual value should be reviewed annually. If a decline in value has occurred which is not temporary, the accounting for the transaction is revised and the resulting reduction in the net investment is recognized as a loss. An upward adjustment of estimated residual value is not made.[14]

The renewal or extension of a sales-type lease, providing the benefits and risks of ownership continue to be substantially transferred to the lessee, would be treated as a direct financing lease. The profit or loss would have been recognized at the inception of the original lease.[15]

Accounting for a Sales-Type Lease Illustrated

To illustrate the accounting for a sales-type lease, assume that on December 31, Year 1, Orr Limited leased equipment (which had a cost of $11,500 and a fair value of $14,000) to LSE, Inc., for four years on the following terms:

1 LSE agreed to make four annual rental payments of $4,000 (excluding executory costs) starting on December 31, Year 1.[16] The economic life of the equipment is six years with an ***unguaranteed*** residual value of $2,500; LSE uses the straight-line method of depreciation.

2 LSE agreed to absorb all maintenance costs, insurance, and property taxes; $800 of initial direct costs were incurred by Orr.

3 LSE was required to return the equipment to Orr at the end of the lease term, December 31, Year 5.

4 Orr's implicit interest rate on December 31, Year 1, for this transaction was 10% a year. LSE had an incremental borrowing rate of 12% a year on December 31, Year 1, and could not obtain sufficient information to determine Orr's implicit interest rate.

There are no abnormal risks associated with the collection of lease payments

13 CICA, ***CICA Handbook***, sec. 3065.47–.48.

14 CICA, ***CICA Handbook***, sec. 3065.49.

15 CICA, ***CICA Handbook***, sec. 3065.50.

16 CICA, ***CICA Handbook***, sec. 3065.13.

from LSE, Inc., and there are no additional unreimbursable costs to be incurred by Orr Limited in connection with the leased machine.

Because the fair value of the equipment ($14,000) exceeds its cost ($11,500); because the present value of the minimum lease payments, $13,947 (see below), is at least 90% of the fair value of the leased property ($14,000 × 0.90 = $12,600); and because of the conditions described in the preceding paragraph, Orr (the lessor) records the lease as a sales-type lease. LSE (the lessee), records the lease as a capital lease because the present value of the minimum lease payments to LSE, $13,607 (see below), meets the 90% of fair value test.

Computation of Lessor's Gross Investment in the Lease

Orr Company's gross investment in the lease with LSE, Inc., is computed as follows:

Computation of lessor's gross investment in sales-type lease

Annual rental payments ($4,000 × 4)	$16,000
Add: Unguaranteed residual value	2,500
Gross investment in lease	$18,500

The computation of the gross investment in the lease provides the amount for the debit to the Lease Receivables ledger account in the journal entry on page 1000.

Computation of Lessor's Net Investment in the Lease

By application of the lessor's implicit rate of 10%, the net investment in the lease is computed below:

Computation of lessor's net investment in sales-type lease

Present value of annual rental payments (minimum lease payments) ($4,000 × 3.486852*)	$13,947
Add: Present value of unguaranteed residual value ($2,500 × 0.683013†)	1,708
Net investment in lease	$15,655

*From Table 4 of Appendix at end of Chapter 5, adjusted for ***annuity due***.
†From Table 2 of Appendix at end of Chapter 5.

The computation of the net investment in the lease provides the remaining amounts necessary to complete the lessor's journal entry at the inception of the lease, as indicated on page 1001.

Computation of Amount to Be Capitalized by Lessee

Because the lessee cannot learn the lessor's implicit interest rate, the lessee uses its incremental borrowing rate, 12% a year, to compute the present value of the minimum lease payments, as follows:

Computation of lessee's present value of minimum lease payments

Present value of annual rental payments (minimum lease payments) ($4,000 × 3.401831*)	$13,607

*From Table 4 of Appendix at end of Chapter 5, adjusted for ***annuity due***.

Journal Entries and Ledger Accounts

The journal entries for both the lessor and the lessee for Years 1 and 2 are presented on page 1001. (The lessee's journal entries are shown for purposes of comparison.) The lessor's ledger accounts for Lease Receivables, Unearned Interest Revenue, and Interest Revenue for the term of the lease are shown below.

Selected ledger accounts of lessor for sales-type lease

Lease Receivables

Date	*Explanation*	*Debit*	*Credit*	*Balance*
Dec. 31/1	Inception of lease.	18,500		18,500 Dr
Dec. 31/1	Receipt of first payment.		4,000	14,500 Dr
Dec. 31/2	Receipt of second payment.		4,000	10,500 Dr
Dec. 31/3	Receipt of third payment.		4,000	6,500 Dr
Dec. 31/4	Receipt of fourth payment.		4,000	2,500 Dr

Unearned Interest Revenue

Date	*Explanation*	*Debit*	*Credit*	*Balance*
Dec. 31/1	Inception of lease ($18,500 – $15,655).		2,845	2,845 Cr
Dec. 31/2	Interest for Year 2 {[($18,500 – $2,845) – $4,000] × 0.10}.	1,166		1,679 Cr
Dec. 31/3	Interest for Year 3 {[($14,500 – $1,679) – $4,000] × 0.10}.	882		797 Cr
Dec. 31/4	Interest for Year 4 {[($10,500 – $797) – $4,000] × 0.10}.	570		227 Cr
Dec. 31/5	Interest for Year 5 {[($6,500 – $227) – $4,000] × 0.10}.	227		–0–

Interest Revenue

Date	*Explanation*	*Debit*	*Credit*	*Balance*
Dec. 31/2	Interest for Year 2.		1,166	1,166 Cr
Dec. 31/2	Closing entry.	1,166		–0–
Dec. 31/3	Interest for Year 3.		882	882 Cr
Dec. 31/3	Closing entry.	882		–0–
Dec. 31/4	Interest for Year 4.		570	570 Cr
Dec. 31/4	Closing entry.	570		–0–
Dec. 31/5	Interest for Year 5.		227	227 Cr
Dec. 31/5	Closing entry.	227		–0–

On December 31, Year 5, the end of the lease term, the lessor's net investment in the lease is $2,500, computed as follows:

Net investment in sales-type lease at end of lease term

Balance of Lease Receivables ledger account	$2,500
Less: Balance of Unearned Interest Revenue ledger account	–0–
Net investment in lease, Dec. 31, Year 5	$2,500

Date	ORR LIMITED (Lessor) Journal Entries (Sales-Type Lease)			LSE, INC. (Lessee) Journal Entries (Capital Lease)		
Year 1 Dec. 31	Lease Receivables	18,500		Leased Equipment—Capital Lease	13,607	
	Cost of Goods Sold ($11,500 − $1,708)	9,792		Obligation Under Capital Lease		13,607
	Unearned Interest Revenue ($18,500 − $15,655)		2,845	To record capital lease at inception. (See page 999 for computation.)		
	Sales		13,947			
	Inventories		11,500			
	To record sales-type lease at inception and cost of leased equipment.					
31	Cost of Goods Sold	800		(No entry.)		
	Cash		800			
	To record payment of initial direct costs incurred under sales-type lease.					
31	Cash	4,000		Obligation Under Capital Lease	4,000	
	Lease Receivables		4,000	Cash		4,000
	To record receipt of first lease payment.			To record lease payment for first year.		
Year 2 Dec. 31	Cash	4,000		Interest Expense [($13,607 − $4,000) × 0.12].	1,153	
	Unearned Interest Revenue [($18,500 − $2,845) − $4,000] × 0.10	1,166		Obligation Under Capital Lease ($4,000 − $1,153)	2,847	
	Lease Receivables		4,000	Cash		4,000
	Interest Revenue		1,166	To record lease payment for second year.		
	To record receipt of second lease payment, and interest earned during Year 2.			Amortization Expense ($13,607 ÷ 4)	3,402	
				Leased Equipment—Capital Lease		3,402
				To record amortization expense (straight-line method) for first year of lease. Four-year term of the lease is used because the lease does not contain a bargain purchase option and does not transfer ownership of the leased property to the lessee.		

The $2,500 is the ***unguaranteed residual value*** that was estimated at the inception of the lease. Had the estimate of the unguaranteed residual value been found to be excessive as a result of periodic reviews during the lease term, a loss would have been recognized by the lessor and the Lease Receivables account would have been credited for the amount of the loss in the period in which the loss was so determined. (An ***upward*** revision of unguaranteed residual value is not made during the lease term; to do so would result in the recognition of an unrealized gain.) Only if the lessor sells the leased property for more than $2,500 at the end of the lease term is a realized gain recognized.

Termination of Sales-Type Lease

If a sales-type lease was to be terminated before the end of the lease term by mutual consent without penalty, the lessee would recognize a gain or a loss. For example, assume that the lease in the foregoing illustration is terminated on December 31, Year 3 (the end of the second year of the lease term), prior to the rental payment due on the date and prior to the recognition of interest expense and depreciation expense for Year 3. The journal entry to record the termination in the accounting records of LSE (the lessee) is as follows:

Lessee's journal entry for termination of capital lease

Interest Expense [($13,607 – $6,847) × 0.12]	811	
Liability Under Capital Lease (net) ($13,607 – $6,847)	6,760	
Depreciation Expense ($13,607 ÷ 4)	3,402	
Gain on Termination of Capital Lease		768
Leased Equipment—Capital Lease ($13,607 – $3,402)		10,205
To record termination of capital lease through mutual consent and depreciation and interest expense for second year of lease.		

The gain recognized by the lessee on termination of the lease results from the lessee's having extinguished a lease liability with a carrying amount of $7,571, including accrued interest ($6,760 + $811 = $7,571) by returning to the lessor the leased equipment with a carrying amount of $6,803 ($10,205 – $3,402 = $6,803). The difference between the two amounts is the $768 realized gain ($7,571 – $6,803 = $768).

On termination of the sales-type lease, the lessor would record the equipment at the ***lowest*** of its original cost, its present fair value, and its present carrying amount,[17] and would recognize any loss represented by the difference from the net investment in the terminated lease. The lessor would not recognize a gain on an early termination of a lease, because the gain would not have been realized.

Sales-Type Lease with Guaranteed Residual Value

A sales-type lease having a ***guaranteed residual value*** requires a slightly different journal entry at the inception of the lease because the guaranteed residual value is part of the ***minimum lease payments***, rather than a separate item, in the computation of the gross investment and the net investment in the lease. For example, if the Orr Limited–LSE, Inc., lease described on page 998 had provided for a

17 CICA, ***CICA Handbook***, sec. 3065.13.

guaranteed, rather than an ***unguaranteed***, residual value of $2,500, the journal entry on December 31, Year 1, for Orr (the lessor) would have been as follows:

Journal entry for sales-type lease with *guaranteed* residual value

Lease Receivables	18,500	
Cost of Goods Sold	11,500	
Unearned Interest Revenue		2,845
Sales		15,655
Inventories		11,500
To record sales-type lease at inception and cost of leased equipment.		

In the foregoing journal entry, both cost of goods sold and sales are $1,708 larger than in the journal entry on page 1001 under the unguaranteed residual value illustration ($11,500 – $9,792 = $1,708; $15,655 – $13,947 = $1,708). The $1,708 difference is the present value of the residual value ($2,500 × 0.683013 = $1,708) which is ***considered to have been sold by the lessor*** to the lessee when it is guaranteed by the lessee under a sales-type lease.

In sales-type leases in which the lessee guarantees a minimum residual value of the property at the end of the lease term, or in which there is a penalty for failure to renew, the lessor's lease receivables at the end of the lease term will be equal to the amount of the guarantee or penalty that becomes effective that date. At the termination of the existing term of a lease being renewed, the net investment in the lease is adjusted to the fair value of the leased property to the lessor on that date, and the net adjustment is debited or credited to Unearned Interest Revenue, which is recognized as interest revenue over the renewal term.

Direct Financing Leases

In direct financing leases, the gross investment in the lease is computed in the same way as for sales-type leases, but the net investment in the lease equals the difference between the gross investment in the lease and the unearned interest revenue. Unearned interest revenue is the difference between the gross investment in the lease and the cost or carrying amount of the leased property. ***Any initial direct costs are expensed, and an equal portion of the unearned interest revenue is recognized as interest revenue in the same accounting period.***[18] The net investment in the lease currently recoverable is classified as a current asset, and any contingent rentals are recognized as revenue when such rentals become receivable.

In direct financing leases containing a residual value guarantee or a penalty for failure to renew, the lessor follows the same procedure as that described for sales-type leases. Similarly, any estimated unguaranteed residual value should be reviewed periodically and, if necessary, adjusted as described for sales-type leases. Because the lessor in a direct financing lease is not selling a product, Sales and Cost of Goods Sold ledger accounts are not used.

18 CICA, *CICA Handbook*, sec. 3065.40.

Illustration of Accounting for a Direct Financing Lease with Initial Direct Costs To illustrate the accounting for a direct financing lease with initial direct costs, assume that on July 31, Year 1, Lessor Corporation leased to Lessee Limited equipment with a cost and fair value of $11,127. The initial direct costs incurred by the lessor were $200. The lease was for seven years at an annual rent (excluding executory costs) of $2,000 payable at the beginning of each year. The economic life of the equipment was nine years, and the estimated ***unguaranteed*** residual value at the end of seven years was $1,200. Lessee uses the straight-line method of amortization. Lease payments were determined at an amount that will give Lessor a 10% annual rate of return on its net investment in the lease, including initial direct costs of $200.

Lessee Limited knows Lessor Corporation's 10% implicit interest rate, which is less than Lessee's 13% incremental borrowing rate. Lessee agreed to pay all executory costs; the risk associated with the collection of rental payments from Lessee Limited is normal when compared with the collection risks associated with similar receivables, and there are no significant future unreimbursable costs to be incurred by Lessor Corporation in connection with the leased equipment. The lessor uses an Equipment Held for Lease ledger account.

This lease meets the criteria for classification as a sales-type lease, ***but because there is no element of profit at the inception of the lease,*** it is recorded as a ***direct financing lease*** by Lessor Corporation and a ***capital lease*** by Lessee Limited. This accounting treatment is appropriate because: (1) the lease term exceeds 75% of the economic life of the equipment (7 ÷ 9 = 0.778); (2) the present value of the minimum lease payments ($2,000 × 5.355261[19] = $10,711) is more than 90% of the fair value of the equipment at the inception of the lease ($11,127 × 0.90 = $10.014); (3) the risks of collectibility are normal and future unreimbursable costs are estimated to be negligible; and (4) there is no element of realized profit at the inception of the lease.

The gross investment in the lease, unearned interest revenue, and the net investment in the lease are computed for the lessor as follows:

Computation of gross investment, unearned interest, and net investment in direct financing lease

Gross investment in lease [($2,000 minimum lease payments × 7) + $1,200 unguaranteed residual value]	$15,200
Unearned interest revenue ($15,200 gross investment in lease − $11,127 cost of leased equipment)	$ 4,073
Net investment in lease ($15,200 gross investment in lease − $4,073 unearned interest revenue)	$11,127

Because the lessee does not obtain rights to the equipment at the end of the lease term and the residual value of the equipment is not guaranteed, only the present value of the minimum lease payments ($10,711) is recorded by the lessee. The journal entries to record this lease in the accounting records of both lessee and lessor for the first two years of the lease term are shown on page 1005 (both

19 From Table 4 of Appendix at end of Chapter 5, adjusted for ***annuity due***.

Date	LESSOR CORPORATION Journal Entries (Direct Financing Lease)			LESSEE LIMITED Journal Entries (Capital Lease)		
Year 1 July 31	Lease Receivables [($2,000 × 7) + $1,200]	15,200		Leased Equipment — Capital Lease ($2,000 × 5.355261*)	10,711	
	Unearned Interest Revenue ($4,073 − $200)		3,873	Obligation Under Capital Lease		10,711
	Equipment Held for Lease		11,127	To record capital lease at inception.		
	Interest Revenue		200	*From Table 4 of Appendix at end of Chapter 5, adjusted for ***annuity due***.		
	To record direct financing lease at inception, and to record interest revenue equal to initial direct costs of lease.					
31	Operating Expenses	200		(No entry.)		
	Cash		200			
	To record payment of initial direct costs of lease.					
31	Cash	2,000				
	Lease Receivables		2,000	Obligation Under Capital Lease	2,000	
	To record receipt of first lease payment.			Cash		2,000
				To record lease payment for first year.		
Year 2 July 31	Cash	2,000		Interest Expense [($10,711 − $2,000) × 0.10]	871	
	Unearned Interest Revenue [($15,200 − $3,873) − $2,000] × 0.10	933		Obligation Under Capital Lease ($2,000 − $871)	1,129	
	Lease Receivables		2,000	Cash		2,000
	Interest Revenue		933	To record lease payment for second year.		
	To record receipt of second lease payment, and interest earned during the year ended July 31, Year 2.			Depreciation Expense ($10,711 ÷ 7)	1,530	
				Leased Equipment—Capital Lease		1,530
				To record depreciation expense (straight-line method) for first year of lease. Seven-year term of lease is used for depreciation because the lease does not transfer ownership of the equipment to the lessee and does not contain a bargain purchase option.		

the lessor and the lessee have a July 31 fiscal year), and the lessor's ledger accounts for Lease Receivables, Unearned Interest Revenue, and Interest Revenue are shown below and on page 1007.

Selected ledger accounts of lessor for direct financing lease

Lease Receivables

Date	*Explanation*	*Debit*	*Credit*	*Balance*
July 31/1	Inception of lease.	15,200		15,200 Dr
July 31/1	Receipt of first payment.		2,000	13,200 Dr
July 31/2	Receipt of second payment.		2,000	11,200 Dr
July 31/3	Receipt of third payment.		2,000	9,200 Dr
July 31/4	Receipt of fourth payment.		2,000	7,200 Dr
July 31/5	Receipt of fifth payment.		2,000	5,200 Dr
July 31/6	Receipt of sixth payment.		2,000	3,200 Dr
July 31/7	Receipt of seventh payment.		2,000	1,200 Dr

Unearned Interest Revenue

Date	*Explanation*	*Debit*	*Credit*	*Balance*
July 31/1	Inception of lease [($15,200 − $11,127) − $200].		3,873	3,873 Cr
July 31/2	Interest for Year 2 {[($15,200 − $3,873) − $2,000] × 0.10}.	933		2,940 Cr
July 31/3	Interest for Year 3 {[($13,200 − $2,940) − $2,000] × 0.10}.	826		2,114 Cr
July 31/4	Interest for Year 4 {[($11,200 − $2,114) − $2,000] × 0.10}.	709		1,405 Cr
July 31/5	Interest for Year 5 {[($9,200 − $1,405) − $2,000] × 0.10}.	580		825 Cr
July 31/6	Interest for Year 6 {[($7,200 − $825) − $2,000] × 0.10}.	437		388 Cr
July 31/7	Interest for Year 7 {[($5,200 − $388) − $2,000] × 0.10}.	281		107 Cr
July 31/8	Interest for Year 8 {[($3,200 − $107) − $2,000] × 0.10}.	107*		-0-

*Adjusted for rounding error.

Interest Revenue

Date	*Explanation*	*Debit*	*Credit*	*Balance*
July 31/1	Revenue to offset initial direct costs.		200	200 Cr
July 31/1	Closing entry.	200		-0-
July 31/2	Interest for Year 2.		933	933 Cr
July 31/2	Closing entry.	933		-0-
July 31/3	Interest for Year 3.		826	826 Cr
July 31/3	Closing entry.	826		-0-
July 31/4	Interest for Year 4.		709	709 Cr
July 31/4	Closing entry.	709		-0-
July 31/5	Interest for Year 5.		580	580 Cr
July 31/5	Closing entry.	580		-0-
July 31/6	Interest for Year 6.		437	437 Cr

July 31/6	Closing entry.	437		-0-
July 31/7	Interest for Year 7.		281	281 Cr
July 31/7	Closing entry.	281		-0-
July 31/8	Interest for Year 8.		107*	107 Cr
July 31/8	Closing entry.	107		-0-

*Adjusted $2 for rounding error.

Note that the initial direct costs of $200 are recognized as operating expenses at the inception of the lease and that an equal amount of interest revenue is recognized in the same accounting period. After the $200 reduction of the unearned interest revenue, the $3,873 balance, when subtracted from the $15,200 gross investment in the lease, yields the $11,327 present value of the lease for the lessor at the lessor's implicit interest rate of 10%, as illustrated below:

Computation of lessor's present value of direct financing lease

Present value of annuity due of 7 rents of $2,000 at 10% (present value of minimum lease payments) ($2,000 × 5.355261*)	$10,711
Add: Present value of unguaranteed residual value ($1,200 × 0.513158†)	616
Present value of lease	$11,327

*From Table 4 of Appendix at end of Chapter 5, adjusted for ***annuity due***.
†From Table 2 of Appendix at end of Chapter 5.

Operating Leases

Rent is recognized as revenue by ***lessors*** over the lease term of an operating lease as it becomes receivable according to the provisions in the lease. However, if the rent payments are not received in level amounts, rent revenue is recognized on a straight-line basis, unless another basis is considered more appropriate. An example of a basis that may be more appropriate than straight-line is hours of usage for a machine. If any initial direct costs relating to an operating lease are material in amount, they are deferred and recognized as expenses over the lease term in the same manner as rent revenue is recognized.

Leased property under operating leases is included by the ***lessor*** in the balance sheet. The leased property is depreciated in accordance with the lessor's normal depreciation policy, and in the balance sheet the accumulated depreciation is deducted from the investment in the leased property.

Disclosure of Leases in Financial Statements of Lessor

When an enterprise's business activities include leasing assets to others, the ***CICA Handbook*** recommends that the following information with respect to these leases be disclosed in the financial statements or notes to the financial statements.[20]

20 Adapted from CICA, ***CICA Handbook***, sec. 3065.54, .58, and .59.

1 For sales-type and direct financing leases:
  a The lessor's net investment separated into current and long-term
  b The amount of financing income
  c The method of computing lessor's investment for purposes of recognizing income

2 For operating leases:
  a The cost of property held for leasing
  b The amount of accumulated depreciation
  c The amount of rental income

The *CICA Handbook* also suggests that it is ***desirable*** to disclose the following ***additional*** information:[21] (1) for sales-type and direct financing leases: the executory costs included in the minimum lease payments, any unguaranteed residual value, the amount of unearned finance income, the aggregate future minimum lease payments receivable, and the term of the lease, together with the amount of minimum lease payments receivable for each of the next five years; (2) for sales-type and direct financing leases and operating leases: the total amount of contingent rentals in the aggregate and for each of the next five years.

An example of note disclosures in the financial statements of a Canadian trust company is shown below, and of Unicorp Canada Corporation on page 1009.

(viii) Leasing transactions
The Company's leasing operations consist principally of the leasing of aircraft, railway rolling stock, and ships. The leases expire over a period of 8 to 12 years. The equipment leasing transactions are recorded as loans receivable and rental payments are treated as blended payments of principal and interest to amortize such loans over the period of the lease.

Any gains resulting from the residual values of leased assets are reflected in income only when realized.

	Sales-type leases	*Operating leases*
	(Dollars in thousands)	
Year 3	$17,848	$223,483
Year 4	12,701	163,643
Year 5	9,589	107,877
Year 6	3,107	62,073
Year 7	1,183	23,226
Laters	481	-0-
Totals	$44,909	$580,302

The Company retains title to all of its leased computer equipment, pays taxes, licences and insurance on such equipment and provides for its general maintenance. At the end of the lease term, the equipment normally is returned to the company.

---

21 CICA, *CICA Handbook*, sec. 3065.54 and .59.

UNICORP

UNICORP CANADA CORPORATION

ANNUAL REPORT 1985

Leases — The Company, as a lessor, has retained substantially all of the risks and benefits of ownership and accounts for its leases as operating leases. Assets held for leasing purposes are classified as income producing properties.

NOTE 15 — RENTAL INCOME

All of the Company's leases are operating leases. The approximate minimum for future rental income due under income producing properties' non-cancellable leases in effect as of December 31, 1985 is as follows:

	thousands
1986	**$ 45,781**
1987	**28,183**
1988	**24,171**
1989	**19,954**
1990	**15,584**
Subsequent years	**172,035**

The above minimum future rental income does not include contingent rentals which may be received under the provisions of the lease agreements. Contingent rentals included in income were approximately $2,100,000 and $3,476,000 in 1985 and 1984, respectively.

OTHER ASPECTS OF ACCOUNTING FOR LEASES

In the preceding pages we have discussed and illustrated the principal aspects of lease accounting. In this section, we shall consider the following topics: leases involving land and buildings, guaranteed and unguaranteed residual value, computation of the lessor's implicit interest rate, and determination of the current portion of lease obligations and receivables.

Leases Involving Land and Buildings

Leases involving ***land only*** are accounted for as capital leases by the lessee if the lease contract includes either of the two conditions stated in the first criterion on page 983. Otherwise, a lease for land is accounted for as an operating lease. Normally, the amount capitalized in the Leased Land — Capital Lease account is not amortized.

The accounting for leases involving ***both land and buildings*** depends on whether one of the conditions stated in the first criterion on page 983 is met. If the terms allow ownership to pass or provide for a bargain purchase option, the lessee would capitalize the land separately from the building. Capitalization would be in proportion to the fair values at the inception of the lease.[22]

When the terms of the lease contain neither the passing of ownership nor a bargain purchase option and the fair value of the land is significant in relation to the total fair value of the leased property, the minimum lease payments would be allocated between the land and the building. The portion of the lease applicable to the land would be classified as an operating lease by both the lessee and the lessor. When the fair value of the land is not a significant portion of the total fair value of the leased property, the land and the building would be considered a ***single unit*** and would be capitalized accordingly. The economic life of the unit would be the economic life of the building.[23]

Guaranteed and Unguaranteed Residual Value

The residual value of a leased asset at the date of termination of the lease may be accounted for differently by the lessor and the lessee. If a lease contains a bargain purchase option, residual value is ignored by ***both*** the lessor and the lessee when accounting for the lease. When there is ***no bargain purchase option***, and there is ***a residual value*** at the end of the lease term, that residual value may be:

1 Unguaranteed

2 Guaranteed by the lessee

3 Guaranteed by a third party related to the lessee

4 Guaranteed by a third party related to the lessor

5 Guaranteed by a third party not related to either the lessor or the lessee

The accounting by the lessor and by the lessee will be different depending on which of the five situations apply. To illustrate the accounting treatments by the two parties to the lease for each of the above five situations, the following information is assumed for Manuco Limited, the lessor, and for Landscape, Inc., the lessee:

a Manuco Limited leased a machine to Landscape, Inc.
b The lease payments are $20,000 per year, in advance.
c The term of the lease is ten years.
d The residual value of the machine at the end of the lease term is estimated to be $10,000.
e The machine cost Manuco Limited $110,000.
f The fair market value of the machine at the inception date of the lease is $129,785.

22 Adapted from CICA, ***CICA Handbook***, sec. 3065.71.

23 CICA, ***CICA Handbook***, sec. 3065.72–.73.

g Landscape's incremental borrowing rate is 10%.
h The implicit interest rate in the lease is 12%.
i The lease does not contain a bargain purchase option.
j The risks associated with the collection of lease payments from Landscape, Inc., are not abnormal.
k There are no additional unreimbursable costs to be incurred by Manuco Limited in connection with the leased machine.

Situation 1: Accounting for the Unguaranteed Residual Value

When the leased asset has an unguaranteed residual value, that portion of the leased asset is ***not sold*** at the inception of the lease. As a result, the selling price (fair market value) and cost of sales (in this sales-type lease) must be reduced by the present value of the unguaranteed residual value. The gross investment in the lease, the sales amount, the cost of sales amount, the unearned interest revenue, and the net investment in the lease are computed as follows:

Computation of gross investment, sales, cost of sales, unearned interest revenue, and the net investment in the lease

Gross investment in lease: ($20,000 minimum lease payment × 10) plus $10,000 unguaranteed residual value	$210,000
Sales: $20,000 × the present value of an annuity due of 10 rents at 12%, 6.328250*	$126,565
Cost of sales: $110,000 cost minus ($10,000 × the present value of the unguaranteed residual value at 12%, 0.321973*	$106,780
Unearned interest revenue: $210,000 gross investment in lease minus $126,565 sales and minus the present value of the unguaranteed residual value, $3,220 ($10,000 × 0.321973)	$ 80,215
Net investment in lease: $210,000 gross investment in lease minus $80,215 unearned interest revenue, or, alternatively, $125,565 sales plus the present value of unguaranteed residual value, $3,220	$129,785

*From Appendix at end of Chapter 5.

The sales amount of $126,565 could have been computed as $129,785 (the fair value of the machine at the inception of the lease) minus $3,220 (the present value of the unguaranteed residual value of $10,000).

The cost of sales cannot be $110,000 because the residual value portion of the machine is retained by the lessor. Manuco Limited will be able to sell or otherwise dispose of the machine at the end of the lease term. Accordingly, the cost of the sale must be the $110,000 minus the residual value at the inception date.

Journal entries in the accounting records of Manuco Limited (the ***lessor***) for the sales-type lease, with an unguaranteed residual value, are as shown in the next illustration at the lease inception date.

Lessor's journal entries at inception date for sales-type lease with unguaranteed residual value

MANUCO LIMITED
Journal Entries

Gross Investment in Lease	210,000	
Cost of Sales	106,780	
Sales		126,565

Unearned Interest Revenue		80,215
Inventory (or Machinery)		110,000
To record the lease of machinery to Landscape, Inc., as a sales-type lease with unguaranteed residual value of $3,220 at the inception of the lease.		
Cash	20,000	
Gross Investment in Lease		20,000
To record first annual lease payment on lease to Landscape, Inc., at inception of lease.		

Landscape, Inc., the ***lessee***, is leasing the machine for the term of the lease and then the machine will be returned to Manuco Limited, the lessor. Accordingly, Landscape, Inc., will record the lease as a capital lease at the present value of the minimum lease payments computed as follows:

Computation of lessee's lease value at date of inception of lease when residual value is unguaranteed

Payment due on inception date	$ 20,000
Add: Present value of ordinary annuity of 9 payments of $20,000 at 10% a year: $20,000 × 5.759024*	115,180
Present value of minimum lease payments (amount to be capitalized by lessee)	$135,180

*Figure obtained from Appendix at end of Chapter 5.

Landscape, Inc.'s, incremental borrowing rate of 10% is used rather than Manuco Limited's implicit interest rate of 12% because the lessee must use the lower of the two rates.

The journal entries in the accounting records of Landscape, Inc., the lessee, for this capital lease with an unguaranteed residual value are as follows at the lease inception date:

Lessee's journal entries at inception date for capital lease with unguaranteed residual value

Leased equipment—Capital Lease	$135,180	
Obligation Under Capital Lease		135,180
To record capital lease at inception of lease.		
Obligation Under Capital Lease	20,000	
Cash		20,000
To record lease payment made on the lease inception date, for the first year.		

Situation 2: Accounting for the Residual Value Guaranteed by the Lessee

When the lessee guarantees the estimated residual value, this is paramount to a sale of the asset as far as the lessor is concerned, because when the asset is sold at the end of the lease term, the lessor is guaranteed ***exactly*** the estimated residual value; any excess received by the lessor must be paid to the lessee; any amount below the guaranteed residual value must be made up by the lessee. Accordingly, based on the information on page 1011, the journal entries for Manuco Limited, the ***lessor***, are:

Lessor's journal entries at inception date for sales-type lease with residual value guaranteed by lessee

Lease Receivable [($20,000 annual lease payment × 10) + $10,000 residual value guaranteed by lessee]	210,000	
Cost of Sales	110,000	
Inventory (or Machinery)		110,000
Sales [($20,000 × 6.328250*) + ($10,000 × 0.321973*)]		129,785
Unearned Interest Revenue [$210,000 lease receivable minus sales (fair value) of $129,785]		80,215
To record the lease of machinery to Landscape, Inc., as a sales-type lease with the residual value guaranteed by the lessee.		
Cash	20,000	
Lease Receivables		20,000
To record first annual lease payment, on lease to Landscape, Inc., in advance, on the inception date.		

*Figure obtained from Appendix at end of Chapter 5.

The ''lease receivables'' of $210,000 is set up in that account because all of that amount is receivable by the lessor. The cost of sales equals the inventory reduction amount because the lessor has ''effectively'' sold the machine to Landscape, Inc., for $210,000. The sale amount will represent the fair value of the leased machine at the inception date. In effect, the entire machine has been sold as far as the lessor is concerned. The amount of unearned interest revenue relates to the minimum lease payments only and therefore does not change.

Landscape, Inc., the ***lessee***, is leasing the machine for the term of the lease and will then return it to the lessor and has guaranteed the lessor $10,000 for the residual value of the machine at that time. Accordingly, the lease will be recorded as a capital lease at the inception date, at a cost including the present value of the minimum lease payments over the term of the lease, plus the present value of the $10,000 guarantee. The journal entries to record the lease at the inception date and to record the first annual lease payment, also at the inception date, will be as shown in the next illustration. The lease equipment and the obligation have both been increased by $3,855 ($10,000 × 0.385543), the present value of the $10,000 residual value guaranteed by the lessee, Landscape, Inc.

Lessee's journal entries at inception date for capital lease with residual value guaranteed by lessee

Lease Equipment—Capital Lease [$125,180 + ($10,000 × present value, at 10%, of residual value 0.385543*)]	129,035	
Obligation Under Capital Lease		129,035
To record capital lease at inception date including guaranteed residual value.		
Obligation Under Capital Lease	20,000	
Cash		20,000
To record lease payment, made on the lease inception date, for the first year.		

*Figure obtained from Appendix at end of Chapter 5.

Situation 3: Accounting for a Lease Guaranteed by a Third Party Related to the Lessee

The lessor treats this situation exactly the same as in situation 2. It makes no difference to the lessor whether the guarantee is directly from the lessee or from a third party related to the lessee. The *lessee* treats this situation in the same manner as if the lessee company had guaranteed the residual value itself.[24] As a result, the entry is exactly the same as in situation 2.

Situation 4: Accounting for the Residual Value Guaranteed by a Third Party Related to the Lessor

In this situation, the *lessor* is responsible for the residual value and thus the lessor has not sold that portion of the leased asset to the lessee. This is equivalent to the unguaranteed residual value where the lessor retains ownership, at the end of the lease term, of the asset at its estimated residual value. Accordingly, the journal entry for the lessor in this case is the same as in situation 1. Since the *lessee* is not purchasing the residual value, situation 1 applies here. The lessee's purchase price includes only the annual lease payments annuity portion of the asset.

Situation 5: Accounting for the Residual Value Guaranteed by a Third Party Who Is Not Related to Either the Lessor or the Lessee

The *lessor* will have ''sold'' the guaranteed residual value at the inception of the lease and will treat this ''sale'' in the same way as under situations 2 and 3. The *lessee* will exclude this guarantee and will treat the lease as in situations 1 and 4.

Computation of Lessor's Implicit Interest Rate

The illustrations of accounting for leases have been simplified by providing the interest rate implicit in the lease. In practice, this rate must be computed by a process of iteration (''trial and error'') involving computers, electronic calculators, or present-value tables. In order to comply with the *CICA Handbook* requirement that the lower of the lessor's implicit rate in the lease and the lessee's incremental borrowing rate be used in the present-value calculations by the lessee, sufficient information must be made available to the lessee. It is not necessary that the lessee be informed of the lessor's implicit interest rate. Sufficient information would be that necessary to allow the computation of the implicit interest rate. As discussed in Chapter 5, the rate of interest may be estimated if the rental period, the amount of periodic rent, and the present value are known—that is, if the lease term, minimum annual lease payments, and fair value of the leased property are known.

However, when the residual value of the leased property or a bargain purchase option is to be included in the calculation, two formulas, the ordinary annuity (for payments at the end of each period) or annuity due (for payment at the inception of the lease and periodically thereafter), and the present-value formula for a single amount (the residual value) must be used. The estimated imputed interest rate can be determined only by trial and error in such situations.

24 CICA, *CICA Handbook*, sec. 3065.03 (q), lessees (ii).

Determination of Current Portion of Lease Obligations and Receivables

The current portion of lease obligations is included in the current liabilities section of the lessee's balance sheet, and the current portion of lease receivables appears in the current asset section of the lessor's balance sheet. Without the assistance of a computer, an electronic calculator, or present-value tables, determination of the current portion of a lease with monthly payments requires separate computations of the principal portion of the next 12 lease payments or receipts.

A short-cut approximation of the current portion is possible by use of the "Rule of 78." (The sum of the digits for 12 consecutive months is 78.) This technique recognizes that the principal portion of each successive monthly fixed lease payment or receipt increases by a nearly uniform amount. For example, the Obligation Under Capital Lease ledger account of Lee Limited on page 986 indicates that almost every monthly principal payment after the first one (which was not affected by interest) was $2 larger than the previous month's payment. Thus, if we multiply this $2 increment by 78 and add the product to 12 times the $191 principal portion of the December 2, Year 1, lease payment, we have an approximation of the current portion of the lease obligation on December 31, Year 1, as shown in the next illustration. This estimate is a reasonably close approximation of the actual current portion of the principal payments (applicable to Year 2), which is $2,442.

Computation of current portion of lease obligation by "Rule of 78"

$2 × 78	$ 156
$191 × 12	2,292
Estimated current portion of lease obligation on Dec. 31, Year 1	$2,448

Appraisal of Current Accounting Standards for Leases

Prior to the issuance of section 3065 of the ***Handbook***, lessees were not required to capitalize leases. Leases often were designed to enable the lessor to record the lease as a sale but at the same time allow the lessee to account for the lease as an operating lease. Thus, billions of dollars of leased assets were not included in the balance sheet of either the lessee or the lessor. Many lessees viewed leasing as an attractive source of "off-balance-sheet financing," because the lease obligation appeared in notes to the financial statements rather than in the liabilities section of the balance sheet. However, users of financial statements considered such accounting practices unsatisfactory. Under current accounting standards, financial statements are more consistent with the conceptual framework of accounting, more informative, and more comparable between those business enterprises that lease assets and business enterprises that purchase assets outright.

For sales-type leases, the residual value can be used to undermine the requirements set forth in section 3065. For example, the use of third-party guarantors not related to either the lessor or the lessee requires the guarantee to be included in the calculation of the present value for the lessor, whereas, for the lessee, this guarantee of the residual value is excluded. As a consequence, there are two different present values to compare to the fair value of the property at the inception of the lease. The third criterion for capital leases detailed on page 983, wherein the present value of the minimum lease payments should be 90% or more of the fair value of the leased asset at the inception of the lease, would not be met and, if the other two criteria also were not met, the lessee would account for the lease as an operating lease (off-balance-sheet financing). This same criterion applies to the lessor: the higher present value to the lessor may comply with the 90% or more of fair value guideline, in which case the lessor would treat the lease as a sale-type lease, recording it as a sale. Such leases, then, are designed to return the lessor and lessee to the pre-section 3065 era, as discussed above. In our opinion the Accounting Standards Committee should consider this issue and make appropriate amendments to the existing recommendations to remedy this apparent oversight.

REVIEW QUESTIONS

1 Define each of the following terms:
- *a* ***Lease***
- *b* ***Sublease***
- *c* ***Sale-leaseback transaction***
- *d* ***Operating lease***

2 Listed below are some terms used in accounting for leases. Give a short definition of each term.
- *a* ***Inception of lease***
- *b* ***Bargain purchase option***
- *c* ***Unguaranteed residual value***
- *d* ***Lessor's implicit interest rate***
- *e* ***Initial direct costs***

3 What are the components of the ***minimum lease payments*** of a typical capital lease of the lessee?

4 To be classified as a ***capital lease*** by the lessee, a lease must meet one of three criteria at its inception. List these three criteria.

5 Briefly describe the accounting procedures that are followed by the lessor and by the lessee for an ***operating lease***.

6 Summarize the procedures followed by the lessee to account for a ***capital lease***.

7 A ***sales-type lease*** (from the standpoint of the lessor) must meet, in addition to one or more of the criteria of a capital lease, two additional criteria. What are these two additional criteria?

8 Differentiate between the accounting procedures used by lessors to account for a ***sales-type lease*** and for a ***direct financing lease***.

9 What disclosures are required for various types of leases in the financial statements or a note to the financial statements of lessees?

10 What disclosures are required for various types of leases in the financial statements or a note to the financial statements of lessors?

11 Marv Company leased a computer for three years at $25,000 a month, with an option to renew the lease for five years at $1,500 a month or to acquire the computer for $20,000 after the lease term of three years. How is this transaction recorded by Marv Company? Explain.

12 Ko Corporation leased an asset under a lease requiring the payment of $24,000 a year in rent. At the end of the current year, when the lease had a remaining term of 10 years, Ko subleased the asset for rent of $36,000 a year for 10 years. When is the gain from this transaction recognized by Ko Corporation? Explain.

13 A lessee's incremental borrowing rate is 18% a year. Unknown to the lessee, the lessor's implicit interest rate is 15%. How do these facts affect the lessee's accounting for a capital lease? Explain.

14 The economic life of leased equipment under a capital lease is 10 years, and the lease term is eight years. How do these facts affect the depreciation of the leased equipment by the lessee? Explain.

15 How does a lessor account for contingent rentals under a direct financing lease?

16 What major reforms in lease accounting were made by the CICA in section 3065 of the ***CICA Handbook***?

EXERCISES

Ex. 20-1 Select the best answer for each of the following multiple-choice questions:

1 On November 1, Year 2, Lessee Limited entered into a 10-year noncancellable lease with Lessor Ltd. for a machine owned by Lessor. The machine had a fair value of $200,000 at inception of the lease, and an economic life of 13 years. Present value of the minimum lease payments is $120,000, and executory costs amounted to $3,000 a year. Lessee is obligated to return the machine to Lessor on expiration of the lease. How much should Lessee record as an asset and corresponding liability at the inception of this lease?

a $0 *b* $120,000 *c* $123,000 *d* $200,000 *e* Some other amount

2 On July 1, Year 5, Lessee Limited sold a machine to Lessor Ltd., and simultaneously leased it back for three years. Pertinent data are:

Economic life, July 1, Year 5	10 years
Sales price	$120,000
Carrying amount, July 1, Year 5	$20,000
Monthly rent under leaseback	$1,266
Interest rate implicit in lease	12%
Present value of lease rentals ($1,266 for 36 months at 12%)	$38,116

How much gain should Lessee recognize on July 1, Year 5, on the sale of the machine?

a $0 *b* $33,333 *c* $61,884 *d* $100,000 *e* Some other amount

3 For an operating lease, the lessee records equal monthly rental payments as:
a Part interest expense and part depreciation expense
b Part interest expense and part reduction of lease liability
c Entirely a reduction of lease liability
d Rent expense

4 On January 2, Year 1, Lessee, Inc., entered into a 10-year noncancellable lease requiring payments of $100,000 a year, beginning January 2, Year 1. Lessee's incremental borrowing rate is 12%, but the lessor's implicit interest rate, which is known to Lessee, is 10%. Present-value factors for an annuity due of 10 rents are 6.75902 at 10% and 6.32825 at 12%. The economic life of the leased property is 12 years, and ownership of the leased property remains with the lessor at expiration of the lease. The amount that Lessee, Inc., capitalizes for the leased property on January 2, Year 1, is:
a $0 *b* $632,825 *c* $675,902 *d* $1,000,000 *e* Some other amount

5 In a lease that is recorded as a sales-type lease by the lessor, the difference between the gross investment in the lease and the sum of the present values of the components of the gross investment is recognized as revenue:
a In full at the lease's expiration
b In full at the lease's inception
c Over the lease term, under the interest method of amortization
d Over the lease term, under the straight-line method of amortization

6 The excess of the fair value of leased property at the inception of the lease over its cost or carrying amount is recorded by the lessor as:
a Unearned revenue from a sales-type lease
b Unearned revenue from a direct financing lease
c Manufacturer's or dealer's profit from a sales type lease
d Manufacturer's or dealer's profit from a direct financing lease

7 On May 1, Year 3, See Limited sold machinery to an unaffiliated enterprise for its current fair value of $275,000. Simultaneously, See leased back the machinery at $750 a month for five years, with no option to renew the lease or to reacquire the machinery. On May 1, Year 3, the machinery had a carrying amount of $250,000 and a remaining economic life of 10 years. See's rent expense for the machinery for the year ended October 31, Year 3, is:
a $0 *b* $2,000 *c* $2,500 *d* $4,500 *e* Some other amount

8 For a capital lease, an amount equal to the present value at the beginning of the lease term of the minimum lease payments during the lease term, excluding the portion of the payments representing executory costs, is recorded by the lessee:
a As an expense
b As a liability but not as an asset
c As an asset but not as a liability
d As an asset and as a liability

9 For a six-year capital lease, the portion of the minimum lease payment in the third year applicable to the reduction of the lessee's lease liability is:
a Less than in the second year
b More than in the second year
c The same as in the fourth year
d More than in the fourth year

Ex. 20-2 Wing Incorporated leased a new machine from Buck Inc. on October 31, Year 5, under a lease concerning which the following data hold:

Lease term	10 years
Annual rent payable each Oct. 31, beginning Oct. 31, Year 5	$200,000
Economic life of machine	15 years
Lessor's implicit interest rate (unknown to lessee)	10%
Lessee's incremental borrowing rate	12%

Wing has an option to acquire the machine on October 31, Year 15, by paying $250,000, which is significantly less than the $500,000 expected current fair value of the machine on the option exercise date. At the inception of the lease, the exercise of the option appears to be reasonably assured.

Compute the amount that Wing Incorporated debits to the Leased Equipment —Capital Lease ledger account on October 31, Year 5. Use the Appendix at the end of Chapter 5 and round all amounts to the nearest dollar.

Ex. 20-3 On November 1, Year 4, Lessee Limited signed a 10-year noncancellable lease for equipment. The lease required annual payments of $15,000 starting November 1, Year 4, with title to the equipment passing to Lessee at the expiration of the lease term. Lessee treated this transaction as a capital lease. The equipment had an economic life of 15 years, with no residual value. Lessee uses the straight-line method of depreciation for its plant assets. Aggregate lease payments were determined to have a present value of $101,385, based on the lessor's implicit interest of 10%, which was known to Lessee.

Compute Lessee Limited's interest expense and amortization expense for the year ended October 31, Year 5, rounded to the nearest dollar.

Ex. 20-4 Arbo Limited leased equipment from Blake Corporation on December 31, Year 6, for a 10-year term (equal to the economic life of the leased property). Payments of $100,000 were due annually, beginning December 31, Year 6, and Arbo guaranteed a residual value of $2,000 for the equipment. Arbo's incremental borrowing rate was 12%; Blake's implicit interest rate, which was unknown to Arbo, was 10%. Arbo made the $100,000 lease payments on December 31, Year 6, and December 31, Year 7.

Compute the balance of Arbo Limited's Obligation Under Capital Lease ledger account on December 31, Year 7, after the lease payment made on that date. Use the Appendix at the end of Chapter 5 and round all amounts to the nearest dollar.

Ex. 20-5 On March 1, Year 4, Lessee Limited entered into a five-year capital lease for equipment with Lessor Limited, with the following details:

Annual rental due each Mar. 1, beginning Year 4	$10,000
Bargain purchase option, Mar. 1, Year 9	$1,000
Economic life of leased equipment	8 years
Executory costs (maintenance) payable each Mar. 1, beginning Year 4	$500
Lessee's incremental borrowing rate	15%

Lessor's implicit interest rate (known to Lessee)	12%
Estimated residual value of equipment at end of lease term	$1,500

Prepare all journal entries for Lessee Limited's capital lease for the year ended February 28, Year 5, assuming Lessee made all payments to Lessor when due. Use the Appendix at the end of Chapter 5 and round all amounts to the nearest dollar.

Ex. 20-6 In its equipment lease with Roddy Limited that expired on July 31, Year 8, Tovar Corporation guaranteed a residual value of $5,000 for the equipment. On July 31, Year 8, Roddy notified Tovar that it had sold the equipment to a third party for $4,600.

Prepare a journal entry for Tovar Corporation on July 31, Year 8, to record its payment of cash to Roddy Limited in settlement of its residual value guarantee.

Ex. 20-7 On January 2, Year 7, Lessee Corporation signed a 10-year noncancellable lease for machinery. The terms of the lease required Lessee to make annual payments of $30,000 for 10 years beginning January 2, Year 7, with title to the machinery to pass to Lessee at the end of this period. The machinery has an economic life of 15 years and no residual value. Lessee uses the straight-line method of depreciation for all its plant assets. Lessee appropriately accounted for the lease transaction as a capital lease, using its incremental borrowing rate of 12% a year.

Compute the following for Lessee Corporation for Year 7 (use the Appendix at the end of Chapter 5 and round all amounts to the nearest dollar):

a Present value of minimum lease payments, January 2, Year 7
b Interest expense for Year 7
c Amortization expense for Year 7

Ex. 20-8 On June 30, Year 4, Day Company, a partnership, sold equipment for $560,000. The equipment had a carrying amount of $500,000 and a remaining economic life of 10 years. That same day, Day leased back the equipment at $11,000 a month for five years, with no option to renew the lease or reacquire the equipment.

Compute Day Company's rent expense for the equipment for the year ended December 31, Year 4.

Ex. 20-9 Widden Corporation leased equipment to Colby, Inc., on January 2, Year 1, for an eight-year term requiring annual payments of $800,000 each January 2, beginning Year 1. The economic life of the equipment was eight years, with no residual value. The equipment was carried in Widden's Inventories ledger account at a cost of $4,200,000. Widden appropriately accounted for the lease as a sales-type lease, using an implicit interest rate of 10%.

Compute Widden Corporation's interest revenue for each of the years ended December 31, Year 1 and Year 2. Use the Appendix at the end of Chapter 5 and round all amounts to the nearest dollar.

Ex. 20-10 Leasing, Inc., leased equipment to Macco Limited on July 1, Year 5, for an eight-year term and annual payments of $600,000 each July 1, beginning Year 5. The equipment was carried in Leasing's Inventories ledger account at a cost of $2,800,000, and Leasing appropriately accounted for the lease as a sales-type lease, using an implicit interest rate of 12%.

Compute the gross profit and interest revenue to be recognized by Leasing, Inc., for the year ended June 30, Year 6. Use the Appendix at the end of Chapter 5 and round all amounts to the nearest dollar.

Ex. 20-11 On January 2, Year 7, Lessor, Inc., entered into a five-year sales-type lease for equipment with Lessee Limited with the following details:

Annual payment due each Jan. 2, beginning Year 7	$10,000
Bargain purchase option, Jan. 2, Year 12	$1,000
Cost of equipment in Lessor's Inventories ledger account	$32,000
Economic life of equipment	8 years
Initial direct costs paid by Lessor, Jan. 2, Year 7	$800
Executory costs (insurance and maintenance) to be paid to Lessor by Lessee each Jan. 2, beginning Year 7	$1,500
Lessee's incremental borrowing rate	15%
Lessor's implicit interest rate (known to Lessee)	12%
Residual value of equipment	None

Lessor uses the perpetual inventory system.

Prepare journal entries for Lessor, Inc., for the year ended December 31, Year 7, assuming Lessee Limited made all lease payments when due. Use the Appendix at the end of Chapter 5 and round all amounts to the nearest dollar.

Ex. 20-12 On January 2, Year 6, Tracy, Inc., leased equipment to Rue Limited at an annual rent of $100,000 receivable at the beginning of each year for 10 years. The first payment was received immediately. The equipment cost $650,000 and had an economic life of 13 years and no residual value. The interest rate implicit in the lease was 12%. Tracy had no other costs associated with the lease. Tracy should have accounted for the lease as a sales-type lease but mistakenly accounted for it as an operating lease.

Compute the effect on income before income taxes during Year 6 as a result of Tracy's (the lessor's) incorrect classification of the lease as an operating lease rather than as a sales-type lease. Use the Appendix at the end of Chapter 5 and round all amounts to the nearest dollar.

Ex. 20-13 Cedar Ltd. retired a machine from production on January 2, Year 5, for the purpose of leasing it. The machine had a carrying amount of $900,000 after 15 years of use and was expected to have four more years of economic life and no residual value. The machine was being depreciated on a straight-line basis. On March 1, Year 5, Cedar leased the machine to Lew Limited for $330,000 a year for a four-year period ending February 28, Year 9. Cedar incurred total maintenance and other related costs under the lease contract of $45,000 relating to the year ended December 31, Year 5. Lew paid $330,000 to Cedar on March 1, Year 5. The lease was classified properly as an operating lease by both Cedar and Lew.

a Compute the income before income taxes derived by Cedar Ltd. from the lease for the year ended December 31, Year 5.

b Compute the amount of rent expense incurred by Lew Limited under the lease for the year ended December 31, Year 5.

Ex. 20-14 Lessor Limited leased equipment to Lessee Limited on May 1, Year 6. At that time the collectibility of the minimum lease payments was not reasonably predictable. The lease expires on May 1, Year 8. Lessee could have acquired the equipment from Lessor for $900,000 instead of leasing it. Lessor's accounting records showed a carrying amount of $800,000 for the equipment on May 1, Year 6. Lessor's depreciation on the equipment in Year 6 was $200,000. During Year 6, Lessee paid $240,000 rent to Lessor. Lessor incurred maintenance and other related costs of $22,000 under the terms of the lease in Year 6. After the lease with Lessee expires, Lessor will lease the equipment to another party for two years.

a Compute Lessor Limited's pre-tax income derived from its operating lease with Lessee Company during Year 6.

b Compute Lessee Limited's pre-tax expense incurred during its operating lease with Lessor Limited during Year 6.

Ex. 20-15 Logo Ltd., a dealer in equipment, leased equipment to Mann, Inc., on July 1, Year 6. The lease was appropriately accounted for as a sales-type lease by Logo and as a capital lease by Mann. The lease was for a 10-year term (the economic life of the equipment) expiring June 30, Year 16. The first of 10 equal annual payments of $500,000 was made on July 1, Year 6. Logo had acquired the equipment for $2,675,000 on January 2, Year 6, and established a selling price of $3,375,000 for the equipment. The present value on July 1, Year 6, of the rent payments over the lease term discounted at 12% (Logo's implicit interest rate, which was known to Mann and was less than Mann's incremental borrowing rate) was $3,164,125.

a Compute the amount of (1) gross profit and (2) interest revenue that Logo Ltd. (lessor) recognizes for the year ended December 31, Year 6. Round all amounts to the nearest dollar.

b Compute the amount of (1) amortization expense (straight-line method, with no residual value) and (2) interest expense that Mann (lessee) recognizes for the year ended December 31, Year 6. Round all amounts to the nearest dollar.

Ex. 20-16 The following information is available for a lease of a machine that is classified as a sales-type lease by Blunt Limited, the lessor, and a capital lease by Easton, Inc., the lessee:

Cost of machine to lessor	$31,000
Initial payment by lessee at inception of lease	1,000
Present value of remaining 47 monthly payments of $1,000 each discounted at 1% a month	37,354

a Record the lease (including the initial receipt of $1,000) and the receipt of the second instalment of $1,000 in the accounting records of Blunt Limited, the lessor. Round all amounts to the nearest dollar.

b Record the lease (including the initial payment of $1,000) and the payment of the second instalment of $1,000 in the accounting records of Easton, Inc., the lessee. Round all amounts to the nearest dollar.

Ex. 20-17 Mell Corporation leased a heavy crane to Canby Corp. on July 1, Year 10, on the following terms:

1 48 payments of $1,500 at the end of each month were to be paid by Canby.

2 The cost of the crane to Mell was $51,064.

Mell appropriately accounted for the lease as a direct financing lease; the difference between total rent receipts, $72,000 ($1,500 × 48 = $72,000), and the cost of the crane, $51,064, was computed to yield a return of 1½% a month over the lease term.

Prepare journal entries for Mell Corporation to record the lease contract and the receipt of the first payment on July 31, Year 10. Record unearned interest revenue of $20,936 ($72,000 – $51,064 = $20,936) and round all amounts to the nearest dollar. Disregard initial direct costs and residual value.

Ex. 20-18 On March 1, Year 1, Lessor, Inc., entered into a direct financing lease with Lessee Limited for a four-year term with annual payments of $10,000 beginning March 1, Year 1. The lease was for equipment carried in Lessor's Equipment Held for Lease ledger account at its cost (and fair value) of $33,239; the equipment had an unguaranteed residual value of $1,500. Lessor's implicit interest rate was 15%, after allowance for initial direct costs of $450 paid by Lessor on March 1, Year 1.

a Compute Lessor's gross investment in the lease, unearned interest revenue, and net investment in the lease. Round all amounts to the nearest dollar.

b Prepare three-column ledger accounts for the Lease Receivables and Unearned Interest Revenue ledger accounts of Lessor, Inc., and post the journal entries for the four-year term of the lease to the accounts. Round all amounts to the nearest dollar.

Ex. 20-19 On October 1, Year 6, Miller Corporation leased equipment carried in its Equipment Held for Lease ledger account at a cost (and fair value) of $20,434 to Naylor Limited on a five-year lease with annual payments of $5,000 beginning on October 1, Year 6, and a guaranteed residual value of $1,000. Miller's implicit interest rate was 12%, after allowance for initial direct costs of $320 paid by Miller on October 1, Year 6.

a Compute Miller Corporation's gross investment in the lease, unearned interest revenue, and net investment in the lease.

b Prepare journal entries for Miller Corporation on October 1, Year 6, to record the inception of the lease, the payment of initial direct costs, and the receipt of the first lease payment from Naylor Limited.

c Compute Miller Corporation's interest revenue (rounded to the nearest dollar) under the lease for the year ended September 30, Year 7.

CASES

Case 20-1 Reuben Limited leased equipment from Traynor Limited. The classification of the lease makes a difference in the amounts included in the balance sheets and income statements of both Reuben and Traynor.

Instructions

a What criteria must be met by the lease in order that Reuben Limited (lessee) classify it as a capital lease?

b What criteria must be met by the lease in order that Traynor Limited (lessor) classify it as a sales-type lease or a direct financing lease?

c Contrast a sales-type lease with a direct financing lease.

Case 20-2 On January 2, Year 7, Nickell Limited, a lessee, entered into three noncancellable leases for equipment, Lease 1, Lease 2, and Lease 3. None of the three leases transfers ownership of the equipment to Nickell at the end of the lease term. For each of the leases, the present value at the beginning of the lease term of the minimum lease payments, excluding the portion representing executory costs, is at least 75% of the fair value of the leased equipment.

Additional Information

1 Lease 1 does not contain a bargain purchase option; the lease term is equal to 80% of the economic life of the equipment.

2 Lease 2 contains a bargain purchase option; the lease term is equal to 50% of the economic life of the equipment.

3 Lease 3 does not contain a bargain purchase option; the lease term is equal to 50% of the economic life of the equipment.

Instructions

a How does Nickell Limited (lessee) classify each of the three leases, and why? Discuss the rationale for your answer.

b What amount, if any, does Nickell Limited record as an obligation at the inception of the lease for each of the three leases?

c Assuming that the minimum lease payments are made on a straight-line basis, how does Nickell Limited record each minimum lease payment for each of the three leases?

Case 20-3 Lindy Corporation entered into a lease contract with Lenore Leasing Corporation for a machine. Lenore's primary business is leasing, and it is not a manufacturer or dealer. Lindy leased the machine for a period of three years, which is 50% of the machine's economic life. Lenore was to take possession of the machine at the end of the initial three-year lease and lease it to an unrelated enterprise. Lindy did not guarantee any residual value for the machine, and the lease did not contain a bargain purchase option.

Lindy's incremental borrowing rate is 10%, and the lessor's implicit interest rate in the lease, 8½%, was not known to Lindy. With either rate, the present value of the minimum lease payments was between 90 and 100% of the fair value of the machine on the date of the lease contract.

Lindy agreed to pay all executory costs directly, and no allowance for these costs was included in the lease payments.

Lenore considers the risk of collectibility of the lease payments normal for its business, and, because Lindy has agreed to pay all executory costs, there are no unreimbursable future costs to be incurred by Lenore.

Instructions

a With respect to Lindy Corporation (the lessee), answer the following questions:

1 What type of lease has been entered into? Explain.
2 How does Lindy compute the amount to be recorded for the lease or asset acquired?
3 What ledger accounts are created or affected by this transaction and how are the lease costs related to the transaction matched with revenue?
4 What disclosures does Lindy make in a note to the financial statements regarding this lease or asset?

b With respect to Lenore Leasing Corporation (the lessor), answer the following questions:

1 What type of lease has been entered into? Explain.
2 How is this lease recorded by Lenore, and how are the amounts determined?
3 How does Lenore determine the amount of revenue to be recognized on receipt of each lease payment?
4 What disclosures does Lenore make in a note to the financial statements regarding this lease?

Case 20-4 *a* Capital leases and operating leases are the two classifications of leases described in section 3065 of the ***CICA Handbook***, from the standpoint of the lessee.

Instructions

1 Describe how a capital lease is accounted for by a lessee, both at the inception of the lease and during the first year of the lease, assuming that the lease transfers ownership of the property to the lessee at the end of the lease term and that equal monthly payments are made by the lessee at the beginning of each month.
2 Describe how an operating lease is accounted for by a lessee, both at the inception of the lease and during the first year of the lease, assuming that equal monthly payments are made by the lessee at the beginning of each month. Describe the change in accounting, if any, when rent payments are not made on a straight-line basis.

You are not asked to discuss the criteria for distinguishing between capital leases and operating leases.

b Sales-type leases and direct financing leases are two of the classifications of leases described in section 3065 of the ***CICA Handbook***, from the standpoint of the lessor.

Instructions

Compare and contrast a sales-type lease with a direct financing lease as follows:

1 Gross investment in the lease
2 Recognition of unearned interest revenue as interest revenue
3 Manufacturer's or dealer's profit

You are not asked to discuss the criteria for distinguishing between the leases described above and operating leases.

Case 20-5 Wingo Aircraft Limited manufactures small single- and multiple-engine aircraft primarily for sale to individuals, flying clubs, and corporations. Wingo is one of the pioneers in the industry and has developed a reputation as a leader in small-craft engineering and marketing innovations.

During the last few years, Wingo has leased profitably an increasing number of aircraft to flying clubs. The leasing activity currently represents a significant portion of Wingo's annual volume. Details of a typical lease contract with flying clubs follow:

1 The flying club signs a long-term lease with Wingo for the aircraft.
2 The lease has a noncancellable term of 6 to 18 years, depending on the aircraft's economic life. The lease term is set at 75% of the economic life of the aircraft leased.
3 The club is required to deposit with Wingo an amount equal to 10% of the total lease rent for the lease term. The deposit is not refundable, but it is used in lieu of rent during the last one-tenth of the lease term.
4 A bank lends Wingo an amount equal to the remaining 90% of the total lease rent after deducting a discount of 14% a year. The net discounted amount is paid immediately to Wingo. The bank-loan contract requires Wingo to use the lease payments from the flying club to repay the loan to the bank.
5 As a condition for the loan, the bank requires Wingo to insure the leased aircraft for an amount equal to the loan.
6 The flying club signs Wingo's bank-loan contract as a guarantor, thus obligating itself if Wingo should default on the loan.
7 When the bank loan is paid in full at the end of the lease term, the flying club may acquire the aircraft and receive title to it by paying Wingo $100.

Instructions

Discuss the criteria and other aspects of Wingo Aircraft Limited's leasing activities that it should consider in determining whether to account for its flying club leases as operating leases or as sales-type leases. In your discussion, identify criteria that are clearly met from the facts presented. For criteria that are not clearly met, indicate what additional information is needed to reach a conclusion with respect to each criterion.

Case 20-6 Apollo Airlines Limited recently acquired eight jetliners for a total cost of $180 million. It plans to depreciate the jets by the sum-of-the-years'-digits method over a 12-year economic life. It is estimated that the jets will have a resale value of $24 million at the end of 12 years. To finance the acquisition of the jets, Apollo borrowed $180 million, payable at the rate of $20 million a year plus interest at 8% on the unpaid balance. The first payment is due one year after the loan is arranged.

Solo Airlines Limited leased from Execucraft, Inc., eight jetliners, of the same type acquired by Apollo, for a 12-year term. Solo does not have an option to acquire the jets at the end of the lease term, and it classified the lease as an operating lease. Lease payments are $22 million a year, payable at the end of each year. The lease payments do not include property taxes, insurance, and maintenance of the jetliners; Solo pays all such expenses. The annual rent was computed to give Execucraft, Inc. (lessor), slightly less than 8% return on investment, taking into account the $24 million resale value of the jets at the end of the 12-year lease term. The lease is noncancellable.

Instructions

a Prepare a working paper to compute annual expenses (depreciation and interest) for Apollo Airlines Limited in connection with the ownership of the eight jetliners. How do annual expenses for Apollo compare with the annual lease rental expense incurred by Solo Airlines Limited? What is the significance of the difference?

b Show the amounts relating to the jets and the related loan that appear in the balance sheet of Apollo Airlines Limited at the end of the first year. In what respect is the balance sheet for Solo Airlines Limited different?

c Do you believe that the classification of the lease as an operating lease by Solo Airlines Limited was in conformity with the provisions of section 3065 of the ***CICA Handbook***? State reasons for your conclusion. (Use the Appendix at the end of Chapter 5 if necessary.)

PROBLEMS

Pr. 20-1 Albany Corporation leases equipment to several lessees. All its leases in effect during Year 5 were operating leases except for a sales-type lease entered into on January 2, Year 5.

Rent revenue from Albany's operating leases totalled $800,000 for Year 5. The cost of the leased equipment was $3,700,000, which was being depreciated by the straight-line method over an estimated economic life of five years with an estimated residual value of $200,000. No equipment leased under operating leases was acquired or constructed during Year 5. Maintenance and repair costs for the equipment leased under operating leases totalled $70,000 during Year 5.

The January 2, Year 5, sales-type lease was for a six-year term expiring on December 31, Year 10. The cost of the leased equipment was $3,500,000, and it had no estimated residual value. Executory costs under the sales-type lease totalling $120,000 were paid by the lessee during Year 5. The first of six equal annual payments of $750,000 under the lease was received by Albany from the lessee on January 2, Year 5. Albany's implicit interest rate under the lease was 10%.

Additional Information

1 Other revenue of Albany for Year 5, exclusive of amounts described in the foregoing paragraphs, totalled $50,000.
2 Other operating expenses of Albany for Year 5, exclusive of amounts described in the foregoing paragraphs, totalled $400,000.
3 Albany's income tax rate is 45%.

Instructions

Prepare a single-step income statement for Albany Corporation (lessor) for Year 5. Show supporting computations. (Use the Appendix at the end of Chapter 5 and round all amounts to the nearest dollar.) Disregard earnings per share.

Pr. 20-2 Coville Corporation had the following leases in effect during Year 7:

1 An operating lease with Wellfry Limited for equipment, dated July 1, Year 7, with monthly rent of $115,000, for the three-year lease term, payable at the inception of the lease and on the first day of each month thereafter. The equipment, which had an eight-year economic life with no residual value, had been carried in the finished goods inventory at cost of $7,000,000 from January 2, Year 7, when it was completed, until it was leased to Wellfry. Maintenance and repair costs paid by Coville for the equipment during the last six months of Year 7 totalled $8,300.
2 A sales-type lease with Yamaki Limited dated January 2, Year 7, for an eight-year term, with annual payments of $600,000 payable beginning on January 2, Year 7. The equipment, which had an economic life of eight years with no residual value, had been carried in Coville's finished goods inventory at cost of $3,000,000. Coville's implicit interest rate under the lease was 10%, which was known to Yamaki and was less than Yamaki's incremental borrowing rate of 12%. Coville paid initial direct costs of $2,300 on October 1, Year 7. Executory costs may be disregarded.

Coville, Wellfry, and Yamaki use the straight-line method of depreciation and/or amortization.

Instructions

a Use the Appendix at the end of Chapter 5 and round all amounts to the nearest dollar when solving the following problems and those in *b*.
  1 Compute Coville Corporation's (lessor's) revenue and expenses related to the operating lease with Wellfry Limited for the year ended December 31, Year 7.
  2 Compute Wellfry Limited's (lessee's) expenses related to the operating lease with Coville Corporation for the year ended December 31, Year 7.

b *1* Compute Coville Corporation's (lessor's) revenue, costs, and expenses related to the sales-type lease with Yamaki Limited for the year ended December 31, Year 7.
  2 Compute Yamaki Limited's (lessee's) expenses related to the capital lease with Coville Corporation for the year ended December 31, Year 7.

Pr. 20-3 During your examination of the financial statements of Dixon Enterprises, a partnership, for the year ended December 31, Year 6, you find that Dixon had erroneously debited two monthly payments of $5,000 each (November 1 and December 1) under a capital lease dated November 1, Year 6, to the Rent Expense ledger account. Your examination of the lease disclosed that it was for a four-year term, included a bargain purchase option of $8,000, and provided that $1,200 of the $5,000 monthly payment was for: insurance, $300; maintenance, $400; and property taxes, $500. You are unable to learn the lessor's implicit interest rate, but you do learn that Dixon's incremental borrowing rate is 12%. The leased equipment under the capital lease had an economic life of six years with a residual value of $6,000. Dixon uses the straight-line method of depreciation for plant assets and recognizes depreciation expense monthly.

Instructions
Prepare a correcting journal entry for Dixon Enterprises (lessee) on December 31, Year 6, to correct the accounting for the capital lease. Use the Appendix at the end of Chapter 5 and round all amounts to the nearest dollar. Disregard income taxes.

Pr. 20-4 On September 30, Year 3, the end of a fiscal year, Lessee Limited entered into a five-year capital lease with Lessor Corporation for equipment with a six-year economic life and a residual value of $2,500. Payments under the lease, excluding executory costs, were $60,000 a year, beginning on September 30, Year 3. Title to the equipment was to be transferred to Lessee on September 30, Year 8. Lessor's implicit interest rate is 12%; Lessee had an incremental borrowing rate of 15% and did not know Lessor's implicit interest rate. On September 30, Year 5, before Lessee made the lease payment due on that date or prepared year-end adjusting entries, the sales-type lease (from the viewpoint of Lessor) was terminated by mutual consent with no penalties.

Instructions
Prepare journal entries related to the capital lease for Lessee Limited on September 30, Year 3, Year 4, and Year 5. Compute amortization expense by the straight-line method. Use the Appendix at the end of Chapter 5 and round all amounts to the nearest dollar. Disregard executory costs.

Pr. 20-5 On December 31, Year 4, Lido Limited leased equipment from Rodeo, Inc., for four annual payments (excluding executory costs) of $10,000, beginning December 31, Year 4. The lease contained a bargain purchase option exercisable by Lido on December 31, Year 8, in the amount of $2,000. The equipment had a five-year economic life with a residual value of $1,000. Because Lido did not know Rodeo's implicit interest rate, Lido used its incremental borrowing rate of 15% to account for the capital lease. Lido depreciates plant assets by the straight-line method.

Instructions

Prepare three-column ledger accounts for Lido Limited's (lessee's) Leased Equipment—Capital Lease and Obligation Under Capital Lease ledger accounts, and post thereto all journal entries related to the capital lease for the five years ended December 31, Year 9. Use the Appendix at the end of Chapter 5 and round all amounts to the nearest dollar. Disregard executory costs.

Pr. 20-6 On July 1, Year 4, Ramer Corporation leased equipment to Gamble Limited. The equipment had been carried in Ramer's Inventories ledger account at a cost of $220,000. Both companies have a June 30 fiscal year. There were no other significant costs associated with the lease and no residual value guarantee by the lessee. The lease was for a noncancellable term of eight years, with $50,000 rent payable by Gamble on each July 1; title to the equipment passes to Gamble at the end of the lease term. Gamble made the first lease payment on July 1, Year 4. Ramer's implicit interest rate, which was known to Gamble and was less than Gamble's incremental borrowing rate of 13%, was 10%, and the present value of an annuity due of eight rents of 1 at 10% is 5.868419. The equipment had an economic life of 12 years with no residual value, and was to be amortized under the straight-line method.

Instructions

(Round all computations to nearest dollar.)

a Prepare journal entries for Ramer Corporation (lessor) on July 1, Year 4, to record the lease transaction as a sales-type lease and receipt of $50,000 from Gamble Limited for the first lease payment.

b Prepare a journal entry for Ramer Corporation (lessor) on June 30, Year 5, to recognize interest revenue for one year.

c Prepare a journal entry for Ramer Corporation (lessor) on July 1, Year 4, to record the lease transaction, but for this part of the problem ***assume that the lease was classified as an operating lease.***

d Compute the expenses relative to the lease for Gamble Limited (lessee) for the year ended June 30, Year 5, assuming that it classified the lease (1) as an operating lease and (2) as a capital lease.

Pr. 20-7 Prado, Inc., was incorporated in Year 1 with a fiscal year ending July 31. Prado's primary product is a sophisticated on-line inventory control system. Its customers pay a fixed fee plus a usage charge for using the system.

Prado leased a large, BIG-I computer system from the manufacturer. The lease required rent of $372,000 a year for the 12-year lease term. The economic life of the computer was 15 years.

Each $372,000 payment included $72,000 for the maintenance on the computer to be performed by the manufacturer. Lease payments were payable beginning on August 1, Year 2, the date the computer was installed and the lease contract was signed.

The lease was noncancellable for its 12-year term. On August 1, Year 14, Prado was to acquire title to the BIG-I system under the lease contract.

The lease was accounted for as a capital lease by Prado, and the computer was to be amortized by the straight-line method with a $140,000 residual value. Borrowed funds for this type of transaction would have cost Prado 12% a year. The lessor's implicit interest rate was unknown to Prado.

Instructions

Prepare journal entries for Prado (lessee) for the year ended July 31, Year 3, relating to the lease. Show supporting computations in the explanation for each journal entry. Use the Appendix at the end of Chapter 5 and round all amounts to the nearest dollar.

Pr. 20-8 On January 2, Year 1, Speeders, Inc., leased a racing car from Seabring Leasing Limited. The fixed noncancellable term of the lease was 24 months, with an option to renew month by month on the basis of a schedule of rents and guarantees of the residual value that decreased over time. The cost, fair value, and economic life of the racing car were as follows:

Cost (carried in Racing Equipment ledger account of Seabring Leasing)	$116,200
Fair value at inception of lease (Jan. 2, Year 1)	$116,200
Economic life	36 months

The lease specified that Speeders was to pay $4,125 on the first day of each month and that it guaranteed a residual value of $36,000 to Seabring Leasing at the end of 24 months (December 31, Year 2).

Speeders was to receive any excess over the guaranteed amount at the end of the lease term. The credit risk associated with the lease was normal when compared to the risk of collection of similar receivables, and no unreimbursable costs were expected to be incurred by Seabring Leasing, which paid $657 initial direct costs of the lease on January 2, Year 1, representing commissions. The rent was deemed to be fair, and the residual value guarantee was expected to approximate actual realizable value. Speeders depreciates other racing cars it owns by the straight-line method, and its incremental borrowing rate generally was 1% a month, which also was the interest rate implicit in the lease. At the end of the lease term, December 31, Year 2, the racing car was sold to a third party by Seabring Leasing for $40,000. The excess of proceeds received over the guaranteed residual value was paid by Seabring Leasing to Speeders.

Instructions

a How is the lease classified by Seabring Leasing Limited (lessor) and Speeders, Inc. (lessee)? Explain in terms of criteria required by section 3065 of the ***CICA Handbook***. Use the Appendix at the end of Chapter 5 to compute the present value of minimum lease payments and round all amounts to the nearest dollar.

b Prepare journal entries at the inception of the lease (including the first lease payment) in the accounting records of (1) Seabring Leasing Limited (lessor), and (2) Speeders, Inc. (lessee).

c Prepare journal entries at the end of the lease term in the accounting records of (1) Seabring Leasing Limited (lessor), and (2) Speeders, Inc. (lessee).

Assume that entries to recognize amortization and/or depreciation expense, interest revenue, or interest expense have been recorded on December 31, Year 2.

Pr. 20-9 Breakers Ballroom entered into a lease on April 1, Year 1, for a sound system from Sound Equipment Leasing Ltd. The fixed noncancellable term of the lease was four years with an option to renew at terms that repesented expected fair value on the option date. The following data relate to the sound system:

Cost to Sound Equipment Leasing Ltd. (carried in Equipment Held for Lease ledger account)	$19,142
Fair value at inception of lease	$19,142
Economic life	4 years

The lease contract specified that Breakers was to pay $489 on the first day of each month, and that it guaranteed a residual value of $2,000 to Sound Equipment Leasing Ltd. at the end of 48 months. Breakers was to receive any excess over the $2,000 guarantee at the end of the lease term.

The collectibility of the lease rentals was considered normal for that type of receivable, and no unreimbursable costs were to be incurred. Initial direct costs of the lease (commissions) paid by Sound Equipment Leasing Ltd. on April 1, Year 1, totalled $854. The rent was deemed to be fair, and the residual value guarantee was expected to approximate the sound system's realizable value at the end of the lease term. Breakers depreciated other plant assets by the straight-line method and had an incremental borrowing rate of 15% compounded monthly. The interest rate implicit in the lease was 1% a month and was known to Breakers.

At the end of the lease term, the sound system was sold by Sound Equipment Leasing Ltd. to a third party for $1,800, and the excess of the residual value guarantee over the sales proceeds was paid by Breakers to Sound Equipment Leasing Ltd.

Instructions

a How is the lease classified by the lessor and the lessee? Explain your conclusion in terms of the classification criteria required by section 3065 of the ***CICA Handbook***. Use the Appendix at the end of Chapter 5 to compute the present value of minimum lease payments and round all amounts to the nearest dollar.

b Prepare the journal entries required at the inception of the lease for (1) Sound Equipment Leasing Ltd. (lessor) and (2) Breakers Ballroom (lessee).

c Prepare the journal entries required at the termination of the lease for (1) Sound Equipment Leasing Ltd. (lessor) and (2) Breakers Ballroom (lessee). Assume that entries to recognize amortization and/or depreciation expense, interest revenue, or interest expense had been recorded on March 31, Year 5.

Pr. 20-10 Craig Limited leased equipment with an economic life of 12 years to Mim Limited on January 2, Year 1, for a period of 10 years. The selling price of the equipment was $288,258, and the unguaranteed residual value at the end of the lease term was estimated at $20,000. Mim was to pay annual rent of $40,000 at the beginning of each year and was responsible for all maintenance, insurance, and property taxes. Craig incurred costs of $197,200 in manufacturing the equipment and $5,000 in negotiating and closing the lease contract. There are no abnormal risks associated with the collection of lease payments from Mim Limited, and no additional, unreimbursable costs were expected to be incurred by Craig. The implicit interest rate for Craig was 9% a year and was known to Mim, which had an incremental borrowing rate of 12%.

Instructions

(Use the Appendix at the end of Chapter 5 and round all amounts to the nearest dollar.)

a How is the lease classified by Craig Limited (lessor)? Explain.

b Assuming that Craig Limited (lessor) classified the lease as a sales-type lease, compute the following at the inception of the lease:

1. Gross investment in lease
2. Net investment in lease
3. Unearned interest revenue
4. Sales proceeds under the lease
5. Cost of goods sold (cost of equipment plus initial direct costs less present value of the unguaranteed residual value)

c Prepare a working paper summarizing the amortization of the net investment in the lease and the recognition of interest revenue over the lease term for Craig Limited (lessor).

d Prepare the journal entries for the first year of the lease for Craig Limited (lessor).

Pr. 20-11 On December 31, Year 1, Maladay, Inc., leased equipment to Fairview Limited. The equipment had a cost and fair value of $278,158. The term of the lease was for seven years, with a $50,000 payment due each December 31 starting in Year 1. The unguaranteed residual value was estimated at $30,000 at the end of the lease term, and the economic life of the equipment was nine years. The terms were designed to give Maladay a 10% annual rate of return on its net investment (including initial direct costs), which had a present value of $283,158.

Fairview was to pay all property taxes, insurance, and maintenance; Maladay paid a commission of $5,000 to a broker for arranging the lease. There were no abnormal risks associated with the collection of lease payments from Fairview Limited, and no significant future unreimbursable costs are expected to be incurred by Maladay, Inc., with respect to the leased equipment.

Instructions

(Use the Appendix at the end of Chapter 5 and round all amounts to the nearest dollar.)

a How is the lease classified by Maladay, Inc. (lessor)? Explain.

b Assuming that Maladay classified the lease as a direct financing lease, compute the following at the inception of the lease:

1. Gross investment in lease

2 Unearned interest revenue
3 Net investment in lease

c Prepare a working paper summarizing the amortization of the $283,158 present value of the lease and the recognition of interest revenue over the lease term for Maladay, Inc. (lessor).

d Prepare the journal entries for Maladay on December 31, Year 1, and on December 31, Year 2, relating to the lease.

Pr. 20-12 On April 1, Year 5, Keel Corporation entered into a five-year, noncancellable equipment lease with Noro Corporation. Annual rent of $10,000 (excluding executory costs) was payable in advance, starting on April 1, Year 5. The lease gave Keel an option to acquire the equipment on March 31, Year 10, for $1,000, and the lease was classified appropriately as a sales-type lease by Noro and as a capital lease by Keel.

The economic life of the equipment was 10 years, and management of Keel estimated that the residual value of the equipment at the end of its economic life would approximate the dismantling and removal costs. The straight-line method of depreciation is used by Keel, and its fiscal year ends on March 31.

The incremental borrowing rate for Keel on April 1, Year 5, was 10% a year. Noro's implicit interest rate also was 10%.

Instructions

(Use the Appendix at the end of Chapter 5 and round all amounts to the nearest dollar.)

a Prepare a summary of the lessee Keel Corporation's minimum lease payments and interest expense for each of the five years of the lease (April 1, Year 5, through March 31, Year 10).

b Prepare journal entries for Keel Corporation relating to the lease for the year ended March 31, Year 6.

c Assuming that the equipment was carried in the lessor Noro Corporation's Inventory of Equipment ledger account at $37,000 and that initial direct costs paid by Noro Corporation totalled $1,200, prepare journal entries for Noro Corporation to record the lease, payment of initial direct costs, and receipt of first lease payment.

Pr. 20-13 In Year 1, Expro Limited negotiated and closed a long-term lease for truck terminals. The terminals had been constructed to Expro's specifications on land owned by Expro. On January 2, Year 2, Expro took possession of the truck terminals.

Although the truck terminals had a composite economic life of 40 years, the noncancellable lease term was for 20 years from January 2, Year 2, with a bargain purchase option available on the expiration of the lease. Expro had an option to acquire the truck terminals for $1,000 on December 31, Year 21. You have determined that the truck terminals and related obligation were to be accounted for as a capital lease by Expro.

The 20-year lease was effective for the period January 2, Year 2, through December 31, Year 21. Rent payments of $1,000,000 were payable to the lessor on January 2 of each of the first 10 years of the lease term. Rent payments of $300,000 were due on January 2 for each of the last 10 years of the lease. Expro also was obligated to make annual payments to the lessor of $95,000 for property taxes and $155,000 for insurance; these payments also were due on January 2. The lease was structured to give the lessor a 10% rate of return, which was known to Expro. The incremental borrowing rate of Expro was 12%.

Instructions

(Use the Appendix at the end of Chapter 5 and round all amounts to the nearest dollar.)

a Prepare a working paper to compute for Expro Limited (lessee) the present value of the minimum lease payments on January 2, Year 2.

b Prepare journal entries for Expro Limited (lessee) to record the:

1 Lease transaction and the payment to the lessor on January 2, Year 2 (separate entries).

2 Amortization of the truck terminals for Year 2, using the straight-line method with a $200,000 residual value.

3 Interest expense for the year ended December 31, Year 2.

4 Payment to the lessor on January 2, Year 3.

Pr. 20-14 Macco Corporation, a lessor of office machines, acquired for $450,000 on December 31, Year 9, a new machine that was delivered the same day to Ranger Limited under a direct financing lease.

Additional Information

1 The lease term was seven years, which was the same as the economic life of the machine, which had an unguaranteed residual value of $60,000.

2 Macco's implicit interest rate of 12% was known to Ranger.

3 Ranger's incremental borrowing rate was 14% on December 31, Year 9.

4 Seven equal annual lease payments were payable each December 31, Year 9 through Year 15.

5 There were no initial direct costs associated with the lease.

6 Ranger appropriately accounted for the lease as a capital lease. Both Macco and Ranger use the calendar year and the straight-line method of depreciation for plant assets.

Instructions

(Use the Appendix at the end of Chapter 5 and round all amounts to the nearest dollar.)

a Compute the annual lease payments under the lease.

b Compute the gross investment in the lease and unearned interest revenue for Macco Corporation (lessor) on December 31, Year 9.

c Compute the expenses of Ranger Limited (lessee) under the lease for the year ended December 31, Year 10.

d Prepare journal entries for Macco Corporation (lessor) on December 31, Year 9, to record the inception of the lease and the first lease payment.

Pr. 20-15 Marcotte, Inc., entered into a lease with Deadwood Corporation for a wood-forming machine. The date of the lease was July 1, 1987, and the lease term was for five years with equal annual payments of $70,000, payable in advance. The equipment had an expected economic life of six years, even though its residual value at the end of five years would have declined to almost zero. The machine could be sold for cash on July 1, 1987, in the amount of $282,800. All repairs and maintenance costs would be borne by Marcotte, Inc., but are not expected to be out of the ordinary. Deadwood Corporation manufactures this type of a machine at an average cost of $200,000 per machine. Marcotte recently borrowed funds from its bank for research and development at a 15% rate.

Instructions

a Prepare the journal entries required at July 1, 1987, to record the lease transactions on that date in the books of Marcotte, Inc., and in the books of Deadwood Corporation. Omit explanations.

b Prepare the journal entries required for each company at December 31, 1987 (the year end for both companies), with respect to the leased asset. (Marcotte, Inc., depreciates like equipment on the straight-line basis.) Omit explanations.

Pr. 20-16 Dieffen Corp. had contracted to manufacture a special rubber extrusion machine which it would lease to Bacher, Inc., for three years. The equipment cost $900,000 to manufacture and in accordance with Dieffen's usual pricing policy would be sold for $1 million. The lease called for delivery of the machine on January 1, 1988, and three equal annual payments of $338,093 to Trillium on January 1, 1988, 1989, and 1990. By the end of 1990, it was not anticipated that the machine would have any operating value but it would have residual value to Dieffen of $100,000. If Bacher, Inc., had intended to purchase the machine the bank would have lent the funds at 8%.

Instructions

a Record the lease transaction for Dieffen Corp. at the date of inception of the lease and at the year-end, December 31, 1988. Omit narratives.

b Record the lease transaction for Bacher Inc. at the date of inception of the lease and at the year-end, December 31, 1988. Omit explanations.

chapter 21

ACCOUNTING FOR INCOME TAXES

THE ROLE OF INCOME TAXES IN INCOME REPORTING

One of the more challenging areas of accounting is the reporting problem created when pre-tax accounting income[1] in a corporation's income statement differs materially from taxable income reported in its income tax return. Our discussion in this chapter relates essentially to corporations, because other business enterprises (such as single proprietorships and partnerships) are not taxable entities.

In the preparation of income statements, accountants are concerned primarily with the measurement of operating results in accordance with generally accepted accounting principles. However, taxable income is a legal concept. In enacting federal tax laws, Parliament is interested not only in meeting the revenue needs of government but also in achieving other economic and social objectives. Because the rules for the measurement of pre-tax accounting income and taxable income were developed with different objectives in mind, it is not surprising that the results are sometimes materially different. In this chapter we discuss some of those differences.

Nature of Income Tax Allocation

Why do differences between pre-tax accounting income and taxable income produce a financial reporting problem? To answer this question, consider the comparative income statements for Amy Limited at the top of page 1038.

In the examination of Amy Limited's comparative income statements, an investor, for example, would want to know why the same pre-tax accounting income resulted in such a large difference in net income for the two years. Corporate

1 The definition of ***pre-tax accounting income*** is that which defines ***accounting income*** in CICA, ***CICA Handbook*** (Toronto), sec. 3470.01 (note 1). Accordingly, these two terms may be used interchangeably in this textbook.

Income taxes expense not determined in accordance with GAAP

AMY LIMITED
Comparative Income Statements
For Years Ended December 31, Year 2 and Year 1

	Year 2	*Year 1*
Sales and other revenue	$9,000,000	$10,000,000
Less: Cost of goods sold and operating expenses	(8,000,000)	(9,000,000)
Income before income taxes	$1,000,000	$ 1,000,000
Income taxes expense	600,000	300,000
Net income	$ 400,000	$ 700,000

income tax rates are changed frequently, but in recent years the rates have been such that a corporation with a pre-tax income of $1 million will pay about 45% of this amount in income taxes. Knowing this, the investor would expect Amy to pay about $450,000 of income taxes each year. It is apparent that Amy's ***taxable income*** in each of the two years differed materially from its pre-tax accounting income, perhaps because $333,333 of Year 1 income was not taxable until Year 2. By analyzing the source of the differences between pre-tax accounting income and taxable income, the investor would be able to determine whether income taxes expense was reported in accordance with generally accepted accounting principles.

Another possible distortion between pre-tax accounting income and income taxes expense may result if, for example, extraordinary items are included in the income statement without a proper allocation of income taxes. To illustrate this point, consider the following partial income statement for Exord Corporation with a pre-tax accounting income of $500,000, including an extraordinary item (a gain) of $300,000, and an effective income tax rate of 45%:

Failure to allocate income taxes violates GAAP

EXORD CORPORATION
Partial Income Statement
For Year Ended September 30, Year 10

	With tax allocation	*Without tax allocation*
Income before income taxes	$200,000	$200,000
Income taxes expense	90,000	225,000
Operating income (loss) before extraordinary item	$110,000	$ (25,000)
Extraordinary item (gain)	165,000	300,000
Net income	$275,000	$275,000

The picture presented in the partial income statement for Exord Corporation without tax allocation obviously is distorted. The income before income taxes absorbs a charge for income taxes at the rate of 112.5%, but the extraordinary item is reported at the pre-tax amount of $300,000. Allocation of income taxes between pre-tax accounting income and the extraordinary item at the effective income tax rate of 45% is consistent with the matching principle and does not distort the relationship between income before income taxes and income taxes expense.

Terminology Used in Accounting for Income Taxes

A brief definition of terms used in accounting for income taxes is necessary at this point.[2]

1 *Income taxes* Taxes based on income as determined under provisions of federal and provincial tax laws. This term also is used to describe the amount of income taxes (income taxes expense) allocated to an accounting period.

2 *Pre-tax accounting income* Income for an accounting period before deduction of income taxes. ***Accounting income*** and ***income before income taxes*** are alternative terms for pre-tax accounting income.

3 *Taxable income* (or *loss*) The excess of taxable revenue over deductible expenses (or the excess of deductible expenses over taxable revenue) for an accounting period. For purposes of this definition, deductible expenses ***do not include*** operating loss carrybacks or carryforwards.

4 *Timing differences* Differences between pre-tax accounting income and taxable income for an accounting period caused by reporting items of revenue or expense in one period for financial accounting and in an earlier or later period for income tax purposes. Timing differences originate in one accounting period and ''reverse'' in future periods. Most timing differences reduce income taxes that otherwise would be payable currently; however, some timing differences increase the amount of income taxes payable currently.

5 *Permanent differences* Differences between pre-tax accounting income and taxable income arising from transactions that, under income tax laws and regulations, ***will not be offset by corresponding differences or reversals in future periods***.

6 *Tax effects* Differences between actual income taxes payable currently and income taxes expense for an accounting period that are attributable to: ***a*** revenue or expense transactions that enter into the measurement of pre-tax accounting income in one accounting period and into the measurement of taxable income in another period; ***b*** deductions or credits that may be carried backward or forward for income tax purposes; and ***c*** prior period adjustments. Permanent differences between pre-tax accounting income and taxable income do not result in tax effects.

7 *Deferred taxes* Tax effects that are postponed for allocation (either as increases or decreases) to income taxes expense in future accounting periods.

8 *Interperiod tax allocation* The process of apportioning income taxes expense among accounting periods.

2 Adapted with some modifications from AICPA, ***APB Opinion No. 11***: ''Accounting for Income Taxes'' (New York: 1967), pp. 158–160.

9 ***Interim-period tax computation*** The computation of income taxes expense for periods, such as fiscal quarters, within a year.

10 ***Tax allocation within an accounting period (intraperiod tax allocation)*** The process of apportioning income taxes expense applicable to an accounting period among income before extraordinary items, extraordinary items, and adjustments applicable to prior periods through retained earnings in the current period.

INTERPERIOD TAX ALLOCATION

Interperiod tax allocation procedures are based on the assumption that income taxes are a business expense and that income taxes will continue in the future. Income measurement under the going-concern principle requires the application of the accrual basis of accounting by matching realized revenue with expired costs (expenses) for each accounting period. Accordingly, income taxes applicable to income recognized in the income statement should be estimated and accrued without regard to the time of payment. Income taxes that must be paid currently but relate to income to be reported in the income statement in future periods should be deferred and recognized as an expense when the related income is reported.

Sources of Differences Between Pre-Tax Accounting Income and Taxable Income

The major sources of differences between pre-tax accounting income and taxable income are:

1 ***Timing differences in the recognition of revenue and expenses*** Certain provisions in the income tax law allow (or sometimes require) taxpayers to recognize revenue and expenses at times different from those appropriate under generally accepted accounting principles. When a corporation has an option, it is likely to choose accounting methods for income tax purposes that delay the recognition of revenue and accelerate the recognition of expenses.

2 ***Legal provisions*** Some types of revenue and expense are recognized for financial accounting but not for income tax purposes; some are recognized in the computation of taxable income but are not included in pre-tax accounting income.

3 ***Carryback and carryforward of operating losses for income tax purposes*** The federal income tax law provides that an operating loss in one year may be offset against taxable income of specified previous and future tax years.[3] As a

3 The current income tax law provides that an ***operating loss*** may be carried back to the third year before the loss and applied until exhausted against taxable income in successive years through the seventh year after the loss. As in the case of taxable income, there are certain differences between the definition of an operating loss for income tax purposes and the financial accounting concept of such a loss.

result, an ***operating loss*** in a year may result in either a refund of income taxes previously paid or a potential reduction of income taxes in future years. For income tax purposes, ***capital losses*** incurred by corporations may be deducted only from capital gains and capital losses in excess of capital gains in one year may be carried back and offset against net capital gains of preceding years. Any unused net capital loss may be carried forward and deducted against net capital gains in future years.

In the following sections we consider the financial accounting implications of each of these three categories. In all illustrations we assume an effective corporate income tax rate of 45% on ordinary income and 30% on net long-term capital gains to simplify the computations.

Timing Differences

In some cases the accounting period in which an item of revenue is taxable or an expense is deductible for income tax purposes differs from the period in which the revenue or expense is recognized in pre-tax accounting income. When pre-tax accounting income in any period differs from taxable income as a result of ***timing differences***, the divergence will be counterbalanced in future periods by opposite variations between pre-tax accounting income and taxable income. When pre-tax accounting income is ***larger*** than taxable income, ***deferred income tax credits*** result; when pre-tax accounting income is ***smaller*** than taxable income, ***deferred income tax debits*** result. Deferred income tax credits and deferred income tax debits are entered in the accounting records through interperiod income tax allocation.

Pre-Tax Accounting Income Exceeds Taxable Income: Deferred Income Tax Credits

Most timing differences produce pre-tax accounting income that is larger than taxable income. The two reasons for such differences are:

1 ***Revenue*** (or ***gain***) ***is recognized later in the income tax return than in the income statement*** An example of this situation occurs when a corporation sells merchandise on the installment plan and recognizes financial accounting income on the accrual basis of accounting when sales are made, but elects to compute taxable income on the basis of cash collections, that is, under the ***instalment method*** of accounting described in Chapter 3. Another example involves construction-type contracts when pre-tax accounting income is measured by the percentage-of-completion method described in Chapter 9, but taxable income is reported only when the contracts are completed (the completed-contract method described in Chapter 9). Finally, the use of the equity method of accounting for investments in common stock generally results in timing differences between taxable income and pre-tax accounting income.

2 ***Expense*** (or ***loss***) ***is recognized earlier in the income tax return than in the income statement*** An example of this situation occurs when a corporation chooses an accelerated method of depreciation or a shorter economic life to depreciate plant assets for income tax purposes but uses the straight-line

method for financial accounting. Another example is the capitalization of interest and property taxes during construction of plant assets but deducting these items currently as expenses in the computation of taxable income.

Taxable Income Exceeds Pre-Tax Accounting Income: Deferred Income Tax Debits The two reasons why taxable income may exceed pre-tax accounting income are explained in the following paragraphs.

1 ***Revenue** (or **gain**) **is recognized earlier in the income tax return than in the income statement*** Parliament is conscious of the fact that taxpaying ability arises when taxpayers have cash to pay the tax. Therefore, the income tax law tends to make ***collection*** of income the general test of tax timing. The accounting test of income recognition depends on whether the business enterprise has earned (realized) the income. Revenue such as rent, royalties, interest, and service fees received in advance is not included in pre-tax accounting income until the earning process is complete, but it usually must be reported for income tax purposes in the period received. For example, suppose that a corporation leases property to others for five years at $30,000 a year and receives the first and last (fifth) year's rent in advance. Assume that, for income tax purposes, the entire $60,000 must be included in income in the year of receipt; for financial accounting, the $30,000 rent for the fifth year is carried as deferred revenue (liability) in the balance sheet until the fifth year, when it will be included in pre-tax accounting income but will not be subject to income taxes because it was included in taxable income in the first year.

2 ***Expense** (or **loss**) **is recognized later in the income tax return than in the income statement*** Generally, estimated expenses or losses relating to outstanding product warranties, pending lawsuits and claims, and unrealized losses on short-term investments in equity securities are recognized in the accounting records when evidence that they have been incurred is reasonably clear. For income tax purposes, more reliable evidence is required. As stated in Chapter 10, business enterprises often guarantee their products against defects for a number of years. On the basis of experience, a corporation knows that, despite its best efforts, a certain portion of the products sold will prove defective, and it must accrue an estimated liability under the product warranty to match the estimated expense with revenue in the year the sale was made. For income tax purposes, this estimated expense is not deductible until it is actually incurred. Pre-tax accounting income therefore is smaller than taxable income in the year the estimated expense is recorded, and the reversal will take place in the year in which customers make claims under the product warranty.

To illustrate the accounting for ***deferred income tax credits***, the example from Chapter 9, Cabot Construction Limited,[4] will be used. Assume Cabot incorporated the percentage-of-completion method into its accounting system and used

4 See Chapter 9, page 429, for gross profits by year, which equals the total of $135,000, used here.

the completed-contract method for its tax return. The effect of these methods on pre-tax accounting income and taxable income is shown below:

Effects of timing differences on pre-tax accounting income and taxable income for deferred income tax credits

December 31:	*Pre-tax accounting income*	*Taxable income*	*Timing difference*
Year 1	$ 25,000	$ -0-	$ 25,000
Year 2	75,000	-0-	75,000
Year 3	35,000	135,000	(100,000)
Totals	$135,000	$135,000	$ -0-

Note that the total pre-tax accounting income and total taxable income are identical over the three-year period. The journal entries to record income taxes are as follows (explanations omitted):

Journal entries for deferred income tax credits arising from timing differences

Year 1			
Dec. 31	Income Taxes Expense ($25,000 × 0.45)	11,250	
	Deferred Income Taxes		11,250
Year 2			
Dec. 31	Income Taxes Expense ($75,000 × 0.45)	33,750	
	Deferred Income Taxes		33,750
Year 3			
Dec. 31	Income Taxes Expense ($35,000 × 0.45)	15,750	
	Deferred Income Taxes ($100,000 × 0.45)	45,000	
	Income Taxes Payable ($35,000 × 0.45) ..		60,750

Deferred income tax credits of $45,000 ($11,250 + $33,750 = $45,000) arise during the first two years, when pre-tax accounting income for this contract exceeds taxable income (which is zero), and are drawn down to zero in the third year, when the reverse is true as the completed contract's income is realized for tax purposes.

It is necessary to disclose, either in the income statement itself or in a note thereto, the portion of income taxes expense which is ***currently payable*** and the amount of income taxes expense which is ***deferred***. In Years 1 and 2, the entire income taxes expense is ***deferred***. However, in Year 3, the income taxes expense of $15,750 represents:

Income taxes payable currently exceeds income taxes expense

Payable currently	$60,750
Less: Deferred income taxes	45,000
Income taxes expense	$15,750

In this case, an examination of the Deferred Income Taxes ledger account shows that the credits were reversed (drawn down) in the third year, as follows:

Deferred Income Taxes ledger account reversal (drawdown) in third year

Date	*Explanation*	*Debit*	*Credit*	*Balance*
Dec. 31, Year 1	Year-end entry.		11,250	11,250 Cr
Dec. 31, Year 2	Year-end entry.		33,750	45,000 Cr
Dec. 31, Year 3	Year-end entry.	45,000		-0-

To illustrate the accounting for deferred income tax debits (charges), assume that Fast Limited sells products that require servicing over a five-year product warranty period. Fast estimates warranty expense as a percentage of sales in each year. However, for income tax purposes the warranty expense is deductible only *as incurred*. The estimated warranty expense and actual servicing costs for the first three years of operations were as follows:

Effects of warranty expense timing differences on pre-tax accounting income and taxable income

Year	*Accounting income before warranty expense*	*Estimated warranty expense*	*Pre-tax accounting income*	*Actual servicing costs*	*Taxable income*
1	$ 600,000	$100,000	$ 500,000	$ 20,000	$ 580,000
2	600,000	100,000	500,000	150,000	450,000
3	600,000	100,000	500,000	70,000	530,000
Totals	$1,800,000	$300,000	$1,500,000	$240,000	$1,560,000

Under interperiod tax allocation procedures, Fast Limited accrues income taxes expense each year on the basis of pre-tax accounting income and records the difference between the current income tax liability and the income taxes expense as deferred income taxes. Journal entries (explanation omitted) to record income taxes at the effective rate of 45% for the three years are as follows:

Journal entries for deferred income tax debits arising from warranty expense timing differences

		Debit	Credit
Year 1	Income Tax Expense ($500,000 × 0.45)	225,000	
	Deferred Income Taxes	36,000	
	Income Taxes Payable ($580,000 × 0.45) ...		261,000
Year 2	Income Taxes Expense ($500,000 × 0.45)	225,000	
	Deferred Income Taxes		22,500
	Income Taxes Payable ($450,000 × 0.45) ...		202,500
Year 3	Income Taxes Expense ($500,000 × 0.45)	225,000	
	Deferred Income Taxes	13,500	
	Income Taxes Payable ($530,000 × 0.45) ...		238,500

In this illustration, pre-tax accounting income and taxable income are not identical over the three-year period, but there is a presumption that the $60,000 ($300,000 – $240,000 = $60,000) excess of estimated warranty expense over actual servicing costs will counterbalance in future years. The debit balance of $27,000 ($36,000 – $22,500 + $13,500 = $27,000) in the Deferred Income Taxes ledger account at the end of Year 3 represents the future income tax benefits that will be realized when the servicing costs actually are incurred and deducted in the computation of taxable income.

In the income statement for Year 1, Fast Limited reports $225,000 of income taxes expense. To meet the required standards of financial reporting, the amount of income taxes ***payable currently*** and ***deferred income taxes*** applicable to future periods are shown separately as illustrated below in the partial income statement for Fast Company for the year ended December 31, Year 1:

Income taxes payable currently exceed income taxes expense

FAST LIMITED
Partial Income Statement
For Year Ended December 31, Year 1

Income before income taxes (operating income)		$500,000
Income tax expense:		
Payable currently	$261,000	
Less: Deferred income taxes	36,000	225,000
Net income		$275,000

To illustrate the accounting for deferred income tax credits and income tax debits, assume that on January 2, Year 1, Slow Limited acquired for $1 million a machine with an economic life of eight years and no residual value. Assume also that the machine was scrapped at the end of the tenth year and was written off then for income tax purposes. Slow used the straight-line method of depreciation for financial accounting and the accelerated depreciation method allowed by Revenue Canada for income tax purposes. Assuming that Slow earned $800,000 each year ended December 31 (before depreciation expense and income taxes expense at 45%), the effect of these procedures on pre-tax accounting income and taxable income, disregarding the effects of the investment tax credit and annual income tax expensing provision, is shown in the next table.

Note that the pre-tax accounting income and total taxable income are identical

Effects of depreciation timing differences on pre-tax accounting income and taxable income

Year ended Dec. 31:	*Financial accounting-ing income before depre-ciation and income taxes*	*Financial accounting depreciation expense (1)*	*Tax return depreciation deduction (2)*	*Pre-Tax accounting income*	*Taxable income*
Year 1	$ 800,000	$ 125,000	$ 200,000(3)	$ 675,000	$ 600,000
Year 2	800,000	125,000	160,000(4)	675,000	640,000
Year 3	800,000	125,000	128,000	675,000	672,000
Year 4	800,000	125,000	102,400	675,000	697,600
Year 5	800,000	125,000	81,920	675,000	718,080
Year 6	800,000	125,000	65,536	675,000	734,464
Year 7	800,000	125,000	52,429	675,000	747,571
Year 8	800,000	125,000	41,943	675,000	758,057

Year 9	800,000	-0-	33,554	800,000	766,446
Year 10	800,000	-0-	134,218	800,000	665,782
Total	$8,000,000	**$1,000,000**	**$1,000,000**	**$7,000,000**	**$7,000,000**

(1) $1,000,000 ÷ 8 = $125,000.
(2) Assume Revenue Canada allows 20% fixed percentage on the declining balance for the ***entire period*** except in Year 10, when the machine is scrapped.
(3) $1,000,000 × 0.20 = $200,000.
(4) ($1,000,000 − $200,000) × 0.20 = $160,000.
(5) [$1,000,000 − ($200,000 + $160,000)] × 0.20 = $128,000; etc.

over the 10-year period because the asset was salvaged (and was the only asset of this type). The journal entries to record income taxes are as follows:

Journal entries for deferred income taxes arising from timing differences

Year 1			
Dec. 31	Income Taxes Expense ($675,000 × 0.45)	303,750	
	Income Taxes Payable ($600,000 × 0.45)		270,000
	Deferred Income Taxes ($75,000 × 0.45)		33,750
Year 2			
Dec. 31	Income Taxes Expense ($675,000 × 0.45)	303,750	
	Income Taxes Payable ($640,000 × 0.45)		288,000
	Deferred Income Taxes ($35,000 × 0.45)		15,750
Year 3			
Dec. 31	Income Taxes Expense ($675,000 × 0.45)	303,750	
	Income Taxes Payable ($672,000 × 0.45)		302,400
	Deferred Income Taxes ($3,000 × 0.45)		1,350
Year 4			
Dec. 31	Income Taxes Expense ($675,000 × 0.45)	303,750	
	Deferred Income Taxes	10,170	
	Income Taxes Payable ($697,600 × 0.45)		313,920
Year 5			
Dec. 31	Income Taxes Expense ($675,000 × 0.45)	303,750	
	Deferred Income Taxes	19,386	
	Income Taxes payable ($718,080 × 0.45)		323,136
Year 6			
Dec. 31	Income Taxes Expense ($675,000 × 0.45)	303,750	
	Deferred Income Taxes	26,759	
	Income Taxes payable ($734,464 × 0.45)		330,509
Year 7			
Dec. 31	Income Taxes Expense ($675,000 × 0.45)	303,750	
	Deferred Income Taxes	32,657	
	Income Taxes Payable ($747,571 × 0.45)		336,407

Year 8			
Dec. 31	Income Taxes Expense ($675,000 × 0.45)	303,750	
	Deferred Income Taxes	37,375	
	Income Taxes Payable ($758,057 × 0.45)		341,125
Year 9			
Dec. 31	Income Taxes Expense ($800,000 × 0.45)	360,000	
	Income Taxes Payable ($766,446 × 0.45)		344,901
	Deferred Income Taxes ($33,554 × 0.45)		15,099
Year 10			
Dec. 31	Income Taxes Expense ($800,000 × 0.45)	360,000	
	Income Taxes Payable ($665,782 × 0.45)		299,602
	Deferred Income Taxes ($134,218 × 0.45) ...		60,398

The total of the 10 years of income taxes expense entries and the total of the 10 years of income taxes payable entries amount to $3,150,000 ($7,000,000 × 0.45 = $3,150,000).

The Deferred Income Taxes ledger account for the above journal entries would be as follows:

Deferred income taxes ledger account for timing differences between financial accounting depreciation and tax return depreciation

Year	*Debit*	*Credit*	*Balance*
1		33,750	33,750 Cr
2		15,750	49,500 Cr
3		1,350	50,850 Cr
4	(a) 10,170		40,680 Cr
5	19,386		21,294 Cr
6	26,759		5,465 Dr
7	32,657		38,122 Dr
8	37,375		75,497 Dr
9		(b) 15,099	60,398 Dr
10		60,398	-0-

(a) This was a drawdown (reversal) from credit entries to a debit entry.
(b) This is a drawdown (reversal) from debit entries to a credit entry.

Capital Gains and Losses

A timing difference will occur when capital gains and losses are included in accounting income in periods different from those for taxable income. Capital losses ***must*** offset capital gains and as a result, although such losses will be recorded as a reduction in accounting income in their year of occurrence, they ***may*** not be allowed as a deduction in the computation of taxable income.

In Slow Limited's income statement for each year, income taxes expense is divided between the amount ***payable currently*** and the amount ***deferred***, as illustrated below in the partial income statement for Slow Limited for the year ended December 31, Year 1:

Income taxes expense is divided between amount payable currently and deferred portion

SLOW LIMITED
Partial Income Statement
For Year Ended December 31, Year 1

Income before income taxes (operating income)		$675,000
Income taxes expense:		
Payable currently	$270,000	
Deferred	33,750	303,750
Net income		$371,250

Alternative Approaches to Interperiod Tax Allocation

Three approaches to the accounting for timing differences have been suggested. These can be summarized as follows:

1 *Deferred method* Under this ***income statement approach***, the income tax effects of current timing differences are computed with ***tax rates in effect when the deferral of taxes takes place***. No adjustments are made to the Deferred Income Taxes ledger account for subsequent changes in income tax rates. The deferred taxes are allocated to income taxes expense when the timing differences reverse. The treatment of timing difference reversals is illustrated on page 1043 in the Cabot Construction example, page 1046 in the Slow Limited example, and on page 1044 in the Fast Limited journal entries.

2 *Accrual method* This is essentially a ***balance sheet approach*** to interperiod tax allocation. Its main objective is the correct measurement of deferred income taxes. If the income tax rates in the year the deferral takes place are different from the expected tax rates in the year in which the payment of income taxes is anticipated, the latter rates are used to measure deferred income taxes. Furthermore, ***subsequent changes in income tax rates require adjustment of deferred income taxes to reflect the new tax rates***.

3 *Net-of-tax method* Interperiod tax allocation under the net-of-tax method views the income tax effects of timing differences as ***valuation accounts*** associated with the related assets and liabilities. ***The tax effects are applied to reduce specific assets or liabilities***. For example, deferred income tax credits arising from the use of an accelerated method depreciation for income tax purposes would be deducted from plant assets in the balance sheet. Similarly, deferred income taxes arising from the use of the instalment method of accounting for income tax purposes would be deducted from instalment accounts receivable in the balance sheet.

The *CICA Handbook*, section 3470, requires the use of the deferred method.[5]

Computational Techniques for Interperiod Tax Allocation

Pre-tax accounting income is that amount which is to be shown in the enterprise's financial statements immediately before income taxes expense and extraordinary

5 CICA, *CICA Handbook*, sec. 3470.19–.20.

items, if applicable. It is the amount of pre-tax income from operations determined following generally accepted accounting principles, in most cases.

Taxable income is that amount of income, before the determination of income taxes payable, that allows for the requirements of the Income Tax Act.

The difference between pre-tax accounting income and taxable income represents the sum of individual timing differences which, when applicable tax rates are applied to each difference or to the aggregate amount, results in the deferred income taxes amount.

Stated in equation form:

Pre-tax accounting income = taxable income + timing difference

and, as a result:

Income taxes expense = income tax payable ± deferred income taxes

The above two equations can be put into work sheet format in which the reasons for differences in a pre-tax accounting income column and a taxable income column, and their income taxes effects, are adequately explained by the details of the timing differences in a timing difference column. (Revenue Canada requires that a company include a reconciliation between income reported in its income statement and taxable income. Timing differences represent the reconciling items, for the most part.)

In the work sheet that follows, the term ''capital cost allowance claimed'' is used. For income tax purposes, the depreciation expense amount used for tax return purposes is called ***capital cost allowance*** (CCA). Also, since only the fixed percentage declining balance method of determining CCA is allowed for tax return purposes, the net book value of the asset used for each successive year's calculation is called the ***undepreciated capital cost*** (UCC) of the asset. In summary, the terminology is as follows:

Financial accounting terminology	***Tax return terminology***
Depreciation expense	Capital cost allowance
Net book value	Undepreciated capital cost

Income tax returns and income statements are prepared annually for government authorities and shareholders respectively. As a consequence, the multiyear examples for Cabot Construction Limited, Slow Limited, and Fast Limited on pages 1042, 1045, and 1044 may be illustrated on an annual basis. Accordingly, a work sheet which provides the necessary information, using the first year of the Slow Limited illustration on page 1045, follows:

Work sheet incorporating timing differences in taxes determinations

SLOW LIMITED
Work Sheet to Compare Income Taxes
For Year 1

	Pre-tax accounting income, (Dr) or Cr	*Taxable income, (Dr) or Cr*	*Timing differences, (Dr) or Cr*
Net income before income taxes	$675,000	$675,000	
Timing differences:			
Remove depreciation expense, not used for tax purposes		125,000	$ (125,000)
Include capital cost allowance claimed		(200,000)	200,000
	$675,000	$600,000	$ 75,000
Income tax rate	45%	45%	45%
Data for journal entry:			
Provision for Income Taxes ($675,000 × 45%)	$303,750		
Income Taxes Payable ($600,000 × 45%)		$270,000	
Deferred Income Taxes ($75,000 ×45%)			$ 33,750

The journal entry at the end of Year 1 to record the above information will be as shown on page 1046. Also, the partial income statement, shown on page 1048, shows the breakdown of the $303,750 provision for income taxes into the above $270,000 (income taxes payable) and $33,750 (deferred income taxes).

The net income before income taxes includes, as a debit, the depreciation expense. Since it does not enter into the computation of taxable income (unless depreciation equals capital cost allowance), it must be removed from the income figure by crediting net income before income taxes in the ''Taxable income'' column. Likewise, capital cost allowance is a deductible ''expense'' for income tax purposes and is therefore debited to net income before income taxes in the ''Taxable income'' column. Accounting income has been determined according to generally accepted accounting principles, and is therefore ''correct.'' Accordingly, a timing difference in the net amount of $75,000 credit results in order for the equation ''accounting income equals taxable income plus or minus timing differences'' to hold true (that is, $675,000 Cr = $600,000 Cr + $75,000 Cr).

Although the entry for the provision for income taxes is at the current year rate, the amount for provision may not be this amount. See pages 1066 and 1067 for an example of a different amount for the provision than that arrived at using only the current rate.

Legal Provisions (Permanent differences)

Accounting income may differ from taxable income because certain revenue and expense is *exempt* from taxation or because allowable tax deductions differ from expenses recognized for financial accounting purposes. These differences are *permanent* in the sense that they arise not from differences in the timing of revenue and expense but because Parliament has used the income tax law to accomplish certain public policy objectives. Some illustrations are given below.

Non-Taxable Revenue

Examples of accounting revenue which is not subject to federal income taxation are life insurance proceeds received by a corporation on the death of its officers and dividends received by a corporation from another taxable Canadian corporation.

Non-Deductible Expenses

Examples of business expenses which are not deductible for federal income tax purposes are premiums paid on life insurance policies for which the corporation is the beneficiary, and certain penalties.

Tax Deductions That Are Not Expenses

The federal income tax law may from time to time allow some deductions for income tax purposes which do not represent actual business expense. The 3% inventory allowance was one prominent example. ***Because permanent differences between taxable and accounting income did not affect other accounting periods, interperiod tax allocation was not appropriate for such differences.*** To illustrate, assume Slow Limited in Year 1 claimed capital cost allowance equal to depreciation expense (no timing difference) and included in income dividends from a taxable Canadian corporation in the amount of $20,000, life insurance premiums of $5,000, and a 3% inventory allowance of $8,000. The work sheet format may be used to compute the provision for income taxes, income taxes payable, and deferred income taxes, as shown below.

Work sheet incorporating permanent differences in taxes determinations

SLOW LIMITED
Work Sheet to Compute Income Taxes
For Year 1

	Pre-tax accounting income, (Dr) or Cr	*Taxable income, (Dr) or Cr*	*Timing differences, (Dr) or Cr*
Net income before income taxes	$675,000	$675,000	
Permanent differences:			
Dividends	(20,000)	(20,000)	
Life Insurance	5,000	5,000	
3% inventory allowance	(8,000)	(8,000)	
Timing differences:			
Depreciation expense		250,000	$ (250,000)
Capital cost allowance claimed		(250,000)	250,000
	$652,000	$652,000	-0-
Income tax rate	45%	45%	
Data for journal entry:			
Provision for Income Taxes ($652,000 × 45%)	$293,400		
Income Taxes Payable ($652,000 × 45%)		$293,400	
Deferred Income Taxes			-0-

The net income before income taxes of $675,000 includes a credit of $20,000 for dividends which will never be taxed creating a permanent rather than a timing difference. The life insurance expense has been included as a debit in the $675,000 and will also never be allowed for tax purposes. The 3% inventory allowance has not been included in the $675,000 figure. It was an amount the tax department allowed as a deduction from income for tax purposes. It could not be reversed in the future and was therefore not a timing but a permanent difference.

Permanent differences affect **both** the "Accounting income" and the "Taxable income" columns. As a result, ***the provision for income taxes and income taxes payable reflect permanent differences.***

The journal entry (explanation omitted) to record the above information is presented below:

Journal entry for determination of income taxes when permanent differences present

Provision for Income Taxes	293,400	
Income Taxes Payable		293,400

The partial income statement for the permanent difference illustration will appear as follows:

Income statement presentation when permanent differences applicable

SLOW LIMITED
Partial Income Statement
For Year 1

Net Income before income taxes	$675,000
Provision for income taxes (all current)	29,340
Net income	$645,660

Shareholders and other users of Slow Limited's financial statements would expect to find the provision for income taxes at an amount of $303,750 ($675,000 × 45%) if they are aware of the corporation income tax rate. However, the provision is $10,350 ($303,750 – $293,400) lower than expected. This is because of the permanent differences totalling $23,000 [($20,000) + $5,000 + ($8,000)], which when multiplied by 45% equals $10,350. The Accounting Standards Committee has considered the matter and concluded that this information would be useful when the amounts are significant.[6]

If the amounts are significant, disclosure may need to be made for:

1 Deductions which may be allowable for tax purposes even though they have no counterpart in the determination of accounting income

2 Items that are nontaxable or nondeductible for income tax purposes on a once-and-for-all basis

6 CICA, *CICA Handbook*, sec. 3470.33.

To illustrate both timing differences and permanent differences, the information for timing differences on page 1045 and for the permanent differences shown in the work sheet on page 1051 will be used. The work sheet will appear as follows:

Work sheet incorporating both permanent and timing differences in taxes determination

SLOW LIMITED
Work Sheet to Compute Income Taxes
For Year 1

	Pre-tax accounting income, (Dr) or Cr	*Taxable income, (Dr) or Cr*	*Timing differences, (Dr) or Cr*
Net income before income taxes	$675,000	$675,000	
Permanent differences:			
Dividends	(20,000)	(20,000)	
Life insurance	5,000	5,000	
3% inventory allowance	(8,000)	(8,000)	
Timing differences:			
Depreciation expense		125,000	(125,000)
Capital cost allowance claimed		(200,000)	200,000
	$652,000	$577,000	$ 75,000
Income tax rate	45%	45%	45%
Data for journal entry:			
Provision for Income Taxes ($652,000 × 45%)	$293,400		
Income Taxes Payable ($577,000 × 45%)		$259,650	
Deferred Income Taxes ($75,000 ×45%)			$ 33,750

An examination of the three worksheets will show that:

1 Permanent differences affect only accounting income and taxable income in the determination of income taxes.

2 Timing differences affect only taxable income and timing differences in the determination of income taxes.

3 The provision for income taxes, therefore, is affected by permanent differences only.

4 Income taxes payable is affected by both permanent and timing differences.

5 Deferred income taxes is affected by timing differences only.

Carryback and Carryforward of Operating Losses

To help ease the income tax burden of corporations that experience losses, federal income tax law provides that operating losses may be carried back against the taxable income of the three preceding years and then forward against taxable income earned in the 7 years following the loss. The effect of this provision is to create either a receivable for a tax refund or a potential future tax savings when an operating loss occurs. When an operating loss is carried back or carried forward, pre-tax accounting income and taxable income (after the operating loss is deducted) differ for the year to which the loss is applied. Thus, ***operating losses create special kinds of tax timing differences***.

Operating Loss Carryback

When an operating loss occurs following a period of profitable operations, a corporation has a claim for a refund of past income taxes that is recognized as an offset to the pre-tax operating loss in the year in which the loss occurs. On this point, the Accounting Standards Committee has made the following recommendation:[7]

> Where a loss for tax purposes gives rise to a recovery of income taxes of the previous period, such recovery should be reflected in the income statement for the period of the loss either before "income (loss) before extraordinary items" or, if it relates to an extraordinary item, as a deduction therefrom.

To illustrate the accounting for an operating loss carryback, assume that Tony Limited reports an operating loss of $100,000 for the year ended June 30, Year 5. Tony is able to carry back the $100,000 loss and offset it against taxable income of prior years, thus claiming a tax refund of $45,000 (assuming a 45% income tax rate). The effect of the loss carry back is recorded at June 30, Year 5, as follows:

Journal entry for operating loss carryback

Income Tax Refund Receivable	45,000	
Provision for Income Taxes		45,000
To record claim for income taxes previously paid ($100,000 × 0.45 = $45,000).		

The lower section of the income statement of Tony Limited for the year ended June 30, Year 5, is presented as follows:

Income statement presentation of operating loss carryback

TONY LIMITED
Partial Income Statement
For Year Ended June 30, Year 5

Operating loss before income tax effect of operating loss carryback	$(100,000)
Less: Provision for income taxes	45,000
Net loss	$ (55,000)

In order for the entire loss of $100,000 to be carried back to a prior period for tax purposes, there must have been taxable income in that prior period to absorb it. To illustrate this important point, assume Tony Limited commenced business July

7 CICA, *CICA Handbook*, sec. 3470.40.

1, Year 3, and had prepared the following work sheet for its year ending June 30, Year 4, income taxes:

Work sheet for computation of year ending June 30, Year 4, income taxes

	Pre-tax accounting income, (Dr) or Cr	*Taxable income, (Dr) or Cr*	*Timing differences, (Dr) or Cr*
Net income before income taxes	$250,000	$250,000	
Permanent differences:	None	None	
Timing differences:			
Depreciation expense		100,000	$(100,000)
Capital cost allowance		(200,000)	200,000
	$250,000	$150,000	100,000
Income tax rate	45%	45%	45%
Data for journal entry:			
Provision for Income Taxes	$112,500		
Income Taxes Payable		$ 67,500	
Deferred Income Taxes			$ 45,000

The taxable income for the year ending June 30, Year 4, was $150,000, as shown above. As a result, the corporation was able to carry back the $100,000 loss as there was sufficient prior period taxable income to absorb this loss.

Assume the taxable loss for the year ending June 30, Year 5 amounted to $400,000.The amount of year ending June 30, Year 4, taxable income ($150,000) is not sufficient to absorb that amount. The income tax department allows a corporation to adjust for deductions claimed in the prior period in order to increase taxable income in that period so as to use up more of the current-year loss as a loss carryback. In this example, by not claiming capital cost allowance for the prior fiscal year, taxable income would be increased by $200,000 to $350,000. The $400,000 loss would then be ''distributed'' for income tax purposes, $350,000 carryback and $50,000 carryforward. Otherwise, the arrangement would have been $150,000 carryback and $250,000 carryforward. It is the taxpayer's decision as to whether deductions claimed for income tax purposes will be adjusted for the prior period (resulting in refiling the prior-period income tax return). When revisions have been made to the deductions claimed in the original income tax return, necessitating the refiling of that year's return, the Accounting Standards Committee recommends:[8]

> Where the recomputation of taxable income for the previous period results in an adjustment to accumulated deferred income taxes, such adjustment should be reflected in the income statement for the period of the loss.

The sole purpose of the recomputation is to adjust the amount of loss that will be available for loss carryforward. The amount which may be shown in the *loss* year, as a result of the loss carryback, *can never exceed the amount of income taxes payable and subsequently paid for the prior period.*

8 CICA, *CICA Handbook*, sec. 3470.42.

Operating Loss Carryforward

If a corporation must depend on future earnings to use a current year's operating loss as a tax deduction, the accounting for income taxes presents a more difficult problem. A question arises as to whether the probability of future income tax benefit is sufficiently high to permit an accounting treatment which ***anticipates*** the income tax benefit of the operating loss carryforward. In a loss year, it is reasonable to expect management to minimize the amount of the net loss. Providing a credit as the income tax provision for the loss carryback partially satisfies the minimization of the loss.

Management would also like to anticipate that sufficient future incomes will be earned in the loss carryforward period to ''use up'' the loss carryforward amount. Thus, income tax payments during this future period will be reduced by the ''using up'' of the loss carryforward multiplied by the tax rate in the year affected. Management would prefer to record these future tax benefits in the loss year, thereby reducing the loss even further.

For example, Tony Limited's $400,000 loss could be carried back in the amount of $350,000 and forward in the amount of $50,000. The loss before recovery of prior periods' income taxes and allowance for the benefit of future years' tax savings was $400,000. This would be reduced by the tax recovery in the loss carryback portion or $157,500 ($350,000 × 0.45) resulting in a loss of $242,500 ($400,000 – $157,500). A further reduction of $22,500 ($50,000 × 0.45) would result if the company were able to anticipate future use of this tax saving. The loss would then be reported as $220,000 ($242,500 – $22,500). Notice that the ***maximum*** reduction of the loss is represented by the tax rate used times the amount of the loss — in this example $180,000 ($400,000 × 0.45).

The Accounting Standards Committee reasons that there would be two situations present to aid in the solution as to whether the tax benefit of loss carryforwards should be recorded in the income statement before or upon realization.

Virtual Certainty When virtual certainty is present, the tax benefit applicable to that portion of the loss carryforward, which is considered virtually certain of application against future taxable income, will be allowed as a reduction in the current year's loss.

Virtual certainty of realizing the loss or a portion thereof in the loss carryforward period (other than capital losses) requires that ***all three*** of the following conditions be present:[9]

1. The loss results from an identifiable and non-recurring cause.
2. A record of profitability has been established over a long period by the corporation, or a predecessor business, with any occasional losses being more than offset by income in subsequent years.
3. There is assurance beyond any reasonable doubt that future taxable income will be sufficient to offset the loss carryforward and will be earned during the carryforward period prescribed by the tax laws. In assessing its ability to earn

9 CICA, *CICA Handbook*, sec. 3470.43.

sufficient future taxable income to offset the loss, a corporation may recognize that it can maximize its taxable income during the loss carryforward period by not claiming certain deductions allowable for tax purposes (e.g., capital cost allowances). This will result either in a reduction of accumulated deferred income tax credits or in the recording of deferred income tax debits during the carryforward period.

The first condition requires the cause of the loss be unusual, such as a lengthy strike. The second condition excludes corporations without a history of profitable operations (which includes relatively new businesses). The third condition requires professional judgement, which may require adjustments in the future carryforward period in the event that anticipated events do not materialize.

If all three of the above conditions are met, the Accounting Standards Committee has recommended the following:[10]

> Where, in the period in which the loss for tax purposes occurs, a corporation is virtually certain of realizing the tax benefit of all or a portion of the resulting loss carryforward for tax purposes, such tax benefit should be reflected in the financial statements of that period. The tax benefit should be reflected in the income statement either before "income (loss) before extraordinary items" or, if it relates to an extraordinary item, as a deduction therefrom. The amount should ordinarily be disclosed separately as an asset in the balance sheet. However, any portion of the tax benefit which is recognized as a result of the assumption that the corporation will not claim certain deductions allowable for tax purposes in the carryforward period should be reflected in the balance sheet either as a reduction of accumulated deferred income tax credits or as deferred income tax debits, as appropriate.

To illustrate a situation wherein virtual certainty is present, assume La Scala, Inc., has conducted profitable operations for a number of years. However, in the current year a lengthy strike closed operations and as a result the corporation suffered a $500,000 loss. The prior periods' taxable incomes amounted to $300,000 and the company decided not to amend CCA claimed on its previous tax returns. As a result, a tax loss of ($500,000 − $300,000) = $200,000 was available for carryforward purposes. Management was virtually certain the corporation would earn in excess of $200,000 taxable income in the loss carryforward period. Assuming the income tax rate remained at 45% La Scala, Inc., will record in the loss year a tax benefit for the loss carryforward of ($200,000 × 45%) = $90,000 to apply against its loss.

The journal entries to record, in the loss year, the refundable tax from the loss carryback and the tax benefit from the loss carryforward are as follows:

Journal entries for loss carryback and loss carryforward when virtual certainty is present

Income Tax Refund Receivable	135,000	
Provision for Income Taxes		135,000
To record claim for income taxes previously paid: $300,000 × 45% = $135,000.		

10 CICA, *CICA Handbook*, sec. 3470.46.

Tax Benefit Available for Application Against Future Income Taxes	90,000	
Provision for Income Taxes		90,000
To record tax benefit of loss carryforward because virtual certainty is present: $200,000 × 45% = $90,000.		

The "tax benefit" account should not be offset against deferred income taxes, but rather should normally be included as an asset in the balance sheet.

The lower section of the corporation's income statement for the year in which the operating loss is incurred appears as follows:

Income statement presentation of operating loss carryback and carryforward

LA SCALA, INC.
Partial Income Statement
For Current Year

Operating loss before recovery of income taxes		$(500,000)
Less: Recovery of income taxes:		
Current	$135,000	
Deferred	90,000	225,000
Net loss		$(275,000)

The taxes refundable from the prior period is ***currently*** receivable. The tax benefits applicable to ***future*** incomes is ***not current*** and therefore is deferred above.

No Virtual Certainty When no virtual certainty is present, the corporation cannot set up, as an asset, the tax benefit account. In fact, the corporation may not be able to include any benefit from future use of the loss carryforward. The loss carryforward in such a case would not be recorded in the accounting records of the corporation. It will be recorded when realized in the future.

For situations in which virtual certainty is not present, the Accounting Standards Committee has made the following recommendation:[11]

> The unrecorded tax benefit of the loss carryforward should be recognized to the extent of any reductions in accumulated deferred income tax credits available in the carryforward period by claiming less capital cost allowances than decpreciation recorded or by making other adjustments of a similar effect. The amount of the reductions recognized in the period in which the loss occurs should be reflected in the income statement before "income before extraordinary items" or, if it relates to an extraordinary item, as a deduction therefrom. It should be reflected in the balance sheet as a reduction of accumulated deferred income tax credits.

An examination of this recommendation reveals the following:

1 The maximum the deferred income taxes balance may be reduced at the end of

11 CICA, *CICA Handbook*, sec. 3470.48.

the loss year is the total amount this account is expected to be reduced during the loss carryforward period.

2. The loss carryforward for tax purposes multiplied by the expected tax rate, if enacted, is the maximum tax benefit that may be recognized in the loss year.
3. Deferred income taxes cannot be placed into debit balance by recognition of the tax benefit of the loss carryforward. Therefore, the maximum will be the credit balance in deferred income taxes at the end of the loss year immediately before consideration of the tax benefit of the loss carryforward.

To illustrate, assume the following for Wilson Limited:

1. The company reports a pre-tax accounting loss of $900,000 for the current year.
2. The balance of deferred income taxes was $400,000 credit at the beginning of the current year. The tax effect of capital cost allowance claimed in excess of depreciation expense represents the entire $400,000.
3. In the current year depreciation expense exceeded capital cost allowance claimed by $50,000.
4. The company reported taxable income of $80,000 in the allowable loss carryback period.
5. The company decided not to amend CCA for the allowable loss carryback period.
6. The income tax rate has been and is expected to be at 45%.
7. The company is unable to satisfy all three conditions of virtual certainty.
8. The company estimated it will expense $700,000 of depreciation in excess of capital cost allowance it will claim during the loss carryforward period.
9. There are no permanent differences in the current year.

The loss for tax purposes will be $900,000 minus the excess of depreciation expense over capital cost allowance claimed of $50,000, or $850,000.

The loss carryforward for tax purposes will be $850,000 minus the loss carryback of $80,000, or $770,000.

The balance in deferred income taxes will be $400,000 minus ($50,000 × 45%) = $377,500 at the end of the loss year before consideration of the tax benefit of the loss carryforward for tax purposes.

The amount of tax benefit that will be recorded by the company for the loss carryforward will be the lower of three maximums set out below.

1. Expected reduction from depreciation in next five years is $700,000 × 45% = $315,000.
2. Tax benefit on loss carryforward is $770,000 × 45% = $346,500.
3. The balance of deferred income taxes at the end of the current year = $377,500.

The company will be able to record a tax benefit for the loss carryforward period of $315,000.

The journal entries to record the information for the current (loss) year with respect to income taxes will be as follows:

Journal entries to record income taxes in the loss year when virtual certainty is not present

Deferred Income Taxes	22,500	
Provision for Income Taxes		22,500
To record the current year timing differences: $50,000 × 45%.		
Income Tax Refund Receivable	36,000	
Provision for Income Taxes		36,000
To record claim for income taxes previously paid: $80,000 × 45% = $36,000.		
Deferred Income Taxes	315,000	
Provision for Income Taxes		315,000
To record the allowable tax benefit arising from the loss carryforward: $700,000 × 45%.		

The company's loss for tax purposes of $850,000 has been accounted for as follows:

Amount of loss carried back	$ 80,000
Amount of loss carried forward	700,000
Amount of loss for tax purposes recorded	$780,000
Total loss for tax purposes	850,000
Unrecorded loss carryforward for tax purposes	$ 70,000

When a corporation has unrecorded loss carryforward for tax purposes at the end of the loss year, it must disclose this fact in the notes to the financial statements as follows:[12]

1 The amount of the loss carryforward for tax purposes (so long as a credit will not be made to deferred income taxes, when that loss carryforward is recognized in the company's accounts)

2 The expiration date of the loss carryforward

The lower section of Wilson Limited's income statement for the loss year appears at the top of page 1061.

The deferred total of $337,500 represents the $22,500 plus $315,000 shown in the journal entries above.

Management of the company would have preferred the $900,000 loss to be reduced by 45% of that amount of $405,000 (which would have been the case had virtual certainty been applicable for the entire loss or if the lowest of the three

12 CICA, *CICA Handbook*, sec. 3470.54.

Income statement presentation of operating loss carryforward when virtual certainty is not present

WILSON LIMITED
Partial Income Statement
For Current Year

Operating loss before recovery of income taxes		$(900,000)
Less: Recovery of income taxes:		
Current	$ 36,000	
Deferred	337,500	373,500
Net loss		$(526,500)

maximums had been the tax effect of the loss carryforward for tax purposes). The difference, $31,500 ($346,500 tax benefit on loss carryforward minus $315,000 expected reduction in deferred income taxes during the loss carryforward period), represents the tax benefit applicable to the unrecorded loss carryforward for tax purposes ($70,000 × 45% = $31,500). The $31,500 or any portion thereof must be included in income as an ***extraordinary item*** in the period in which it is realized so long as it is able to be realized within the loss carryforward period.[13]

When virtual certainty is not present in the loss year, and there is ***no*** deferred income tax ***credit*** balance, the loss carryforward tax benefit will not be recorded in the accounts. However, it is reasonable to expect management not to take capital cost allowance in a loss year, as doing so increases taxable loss. However, depreciation expense must be recorded in conformity with generally accepted accounting principles. The result is a ***debit timing difference***. If the requirement that deferred income taxes not be in debit balance were followed, no provision for income taxes would be allowed for the depreciation expense. Capital cost allowance may be claimed well beyond the loss carryforward period, and, as a consequence, if there is ***reasonable assurance*** that the debit balance in deferred income taxes ***arising in the loss year*** (for example, by not claiming capital cost allowances) will reverse in the future (not restricted to the loss carryforward period), it will be allowed. This exception (***reasonable assurance***) may only occur in the loss period. If in a subsequent period there no longer is ***reasonable assurance***, deferred income tax debits arising from prior loss periods are to be written off to income where they will appear as an extraordinary item.[14]

To illustrate, assume the following for Start-Up, Inc., which commenced business on January 1, 19X1:

	Years ending December 31:	
	19X1	*19X2*
Income (Loss) before income taxes	$(300,000)	$600,000
Depreciation booked	40,000	40,000
Capital cost allowance claimed	—	100,000
Income tax rate	45%	45%

13 CICA, *CICA Handbook*, sec. 3470.56.

14 CICA, *CICA Handbook*, sec. 3470.52.

For the 19X1 year, the work sheet would include the following:

Work sheet for "reasonable assurance" example, 19X1

	Pre-tax accounting income, (Dr) or Cr	*Taxable income, (Dr) or Cr*	*Timing differences, (Dr) or Cr*
Loss before income taxes	$(300,000)	$(300,000)	
Timing differences:			
Depreciation		40,000	$(40,000)
CCA		—	—
	$(300,000)	$(260,000)	($40,000)

Since this is the first year of operations, Start-Up, Inc., will have no deferred income taxes balance. Accordingly, if the debit timing difference was allowed to affect the deferred income tax, a debit of $18,000 ($40,000 × 0.45 = $18,000) would be recorded by the company. This entry is permissible, in a loss year, if there is ***reasonable assurance*** that ***sometime*** in the future, the company will earn sufficient taxable income to require that capital cost allowance be taken in excess of depreciation booked such that the deferred income taxes debit balance is ***reversed***.

Assuming ***reasonable assurance is present***, the entry to record the 19X1 income taxes is as follows:

Deferred Income Taxes	18,000	
Provision for Income Taxes		18,000

There will also be a footnote stating there is a loss carryforward of $260,000 which expires in 19X8.

Assuming ***reasonable assurance is not present***, no entry is recorded in 19X1 for income tax purposes. A footnote would indicate a loss carryforward of $260,000 and an unrecorded $40,000 timing difference.

The work sheet and journal entries for Year 19X2 when ***reasonable assurance was present in 19X1***, is as follows:

Work sheet for "reasonable assurance" example, Year 19X2, when reasonable assurance was present in Year 19X1

	Pre-tax accounting income, (Dr) or Cr	*Taxable income, (Dr) or Cr*	*Timing differences, (Dr) or Cr*	*Extraordinary item, (Dr) or Cr*
Income before income taxes	$600,000	$600,000		
Timing differences:				
Depreciation		40,000	$(40,000)	
CCA		(100,000)	100,000	
	$600,000	$540,000	$ 60,000	
Loss carryforward		(260,000)		$260,000
	$600,000	$280,000	$ 60,000	$260,000

Data for journal entry:				
Provision for Income Taxes	$270,000			
Income Tax Payable		$126,000		
Deferred Income Taxes			$ 27,000	
Extraordinary Item				$117,000

Under ***reasonable assurance***, the 19X2 journal entry will be:

Provision for Income Taxes	270,000	
Income Taxes Payable		126,000
Deferred Income Taxes		27,000
Extraordinary Item		117,000

Where ***reasonable assurance was not present in 19X1***, the work sheet and journal entries in 19X2 will be as follows:

Work sheet for "reasonable assurance" example, Year 19X2, when reasonable assurance was *not* present in 19X1

	Pre-tax accounting income, (Dr) or Cr	*Taxable income, (Dr) or Cr*	*Timing differences, (Dr) or Cr*	*Extraordinary item, (Dr) or Cr*
Income before income taxes	$600,000	$600,000		
Timing differences:				
Depreciation		40,000	$(40,000)	
CCA		(100,000)	100,000	
	$600,000	$540,000	$ 60,000	
Loss carryforward		(260,000)	(40,000)	$300,000
	$600,000	$280,000	$ 20,000	$300,000
Data for journal entry:				
Provision for Income Taxes	$270,000			
Income Taxes Payable		$126,000		
Deferred Income Taxes			$ 9,000	
Extraordinary Item				$135,000

When ***no reasonable assurance was present in Year 19X1***, the journal entry for 19X2 will be:

Provision for Income Taxes	270,000	
Income Taxes Payable		126,000
Deferred Income Taxes		9,000
Extraordinary Item		135,000

In the ***reasonable assurance*** example, the deferred tax debit was ***reversed*** in the 19X2 year. Note that the sum of the 19X1 deferred income taxes and the 19X2 deferred income taxes amounted to $9,000 [$(18,000) + $27,000 = $9,000], the same end-of-year 19X2 balance as when ***no reasonable assurance*** was present. The assumption that reasonable assurance was present was sound in this illustration.

Note also that the loss in 19X1 was reduced by the provision for income taxes in 19X1 ($18,000) when reasonable assurance was present. This amount represents the increase in the extraordinary item credit in 19X2 for the ''no reasonable assurance'' example ($135,000 − $117,000 = $18,000). The total of the two years' incomes is the same; only the ***timing*** of the recording of income is different.

The lower portion of the income statement for 19X1 and 19X2, and the total for the two years, in both situations is shown below.

Reasonable assurance present in 19X1 year

	19X1		*19X2*		*Total (19X1 + 19X2)*	
Income (loss) before extraordinary item and income taxes ...		$(300,000)		$600,000		$300,000
Provison for income taxes:						
Deferred	$(18,000)		$ 27,000		$ 9,000	
Current	—	18,000	243,000	270,000	243,000	252,000
Income before extraordinary item		$(282,000)		$330,000		48,000
Extraordinary item ..				117,000		117,000
Net income		$(282,000)		$447,000		$165,000

No reasonable assurance present in 19X1 year

	19X1		*19X2*		*Total (19X1 + 19X2)*	
Income (loss) before extraordinary item and income taxes ...		$(300,000)		$600,000		$300,000
Provison for income taxes:						
Deferred	—		$ 27,000		$ 27,000	
Current	—	—	243,000	270,000	243,000	270,000
Income before extraordinary item		$(300,000)		$330,000		30,000
Extraordinary item ..				135,000		135,000
Net income		$(300,000)		$465,000		$165,000

Carryback and Carryforward of Capital Losses

In order for a capital loss in a year to be reduced by the applicable (provision for income tax credit) benefit, there must be virtual certainty that the capital loss will be offset by capital gains in the foreseeable future. Section 3470.44 of the ***CICA Handbook*** sets out the requirements with respect to capital losses, as follows:

> The fact that allowable capital losses can be carried forward indefinitely does not ensure the realization of the tax benefit. There cannot be an assumption that allowable capital losses will be eventually offset by taxable capital gains unless there are circumstances present indicating that there is virtual certainty that sufficient taxable capital gains will be realized in the foreseeable future. Virtual certainty requires all three of the following conditions to be present:
> **(i)** a potential capital gain is present in unrealized form and in assets which are not essential to the future operations of the corporation;
> **(ii)** the balance of the unrealized capital gain, after allowance for possible decline before disposal, is sufficient to offset the loss in question; and
> **(iii)** there is satisfactory evidence of an intent to dispose of the particular assets in the foreseeable future and thus realize the potential capital gain.

Assuming these requirements are met, and that one-half of the capital losses will represent a ***permanent difference***, then one-half of all capital gains is exempt from tax and the other half is taxable at the current income tax rate. As a result, the one-half of the loss which is to be used to offset the taxable future capital gains will be reduced by the tax saving thereon at the future tax rate, if such is enacted — otherwise at the current tax rate. It should be noted that in ***all*** virtual certainty situations, when the tax rate changes, the tax benefit asset account and the provision for income taxes will be adjusted so as to reflect the new rate. This represents the accrual rather than the deferral concept.

Summary of Timing Differences

A proper accounting for deferred income taxes requires a continuous accounting for its components. Two reasons why a summary of timing differences and its related deferred income taxes should be maintained by a corporation are (1) to be able to separate current deferred income taxes from long-term deferred income taxes for financial statement purposes,[15] and (2) to properly account for changing tax rates. The accounting for changes in tax rates, as detailed under item **1** on page 1048, requires some method of removing items from deferred income taxes when a drawdown occurs and the increases to that account have been at different tax rates over time. The Accounting Standards Committee suggests the following:[16]

> Where the difference between accounting and taxable income in a period gives rise to a transfer to income from the tax allocation balance accumulated in prior periods,

15 CICA, ***CICA Handbook***, sec. 3470.24, .26, .27.

16 CICA, ***CICA Handbook***, sec. 3470.18.

such transfer will be computed at the rate of accumulation. Where there are practical difficulties in identifying the specific components, the transfer may be calculated at the effective average rate of accumulation, i.e., the proportion that the accumulated deferred credit or charge bears to the accumulated difference between taxable and accounting income. This calculation might be made either by types of differences or in the aggregate.

To illustrate a suitable summary of timing differences, together with related deferred income taxes, assume the following information for Easy Corporation:

Timing differences:	*Year 1*	*Year 2*	*Year 3*
Warranty expense	$100,000	$150,000	$100,000
Warranty payments	50,000	100,000	150,000
Depreciation expense	200,000	200,000	200,000
Capital cost allowance claimed	400,000	200,000	150,000
Tax rate	40%	45%	50%

The income tax department allows warranty payments as expense for tax purposes and disallows warranty expense based on estimated warranty costs.

An analysis of the summary of timing differences shown below and the work sheet shown on page 1067 for the three years indicates the following:

1 In Years 1 and 2, while the entries to the summary *increase* the balance, even though the tax rate changes, the net deferred income tax effect is at the current rate each year as shown in the work sheet for each year.

2 In Year 3 there is a drawdown in each category. The *deferred method* requires this drawdown be at the specific or average tax rate. The average tax rate (determined by dividing the deferred income taxes by their timing difference for each category) is used in this illustration.

EASY CORPORATION
Summary of Timing Differences

	Current Year 1	*Opening balance, Year 2*	*Current Year 2*	*Opening balance, Year 3*	*Current Year 3*	*Closing balance, Year 3*
Depreciation expense/Capital cost allowance	$200,000	$200,000	-0-	$200,000	$(50,000)	$150,000
Income tax rate	40%	40%	45%	40%	40%	40%
Deferred income tax	80,000	80,000	-0-	80,000	(20,000)	60,000
Warranty expense/Warranty payments	(50,000)	(50,000)	(50,000)	(100,000)	50,000	(50,000)
Income tax rate	40%	40%	45%	42.5%	42.5%	42.5%
Deferred income taxes	(20,000)	(20,000)	(22,500)	(42,500)	21,250	(21,250)

3 The result is that although net timing differences are nil (see work sheet Year 3), there is a net deferred income tax credit of $1,250 which must result in an adjustment to the provision for income taxes therefor. Under such circumstances the amount of the provision for income taxes is presented as an amount necessary to balance the entries to income taxes payable and deferred income taxes.

The work sheet for the timing differences items listed on page 1066 and used in the determination of taxable income would appear as follows:

Work sheet for timing differences in determination of taxable income or loss

EASY CORPORATION
Partial Work Sheet to Compute Income Taxes
For Years 1, 2, and 3

	Pre-tax accounting income, (Dr) or Cr	*Taxable income, (Dr) or Cr*	*Timing differences, (Dr) or Cr*
Year 1:			
Net income before income taxes	$XXX	$ XXX	
Timing differences:			
Warranty expense		100,000	$(100,000)
Warranty payments		(50,000)	50,000
Depreciation expense		200,000	(200,000)
Capital cost allowance claimed		(400,000)	400,000
			$ 150,000
Tax rate (40%)			
Deferred income tax credit (See summary of timing differences)			$ 60,000
Year 2:			
Net income before income taxes	$XXX	$ XXX	
Timing differences:			
Warranty expense		150,000	$(150,000)
Warranty payments		(100,000)	100,000
Depreciation expense		200,000	(200,000)
Capital cost allowance claimed		(200,000)	200,000
			$ 50,000
Tax rate (45%)			
Deferred income tax (See summary of timing differences)			$ (22,500)
Year 3:			
Net income before income taxes	$XXX	$ XXX	
Timing differences:			
Warranty expense		100,000	$(100,000)
Warranty payments		(150,000)	150,000
Depreciation expense		200,000	(200,000)
Capital cost allowance claimed		(150,000)	150,000
			-0-
Tax rate (50%)			
Deferred income taxes (See summary of timing differences)			$ 1,250

Evaluation of Interperiod Tax Allocation

We have seen that differences between accounting income and taxable income arise from several sources. No allocation problem arises from permanent differences between accounting income and taxable income, as they affect both equally. The ***intra***period allocation of income taxes to extraordinary items and to adjustment applicable to prior periods (discussed on pages 1070–1074) is widely accepted. The controversy over income tax allocation centres on ***inter***period tax allocation.

Arguments in Favour of Interperiod Tax Allocation

The two major arguments in favour of interperiod tax allocation may be stated as follows:

1 Income taxes result from the earning of income. The tax expense to be applied in the measurement of periodic income is the tax caused by each period's earnings, independent of the time of payment. Failure to match income taxes against income when it is included in the income statement causes misleading fluctuations in net income.

2 Timing differences are temporary and create liabilities or assets. A tax saving attributable to a timing difference is only a postponement of the income tax, and a highly probable future cash outlay based on a past event is created. Similarly, a tax payment based on income which will be recognized in the accounting records at some later date makes it highly probable that a corporation will earn tax-free income in future years, creating an expected future economic benefit. Consequently, these highly probable future outlays and benefits meet the accounting definitions of liabilities and assets. For these future outlays and benefits to be highly probable, it must be assumed that future income tax rates will remain at similar levels and that a corporation will earn taxable income in future years. Experience in past years has tended to support the assumption as to income tax rates; the assumption as to profitable continuity has proved applicable to most major corporations, especially with liberal operating loss carryback and carryforward provisions in the income tax law.

Arguments Against Interperiod Tax Allocation

Opposition to interperiod tax allocation is based primarily on the nature of income taxes and the possibility that timing differences may not be temporary. These arguments are summarized below:

1 Income taxes by their nature differ from most expenses. First, income taxes expense (provision for income taxes) emerges only if income is earned; secondly, income taxes expense is based on taxable income, which differs from accounting income in a number of respects. This line of reasoning leads to the conclusion that income taxes are not an expense but an involuntary payment to government units. Furthermore, critics of interperiod tax allocation argue that the provision for income taxes for an accounting period should be the legal tax liability for that period because income taxes are based on the legal concept of taxable income rather than on accounting income.

2 When we view the taxable income of a corporation as a whole, the shifting of income taxes in time (particularly the postponement of taxes) tends to be a permanent rather than a temporary shift, because when one deferral is reversed another arises to take its place. This argument is raised most frequently with respect to one area of timing differences — the case in which a corporation adopts the fixed percentage declining balance method of depreciation for income tax purposes, but not for financial accounting. For example, a corporation acquiring about the same amount of plant assets each year realizes a tax postponement each year, and this postponement is never offset in future years as long as the plant assets are replaced at a steady rate. If a corporation acquires a larger amount of plant assets each year, the total difference between tax depreciation and depreciation expense recognized in the accounting records continues to increase.

Partial Allocation Versus Comprehensive Allocation

In an effort to find a compromise position in the arguments for and against interperiod tax allocation, some accountants have recommended ***partial allocation*** of timing differences. Supporters of partial interperiod tax allocation argue that when recurring differences between pre-tax accounting income and taxable income appear to cause an indefinite postponement of income tax payments, tax allocation is not required for such differences. For example, assume that a corporation with a growing investment in plant assets uses straight-line depreciation for financial accounting purposes and declining balance depreciation for income tax purposes. Under the partial allocation approach, the provision for income taxes for the corporation would be the income tax actually payable for the accounting period.

Advocates of partial allocation thus make a general presumption that the provision for income taxes for financial accounting purposes should be the income tax payable for the accounting period, except for cases in which nonrecurring timing differences between taxable income and accounting income cause material misstatement of the provision for income taxes and net income. Such an exception is illustrated by the instalment sale of an asset at a gain, which is reported in accounting income of the current accounting period but is not taxable until future periods.

The more widely accepted position is that all timing differences between accounting income and taxable income require ***comprehensive allocation*** of income taxes. Under comprehensive allocation, the provision for income taxes for an accounting period includes all accruals, deferrals, and estimates necessary to adjust the income taxes actually payable for the period in order to recognize the tax effects of transactions included in accounting income for that period. Tax effects of initial timing differences are recognized and allocate to those periods in which the initial differences ***reverse***. Comprehensive allocation thus associates tax effects with related transactions as they are reported in the income statement.

The Accounting Standards Committee did not directly address the issue of comprehensive versus partial tax allocation. However, comprehensive tax allocation is recommended because of the pronouncement in section 3470.13 of the ***CICA Handbook*** which states:

> *When timing differences occur* between accounting income and taxable income, income taxes should be accounted for on the allocation basis for all corporations with the exception of certain regulated and similar enterprises.... [Emphasis added]

Although sections 3470 and 3471 of the *CICA Handbook* established workable standards for interperiod tax allocation, they by no means eliminated the conceptual controversies associated with this subject. Many accountants and business executives continue to favour the accrual method, partial allocation of income taxes, and the net-of-tax method for balance sheet presentation of deferred income tax accounts. Interperiod tax allocation probably will continue to be a controversial topic as long as taxes on corporate income continue to be levied at high rates.

TAX ALLOCATION WITHIN A PERIOD (INTRAPERIOD TAX ALLOCATION)

The need for tax allocation within an accounting period (also known as ***intraperiod tax allocation***) arises, for example, when extraordinary items are included in net income or an adjustment applicable to prior periods is recorded in the current period. If extraordinary items and these prior period adjustments are taxable or are deductible for income tax purposes, income taxes (or tax refunds) are apportioned between income before extraordinary items, extraordinary items, and these prior period adjustments. Income taxes applicable to income before extraordinary items are based on the difference between revenue and expenses before giving effect to the income tax consequences of extraordinary items. Extraordinary items and adjustments applicable to prior periods are reported ***net*** of the income tax effect in the income statement and the statement of retained earnings respectively.

Extraordinary Gain and Adjustments Applicable to Prior Periods

To illustrate a situation involving an extraordinary gain and an adjustment applicable to a prior period, assume that Lyman Limited reported the following for Year 4:

Data for illustration

Income before income taxes and extraordinary item (fully taxable at 45%)	$300,000
Extraordinary long-term capital gain (taxable at 22½%)	800,000
Prior period accounting error: Increase in earnings for Year 1 as a result of an error (fully taxable at 45%)	200,000

The presentation of these items in the income statement and the statement of retained earnings with and without intraperiod tax allocation is shown on page 1071.

Failure to apply intraperiod tax allocation procedures in this case distorts the income statement and also understates net income by $90,000, the income tax applicable to the prior period error adjustment.

Assuming that the extraordinary gain and the prior period error adjustment

Presentation of extraordinary gain and prior period error adjustment with and without intraperiod tax allocation

	With tax allocation	*Without tax allocation*
Income statement:		
Income before income taxes and extraordinary gain	$300,000	$ 300,000
Provision for income taxes	135,000	405,000*
Income (loss) before extraordinary gain	$165,000	$ (105,000)
Extraordinary gain:		
(Net of income tax)	620,000	
Without tax allocation		800,000
Net income	$785,000	$695,000
Statement of retained earnings:		
Prior period error adjustment: Increase in beginning balance of retained earnings	$110,000	$ 200,000

*Income taxes expense: $300,000 × 45%	$135,000
Tax on long-term capital gain: $800,000 × 22½%	180,000
Tax on prior period error adjustment: $200,000 × 45%	90,000
Total income taxes currently payable	$405,000

had already been recorded (before recognition of the income tax effects), income taxes for Year 4, with intraperiod tax allocation, should be recorded by Lyman Limited as in the next illustration.

Journal entry for intraperiod tax allocation to extraordinary gain and to prior period error adjustment

Provision for Income Taxes	135,000	
Extraordinary Gain (income tax effect)	180,000	
Prior Period Error Adjustment (income tax effect)	90,000	
Income Taxes Payable		405,000
To record income tax effects on operating income extraordinary gain, and prior period error adjustment (correction of error).		

Extraordinary Loss

To illustrate a situation involving an extraordinary loss, assume that in Year 5 Lyman Limited reported accounting income of $600,000 and incurred a fully deductible extraordinary loss of $500,000. The tax rate is 45%, and the company's liability for income taxes is $45,000 (45% of taxable income of $100,000). The comparative summary on page 1072 shows how Lyman's income statement appears with and without intraperiod tax allocation.

The greater clarity obtained with intraperiod tax allocation is apparent. The presentation shows the after-tax effect of the extraordinary loss and the normal impact of income taxes on income before income taxes. If tax allocation is not used, the user of the income statement will question the relationship between the pre-tax income of $600,000 and the disproportionately low provision for income taxes of $45,000. Without tax allocation, both the amount of income before extraordinary loss and the amount of the extraordinary loss are overstated by $225,000

Presentation of extraordinary loss with and without intraperiod tax allocation

	With tax allocation	*Without tax allocation*
Income statement:		
Income before income taxes and extraordinary loss	$600,000	$600,000
Provision for income taxes	270,000	45,000*
Income before extraordinary loss	$330,000	$555,000
Extraordinary loss:		
(Net of income tax)	275,000	
Without tax allocation		500,000
Net income	$ 55,000	$ 55,000

*Income taxes expense: $600,000 × 45%	$270,000
Income tax credit on extraordinary loss: $500,000 × 45%	225,000
Total income taxes currently payable	$ 45,000

($500,000 × 45%), the tax effect of the extraordinary loss. With intraperiod tax allocation, income taxes are recorded as shown below.

Journal entry for intraperiod tax allocation to extraordinary loss

Provision for Income Taxes ($600,000 × 45%)	270,000	
Extraordinary Loss (income tax effect)		225,000
Income Taxes Payable		45,000
To record income tax effects on pre-tax income and extraordinary loss.		

Note that the income tax effect is recorded as an offset to the Extraordinary Loss account, which we have assumed had already been recorded at $500,000; it would be possible to record the income tax effect in a separate ledger account. In either case, the extraordinary loss is reported in the income statement ***net of income taxes***, that is, at $275,000, with appropriate disclosure of the current income tax liability and the income tax effect of the loss.

Because extraordinary items and adjustments applicable to prior periods create certain income tax consequences, intraperiod tax allocation is an effort to match income taxes (or tax credits) with these special items. In this way, extraordinary items and adjustments applicable to prior periods are reported net of income taxes — that is, at amounts representing the net ***economic impact*** of such items.

PRESENTATION OF INCOME TAX ACCOUNTS IN THE BALANCE SHEET

Thus far we have assumed that income tax allocation that stems from differences in the timing of revenue and expense results in either a liability or an asset. Whether these deferred income tax credits and debits meet the definition of liabilities and assets is an issue worth considering.

Deferred income tax credits arise when a corporation recognizes income in its income statement before it is taxed. There is no existing debt to the government for taxes on future earnings that may or may not materialize. However, we previously defined liabilities to include future outlays that result from current or past events and may be measured with reasonable accuracy. Assuming continuing profitability, it is reasonable to include in this definition the increased taxes that will follow from having recognized income before it is taxed. Even though the deferred income tax ''liability'' may not be paid for many years, the Accounting Standards Committee has stated that ''tax allocation amounts should not be calculated on a discounted basis.''[17]

The classification of deferred income taxes as an asset rests on the assumption that there will be a future income tax benefit to the corporation. At some later time the corporation will realize revenue that will not be subject to income tax, or it will have a tax deduction that will not be recognized as an accounting expense. The asset represents the amount of tax that has already been paid on income to be reported in the income statement in future accounting periods.

The Accounting Standards Committee emphasized the ''deferred'' characteristics of the tax accounts resulting from interperiod tax allocation procedures when they established the following guidelines for presentation of such accounts in the balance sheet:[18]

> The balance representing accumulated tax allocation credits and/or debits may include current and non-current items. The classification of accumulated tax allocation debits or credits in the balance sheet should be based on the classification of the assets or liabilities to which the timing differences relate. For example, where a company classifies instalment receivables or construction holdback receivables as current assets, any tax allocation credit relating thereto should be included in the current liability section. On the other hand, tax allocation balances arising from timing differences between recorded depreciation and capital cost allowances should be shown as non-current, because the related depreciable assets are non-current. Where there are both tax allocation debits and credits, the usual treatment would be to show the net total of the current items and the net total of the non-current items.
>
> Appropriate terminology to identify accumulated tax allocation debits or credits would be ''Deferred Income Taxes.'' In most cases, it will be desirable to show only the net current deferred taxes and the net non-current deferred taxes rather than separating the debits and credits in each category.

In addition the ''deferred'' portion of the current income tax provision must be disclosed as follows:[19]

> The amount by which the current income tax provision has been increased or decreased as a result of tax deferrals would frequently be evident from the financial statements themselves (e.g., where the amount is set out in the statement of changes in financial position). Where this is not the case, appropriate disclosure should be made.

17 CICA, *CICA Handbook*, sec. 3470.22.

18 CICA, *CICA Handbook*, sec. 3470.23 and .25.

19 CICA, *CICA Handbook*, sec. 3470.28.

This could be done by showing the current and deferred portions of the income tax provision separately in the income statement or by means of a note to the financial statements.

The requirements for reporting income tax accounts in the balance sheet are summarized in the next illustration.

Current assets:	*Current liabilities:*
1 Prepayments of deferred income taxes (related to current liabilities such as estimated product warranties outstanding which will be satisfied within one year or the next operating cycle of the corporation)	*1* Deferred income taxes (related to current assets such as receivables from instalment sales or construction contracts in progress)
2 Claim for refund of income taxes previously paid (loss carryback)	*2* Current income tax liability (balance of tax due on income taxable currently)
3 Potential income tax benefit of operating loss carryforward (if current benefits are virtually certain of being realized)	
Noncurrent assets:	*Noncurrent liabilities:*
1 Prepayments of deferred income taxes (related to noncurrent liabilities such as the situation when pension expense exceeds pension funding)	*1* Deferred income taxes (related to timing differences, such as those caused by use of an accelerated depreciation method for income tax purposes)

The items listed first under each of the two current categories are offset and reported as a single amount. Similarly, the items listed first under each of the two noncurrent categories are offset and reported as a single amount.

The income taxes currently payable, the tax effects of timing differences, and the tax effects of operating loss carrybacks and carryforwards are disclosed in the income statement or in notes to the financial statements. These amounts are allocated to income before extraordinary items and to extraordinary items. As previously stated, the income tax benefit of an operating loss carryforward not previously recorded is reported as an extraordinary item in the accounting period in which it is realized. In addition, as stated earlier, notes to the financial statements include disclosure of unused operating loss carryforwards for tax purposes (along with expiration dates), reasons for significant variations in the customary relationships between provision for income taxes and accounting income due to permanent differences and any other factors relating to income taxes that users of financial statements would find helpful in evaluating current and future earnings of the corporation.

OTHER TAX ACCOUNTING TOPICS

The primary focus of our discussion thus far has been on accounting for interperiod and intraperiod income tax allocation. Accounting for income taxes is complicated by the need to measure income taxes expense for interim periods and by many technical tax laws relating to tax credits, laws designed, for example, to stimulate domestic and foreign investments, to create jobs, and to encourage common stock ownership by employees. Also, the purchase and sale of income tax benefits (such as investment tax credits and depreciation deductions) may create difficult financial accounting problems.

The accounting for the investment tax credit and the allocation of income taxes to interim periods are discussed in the rest of this chapter.

Investment Tax Credit

Federal income tax statutes have, from time to time, provided for a reduction of income taxes paid by individuals and corporations by an amount known as the ***investment tax credit*** (ITC). To illustrate, if a corporate enterprise acquired for $100,000 a plant asset that qualified for an ITC of 10%, it would be entitled to a reduction of $10,000 ($100,000 × 0.10 = $10,000) in its federal income taxes payable.

Two methods have been used to recognize the effect of the investment tax credit in the accounting records.

1 The ***flow-through method***, which reduces income taxes expense by the amount of the investment tax credit in the year the plant asset is acquired. This method has been favoured by most business executives on grounds that immediate tax reduction is the intent of the federal income tax law. Because income taxes expense is reduced in the year depreciable plant assets are acquired, this method allows business enterprises to increase net income by acquiring depreciable plant assets that qualify for the investment tax credit.

2 The ***cost reduction method***, which requires the amortization of the benefit arising from the ITC over the economic life of the depreciable plant asset acquired. Under this method the investment tax credit is viewed as a reduction in the effective cost of the asset, although it generally is reported as a deferred credit in the balance sheet and is amortized by periodic credits to the Income Taxes Expense ledger account.

The cost reduction method is favoured by most accountants and should be used for ''reporting purposes'' because it avoids an immediate increase in net income as a result of acquisition of plant assets, and thus provides a more meaningful measurement of net income. It treats the ITC as set out in ***CICA Handbook*** section 3805.12, which requires that investment tax credits be accounted for using the cost reduction approach. Those ITCs relating to the acquisition of assets would be either:[20]

a deducted from the related assets with any depreciation or amortization calculated on the net amount; or
b deferred and amortized to income on the same basis as the related assets.

20 CICA, ***CICA Handbook***, sec. 3805.13.

In either event, the ITCs should only be accrued when there is reasonable assurance that the credits will be realized.

To illustrate these two methods of accounting for the ITC, assume the following facts for the year ended December 31, Year 3:

1 The net book value and undepreciated capital cost of the fixed assets of Master Ltd. was $500,000. Master purchased $1,000,000 of fixed assets in January of Year 3. These purchases allowed the company an ITC of $30,000.

2 Master Ltd. depreciated its assets at 10% of their net book value. Capital cost allowance was claimed at 20% on the opening undepreciated capital cost (UCC) and 10% on current-year additions.

3 Income before depreciation for Year 3 totalled $1,200,000.

The effect of using the ***cost reduction method*** on pre-tax accounting income and taxable income is shown below:

Effect of using the cost reduction method in accounting for the investment tax credit

	Pre-tax accounting income	*Taxable income*	*Timing difference*
Net income before depreciation and income taxes	$1,200,000	$1,200,000	
Depreciation	(1) (147,000)	(147,000)	
Net income before income taxes	$1,053,000	$1,053,000	
Timing differences:			
Depreciation		147,000	$(147,000)
CCA		(1) (197,000)	197,000
	$1,053,000	$1,003,000	$ 50,000

(1) Calculation of depreciation and CCA:

	Book	*Tax*
Opening balance	$ 500,000	$ 500,000
Additions in Year 3	1,000,000	1,000,000
Investment tax credit	(30,000)	(30,000)
Depreciation: 10%	147,000	
CCA: 20%		197,000
Closing balances	$1,323,000	$1,273,000

Journal entries (explanations omitted) to record income taxes at the effective rate of 45% for Year 3 are as follows:

Journal entries for recording income taxes when the cost reduction method is used to account for the investment tax credit

Income Taxes Expense ($1,053,000 × 0.45)	473,850	
Income Taxes Payable ($1,003,000 × 0.45)		451,350
Deferred Income Taxes ($50,000 × 0.45)		22,500

Income Taxes Payable (ITC)	30,000	
Fixed Assets		30,000

The effect of using the ***flow-through method*** on pre-tax accounting income and taxable income is shown below:

Effect of using the flow-through method in accounting for the investment tax credit

	Pre-tax accounting income	*Taxable income*	*Timing difference*
Net income before depreciation and income taxes	$1,200,000	$1,200,000	
Depreciation	(150,000)	(150,000)	
Net income before income taxes	$1,050,000	$1,050,000	
Depreciation	3,000	150,000	$(147,000)
CCA		(197,000)	197,000
	$1,053,000	$1,003,000	$ 50,000

Calculation of depreciation and CCA:

	Book	*Tax*
Opening balance	$ 500,000	$ 500,000
Additions in Year 3	1,000,000	1,000,000
Investment tax credit		(30,000)
	$1,500,000	$1,470,000
Depreciation: 10%	150,000	
CCA: 20% and 10%		197,000
	$1,350,000	$1,273,000

The effect of each method on the timing difference and calculation of deferred income taxes follows:

Effect of each method on deferred income taxes

	Cost reduction method	*Flow-through method*
NBV*, December 31, Year 3	$1,323,000	$1,350,000
UCC, December 31, Year 3	1,273,000	1,273,000
Timing differences	$ 50,000	$ 77,000
Investment tax credit remaining ($30,000 – $3,000)		27,000
	$ 50,000	$ 50,000
Year 3 tax rate	45%	45%
Deferred income taxes	$ 22,500	$ 22,500

*Net book value.

Allocation of Income Taxes Expense to Interim Periods

Most publicly owned corporations issue earnings reports on a quarterly basis. Determination of the provision for income taxes for such interim accounting periods involves two classes of problems — estimating of appropriate income tax rates and the treatment of losses.

Estimation of Appropriate Income Tax Rates

The estimation of the appropriate income tax rate requires consideration of the effect of rate differentials, permanent differences between accounting income and taxable income, expected investment tax credits and other government allowances, etc. As well, management must assess the impact of differing treatments of capital gains and goodwill on the rate of tax eventually used, as well as the intrastatement tax effect on extraordinary items and retained earnings. Section 1750 of the ***CICA Handbook***, ''Interim Financial Reporting to Shareholders,'' addresses the problem of rate differentials with respect to the provision for income taxes.[21] There, the Accounting Standards Committee has suggested that either of two methods be used: (1) the allocation of the low rate of tax may be made evenly over the interim periods, and (2) the determination of the effective rate of tax for the entire period up to then may be applied to the interim periods.

To illustrate each of the above methods, assume that Interim Limited is subject to income taxes at 20% on the first $50,000 of taxable income and at 50% on taxable income in excess of $50,000. Capital expenditures yielding $10,000 in investment tax credits are planned for the current fiscal year. Income before income taxes for the first quarter was $20,000, and when the income statement for the first quarter was being prepared, income before income taxes for the entire fiscal year was expected to be $100,000. There were no extraordinary items or timing differences. The provision for income taxes for the first quarter is computed below.

1 Allocation of low rate of taxes evenly over the interim periods:

Computation of provision for income taxes for first quarter of fiscal period: first method

First-quarter share of income attributable to the low rate of tax: ($50,000 × ¼)	$12,500
Income tax rate on first $50,000	20%
Income tax on first $12,500 income	$ 2,500
First-quarter share of income attributable to the high rate of tax and tax thereon: ($20,000 − $12,500) × 50%	3,750
	$ 6,250
First-quarter share of investment tax credits ($10,000 × ¼)	2,500
Provision for income taxes for the first quarter	$ 3,750

2 Determination of annual effective tax rate to be applied to the first-quarter income:

21 CICA, ***CICA Handbook***, sec. 1750.17(a).

Computation of provision for income taxes for first quarter of fiscal year: second method

Provision for income taxes estimated for the year: ($50,000 × 20%) + ($50,000 × 50%)	$35,000
Less: Anticipated investment tax credits	10,000
Net estimated provision for income taxes for the year	$25,000
Estimated effective income tax rate for the year ($25,000 ÷ $100,000)	25%
Provision for income taxes for the first quarter ($20,000 × 25%)	$ 5,000

Under the second method for subsequent quarters the year-to-date provision for income taxes is computed with a current estimate of the effective tax rate. The provision for taxes for the quarter is the difference between the new year-to-date provision and the tax previously recognized up to the beginning of the quarter. If Interim Limited had income before income taxes of $30,000 for the second quarter, and now expected income before income taxes for the year of $110,000 instead of $100,000 and investment tax credits of $9,200 instead of $10,000, the provision for income taxes for the second quarter is computed as follows:

Computation of provision for income taxes for second quarter of fiscal year: second method

Estimated provision for income taxes for the year: ($50,000 × 20%) + ($60,000 × 50%)	$40,000
Less: Anticipated investment tax credits	9,200
Net estimated provision for income taxes for the year	$30,800
Estimated effective income tax rate for the year ($30,800 ÷ $110,000)	28%
Provision for income taxes for the second quarter:	
Year-to-date income before income taxes ($20,000 + $30,000)	$50,000
Estimated effective income tax rate	0.28
Year-to-date provision for income taxes	$14,000
Less: Provision for income taxes accrued for the first quarter	5,000
Provision for income taxes for the second quarter	$ 9,000

Extraordinary items are included in income in the period in which they occur.[22]

Treatment of Losses

Treatment of situations involving losses in interim periods is similar to the treatment of operating loss carrybacks, and carryforwards under virtual certainty in annual reporting. Regarding seasonal fluctuations in interim earnings, the Accounting Standards Committee has stated:[23]

> Where the pattern of earning fluctuates from one interim period to another, such as in a seasonal business where there may be a profit in one interim period and a loss in another, profitable periods should normally show income tax provisions and unprofitable periods should show income tax recoveries provided such recoveries are virtually certain of realization.

22 CICA, *CICA Handbook*, sec. 1750.07.

23 CICA, *CICA Handbook*, sec. 1750.18(b).

Concerning the case when, for the interim period, there are profits to which loss carryforward from prior years may be applied or there is a loss which may be carried back to a previous annual period, the Accounting Standards Committee has stated:[24]

> The existence of loss carryforwards from prior years for which a tax recovery has not been recognized in the accounts would raise the question of how they should be applied to the current year's interim periods. Loss carryforwards may be treated as final interim period items since tax assessments are based on a taxation year and the benefits of loss carryforwards from prior years are only realizable on an annual basis. Another method would be to prorate the loss carryforward over the year to the extent that it is virtually certain of realization due to the earning of profits within the year. This method is not considered to be the proration of an extraordinary item but rather the progressive recognition during the year of the tax reduction associated with a loss carryforward which is reflected as an extraordinary item.
>
> Where the loss in the interim period is less than or equal to the income for the prior annual period, recognition of the tax recovery due to loss carryback provisions to the extent of the entire loss for the interim period is appropriate.
>
> Where the loss in the interim period is in excess of the income for the prior annual period, it is appropriate to recognize the tax recovery due to loss carryback provisions, but the potential tax recovery due to loss carryforward provisions is not to be recognized in the interim period unless it appears virtually certain that the carryforward benefit will be realized within the carryforward period allowed by the tax authorities.

In situations in which management is given a choice as to the method to be followed, such methods should be both "mutually consistent" and "consistent from period to period,"[25] according to the Accounting Standards Committee.

REVIEW QUESTIONS

1. What is the objective of generally accepted accounting principles in their application to the income statement? What are the objectives of income tax laws?
2. Define ***interperiod tax allocation, intraperiod tax allocation***, and ***interim-period tax computation***.
3. What assumptions are necessary in the implementation of income tax allocation for financial accounting?
4. What are three sources of differences between pre-tax accounting income and taxable income?
5. Describe two situations that result, under interperiod tax allocation procedures, in deferred income tax credits for financial accounting.
6. Describe two situations that result, under interperiod tax allocation procedures, in deferred income tax debits for financial accounting.

24 CICA, *CICA Handbook*, sec. 1750.19(c), (d).

25 CICA, *CICA Handbook*, sec. 1750.16.

7 Explain the following interperiod tax allocation approaches:
 a ***Deferred method***
 b ***Accrual method***
 c ***Net-of-tax method***

8 Describe what ***drawdown*** or ***reversal*** means when considering deferred income taxes.

9 What is meant by an ***operating loss carryback*** and an ***operating loss carryforward***?

10 Explain the different accounting problems that arise in accounting for an operating loss carryback and for an operating loss carryforward.

11 Describe three situations that produce a permanent difference between taxable income and pre-tax accounting income. Give an example of each.

12 Briefly summarize the arguments for and against interperiod income tax allocation.

13 Explain how each of the following ledger accounts is classified (for example, ''current asset'' or ''current liability'') in the balance sheet:
 a Deferred Income Tax (credit balance)
 b Deferred Income Tax (debit balance)
 c Income Tax Refund Receivable
 d Tax Benefit Available for Application Against Future Income Taxes

14 What information regarding an unrecorded loss carryforward for tax purposes is included in a note to the financial statements?

15 What two approaches may be considered in accounting for the investment tax credit (ITC)? Briefly describe each method and indicate which is required.

16 Identify and briefly explain some of the problems involved in the estimation of income taxes expense for interim accounting periods.

17 Management may determine the effective tax rate for the entire period and then apply that rate to the interim periods. Explain why the effective income tax rate for each quarter of a fiscal year may differ significantly from the actual income tax rate for the year.

EXERCISES

Ex. 21-1 Select the best answer for each of the following multiple-choice questions:

1 At the most recent year-end, Lane Limited's deferred income tax debit related to a noncurrent liability exceeded a deferred income tax credit related to a current asset. Which of the following is reported in Lane's most recent year-end balance sheet?
 a The deferred income tax debit as a current asset
 b The excess of the deferred income tax debit over the deferred income tax credit as a current asset
 c The deferred income tax debit as a noncurrent asset and the deferred income tax credit as a current liability
 d The excess of the deferred income tax debit over the deferred income tax credit as a noncurrent asset

2 The amount of income taxes applicable to transactions that are reported with intraperiod income tax allocation is computed:
   a By multiplying the item by the effective income tax rate
   b As the difference between the income taxes computed based on taxable income excluding the item and the taxes computed based on taxable income including the item
   c As the difference between the income taxes computed on the item based on the amount used for financial accounting and the amount used in the computation of taxable income
   d By multiplying the item by the difference between the effective income tax rate and the statutory income tax rate
3 An example of an item requiring intraperiod income tax allocation is:
   a Interest revenue on bonds
   b Estimated expenses for major repairs accrued for financial accounting in one year, but deducted for income tax purposes when paid in a subsequent year
   c Rent revenue included in income for income tax purposes when collected, but deferred for financial accounting until realized in a subsequent year
   d Reporting a prior period adjustment in the statement of retained earnings
4 Which of the following requires intraperiod income tax allocation?
   a Dividends received from a taxable Canadian corporation and included in income
   b The excess of capital cost allowance (CCA) claimed for income tax purposes over straight-line depreciation for financial accounting
   c Extraordinary gains and losses
   d All differences between taxable income and pre-tax accounting income
5 A Tax Benefit Available for Application Against Future Income Taxes ledger account is presented in a corporation's:
   a Income statement as a reduction of pre-tax operating loss
   b Balance sheet as an asset
   c Income statement as an extraordinary item
   d Balance sheet as a contra to deferred income tax credits
6 Rollo Corporation had dividend income from taxable Canadian corporations of $200,000 in Year 2. For financial accounting, Rollo included the $200,000 in its income statement. For income tax reporting, the $200,000 was exempt income. Assuming an income tax rate of 45%, what is reported in the provision for deferred income taxes relative to the interest revenue in Rollo's income statement for the year ended December 31, Year 2?
   a $0 *b* $90,000 credit *c* $90,000 debit *d* $200,000 debit
   e Some other amount
7 Agard Limited's effective income tax rate is 45%. For the year ended December 31, Year 1, Agard's income statement included depreciation of $1,000,000 in cost of goods sold. However, Agard properly deducted $4,000,000 for capital cost allowance claimed in its Year 1 income tax return. What amount is reported as provision for deferred income tax credits in

Agard's Year 1 financial statements?
a \$0 *b* \$450,000 *c* \$1,350,000 *d* \$1,800,000 *e* Some other amount

8 On December 31, Year 3, Tower Corporation accrued for financial accounting an estimated loss of \$100,000 on disposal of obsolete plant assets. During Year 3, Tower collected \$150,000 in royalties, of which \$80,000 was unrealized on December 31, Year 3. Assuming an effective income tax rate of 45%, what amount does Tower record as deferred income tax credits to income for Year 3?
a \$9,000 *b* \$36,000 *c* \$45,000 *d* \$81,000 *e* Some other amount

9 Bishop Corporation began operations in Year 1 and had operating losses of \$200,000 in Year 1 and \$150,000 in Year 2. For the year ended December 31, Year 3, Bishop had pre-tax accounting income and taxable income of \$300,000. For the three-year period Year 1 through Year 3, assume an income tax rate of 45% and no permanent or timing differences between pre-tax accounting income and taxable income. In Bishop's Year 3 income statement, what amount is reported as income taxes expense?
a \$0 *b* \$45,000 *c* \$67,500 *d* \$135,000 *e* Some other amount

10 On January 2, Year 5, Clark Limited acquired a building for \$1,500,000. The building was to be depreciated \$50,000 a year under the straight-line method for financial accounting. For income tax purposes, Clark claimed CCA in the amount of \$200,000 for Year 5. Assuming an income tax rate of 45%, what amount is credited to Clark's Deferred Income Tax Credits ledger account on December 31, Year 5?
a \$22,500 *b* \$67,500 *c* \$90,000 *d* \$150,000 *e* Some other amount

Ex. 21-2 Martin Limited began operations on January 3, Year 1, and a substantial part of its sales were made on the instalment plan. For financial accounting Martin recognized revenue from all sales on the accrual basis. However, in its income tax returns, Martin reported revenue from instalment sales on the instalment method. Information concerning pre-tax income from instalment sales under each method is as follows:

Year	*Accrual basis*	*Instalment method*
1	\$400,000	\$150,000
2	650,000	350,000
3	500,000	600,000

The effective income tax rate for both years was 45%, and there were no other timing differences.

Prepare journal entries for Martin Limited to record income taxes expense for each year (omit explanations).

Ex. 21-3 For the year ended December 31, Year 1, Rex Corporation reported pre-tax accounting income of \$1,000,000. The following information is available for Year 1:

Dividend revenue from taxable Canadian corporations	$ 80,000
Capital cost allowance claimed in tax return in excess of depreciation expense in income statement	140,000
Warranty expense on the accrual basis of accounting	65,000
Actual warranty expenditures	35,000

Rex's effective income tax rate is 45% for Year 1.

Prepare a journal entry for Rex Corporation to record income taxes expense for the year ended December 31, Year 1 (omit explanation).

Ex. 21-4 Sunrise, Inc., uses the deferral method of accounting for the investment tax credit. In Year 5, Sunrise had a $37,800 investment tax credit as a result of acquisitions early in Year 5 of plant assets with a 10-year economic life. On December 31, Year 5, Sunrise's accountant recorded an income tax liability of $160,000 before recognition of the investment tax credit.

Prepare journal entries for Sunrise, Inc., on Decembver 31, Year 5, and on December 31, Year 6, to adjust income taxes expense for the effect of the investment tax credit.

Ex. 21-5 Samore Corporation acquired a machine on January 2, Year 8, for $5,500,000. The machine had an estimated economic life of 10 years with no residual value. Capital cost allowance was claimed at a 20% rate in Year 8 for income tax purposes and by the straight-line method for financial accounting. The income tax rate is 45%.

Compute the amount credited by Samore Corporation to the Deferred Income Taxes ledger account on December 31, Year 8.

Ex. 21-6 Shadi Corporation reported the following operating results for the two years ended December 31, Year 8 and Year 7:

	Year 8	*Year 7*
Pre-tax accounting income	$1,500,000	$800,000
Taxable income	1,800,000	320,000

The disparity between pre-tax accounting income and taxable income was attributable to timing differences. The income tax rate is 45%.

Compute Shadi Corporation's income taxes expense for Year 8, divided between current and deferred portions.

Ex. 21-7 Acosta Corporation's accounting records for the year ended December 31, Year 9, showed pre-tax accounting income of $400,000. In the computation of taxable income, the following timing differences were taken into acount:

Depreciation deducted for income tax purposes in excess of depreciation recognized in income statement	$80,000

Income from instalment sales reported for income tax purposes in excess of income recognized in income statement	60,000

The income tax rate is 45%.

Compute Acosta's current income tax liability on December 31, Year 9.

Ex. 21-8 In Year 5, Kane Limited reported $300,000 of pre-tax accounting income, but only $80,000 in its income tax return. In Year 6, pre-tax accounting income was $350,000 and taxable income was $450,000.

Prepare Kane Limited's journal entry to record income taxes expense and income taxes payable for Year 6, assuming that the reversal of timing differences was responsible for the disparity between pre-tax accounting income and taxable income. The income tax rate is 45%.

Ex. 21-9 The pre-tax accounting income and taxable income for Mejia Limited for a three-year period were as follows:

Year	*Pre-tax accounting income*	*Taxable income*
1	$70,000	$72,500
2	70,000	63,400
3	70,000	64,100

The differences between pre-tax accounting income and taxable income were due solely to the fact that CCA claimed differed from depreciation expense each year. Income tax rates are 20% on the first $50,000 of pre-tax income and 45% on pre-tax income in excess of $50,000.

Prepare Mejia Limited's journal entries for each year to allocate income taxes resulting from timing differences in accounting for depreciation expense.

Ex. 21-10 The pre-tax accounting income and taxable income for Otake Corporation over a three-year period are presented below:

Year	*Pre-tax accounting income*	*Taxable income*
1	$100,000	$140,000
2	100,000	95,000
3	100,000	95,000

The differences between pre-tax accounting income and taxable income are explained as follows:

1 Taxable income in Year 1 included $45,000 of rent revenue that was recognized in the accounting records at the rate of $15,000 a year.

2 Amortization of goodwill at the rate of $20,000 a year was recognized in the accounting records but $10,000 was deductible in the computation of taxable income. The difference of $10,000 is a permanent difference.

Prepare journal entries for Years 1, 2, and 3 to record Otake Corporation's income taxes. Assume that income taxes are 45% of taxable income.

Ex. 21-11 Income statements for Peter Corporation show the following pre-tax results for the first three years of its operations:

Year 1: Operating loss	$(100,000)
Year 2: Operating income	240,000
Year 3: Operating loss	(200,000)

Peter operates in a cyclical and highly competitive capital goods industry. Peter Corporation has not claimed capital cost allowance in any of the three years.

Prepare Peter Corporation's journal entries for each year to record the tax effects of operating loss carryforwards or carrybacks. Assume that operating losses as reported in the income statements are allowable in full for income tax purposes and that the income tax rate is 45%. Assume there is no reasonable assurance in either loss year that deferred income tax debits will reverse in the future.

Ex. 21-12 Lui Corporation reported pre-tax accounting income of $300,000 and an extraordinary gain of $1.2 million for the year ended March 31, Year 4.

Prepare a journal entry to record the tax effect of the pre-tax accounting income and of the extraordinary gain. (Record the tax effect of the gain as a debit to the Extraordinary Gain ledger account.) Show how the foregoing information is presented in the income statement for the year ended March 31, Year 4. (The income tax rate is 45% on income before income taxes and on the extraordinary gain.)

Ex. 21-13 Aki Corporation issues financial statements on a quarterly basis. During Year 1, its actual quarterly results and its expectations were as follows:

	Pre-tax accounting income		*Pre-tax accounting income expected in year*
	Quarter	*Year to date*	
End of 1st quarter	$20,000	$ 20,000	$ 80,000
End of 2nd quarter	10,000	30,000	60,000
End of 3rd quarter	40,000	70,000	90,000
End of year	30,000	100,000	100,000

Assuming that Aki's income tax rate is 20% on the first $50,000 of taxable income and 45% on taxable income above $50,000, and that taxable income is the same as pre-tax accounting income, compute: ***a*** the estimated effective income tax rate for each quarter; ***b*** the year-to-date income taxes expense at the end of each quarter; and ***c*** the income taxes expense for each quarter.

CASES

Case 21-1 Plaga Limited was organized on January 2, Year 1, and adopted the accrual basis of accounting for financial accounting. For income tax purposes, Plaga adopted the cash basis of accounting because accounts receivable were expected to exceed accounts payable by a significant amount each year. Thus, Plaga could defer the payment of income taxes through the use of the cash basis of accounting for income tax purposes.

You were engaged to examine the financial statements of Plaga for the year ended December 31, Year 1. In a discussion of interperiod tax allocation procedures with you, Laura Dykes, controller, objected to the use of comprehensive tax allocation for all differences between Plaga's pre-tax accounting income and taxable income. She stressed that forecasts of Plaga's future operations indicated an ever-increasing deferred income tax liability from comprehensive tax allocation because of the growth of accounts receivable in relation to accounts payable.

Instructions

How would you respond to the controllers' objections? Explain.

Case 21-2 A partial income statement and the related note to the financial statements of Edmund, Inc., for the year ended June 30, Year 4, are shown below:

Income before income taxes	$8,400,000
Provision for income taxes (**NOTE 1**)	3,780,000
Income before extraordinary item	$4,620,000
Extraordinary item arising from benefit of operating loss carryforward (**NOTE 1**)	3,780,000
Net income	$8,400,000

NOTE 1—Income Taxes: No income taxes are payable because of an available operating loss carryforward from prior years. However, in the income statement, a provision for income taxes that would have been paid in the absence of the operating loss carryforward benefit has been deducted to determine income before extraordinary item, and the benefit of the operating loss carryforward was reported as an extraordinary item.

Instructions

a Present an argument in support of the procedure used by Edmund, Inc., to account for the tax effect of the operating loss carryforward.

b Prepare a journal entry to record the tax effect of the operating loss carryforward of Edmund, Inc. Use the account titles as they appear in the income statement of Edmund, Inc.

c Assume that Edmund, Inc., had recognized the full potential income tax benefit of the operating loss in prior years. How would Edmund's income statement differ for the year ended June 30, Year 4?

Case 21-3 Nelson Construction Corporation was organized early in Year 1 after Rick Nelson was awarded a contract to build a major section of a highway in the Yukon. The completion of the contract will take four years, and Nelson does not plan to bid on additional contracts. All costs incurred by Nelson are chargeable to the highway contract; thus, Nelson will not record any selling and administrative expenses. Assume that the income tax rate is 20% on the first $50,000 and 45% on any excess.

The pre-tax profit on the construction-type contract is estimated at $200,000. Under the percentage-of-completion method of accounting, $50,000 of the profit will be recognized in each of the four years. Income taxes of $10,000 ($50,000 × 0.20 = $10,000) will be paid on March 15 of each year starting in Year 2 if the percentage-of-completion method is adopted for income tax purposes. If the completed-contract method is adopted for income tax purposes, income taxes in the amount of $77,500 [($200,000 × 0.45) – ($50,000 × 0.25) = $77,500] will be paid on March 15, Year 5.

Instructions

a Assume that Nelson Construction Corporation considers 8% a fair rate of return after income taxes. Prepare a working paper to show whether Nelson should use the completed-contract method or the percentage-of-completion method of accounting for income tax purposes. Compute the net advantage of the method you recommend, in terms of dollar savings as of March 15, Year 5. (The amount of an ordinary annuity of four rents of 1 at 8% is 4.5061.)

b Assume that Nelson Construction Corporation had a large amount of income each year from other sources and that the entire profit on the construction-type contract is taxed at the marginal rate of 45%. What method of accounting do you recommend for income tax purposes? What is the net advantage for Nelson Construction as of March 15, Year 5, if money is worth 8%?

Case 21-4 In Year 10, Alta Limited received $50,000 as an advance rental on one of its mining properties. The rent advance was subject to income taxes in Year 10, although Alta did not recognize rent revenue for financial accounting until Year 11.

In Year 10, Alta reported taxable income of $250,000, paying income taxes of $100,000 (20% on the first $50,000 of taxable income and 45% on the balance of $200,000). The controller reported $200,000 as Alta's pre-tax accounting income for Year 10 and $22,500 of income taxes applicable to the rent advance ($50,000 × 0.45 = $22,500) as an asset (deferral income taxes) in the balance sheet.

In Year 11, Alta suffered a decline in income as a result of declining metal prices, and its operations resulted in pre-tax accounting income of only $50,000, including the rent advance received in Year 10. When the controller presented Alta's Year 11 income statement to the president, the latter commented, "I thought you said the effect of interperiod tax allocation was to show in each year a tax expense that bore a normal relationship to pre-tax accounting income. You report pre-tax accounting income of $50,000 and show income taxes of $22,500. If we had taxable income of only $50,000 we would pay only $10,000 in income taxes. I realize we broke even in the income tax return this year and won't actually pay any income tax, but I think your tax allocation procedure is incorrect.''

Instructions

a Prepare partial comparative income statements for Alta Limited for Years 10 and 11, starting with income before income taxes and following the controller's approach.

b What is the issue implicit in the president's comment? How would you reply if you were the controller?

PROBLEMS

Pr. 21-1 This problem consists of three independent parts.

a Turley Corporation's income statement for the year ended December 31, Year 10, showed pre-tax accounting income of $500,000. The following items for Year 10 were treated differently in the income tax return from the way they were treated in the accounting records:

	Income tax return	*Accounting records*
Rent revenue	$ 60,000	$ 40,000
Depreciation expense	160,000	100,000
Advertising on a foreign television station		30,000
Interest revenue*	30,000	40,000

*Permanent differences between pre-tax accounting income and taxable income

Assume that Turley's effective income tax rate is 45% for Year 10.

Instructions

Prepare a journal entry for Turley Corporation to record income taxes expense for the year ended December 31, Year 10.

b Dugan Corporation began operations on January 5, Year 8. Dugan recognized income on construction-type contracts under the percentage-of-completion method in its financial statements but used the completed-contract method for income tax purposes. Income before income taxes under each method was as follows:

Year	*Percentage-of-completion*	*Completed-contract*
8	$400,000	$100,000
9	650,000	350,000
10	800,000	90,000

For all years, Dugan's effective income tax rate was 45%, and there were no other timing differences.

Instructions
Prepare a journal entry for each year to record income taxes expense for Dugan Corporation.

c The income statement for Yamamura Corporation for the year ended June 30, Year 5, included the following pre-tax amounts:

Income from continuing operations	$1,750,000
Depreciation expense, which was $100,000 less than the amount reported in the income tax return	600,000
Insurance expense (premiums on life insurance policies on which Yamamura was the beneficiary)	50,000
Loss from disposal of a discontinued business segment (an extraordinary loss)	800,000
Extraordinary gain (extinguishment of long-term debt)	500,000

Yamamura recorded payments of $480,000 on estimated income taxes in the Income Taxes Expense ledger account during the year ended June 30, Year 5. The effective income tax rate for Yamamura was 45%.

Instructions
Prepare a journal entry to adjust Yamamura Corporation's Income Taxes Expense ledger account for the year ended June 30, Year 5.

Pr. 21-2 Pre-tax accounting income of Westlake Corporation, after all adjustments and corrections, was $280,000 for Year 1, $212,000 for Year 2, and $252,000 for Year 3. The income tax rate was 45% in each of the three years. Depreciation expense, rent revenue, and dividend income have been included in pre-tax accounting income and taxable income for Years 1, 2, and 3, as follows:

	Pre-tax accounting income	*Taxable income*
Depreciation expense:		
Year 1	$50,000	$70,000
Year 2	54,000	71,000
Year 3	58,000	68,000
Rent revenue:		
Year 1	9,000	9,500
Year 2	9,000	8,500
Dividend income from taxable Canadian corporations:		
Year 1	8,000	
Year 2	4,000	
Year 3	3,800	

Instructions

a Compute the amount of income taxes payable for Westlake Corporation on December 31, Years 1, 2, and 3.

b Compute the amount of income taxes expense for Westlake Corporation for Years 1, 2, and 3.

c Prepare a journal entry to record income taxes of Westlake Corporation for each year (omit explanations).

Pr. 21-3 Lake Corporation had pre-tax accounting income of $400,000 for Year 1 and was subject to income taxes of 45%. The following items were treated in one way in the computation of the $400,000 pre-tax accounting income but differently in the computation of taxable income:

1 Lake recorded $70,000 in product warranty expense; for income tax purposes only $44,000 of warranty costs actually incurred was deductible. The warranty liability account was classified as current.

2 $80,000 of profits on construction-type contracts was included by Lake in pre-tax accounting income on the percentage-of-completion basis. Only one-fourth of this amount was taxable in Year 1; the balance was to be taxed in Year 2 when the remaining construction-type contracts were completed.

3 A lease deposit of $40,000 was received by Lake and credited to a long-term liability ledger account. It was taxable in Year 1 but would not be realized for financial accounting until Year 5.

4 Lake recorded $130,000 depreciation expense in its accounting records by the straight-line method. Capital cost allowance totalling $150,000 was claimed in the income tax return.

Instructions

a Compute the income taxes expense to be included in Lake Corporation's Year 1 income statement, and the amount of income taxes currently payable.

b Prepare a journal entry to record Lake Corporation's income taxes expense and related deferred income taxes on December 31, Year 1.

c Prepare a partial income statement for Lake Corporation on December 31, Year 1, beginning with income before income taxes.

d Indicate the amount and classification of any income tax items in Lake Corporation's balance sheet on December 31, Year 1. Deferred income tax debits and credits should be classified in two categories—the ***net current amount*** and the ***net noncurrent amount***.

Pr. 21-4 Zeno Corporation was subject to income taxes at 45% of taxable income and had made estimated income tax payments of $310,000 during Year 4. No computation of taxable income had been made for Year 4, but the pre-tax accounting income for Year 4 was stated correctly at $900,000. The following items required consideration in the reconciliation of pre-tax accounting income and taxable income for the year ended December 31, Year 4:

1 Zeno included in pre-tax accounting income dividends received from taxable Canadian corporations in the amount of $15,000.

2 Gross profit on instalment sales had been recognized in the amount of

$250,000 in the accounting records. For income tax purposes, only $150,000 of gross profit was reportable in Year 4. All instalment accounts receivable were current assets.

3 Pension expense accrued during Year 4 amounted to $74,000; only the $30,000 cash deposited in a pension trust fund was deductible in the Year 4 income tax return. The related pension plan liability was to be paid in Year 5.

4 Interest expense for Year 4 was $120,000 after $3,000 amortization of bond premium. Zeno did not amortize bond premium for income tax puroposes.

5 Straight-line depreciation of $190,000 had been recognized in the accounting records; however, $240,000 in capital cost allowance will be claimed in the income tax return.

Instructions

a Compute the additional income taxes to be paid by Zeno Corporation for the year ended December 31, Year 4.

b Prepare a journal entry to record Zeno Corporation's remaining income taxes expense for Year 4, assuming that the estimated tax payments were debited to the Income Taxes Expense ledger account during the year.

c Prepare a partial income statement for Zeno Corporation for the year ended December 31, Year 4. Start with the $900,000 income before income taxes.

d Show Zeno Corporation's balance sheet presentation of all income tax items on December 31, Year 4. Show deferred charges and credits as one ***net current amount*** and another ***net noncurrent amount***.

Pr. 21-5 Roadman Limited began operations in Year 1. Anticipating a growth in traffic, Roadman has developed plans for the acquisition of trucks during the next six years. The controller of Roadman is studying the question of depreciation policies, and feels that, even though the fixed percentage declining balance method must be used for income tax purposes, the straight-line method of depreciation is preferable for financial accounting. The controller has prepared the data below, using a five-year economic life for the trucks:

	Year 1	*Year 2*	*Year 3*	*Year 4*	*Year 5*	*Year 6*
Cost of new trucks acquired	$100,000	$220,000	$300,000	$ 50,000	$ 10,000	$ 25,000
Residual value	10,000	25,000	30,000	5,000	1,000	2,500
CCA claimed	15,000	58,500	118,950	135,765	104,036	78,074
Straight-line depreciation	18,000	57,000	111,000	120,000	121,800	108,300

Instructions

a Compute the balance of Roadman Limited's Deferred Income Taxes ledger account on December 31, Year 6, if an income tax rate of 45% is applicable. State how this amount is classified in the balance sheet.

b Assuming that Roadman's accounting records show pre-tax accounting income of $150,000 in Year 1 and $209,600 in Year 6, prepare partial income statements (starting with income before income taxes) for those two years. In the income statements or in a note to the financial statements show the taxes currently payable, the tax effects of timing differences, and the reason for the timing differences.

c Compare Roadman Limited's net incomes for Year 1 and for Year 6 as computed in ***b*** with the net income that would result if income tax allocation procedures were not followed. Make the comparison both in terms of dollars and as a percentage of pre-accounting income.

Pr. 21-6 Gerald Finnell is president and sole shareholder of Jerry's, Inc., a successful restaurant. During the year ended December 31, Year 8, confident of the competence and integrity of the assistant manager, Finnell left for a six-month trip to Africa. On returning he found that the manager had been stealing from the restaurant to cover gambling losses and that the quality (and patronage) of the restaurant had suffered. As a result, a pre-tax operating loss of $300,000 was incurred in Year 8. On the basis of prior success, Finnell believed that, under his personal direction, the restaurant would be restored to profitability immediately. The pre-tax operating income for Year 9 was $220,000. The income tax rate for all years involved was 45%.

Instructions

a Prepare journal entries to record income taxes of Jerry's, Inc., for the years ended December 31, Year 8 and Year 9. Assume that of the $300,000 operating loss for Year 8, only $200,000 could be carried back to preceding years and that no recognition would be given to the potential income tax benefit of the $100,000 ($300,000 – $200,000 = $100,000) operating loss carryforward in the financial statements for Year 8.

b Prepare partial comparative income statements for Jerry's, Inc., for the years ended December 31, Year 8 and Year 9.

c Using the assumptions in ***a*** and ***b***, ***except*** that you are to assume that the potential income tax benefit of the $100,000 operating loss carryforward was recognized in the financial statements for Year 8 because of the assumption of virtual certainty for the entire $100,000 amount, prepare journal entries for Jerry's, Inc., to record income taxes for Year 8 and Year 9, and partial comparative income statements for the years ended December 31, Year 8 and Year 9. Assume depreciation booked equalled capital cost allowance claimed in all years.

Pr. 21-7 The comparative income statements shown on page 1094 were presented to Kay Park, president of Park Corporation.

After examining the statements, Park frowned, "When I send these statements to my father, who owns 30% of the common stock, he will never understand why net income fell in the face of a substantial increase in income before income taxes."

"There are two reasons," commented the controller. "You will remember that last year we took a $40,000 fully deductible earthquake loss on the East Bend warehouse, and this year we had a capital gain of $120,000 (taxed at 30%) when we sold our Cable Limited common stock, our only investment, and used the

PARK CORPORATION
Comparative Income Statements
For Years Ended December 31, Year 6 and Year 5

	Year 6	*Year 5*
Net sales	$1,090,000	$1,000,000
Cost of goods sold	690,000	630,000
Gross profit on sales	$ 400,000	$ 370,000
Operating expenses	250,000	280,000
Income before income taxes	$ 150,000	$ 90,000
Income taxes expense	92,000	10,000
Net income	$ 58,000	$ 80,000

proceeds to build a new warehouse. Both these transactions were reported in the statement of retained earnings, but their tax effects were included in income taxes expense for the year ended December 31, Year 6.''

''I'll have trouble getting that across to my father,'' Park replied. ''He knows we're subject to federal taxes of 46% on all income over $50,000 and 20% on the first $50,000. An 820% increase in income taxes in the income statement is going to be confusing. Can't you revise the income statement so that the reasons for these odd tax amounts will be apparent?''

Instructions

a Prepare revised comparative income statements for Park Corporation that will, in your opinion, meet the objections raised by Kay Park. Assume that both the earthquake loss and the gain on the sale of Cable Limited common stock are extraordinary items.

b Prepare a correcting entry for Park Corporation on December 31, Year 6, to restate the ledger account balances (assume that the accounting records for the year ended December 31, Year 6, have not been closed).

Pr. 21-8 Kenneth Helwig, controller of Ken Corporation, has summarized the following data with respect to Ken's operations for the year ended December 31, Year 5:

Sales	$1,500,000
Extraordinary gain resulting from a successful antitrust suit for treble damages (taxable at ordinary income tax rates)	300,000
Cost of goods sold	1,000,000
Operating expenses (Includes $40,000 amortization of goodwill, half of which is a permanent difference)	285,000
Correction of error resulting from double-counting items in inventories on Dec. 31, Year 4	60,000

Because Helwig is busy with problems arising in connection with a newly installed computer system, he has asked you, as an independent consultant, to assist him in the preparation of the income statement for Year 5. There were no timing differences in Year 5.

Instructions

a Compute the income taxes of Ken Corporation for Year 5 applicable to current operations, to the extraordinary gain, and to the prior-period adjustment. The income tax rate for Year 5 is 45%; for Year 4 it was 42%.

b Prepare Ken Corporation's condensed income statement for Year 5. Disregard earnings per share.

c Prepare Ken Corporation's statement of retained earnings for Year 5. The balance of retained earnings reported on December 31, Year 4 (without correction for the error in inventories), was $720,000, and cash dividends of $110,000 were declared in Year 5.

Pr. 21-9 Keith Renken, the controller of Sells Limited, handed an assistant a sheet of paper on which appeared the information shown below, saying, ''Here's the story on our accounting and taxable income for the current year; I'd like you to put these amounts together in an income statement and a statement of retained earnings.''

SELLS LIMITED
Computation of Pre-Tax Accounting Income
For Year Ended March 31, Year 8

	Debit	*Credit*
Sales (net)		$869,000
Dividend income from taxable Canadian corporations		10,000
Prior period adjustment: refund of income taxes as a result of income tax reassessment		30,000
Cost of goods sold	$519,000	
Operating expenses	128,000	
Earthquake loss (not covered by insurance), before income tax effect	142,000	
Gain on extinguishment of debt, before income tax effect		90,000
Subtotals	$789,000	$999,000
Prior period adjustment (See above)	30,000	
Income taxes payable (See below)	51,750	
Net income	128,250	
Totals	$999,000	$999,000

SELLS LIMITED
Computation of Income Taxes Payable
For Year Ended March 31, Year 8

Sales (net)		$869,000
Gain on extinguishment of debt (fully taxable)		90,000
Total revenue		$959,000
Less:		
Cost of goods sold	$519,000	
Operating expenses	128,000	
Earthquake loss (fully deductible)	142,000	

Excess of capital cost allowance claimed over straight-line depreciation used for financial accounting	55,000	844,000
Taxable income		$115,000
Income tax rate		0.45
Income taxes payable		$ 51,750

The amount of income taxes payable for the year ended March 31, Year 8, was computed correctly.

Instructions

a Prepare a journal entry for Sells Limited to record income taxes expense, deferred income taxes, and intraperiod allocation of taxes. Assume that the earthquake loss and the gain on extinguishment of debt qualify as extraordinary items for financial accounting.

b On the basis of this information, and assuming an income tax rate of 45%, prepare an income statement and a statement of retained earnings for Sells Limited for the year ended March 31, Year 8. Sells reported a retained earnings balance of $1,917,200 on March 31, Year 7, and declared cash dividends of $75,000 during the year ended March 31, Year 8. Disregard earnings per share.

Pr. 21-10 In Year 5, Queen Limited had sales of $800,000 and pre-tax accounting income of $300,000. Straight-line depreciation expense of $80,000 was recorded for financial accounting, but capital cost allowance claimed for income tax purposes amounted to $124,000. Cost depletion of $100,000 was deducted to compute pre-tax accounting income, but a deduction for depletion equal to 22% of sales was allowed in the income tax return.

Pre-tax accounting income did not include a gain of $440,000 from the disposal of land on the instalment basis, which was reported as an extraordinary item. The gain from the disposal of the land was reported as an extraordinary item because it resulted from the only disposable parcel of land that Queen owned. Only one-fourth of the selling price was collected in Year 5; therefore, only $110,000 of the gain was taxable at 30% in Year 5.

Pre-tax accounting income was taxed at 20% of the first $50,000 and 46% of the balance. An unrecorded operating loss carryforward of $50,000 and a capital loss of $8,000 were carried forward from Year 4, and are available to reduce the income tax liability for Year 5; the capital loss carryforward was to be offset against the gain from the disposal of land in Year 5.

Instructions

a Prepare a journal entry for Queen Limited to record income taxes for Year 5. Deferred taxes are to be recognized for the timing differences between pre-tax accounting income and taxable income.

b Prepare Queen Limited's income statement for Year 5. Disregard earnings per share.

c Show how the deferred income taxes appear in Queen Limited's balance sheet on December 31, Year 5. Assume that on January 1, Year 5, the Deferred Income Taxes—Noncurrent ledger account showed a credit balance of $245,000 (there was no current balance) and that one-fourth of the selling price of the land was to be collected in Year 6.

Pr. 21-11 Juan Cortez, controller of Madera Corporation, was injured in an accident shortly after the end of Year 5. In his absence, the accountant for Madera prepared the following income statement for use in connection with the Year 5 audit:

MADERA CORPORATION
Income Statement
For Year Ended December 31, Year 5

Sales		$2,000,000
Rent revenue (An additional $5,000 advance rent was received and is taxable in Year 5 but will not be recognized as revenue until Year 6)		45,000
Other revenue (including $6,000 tax-free dividend income)		14,000
Total revenue		$2,059,000
Cost of goods sold	$1,400,000	
Operating expenses (including straight-line depreciation of $45,000) (Capital cost allowance for income tax purposes is $60,000)	500,000	
Extraordinary loss: Seizure of shipment of goods by foreign terrorists (fully deductible for income tax purposes)	250,000	
Additional depreciation expense recognized this year attributable to error in computation of depreciation for Year 4 (Same error was included in the income tax return for Year 4)	49,000	
Total costs and expenses		2,199,000
Loss before income tax effect		$ (140,000)

The income tax rate in effect for Years 1 through 5 was 45%; taxable income amounted to more than $200,000 each year in Years 2, 3, and 4.

Instructions

a Compute all essential income tax amounts in connection with Madera Corporation's income statement for the year ended December 31, Year 5.

b Prepare Madera Corporation's journal entry to record income taxes on December 31, Year 5. Assume that the operating loss for Year 5 is carried back to Year 2.

c Prepare Madera Corporation's combined statement of income and retained earnings for the year ended December 31, Year 5. The retained earnings balance as previously reported on December 31, Year 4, was $1,543,000; cash dividends of $85,000 were declared on December 10, Year 5.

Pr. 21-12 The Noro, Inc., bookkeeper was unable to determine the balances of the income tax accounts for the company because she was unable to make the appropriate journal entries. The president of the company, Mrs. Norma Johnston, has requested that you, as the company's accountant, prepare the necessary information. You are able to get the following information from the company records:

	Year 6	*Year 7*	*Year 8*
Accounting income (lost)	$100,000	$(110,000)	$150,000
Capital cost allowance claimed	75,000	–0–	75,000
Depreciation expense	50,000	50,000	50,000

The company's income tax rate has always been 45% and is expected to remain there for the forseeable future. At the end of Year 5 the balance in the deferred income tax account was $135,000 credit, representing the excess of capital cost allowance claimed for tax purposes over depreciation taken for financial accounting purposes. The company will not adjust CCA claimed in any year.

Instructions

a Prepare the journal entries to record income taxes for Year 6, Year 7, and Year 8.

b Prepare a partial income statement for Year 7 starting with ''Loss Before Income Taxes.''

c Prepare a ''Summary of Timing Differences'' for the three-year period.

Pr. 21-13 New Method Corporation has provided the following information for income tax purposes:

	Year 11	*Year 12*	*Year 13*
Net income (loss) before income taxes	$100,000	$(180,000)	$170,000
Permanent differences:			
3% inventory tax allowance	13,000	14,000	11,000
Dividends from taxable Canadian company (included in income)	15,000	15,000	15,000
Income tax penalty for late filing of tax return	8,000	9,000	6,000
Timing differences:			
Depreciation expense	40,000	40,000	40,000
Capital cost allowance claimed	60,000	–0–	60,000
Income tax rate	45%	45%	45%

The opening deferred tax timing difference of $200,000 has been accumulated because capital cost allowance claimed for tax purposes has exceeded depreciation taken for financial accounting purposes at a tax rate of 45%. The tax rate is expected to remain at 45% into the forseeable future.

Instructions

Assuming virtual certainty is ***present***:

a Prepare journal entries to record income taxes for the three years.

b Prepare partial income statements for the three years, and describe the accounts and amounts which would appear on the balance sheet at the end of each of the three years.

c Prepare a summary of timing differences for the three-year period.

Assuming virtual certainty is ***not present*** and the Year 10 income tax return will not be refiled, repeat the above three instructions.

Pr. 21-14 From the information given for New Method Corporation in the previous problem, assume that there is no virtual certainty and that the prior-period tax return is refiled claiming no capital cost allowance.

Instructions

a Prepare journal entries to record income taxes for the three years.

b Prepare partial income statements and balance sheet disclosure requirements for the three years.

c Prepare a summary of timing differences for the three-year period.

Pr. 21-15 Nuco Corporation commenced business January 1, Year 1. Information with respect to income and income taxes for the five years ending December 31, Year 5, is given below:

Year	*Pre-tax accounting income before depreciation & tax*	*Depreciation booked*	*CCA claimed*
1	$ -0-	$200,000	$ -0-
2	-0-	200,000	-0-
3	100,000	200,000	100,000
4	400,000	200,000	350,000
5	400,000	200,000	300,000

The income tax rate remained at 40% for the 5 years.

Instructions

a Prepare the journal entry for income taxes at the end of each year assuming reasonable assurance is present.

b Prepare a ''Summary of Timing Differences'' schedule for the five-year period, assuming there is reasonable assurance.

c h a p t e r 2 2

ACCOUNTING CHANGES, ERRORS, AND INCOMPLETE RECORDS

As generally accepted accounting principles change in response to changes in the economic and social environment, accountants must find ways to implement the new principles in financial reporting. Placing new principles and new accounting estimates into the stream of financial statements may make current-period statements inconsistent with those of prior accounting periods. However, new and improved principles and estimates should not be ignored simply to maintain consistency with the financial reporting of the past. In this chapter we explore some approaches to the adoption of new accounting principles and estimates with the goal of maintaining the maximum degree of comparability and, at the same time, gaining the advantages inherent in a change to improved or preferable accounting principles and estimates.

In this chapter we also discuss methods of correcting and reporting errors that are discovered in previously issued financial statements. Finally, we consider ways in which accountants may develop financial statements from incomplete accounting records.

ACCOUNTING CHANGES

In the past, questions often were raised as to how certain accounting changes should be reported in the financial statements while at the same time preserving the consistency and comparability of the statements. By changing its accounting practices, a business enterprise might affect significantly the presentation of its financial position and results of operations. The change also might distort the earnings trend reported in income statements for earlier years.

For example, suppose that Romm Limited acquired equipment early in Year 1 for $500,000. The equipment had an economic life of eight years and a net residual value of $50,000. For two years the equipment was depreciated by the straight-line method. Early in Year 3, Romm revised its original estimates and concluded that the equipment had a remaining economic life of 10 years and a revised net residual value of $100,000. During Year 3, Rommn also changed from the straight-line method to an accelerated method of depreciation and merged with Poo Ling Inc. in a business combination accounted for as a pooling of interests. It is evident that the financial statements prepared by Romm at the end of Year 3 would not be comparable with the financial statements issued in Years 1 and 2, unless the changes that took place were reported in a manner designed to preserve comparability.

The foregoing illustration has examples of (1) a ***change in accounting estimate*** (the revisions of estimated economic life and net residual value of the equipment), (2) a ***change in accounting policy*** (the change from the straight-line method to an accelerated method of depreciation), and (3) a ***change in reporting entity*** (the inclusion of Poo Ling Inc. in the financial statements for Year 3). Thus, accountants must find appropriate methods of reporting these accounting changes to users of financial statements so that the statements are not misleading and so that a meaningful comparison of earnings for the three-year period may be made.

For many years, the disclosures of accounting changes often were incomplete and obscure and resulted in suggestions by some critics that such changes were used by management to manipulate reported earnings. Many users of financial statements not only misunderstood the reasons for accounting changes but also failed to grasp their full impact. In an effort to establish principles for measuring and reporting the effects of accounting changes on financial statements, the Accounting Standards Committee defined the different types of accounting changes and established guidelines for reporting such changes in financial statements.[1]

Types of Accounting Changes

Section 1506 of the ***CICA Handbook***, "Accounting Changes," focusses on the accounting and reporting issues of: (1) changes in accounting policies, (2) changes in accounting estimates, and (3) corrections of errors in prior period financial statements.

A ***change in accounting policy*** results from the adoption of a generally accepted accounting principle or method which is more appropriate than the one used previously for financial reporting. Thus, the term ***accounting policy*** encompasses the specific accounting principles as well as the methods used in the application of accounting principles. Examples of changes in accounting policy are a change in the method of computing depreciation (such as a change to an accelerated depreciation method from a straight-line method) and a change in the method of valuing inventory (such as a change from lifo to fifo).

A ***change in accounting estimate*** may be required as new events occur and as better information becomes available about the probable outcome of future events.

1 CICA, ***CICA Handbook*** (Toronto), sec. 1506.

Examples of changes in accounting estimates are an increase in the percentage used to estimate doubtful or uncollectible accounts expense from 2 to 5% of sales; a major write-down of inventories because of obsolescence; a change in the estimated economic life of plant assets; a change in the recoverable units of natural resources; and a revision in the amount of estimated liability for outstanding product warranties.

A ***correction of an error*** is required when errors are discovered in prior period financial statements. A correction of an error is different from a change in accounting policies or in accounting estimates. Errors may result from inaccurate computations, mistakes in the application of accounting principles or methods, or an oversight or misuse of facts that existed at the time the financial statements were prepared. Corrections of errors may follow the discovery that material amounts of depreciation were not recorded in prior accounting periods, or the decision to change from an accounting principle that is not generally accepted to one that is generally accepted.

Change in Accounting Policy

At first glance, a change in accounting policy seems to violate the assumption that financial statements are prepared ''in accordance with generally accepted accounting principles applied on a basis consistent with that of the preceding year.'' In the preparation of financial statements there is a presumption that accounting policies, once adopted, should not be changed so that meaningful comparisons of successive financial statements can be made. Consequently, section 1506 of the ***CICA Handbook*** states that a change in accounting policy may be made to conform to new recommendations of the Accounting Standards Committee or legislative requirements or when the change is an adoption of a ***more appropriate, alternative*** generally accepted accounting principle or method. Such a change enables an enterprise to present more appropriately its financial position and operating results.

Section 1506 also states, however, that changes in accounting policy do not include: (1) the initial adoption or alteration of an accounting policy created by situations substantially different from those in the prior periods, (2) the initial adoption of an accounting policy for a new situation or a situation previously considered immaterial, and (3) a change in the classification of an item in the financial statements. As stated earlier, a change from an unaccepted accounting principle or method to a principle or method that is generally accepted is not a change in accounting policy but a correction of an error made in prior period financial statements.

How should a change in accounting policy be implemented in order to preserve the comparability between future financial statements and those of the prior periods? In its deliberations on this issue, the Accounting Standards Committee considered the following three methods:

1 ***Retroactive application with restatement of prior periods (retroactive restatement)*** Under this method, the effect of an accounting policy change is reflected ***retroactively*** in those prior period financial statements affected by the change. Thus, each of these prior period financial statements presented for compara-

tive purposes is to be ***restated*** to reflect the change. In addition, the cumulative effect of the change on the periods preceding the earliest period included in the comparative financial statements is treated as an adjustment to the beginning balance of retained earnings of the earliest period.

2 ***Retroactive application with no restatement of prior periods*** Under this method, the total cumulative effect of those prior period financial statements affected by an accounting policy change is treated either as an item in the income statement or as an adjustment to the beginning balance of retained earnings of the period in which the change is made. Prior period financial statements presented for comparative purposes are ***not*** restated to reflect the effect of the change in accounting policy.

3 ***Prospective application*** Under this method, the effect of the new accounting policy is reflected in the period in which the change is made. It requires ***no*** cumulative adjustments to, or restatement of, prior periods.

A survey of 325 companies indicated that, prior to the Committee's recommendations, all these methods were in use. Of the 52 companies with changes in accounting policy in 1980, 21 applied the changes retroactively, 29 did not apply the changes retroactively, and 2 applied the changes both retroactively and non-retroactively.[2] Also, 3 of the 64 companies in 1979 applied the cumulative effect of the changes in the income statements.[3]

After weighing the merits of the three methods, the Accounting Standards Committee recommended in section 1506 that the first method, ***retroactive restatement***, should be used. The rationale for this is that this method provides consistency in accounting policies from one period to another and thus makes the evaluation of earnings trends more meaningful. Accordingly, the benefits derived from such consistency and comparability outweigh any perceived loss in confidence that may result from the restatement of prior period financial statements.[4] In addition, the committee also stipulated in section 1506 the following disclosure requirements for the retroactive restatement of an accounting policy change: (1) a description of the change, (2) a description of the effect of the change on the financial statements of the current period, and (3) a disclosure of the fact that prior period financial statements presented for comparative purposes have been restated and of the effect of the change on those prior periods.[5] Of course, additional disclosures such as the reasons for the change, the related income tax effect, and the effect of the change on earnings per share and working capital, would be desirable.

To illustrate how a change in accounting policy would be reported under the retroactive-restatement method, let us assume the following:

1 Alta Limited, which owns and operates office buildings, decided in Year 5 to change from the straight-line method to an accelerated method of depreciation.

2 CICA, *Financial Reporting in Canada*, 14th ed (1981), p. 19.

3 CICA, *Financial Reporting in Canada*, p. 19.

4 CICA, *CICA Handbook*, sec. 1506.09.

5 CICA, ***CICA Handbook***, sec. 1506.15–.16.

2 The accelerated method, which has been used for income tax purposes, was considered more appropriate for financial reporting because the revenue-producing capacity of the office buildings tended to decline as the buildings became older. Moreover, the change would make the company's operating results more comparable with other companies in the office rental business since most competitors used the accelerated method of depreciation.

3 The depreciation computed under the two methods was:

	Year 5	*Year 4*	*Prior to Year 4*
Straight-line	$ 90,000	$ 90,000	$200,000
Accelerated	130,000	160,000	500,000

4 The net income before depreciation for Year 5 is $270,000 and for Year 4 was $290,000. The net income after depreciation for Year 4 was $200,000 ($290,000 − 90,000).

5 The beginning balances of retained earnings for Years 5 and 4 were $1,800,000 and $1,600,000 respectively.

6 Ignore income tax implications. (If income tax is considered, there will be adjustments to the deferred income tax liability account for the prior years.)

On the basis of these assumptions, the statements of retained earnings for Years 5 and 4 and the income statements for Years 5 and 4 are shown below and on the next page.

The change in depreciation method as illustrated also affects the balance sheet and the statement of changes in financial position. Thus, both balance sheet and the statement of changes in financial position of the prior period presented for

ALTA LIMITED
Statement of Retained Earnings
For Years Ended December 31, Year 5 and Year 4

	Year 5	*Year 4 (restated; see NOTE)*
Beginning balance	$1,800,000	$1,600,000
Less: cumulative effect on prior years of change from the straight-line method to an accelerated method of depreciation applied retroactively	370,000	300,000
Beginning balance restated	$1,430,000	$1,300,000
Add: Net income	140,000	130,000
Ending balance	$1,570,000	$1,430,000

NOTE: During the year ended December 31, Year 5, the company changed its accounting for depreciation from the straight-line method to an accelerated method. The new method is a generally accepted one and is commonly used in the industry. The company believed that its operating results under this new method would be more meaningful and more comparable with those of other companies in the industry. The effects of the change for the Years 5 and 4 were decreases in net income of $40,000, and $70,000, and decreases in earnings per share of $0.40 and $0.70. The cumulative effect of the change for the years prior to Year 4 was $300,000 and was reported as an adjustment to the beginning balance of retained earnings of Year 4. The financial statements for Year 4 presented for comparative purposes have been retroactively restated to reflect the effect of the change.

ALTA LIMITED
Partial Income Statements
For Years Ended December 31, Year 5 and Year 4

	Year 5	*Year 4 (restated; see NOTE above)*
Net income before depreciation	$270,000	$290,000
Depreciation expense	130,000	160,000
Net income	$140,000	$130,000
Earnings per share	$1.40	$1.30

comparative purposes should be restated to reflect the effect of the change.

When an accounting policy change is to conform to new recommendations of the Accounting Standards Committee or legislative requirements, the retroactive-restatement method is encouraged even though such treatment is not stipulated in the recommendations or the legislation.[6]

It should be recognized that the application of the retroactive-restatement method may ***not*** be practicable under certain circumstances. In some cases, the effect of an accounting policy change for specific prior periods may not be reasonably determinable even though the total cumulative effect of the change on these prior periods can be determined. This may occur when the method of accounting for long-term contracts is changed from the completed-contract to the percentage-of-completion basis. In such a case, section 1506 recommends that the retroactive effect of the accounting policy change be treated as a cumulative adjustment to the beginning balance of retained earnings of the period in which the change is made. Also, financial statement disclosure should include: (1) the fact that the prior-period financial statements presented for comparative purposes have ***not*** been restated and (2) the fact that the cumulative adjustment has been made to the beginning balance of the retained earnings of the ***current*** year.

There are also circumstances in which it may be extremely difficult to obtain the necessary financial data for the retroactive application of an accounting policy change. In such cases, section 1506 recommends that the new accounting policy should be applied ***prospectively*** and disclosure should be made to indicate that the accounting policy change has not been applied retroactively.

The reporting and disclosure requirements of an accounting policy change depend on its materiality. In considering materiality, not only the current period but also both the prior and future periods should be included. Thus, if the effect of the change does not have a material effect in the current period but is likely to have a material effect in future periods, section 1506 recommends that the change be disclosed in the financial statements of the current period.

Change in Accounting Estimate

Much of accountants' work involves subjective judgement. That is, accountants often are relied on to estimate such things as the economic life and residual value

6 CICA, *CICA Handbook*, sec. 1506.11.

of plant assets, the amount of probable uncollectible accounts receivable, and inventory obsolescence, and to make other decisions which require the estimate of the effects of future events. As time passes, new events and better information may require that the original estimate of economic life or residual value of plant assets, for example, be revised to reflect these new developments.

For example, assume that management had estimated the economic life of a plant asset at 10 years, with no residual value at the end of that period. The cost of the asset, $20,000, has been depreciated at the rate of $2,000 a year for seven years. At the beginning of the eighth year, management determined that the asset had a remaining economic life of five years and that its residual value would be $500 at the end of 12 years of use. The revised annual depreciation expense over the remaining economic life of the asset is determined as shown in the next illustration.

The change in estimated economic life and residual value affects only the remaining years of economic life (Years 8 through 12); ***no correction of the previously reported earnings for Years 1 through 7 is required***. Because accounting measurements based on estimates are imperfect, and some disparity between past and subsequent estimates cannot be avoided, retroactive restatements of previously reported earnings as a result of changes in accounting estimates may cast suspicion on both the original and the revised earnings amounts. The information used to revise the service potential of the plant asset could not have been anticipated at the time the asset was acquired. Revised estimates are based on present conditions and management policies. Therefore, a reasonable approach is to allocate the unexpired service potential of the plant asset over its remaining economic life based on the latest information.

Computation of revised annual depreciation for plant asset with changed estimates of economic life and residual value

Cost of plant asset	$20,000
Less: Depreciation for Years 1–7 at $2,000 a year	14,000
Undepreciated cost at beginning of Year 8 (carrying amount)	$ 6,000
Less: Estimated residual value at end of Year 12	500
Amount to be depreciated in Years 8–12 (5 years)	$ 5,500
Revised annual depreciation for Years 8–12; $5,500 ÷ 5 years of remaining economic life	$ 1,100

A change in an accounting estimate occurs because new or better information has come to light in the current accounting period. Thus, it is logical that the resulting change should affect the computation of net income for the accounting period in which the change is made; if the change has a continuing effect, it should be consistently applied to the periods following the period of the change. Accordingly, section 1506 of the ***CICA Handbook*** recommends that the effect of a change in an accounting estimate be accounted for in the period of change, or in the period of change and the applicable future periods, according to whether the change affects one or more periods. ***A change in accounting estimate does not require (as does a change in accounting policy) the recording of the cumulative effect of the change in the current accounting period or the retroactive restatement of financial statements for prior periods.*** Disclosure is not necessary for changes in estimates which are made in the ordinary course of accounting for items such as doubtful accounts expense or inventory obsolescence. However, the nature and effect of a change in an accounting estimate should be disclosed *if* the change is rare or unusual and may affect the current and future periods, such as a change in the estimated economic life of a plant asset.[7]

A revision of the estimated economic life or residual value of a plant asset, as described above, is a change in accounting estimate. A change in the method of computing depreciation on a previously recorded asset is a change in accounting principle. But what if a business enterprise acquired a new plant asset and decided that the output method of depreciation is the most appropriate method for the asset? As long as it continued to depreciate its previously recorded assets by the same method as before, there is no need for a cumulative adjustment in the income statement because there was no change in accounting principle for those assets. However, methods of depreciation should be disclosed.

In certain instances, a change in accounting principle may be accompanied by a change in accounting estimate. In such cases ***it is difficult to separate the effect of the change in principle from the effect of the change in estimate***. For example, a business enterprise that has been deferring and amortizing certain costs might decide to change to a policy of recognizing such costs as expenses because the future benefits of the costs have become doubtful. This type of change often is related to the process of obtaining additional information that calls for a revision of the original judgement that the costs will provide future benefits. Because the new accounting method was adopted as a result of the change in estimated future benefits, ***such a change is accounted for as a change in accounting estimate***.[8]

Change in Reporting Entity

A business combination of two or more companies accounted for as a ***pooling of interests*** (see Chapter 16, page 807), results in financial statements that are in effect the statements of a ***different reporting entity***. This change in reporting entity is viewed as a special type of change in accounting principle that ***requires the restatement of the financial statements of all prior accounting periods as though the combined enterprise had existed all along***.

The condensed two-year financial statements of Combinor Corporation and Combinee Limited shown on page 1108 are used to illustrate a change in reporting entity resulting from a business combination accounted for as a pooling of interests. The financial statements were prepared immediately prior to a pooling-type business combination of the two enterprises on December 31, Year 2.

On December 31, Year 2, Combinor Corporation issued 40,000 shares of its no-par-value common stock to shareholders of Combinee Limited for all 50,000 shares of Combinee's outstanding no-par-value common stock. The market value of Combinor Corporation common shares, at the date of the share exchange,

7 CICA, ***CICA Handbook***, sec. 1506.24.

8 CICA, ***CICA Handbook***, sec. 1506.22.

COMBINOR CORPORATION AND COMBINEE LIMITED
Condensed Financial Statements Prior to Business Combination
For Years Ended December 31, Year 2 and Year 1

	Combinor Corporation, Year ended Dec. 31:		*Combinee Limited, Year ended Dec. 31:*	
	Year 2	*Year 1*	*Year 2*	*Year 1*
Income statements:				
Revenue	$ 800,000	$ 600,000	$400,000	300,000
Costs and expenses	600,000	500,000	250,000	200,000
Net income	$ 200,000	$ 100,000	$150,000	$100,000
Statements of retained earnings:				
Retained earnings, beginning of year	$ 400,000	$ 300,000	$250,000	$150,000
Net income	200,000	100,000	150,000	100,000
Retained earnings, end of year	$ 600,000	$ 400,000	$400,000	$250,000
Balance sheets:				
Total assets	$1,600,000	$1,300,000	$800,000	$600,000
Liabilities	$ 900,000	$ 800,000	$350,000	$300,000
Common stock, no par value	100,000	100,000	50,000	50,000
Retained earnings	600,000	400,000	400,000	250,000
Total liabilities & shareholders' equity	$1,600,000	$1,300,000	$800,000	$600,000

Illustration of change in reporting entity

COMBINOR CORPORATION
Condensed Financial Statements
For Years Ended December 31, Year 2 and Year 1
(Restated for effects of pooling-of-interests business combination)

	December 31:	
	Year 2	*Year 1*
Income statements:		
Revenue	$1,200,000	$ 900,000
Costs and expenses	850,000	700,000
Net income	$ 350,000	$ 200,000
Statements of retained earnings:		
Retained earnings, beginning of year:		
As previously reported	$ 400,000	$ 300,000
Add: Adjustment to reflect pooling of interests with Combinee Company	250,000	150,000
As restated	$ 650,000	$ 450,000
Net income	350,000	200,000
Retained earnings, end of year	$1,000,000	$ 650,000
Balance sheets:		
Total assets	$2,400,000	$1,900,000
Liabilities	$1,250,000	$1,100,000
Common stock, no par value	150,000	150,000
Retained earnings	1,000,000	650,000
Total liabilities & shareholders' equity	$2,400,000	$1,900,000

was $1.25 per share. (Out-of-pocket costs of the business combination are disregarded in this illustration.) As a result of this combination, which was accounted for as a pooling of interests, Combinee was liquidated and Combinor acquired Combinee's net assets. Combinor Corporation issues the following restated financial statements of the ***new reporting entity*** for Year 2 and Year 1:

Under pooling-of-interests accounting, the business combination of Combinor Corporation and Combinee Limited is considered to have taken place on January 1, Year 1, the beginning of the earliest accounting period covered by Combinor's financial statements on page 1108, rather than on December 31, Year 2. Accordingly, the income statement and balance sheet show ***combined amounts*** for all elements — revenue, expenses, assets, liabilities, and shareholders' equity.

CORRECTION OF ERRORS

In previous chapters we have noted the difficulties inherent in any attempt to determine the periodic income of a business enterprise. At best, accountants can only measure the impact of the past transactions and events and make informed estimates of the present effect of probable future events. In addition, ***errors*** in financial statements may result from mathematical mistakes, mistakes in the application of accounting principles, or the oversight or misuse of facts that existed at the time the financial statements were prepared. An example of a correction of an error is the discovery that material amounts of depreciation were not recorded in prior periods.

Correction of an Error in Prior Period Financial Statements

When a material error in prior period financial statements is discovered, section 1506 of the ***CICA Handbook*** recommends that the correction of the error be accounted for ***retroactively*** and the financial statements of all these prior periods presented for comparative purposes be ***restated***. In addition, it requires disclosure in the current period regarding: (1) the nature of the error, (2) the effect of the correction on the financial statements of the current and prior periods, and (3) the fact that the prior period financial statements presented for comparative purposes have been restated. The disclosure of the effect of the correction on such significant items as net income, earnings per share, and working capital may be appropriate as well.

These requirements are logical because they make comparisons of performance of a business enterprise over a number of periods more meaningful, and prevent them from being misleading. Anyone who attempts to assess the probable future earnings and financial position of an enterprise relies on past information. An error that causes a material misstatement of net income for any recent period results in a misleading picture of the earnings pattern of the enterprise, and can affect the decisions of those who rely on financial statements for investment information.

Correction of Previously Issued Financial Statements Illustrated

To illustrate the correction of a material error, assume that Trevor Corporation acquired a machine on January 2, Year 1 for $100,000. The machine had an economic life of 10 years with no net residual value, and was being depreciated by the accelerated depreciation method. The accountant incorrectly recorded (for financial accounting and in income tax returns) annual depreciation expense for Year 1 through Year 4 at $2,000, $1,800, $1,620, and $1,458 respectively, rather than at the correct amounts of $20,000, $18,000, $16,200, and $14,580 respectively because of a computation error. Thus, depreciation expense was understated by $18,000, $16,200, $14,580, and $13,122 for Year 1 through Year 4 respectively. The error, totalling $61,902, was discovered early in Year 5, after the following condensed financial statements ***had been issued:***

TREVOR CORPORATION
Comparative Income Statements
(Before correction)
For Year 4 and Year 3

	Year 4	*Year 3*
Sales	$300,000	$280,000
Costs and expenses	270,000	260,000
Net income	$ 30,000	$20,000
Earnings per share of common stock (10,000 shares)	$ 3.00	$ 2.00

TREVOR CORPORATION
Statement of Retained Earnings
(Before correction)
For Year 4 and Year 3

	Year 4	*Year 3*
Beginning balance	$200,000	$180,000
Add: Net income	30,000	20,000
Ending balance	$230,000	$200,000

TREVOR CORPORATION
Comparative Balance Sheets
(Before correction)
End of Year 4 and Year 3

	Year 4	*Year 3*
Assets		
Other assets	$260,000	$225,000
Machinery	320,000	290,000
Less: Accumulated depreciation	(80,000)	(65,000)
Total assets	$500,000	$450,000
Liabilities & Stockholders' Equity		
Liabilities	$170,000	$150,000
Common stock, no par value	100,000	100,000
Retained earnings	230,000	200,000
Total liabilities & shareholders' equity	$500,000	$450,000

Assuming an income tax rate of 50%, the following correcting journal entry is required for Trevor Corporation early in Year 5:

Journal entry to correct computational error of prior periods

Income Tax Refund Receivable ($61,902 × 0.50)	30,951	
Retained Earnings ($61,902 − $30,951)	30,951	
Accumulated Depreciation of Machinery		61,902
To correct error in computation of depreciation expense for Year 1 through Year 4, and to establish receivable for income taxes overpaid for those years.		

If corrected financial statements for prior years are not issued in Year 5, the ***prior periods adjustment*** totalling $30,951 is reported in the statement of retained earnings for Year 5 as a correction to retained earnings at the beginning of Year 5. When corrected financial statements for prior years are issued in Year 5, the beginning and ending balances for retained earnings are ***corrected retroactively*** for each prior year for which corrected financial statements are issued. As an example, the corrected comparative financial statements of Trevor Corporation for Year 4 and Year 3 are presented below and on page 1112.

In the corrected income statements, costs and expenses of each year are increased retroactively by the understatement in each year's depreciation expense net of the 50% income taxes. For Year 3, the correction in depreciation expense of $14,580, less income tax saved at 50% in the amount of $7,290, equals a net

TREVOR CORPORATION
Comparative Income Statements
(After correction)
For Year 4 and Year 3

	Year 4	*Year 3*
Sales	$300,000	$280,000
Costs and expenses	276,561	267,290
Net income	23,439	12,710
Earnings per share of common stock (10,000 shares)	$ 2.34	$ 1.27

TREVOR CORPORATION
Statement of Retained Earnings
(After correction)
For Year 4 and Year 3

	Year 4 (restated)	*Year 3 (restated)*
Beginning balance	$200,000	$180,000
Less: Error in computing depreciation starting Year 1 ..	24,390	17,100
Beginning balance restated	$175,610	$162,900
Add: Net income	23,439	12,710
Ending balance	$199,049	$175,610

TREVOR CORPORATION
Comparative Balance Sheets
(After correction)
End of Year 4 and Year 3

	Year 4	*Year 3*
Assets		
Other assets	$290,951	$249,390
Machinery	320,000	290,000
Less: Accumulated depreciation	(141,902)	(113,780)
Total assets	$469,049	$425,610
Liabilities & Shareholders' Equity		
Liabilities	$170,000	$150,000
Common stock, no par value	100,000	100,000
Retained earnings	199,049	175,610
Total liabilities & shareholder's equity	469,049	$425,610

increase in costs and expenses of $7,290 ($260,000 + $7,290 = $267,290). For Year 4, the correction in depreciation expense of $13,122, less income tax saved at 50% in the amount of $6,561, equals the increase in costs and expenses of $6,561 ($270,000 + $6,561 = $276,561). Thus net income in Year 3 is decreased by $7,290 and in Year 4 by $6,561.

The balance sheet items requiring correction at the end of Year 4 and Year 3 are other assets (for income tax receivable), accumulated depreciation, and retained earnings. The cumulative effect of Years 1, 2, and 3 depreciation adjustments in the amount of $48,780 ($18,000 + $16,200 + $14,580 = $48,780) is credited to accumulated depreciation at the end of Year 3. Likewise, 50% of $48,780 or $24,390 is debited to other assets as income tax receivable on the under-expensing of depreciation to the end of Year 3. Retained earnings, at the beginning of Year 3, must be adjusted for the after-tax effect for Years 1 and 2. Year 3 will flow through the income statement. As a result, the Year 3 ending retained earnings will have been adjusted by $24,390 [($18,000 + $16,200) × 0.50 + ($14,580 × 0.50)] = ($17,100 + $7,290) = $24,390, and ($200,000 − $24,390) = $175,610. Consequently, Year 4 retained earnings will be adjusted by $24,390 at the beginning of the year and by an adjustment to Year 4 income of $6,561 ($13,122 × 0.50 = $6,561). Accordingly, the total adjustment to the end of Year 4's retained earnings will be $30,951 ($24,390 + $6,561 = $30,951).

Types of Errors

Many accounting errors are brought to light by the controls in the double-entry accounting system. Independent accountants, internal auditors, and Revenue Canada auditors may uncover errors during an examination of the accounting records. The installation of an improved accounting system may uncover material errors resulting from the inadequacies of the previous system. Thus, the need to correct errors is more likely to occur in a small business enterprise than in a large publicly owned corporation.

The problem of dealing with errors of the same type may be generalized to some extent. Once the nature of the distortion created by a class of error is understood,it is possible to determine the effect of similar errors.

Errors Affecting Only Balance Sheet Amounts

An error that affects only balance sheet amounts may arise because (1) journal entries were made to the wrong ledger account, (2) transactions were omitted from the journal, or (3) the amounts of certain journal entries were wrong. For example, if Accounts Payable is debited instead of Accounts Receivable, total assets and total liabilities are understated by the same amount. When the error is discovered, only balance sheet amounts require correction.

Errors Affecting Only Income Statement Amounts

An error that is confined to income statement amounts has no effect on net income. Such errors generally arise through misclassification; for example, an expense or revenue item may be debited or credited to the wrong ledger account.

Errors Affecting Both the Balance Sheet and the Income Statement

Errors that affect both the balance sheet and the income statement fall into two categories: (1) errors that will be counterbalanced in the next accounting period, and (2) errors that will not be counterbalanced in the next period.

Some errors, if not discovered, ***will be counterbalanced*** in the course of the next period's accounting. The typical counterbalancing error causes a misstatement of the net income of one accounting period and the balance sheet at the end of that period, which is offset by a misstatement of income in the ***opposite direction*** in the following period. The balance sheet at the end of the second period and the net income of subsequent periods are not affected by the error, which has in a sense ''corrected itself'' over the two periods.

An example of a counterbalancing error is the failure to record accrued wages at the end of an accounting period. The liability wages payable is understated at the end of the period, and because wages expense is understated, net income is overstated in the period the error is made. In the following period, the payment of the unrecorded accrued wages is debited to expense; thus, wages expense for the second period is overstated. As a result, net income of the second period is understated by an amount equal to the overstatement of the previous period. If proper wage accruals are made at the end of the second period, the wages payable in the balance sheet on that date is correct. The balance of retained earnings also is correctly stated at the end of the second period.

Other errors affect both the balance sheet and the income statement, but ***are not counterbalanced*** in the next accounting period. For example, suppose an acquisition of equipment is debited to expense by mistake. Because an expense is overstated in the period the error is made, net income for that period is understated by an amount equal to the cost of the equipment less the depreciation expense that should have been recognized. Net income also is overstated in subsequent periods by the amount of unrecorded deprecation expense on the equipment while it is in service. Equipment in the balance sheet is understated throughout its economic life.

Analyzing the Effect of Errors

When an error is discovered, the accountant must analyze the effect of the error on financial data for prior, current, and subsequent accounting periods. Because it is not feasible to discuss every possible error that might occur, in this section we will discuss only the reasoning used in the determination of the effect of errors. The illustrations are designed to show corrections required to produce revised income statements of prior periods, and do not purport to illustrate the application of any *CICA Handbook* recommendations. In other words, we are concerned primarily with omissions and other errors that may occur in a ***small business enterprise that does not issue financial statements to the public***.

As an example, let us trace the effect of an error in the determination of the amount of inventories at the end of an accounting period. Assume that we discover that the inventories on December 31, Year 4, are overstated by $3,400, and that the ***periodic inventory system is used***. We may analyze the effect of this error (disregarding income taxes) as illustrated at the bottom of this page.

The action to be taken on discovery of this error depends on when the error is discovered and the extent of the revision of financial statements that is desired.

Discovery in Year 4

If the error is discovered in Year 4 before the ledger accounts are closed, a separate correcting journal entry is not necessary. The ending inventories under the ***periodic inventory system*** are recorded at the time closing entries are made, and it is a simple matter to use the revised inventories amount in the closing (or adjusting) entries. The ending inventories in the income statement for Year 4 are decreased by $3,400, and net income is decreased by this amount.

Discovery in Year 5

If the error is discovered at any time prior to the closing of the ledger accounts for Year 5, the correcting entry is as shown on page 1115.

Analysis of effect of overstatement of inventories at end of Year 4

Year 4	*Year 5*	*Year 6*
	Income Statement	
Net income is overstated by $3,400. (Cost of goods sold is understated, because ending inventories were overstated.)	Net income is understated by $3,400. (Cost of goods sold is overstated, because beginning inventories were overstated.)	Error has fully counterbalanced; no correction is required.
	Balance Sheet	
Assets are overstated by $3,400. (Ending inventories are overstated.) Retained earnings is overstated by $3,400. (Net income was overstated.)	Balance sheet items are properly stated, because Dec. 31, Year 5, inventories are correct, and overstatement of retained earnings in Year 4 has been offset by understatement of net income in Year 5.	No correction is required.

Journal entry to correct error in ending inventories of prior accounting period

Retained Earnings (net income, Year 4)	3,400	
Inventories (Dec. 31, Year 4)		3,400
To correct overstatement in beginning inventories (income tax effects are disregarded).		

The purpose of this entry is to correct the financial statements for Year 5. Both the net income for Year 5 and the balance sheet at the end of Year 5 are stated correctly after the prior period adjustment of $3,400 (correction of net income for Year 4) is recorded in the Retained Earnings ledger account. In the statement of retained earnings for Year 5, the adjustment for the prior period error is reported as a correction of the beginning balance of retained earnings.

Discovery in Year 6

If the error in the inventories at the end of Year 4 is not discovered until Year 6, no correcting entry is required, because the error has been fully counterbalanced. If the Year 4 and Year 5 financial statements were to be corrected retroactively, this could be accomplished by changing the inventories and retained earnings amounts in these statements or by the use of a working paper. As of the beginning of Year 6, however, all balance sheet ledger accounts are free of this error.

Working Paper for Analysis of Errors

The first procedure in the correction of errors is to analyze the effect of the errors on financial data. The next procedure is to prepare the necessary correcting journal entries. In the course of an audit or when an accountant is assigned to correct accounting records that had not been maintained correctly, a substantial number of errors, affecting several accounting periods, may be discovered. In such cases it may be helpful to use a working paper to analyze the errors and their effects on financial statements. The working paper also serves as the underlying support for a single correcting journal entry to bring the accounting records up to date. There is no standard form of working paper; one form that has proved useful for this purpose is illustrated in the following example.

Illustration

An audit of the accounting records of Lam Trading Limited early in Year 8 disclosed the following errors affecting the financial statements for Year 6 and Year 7:

1 Unexpired insurance was omitted from the accounting records; insurance premiums were debited to Insurance Expense at the time of payment. The correct amount of unexpired insurance at the end of Year 6 was $550; at the end of Year 7, it was $980.

2 No journal entry had been made to accrue interest on notes payable at the end of the year. Interest was debited to Interest Expense at the time of payment. Interest payable at the end of Year 6 was $1,700; at the end of Year 7, it was $480.

3 Interest on notes receivable was credited to Interest Revenue when received. At the end of Year 6, interest receivable amounted to $450; at the end of Year 7, it was $840.

4 Lam rented part of its land, receiving rent in advance; receipts were credited to Rent Revenue. Unearned rent at the end of Year 6 was $1,800; at the end of Year 7, it was $740.

5 Lam is subject to federal income taxes at a rate of 45% of taxable income. There are no differences between taxable income and pre-tax accounting income. It is assumed that Year 6 income tax returns will be amended to reflect corrections of the foregoing errors, and that Lam will claim a refund for excess income taxes paid in Year 6, or will pay any tax deficiency.

Lam Trading Limited reported net income of $20,000 for Year 6, and $16,000 for Year 7. We wish to determine the extent of the errors in the net income for Year 6 and Year 7, and to correct the accounting records as of December 31, Year 7. The working paper on page 1117 illustrates a procedure that may be followed.

Let us assume that the ledger accounts ***have been closed*** at the end of Year 7. On the basis of our working paper analysis, the following journal entry corrects the ledger accounts as of December 31, Year 7:

Journal entry to correct ledger accounts for errors *after* accounts are closed

Unexpired Insurance	980	
Interest Receivable	840	
Income Tax Refund Receivable	1,125	
Retained Earnings (net income, Years 6 and 7)		330
Interest Payable		480
Unearned Rent		740
Income Taxes Payable		1,395
To correct errors revealed by audit in Year 8 after the ledger accounts had been closed for Year 7.		

Trace the amounts in this journal entry to the working paper and you will see that all the data necessary for the entry were developed in the working paper. To prepare a corrected income statement for Year 7, it is necessary to revise the specific expense and revenue ledger accounts to reflect the total increase of $1,705 in Year 7 net income. If the ledger accounts ***had not been closed*** at the time the correcting entry was made, it would be necessary to expand the correcting journal entry to include corrections to revenue and expense accounts for Year 7, as shown on page 1118.

The analysis of errors in the working paper indicates that net income for Year 7 was understated by $1,705. If Year 7 revenue and expense ledger accounts are to be corrected, it is necessary to look at the details in the column headed ''Net income for Year 7'' and determine the specific revenue and expense accounts that require correction. All the necessary amounts appear in this column, but the working paper does not show the ledger accounts involved. It is possible to add a column or two to the working paper and enter the account titles at the time the working paper is prepared. However, it usually is easier to determine the appropriate revenue or expense account by noting the description of the error in the explanation column. For example, when we see that unexpired insurance was omitted at the end of both Year 6 and Year 7, it is apparent that the correction involves insurance expense. Unexpired insurance increased from $550 to $980

LAM TRADING LIMITED
Working Paper for Analysis of Errors
December 31, Year 7

Explanation	*Net income for Year 6* (Dr) Cr*	*Net income for Year 7* (Dr) Cr*	*Balance sheet ledger accounts requiring correction, Dec. 31, Year 7* (Dr) Cr*	Ledger accounts
1 Unexpired insurance omitted:				
Dec. 31, Year 6	$ 550	$ (550)		
Dec. 31, Year 7		980	$(980)	Unexpired Insurance
2 Accrued interest on notes payable omitted:				
Dec. 31, Year 6	(1,700)	1,700		
Dec. 31, Year 7		(480)	480	Interest Payable
3 Accrued interest on notes receivable omitted:				
Dec. 31, Year 6	450	(450)		
Dec. 31, Year 7		840	(840)	Interest Receivable
4 Unearned rent omitted:				
Dec. 31, Year 6	(1,800)	1,800		
Dec. 31, Year 7		(740)	740	Unearned Rent
Increase (or decrease) in income before income taxes	$ (2,500)	$ 3,100		
5 Revision of income taxes (45%):				
Year 6 income taxes expense overstated	1,125		(1,125)	Income Tax Refund Receivable
Year 7 income taxes expense understated		(1,395)	1,395	Income Taxes Payable
Increase (or decrease) in net income	$(1,375)	$ 1,705	330	Retained Earnings
Net income as originally reported	20,000	16,000		
Corrected net income	$18,625	$17,705		

*Separate columns for debit and credit amounts may be used.

during Year 7; therefore, it is clear that insurance expense was overstated by $430 ($980 – $550 = $430) because an increase in assets in this amount was incorrectly recognized as an expense. This reasoning is used to determine the credit of $430 to Insurance Expense in the correcting journal entry above.

The working paper for analysis of errors illustrated above is helpful in tracing the effect of errors on net income for several years and in providing the basis for the necessary journal entry or entries to correct ledger account balances at the end of the latest year. Once the necessary journal entries have been recorded, the balance sheet and income statement for the latest year may be prepared.

Journal entry to correct ledger accounts for errors *before* accounts are closed

Account	Debit	Credit	
Unexpired Insurance	980		
Interest Receivable	840		
Income Tax Refund Receivable	1,125		
Retained Earnings (net income, Year 6)	1,375		
Income Taxes Expense (Year 7)	1,395		
Insurance Expense ($980 − $550)		430	Correction of revenue and expense ledger accounts to reflect $1,705 increase in net income for Year 7
Interest Expense ($1,700 − $480)		1,220	
Interest Revenue ($840 − $450)		390	
Rent Revenue ($1,800 − $740)		1,060	
Interest Payable		480	
Unearned Rent		740	
Income Taxes Payable		1,395	
To correct errors revealed by audit in Year 8. Ledger accounts had not been closed on Dec. 31, Year 7.			

If comparative financial statements are to be prepared, there remains the problem of revising the financial statements of prior years to reflect the correction of errors. A correcting entry always revises balance sheet ledger accounts to their corrected balances at the end of the current year, but it does not correct account balances on any prior date. Similarly, once the revenue and expense accounts for a year have been closed, a journal entry to correct errors has no effect on any revenue and expense accounts for that year.

If there are few errors affecting data for prior years, it is usually a simple matter to make the necessary changes in amounts appearing in financial statements for prior years. However, when there are numerous errors, or when the correcting entries are complex, it may be desirable to use a working paper to correct the financial statements for prior years. A working paper that provides two columns for the original ledger account balances, two columns for the correcting entries, and two columns each for the corrected income statement and balance sheet amounts serves this purpose, and also serves as a permanent record for the accounting files.

FINANCIAL STATEMENTS FROM INCOMPLETE RECORDS

The heart of the double-entry accounting system is the analysis of the effect of each business transaction or event on the accounting equation: Assets = liabilities + owners' equity. Many small business enterprises operate with varying degrees of success with only minimal accounting records and without the benefit of a complete accounting system. A system (or lack of system) in which transactions are not analyzed and recorded in the double-entry framework sometimes is called a ***single-entry accounting system***. The accounting records of social clubs, civic organizations, and small business enterprises often are maintained on a single-entry basis.

At some time after the data have been well muddled, an accountant is likely to be called on to sift through the accounting records and gather enough information to complete an income tax return and to prepare financial statements. Thus, the process of recasting single-entry accounting information into the double-entry framework is a practical analytical exercise.

Balance Sheet from Incomplete Accounting Records

A business enterprise having no formal accounting system still must record certain basic information. For example, a record of cash received and cheques written and a record of amounts receivable from customers and amounts payable to creditors is essential. It is possible to prepare a balance sheet on any date for such an enterprise from various sources of information. Cash may be determined by count and by reconciliation of bank statements. Amounts receivable from customers may be summarized from unpaid sales invoices. Inventories may be counted, weighed, or measured, and their cost determined from suppliers' invoices. The cost of plant assets owned similarly may be established. Amounts payable to creditors may be determined from invoices and monthly statements. Ownership equity is the difference between the amounts assigned to assets and to liabilities.

Computation of Net Income from Single-Entry Accounting Records

One way to measure net income from single-entry accounting records is to analyze the change in owners' equity during an accounting period. We know that owners' equity is the residual interest in the net assets of a business enterprise and that it is increased by net income and additional investments, and decreased by net losses and withdrawals by owners. By the process of elimination, if we know the beginning and ending balance of owners' equity and the amount of any additional investments or withdrawals by owners, we may compute the change in owners' equity attributable to the net income or loss during an accounting period as follows:

Computation of net income or net loss by analysis of changes in owners' equity

	Example A (net income)	*Example B (net loss)*
Owners' equity at end of accounting period	$22,000	$20,000
Less: Owners' equity at beginning of period	18,500	25,000
Total increase (decrease) in owners' equity	$ 3,500	$ (5,000)
Add: Amounts withdrawn by owners	4,800	2,600
Less: Additional investments by owners	(1,000)	(500)
Net income (loss) for period	$ 7,300	$ (2,900)

For most purposes, a more complete picture of operations is needed than that conveyed by the net income amount. Revenue Canada requires details of revenue and expenses in income tax returns. For even the most elementary budgeting and managerial control purposes, information is required as to how net income was computed. The objective, then, is to develop revenue and expenses from single-entry accounting records. Because cash transactions are of major importance in any business enterprise, a detailed record of cash receipts and payments is a valuable source of information. This is demonstrated below:

From a detailed list of cash receipts we may determine:	*From a detailed list of cash payments we may determine:*
Cash receipts from sales and other revenue	Cash paid for purchases of merchandise and operating expenses
Collections on customers' accounts	Payments to trade creditors
Proceeds from disposal of plant assets	Cash paid to acquire plant assets
Amounts borrowed	Payments on loans
Cash investments by owners	Cash withdrawals by owners

If, in addition to cash receipts and payments data, we have (1) a list of assets at the beginning and end of the accounting period, and (2) a list of liabilities at the beginning and end of the period, we may compute the owners' equity at the beginning and end of the period, and prepare comparative balance sheets. From this information, plus some help from miscellaneous sources, we may reconstruct the major components of the income statement. In the sections that follow are some examples to illustrate how the various revenue and expense items may be derived from information available in single-entry accounting records.

Illustration: Income Statement from Incomplete Accounting Records

To illustrate the preparation of an income statement, we assume a relatively simple situation. The balance sheet on December 31, Year 1, summary of operations for Year 2, ledger account balances on December 31, Year 2, and additional information for Joe's Place, a single proprietorship, presented below and on page 1121, serve as a basis for our illustration.

JOE'S PLACE
Balance Sheet
December 31, Year 1
(Prepared from incomplete accounting records)

Assets		*Liabilities & Proprietor's Capital*	
Cash	$ 4,680	Accounts payable	$ 9,400
Notes receivable	12,000	Salaries payable	1,100
Accounts receivable	4,000	Unearned rent	600
Interest receivable	320	Total liabilities	$ 11,100
Inventories	18,000		
Unexpired insurance	500		
Land	50,000		
Building and equipment	140,000		
Less: Accumulated depreciation	(62,500)	Joe Palermo, capital	155,900
Total assets	$167,000	Total liabilities & capital	$167,000

JOE'S PLACE
Summary of Operations
For Year Ended December 31, Year 2
(From cash and supplementary records)

Cash receipts:		
Collections on accounts receivable	$35,000	
Sales for cash	42,000	
Interest revenue	540	
Rent revenue	3,600	$81,140
Cash payments:		
Accounts payable for merchandise (including freight-in)	$53,400	
Insurance premiums	940	
Salaries	10,700	
Other operating expenses	3,000	
Drawings by owner	6,000	74,040
Sales returns and allowances (all applicable to Year 2 sales)		1,800
Cash discounts taken by customers (sales discounts)		600
Accounts receivable written off as uncollectible during Year 2		300
Cash discounts taken on purchases (purchases discounts)		1,100
Purchases returns and allowances (all applicable to Year 2 purchases)		970

JOE'S PLACE
Ledger Account Balances
December 31, Year 2
(From supplementary analysis)

Cash (verified through count and bank reconciliations)	$11,780
Notes receivable (no change during Year 2)	12,000
Accounts receivable	7,600
Interest receivable	530
Inventories	25,000
Unexpired insurance	700
Accounts payable	8,500
Salaries payable	1,900
Unearned rent	450

Additional Information

1 No acquisitions or disposals of plant assets were made in Year 2.

2 Depreciation expense is computed at $12,800 for Year 2.

3 Payroll taxes and income tax withholdings are disregarded.

4 The direct write-off method is used to record doubtful accounts expense.

Computation of Gross Sales

Sales are from two sources, cash receipts from customers and gross increases in accounts receivable. Because accounts receivable on December 31, Year 1, reflect revenue collected in prior years, cash collections of these receivables during Year 2 have no connection with the revenue of that year. Therefore, the beginning balance of accounts receivable must be deducted from the total cash collections to compute sales for Year 2 that were collected in cash. Conversely, accounts receivable on December 31, Year 2, represent sales that were not included in cash receipts of Year 2 and therefore must be added to cash receipts to compute the sales for that year. Accounts receivable included in this computation should include only accounts arising from the sale of goods and services.

Sales returns and allowances, sales discounts, and accounts receivable written off during Year 2 represent sales during that year that were not collected in cash and are not included in accounts receivable on December 31, Year 2. However, these amounts should be included in the computation of gross sales for Year 2. Applying this reasoning, the computation of gross sales for Joe's Place is shown below.

JOE'S PLACE
Computation of Gross Sales
For Year Ended December 31, Year 2

Sales on credit for Year 2:		
Collections on accounts receivable	$35,000	
Accounts receivable written off as uncollectible	300	
Sales returns and allowances (all applicable to Year 2 sales)	1,800	
Cash discounts taken by customers	600	
Accounts receivable, Dec. 31, Year 2	7,600	
Less: Accounts receivable, Dec. 31, Year 1	(4,000)	$41,300
Add: Sales for cash		42,000
Gross sales		$83,300

Computation of Other Revenue

The amount of other revenue, such as interest revenue and rent revenue, may be computed from comparative balance sheets and cash receipts data as illustrated below:

JOE'S PLACE
Computation of Other Revenue
For Year Ended December 31, Year 2

	Interest revenue	*Rent revenue*
Revenue received in cash in Year 2	$540	$3,600
Less: Revenue received in cash but not realized in Year 2:		
Unearned rent, Dec. 31, Year 2		450
Interest receivable, Dec. 31, Year 1	320	
Cash receipts representing revenue for Year 2	$220	$3,150
Add: Revenue realized in Year 2 but not included in cash receipts:		
Unearned rent, Dec. 31, Year 1		600
Interest receivable, Dec. 31, Year 2	530	
Revenue	$750	$3,750

Computation of Cost of Goods Sold

The cost of goods sold is derived from information about purchases and inventories. The amount of ending inventories may be determined by counting, weighing, or measuring. Presumably, the amount of beginning inventories was determined comparably; if not, an estimated amount must be used.

The amount of purchases may be computed from cash payments and accounts payable at the beginning and end of Year 2. The balance of accounts payable on December 31, Year 1, includes purchases during prior years that were not a part of the operating results of Year 2. Therefore, from total cash payments to suppliers we must deduct the December 31, Year 1, balance of accounts payable to compute the cash outlays for purchases applicable to Year 2. Accounts payable on December 31, Year 2, represent credit purchases during Year 2 that must be added to compute the total amount of purchases for that year. An analysis of invoices provides information as to the cash discounts taken and the credits received for purchases returns and allowances during Year 2.

The following illustration for Joe's Place demonstrates how reasoning and a systematic organization of the available data are used to compute the cost of goods sold. The first step is to compute the amount of gross purchases for Year 2, as shown below:

JOE'S PLACE
Computation of Gross Purchases
For Year Ended December 31, Year 2

Payments on accounts payable during Year 2 (including freight-in)	$53,400
Add: Cash discounts taken on purchases	1,100
Purchases returns and allowances (all applicable to Year 2 purchases)	970
Accounts payable, Dec. 31, Year 2	8,500
Less: Accounts payable, Dec. 31, Year 1	(9,400)
Gross purchases	$54,570

In the computation of gross purchases, only liabilities relating to merchandise purchases should be included. This analysis, together with the amounts for inventories, provides the information necessary to compute cost of goods sold as shown below:

JOE'S PLACE
Computation of Cost of Goods Sold
For Year Ended December 31, Year 2

Inventories, Dec. 31, Year 1		$18,000
Add: Gross purchases (see above)	$54,570	
Less: Cash discounts taken on purchases	(1,100)	
Purchases returns and allowances	(970)	
Net purchases		52,500
Cost of goods available for sale		$70,500
Less: Inventories, Dec. 31, Year 2		25,000
Cost of goods sold		$45,500

Computation of Operating Expenses

Expenses arise from cash payments, from purchases of goods and services on credit, and from the consumption of assets. Because cash payments during an accounting period may involve the acquisition of assets or the payment of liabilities that relate to expenses of prior periods, computation of expenses of the current period requires an analysis of both asset and liability ledger account balances, as well as of cash payments.

The balance of any asset account that is subject to amortization increases as a result of the acquisition of additional assets, and decreases as the assets are used up. The normal process for the computation of the ending balance of such an asset account is: Beginning account balance, plus acquisitions of assets, less assets consumed, equals ending account balance. In the computation of expenses, we usually are able to compute the beginning and ending balance of the related asset account and the cost of new acquisitions during the accounting period (through an analysis of cash payments and credit transactions). We may convert this information to the amount of expense for the period as follows:

Reconstruction of expense through analysis of related asset account

Assets acquired during accounting period	$ XX
Less: Asset account balance at end of period	(XX)
Add: Asset account balance at beginning of period	XX
Expense for period	$XXX

The computation of expenses by analysis of accrued liability balances and related cash payments is a similar process. The beginning balance of the accrued liability account is deducted from the total cash payments during the current

JOE'S PLACE
Computation of Operating Expenses
For Year Ended December 31, Year 2

	Insurance expense	*Salaries expense*	*Other operating expenses*	*Depreciation expense*
Cash payments during Year 2	$940	$10,700	$3,000	
Less: Amounts included in cash payments but not expenses of Year 2:				
Prepayments, Dec. 31, Year 2........	(700)			
Accrued liability, Dec. 31, Year 1....		(1,100)		
Add: Amounts not included in cash payments but allocable to operations of Year 2:				
Prepayments, Dec. 31, Year 1	500			
Accrued liability, Dec. 31, Year 2....		1,900		
Depreciation expense (as computed)				$12,800
Operating expenses	$740	$11,500	$3,000	$12,800

period to compute the cash payments relating to the current period's expense. Adding to this amount the balance of the accrued liability account at the end of the period produces the expense for the current period.

Computation of operating expenses for Joe's Place is illustrated at the bottom of page 1124.

Working Paper for Preparation of Financial Statements from Incomplete Accounting Records

The foregoing computations and other information derived from incomplete accounting records may be used to prepare financial statements. Many accountants prefer to summarize the information in a working paper, as illustrated on pages 1126–1127 for Joe's Place. Financial statements may be prepared from the information in the last four columns of the working paper. Alternative forms of the working paper may be used; for example, a pair of columns for a trial balance on December 31, Year 2, may be added following the "Transactions for Year 2" columns in the working paper illustrated.

The income statement and the balance sheet prepared for Joe's Place from the working paper have no unusual features and are not illustrated here; the statement of changes in proprietor's capital for the year ended December 31, Year 2, is as follows:

JOE'S PLACE
Statement of Proprietor's Capital
For Year Ended December 31, Year 2

Proprietor's capital, beginning of year	$155,900
Add: Net income	11,560
Subtotal	$167,460
Less: Drawings	6,000
Proprietor's capital, end of year	$161,460

REVIEW QUESTIONS

1 Briefly describe the purpose of section 1506 of the *CICA Handbook*, "Accounting Changes," issued by the Accounting Standards Committee.
2 What are two types of ***accounting changes***? Briefly describe each type.
3 Describe when a ***change in accounting policy*** is considered proper.
4 Briefly describe the following methods relating to changes in accounting policy:
   a Retroactive application with restatement of prior periods
   b Retroactive application with no restatement of prior periods
   c Prospective application
5 How is the ***cumulative effect*** of a change in accounting policy determined and reported when the change is applied on a retroactive-restatement basis?

JOE'S PLACE
Working Paper for Preparation of Financial Statements from Incomplete Accounting Records
For Year Ended December 31, Year 2

Accounts	*Balance sheet, Dec. 31, Year 1*		*Transactions for Year 2*		*Income statement for Year 2*		*Balance sheet Dec. 31, Year 2*	
	Debit	*Credit*	*Debit*	*Credit*	*Debit*	*Credit*	*Debit*	*Credit*
Cash	4,680		(1) 42,000	(5) 53,400			11,780	
			(2) 35,000	(6) 14,640				
			(3) 4,140	(8) 6,000				
Notes receivable	12,000						12,000	
Accounts receivable	4,000		(1) 41,300	(2) 37,700			7,600	
Interest receivable	320		(3) 210				530	
Inventories, Dec. 31, Year 1	18,000				18,000			
Unexpired insurance	500		(6) 200				700	
Land	50,000						50,000	
Building and equipment	140,000						140,000	
Accumulated depreciation		62,500		(7) 12,800				75,300
Accounts payable		9,400	(5) 55,470	(4) 54,570				8,500
Salaries payable		1,100		(6) 800				1,900
Unearned rent		600	(3) 150					450
J. Palermo, capital		155,900						155,900
J. Palermo, drawings			(8) 6,000				6,000	

Sales				(1) 83,300		83,300		
Sales ret. and allow.			(2) 1,800		1,800			
Sales discounts			(2) 600		600			
Doubtful accounts expense			(2) 300		300			
Interest revenue				(3) 750		750		
Rent revenue				(3) 3,750		3,750		
Purchases			(4) 54,570		54,570			
Purchases ret. and allow.				(5) 970		970		
Purchases discounts				(5) 1,100		1,100		
Insurance expense			(6) 740		740			
Salaries expense			(6) 11,500		11,500			
Other operating expenses			(6) 3,000		3,000			
Depreciation expense			(7) 12,800		12,800			
Inventories, Dec. 31, Year 2						25,000	25,000	
Subtotals					103,310	114,870	253,610	242,050
Net income					11,560			11,560
Totals	229,500	229,500	269,780	269,780	114,870	114,870	253,610	253,610

Explanation of transactions and events for Year 2:

(1) Gross sales, $42,000 in cash and $41,300 on credit.
(2) Collections on accounts receivable; sales returns and allowances, sales discounts, and doubtful accounts expense.
(3) Collection of interest and rent revenue; adjustment of interest receivable and unearned rent.
(4) Gross purchases.
(5) Payments on accounts payable; purchases returns and allowances and purchases discounts.
(6) Payments to expenses; adjustment of unexpired insurance and salaries payable.
(7) Depreciation expense.
(8) Owner's drawings.

6 List the disclosure requirement for changes in accounting policy where there is a retroactive restatement of financial statements for prior periods.

7 Lundy Company wrote down its plant assets by $15 million in Year 2. The reasons given were "to reduce excess capacity by closing inefficient plants and to recognize obsolescence attributed to new technological developments and a shift in the demand for the company's products."
How should the write-down be reported in Lundy's financial statements?

8 Seafaring Corporation debited $87.9 million to operating expense as a result of write-down of its tanker fleet. Included in this amount was $65 million "for possible losses in the future." Evaluate the accounting treatment of this write-down.

9 How is a material error in prior period financial statements reported in the accounting period the error is discovered?

10 Briefly describe the following items and give an example to support each of your answers:
a A change in an accounting policy
b A change in an accounting estimate
c A correction of an error in prior period financial statements

11 Which of the following should be treated as errors under section 1506 of the *CICA Handbook*?
a A depreciable asset which was estimated to have an economic life of four years is now estimated to have an economic life of six years.
b A substantial deficiency in income taxes relating to the income of two years ago is assessed by Revenue Canada as a result of an error in computing the amount of income taxes.
c An analysis of credit experience indicates that actual doubtful accounts expense over the past three years has exceeded the provision for such expense made at the rate of 1% of sales.
d A substantial amount of merchandise in transit at the close of the previous year was included in purchases but was not included in the ending inventory.
e An audit reveals that a substantial purchase of a depreciable asset was inadvertently debited to expense last year.

12 Errors affecting both the balance sheet and the income statement may be classified into two major types. Identify and define each type.

13 Why is it important to correct material errors even after they have counterbalanced?

14 Explain what is meant by the term ***single-entry accounting system***.

15 Briefly describe two methods that may be used to compute the amounts required to prepare financial statements from incomplete accounting records.

EXERCISES

Ex. 22-1 Select the best answer for each of the following multiple-choice questions.

1 On November 1, Year 3, Tom Company acquired machinery at a cost of $150,000. The machinery was being depreciated by the double-declining-

balance method over an economic life of 10 years, with no residual value. On November 1, Year 5, Tom decided to change to the straight-line method of depreciation. Disregarding income taxes, the cumulative effect of this accounting change is:
a $0 *b* $24,000 *c* $28,200 *d* $54,000 *e* Some other amount

2 Which of the following is (are) the proper time period(s) to record a change in accounting estimate which affects prior as well as future periods?
   a Current accounting period and prospectively
   b Current accounting period and retroactively
   c Retroactively only
   d Current accounting period only

3 A business enterprise changed from the double-declining-balance method of depreciation for previously recorded plant assets to the straight-line method. The cumulative effect of the change on the amount of retained earnings at the beginning of the accounting period in which the change is made is reported separately as:
   a An extraordinary item
   b A component of income after any extraordinary items
   c A component of income from continuing operations
   d A retroactive application adjustment

4 The correction of a material error in the financial statements of a prior accounting period is included, net of applicable income taxes, in the current period's:
   a Income statement after income from continuing operations and before any extraordinary items
   b Income statement after income from continuing operations and after any extraordinary items
   c Statement of retained earnings as an adjustment of the beginning balance
   d Statement of retained earnings after net income but before dividends

5 The typical counterbalancing error that affects both the income statement and the balance sheet of an accounting period:
   a Is offset by a misstatement, in the opposite direction, of net income of the succeeding period
   b Also misstates net income of several succeeding accounting periods
   c Is offset by a misstatement, in the opposite direction, of total owners' equity in the balance sheet of the succeeding period
   d Is offset by a misstatement, in the opposite direction, of both net income and total owners' equity in the financial statements of the succeeding period

6 During the year ended October 31, Year 8, Lou Company, which uses the periodic inventory system, discovered a $50,000 understatement of the inventory of October 31, Year 6. No other errors were found. The accounting records have not been closed for the year ended October 31, Year 8. Disregarding income taxes, Lou Company's appropriate action is to prepare:
   a A journal entry debiting Retained Earnings and crediting Prior Period Adjustment (net income, fiscal Year 6) for $50,000
   b A journal entry debiting Prior Period Adjustment (net income, fiscal

Year 7) and crediting Prior Period Adjustment (net income, fiscal Year 6) for $50,000

c A journal entry debiting Cost of Goods Sold (fiscal Year 7) and crediting Cost of Goods Sold (fiscal Year 6) for $50,000

d No journal entry

7 A change in the net residual value of a plant asset, depreciated by the straight-line method, that was made because additional information had been obtained is:

a An accounting change reported in both the accounting period of the change and future periods, if the change affects future periods

b An accounting change reported by restatement of the financial statements of all prior accounting periods presented

c A correction of an error of prior accounting periods

d Not an accounting change

8 Webster Company acquired a machine on January 2, Year 4, for $480,000. On the date of acquisition the machine had an economic life of six years with no residual value. The machine was being depreciated under the straight-line method. On January 2, Year 7, Webster determined, as a result of additional information, that the machine had an economic life of eight years from the date of acquisition, with no residual value. An accounting change was made for the year ended December 31, Year 7, to reflect this additional information. What is the amount of depreciation expense for the machine for the year ended December 31, Year 7?

a $0 *b* $30,000 *c* $48,000 *d* $60,000 *e* Some other amount

9 When a cumulative-effect-type change in accounting principle is made during a year, the cumulative effect on retained earnings is computed:

a During the year using a weighted-average method

b As of the date of the change

c As of the beginning of the year in which the change is made

d As of the end of the year in which the change is made

e In some other manner

Ex. 22-2 Corb Company, which began operations on January 2, Year 3, used an accelerated method of depreciation for machinery until January 2, Year 5. On that date, Corb adopted the straight-line method of depreciation for both newly acquired and previously acquired machinery. Information concerning depreciation expense under each method follows:

	Depreciation expense	
Year ended Dec. 31:	***Accelerated method***	***Straight-line method***
Year 3	$400,000	$300,000
Year 4	530,000	375,000
Year 5	600,000	400,000

The direct effects of Corb's accounting change are on depreciation expense and income taxes expense only. The income tax rate for Year 3 through Year 5 was 45%.

Compute the cumulative effect of Corb Company's change in accounting principle for its income statement for Year 5.

Ex. 22-3 Naomi Company began operations on January 2, Year 6, and used the first-in, first-out method to value its inventories. Management is contemplating a change to the last-in, first-out method in Year 7 and is interested in determining what effect such a change will have on net income. Accordingly, the following information has been accumulated:

	Year 6	*Year 7*
Ending inventories:		
First-in, first-out method	$240,000	$270,000
Last-in, first-out method	200,000	210,000
Net income (computed under the first-in, first-out-method	120,000	170,000

Compute net income of Naomi Company for Year 7, assuming that the change to the last-in, first-out method of inventory valuation was effected in Year 7. The income tax rate was 45% in both Year 6 and Year 7.

Ex. 22-4 Remo Company included the following assets in its balance sheet on December 31, Year 5:

Equipment	$3,780,000	
Less: Accumulated depreciation	1,260,000	$2,520,000
Goodwill (net)		1,225,000

Both assets were acquired early in Year 1. The equipment had been depreciated over an economic life of 15 years with no residual value, and the goodwill had been amortized over a period of 20 years. Late in Year 6, Remo decided that the total economic life of the equipment should be reduced to 12 years and that goodwill should be amortized over a period of 30 years from the date of acquisition.

Compute Remo Company's annual depreciation expense on the equipment and amortization of goodwill for Year 6, assuming that the net residual value of the equipment was estimated at $210,000 late in Year 6.

Ex. 22-5 During the year ended October 31, Year 13, the following occurred for Hardy Company, which uses the periodic inventory system:

1 A change in the estimated economic life of Hardy's building to 30 years from

40 years (the estimated net residual value of the building remained unchanged at $40,000). The building had been acquired on October 31, Year 2, at a cost of $840,000. Hardy used the straight-line method of depreciation for the building.

2 The discovery on March 18, Year 13, of a $60,000 understatement of Hardy's inventories of October 31, Year 12. This error resulted in a $27,000 understatement of Hardy's income tax liability for the year ended October 31, Year 12.

Prepare journal entries for Hardy Company (1) on March 18, Year 13, to correct the error in the October 31, Year 12, inventories, and (2) on October 31, Year 13, to reflect the accounting change. Hardy's income tax rate is 45%, and it will file an amended income tax return for the year ended October 31, Year 12.

Ex. 22-6 On December 31, Year 1, Trace Company's accountant recorded the cost of patents acquired from an inventor, intending to amortize the cost over five years. At the end of Year 3, it was discovered that the sales manager's Year 1 salary of $40,000 had been recorded in the Patents ledger account on December 31, Year 1. Trace is subject to a 45% income tax rate and intends to file amended income tax returns for Year 1 and Year 2.

Prepare a journal entry for Trace Company to correct this error on December 31, Year 3, after adjusting entries have been made but before the ledger accounts have been closed for Year 3.

Ex. 22-7 The following errors in the accounting records of the Foss & Grable Partnership were discovered on January 18, Year 4:

Year of error	*Ending inventories overstated*	*Depreciation understated*	*Accrued rent revenue not recorded*	*Accrued interest expense not recorded*
1	$10,000		$ 3,000	
2		$2,500	11,000	
3	14,000			$1,500

The partners share net income and losses equally.

a Prepare a correcting journal entry on January 18, Year 4, assuming that the ledger accounts were closed for Year 3.

b Prepare a correcting journal entry on January 18, Year 4, assuming that the ledger accounts are still open for Year 3 and that the partnership uses the perpetual inventory system.

Ex. 22-8 Rio Company's financial statements contained the following errors:

	Dec. 31, Year 3	*Dec. 31, Year 4*
Ending inventories (periodic system) ..	$2,000 understated	1,800 overstated
Depreciation expense	400 understated	No error

Net income as determined by Rio was $25,000 in Year 3 and $30,000 in Year 4. An insurance premium of $1,500 was prepaid in Year 3 covering Year 3, Year 4, and Year 5. The entire amount was debited to Insurance Expense. In addition, on December 31, Year 4, a fully depreciated machine was sold for $3,400, but the disposal was not recorded until January 4, Year 5. There were no other errors during Year 3 or Year 4, and no corrections have been made for any of the errors. Income taxes may be disregarded.

a Compute Rio Company's corrected net income under the accrual basis of accounting for Year 4.

b Compute the total effect of the errors on Rio Company's working capital on December 31, Year 4.

c Prepare a journal entry to correct Rio Company's accounting records on January 15, Year 5. Assume that ledger accounts have been closed for Year 4. (The gain on the disposal of the fully depreciated machine was recognized, but in the wrong year.)

Ex. 22-9 The cash records of Zwick Corporation show that $28,400 was collected in July, Year 7, from credit customers and $12,400 was received from cash sales. The amount due from credit customers increased from $7,300 at the beginning of July to $9,150 at the end of July. In July the credit manager had written off $1,090 of trade accounts receivable as uncollectible.

From the foregoing information, compute the gross sales of Zwick Corporation for July, Year 7.

Ex. 22-10 Placer Company sells television cable services to customers, who may choose to pay $25 a month for the service or may pay in advance a yearly charge of $250 for 12 months of service. During Year 8, Placer collected $160,700 from customers. Here is additional information for Year 8:

	Jan. 1, Year 8	*Dec. 31, Year 8*
Advance payments by customers	$3,500	$5,700
Accounts receivable from customers	6,820	6,970

From the information given, compute the total cable revenue of Placer Company for Year 8.

Ex. 22-11 The inventories of Moll Company increased by $18,500 during Year 4, and the accounts payable to merchandise suppliers increased by $9,600. During Year 4, Moll paid $130,200 to suppliers and $7,200 freight-in charges on merchandise. Moll also purchased $5,800 of merchandise for cash.

Compute Moll Company's cost of goods sold for Year 4.

Ex. 22-12 The following information was taken from the accounting records of Toma Corporation for Year 1:

	Jan. 1	*Dec. 31*
Shareholders' equity (no capital stock was issued or retired)	$98,000	$117,000
Cash	6,000	12,400
Inventories	20,000	14,000
Payable to merchandise suppliers	8,000	8,500
Trade accounts receivable	14,200	18,200
Cash paid to merchandise suppliers		70,000
Operating expenses and income taxes paid (including $800 prepaid on December 31)		32,000
Year 1 sales written off as uncollectible (an additional allowance of $750 is required on Dec. 31)		500
Dividends declared and paid		20,000
Depreciation expense		6,200
Other assets	77,800	82,350
Other liabilities	12,000	22,000

Prepare an income statement for Toma Corporation for Year 1 on the accrual basis of accounting. Show supporting computations for sales, cost of goods sold, and total operating expenses and income taxes. ***Hint:*** First compute net income and work back to sales.

CASES

Case 22-1 It is important to differentiate among the various types of accounting changes and to report such changes in the financial statements in conformity with generally accepted accounting principles.

Instructions

a What type of accounting change is a change from an accelerated method of depreciation to the straight-line method of depreciation for plant assets? Discuss the propriety of such a change.

b What type of accounting change is a change in the economic lives of plant assets? Include in your discussion how such a change is reported in the income statement for the accounting period in which the change is made and disclosed in a note to the financial statements for that period.

c A business combination accounted for as a pooling of interests results in a change in reporting entity. Describe the accounting change and the means by which it is reported in the financial statements.

Case 22-2 A business enterprise may change its method of accounting for certain items. The change may be classified as a change in accounting policy, or a change in accounting estimate. Listed below are two independent situations relating to accounting changes.

a Wister, Inc., determined that the economic lives of its plant assets were too long to match the cost of the plant assets with the revenue produced.

Therefore, Wister decided in January, Year 7, to reduce the economic lives of all of its existing plant assets by five years.

b Lorraine Limited decided in January, Year 4, to adopt the straight-line method of depreciation for plant assets. The straight-line method would be used for new acquisitions as well as for previously acquired plant assets for which depreciation had been computed by an accelerated method.

Instructions

For each situation described above, provide the following information. Complete your discuss of the first situation before discussing the second situation.

1 Type of accounting change

2 Manner of reporting the change under generally accepted accounting principles, including a discussion, where applicable, of how amounts are computed

3 Effect of the change on the balance sheet, the income statement, and the Statement of Retained Earnings

4 Additional disclosure required in a note to the financial statements

Case 22-3 Various types of accounting changes can affect the reporting standard of generally accepted auditing standards which requires that the audit report shall state whether accounting principles have been consistently observed in the current period in relation to the preceding period.

Assume that the following list describes changes which ***have a material effect*** on a corporation's financial statements for the current year.

1 A change from the completed-contract method to the percentage-of-completion method of accounting for long-term construction contracts

2 A change in the estimated economic life of previously recorded plant assets based on newly acquired information

3 A correction of an error in inventory pricing made in a prior period

4 A change from deferring and amortizing preproduction costs to recording such costs as an expense when incurred because future benefits of the costs have become doubtful. The new accounting method was adopted in recognition of the change in estimated future benefits.

5 A change from the fifo method to the weighted-average method of inventory valuation.

Instructions

Identify the type of change described in each item above and state whether the prior year's financial statements should be restated when presented in comparative form with the current year's statements.

Case 22-4 Vitale Corporation, which is closely held, plans to issue additional shares of common stock to the public to finance an expansion program. The corporation has been in operation for five years and has never had an audit. To meet the requirements of the corporations and securities legislation, the corporation has hired a firm of CAs to audit its financial statements for the end of Year 10.

In its financial statements for the past five years, Vitale has reported the following earnings and shareholders' equity:

Year	*Net income*	*Earnings per share of common stock*	*Shareholders' equity*
6	$368,000	$1.84	$4,945,000
7	390,000	1.95	5,195,000
8	435,000	2.18	5,350,000
9	470,000	2.35	5,620,000
10	510,000	2.55	5,870,000

The auditors discovered in the course of their examination that the corporation consistently had omitted merchandise in a warehouse in Halifax from its ending inventories in each of the five years. This warehouse operation had not proved successful and had been discontinued in Year 10; therefore, the inventories at the end of Year 10 were not affected by the error. Warehouse records show that the inventory of merchandise in the warehouse at the end of each year, stated at lower of average cost and market, was as follows: Year 6, $190,000; Year 7, $90,000; Year 8, $220,000; Year 9, $115,000. The auditors also discovered that because the sales report from the warehouse was late in arriving at the end of Year 7, $80,000 of sales applicable to Year 7 operations were not recorded as revenue until Year 8.

When the auditors insisted that these errors be corrected retroactively in the presentation of income data for the five-year period in the statement to the securities commissions, Vitale's controller objected: ''The warehouse has been discontinued. There is no inventory there now. All these errors you have dug up have washed themselves out in the accounting records, and there is no point in going back and raking over the dead coals of past history. There's nothing wrong with our balance sheet at the end of Year 10 or our income statement for Year 10, and that's what the people who acquire our common stock are interested in.''

Instructions

Determine the effect of the errors discovered by the auditors on the financial statements of Vitale Corporation. You may ignore income taxes. What position would you take with respect to the controller's objection?

PROBLEMS

Pr. 22-1 On January 2, Year 5, Maxey Corporation acquired for $240,000 a machine with an economic life of 10 years and a net residual value of $20,000. Maxey used the straight-line method of depreciation for Year 5 through Year 7. On January 2, Year 8, Maxey appropriately changed to the double-declining-balance method of depreciation for the machine. Maxey wished to have no deferred income taxes with respect to this machine. Assume Maxey has claimed the maximum allowable CCA in each year.

a Compute the carrying amount of Maxey Corporation's machine on December 31, Year 8.

b Compute the cumulative effect on opening retained earnings of Maxey Corporation's accounting change for the year ended December 31, Year 8. The income tax rate has been 45% for the entire period.

c Prepare a journal entry for Maxey Corporation on January 2, Year 8, to record the accounting change.

Pr. 22-2 The financial statements of Kirby Limited, which began operations on January 2, Year 4, showed pre-tax accounting income of $4,030,000 for Year 5 and $3,330,000 for Year 4.

Additional Information

1 Expenditures for plant assets were $2,800,000 in Year 5 and $4,000,000 in Year 4. Included in the Year 5 expenditures was $1,000,000 for equipment acquired on January 2, Year 5, with no residual value. Kirby used the straight-line method of depreciation and a 10-year economic life for the equipment in Year 5. On December 31, Year 5, Kirby determined that the equipment had only an eight-year economic life when acquired.

2 On January 2, Year 5, Kirby paid $180,000 for insurance premiums and debited the entire amount to Insurance Expense. The premiums applied entirely to Year 4, and the amount is material.

3 Kirby's Allowance for Doubtful Accounts ledger account had a credit balance of $7,000 on December 31, Year 5, and a credit balance of $97,000 on December 31, Year 4. During Year 5, trade accounts receivable totalling $90,000 had been written off to the allowance account as uncollectible, Kirby had used 0.2% of net credit sales to compute doubtful accounts expense in prior years, but had not yet made the computation for Year 5. Kirby's net credit sales were $58,500,000 for Year 5 and $49,230,000 for Year 4.

4 Kirby's Liability under Product Warranty ledger account had a credit balance of $230,000 on December 31, Year 5. An analysis indicated that the balance should be $400,000 on that date.

5 Prior to Year 5, Kirby had debited the cost of relining its blast furnaces to Maintenance and Repairs Expense. In Year 5, Kirby changed to a policy of capitalizing and depreciating relining costs over a five-year economic life, with no residual value. This accounting change met the requirements for a change in accounting policy. Prior to the accounting change, Kirby had expensed relining costs of $280,000 on January 2, Year 4, and $300,000 on January 2, Year 5.

Instructions

a Prepare a working paper to compute Kirby Limited's correct pre-tax accounting income for Year 5 and Year 4. Show supporting computations, and disregard income taxes. The final amount in your working paper is to be labelled "Income before income taxes."

b Compute the cumulative effect, disregarding income taxes, of Kirby Limited's accounting change on Year 5 opening retained earnings.

Pr. 22-3 During the year ended December 31, Year 3, Joliet Limited, which had been organized in Year 1, changed its method of accounting for property taxes during construction of plant assets from expensing property taxes to capitalizing them as building costs. The data below are taken from Joliet's accounting records:

	Year 3	*Year 2*	*Year 1*
Retained earnings, beginning of year before cumulative effect of accounting change in Year 3	$720,000	$450,000	$300,000
Income before reflecting effect of accounting change in Year 3	400,000	270,000	150,000
Property taxes during construction	125,000	75,000	24,500
Depreciation of buildings, based on expensing all property taxes	50,000	35,000	30,000
Depreciation of buildings, based on capitalizing all property taxes	59,000	39,000	30,980
Earnings per share as reported, before cumulative effect of accounting change in Year 3	2.00*	1.35	0.75

*The income for Year 3 was measured under the newly adopted accounting policy. The number of shares of common stock outstanding during the entire three-year period was 200,000.

Joliet accounted for the accounting change retroactively with restatement.

Instructions

a Compute the cumulative effect of the change in accounting policy to be included in Joliet Limited's comparative statement of retained earnings at the end of Year 3. Assume a 45% income tax rate. Round all amounts to the nearest dollar.

b Compute the effect of the change in accounting policy on earnings per share of Joliet Limited for each of Years 1 and 2, rounded to the nearest cent.

c Prepare partial comparative income statements for Joliet Limited for Years 1, 2, and 3. The income statements should include the earnings per share.

d Prepare the comparative statement of retained earnings for the three years ending December 31, Year 3.

Pr. 22-4 The following fragmentary information relates to the financial position of May's Shop, a single proprietorship, at the beginning and at the end of Year 6:

	Jan. 1, Year 6	*Dec. 31, Year 6*
Owner's equity (May Day, capital)	$81,900	$97,800
Inventories	15,800	27,320
Accounts payable (to suppliers)	40,000	25,000
Short-term prepayments	1,800	2,400
Accrued liabilities	3,150	2,850

A summary of cheques written shows that $200,000 was paid to suppliers during Year 6, $67,000 was paid for operating expenses, and $17,400 cash was withdrawn by May Day. Depreciation expense for Year 6 is $8,400, and the provision for doubtful accounts expense is 2% of gross sales.

Instructions

On the basis of the foregoing information, prepare an income statement for May's Shop for Year 6. Show supporting computations, rounded to the nearest dollar.

Pr. 22-5 Kinder, Inc., has used the completed-contract method of accounting for its construction-type contracts for 10 years. In Year 11, Kinder decided to change to the percentage-of-completion method to achieve a better matching of contract costs and contract revenue in its income statements. Kinder had recently hired an expert in cost estimation, and management believed that it would be possible to make reasonably accurate estimates of costs to be used in the determination of the percentage of completion on each contact. In addition, management decided that it would be unfair to stockholders to report a decrease in earnings for Year 11, which was attributed to the following two factors:

1. Several major contracts were completed in Year 10, which resulted in an unusually large net income.
2. Few contracts were completed in Year 11, although Kinder had 40% more work under construction in Year 11 than it did in Year 10, and had 30% more employees on the payroll.

A summary of results for the last two years under the completed-contract method follows:

	Year 11	*Year 10*
Contract revenue	$6,000,000	$18,600,000
Cost of contract revenue	4,500,000	14,700,000
Operating expenses	1,050,000	900,000
Income taxes expense (45%)	202,500	1,350,000
Net income	247,500	1,650,000

Application of the percentage-of-completion method to the operations of the last two years would have given the following results:

	Year 11	*Year 10*
Contract revenue	$17,400,000	$9,300,000
Cost of contract revenue	14,100,000	7,500,000

Operating expenses under the percentage-of-completion method are the same as reported under the completed-contract method. The completed-contract method will continue to be used for income tax purposes. Income tax allocation procedures for timing differences will be used in the preparation of revised financial statements, giving retroactive effect to the change in accounting principles. Assume that income taxes are 45% of pre-tax accounting income.

Instructions

Restate the comparative income statements for Kinder, Inc., for Year 10 and Year 11, giving retroactive recognition to the change in accounting principle. Assume that 300,000 shares of common stock were outstanding during the two-year period. Prepare a note to the financial statements that explains the reason for the change in accounting principle and the effect of the change on net income and earnings per share. Disregard deferred income credits.

Pr. 22-6 Condensed statements of income and retained earnings of Nubo Corporation for the years ended December 31, Year 4, and December 31, Year 3, are as follows:

NUBO CORPORATION
Condensed Statements of Income and Retained Earnings
For Years Ended December 31, Year 4 and Year 3

	Year 4	*Year 3*
Sales	$3,000,000	$2,400,000
Cost of goods sold	1,300,000	1,150,000
Gross profit on sales	$1,700,000	$1,250,000
Operating expenses	$ 450,000	$ 500,000
Income taxes expense (45%)	562,500	337,500
Total expenses	$1,012,500	$ 837,500
Income before extraordinary item (loss)	$ 687,500	$ 412,500
Extraordinary item (loss) (net of income tax credit $450,000)	(550,000)	
Net income	$ 137,500	$ 412,500
Retained earnings, beginning of year	862,500	450,000
Retained earnings, end of year	$1,000,000	$ 862,500

The following three ***unrelated*** situations involve accounting changes and classification of certain items as ordinary or extraordinary. Each situation is based on the above statements, and requires revisions to them.

Situation A

On January 2, Year 2, Nubo acquired machinery at a cost of $150,000. Nubo adopted the double-declining-balance method of depreciation for this machinery for both financial accounting and income taxes, and had been recording depreciation over an estimated economic life of 10 years, with no residual value. At the beginning of Year 4, the straight-line method of depreciation was adopted for financial accounting. Due to an oversight, however, the double-declining-balance method was used for Year 4. For financial accounting, depreciation expense is included in operating expenses.

The extraordinary item for Year 4 related to shutdown expenses incurred during a labor strike in Year 4.

Situation B

At the end of Year 4, Nubo's management decided that the estimated rate of doubtful accounts expense was too low. The rate used for Years 3 and 4 was 1% of total sales, and due to an increase in the write-off of uncollectible accounts, the rate for Year 4 was increased to 3% of total sales. The amount recorded as doubtful accounts expense (included in operating expenses) was $30,000 for Year 4 and $24,000 for Year 3.

The extraordinary item for Year 4 related to a loss incurred in the abandonment of obsolete equipment.

Situation C

The extraordinary item for Year 4 represented a correction of a material error (after income taxes) in the computation of cost of goods sold. Of the total amount, $467,500 related to Years 1 and 2 and $82,500 related to Year 3.

Instructions

For each of situations A, B, and C (which, again, are ***not*** related to one another), prepare revised condensed statements of income and retained earnings of Nubo Corporation for the years ended December 31, Year 4, and December 31, Year 3. Each answer should recognize the appropriate accounting changes and other items outlined in the situation. Disregard earnings-per-share computations.

Pr. 22-7 Mona Meadows started a single proprietorship, Mona's Boutique, on July 10, Year 1, by investing $75,000 in cash and merchandise. Net income for the remainder of Year 1 was $30,000, and for Year 2 it was $56,250. Meadows made no additional investments and made no withdrawals since July 10, Year 1. Comparative balance sheets prepared by Meadows are as shown in the next illustration.

MONA'S BOUTIQUE
Balance Sheets
December 31, Year 2 and Year 1

	Year 2	*Year 1*
Assets		
Cash	$ 22,650	$ 16,650
Accounts receivable	67,500	48,750
Inventory	60,000	42,600
Equipment	55,000	45,000
Total assets	$205,150	$153,000
Liabilities & Owner's Equity		
Notes payable to bank	$ 10,000	$ 15,000
Accounts payable	33,900	33,000
Mona Meadows, capital	161,250	105,000
Total liabilities & owner's equity	$205,150	$153,000

The following errors were discovered by the auditor engaged on January 20, Year 3, to examine the financial statements of Mona's Boutique:

1 Inventory was overstated by $4,500 on December 31, Year 1.
2 Interest payable of $1,800 was not recorded on December 31, Year 1, and interest payable of $1,200 was not recorded on December 31, Year 2.
3 Inventory of supplies of $1,050 was not recorded as an asset on December 31, Year 1, and inventory of supplies of $450 on December 31, Year 2, had been expensed.
4 A credit sale of $1,200 on December 31, Year 2 was not recorded in Year 2.
5 Accounts receivable of $2,500 resulting from sales in Year 1 were uncollectible on December 31, Year 2, but there had been no write-offs of accounts receivable in either Year 1 or Year 2. An allowance for doubtful accounts equal to 6% of the corrected amount of accounts receivable (after the write-off of $2,500 on December 31, Year 2) should have been established at the end of each year.
6 Depreciation expense of $1,500 was not recorded in Year 1 and depreciation expense of $3,000 was not recorded in Year 2.

Instructions

a Prepare a working paper for analysis of errors to correct the net income of Mona's Boutique for Year 1 and for Year 2.
b Prepare a correcting journal entry for Mona's Boutique on January 20, Year 3, assuming that the ledger accounts are closed for Year 2.
c Prepare corrected comparative balance sheets for Mona's Boutique on December 31, Year 1 and Year 2. ***Note:*** Be sure that capital for Meadows on December 31, Year 1 is equal to the original investment plus the corrected net income for Year 1; similarly, the capital for Meadows on December 31, Year 2, should equal the original investment plus the total corrected net income for Years 1 and 2.

Pr. 22-8 The office manager of Cue Corporation, a closely held corporation, prepared the following balance sheet on December 31, Year 3:

CUE CORPORATION
Balance Sheet
December 31, Year 3

Assets		*Liabilities & Shareholders' Equity*	
Cash	$ 9,800	Accounts payable	$ 25,600
Accounts receivable (net)	37,000	Income taxes payable	2,700
Inventory	45,000	Common stock, no par	40,000
Furniture and equipment (net)	38,000	Retained earnings	61,500
Total assets	$129,800	Total liabilities & shareholders' equity	$129,800

Cue began operations early in Year 1, and income statements prepared by the office manager showed the following net income for the three-year period:

Year 1, $26,000; Year 2, $19,200; Year 3, $16,300.

Carl Cue, the president of Cue Corporation, was concerned about this income trend, and asked an accounting firm to examine Cue's financial statements. This review disclosed that the following errors and omissions had not been corrected during the applicable years:

End of:	*Inventory overstated*	*Inventory understated*	*Prepaid rent omitted*	*Unearned revenue omitted*	*Accrued expenses (misc. payables) omitted*	*Accrued revenue (misc. receivables) omitted*
Year 1	$8,700		$ 950		$1,400	
Year 2	6,500		1,100	$ 800	1,200	$ 400
Year 3		$4,900	1,300	1,250	900	2,700

Income taxes were 45% of pre-tax accounting income. Cue Corporation will file amended income tax returns for Years 1 and 2; the income tax return for Year 3 had not been filed at the time the foregoing errors were discovered. No dividends had been declared by Cue during the first three years of its operations.

Instructions

a Prepare a working paper for analysis of errors to correct Cue Corporation's net income for Year 1, Year 2, and Year 3. Round all amounts to the nearest dollar.

b Assuming that the ledger accounts have been closed on December 31, Year 3, prepare a journal entry for Cue Corporation to correct the accounting records as of December 31, Year 3.

c Prepare a corrected balance sheet for Cue Corporation on December 31, Year 3.

d If you were presented with revised income statements for Cue Corporation for the past three years, would your conclusions regarding its earnings trend be changed substantially? Comment.

Pr. 22-9 Robert Lin began RL Company, a single proprietorship, several years ago. For a number of years Lin's wife maintained the accounting records, but early in Year 5, she became seriously ill. Lin consulted a bookkeeping service whose manager told him, "You keep a record of your cash receipts and payments, and a list of your assets and liabilities at the beginning and end of the year, and I'll prepare financial statements for you at the end of the year."

At the close of Year 5, Lin presented the data given on page 1144 to the manager of the bookkeeping service.

Lin reported that all accounts and notes receivable were from merchandise sales and that $1,400 of accounts receivable had been written off during Year 5, of which $850 was from sales prior to Year 5. Lin estimated that $1,420 of the December 31 receivable may be uncollectible. Only purchases of merchandise were recorded in accounts payable.

RL COMPANY
Analysis of Cash Receipts and Cash Payments for Year 5

Cash receipts:		*Cash payments:*	
Jan. 1, Year 5, cash balance	$ 18,460	Accounts payable (net of $6,480 cash discounts)	$225,650
Proceeds of bank loan	40,000	Acquisition of equipment	25,000
Cash sales	87,300	Operating expenses	47,610
Interest received	1,590	Insurance policy premium	980
Notes receivable	13,000	Freight-in on purchases	12,400
Equipment rental	7,000	Notes payable (including interest of $600)	15,600
Accounts receivable (net of $4,130 cash discounts)	177,690	Dec. 31, Year 5, cash balance	17,800
Total cash receipts	$345,040	Total cash payments	$345,040

RL COMPANY
List of Assets and Liabilities on January 1 and December 31, Year 5

	Jan. 1	*Dec. 31*
Cash	$ 18,460	$ 17,800
Notes receivable	15,000	2,000
Interest receivable	900	500
Accounts receivable	43,560	64,320
Inventory	38,900	43,400
Unexpired insurance	1,900	1,500
Equipment (net of accumulated depreciation)	124,000	136,000
Total assets	$242,720	$265,520
Notes payable	$ 10,000	$ 35,000
Interest payable	500	1,750
Accounts payable	47,500	52,300
Other liabilities	3,400	6,300
Unearned rent	1,200	1,800
Total liabilities	$ 62,600	$ 97,150

Instructions

a On the basis of the foregoing information, prepare an income statement for RL Company for Year 5. Prepare exhibits in support of the revenue and expenses included in the income statement.

b Prepare a statement of changes in proprietor's capital for RL Company for Year 5.

Pr. 22-10 Panich Corporation was organized on July 1, Year 1, with authorized stock of 200,000 shares of no-par common stock and 10,000 shares of no-par, $12 dividend preferred stock. John Panich was given 200 shares of preferred stock and 2,000 shares of common stock for services and expenses totalling $30,000 incurred in organizing and promoting Panich Corporation. Preferred stock was credited with $20,000 and common stock with $10,000. Attorneys' fees of $1,800, incurred in connection with the formation of Panich Corporation, had not been paid as of September 30, Year 1.

Additional Information

1 On July 15, Year 1, John Panich transferred assets from his single proprietorship to Panich Corporation in exchange for 6,000 shares of preferred stock. The current fair values of the assets were as follows: notes receivable, $360,000; inventories, $60,000; equipment, $180,000. Panich Corporation did not begin operations until August 1, Year 1, but interest of $900 accrued on the notes receivable between the time they were transferred to Panich Corporation and July 31, Year 1. This amount was debited to Interest Receivable on July 31.

2 On July 31, Year 1, 160,000 shares of common stock were issued for $800,000 cash, of which $150,000 was used to acquire land and $600,000 was applied to the cost of a building on the land. The building cost $1,340,000; the unpaid balance was represented by a 15% mortgage note payable due in 10 years. Interest on the mortgage note payable did not begin accruing until August 1, Year 1, and was payable monthly.

3 On September 30, Year 1, the accountant for Panich Corporation prepared a summary of all transactions completed by Panich Corporation during August and September, Year 1, in the form of ''net'' debit and credit *changes in ledger account balances*. This information, which includes all adjusting entries, except for ending inventories (periodic inventory system) and income taxes, is shown in the next illustration.

	Net changes in ledger account balances, Aug. 1 to Sept. 30, Year 1	
	Debits	*Credits*
Cash		$ 28,300
Accounts receivable	$ 76,285	
Allowance for doubtful accounts		1,250
Interest receivable	3,600	
Accumulated depreciation of building		8,375
Accumulated depreciation of equipment		6,500
Organization costs		1,060
Accounts payable		18,500
Sales		164,800
Purchases	110,000	
Operating expenses (including depreciation, amortization of organization costs, and doubtful accounts expense)	24,000	
Interest expense	18,500	
Interest revenue (does not include $900 earned in July, Year 1)		3,600
Totals	$232,385	$232,385

The organization costs (an asset) was being amortized over 60 months, starting August 1, Year 1. The inventories on September 30, Year 1, amounted to $68,200.

Instructions

a Prepare the balance sheet of Panich Corporation on July 31, Year 1. Income taxes expense should be provided at the rate of 45% on the interest revenue recognized in July. This was the only item of revenue or expense through July 31, Year 1.

b Prepare an income statement for Panich Corporation for the two months ended September 30, Year 1. Income taxes expense is 45% of pre-tax accounting income. Do not compute earnings per share.

c Prepare the balance sheet of Panich Corporation on September 30, Year 1.

d Prepare an analysis of cash receipts and cash payments of Panich Corporation to reconcile the decrease of $28,300 in the Cash ledger account during the two-month period ended September 30, Year 1.

Pr. 22-11 Yolo Corporation decided that in the preparation of its Year 3 financial statements two accounting changes would be made from the methods used in prior years:

1 ***Depreciation*** For plant assets Yolo previously had used the declining-balance method for both income taxes and financial accounting, but decided to change during Year 3 to the straight-line method for financial accounting only. The excess of accelerated depreciation over straight-line depreciation is summarized below:

Prior to Year 2	$1,300,000
Year 2	101,000
Year 3	99,000
Total	$1,500,000

Depreciation expense is allocated to cost of goods sold and to selling and administrative expenses in the ratio of 75% and 25% respectively.

2 ***Doubtful accounts expense*** In the past Yolo had recorded doubtful accounts expense equal to 1.5% of net sales. After a careful analysis, Yolo decided that a rate of 2% was more appropriate for Year 3. Doubtful accounts expense is included in operating expenses.

The financial statements below are preliminary, prepared before giving effect to the two accounting changes.

YOLO CORPORATION
Income Statements
For Years Ended December 31, Year 3 and Year 2

	Year 3	*Year 2*
Net sales	$80,520,000	$78,920,000
Cost of goods sold	54,847,000	53,074,000
Gross profit on sales	$25,673,000	$25,846,000
Operating expenses	19,540,000	18,411,000
Income from operations	$ 6,133,000	$ 7,435,000
Other revenue (expense), net	(1,198,000)	(1,079,000)

Income before income taxes	$ 4,935,000	$ 6,356,000
Income taxes expense	2,368,800	3,050,880
Net income	$ 2,566,200	$ 3,305,120

YOLO CORPORATION
Balance Sheets
December 31, Year 3 and Year 2

	Year 3	*Year 2*
Assets		
Current assets	$43,561,000	$43,900,000
Plant assets, at cost	45,792,000	43,974,000
Less: Accumulated depreciation	(23,761,000)	(22,946,000)
Total assets	$65,592,000	$64,928,000
Liabilities & Shareholders' Equity		
Current liabilities	$21,124,000	$23,650,000
Long-term debt	15,154,000	14,097,000
Common stock, $10 par	11,620,000	11,620,000
Retained earnings	17,694,000	15,561,000
Total liabilities & shareholders' equity	$65,592,000	$64,928,000

There have been no timing differences between pre-tax accounting income and taxable income prior to the two accounting changes. The income tax rate is 48%. Dividends totalling $433,200 were declared and paid in Year 3.

Instructions

Compute for the items listed below the amounts to be included in the Year 3 and Year 2 financial statements of Yolo Corporation after adjustment for the two accounting changes. Show amounts for both Year 3 and Year 2, and include supporting computations.

a Accumulated depreciation
b Deferred income tax liability
c Operating expenses
d Total income taxes expense
e Deferred portion of income taxes expense
f Retained earnings
g Net income restated

Pr. 22-12 You have been engaged to examine the financial statements of Bart Corporation for the year ended December 31, Year 6. In the course of your examination you ascertained the following information:

1 A cheque for $1,500 representing the repayment of an unused employee expense advance was received on December 29, Year 6, but was not recorded until January 2, Year 7.
2 Bart used the allowance method of accounting for doubtful accounts expense. The allowance was based on 3% of past-due accounts receivable

(over 120 days) and 1% of current accounts at the close of each month. Because of changing economic conditions, the amount of past-due accounts increased significantly, and management decided to increase the percentage based on past-due accounts to 5%. The following balances were available:

	Nov. 30, Year 6, Dr (Cr)	*Dec. 31, Year 6, Dr (Cr)*
Accounts receivable	$390,000	$430,000
Past-due accounts included in accounts receivable	12,000	30,000
Allowance for doubtful accounts	(28,000)	9,000

3 The inventory on December 31, Year 5 did not include merchandise costing $7,000 that was stored in a public warehouse. Merchandise costing $3,000 was erroneously counted twice and included twice in the inventory on December 31, Year 6. Bart used the periodic inventory system.

4 On January 2, Year 6, Bart acquired a new machine costing $97,000. The machine was being depreciated by the straight-line method over an economic life of 10 years, with no residual value. When the machine was installed, Bart paid for the following items, which were not included in the cost of the machine, but were debited to Repairs and Maintenance Expense:

Delivery costs	$ 2,500
Installation costs	8,000
Rearrangement of related equipment	4,000
Total	$14,500

5 On January 2, Year 5, Bart leased a building for 10 years under an operating lease at a monthly rent of $12,000. On that date, Bart paid the lessor the following amounts:

Rent deposit	$ 6,000
First month's rent	12,000
Last month's rent	12,000
Installation of new walls and offices	80,000
Total	$110,000

The entire amount of $110,000 was debited to Rent Expense in Year 5.

6 In January, Year 5, Bart issued $200,000 of 8%, 10-year bonds at 97 (97% of face amount). The discount was debited to Interest Expense in Year 5. Interest on the bonds was payable on December 31 of each year. Bart recognized interest expense of $22,000 for Year 5 and $16,000 for Year 6. Bart planned to amortize the discount on bonds payable by the straight-line method.

7 On May 3, Year 6, Bart exchanged 500 shares of treasury stock (its no-par-value common stock) for land to be used as a site for a new factory. The

treasury stock had cost $70 a share when it was acquired, and on May 3, Year 6, it had a current fair value of $80 a share. Bart received $2,000 when an existing building on the land was sold for scrap. The land was recorded at $40,000, the $2,000 received for scrap was credited to Other Revenue, and Bart recognized a gain of $5,000 on the reissuance of the treasury stock.

8 The Advertising and Promotion Expense ledger account included an amount of $75,000, which represented the cost of printing sales catalogues for a special promotional campaign in January, Year 7.

9 Bart was a defendant in a lawsuit by a former customer. Bart's legal counsel advised management that Bart had a good defence. Bart's counsel did not anticipate any impairment of Bart's assets or that any significant liabilities would be incurred as a result of the lawsuit. However, management established a loss contingency of $100,000 by a debit to an expense ledger account.

Instructions

Prepare a working paper to show the effect of errors on Bart Corporation's financial statements for Year 6. The items in the working paper are to be presented in the same sequence as the facts are given, with corresponding numbers *1* through *9*. Use the following columnar headings for the working paper:

		Income statement	*Balance sheet, Dec. 31, Year 6*	
No.	*Explanation*	*Dr (Cr)*	*Dr (Cr)*	*Ledger accounts*
(1)				

Pr. 22-13 Following are financial statements of Helena Corporation for the end of its first year of operations:

HELENA CORPORATION
Statement of Income and Retained Earnings
For Year Ended December 31, Year 1

Net sales		$2,950,000
Costs and expenses:		
Cost of goods sold	$1,670,000	
Depreciation expense	40,000	
Research and development expense	30,000	
Other operating expenses	650,000	
Total costs and expenses		2,390,000
Income before income taxes		$ 560,000
Income taxes expense		252,000
Net income and retained earnings, end of year		$ 308,000

HELENA CORPORATION
Balance Sheet
December 31, Year 1

Assets	
Current assets:	
Cash	$ 150,000
Short-term investments, at cost	60,000
Accounts receivable, less allowance for doubtful accounts of $59,000	391,000
Inventories	430,000
Unexpired insurance	15,000
Total current assets	$1,046,000
Plant assets, less accumulated depreciation of $40,000	386,000
Research costs	120,000
Total assets	$1,552,000
Liabilities & Shareholders' Equity	
Current liabilities:	
Accounts payable and accrued liabilities	$ 592,000
Income taxes payable	252,000
Total current liabilities	$ 844,000
Shareholders' equity:	
Common stock, no par, authorized, issued, and outstanding 40,000 shares	$ 400,000
Retained earnings	308,000
Total shareholders' equity	$ 708,000
Total liabilities & shareholders' equity	$1,552,000

Additional Information

1 The short-term investments are marketable equity securities with an aggregate market value of $55,000 on December 31, Year 1.

2 An aging of accounts receivable on December 31, Year 1, indicated that accounts totalling $36,000 were doubtful of collection.

3 Merchandise costing $12,000 that was out on consignment had been omitted from the physical inventory on December 31, Year 1.

4 A $3,000 insurance premium paid on December 31, Year 1, and debited to Insurance Expense applied to a policy that expired on December 31, Year 2.

5 Helena had adopted a funded, noncontributory pension plan for eligible employees on July 1, Year 1. Current service costs for the first year of the plan, which had not been funded as of December 31, Year 1, were estimated at $45,000.

6 The cost of a machine acquired for $24,000 on July 1, Year 1, had been debited to Repairs and Maintenance Expense and closed to Cost of Goods Sold. Helena uses the straight-line method of depreciation, no net residual value, and a five-year economic life for machines of this type.

7 Helena incurred research costs of $150,000 during Year 1 in researching a possible invention that Helena hopes will develop into a patentable product in Year 2. Helena initiated a five-year amortization period for the research costs, beginning in Year 1.

8 During January, Year 2, a competing business enterprise filed a patent infringement suit against Helena, claiming $200,000 damages. Helena's legal counsel considers it probable that Helena will be held liable for $50,000 damages by the court.

9 Helena's income tax rate is 45%.

Instructions

Prepare a working paper, with accounts listed in ledger sequence, to correct Helena Corporation's ledger account balances on December 31, Year 1. Explain corrections at the bottom of the working paper. Show supporting computations. Disregard deferred income tax credits.

p a r t   s i x

ANALYTICAL PROCEDURES AND STATEMENTS

The purpose and the preparation of the statement of changes in financial position, analysis of financial statements, and accounting for the effects of inflation constitute the subject matter of Part Six of this book. The statement of changes in financial position is now firmly established as a major financial statement. Because the statement of changes in financial position should be prepared on the cash and cash equivalents basis, this approach will be thoroughly discussed and illustrated. Analysis of financial statements provides an opportunity to integrate much of the subject matter of this book and to develop relationships useful for business and investment decisions. Despite the abatement in the level of inflation in recent years, its impact on net income and on financial statements generally continues to be a topic of considerable importance to accountants and users of financial statements.

c h a p t e r 2 3

STATEMENT OF CHANGES IN FINANCIAL POSITION

HISTORICAL PERSPECTIVE

For many years the basic financial statements of business enterprises were a balance sheet and an income statement. Many enterprises also prepared a third financial statement, called a ***statement of source and application of funds***, or simply a ***funds statement***. This statement originally was developed as a means of explaining to creditors why net income was not accompanied by a corresponding increase in cash or working capital. The inclusion of such a financial statement in annual reports issued by corporations to their shareholders was optional for many years, and even among those enterprises that prepared funds statements, the content and terminology varied considerably. It was recognized that the term ***funds*** might be interpreted solely as ***cash*** or ***cash equivalents***. A funds statement based on this narrow definition was essentially a statement of cash receipts and cash payments. However, most publicly owned companies defined ***funds*** more broadly as ***working capital***. A funds statement prepared on the working capital concept usually included only transactions that directly increased or decreased current assets and current liabilities.

The format of this "funds" statement normally segregated ***sources*** of funds from their ***uses*** and denoted the difference between the two as an increase or decrease in "funds" (usually defined as working capital). Net income before extraordinary items was separately disclosed, if positive, as a source, or a use if negative. Adjustments to income which did not affect "funds" were removed in the statement itself to arrive at a net income figure which did affect "funds." Accordingly, the "Source and Use of Funds Statement" basically listed and accumulated sources of funds and uses of funds. This narrow definition of funds did not provide an explanation to statement users of all of the transactions occurring in the year which affected the financing and investing activities of the enterprise. For example, the issuance of common stock directly to the owner of a building for the building had no effect on the current assets and/or current liabilities, and therefore would be excluded from the funds statement even though it constituted both a financing activity (issuance of common shares) and an investing activity (purchase of a building).

In August 1974 the Accounting Standards Committee issued a revised section 1540 of the ***CICA Handbook***, in which they changed the name of the statement to "Statement of Changes in Financial Position," because it was expanded to portray all aspects of the enterprise's ***financing*** and ***investing*** activities undertaken during the period covered by the statement (a total resources perespective). This is commonly known as the ***all-financial-resources*** concept of funds flows. The committee also indicated that the term "funds" referred to ***working capital*** whenever current assets and current liabilities were segregated on the balance sheet. They did indicate, however, that where working capital was not considered to be an appropriate definition of funds, cash and cash equivalents, or cash, cash equivalents, and such other assets less liabilities which constitute current resources[1] could be used. Further, in September 1974 the committee issued section 1500.05 of the ***CICA Handbook***, which read as follows:

> Any information required for fair presentation of financial position, results of operations, or changes in financial position, should be presented in the financial statements including notes to such statements and supporting schedules to which the financial statements are cross-referenced.

It became apparent that:

a The statement would include ***all financing and investing activities*** of the enterprise regardless of whether or not such activities affected working capital directly.

b ***Statement of Changes in Financial Position*** would be the new heading for the funds statement.

c The statement would ***normally be included*** in the enterprise's set of financial statements.

The primary objective at that time was stated in section 1540.03 as follows:

> The objective of the statement of changes in financial position is to provide information as to how the activities of the enterprise have been financed and how its financial resources have been used during the period covered by the statement.

Finally, in December 1983 the committee issued a new (revised) section 1540 of the ***CICA Handbook***, in which ***cash and cash equivalents***[2] became the definition

1 CICA, ***CICA Handbook*** (Toronto), sec. 1540.07 (Aug. 1974), now superseded.

2 Sec. 1540.03 of the ***CICA Handbook*** states that cash and cash equivalents would normally include cash, net of short-term borrowings, and temporary investments. Because of the variations available, section 1540.06 stated that the components of cash and cash equivalents should be disclosed.

of funds. Further, the ***format*** of the statement should normally classify, ***separately***, cash flows (funds) with respect to ***operating***, ***financing***, and ***investing activities***, as stated in section 1540.18:

> Cash flows presented in the statement of changes in financial position should normally be classified by operating activities, financing activities and investing activities.

Also, noncash financing and investing activities were addressed in section 1540.20 as follows:

> Certain financing and investing activities may not involve the cash resources of an enterprise. Examples include the acquisition of assets in exchange for other assets or the acquisition of assets financed by debt (e.g., the acquisition of property and the assumption of a mortgage, or the acquisition of property under a capital lease), the exchange of one form of financing instrument for another (e.g., the conversion of debt into share capital), and stock dividends where the shareholder has the option of receiving cash or shares. The effect of these transactions is similar to a cash inflow followed immediately by a cash outflow, or vice versa. These transactions, which are part of the financing and investing activities of an enterprise, affect its capital and asset structure and therefore need to be disclosed. The financing and investing aspects of the transaction would be disclosed separately in a manner that indicates the nature of their relationship.

As a result, the definition of ''funds'' and the ''format'' of the statement were materially altered. The all-financial-resources concept of funds flows was retained; however, those exchange transactions should now be segregated between financing and investing activities.

For example, the issuance of 10,000 shares of common stock with a current fair value of $60 a share in exchange for patents may be reported in a statement of changes in financial position as follows:

Exchange transaction: *investing* in patents *financed* by issue of common shares

Investing activities:	
Acquisition of patents in exchange for common stock	$600,000
Financing activities:	
Issuance of common stock in exchange for patents	600,000

Similarly, the conversion of $5,000,000 of bonds payable to common stock may be reported in a statement of changes in financial position as follows:

Exchange transaction: replacing one form of *financing* with another form of *financing*

Financing activities:	
Issuance of common stock pursuant to conversion of bonds	$ 5,000,000
Extinguishment of bonds payable through conversion to common stock	(5,000,000)

Although neither of the foregoing exchange transactions affected cash (cash and cash equivalents) directly, they were interpreted for inclusion in the statement of changes in financial position respectively as (1) the issuance of common stock for cash (a ***financing*** activity) and the use of the cash to invest in a patent (an ***investment*** activity), and (2) to extinguish bonds payable (a ***financing*** repayment activity). Other examples of such exchange transactions are: refunding of bonds payable (***financing*** repayment activity) with the issue of new bonds payable (***financing*** activity), exchange of one property for another (both ***investing*** type activities), contracts for capital leases by lessee (***investing*** in capital assets ***financed*** by long-term obligation), and donation of plant assets to a business enterprise (***investing*** in plant asset donated—***financed***—by outsider). However, such transactions as nonoptional stock dividends, stock splits, write-offs of noncurrent assets, and appropriations of retained earnings are not a type of (barter) exchange transaction because they cannot conceptually be broken down into two transactions, one representing the inflow of cash and the other an outflow. Accordingly, their effects on noncurrent ledger account balances are not included in the statement of changes in financial position.

The definition of the objective of the statement was expanded, as follows.[3]

> The objective of the statement of changes in financial position is to provide information about the operating, financing and investing activities of an enterprise and the effects of those activities on cash resources. The statement of changes in financial position assists users of financial statements in evaluating the liquidity and solvency of an enterprise, and in assessing its ability to generate cash from internal sources, to repay debt obligations, to reinvest and to make distributions to owners. This information is not provided or is only indirectly provided in the balance sheet, income statement and statement of retained earnings. Thus, the statement of changes in financial position complements, and presents information different from that provided in, the other financial statements.

The rationale for changing the definition of ''funds'' from working capital to cash and cash equivalents was to focus on the liquid financial resources readily available to the enterprise. In this way the statement is expected to provide a better indication of ***liquidity*** and ***solvency*** and ***an enterprise's ability to generate cash resources*** than previous statements.[4]

The format of the statement of changes in financial position, previously showing sources of and applications of funds, is now normally classified into the three activity areas of operating, financing, and investing. The operating activities area denotes the cash flow (cash and cash equivalents) resulting from operations. The Accounting Standards Committee has offered no definition of ''operations'' per se. Cash flows from financing activities (investment and disinvestment transactions) would represent investment in assets and proceeds from disposals of assets. Cash flows from financing activities would include the issue and purchase of previously issued debt and share capital. Cash flows resulting from the payment of dividends have not been classified under any of the three activities. Accordingly, enterprises might report these cash flows in operating or financing

3 CICA, ***CICA Handbook***, sec. 1540.01.

4 CICA, ***CICA Handbook***, sec. 1540.02.

activities or set this activity out separately in the ''funds'' statement. Cash flows resulting from extraordinary items would be included in that activity to which the extraordinary item related. If it related to operating activities, the cash flow with respect to the extraordinary item would be reported separately, as is currently how it is reported in the income statement.

The Accounting Standards Committee has set out the ***minimum*** disclosure requirements for the statement of changes in financial position as follows:

> The statement of changes in financial position should disclose at least the following items:
>
> **a** cash from operations: the amount of cash from operations should be reconciled to the income statement or the components of cash from operations should be disclosed;
>
> **b** cash flows resulting from extraordinary items;
>
> **c** outlays for acquisition and proceeds on disposal of assets, by major category, not included in **a** or **b** above;
>
> **d** the issue, assumption, redemption and repayment of debt not included in **a** or **b** above;
>
> **e** the issue, redemption and acquisition of share capital; and
>
> **f** the payment of dividends, identifying separately dividends paid by subsidiaries to minority interests.

Generally speaking, the normal segregation of items into operating, financing, and investing activities, would have ***a*** and ***b*** in operating activities, ***c*** in investing activities, and ***d*** and ***e*** in financing activities. The aggregate of items ***a*** to ***f*** would equal the increase or decrease in cash (cash and cash equivalents) for the period.

Because of the change in focus from the ***working capital*** basis to the ***cash*** basis, we will first describe the preparation of a statement of changes in financial position on the cash basis, incorporating the operating, financing, and investing activities concept. We will then describe, using the same example, the preparation of the statement using the working capital basis. In this way the extension of cash and cash equivalents to the point of including all current assets and current liabilities is accomplished. Also, in this way the reader may feel more comfortable moving to the cash basis from the working capital basis of disclosure.

We will then give a more extensive illustration encompassing some of the special problems that may be encountered in practice.

STATEMENT OF CHANGES IN FINANCIAL POSITION: CASH BASIS

When ***funds*** are viewed as ***cash*** and ***cash equivalents***, the statement of changes in financial position is ***more than a cash flow statement***, that is, a listing of cash receipts and cash payments, because financing and investing activities that do not directly involve cash also are listed as such. Adoption of cash as the definition of funds may be justified on the grounds that a statement of changes in financial position on the cash basis provides useful ***predictive information*** for decision makers. Management and outside users of financial statements are concerned with the ability of a business enterprise to meet maturing obligations and remain solvent. A statement of cash flows that includes other significant financing and investing activities is viewed by many users of financial statements as a useful barometer of a business enterprise's financial strength.

Sources and Uses of Cash

The principal sources and uses of cash of a corporation are summarized in a "T" form of ledger account as follows:

Summary of principal sources and uses of cash

Cash	
Sources	*Uses*
1 Cash provided from operations (unprofitable operations result in a ***negative source*** of cash)	1 Acquisition of noncurrent assets
2 Disposal of noncurrent assets	2 Extinguishment of long-term debt and current debt
3 Borrowings (other than temporary and other than from suppliers)	3 Distributions to shareholders, including cash dividends, acquisition of treasury stock, and redemption of preferred stock
4 Issuance of equity securities	

In the preparation of a statement of changes in financial position on the cash basis, all the foregoing sources and uses of cash except profitable operations are readily obtained from the accounting records and the statement of shareholders' equity. The determination of cash provided from profitable operations is more complicated, because an income statement prepared under the accrual basis of accounting includes many expenses and contra-revenue items that did not require cash payments and some revenue and contra expenses that did not involve cash receipts. The easiest method of reconciling cash provided from operations to the income statement is to begin the statement with the figure for net income before extraordinary items. Consequently, the noncash expenses and contra revenue and noncash revenue and contra expenses that are related to ***noncurrent assets*** and ***liabilities*** must be added to or deducted from income before extraordinary items, as appropriate, in the computation of cash provided from operations. In addition, changes in ***current assets*** (other than cash and cash equivalents) and in ***current liabilities*** enter into the computation of cash provided from operations because such items respectively generate and deplete cash during a business enterprise's operating cycle.

Cash Provided from Operations

Noncash Revenue and Expenses

The noncash revenue and expense items included in an income statement typically are produced by adjusting entries at the end of an accounting period. The list on page 1160 summarizes the noncash items that affect noncurrent assets and liabilities.

A decrease in long-term deferred income tax credits, the amortization of investment tax credit or long-term unearned revenue, and the amortization of premium on bonds payable all represent increases in net income and decreases in long-term liabilities. Because these items ***increase net income*** but are not sources of cash, they are ***deducted from*** income before extraordinary items in the computation of cash provided from operations. The accumulation of discount on long-term investment in bonds and the income accrued on investments in common stock under the equity method of accounting represent increases in long-term investments and net income but are not a source of cash; therefore, these items also are ***deducted from*** income before extraordinary items to measure cash provided from operations.

Noncash revenue and expenses that affect noncurrent assets and liabilities

Noncash revenue or contra expenses	*Noncash expenses or contra revenue*
Revenue:	Expenses:
Amortization of long-term unearned revenue	Depreciation expense
Investment income under the equity method of accounting	Amortization expense (intangible assets and deferred charges such as bond issue costs)
Accumulation of discount on long-term investment in bonds	Amortization of discount on bonds payable
Contra expenses:	Investment loss under the equity method of accounting
Decrease in long-term deferred income tax credits	Increase in long-term deferred income tax credits
Amortization of investment tax credit under deferral method	Contra revenue:
Amortization of premium on bonds payable	Amortization of premium on long-term investment in bonds

Depreciation expense, an increase in long-term deferred income tax credits, the amortization of intangible assets and deferred charges, and the amortization of bond discount all ***reduce net income*** without reducing cash and therefore are ***added to*** income before extraordinary items in the computation of cash provided from operations. Similarly, the amortization of a premium on long-term investment in bonds and the loss accrued on investments in common stock under the equity method of accounting reduce long-term investments and net income but have no effect on cash; therefore, these items also are ***added to*** income before extraordinary items to measure the cash provided from operations.

Changes in Other Current Assets and Liabilities

In the computation of cash provided from operations, changes also must be considered in most current assets and liabilities excepting cash and cash equivalents, temporary investments and short-term borrowings, and dividends payable. During the operating cycle, cash inflows result from the collection of trade accounts receivable for sales of goods and services, and cash outflows result from payments of trade accounts payable and accrued liabilities incurred in the purchase of goods and services. Liabilities for dividends payable are not a result of operations and thus are excluded in the computation of cash provided from operations.

The following table summarizes the additions to and deductions from income before extraordinary items for changes in current assets and liabilities other than cash and cash equivalents and dividends payable.

Changes in current assets and liabilities included in the computation of cash provided from operations

Additions to income before extraordinary items	*Deductions from income before extraordinary items*
Decreases in net trade accounts and loans receivable from customers	Increases in net trade accounts and loans receivable from customers
Decreases in inventories and short-term prepayments	Increases in inventories and short-term prepayments
Increases in trade accounts and loans payable to suppliers	Decreases in trade accounts and loans payable to suppliers
Increases in accrued liabilities (including income taxes payable)	Decreases in accrued liabilities (including income taxes payable)

Decreases in net trade accounts and loans receivable from customers during an accounting period indicate that more cash was collected from customers than was reported as revenue in the income statement; increases in these accounts indicate that less cash was collected from customers than was reported as revenue in the income statement.

Decreases in inventories and short-term prepayments indicate that a portion of the cost of goods sold and expenses resulted from the use of assets previously paid for and not from current cash outlays; increases in inventories and short-term prepayments indicate that cash was used to accumulate these assets.

Increases in trade accounts and loans payable to suppliers and accrued liabilities indicate that portions of cost of goods sold and expenses included in the income statement were not paid; decreases in trade accounts and loans payable to suppliers and accrued liabilities indicate that more cash was paid for these items than was included as expenses in the income statement.

The amount of cash provided from operations ***should not be viewed as a substitute for net income***. Cash flow from operations is essentially the amount of net income on a cash basis of accounting; it is not a summary of revenue realized and expenses incurred. The profitability of a business enterprise is measured by comparing expired costs with realized revenue, not by measuring net income on the cash basis of accounting.

Illustration of Statement of Changes in Financial Position: Cash Basis

An income statement, a statement of shareholders' equity or retained earnings, and comparative balance sheets provide the basis information for preparing a statement of changes in financial position. With this information, the major movements of cash and cash equivalents may be identified for the accounting period under consideration.

When the cash and cash equivalents[5] basis is adopted, ***changes in all other balance sheet accounts represent potential inflow and outflow of cash***. Balance sheet accounts are analyzed to obtain specific amounts of cash inflows and outflows, resulting in a reconciliation of the beginning balance with the ending balance of cash.

The financial statements and additional information below and on page 1163 for Elwood Supply Limited are used to illustrate the preparation of a statement of changes in financial position on the cash basis, without the use of a working paper.

ELWOOD SUPPLY LIMITED
Income Statement
For Year Ended December 31, Year 2

Sales (net)		$107,000
Cost of goods sold:		
Inventories, Jan. 1, Year 2	$40,000	
Purchases (net)	50,000	
Cost of goods available for sale	$90,000	
Less: Inventories, Dec. 31, Year 2	30,000	
Cost of goods sold		60,000
Gross profit on sales		$ 47,000
Expenses:		
Operating (excluding depreciation)	$10,000	
Depreciation	7,500	
Interest	1,500	19,000
Income before income taxes		$ 28,000
Income taxes expense		7,000
Net income		$ 21,000

ELWOOD SUPPLY LIMITED
Statement of Shareholders' Equity
For Year Ended December 31, Year 2

	Common stock, no par	*Retained earnings*	*Total*
Balances, beginning of year	$110,000	$30,000	$140,000
Issuance of 1,000 shares of common stock in exchange for equipment	12,000		12,000
Net income		21,000	21,000
Cash dividends declared ($0.45 a share)		(5,000)	(5,000)
Balances, end of year	$122,000	$46,000	$168,000

5 Hereafter, the term ***cash*** will denote cash, temporary investments (short-term investments), and short-term borrowings if any are applicable.

ELWOOD SUPPLY LIMITED
Comparative Balance Sheets
December 31, Year 2 and Year 1

	Dec. 31, Year 2	*Dec. 31, Year 1*	*Net change increase (decrease)*
Assets			
Cash	$ 29,900	$ 14,000	$15,900
Accounts receivable (net)	33,000	27,000	6,000
Inventories	30,000	40,000	(10,000)
Short-term prepayments	1,600	1,000	600
Equipment	130,000	100,000	30,000
Less: Accumulated depreciation	(19,500)	(12,000)	7,500*
Total assets	$205,000	$170,000	$35,000
Liabilities & Shareholders' Equity			
Accounts payable	$ 15,500	$ 23,400	$ (7,900)
Interest payable	1,500		1,500
Income taxes payable	7,000	6,600	400
Dividends payable	5,000		5,000
Long-term notes payable, due in Year 5	8,000		8,000
Common stock, no par value	122,000	110,000	12,000
Retained earnings	46,000	30,000	16,000
Total liabilities & shareholders' equity	$205,000	$170,000	$35,000

*An *increase* in accumulated depreciation and a *decrease* in total assets.

Additional Information for Year 2

1 Equipment was acquired for $18,000 cash.

2 Cash of $8,000 was borrowed from a bank on a long-term promissory note due in Year 5.

Statement of Changes in Financial Position on the Cash Basis

When a statement of changes in financial position is prepared on the cash basis, it contains a summary of all cash receipts and payments, as well as the effect of exchange transactions. This form is a useful analytical tool for management and other users of financial statements because it provides answers to questions such as the following: How much cash was generated from operations last accounting period? What use was made of cash receipts? How much cash was received from nonrecurring sources? Why is the company short of cash? Can the current level of cash dividend payments be maintained? The statement of changes in financial position on the cash basis for Elwood Supply Limited is illustrated on the top of the next page.

ELWOOD SUPPLY LIMITED
Statement of Changes in Financial Position
For Year Ended December 31, Year 2

Operating activities:		
Net income		$21,000
Add: Depreciation expense		7,500
Decrease in inventories		10,000
Increase in interest payable		1,500
Increase in income taxes payable		400
Less: Increase in net accounts receivable	$ 6,000	
Increase in short-term prepayments	600	
Decrease in accounts payable	7,900	(14,500)
Cash provided from operations		$25,900
Financing activities:		
Borrowing on long-term promissory note	$ 8,000	
Issuance of common stock in exchange for equipment	12,000	
Cash provided from financing activities		$20,000
Investing activities:		
Acquisition of equipment for cash	$18,000	
Acquisition of equipment in exchange for common stock	12,000	
Cash used in investing activities		(30,000)
Increase in cash*		$15,900

**Cash itself* is the definition of funds in this statement.

The following features of the foregoing statement should be noted:

1 The statement begins with net income, absent any extraordinary items. To net income is added depreciation expense, which is the only noncash revenue or expense item of Elwood Supply Limited that affects noncurrent assets or liabilities. Net income and depreciation expense thus are the only items in the statement of changes in financial position that were taken from the income statement.

2 The comparative balance sheets provided the increases and decreases in current assets (other than cash) and current liabilities for inclusion in the statement of changes in financial position.

3 The increase in the dividends payable current liability is not an adjustment to net income because dividends are not an operating item. Because the dividends were not ***paid*** during Year 2, the $5,000 amount is not included in the statement of changes in financial position.

4 Once the ''Cash provided from operations'' section of the statement is completed, a review of the increases and decreases in noncurrent assets and liabilities and shareholders' equity in the comparative balance sheets and the statement of shareholders' equity, together with the other information for Year 2, provides information required for completion of the statement. The

issuance of common stock for equipment, disclosed in the statement of shareholders' equity, is an ***exchange transaction*** that does not directly affect cash. However, following the all-inclusive financing/investing basis (the ***all-financial-resources*** concept), the transaction is included as both a financing activity and an investing activity.

5 The statement shows the increase in cash as the final amount, thereby separately disclosing the change in cash for the period.

Alternative Approach: Cash-Basis Net Income

Instead of reporting the cash provided from operations in the statement of changes in financial position as shown on page 1164, the income statement may be converted from the accrual basis of accounting to the cash basis of accounting to show actual cash receipts and payments from operations (see page 29 in Chapter 1). Receipts from customers, payment to suppliers, and payments for specific expenses thus are reported with other operating items provided and applied in the statement of changes in financial position on a cash basis. This approach is illustrated below and on page 1165 for Elwood Supply Limited.

Neither depreciation expense nor interest expense required the payment of cash in Year 2; therefore, both amounts were eliminated in the conversion of the income statement to the cash basis of accounting.

ELWOOD SUPPLY LIMITED
Conversion of Income Statement from Accrual Basis to Cash Basis of Accounting
For Year Ended December 31, Year 2

	Income statement (accrual basis)	*Add (deduct)*	*Income statement (cash basis)*
Sales	$107,000		
Less: Increase in net accounts receivable		$ (6,000)	$101,000
Cost of goods sold	60,000		
Add: Decrease in accounts payable		7,900	
Less: Decrease in inventories		(10,000)	57,900
Gross profit on sales	$ 47,000		$ 43,100
Expenses:			
Operating expenses (excluding depreciation)	$ 10,000		
Add: Increase in short-term prepayments		600	$ 10,600
Depreciation expense	7,500	(7,500)	
Interest expense	1,500	(1,500)	
Income taxes expense	7,000		
Less: Increase in income taxes payable		(400)	6,600
Total expenses	$ 26,000		$ 17,200
Net income, accrual basis	$ 21,000		
Net income, cash basis (cash provided from operations as reported on page 1164)			$ 25,900

ELWOOD SUPPLY LIMITED
Statement of Changes in Financial Position
For Year Ended December 31, Year 2

Operating activities:		
Collections from customers		$101,000
Deduct: Merchandise purchases	$57,900	
Operating expenses	10,600	
Income taxes expense	6,600	75,100
Cash provided from operations		$ 25,900
Financing activities:		
Borrowing on long-term promissory note	$ 8,000	
Issuance of common stock in exchange for equipment	12,000	20,000
Investing activities:		
Acquisition of equipment for cash	$18,000	
Acquisition of equipment in exchange for common stock	12,000	(30,000)
Increase in cash*		$ 15,900

**Cash itself* is the definition of funds in this statement.

STATEMENT OF CHANGES IN FINANCIAL POSITION: WORKING CAPITAL BASIS

The *working capital* of a business enterprise is the amount by which current assets exceed current liabilities. The amount of working capital is a measure of the safety factor that exists for the protection of short-term creditors. Working capital also may be viewed as funds available for investment in noncurrent assets or to liquidate noncurrent liabilities. Increases in working capital occur when noncurrent assets are decreased (sold) and when noncurrent liabilities and shareholders' equity are increased (as by additional financing activities). Decreases in working capital occur when noncurrent assets are increased (acquired) and when noncurrent liabilities and shareholders' equity are decreased (as by extinguishment of long-term debt, acquisition of treasury stock, or declaration of cash dividends). The major sources and uses of working capital for a corporation are the same as those outlined for cash on page 1159. However, working capital provided from operations generally differs significantly from cash provided from operations.

When the working capital basis is used for a statement of changes in financial position, the noncurrent assets of a business enterprise represent the financial resources in which working capital has been invested; the noncurrent liabilities and the shareholders' equity represent the financial sources from which working capital was provided. The first clue to an inflow or outflow of working capital, therefore, is changes in noncurrent accounts during the accounting period. The income statement and the statement of shareholders' equity or retained earnings help to explain the change in financial position that resulted from operations and from transactions with shareholders. The difference between the inflow and the outflow of financial resources during the accounting period ***must equal*** the increase or decrease in working capital during the accounting period. These inflows and outflows of financial resources are shown as operating, financing, and investing activities.

Working Capital Provided from Operations

Working capital provided from operations differs from cash provided from operations in the treatment of changes in current assets and current liabilities. Such changes, which are an integral part of ***cash*** provided from operations, are not relevant to ***working capital*** provided from operations, because working capital is the difference between current assets and current liabilities.

Illustration of Statement of Changes in Financial Position: Working Capital Basis

To illustrate the preparation of a statement of changes in financial position on the working capital basis, we return to the income statement, statement of shareholders' equity, and comparative balance sheets of Elwood Supply Limited on pages 1162–1163. Elwood's working capital increased $13,500 during Year 2. The increase in working capital for Elwood Supply Limited may be viewed as a ***result*** that is to be explained by analyzing the changes in non–working capital ledger accounts. In other words, the ***causes*** of the increase in working capital may be found only in the changes that took place in the noncurrent accounts. However, not all changes in noncurrent accounts cause changes in working capital. For example, an ***exchange transaction*** causes changes in noncurrent accounts but does not change working capital. However, exchange transactions, such as the issuance of common stock for equipment by Elwood Supply, are treated in the same manner here as they were in using the cash basis for preparation of the statement of changes in financial position.

A statement of changes in financial position on the working capital basis for Elwood Supply Limited is illustrated below. This format highlights the $13,500 increase in working capital.

ELWOOD SUPPLY LIMITED
Statement of Changes in Financial Position
For Year Ended December 31, Year 2

Operating activities:		
Net income		$21,000
Add: Depreciation expense		7,500
Working capital provided from operations		$28,500
Financing activities:		
Borrowing on long-term promissory note	$ 8,000	
Issuance of common stock in exchange for equipment	12,000	20,000
Investing activities:		
Acquisition of equipment for cash	$18,000	
Acquisition of equipment in exchange for common stock	12,000	(30,000)
Declaration of cash dividends		(5,000)
Increase in working capital		$13,500

Note in the foregoing statement that the ***declaration*** of cash dividends is an application of working capital because it increases current liabilities. (The ***payment*** of the cash dividend will not affect working capital because current assets and current liabilities will be reduced by the same amount.)

SPECIAL PROBLEMS IN PREPARATION OF STATEMENT OF CHANGES IN FINANCIAL POSITION

When a statement of changes in financial position is prepared from detailed accounting records, all the necessary information may be obtained from ledger account balances or from computer printouts. The task is more difficult when the statement must be prepared from comparative balance sheets, an income statement, a statement of shareholders' equity (or a statement of retained earnings), and other sources. Some special problems involved in the preparation of the statement of changes in financial position are described in the following sections.

Doubtful Accounts Expense

Neither the recording of doubtful accounts expense nor the write-off of uncollectible ***current*** accounts receivable requires any action in the preparation of a statement of changes in financial position. The recording of doubtful accounts expense reduces net current accounts receivable and is reflected as deduction from revenue in the measurement of cash or working capital provided from operations. A write-off of a current account receivable does not reduce net current accounts receivable and thus has no effect on cash or working capital.

In contrast, the recording of doubtful accounts expense on ***noncurrent*** accounts receivable does not reduce cash or working capital; therefore, such expense is added to net income in the computation of cash or working capital provided from operations.

Gain or Loss on Disposal (or Write-Down) of Short-Term Investments

When short-term (temporary) investments that are classified as current assets are sold at a gain, cash and working capital include the amount of the gain; if short-term investments are sold at a loss, cash and working capital include the amount of the loss. Unrealized gains and losses recorded on short-term (temporary) marketable equity securities whose aggregate market value differs from cost are included in the measurement of net income and change the amount of cash and cash equivalents and of working capital. However, because temporary marketable securities generally are acquired to obtain a return on cash not currently needed in operations, ***such gains and losses generally are included in net income that is a part of the computation of cash or working capital provided from operations***.

Purchase-Type Business Combination

When a purchase-type business combination (see Chapter 16, page 807) is completed, the effect of the acquisition on financial resources requires careful analysis. For example, assume the following transaction:

Journal entry to record purchase-type business combination

Current Assets	200,000	
Noncurrent Assets	500,000	
Current Liabilities		50,000
Cash		150,000
Common Stock, no par value		500,000
To record acquisition of a business enterprise in a purchase-type business combination.		

The $150,000 cash paid in the business combination requires no separate disclosure in a statement of changes in financial position on the cash basis. However, the net assets, other than cash and cash equivalents, would be classified as an investing activity, and the financing activity would be reported separately. Section 1540.22 of the ***CICA Handbook*** states, in part:

> On acquisition of an entity which is to be consolidated, the net assets acquired, other than cash and cash equivalents, would be classified as an investing activity and the financing aspect would be disclosed separately. The increase or decrease in the consolidated cash and cash equivalents resulting from the acquisition, and the assigned costs of the other assets and liabilities acquired, including any goodwill arising from the transaction, would also be disclosed to portray the components of the net assets acquired. The disclosure would be made either in the body of the statement of changes in financial position or in a note to the financial statements.

The acquisition of current assets in the amount of $200,000 in this example does not affect working capital, because current liabilities were increased by $50,000 and cash was decreased by $150,000.

The net effect was to increase both the current assets and the current liabilities by $50,000. The exchange of common stock for noncurrent assets is reported as both a financing activity and an investing activity, in the amount of $500,000, under both the cash basis and the working capital basis.

Reclassification of Assets and Liabilities

When a long-term debt matures within a year, it is reclassified as a current liability. For example, serial bonds and mortgage notes payable that mature within one year generally are reclassified from long-term debt to the current liabilities category. This reclassification decreases the amount of working capital and thus represents a use of working capital. Similarly, a long-term receivable that matures within one year from the end of the current accounting period is reclassified as a current asset, thus increasing working capital under the working capital basis. Neither of the transactions affects the cash basis, however.

A reclassification of a current asset to the noncurrent category (such as an extension of maturity dates on receivables) reduces the amount of working capital; a reclassification of a current liability to long-term debt (through a troubled debt restructuring, for example) increases the amount of working capital. Consequently, such reclassifications are reported in the statement of changes in financial position prepared on the working capital basis. Again, these transactions have no effect on the cash basis.

Analysis of Changes in Plant Asset Ledger Accounts

When numerous transactions were recorded in plant asset ledger accounts, it is helpful to analyze these accounts before isolating the effect on cash or working capital. For example, assume that the following information relating to equipment is available from comparative financial statements:

Effect of transactions relating to equipment

	Dec. 31, Year 5	*Dec. 31, Year 4*
Equipment	$540,000	$620,000
Accumulated depreciation of equipment	230,000	195,000
Depreciation expense	60,000	
Loss on disposal of equipment	40,000	

Equipment that cost $130,000 and had a carrying amount of $105,000 was sold for $65,000 cash, and equipment was acquired for $50,000 cash in Year 5. The analyses of the Equipment and Accumulated Depreciation of Equipment ledger accounts shown below identify the transactions that caused the changes in these two accounts and affected cash or working capital:

More detailed analysis of changes in plant asset ledger accounts . . .

	Equipment, Dr (Cr)	*Accumulated Depreciation of Equipment, Dr (Cr)*
Balances, beginning of Year 5	$620,000	$(195,000)
Sale of equipment for $65,000 cash	(130,000)	25,000
Acquisition of equipment for cash	50,000	
Depreciation expense		(60,000)
Balances, end of Year 5	$540,000	$(230,000)

The journal entries prepared at the time of each transaction, and the corresponding effect on the statement of changes in financial position prepared on either the cash basis or the working capital basis, are summarized on page 1171.

The analyses above fully explain the changes in the Equipment and Accumulated Depreciation of Equipment ledger accounts: Net income is increased by $100,000 to cancel the effects of noncash expenses (loss on disposal of equipment of $40,000 and depreciation expense of $60,000), and the amounts to be reported as financial resources provided ($65,000) and applied ($50,000) in the investing activities section of the statement of changes in financial position prepared on the cash basis or the working capital basis.

Stock Dividends

Dividends in shares of preferred stock or common stock of the issuer do not affect cash or working capital and are not exchange transactions. Therefore, stock dividends are not reported in a statement of changes in financial position.

... and journal entries causing changes in plant asset ledger accounts

Journal entries to record transactions			*Effect on statement of changes in financial position*
Cash	65,000		*Negative investment activity:*
Accumulated Depreciation of Equipment	25,000		Sale of equipment, $65,000.
Loss on Disposal of Equipment ..	40,000		The loss on disposal of equipment, $40,000, is added to net income to measure the amount of cash or working capital provided from operations.
Equipment		130,000	
To record sale of equipment.			
Equipment	50,000		*Positive investing activity:*
Cash		50,000	Acquisition of equipment, $50,000.
To record acquisition of equipment.			
Depreciation Expense	60,000		Depreciation of $60,000 is added to net income to measure the amount of cash or working capital provided from operations.
Accumulated Depreciation of Equipment		60,000	
To record depreciation expense.			

Capital Leases

A lease contract that meets the criteria for a capital lease is recorded by the lessee as a debit to a noncurrent asset and a credit to a liability account, a portion of which is payable on the date of the lease. To illustrate, assume that Lessee Company recorded a capital lease requiring ten annual payments of $10,000 beginning on December 31, Year 1, the date of the lease, at the lessee's incremental borrowing rate of 12%, as follows:

Journal entries to record capital lease by lessee

Leased Equipment Under Capital Lease ($10,000 × 6.328250*)..	63,283	
Liability Under Capital Lease (net)		63,283
To record capital lease at inception of lease.		
Liability Under Capital Lease	10,000	
Cash		10,000
To record first lease payment.		

*From Table 4 in the Appendix at the end of Chapter 5, adjusted for *annuity due*.

In a statement of changes in financial position on the cash basis for the year ended December 31, Year 1, the lease contract is reported by Lessee Company as follows:

Financing activities:	
Long-term borrowing under capital lease	$63,283
Initial payment on liability under capital lease	(10,000)
Investing activities:	
Acquisition of equipment under capital lease	$63,283

What part of the foregoing journal entry is an "exchange"? (The execution of the lease contract and acquisition of equipment constitute the "exchange.")

Elwood Supply Limited provided a simple example of statements of changes in financial position. In the next section we illustrate an example that necessitates the preparation of a working paper to analyze transactions before the statement of changes in financial position is completed. The income statement (excluding earnings per share), statement of shareholders' equity, comparative balance sheets, and additional information for Rose Corporation appear below and on page 1173.

ROSE CORPORATION
Income Statement
For Year Ended December 31, Year 5

Revenue:		
Sales		$313,600
Investment income		13,250
Total revenue		$326,850
Costs and expenses:		
Cost of goods sold	$158,000	
Depreciation expense	30,000	
Other operating expenses	28,000	
Interest expense	11,250	
Income taxes expense ($10,000 deferred)	48,300	
Total costs and expenses		275,550
Income before extraordinary item		$ 51,300
Extraordinary item (gain on condemnation of building), net of income tax effect of $22,500		27,500
Net income		$ 78,800

ROSE CORPORATION
Statement of Shareholders' Equity
For Year Ended December 31, Year 5

	Common stock, no par	*Retained earnings*	*Treasury stock*	*Total*
Balances, beginning of year (10,000 shares)	$158,000	$198,500		$356,500
Issuance of 4,640 shares of common stock in exchange for equipment	92,800			92,800

Acquisition of 1,000 shares of common stock for the treasury			$(17,500)	(17,500)
Net income		78,800		78,800
Dividends:				
Cash ($3 a share)		(42,000)		(42,000)
Stock, 4% (360 shares)	5,400	(5,400)		
Balances, end of year	$256,200	$229,900	$(17,500)	$468,600

ROSE CORPORATION
Comparative Balance Sheets
December 31, Year 5 and Year 4

	Dec. 31, Year 5	*Dec. 31, Year 4*	*Increase (decrease)*
Assets			
Cash	$ 7,100	$ 52,800	$ (45,700)
Notes receivable	50,000	30,000	20,000
Accounts receivable (net)	36,900	50,400	(13,500)
Inventories	96,050	57,300	38,750
Short-term prepayments	12,600	9,600	3,000
Investment in Zola Limited common stock, 25%, at equity	53,250	40,000	13,250
Land	150,000		150,000
Buildings and equipment	554,000	826,000	(272,000)
Accumulated depreciation of buildings and equipment	(185,000)	(355,000)	(170,000)*
Total assets	$774,900	$711,100	$163,800
Liabilities & Shareholders' Equity			
Accounts payable	$ 22,150	$ 31,300	$ (9,150)
Dividends payable	22,000		22,000
Income taxes payable	42,800	17,000	25,800
Other current liabilities	17,600	16,300	1,300
8% bonds payable (due Jan. 1, Year 15)	150,000	200,000	(50,000)
Premium on bonds payable	6,750	10,000	(3,250)
Deferred income tax credits	45,000	80,000	(35,000)
Common stock, no par value	256,200	158,000	98,200
Retained earnings	229,900	198,500	31,400
Treasury stock, 1,000 shares at cost	(17,500)		17,500†
Total liabilities & shareholders' equity	$774,900	$711,100	$ 63,800

*A *decrease* in accumulated depreciation and an *increase* in total assets.
†An *increase* in treasury stock and a *decrease* in total liabilities & shareholders' equity.

Additional Information for Year 5

1 Land was acquired for $150,000 cash.

2 An analysis of the changes in the Buildings and Equipment and Accumulated Depreciation of Buildings and Equipment ledger accounts during Year 5 is shown on page 1174.

Changes in plant asset accounts

	Buildings and Equipment	*Accumulated Depreciation of Buildings and Equipment*
Balances, Dec. 31, Year 4	$826,000	$355,000
Condemnation of building	(400,000)*	(200,000)
Acquisition of equipment	128,000†	
Depreciation expense		30,000
Balances, Dec. 31, Year 5	$554,000	$185,000

*The condemnation of the building in Year 5 was recorded as follows:

Cash	250,000	
Accumulated Depreciation of Buildings and Equipment	200,000	
Deferred Income Tax Credits	45,000	
Buildings and Equipment		400,000
Extraordinary Item (gain on condemnation of building), net of income tax effect $22,500		27,500
Income Taxes Payable ($45,000 + $22,500)		67,500
To record proceeds received from condemnation of building on leased land.		

†Acquired in an exchange transaction through issuance of 4,640 shares of common stock with a current fair value of $92,800 and $35,200 cash, a total of $128,000.

3 On January 2, Year 5, $50,000 of bonds payable were called at 105 and extinguished. Unamortized premium of $2,500 ($10,000 × ¼ = $2,500) on bonds payable was written off, resulting in neither a gain nor a loss on the extinguishment. The balance of the Premium on Bonds Payable ledger account, $7,500 ($10,000 − $2,500 = $7,500) was being amortized at an amount of $750 a year under the straight-line method.

Working Paper for Statement of Changes in Financial Position

The working paper for statement of changes in financial position on pages 1176–1177 is organized to facilitate the preparation of the statement on either the cash concept or the working capital concept. Thus, it first shows the beginning balance, ending balance, and net change (coded X) for cash; then it has the beginning and ending totals for other current assets less current liabilities other than dividends payable (only dividends ***paid*** are included in a statement of changes in financial position on the cash concept). Dividends payable is the next item in the working paper so that a subtotal for beginning and ending working capital may be provided. The top portion of the working paper is completed by entering beginning and ending balances of noncurrent assets and liabilities and shareholders' equity.

Our objective in completing the working paper is to explain the $45,700 decrease in cash of Rose Corporation during the year ended December 31, Year 5, by analysis of its operations and its investing and financing activities. The analyses of the transactions completed by Rose are explained below. (The numbers correspond to the numbers used in the working paper.)

Operations (Cash Basis)

1 The net income of $78,800 is closed to the Retained Earnings ledger account. Net income represents an increase in shareholders' equity and is a major source of cash for most companies. However, net income is only the starting point in the computation of the increase in cash from operations because not all revenue and expense items represent sources and uses of cash. Furthermore, any extraordinary items and material nonoperating gains and losses are eliminated from net income because the transactions giving rise to such items are ***reported separately***.

2 Depreciation expense has no effect on cash. Therefore, the depreciation expense of $30,000 for Year 5 is added to net income and is credited to Accumulated Depreciation of Buildings and Equipment. In other words, because depreciation is a noncash expense, the cash provided from operations (assuming no other noncash items) is equal to the amount of net income plus depreciation expense.

3 Depreciation was not the only expense that did not reduce cash. The income taxes expense of $48,300 includes $10,000 not payable currently, which resulted in an increase in the Deferred Income Tax Credits ledger account, which is noncurrent. The $10,000 portion of income taxes expense is added to net income because it did not reduce cash during Year 5.

4 The net income for Year 5 includes $13,250 of income on the investment in the common stock of Zola Limited. The investment income ***was recorded under the equity method of accounting*** as follows:

Journal entry to record investment income

Investment in Zola Limited Common Stock	13,250	
Investment Income		13,250

In the working paper, this journal entry is recorded as a debit to the investment-account and a credit (reduction) to "operations," because the investment income did not generate cash. After this journal entry is entered in the working paper, the ending balance of $53,250 of the Investment in Zola Limited Common Stock ledger account is verified by adding $13,250 to the balance of $40,000 at the beginning of Year 5.

5 The amortization of the premium on bonds payable was recorded on December 31, Year 5, as follows:

Journal entry to amortize premium on bonds payable

Premium on Bonds Payable	750	
Interest Expense		750

The working paper analysis of this adjusting entry is to debit the Premium on Bonds Payable ledger account and to record a reduction in cash provided from operations, because the credit to Interest Expense increased net income

ROSE CORPORATION
Working Paper for Statement of Changes in Financial Position
For Year Ended December 31, Year 5

	Balances, Dec. 31, Year 4	*Transactions for Year 5*		*Balances Dec. 31, Year 5*
		Debit	*Credit*	
Cash	52,800		(X) 45,700	7,100
Other current assets less current liabilities other than dividends payable	82,700	(6) 30,300		113,000
Dividends payable		(16) 20,000	(14) 42,000	(22,000)
Working capital	135,500	50,300	87,700	98,100
Investment in Zola Limited common stock	40,000	(4) 13,250		53,250
Land		(7) 150,000		150,000
Buildings and equipment	826,000	(8) 35,200 (9) 92,800	(10) 400,000	554,000
Treasury stock		(12) 17,500		17,500
Totals	1,001,500			872,850
Accumulated depreciation of buildings and equipment	355,000	(10) 200,000	(2) 30,000	185,000
8% bonds payable	200,000	(13) 50,000		150,000
Premium on bonds payable	10,000	(5) 750 (13) 2,500		6,750
Deferred income tax credits	80,000	(10) 45,000	(3) 10,000	45,000
Common stock	158,000		(11) 92,800 (15) 5,400	256,200
Retained earnings	198,500	(14) 42,000 (15) 5,400	(1) 78,800	229,900
Totals	1,001,500	704,700	704,700	872,850

Operating activities:					
Net income	(1)	78,800			Cash provided from operations, $47,000*
Add: Depreciation expense	(2)	30,000			
Increase in deferred income tax credits	(3)	10,000			
Less: Investment income			(4)	13,250	
Amortization of premium on bonds payable			(5)	750	
Extraordinary item (gain)			(10)	27,500	
Increase in net current assets			(6)	30,300	
Cash dividends paid			(16)	20,000	Dividends paid, $20,000
Financing activities:					
Issuance of common stock in exchange for equipment	(11)	92,800			Net financing activities, $22,800
Acquisition of treasury stock			(12)	17,500	
Extinguishment of bonds payable			(13)	52,500	
Investing activities:					
Acquisition of land			(7)	150,000	Net investing activities, $(95,500)
Acquisition of equipment for cash			(8)	35,200	
Acquisition of equipment in exchange for common stock			(9)	92,800	
Proceeds on condemnation of building (net of income taxes)	(10)	182,500			
Total financial resources provided and applied		394,100		439,800	
Decrease in cash	(X)	45,700			
Totals		439,800		439,800	

*Working capital provided from operations: $47,000 + $30,300 = $77,300.

without increasing cash. The amount of bond interest ***paid*** in Year 5 was \$12,000 (\$150,000 × 0.08 = \$12,000), not \$11,250 reported as interest expense in the income statement.

6 The \$30,300 increase in current assets other than cash less current liabilities other than dividends payable, represents a decrease in cash provided from operations, as explained on pages 1160–1161. This ***increase in net current assets*** is obtained from the comparative balance sheets of Rose Corporation on page 1173 as follows:

Increase (decrease) in current assets other than cash:		
Notes receivable	\$20,000	
Accounts receivable (net)	(13,500)	
Inventories	38,750	
Short-term prepayments	3,000	\$48,250
Less: Increase (decrease) in current liabilities other than dividends payable:		
Accounts payable	\$ (9,150)	
Income taxes payable	25,800	
Other current liabilities	1,300	17,950
Increase in net current assets		\$30,300

The remaining component of the computation of cash provided from operations (the extraordinary gain on condemnation of building) is explained in ***12*** under ***Financing Activities***.

Investing Activities

7 Land was acquired for \$150,000 in Year 5. This is a reduction in cash and is listed in the working paper as an investing activity.

8 and **9** The acquisition of equipment for cash of \$35,200 and 4,640 shares of common stock was recorded by Rose Corporation as follows:

Journal entry to record acquisition of plant assets

Buildings and Equipment	128,000	
Cash		35,200
Common Stock, no par value		92,800

Although this transaction actually reduced cash by only \$35,200, the total cost of the equipment acquired is reported as an investing activity (\$35,200 + \$92,800 = \$128,000). The reason for this is that the issuance of common stock valued at \$92,800 is included under ***Financing activities*** (**11** shown below).

10 The journal entry to record the condemnation of the building on leased land in Year 5 is shown on page 1174. In the working paper, the condemnation is recorded as a source of cash of \$182,500 (cash received of \$250,000 less current income taxes of $67,500 paid in Year 5). The accumulated depreciation applicable to the building, $200,000, is debited to the Accumulated Depreciation of Buildings and Equipment ledger account, and the deferred tax of $45,000 relating to the building is debited to the Deferred Income Tax Credits account. The extraordinary item (gain) of $27,500 is deducted from net income so that the proceeds (net of the income taxes of $22,500 on the gain paid in Year 5) may be listed as a source of cash. The cost of the building, $400,000, is credited to the Buildings and Equipment ledger account to complete the transaction in the working paper. Note that when the increase of $30,000 for depreciation expense and the decrease of $200,000 on the condemnation of the building are combined with the beginning balance of $355,000, the ending balance of $185,000 in the Accumulated Depreciation of Buildings and Equipment ledger account is obtained. Finally, the debit of $128,000 in the Buildings and Equipment ledger account in investing activities **8** and **9**, less the credit of $400,000 in this investing activity **12**, explains the net decrease in that account in Year 5 from $826,000 to $554,000.

Financing Activities

11 As explained for **8** and **9** under ***Investing activities***, the issuance of 4,640 shares of common stock (together with cash) is interpreted as a financing activity of $92,800, the current fair value of the stock. In the working paper, the $92,800 is credited to the Common Stock ledger account.

12 The acquisition of treasury stock for $17,500 is recorded in the working paper as a debit to the Treasury Stock ledger account, thus establishing the ending balance in that account, and as a credit under ***Investing activities*** to the Acquisition of Treasury Stock ledger account.

13 At the beginning of Year 5, bonds payable were called at 105 (the carrying amount) and retired, as illustrated in the journal entry below:

Journal entry to record call and extinguishment of bonds payable

8% Bonds Payable	50,000	
Premium on Bonds Payable	2,500	
Cash		52,500

This transaction is recorded in the working paper by a debit of $50,000 to 8% Bonds Payable, a debit of $2,500 to Premium on Bonds Payable, and a credit of $52,500 under ***Financing activities*** to the Extinguishment of Bonds Payable ledger account. At this point we have accounted for the decrease in the 8% Bonds Payable ledger account from $200,000 to $150,000. In addition, the debit of $750 to the Premium on Bonds Payable account in entry **5** under ***Operations***, combined with the debit of $2,500 in this transaction, **13**, explains the decrease in that account, from a balance of $10,000 on December 31, Year 4, to a balance of $6,750 on December 31, Year 5.

Treatment of Cash and Stock Dividends: Completion of Working Paper

14 The declaration of the cash dividend, $42,000, is entered in the working paper as a debit to Retained Earnings and a credit to Dividends Payable. The $22,000 balance in the Dividends Payable account means cash dividends in the amount of $20,000 were paid in Year 5. The paid dividends will be set up separately in the statement of changes in financial position, in this example.

15 The declaration of a stock dividend required a transfer from Retained Earnings to paid-in capital ledger accounts. A stock dividend has no effect on cash and is not considered as a financing or investing activity under the all-financial-resources concept of funds flows. The working paper entry for the 4% stock dividend (360 shares valued at $15 a share) requires a debit to Retained Earnings for $5,400 and a credit to Common Stock for $5,400. After this transaction is entered in the working paper, the December 31, Year 5, balances in the Common Stock and Retained Earnings ledger accounts have been substantiated.

16 For cash dividend paid in the current year, $20,000, see entry **14**.

X The working paper for statement of changes in financial position is completed as follows:

1 Total the debit and credit ''Transactions for Year 5'' columns in the top portion of the working paper to make certain all transactions (including the net change in cash) have been entered correctly. The equality of the $704,700 amounts indicates that amounts were entered correctly.

2 Total the debit and credit ''Transactions for Year 5'' columns in the bottom portion of the working paper and enter the totals ($394,100 debit column and $439,800 credit column).

3 Compute the difference between the totals of the two columns computed in **2**; the difference should equal the net change in cash coded **X** in the top portion of the working paper. The $439,800 total of the credit column, which is total ***uses*** of cash for Year 5, minus the $394,100 total of the debit column, which is total ***sources*** of cash for Year 5, equals $45,700, the decrease in cash already entered in the top portion of the working paper. The $45,700 decrease in cash, also coded **X**, is entered in the bottom portion of the ''Transactions for Year 5'' debit column, and the debit and credit columns are again totalled to show their equality in the amount of $439,800.

4 Compute the net amounts in the debit and credit ''Transactions for Year 5'' columns for ***Operations*** ($47,000 net debits), ***Investing activities*** ($95,500 net credits), ***Financing activities*** ($22,800 net debits), and ***Dividends paid*** ($20,000 credit). The net of these four amounts is a credit of $45,700 ($95,500 + $20,000 − $47,000 − $22,800 = $45,700), and measures the decrease in cash of Rose Corporation during the year ended December 31, Year 5.

The completed statement of changes in financial position appears on page 1181.

ROSE CORPORATION
Statement of Changes in Financial Position
For Year Ended December 31, Year 5

Operating activities:		
Income before extraordinary item	$ 51,300	
Add (Deduct) items not involving a flow of cash:		
Depreciation expense	30,000	
Increase in deferred income tax credits	10,000	
Investment income-equity method	(13,250)	
Amortization of premium on bonds payable	(750)	$ 77,300
Changes in noncash operating working capital:		
Decrease in accounts receivable (net)	$ 13,500	
Increase in income taxes payable	25,800	
Increase in other current liabilities	1,300	
Increase in notes receivable	(20,000)	
Increase in inventories	(38,750)	
Increase in short-term prepayments	(3,000)	
Decrease in accounts payable	(9,150)	(30,300)
Cash provided from operations		$ 47,000
Financing activities:		
Issuance of common stock in exchange for equipment	$ 92,800	
Acquisition of treasury stock	(17,500)	
Extinguishment of bonds payable	(52,500)	
Cash provided from financing activities		22,800
Investing activities:		
Acquisition of land	$(150,000)	
Acquisition of equipment for cash	$(35,200)	
Acquisition of equipment in exchange for common stock	(92,800)	
Proceeds on condemnation of building (net of income taxes)	182,500	
Cash used for investing activities		(95,500)
Dividends paid in current year		(20,000)
Decrease in cash*		$(45,700)
Cash at beginning of year		52,800
Cash at end of year		$ 7,100

*Cash position comprises cash only.

Statement of Changes in Financial Position on the Working Capital Basis

With the following modifications, the working paper on pages 1176–1177 may be used as the basis for preparation of a statement of changes in financial position on the working capital basis:

1 Compute the change in working capital during Year 5 from the ''Working capital'' line by deducting the $30,300 subtotal of the ''Transactions for Year 5'' debit column from the $67,700 subtotal of the credit column. The difference of $37,400 ($67,700 – $30,300 = $37,400) is the decrease in working capital for Year 5. The decrease in working capital also may be computed by subtracting

the working capital on December 31, Year 5, from the working capital on December 31, Year 4 ($135,500 − $98,100 = $37,400).

2 Convert cash provided from operations ($47,000) to working capital provided from operations by adding the $30,300 increase in net current assets, which are a part of working capital ($47,000 + $30,300 = $77,300 working capital provided from operations).

3 Include cash dividends ***declared***, $42,000, as a use of working capital in the statement of changes in financial position on the working capital concept. As indicated on page 1180, cash dividends must be paid to be a ***use of cash*** in a statement of changes in financial position on the cash basis. However, the declaration of cash dividends is a ***use of working capital***, because a current liability is increased.

The statement of changes in financial position on the working capital basis for Rose Corporation is illustrated below.

ROSE CORPORATION
Statement of Changes in Financial Position
For Year Ended December 31, Year 5

Operating activities:		
Net income before extraordinary item	$ 51,300	
Add (deduct) items not affecting cash:		
Depreciation expense	30,000	
Increase in deferred income tax credits	10,000	
Investment income on equity basis	(13,250)	
Amortization of premium on bonds payable	(750)	
Working capital provided from operations		$ 77,300
Cash dividends declared		(42,000)
Financing activities:		
Issuance of common stock in exchange for equipment	$ 92,800	
Acquisition of treasury stock	(17,500)	
Extinguishment of bonds payable	(52,500)	
Working capital provided from financing activities		22,800
Investing activities:		
Acquisition of land	$150,000	
Acquisition of equipment for cash	35,200	
Acquisition of equipment in exchange for common stock	92,800	
Proceeds from condemnation of building (net of income taxes)	(182,500)	
Working capital used for investing activities		(95,500)
Decrease in working capital		$ (37,400)
Balance at beginning of the year		135,500
Balance at end of the year		$ 98,100

Concluding Comments

The statements of changes in financial position illustrated in this chapter are not indicative of all the formats that might be used. Examples of statements of changes in financial position incorporating the operating, financing, and investing activities requirements follow on pages 1183–1189. Notice the location of dividends paid, the details included in the determination of cash from operations, and the placement of extraordinary items (if appropriate).

PARKLAND INDUSTRIES LTD.

CONSOLIDATED STATEMENT OF CHANGES IN FINANCIAL POSITION

(YEAR ENDED JUNE 30, 1987)

	1987	1986
	(thousands of dollars)	
Cash Provided By (Used For):		
Operations:		
Net Earnings	$ 3 919	$ 3 712
Add (Deduct) Items Not Involving Operating Cash:		
Depreciation, Depletion and Amortization	3 209	2 545
Deferred Income Taxes	877	1 471
Extraordinary Item	–	(910)
	8 005	6 818
Changes in Non-Cash Working Capital:		
Accounts Receivable	(594)	890
Inventories	(874)	(76)
Prepaid Expenses	(24)	(175)
Accounts Payable	1 265	(170)
Corporate Taxes Payable	1 772	1 315
Cash From Operations (Note 9)	9 550	8 602
Financing:		
Issue of Capital Stock	14 738	–
Net Cost of Issuing Capital Stock	(450)	–
Proceeds from Long-Term Debt	1 815	4 159
Long-Term Debt Payments	(14 692)	(5 568)
Extraordinary Item	–	910
Deferred Income Taxes on Extraordinary Item	–	228
Cash From (Used For) Financing Activities	1 411	(271)
Investments:		
Purchase of Fixed Assets	(6 044)	(7 363)
Proceeds on Sale of Fixed Assets	212	118
Investment in Other Assets	(72)	(173)
Cash (Used For) Investment Activities	(5 904)	(7 418)
Increase During the Year	5 057	913
Cash, Beginning of Year	3 346	2 433
Cash, End of Year	$ 8 403	$ 3 346
Cash Comprised of:		
Cash on Hand	$ 8 403	$ 3 346

Imasco Limited
For the years ended March 31

Consolidated Statement of Changes in Financial Position

	1987	1986	1985
	Thousands of dollars		
Operating activities			
Earnings before extraordinary items	212,646	261,745	234,108
Items not affecting working capital	55,656	147,543	125,376
Working capital provided from operations	268,302	**409,288**	**359,484**
Decrease (increase) in non-cash operating working capital	12,794	19,201	(236,462)
Deferred charges	(19,738)	(17,971)	(9,375)
Unrealized foreign exchange	10,153	(2,799)	(6,058)
Total cash from operating activities	271,511	**407,719**	**107,589**
Financing activities			
Issue of shares, net of issue costs	539,636	—	157,250
Issue of long term debt	3,261,071	85,151	93,092
Repayment of long term debt	(1,408,751)	(72,399)	(50,915)
Payments under capital leases	(4,381)	(4,576)	(3,580)
Treasury shares issued in excess of (less than) common shares purchased for cancellation	362	313	(287)
Total cash from financing activities	2,387,937	**8,489**	**195,560**
Investing activities			
Business acquisitions	(2,605,032)	(22,435)	(173,735)
Additional investment in Imasco Enterprises Inc.	(22,372)	—	—
Extraordinary items	(2,393)	66,536	—
Purchases of fixed assets	(233,860)	(184,109)	(202,078)
Proceeds from disposal of fixed assets	14,436	20,074	28,350
Disposal of investments and receivables collected	29,828	31,003	28,824
Increase in investments and receivables	(51,505)	(54,571)	(13,033)
Total cash used for investing activities	(2,870,898)	**(143,502)**	**(331,672)**
Cash and cash equivalents			
From operating activities	271,511	407,719	107,589
From financing activities	2,387,937	8,489	195,560
(For) investing activities	(2,870,898)	(143,502)	(331,672)
(For) dividends	(112,247)	**(82,018)**	**(67,421)**
Increase (decrease) for year	(323,697)	190,688	(95,944)
Beginning of year	126,497	(64,191)	31,753
End of year	(197,200)	**126,497**	**(64,191)**

Cash and cash equivalents include cash and short term investments, net of bank and other short term loans.

Silcorp Limited

CONSOLIDATED STATEMENT OF CASH FLOWS

Year ended December 28, 1986
(With comparative amounts for the years ended December 29, 1985
and December 30, 1984)

(In 000's of dollars)

	1986	1985	1984
Cash provided by (used in) operating activities:			
Net earnings	$ 2,304	$ 2,281	$ 2,715
Charges to net earnings which do not affect cash:			
Depreciation and amortization	10,398	8,330	6,449
Deferred income taxes	2,320	750	20
Cash flow from operations	15,022	11,361	9,184
Net change in non-cash working capital	2,031	(14,200)	(7,561)
Other	75	(258)	1,250
Cash provided by (used in) operating activities	17,128	(3,097)	2,873
Cash provided by (used in) investment activities:			
Additions to fixed assets	(16,224)	(21,323)	(17,049)
Acquisition of Convenience Services Limited.	(6,825)		
Purchase of goodwill		(86)	(57)
Net proceeds from disposal of fixed assets	3,087	3,448	4,028
Cash provided by (used in) investment activities	(19,962)	(17,961)	(13,078)
Cash provided by (used in) financing activities:			
Issue of convertible subordinated debentures.	57,837		
Issue of capital stock		1,387	
Net change in long-term debt	(19,687)	(2,012)	(4,632)
Net change in capital lease obligations	(3,623)	(689)	(722)
Dividends to shareholders	(836)	(807)	(807)
Cash provided by (used in) financing activities	33,691	(2,121)	(6,161)
Net increase (decrease) in cash during the year	30,857	(23,179)	(16,366)
Cash position, beginning of year	(17,402)	5,777	22,143
Cash position, end of year	$ 13,455	$(17,402)	$ 5,777
Represented by:			
Cash and short-term investments	$ 13,455	$ 11,182	$ 9,608
Bank indebtedness		(28,584)	(3,831)
	$ 13,455	$(17,402)	$ 5,777

George Weston Limited

Consolidated Cash Flow Statement

Year ended December 31, 1986

(In millions of dollars)	1986	1985	1984
Operations and working capital			
Earnings before minority interest	**$ 143.5**	$ 121.1	$ 107.3
Depreciation	**153.4**	135.5	131.2
Income taxes not requiring cash	**28.4**	16.2	17.2
Gain on sale of fixed assets	**(19.8)**	(12.1)	(3.8)
Other	**(5.3)**	.9	(.5)
Cash flow from operations	**300.2**	261.6	251.4
Provided from (used for) working capital	**(10.7)**	(28.9)	(69.0)
	289.5	232.7	182.4
Investment			
Purchase of owned fixed assets	**(389.7)**	(247.0)	(206.4)
Acquisition of subsidiary companies	**(81.5)**	(33.2)	
Proceeds from sale of fixed assets	**61.5**	40.8	30.6
Net decrease (increase) in properties held for development	**10.5**	(9.9)	1.3
Net decrease (increase) in other investments and sundry	**(10.3)**	(27.2)	1.4
	(409.5)	(276.5)	(173.1)
Financing			
Increase in long term debt	**211.7**	122.6	84.5
Reduction in long term debt	**(120.2)**	(88.7)	(48.4)
Proceeds from issue of share capital	**100.8**	.8	.3
Proceeds from issue of subsidiary's share capital	**75.4**	.8	.2
Reduction in obligations under capital leases	**(13.8)**	(9.5)	(6.3)
Purchase of minority interest	**(.6)**	(1.5)	(8.1)
	253.3	24.5	22.2
Dividends			
To shareholders	**(34.2)**	(30.9)	(29.2)
To minority shareholders in subsidiary companies	**(8.7)**	(6.3)	(6.1)
	(42.9)	(37.2)	(35.3)
Increase (decrease) in cash position*	**$ 90.4**	$ (56.5)	$ (3.8)

**Cash position is defined as cash and short term investments net of bank advances and notes payable.*

CONSOLIDATED STATEMENT OF CHANGES IN FINANCIAL POSITION

CAMPEAU CORPORATION

Year Ended December 31, 1986
(In Thousands)

	Notes	1986	1985
Operating Activities:			
Net earnings from continuing operations		$ 84,951	32,357
Items not requiring a current outlay of cash:			
Deferred income taxes		15,712	24,293
Depreciation and amortization		31,488	12,313
Amortization of financing cost		12,259	1,347
Amortization of goodwill		5,643	—
		150,053	70,310
Net changes in non-cash working capital balances related to operations:			
Accounts receivable		(193,117)	8,081
Merchandise inventory		109,742	—
Prepaid expenses		19,482	(1,097)
Accounts payable		(160,948)	2,135
Income taxes payable		92,927	—
		(131,914)	9,119
Cash provided by continuing operations		18,139	79,429
Cash provided by assets for sale	2	7,591	—
Cash applied to discontinued business assets	15	—	(7,328)
Cash provided by operating activities		25,730	72,101
Financing Activities:			
Issue and repurchase of capital stock		109,889	19,834
Short term debt related to real estate		34,066	(67,895)
Accounts payable related to development activity		56,143	6,451
Debt issued		4,646,804	613,390
Debt issue cost		(245,655)	(1,696)
Debt repaid		(4,164,118)	(286,366)
Debt issued on acquisition	2	4,810,539	—
Cash provided by financing activities		5,247,668	283,718
Investment Activities:			
Properties and equipment		38,863	—
Rental properties		60,961	144,773
Rental properties under development		137,857	186,215
Land held for development		41,425	33,719
Costs recovered from sale of properties		(27,273)	(13,375)
Acquisition of Allied Stores Corporation	2	4,957,000	—
Other		10,649	(23,157)
Assets for sale		18,374	—
Discontinued business assets	15	(15,375)	23,532
Cash applied to investment activities		5,222,481	351,707
Dividends:		11,662	4,283
Increase (decrease) in cash during year		39,255	(171)
Cash — Beginning of Year:		3,167	3,338
Cash Deficiency Acquired:		(288,720)	—
Cash — End of Year:		$ (246,298)	3,167

Cash is comprised of cash and short term investments, bank overdrafts and revolving operating facilities.

MARK RESOURCES INC.

Consolidated Statements of Changes in Financial Position

	For the year ended December 31,		
	1986	1985	1984
	(Thousands of dollars)		
Operating Activities			
Earnings (loss) before write-down	$ **(2,011)**	$ 7,319	$ 5,640
Add (deduct) items not affecting working capital			
Depletion and depreciation	**9,165**	6,798	5,579
Deferred taxes	**1,445**	8,478	8,993
Other	**229**	(1)	(20)
Working capital derived from operations	**8,828**	22,594	20,192
Net change in non-cash working capital balances related to operating activities	**1,370**	2,412	(523)
	10,198	25,006	19,669
Financing Activities			
Share capital — preferred	—	(20,000)	25,000
— common (Notes 4c and 9)	**72,704**	737	254
Long-term debt	**15,219**	6,804	(199)
Deferred revenue	**4,872**	6,678	52
Dividends on preferred shares	**(1,729)**	(2,840)	(3,488)
Other	—	(97)	(203)
Net change in non-cash working capital balances related to financing activities	**(6,291)**	3,944	47
	84,775	(4,774)	21,463
Cash Resources Provided from Operating and Financing Activities	**94,973**	20,232	41,132
Investing Activities			
Property, plant and equipment	**25,294**	42,137	44,018
Government incentive grants and credits	**(3,667)**	(4,663)	(5,449)
	21,627	37,474	38,569
Acquisition of Precambrian Shield Resources Limited (Note 9)	**72,639**	—	—
Investments and other assets	**41**	28	—
Net change in non-cash working capital balances related to investing activities	**867**	526	(1,221)
	95,174	38,028	37,348
Increase (Decrease) in Cash Resources	**(201)**	(17,796)	3,784
Cash Resources at Beginning of Year	**(830)**	16,966	13,182
Cash Resources at End of Year	**$ (1,031)**	$ (830)	$ 16,966
Cash Resources are Comprised of:			
Cash and short-term deposits	**$ —**	$ —	$ 17,374
Short-term bank loans	**(1,031)**	(830)	(408)
	$ (1,031)	$ (830)	$ 16,966

AIR CANADA

CONSOLIDATED STATEMENT OF CHANGES IN FINANCIAL POSITION

YEAR ENDED DECEMBER 31 (In thousands of dollars)

	1986	1985
Cash provided by (used for):		
Operations		
Net income (loss) before extraordinary items	**$ 35 941**	$(21 895)
Extraordinary items	**6 456**	(5 062)
Non-cash items included in net income (loss)	**148 340**	129 122
Income results	**190 737**	102 165
Change in net trade balances	**11 873**	(33 464)
Increase in advance ticket sales	**16 074**	18 075
Increase in spare parts, materials and supplies	**(12 685)**	(18 925)
Other	**(15 977)**	(3 231)
	190 022	64 620
Financing		
Subordinated perpetual bonds	**336 000**	–
Debt defeasance	**(268 671)**	–
Long-term borrowings	**9 129**	136 545
Repayment of long-term debt	**(111 129)**	(113 503)
Repayment of capital lease obligations	**(18 183)**	(22 814)
Other	**(9 150)**	15 933
	(62 004)	16 161
Investments		
Additions to fixed assets	**(87 127)**	(104 169)
Proceeds from disposal of fixed assets	**294 244**	36 491
Investment in affiliated companies	**(18 554)**	(3 884)
Dividends received from affiliated companies	**3 548**	2 390
	192 111	(69 172)
Increase in cash position	**320 129**	11 609
Cash position at beginning of year	**62 293**	50 684
Cash position at end of year	**$382 422**	$ 62 293

Cash position consists of cash and short-term investments.

APPENDIX: T-ACCOUNT METHOD FOR THE PREPARATION OF STATEMENT OF CHANGES IN FINANCIAL POSITION

The ***T-account method*** utilizes ''T accounts'' to capture the same information as the working paper method illustrated in the chapter. Thus, all the accounts required for the preparation of the statement of changes in financial position are set up in a T-account format rather than in the working paper format. The differences between the beginning and ending balances for these accounts are noted in the T accounts. (With the working paper method, the beginning and ending balances rather than their differences are noted.) These differences are accounted for by reconstructing the entries posted to these accounts during the period. (With the working paper method, the beginning and ending balances are reconciled by reconstructing the entries posted to these accounts.) The examples shown on page 1191, selected from the illustration for Rose Corporation, delineate these three basic differences.

A careful study of these examples shows clearly that the working paper and the T accounts contain the same information—that needed for the preparation of the statement of changes in financial position. The essential difference is really the format in which the information is presented. In the following example, one item from each of investing, financing, and financing activities areas of the working paper on pages 1176–1177 has been chosen. Notice that these three items go to their respective ''activity'' T account. Similar parallels can be drawn for all the other accounts in the Rose Corporation illustration. The T-account method may be more efficient, particularly for solving relatively simple problems.

The T-account method generally involves the following steps:

1 Open a T account for cash or cash and cash equivalents and debit or credit the account with the increase or decrease (change) in ''cash.'' Draw a line under this amount.

2 Open a T account for each noncurrent account with the difference between the beginning and ending balance and debit or credit the differences to these accounts. Underline each of these differences. Do the same for each current asset and current liability account not included in **1**.

3 Add the debits and credits of the T accounts. The equality of the debit and credit totals proves that the amounts have been correctly noted in these accounts (unless there are exactly offsetting errors which are usually unlikely).

4 Open a T account for ''Operating Activities'' for the reconstruction of the postings of entries related to cash from operations such as net income, extraordinary items, and items included in the income statement that do not provide cash or require the use of cash (e.g., amortization of premium on bonds payable or depreciation), and to record changes in operating net current assets accounts. This operating activities T account shows the details of cash provided from or used for operating activities.

5 Open a T account for each of ''Financing Activities'' and ''Investing Activities'' for the reconstruction of entries affecting cash and each of these activities, and also to reflect exchange-type transactions. These two T accounts

T-Account Method

Land

(Change)	150,000	
(7) Acquisition of land	150,000	

Investment in Common Stock of Z Limited (Equity method)

(Change)	13,250	
(4) Investment income	13,250	

Treasury Stock

(Change)	17,500	
(10) Acquisition of treasury stock	17,500	

Operating Activities

	13,250 (4) Investment income from Zola Limited

Financing Activities

	17,500 (10) Acquisition of treasury stock

Investing Activities

	150,000 (7) Acquisition of land

Working Paper Method

	Balances, Dec. 31, Year 4	*Transactions for Year 5*		*Balances, Dec. 31, Year 5*
		Debit	*Credit*	
Land	-0-	(7) 150,000		150,000
Investment in Common Stock of Zola Limited (equity method)	40,000	(4) 13,250		53,250
Treasury stock, 1,000 shares	-0-	(10) 17,500		17,500
Operating activity:				
Investment Income from Z Limited			(4) 13,250	
Investing activity:				
Acquisition of land			(7) 150,000	
Financing activity:				
Acquisition of treasury stock			(10) 17,500	

will collectively contain all sources and uses of cash and all exchange transactions for the reconstruction of the postings of entries affecting cash, other than the details of cash provided from or used by operations as described in **4**.

6 Analyze all available information and reconstruct the postings to account for the differences in the T accounts.

7 Check that the underlined difference in each financial statement T account other than the cash T account has been accounted for.

8 Add the ''Operating Activities'' T account and transfer the balance (this is the amount of cash provided from or used by operations) to the cash T account.

9 Add the ''Financing Activities'' T account and transfer the balance (this is the amount of cash provided by financing activities) to the cash account.

10 Add the ''Investing Activities'' T account and transfer the balance (this represents the cash used for investing activities) to the cash T account.

11 If the ''Cash Dividends Paid'' are to be shown separately in the statement, they will have a separate T account. Transfer the balance of this account to the cash T account.

12 Check that the cash T account's underlined balance is the same amount and is of the same sign as the debits and/or credits from steps **8**, **9**, **10**, and **11**.

13 Prepare the statement of changes in financial position from:
  a The ''Operating Activities'' T account, which provides all the details of cash provided from or used by operations
  b The ''Financing Activities'' T account, which provides all the details of the cash provided by financing activities
  c The ''Investing Activities'' T account, which provides all the details of cash used for investing activities
  (Review all the noncurrent T accounts to ensure that all exchange transactions have been accounted for and disclosed in the statement.)

In the section that follows, these steps are applied to the case of Rose Corporation presented earlier.

1 The information contained in the T accounts after steps **1** to **5** is as follows (the total of debits, $509,900, equals the total of credits, $509,900:

Cash		*Notes Receivable*		*Accounts Receivable*		*Inventories*	
	45,700	20,000			13,500	38,750	

Short-Term Prepayments	
3,000	

Dividends Payable	
	22,000

Accounts Payable	
9,150	

Income Taxes Payable	
	25,800

Other Current Liabilities	
	1,300

Investment in Zola Limited (Equity method)	
13,250	

Land	
150,000	

Building and Equipment	
	272,000

Treasury Stock	
17,500	

Accumulated Depreciation	
170,000	

8% Bonds Payable	
50,000	

Premium on Bonds Payable	
3,250	

Deferred Income Taxes	
35,000	

Common Stock	
	98,200

Retained Earnings	
	31,400

Operating Activities	

Financing Activities	

Investing Activities	

2 After analyzing all available information and reconstructing the postings to account for the differences in the T accounts as required by step **6**, the T accounts presented in **2** above will be as follows:

Cash	
	45,700

Notes Receivable	
20,000	
(6) 20,000	

Accounts Receivable	
	13,500
	13,500 (6)

Inventories	
38,750	
(6) 38,750	

Short-Term Prepayments	
3,000	
(6) 3,000	

Dividends Payable	
	22,000
	42,000 (14)
(16) 20,000	

Accounts Payable	
9,150	
(6) 9,150	

Income Taxes Payable	
	25,800
	25,800 (6)

Other Current Liabilities	
	1,300
	1,300 (6)

Investment in Zola Limited (Equity Method)	
13,250	
(4) 13,250	

Land	
150,000	
(7) 150,000	

Building and Equipment	
	272,000
(8) 35,200	400,000 (10)
(9) 92,800	

Treasury Stock	
17,500	
(12) 17,500	

Accumulated Depreciation	
170,000	
(10) 200,000	30,000 (2)

8% Bonds Payable	
50,000	
(13) 50,000	

Premium on Bonds Payable	
3,250	
(13) 2,500	
(5) 750	
3,250	

Deferred Income Taxes	
35,000	
(10) 45,000	10,000 (3)

Common Stock	
	98,200
	92,800 (11)
	5,400 (15)

Retained Earnings	
	31,400
(14) 42,000	78,800 (1)
(15) 5,400	

*Cash Dividends Paid**	
	20,000 (16)

*"Cash dividends paid" may be included in either operating activities or financing activities, or be separately disclosed, in the statement of changes in financial position. In this example, they are separately disclosed, necessitating a separate T account for them.

Operating Activities

	Debit	Credit	
(1) Net income	78,800	27,500	(10) Extraordinary gain
Income before extraordinary gain	51,300	13,250	(4) Investment income
(2) Depreciation expense	30,000	750	(5) Amortization of premium on bonds payable
(3) Deferred income taxes	10,000		
(6) Decrease in accounts receivable	13,500	20,000	(6) Increase in notes receivable
(6) Increase in income taxes payable	25,800	38,750	(6) Increase in inventories
		3,000	(6) Increase in short-term prepayments
(6) Increase in other current liabilities	1,300	9,150	(6) Decrease in accounts payable

Financing Activities

	Debit	Credit	
(11) Issuance of common stock in exchange for equipment	92,800	17,500	(10) Acquisition of treasury stock
		52,500	(13) Extinguishment of bonds payable

Investing Activities

	Debit	Credit	
(10) Proceeds on condemnation of building (net of income taxes)	182,500	150,000	(7) Acquisition of land
		35,200	(8) Acquisition of equipment
		92,800	(9) Acquisition of equipment for common stock

3 Add the ''Operating activities,'' ''Financing activities,'' ''Investing activities,'' and ''Cash dividends paid'' T accounts and transfer their balances to the ''Cash'' T account as indicated in steps **8** to **11**. Check that the ''Cash'' T account is in balance (step 12). These five T accounts, after the steps have been performed, are as follows:

Cash

Debit	Credit
	45,700
(17) 47,000	95,500 (19)
(18) 22,800	20,000 (20)

Cash Dividends Paid

Debit	Credit
	20,000 (16)
(20) Transfer to Cash account 20,000	

Operating Activities

	Debit	Credit	
(1) Net income	78,800	27,500	(10) Extraordinary gain
Income before extraordinary gain	51,300	13,250	(4) Investment income
(2) Depreciation expense	30,000	750	(5) Amortization of premium on bonds payable
(3) Deferred income taxes	10,000		
(6) Decrease in accounts receivable	13,500	20,000	(6) Increase in notes receivable
(6) Increase in income taxes payable	25,800	38,750	(6) Increase in inventories
(6) Increase in other current liabilities	1,300	3,000	(6) Increase in short-term prepayments
		9,150	(6) Decrease in accounts payable
	131,900	84,900	
		47,000	(17) Transfer to Cash account
	131,900	131,900	

Financing Activities

	Debit	Credit	
(11) Issuance of common stock in exchange for equipment	92,800	17,500	(10) Acquisition of treasury stock
		52,500	(13) Extinguishment of bonds payable
	92,800	70,000	
		22,800	(18) Transfer to Cash account
	92,800	92,800	

Investing Activities

	Debit	Credit	
(10) Proceeds on condemnation of building (net of income taxes)	182,500	150,000	(7) Acquisition of land
		35,200	(8) Acquisition of equipment
		92,800	(9) Acquisition of equipment for common stock
	182,500	278,000	
(19) Transfer to Cash account	95,500		
	278,000	278,000	

4 Review all the noncurrent T accounts to ensure that all exchange-type transactions have been accounted for.

5 Use the information in the ''Activities'' and ''Cash Dividends Paid'' T accounts to prepare the statement of changes in financial position. This statement will be the same as that on page 1181.

Note: While the following entries are not required for the T-account method, they further explain the reconstruction of the transactions posted to the T accounts and are very useful as an educational methodology. The entries are numbered in the same manner as the postings.

	Account	Debit	Credit
1	Operating Activities (Net Income)	78,800	
	Retained Earnings		78,800
2	Operating Activities (Depreciation Expense)	30,000	
	Accumulated Depreciation		30,000
3	Operating Activities	10,000	
	Deferred Income Taxes		10,000
4	Investment in Zola Limited Common Stock	13,250	
	Operating Activities (Investment Income)		13,250
5	Premium on Bonds Payable	750	
	Operating Activities (Interest Expense)		750
6	Operating Activities (Accounts Receivable)	13,500	
	Operating Activities (Income Taxes Payable)	25,800	
	Operating Activities (Other Current Liabilities)	1,300	
	Notes Receivable	20,000	
	Inventories	38,750	
	Short-Term Prepayments	3,000	
	Accounts Payable	9,150	
	Accounts Receivable		13,500
	Income Taxes Payable		25,800

		Debit	Credit
	Other Current Liabilities		1,300
	Operating Activities:		
	Notes Receivable		20,000
	Inventories		38,750
	Short-Term Prepayments		3,000
	Accounts Payable		9,150
7	Land	150,000	
	Investing Activities		150,000
8	Buildings and Equipment	35,200	
	Investing Activities		35,200
9	Buildings and Equipment	92,800	
	Investing Activities		92,800
10	Investing Activities	182,500	
	Accumulated Depreciation	200,000	
	Deferred Income Taxes	45,000	
	Buildings and Equipment		400,000
	Operating Activities (Extraordinary Item)		27,500
11	Financing Activities	92,800	
	Common Stock		92,800
12	Treasury Stock	17,500	
	Financing Activities		17,500
13	8% Bonds Payable	50,000	
	Premium on Bonds Payable	2,500	
	Financing Activities		52,500
14	Retained Earnings	42,000	
	Dividends Payable		42,000
15	Retained Earnings	5,400	
	Common Stock		5,400
16	Dividends Payable	20,000	
	Cash Dividends Paid		20,000
17	Cash	47,000	
	Operating Activities		47,000
18	Cash	22,800	
	Financing Activities		22,800
19	Investing Activities	95,500	
	Cash		95,500
20	Cash Dividends Paid	20,000	
	Cash		20,000

REVIEW QUESTIONS

1. What are some meanings that have been given to the term ***funds*** in the preparation of a statement of changes in financial position?
2. Briefly describe the ***all-financial-resources*** concept of funds flows, and give some examples of ***exchange transactions***.
3. Why has the Accounting Standards Committee adopted the cash and cash equivalents definition of funds?
4. Could cash and cash equivalents represent cash only? Explain.

5 Give an example of each of the following situations, assuming preparation of a statement of changes in financial position on the cash flow basis.
   a A decrease in a noncurrent asset that is ***not*** a source of cash
   b A decrease in a noncurrent asset that ***is*** a source of cash
   c An increase in a noncurrent liability that is ***not*** a source of cash
   d A decrease in shareholders' equity that ***is*** a use of cash
   e An increase in shareholders' equity that is ***not*** a source of cash
   f An increase in a noncurrent asset that is ***not*** a use of cash
   g A decrease in a noncurrent liability that is ***not*** a use of cash
6 Explain how each of the following enters into the computation of cash provided from operations in a statement of changes in financial position on the cash flow basis:
   a Increases in inventories and short-term prepayments
   b Increases in accrued liabilities (including income taxes payable)
   c Decreases in accounts and notes payable to suppliers
   d Increase in dividends payable (from zero in the preceding year)
7 "Last year, Elixir Oil Limited earned $8 a share on sales of $250 million. Its cash flow for the year, a generous $60 million, represented a high return on equity capital." Comment on the implications of this quotation.
8 The following transaction was recorded by Dover Limited in Year 6:

Land	35,000	
Buildings	450,000	
Mortgage Note Payable (Long-Term)		380,000
Short-Term Investments		50,000
Cash		55,000
To record acquisition of land and buildings.		

Describe how this transaction may be reported in Dover Limited's statement of changes in financial position that lists operating, financing, and investing activities separately for Year 6 on the cash flow basis.
9 Garr Limited has outstanding a $5 million issue of serial bonds. The first series of bonds, in the amount of $500,000, matures in July, Year 10. In preparing Garr's statement of changes in financial position on the working capital basis for calendar Year 9, Garr's accountant recorded a use of working capital of $500,000 relating to these bonds. Is this correct? Explain. What disposition of this item would have occurred if the statement were prepared on the cash flow basis?
10 How is the extinguishment of bonds payable reported in a statement of changes in financial position on the cash flow basis, assuming that sinking-fund investments are liquidated and the proceeds are used to extinguish the bonds?
11 Explain how the ***declaration*** and the ***payment*** of cash dividends are handled in the preparation of a statement of changes in financial position on the:
   a Cash basis
   b Working capital basis

12 Does doubtful accounts expense enter into the computation of cash provided from operations? Explain.

13 Under the ***all-financial-resources*** concept of funds flows, the accountant for Everly Limited reported a 5% common stock dividend distributed with a current market value of $18,000 as a financing activity on the cash flow basis in the statement of changes in financial position. Is this treatment correct? Explain.

14 State in which one, if any, of the categories ***operations***, ***investing activities***, and ***financing activities*** each of the following would be included for a statement of changes in financial position on the cash basis:

a Extraordinary item (gain) relating to operations
b Acquisition of equipment in exchange for long-term promissory note
c Reissuance of treasury stock
d Classification of current portion of long-term debt as a current liability

15 State how ***cash provided from operations*** appearing in a statement of changes in financial position on the cash basis, wherein cash, temporary investments, and temporary loans are included in the definition of cash flow, may be converted to ***working capital provided from operations***.

EXERCISES

Ex. 23-1 Select the best answer for each of the following multiple-choice questions:

1 Which of the following is disclosed in a statement of changes in financial position on the cash basis as both a financing and an investing activity?
a Acquisition of plant assets in exchange for common stock
b Distribution of common stock dividend
c Refunding of a bond issue
d Conversion of convertible bonds to common stock
e None of the foregoing

2 How is the amortization of discount on bonds payable disclosed in a statement of changes in financial position on the cash and cash equivalents basis?
a It is not disclosed
b As an investing activity
c As an expense not requiring the use of cash, in the operating activities area
d None of the foregoing

3 In the preparation of a statement of changes in financial position on the cash basis, an increase in inventories is an adjustment to net income because:
a Cash was increased, inventories being a current asset
b Inventories are an expense in the measurement of net income, but do not require the use of cash
c The increase in inventories resulted from purchases in excess of cost of goods sold, and thus is an assumed use of cash
d All changes in noncash ledger accounts are disclosed under the all-financial-resources concept

4 In a statement of changes in financial position on the cash and cash equivalents basis including accounts receivable and accounts payable in the definition of cash equivalents, is doubtful accounts expense added to net income if it relates to current accounts receivable? Long-term accounts receivable? Answer *a*, *b*, *c*, or *d* according to the following table.

	Current accounts receivable	*Long-term accounts receivable*
a	Yes	Yes
b	Yes	No
c	No	No
d	No	Yes

5 Nolo Corporation uses the allowance method of accounting for doubtful current accounts receivable. During Year 7, Nolo debited Doubtful Accounts Expense for $30,000 and debited Allowance for Doubtful Accounts for uncollectible accounts receivable totalling $25,200. In Nolo's statement of changes in financial position on the cash basis, these journal entries are treated as a decrease in cash of:
a $0 *b* $4,800 *c* $25,200 *d* $30,000 *e* Some other amount

6 Patents amortization expense is presented in a statement of changes in financial position on the cash flow basis as:
- *a* A financing and an investing activity
- *b* A financing activity
- *c* An addition to net income
- *d* A deduction from net income

7 A loss on the disposal of machinery is presented in a statement of changes in financial position on the cash flow basis as:
- *a* A deduction from net income
- *b* An addition to net income
- *c* A financing activity
- *d* An investing activity

8 Kregar Limited sold a computer in Year 2 for $70,000. The cost of the computer was $250,000, and the accumulated depreciation on the date of sale was $200,000. If ***funds*** are defined as cash and cash equivalents, the sale of the computer appears in Kregar's Year 2 statement of changes in financial position as:
- *a* A deduction from net income of $20,000 and a financing activity item in the amount of $50,000
- *b* An addition to net income of $20,000 and a financing activity item in the amount of $50,000
- *c* A deduction from net income of $20,000 and an investing activity item in the amount of $70,000
- *d* A financing activity item in the amount of $70,000
- *e* Some other item

9 Which of the following is presented in a statement of changes in financial position only because of the ***all-financial-resources*** concept of funds flows?

a Conversion of preferred stock to common stock
b Acquisition of treasury stock for cash
c Issuance of common stock for cash
d Declaration of cash dividend

10 Which of the following is an operating activities item?
a Disposal of plant assets for cash
b Writeoff of trade account receivable against the allowance for doubtful accounts
c Long-term borrowing
d None of the foregoing

11 An example of an addition to income before extraordinary item made in the computation of cash provided from operations in a statement of changes in financial postion is:
a Increase in net accounts receivable
b Decrease in accounts payable
c Decrease in short-term prepayments
d Increase in inventories
e None of the foregoing

12 Do cash dividends declared in the preceding accounting period and paid in the current period appear in a statement of changes in financial position for the current period prepared on the working capital basis? Cash basis? Answer ***a***, ***b***, ***c***, or ***d*** according to the following table.

	Working capital basis	*Cash basis*
a	Yes	Yes
b	Yes	No
c	No	Yes
d	No	No

Ex. 23-2 Enderle Limited's statement of changes in financial position shows operating, financing, and investing activities on the cash basis. Here is selected accounting information for Enderle for Year 6:

Cash provided from operations	$1,500,000
Mortgage note payable issued in exchange for land and building	1,800,000
Common stock issued pursuant to conversion of preferred stock	500,000
Cash from disposal of equipment at a gain of $60,000	400,000
Cost of equipment acquired for cash	200,000

Compute Enderle Company's total investing activities for Year 6.

Ex. 23-3 From the following data for Murdoch, Inc., compute the amount of cash provided from operations during Year 5:

	Dec. 31, Year 5	Jan. 1, Year 5
Accounts receivable (net)	$20,200	$15,200
Accounts payable	15,000	24,000
Accumulated depreciation (no plant assets were retired during the year)	32,000	26,000
Inventories	30,000	27,500
Other current liabilities	3,600	1,600
Short-term prepayments	2,200	3,000
Net income	41,300	

Ex. 23-4 The following data are taken from the latest comparative balance sheets of Avila Corporation:

	June 30, Year 2	June 30, Year 1
Cash	$ 20,000	$ 15,000
Short-term investments (marketable equity securities, net of allowance)	40,000	55,000
Accounts receivable (net)	50,000	30,000
Inventories	70,000	60,000
Short-term prepayments	5,000	3,000
Noncurrent assets (net)	242,500	209,000
Notes payable (current)	25,000	40,000
Accounts payable	60,000	30,000
Other current liabilities	2,500	2,000
Long-term debt and shareholders' equity	340,000	300,000

Compute the change in non-cash operating working capital to be included in Avila Corporation's statement of changes in financial position on the cash and cash equivalents basis for the year ended June 30, Year 2.

Ex. 23-5 Venice Corporation reported net income of $50,000 and declared and paid dividends of $25,000 in Year 2. Here are balance sheets on December 31, Year 2 and Year 1:

VENICE CORPORATION
Balance Sheets
December 31, Year 2 and Year 1

	Year 2	Year 1
Assets		
Cash	$ 82,500	$ 12,500
Accounts receivable (net)	67,500	37,500
Inventories	80,000	100,000
Equipment (net)	380,000	300,000
Total assets	$610,000	$450,000

Liabilities & Shareholders' Equity		
Accounts payable	$ 40,000	$ 25,000
Bonds payable (due in Year 15)	80,000	100,000
Common stock, no par value	290,000	150,000
Retained earnings	200,000	175,000
Total liabilities & shareholders' equity	$610,000	$450,000

Equipment was acquired for $75,000 cash, common stock with a current fair value of $40,000 was issued in exchange for equipment, and additional common stock was issued for cash.

Prepare Venice Corporation's statement of changes in financial position on the cash basis for Year 2. Dividends are to be shown separately.

Ex. 23-6 The following are condensed comparative balance sheets of Marquess Limited for Years 7 and 6 ended December 31:

MARQUESS LIMITED
Balance Sheets
December 31, Year 7 and Year 6

	Year 7	*Year 6*
Assets		
Current assets	$ 474,000	$ 320,000
Equipment	1,230,000	1,200,000
Accumulated depreciation of equipment	(436,000)	(420,000)
Goodwill (net)	480,000	500,000
Total assets	$1,748,000	$1,600,000
Liabilities & Shareholders' Equity		
Current liabilities	$ 360,000	$ 161,000
Bonds payable	400,000	600,000
Discount on bonds payable	(12,000)	(21,000)
Common stock, no par value	1,112,000	1,112,000
Retained earnings (deficit)	(112,000)	(252,000)
Total liabilities & shareholders' equity	$1,748,000	$1,600,000

During Year 7, Marquess sold, at no gain or loss, equipment with a carrying amount of $76,000, and acquired equipment for $150,000 cash. On January 2, Year 7, Marquess extinguished, again at no gain or loss, long-term bonds payable with a face amount of $200,000. No dividends were declared or paid in Year 7.

a Compute working capital provided from operations for Marquess Company for the year ended December 31, Year 7.

b Assuming that bonds with a face amount of $100,000 became current on December 31, Year 7, compute Marquess Limited's increase or decrease in working capital for the year ended December 31, Year 7.

Ex. 23-7 Cash and cash equivalents of Orrum Limited on December 31, Year 3, was $10,000,000. Here is selected information for Orrum for Year 4:

Cash provided from operations	$1,700,000
Acquisitions of plant assets for cash	3,000,000
Proceeds from short-term borrowings	1,000,000
Proceeds from long-term borrowings on bonds	2,000,000
Payments of short-term borrowings	500,000
Payments of long-term borrowings on bonds	600,000
Cash from issuance of common stock	1,400,000
Dividends declared and paid on common stock	800,000

Compute Orrum Limited's cash and cash equivalents balance on December 31, Year 4. Orrum does ***not*** consider short-term borrowings to be a cash equivalent item.

Ex. 23-8 Ledger account balances of Fortune Corporation relating to equipment during Year 8 follow:

	Dec. 31, Year 8	*Jan. 1, Year 8*
Equipment	$210,000	$96,000
Less: Accumulated depreciation	38,000	30,000

Equipment with a carrying amount of $10,000 and cost of $25,000 was sold during Year 8 at a gain of $4,000.

Compute the following for Fortune Corporation for Year 8:

a Cash provided from disposal of equipment
b Cash used to acquire equipment
c Depreciation expense added to net income in the computation of cash provided from operations

Ex. 23-9 Explain how each of the following transactions is shown in a statement of changes in financial position for Year 10, prepared on the cash basis.

a Cash dividends of $200,000 were declared on December 11, Year 10, payable on January 14, Year 11.
b A 5% common stock dividend was distributed; the market value of the dividend shares, $1,020,000, was transferred from Retained Earnings to Common Stock.
c Mining properties valued at $380,000 were acquired on January 2, Year 10, in exchange for bonds payable with a face amount of $400,000. The bonds were to mature on December 31, Year 19. The straight-line method is used for amortization of bond discount.
d An additional income tax assessment of $98,000 was debited to the Retained Earnings ledger account as a prior-period adjustment. The assessment,

which was paid in Year 10, resulted from a material error in the preparation of prior years' income tax returns.

e Oil exploration costs of $200,000 were deferred in Year 9 for financial accounting but were deducted in the computation of taxable income. As a result, the Deferred Income Tax Credits ledger account was credited for $90,000. In Year 10, the deferred oil exploration costs were written off as follows:

Oil Exploration Expenses	110,000	
Deferred Income Tax Credits	90,000	
Deferred Oil Exploration Costs		200,000
To write off deferred oil exploration costs.		

Ex. 23-10 Widmark Limited had net income of $80,600 for Year 5. The following items were included in the measurement of net income:

Compensation expense (value of compensatory stock options)	$ 24,000
Amortization of premium on bonds payable	5,000
Investment loss from 25%-owned investee	120,000
Depreciation expense	45,000
Doubtful accounts expense (current accounts receivable)	11,200
Unrealized loss in value of marketable equity securities (current portfolio)	25,000
Amortization of organization costs	3,000
Write-down of obsolete inventories to cost of goods sold	18,000
Income taxes expense, of which $27,000 was deferred to Year 8	70,000
Gross profit recognized on construction-type contracts in process	35,000
Extraordinary item (gain), net of income tax effect of $33,750	41,250

Compute the amount of working capital provided from operations for Widmark Limited in Year 5.

Ex. 23-11 Here are comparative balance sheets for Job Limited on December 31, Year 2, and Year 1:

JOB LIMITED
Comparative Balance Sheets
December 31, Year 2 and Year 1

	Year 2	*Year 1*
Assets		
Cash	$ 52,500	$ 65,000
Accounts receivable (net)	100,000	90,000
Inventories	97,500	40,000
Plant assets	260,000	155,000
Less: Accumulated depreciation of plant assets	(80,000)	(50,000)
Total assets	$430,000	$300,000

Liabilities & Shareholders' Equity		
Accounts payable	$ 70,000	$ 55,000
Common stock, no par value	305,000	200,000
Retained earnings	55,000	45,000
Total liabilities & shareholders' equity	$430,000	$300,000

On June 15, Year 2, Job issued 8,000 shares of common stock in exchange for equipment. There were no disposals of plant assets in Year 2. Dividends of $25,000 were declared and paid to shareholders during Year 2. The allowance for doubtful accounts was reduced by $3,000 during Year 2 as a result of writing off accounts receivable known to be uncollectible, and increased by $5,000 on December 31, Year 2, to record doubtful accounts expense. The net income may be derived from the data given.

Prepare Job Limited's statement of changes in financial position on the cash basis showing operating, investing, and financing activities for Year 2, without using a working paper.

Ex. 23-12 A summary of the financial position of Nansen Limited on February 28, Year 10 and Year 9, is shown below:

	Feb. 28, Year 10	*Feb. 28, Year 9*
Working capital	$ 87,500	$ 96,000
Noncurrent assets:		
Investment in Tolliver, Inc., common stock (equity method)	82,500	75,000
Land	60,000	45,000
Buildings	120,000	100,000
Less: Accumulated depreciation of buildings	(50,000)	(46,000)
Totals	$300,000	$270,000
Long-term debt & shareholders' equity:		
Notes payable, due Feb. 28, Year 15	$ 20,000	
Common stock, no par value	200,000	$200,000
Retained earnings	80,000	70,000
Totals	$300,000	$270,000

The net income of $25,000 (after depreciation expense of $4,000) included investment income (equity method) of $7,500 from Tolliver, Inc. A cash dividend was declared and paid during the year ended February 28, Year 10.

Prepare Nansen Limited's statement of changes in financial position on the working capital basis showing operating, investing, and financing activities, without using a working paper.

Ex. 23-13 The following illustration shows selected financial statements of Willard Corporation. Total assets in Willard Corporation's balance sheet on December 31, Year 1, were $110,000. Accumulated depreciation on the equipment disposed of was $6,000.

On the basis of information available from the balance sheet on January 1, Year 1, and the statement of changes in financial position for Year 1, prepare a balance sheet for Willard Corporation on December 31, Year 1.

WILLARD CORPORATION
Balance Sheet
January 1, Year 1

Assets	
Current assets	$ 37,000
Equipment	48,000
Less: Accumulated depreciation of equipment	(15,000)
Patents (net)	5,000
Total assets	$ 75,000
Liabilities & Shareholders' Equity	
Current liabilities	$ 12,000
Common stock, no par value	27,000
Retained earnings	36,000
Total liabilities & shareholders' equity	$ 75,000

WILLARD CORPORATION
Statement of Changes in Financial Position
For Year Ended December 31, Year 1

Working capital, Jan. 1, Year 1		$ 25,000
Operating activities:		
Net income	$ 24,000	
Add: Depreciation expense	10,000	
Amortization expense (patents)	1,000	
Less: Gain in disposal of equipment	(4,000)	
Working capital provided from operations		31,000
Financing activities:		
Issuance of common stock		13,000
Investing activities:		
Disposal of equipment	$ (7,000)	
Acquisition of land	14,000	
Acquisition of equipment	30,000	37,000
Dividend declared		12,000
Working capital, Dec. 31, Year 1		$ 20,000

CASES

Case 23-1 Cody Engineering Limited is a growing manufacturer of electronic instruments and technical equipment. You have been retained by Cody to advise it in the preparation of a statement of changes in financial position on the cash basis, showing operating, investing, and financing activities. For the year ended October 31, Year 2, you obtained the following information concerning certain transactions and events relating to Cody:

1 Net income for the year was $800,000, which included a deduction for an extraordinary loss of $93,000 (see item *5* below).
2 Depreciation expense of $240,000 was included in the income statement.
3 Uncollectible accounts receivable of $30,000 were written off against the allowance for doubtful accounts. Also, $37,000 of doubtful accounts expense was included in the measurement of net income for the year, and the same amount was added to the allowance for doubtful accounts.
4 A gain of $4,700 was recognized on the disposal of a machine having a cost of $75,000, of which $25,000 was undepreciated on the date of sale.
5 On April 1, Year 2, a freak lightning storm caused an uninsured inventories loss of $93,000 ($180,000 loss, less reduction in income taxes of $87,000). This extraordinary loss was included in net income as indicated in *1* above.
6 On July 3, Year 2, land and building were acquired for $600,000; Cody gave in payment $100,000 cash, $200,000 current fair value of its unissued common stock, and a $300,000 mortgage note payable due in three years.
7 On August 3, Year 2, $700,000 face amount of Cody's 10% convertible debentures were converted under the carrying amount (book value) method to no-par-value common stock. The bonds had been issued at face amount.
8 Cody's board of directors declared a $320,000 cash dividend on October 20, Year 2, payable on November 15, Year 2, to stockholders of record on November 5, Year 2.

Instructions

State whether each of the eight items above is a source or a use of cash and explain how it is disclosed in Cody Engineering Limited's statement of changes in financial position on the cash basis for the year ended October 31, Year 2. If an item is neither a source nor a use of cash, explain why it is not and indicate the disclosure, if any, that is made of the item in Cody's statement of changes in financial position for the year ended October 31, Year 2.

Case 23-2 Information concerning the debt and shareholders' equity of Worthy Limited for the year ended December 31, Year 5, is shown below.

Short-term borrowings:	
Balance, Dec. 31, Year 4	$ 1,200,000
Proceeds from borrowings in Year 5	1,500,000
Payments made in Year 5	(1,400,000)
Balance, Dec. 31, Year 5	$ 1,300,000
Current portion of long-term debt:	
Balance, Dec. 31, Year 4	$ 5,500,000
Transfers from caption "Long-term debt"	6,000,000
Payments made in Year 5	(5,500,000)
Balance, Dec. 31, Year 5	$ 6,000,000
Long-term debt:	
Balance, Dec. 31, Year 4	$ 42,500,000

Proceeds from borrowings in Year 5	18,000,000
Transfers to caption "Current portion of long-term debt"	$ (6,000,000)
Payments made in Year 5	(10,000,000)
Balance, Dec. 31, Year 5	$ 44,500,000

Shareholders' equity, Dec. 31, Year 4:	
Convertible preferred stock, no par value, each share convertible to two shares of common stock, authorized 60,000 shares, issued and outstanding 55,000 shares	$ 1,100,000
Common stock, no par value, authorized 3,000,000 shares, issued and outstanding 2,000,000 shares	24,225,000
Retained earnings	10,650,000
Total shareholders' equity	$ 35,975,000

During Year 5, 30,000 shares of the convertible preferred stock were converted to common stock. Also during Year 5, 100,000 shares of common stock were issued for cash at $25 a share.

Instructions

a Assuming that ***funds*** are defined as cash and short-term borrowings, show how the above information is presented in Worthy Limited's statement of changes in financial position listing "financing activities" and "investing activities," if appropriate, for the year ended December 31, Year 5.

b Explain why each change in the accounts listed above is included in or excluded from the statement of changes in financial position for Year 5. Disregard "operating activities" and dividends declared for Year 5.

Case 23-3 The statement of changes in financial position on page 1210 was improperly prepared by the accountant for Mercer Limited. The accountant was unaware that the "cash basis" was now used.

Helen Breen, the president of Mercer, is upset because she had hoped to increase cash during Year 1 by at least $100,000. Furthermore, she is somewhat confused with the arrangement of the statement and wonders if she should plan to issue additional shares of common stock early in Year 2 to "replenish cash."

Instructions

a Identify and discuss the weaknesses in the presentation of the foregoing statement of changes in financial position of Mercer Limited for Year 1. Your discussion should explain why you consider the items to be weaknesses and suggest the proper treatment of any item improperly presented.

b Prepare a revised statement of changes in financial position on the cash basis, according to section 1540 of the ***CICA Handbook***, and advise Helen Breen, the president, whether Mercer Limited should issue additional shares of common stock to replenish cash.

MERCER LIMITED
Statement of Changes in Financial Position
December 31, Year 1

Funds provided:	
Acquisition of land	$105,000
Credit change in operating working capital in Year 1, excluding cash and other current items listed separately in this statement	30,000
Stock dividend distributed	50,000
Acquisition of equipment	15,000
Acquisition of marketable equity securities as short-term investments	150,000
Total funds provided	$350,000
Funds applied:	
Net income (including gain of $20,000 on disposal of equipment, net of income taxes)	$120,000
Short-term borrowings	85,000
Depreciation and amortization expense	60,000
Disposal of equipment—carrying amount (disposed of at gain of $20,000, net of income taxes)	10,000
Distribution of common stock as a stock dividend	$ 50,000
Decrease in working capital	25,000
Total funds applied	$350,000

Case 23-4 The income statement for Weatherby Limited for Year 3 included the following items:

Net income	$459,500
Deferred income taxes expense	20,000
Depreciation expense	160,000
Discount on long-term investment in bonds	1,000
Amortization of discount on bonds payable	1,500
Doubtful accounts expense (relating to current accounts receivable)	7,600
Realized gross profit on installment sales made in Years 1 and 2	62,000
Gain on disposal of equipment	102,000
Interest revenue	4,800
Expenses for Year 3 that will be paid in Year 4	12,000
Amortization of deferred investment tax credit	4,000
Investment income on investment in Allen Limited common stock (equity method of accounting)	5,000

Instructions

a Determine the amount of Weatherby Limited's working capital provided from operations for Year 3, assuming that the effects of nonoperating transactions on working capital are reported separately.

b Briefly explain the effect on Weatherby Limited's working capital of each of the foregoing items.

Case 23-5 The statement of changes in financial position for Allen Archer Corporation is shown in the next illustration.

ALLEN ARCHER CORPORATION
Statement of Changes in Financial Position
For Year Ended March 31, Year 10
(In thousands of dollars)

Financial resources provided:				
Operations—income before gain on disposal of aircraft (extraordinary item)			$ 3,700	(1)
Add: Decrease in net current assets			5,380	(20)
Depreciation			6,000	(2)
Deferred income taxes, amortization of investment tax credit, and deferred bond issue costs			1,400	(3)
Net loss of unconsolidated subsidiaries			450	(4)
Cash provided from operations			$ 17,000	(5)
Gain on disposal of aircraft, including $1 million of deferred income taxes			2,100	(6)
Addition to long-term debt			40,000	(7)
Issuance of common stock			5,800	(8)
Disposal of aircraft (carrying amount)			1,800	(9)
Increase in current portion of contracts receivable on aircraft leases			1,200	(10)
Total financial resources provided			$ 67,900	
Financial resources applied:				
Dividends paid on common stock	$ 610	(11)		
Addition to long-term contracts receivable, excluding aircraft reclassifications	3,205	(12)		
Long-term investment of funds held for acquisition of aircraft	4,785	(13)		
Additions to flight equipment, other equipment, and deposits on aircraft acquisition contracts	62,100	(14)		
Long-term debt refinanced	12,000	(15)		
Provision for current portion of long-term debt	8,500	(16)		
Long-term advances to unconsolidated subsidiaries	2,250	(17)		
Total financial resources applied			93,450	
Increase (decrease) in cash			$ (25,550)	(18)
Cash, end of year			$ 12,600	(19)

Instructions

a Briefly explain items 1 to 20 and comment on their inclusion in the foregoing statement of changes in financial position.

b Prepare a statement of changes in financial position in accordance with the requirements of section 1540 of the ***CICA Handbook***.

PROBLEMS

Pr. 23-1 Financial statements of Werther Limited for the year ended November 30, Year 3, ***its first year of operations***, are presented in the next illustrations.

WERTHER LIMITED
Statement of Income and Retained Earnings
For Year Ended November 30, Year 3

Net sales		$700,000
Costs and expenses:		
Cost of goods sold	$350,000	
Operating expenses	160,000	
Interest expense	20,000	530,000
Income before income taxes		$170,000
Income taxes expense:		
Current	$ 72,000	
Deferred	4,500	76,500
Net income		$ 93,500
Less: Cash dividends declared and paid ($0.60 a share)		30,000
Retained earnings, end of year		$ 63,500

WERTHER LIMITED
Balance Sheet
November 30, Year 3

Assets		
Current assets:		
Cash		$ 25,000
Accounts receivable (net)		60,000
Inventories		95,000
Short-term prepayments		1,500
Total current assets		$181,500
Plant assets (net of $60,000 accumulated depreciation)		480,000
Total assets		$661,500
Liabilities & Shareholders' Equity		
Current liabilities:		
Accounts payable		$ 30,000
Income taxes payable		72,000
Current portion of long-term debt		40,000
Total current liabilities		$142,000
Long-term debt:		
10% note payable, due $40,000 a year with interest on unpaid balance	$120,000	
Deferred income tax credits	4,500	124,500
Total liabilities		$266,500
Shareholders' equity:		
Common stock, no par value, authorized 100,000 shares, issued and outstanding 50,000 shares	$331,500	
Retained earnings	63,500	395,000
Total liabilities & shareholders' equity		$661,500

Additional Information for Year Ended November 30, Year 3

1 On December 1, Year 2, Werther Limited (1) issued 50,000 shares of common stock at $6.63 a share; (2) borrowed $200,000 from a bank on a 10% long-term note payable, which was due $40,000 a year plus interest on the unpaid balance, beginning November 30, Year 3; and (3) acquired plant assets costing $540,000 for cash of $531,500 and an account payable of $8,500. There were no other acquisitions or disposals of plant assets during the year ended November 30, Year 3. Werther began operations on December 1, Year 2.
2 On November 30, Year 3, Werther (1) declared and paid a cash dividend of $0.60 a share to the common shareholders; and (2) paid $40,000 principal and $20,000 interest ($200,000 × 0.10 = $20,000) to the bank.
3 Deferred income taxes resulted from Werther's use of the straight-line method of depreciation for financial accounting and the accelerated method for income taxes.
4 Werther management consider dividend payments to be a financing activity.

Instructions

Prepare a statement of changes in financial position for Werther Limited for the year ended November 30, Year 3, on the cash basis. A working paper is not required.

Pr. 23-2 Financial statements of Bradstone Corporation for the year ended December 31, Year 4, were as follows:

BRADSTONE CORPORATION
Income Statement
For Year Ended December 31, Year 4

Revenue	$427,000
Costs and expenses (including depreciation expense, $30,000)	357,000
Net income	$ 70,000

BRADSTONE CORPORATION
Statement of Shareholders' Equity
For Year Ended December 31, Year 4

	Common stock, no par	*Retained earnings (deficit)*	*Total*
Balances, beginning of year	$550,000	$(126,000)	$424,000
Issuance of common stock in exchange for equipment	125,000		125,000
Net income		70,000	70,000
Balances, end of year	$675,000	$ (56,000)	$619,000

BRADSTONE CORPORATION
Balance Sheets
December 31, Year 4 and Year 3

	Year 4	*Year 3*
Assets		
Cash	$ 30,600	$ 22,000
Accounts receivable	50,000	30,000
Inventories	150,000	100,000
Equipment	740,000	600,000
Accumulated depreciation of equipment	(218,000)	(210,000)
Goodwill (net)	240,000	250,000
Total assets	$992,600	$792,000
Liabilities & Shareholders' Equity		
Accounts payable	$150,000	$ 60,000
Accrued expenses	30,000	20,000
Bonds payable (due Dec. 31, Year 8)	200,000	300,000
Discount on bonds payable	(6,400)	(12,000)
Common stock, no par or stated value	675,000	550,000
Retained earnings (deficit)	(56,000)	(126,000)
Total liabilities & shareholders' equity	$992,600	$792,000

Additional Information for Year 4

1 Equipment was sold at its carrying amount of $38,000, and equipment was acquired for $75,000 cash.

2 On January 2, bonds with a face amount of $100,000 were extinguished at 101. Discount on bonds payable was being amortized by the straight-line method.

Instructions

Prepare Bradstone Corporation's statement of changes in financial position for the year ended December 31, Year 4, on the cash basis, without using a working paper.

Pr. 23-3 Comparative income statements and balance sheets and a statement of shareholders' equity of Orca Limited are shown in the next illustrations.

ORCA LIMITED
Income Statements
For Years Ended December 31, Year 5 and Year 4

	Year 5	*Year 4*
Net sales	$3,250,000	$2,000,000
Cost of goods sold	2,500,000	1,600,000
Gross profit on sales	$ 750,000	$ 400,000
Operating expenses and income taxes expense	540,000	260,000
Net income	$ 210,000	$ 140,000

ORCA LIMITED
Statement of Shareholders' Equity
For Year Ended December 31, Year 5

	Common stock, no par	*Retained earnings*	*Total*
Balances, beginning of year	$450,000	$165,000	$615,000
Issuance of common stock for cash	150,000		150,000
Net income		210,000	210,000
Cash dividends declared		(120,000)	(120,000)
Balances, end of year	$600,000	$255,000	$855,000

ORCA LIMITED
Balance Sheets
December 31, Year 5 and Year 4

	Year 5	*Year 4*
Assets		
Current assets:		
Cash	$ 120,000	$100,000
Short-term investments	40,000	
Accounts receivable (net)	420,000	290,000
Inventories	330,000	210,000
Short-term prepayments	50,000	25,000
Total current assets	$ 960,000	$625,000
Plants assets	565,000	300,000
Accumulated depreciation of plant assets	(55,000)	(25,000)
Total assets	$1,470,000	$900,000
Liabilities & Shareholders' Equity		
Current liabilities:		
Accounts payable	$ 265,000	$220,000
Dividends payable	30,000	
Other current liabilities	70,000	65,000
Total current liabilities	$ 365,000	$285,000
Note payable, due June 30, Year 8	250,000	
Total liabilities	$ 615,000	$285,000
Shareholders' equity:		
Common stock, no par value	600,000	450,000
Retained earnings	255,000	165,000
Total liabilities & shareholders' equity	$1,470,000	$900,000

Additional Information for Year 5

1 The note payable due June 30, Year 8, was issued in exchange for equipment.
2 There were no disposals of plant assets.
3 The payment of cash dividends is not to be included in operating, financing, or investing activities.

Instructions

Prepare a statement of changes in financial position for Orca Limited on the cash basis for the year ended December 31, Year 5. A working paper is not required.

Pr. 23-4 Shown below is a statement of changes in financial position on the working capital basis for Lucky's, a single proprietorship:

LUCKY'S
Statement of Changes in Financial Position
For Year Ended July 31, Year 10

Financial resources provided:		
Operations—net income		$62,300
Add: Charges that did not reduce working capital (depreciation expense, $13,900, and loss on disposal of equipment, $1,600)		15,500
Working capital provided from operations		$77,800
Disposal of equipment		2,000
Total financial resources provided		$79,800
Financial resources applied:		
Acquisition of equipment	$35,900	
Drawings by proprietor	30,000	
Total financial resources applied		65,900
Increase in financial resources (working capital)		$13,900

Composition of working capital:

	July 31, Year 10	*July 31, Year 9*	*Increase (decrease)*
Current assets:			
Cash	$ 62,400	$ 32,300	$30,100
Accounts receivable (net)	81,600	89,400	(7,800)
Inventories	127,200	140,200	(13,000)
Total current assets	$271,200	$261,900	$ 9,300
Current liabilities:			
Accounts payable	$ 76,400	$ 81,400	$ (5,000)
Other current liabilities	2,700	2,300	400
Total current liabilities	$ 79,100	$ 83,700	$ (4,600)*
Working capital	$192,100	$178,200	$ 13,900

*A *decrease* in current liabilities and an *increase* in working capital.

Instructions

Prepare a statement of changes in financial position for Lucky's for the year ended July 31, Year 10, on the cash basis. The drawings of the proprietor should be shown separately.

Pr. 23-5 Shown below and on the next two pages are financial statements for Monte Evans, Inc.:

MONTE EVANS, INC.
Income Statement
For Year Ended December 31, Year 5

Net sales		$1,616,918
Costs and expenses:		
Cost of goods sold	$420,600	

Depreciation expense	225,000	
Amortization expense	10,000	
Other operating expenses	215,000	
Interest expense	14,500	
Income taxes expense	329,318	
Total costs and expenses		1,214,418
Net income		$ 402,500

MONTE EVANS, INC.
Statement of Shareholders' Equity
For Year Ended December 31, Year 5

	Preferred stock, no par	*Common stock, no par*	*Retained earnings*	*Total*
Balances, beginning of year, as previously reported	$240,000	$1,470,000	$3,300,000	$5,010,000
Prior period adjustment:				
Claim for refund of Year 3 income taxes			12,500	12,500
Balances, beginning of year, as adjusted	$240,000	$1,470,000	$3,312,500	$5,022,500
Redemption of preferred stock	(240,000)		(11,400)	(251,400)
Net income			402,500	402,500
Dividends:				
Cash			(210,000)	(210,000)
5% common stock		105,000	(105,000)	
Balances, end of year	$ -0-	$1,575,000	$3,388,600	$4,963,600

MONTE EVANS, INC.
Balance Sheets
December 31, Year 5 and Year 4

	Year 5	*Year 4*
Assets		
Cash	$ 86,000	$ 60,450
Accounts receivable	280,200	260,200
Allowance for doubtful accounts	(42,500)	(40,000)
Income tax refund receivable	12,500	
Inventories	1,449,450	1,426,900
Equipment	3,981,600	3,831,600
Accumulated depreciation of equipment	(308,200)	(243,200)
Goodwill (net)	250,000	260,000
Total assets	$5,709,050	$5,555,950
Liabilities & Shareholders' Equity		
Accounts payable	$ 241,632	$ 298,350
Income taxes payable	329,318	247,600
Interest payable	15,000	
10% bonds payable, due Jan. 2, Year 25	150,000	

Premium on bonds payable	9,500	
Preferred stock, no par value		240,000
Common stock, no par value	1,575,000	1,470,000
Retained earnings	3,388,600	3,300,000
Total liabilities & shareholders' equity	$5,709,050	$5,555,950

Additional Information for Year 5

1 Uncollectible accounts receivable of $20,000 were written off.
2 Equipment costing $200,000, which had accumulated depreciation of $160,000, was sold at carrying amount. New equipment was acquired for cash and in exchange for the 10% bonds payable, which were issued for $160,000 on January 2, Year 5, with interest payable annually.
3 Premium on bonds payable was amortized by the straight-line method.
4 Management consider the payment of dividends to be an operating activity.

Instructions

Prepare a statement of changes in financial position on the cash basis for Monte Evans, Inc., for the year ended December 31, Year 5. A working paper is not required.

Pr. 23-6 Following are financial statements of Fowler Corporation:

FOWLER CORPORATION
Income Statement
For Year Ended December 31, Year 2

Revenue	$380,000
Costs and expenses, including $1,200 loss (not considered material) on extinguishment of long-term debt	315,000
Net income	$ 65,000

FOWLER CORPORATION
Statement of Shareholders' Equity
For Year Ended December 31, Year 2

	Common stock, no par	*Retained earnings*	*Total*
Balances, beginning of year	$240,000	$95,000	$335,000
Issuance of 800 shares of common stock in exchange for land	50,000		50,000
Net income		65,000	65,000
Dividends:			
Cash		(44,000)	(44,000)
5% stock, 400 shares	25,000	(25,000)	
Balances, end of year	$315,000	$91,000	$406,000

FOWLER CORPORATION
Balance Sheets
December 31, Year 2 and Year 1

	Year 2	*Year 1*
Assets		
Cash	$ 44,220	$ 35,800
Accounts receivable (net)	40,400	24,000
Inventories	37,600	36,800
Short-term prepayments	4,180	4,400
Land	69,000	19,000
Buildings	276,000	250,000
Accumulated depreciation of buildings	(92,000)	(80,000)
Equipment	381,600	360,000
Accumulated depreciation of equipment	(238,000)	(220,000)
Patents (net)	32,000	40,000
Total assets	$555,000	$470,000
Liabilities & Shareholders' Equity		
Accounts payable	$ 64,000	$ 30,000
Other current liabilities	20,000	10,000
Long-term debt, due Dec. 31, Year 10	65,000	95,000
Common stock, no par value	315,000	240,000
Retained earnings	91,000	95,000
Total liabilities & shareholders' equity	$555,000	$470,000

Additional Information for Year 2

1 There were no disposals of buildings or equipment.
2 No patents were acquired.
3 Fowler Corporation wants dividends paid to appear immediately following ''Working capital provided from operations'' or ''Cash provided from operations.''

Instructions

a Prepare Fowler Corporation's statement of changes in financial position for Year 2 on the working capital basis, showing operating, investing, and financing activities. Preparation of a working paper is not required.
b Prepare Fowler Corporation's statement of changes in financial position for Year 2 on the cash basis. Preparation of a working paper is not required.

Pr. 23-7 Financial statements of Liddy Corporation are shown in the next illustrations.

Additional Information for Year 6

1 On January 2, Year 6, Liddy acquired 90% (45,000 shares) of the outstanding common stock of Merrill Limited in a business combination accounted for as a purchase. To consummate this transaction, Liddy paid $72,000 cash and issued 3,500 shares of its preferred stock and 2,400 shares of its common stock. The consideration paid was equal to the underlying carrying amount of the assets acquired. The current fair value of Liddy's preferred stock on the date of the transaction was $3 a share, and the current fair value of its common stock was $12 a share.

LIDDY CORPORATION
Income Statement
For Year Ended December 31, Year 6

Revenue:		
Net sales		$2,450,000
Investment income		135,000
Total revenue		$2,585,000
Cost and expenses:		
Cost of goods sold	$1,252,276	
Depreciation expense	66,600	
Amortization expense	3,000	
Other operating expenses	347,106	
Loss on disposal of Rupp Limited common stock	13,000	
Loss on disposal of plant assets	1,200	
Income taxes expense	405,818	
Total costs and expenses		2,089,000
Net income		$ 496,000

LIDDY CORPORATION
Statement of Shareholders' Equity
For Year Ended December 31, Year 6

	Preferred stock, no par	*Common stock, no par*	*Retained earnings*	*Total*
Balances, beginning of year	$55,500	$709,600	$420,100	$1,185,200
Issuance of preferred and common stock in business combination with Merrill Company	10,500	28,800		39,300
Net income			496,000	496,000
Dividends:				
Cash			(181,000)	(181,000)
4% common stock		33,600	(33,600)	
Balances, end of year	$66,000	$772,000	$701,500	$1,539,500

LIDDY CORPORATION
Balance Sheets
December 31, Year 6 and Year 5

	Year 6	*Year 5*
Assets		
Current assets:		
Cash	$ 450,000	$ 287,000
Notes receivable	45,000	50,000
Accounts receivable (net)	479,200	380,000
Inventories	460,000	298,00
Total current assets	$1,434,200	$1,015,000

Investments:		
Rupp Limited common stock (3%), at cost		39,000
Merrill Limited common stock (90%), at equity	246,300	
Plant assets	455,000	381,000
Accumulated depreciation	(193,000)	(144,000)
Patents (net)	26,000	19,000
Total assets	$1,968,500	$1,310,000
Liabilities & Shareholders' Equity		
Current liabilities:		
Accounts payable	$ 156,000	$ 40,800
Dividends payable	181,000	
Other liabilities	92,000	84,000
Total current liabilities	$ 429,000	$ 124,800
Shareholders' equity:		
Preferred stock, no par	60,000	53,000
Common stock, no par	752,000	700,000
Retained earnings	701,500	420,100
Total liabilities & shareholders' equity	$1,968,500	$1,310,000

Merrill was considered to be an unrelated business and not compatible with Liddy's operations. Therefore, consolidated financial statements for the two companies were not required. For the year ended December 31, Year 6, Merrill had net income of $150,000 and declared no dividends.

2 A plant asset that was acquired in Year 1 at a cost of $22,000 was sold as scrap for $3,200. On the date of disposal the plant asset had a carrying amount of $4,400.

In addition, Liddy acquired new plant assets at a cost of $81,000. The remaining increase in plant assets resulted from major improvements that were recorded as capital expenditures.

3 A new patent was acquired for cash.

4 Liddy management consider dividends paid out to be financing activities.

Instructions

Prepare Liddy Corporation's statement of changes in financial positon on the cash basis for the year ended December 31, Year 6. Preparation of a working paper is not required.

Pr. 23-8 Financial statements of Argent Corporation are shown on pages 1222–1223.

Additional Information for Year 7

1 New machinery and equipment were acquired for $386,000. In addition, machinery with a carrying amount of $61,000 was sold for $48,000.

2 Legal costs of $2,000 were incurred in the successful defence of a patent.

3 Income taxes for Year 7 and bond interest were paid on December 31, Year 7.

Instructions

Prepare Argent Corporation's statement of changes in financial position for the year ended December 31, Year 7, on the cash basis. Preparation of a working paper is not required.

ARGENT CORPORATION
Income Statement
For Year Ended December 31, Year 7

Net sales		$946,200
Costs and expenses:		
Cost of goods sold	$394,015	
Depreciation expense	89,000	
Amortization expense	13,200	
Loss on disposal of machinery	13,000	
Other operating expenses	82,440	
Income taxes expense	159,545	
Total costs and expenses		751,200
Net income		$195,000

ARGENT CORPORATION
Statement of Shareholders' Equity
For Year Ended December 31, Year 7

	Preferred stock, no par	*Common stock, no par*	*Retained earnings*	*Total*
Balances, beginning of year	$100,000	$500,000	$268,000	$ 868,000
Redemption of preferred stock	(10,000)		(1)00-	(11,000)
Net income			195,000	195,000
Cash dividends			(40)00-	(40,000)
Balances, end of year	$ 90,000	$500,000	$422,000	$1,012,000

ARGENT CORPORATION
Balance Sheets
December 31, Year 7 and Year 6

	Year 7	*Year 6*
Assets		
Cash	$ 145,000	$ 186,000
Accounts receivable	253,000	273,000
Allowance for doubtful accounts	(14,000)	(17,000)
Inventories	483,000	538,000
Long-term investments	150,000	
Leasehold improvements (net)	29,000	38,000
Machinery and equipment	927,000	647,000
Accumulated depreciation of machinery and equipment	(416,000)	(372,000)
Patents (net)	27,800	30,000
Total assets	$1,584,800	$1,323,000
Liabilities & Shareholders' Equity		
Accounts payable	$ 232,800	$ 105,000
Dividends payable	40,000	
Current portion of 10% serial bonds payable	50,000	50,000
10% serial bonds payable, less current portion	250,000	300,000

Preferred stock, no par value	90,000	100,000
Common stock, no par value	500,000	500,000
Retained earnings	422,000	268,000
Total liabilities & shareholders' equity	$1,584,800	$1,323,000

Pr. 23-9 Garfield Limited's statement of changes in financial position on the working capital basis for the year ended December 31, Year 10, is shown in the next illustration.

GARFIELD LIMITED
Statement of Changes in Financial Position
For Year Ended December 31, Year 10

Financial resources provided:		
Operations—net income		$183,410
Add: Charges that did not reduce working capital:		
Depreciation expense	$ 40,300	
Amortization of discount on bonds payable	1,200	
Less: Gain on disposal of machinery	(9,400)	32,100
Working capital provided from operations		$215,510
Proceeds from disposal of machinery		13,600
Proceeds from exercise of common stock options		140,000
Issuance of preferred stock in exchange for machinery		100,000
Total financial resources provided		$469,110
Financial resources applied:		
Acquisition of machinery for cash	$ 45,000	
Acquisition of machinery in exchange for preferred stock	100,000	
Acquisition of land	63,500	
Bonds payable reclassified as current liability	28,000	
Cash dividends declared on preferred stock	20,000	
Total financial resources applied		256,500
Increase in financial resources (working capital)		$212,610

Composition of working capital:

	Dec. 31, Year 10	*Dec. 31, Year 9*	*Increase (decrease)*
Current assets:			
Cash	$104,370	$ 43,260	$ 61,110
Accounts receivable (net)	218,300	142,300	76,000
Inventories	464,500	427,500	37,000
Short-term prepayments	19,200	18,200	1,000
Total current assets	$806,370	$631,260	$175,110
Current liabilities:			
Notes payable to suppliers	$115,000	$130,000	$ (15,000)
Current portion of bonds payable	28,000	28,000	
Accounts payable	126,820	182,320	(55,500)
Dividends payable	20,000		20,000
Other liabilities	92,940	79,940	13,000
Total current liabilities	$382,760	$420,260	$ (37,500)*
Working capital	$423,610	$211,000	$212,610

*A *decrease* in current liabilities and an *increase* in working capital.

Instructions

Prepare a statement of changes in financial position for Garfield Limited for the year ended December 31, Year 10, on the cash basis.

Pr. 23-10 Financial statements of Ulster Corporation are shown in the next three illustrations.

Additional Information for Three Months Ended March 31, Year 4

1 On January 8, Year 4, Ulster sold short-term investments for cash at their carrying amount. The investments had been owned for less than one year.
2 On January 17, Year 4, land was sold for $32,000 cash.
3 On March 25, Year 4, Ulster acquired equipment for cash.
4 On March 31, Year 4, additional bonds payable were issued at face amount for cash. Discount on the bonds payable was amortized by the straight-line method.
5 The carrying amount of the investment in Wardell Limited common stock

ULSTER CORPORATION
Income Statement
For Three Months Ended March 31, Year 4

Revenue:		
Sales		$245,207
Investment income		5,880
Gain on disposal of land		10,700
Total revenue		$261,787
Costs and expenses:		
Cost of goods sold	$138,407	
Depreciation expense	1,250	
Other operating expenses	22,010	
Interest expense	1,150	
Income taxes expense ($336 deferred)	34,952	
Total costs and expenses		197,769
Net income		$ 64,018

ULSTER CORPORATION
Statement of Shareholders' Equity
For Three Months Ended March 31, Year 4

	Convertible preferred stock, no par	*Common stock, no par*	*Retained earnings*	*Total*
Balances, beginning of period	$ 30,000	$ 80,000	$ 83,100	$193,100
Conversion of preferred stock	(30,000)	30,000		
Net income			64,018	64,018
Cash dividends declared			(8,000)	(8,000)
Balances, end of period	$ -0-	$110,000	$139,118	$249,118

ULSTER CORPORATION
Balance Sheets
March 31, Year 4 and December 31, Year 3

	Mar. 31, Year 4	*Dec. 31, Year 3*
Assets		
Current assets:		
Cash	$ 87,400	$ 25,300
Short-term investments	7,300	16,500
Accounts receivable (net)	49,320	24,320
Inventories	48,590	31,090
Total current assets	$192,610	$97,210
Investment in Wardell Limited common stock, at equity	$ 67,100	$ 61,220
Land	18,700	40,000
Building	250,000	250,000
Equipment	81,500	
Accumulated depreciation of building and equipment	(16,250)	(15,000)
Other assets	15,100	15,100
Total assets	$608,760	$448,530
Liabilities & Shareholders' Equity		
Current liabilities:		
Accounts payable	$ 17,330	$ 21,220
Dividends payable	8,000	
Income taxes payable	34,616	
Total current liabilities	$ 59,946	$ 21,220
Bonds payable	115,000	50,000
Discount on bonds payable	(2,150)	(2,300)
Deferred income tax credits	846	510
Other long-term liabilities	186,000	186,000
Convertible preferred stock, no par value	-0-	30,000
Common stock, no par value	110,000	80,000
Retained earnings	139,118	83,100
Total liabilities & shareholders' equity	$608,760	$448,530

included an amount attributable to goodwill of $3,220 on December 31, Year 3. Goodwill was being amortized at an annual rate of $480.

Instructions

Prepare Ulster Corporation's statement of changes in financial position for the three months ended March 31, Year 4, on the cash basis. A working paper is not required.

Pr. 23-11 Financial statements of Rulo, Inc., are shown on pages 1226–1227.

Additional Information for Year 2

1. Equipment costing $60,000 was sold for its carrying amount of $30,000. Additional equipment was acquired for cash.
2. On July 1, Year 2, 10% bonds payable with a face amount of $200,000 were called at 102 and extinguished.

RULO, INC.
Income Statement
For Year Ended December 31, Year 2

Revenue:		
Net sales		$ 860,400
Gain on disposal of long-term investments		80,000
Total revenue		$ 940,400
Costs and expenses:		
Cost of goods sold	$680,800	
Depreciation expense	120,000	
Interest expense	99,000	
Other operating expenses	140,490	
Loss on disposal of short-term investments	2,110	
Loss on extinguishment of bonds payable	8,000	
Total costs and expenses		$1,050,400
Net loss		$ (110,000)

RULO, INC.
Statement of Shareholders' Equity
For Year Ended December 31, Year 2

	Convertible preferred stock, no par	*Common stock, no par*	*Retained earnings*	*Total*
Balances, beginning of year	$300,000	$ 840,000	$725,000	$1,865,000
Issuance of 7,000 shares of common stock for cash		308,000		308,000
Conversion of 500 shares of preferred stock to 1,500 shares of common stock	(50,000)	50,000		
Net loss			(110,000)	(110,000)
Cash dividends declared and paid on preferred stock			(40,000)	(40,000)
Balances, end of year	$250,000	$1,198,000	$575,000	$2,023,000

RULO, INC.
Balance Sheets
December 31, Year 2 and Year 1

	Year 2	*Year 1*
Assets		
Cash	$ 76,000	$ 170,000
Short-term investments		30,000
Accounts receivable (net)	435,000	260,000
Inventories	493,000	400,000
Long-term investments, at cost	520,000	610,000
Equipment (net)	1,953,000	1,700,000
Total assets	$3,477,000	$3,170,000

Liabilities & Shareholders' Equity		
Bank overdraft	$ 1,000	
Notes payable to suppliers	350,000	$ 40,000
Accounts payable	315,000	290,000
10% bonds payable, due June 30, Year 4	800,000	1,000,000
Discount on 10% bonds payable	(12,000)	(25,000)
Convertible preferred stock, no par value	250,000	300,000
Common stock, no par value	1,198,000	840,000
Retained earnings	575,000	725,000
Total liabilities & shareholders' equity	$3,477,000	$3,170,000

3 Rulo wish cash dividends to be disclosed separately.
4 The definition of cash is to include cash, short-term investments, and bank overdraft.

Instructions

a Prepare a working paper for statement of changes in financial position for Rulo, Inc., for the year ended December 31, Year 2, suitable for both the cash basis and the working capital basis, showing operating, investing, and financing activities.
b Prepare Rulo's statement of changes in financial position for the year ended December 31, Year 2, on the cash basis.

Pr. 23-12 Shown in the next three illustrations are financial statements of Nix Limited.

Additional Information for Year 2

1 On January 2, Year 2, Nix sold equipment costing $45,000, with a carrying amount of $24,000, for $19,000 cash.
2 On July 1, Year 2, Nix acquired equipment for $63,000 cash.
3 On December 31, Year 2, land with a current fair value of $150,000 was acquired through the issuance of a long-term promissory note in the amount of $150,000. The note bore interest at the rate of 15% and was due on December 31, Year 7.
4 Deferred income tax credits represented timing differences primarily relating to the use of the accelerated method of depreciation for income taxes and the straight-line method of depreciation for financial accounting.
5 Dividend payments are considered by Nix management to be operating activities.

Instructions

a Prepare a working paper for statement of changes in financial position for Nix Limited for the year ended December 31, Year 2, suitable for the cash basis, showing operating, investing, and financing activities.
b Prepare Nix Limited's statement of changes in financial position for the year ended December 31, Year 2, on the cash basis.

NIX LIMITED
Income Statement
For Year Ended December 31, Year 2

Revenue:		
Net sales		$1,950,000
Investment income		13,000
Total revenue		$1,963,000
Costs and expenses:		
Cost of goods sold	$1,150,000	
Depreciation expense	53,000	
Amortization expense	4,000	
Other operating expenses	505,000	
Interest expense	15,000	
Loss on disposal of equipment	5,000	
Income taxes expense ($11,000 deferred)	90,000	
Total costs and expenses		1,822,000
Net income		$ 141,000

NIX LIMITED
Statement of Shareholders' Equity
For Year Ended December 31, Year 2

	Common stock, no par	*Retained earnings*	*Treasury stock*	*Total*
Balances, beginning of year	$575,000	$334,000	$ (17,000)	$ 892,000
Issuance of common stock for cash	31,000			23,000
Conversion of $50,000 face amount of convertible bonds	50,000			50,000
Reissuance of treasury stock			17,000	25,000
Net income		141,000		141,000
Cash dividends declared and paid		(43,000)		(43,000)
Balances, end of year	$656,000	$432,000	$ -0-	$1,088,000

NIX LIMITED
Balance Sheets
December 31, Year 2 and Year 1

	Year 2	*Year 1*
Assets		
Cash	$ 275,000	$ 180,000
Accounts receivable (net)	295,000	305,000
Inventories	549,000	431,000
Investment in Race Limited common stock (at equity)	73,000	60,000
Land	350,000	200,000
Other plant assets	624,000	606,000
Accumulated depreciation of other plant assets	(139,000)	(107,000)

Goodwill (net)	16,000	20,000
Total assets	$2,043,000	$1,695,000
Liabilities & Shareholders' Equity		
Accounts payable and accrued liabilities	$ 604,000	$ 563,000
Note payable (long-term)	150,000	
Bonds payable	160,000	210,000
Deferred income tax credits	41,000	30,000
Common stock, no par value	656,000	575,000
Retained earnings	432,000	334,000
Treasury stock (at cost)		(17,000)
Total liabilities & shareholders' equity	$2,043,000	$1,695,000

Pr. 23-13 Financial statements of Brinker Limited are shown in the next illustrations.

Additional Information for Year 6

1 On December 31, Year 6, Brinker borrowed $450,000 on a 15% promissory note payable $150,000 a year beginning December 31, Year 7.

2 On June 15, Year 6, Brinker acquired equipment for $392,000 cash. On July 1, Year 6, Brinker sold for $33,000 cash equipment costing $52,000 that had a carrying amount of $28,000.

3 On December 31, Year 6, Brinker leased equipment under a 10-year capital lease with equal annual payments of $25,000 due each December 31, beginning in Year 6. The $25,000 lease payment due on December 31, Year 7, will consist of $16,000 interest and $9,000 principal.

4 The company wishes to show dividend payments and the Year 4 income tax assessment separately, in the statement of changes in financial position.

BRINKER LIMITED
Income Statement
For Year Ended December 31, Year 6

Revenue:		
Net sales		$942,300
Dividends		5,500
Gain on disposal of long-term investments		20,000
Gain on disposal of equipment		5,000
Total revenue		$972,800
Costs and expenses:		
Cost of goods sold	$198,200	
Depreciation expense	149,000	
Other operating expenses	71,600	
Interest expense	48,000	
Income taxes expense ($15,000 deferred)	253,000	
Total costs and expenses		719,800
Net income		$253,000

BRINKER LIMITED
Statement of Shareholders' Equity
For Year Months Ended December 31, Year 6

	Common stock, no par	*Retained earnings*	*Total*
Balances, beginning of year, as previously reported	$844,000	$408,000	$1,252,000
Prior period adjustment: Additional income tax assessment paid for Year 4		(20,000)	(20,000)
Balances, beginning of year, as adjusted	$844,000	$388,000	$1,232,000
Issuance of 2,000 shares of common stock in exchange for land	100,000		100,000
Net income		253,000	253,000
Cash dividends declared and paid		(30,000)	(30,000)
Balances, end of year	$944,000	$611,000	$1,555,000

BRINKER LIMITED
Balance Sheets
December 31, Year 6 and Year 5

	Year 6	*Year 5*
Assets		
Cash	$ 541,000	$ 308,000
Accounts receivable (net)	585,000	495,000
Inventories	895,000	780,000
Long-term investments, at cost	180,000	255,000
Land	350,000	250,000
Buildings and equipment	1,060,000	720,000
Accumulated depreciation of building and equipment	(295,000)	(170,000)
Leased equipment under capital lease	158,000	
Total assets	$3,474,000	$2,638,000
Liabilities & Shareholders' Equity		
Accounts payable and accrued liabilities	$ 760,000	$ 823,000
Current portion of long-term debt	159,000	
Notes payable, long-term	300,000	
10% bonds payable	500,000	500,000
Premium on bonds payable	16,000	18,000
Liability under capital lease	124,000	
Deferred income tax credits	60,000	45,000
Common stock, no par value	944,000	844,000
Retained earnings	611,000	408,000
Total liabilities & shareholders' equity	$3,474,000	$2,638,000

Instructions

a Prepare a working paper for statement of changes in financial position for Brinker Limited for the year ended December 31, Year 6, suitable for the cash basis, showing operating, investing, and financing activities.

b Prepare Brinker Limited's statement of changes in financial position for the year ended December 31, Year 6, on the cash basis.

chapter 24

ANALYSIS OF FINANCIAL STATEMENTS

Many groups outside a business enterprise — creditors, investors, regulatory agencies, financial analysts, labour union leaders — are interested in its financial affairs. This is particularly true for publicly owned corporations. Management also is interested in the results and relationships reported in financial statements. Outsiders do not have access to the detailed data available to management and must rely on published information in making business decisions. In this chapter we consider the analysis of financial statements as a basis for decision making by outsiders.

Management makes operating and financial decisions on the basis of a wide variety of reports that are either generated by the enterprise's own information system or available from other sources. Management's use of financial information is mentioned in many of the preceding chapters. More sophisticated analyses of profit-volume relationships, make-or-buy decisions, differential costs, financial forecasts, product line profitability, gross profits, distribution costs, and rates of return on investments usually are covered in cost and management accounting courses and for that reason are not discussed in this chapter.

Sources of Financial Information Available to Outsiders

The first procedure in financial analysis is to obtain useful information, at least cost, including some information not found in financial statements. The major sources of financial information for publicly owned corporations are described in the following sections.

Published Reports

As stated in Chapter 4, corporations whose stock is publicly owned issue annual and quarterly reports. Annual reports of public corporations contain comparative financial statements and notes to the financial statements, supplementary financial information, and management's discussion and analysis of the comparative years' operations and prospects for the future. Annual reports are made available to the public as well as to shareholders.

Credit and Investment Advisory Services

Organizations such as Moody's Investors Service and Standard & Poor's Corporation compile financial information for investors in annual volumes and periodic supplements. A wide variety of data relating to business enterprises, particularly small and medium-sized enterprises, is published by such organizations as Dun & Bradstreet of Canada and Financial Post. Many trade associations collect and publish financial ratios for enterprises in various industries. Major brokerage firms and investment advisory services compile financial information about public corporations and make it available to their customers. In addition, most brokerage firms maintain a staff of analysts who study business conditions and review published financial statements; visit plants and meet with executives to obtain information on new products, industry trends, and management changes; and interpret all this information for investors.

Audit Reports

When an independent CA firm performs an audit, its report is addressed to the shareholders of the audited enterprise. The CA firm's opinion on financial statements is included in annual reports.

What is Financial Analysis?

Knowing what to look for and how to interpret it is the essence of the art of financial analysis. Financial analysis is a process of ***selection, relation, and evaluation***. The first procedure is to select from the total information available about a business enterprise the information relevant to the decision under consideration. The second procedure is to arrange the information in a way that will bring out significant relationships. The final procedure is to study these relationships and interpret the results.

Financial statements themselves are organized summaries of detailed information, and are thus a form of analysis. The types of financial statements accountants prepare, the way they arrange items in the statements, and their standards of disclosure are influenced by a desire to provide information in convenient and useful form. In using financial statements, analysts focus their attention on key amounts and relationships, then extend their investigation to ascertain why the conditions revealed by the financial statements exist.

Procedure of Analysis

Financial analysis is not primarily a matter of making computations. The important part of the analytical process begins when the computational task is finished.

However, there are some analytical procedures that are useful in highlighting important relationships and reducing masses of detail to convenient numerical form so that the essential facts may be grasped quickly.

Ratios

Ratios may be expressed as percentages, as fractions, or as a stated comparison between two amounts. For example, we might describe the relationship between $120 million of sales and $24 million of operating income as: (1) operating income is 20% of sales; (2) operating income is ⅕ of sales; (3) the ratio of sales to operating income is 5 to 1; (4) for every dollar of sales the enterprise earned 20 cents in operating income. Each of these ratios describes the relationship between sales and operating income. The computation of a ratio does not add any information not already inherent in the amounts under study. A useful ratio may be computed only when a significant relationship exists between two amounts; a ratio of two unrelated amounts is meaningless.

A ratio, once computed, is best interpreted by comparing it with the same ratio for recent accounting periods and for other business enterprises, and with an appropriate industry standard. Such comparisons are discussed on pages 1257–1259.

Component Percentages: Common-Size Financial Statements

The ratio of one amount in a financial statement to the total that includes that amount is called a ***component percentage***. Reducing data to component percentages helps the analyst to visualize both the relative importance of the amounts in the financial statements and the changes from period to period.

Financial statements expressed in component percentages are sometimes called ***common-size financial statements***. Two examples, one for Ara Company and one for Ali Company and Bry Company, are presented in the next two illustrations.

In the first example for Ara Company, reducing the operating data to component percentages helps the analyst to see the major factors that brought about an increase in the rate of earnings per dollar of sales. In the second example, component percentages highlight the difference in the asset and capital structures; Ali Company has a larger proportion of debt and a relatively larger amount of current

Each item in the income statements is reported as a percentage of net sales

ARA COMPANY
Common-Size Income Statements
For Years Ended December 31, Year 2, and Year 1

	Year 2	*Year 1*
Net sales	100.0%	100.0%
Cost of goods sold	63.2	66.4
Gross profit on sales	36.8%	33.6%
Operating expenses	23.2	24.2
Income before income taxes	13.6%	9.4%
Income taxes expense	5.0	3.2
Net income	8.6%	6.2%

Items in the balance sheets are reported as a percentage of total assets

ALI COMPANY and BRY COMPANY
Common-Size Balance Sheets
December 31, Year 1

	Ali Company	*Bry Company*
Assets		
Current assets	56.4%	43.2%
Plant assets (net)	38.7	50.1
Other assets	4.9	6.7
Total assets	100.0%	100.0%
Liabilities & Shareholders' Equity		
Current liabilities	36.2%	20.5%
Long-term debt	24.0	12.6
Total liabilities	60.2%	33.1%
Shareholders' equity	39.8	66.9
Total liabilities & shareholders' equity	100.0%	100.0%

assets; Bry Company is financed to a larger degree by use of equity capital and has a relatively larger investment in plant assets.

When information is reduced to simple terms, there may be some loss of completeness, but there may be some gains. Component percentages emphasize relative size rather than absolute amounts. For example, if Ara Company has managed to increase its net income from 6.2% to 8.6% of sales only by reducing sales volume in half, there is no hint of this in the common-size income statements. Similarly, the common-size balance sheets will not reveal, for example, that Ali Company may be 10 times as large as Bry Company.

Changes over Time

The analytical information that may be gleaned from the financial statements of only one year is limited. Previous chapters describe the difficulty of measuring income and financial position accurately. Futhermore, an enterprise's experience in a single year may not be typical. Investigating performance over a reasonable number of years is a useful form of financial analysis.

Example of a 5-year summary

WALT DISNEY PRODUCTIONS
Revenues, Net Income, and Dividends
For Years Ended September 30, 1980 Through 1984

	1984	*1983*	*1982*	*1981*	*1980*
Revenues (millions)	$1,656	$1,307	$1,030	$1,005	$915
Net income (millions)	98*	93	100	121	135
Earnings per share (dollars)	2.73	2.70	3.01	3.72	4.16
Cash dividends per share (dollars)	1.20	1.20	1.20	1.00	0.72

*Includes $76 million from change in accounting for investment tax credit.

Public corporations' annual reports usually include a five- to ten-year summary of selected financial data. For example, the data at the bottom of page 1235 are taken from the annual report of Walt Disney Productions. We note that the revenues and cash dividends per share of Walt Disney Productions generally have been growing steadily, but that net income and earnings per share generally have declined.

There are a number of ways this five-year record may be presented to facilitate analysis. In the summary below relating to sales and net income, the dollar change each year from the previous year, the percentage change from the previous year, and the *trend percentage* in relation to the first year in the series are shown for Walt Disney Productions:

Summary of increases and trend percentages revenues and net income

WALT DISNEY PRODUCTIONS
Analysis of Changes
For Years Ended September 30, 1980 Through 1984

	Dollar change from previous year (in millions of dollars)		*Percentage change from previous year*		*Trend percentage in relation to 1980*	
Year	*Revenues*	*Net income*	*Revenues*	*Net income*	*Revenues*	*Net income*
1980					100.0%	100.0%
1981	+ 90	−14	+ 9.8	−10.4	109.8	89.6
1982	+ 25	−21	+ 2.5	−17.4	112.6	74.1
1983	+277	− 7	+26.9	− 7.0	142.8	68.9
1984	+349	+ 5	+26.7	+ 5.4	181.0	72.6

Each of these computations points out the change in revenues and net income over the five-year period in a slightly different way. If the analyst is primarily interested in absolute change, the dollar changes tell the story. The percentage of increase or decrease year by year expresses growth or decline in comparison with the prior year's performance. Trend percentages (computed by dividing the amount for each year by the amount for the base year) reveal a total growth of 81.0% (181.0% − 100.0% = 81.0%) in revenues and a decline of 27.4% (100.0% − 72.6% = 27.4%) in net income over a period of four years for Walt Disney Productions.

Analytical Objectives

The outcome of business decisions (to acquire or dispose of a company's securities or to extend or refuse to extend credit, for example) naturally depends on future events. Financial statements are essentially a record of the past. Therefore, analysts study financial statements as evidence of past performance that may be useful in making predictions of future performance. The management of a company is responsible for earning as large a return as possible on the resources invested in the company consistent with the objectives of maintaining a sound financial condition, meeting social responsibilities, and doing business in accordance with high ethical standards. Insofar as the attainment of these objectives may be measured quantitatively (and quantitative information usually is only a part of the basis for any business decision), financial statements provide useful information.

In looking at past performance and present position, the financial analyst seeks answers to two primary questions: (1) What is the company's earnings performance, and (2) is the company in sound financial condition? We may examine the process of analysis within the framework of these two questions.

ANALYSIS OF EARNINGS PERFORMANCE

Unfortunately, an outside analyst usually does not have access to many of the important details that underlie reported net income. Most published income statements are highly condensed, and the outsider must be satisfied with a general review of the relationship between revenue, cost of goods sold, total operating expenses, and net income. This requires a careful analysis of gross profit percentages and ***operating expense ratios*** (total operating expenses divided by net sales) over a number of years. Also, the analyst will review any items of nonoperating revenue and expense, extraordinary items, accounting changes, and disposals of business segments, in order to predict the likely normal earning power of a business enterprise.

Net Income and Accounting Practices

The point is made throughout this book that the amount of net income reported in an accounting period may be affected by the accounting practices followed. These practices are selected by management; independent auditors merely inform users that the financial statements were prepared "in conformity with generally accepted accounting principles consistently applied." Unfortunately, a wide variety of accounting principles may be considered "generally accepted," and financial analysts must determine the accounting practices and principles used, especially for the recognition of revenue and expenses, and then evaluate their impact on reported net income. In other words, financial analysts are concerned with the ***quality of reported earnings***.

In recent years significant progress has been made in reducing areas of differences in financial accounting and reporting, and additional reforms are contemplated by authoritative bodies. The required inclusion in annual reports of a description of the accounting policies used in the preparation of financial statements was an important development.[1] The accounting policies for revenue recognition, depreciation, inventories, leases, pension plans, consolidation of subsidiaries, business combinations, and income taxes, for example, are especially significant to financial analysts. In addition, the notes to the financial statements provide useful information on these and other financial accounting and reporting matters.

1 CICA, ***CICA Handbook*** (Toronto), sec. 1505.

Trend in Earnings

The analysis of earnings should always cover several years, not only because of the difficulty of measuring income year by year but also because it is important to know how a company performs in periods of prosperity and adversity. Net income may be satisfactory in one year and decline substantially in the following year, because of unfavourable business conditions.

One of the first things an analyst looks for is the trend of revenue (sales) over a number of years. A rising trend of revenue usually is a sign of expansion. Obviously, the revenue trend is not the whole story, because a growth in revenue is not always accompanied by a corresponding increase in net income. The ideal situation is to find a company maintaining a constant or increasing ***rate*** of net income on a rapidly growing revenue.

The pattern of revenue and net income throughout the business cycle is also an important factor. There is obviously greater risk in investing in (or lending to) a company whose net income fluctuates widely with changes in business conditions than in an enterprise able to show ***stability*** of earnings throughout all phases of the business cycle. An enterprise that must reduce operations severely during recessions inevitably suffers in terms of such factors as effective product planning and employee morale, and may find it difficult to cover its fixed expenses. Furthermore, earnings tend to decline faster than revenue because some expenses are fixed. Investors are interested in identifying a ***cyclical*** company, not only because the risk of investment is higher, but also because the timing of their investment will depend on the company's performance in relation to cyclical trends. A shift by investors to ***defensive stocks*** (common stocks of companies that perform well in all phases of the business cycle) when a recession is in the offing and a shift to stocks of cyclical companies at the first sign of an economic upturn are popular investment strategies.

Return on Investment

Business executives invest capital with the objective of earning a satisfactory rate of return. The rate of return depends on numerous factors, including the nature of competition and the risks inherent in an industry. Management often is evaluated in terms of the rate of return it is able to earn on invested capital. Although outsiders cannot determine the rate of return on the investment for particular divisions or segments of a business enterprise, they may make some overall estimates of the rate. This rate may serve as a valuable index in evaluating the relative profitability of a particular company and the quality of its management.

The ***rate of return on investment*** for any period is determined by dividing "income" by average investment. The appropriate income amount to be used depends on the related concept of ***investment***. This idea is illustrated in the next table.

In each case net income excludes any extraordinary items, discontinued operations, or cumulative effect of change in accounting policy, and the investment is computed as an average for the period. Ratio **1** is a measure of the earnings (after interest and income taxes) that relate to the total economic resources employed by

Three different rates of return

Appropriate income amount		*Concept of investment (in all cases an average for the period covered by the income amount)*
1 Return on total assets: Net income	÷	Total assets
2 Return on total shareholders' equity: Net income	÷	Total shareholders' equity
3 Return on common shareholders' equity: Net income applicable to common stock	÷	Common shareholders' equity

a company. It is possible to add interest expense to net income to compute an approximation of earnings before payment of interest to creditors but after income taxes. Some analysts prefer to compute return on total assets ***before interest and income taxes***, in which case a ratio of operating income to total assets is used. If total assets include some idle plant assets, bond sinking funds, or long-term investments, such assets and the related earnings generated by the assets are excluded from rate of return computations.

Ratios **2** and **3** are computed from the viewpoint of shareholders, and the approach used depends on whether the analyst is interested in the rate of return on total shareholders' equity or on common shareholders' equity. In the computation of the rate of return on common shareholders' equity, dividends on cumulative preferred stock for each period are deducted from net income to obtain ***net income applicable to common stock***. The data for Barker Limited shown below (in millions of dollars) are used to compute the three rate-of-return ratios:

Rates of return computed in next table are based on these data

BARKER LIMITED
Data for Analysis
(In millions of dollars)

Income statement data	*Year 2*	*Year 1*	*Balance sheet data*	*Year 2*	*Year 1*	*Year 0*
Net sales	$130	$ 95	Current assets	$19	$20	$18
Other revenue	10	5	Noncurrent assets	61	60	56
Total revenue	$140	$100	Total assets	$80	$80	$74
Cost of goods sold	$ 95	$ 65				
Operating expenses	26	20	Current liabilities	$ 6	$10	$ 9
Interest expense	1	1	Long-term debt	19	20	21
Income taxes expense (50%)	9	7	Preferred stock	16	16	16
Total expenses	$131	$ 93	Common shareholders' equity	39	34	28
Net income	$ 9	$ 7				
Less: Preferred stock dividends	1	1	Total liabilities & shareholders' equity	$80	$80	$74
Available for common stock	$ 8	$ 6				

The rates of return described in the outline on page 1239 are computed below for Barker Company (all dollar amounts are stated in millions):

Computation of rates of return

Measurement	Computation: Year 2	Computation: Year 1
1 Return on total assets	$\frac{\$9}{½(\$80 + \$80)} = \frac{\$9}{\$80} = 11.2\%$	$\frac{\$7}{½(\$80 + \$74)} = \frac{\$7}{\$77} = 9.1\%$
2 Return on total shareholders' equity	$\frac{\$9}{½(\$55 + \$50)} = \frac{\$9}{\$52.5} = 17.1\%$	$\frac{\$7}{½(\$50 + \$44)} = \frac{\$7}{\$47} = 14.9\%$
2 Return on common shareholders' equity..	$\frac{\$8}{½(\$39 + \$34)} = \frac{\$8}{\$36.5} = 21.9\%$	$\frac{\$6}{½(\$34 + \$28)} = \frac{\$6}{\$31} = 19.4\%$

Interpreting Return on Investment

Each of the measures of return on investment for Barker Limited shows an improved performance in Year 2. If we consider the underlying factors — the revenue generated per dollar of investment (***asset turnover rate***) and the net income per dollar of revenue — we obtain some additional insight:

Asset turnover rate × percentage earned on total revenue equals...

	Year 2	Year 1
Revenue generated per dollar of assets:		
$\frac{\text{Total revenue}}{\text{Average investment (total assets)}}$	$\frac{\$140}{\$80} = \$1.75$	$\frac{\$100}{\$77} = \$1.30$
Net income per dollar of revenue:		
$\frac{\text{Net income}}{\text{Total revenue}}$	$\frac{\$9}{\$140} = 6.4\%$	$\frac{\$7}{\$100} = 7.0\%$

Although Barker earned a smaller margin of income per dollar of total revenue in Year 2, it was able to improve its volume of revenue per dollar of investment from $1.30 to $1.75. This ratio may be viewed as the ***number of times total assets are turned over*** and may be used to verify the rates of return on total assets as follows:

...rate of return on total assets

Year 2: $1.75 × 6.4% = 11.2 cents per dollar of assets, or 11.2%
Year 1: $1.30 × 7.0% = 9.1 cents per dollar of assets, or 9.1%

What we have done here is simply multiply the rate earned on revenue by the asset turnover rate to measure the earnings rate on assets. This concept is really a truism: If a profit of 3%, for example, is earned on sales, and $10 of sales is generated by each $1 of assets, then the rate earned on assets is 10 × 3%, or 30%.

Trading on the Equity

When a business enterprise borrows money for long-term purposes, it is ***trading on the equity***, or ***using financial leverage***. The results from trading on the equity may be favourable or unfavourable to common shareholders. If the rate earned before interest and income taxes on total assets is higher than the interest rate paid for the use of money, the common shareholders will gain; if the interest rate is higher than the earnings rate on assets, then a loss to common shareholders results from trading on the equity. Issuance of preferred stock produces similar results but is more ''expensive'' to the common shareholders, because dividends paid on preferred stock are not deductible in the computation of taxable income.

The fact that the return on common shareholders' equity for Barker Limited is higher than the return on total assets is significant. Barker is successfully trading on the equity; that is, the total of interest on bonds and dividends on preferred stock is less than the earnings on capital raised through these ***senior securities***. Barker has about $20 million in long-term debt at an interest cost of about 5% before income taxes ($1 million ÷ $20 million = 0.05) and 2½% after income taxes at 50%, and it has $16 million in preferred stock paying dividends of approximately 6.3% ($1 ÷ $16 = 0.063). Barker earned 11.2% after income taxes on its total assets during Year 2. Therefore, the funds raised through the issuance of senior securities earned a much higher rate than the fixed interest and dividends paid by Barker. This excess accrued to Barker's common shareholders, resulting in a 21.9% rate earned on common shareholders' equity in Year 2 and 19.4% in Year 1.

Earnings, Dividends, and Equity (Book Value) per Share

Because shareholders think in terms of the number of shares they own or plan to acquire or dispose of, reducing corporate financial information to per-share terms puts it into useful perspective for shareholders. Perhaps the most commonly used statistics relating to common stocks are ***earnings*** (or ***loss***) ***per share*** and ***dividends per share***. These appear widely in financial press releases, prospectuses, proxy materials, and various reports to shareholders.

Comparative earnings-per-share data, supported by complete financial statements, are useful in evaluating the performance of a company from the common shareholders' point of view. There is little doubt that earnings (or loss) per share is a highly significant summary amount, but it has some serious limitations; and there are dangers in focussing too much attention on it.

The manner of computing and reporting of earnings per share has been a major concern not only of the accounting profession but also of the securities commissions and the major stock exchanges. The technical aspects of computing and reporting ***basic*** and ***fully diluted*** earnings per share are discussed and illustrated in Chapter 18.

Dividends on common stock represent historical facts and should be reported at amounts actually paid, except in cases following stock splits or stock dividends. In such cases, they should be reported on the same ''weighted-average number of shares outstanding'' basis as is followed for the earnings-per-share calculation.

Dividend Payout Ratio, Dividend Yield, and Price-Earnings Ratio

Investors in common stock are more interested in earnings and dividends in relation to the ***market price*** of their shares than in relation to the equity (book value) of their shares, because market price measures the amount of money they forgo at any specific time by a decision to continue owning the common stock. To illustrate, suppose that Jane Adams owns one share of common stock of Solo Limited that currently earns $5 a share and pays a dividend of $2 a share. The equity (book value) is $40 a share and the current market price of Solo's common stock is $50. The fact that Solo is earning a return of 12½% on shareholders' equity ($5 ÷ $40 = 0.125) is of secondary interest to Adams, because she gives up the use of $50 by the decision to own this share. Thus, Adams views this investment as one producing an ***earnings yield*** of 10% ($5 ÷ $50 = 0.10), a ***dividend payout ratio*** of 40% ($2 ÷ $5 = 0.40), and a ***dividend yield*** of only 4% ($2 ÷ $50 = 0.04). In investment circles the earnings yield usually is expressed in reverse as a ***price-earnings ratio***[2] of ***ten times earnings*** or simply 10 to 1 ($50 ÷ $5 = 10).

Serious investors monitor the relationships among earnings, dividends, and the market prices of common stock and seek to evaluate such relationships by analyzing the financial data available to them. The table below shows these relationships for three hypothetical companies:

Note differences in dividend payout ratios, yields, and price-earnings ratios

	Coy Limited	*Day Limited*	*Elm Limited*
Earnings per share in Year 5	$1.00	$2.50	$5.00
Dividends per share in Year 5	$0.60	$2.00	$2.00
Market price per share during Year 5:			
High	$7	$50	$110
Low	$3	$35	$ 96
Ending	$5	$40	$100
Dividend payout ratio	60%	80%	40%
Dividend yield on market price, Dec. 31, Year 5	12%	5%	2%
Price-earnings ratio, Dec. 31, Year 5	5 to 1	16 to 1	20 to 1

This divergence in price-earnings and yield ratios (an even wider spread often exists among listed common stocks) suggests that investors assess the risks and future prospects of these three investments in quite different terms. Coy Limited, for example, may be a marginal producer in its industry, with highly volatile earnings and low growth prospects. As a result, its common stock trades at a low price-earnings ratio of ***five times earnings*** and yields 12%. The common stock of Day Limited trades at a much higher multiple of earnings and yields 5%. In contrast, Elm Limited appears to be a "growth company"; the price-earnings ratio for its common stock is ***twenty times earnings*** and the yield is 2% because only 40% of its net income is distributed to shareholders.

2 The price-earnings ratios generally are determined using basic earnings per share for the latest 12 months, excluding extraordinary items. The price-earnings ratios for stocks traded on the stock exchanges are reported in most daily newspapers, along with the annual price range, the daily high and low prices, the closing price, and the net price change from the previous day's closing price.

An investor who tries to determine whether the market price of a common stock is reasonable must consider a variety of factors. All, however, relate to an estimate of the ultimate return on investment; this return depends on the dividends received during the period the common stock is held and the price obtained when the stock is sold, both of which are difficult to project with any degree of precision.

Earnings and Fixed Charges

A company that finances its operations with long-term debt or preferred stock is committed to pay a fixed return to the holders of these securities. The commitment on long-term debt is stronger than on preferred stock, because in the latter case the obligation is only that preferred dividends will be paid before any dividends on common stock are declared. A company that ***passes*** a preferred dividend has impaired its financial reputation to some degree, but a company that cannot pay interest on its debt is in serious financial trouble.

Bondholders and preferred shareholders have learned from experience that the relationships between earnings and fixed charges are useful measures of the safety of their investment. The data below for Foy Limited and Glo Limited are used to illustrate two ratios that measure these relationships:

Data used to compute times fixed charges are earned

	Foy Limited	*Glo Limited*
Operating income	$600,000	$900,000
Less: Interest on long-term debt	200,000	100,000
Income before income taxes	$400,000	$800,000
Less: Income taxes expense	200,000	400,000
Net income	$200,000	$400,000
Less: Preferred stock dividends	50,000	200,000
Net income available for common stock	$150,000	$200,000

Times Interest Earned

The times interest earned ratio may be computed in two ways as shown below and at the top of page 1244.

Because interest expense is deductible for income taxes, logic would seem to support method 1. Business executives and investors are strongly conditioned to an after-tax view of corporate affairs, however, which may explain why method 2 generally is used in practice. The after-tax computation always results in a more conservative measurement for coverage of interest expense.

Alternative methods for computing times interest earned

	Foy Limited	*Glo Limited*
Method 1:		
Times interest earned before income taxes:		
(a) Operating income	$600,000	$900,000
(b) Interest expense	$200,000	$100,000
Times interest earned (a ÷ b)	3 times	9 times

Method 2:		
Times interest earned after income taxes:		
Net income	$200,000	$400,000
(a) Add: Interest expense	200,000	100,000
(b) Income before interest charges	$400,000	$500,000
Times interest earned (b ÷ a)	2 times	5 times

Times Preferred Stock Dividends Earned

The computation of the number of times preferred stock dividends are earned also may be made in two ways, as illustrated below:

Are the dividends on the preferred stock of Foy Company more assured?

	Foy Limited	*Glo Limited*
Method 1:		
Net income available for preferred stock dividends:		
(a) Net income	$200,000	$400,000
(b) Preferred stock dividend requirement	$ 50,000	$200,000
Times preferred stock dividends earned (a ÷ b)	4 times	2 times

These ratios make it appear that preferred stock dividends of Foy Limited are better protected by earnings than its interest expense; yet interest obviously has a prior claim. To overcome this objection, the test of preferred stock dividend safety most often used is the ***number of times combined interest expense and preferred stock dividends are earned***. This is illustrated for Foy Limited and Glo Limited below:

No, based on this computation!

	Foy Limited	*Glo Limited*
Method 2:		
Times interest expense and preferred stock dividends are earned:		
Interest expense	$200,000	$100,000
Preferred stock dividend requirement	50,000	200,000
(a) Total interest expense and preferred stock dividend requirement	$250,000	$300,000
(b) Net income (after taxes) plus interest expense	$400,000	$500,000
Number of times interest expense and preferred stock dividends are earned (b ÷ a)	1.6 times	1.7 times

"Times-earned" ratios are useful not only to creditors and preferred shareholders but also to common shareholders. Common shareholders know that a company that has to forgo paying either interest or preferred stock dividends will suffer financial embarrassment at the least; furthermore, they are concerned about a sufficiency of earnings and cash to allow for common stock dividends. There is little mystery in interpreting times-earned ratios — the higher the ratio the more favourable for bondholders and preferred shareholders. The more difficult question is: How large should the ratios be to satisfy these two groups without being detrimental to the common shareholders? In general, the answer to this question depends on the stability of past and potential earnings over the business cycle; if earnings are stable, lower times-earned ratios may be viewed as satisfactory.

In the analysis of financial statements, the coverage of fixed charges logically should be expanded to include ***all*** fixed obligations of a company. For example, a company must make regular payments on long-term operating leases, property taxes, and other fixed commitments, in addition to interest on debt, before dividends may be declared. The ability of a company to generate sufficient revenue in excess of variable expenses to cover fixed charges is one of the most important considerations to the analyst.

Equity (Book Value) per Share

The term ***equity*** (or ***book value***) ***per share*** often is used in negotiations for the sale of a business enterprise. In closely held corporations, it is not unusual for one common shareholder to have a contractual right to acquire the common stock of other shareholders at a price equal to the equity per share of the common stock. Computation of equity per share generally is based on going-concern value, not on the assumption of liquidation. ***Equity per share is the amount of net assets applicable to each share of outstanding capital stock.*** When a corporation has only common stock outstanding, equity per share is computed by dividing the total shareholders' equity by the number of shares of stock outstanding, as illustrated below:

Equity (book value) per share of common stock

$$\frac{\text{Total shareholders' equity}}{\text{Number of shares outstanding}} = \frac{\$2{,}500{,}000}{100{,}000} = \$25 \text{ equity per share}$$

If a corporation has treasury stock, the debit balance in the Treasury Stock ledger account is deducted to measure the total shareholders' equity, and the number of shares outstanding does not include the shares of treasury stock.

Equity per share is used to some extent as a guide for investors, but usually with recognition that other measurements, such as earnings per share, are more important determinants of market prices for common stocks. The equity per share as traditionally computed may be far different from the per-share ***current fair value*** of net assets. Even though common stocks often trade at prices far above or far below the equity per share, some investors feel that the equity per share should be considered, along with other information, in making investment decisions.

The concept of "equity per share" is more meaningful and more widely used for common stock than for preferred stock; however, if a corporation has both types of stock outstanding, the total equity of the preferred stock must be determined as a preliminary step in the computation of the equity per share of the common stock, as illustrated in the following example:

Equity (book value) per share — two classes of capital stock outstanding

Total shareholders' equity (net of cost of treasury stock)	$9,280,000
Less: Amount applicable to $10, no-par-value preferred stock: 10,000 shares outstanding (callable at 108)	1,080,000
Equity applicable to no-par-value common stock: 1,000,000 shares outstanding (not including treasury stock)	$8,200,000
Equity (book value) per share of common stock: $8,200,000 ÷ 1,000,000 shares	$ 8.20

The equity of the preferred stock in this example is $108 a share. In the computation of the equity of the preferred stock, consideration must be given to any ***cumulative dividends in arrears*** and other contractual limitations on the equity of preferred shareholders in the net assets of the corporation. On a going-concern basis, is it (1) par (or stated) value, (2) call price, or (3) liquidation price that is most significant in measuring the equity of the preferred stock? Nearly all preferred stocks contain a call provision; this call price usually is the maximum claim against net assets under the preferred stock contract. Although there may be no immediate prospect that the preferred stock will be called, the call price probably is more significant from the viewpoint of the going concern than is the liquidation price. Therefore, we favour using the call price of the preferred stock as the most appropriate measure of the equity applicable to preferred stock.

Significant changes in the equity per share of common stock may result from transactions such as conversions of bonds payable or preferred stock to common stock, issuances of additional shares of common stock, business combinations, and quasi-reorganizations. Some examples of events that change the equity per share of common stock are listed below:

- ***Increases in equity per share*** Net income, reverse splits, issuance of additional common stock at prices in excess of the present equity per share, acquisition of common stock for the treasury at prices less than the present equity per share, and redemption of preferred stock at prices less than the present equity per share of the preferred stock.
- ***Decreases in equity per share*** Net loss, cash dividends (including any dividends in arrears on cumulative preferred stock), stock dividends, stock splits, issuance of additional common stock at prices less than the present equity per share, acquisition of common stock for the treasury at prices in excess of the present equity per share, and redemption of preferred stock at prices in excess of the present equity per share of the preferred stock.

ANALYSIS OF FINANCIAL STRENGTH

A strong earnings record usually accompanies a strong financial position. Furthermore, an unsatisfactory financial position appears much less unfavourable in the presence of a good earnings record; a company with proved earning power usually works out its financial problems. However, a good earnings record is not the whole story. A company's ability to meet its obligations, to cope with economic adversity, to shift resources to meet changing conditions — in short, its financial strength — is an important factor to continuing survival and growth. In seeking evidence of financial strength, analysts consider first the relationship between assets and liabilities. They ask questions such as: Will the company be able to pay its liabilities when they are due? Does the company have the resources to meet current commitments and future demands for cash necessary to conduct its business successfully?

Ability to Pay Short-Term Debt

A company's short-term financial strength (or ***liquidity***) is dependent on two primary factors: its working capital position and the speed with which it generates liquid assets. We provide the selected financial data for Strength Limited below as a basis for discussion of these factors.

Working Capital Position

The amount by which current assets exceed current liabilities is the ***working capital*** of a business enterprise. Changes in the amount of working capital from

Data used to analyze working capital position

STRENGTH LIMITED
Selected Financial Data
For Year 1 Through Year 3
(In thousands of dollars)

	Year 3	*Year 2*	*Year 1*
Current assets:			
Cash	$ 50	$ 80	$ 60
Short-term investments		50	150
Accounts receivable (net)	500	400	300
Inventories (first-in, first-out cost)	1,100	700	500
Short-term prepayments	70	60	50
Total current assets	$ 1,720	$ 1,290	$ 1,060
Current liabilities:			
Notes payable	$ 120	$ 100	
Accounts payable	680	330	$ 170
Other current liabilities	220	170	140
Current portion of long-term debt	180	200	200
Total current liabilities	$ 1,200	$ 800	$ 510
Net sales	$ 3,500	$ 3,000	$ 2,600
Cost of goods sold	(2,600)	(2,000)	(1,900)
Operating expenses	(600)	(500)	(400)
Interest expense	(48)	(49)	(50)
Income before income taxes	$ 252	$ 451	$ 250
Income taxes expense	122	231	125
Net income	$ 130	$ 220	$ 125

one accounting period to another are significant, because the amount of working capital is a useful indicator of short-term debt-paying ability.

In addition to the dollar amount of working capital, two analytical ratios of working capital position often are computed. The ***current ratio*** (current assets divided by current liabilities) helps put the amount of working capital in perspective by showing the relationship between current resources and short-term debt. The ***quick ratio*** (sometimes called the ***acid-test ratio***) focusses on immediate liquidity. Inventories and short-term prepayments, the least liquid current assets, are excluded in the computation of the quick ratio. ***Quick assets*** consists of cash, short-term investments, and short-term receivables; and the quick ratio is computed by dividing quick assets by current liabilities. The working capital position of Strength Limited is summarized below:

Current ratio and quick ratio

STRENGTH LIMITED
Analysis of Working Capital Position
For Year 1 Through Year 3
(In thousands of dollars)

	Year 3	*Year 2*	*Year 1*
(a) Current assets	$1,720	$1,290	$1,060
(b) Current liabilities	1,200	800	510
Working capital (a − b)	$ 520	$ 490	$ 550
Current ratio (a ÷ b)	1.4	1.6	2.1
(c) Total quick assets (cash, short-term investments, and accounts receivable)	$ 550	$ 530	$ 510
Quick ratio (c ÷ b)	0.5	0.7	1.0

Each measurement presented above contributes something to the analysis of Strength Limited's working capital position. Strength has maintained its working capital at about $500,000 during the three-year period. However, its relative short-term liquidity has worsened, as indicated by the steady decline in the current ratio from 2.1 to 1.4 and in the quick ratio from 1.0 to 0.5 from Year 1 to Year 3. This is a picture of a company that may be heading toward financial difficulty, unless these trends are reversed. The increase in accounts payable from $170,000 to $680,000 during the last two years suggests that payments to creditors may be falling behind schedule. Thus, the analysis has brought to light a potential trouble spot in Strength's financial position. However, if the increase in accounts payable is the result of large current expenditures for research and development, or for inventories in anticipation of a significant increase in sales, then the trend must be evaluated in a more favourable light.

Need for Working Capital

A business enterprise generates working capital through a series of events called the ***operating cycle***. The operating cycle refers to the process of investing cash in inventories, converting the inventories to accounts receivable through sales, and collecting the receivables in cash, which in turn is used to pay current liabilities incurred in operations and to replace inventories. The average length of time necessary to complete this cycle is important in determining an enterprise's working capital needs. An enterprise with a short operating cycle may manage comfortably on a relatively small amount of working capital and with relatively small quick and current ratios. A long operating cycle requires a larger margin of current assets and larger quick and current ratios unless the credit terms of suppliers can be extended accordingly. The average length of the operating cycle may be estimated by adding the number of days' sales in average inventories to the average age of accounts receivable.

Inventories Turnover

The total cost of all goods that have been moved out of inventories during a year is represented by the cost of goods sold amount in the income statement. Therefore, the ratio of cost of goods sold to the average inventories during an accounting period is a measure of the number of times that inventories turn over on the average and must be replaced. The larger this turnover, the shorter the average time between investment in inventories and sales transactions.

Average inventories generally are determined by averaging monthly or quarterly inventory amounts. This information usually is not available to external analysts, however, and therefore only an average of the inventories at the beginning and end of the year is used. Because many companies adopt a fiscal year that ends when inventories are at a minimum, inventories turnover computed in this manner may appear larger than it really is.

Dividing the annual cost of goods sold by average inventories produces a "times per year" turnover rate. Turnover may be expressed in days by dividing 365 by the number of turnovers per year.[3] An additional useful measure is the ***number of days' sales in ending inventories***, computed by multiplying 365

Inventories turnover and days' sales in inventories

STRENGTH LIMITED
Analysis of Inventories
For Year 1 Through Year 3
(In thousands of dollars)

	Year 3	*Year 2*	*Year 1*
(a) Cost of goods sold	$2,600	$2,000	$1,900
Inventories, beginning of year	$ 700	$ 500	$ 540*
Inventories, end of year	1,100	700	500
(b) Average inventories	$ 900	$ 600	$ 520
(c) Turnover per year (a ÷ b)	2.9 times	3.3 times	3.7 times
Number of days' sales in *average* inventories (365 ÷ c)	126 days	111 days	99 days
Number of days' sales in *ending* inventories	154 days†	128 days	96 days

*Assumed.
†365 × $1,100/$2,600 = 154.

3 A year is sometimes viewed as consisting of 300 business days in the computation of the number of days of sales in inventories or receivables.

days by the fraction of which the ending inventories is the numerator and cost of goods sold is the denominator. The three-year analysis of inventories for Strength Limited is shown in the illustration on page 1249.

These computations show that inventories turnover has slowed during the three-year period from a little over three months to about four months, and that there are enough inventories on hand at the end of Year 3 to meet sales requirements at current levels for approximately five months (154 days).

For a manufacturing enterprise, the overall inventories turnover may be estimated by dividing cost of goods sold by the average amount of the three inventories: material, goods in process, and finished goods. Alternatively, three separate turnover rates may be computed: (1) cost of goods sold divided by average finished goods inventory, (2) cost of goods manufactured divided by average goods in process inventory, and (3) material used divided by average material inventory.

It should be pointed out that the foregoing computations would be misleading if the current cost of inventories were substantially higher than historical cost. In such cases, alternative measurements should be used to anlayze inventories.

Accounts Receivable Turnover

The turnover of accounts receivable may be computed in a manner comparable to that for inventories. Unless a business enterprise has a large amount of cash sales, sales for an accounting period produce inflows of accounts receivable. When net sales is divided by the average balance of accounts receivable during the period, the result is a rough indication of the average length of time necessary to convert accounts receivable to cash. Ideally, only credit sales should be included in the sales amount, and an average monthly balance of ***gross*** accounts receivable should be used. However, these refinements may not be possible in external analysis, and a less exact computation may serve the purpose of indicating favourable or unfavourable trends. The reasonableness of the ending balance of accounts

Receivables turnover and days' sales in receivables

STRENGTH LIMITED
Analysis of Accounts Receivable
For Year 1 Through Year 3
(In thousands of dollars)

	Year 3	*Year 2*	*Year 1*
(a) Net sales	$3,500	$3,000	$2,600
Accounts receivable, beginning of year	$ 400	$ 300	$ 280*
Accounts receivable, end of year	500	400	300
(b) Average accounts receivable	$ 450	$ 350	$ 290
(c) Accounts receivable turnover (a ÷ b)	7.8 times	8.6 times	9.0 times
Number of days' sales in ***average*** accounts receivable (365 ÷ c)	47 days	42 days	41 days
Number of days' sales in ***ending*** accounts receivable	52 days†	49 days	42 days

*Assumed.
†365 × $500/$3,500 = 52.

receivable may be evaluated by computing the ***number of days' sales in ending accounts receivable***. The accounts receivable of Strength Limited are analyzed at the bottom of page 1250 (dollar amounts are in thousands).

It is evident that, absent a change in credit terms, collections have slowed down over the three-year period. The trend is unfavourable; interpretation of the absolute amounts depends on the credit terms and policies of Strength Limited.

Length of Operating Cycle

As stated on page 1249, an estimate of the average length of the operating cycle may be computed by adding the average days' sales in inventories and in accounts receivable. This is illustrated below for Strength Limited:

Length of operating cycle for Strength Limited

	Year 3	*Year 2*	*Year 1*
Average days to dispose of inventories	126	111	99
Average days to collect accounts receivable	47	42	41
Average days in operating cycle	173	153	140

The operating cycle of Strength has increased by more than a full month (33 days) from Year 1 to Year 3. If this has happened inadvertently, it may explain the unfavourable trend in the current and quick ratios. If the change is the result of company policy, it indicates the need for a larger amount of working capital to finance current operations.

Number of Days' Operations to Cover Negative Working Capital

When current liabilities exceed current assets, management may estimate the length of time it will take to eliminate the negative working capital as a result of generating liquid assets from operations. For example, assume that the current liabilities of Lomax Corporation on March 31, Year 6, exceeded its current assets by $20,000. Assume further that Lomax's operations are relatively stable during a calendar year and normally generate working capital as follows:

Working capital provided from operations...

Net income	$ 75,000
Add: Depreciation expense and other expenses that do not require use of working capital	45,000
Working capital normally provided from operations over 12-month period	$120,000

From the foregoing information we may estimate that the negative working capital of $20,000 will be eliminated in approximately two months:

...will eliminate the working capital deficit in two months

$$\frac{\$20{,}000 \text{ (negative working capital)}}{\$120{,}000 \text{ (annual working capital provided from operations)}} \times 365 \text{ days} = \underline{\underline{61 \text{ days}}}$$

Interpreting the Analysis of Liquidity

The following factors should be considered in interpreting the liquidity of a company as shown by the analytical procedures just described:

1. Creditors tend to believe that the larger the current and quick ratios and the shorter the operating cycle, the better. From the viewpoint of company performance, there are limits. It is possible for a company to accumulate working capital in excess of the amount that may be employed profitably. Thus, excessive current and quick ratios are unfavourable indicators. Similarly, an unusually high rate of inventories turnover may indicate that a company is losing business by failing to maintain adequate inventories to serve customers' needs. A rapid turnover of accounts receivable may indicate overly severe credit policies that reduce revenue below levels that could be achieved by more liberal credit terms.

2. Because creditors and other outsiders emphasize a company's working capital position as evidence of short-run solvency, there is a temptation for managers to take action just before the end of an accounting period to make the working capital relationships appear more favourable than they are. This process is called ***window dressing***. By postponing purchases, allowing inventories to decrease below normal levels, using all available cash to pay current liabilities, and pressing collections on accounts receivable, a company may artificially improve its current and quick ratios, as well as its inventories and accounts receivable turnover rates. Decreases in accounts receivable and inventories will increase turnover rates. Any equal decrease in both current assets and current liabilities will improve a current ratio that already is more than 1 to 1.

3. Even when no deliberate attempt has been made to present an artificially favourable picture, the working capital position shown by year-end financial statements is probably more favourable than at any other time of the year. This is particularly true when a company has adopted a ***natural business year*** that ends during an ebb in the seasonal swing of business activity. At times of peak activity, accounts receivable, inventories, and current liabilities tend to be at higher levels. There are many reasons why a natural business year is desirable, and accountants generally encourage companies to adopt such an accounting period.

Analysis of Capital Structure

The way in which a business enterprise meets its financing needs, as reflected in its ***capital structure***, is an important factor in assessing its financial strength and the use of ***financial leverage***. The most common approach for this purpose is to restate the major elements of the liabilities and shareholders' equity to component percentages of total assets, as shown on page 1253.

Debt and Equity Ratios

Analysts often condense the essence of the capital structure of a company into one or more of three ratios. The ***debt ratio*** is the ratio of total liabilities to total

Three ways to measure relationship between debt and equity

Component percentages				*Debt and equity ratios*	
Total assets		100%			
Sources of financing:					
Current liabilities		10%			
Long-term debt		18%			
Total liabilities		28%	→	Debt ratio	28%
Preferred stock	9%				
Common shareholders' equity	63%	72%	→	Equity ratio	72%
Total liabilities & shareholders' equity		100%		Debt-to-equity ratio (28 ÷ 72) ..	39%

assets; the ***equity ratio*** is the ratio of shareholders' equity to total assets; and the ***debt-to-equity ratio*** is the ratio of total liabilities to shareholders' equity. Any one of these ratios tells the essential story about the debt-equity relationship for a company.

Financial analysts compute other ratios to aid in evaluating capital structure. For example, the ratio of total plant assets to shareholders' equity sometimes is used as a test of the adequacy of equity capital. If the investment in plant assets is substantial relative to shareholders' equity, this indicates that a company has borrowed heavily to invest in nonliquid assets, which may lead to difficulties should earnings not prove satisfactory.

Evaluating Capital Structure

What factors should be considered in evaluating the capital structure of a company? The answer to this question depends on the concerns of creditors and shareholders.

Creditors' View

Creditors are primarily concerned with the safety of their claims. They view a relatively low debt ratio as a favourable factor because it indicates a substantial cushion of protection against a shrinkage in asset values. Because the source for payment of debt is either new borrowing or internal cash flow, all creditors are interested in long-run financial strength and a healthy earnings record. The debt ratio and the times-interest-earned ratio are the prime indicators of financial strength from the creditor's viewpoint.

Shareholders' View

Present or prospective shareholders are concerned with a company's ability to meet its long-term debt obligations, because failure to pay interest or current maturities of debt is a serious matter affecting adversely both the credit standing of the company and the position of shareholders. A low debt ratio, or the absence of long-term debt, is not necessarily to the shareholders' advantage. To the extent that a company is able to earn a return in excess of the interest rate on its long-term debt, its shareholders' benefit from the ***leverage factor***. However, this benefit may be more than offset by the increased risks and costs of the various restrictive covenants included in the borrowing contract by the lender, which may limit management's freedom of action.

It has been argued that the existence of long-term debt or other senior securities increases the risk borne by common shareholders and causes the common stock to trade at a lower price-earnings ratio. In a well-managed and profitable company, it is doubtful whether a reasonable amount of debt increases the common shareholders' risk sufficiently to be reflected in the price-earnings ratio of the common stock. If the amount of long-term debt is excessive and earnings are not increasing, it is likely that the advantage of ***trading on the equity*** will be offset by the dampening effect of the large debt on the market price of the company's common stock.

Capacity of Additional Investment and Growth in Earnings

A business enterprise seldom is able to maintain a stable position over a long period of time; it either changes and grows, or stagnates and dies. A healthy company must be able to finance the development of new products as old ones lose their profit potential, and to move in new directions as demand and technology change. An important element of financial strength is the ability to generate additional cash when needed.

In part, this means the ability to borrow or to obtain new capital from owners. Another major source of investment capital is earnings retained for use in business operations. Many enterprises typically generate more cash and cash equivalents each period than the amount of net income (see Chapter 23). The amount of cash provided from operations, less dividend and sinking-fund requirements, offers a rough indicator of the internally generated funds available to expand the level of operations (expand plant capacity, develop new products, enter new markets, undertake business combinations) or to retire long-term debt.

Standards for Comparison

When analysts have computed the significant dollar and percentage changes and ratios and have reduced the mass of financial data to digestible form, they need some criteria as a guide in evaluating these findings and in making business and investment decisions. Three possibilities are discussed in the following sections.

Past Record of the Company

A comparison of analytical data over time (sometimes called ***horizontal analysis***, in contrast to ***vertical analysis***, which deals with single-year financial statements) may reveal trends in performance and position that will aid in determining progress or lack of progress and may help in assessing future prospects. Many companies present trends in sales, earnings, and other data in the form of a graph. (For some examples, see pages 204, 205, and 206 of Chapter 4.) As a basis for forecasting, the projecting of past trends into the future has serious limitations, because changes may reverse direction at any time. However, knowing that the trend is favourable or unfavourable leads to further inquiry as to the underlying reasons.

Another limitation of horizontal analysis is that the past record of a company does not afford a basis for comparison with similarly situated companies. For example, if the sales of a company have increased 10%, but industry sales have increased 50%, the 10% increase may appear to be favourable, but the company's sales performance in its industry is poor.

Comparison with Competitors or Industry as a Whole

Perhaps the best way to put a company's performance in perspective is to compare its position and operating results with those of competitors. For example, a study by Dun & Bradstreet, Inc., of the financial statements of drug companies showed the following:

Example of financial statistics for an industry

	Current ratio	*Net profits on net sales*	*Return on owners' investment*	*Total debt to owners' equity*	*Net sales to inventories (times)*
Upper quartile	3.5	11.3%	20.4%	35.8%	9.1
Median	2.6	6.8	15.4	43.5	6.3
Lower quartile	1.8	2.9	5.5	63.6	4.6

On the basis of this kind of information, an analyst examining the financial statements of a drug company obtains some idea of the position of the company in relation to others in the industry. Note that Dun & Bradstreet, Inc., apparently computes ''inventories turnover'' by dividing net sales by the amount of average inventories. Although this procedure often is used by financial analysts as a matter of convenience, it does not measure ''turnover,'' but simply relates the average level of inventories (at cost) to the sales volume for the year (at selling prices).

One of the difficulties in making comparisons among business enterprises is that some companies that appear to be in the same industry are not comparable because industries are difficult to define. For example, many companies have diversified their activities by moving into new fields or acquiring other companies whose business activities are not closely related, with the result that companies falling roughly within the same industry are no longer comparable in many respects. When ***diversified enterprises*** report industry segment sales and profitability figures, it is much easier to analyze their financial statements.

In the ***CICA Handbook***, section 1700, ''Segmented Information,'' the Accounting Standards Committee established standards for disclosure of information about the reporting corporation's operations in different industries, its foreign operations, and its export sales.[4] Also, in section 3840.18, the committee recommended disclosures with respect to economic dependence on another party with whom the corporation conducts business. Section 1700 also required that a corporation operating predominantly in a single industry disclose that fact ***together with ''a***

4 CICA, ***CICA Handbook***, sec. 1700.

general description of products and services from which revenue is derived."[5] The information to be reported for each industry segment includes:[6]

> A general description of the products and services from which each reportable industry segment derives its revenue should be provided. Disclosure of the following data should be made for each reportable industry segment and, in aggregate, for the remainder of the enterprise's industry segments:
> 1 segment revenue derived from sales to customers outside the enterprise;
> 2 segment revenue derived from inter-segment sales or transfers and the basis of accounting therefor;
> 3 segment operating profit or loss, the amount of depreciation, amortization and depletion expense, and any unusual items included in determining segment operating profit or loss; and
> 4 total carrying amount of identifiable assets at the end of the fiscal year and the amount of capital expenditure for the period.
>
> A reconciliation of the aggregate segment revenue, aggregate segment operating profit or loss and aggregate identifiable assets to the sales, net income and total assets reported in the financial statements of the enterprise should be provided.

A ***reportable industry segment*** is one which[7] **1** includes 10% or more of the combined identifiable assets of the corporation, **2** generates 10% or more of the corporation's revenue, or **3** generates 10% or more, in absolute terms, of the corporation's segments' operating incomes and losses. The purpose of disclosure of segment information is to help users of financial statements to analyze and understand the corporation's past performance and future prospects. For a complete discussion of segment reporting the student should consult an advanced accounting text.

Comparison with Independent Statistical Measures

It often is useful to relate certain financial indexes for a business enterprise to statistical measures. For example, a comparison of the trend of sales or net income with an ***index of industrial production*** may show whether the enterprise is growing more slowly or faster than the economy. Similarly, indexes may be developed for sales and net income, for example, comparing the performance of a single enterprise with the industry performance index during the same period. Price indexes may be used to deflate sales in dollars to determine whether the growth in sales is a growth in physical volume or the result of inflation. It also may be possible to relate financial data to physical measures of production or output. For example, statistics such as the average freight haul in miles per ton, or the average revenue per ton-mile, give a useful basis for comparing the operating performance of difference railroad companies.

5 CICA, ***CICA Handbook***, sec. 1700.34.

6 CICA, ***CICA Handbook***, sec. 1700.33.

7 CICA, ***CICA Handbook***, sec. 1700.23.

Inflation and Analysis of Financial Statements

Financial statements prepared on the basis of historical cost do not reflect fully the economic resources or the ***real*** income (in terms of purchasing power) of a business enterprise. Financial analysts must attempt to evaluate the impact of inflation on the financial position and results of operations of the enterprise they are evaluating. They should raise questions such as: How much of the income is attributable to price increases? Are expenses (such as depreciation) understated in terms of current price levels? Is the enterprise gaining or losing from inflation because of the composition of its assets and the amount of its liabilities? Financial statements adjusted for price level changes are illustrated in Chapter 25.

Summary of Ratios and Other Analytical Measurements

The more widely used ratios and other measurements discussed in this chapter and their significance are summarized below and on pages 1258–1259.

Summary of ratios and other analytical measurements

	Ratio or other measurement	*Method of computation*	*What it shows*
Earnings performance	1 Return on total assets	$\frac{\text{Net income + interest expense}}{\text{Average investment in assets}}$	Productivity of assets
	2 Return on common shareholders' equity	$\frac{\text{Net income − preferred stock dividends}}{\text{Average common shareholders' equity}}$	Earning power on residual owners' equity
	3 Earnings per share of common stock	$\frac{\text{Net income − preferred dividends}}{\text{Average number of shares of common stock outstanding}}$	Amount earned on each share of common stock
	4 Price-earnings ratio for common stock	$\frac{\text{Market price per share}}{\text{Earnings per share}}$	Whether market price of common stock is in line with earnings
	5 Dividend yield on common stock	$\frac{\text{Dividends per share}}{\text{Market price per share}}$	Return to common shareholders based on current market price of common stock
	6 Dividend payment ratio for common stock	$\frac{\text{Dividends per share}}{\text{Earnings per share}}$	Percentage of earnings distributed as dividends
	7 Number of times interest earned (before income taxes)	$\frac{\text{Operating income}}{\text{Annual interest expense}}$	Coverage of interest expense (particularly on long-term debt)
	8 Times preferred stock dividends earned	$\frac{\text{Net income}}{\text{Annual preferred stock dividends}}$	Adequacy of earnings to pay preferred stock dividends

	Ratio	Formula	Significance
Financial strength—liquidity and leverage	9 Equity (book value) per share of common stock	Common shareholders' equity / Number of shares of common stock outstanding	Amount of net assets allocable to each share of common stock
	10 Current ratio	Current assets / Current liabilities	Short-run debt-paying ability
	11 Quick (acid-test) ratio	Quick assets / Current liabilities	Short-term liquidity
	12 Inventories turnover	Cost of good sold / Average inventories	Ability to control investment in inventories
	13 Accounts receivables turnover	Net sales on credit / Average accounts receivable	Possible excessive accounts receivable; effectiveness of collection policy
	14 Debt ratio	Total liabilities / Total assets	Extent of borrowing and trading on the equity (financial leverage)
	15 Equity ratio	Total shareholders' equity / Total assets	Protection to creditors and extent of trading on the equity (financial leverage)
	16 Debt-to-equity ratio	Total liabilities / Total shareholders' equity	Relationship between borrowed capital and equity capital

The relevance of any of the foregoing measurements depends on the direction of its trend and on its comparison with a predetermined standard. The information available in financial statements may be useful in appraising a company's financial position, in predicting its earnings, and in making other predictive judgements about the company. Relationships among reported data may be quite informative. However, we must remember that financial statements have limitations and that qualitative factors may be far more important than "cold figures." For example, factors such as the following should be considered by analysts in predicting the likely earnings performance of a company: (1) source of markets for the company's products and services; (2) growth potential for its products and services; (3) market share in its industry; (4) patent protection, if any, for its major products; (5) sensitivity of its earnings to economic fluctuations; (6) effect of technological and environmental changes on its business activities; and, perhaps the most important factor, (7) the quality of its management.

Analysts should keep in mind that, although a balance sheet is a statement of assets and claims against these assets,most assets are stated at historical cost, and not all elements of value are included in the balance sheet (for example, capable management, good credit standing, potential new products, internally developed goodwill, and the appreciation in the value of assets, especially natural resources). Furthermore, the ***quality of assets and earnings*** must be carefully evaluated. An income statement is a product of matching expired costs with realized revenue and covers only a brief period of a company's life. Consequently, the income statement does not necessarily measure the ***improvement in the company's economic wealth*** during the accounting period. The dangers of attaching too much significance to either the balance sheet or the income statement should be recognized by those undertaking an analysis of financial statements.

REVIEW QUESTIONS

1 Describe four sources from which an outsider might obtain financial information about a business enterprise.

2 Explain what is meant by the following terms:

a ***Trend percentage***
b ***Common-size statements***
c ***Trading on the equity***
d ***Capital structure***
e ***Dividend payout ratio***
f ***Price-earnings ratio***

3 *a* Discuss some limitations of single-year financial statements for purposes of analysis and interpretation.
b To what extent are these limitations overcome by the use of comparative financial statements?
c In what ways may a five-year summary of financial data be misleading?

4 Describe the effect of each of the following transactions on the indicated ratios. Will the ratio increase, decrease, or remain unchanged?

	Transaction		*Ratio*
a	Purchase of merchandise for cash	*a*	Current ratio of 2 to 1
b	Payment of accounts payable	*b*	Quick ratio of 0.6 to 1
c	Accounts receivable written off against Allowance for Doubtful Accounts ledger account	*c*	Average age of accounts receivable of 60 days
d	Declaration of cash dividend on preferred stock	*d*	Equity ratio of 60%
e	Distribution of a 10% common stock dividend	*e*	Loss per share of common stock, $1.20
f	Conversion of long-term debt to common stock	*f*	Return on total long-term capital
g	Change from fifo to lifo method of inventories valuation during period of rising prices	*g*	Inventories turnover

5 Each of the following ratios has been used at times by financial analysts. Explain what each indicates, and why it is or is not significant.

a Ratio of plant assets to long-term debt
b Ratio of net sales to working capital (working capital turnover)
c Ratio of current liabilities to inventories
d Ratio of total operating expenses to current liabilities

e Ratio of plant assets to shareholders' equity
f Ratio of long-term debt to working capital
g Ratio of net sales to shareholders' equity
h Ratio of net income to current assets

6 In an analysis of the financial position and operations of a business enterprise, it is necessary to have some standards or criteria for comparison. Suggest several standards that may be employed for this purpose.

7 An estimate of inventories turnover sometimes is made by dividing net sales by average inventories. Evaluate this method of computing inventories turnover.

8 What procedures are required to compute the equity (book value) per share of common stock in each of the following cases?
a Both preferred stock and common stock are outstanding
b Treasury stock (common) has been acquired

9 The equity (book value) of 100,000 shares of common stock is $40 a share. Indicate the effect of each of the following four transactions on the equity per share:
a Issuance of additional shares of common stock at $10 a share pursuant to stock option contract
b Issuance of additional shares of common stock at $60 a share through rights offering
c Acquisition of common stock for treasury at $75 a share
d Conversion of bonds at 20 shares of common stock for every $1,000 bond

10 Two companies have the same amount of working capital. The current debt-paying ability of one company is much weaker than the other. Explain how this could occur.

11 Explain how you would evaluate the ability of a business enterprise to make required payments on long-term debt or to finance replacements of plant assets, assuming that you had available financial statements of the enterprise for the last five years.

12 If you were asked to make three analytical computations (ratios, percentages, etc.) that would be most useful in appraising the financial statements of a corporation from the viewpoint of the following parties, which computations would you make, and why do you feel these are of prime importance?
a Short-term creditor
b Long-term creditor
c Prospective investor in the corporation's preferred stock
d Prospective investor in the corporation's common stock

13 In response to a request that its ***profit margins on different products*** be disclosed, the management of Raines Limited responded, ''Public disclosure would cause us to suffer at the hands of our competitors, particularly in regard to a product that accounts for 90% of our sales.'' In what ways would the disclosure of this information possibly be detrimental to Raines?

14 The following comments by an oil company executive appeared in an article in a financial journal:

In seeking textbook ratios between current assets and current liabilities, some companies may be going overboard on building up cash. These ratios may not mean much any more. In the old days, when these ratios were established, credit facilities weren't so readily available as they are today. There are elements of liquidity that don't show up in the balance sheet, such as a contractual line of bank credit, which may be just as solid as a savings account. But to some extent, we're stuck with archaic ratios that the investment community likes to see.

Evaluate these comments.

15 In the ***CICA Handbook***, section 1700, ''Segmented Information,'' the Accounting Standards Committee established standards for disclosure of information about the reporting enterprise's operations in different industries, its foreign operations, and its export sales. Define a ***reportable industry segment*** and indicate the type of information that is reported for each such segment.

EXERCISES

Ex. 24-1 Select the best answer for each of the following multiple-choice questions:

1 Are inventories included in the computation of the quick (acid-test) ratio? Current ratio? Answer ***a***, ***b***, ***c***, or ***d*** in accordance with the following table.

	Quick (acid-test) ratio	*Current ratio*
a	Yes	Yes
b	Yes	No
c	No	Yes
d	No	No

2 How are the following used in the computation of the dividend payout ratio for a corporation with only common stock outstanding?

	Dividends per share	*Earnings per share*	*Equity per share*
a	Denominator	Numerator	Not used
b	Denominator	Not used	Numerator
c	Numerator	Denominator	Not used
d	Numerator	Not used	Denominator

3 A corporation's dividend yield for an accounting period is computed by dividing:

a Dividends declared per share by earnings per share
b Dividends declared per share by equity (book value) per share
c Dividends declared per share by end-of-period market price per share
d Earnings per share by dividends per share

4 The number of days' sales in average accounts receivable is computed by:
   a Multiplying the accounts receivable turnover by 30
   b Dividing the accounts receivable turnover by 30
   c Multiplying the accounts receivable turnover by 365
   d Dividing 365 by the accounts receivable turnover

5 Sato Ltd. has total liabilities of $600,000 and total shareholders' equity of $900,000. Sato's equity ratio is:
   a 150.0% *b* 66.7% *c* 60.0% *d* 40.0% *e* Some other percentage

6 The ratio of an amount in a financial statement to the total that includes the amount is a:
   a Component percentage
   b Common-size percentage
   c Trend percentage
   d Turnover percentage

7 In comparing the current ratios of two companies, why is it inappropriate for the analyst to assume that the company with the larger current ratio is more successful than the other company?
   a The current ratio includes assets other than cash
   b A large current ratio may indicate inadequate inventories
   c A large current ratio may indicate inefficient management of current assets and current liabilities
   d the two companies may define ***working capital*** differently

8 Which of the following transactions increases a current ratio of at least 1:1?
   a Disposal of short-term investments at a loss
   b Use of the equity method of accounting for an influenced investee
   c Borrowing cash on a short-term promissory note
   d Paying the principal of a short-term promissory note

9 Ander, Inc., was organized on January 2, Year 1, with the following capital structure:

10% cumulative preferred stock, par and liquidation value $100, callable at 110, authorized, issued, and outstanding 1,000 shares	$100,000
Common stock, no par value, authorized 20,000 shares, issued and outstanding 10,000 shares	50,000

Ander's net income for the year ended December 31, Year 1, was $450,000, but no dividends were declared. How much was Ander's common shareholders' equity (book value) per share on December 31, Year 1?
   a $44 *b* $45 *c* $49 *d* $50 *e* Some other amount

Ex. 24-2 Trend percentages and common-size percentages for Westward Corporation for the years ended December 31, Year 2 and Year 1, are shown in the next table.
   a Compute the missing trend percentages and common-size percentages for Westward Corporation.

	Year 2	*Year 1*
Trend percentages:		
Net sales	120%	100%
Cost of goods sold	?	100
Gross profit on sales	?	100
Operating expenses and income taxes expense	?	100
Net income	?	100
Common-size percentages:		
Net sales	100%	100%
Cost of goods sold	?	?
Gross profit on sales	45%	? %
Operating expenses and income taxes expense	27.5	30
Net income	? %	10%

b If the net income for Year 1 amounted to $10,000, compute the net income of Westward Corporation Company for Year 2.

Ex. 24-3 The following common-size income statements are available for Lewis Corporation for the two years ended December 31, Year 5 and Year 4:

	Year 5	*Year 4*
Net sales	100%	100%
Cost of goods sold	55	70
Gross profit on sales	45%	30%
Operating expenses (including income taxes expense)	20	18
Net income	25%	12%

The trend percentages for sales are as follows:

Year 5	125%
Year 4	100%

Compute the trend percentage for gross profit on sales of Lewis Corporation for Year 5, rounded to the nearest tenth.

Ex. 24-4 The information in the next table (in thousands of dollars) for three companies is presented to you on December 31, Year 10.

Compute the following for each company for Year 10:

a Number of times interest was earned (before income taxes), to the nearest hundredth; the income tax rate is 45%

b Rate earned on ending shareholders' equity, to the nearest tenth

c Rate earned on total assets on December 31, Year 10 (before interest expense and income taxes of 45%), to the nearest tenth

	Alb Limited	*Bur Limited*	*Con Limited*
Total assets	$140,000	$140,000	$140,000
Current liabilities	$ 20,000	$ 50,000	$ 20,000
10% bonds payable, due in Year 15	40,000		
12% bonds payable, due in Year 20		10,000	
10% bonds payable, due in Year 22			80,000
Shareholders' equity	80,000	80,000	40,000
Total liabilities & shareholders' equity	$140,000	$140,000	$140,000
Net income	$ 14,025	$ 12,650	$ 9,790

Ex. 24-5 Quigley, Inc., has the following capital structure (in millions): 10% bonds, $12.5; 11% preferred stock, $30.0; common stock (contributed capital and retained earnings), $50.0. Income before interest and income taxes at 45% for Year 6 was $15 million.

Compute the amount of Year 6 earnings of Quigley, Inc., available for common stock.

Ex. 24-6 Exeter Corporation reported earnings per share for Year 4 of $4.20 on 100,000 shares of common stock outstanding during the entire year. On April 1, Year 5, Exeter declared a 50% common stock dividend, and on October 1 it issued 60,000 shares of common stock for cash. Net income for Year 5 was $528,000. No preferred stock was outstanding.

Compute the increase or decrease in earnings per share of common stock of Exeter Corporation in Year 5.

Ex. 24-7 Silvio Corporation had total shareholders' equity of $35,500,000, including $10,750,000 of retained earnings. The capital stock included in shareholders' equity on April 30, Year 5, follows:

12% preferred stock, no par value, callable at $53 a share, 200,000 shares issued and outstanding (no dividends in arrears)	$10,000,000
Common stock, no par value, 5,000,000 shares authorized, 1,550,000 shares issued, 1,500,000 shares outstanding (50,000 shares, cost $750,000, in treasury)	15,500,000

Compute the equity (book value) per share of common stock of Silvio Corporation on April 30, Year 5.

Ex. 24-8 Comparative balance sheets and other financial information for Winsett Limited, a retail enterprise, are presented on page 1265. Dollar amounts are in thousands. Sales for Year 2 were $100 million, and cost of goods sold amounted to $58 million. Other items from the income statement for Year 2 were: interest expense, $2 million; income taxes expense, $9.9 million; and net income, $12.1 million.

WINSETT COMPANY
Comparative Balance Sheets
December 31, Year 2 and Year 1
(In thousands of dollars)

	Year 2	*Year 1*
Assets		
Cash	$ 7,000	$ 4,000
Short-term investments	2,000	4,000
Accounts receivable (net)	13,000	9,000
Inventories	9,000	7,000
Plant assets (net)	69,000	66,000
Total assets	$100,000	$90,000
Liabilities & Shareholders' Equity		
Current liabilities	$ 14,000	$16,000
Bonds payable, due in Year 15	24,000	20,000
Common stock, no par value	30,000	30,000
Retained earnings	32,000	24,000
Total liabilities & shareholders' equity	$100,000	$90,000

Show how you would compute the following ratios (or measurements) for Winsett Limited for Year 2 by listing the appropriate dollar or other amounts to be used in computing each item. For example: debt ratio, $38,000 ÷ $100,000.

a Current ratio
b Quick (acid-test) ratio
c Times interest earned (before income taxes)
d Rate of gross profit on sales
e Earnings per share of common stock

Ex. 24-9 Information for Hovack Limited is presented below for the two years ended December 31, Year 2 and Year 1:

	Year 2	*Year 1*
Cash	$ 30,000	$ 30,000
Accounts receivable	60,000	40,000
Less: Allowance for doubtful accounts	(5,000)	(4,000)
Inventories	45,000	35,000
Plant assets (net)	230,000	189,000
Totals	$360,000	$290,000
Accounts payable	$ 50,000	$ 40,000
12% bonds payable	100,000	100,000
Common stock, no par value	130,000	100,000
Retained earnings	80,000	50,000
Totals	$360,000	$290,000
Sales (all on credit)	$180,000	$120,000
Cost of goods sold	100,000	70,000
Gross profits on sales	$ 80,000	$ 50,000

Operating expenses and income taxes expense	50,000	30,000
Net income	$ 30,000	$ 20,000

Compute each of the following for Hovack Limited for Year 2 (show computations):

a Quick (acid-test) ratio
b Number of days' sales in gross accounts receivable at year-end
c Inventories turnover
d Equity (book value) per share of common stock at year-end
e Number of days' sales in inventories at year-end

Ex. 24-10 Selected amounts from the comparative balance sheets of Quebec Corporation are as follows:

	Dec. 31, Year 2	*Dec. 31, Year 1*
Current assets	$4,224,000	$3,500,000
Other assets	5,376,000	6,500,000
Current liablities	1,920,000	2,500,000
Bonds payable, due in Year 7	1,680,000	2,000,000
Common stock, $10 par	3,600,000	3,600,000
Retained earnings	2,400,000	1,900,000

Dividends of $220,000 were declared in Year 2. Dividends and net income accounted for the change in retained earnings. There was no preferred stock outstanding.

Compute the following for Quebec Corporation (show computations):

a Current ratio, December 31, Year 1
b Working capital, December 31, Year 2
c Equity ratio, December 31, Year 1
d Debt ratio, December 31, Year 2
e Earnings per share of common stock for Year 2
f Equity (book value) per share, December 31, Year 2

Ex. 24-11 Selected financial data for Menzies Corporation follow:

	Dec. 31, Year 2	*Dec. 31, Year 1*
Cash	$ 10,000	$ 80,000
Short-term investments	30,000	10,000
Accounts receivable (net)	50,000	150,000
Inventories	90,000	150,000
Plant assets (net)	340,000	360,000
Notes payable (current)	20,000	40,000
Accounts payable	70,000	110,000
Mortgage note payable (due in Year 5)	280,000	280,000
Cash sales	1,800,000	1,600,000

Credit sales	500,000	800,000
Cost of goods sold	1,000,000	1,400,000

Compute the following for Menzies Corporation for Year 2 (show supporting computations):

a Quick (acid-test) ratio
b Accounts receivable turnover
c Inventories turnover
d Current ratio

Ex. 24-12 *a* Lopar Corporation's net accounts receivable totalled $250,000 on December 31, Year 1, and $300,000 on December 31, Year 2. Net cash sales for Year 2 totalled $100,000, and the accounts receivable turnover for Year 2 was 5.
Compute Lopar Corporation's total net sales for Year 2.

b Selected financial information for Capper Corporation follows:

	Year 2	*Year 1*
8% noncumulative, nonconvertible preferred stock, $100 par and liquidation value	$125,000	$125,000
Common stock	400,000	300,000
Retained earnings	185,000	75,000
Dividends declared and paid on preferred stock	10,000	10,000
Net income	120,000	60,000

Compute Capper Corporation's return on shareholders' equity for Year 2.

c Proteus Limited's shareholders' equity on December 31, Year 7, was as follows:

$6 cumulative preferred stock, no par value, 1,000 shares authorized, issued, and outstanding (dividends in arrears for Year 3 through Year 7)	$100,000
Common stock, no par value, 300,000 shares authorized, 50,000 shares issued and outstanding	500,000
Retained earnings	90,000

Compute Proteus Limited's equity (book value) per share of common stock on December 31, Year 7.

d Vance Corporation had 100,000 shares of no-par-value common stock issued and outstanding throughout Year 8. Total shareholders' equity on December 31, Year 8, was $2,800,000, and net income for the year ended December 31, Year 8, was $800,000. During Year 8 Vance declared and paid dividends of $3 a share on the common stock. Market price of Vance's common stock was $24 on December 31, Year 8.
Compute the price-earnings ratio of Vance Corporation's common stock for the year ended December 31, Year 8.

CASES

Case 24-1 Financial statements and notes to the financial statements prepared by the accountant of Romo Limited for the year ended October 31, Year 8, follow:

ROMO LIMITED
Income Statement
For Year Ended October 31, Year 8

Sales		$1,000,000
Cost of goods sold		750,000
Gross profit on sales		$ 250,000
Expenses:		
Doubtful accounts expense	$ 7,000	
Insurance	13,000	
Lease expenses (**NOTE 1**)	40,000	
Repairs and maintenance	30,000	
Pensions (**NOTE 2**)	12,000	
Salaries	60,000	162,000
Earnings before income taxes		$ 88,000
Income taxes expense		28,740
Net income		$ 59,260
Earnings per share		$ 0.5926

ROMO LIMITED
Statement of Retained Earnings
For Year Ended October 31, Year 8

Retained earnings, beginning of year	$150,000
Add: Extraordinary item (gain), net of income tax effect	25,000
Net income	59,260
Subtotal	$234,260
Less: Dividends ($0.3426 a share)	34,260
Retained earnings, end of year	$200,000

ROMO LIMITED
Balance Sheet
October 31, Year 8

Assets

Cash	$ 15,000
Accounts receivable (net)	150,000
Inventories	120,000
Total current assets	$285,000
Land	125,000
Trademark (**NOTE 3**)	250,000
Total assets	$660,000

Liabilities & Shareholders' Equity

Accounts payable		$ 80,000
Other current liabilities		20,000
Deferred income tax credits (**NOTE 4**)		80,000
Common stock, no par value (**NOTE 5**)	$280,000	
Retained earnings	200,000	480,000
Total liabilities & shareholders' equity		$660,000

NOTE 1—Long-Term Lease: Under the terms of a five-year noncancellable lease for buildings and equipment, the company is obligated to make annual rental payments of $40,000 in each of the next four fiscal years. At the conclusion of the lease term, the company has an option to acquire the leased assets for $20,000 (a bargain purchase option) or to renew the lease for another five-year term at an annual rental of $5,000.

NOTE 2—Pension Plan: Substantially all employees are covered by the company's pension plan. Pension expense is equal to the total of pension benefits paid to retired employees during the year.

NOTE 3—Trademark: The company's trademark was acquired from Apex Corporation on January 2, Year 6, for $250,000.

NOTE 4—Deferred Income Tax Credits: The entire amount of the deferred income tax credits resulted from dividends received from taxable Canadian corporations in the previous year, giving rise to a difference between taxable income and reported net income for the year ended October 31, Year 7. The deferred income tax credits amount was computed on the basis of expected tax rates in future years.

NOTE 5—Warrants: On January 2, Year 7, one common stock warrant was issued to shareholders of record for each share of common stock owned. An additional share of common stock is to be issued on exercise of 10 stock warrants and receipt of an amount of $1 per share. For the six months ended October 31, Year 8, the average market price for the company's common stock was $5 a share, and no warrants were exercised.

NOTE 6—Contingency: On October 31, Year 8, the company was contingently liable for product warranties in an amount estimated to aggregate $75,000. This loss contingency was not recognized in the accounting records.

Instructions

Review the foregoing financial statements of Romo Limited for the year ended October 31, Year 8, and the notes to the financial statements. Identify any inclusions or exclusions from them that are in violation of generally accepted accounting principles, and indicate corrective action to be taken. Do not comment as to format or style. Respond in the following order:

- Income statement
- Statement of retained earnings
- Balance sheet
- Notes to the financial statements
- General

Case 24-2 Lindell Corporation needs additional capital for plant expansion. The board of directors is considering obtaining the funds by issuing additional short-term promissory notes, long-term bonds, preferred stock, or common stock.

Instructions

a What primary factors should the board of directors of Lindell Corporation consider in selecting the best method of financing plant expansion?

b One member of the board of directors suggests that Lindell should maximize trading on the equity, that is, using shareholders' equity as a basis for borrowing additional funds at a lower rate of interest than the expected earnings rate from the use of the borrowed funds.

1 Explain how trading on the equity affects earnings per share of common stock.
2 Explain how a change in income tax rates affects trading on the equity.
3 Under what circumstances should a corporation seek to trade on the equity to a substantial degree?

c Two specific proposals under consideration by the board of directors are to issue 14% subordinated income bonds, or to issue 14% cumulative, nonparticipating, nonvoting preferred stock, callable at par. In discussing the impact of the two proposals on the debt-to-equity ratio, one member of the board of directors stated that the resulting debt-to-equity ratio would be the same under either alternative because the income bonds and preferred stock should be included in the same balance sheet classification. What are the arguments (1) for (and (2) against inclusion of the subordinated income bonds and the preferred stock in the same balance sheet classification?

Case 24-3 The following information was extracted from annual reports to shareholders of three large corporations:

1 ***Local Gas Limited*** Revenue has increased steadily for the past few years and last year rose 10% over that for the previous year to a record $1.6 billion. Earnings from operations rose 19% to $134.2 million, or $3.95 per common share after preferred dividends. Our profits have grown steadily for the last five years and have exceeded industry growth; the 19% increase in profits compares with 12% for the gas industry and 9% for all industries.
2 ***Won Steel Corporation*** Income reinvested in the business, which also is to the benefit of shareholders, was $130.1 million, or $2.40 per common share.
3 ***Lick Limited*** See the table below.

	Year 3 (millions)	*Year 2 (millions)*	*Year 1 (millions)*
Gross revenue	$133	$ 99	$70
Net income	$ 28	$ 18	$12
Working capital	$ 34	$ 52	$87
Current ratio	2 to 1	5 to 1	10 to 1
Plant assets (net)	$275	$145	$92

Instructions

a Do you consider the information regarding the company's growth compared with industry growth presented by Local Gas Limited useful to shareholders? Is there a possibility that the information may be misleading?

b Comment on the information taken from the annual report of Won Steel Corporation in view of the following additional facts for the latest year:
1 Earnings amounted to $4.60 per share compared with an average of $6.59 per share 8 to 10 years ago.
2 The rate earned on shareholders' equity amounted to less than 8%.
3 The balance sheet included over $1.28 billion of short-term investments and over $268 million in cash.

c As a shareholder, would you be concerned about the decrease in the current ratio of Lick Limited? Explain.

Case 24-4 As the consultant to the president of Coleman Corporation, you are asked to compute some key ratios based on the information in the comparative financial statements. These key ratios will be used by the president to convince creditors that Coleman is solvent and to support the use of going-concern valuation procedures in the financial statements. The president wants to save time by concentrating on only these key ratios.

The data requested and the computations taken from the financial statements follow:

	Year 7	*Year 6*
Current ratio	2.5:1	2.0:1
Quick (acid-test) ratio	0.7:1	1.2:1
Plant assets to shareholders' equity	2.6:1	2.3:1
Sales to shareholders' equity	2.5:1	2.8:1
Net income	Up 30%	Down 10%
Earnings per share of common stock	$3.12	$2.40
Equity (book value) per share of common stock	Up 5%	Up 8%

Instructions

a The president asks that you prepare a list of brief comments stating how each of these items supports the solvency and going-concern status of Coleman Corporation. These comments are to be used in the presentation of data to creditors. Prepare the comments requested, giving the implications and the limitations of each item separately and then the collective inference one may draw from them about the solvency and going-concern status of Coleman.

b After doing as the president requested in part ***a***, prepare a list of additional ratio-analysis-type data for the president that you think the creditors will request to supplement the data provided in part ***a***. Explain why you consider the additional data to be helpful to creditors in evaluating the solvency of Coleman Corporation.

c What warnings would you offer creditors of Coleman Corporation about the limitations of using ratio analysis to evaluate solvency and the going-concern valuations of assets?

Case 24-5 Doris Simpson, executive vice president of Cannon Corporation, was having lunch with three students who were being considered for a position as her assistant. Simpson pointed out that many of her clients were active in acquiring other companies and that "the person who will be hired should be able to make effective overall analyses of the financial position and operating results of companies that are for sale." In order to get a better line on the business and financial acumen of the three students, she posed the following question to them:

"Suppose that I called one of you at 10 P.M. one evening and asked you to fly to

Halifax the next morning to investigate the operations and financial position of Todd Corporation, which is for sale at a price of $5 million. I would like to have a preliminary report by phone before 5 P.M. on that same day and a final report within a week. Arrangements have been made for you to visit the corporate offices of Todd. What approach would you take in preparing these reports?''

The three students then proceeded to summarize their approach to this hypothetical assignment.

Instructions

Assuming that you are one of the three students being considered for the position as assistant to the executive vice president of Cannon Corporation, write a brief report summarizing the areas you would evaluate and the approach you would take in preparing the preliminary and the final reports.

Case 24-6 The complete set of financial statements and notes to the financial statements for Le Bow Corporation is shown in the next two illustrations.

Instructions

Identify and explain the deficiencies in the presentation of Le Bow Corporation's financial statements for the year ended August 31, Year 6. If an item appears in

LE BOW CORPORATION
Statement of Income and Retained Earnings
For Year Ended August 31, Year 6

Sales		$3,500,000
Less: Returns and allowances		35,000
Net sales		$3,465,000
Less: Cost of goods sold		1,039,000
Gross profit on sales		$2,426,000
Less: Selling expenses	$1,000,000	
General and administrative expenses (**NOTE 1**)	1,079,000	2,079,000
Operating earnings		$ 347,000
Other revenue:		
Purchases discounts	$ 10,000	
Gain from increase in value of investments in real estate	100,000	
Gain on reissuance of treasury stock	200,000	
Correction of error in prior year's income statement	90,000	400,000
Ordinary earnings		$ 747,000
Add: Extraordinary item (gain on disposal of plant assets)		53,000
Income before incomes taxes		$ 800,000
Less: Income taxes expense		380,000
Net income		$ 420,000
Add: Retained earnings, beginning of year		2,750,000
Subtotal		$3,170,000
Less: Dividends (12% stock dividend declared but not distributed)	$ 120,000	
Appropriated for contingency (**NOTE 4**)	300,000	420,000
Unappropriated retained earnings, end of year		$2,750,000

LE BOW CORPORATION
Balance Sheet
August 31, Year 6

Assets

Current assets:		
Cash		$ 80,000
Accounts receivable (net)		110,000
Inventories		130,000
Total current assets		$ 320,000
Other assets:		
Investments in real estate (current fair value)	$1,508,000	
Investment in Cobb Ltd., at cost (**NOTE 2**)	160,000	
Plant assets (net)	4,000,000	
Goodwill (**NOTE 3**)	250,000	
Discount on bonds payable	42,000	
Total other assets		5,960,000
Total assets		$6,280,000

Liabilities & Shareholders' Equity

Current liabilities:		
Accounts payable		$ 140,000
Income taxes payable		320,000
Stock dividend payable		120,000
Total current liabilities		$ 580,000
Other liabilities:		
Payable to Oldham Limited (**NOTE 4**)	$ 300,000	
Liability under employee pension plan	450,000	
Bonds payable (including portion due in one year)	1,000,000	
Deferred income tax credits	58,000	
Total other liabilities		1,808,000
Total liabilities		2,388,000
Shareholders' equity:		
Common stock	$1,142,000	
Unappropriated retained earnings	2,750,000	
Total shareholders' equity		3,892,000
Total liabilities & shareholders' equity		$6,280,000

NOTES TO FINANCIAL STATEMENTS:

1 Depreciation expense is included in general and administrative expenses. During the year, the company changed from the straight-line method of depreciation to the declining balance method.

2 The company owns 40% of the outstanding common stock of Cobb Ltd. Because the ownership is less than 50%, consolidated financial statements with Cobb are not presented.

3 Because of company policy, goodwill is not amortized. The goodwill was acquired in Year 3.

4 The amount payable to Oldham Limited is contingent on the outcome of a lawsuit that is currently pending. No loss is expected; however, the maximum loss would not exceed $300,000, and that amount was appropriated by a debit to the Retained Earnings ledger account.

both financial statements, identify the deficiencies for each financial statement separately. There are no arithmetical errors in the statements. Organize your answer as follows:

a Deficiencies in the statement of income and retained earnings
b Deficiencies in the balance sheet
c Other deficiencies

PROBLEMS

Pr. 24-1 Financial statements of Braley Corporation for the two years ended December 31, Year 2, follow:

BRALEY CORPORATION
Income Statements
For Years Ended December 31, Year 2 and Year 1

	Year 2	*Year 1*
Net sales	$6,300,000	$4,000,000
Cost and expenses:		
Cost of goods sold	$4,900,000	$3,200,000
Loss on disposal of plant assets	10,000	
Operating expenses and income taxes expense	690,000	630,000
Total costs and expenses	$5,600,000	$3,830,000
Net income	$ 700,000	$ 170,000

BRALEY CORPORATION
Statements of Shareholders' Equity
For Years Ended December 31, Year 1 and Year 2

	Common stock, no par	*Retained earnings*	*Total*
Balances, Jan. 1 Year 1	$1,000,000	$250,000	$1,250,000
Net income		170,000	170,000
Cash dividends ($1 a share)		(90,000)	(90,000)
Balances, Dec. 31, Year 1	$1,000,000	$330,000	$1,330,000
Issuance of 10,000 shares of common stock for cash, Apr. 1, Year 2	125,000		125,000
Net income		$700,000	700,000
Dividends:			
Cash ($1.25 a share)		(125,000)	(125,000)
Stock (20,000 shares)	275,000	(275,000)	
Balances, Dec. 31, Year 2	$1,400,000	$630,000	$2,030,000

BRALEY CORPORATION
Balance Sheets
December 31, Year 2 and Year 1

	Year 2	*Year 1*
Assets		
Current assets:		
Cash	$ 480,000	$ 220,000
Accounts receivable (net)	840,000	560,000
Inventories	760,000	470,000
Total current assets	$2,080,000	$1,250,000
Plant assets	$1,330,000	$ 800,000

Less: Accumulated depreciation of plant assets	210,000	150,000
Total plant assets	$1,120,000	$ 650,000
Total assets	$3,200,000	$1,900,000
Liabilities & Shareholders' Equity		
Current liabilities:		
Accounts payable	$ 830,000	$ 440,000
Dividends payable	40,000	
Other current liabilities	300,000	130,00
Total current liabilities	$1,170,000	$ 570,000
Shareholders' equity:		
Common stock, no par value	$1,400,000	$1,000,000
Retained earnings	630,000	330,000
Total shareholders' equity	$2,030,000	$1,330,000
Total liaiblities & shareholders' equity	$3,200,000	$1,900,000

Additional Information for Year 2

1 Braley disposed of plant assets with a cost of $100,000 and a carrying amount of $30,000.

2 Braley acquired for cash plant assets costing $630,000.

Instructions

Compute the following for Braley Corporation for the year ended December 31, Year 2 (show computations):

a Cash provided from operations
b Earnings per share of common stock (round to the nearest cent)
c Cash dividends payout ratio for common stock (round to the nearest percent)
d Accounts receivable turnover (round to the nearest whole number)
e Inventories turnover (round to the nearest whole number)
f Quick (acid-test) ratio (round to the nearest tenth)

Pr. 24-2 The shareholders' equity section of Ramo Limited's December 31, Year 7, balance sheet follows:

RAMO LIMITED
Shareholders' Equity Section of Balance Sheet
December 31, Year 7

Shareholders' equity:	
Common stock, no par value, authorized 40,000,000 shares, issued and outstanding 20,000,000 shares	$242,000,000
Retained earnings	280,000,000
Total shareholders' equity	$522,000,000

Additional Information for Year 8

1 On January 15, Year 8, Ramo declared a 10% common stock dividend; the market price of Ramo's common stock was $10 a share on that date.

2 On July 1, Year 8, Ramo acquired 500,000 shares of its common stock for the treasury for $12 a share.

3 On October 22, Year 8, Ramo discovered a $24,000,000 understatement of its December 31, Year 7, inventories. Ramo's income tax rate is 45%.

4 On December 15, Year 8, Ramo declared a cash dividend of $1 a share on the common stock outstanding.

5 Ramo's net income for the year ended December 31, Year 8, was $55,000,000, after giving effect to the error in item *3* above.

Instructions

a Prepare Ramo Limited's statement of shareholders' equity for the year ended December 31, Year 8, in thousands of dollars.

b Compute the following for Ramo Limited for Year 8 (show computations):

1. Earnings per share of common stock, rounded to the nearest cent
2. Dividend payout ratio, rounded to the nearest tenth of a percent
3. Equity (book value) per share, rounded to the nearest cent
4. Return on common shareholders' equity, rounded to the nearest tenth of a percent

Pr. 24-3 The principal shareholders of Calgary Corporation are concerned about Calgary's current financial position and return on investment. They requested your assistance in analyzing the following financial statements:

CALGARY CORPORATION
Statement of Working Capital Deficit
December 31, Year 2

Current liabilities		$223,050
Less: Current assets:		
Cash	$ 5,973	
Accounts receivable (net)	70,952	
Inventories	113,125	190,050
Working capital deficit		$ 33,000

CALGARY CORPORATION
Income Statement
For Year Ended December 31, Year 2

Sales	$760,200
Cost of goods sold	452,500
Gross profit on sales	$307,700
Operating expenses (including $27,980 depreciation expense)	155,660
Income before income taxes	$152,040
Income taxes expense	68,418
Net income	$ 83,622

Assets other than current assets consisted of plant assets with a carrying amount of $443,450 on December 31, Year 2.

Instructions

Compute the following for Calgary Corporation for the year ended December 31, Year 2 (show computations):

a Number of days' sales uncollected (Accounts receivable [net] on December 31, Year 1, were $66,456)
b Inventories turnover (The inventories on December 31, Year 1, were $126,273)
c Number of days' operations required to cover the working capital deficit
d Return on total assets as a product of assets turnover rate and net income per dollar of revenue (Total assets on December 31, Year 1, amounted to $648,220)

Pr. 24-4 Comparative balance sheets of Naylor Corporation follow:

NAYLOR CORPORATION
Comparative Balance Sheets
December 31, Year 2 and Year 1

	Year 2	*Year 1*
Assets		
Cash	$ 18,000	$ 12,000
Short-term investments (at cost, which is less than market value)	6,000	12,000
Accounts receivable	42,000	30,000
Less: Allowance for doubtful acounts	(12,000)	(6,000)
Inventories	27,000	21,000
Plant assets	270,000	261,000
Less: Accumulated depreciation of plant assets	(69,000)	(60,000)
Total assets	$282,000	$270,000
Liabilities & Shareholders' Equity		
Accounts payable	$ 12,000	$ 15,000
Other current liabilities	9,000	3,000
8% long-term note payable, due in Year 12	60,000	60,000
$9 preferred stock, no par value (150 shares issued)	15,000	30,000
Common stock, no par value (3,000 shares issued)	120,000	120,000
Retained earnings	66,000	42,000
Total liabilities & shareholders' equity	$282,000	$270,000

All sales were made on credit and amounted to $450,000 in Year 2. Gross profit on sales was 40% of sales, and net income was 10% of sales. Income taxes expense was 45% of pre-tax income.

Instructions

Compute the following for Year 2:

a Return (before income taxes expense and interest expense on the 8% long-term note payable) on total assets, December 31, Year 2
b Accounts receivable turnover (gross basis)
c Inventories turnover
d Current ratio
e Quick ratio
f Times interest earned on the 8% long-term note payable (before income taxes)

Pr. 24-5 Selected statistics for Widd Company, Inc., for the three most recent years appear below:

	Year 3	*Year 2*	*Year 1*
Gross profit percentage	36%	33⅓%	30%
Inventories turnover	20 times	25 times	14 times
Average inventories	$ 19,200	$18,000	$35,000
Average accounts receivable (net)	$100,000	$84,375	$43,750
Income tax rate	45%	45%	45%
Net income as percentage of sales	12%	7%	6%
Maximum credit period allowed to customers	60 days	60 days	30 days

Instructions

a Prepare income statements for Widd Company, Inc., for Year 1, Year 2, and Year 3.

b Comment on the trend in sales volume, the gross profit percentage, and the net income percentage.

c Compute the accounts receivable turnover rates and comment on the trend in view of the change in credit terms in Year 2. All sales were made on credit.

Pr. 24-6 You have been assigned by the acquisitions committee of a diversified enterprise to examine a potential acquisition, Ginger, Inc. Ginger is a merchandiser that was offered for sale because of the death of its founder and principal shareholder. Recent financial statements of Ginger are shown below and on page 1279.

Instructions

For Ginger, Inc., for the years ended January 31, Year 3 and Year 2:

a Compute the inventories turnover rates for Year 2 and for Year 3.

GINGER INC.
Income Statements
For Years Ended January 31, Year 3 and Year 2

	Year 3	*Year 2*
Sales	$3,000,000	$2,600,000
Less: Costs and expenses:		
Cost of goods sold	$2,256,000	$2,002,000
Wages	360,000	271,000
Supplies	43,600	34,600
Depreciation	100,000	75,000
Interest	22,400	22,400
Loss on disposal of plant assets	65,000	105,000
Total costs and expenses	$2,847,000	$2,510,000
Income before income taxes	$ 153,000	$ 90,000
Income taxes expenses	68,000	40,000
Net income	$ 85,000	$ 50,000
Earnings per share of common stock	$ 3.08	$ 1.81

GINGER, INC.
Balance Sheets
January 31, Year 3, Year 2, and Year 1

	Year 3	*Year 2*	*Year 1*
Assets			
Cash	$ 130,000	$ 120,000	$ 100,000
Accounts receivable (net)	430,000	470,000	300,000
Inventories	400,000	300,000	200,000
Plant assets	900,000	800,000	700,000
Less: Accumulated depreciation	(325,000)	(250,000)	(200,000)
Total assets	$1,535,000	$1,440,000	$1,100,000
Liabilities & Shareholders' Equity			
Accounts payable	$ 300,000	$ 260,000	$ 220,000
8% notes payable, due Jan. 31, Year 11	280,000	280,000	
Common stock, $25 par	690,000	690,000	690,000
Retained earnings	265,000	210,000	190,000
Total liabilities & shareholders' equity	$1,535,000	$1,440,000	$1,100,000

GINGER INC.
Statements of Changes in Financial Position
For Years Ended January 31, Year 3 and Year 2

	Year 3	*Year 2*
Operating activities:		
Net income	$ 85,000	$ 50,000
Add: Depreciation expense	100,000	75,000
Loss on disposal of plant assets	65,000	105,000
Working capital provided from operations	$250,000	$230,000
Financing activities:		
Notes payable issued for cash		$280,000
Dividends declared and paid	$ (30,000)	(30,000)
	$ (30,000)	$250,000
Investing activities:		
Disposal of plant assets	$ (10,000)	
Plant assets acquired	200,000	$230,000
	$190,000	$230,000
Increase in working capital	$ 30,000	$250,000

b Compute the current ratio on January 31, Year 3.
c Compute the rate of return on average shareholders' equity for Year 3.
d Summarize the cash flow for Year 3 by restating the statement of changes in financial position on the cash basis.
e Comment on the operating results of Ginger, Inc. for Year 3.

Pr. 24-7 Carr Corporation has asked for a line of trade credit from Ball Ltd. It is estimated that sales to Carr by Ball will amount to $2,000,000 each year. Ball is a wholesaler that sells nationally, and Carr is a retailer that has a number of stores in Ontario. Ball has had a gross profit of 60% in recent years and expects to have a similar gross profit on sales to Carr. The sales to Carr will be approximately 15% of Ball's present sales volume. Recent financial statements of Carr are presented below and on page 1281.

CARR CORPORATION
Income Statements
For Years Ended December 31, Years 10, 9 and 8
(In thousands of dollars)

	Year 10	*Year 9*	*Year 8*
Net sales	$24,900	$24,500	$24,200
Cost of goods sold	18,000	17,200	16,900
Gross profit on sales	$ 6,900	$ 7,300	$ 7,300
Selling expenses	$ 4,600	$ 4,400	$ 4,300
Administrative expenses	2,700	2,400	2,300
Total expenses	$ 7,300	$ 6,800	$ 6,600
Income (loss) before income taxes expense or credit	$ (400)	$ 500	$ 700
Income taxes expense (credit)	(180)	225	315
Net income (loss)	$ (220)	$ 275	$ 385

CARR CORPORATION
Balance Sheets
December 31, Years 10, 9, and 8
(In thousands of dollars)

	Year 10	*Year 9*	*Year 8*
Assets			
Current assets:			
Cash	$ 1,600	$ 1,800	$ 2,600
Short-term investments (at cost)		200	400
Accounts receivable (net)	8,480	8,500	8,000
Inventories	2,800	3,200	2,800
Short-term prepayments	600	600	700
Total current assets	$13,480	$14,300	$14,500
Plant assets (net)	5,900	5,400	4,300
Total assets	$19,380	$19,700	$18,800
Liabilities & Shareholders' Equity			
Current liabilities:			
Notes payable	$ 4,200	$ 3,700	$ 3,200
Accounts payable	4,100	3,700	2,800
Other	1,000	1,125	915
Total current liabilities	$ 9,300	$ 8,525	$ 6,915
Long-term debt, 8% ($1 million extinguished on Dec. 31, Year 9 and Year 10)	1,000	2,000	3,000
Total liabilities	$10,300	$10,525	$ 9,915
Shareholders' equity	9,080	9,175	8,885
Total liabilities & shareholders' equity	$19,380	$19,700	$18,800

CARR CORPORATION

Statements of Changes in Financial Position
For Years Ended December 31, Years, 10, 9, and 8
(In thousands of dollars)

	Year 10	*Year 9*	*Year 8*
Operating activities:			
Net income (loss)	$ (220)	$ 275	$ 385
Add (deduct): Depreciation expense	500	500	400
Change in accounts receivable (net)	20	(500)	100
Change in inventories	400	(400)	100
Change in short-term prepayments	—	100	—
Change in notes payable	500	500	500
Change in accounts payable	400	900	200
Other current liabilities	(125)	210	115
Cash provided from operations	$1,475	$ 1,585	$1,800
Financing activities:			
Reissuance of treasury stock	$ 125	$ 115	—
Extinguishment of long-term debt	(1,000)	(1,000)	—
Cash used in extinguishing financing	$ (875)	$ (885)	—
Investing activities:			
Disposal of plant assets			$ (200)
Acquisition of plant assets	$1,000	$ 1,600	1,200
Cash used in investing activities	$1,000	$ 1,600	$1,000
Dividends declared and paid		$ 100	$ 100
Increase (decrease) in cash*	$ (400)	$(1,000)	$ 700
Cash at beginning of year	2,000	3,000	2,300
Cash at end of year	$1,600	$ 2,000	$3,000

*Cash comprises cash and short-term investments.

Instructions

a Compute the following ratios or other measurements for Carr Corporation for Year 10:

1. Rate of return on average total assets (before interest expense on long-term debt and income taxes credit)
2. Rate of return on sales
3. Quick (acid-test) ratio
4. Current ratio
5. Inventories turnover

b As part of the analysis to determine whether or not Ball Ltd. should extend credit to Carr Corporation, ***assume*** that the ratios below were computed from Carr's financial statements. For each ratio indicate whether it is favourable, unfavourable, or neutral in the decision to grant credit to Carr. Briefly explain your choice for each ratio.

	Year 10	*Year 9*	*Year 8*
1 Rate of return on total assets	(0.87)%	1.12%	1.96%
2 Rate of return on sales	(0.69)%	0.99%	1.69%
3 Quick (acid-test) ratio	1.19 to 1	1.36 to 1	1.73 to 1
4 Current ratio	1.67 to 1	1.92 to 1	2.39 to 1

5 Inventories turnover (times)	4.52	4.32	4.41
6 Equity relationships:			
Current liabilities	48.0%	43.0%	36.0%
Long-term liabilities	5.0	10.5	16.0
Shareholders' equity	47.0	46.5	48.0
Totals	100.0%	100.0%	100.0%
7 Asset relationships:			
Current assets	69.5%	72.5%	77.0%
Plant assets	30.5	27.5	23.0
Totals	100.0%	100.0%	100.0%

c Should Ball Ltd. grant credit to Carr Corporation? Support your answer with facts given in the problem.

d What additional information, if any should Ball Ltd. obtain before making a final decision on Carr Corporation's request for credit?

Pr. 24-8 Selected information taken from the financial statements for Barstow Corporation for the past four years is as follows:

	Year 10	*Year 9*	*Year 8*	*Year 7*
Net sales	$800,000	$642,000	$624,000	$580,000
Cost of goods sold	560,000	417,300	411,840	400,200
Gross profit on sales	240,000	224,700	212,160	179,800
Net income	56,000	25,680	30,000	34,500
Accounts receivable (net)	88,000	45,000	50,000	40,000
Inventories (first-in, first-out)	80,000	125,000	82,400	102,000
Industry sales index (Year 7 = 100)	118	112	110	100

All sales were on credit terms of 2/10, n/30.

Instructions

a For each of Years 7 through 10, compute the following for Barstow Corporation and present in tabular form:

1. Gross profit percentage
2. Net income percentage
3. Expenses (including income taxes but excluding cost of goods sold) as percentage of net sales
4. Number of days' sales in ending inventories (nearest day)
5. Number of days' sales in ending accounts receivable (nearest day)
6. Index of Barstow Corporation's sales to industry sales index

b **Briefly comment on the trend in items *1* to *6* in part *a*.**

Pr. 24-9 The preferred and common stocks of Columbia Limited are listed on the Vancouver Stock Exchange. The market price of the common stock was $19¾ a share on December 31, of both Year 5 and Year 4. Columbia's financial statements for the years ended December 31, Year 5 and Year 4, are in the next two illustrations.

COLUMBIA LIMITED
Statements of Income and Retained Earnings
For Years Ended December 31, Year 5 and Year 4
(In thousands of dollars)

	Year 5	*Year 4*
Net sales	$600,000	$500,000
Costs and expenses:		
Cost of goods sold	$490,000	$400,000
Operating expenses	66,000	60,000
Other expenses	7,000	6,000
Total costs and expenses	$563,000	$466,000
Income before income taxes	$ 37,000	$ 34,000
Income taxes expense	16,650	15,300
Net income	$ 20,350	$ 18,700
Retained earnings, beginning of year	134,500	126,200
Dividends:		
Preferred stock	(400)	(400)
Common stock	(11,800)	(10,000)
Retained earnings, end of year	$142,650	$134,500

COLUMBIA LIMITED
Balance Sheets
December 31, Year 5 and Year 4
(In thousands of dollars)

	Year 5	*Year 4*
Assets		
Current assets:		
Cash	$ 3,500	$ 3,600
Short-term investments (at cost, which approximates market value)	13,000	11,000
Accounts receivable (net)	105,000	95,000
Inventories (at lower of first-in, first-out cost and market)	126,000	154,000
Short-term prepayments	2,500	2,400
Total current assets	$250,000	$266,000
Investments in common stock (at equity)	2,000	3,000
Plant assets (net)	311,000	308,000
Goodwill and patents (net)	6,000	6,500
Other assets	21,000	24,500
Total assets	$590,000	$608,000
Liabilities & Shareholders' Equity		
Current liabilities:		
Notes payable	$ 5,000	$ 15,000
Accounts payable	38,000	48,000
Income taxes payable	350	500
Other current liabilities	24,500	27,000

Payments due within one year on long-term debt	6,500	7,000
Total current liabilities	$ 74,350	$ 97,500
Long-term debt	169,000	180,000
Deferred income tax credits	74,000	67,000
Other liabilities	9,000	8,000
Total liabilities	$326,350	$352,500
Shareholders' equity:		
$10 cumulative, nonparticipating, no-par-value preferred stock, $100 call price, authorized 50,000 shares, issued and outstanding 40,000 shares	$ 4,000	$ 4,000
Common stock, no par value, authorized 20,000,000 shares, issued and outstanding 10,000,000 shares	117,000	117,000
Retained earnings	142,650	134,500
Total shareholders' equity	$263,650	$255,500
Total liabilities & shareholders' equity	$590,000	$608,000

Instructions

From the foregoing information, compute items ***a*** through ***h*** for Columbia Limited for Year 5 (show supporting computations).

a Current ratio
b Quick (acid-test) ratio
c Number of days' sales in average net accounts receivable, assuming all sales were on credit
d Inventories turnover rate
e Equity (book value) per share of common stock
f Earnings per share of common stock
g Price-earnings ratio for common stock
h Dividend payout ratio (for preferred stock and common stock combined)

Pr. 24-10 The income statement, unclassified balance sheet, and additional information for Maddox Limited are shown in the next two illustrations.

Additional Information for Year 1

1 There were no preferred dividends in arrears, and the balances in the Accounts Receivable and Inventories ledger accounts were unchanged.
2 There were no changes in the Bonds Payable, Preferred Stock, Treasury Stock, or Common Stock ledger accounts.
3 All sales were on credit.

Instructions

From the foregoing information, compute the following for Maddox Limited to the nearest tenth:

a The current ratio on December 31, Year 1
b The number of times bond interest was earned during Year 1, using the theoretically preferable method
c The number of days' sales in inventories on December 31, Year 1
d The average number of days in the operating cycle during Year 1
e The equity (book value) per share of common stock on December 31, Year 1
f The rate of return on year-end common shareholders' equity for Year 1

MADDOX LIMITED
Income Statement
For Year Ended December 31, Year 1

Net sales	$1,500,000
Cost of goods sold	900,000
Gross profit on sales	$ 600,000
Operating expenses and interest expense	498,000
Income before income taxes	$ 102,000
Income taxes expense	45,900
Net income	$ 56,100
Earnings per share of common stock	$ 0.90

MADDOX LIMITED
Balance Sheet
December 31, Year 1

Assets	
Cash	$ 174,000
Accounts receivable (net)	566,000
Inventories	320,000
Plant assets (net)	740,000
Patents (net)	26,000
Other intangible assets (net)	14,000
Total assets	$1,840,000
Liabilities & Shareholders' Equity	
Accounts payable	$ 194,000
Income taxes payable	32,000
Miscellaneous liabilities	38,000
10% bonds payable, due Year 18	300,000
$7 cumulative, nonparticipating, no-par preferred stock, callable at $110, 2,000 shares issued, 1,600 outstanding	200,000
Common stock, no par, 50,000 shares authorized, issued, and outstanding	400,000
Retained earnings	720,000
Treasury stock, 400 shares of preferred stock	(44,000)
Total liabilities & shareholders' equity	$1,840,000

g The debt ratio on December 31, Year 1
h The equity ratio on December 31, Year 1

Pr. 24-11 Ratio analysis often is applied to test the reasonableness of the relationships among current financial data against those of prior-year financial data. Given prior financial relationships and a few key amounts, a CA may prepare estimates of current financial data to test the reasonableness of data furnished by a client.

Carlson Corporation has in recent years maintained the following relationships among the data in its financial statements:

1 Gross profit rate on net sales	40%
2 Net income rate on net sales	10%
3 Selling expenses as a percentage of net sales	15%
4 Accounts receivable turnover	8 per year
5 Inventories turnover	6 per year
6 Quick (acid-test) ratio	2 to 1
7 Current ratio	3 to 1
8 Quick-asset composition:	
Cash	8%
Short-term investments	32%
Accounts receivable (net)	60%
9 Assets turnover	2 per year
10 Ratio of total assets to intangible assets	20 to 1
11 Ratio of accumulated depreciation to cost of plant assets	1 to 3
12 Ratio of accounts receivable (net) to accounts payable	1.5 to 1
13 Ratio of working capital to shareholders' equity	1 to 1.6
14 Ratio of total liabilities to shareholders' equity	1 to 2

Carlson had net income of $120,000 for Year 15, after income taxes at the rate of 45%, which resulted in earnings of $2.60 per share of common stock.

Additional Information

1 Capital stock authorized, issued (all in Year 2), and outstanding: preferred, 6% cumulative, nonparticipating, $50 par, issued at 10% in excess of par; common, $5 par, issued at 10% in excess of par.

2 Market price of common stock on December 31, Year 15, $31.25 a share.

3 Preferred dividends declared in Year 15, $3,000.

4 Times interest earned in Year 15, 16 times (after interest and income taxes).

5 The amounts of the following were the same on December 31, Year 15, as on January 1, Year 15: inventories, accounts receivable, 10% bonds payable—due Year 27, and total shareholders' equity.

6 All purchases and sales were on credit.

Instructions

a Prepare a condensed income statement and a balance sheet for the year ended December 31, Year 15, presenting the amounts that should appear in Carlson Corporation's financial statements. Captions appearing in the balance sheet are: Current Assets, Plant Assets, Intangible Assets, Current Liabilities, Long-Term Debt, and Shareholders' Equity. In addition to the ledger accounts given in the problem, you should include accounts for Short-Term Prepayments, Other Current Liabilities, and Administrative Expenses. Show supporting computations.

b Compute the following for Year 15 (show computations): (1) rate of return on shareholders' equity, (2) price-earnings ratio for common stock, (3) dividends declared per share of common stock, and (4) dividends declared per share of preferred stock.

Pr. 24-12 The shareholders' equity of Ramon Limited on December 31, Year 1, was as follows:

$9 cumulative, convertible preferred stock, no par and $50 liquidation value, 600,000 shares authorized, no shares issued	–0–
Common stock, no par, 6,000,000 shares authorized, 2,000,000 shares issued and outstanding	$27,500,000
Retained earnings	6,500,000
Total shareholders' equity	$34,000,000

Additional Information

1 On January 2, Year 2, Ramon issued 100,000 shares of the $9 cumulative, convertible preferred stock for $54 a share. Each share of the preferred stock was convertible to four shares of Ramon's common stock.

2 On February 1, Year 2, Ramon acquired for the treasury 20,000 shares of its outstanding common stock at $16 a share.

3 On May 1, Year 2, Ramon issued 500,000 shares of previously unissued common stock at $17 a share.

4 On November 1, Year 2, Ramon reissued 10,000 shares of treasury stock at $21 a share.

5 On December 14, Year 2, Ramon declared the yearly cash dividend on the $9 preferred stock and a $1 per share dividend on the common stock, both payable January 14, Year 3, to shareholders of record on December 31, Year 2.

6 On January 20, Year 3, before the nominal ledger accounts were closed for Year 2, Ramon discovered that the inventories for December 31, Year 1, had been understated by $300,000 (after-income taxes effect on Year 1 net income was $165,000). An appropriate correcting journal entry was recorded.

7 After correction of the beginning inventories, net income of Ramon for Year 2 was $4,500,000.

Instructions

a Prepare a statement of shareholders' equity for Ramon Limited for the year ended December 31, Year 2.

b Prepare the shareholders' equity section of Ramon Limited's balance sheet on December 31, Year 2.

c Compute the following for Ramon Limited for Year 2 (show computations):
  1. Equity (book value) per share of common stock, December 31, Year 2
  2. Return on average common shareholders' equity for Year 2
  3. Earnings per share of common stock for Year 2.

c h a p t e r 2 5

ACCOUNTING FOR INFLATION

One of the primary purposes of financial statements is to provide information for decision making. Decision makers such as investors, creditors, and management realize that financial statements prepared under generally accepted accounting principles may not reflect current economic values. As a result, it has been suggested that financial statements would be more useful if historical costs were adjusted for the changing value of the dollar, or if historical costs were abandoned entirely and replaced with current fair values or with current costs.

In this chapter we describe some conceptual issues that are faced by accountants and users of financial statements when changes in the general price level or changes in the current costs of assets are incorporated in the accounting model. The latter sections of this chapter include a discussion and illustration of section 4510 of the ***CICA Handbook***, "Reporting the Effects of Changing Prices," which requires disclosure, as supplementary information, of certain constant-dollar and ***current-cost*** information by some large publicly owned corporations.

FINANCIAL STATEMENTS RESTATED FOR CHANGES IN THE GENERAL PRICE LEVEL

Needed: A Stable Measurement Unit

Money is the measuring unit used in the preparation of financial statements. The dollar, or any other monetary unit, represents a unit of value; it measures the amount of purchasing power available to acquire goods and services. Implicit in the use of money as a measuring unit is the assumption that the dollar is a stable unit of value, just as the kilometre is a stable unit of distance and a hectare is a stable unit of area. But unlike the kilometre and the hectare, the dollar is not in fact a stable measurement unit.

For many years the prices of goods and services in our economy have been rising. When the general price level rises, the value of money decreases. The ***general price level*** is the weighted average of the prices of goods and services in the economy and is measured by an ***index*** with a base year assigned a value of 100. The reciprocal of the general price-level index represents the ***purchasing power*** of the dollar. Thus, if the general price-level index in Year 1 is 100 and in Year 5 is 125, the current (Year 5) purchasing power of the dollar amounts to only 80% (100 ÷ 125 = 0.80) of the base-year dollar; in other words, prices have risen 25%, and purchasing power of the dollar has decreased by 20%. The most common measurements of the general price level are the ***Consumer Price Index*** and the ***Gross National Product Implicit Price Deflator***. Both of these indexes are published by Statistics Canada. The ***CICA*** allows the use of either for the computation of information on a constant-dollar basis.[1]

Despite the steady erosion in the purchasing power of the dollar in our economy for nearly 50 years, accountants generally have continued to assume that the value of the dollar is stable. Income tax laws have to a large extent ignored changes in the purchasing power of the dollar. This unrealistic assumption is one of the reasons why traditional financial statements are considered by many users to be potentially misleading. Consequently, proposals have been made to restate the ***historical-cost/nominal-dollar*** financial statements, or certain selected financial information therefrom, to ***constant dollars*** by use of an appropriate general price-level index.

Historical Cost Versus Current Fair Value

Even if the historical-cost/nominal-dollar financial statements were restated to reflect the changing value of the dollar, the resulting statements for information would still be presented in terms of historical costs and would not reflect the current fair values of assets. For example, a tract of land that cost $1 million would be restated at $1.5 million if the general price level had risen by 50%. However, the current fair value of the land might be $5 million because the price of land had risen more than the general price level. Historical cost reflects the current fair value of a plant asset on the date of acquisition; but a significant change in the current fair value of the asset after acquisition tends to make historical cost misleading for decision-making purposes. As a result, some users of financial statements have argued that ***current fair values*** of assets should replace historical costs as a valuation basis used in the preparation of general-purpose financial statements.

Effects of Inflation on Financial Statements

As stated earlier, our economy has experienced persistent inflation (increase in the general level of prices) for many years. In other words, the value of the dollar has been falling. How does inflation affect the measurement of income and the presentation of financial position for a business enterprise? Suppose that Reyes Limited acquired a building for $1 million early in Year 1 when the general

1 CICA, ***CICA Handbook*** (Toronto), sec. 4510.49.

price-level index was 100. The building had an estimated economic life of 20 years with no residual value and had been depreciated at the rate of $50,000 a year. Assume that the general price-level index at the end of Year 5 is 200; thus, the cost of the building in end-of-Year-5 dollars is $2 million. ***The higher constant-dollar cost of the building is attributed entirely to the decrease in the purchasing power of the dollar***; a doubling in the general price-level index means that a dollar at the end of Year 5 can buy only half as much as in Year 1. Financial statements prepared in accordance with generally accepted accounting principles at the end of Year 5 would include the following information relating to the building:

Data from historical-cost/ nominal-dollar financial statements

REYES LIMITED
Data from Historical-Cost/Nominal-Dollar Financial Statements
For Year 5

In balance sheet		*In income statement*	
Building	$1,000,000	Depreciation expense	$50,000
Less: Accumulated depreciation	250,000		
Carrying amount of building	$ 750,000		

Is this a meaningful portrayal of economic facts? Clearly it is not. Giving effect to the 50% reduction in the purchasing power of the dollar (100% increase in the general price-level index), the information may be presented more meaningfully as follows:

Data from historical-cost/ constant-dollar financial statements

REYES LIMITED
Data from Historical-Cost/Constant-Dollar Financial Statements
For Year 5

In balance sheet		*In income statement*	
Building	$2,000,000	Depreciation expense	$100,000
Less: Accumulated depreciation	500,000		
Carrying amount of building	$1,500,000		

Both presentations are stated in terms of historical cost; however, in the latter the historical cost is adjusted to reflect the current general price-level index. The increase of $750,000 in the carrying amount of the building would be reflected in the shareholders' equity section of the balance sheet. When financial statements are not adjusted for increases in the general price-level index, carrying amounts of depreciable plant assets and depreciation expense may be significantly understated; similarly, inventories, cost of goods sold, other nonmonetary assets, and various other expenses also may be misstated. When the effects of changes in the general price-level index are ignored, net income is measured by matching costs and revenue expressed in ***nominal dollars*** having ***different purchasing power***.

Income Measurement and Maintenance of Capital

Suppose you purchase 1,000 kilograms of sugar for $400 when the general price level is 100 and sell the sugar for $430 when the general price level is 110. How much gross profit did you realize on the transaction? By comparing your cost of $400 with the sales proceeds of $430 you conclude that you have realized a gross profit of $30. However, in reaching this conclusion, you are using different types of dollars. It would be more logical to say that your investment of $400 is now equivalent to $440 in terms of current purchasing power ($400 × 1.10 = $440) and that you have actually lost $10 ($440 − $430 = $10) on the transaction because you cannot purchase another 1,000 kilograms of sugar for $400 today to restock your inventory. In other words, you have failed to recover your investment and thus incurred an ***economic loss*** of $10 on the transaction.

To illustrate this point with another example, suppose that a business enterprise acquired land in Year 1 for $100,000 and sold it for $200,000 in Year 11. If the general price-level index doubled during that 10-year period, thus cutting the value of money in half, the enterprise is not "better off" as a result of these two transactions; the $200,000 received for the land in Year 11 is equal to the $100,000 invested in Year 1. In terms of the dollar as a measuring unit, however, accountants recognize a gain of $100,000 ($200,000 − $100,000) in Year 11 under historical-cost/nominal-dollar accounting, and the government may levy a tax on the "gain." Thus, by combining the Year 1 and Year 11 transactions in dollar terms, accountants conclude that the enterprise is "better off" (by recognizing a gain) if it recovers more than the original ***number of dollars*** invested in the land.

Failure to consider the changing value of money in the preparation of financial statements in a period of inflation means that what is reported as income may be, in part, a ***recovery of capital***. The amount of ***original capital invested in the business enterprise would not be maintained***, and taxable income, income taxes expense, and net income may be overstated. Taxable income may be overstated because depreciation expense is not large enough to offset the inflation in the prices of plant assets. This characteristic of traditional financial statements is perhaps the major argument in favour of ***constant-dollar*** accounting. However, failure to recognize the effect of price-level changes during a period of inflation does not necessarily result in an overstatement of net income, because there may be an offsetting purchasing power gain from borrowing. This point is explained in the following section.

Monetary Items and Purchasing Power Gains and Losses

In discussions of the changing value of the dollar, balance sheet items are classified either as monetary or as nonmonetary items. Cash, certificates of deposit, notes receivable, accounts receivable, investments in nonconvertible bonds that will be held to maturity, and most liabilities are examples of ***monetary items*** because they represent current buying power or obligations to pay a fixed number of dollars. All other balance sheet items (inventories, investments in common stocks, plant assets, intangible assets, and shareholders' equity) are examples of ***nonmonetary items***.[2]

2 Sec. 4510 of the ***CICA Handbook*** considers nonparticipating preferred stock a monetary item.

Changes in the general price level give rise to ***purchasing power gains and losses*** as a result of an enterprise's holding monetary items. The ownership of cash or claims to cash in the form of notes receivable and accounts receivable result in a loss of purchasing power when the general price level is rising; in contrast, owing money during a period when the general price level is rising results in a gain of purchasing power because the monetary liabilities may be paid with cheaper dollars. We may summarize this point as follows: When the general price level is rising, it is advantageous to be in a ***negative monetary position***, that is, to hold an excess of monetary liabilities over monetary assets; a ***positive monetary position*** (excess of monetary assets over monetary liabilities) results in a loss of purchasing power when the general price level is rising. To illustrate, assume the following balance sheets (in millions of dollars) for two companies at the end of Year 1:

Comparative balance sheets: historical-cost/nominal-dollar accounting

	X Limited	*Y Limited*
Cash and notes and accounts receivable	$600	$100
Inventories and plant assets (net)	300	800
Total assets	$900	$900
Liabilities (current and long-term)	$200	$650
Shareholders' equity	700	250
Total liabilities & shareholders' equity	$900	$900

If at the end of Year 2 the general price-level index had increased by 10% (from 120 to 132, for example) and the foregoing ***balance sheets remained unchanged***, the balance sheets would be restated to constant purchasing power as follows:

Comparative balance sheets: historical-cost/constant-dollar accounting

	X Limited	*Y Limited*
Cash and notes and accounts receivable	$600	$100
Inventories and plant assets (net)	330 ($300 × 1.1)	880 ($800 × 1.1)
Total assets	$930	$980
Liabilities (current and long-term)	$200	$650
Shareholders' equity	770 ($700 ×1.1)	275 ($250 × 1.1)
Purchasing power gain or (loss)	(40)*	55†
Total liabilities & shareholders' equity	$930	$980

*Loss from holding cash and receivables, $60 ($600 × 0.10 = $60), reduced by the gain from borrowing, $20 ($200 × 0.10 = $20) = $40. X Company has a positive monetary position.

†Gain from borrowing, $65 ($650 × 0.10 = $65), reduced by the loss from holding cash and receivables, $10 ($100 × 0.10 = $10) = $55. Y Company has a negative monetary position.

The nonmonetary items (inventories, plant assets, and shareholders' equity) are restated to constant purchasing power by use of a ***conversion factor*** of 1.1

(132 ÷ 120 = 1.1).[3] To put it another way, the current general price-level index is equal to 110% of the index on the date when inventories and plant assets were acquired. ***Monetary items are not restated because these items are stated in terms of constant purchasing power.***

To illustrate the fundamental effects of inflation on the financial statements of the two companies we have admittedly used a static and oversimplified example: we have assumed that all assets and liabilities remained unchanged while the general price-level index was rising by 10%. The effects of general price-level changes on monetary assets and liabilities are further illustrated in a subsequent section of this chapter.

FAIR-VALUE ACCOUNTING

Significance of Changes of Value

The restatement of historical-cost/nominal-dollar financial statements for price-level changes recognizes the fact that the value of the dollar is not stable. Such financial statements require no other departures from generally accepted accounting principles. Many accountants believe that an additional departure is needed to add relevance and usefulness to financial statements. In their view, historical costs and completed transactions should be replaced by ***fair-value accounting***. They argue that financial statements showing current fair values of assets and the changes in such values convey a more meaningful picture of the financial position and earning power of business enterprises.

To illustrate, suppose that a business enterprise acquired land for $100,000 and a factory building for $600,000. The building is being depreciated over a 30-year economic life with no residual value, or $20,000 a year. During the first 10 years the current fair values of the land and building increased substantially. At the end of the 10-year period (during which the general price level remained stable), it was apparent that the land and building were worth considerably more than their carrying amounts. As a result, the financial statements for the enterprise in the eleventh year showed: (1) assets and shareholders' equity that were substantially below current fair value; (2) net income that was overstated because the full economic cost of using the building was not recognized in annual depreciation expense; and (3) rates of return (on assets and shareholders' equity) that were overstated, because what essentially was capital recovery in terms of current prices was being reported as a part of net income and because assets and shareholders' equity were understated.

Assuming that at the beginning of the eleventh year the current fair value of the land was $180,000 and the current fair value of the building was $1,000,000 (cost if

3 The adjustment of financial statements for changes in the general price-level index is sometimes facilitated by computing the relationship between the current index and the base-year index as a ***conversion factor*** in decimal form. For example, a current index of 126.9 and a base-year (or date-of-transaction) index of 90 gives a conversion factor of 1.41 (126.9 ÷ 90 = 1.41). In this chapter, however, the ***fractional conversion factor*** (***not*** in decimal form) will be used.

new of $1,500,000 less depreciation to date on such cost of $500,000), the appraisal *might* be recorded as illustrated below.

Possible journal entry to record current fair values of plant assets

Land—Appraisal Increase ($180,000 – $100,000)	80,000	
Building—Appraisal Increase ($1,500,000 – $600,000)	900,000	
Accumulated Depreciation of Building—Appraisal Increase [$500,000 – ($20,000 × 10)]		300,000
Appraisal Increment from Land and Building ...		680,000
To record appraisal of land and building to current fair value.		

The annual depreciation expense on the building would be $50,000 ($1,500,000 ÷ 30 years = $50,000) to reflect the current cost of building services consumed each year. The balance sheet would show land and building at amounts approximating current fair value, and net income would represent the amount by which the enterprise was "better off" after recovering the current fair value of the remaining building services over the next 20 years, assuming that no further value changes occurred during that period.

Relationship Between Constant-Purchasing-Power Accounting and Fair-Value Accounting

The use of fair-value accounting does not mean that changes in the general price level would be ignored. Constant-dollar accounting and fair-value accounting are complementary responses to different measurement problems. ***The two approaches are not mutually exclusive alternatives***. Dealing with one is not a substitute for dealing with the other, and either or both approaches may be adopted in financial statements. Restatement of financial statements for general price-level changes does not deal with specific price changes, and fair-value accounting does not deal specifically with inflation. The different alternatives that may be followed in the preparation of financial statements are:

1 Historical cost/nominal dollars

2 Historical cost/constant dollars

3 Current fair value, without separate identification of the effects of general price-level changes

4 Current fair value, with the effects of general price-level changes shown separately

Financial statements adjusted for changes in the general price level are based on historical cost; however, the unit of measurement (the dollar) is adjusted to reflect changes in its general purchasing power. In contrast, ***fair-value accounting***

is a departure from historical cost because the current fair values for assets are derived from appraisals that reflect both changes in the general price level and changes in the relative price levels of specific goods. Thus, fair-value accounting represents a clear break from historical cost for a particular business enterprise. For example, if M Limited and N Limited acquired identical assets on different dates and at different prices, historical-cost/constant-dollar accounting would give different adjusted values for the assets of each enterprise. However, fair-value accounting would give the ***same value*** for the assets of both enterprises because fair-value accounting is not tied to historical costs.

If changes in the general price level are ***not*** incorporated in fair-value financial statements, the difference between historical costs and current fair values of assets is referred to as an ***unrealized holding gain or loss***; the unrealized holding gain or loss is reported as a separate item in the income statement. If changes in the general price level ***are*** incorporated in fair-value financial statements, the unrealized holding gain or loss (difference between historical costs and current fair values of assets) consists of (1) a net purchasing power gain or loss and (2) the net gain or loss resulting from changes in the relative values of specific assets. These two distinct types of net gains or losses would be reported separately in the income statement.

Use of Current Fair Values in Financial Statements of Business Enterprises

Proposals to incorporate current fair values in accounting measurements are not new. For example, fair values are used in the application of the lower-of-cost-and-market rule to the valuation of inventories and marketable equity securities, and assets may be written down to current fair value in a reorganization. In such cases the use of current fair values results in a reduction in the carrying amounts of assets ***below*** cost (or carrying amount in terms of historical cost). However, current fair values also are used when such values exceed historical cost. For example, marketable securities held by mutual funds and inventories of certain metals and agricultural products frequently are reported at current fair (or market) value.

Estimates of Current Fair Value

Thus far, we have mentioned the possibility of replacing historical costs of assets with current fair values without specifying how these values might be determined. The concept of current fair value most widely referred to in legal proceedings is "an exchange price that a willing and informed purchaser and an equally willing and informed seller would reach through negotiation." This should not be confused with ***market value***, which is the price obtainable currently for any asset. No single method of estimating current fair value is entirely satisfactory; therefore, in order to be able to evaluate intelligently the arguments for and against fair-value accounting, it may be helpful to identify some of the methods used to estimate current fair value.

Capitalization of Net Cash Inflows

In theory, the ideal way to estimate the current fair value or ***economic value*** of an asset is to compute the present discounted amount of the probable future net cash inflows expected to result from the use of the asset. This is known as ***direct valuation***. A limitation of the direct valuation approach is that estimates of future net cash inflows are likely to be highly subjective. More importantly, the earnings and cash inflows of a business enterprise are a joint product of all its resources, and it is virtually impossible to identify the contribution to earnings and cash inflows of a particular asset. The concept of direct valuation, although somewhat impractical for the valuation of specific assets, is useful for appraising the merits of two ***indirect valuation*** methods discussed below.

Exit Values

The ***current exit value*** of an asset is the amount that could be realized from its current sale; the ***expected exit value*** of an asset is the amount of cash to which the asset is expected to be converted in the course of operations. Exit values may be viewed as current fair values only for assets that are in fact offered for sale, and as minimum values for assets that are continued in use. However, in some cases the current fair values of assets may be materially above exit values. Exit values are related to, but are not identical to, market values because exit values may imply an urgent need to sell. Although reasonable estimates of exit values may be made for assets such as investments in marketable equity securities and inventories, estimates of exit values for plant assets and intangible assets, for example, may be quite difficult to obtain.

Current Cost

The ***current cost*** of an asset is the estimated cost of acquiring a ***new*** and substantially ***equivalent*** asset at current prices, adjusted for estimated depreciation since acquisition and for any operating advantages (or disadvantages) of the asset due to technological change. Current cost can be approximated by applying an appropriate ***specific-price index*** to the historical cost of assets, particularly plant assets. Specific-price indexes are available for broad categories of plant assets. The application of specific-price indexes to estimate the current cost of plant assets is illustrated as follows:

The building was acquired for $200,000 when the specific-price index for building construction in this industry was 100. Because the index now is 125, the historical cost of the building is restated to current cost of $250,000 ($200,000 × $^{125}/_{100}$ = $250,000); accumulated depreciation similarly is adjusted. The specific-price index of land costs in the geographical area where the land is located increased from 120 to 168 since the land was acquired; therefore, the historical cost of the land, $400,000, is multiplied by $^{168}/_{120}$ to estimate the current cost of $560,000 ($400,000 × $^{168}/_{120}$ = $560,000).

This discussion, though brief, should serve to point out that much sharper asset valuation techniques must be developed before fair-value accounting becomes a practical alternative for historical cost in the preparation of general-purpose financial statements.

Estimates of current cost of plant assets by use of specific-price indexes

Assets	*Historical cost*	*Specific-price indexes on date of acquisition*	*Current specific-price indexes*	*Conversion factors*	*Current cost*
Building	$200,000	100	125	125/100	$250,000
Less: Accumulated depreciation	60,000	100	125	125/100	75,000
Carrying amount of building	$140,000				$175,000
Land	400,000	120	168	168/120	560,000

THE CICA'S APPROACH TO ACCOUNTING FOR INFLATION

In section 4510 of the ***CICA Handbook***, ''Reporting the Effects of Changing Prices,'' the CICA adopted certain components of both constant-dollar accounting and current-cost accounting as ***supplementary information*** to be included by large publicly owned corporations in their ***annual*** reports, together with conventional historical-cost financial statements. Corporations are subject to the requirements of section 4510 if they have total assets (after the related accumulated depreciation, depletion, and amortization) of $350 million or more, or if inventories and property, plant, and equipment (before the related accumulated depreciation, depletion, and amortization) total $50 million or more. These total amounts are the beginning balances of the historical-cost financial statements. The recommended disclosure requirements for the ***supplementary*** information are summarized as follows:[4]

A The supplementary information should be presented in the corporation's ***annual*** report containing the historical-cost financial statements.

B The ***supplementary*** information should include:

1 The current-cost amounts of (a) cost of goods sold and depreciation, depletion, and amortization expenses, (b) inventory and property, plant, and equipment at the end of the period, and (c) net assets at the end of the period.

The amount of current cost of goods sold is measured at the lower of current cost and recoverable amount at the date of commitment to or use for a specific contract. The amounts of depreciation, depletion, and amortization expenses are measured at the average current cost or lower recoverable amount of the assets' service potential during the period.

The amount of current cost of inventory is measured at the lower of current cost and recoverable amount at the balance sheet date. Similarly,

4 CICA, ***CICA Handbook***, sec. 4510, paras. 17, 18, 21, 24, 26, 28, 30, 31, 38, 40, 42, and 48.

the amounts of current cost of property, plant, and equipment are measured at the lower of current cost and recoverable amount of the assets' remaining service potential at the balance sheet date, with any reduction from current cost to lower recoverable amount identified.

The amount of current cost of net assets is equal to the amount of shareholders' equity (excluding any nonparticipating preferred shares), after restating inventory and property, plant, and equipment at the lower of current cost and recoverable amount at the end of the period.

2 The changes in the current-cost amounts of inventory and property, plant, and equipment during the period, identifying any reduction from current cost to lower recoverable amount.

3 The current and deferred amounts of income taxes expense for the period. The amount of the income taxes expense is to be the same as that charged against income before extraordinary items in the historical-cost financial statements.

4 The income before extraordinary items, after reflecting the current-cost amounts of cost of goods sold and of depreciation, depletion, and amortization expenses of property, plant, and equipment, and the current and deferred income taxes expense. This income amount is called ***income on a current-cost basis***.

5 The amount of the financing adjustment, identifying separately the portion charged against income during the period. The term financing adjustment is the total amount of changes in the current costs of inventory and property, plant, and equipment during the period that, according to the existing relationship between debt and equity, need not be charged against present and future revenues in maintaining the common shareholders' proportionate interest in the operating capability of the enterprise.

The amount of the financing adjustment is determined by multiplying (a) the total amount of the changes in the current costs of inventory and property, plant, and equipment with (b) a fraction whose numerator is the net monetary liabilities on a historical-cost basis and whose denominator is the aggregate of the net monetary liabilities on a historical basis and the ***common*** shareholders' equity on a current-cost basis.

This financing adjustment consists of the ***realized*** and the ***unrealized*** portions. The portion that is realized is the amount charged against income during the period. The realized portion is to be disclosed separately. The portion that is unrealized is the amount ***not*** charged against income during the period and it need not be disclosed separately.

6 The amount of the changes in the current costs of inventory and property, plant, and equipment during the period attributable to the effects of general inflation (that is, the change in the general price level or the purchasing power of the dollar).

7 The amount of the gain or loss in the purchasing power (due to the effect of general inflation) resulting from holding net monetary items (the excess

of monetary liabilities over monetary assets or vice versa) during the period.
The index used to calculate the amounts for item **6** above and item **7** is either the Consumer Price Index for Canada or the Gross National Expenditure Implicit Price Deflator published by Statistics Canada.

8 The amounts described in the above seven items are to be presented on a comparative basis with the preceding period. The amounts of the corresponding preceding period are to be ***restated*** for the change in the general purchasing power of the dollar (that is, the effect of general inflation), using either the Consumer Price Index for Canada or the Gross National Expenditure Implicit Price Deflator.

9 An explanation of the supplementary information disclosed, a description of the bases and methods used in the preparation of the supplementary information, and a narrative discussion of the significance of the supplementary information disclosed.

In addition to these recommended ***disclosure*** requirements, section 4510 of the ***CICA Handbook*** provides a number of other recommendations.[5]

1 The accounting principles and methods used in computing income on a ***current-cost basis*** should be consistent with those used in computing income on a historical-cost basis, unless such exceptions are expressly provided under section 4510 (these exceptions are related mainly to the recommendations for specialized assets and industries and they are not covered in this chapter).

2 When supplementary information ***in addition to*** that recommended is presented on a current-cost basis, the enterprise should include an explanation of such information, a description of the bases and methods used in its preparation, and a narrative description of its significance.

3 Disclosure of the corresponding amounts for the preceding period on a comparative basis is not required for an enterprise adopting the recommendations for the first time.

4 The recommendations do ***not*** apply to banks, trust and insurance companies, and income-producing real estate assets.

5 Additional disclosure requirements are recommended for specialized assets and industries such as mining, gas, and oil because of their unique nature. Since these recommendations deal with highly complex and specialized issues, they are not included in the discussions here but should be covered in an advanced accounting text.

5 CICA, ***CICA Handbook***, sec. 4510, paras. 14, 29, 30, 31, and 50 to 67.

Section 4510 of the ***CICA Handbook*** includes two ***conditional*** recommendations concerning the proper disclosure when an enterprise presents income attributable to common shareholders on a current-cost basis under (a) the operating capability concept of capital and (b) the financial concept of capital measured in constant dollars.[6]

1 When an enterprise chooses to disclose ''income attributable to common shareholders on a current cost basis under an ***operating capability concept*** of capital..., income on a current cost basis should be adjusted by dividends on non-participating preferred shares and the financing adjustment.''[7] Also, if an enterprise chooses ''to exclude unrealized changes in current cost from income attributed to common shareholders, the amount of the financing adjustment would be based on the current cost adjustments made to income for the period''[8] (that is, the realized portion of the financing adjustment).

2 When an enterprise chooses to disclose ''income attributable to common shareholders on a current cost basis under a ***financial concept*** of capital measured in constant dollars..., income on a current cost basis should be adjusted by dividends on non-participating preferred shares, the amount of changes during the reporting period in the current cost amounts of inventory and property, plant and equipment,''[9] including the portion that is attributable to the effect of general inflation (that is, the changes in the general price level on the purchasing power of the dollar), and the amount of the gain or loss in general purchasing power resulting from holding net monetary items during the period.

A number of technical concepts and terms included in section 4510 have been introduced in the preceding paragraphs. A sound understanding of these and other technical concepts and terms is essential to a full comprehension of the recommendations of section 4510 of the ***CICA Handbook***. The explanations and definitions of the relevant concepts and terms are provided below:[10]

1 ***Maintenance of operating capability of the enterprise*** To maintain its operating capability (capacity to provide goods and services), an enterprise typically needs to hold a certain minimum quantity of inventory, property, plant and equipment, and other assets. When the prices of those assets are rising, the money amount of the investment required to maintain operating capability increases. Information on the current costs of resources that are used to generate revenues shows the extent to which those revenues are sufficient to enable an enterprise to maintain its operating capability.

6 CICA, ***CICA Handbook***, sec. 4510, paras. 22 and 25.

7 CICA, ***CICA Handbook***, sec. 4510, para. 22. Emphasis added.

8 CICA, ***CICA Handbook***, sec. 4510, para. 22.

9 CICA, ***CICA Handbook***, sec. 4510, para. 25. Emphasis added.

10 Adapted from paras. 6 and 15 of sec. 4510 of the ***CICA Handbook***.

2 *Maintenance of operating capability financed by common shareholders*[11] The capital required to maintain the operating capability of an enterprise may be provided entirely from shareholders' funds or by a combination of shareholders' funds and borrowed funds. In the latter case, the common shareholders' proportionate interest in the operating capability of an enterprise can be preserved without charging against present and future revenues the entire amount of increases in the current costs of assets. The amount of increases in the current cost of assets during the period that, on the basis of the existing relationship between debt and equity, need not be charged against revenues for the purposes of computing income attributable to common shareholders under an operating capability concept of capital is described as a financing adjustment. The financing adjustment shows income attributable to common shareholders on the basis of an operating capability concept of capital, thus allowing the return generated on capital invested by common shareholders to be measured.

3 *Maintenance of general purchasing power of capital* When general price levels are increasing, larger amounts of money are required to maintain a fixed amount of general purchasing power. Financial information that reflects changes in the general purchasing power of money indicates whether an enterprise has maintained the general purchasing power of its capital, that is, the financial concept of capital measured in constant dollars.

4 *Current cost* is the amount of cash or other consideration that would be needed currently to acquire an asset having the same service potential as embodied by the asset owned and, depending on the extent of technological change, would be determined by reference to either current reproduction cost or current replacement cost.

5 *Current reproduction cost* is the amount of cash or other consideration that would be needed currently to acquire a used asset of the same age, in the same location, and in the same condition as that owned or the amount of cash or other consideration that would be needed currently to acquire a new asset that has the same service potential as the existing asset had when it was new, adjusted for depreciation or amortization. Current reproduction cost is generally an appropriate measurement of current cost when the function performed by the asset has not been subject to significant technological change.

6 *Current replacement cost* is the amount of cash or other consideration that would be needed currently to acquire the best available asset to undertake the function of the asset owned, adjusted for depreciation or amortization if appropriate. Current cost may be determined by reference to current replacement cost when the function performed by the asset has been subject to significant technological change.

11 When an enterprise has participating preferred shares outstanding, the term *common shareholders* should be read to include participating preferred shareholders.

7 ***Service potential*** is used to describe the output or service capacity of an asset and is normally determined by reference to the attributes of the asset owned, that is, physical output capacity, associated operating costs, service life, and quality of output.

8 ***Recoverable amount*** is the current worth of the net amount of cash expected to be recovered from the use or sale of an asset, being value in use and net realizable value respectively.

9 ***Value in use*** is the present value of future net cash flows expected to result from the use of an asset by the enterprise and from its ultimate disposition.

10 ***Net realizable value*** of an asset is its estimated selling price in the ordinary course of business less reasonably predictable costs of completion and disposal.

11 ***Monetary items*** are money and claims to money the value of which, in terms of the monetary unit, whether foreign or domestic, is fixed by contract or otherwise. (Deferred income taxes are classified as nonmonetary.) The amount of net monetary items is the excess of monetary assets over monetary liabilities.

12 ***Financing adjustment*** is the term used to describe the amount of changes during a reporting period in the current cost of assets held by an enterprise that, on the basis of the existing relationship between debt and equity, does not need to be charged against present and future revenues to provide for maintenance of the ***common*** shareholders' proportionate interest in the operating capability of the enterprise.

13 ***Nominal dollars*** are actual money amounts used to measure financial statement items without adjustment for the fact that the general purchasing power of the dollar varies over time.

14 ***Constant dollars*** are units of constant general purchasing power used to measure financial statement items in terms of the general purchasing power of the dollar at a specified date.

15 ***Net assets*** is equal to the amount of shareholders' equity, ***excluding*** any nonparticipating preferred shares.

Now that we have presented the relevant recommendations and other related information of section 4510 of the ***CICA Handbook*** on reporting the effects of changing prices, we may appropriately ask: What is the objective of these recommendations? The objective is to provide information about the effect on an enterprise's financial position and operating results that are caused by (1) changes in prices of specific goods and services purchased, produced, and used and (2) changes in the general purchasing power of the monetary unit in which transactions are measured.[12] Thus, section 4510 is concerned with both the concepts of specific price level changes (that is, fair-value or current-cost accounting) and

12 CICA, *CICA Handbook*, sec. 4510.04.

general price-level changes (that is, purchasing-power-of-dollar or constant-dollar accounting). The distinction between these two was discussed in the first part of this chapter. Students should keep this distinction in mind when they study the material presented in this chapter.

Illustration of Reporting on the Effects of Changing Prices

The purpose of this section is to illustrate the application of the *CICA Handbook* recommendations presented earlier. To ensure a better understanding of the application of these recommendations, the information from a relatively simple set of financial statements of Baker Limited will be used for the illustration, even though, technically, a small company such as Baker Limited is not subject to these recommendations.

Baker Limited was organized on December 31, Year 4, as a result of combining several separate business enterprises that had operated as partnerships and single proprietorships. All assets were recorded by Baker Limited at current cost (current fair values) on December 31, Year 4. The Consumer Price Index (CPI) and the related conversion factors for Year 5 are presented below:

Indexes and conversion factors for Year 5

	CPI	*Conversion factor to restate to average Year 5 dollars*
End of Year 4 (and beginning of Year 5)	150.0	157.5/150.0
Average for Year 5 (also on July 1)	157.5	159.5/157.5
End of Year 5	163.8	157.5/163.8

The comparative historical-cost/nominal-dollar balance sheets at the end of Year 4 and Year 5 for Baker Limited are as follows:

BAKER LIMITED
Comparative Balance Sheets (Historical-Cost/Nominal-Dollar Basis)
End of Year 4 and Year 5

	End of Year 4	*End of Year 5*
Assets		
Monetary assets (cash and receivables)	$200,000	$260,000
Inventories (fifo method)	150,000(1)	141,000(2)
Land	40,000	40,000
Equipment	210,000	270,000
Less: Accumulated depreciation	-0-	(24,000)
Total assets	$600,000	$687,000
Liabilities & Shareholders' Equity		
Current liabilities	$ 80,000	$ 20,000
Long-term liabilities	100,000	116,000
Preferred stock, nonparticipating	140,000	140,000
Common stock, no par	280,000	280,000

Retained earnings	–0–	131,000
Total liabilities & shareholders' equity	$600,000	$687,000

(1) 3,750 units. Recoverable amount $150,000.
(2) 3,000 units. Recoverable amount $146,000.

The historical-cost/nominal-dollar statement of income and retained earnings for Baker Limited for Year 5 (the first year of operations) is as follows:

BAKER LIMITED
Statement of Income and Retained Earnings
(Historical-Cost/Nominal-Dollar Basis)
For Year 5 (the first year of operations)

Sales (14,000 units)		$923,000
Cost of goods sold:		
Inventory at December 31, Year 4	$150,000	
Purchases, current year*	583,000	
	$733,000	
Inventory at December 31, Year 5	141,000	
Cost of goods sold		592,000
Gross profit on sales		$331,000
Operating expenses (excluding depreciation)	$ 96,000	
Depreciation expense	24,000	120,000
Income before income taxes		$211,000
Income taxes expense		70,000
Net income		$141,000
Less: Dividends on preferred stock		10,000
Retained earnings, end of Year 5		$131,000

*Purchase of 13,250 units at a total cost of $583,000

Equipment costing $60,000 was acquired on July 1, Year 5, when the CPI stood at 157.5. Historical-cost/nominal-dollar depreciation expense for Year 5 was computed as follows:

Computation of historical-cost/ nominal-dollar depreciation expense for Year 5

$210,000 × 10%	$21,000
$60,000 × 5% (one-half of year)	3,000
Total depreciation expense for Year 5	$24,000

or:

Historical cost of equipment:	
Dec. 31, Year 4	$210,000
Dec. 31, Year 5	270,000
Average historical cost for Year 5 [($210,000 + $270,000) ÷ 2]	240,000
Average historical cost of depreciation expense for Year 5 ($240,000 × 0.10)	$24,000

Sales, purchases, and operating expenses (excluding depreciation) took place evenly throughout the year. Inventories are priced on a first-in, first-out basis; goods in ending inventories were acquired in the last purchases of merchandise for Year 5 at an average price of $47 per unit for the 3,000 units. The dividend on nonparticipating preferred stock of $10,000 was paid near the end of Year 5.

Section 4510 of the ***CICA Handbook*** does not specify the format for the recommended disclosure requirements and encourages corporations to experiment with different forms of presentation. However, its Appendix B provides guidance on the manner in which the disclosure ***may*** be presented. Our illustration follows closely the format suggested in that appendix.

The supplementary information on the effects of changing prices, based on the financial statements of Baker Limited and on the recommendations summarized on pages 1297–1300, is presented in Exhibit 1.

Exhibit 1

BAKER LIMITED

Statement of Income on a Current-Cost Basis and Other Supplementary Information
For Year 5 (the first year of operations)

	Current-cost basis	*Historical-cost nominal-dollar basis*
Sales	$923,000	$923,000
Cost of goods sold	616,000	592,000
Gross profit on sales	$307,000	$331,000
Less: Operating expenses (excluding depreciation)	(96,000)	(96,000)
Depreciation expense	(31,700)	(24,000)
Income before income taxes	$179,300	$211,000
Income taxes expense	70,000	70,000
Income	$109,300	$141,000

Other supplementary information:

1 Assets on a current-cost basis, December 31, Year 5:

	Current-cost basis	*As reported in the historical-cost statements, Year 5*
Inventories (page 1308)	$144,000	$141,000
Land and equipment — net of accumulated depreciation (page 1308)	$442,000	$286,000
Net assets (common shareholders' equity) (page 1309)	$570,000	$411,000

	Year 5
2 a Increase in the current-cost amounts of inventories and land and equipment (Exhibit 2)	$190,700
b Effects of general inflation (Exhibit 3)	42,472
c Excess of increase in current cost over the effect of general inflation	$148,288
3 Gain in general purchasing power from having net monetary liabilities (Exhibit 4)	$ 6,230
4 Financing adjustment (Exhibit 5)	$ 26,317
5 Amount of financing adjustment based on current cost charged against income during the year (Exhibit 6)	$ 4,375

A brief explanation of each of the items affecting the computation of income on a current-cost basis and of the five other supplementary information items as shown in Exhibit 1 is presented in the following sections.

Sales, Operating Expenses, and Income Taxes Expense

These items are stated at the same amounts in the statement of income on the current-cost basis and on the historical-cost/nominal-dollar basis. Since sales and operating expenses are assumed to have occurred evenly throughout the year, they are already stated at the average price for the year and thus no adjustment is required. The reasons for not adjusting the income taxes expense from the historical-cost basis to the current-cost basis, as explained in section 4510A.40-43 of the ***CICA Handbook***, are primarily based on practical rather than conceptual considerations. The Accounting Standards Committee believes that in view of the present stage of development of current-cost concepts and the partial nature of the application of these concepts, the inclusion of such an undue complexity of adjusting income taxes expense on a current-cost basis may detract from rather than enhance the understanding of the current-cost information.

Cost of Goods Sold

The current cost of goods sold of $616,000, based on the ***average*** current cost per unit of the beginning and ending inventories of Year 5, may be computed as follows:

Computation of average current cost of goods sold

Inventories, Dec. 31, Year 4:	
Current cost	$150,000
Number of units (page 1304, note 1)	3,750
Average unit current cost ($150,000 ÷ 3,750)	$ 40
Inventories, Dec. 31, Year 5:	
Current cost (page 1308)	$144,000
Number of units (page 1304, note 2)	3,000
Average unit current cost ($144,000 ÷ 3,000)	$ 48
Average of current cost of inventories on Dec. 31, Year 4, and Dec. 31, Year 5 [$40 + $48) ÷ 2]	$ 44
Number of units sold during Year 5 (page 1304)	14,000
Average current cost of goods sold (14,000 × $44)	$616,000

Or it may be computed as follows:

1 Compute as below the current cost per unit of opening inventory and closing inventory and determine the average per-unit cost for the period therefrom.

Computation of average current cost of goods sold

Unit cost of opening Year 5 inventory [$150,000 ÷ 3,750 units (page 1304)]	$40
Unit cost of closing Year 5 inventory [$144,000 (page 1308) ÷ 3,000 units (page 1304)]	48
Average current cost of inventories [($40 + $48) ÷ 2]	44

2 Convert the opening and closing inventories to average current cost and calculate current cost of goods sold, as follows:

Computation of current cost of goods sold and cost of goods sold adjustment

Inventory	*Current cost*		*Conversion factor*	*Average current cost*
Balance at December 31, Year 4.	$150,000	×	44/40	$165,000
Purchases for year (page 1304)..	583,000	×	44/44	583,000
Balance at December 31, Year 5..	(141,000)	×	44/47	(132,000)
Cost of goods sold on a current-cost basis				$616,000
Cost of goods sold on a historical-cost basis (page 1304)				592,000
Cost of goods sold adjustment				$ 24,000

Since it was assumed that Baker's sales took place evenly throughout the year (page 1305), this simple ''average method'' is appropriate. Ideally, the computation of current cost of goods sold should be based on the current cost at the time the units are sold or on the monthly or quarterly current-cost average. However, when such information is not available, or not available at reasonable cost, the simple ''average method'' can be used as a practical alternative.

Depreciation and Accumulated Depreciation

The current cost of depreciation of $31,700, based on the ***average*** current cost of equipment, is computed as follows:

Computation of average current cost of depreciation expense for Year 5

Current cost of equipment:	
Dec. 31, Year 4 (page 1303)	$210,000
Dec. 31, Year 5 (page 1309)	424,000
Average current cost for Year 5 [($210,000 + $424,000) ÷ 2]	317,000
Average current cost of depreciation expense for Year 5 ($317,000 × 0.10)	$ 31,700

Appendix B to section 4510 suggests that, for practical purposes, the above simple ''average method'' would usually be used, unless it is clearly inappropriate because of movement patterns of plant assets. Ideally, the current cost of depreciation should be based on the amount prevailing at the date of consumption of the plant assets.

There was no accumulated depreciation of plant assets on December 31, Year 4, the date the assets were acquired by Baker Limited. The current cost of accumulated depreciation of equipment on December 31, Year 5, of $38,000 is computed as shown at the top of page 1308.

The current cost of Baker's depreciation expense for Year 5 could be stated at $38,000, the same amount as the current cost of Baker's accumulated depreciation on December 31, Year 5. However, section 4510 of the ***CICA Handbook*** suggests that the current cost of depreciation expense may be computed by reference to average current cost of the related assets. The technique was illustrated earlier and the amount computed was $31,700. The difference between the amount of

Computation of current cost of accumulated depreciation of equipment, end of Year 5

Date acquired	*Current cost, Dec. 31, Year 5 (p. 1309)*	*Percent depreciated, Dec. 31, Year 5 (p. 1304)*	*Current cost of accumulated depreciation, Dec. 31, Year 5*
Dec. 31, Year 4	$336,000	10%	$33,600
July 1, Year 5	88,000	5	4,400
Totals	$424,000		$38,000

accumulated depreciation and the amount of depreciation is $6,300 ($38,000 − $31,700 = $6,300). This amount of $6,300 is called ''backlog depreciation'' (see page 1310).

Income on a Current-Cost Basis

The income on a current-cost basis of $109,300 is determined after deducting the current cost amounts of cost of goods sold ($616,000) and depreciation ($31,700).

Current Cost of Inventories, Land and Equipment, and Net Assets

The current-cost amount of inventories of $144,000 at December 31, Year 5, is determined by reference to applicable vendors' invoices and price listings. The December 31, Year 4, inventories (beginning inventories) of $150,000 were already stated at current cost at that date. The recoverable amounts (net realizable value) of the beginning and ending inventories are determined to be $150,000 and $146,000 respectively. Because the recoverable amounts of both the beginning and ending inventories are either equal to or more than the current-cost amounts, the latter amounts are used for the supplementary information as required by section 4510 of the ***CICA Handbook***.

The total current-cost amount of land and equipment (after deducting accumulated depreciation of $38,000) of $442,000 at December 31, Year 5, is determined by reference to appropriate specific-price indexes.

The applicable specific-price indexes for land and equipment were as follows:

Specific-price indexes for land and equipment

Land:	
End of Year 5	154
End of Year 4	110
Equipment:	
End of Year 5	176
July 1, Year 5	120
End of Year 4	110

The computation of the total current-cost amount of land and equipment (net of accumulated depreciation) is as shown at the top of page 1309. The December 31, Year 4, amounts for land and equipment were already stated at current cost at that date. By the use of appropriate present-value techniques for measuring ***value in use***, it is determined that the recoverable amounts for land and equipment at December 31, Year 4 and Year 5, are in excess of current costs. Therefore, current-cost amounts are used for the supplementary information as required by section 4510.

Computation of current cost of land and equipment

	Carrying amount	*Conversion factors*	*Current cost, Dec. 31, Year 5*
Land	$ 40,000	154/110 (a)	$ 56,000
Equipment:			
Dec. 31, Year 4, acquisition	$210,000	176/110 (b)	$336,000
July 1, Year 5, acquisition	60,000	176/120 (c)	88,000
Total equipment	$270,000		$424,000
Total plant assets	$310,000		$480,000
Less: Accumulated depreciation, Dec. 31, Year 5			38,000
Land and equipment (net of accumulated depreciation)			$442,000

(a) The specific-price index for the land at the end of Year 5 (154), divided by the specific-price index for the land at the end of Year 4 (110).
(b) The specific-price index for the equipment at the end of Year 5 (176), divided by the specific-price index for the equipment at the end of Year 4 (110).
(c) The specific-price index for the equipment at the end of Year 5 (176), divided by the specific-price index on July 1, Year 5 (120).

The current-cost amount of net assets (***common*** shareholders' equity) of $570,000 at December 31, Year 5, is determined by adding to the historical cost amount of ***common*** shareholders equity at December 31, Year 5, the amount of increase of current cost over historical cost of inventories and land and equipment (net of accumulated depreciation). This amount is computed as follows:

Computation of current-cost amount of net assets at December 31, Year 5

Common shareholders' equity at December 31, Year 5 (common stock $280,000 and retained earnings $131,000)	$411,000
Increase of current cost from historical cost of:	
Inventories (current cost $144,000 − historical cost $141,000)	3,000
Land and equipment (net current cost $442,000 − net historical cost $286,000)	156,000
Net assets (common shareholders' equity) on a current cost basis at December 31, Year 5	$570,000

Increase in Current-Cost Amounts of Inventories and Land and Equipment

The increase in the current cost of inventories and land and equipment of $190,700 is computed in Exhibit 2.

Exhibit 2

BAKER LIMITED

Increase in the Current-Cost Amounts of Inventories and Land and Equipment
For Year 5

Increase in the current costs of:	
Inventories	$ 27,000
Land and equipment	163,700
Total increase	$190,700

Inventories

The increase of $27,000 in the current cost of inventories is determined as the balancing item in the inventories account after reflecting all entries at current cost as shown in the next illustration.

Computation of increase in current cost of inventories for Year 5

Balance, December 31, Year 5	$144,000
Cost of goods sold (14,000 × $44)	616,000
	$760,000
Less: Purchases for the year (page 1304)	583,000
	$177,000
Less: Balance, December 31, Year 4	150,000
Increase in the current cost of inventories	$ 27,000

Land and Equipment

The increase of $163,700 in the current cost of land and equipment is determined as the balancing item in the land and equipment accounts after reflecting all entries at current cost:

Computation of increase in current cost of land and equipment for Year 5

	Gross current cost	*Accumulated depreciation*	*Net current cost*
Balance, December 31, Year 5	$480,000	$38,000	$442,000
Depreciation expense		(31,700)	31,700
Addition—July 1, Year 5	(60,000)		(60,000)
Balance, December 31, Year 4	(250,000)	-0-	(250,000)
"Backlog depreciation" adjustment	$ 6,300	$ 6,300	
Net increase in the current cost of land and equipment	$163,700		$163,700

Effect of General Inflation on the Increase in Current Costs of Inventories and Land and Equipment

The amount of increase in the current costs of inventories and land and equipment consists of the portion that is attributable to the effect of general inflation. The portion attributable to the effect of general inflation for inventories of $12,972 and for land and equipment of $29,500 is computed in Exhibit 3.

In Exhibit 3, current-cost data for inventories, purchases, and cost of goods sold are ***restated*** from nominal dollars to ***average*** Year 5 dollars by the use of appropriate conversion factors. The resultant current-cost/constant-dollar increase in inventories during Year 5 is subtracted from the related current-cost/nominal-dollar amount; the difference of $12,972 represents the amount of the increase in current cost of inventories that is attributable to the effect of general inflation (changes in the general price level) and is referred to as the ***general inflation component***.

The general inflation component of the increase in the current cost of land and equipment is computed on the same basis as inventories. In Exhibit 3, current-cost data for land and equipment, additions, and depreciation are ***restated*** from

Exhibit 3

BAKER LIMITED

Computation of Effects of General Inflation on the Increase in the Current Costs of Inventories and Land and Equipment for Year 5

	Increase in current cost	*Effect of general inflation*
Inventories	$ 27,000	$12,972 (A)
Land and equipment	163,700	29,500 (B)
	$190,700	$42,472

A: Inventories:

	Current cost at nominal dollars	*Conversion factors*	*Current cost at average Year 5 dollars*
Balance, December 31, Year 5	$144,000	157.5/163.8 (a)	$138,528
Cost of goods sold	616,000		616,000
	$760,000		$754,528
Purchases for the year (page 1304)	(583,000)	(b)	(583,000)
	$177,000		$171,528
Balance, December 31, Year 4	(150,000)	157.5/150.0 (c)	(157,500)
Increase in inventories	$ 27,000		$ 14,028
	14,028 ←		
Effects of general inflation	$ 12,972		

(a) The average CPI during Year 5 (157.5) divided by the CPI at the end of Year 5 (163.8). (See page 1303 for these conversion factors.)
(b) Assume that purchases took place evenly throughout the year as stated on page 1305. Thus, it was already in average Year 5 dollars.
(c) The average CPI during Year 5 (157.5) divided by the CPI at the end of Year 4 (150). (See page 1303.)

B: Land and equipment:

	Current cost at nominal dollars	*Conversion factors*	*Current cost at average Year 5 dollars*
Balance, December 31, Year 5	$442,000 (a)	(b)	$425,000
Less: balance, December 31, Year 4	$250,000	(c)	$262,500
Add: Additions	60,000	(d)	60,000
	$310,000		$322,500
Less: Depreciation expense (page 1307)	31,700	(e)	31,700
	$278,300		$290,800
Increase in land and equipment ...	$163,700		$134,200
	134,200 ←		
Effects of general inflation	$29,500		

(a) $480,000 current cost of plant assets (page 1309) less $38,000 current cost of accumulated depreciation (page 1308) = $442,000.
(b) The average CPI during Year 5 (157.5) divided by the CPI at the end of Year 5 (163.8).
(c) The average CPI during Year 5 (157.5) divided by the CPI at the end of Year 4 (150).
(d) Assume that the addition was in average Year 5 dollars as stated on page 1304.
(e) Assume that the depreciation took place evenly throughout the year and that thus it was already in average Year 5 dollars.

nominal dollars to ***average*** Year 5 dollars by the use of appropriate conversion factors. The resultant current-cost/constant-dollar increase in land and equipment during Year 5 is subtracted from the related current-cost/nominal-dollar amount; the difference of $29,500 represents the amount of increase in current cost of land and equipment that is attributable to the effect of general inflation (changes in the general price level).

Gain in General Purchasing Power from Having Net Monetary Liabilities
The gain in general purchasing power of $6,230 as a result of monetary liabilities in excess of monetary assets is computed in Exhibit 4a. A summary computation is shown in Exhibit 4.

Exhibit 4

BAKER LIMITED
Computation of Gain in General Purchasing Power
For Year 5
(In average Year 5 dollars)

	Nominal dollars	*Conversion factors*	*Average Year 5 dollars*
Net monetary liabilities:			
Balance, December 31, Year 4	$120,000 (A)	(a)	$126,000
Decrease during year	104,000	(b)	104,000
			$ 22,000
Balance, December 31, Year 5	$ 16,000 (A)	(c)	15,385
Gain in general purchasing power from having net monetary liabilities during the year			$ 6,615

(a) The average CPI during Year 5 (157.5) divided by the CPI at the end of Year 4 (150.0).
(b) Assume the change to have taken place evenly throughout the year and that thus it was already in average Year 5 dollars.
(c) The average CPI during Year 5 (157.5) divided by the CPI at the end of Year 5 (163.8).

A: Net monetary liabilities:

	Balance, December 31:	
	Year 4	*Year 5*
Monetary liabilities:		
Current	$ 80,000	$ 20,000
Long-term	100,000	116,000
Nonparticipating preferred stock	140,000	140,000
	$320,000	$276,000
Monetary assets	200,000	260,000
Net monetary liabilities	$120,000	$ 16,000

After the net monetary liabilities have been determined (note that the nonparticipating preferred stock is included as a monetary liability), the ending balances of net monetary liabilities for Year 4 and Year 5 and the decrease in net monetary liabilities during Year 5 are ***restated*** from nominal dollars to ***average*** Year 5 dollars by the use of appropriate conversion factors. The difference between the restated amount of the Year 4 ending balance and the restated total of the decrease during Year 5 and the Year 5 ending balance (adjusted to ***average*** Year 5 dollars) is the gain in general purchasing power.

The Baker Limited example above computes the purchasing power gain using average Year 5 dollars and assuming that sources and uses of monetary items occurred uniformly (evenly) during Year 5. The computation could have been to the end of Year 5, in which case the conversion ratio would have had 163.8 as the numerator. The measurement of the purchasing power gain or loss is an assessment of management's ability to finance and invest through the use of monetary items in an inflationary or deflationary economy. A ***detailed working paper***, analyzing the sources and uses of monetary items for Baker Limited, is shown in Exhibit 4a so that you may understand the basics of this computation should the uniformity of sources and uses of monetary items not be present. As in Exhibit 4, Exhibit 4a shows the result in average Year 5 dollars.

Exhibit 4a

BAKER LIMITED
Computation of Gain in General Purchasing Power
For Year 5
(In ***average*** Year 5 dollars)

Net monetary items, Jan. 1, Year 5:				
Monetary assets (cash and receivables)	$200,000			
Less:				
Current liabilities	(8,000)			
Long term liabilities	(10,000)			
Preferred shares	(140,000)			
Net monetary items, Jan. 1, Year 5		$(120,000)	157.5/150.0	$(126,000)
Source of monetary items, Year 5:				
Sales		923,000		923,000
		$ 803,000		$ 797,000
Uses of monetary items, Year 5:				
Purchases	$583,000			$583,000
Operating expenses (excluding depreciation expense)	96,000			96,000
Income taxes expense	70,000			70,000
Dividends on preferred shares	10,000		157.5/163.8	9,615
Acquisition of equipment	60,000			60,000
Total uses of monetary items		819,000		$ 818,615
Net monetary items as restated, Dec. 31, Year 5, if there were no purchasing power gain or loss ($797,000 – $818,615)				$ (21,615)

Net monetary items on hand, Dec. 31, Year 5:				
Monetary assets (cash and receivables	$ 260,000			
Less:				
Current liabilities	(20,000)			
Long term liaibilities	(116,000)			
Preferred shares	(140,000)	$ (16,000)	157.5/163.8	(15,385)
Purchasing power gain				$ 6,230

NOTE: Exhibit 4 computations assumed uniformity of sources and uses of monetary items, whereas in fact the preferred dividend was paid near the end of Year 5.

Exhibit 4 purchasing power gain	$6,615
Preferred shares dividend change ($10,000 − $9,615)	(383)
Exhibit 4a purchasing power gain	$6,230

Financing Adjustment

The financing adjustment of $26,317 is computed by multiplying the debt financing ratio of 0.138 with the increase of $190,700 in current costs of inventories and land and equipment. The debt financing ratio is determined by dividing the average net monetary liabilities on a historical-cost basis with the aggregate of the average net monetary liabilities on a historical-cost basis and the average common shareholders' equity on a current-cost basis. Exhibit 5, including parts *A* to *D*, shows the details of the financing adjustment computation. ***In those cases where monetary assets are in excess of monetary liabilities, no financing adjustment would be required, because inventory and property, plant, and equipment are considered to be financed entirely with common shareholders' equity.***

Exhibit 5

BAKER LIMITED
Computation of Financing Adjustment
For Year 5

Financing adjustment:

Debt financing ratio	×	Increase in current costs of inventories and land and equipment	=	Financing adjustment
0.138 (A)	×	$190,700 (Exhibit 2)	=	$26,317

A: Debt financing ratio:

	Net monetary liabilities (B)	*Common shareholders' equity on current-cost basis*
Balance, December 31, Year 4	$120,000	$280,000 (C)
Balance, December 31, Year 5	16,000	570,000 (D)
Totals	$136,000	$850,000
Average for the year (total ÷ 2)	$ 68,000	$425,000

Debt financing ratio [$68,000 ÷ ($68,000 + $425,000)] .. 0.138

B: (See Exhibit 4.)

C: (See page 1303.)

D: Common shareholders' equity on current-cost basis:

			Balance, December 31, Year 5
Common shareholders' equity (net assets) on a historical basis (page 1303):			
Common stock			$280,000
Retained earnings			131,000
			$411,000
Difference between current costs and historical costs of:			
	Current cost	*Historical cost*	
Inventories	$144,000	$141,000	3,000
Land and equipment (net of accumulated depreciation of $38,000 and $24,000)	$442,000	$286,000	156,000
Common shareholders' equity (net assets) on a current-cost basis			$570,000

Amount of Financing Adjustment Based on Current Cost Charged Against Income During the Year

This amount of $4,375 is the portion of the financing adjustment realized during Year 5. It is computed by multiplying the debt financing ratio of 0.138 (Exhibit 5) with the amount of increase of $31,700 in current cost from historical cost of cost of goods sold and depreciation, as shown in Exhibit 6.

Exhibit 6

BAKER LIMITED

Computation of Amount of Financing Adjustment Based on Current Cost Charged Against Income
For Year 5

Amount of financing adjustment based on current cost charged against income during Year 5:

Debt financing ratio	×	Current cost adjustments of cost of goods sold and depreciation	=	Financing adjustment
0.138 (Exhibit 5)	×	$31,700 (A)	=	$4,375

A: Current-cost adjustments:

	Current cost	*Historical cost*	*Current-cost adjustment*
Cost of goods sold (Exhibit 1)	$616,000	$592,000	$24,000
Depreciation (Exhibit 1)	$ 31,700	$ 24,000	7,700
			$31,700

Concluding Remarks

It should be noted that this illustration thus far does not include the recommendations regarding (1) the presentation of comparative amounts of the corresponding preceding period and (2) management commentary on the supplementary information.

The supplementary information was not presented because this is Baker Limited's first year of operation. In Year 6, the second year of operation, Baker Limited would be required to present the supplementary information of Year 6 on a comparative basis with Year 5 and ***the amounts for Year 5 would be restated for the change in the general purchasing power of the dollar*** by using either the Consumer Price Index or the Gross National Expenditure Implicit Price Deflator. Thus, the Year 5 supplementary information would be reported in terms of Year 6 dollars. To illustrate this restatement process, assume that the average Consumer Price Indexes for Year 5 and Year 6 are 157.5 and 176.4 respectively. The amounts for Year 5 would be ***restated*** by a conversion factor of 176.4 ÷ 157.5. For example, the sales and cost of goods sold for Year 5 would be restated as shown in the next illustration.

Sales	$923,000 × 176.4/157.5 = $1,033,760
Cost of goods sold	$616,000 × 176.4/157.5 = $ 689,920

The management commentary on the supplementary information would include an explanation of the supplementary information disclosed and its significance, as well as a description of the bases and methods used in the preparation of the supplementary information. For example, an explanation of financing adjustment and maintenance of the general purchasing power of common shareholders' equity for Baker Limited may be worded as follows:[13]

Financing Adjustment

In periods of increasing prices the enterprise will require additional capital to offset the effect of increases in the specific prices of its productive physical assets (that is, inventory and property, plant, and equipment). This is referred to as maintenance of the operating capability of the enterprise. The capital required to maintain the operating capability of the enterprise is provided by a combination of shareholders' funds and borrowed funds. The financing adjustment of $26,317 represents the increase in current cost amounts of that portion of inventory and land and equipment financed by debt. The use of debt to finance these assets reduces the amount of the increase in their current cost that must be charged against revenues in determining income attributable to common shareholders.

Maintenance of the General Purchasing Power of Common Shareholders' Equity

The general purchasing power of common shareholders' equity is eroded by increases in general price levels. The increase in current cost amounts of inventory and land

13 Adapted from sec. 4510B.3 of the *CICA Handbook*.

and equipment attributable to the effects of general inflation of $42,472 less the general purchasing power gain from having net monetary liabilities of $6,230 provides a measure of this erosion. However, this erosion is offset by the increase in the current cost amounts of inventory and land and equipment of $190,700.

Also, this illustration has so far not included the two ***conditional*** recommendations on the disclosure of income attributable to common shareholders on a current-cost basis under (1) the operating capability concept of capital and (2) the financial concept of capital measured in constant dollars. These two recommendations will now be discussed.

Under the ***operating capability of capital***, the income attributable to common shareholders on a current-cost basis of $125,617 is computed by adding the financing adjustment of $26,317 to, and deducting the dividends of $10,000 on nonparticipating preferred stock from, the income on a current-cost basis of $109,300 (Exhibit 1) as shown in Exhibit 7 on page 1318.

The main differences between Exhibit 7 (Statement of Income Attributable to Common Shareholders on a Current-Cost Basis Under an Operating Capability Concept of Capital and Other Supplementary Information) and Exhibit 1 (Statement of Income on a Current-Cost Basis and Other Supplementary Information) are:

1 The financing adjustment of $26,317 is presented as an addition to the income on a current basis in the body of the statement rather than as an item under "Other Supplementary Information."

2 The dividends of $10,000 on nonparticipating preferred stock are presented as a deduction from the income on a current-cost basis in the body of the statement rather than excluded from the statement and the other supplementary information.

Consequently, the other supplementary information in Exhibit 7 shows only four items: the assets on a current-cost basis at December 31, Year 5, the increase in the current-cost amounts of inventories and land and equipment together with the portion attributable to the effect of general inflation, the gain in general purchasing power from having net monetary liabilities, and the amount of financing adjustment based on current cost charged against income during the year.

The rationale for presenting the income attributable to common shareholders on a current basis under the operating capability concept of capital of $125,617 is to show the maximum amount of income ($125,617) that Baker Limited, under the existing debt and equity structure, can distribute to its common shareholders and still maintain its present operating capability. It should be noted that the financing adjustment of $26,317 includes an unrealized portion of $21,929 ($26,317 − $4,375). It would seem more prudent to add to the income on a current-cost basis only the realized portion ($4,375) of the financing adjustment. Under this alternative, the amount of income attributable to common shareholders would be $103,675 ($109,300 + $4,375 − $10,000 or $125,617 − $26,317 + $4,375); the amount of financing adjustment based on current cost charged against income during the year of $4,375 would be shown as an addition to the income on a

Exhibit 7

BAKER LIMITED

Statement of Income Attributable to Common Shareholders on a Current-Cost Basis Under an Operating Capability Concept of Capital and Other Supplementary Information For Year 5 (the first year of operations)

	Current-cost basis	*Historical-cost/ nominal-dollar basis*
Sales	$923,000	$923,000
Cost of goods sold	616,000	592,000
Gross profit on sales	$307,000	$331,000
Less: Operating expenses (excluding depreciation)	(96,000)	(96,000)
Depreciation expense	(31,700)	(24,000)
Income before income taxes	$179,300	$211,000
Income taxes expense	70,000	70,000
	$109,300	$141,000
Financing adjustment	26,317	
Dividends on nonparticipating preferred stock	(10,000)	
Income attributable to common shareholders on a current-cost basis under an operating capability concept of capital	$125,617	

Other supplementary information:

1 Assets on a current-cost basis, December 31, Year 5:

	Current-cost basis	*As reported in the historical-cost statements, Year 5*
Inventories (page 1308)	$144,000	$141,000
Land and equipment, net of accumulated depreciation (page 1308)	$442,000	$286,000
Net assets (common shareholders' equity) (page 1309)	$570,000	$411,000

	Year 5
2 a Increase in the current-cost amounts of inventories and land and equipment (Exhibit 2)	$190,700
b Effect of general inflation (Exhibit 3)	42,472
c Excess of increase in current cost over the effect of general inflation	$148,228
3 Gain in general purchasing power from having net monetary liabilities (Exhibit 4)	$ 6,230
4 Amount of financing adjustment based on current cost charged against income during the year (Exhibit 6)	$ 4,375

current-cost basis and the financing adjustment of $26,317 would be shown in the other supplementary information. Both alternatives are sanctioned by section 4510.22 of the *CICA Handbook*.

Under the ***financial concept of capital measured in constant dollars***, the income attributable to common shareholders on a current-cost basis of $253,758 is computed by adding the increase in the current-cost amounts of inventories and land and equipment of $190,700 and the gain in general purchasing power from having net monetary liabilities (using the amount computed in Exhibit 4a) of $6,230 to, and deducting the dividends of $10,000 on nonparticipating preferred stock and the increase in current-cost amounts of inventories of land and equipment attributable to the effect of general inflation of $42,472 from, the income on a current-cost basis of $109,300 (Exhibit 1) as shown in Exhibit 8 on page 1320.

The main differences between Exhibit 8 (Statement of Income Attributable to Common Shareholders on a Current-Cost Basis Under a Financial Concept of Capital and Other Supplementary Information) and Exhibit 1 (Statement of Income on a Current-Cost Basis and Other Supplementary Information) are:

1 The increase of $190,700 in the current-cost amounts of inventories and land and equipment is presented as an addition to the income on a current-cost basis in the body of the statement rather than as an item in the other supplementary information.

2 The dividends of $10,000 on nonparticipating preferred stock is presented as a deduction from the income on a current-cost basis in the body of the statement rather than excluded from both the statement and the other supplementary information.

3 The increase of $42,472 in current-cost amounts of inventories and land and equipment attributable to the effect of general inflation is presented as a deduction from the income on a current-cost basis in the body of the statement rather than as an item in the other supplementary information.

4 The gain of $6,230 in general purchasing power from having net monetary liabilities is presented as an addition to the income on a current-cost basis in the body of the statement rather than as an item in the other supplementary information.

Consequently, the other supplementary information in Exhibit 8 shows only three items: the assets on a current-cost basis at December 31, Year 5, the financing adjustment, and the amount of financing adjustment based on current cost charged against income during Year 5.

The rationale for presenting the income attributable to common shareholders on a current-cost basis under the financial concept of capital measured in constant dollars of $253,758 is to show the maximum amount of income ($253,758) that Baker Limited can distribute to its common shareholders and still maintain its financial capital measured in constant dollars. It is suggested that such a concept of reporting income provides "a useful basis for users to assess whether an

Exhibit 8

BAKER LIMITED

Statement of Income Attributable to Common Shareholders on a Current-Cost Basis Under a Financial Concept of Capital and Other Supplementary Information For Year 5 (the first year of operations)

	Current-cost/ constant-dollar basis	*Historical-cost/ nominal-dollar basis*
Sales	$923,000	$923,000
Cost of goods sold	616,000	592,000
Gross profit on sales	$307,000	$331,000
Less: Operating expenses (excluding depreciation)	(96,000)	(96,000)
Depreciation expense	(31,700)	(24,000)
Income before income taxes	$179,300	$211,000
Income taxes expense	70,000	70,000
	$109,300	$141,000
Increase in the current-cost amounts of inventory and land and equipment held during the year	190,700	
Dividends on nonparticipating preferred stock	(10,000)	
Income attributable to common shareholders on a current-cost basis in nominal dollars	$290,000	
General purchasing power adjustments:		
Increase in current-cost amounts of inventories and land and equipment attributable to the effect of general inflation	(42,472)	
Gain in general purchasing power from having net monetary liabilities	6,230	
Income attributable to common shareholders on a current-cost basis under a financial concept of capital	$253,758	

Other supplementary information:

1 Assets on a current-cost basis December 31, Year 5:

	Current-cost basis	*As reported in the historical-cost statements, Year 5*
Inventories (page 1308)	$144,000	$141,000
Land and equipment, net of accumulated depreciation (page 1308)	$442,000	$286,000
Net assets (common shareholders' equity) (page 1309)	$570,000	$411,000

	Year 5
2 Financing adjustment (Exhibit 5)	$ 26,317
3 Amount of financing adjustment based on current cost charged against income during the year (Exhibit 6)	$ 4,375

enterprise has maintained the general purchasing power of its capital and whether returns earned are sufficient to enable the enterprise to maintain the general purchasing power of distributions to shareholders over time.''[14] Exhibit 9 compares the presentations of the section 4510 disclosure formats.

Exhibit 9

BAKER LIMITED
Comparison of Presentations

	Exhibits 1, 7, & 8	*Exhibit 1*	*Exhibit 7*	*Exhibit 8*
Sales	$923,000	$923,000	$923,000	$923,000
Cost of goods sold	592,000	616,000	616,000	616,000
Gross profit on sales	$331,000	$307,000	$307,000	$307,000
Operating expenses (no depreciation)	$ 96,000	$ 96,000	$ 96,000	$ 96,000
Depreciation expense	24,000	31,700	31,700	31,700
	$120,000	$127,700	$127,700	$127,700
Income before income taxes	$211,000	$179,300	$179,300	$179,300
Income taxes expense	70,000	70,000	70,000	70,000
(A) Income; (B) Income on a current cost basis	(A) $141,000	(B) $109,300	(B) $109,300	(B) $109,300
Financing adjustment			26,317	
Dividends on nonparticipating preferred shares			(10,000)	(10,000)
Income attributable to common shareholders under an operating capability concept of capital			$125,617	
Increase in current-cost amounts of inventory and land and equipment held during year				190,700
Income attributable to common shareholders on current-cost/nominal-dollar basis				290,000
Increase in land, building, and equipment current cost due to inflation				(42,472)
Gain in purchase power, net of monetary liabilities				6,230
Income attributable to common shareholders on a current-cost basis under a financial concept of capital				253,758
Other supplementary information:				
1 Assets on a current-cost basis:				
Inventories	$141,000	$144,000	$144,000	$144,000

14 CICA, ***CICA Handbook***, sec. 4510A.33.

Land and equipment (net of accumulated depreciation)	286,000	442,000	442,000	442,000
Net assets (common shareholders' equity)	411,000	570,000	570,000	570,000
2 a Increase in current-cost amounts of inventories and land and equipment		190,700	190,700	
b Effects of general inflation		42,472	42,472	
c Excess of increase in current costs over effects of general inflation		$148,228	$148,228	
3 Gain in general purchasing power, net of monetary liabilities		$ 6,230	$ 6,230	
4 Financing adjustment		26,317		26,317
5 Amount of financing adjustment based on current cost charged against income during the year		4,375	4,375	4,375

Appraisal of Section 4510 of the *CICA Handbook*

In section 4510, the Accounting Standards Committee of the CICA took a compromise position between two views on accounting for inflation. One view is that historical-cost/constant-dollar financial statements are the most meaningful indicators of the effect of inflation on a business enterprise. Proponents of this view argue that constant-dollar data are more reliable than current-cost data, because constant-dollar amounts are computed with a uniform measure—the Consumer Price Index, or the Gross National Product Implicit Price Deflator.

Another view is that constant-dollar data are not as meaningful as current-cost data because of shortcomings of general price-level indexes such as the CPI. Such indexes are misleading, the critics claim, because of their assumption of a ''mix'' of goods and services in the computation of the indexes. Supporters of current-cost measures of inflation argue that current-cost amounts of the resources of a business enterprise provide more relevant data for decision makers than constant-dollar amounts.

In issuing section 4510, the Accounting Standards Committee acknowledged that it represented a first step in the search for the most meaningful presentation of the effect of inflation on a business enterprise and that business enterprises should be ''encouraged to experiment with the disclosure of other assets and liabilities and related expenses measured on a current cost basis.''[15] The committee is committed to a comprehensive review of section 4510 within five years of its release and to make such appropriate revisions as considered necessary.

15 CICA, *CICA Handbook*, sec. 4510.08.

It should be noted that the recommendations of section 4510 do not carry the same force of compliance by business enterprises as other recommendations of the ***CICA Handbook*** because the former are related to supplementary information in the annual report and not necessarily part of the annual financial statements. Consequently, these recommendations are essentially voluntary in nature. The extent to which business enterprises have adopted these recommendations has depended largely on whether the enterprises are convinced that the benefits exceed the cost involved in providing the supplementary information, and whether they are Securities and Exchange Commission (SEC—United States) registrants where supplementary disclosure was compulsory under ***FASB Statement No. 33***.

The Canadian Institute of Chartered Accountants issued a report on the third year's experience with section 4510 of the ***CICA Handbook*** in October 1986. This booklet represents a continuation of the monitoring process undertaken by the Accounting Standards Committee as part of the ''data gathering process'' considered necessary in order to comply with its mandate to undertake a comprehensive review of section 4510 within five years of the release of the recommendations (December 1982).

The extent of implementation of section 4510 by the companies that fall within its scope of application was:

	1985	*1984*	*1983*
Total number of companies	275	323	321
Number of companies presenting information as recommended in section 4510	43	59	62
Percent of total	15.6%	18.3%	19.3%

In addition, one company that did ***not*** fall within the scope of application of the section reported according to recommendations in section 4510 in 1985. (The figures for the other years were: 1984, two; 1983, three.)

The 44 companies' presentations of information according to section 4510, can be summarized as follows:

	No. of Companies
Income statement format similar to that illustrated in Appendix B to section 4510	20
Reconciliation between historical-cost and current-cost income	20
Information for selected items only: historical cost and current cost	4
	44

In summary, the number of companies reporting according to the recommendations of section 4510 has been disappointingly low (and has decreased both over the three-year monitoring period and to date). Experience in the United States and the United Kingdom, where similar supplementary information has been required, has been similar. In the United Kingdom, the standard (***Statement***

of Standard Accounting Practice No. 16: ''Current Cost Accounting'') was suspended and therefore is no longer mandatory. In early 1986, the U.K.'s Accounting Standards Committee issued a statement, ***TR604***, in which it concluded that ''if a general practice of even modest minimum disclosure is to be established, it is presently beyond the accounting profession alone,'' and proposed that ***Statement No. 16*** be withdrawn. In the United States, the FASB has eliminated the requirement to report historical-cost/constant-dollar information in financial statements for 1984 and beyond. It has subsequently removed its mandatory requirements, thus making supplementary changing prices disclosures voluntary.

It has become more and more apparent that, for one reason or another, companies do not wish to report the effects of changing prices under the present section 4510 supplementary disclosure requirements. The low inflation rate in recent years has lowered the interest in inflation accounting. This situation cannot be expected to continue indefinitely. It is hoped that the Accounting Standards Committee will be better prepared to address ''accounting for inflation'' when the inflation rate again becomes a significant issue.

REVIEW QUESTIONS

1 What evidence can you offer in support of the assertion that ''the dollar is not a stable unit of value''?

2 List the indexes selected by the CICA as a measure of the general movement in prices.

3 Evaluate the following quotation: ''If historical-cost/nominal-dollar financial statements were restated to reflect the changing value of the dollar, assets would be stated at current fair value and net income would not be determined by matching realized revenue with expired costs.''

4 Explain how the use of generally accepted accounting principles may result in reporting as a part of net income what is in reality a recovery of capital.

5 Explain each of the following:

a Monetary items

b Positive monetary position

c Negative monetary position

d Purchasing power gains and losses

6 What is meant by the expression ***conversion factor***? Set up the conversion factor for land if the general price-level index was 80 on the date the land was acquired and is 144 today, using an example.

7 To what extent have current fair values been used by accountants in the preparation of financial statements?

8 What is a ***holding gain or loss***? How is it measured?

9 The basic method of valuation used in accounting for plant assets is historical cost (nominal dollars) less depreciation. At various times during their economic life it is possible to estimate the current fair value of such assets by use of one of the following methods:

a Capitalization of net cash inflows (or direct valuation)
b Exit values (both current and expected)
c Current cost

Explain the meaning of the term ***current fair value*** and define each of the three methods of estimating current fair value listed above.

10 Evaluate the following quotation: ''Accounting is no more than the recording and reporting of transactions. Recognition of the current fair values of assets in the financial statements is neither feasible nor useful; besides, it lacks objectivity.''

11 State the objective of section 4510 of the ***CICA Handbook*** on reporting the effects of changing prices.

12 State the criteria under which corporations are subject to the recommendation of section 4510 of the ***CICA Handbook***.

13 List the supplementary information disclosure requirements of section 4510 of the ***CICA Handbook***.

14 Define the term ***income on a current cost basis*** as used in section 4510 of the ***CICA Handbook***.

15 What are the two ***conditional*** recommendations of section 4510 of the ***CICA Handbook*** and what is the rationale underlying each of these two recommendations?

16 Define the term ***financing adjustment*** as used in section 4510 of the ***CICA Handbook*** and explain how it is determined. Distinguish the realized portion from the unrealized portion of the financing adjustment.

17 Explain the following concepts:
a Maintenance of operating capability
b Maintenance of operating capability financed by common shareholders
c Maintenance of general purchasing power of capital

18 Define the following terms:
a Recoverable amount
b Value in use
c Net realizable value

19 Explain how the supplementary information of a corresponding preceding period is presented on a comparative basis with the supplementary information of the current year.

20 The recoverable amount of Wight Corporation's land on March 31, Year 6, is $1,482,000. Current cost of the land on that date is $1,843,000. How do these facts affect the preparation of current-cost supplementary information for Wight's annual report for the year ended March 31, Year 6? Explain.

EXERCISES

Ex. 25-1 Select the best answer for each of the following multiple-choice questions:

1 The Accounting Standards Committee requires that the current cost of inventories be measured as the:

a Recoverable amount, regardless of the current cost
b Current cost, regardless of the recoverable amount
c Higher of current cost or recoverable amount
d Lower of current cost or recoverable amount

2 In the computation of information on a historical-cost/constant-dollar basis, which of the following is classified as ***nonmonetary***?
a Cash surrender value of life insurance
b Long-term accounts receivable
c Allowance for doubtful accounts
d Deferred income taxes

3 Do purchasing power gains and losses result from monetary assets and liabilities? Nonmonetary assets and liabilities? Answer ***a***, ***b***, ***c***, or ***d*** according to the table below.

	Monetary	*Nonmonetary*
a	Yes	Yes
b	Yes	No
c	No	No
d	No	Yes

4 The Consumer Price Index is used to compute information on:
a A historical-cost basis
b A current-cost basis
c A constant-dollar basis
d A nominal-dollar basis

5 In the computation of information on a historical-cost/constant-dollar basis, which of the following is classified as ***monetary***?
a Obligations under product warranties
b Inventories carried on fifo basis
c Trademarks
d Short-term investments in common stocks
e None of the foregoing

6 A method of accounting based on measures of current cost or lower recoverable amount, without restatement to units of the same general purchasing power, is:
a Historical-cost/constant-dollar accounting
b Historical-cost/nominal-dollar accounting
c Current-cost/constant-dollar accounting
d Current-cost/nominal-dollar accounting

Ex. 25-2 LeMons Limited's plant assets on December 31, Year 6, were composed of the following:

Year acquired	*Percent depreciated*	*Historical cost*
Year 4	30%	$30,000
Year 5	20	20,000

Year 6	10	10,000
Total plant assets		$60,000

LeMons uses the straight-line method, no residual values, and a 10-year economic life for depreciation of all plant assets, and takes a full year's depreciation in the year of acquisition of plant assets. There were no disposals of plant assets in Year 6. Average Consumer Price Indexes were as follows: Year 4, 100; Year 5, 120; Year 6, 150.

Compute the amount of depreciation expense for LeMons Limited's historical-cost/constant-dollar income statement for the year ended December 31, Year 6.

Ex. 25-3 Reno Corporation prepared the following nominal-dollar data for the computation of its purchasing power gain or loss on net monetary items for inclusion in its supplementary information for Year 4:

	Dec. 31, Year 3	*Dec. 31, Year 4*
Monetary liabilities	$1,566,000	$2,449,000
Less: Monetary assets	600,000	1,000,000
Net monetary liabilities	$ 966,000	$1,449,000

Consumer Price Indexes were as follows: December 31, Year 3, 210; December 31, Year 4, 230; average for Year 4, 220.

Compute Reno Corporation's purchasing power gain or loss (expressed in average Year 4 constant dollars) on net monetary items for the year ended December 31, Year 4. ***Hint:*** Compare the ***nominal-dollars*** increase in net monetary liabilities with the increase expressed in ***constant dollars***.

Ex. 25-4 Lexx Limited acquired a machine in Year 8 when the Consumer Price Index was 180. The CPI was 190 for Year 9 and 200 for Year 10. Depreciation expense for the machine was $200,000 a year.

Compute historical-cost/constant-dollar depreciation expense for Lexx Limited's machine for Year 10.

Ex. 25-5 Levi Limited was organized on January 2, Year 7. Selected balances from the historical-cost/nominal-dollar balance sheet on December 31, Year 7, were as follows:

Cash	$50,000
Short-term investments, common stocks (acquired on Jan. 2, Year 7)	70,000
Short-term investments, bonds, (acquired on Jan. 2, Year 7, and held for speculation)	80,000
Long-term note receivable	90,000

The Consumer Price Index was 100 on December 31, Year 6 (and January 2, Year 7), and 110 on December 31, Year 7.

Compute the amounts at which the foregoing items would be presented in Levi Limited's historical-cost/constant-dollar balance sheet on December 31, Year 7.

Ex. 25-6 Oro, Inc., was organized on January 2, Year 3, when common stock was issued for cash of $50,000 and for land with a current fair value of $200,000. Oro did not begin operations until Year 4, and no transactions occurred in Year 3, except the issuance of the common stock. The Consumer Price Index was 100 on December 31, Year 2, and 110 on December 31, Year 3.

Compute the purchasing power gain or loss to be included in a historical-cost/constant-dollar income statement for Oro, Inc., for Year 3.

Ex. 25-7 For each *independent* situation below, compute the purchasing power gain or loss, assuming that assets and liabilities remained unchanged during the entire accounting period and that the Consumer Price Index rose by 7% during the period.

a	Monetary assets	$220,000
	Monetary liabilities	60,000
b	Monetary assets	$260,000
	Current monetary liabilities	100,000
	Long-term monetary liabilities	300,000
c	Cash	$140,000
	Short-term investments in common stocks	200,000
	Notes receivable	90,000
	Accounts receivable	60,000
	Inventories	100,000
	Plant assets (net of accumulated depreciation)	600,000
	Monetary liabilities	475,000
	Shareholders' equity	625,000

Ex. 25-8 The following information is taken from the accounting records of Lambert Corporation.

Inventories:	
December 31, Year 1	$100,000
December 31, Year 2	120,000
Purchases for Year 2	600,000

The cost of goods sold for Year 2 at current cost was $632,000. The current cost of inventories at December 31, Year 1 and Year 2, were $110,000 and $146,000 respectively. Sales and purchases took place evenly throughout Year 2. Inventories are priced on a first-in, first-out basis.

The Consumer Price Indexes were:

End of Year 1	120
Average during Year 2	126
End of Year 2	130

Compute the increase or decrease in the current cost of inventories during Year 2 and the effect of general inflation on the increase or decrease in the current cost of inventories during Year 2.

Ex. 25-9 Pak Corporation paid $1,200,000 in December, Year 6, for certain items of its inventory. In December, Year 7, one-half of the items were sold for $1,100,000 when the current fair value of the entire group of items was $1,400,000.

Compute the amount to be shown as the total gain resulting from the above facts in Pak Corporation's current fair value income statement for Year 7. Disregard income taxes.

Ex. 25-10 Duran Corporation acquired a machine for $2,000,000 in Year 4 when the specific-price index was 180. The applicable specific-price index was 190 on December 31, Year 5, and 200 on December 31, Year 6. Depreciation expense on a historical-cost/nominal-dollar basis was $200,000 a year.

Compute Duran Corporation's average current cost of depreciation expense for Year 6.

Ex. 25-11 Toland Ltd. acquired a machine on December 31, Year 7, for $200,000. The machine was being depreciated on the straight-line basis with no residual value and a five-year economic life. There was an increase in current cost of the machine of 10% during Year 8 and 10% during Year 9 (based on the December 31, Year 8, current cost).

Compute accumulated depreciation on a current-cost basis for inclusion in Toland Ltd.'s supplementary current-cost information for Year 9.

Ex. 25-12 Villar Limited's plant assets on December 31, Year 8, were composed of the following:

Year acquired	*Percent depreciated*	*Historical cost*	*Current cost*
Year 6	30%	$50,000	$ 70,000
Year 7	20	15,000	19,000
Year 8	10	20,000	22,000
Total plant assets		$85,000	$111,000

Villar uses the straight-line method, no residual values, and a 10-year economic life for depreciation of all plant assets, and takes a full-year's depreciation in the year of acquisition of plant assets.

Compute the net current cost (after accumulated depreciation) of Villar Limited's plant assets on December 31, Year 8.

Ex. 25-13 Details of Windsor Corporation's cost of goods sold for Year 3 were as follows:

	Units	*Historical costs*
Finished goods inventory, Jan. 1, Year 3	10,000	$ 530,000
Add: Cost of goods manufactured	45,000	2,790,000
Cost of goods available for sale	55,000	$3,320,000
Less: Finished goods inventory, Dec. 31, Year 3	15,000	945,000
Cost of goods sold	40,000	$2,375,000

Estimated current cost of Windsor's finished goods inventory was $58 a unit on January 1, Year 3, and $72 a unit on December 31, Year 3.

Compute the average current cost of Windsor Corporation's cost of goods sold for Year 3.

Ex. 25-14 Valuation to reflect constant dollars, as opposed to current cost, yields differing amounts for a business enterprise's financial statements. Several transactions concerning one asset of Roebuck Corporation, a calendar-year enterprise, are summarized below:

Year 4: Acquired land for $400,000 cash on December 31; current cost at year-end was $400,000.
Year 5: Owned this land all year; current cost at year-end was $520,000.
Year 6: Sold this land for $690,000 on October 31.

The average Consumer Price Index for each year was as follows:

Year 4	100
Year 5	110
Year 6	120

On your working paper, set up the format below and complete the information on the basis of the transactions described above for Roebuck Corporation. Assume that holding gains and losses are included in current-cost data.

	Historical-cost/ constant-dollars	*Current-cost*
Valuation of land in balance sheet:		
Dec. 31, Year 4	$	$
Dec. 31, Year 5		
Gain in income statement:		
Year 4	$	$
Year 5		
Year 6		
Totals	$	$

CASES

Case 25-1 Financial reporting should provide information to help investors, creditors, and other users of financial statements. The Accounting Standards Committee of the *CICA* requires large publicly owned corporations to disclose certain supplementary information.

Instructions

a Describe the historical-cost/constant-dollar method of accounting. Include in your discussion how historical-cost amounts are used to make historical-cost/constant-dollar measurements.

b Describe the principal advantage of the historical-cost/constant-dollar method of accounting over the historical-cost/nominal-dollar method of accounting.

c Describe the current-cost method of accounting.

d Why would depreciation expense for a specific year differ under the current-cost method of accounting as compared with the historical-cost method of accounting? Include in your discussion whether depreciation expense is likely to be higher or lower under the current-cost method of accounting as compared with the historical-cost/nominal-dollar method of accounting in a period of rising prices, and why.

Case 25-2 Advocates of fair-value accounting propose several methods for estimating the approximate current fair values of assets. Two of the methods proposed are ***current cost*** and ***present value of future cash inflows***.

Instructions

Describe each of the two methods (without reference to section 4510 of the ***CICA Handbook***) and discuss the advantages and disadvantages of the various procedures used to estimate the valuation of assets for each method.

Case 25-3 Jean Daily, the controller of Exeter Limited, was discussing a comment you made in the course of presenting your audit report:

"... And frankly," Daily continued, "I agree that we, too, are responsible for finding ways to produce more relevant financial statements that are as reliable as the ones we now produce.

"For example, suppose we acquired an item of inventory for $400 when the general price-level index was 110. And, later, the item was sold for $750 when the general price-level index was 121 and the current cost was $540. We could compute and report a 'holding gain' of $100."

Instructions

a Explain to what extent and how current costs are used under generally accepted accounting principles to value inventories.

b Explain how Jean Daily computed the holding gain of $100.

Case 25-4 Valuation of assets is an important topic in accounting theory. Suggested valuation methods include the following:

- Historical-cost/nominal-dollar

- Historical-cost/constant-dollar
- Discounted-cash-inflows
- Market price (current selling prices)
- Current cost (current purchase prices)

Instructions

a Why is the valuation of assets a significant issue?

b Explain the basic theory underlying each of the valuation methods listed above. Do not discuss advantages and disadvantages of the methods and do not make specific reference to section 4510 of the ***CICA Handbook***.

Case 25-5 A common objective of accountants is to prepare useful financial statements. To attain this objective many accountants maintain that the financial statements must be adjusted for changes in the general price level. Other accountants believe that financial statements should continue to be prepared on the basis of unadjusted historical cost.

Instructions

a List arguments for adjusting financial statements for changes in the general price level.

b List arguments for preparing financial statements only on the basis of unadjusted historical cost.

c In their discussions about accounting for changes in the general price level and the methods of measuring them, uninformed individuals frequently have failed to distinguish between adjustments for changes in the price levels of specific goods and services and adjustments for changes in the purchasing power of the dollar. What is the distinction? Discuss.

Case 25-6 Financial statements are tools for the communication of quantifiable economic information to users as one of the factors for a variety of management and investment decisions. To fulfill this function, accounting data should be quantifiable and relevant for the kinds of decisions to be made. They should be reliable and free from bias. Many accountants believe that for some purposes current cost is a more useful measure than historical cost and recommend that dual financial statements be prepared showing both historical costs and current costs.

Instructions

a Discuss the ways in which historical costs and current costs conform to the standards of ***reliability*** and ***freedom from bias***.

b Describe briefly how the current cost of the following assets might be determined:

1 Inventories
2 Investments in marketable securities
3 Equipment
4 Natural resources

PROBLEMS

Pr. 25-1 Select the best answer for each of the following multiple-choice questions relating to historical-cost/constant-dollar accounting.

1 Roy Company reported sales of $2,000,000 in Year 3 and $3,000,000 in Year 4. Sales were made evenly throughout each year. The general price-level index during Year 2 remained constant at 100, and at the end of Year 3 and Year 4 it was 102 and 104 respectively. What amount does Roy Company report as sales for Year 4 in terms of end-of-Year-4 purchasing power?
a $3,000,000 *b* $3,029,126 *c* $3,058,821 *d* $3,120,000

2 On January 2, Year 5, Noone Corporation mortgaged one of its properties as collateral for a $1,000,000, 15%, five-year loan. During Year 5, the general price level increased evenly, resulting in a 5% increase for the year.
In a historical-cost/constant-dollar balance sheet on December 31, Year 5, at what amount does Noone Corporation report its mortgage note payable?
a $950,000 *b* $1,000,000 *c* $1,025,000 *d* $1,050,000

3 If land was acquired in Year 10 for $150,000 when the general price-level index was 100 and sold on December 31, Year 19, for $240,000 when the index was 170, the historical-cost/constant-dollar income statement for Year 19 shows:
a A purchasing power gain of $105,000 and a loss on disposal of land of $15,000
b A gain on disposal of land of $90,000
c A purchasing power loss of $15,000
d A loss on disposal of land of $15,000
e None of the foregoing

4 A business enterprise was organized on January 2, Year 2. Selected items from the historical-cost/nominal-dollar balance sheet on December 31, Year 2, had the following amounts:

Accounts receivable (net)	$ 70,000
Accounts payable	60,000
Long-term debt	110,000
Common stock	100,000

At what amounts are these selected items shown in a historical-cost/constant-dollar balance sheet on December 31, Year 2, if the general price-level index was 100 on December 31, Year 1, and 110 on December 31, Year 2? Answer ***a, b, c,*** or ***d*** according to the following table.

	Accounts receivable	*Accounts payable*	*Long-term debt*	*Common stock*
a	$70,000	$60,000	$110,000	$100,000
b	$70,000	$60,000	$110,000	$110,000
c	$70,000	$60,000	$121,000	$110,000
d	$77,000	$66,000	$121,000	$110,000

5 If the base year is Year 1 (when the general price-level index was 100) and land is acquired for $50,000 in Year 5 when the general price-level index is 108.5, the cost of the land restated to Year 1 purchasing power (rounded to the nearest dollar) is:
a $54,250 *b* $50,000 *c* $46,083 *d* $45,750 *e* Some other amount

6 Assume the same facts as in the previous question. The cost of the land restated to December 31, Year 10, purchasing power when the general price-level index is 119.2 (rounded to the nearest dollar) is:
a $59,600 *b* $54,931 *c* $46,083 *d* $45,512 *e* Some other amount

7 If land is acquired at a cost of $120,000 in January, Year 13, when the general price-level index was 120 and is sold in December, Year 19, when the index was 150, the selling price that results in no gain or loss in historical-cost/constant-dollar financial statements is:
a $180,000 *b* $144,000 *c* $120,000 *d* $150,000 *e* Some other amount

8 Equipment acquired for $120,000 on January 2, Year 1, when the general price-level index was 100, was sold on December 31, Year 3, at a price of $85,000. The equipment had an economic life of six years, with no residual value, and was depreciated by the straight-line method. The general price-level index on December 31, Year 1, was 120, on December 31, Year 2, was 150, and on December 31, Year 3, was 175.

In historical-cost/constant-dollar comparative financial statements for Year 1 and Year 2, the Year 1 financial statements show equipment (net of accumulated depreciation) at:
a $150,000 *b* $125,000 *c* $100,000 *d* $80,000 *e* Some other amount

9 Assume the information given in the previous question.

The historical-cost/constant-dollar financial statements for Year 2 include depreciation expense of:
a $35,000 *b* $30,000 *c* $25,000 *d* $20,000 *e* Some other amount

10 Assume the information given in the previous question.

The historical-cost/constant-dollar income statement at the end of Year 3 includes:
a A gain of $35,000 *b* A gain of $25,000 *c* No gain or loss *d* A loss of $20,000 *e* Some other amount

Pr. 25-2 Daniel Limited sells a single product, which it values at first-in, first-out cost in historical-cost/nominal-dollar financial statements. Daniel's perpetual inventory records showed the following information for Year 6:

	Units	*Amount*
Balance, Dec. 31, Year 5	10,000	$ 60,000
Add: Purchases during Year 6	510,000	4,472,000
Subtotals	520,000	$4,532,000
Less: Sales during Year 6	502,000	4,391,600
Balance, Dec. 31, Year 6	18,000	$ 140,400

Unit price quotations from three of Daniel's vendors were as follows:

Dec. 31, Year 5	$6.70, $6.80, $7.00
Dec. 31, Year 6	$8.10, $8.30, $8.35

Daniel generally purchases from the vendor quoting the lowest unit cost.
Daniel's selling expenses generally amount to 10% of net sales. Expected unit selling prices of Daniel's product were as follows:

Dec. 31, Year 5	$10.40
Dec. 31, Year 6	12.60

Instructions
Prepare a working paper to compute Daniel Limited's average current cost of goods sold for Year 6, and the current cost of its inventory on December 31, Year 6, based on the recommendations of section 4510 of the ***CICA Handbook***.

Pr. 25-3 Nikko Limited was organized and began operations on June 1, Year 1, and adopted a fiscal year ending May 31. Nikko rented land and a building under an operating lease on June 1, Year 1. Nikko's equipment acquisitions and related specific-price indexes during the year ended May 31, Year 2, were as follows:

	Cost	*Specific-price index*
June 1, Year 1	$ 48,000	120
Dec. 1, Year 1	39,000	130
Mar. 1, Year 2	50,000	150
Total	$137,000	

Nikko depreciates equipment to the nearest month by the straight-line method over a 10-year economic life with no residual value.
The specific-price index for Nikko's equipment on May 31, Year 2, was 160. Nikko computed value in use for its equipment as follows:

June 1, Year 1	$ 70,000
May 31, Year 2	175,000

Instructions

a Prepare a working paper to compute the current cost of Nikko Company's equipment and related accumulated depreciation on May 31, Year 2, and the average current cost of its depreciation expense for the year ended May 31, Year 2. Use fractions for conversion factors and round computations to the nearest dollar.

b Prepare a working paper to compute the amount of the increase in the current cost of equipment during the year that is attributable to the effect of general inflation. Assume that the purchases of equipment on December 1, Year 1, and March 1, Year 2, and the depreciation are at the average Consumer Price Index during the year of 106.

Pr. 25-4 Financial statements of Langer Limited for the year ended June 30, Year 3, its first year of operations, are presented below.

LANGER LIMITED
Statement of Income and Retained Earnings
For Year Ended June 30, Year 3

Net sales		$1,400,000
Costs and expenses:		
Cost of goods sold	$700,000	
Operating expenses	320,000	
Interest expense	40,000	1,060,000
Income before income taxes		$ 340,000
Income taxes expense:		
Current	$144,000	
Deferred	9,000	153,000
Net income		$ 187,000
Less: Dividends ($0.60 a share)		60,000
Retained earnings, end of year		$ 127,000

LANGER LIMITED
Balance Sheet
June 30, Year 3

Assets

Current assets:	
Cash	$ 50,000
Accounts receivable (net)	120,000
Inventories (first-in, first-out cost)	190,000
Short-term prepayments	3,000
Total current assets	$ 363,000
Plant assets (net of $120,000 accumulated depreciation)	960,000
Total assets	$1,323,000

Liabilities & Shareholders' Equity

Current liabilities:	
Accounts payable	$ 60,000
Income taxes payable	144,000
Current portion of long-term debt	80,000
Total current liabilities	$ 284,000
10% note payable, due $80,000 a year with interest on unpaid balance	240,000
Deferred income tax credits	9,000
Total liabilities	$ 533,000

Shareholders' equity:	
Common stock, no par value, authorized 200,000 shares, issued and outstanding 100,000 shares	$ 663,000
Retained earnings	127,000
Total shareholders' equity	$ 790,000
Total liabilities & shareholders' equity	$1,323,000

Additional Information

1 On June 30, Year 2, Langer completed the following transactions:
- Issued 100,000 shares of common stock to the public at $6.63 a share.
- Borrowed $400,000 from a bank on a 10% promissory note, which was due $80,000 a year plus interest on the unpaid balance, beginning on June 30, Year 3, and was guaranteed by an affiliated enterprise.
- Acquired plant assets costing $1,080,000 for cash of $1,000,000 and an account payable of $80,000.

2 Langer began operations on July 1, Year 2.

3 There were no other plant asset acquisitions or disposals during the year ended June 30, Year 3.

4 On June 30, Year 3, Langer completed the following transactions:
- Declared and paid a cash dividend of $0.60 a share to common shareholders.
- Paid $80,000 principal and $40,000 interest ($400,000 × 0.10 = $40,000) to the bank.

5 The deferred income tax credits resulted from Langer's use of the straight-line method of depreciation for financial accounting and the double-declining-balance method for income taxes.

6 The Consumer Price Index was as follows for the year ended June 30, Year 3:

July 1, Year 2	100
June 30, Year 3	120
Average for year	110

Instructions

Prepare for Langer Limited a detailed working paper to compute Langer's purchasing power gain or loss on net monetary items for the year ended June 30, Year 3. Round all amounts to the nearest dollar. The conversion should be in June 30, Year 3, dollars.

Pr. 25-5 The historical-cost/nominal-dollar income statement for Tilton Limited for the year ended December 31, Year 2, its first year of operations, follows:

TILTON LIMITED
Income Statement
For Year Ended December 31, Year 2

Net sales	$900,000
Cost of goods sold	690,000
Gross profit on sales	$210,000

Expenses:		
Depreciation	$ 15,000	
Other (including interest and income taxes)	120,000	135,000
Net income		$ 75,000

Sales generally averaged $75,000 a month during Year 2, and expenses (including income taxes) were incurred at a relatively even rate throughout Year 2. Both cost of goods sold and the ending inventory consist of a representative sample of goods purchased during Year 2.

Historical-cost/nominal-dollar balance sheets on December 31, Year 1, and on December 31, Year 2, are shown below:

TILTON LIMITED
Balance Sheets
December 31, Year 1 and Year 2

	Year 1	*Year 2*
Assets		
Monetary assets	$127,500	$ 22,500
Investment in common stock of Louis Ltd.		100,000
Inventories (first-in, first-out cost)		160,000
Land	60,000	60,000
Building (net)	150,000	144,000
Equipment (net)	112,500	103,500
Total assets	$450,000	$590,000
Liabilities & Shareholders' Equity		
Current liabilities	$ 25,000	$135,000
Long-term notes payable	175,000	150,000
Common stock, no par value	250,000	250,000
Retained earnings		55,000
Total liabilities & shareholders' equity	$450,000	$590,000

On April 30, Year 2, Tilton invested $100,000 in the common stock of Louis Ltd. Also on April 30, Year 2, Tilton declared a dividend of $20,000.

The changes in the Consumer Price Index during Year 2 are summarized below:

	CPI	*Conversion factor to restate to end-of-Year-2 purchasing power*
Dec. 31, Year 1	110	1.100
Apr. 30, Year 2	112	1.080
July 1, Year 2 (also average for Year 2)	115	1.052
Dec. 31, Year 2	121	1.000

Instructions

(Use the conversion factor numbers in computations.)

a Prepare a working paper to restate Tilton Limited's income statement for the year ended December 31, Year 2, to the historical-cost/constant-dollar basis using end-of-Year-2 purchasing power. Compute any purchasing power gain or loss in a supporting exhibit (Exhibit 1). (Use the ***detailed*** method.)

b Prepare a working paper to restate Tilton Limited's balance sheets on December 31, Year 1 and Year 2, to the historical-cost/constant-dollar basis.

c Verify the amount of retained earnings needed in part ***b*** to balance total assets (as restated) with total liabilities and shareholders' equity (as restated) by preparing Tilton Limited's statement of retained earnings for the year ended December 31, Year 2, on the historical-cost/constant-dollar basis.

Pr. 25-6 Selected current-cost data for Lucinda Corporation's inventories and net plant assets during Year 8 are presented below:

	Inventories	*Net plant assets*
Balances, Dec. 31, Year 7	$120,000	$1,240,000
Purchases or additions (at average Year 8 purchasing power)	870,000	70,000
Cost of goods sold or depreciation expense	920,000	120,000
Balances, Dec. 31, Year 8	180,000	1,650,000

Consumer Price Indexes were as follows:

Dec. 31, Year 7	120
Average for Year 8	140
Dec. 31, Year 8	150

Instructions

Prepare working papers to compute the following for Lucinda Corporation (assume that the current cost of merchandise purchases, costs of goods sold, additions to plant assets, and depreciation expense are stated in average Year 8 purchasing power):

a Increase in current cost of inventories, net of inflation, measured in average Year 8 purchasing power.

b Increase in current cost of net plant assets, net of inflation, measured in average Year 8 purchasing power.

Pr. 25-7 Ozawa Limited was organized on December 31, Year 9. Ozawa's management has decided to supplement its Year 12 historical-cost/nominal-dollar financial statements with historical-cost/constant-dollar financial statements. The following general ledger trial balance (historical-cost/nominal-dollar basis) and additional information are available:

OZAWA LIMITED
Trial Balance
December 31, Year 12

	Debit	*Credit*
Cash and accounts receivable (net)	$ 540,000	
Short-term investments (common stock)	500,000	
Inventories	440,000	
Equipment	650,000	
Accumulated depreciation of equipment		$ 164,000
Accounts payable		400,000
15% bonds payable, due in Year 30		500,000
Common stock, no par value		1,000,000
Retained earnings, Dec. 31, Year 11	46,000	
Sales		1,900,000
Cost of goods sold	1,508,000	
Depreciation expense	65,000	
Other operating expenses, interest expense, and income taxes expense	215,000	
Totals	$3,964,000	$3,964,000

Additional Information

1 Monetary assets (cash and accounts receivable) exceeded monetary liabilities (accounts payable and bonds payable) by $445,000 on December 31, Year 11. The amounts of monetary items are fixed in terms of numbers of dollars, regardless of changes in specific prices or in the Consumer Price Index.

2 Purchases ($1,840,000 in Year 12) and sales were made evenly during Year 12.

3 Depreciation expense was computed by the straight-line method, with a full year's depreciation taken in the year of acquisition and none in the year of retirement. The depreciation rate is 10%, and no residual value of plant assets is anticipated. Acquisitions and retirements of plant assets have been made evenly during each year, and the retirements in Year 12 consisted of assets acquired during Year 10. An analysis of the Equipment ledger account follows:

Year	*Beginning balance*	*Acquisitions*	*Retirements*	*Ending balance*
10		$550,000		$550,000
11	$550,000	10,000		560,000
12	560,000	150,000	$60,000	650,000

4 The 15% bonds payable were issued in Year 10, and the short-term investments were acquired at regular intervals during Year 12. Other operating expenses and interest expense were incurred evenly during Year 12.

5 Assume that Consumer Price Indexes (Year 4 = 100) were as follows:

Annual averages	*CPI*	*Conversion factors**
Year 9	113.9	1.128
Year 10	116.8	1.100
Year 11	121.8	1.055
Year 12	126.7	1.014
Quarterly averages		
Year 11:		
4th	123.5	1.040
Year 12:		
1st	124.9	1.029
2nd	126.1	1.019
3rd	127.3	1.009
4th	128.5	1.000

*Average index for 4th quarter of Year 12 (128.5) divided by the index for any preceding period. For example, the conversion factor for Year 9 is 1.128 (128.5 ÷ 113.9 = 1.128). (Use these conversion factors in your computations.)

Instructions

a Prepare a working paper to restate Ozawa Limited's Equipment ledger account balance on December 31, Year 12, from historical-cost/nominal-dollars to historical-cost/constant-dollars.

b Prepare a working paper to analyze in historical-cost/nominal-dollars Ozawa Limited's Accumulated Depreciation of Equipment ledger account for Year 12.

c Prepare a working paper to analyze (in historical-cost/constant-dollars) Ozawa Limited's Accumulated Depreciation of Equipment ledger account for Year 12.

d Prepare a working paper to compute Ozawa Limited's purchasing power gain or loss on its net monetary items for Year 12 (disregard income taxes). The working paper should give consideration to appropriate items in (or related to) the balance sheet and the income statement. Present a ***detailed working paper***.

Pr. 25-8 Yolie Corporation was organized on December 31, Year 4, and issued 100,000 shares of no-par-value common stock for $500,000. On January 2, Year 5, Yolie completed the following transaction:

Land	80,000	
Buildings	200,000	
Equipment	150,000	
Cash		300,000
Long-Term Notes Payable		130,000
To record acquisition of assets valued at current fair value in exchange for cash and long-term notes payable.		

The changes in the Consumer Price Index during Year 5 are summarized below:

	CPI	*Conversion factor to restate to end-of-Year-5 purchasing power*
Dec. 31, Year 4 (also for Jan. 1, Year 5)	100	1.232
July 1, Year 5 (also the average for Year 5)	110	1.120
Sept. 30, Year 5	115.5	1.067
Dec. 31, Year 5	123.2	1.000

On September 30, Year 5, Yolie paid a cash dividend of 50 cents a share and issued 10,000 additional shares of common stock at $8 a share.

The balance sheet on December 31, Year 5, and the statement of income and retained earnings for Year 5, on the historical-cost/nominal-dollar basis, are as follows:

YOLIE CORPORATION
Balance Sheet
December 31, Year 5

Assets		*Liabilities & Shareholders' Equity*	
Monetary assets	$390,000	Current liabilities	$110,000
Inventories	100,000	Long-term notes payable	130,000
Land	80,000	Common stock, no par value	580,000
Buildings (net)	192,000	Retained earnings	80,000
Equipment (net)	138,000		
Total assets	$900,000	Total liabilities & shareholders' equity	$900,000

YOLIE CORPORATION
Statement of Income and Retained Earnings
For Year Ended December 31, Year 5

Net sales		$1,260,000
Cost of goods sold		920,000
Gross profit on sales		$ 340,000
Expenses:		
Depreciation	$ 20,000	
Other (including interest and income taxes)	190,000	210,000
Net income		$ 130,000
Less: Dividends ($0.50 a share)		50,000
Retained earnings, end of year		$ 80,000

Sales amounted to approximately $105,000 a month, and expenses accrued at the rate of $17,500 a month. Both the cost of goods sold and the ending inventories consist of a representative cross section of merchandise purchased throughout Year 5. All liabilities are monetary.

Instructions

a Prepare a working paper to restate Yolie Corporation's statement of income and retained earnings for Year 5 to a historical-cost/constant-dollar basis. Compute the purchasing power gain or loss in a supporting detailed working paper.

b Prepare a working paper to restate Yolie Corporation's December 31, Year 5, balance sheet to a historical-cost/constant-dollar basis.

Pr. 25-9 The financial statements and other information related to Hercules Limited are given below:

HERCULES LIMITED
Income Statement (Historical-Cost/Nominal-Dollar Basis)
For Year Ended December 31, Year 11

Sales		$760,000
Cost of goods sold		495,000
Gross profit on sales		$265,000
Operating expenses:		
Depreciation	$38,000	
Other	47,000	85,000
Income before income taxes		$180,000
Income taxes expense		75,000
Net income		$105,000

HERCULES LIMITED
Comparative Balance Sheets (Historical-Cost/Nominal-Dollar Basis)
December 31, Year 10 and Year 11

	December 31, Year 10	*December 31, Year 11*
Assets		
Monetary assets	$160,000	$190,000
Inventories (fifo)	100,000	220,000
Equipment	380,000	380,000
Less: Accumulated depreciation	-0-	(38,000)
Total assets	$640,000	$752,000
Liabilities & Shareholders' Equity		
Current liabilities	$ 90,000	$ 97,000
Long-term liabilities	220,000	220,000
Common stock	330,000	330,000
Retained earnings	-0-	105,000
Total liabilities & shareholders' equity	$640,000	$752,000

Hercules Limited was organized on December 31, Year 10, by acquiring the assets and assuming the liabilities of another company. Thus, the assets at December 31, Year 10, were stated at current cost on that date.

Sales, purchases, and other operating expenses took place evenly throughout Year 11. The company had beginning inventory of 5,000 units at a cost of $20 per unit, purchased 30,000 units at a total cost of $615,000, and had 10,000 units in inventory at December 31, Year 11.

The following was the current cost at December 31, Year 11 for:

Inventories (10,000 units)	$260,000
Equipment	460,000

The annual depreciation rate for the equipment was 10% and the equipment has no residual value.

The Consumer Price Indexes were:

End of Year 10	120
Average during Year 11	126
End of Year 11	130

Instructions

Assuming Hercules Limited is required to follow the recommendations of section 4510 of the ***CICA Handbook***, prepare a statement of income on a current-cost basis and other supplementary information for Year 11, using the format illustrated in the chapter (including restating in ***average*** dollars for the year).

Pr. 25-10 Using the information given in Problem **25-9** for Hercules Limited, prepare a statement of income attributable to common shareholders on a current-cost basis under:

a An operating capability concept of capital and other supplementary information

b A financial concept of capital and other supplementary information

Pr. 25-11 Isabelle Limited was organized on December 31, Year 1 by acquiring a number of companies in the merchandising business. Its historical-cost/nominal-dollar income statement for the year ended December 31, Year 2, the first year of operations, is given below:

ISABELLE LIMITED
Income Statement
For Year Ended December 31, Year 2
(In thousands of dollars)

Sales	$290,000
Cost of goods sold	149,000
Gross profit on sales	141,000

Operating expenses:		
Depreciation	$34,000	
Other	42,000	76,000
Income before income taxes		$ 65,000
Income taxes:		
Current	$20,000	
Deferred	9,000	29,000
Net income		$ 36,000

Sales, purchases, other operating expenses, and sources and uses of monetary items took place evenly throughout the year. The total purchases for Year 2 were $154,000 (in thousands of dollars). The quantities of merchandise (in thousands of units) for the year were: sales, 7,050; purchases, 7,000; inventories, December 31, Year 1, 1,250; inventories, December 31, Year 2, 1,200.

Historical-cost/nominal-dollar comparative balance sheets on December 21, Year 1 and Year 2, are as follows:

ISABELLE LIMITED
Comparative Balance Sheets
December 31, Year 1 and Year 2
(In thousands of dollars)

	December 31, Year 1	*December 31, Year 2*
Assets		
Cash	$ -0-	$ 2,000
Marketable securities, at lower of cost and market	-0-	18,000
Accounts receivable (net)	16,000	25,000
Inventories (fifo method)	25,000	30,000
Land	100,000	100,000
Buildings	300,000	380,000
Less: Accumulated depreciation	(-0-)	(34,000)
Total assets	$441,000	$521,000
Liabilities & Shareholders' Equity		
Current liabilities	$ 12,000	$ 31,000
Long-term liabilities	80,000	110,000
Preferred stock, participating	200,000	200,000
Preferred stock, nonparticipating	100,000	100,000
Common stock	49,000	49,000
Retained earnings	-0-	31,000
Total liabilities & shareholders' equity	$441,000	$521,000

The assets were transferred to Isabelle Limited from the acquired companies at current cost at December 31, Year 1. The recoverable amounts of these assets on December 31, Year 1 were equal to their current cost. The liabilities of the acquired companies were assumed by Isabelle on December 31, Year 1.

Isabelle Limited, by reference to applicable vendor's invoices and price lists, developed a current cost of $36,000 for inventories on December 31, Year 2. The recoverable amount of the December 31, Year 2, inventories was determined as $38,500. (These amounts are in thousands of dollars.)

A building costing $80,000 (in thousands of dollars) was purchased on July 1, Year 2, when the specific-price index was at 120. The specific-price index for this building at December 31, Year 2, was 126. All buildings were depreciated at the rate of 10% a year except for additions during the year which were depreciated at 5%. The specific-price indexes were as shown in the next illustration.

	Dec. 31, Year 1	*Dec. 31, Year 2*
Land	100	121
Buildings	120	138

The company, using appropriate present-value methods for measuring value in use, determined the recoverable amount for land and buildings to be in excess of their current costs.

The company declared and paid $5,000 (in thousands of dollars) dividends to the nonparticipating preferred shareholders near the end of Year 2. No dividends were declared for the participating preferred and common shareholders.

The Consumer Price Indexes were:

End of Year 1	160
Average during Year 2	168
End of Year 2	175

Instructions

Prepare a statement of income on a current-cost basis and other supplementary information as required by section 4510 of the ***CICA Handbook***, using the format illustrated in this chapter. Show all supporting computations. (The two ***conditional*** recommendations are not required for this problem.)

Pr. 25-12 Using the information given in Problem **25-11** for Isabelle Limited, prepare a statement of income attributable to common shareholders on a current-cost basis under:

a An operating capability concept of capital and other supplementary information

b A financial concept of capital and other supplementary information

I N D E X

I N D E X

CUT HERE

STUDENT REPLY CARD

In order to improve future editions, we are seeking your comments on this book.

After you have read ***Intermediate Accounting***, Fifth Canadian Edition, by Mosich, Larsen, Lam, and Johnston, please answer the following questions and return this form via Business Reply Mail.

Thanks in advance for your feedback!

1. Name of your college or university: ______________________________
2. Your major program of study: ______________________________
3. Your instructor for this course: ______________________________
4. Were any sections of this text ***not*** assigned as course reading? If so, please specify the chapters or portions: ______________________________

____

____

5. How would you rate the overall accessibility of the content? (Please feel free to comment on reading level, writing style, terminology, layout and design features, and such learning aids as chapter objectives, summaries, and appendixes.) ______________________________

____

____

____

____

____

____

____

____

6. What did you like ***best*** about this book? ______________________________

____

____

____

____

7. What did you like ***least***? ______________________________

____

____

____

If you'd like to say more, we'd love to hear from you. Please write to us at the address shown on the reverse of this form.

CUT HERE

CUT HERE

CUT HERE

FOLD HERE

BUSINESS REPLY MAIL

No Postage Stamp
Necessary If Mailed
in Canada

Postage will be paid by

Attn: Sponsoring Editor, Business and Economics

The College Division
McGraw-Hill Ryerson Limited
330 Progress Avenue
Scarborough, Ontario
M1P 9Z9

TAPE SHUT